The Law of Environmental Justice

Theories and Procedures to Address Disproportionate Risks

Michael B. Gerrard, Editor

For updates: http://www.abanet.org/abapubs/envirolaw.html

ABA SECTION OF ENVIRONMENT ENERGY AND RESOURCES

Section of Environment, Energy, and Resources
American Bar Association

Defending Liberty
Pursuing Justice

Cover design by Lisa Empleo.

Printed in the United States of America.

03 02 01 00 99   5 4 3 2 1

Law of environmental justice / Michael B. Gerrard, editor.
p. cm.
Includes index.
ISBN 1-57073-680-4
1. Environmental law—United States. 2. Environmental justice—United States. 3. Race discrimination—Law and legislation—United States. I. Gerrard, Michael. II. American Bar Association. Section of Environment, Energy, and Resources.
KF3775.E4667 1999
344.73'046—dc21 99-33273
CIP

www.abanet.org/abapubs/envirolaw.html

SUMMARY CONTENTS

PART II: Legal Procedures

PART III: Legal Objectives

CONTENTS

ABOUT THE EDITOR

Michael B. Gerrard, General Editor of this book, is a partner in the New York office of Arnold & Porter, where he is involved in environmental litigation (civil, criminal, and administrative), project development, regulatory compliance counseling, and transactional services. He has practiced environmental law in New York City since 1978. He has served as chairman of the Executive Committee of the 21,000-member Association of the Bar of the City of New York, and as chairman of the Environmental Law Section of the New York State Bar Association, and is Strategic Planning Chair of the American Bar Association's Environment, Energy, and Resources Section. Gerrard also teaches environmental law as a member of the adjunct faculties of Columbia Law School and the Yale School of Forestry and Environmental Studies.

Since 1986, Gerrard has written the environmental law column for the *New York Law Journal,* and since 1989 he has been editor of a monthly newsletter, *Environmental Law in New York.* He is author or editor of four prior books, two of which were named Best Law Book of the Year by the Association of American Publishers: *Environmental Law Practice Guide* (eight volumes, 1992) and *Brownfields Law and Practice: The Cleanup and Redevelopment of Contaminated Land* (two volumes, 1998). His other books are *Environmental Impact Review in New York* (two volumes, 1990, with Ruzow and Weinberg) and *Whose Backyard, Whose Risk: Fear and Fairness in Toxic and Nuclear Waste Siting* (1994).

Gerrard also serves on the boards of the Council on the Environment of New York City; New York Environmental Advocates; INFORM, Inc.; and the Westchester Land Trust, and is General Counsel of the Municipal Art Society. He received his B.A. from Columbia University and his J.D. from New York University School of Law.

ABOUT THE AUTHORS

Chuck D. Barlow serves as Chief of the Legal Division of the Mississippi Department of Environmental Quality. From 1990 through 1996 he was associated with the Jackson office of Phelps Dunbar, L.L.P., where he practiced environmental law and general litigation. Previously, Mr. Barlow clerked for former Chief Judge Charles Clark of the United States Court of Appeals for the Fifth Circuit. He received his undergraduate degree from Mississippi College and his law degree from the Mississippi College School of Law. He holds a Master of Laws in environmental and natural resource law from the Northwestern School of Law of Lewis & Clark College, and a Master of Arts in English from the University of Virginia. He is currently a vice-chair of the American Bar Association's Section of Environment, Energy, and Resources Special Committee on Agricultural Management.

Ellen P. Chapnick is Assistant Dean and Director of the Center for Public Interest at Columbia Law School and has focused her current work on environmental justice issues that affect communities and workers. Ms. Chapnick received her Juris Doctor from Georgetown University Law Center and her undergraduate degree from Cornell University College of Arts and Sciences.

Carl F. Cranor is a professor of philosophy and Associate Dean at the College of Humanities, Arts, and Social Sciences at the University of California, Riverside. Specializing in the philosophy of regulatory law and science and the philosophy of risk assessment, Mr. Cranor's work has been the subject of several publications. He earned his undergraduate degree from the University of Colorado, his Ph.D. from

UCLA, and his Master of Studies in Law from Yale Law School. Among other positions, he has held American Council of Learned Societies, Yale's Master of Studies in Law, Congressional, and NSF Fellowships. In 1998 he was elected a Fellow of the American Association for the Advancement of Science.

Colin Crawford is an associate professor at Thomas Jefferson School of Law in San Diego and a graduate of Columbia and Cambridge Universities and Harvard Law School. His book of narrative nonfiction, *Uproar at Dancing Rabbit Creek: Battling Over Class, Race and the Environment* (Addison Wesley, 1996) examined the struggle of one poor, predominantly African-American community over the possible siting of the nation's largest hazardous waste dump. Environmental justice has been the subject of Mr. Crawford's writing in academic journals as well.

Sheila Foster is an associate professor of law at Rutgers University in Camden, New Jersey, where she specializes in the intersection of race and legal theory, particularly as it relates to contemporary problems of racial inequality. Ms. Foster received her Bachelor of Arts from the University of Michigan and her Juris Doctor from Boalt Hall School of Law at the University of California-Berkeley. She is the author of numerous articles, the most recent of which is "Intent and Incoherence" in the *Tulane Law Review* (1998).

Jeffrey B. Gracer is a member of the firm at Lowenstein Sandler, in Roseland, New Jersey. His practice encompasses a wide array of environmental matters, including contaminated site remediation, solid and hazardous waste regulation, and environmental litigation. Before entering private practice, Mr. Gracer was a staff attorney in the national office of the American Civil Liberties Union. He was appointed by Commissioner Robert Shinn to the New Jersey Department of Environmental Protection's Environmental Equity Task Force, and is the author of *Taking Environmental Claims Seriously,* 28 ELR 10373 (July 1998). Mr. Gracer received his B.A. from Columbia College and his Juris Doctor from Columbia University School of Law. He is currently a member of the section of International Law and Practice of the American Bar Association, the Environmental Law Committee of the Inter-American Bar Association, and the Inter-American Affairs Committee of the New York City Bar Association.

Allan Kanner received his undergraduate degree from the University of Pennsylvania and his law degree from Harvard Law School. He is a member of Allan Kanner & Associates, P.C. in New Orleans.

His national practice in environmental, toxic tort and commercial fraud litigation includes extensive experience in complex litigation.

Mr. Kanner's career includes a number of leading cases, such as the *Three Mile Island Litigation,* the *Louisville Sewer Explosion Litigation,* and the first successful private party case under Superfund, *Walls v. Waste Resources.*

In 1988 he sued Georgia Gulf on behalf of the African-American residents of Revelletown in a groundbreaking case. In 1992, he used a prospective nuisance theory to help stop Formosa Chemical from building a major facility in St. John Baptist Parish, Louisiana, without prior proof that the facility would operate safely and without causing a nuisance.

Since 1990, he has been an Adjunct Professor of Law at the Tulane Law School, and currently serves as a member of the advisory board of BNA's *Toxic Law Reporter* and the editorial board of ELI's *Environmental Law Reporter.* Mr. Kanner is the author of ENVIRONMENTAL AND TOXIC TORT TRIALS (Michie Co., 1997 Supp.), as well as numerous articles on complex litigation, toxic torts, and environmental law. He serves on the Louisiana Supreme Court's Complex Litigation Committee and helped draft the new LOUISIANA JUDGES' COMPLEX LITIGATION BENCH BOOK (1997).

A much earlier draft of his chapter was presented at the Southwest Indigenous People's Uranium Forum on September 23–24, 1993 in Paguate, Laguna Pueblo, New Mexico.

Barnett Lawrence is an Environmental Law Specialist for the firm of Arnold & Porter in Washington, D.C., where he specializes in environmental and workplace safety law. His past experience in environmental law includes working for the Environmental Law Institute as Senior Associate Editor of the Environmental Law Reporter. Mr. Lawrence received his Juris Doctor from the Georgetown University Law Center.

Bradford C. Mank is a professor of law at the University of Cincinnati College of Law where he teaches in the areas of environmental law and property. Mr. Mank received his undergraduate degree from Harvard University and his law degree from Yale Law School, where he served as an editor of the *Yale Law Journal.* After graduation, he clerked for Justice David Shea of the Connecticut Supreme Court. He practiced environmental law with a private law firm in Hartford, Connecticut and as an Assistant Attorney General with the State of Connecticut. He has been published in the *Ecology Law Quarterly, Columbia Journal of Environmental Law, Tulane Law Review, Washington & Lee Law Review,* and *Ohio State Law Journal.*

Barbara J. Olshansky is Assistant Legal Director of the Center for Constitutional Rights in New York, where she assists in all phases of case development and litigation as well as political advocacy in the areas of civil, constitutional, and international human rights. She came to the Center from the Environmental Defense Fund, a national, not-for-profit environmental organization. She was instrumental in incorporating environmental justice concerns into the EDF's docket and worked on a number of environmental justice cases. She has published articles in various industry newsletters and journals. Olshansky graduated from Stanford Law School in 1985 and clerked for two years for Justice Rose E. Bird, then Chief Justice of the California Supreme Court. In 1982, she graduated from the University of Rochester, summa cum laude, with a B.A. in both European history and political science.

Heidi Gorovitz Robertson is assistant professor of Law at the Cleveland-Marshall College of Law at Cleveland State University. She practiced environmental law with the law firm of Pillsbury Madison & Sutro, served as an Associate in Law at Columbia Law School, and was an articles editor on the *Columbia Journal of Environmental Law.* In addition, she served as a consulting attorney for the World Wildlife Fund and on the editorial board of the *California Environmental Law Reporter.* Ms. Robertson received her J.D. from the University of Wisconsin-Madison and her L.L.M. from Columbia Law School. Her current research interests concern equity issues in the distribution of environmental risk and barriers to the redevelopment of urban brownfields land.

Judith V. Royster is a professor of law and Co-Director of the Native American Law Program at the University of Tulsa College of Law. She teaches in the areas of federal Indian law, natural resources law, and constitutional law, and writes and lectures primarily on environmental and natural resources issues in Indian country. She received her B.A., M.A., and J.D. degrees from the University of Wisconsin.

Irma S. Russell is an associate professor of law at the Cecil C. Humphreys School of Law at the University of Memphis, where she teaches environmental law. In practice, Ms. Russell has represented potentially responsible parties on issues arising under CERCLA in Superfund negotiations as well as representing lenders and other clients on issues involving wetlands designation and site mitigation, the Clean Water Act, asbestos regulations and other environmental issues. Ms. Russell received her Juris Doctor degree from the University of Kansas School of Law. In addition to working on numerous legal publications, she is a member of the Judicial Conference of the Tenth Judicial Circuit, and the Memphis, Tennessee, and American Bar Associations.

Larry Schnapf is an environmental attorney based in New York City and is the founder of the Schnapf Environmental Law Center. He has more than 15 years of national environmental experience with Fortune 500 corporations and a number of major New York-based law firms. Mr. Schnapf concentrates his practice on environmental issues associated with corporate acquisitions, commercial lending and financing, real estate transactions and bankruptcy matters as well as preparing environmental disclosures for SEC and private placement offerings. He is an adjunct professor of environmental law at New York Law School, and has written many articles and authored several publications on environmental law. Mr. Schnapf is the co-chair of the New York State Bar Association's Hazardous Site Remediation Committee, chairman of the Brownfield Task Force, and a member of the ASTM Task Group on Access and Land Use Controls.

Elizabeth A. Stringer is an environmental lawyer at the law firm of Arnold & Porter in Washington, D.C. She earned her Juris Doctor from Northwestern School of Law of Lewis & Clark College, with a specialty certificate in environmental and natural resources law. Ms. Stringer is a member of the Colorado, Oregon, and Washington, D.C., Bar Associations.

Kenneth J. Warren is a partner in the Bala Cynwyd, Pennsylvania, law firm of Manko, Gold & Katcher, LLP, an environmental practice with offices in Pennsylvania and New Jersey. He handles environmental litigation and directs the firm's litigation practice. Mr. Warren is a member of the governing council of the American Bar Association's Section of Environment, Energy, and Resources and chair of its Rapid Response Committee. He has been published in BNA's *Toxic Law Reporter* and *Environment Reporter,* and is a monthly contributor to the *Philadelphia Legal Intelligencer.* Mr. Warren graduated in 1975 from Brown University, magna cum laude in history, and in 1979 from the University of Pennsylvania School of Law, magna cum laude, where he served as an associate editor of the law review.

Philip Weinberg teaches constitutional law and environmental law at St. John's University School of Law in Queens, New York. Prior to joining the faculty, Mr. Weinberg was Assistant Attorney General in charge of the Environmental Protection Bureau in the New York State Attorney General's office. He argued numerous appeals, including three at the U.S. Supreme Court. A graduate of Columbia Law School, Mr. Weinberg writes practice commentary to *McKinney's New York Environmental Conservation Law* and is the author of an environmental law casebook, as well as several articles on environmental and constitutional law. He has been chair of the New York State Bar Association's Environmental Law Section and of the Committee on Environmental Law and the Committee on Transportation of the Association of the Bar of the City of New York.

Bernard A. Weintraub is an attorney with the New York office of Shearman & Sterling, where he practices in both the Environmental and Real Estate Practice Groups. While involved in all aspects of environmental and real estate practice, his particular expertise and interest involves redevelopment of environmentally contaminated property. After receiving a B.S. and an A.B. degree from Cornell University, Mr. Weintraub earned his Master's degree from Yale University and his J.D. degree from New York University School of Law. He currently serves as co-chair of the Environmental Law Committee of the New York County Lawyers' Association and has served as Chairman of the Environmental Justice Subcommittee of the Association of the Bar of the City of New York's Environmental Law Committee. Mr. Weintraub has written numerous articles on environmental matters and is a member of the New York City Mayor's Task Force on Brownfield Development.

PREFACE

There is no universally accepted definition of environmental justice. I define it as the idea that minority and low-income individuals, communities, and populations should not be disproportionately exposed to environmental hazards, and that they should share fully in making the decisions that affect their environment.

This notion has been around for years. I can recall attending the National Conference on the Urban Environment in New York City in 1975, and the Urban Environment Conference in Detroit in 1978, which focused on issues of pollution in the central cities. The suggestion that this pollution was distributed in a systematically unfair manner was not widely discussed, however, until the landmark 1987 report, *Toxic Wastes and Race in the United States,* from the Commission of Racial Justice of the United Church of Christ. Many groups organized after that report, and they came together at the First National People of Color Environmental Leadership Summit in Washington, D.C., October 24–27, 1991. I attended that conference as well, and saw the leaders of several national environmental organizations sitting in the front row and being lectured by the conference organizers for allegedly devoting too little attention to the environmental concerns of communities of color.

Much legal activity occurred, both before and after the 1991 Summit, aimed at establishing environmental justice as an enforceable right. This litigation was almost invariably unsuccessful in court (though not necessarily politically), because the plaintiffs were unable to prove that there had been intentional discrimination, which seemed to be a prerequisite. In 1993 the American Bar Association's House of Delegates adopted a resolution endorsing the principles of environmental justice, and in 1994 President Clinton issued Executive Order 12,898, "Federal Actions to Address Environmental Justice in Minority Populations and Low-Income Populations." It was not until 1997 that plaintiffs began winning cases on environmental justice grounds, mostly through emerging doctrines that did not require proof of intent.

Thus a series of judicial and administrative decisions in 1997 and 1998, and the cancellation of several large projects that had come under fire on environmental justice grounds, demonstrated that these claims can have serious legal consequences, and that the time had become ripe for a book-length treatise on the law of environmental justice.

This book is organized in three parts. Part I, Legal Theories, covers the sources of environmental justice law: the equal protection clause of the U.S. Constitution, the Civil Rights Act of 1964, the 1994 Executive Order, relevant state laws, and Native American law. Part II, Legal Procedures, concerns the methods by which parties can utilize environmental justice law—through participation in administrative proceedings, access to information, use of the impact assessment and risk assessment processes, and access to the courts—as well as issues of evidence and legal ethics. Part III, Legal Objectives, discusses how the law can be used to achieve many of the goals of environmental justice: stopping (or building) new facilities, controlling ongoing pollution, cleaning up or redeveloping old facilities, controlling residential and occupational exposure, assisting injured individuals, and protecting citizens of other countries.

The intended audience for this book is lawyers on all sides of environmental justice controversies: those representing community groups, corporations, and government agencies. Similarly, the chapter authors come from a diversity of viewpoints, and I have asked them to strive for a neutral, balanced tone and to present the legal bases for defenses as well as for claims. Needless to say, the views expressed do not necessarily reflect the opinions of the authors' (or the editor's) employers or clients, or of the American Bar Association. Nor is this book a substitute for legal advice; it aims to help lawyers find the law that they can apply to particular situations.

This book attempts to be current through early 1999. The field is developing so quickly that the importance of checking for more recent cases and other events cannot be overemphasized. The ABA is in the process of creating an update service that will make information about new developments available on the World Wide Web. This service can be accessed through this web site: www.abanet.org/abapubs/envirolaw.html.

Many people played vital roles in the development of this book. Most important are the chapter authors who, acting on tight deadlines, gave so generously of their time and talents. A team of peer reviewers led by William Penny and including Brian M. Babb, Elizabeth C. Barton, Elizabeth B. Davis, William H. Gelles, W. Thomas Lavender, Jr., S. Wayne Rosenbaum, Dean B. Suagee, Peter Van Oot, Catherine Ward, and Patrick Zaepfel, read draft chapters and contributed invaluable suggestions. Rick Paszkiet and his staff at ABA Publishing were extremely helpful throughout. George Knapp, Chair of the ABA's Section on Environment, Energy, and Resources, and J.B. Ruhl, Section Publications Officer, and Mark Squillace, Chair of the Section's Book Publications Committee, were completely supportive. My colleagues in the New York, Washington, D.C., Denver, and Los Angeles offices of Arnold & Porter were helpful and indulgent, and my secretary, Dolia Christoffersen, was efficient and cheerful as always.

My wonderful family—my wife, Barbara, and our sons, David and William—continue, for reasons that still mystify me, to put up with the extracurricular activities, like this, that I undertake.

I dedicate this book to the memories of my parents, Dr. Nathan L. Gerrard and Dr. Louise Burr Gerrard, whose enthusiastic support of the civil rights movement during my childhood in the 1960s left me with an abiding sense of the importance of the issues discussed here.

M.B.G.
New York, New York
January 1999

PART I

Legal Theories

CHAPTER 1

EQUAL PROTECTION

PHILIP WEINBERG

Generally; Historical Perspective

The Constitutional basis for environmental justice and all other challenges to governmental discrimination lies in the Equal Protection Clause. The Fourteenth Amendment expressly provides that the states may not "deny to any person within [their] jurisdiction the equal protection of the laws."[1] The notion of equality is imbedded even more deeply in American law, since the Declaration of Independence stated in ringing terms that "all men are created equal."

The Supreme Court has laid down several basic principles implementing equal protection. First, a governmental action must be involved for the clause to be violated. Private discrimination, unless somehow mandated or abetted by state law, does not constitute a denial of equal protection.[2] However, if the state furthers private action, as, for example, by court enforcement of a private racially-discriminatory agreement, that action triggers the Equal Protection Clause.[3] Second, although the Clause by its terms applies to the states (thus including local governments as well), the courts use the Fifth Amendment's Due Process Clause to bar discriminatory action by the federal government.[4] The standards in suits against states and the federal government asserting race-based discrimination are essentially the same.

All statutory classifications in some way discriminate, by distinguishing between different forms of conduct or classes of people. It is only invidious—that is, unjustifiable—discrimination that the Equal Protection Clause prohibits. In other words, to show a violation of equal protection, one must prove that persons similarly situated are treated differently.[5] Finally, a denial of equal protection requires proof of intent to discriminate, as discussed in "The Need to Prove Intent to Discriminate," beginning on page 6.

Although the Equal Protection Clause may be used to challenge acts of government that unconstitutionally discriminate on any basis, its origin in 1868 was in curbing the widespread discrimination based on race throughout the South in the aftermath of the Civil War. Indeed, the Supreme Court at first ruled that the Clause only barred racial discrimination against blacks, and could not be invoked in other situations.[6] However, the Court soon broadened its reading of the Clause, in keeping with the sweep of its wording, and held as early as 1897 that it barred discrimination by states whether or not based on color.[7] That case declared violative of Equal Protection a statute that awarded lawyers' fees in successful actions against railroad companies, though not against other defendants.

Racial discrimination, generally the prime issue in environmental justice assertions, was held as early as 1879 to violate the Equal Protection Clause. *Strauder v. West Virginia*[8] overturned a statute that barred blacks from serving on juries. Significantly, the Supreme Court noted that a statute that barred whites would be just as violative of Equal Protection. Unfortunately, the Court ruled soon thereafter that the infamous separate but equal doctrine was valid. *Plessy v. Ferguson*[9] sustained a Louisiana law that required the races to travel in separate railroad cars, concluding that the statute's mandate for "equal but separate accommodations" did not "stamp[] the colored race with a badge of inferiority." The eloquent dissent by the first Justice Harlan maintained the statute's purpose was "to exclude colored people" and that "it interferes with the personal freedom of citizens." In language often echoed since, he observed that "[o]ur Constitution is color-blind."

It was only in 1954, in *Brown v. Board of Education*,[10] that the Court squarely overruled *Plessy* and rejected separate but equal as inherently unequal. Since *Brown*, the courts have consistently overturned statutes enforcing or mandating discrimination against racial minorities. In more recent years, the Supreme Court has had to wrestle with the complex issue of affirmative action statutes and regulations designed to benefit, rather than injure, racial minorities[11]—an issue beyond the scope of this book.

The states have equal protection provisions in their constitutions as well. Since it is well-settled that the states are free to furnish greater (though not less) protection to individual rights than the United States Constitution accords,[12] state constitutions may be invoked as well as the Fourteenth Amendment in seeking environmental justice. These issues are examined in Chapter 5, "State Environmental Justice Programs and Related Authorities."

Standards of Judicial Scrutiny

Rational Basis Test

The ordinary measure of judicial review under the Equal Protection Clause is the familiar rational basis test. Unless either a suspect classification such as race or a fundamental right like free speech is involved, the courts will uphold a statutory classification as long as some reasonable basis exists for it.

In one noted decision, the Supreme Court sustained a ban on commercial advertisements on the sides of trucks, even though the law exempted ads for the truck owner's own business.[13] The Court ruled it was rational to control advertising for hire although advertisements by the owner of the vehicle were not restricted. (Today, with commercial speech regarded as protected by the First Amendment, the Court would subject this law to a higher degree of scrutiny for that reason.)

In another case, the Court upheld a federal regulation of cable television operators that excluded from its terms facilities serving only one or more buildings under common ownership.[14] Holding that "[w]here there are 'plausible reasons' for Congress' action, 'our inquiry is at an end,'" it ruled the greater bargaining power of buildings under common ownership as against the cable operator, in contrast to separately owned buildings, was sufficient to justify the exclusion.[15]

One notable land-use decision is representative of the few that have invalidated classifications as irrational. In *City of Cleburne v. Cleburne Living Center,*[16] the Supreme Court held that though the mentally retarded are not a suspect class like racial minorities, a zoning law excluding a group home for retarded persons nonetheless was invalid since it lacked a rational basis. The ordinance permitted all manner of residences, including apartments, boarding houses, dormitories, and even nursing homes for the aged or convalescents, yet excluded homes for retarded or mentally ill persons. The Court sensibly found the provision "appears to us to rest on an irrational prejudice against the mentally retarded," and set it aside.

The genesis of the higher judicial scrutiny accorded suspect classifications like race, as well as laws interfering with speech, voting, access to justice, and other fundamental rights, is in a footnote by Justice Stone in a 1938 decision, *United States v. Carolene Products Co.*[17] In upholding a federal law prohibiting the interstate shipment of "filled milk" (containing certain non-milk products designed to resemble milk), the Court held the statute had a rational basis since it was designed to prevent deception of consumers. The famous footnote 4 then noted that judicial scrutiny might well be stricter where laws are "directed at particular religions or national or racial minorities" or interfere with rights such as free speech and thus impede the political process.

Footnote 4, described by Justice Powell as "the most celebrated footnote in constitutional law,"[18] led to the courts requiring strict scrutiny where a statute or regulation employs a suspect classification like race or restricts free speech or some other right deemed to be fundamental. Strict scrutiny requires the government to show the regulation is narrowly tailored to serve a compelling governmental interest, as the next subsection describes.

Strict Scrutiny for Racial Discrimination

Since the *Carolene Products* decision six decades ago,[19] the Supreme Court has employed strict scrutiny for statutes, regulations, and similar governmental acts that discriminate based on race or national origin. In these situations, the burden shifts to government to prove the law is narrowly tailored to serve a compelling state interest.[20]

Since the landmark decision in *Brown v. Board of Education* outlawing race discrimination in the public schools,[21] the courts have invariably ruled that laws discriminating against racial minorities fail to satisfy the heavy burden imposed by the strict scrutiny test. In the wake of *Brown,* the Supreme Court has overturned attempts to maintain segregated public schools by indirect or subtle techniques,[22] as well as laws prohibiting interracial marriage[23] and efforts to retain segregated public universities through using higher test scores for entry to formerly all-white campuses.[24]

However, laws that discriminate outright against minorities on the basis of race are unlikely to resurface. (Affirmative action programs that arguably discriminate in favor of minorities are, as noted earlier, beyond the scope of this book.) The focus, particularly in the environmental and land-use areas, has shifted to laws, neutral on their face, that are claimed to have been unequally applied. These are discussed in the section immediately following.

The Need to Prove Intent to Discriminate

As noted in the previous two sections, a violation of the Equal Protection Clause requires proof of governmental intent to discriminate. Mere evidence of a disparate, or greater, impact on one class than another will not suffice. This necessity to prove intent takes on deeper significance where, as in environmental justice litigation, the plaintiffs claim discrimination based on race or national origin, since, as just shown, those claims require government to meet strict scrutiny. In a series of cases commencing with *Washington v. Davis*[25] in 1976, the Supreme Court has made clear that proof that a law falls with greater weight on one racial group than another, without proof of intent to discriminate, does not make out a claim of denial of equal protection.

Washington v. Davis

This decision, a watershed case in equal protection law, dealt with a written test given applicants to the District of Columbia's police department. The plaintiffs showed that four times as many black applicants failed this test as did whites. The test was designed to show likelihood of success in the training program, and there was no proof it was culturally slanted to favor whites. The Court of Appeals for the District of Columbia Circuit found the proof of vastly disproportionate impact showed a denial of equal protection, in the absence of further proof by the District that the test measured actual performance, as opposed to success in the training program. But the Supreme Court unanimously reversed. In an opinion by Justice White, it held "the invidious quality of a law claimed to be racially discriminatory must ultimately be traced to a racially discriminatory purpose." The disparity alone was, in the absence of any proof of such an intent to discriminate, insufficient to trigger a violation of equal protection.

The necessity of showing intent was heightened by proof that the police were actively seeking and recruiting minority applicants. As the Court pointed out,

> A rule that a statute designed to serve neutral ends is nevertheless invalid, absent compelling justification, if in practice it benefits or burdens one race more than another would be far-reaching and would raise serious questions about, and perhaps invalidate, a whole range of tax, welfare, public service, regulatory, and licensing statutes that may be more burdensome to the poor and to the average black than to the more affluent white.

The Court rejected the plaintiffs' further argument that it should examine the defendants' motive—as opposed to their intent or purpose. As Justice Stevens, concurring, observed, the courts ought not "invalidate otherwise legitimate action simply because an improper motive affected the deliberation of a participant in the decisional process. A law conscripting clerics should not be invalidated because an atheist voted for it."[26]

Note that statutes may, and often do, make discriminatory action unlawful on proof of disparate impact alone, without proof of discriminatory intent. Title VII of the 1964 Civil Rights Act[27] so provides in the context of employment discrimination. In the environmental justice area itself, the EPA's Title VI regulations likewise dispense with the need to prove intent to discriminate. (See Chapter 3, "Other Civil Rights Titles.")

Village of Arlington Heights: Circumstantial Proof of Intent

Following *Washington v. Davis,* described in the previous subsection, the Supreme Court in 1977 reaffirmed the need to prove a discriminatory purpose in equal protection cases asserting discrimination based on race. In *Village of Arlington Heights v. Metropolitan Housing Development Co.,*[28] one-family zoning in a Chicago suburb was challenged as racially motivated since it excluded apartments. The plaintiff, which sought permission to build racially integrated multifamily buildings, claimed the village's denial of permission to rezone its parcel constituted racial discrimination.

However, the Supreme Court found a lack of either direct or circumstantial evidence of an intent to discriminate based on race. Noting that "[t]he legislative or administrative history may be highly relevant," it ruled there was no proof that the refusal to rezone was racially motivated. The property had been zoned one-family when zoning was enacted two decades earlier. Had the village rezoned the parcel from multifamily to one-family when it became aware of the plan for integrated housing, the Court observed, "we would have a far different case." Similarly, "[d]epartures from the normal procedural sequence also might afford evidence [of] improper purposes." But none of this was present. And without evidence of racially discriminatory intent, the rezoning should be sustained, it ruled, as long as it is supported by a rational basis.

It is noteworthy, however, that following dismissal of the equal protection claim, the plaintiffs succeeded in showing that the racially disparate impact of the zoning violated the Fair Housing Act.[29]

As indicated in *Arlington Heights,* the courts make clear in interpreting the Equal Protection Clause that the requisite showing of intent to discriminate may be proven circumstantially. This may be accomplished either by showing that a law seemingly neutral on its face either has been applied in a discriminatory fashion or was in fact enacted with a discriminatory purpose.

Discriminatory Enforcement

Proof of discriminatory enforcement of a neutral statute has sufficed to show a violation of equal protection since the 1886 decision in *Yick*

Wo v. Hopkins.[30] A San Francisco local ordinance barred laundries from operating in wooden buildings because of the risk of fire. But this neutral law was enforced solely against persons of Chinese ancestry. Of 320 laundries in the city, all but ten built of wood, 240 were owned by Chinese, and of those over 150 had been prosecuted under the ordinance. In contrast, not one of the other 80 had been charged. The Supreme Court unanimously reversed the conviction, holding "the conclusion cannot be resisted that no reason for [the discrimination] exists except hostility to [the defendant's] race and nationality."

Similarly, the exercise of peremptory challenges to jurors to exclude all jurors of a particular race or national origin violates equal protection.[31] Here, too, a law neutral on its face may be unconstitutional as applied, if sufficient proof exists.

However, statistical proof of disparity is not enough unless it supports an inference of intent to discriminate. For example, proof that over four times as many defendants in Georgia were sentenced to death where the murder victim was white rather than black was ruled insufficient to prove purposeful racial discrimination.[32] As the Court noted, "each particular decision to impose the death penalty is made by a [jury] unique in its composition" and "rest[s] on consideration of innumerable factors that vary according to the characteristics of the individual defendant and the facts of the particular capital offense." There was no concerted purpose to discriminate as in *Yick Wo* or in the use of peremptory challenges by a particular prosecutor.

Other Circumstantial Proof of Intent

A law that appears neutral may be shown to have been enacted with a racially hostile purpose. In *Gomillion v. Lightfoot,*[33] the Alabama legislature altered the boundaries of the largely black city of Tuskegee to exclude nearly all of its black voters. This blatant racial gerrymander was found to lead, if proven at trial, to a "conclusion [that] would be irresistible, tantamount for all practical purposes to a mathematical demonstration, that the legislation is solely concerned with . . . fencing Negro citizens out of town . . . to deprive them of their preexisting municipal vote."

Another dramatic instance is *Lane v. Wilson.*[34] After the Supreme Court had held in a 1915 case[35] that Oklahoma's law requiring literacy tests for voters, but exempting those whose grandfathers had voted, discriminated based on race, the state passed a law allowing all voters already registered to be permanently eligible to vote. All others, though, had to register within 12 days or be rendered permanently ineligible to vote. The Court found the barely concealed racially discriminatory intent and set the law aside as violative of the

Fifteenth Amendment (which bars states from denying the vote based on race).

As these cases show, the requisite showing of intent to discriminate may be proven if the circumstantial evidence is strong—like the proverbial proof that milk was watered by finding "a trout in the milk."

Recent Cases

The Supreme Court has most recently considered these issues in *Crawford-El v. Britton*,[36] a First Amendment suit brought under 42 U.S.C. § 1983. The plaintiff claimed that while he was being transferred from one prison to another the defendant corrections officer intentionally misdirected his clothing and legal materials, "to punish him for exercising his First Amendment rights and to deter similar conduct in the future." He sued to recover the costs incurred by the delay and for emotional distress. Since the plaintiff had to prove an intent to deprive him of his First Amendment right of free speech, the District of Columbia Circuit Court of Appeals held he had to prove this unconstitutional motive by clear and convincing proof. The Supreme Court reversed, holding that was too high a hurdle for plaintiffs in such suits. It pointed out that the unjustifiable heightened standard would govern equal protection claims as well. It distinguished earlier rulings that mandated a heightened standard to overcome a qualified immunity defense,[37] noting that those cases "provide[] no support for making any change in the nature of the plaintiff's burden of proving a constitutional violation." That burden continues to be the conventional one of proving intent to discriminate by a preponderance of the evidence. In addition, the plaintiff must show that the government's action lacks a rational basis, unless, as discussed earlier in the subsection "Strict Scrutiny for Racial Discrimination" (page 6), strict scrutiny is required.

Environmental Justice Suits Asserting Denial of Equal Protection

Several federal courts have looked at environmental justice claims based on denial of equal protection and, using the need to prove discriminatory intent and related issues discussed earlier in this chapter, essentially rejected those claims.

Bean v. Southwestern Waste Management

The first important decision based on an equal protection claim in the environmental justice area, *Bean v. Southwestern Waste Management Corp.*,[38] concerned a challenge to a state permit for a solid waste landfill on the outskirts of Houston. The plaintiffs asserted the permit approval was part of a pattern of discrimination by the Texas Department of Health (TDH) in approving solid waste sites. However, the data showed 59 percent of the 17 such sites in Houston were in areas of under 25 percent minority population when the facilities opened, and 82 percent were in areas then less than 50 percent minority. Even in the immediate area surrounding the site, the only other site approved by TDH was in a census tract less than 10 percent minority when it opened.

The plaintiffs offered further proof that over two thirds (68 percent) of Houston's solid waste sites were in the city's eastern half, where 62 percent of its minority population lives. But, as the court found, many of these sites were licensed by a different agency, the Texas Department of Water Resources, and were located there "because that is where Houston's industry is, not because that is where Houston's minority population is." Besides, the proportion of total sites approved by both agencies in fact closely paralleled the racial mix: 42.3 percent of the sites were in the 42.5 percent of tracts with a largely minority population, and 57.7 percent were in the 57.5 percent of largely nonminority tracts.

For these reasons the court ruled the plaintiffs' proof fell far short of the substantial likelihood of success needed for the preliminary injunction they sought (see Chapter 14, "Stopping or Building New Facilities"). Although the court criticized TDH for approving a site close to a high school and residential neighborhood, it denied the preliminary injunction sought on a racial discrimination claim. The Fifth Circuit affirmed without opinion. The proof fell short of the "smoking gun" proof of race hostility mandated by *Washington v. Davis* and *Arlington Heights* (see pages 6–8).

East Bibb Twiggs v. Macon Planning and Zoning Commission

A decade after *Bean, East Bibb Twiggs Neighborhood Association v. Macon-Bibb County Planning and Zoning Commission*[39] was decided. Like *Bean,* it involved an equal protection suit to enjoin a landfill in a largely minority community. And, as in *Bean,* the attempt failed, this time after trial. Although the Planning and Zoning Commission had approved this site to dispose of wood waste from a tree service—a relatively benign form of solid waste—the only other private landfill in the county was in a heavily white area.

The Commission had originally denied the tree service's application since the site was near a residential area. It then approved an amended application that prohibited the burning of waste and open dumping and increased the buffer zone protecting nearby residences from its original 100 feet to 150 feet.

The court found no intent to discriminate here. It noted that the location of the only other private landfill in a predominantly white neighborhood "tend[s] to undermine the development of a 'clear pattern, unexplainable on grounds other than race . . .'" (quoting from *Arlington Heights*).

In addition, there was found to be no pattern of locating unwanted land uses in minority areas, as the plaintiffs contended. The court pointed out that the Commission does not solicit landfill applications, but "reacts to applications from private landowners"—though that seems immaterial to the plaintiffs' claims. Again as in *Bean*, the court refused to consider objectionable land uses approved by agencies other than the defendant. Perhaps the plaintiffs in both suits should have sued the state or county governments more generally—though that would likely have led to motions to dismiss the agencies not directly responsible for the challenged permits. In addition, suit against the state itself in *Bean*, as opposed to its Department of Health, might have run afoul of the Eleventh Amendment, which bars direct suits against states in federal courts.[40]

The court also rejected the plaintiffs' reliance on the Commission's land-use study recognizing that racial discrimination in housing existed in the county, noting that "[t]he Commission's recognition of the situation does not constitute its adoption. Indeed, such recognition probably encourages that Commission to exercise vigilance in guarding against such unprincipled influence."

Finally, the court turned away claims of deviations from the Commission's normal procedures and statements by commissioners as evidence of an intent to discriminate. These issues are discussed later in this chapter, in subsections entitled "Shifts in Procedure" and "Statements by Officials or Witnesses," pages 17–18.

The Court of Appeals affirmed, holding the plaintiffs failed to prove either specific intent to discriminate or a history of discrimination by the Commission.[41]

R.I.S.E. v. Kay

A third important equal protection decision, also concerning a landfill, was *R.I.S.E., Inc. v. Kay*.[42] The plaintiff organization, an acronym for Residents Involved in Saving the Environment, contended the county board of supervisors denied its members equal protection when it granted a permit for a regional landfill in a predominantly black northern Virginia community. The plaintiffs viewed this as the most recent in a series of landfills established in minority areas. The current facility, privately run but agreeing to accept the county's waste, was to be in an area 64 percent black. The three smaller county landfills it was to replace were in areas 95 percent to 100 percent black. Another private landfill, King Land, had operated for a year, until closed by the county for zoning and environmental violations, and in a mainly white district.

The court, as in *Bean* and *East Bibb*, found the landfill's opponents had failed to prove purposeful racial discrimination. It held "[t]he Board's opposition to the King Land landfill and its approval of the proposed landfill was [sic] based not on the racial composition of the respective neighborhoods . . . but on the relative environmental suitability of the sites." The court emphasized King Land's repeated ignoring of environmental and safety concerns, which led to its closure. Nor was there any unusual procedure before the Board that might imply deliberate bias.

Other Decisions

Two more recent decisions similarly rejected equal protection environmental claims. *Boyd v. Browner*[43] was a suit by black residents of an area in Texarkana, Texas, found to be contaminated with toxic chemicals. The federal government offered to purchase their land at its value as if it were not contaminated, and wrote each home owner:

> If we are unable to negotiate a direct purchase from you, it will be necessary to acquire the property through condemnation proceedings . . . based on the value of the property [at] its actual condition [reflecting] the fact that the property is located within an environmentally unsafe area. This, in all probability, would lower the appraised value of your property.

The plaintiffs regarded these letters as "threats" that, they asserted, "had not been made to residents of non-minority communities," such as Times Beach, Missouri, where homes on contaminated land were also purchased by the government. But, as the plaintiffs themselves conceded, there were "differences in offers, acquisition practices or other dissimilarities" at those sites. The court therefore found that they had failed to satisfy the basic requirement that persons similarly situated be treated differently (see text on pages 3–4 and accompanying n.5). In addition, the court added in dicta that they had failed to offer any proof of intent to discriminate, since the letters were "nonthreatening." It granted summary judgment to the defendant government officials, and the Court of Appeals affirmed with an unpublished explanatory memorandum.

Rozar v. Mullis[44] again involved a county landfill, this one in Georgia. However, the plaintiffs' equal protection arguments misfired. Their claims against the county, which had assertedly rejected a site in a white area and voted to build the landfill in a black one, were found to be time-barred. (This issue is discussed on pages

19–20, "Statute of Limitations"). Their remaining claims against state officials were then held, though timely, dismissable since they had failed to assert discrimination while the state agency was considering the permit required for the landfill; and, in any event, the county chose the site. The state merely examined its technical suitability. The court ruled the plaintiffs failed even to claim, let alone show, a pattern of intentional discrimination.

Proving Intent

Several avenues lead to the required proof of intent to discriminate discussed in "The Need to Prove Intent to Discriminate," pages 6–10. Justice Powell's opinion in *Arlington Heights* enumerates several of these: circumstantial proof of sufficiently disparate impact, discrimination in applying statutory criteria, shifts in agency procedure, and statements evincing an intent to discriminate. These are all, if proven, ways of meeting this burden.[45] This subsection examines each of these four elements.

Greatly Disparate Impact

As the Supreme Court held in *Yick Wo* and *Gomillion,* described on pages 8–10, a sufficiently disparate impact on different races is strong circumstantial proof of intent to discriminate. In *Yick Wo,* prosecuting 150 of 240 Chinese and none of 80 of other races was such clearly selective enforcement that it proved a denial of equal protection. Likewise, the blatant gerrymandering of city boundaries in *Gomillion* to deprive virtually all the city's black residents of the vote constituted proof of intent to discriminate.

This sort of proof of egregious disparity has been hard to adduce in equal protection-based environmental justice cases. In *Bean* (pages 10–11) the landfills licensed by the defendant agency were shown to be chiefly in nonminority neighborhoods when opened. Although 68 percent of Houston's total number of solid waste disposal sites (including several licensed by another agency) were in the predominantly minority eastern half of the city, the court found that was so "because that is where Houston's industry is, not because that is where Houston's minority population is."

Similarly, in *East Bibb* (pages 11–12) the two landfills in the area were evenly split—one in a mainly minority neighborhood, the other not. The court again did not weigh the impact of other assertedly noxious land uses permitted by agencies other than the defendant planning and zoning commission. These cases show the unwillingness of courts to examine general land use patterns in suits claiming a denial of equal protection, where the plaintiff must prove intent to discriminate on the part of the defendant agency, not society generally. The courts have consistently held that societal discrimination (or discrimination by other agencies) does not constitute proof of a denial of equal protection by a particular governmental entity. The Supreme Court so held in *Personnel Administrator of Massachusetts v. Feeney*,[46] rejecting a claim that a civil service test preference for veterans discriminated against females, and stating "[t]he enlistment policies of the Armed Services may well have discriminated on the basis of sex. But the history of discrimination against women in the military is not on trial in this case."

The best-documented factual showing of disparate impact in an environmental justice suit based on equal protection was in *R.I.S.E v. Kay* (pages 12–13). Here all three existing county landfills were in overwhelmingly minority communities, and the one designed to replace all three was also in a mainly minority area. Only one short-lived private landfill had been in a chiefly white community, and the plaintiffs argued its prompt closure was itself proof of discriminatory intent. But the court nonetheless found the closure of that landfill and selection of the new one challenged by the plaintiffs were based not on race but on their environmental suitability.

In contrast, proof of severely disparate impact has sufficed to show a denial of equal protection in suits about unequal municipal services. In *Hawkins v. Town of Shaw*,[47] a showing that 98 percent of homes on unpaved streets were lived in by blacks, where the total population was 60 percent black, made out an equal protection claim. Similarly, 99 percent of whites and 80 percent of blacks were served by sanitary sewers—again sufficient proof of a denial of equal protection. Likewise, in *Ammons v. Dade City*[48] proof that 29.5 percent of streets in black neighborhoods were unpaved, as against 18.1 percent in white areas, was held to show a denial of equal protection. While 28 percent of white homes lacked sewers, 50 percent of black homes were without them. The court enjoined these failures to furnish paved streets and sewers, inferring the required intent to discriminate.

Discrimination in Applying Statutory Standards

The environmental justice suits asserting denial of equal protection have thus far failed to show discrimination in applying statutory standards for locating landfills and the like sufficient to trigger a violation of the Clause. In *Boyd v. Browner* (page 13), the plaintiffs claimed the letters they received from the government with a take-it-or-leave-it condemnation offer were more threatening than those sent in non-minority areas. In the end, though, they acknowledged that "dissimilarities" existed at those sites so that comparison was useless. And in *R.I.S.E. v. Kay* (pages 12–13), the closing of a landfill in a white community shortly before approving one in a minority area was, the court found, "based not on the racial composition of the respective neighborhoods . . . but on the relative environmental suitability of the sites."

In *Beasley v. Potter*,[49] a court similarly turned away claims of racial bias in zoning where the plaintiffs asserted different standards were applied to them. An asphalt company owned by blacks, denied permission to build a plant, contended a white-owned company had been granted a permit under the same zoning ordinance. However, the court emphasized that unlike the white-owned company, the plaintiffs sought to build in an agricultural district. In addition, the white-owned plant antedated the zoning and was a protected nonconforming use.

Again, in *Walker v. City of Bogalusa*,[50] a claim was rejected that police and fire department officials denied equal protection to the plaintiffs by evacuating black residents after whites following a chemical leak from a freight car. The record showed areas downwind of the leak were evacuated first, and these areas happened to be predominantly white. Blacks were evacuated from schools and shopping centers in these areas along with whites. The areas not immediately threatened were evacuated later. There was no showing that "the decisionmaker selected . . . a particular course of action at least in part 'because of,' not merely 'in spite of' its adverse effects upon a particular group."[51]

However, suits claiming discrimination in providing housing and other governmental services have succeeded on proof that the locality employed the same criteria differently. For example, *United States v. Yonkers Board of Education*[52] enjoined municipal housing policies where, using the same statutory standards, "over a period of more than three decades, the City approved no [public] housing for minorities in any area that was not in or close to an already heavily minority area." And in *Atkins v. Robinson*,[53] a county vetoed an application to build a low-income housing development that would have largely housed minority members, though the county had much substandard housing, disregarding national and state criteria that likely would have justified the development.

Shifts in Procedure

Arlington Heights (pages 6–8) expressly noted that "[d]epartures from the normal procedural sequence also might afford evidence that improper purposes are playing a role" in decision-making. Proof of this was attempted in *East Bibb* (pages 11–12), but was found wanting. The plaintiffs there contended the Planning and Zoning Commission sought the views of city and county officials concerning the proposed landfill. The court, however, credited the statements of the commissioners that they had "concerns about accountability to the public for certain controversial governmental decisions and about centralized planning for the area's present and future waste disposal problems." Similarly, the fact that the Commission first denied the application and then granted it on rehearing was not, without more, the sort of procedural departure that would support an inference of discriminatory intent.

This is in contrast to the *Yonkers* case (page 16) where the city rezoned parcels as soon as the prospect of public housing surfaced. Maneuvers by Southern cities and counties to evade public school desegregation, including imaginative techniques such as tuition grants to private "academies" and "freedom-of-choice" plans allowing whites to skirt integrated schools,[54] are other instances of novel departures from standard operating procedures that properly drew inferences of racially discriminatory intent. Similarly, in *Ammons* (page 15), city officials who had consistently paid to pave streets in white neighborhoods told black residents the home owners would have to advance the funds for paving.

Statements by Officials or Witnesses

A final method of proving intent is through the mouths of public officials themselves, or of witnesses at hearings. The Supreme Court decision in *Arlington Heights* (page 8) explicitly declared "highly relevant" the "contemporary statements by members of the decisionmaking body, minutes of its meetings," and the like. The Court noted, however, the difficulty in actually requiring officials to testify in suits asserting denials of equal protection. It suggested that actual testimony be limited to "extraordinary instances," since "such testimony frequently will be barred by privilege" and, in any event, would "represent a substantial intrusion into the workings of other branches of government[,] 'usually to be avoided.'"

In *East Bibb* (pages 11–12) the court remained unpersuaded by evidence that came from statements of the decisionmaking commissioners that, the plaintiffs argued, proved a discriminatory purpose. These statements focused on the commission's reversal on rehearing of its original denial of the landfill permit. However, the commissioners' statements, typified by a comment that the site "is an adequate site and in my most difficult decision to date I will vote to support the resolution," were found to buttress the commission's insistence that its decision was not racially motivated.

Similarly, in *Kawaoka v. City of Arroyo Grande*,[55] a city's temporary moratorium on water use in subdivision developments was held not discriminatory as applied to a property owner of Japanese ancestry, despite a council member's comment that "[W]hy should these Japanese people make all that money?" The court found this remark insufficient without proof that other council members were racially motivated. The vote for the moratorium had been unanimous, and the court held it to be justified by the city's stated reasons to preserve agriculture and its small-town ambiance, as well as water conservation.

Likewise, in *Board of Managers of Glen Mills Schools v. West Chester Areas School District*,[56] a court rejected claims of racial animus when a school board refused to sell an unused building to a private school for delinquents, primarily black and Latino. The court was not persuaded by testimony that a student from the private school had been caught undressing in a bedroom of a nearby home, which led to an "uproar" by local residents. (Though it dismissed the school's equal protection claims, the court allowed a related due process claim of "arbitrary use of government power" to go to trial.)

Contrast this with some of the flagrant statements in other cases. In *Ammons v. Dade City*,[57] city officials said the "black community just doesn't need more drainage." In *United States v. Yonkers Board of Education*[58] "[v]irtually all councilmen from East Yonkers stated that they were concerned about community opposition to low-income housing in their areas; many acknowledged explicitly that that opposition was race related." One council member testified that some constituents told him "they didn't want the housing because they didn't want any blacks there."

As public officials become more aware of, and more acclimated to, environmental justice issues, the likelihood of this sort of direct testimony will probably diminish.

Procedural Issues

Federal and State Courts

Equal protection claims may be litigated in both state and federal courts.[59] They may be joined, most appropriately in state courts, with claims based on the equal protection provisions of state constitutions. This issue is discussed in Chapter 5, "State Environmental Justice Programs and Related Authorities." It should be remembered, though, that the states are free to construe their own constitutional provisions safeguarding individual rights more broadly (though not more narrowly) than the federal courts have interpreted the United States Constitution.[60]

As a dramatic example, state courts in several states have ruled, in contrast to the United States Supreme Court, that the unequal funding of public schools from districts with varying amounts of taxable real property amounts to a denial of equal protection under state constitutional guarantees.[61]

Most environmental justice suits, however, have been brought in federal courts where equal protection contentions may be readily joined with claims under Civil Rights Act Title VI, the Fair Housing Act, the Presidential Executive Order, and the like (see Chapters 2–4).

Asserting Equal Protection Claims

The most common procedural vehicle for the assertion of equal protection claims is a suit under 42 U.S.C. § 1983. This statute, enacted in 1871, makes any "person who, under color of any statute, ordinance, regulation, custom, or usage, of any State . . . , subjects, or causes to be subjected, any citizen . . . to the deprivation of any rights . . . secured by the Constitution and laws, . . . liable . . . in an action at law [or] equity . . ."

Section 1983 may be used in an action against a municipality[62] or a state agency.[63] The Eleventh Amendment bars any suit in federal court by a person or corporation against a state; but, as discussed in the subsection on *East Bibb* at n. 40 (see pages 11–12), since the Supreme Court's 1908 decision in *Ex Parte Young,* state officials and agencies may be sued in federal courts, although not the state itself. Although the Eleventh Amendment generally prevents recovering damages against states,[64] injunctive relief is available, and damages have been awarded as well in actions under statutes, such as Title VII of the Civil Rights Act of 1964,[65] which were enacted to enforce the Fourteenth Amendment.[66]

Public officials are clothed in varying degrees of immunity from suits for damages. Most have qualified immunity, protecting them from actions unless their conduct was willful.[67] Judges, as well as prosecutors and other law enforcement officials, have absolute immunity from damages.[68] Most environmental justice suits, however, seek injunctive relief or the annulment of agency determinations, not damages. In these cases, the Eleventh Amendment is not a bar as long as the suit is brought against a municipality or a state official or agency.

Although Section 1983 does not apply to suits against federal officials, the Supreme Court has recognized equivalent claims under federal common law, governed by essentially the same standards.[69]

Statute of Limitations

Actions under Section 1983 are subject to the state's statute of limitations.[70] In general, the statute governing tort actions for personal injury applies. Statutes imposing shorter periods of limitation for suits against public officials are not applicable.[71] The action accrues when the plaintiff knows, or has reason to know, of the injury.[72]

In Section 1983 suits relating to the use of real property, as most environmental justice actions are, the period of limitations runs from the making of the final decision with regard to the parcel.[73]

Standing

While issues relating to standing are dealt with in detail in Chapter 11, "Evidentiary Issues," it is appropriate to briefly discuss them here as well, since the Supreme Court has had much to say on this complex subject.

In general, standing to raise constitutional claims requires a showing of actual or imminent injury. The injury need not be pecuniary, but it must be direct. For example, parents of public school students may not challenge the failure of the Internal Revenue Service to adopt standards by which to deny tax-exempt status to segregated schools. Even though the parents asserted that this impeded the desegregation of the schools their children attended, the Supreme Court found the harm not directly enough related to the claimed unlawful conduct.[74]

On the other hand, after Congress explicitly forbade racial discrimination in housing, a claim based on the plaintiff's interest in residing in a racially integrated community was held sufficient to confer standing.[75]

An organization, such as the plaintiffs in *East Bibb* and *R.I.S.E.* (pages 11–13), may assert injury on behalf of its members. But the group must show actual or threatened injury to those members.[76] This rule has been held to confer standing on civil rights organizations.[77] On the other hand, injury to an organization does not, without more, provide standing to its executive director to bring suit.[78]

Notes

* The author is indebted to Lisa Chun (St. John's Law School 2000) for research assistance in preparing this chapter.

1. U.S. CONST., amend. XIV, § 1.
2. Evans v. Abney, 396 U.S. 435 (1970).
3. Shelley v. Kraemer, 334 U.S. 1 (1948).
4. Washington v. Davis, 426 U.S. 229 (1976); Buckley v. Valeo, 424 U.S. 1 (1976).
5. Plyler v. Doe, 457 U.S. 202, 216 (1982).
6. The Slaughter-House Cases, 83 U.S. 36, 72 (1872).
7. Gulf, C. & S. F. Ry. Co. v. Ellis, 165 U.S. 150 (1897).

8. 100 U.S. 303 (1879).

9. 163 U.S. 537 (1896).

10. 347 U.S. 483 (1954).

11. *See, e.g.*, Regents of University of California v. Bakke, 438 U.S. 265 (1978); Adarand Constructors, Inc. v. Pena, 515 U.S. 200 (1995).

12. Pruneyard Shopping Center v. Robins, 447 U.S. 74 (1980).

13. Railway Express Agency, Inc. v. People of State of New York, 336 U.S. 106 (1949).

14. Federal Communications Commission v. Beach Communications, Inc., 508 U.S. 307 (1993).

15. *Id.* at 314, *quoting* United States Railroad Retirement Board v. Fritz, 449 U.S. 166, 179 (1980).

16. 473 U.S. 432 (1985).

17. 304 U.S. 144, 153, n.4 (1938).

18. Justice Lewis Powell, *Carolene Products Revisited*, 82 COLUM. L. REV. 1087 (1982).

19. *See supra* note 17.

20. Loving v. Virginia, 388 U.S. 1 (1967).

21. 347 U.S. 483 (1954).

22. Keyes v. School Dist. No. 1, 413 U.S. 189 (1973) (racially gerrymandered school district lines); Swann v. Charlotte-Mecklenburg Bd. of Educ., 402 U.S. 1 (1971) (Court directed racial quotas until vestiges of segregation ended).

23. *Loving, supra* note 20.

24. United States v. Fordice, 505 U.S. 717 (1992).

25. 426 U.S. 229 (1976).

26. *See also* United States v. O'Brien, 391 U.S. 367, 383 (1968); Michael M. v. Superior Court, 450 U.S. 464, 472 n.7 (1981).

27. 42 U.S.C.A. §§ 2000e–2000e(17).

28. 429 U.S. 252 (1977).

29. Metropolitan Housing Development Co. v. Village of Arlington Heights., 558 F.2d 1283 (7th Cir. 1977), *cert. denied*, 434 U.S. 1025 (1978). The Fair Housing Act is codified at 42 U.S.C.A. §§ 3601–3631.

30. 118 U.S. 356 (1886).

31. Batson v. Kentucky, 476 U.S. 79 (1986).

32. McCleskey v. Kemp, 481 U.S. 279 (1987).

33. 364 U.S. 339 (1960).

34. 307 U.S. 268 (1939).

35. Guinn v. United States, 238 U.S. 347 (1915).

36. 118 S. Ct. 1584 (1998).

37. *See* Harlow v. Fitzgerald, 457 U.S. 800 (1982).

38. 482 F. Supp. 673 (S.D. Tex. 1979), *aff'd without opinion*, 782 F.2d 1038 (5th Cir. 1986).

39. 706 F. Supp. 880 (M.D.Ga. 1989), *aff'd*, 896 F.2d 1264 (11th Cir. 1989).

40. Seminole Tribe v. Florida, 116 S. Ct. 1114 (1996). *Ex Parte Young*, 209 U.S. 123 (1908), allowed suits against state officials, as opposed to the state itself.

41. 896 F.2d 1264, 1267 (11th Cir. 1989).

42. 768 F. Supp. 1144 (E.D.Va. 1991), *aff'd without opinion*, 977 F.2d 573 (4th Cir. 1992).

43. 897 F. Supp. 590 (D.D.C. 1995), *aff'd,* 107 F.3d 922 (D.C. Cir. 1996), *cert. denied,* 118 S. Ct. 364 (1997).

44. 85 F.3d 556 (11th Cir. 1996).

45. *See Arlington Heights, supra* note 28, 429 U.S. at 266–68.

46. 442 U.S. 256, 278 (1979).

47. 437 F.2d 1286 (5th Cir. 1971), *aff'd en banc,* 461 F.2d 1171 (5th Cir. 1972).

48. 594 F. Supp. 1274 (M.D. Fla. 1984), *aff'd,* 783 F.2d 982 (11th Cir. 1986).

49. 493 F. Supp. 1059 (W.D. Mich. 1980).

50. 1997 WL 423102 (E.D. La. 1997).

51. *Feeney, supra* note 46, 442 U.S. at 279.

52. 837 F.2d 1181, 1220 (2d Cir. 1987), *cert. denied,* 486 U.S. 1055 (1988).

53. 545 F. Supp. 852 (E.D. Va. 1982), *aff'd,* 733 F.2d 318 (4th Cir. 1984).

54. Griffin v. Prince Edward County Bd. of Educ., 377 U.S. 218 (1964); Green v. County School Bd., 391 U.S. 430 (1968).

55. 17 F.3d 1227 (9th Cir. 1994), *cert. denied,* 513 U.S. 870 (1994).

56. 838 F. Supp. 1035 (E.D. Pa. 1993), *reversed in part, aff'd in part without opinion,* 52 F.3d 313 (3d Cir. 1995).

57. *Supra* note 48.

58. *Supra* note 52.

59. *See* Coffman v. Wilson Police Dept., 739 F. Supp. 257 (E.D. Pa. 1990); Gumpl v. Bost, 611 N.E.2d 343 (Ohio App. 1992), *cert. denied,* 510 U.S. 1055 (1994).

60. *See* note 12 and accompanying text.

61. *See* San Antonio Independent School Dist. v. Rodriguez, 411 U.S. 1 (1973) (rejecting argument under Fourteenth Amendment); Serrano v. Priest, 487 P.2d 1241 (Calif. 1971); Edgewood School Dist. v. Kirby, 777 S.W.2d 391 (Tex. 1989).

62. Monell v. Department of Social Services, 436 U.S. 658 (1978).

63. United States v. Gillock, 445 U.S. 360 (1980).

64. Quern v. Jordan, 440 U.S. 332 (1979).

65. 42 U.S.C.A. §§ 2000e–2000e(17).

66. Fitzpatrick v. Bitzer, 427 U.S. 445 (1976).

67. Scheuer v. Rhodes, 416 U.S. 232 (1974).

68. Imbler v. Pachtman, 424 U.S. 409 (1976).

69. Bivens v. Six Unknown Named Agents, 403 U.S. 388 (1971).

70. Owens v. Okure, 488 U.S. 235 (1989).

71. Meiselman v. Richardson, 743 F. Supp. 143 (E.D.N.Y. 1990).

72. Clay v. LaPorta, 815 F. Supp. 911 (E.D. Va. 1993), *aff'd,* 36 F.3d 1091 (4th Cir. 1994).

73. Norco Construction, Inc. v. King County, 801 F.2d 1143 (9th Cir. 1986).

74. Allen v. Wright, 468 U.S. 737 (1984).

75. Trafficante v. Metropolitan Life Ins. Co., 409 U.S. 205 (1972).

76. Sierra Club v. Morton, 405 U.S. 727 (1972).

77. NAACP v. Button, 371 U.S. 415 (1963).

78. North Florida Educational Development Corp. v. Woodham, 942 F. Supp. 542 (N.D. Fla. 1996).

CHAPTER 2

Title VI

BRADFORD C. MANK

Introduction

Title VI of the Civil Rights Act of 1964,[1] which forbids discrimination by programs receiving federal financial assistance, offers the best opportunity for private citizens to bring environmental inequity challenges against state or local agencies. Because virtually every state environmental agency receives some funding from the EPA, almost all state permit decisions are potentially subject to Title VI's jurisdiction. Title VI cases are typically brought against state or local government recipient agencies rather than private permit applicants, but challenges to environmental permits also indirectly involve the permittee who has received initial approval for siting a facility. Title VI does not normally apply directly against federal agencies.

Section 601[2] of Title VI has been ineffective at preventing environmental inequities because the Supreme Court has held that both Section 601 of Title VI and the Equal Protection Clause require proof of discriminatory intent, and environmental justice plaintiffs usually cannot prove that government or industry has consciously discriminated against minority groups.[3] In *Guardians Ass'n v. Civil Service Commission,* a deeply divided Supreme Court ruled that Section 601 of Title VI requires proof of intentional discrimination, but that federal grant agencies may promulgate regulations under Section 602[4] prohibiting recipient state or local agencies from engaging in practices causing discriminatory effects.[5]

Pursuant to Section 602 of Title VI, a number of federal agencies have promulgated Title VI implementing regulations that prohibit recipient agencies from engaging in practices or distributing funds in ways that cause disparate impacts.[6] The EPA has promulgated regulations under Section 602 of Title VI that prohibit recipient agencies from engaging in practices creating discriminatory effects or locating a facility where it will have discriminatory effects, including state agencies granting environmental permits.[7] EPA's Title VI regulations offer the best way to bring legal challenges to state or local permits on environmental justice grounds.

It is unclear, however, whether agency regulations based on Section 602 of Title VI create private rights of action allowing plaintiffs to file suit in federal courts, or merely allow the public to file an administrative complaint with a federal agency that is subject to very limited judicial review of the agency's administrative decision.[8] In *Guardians,* the Supreme Court clearly recognized a private right of action under Section 601 of the statute, but did not explicitly address whether there is a similar right under Section 602 regulations. In 1998, the Supreme Court in *Seif v. Chester Residents Concerned for Quality Living* granted certiorari to examine the issue of private lawsuits under Section 602, but the case became moot before the Court could decide the issue.[9]

Regardless of how courts eventually resolve the contentious issue of whether there are private rights of action under EPA's Title VI regulations, citizens can still file an administrative complaint with EPA. In February 1998, EPA promulgated a controversial *Interim Guidance for Investigating Title VI Administrative Complaints Challenging Permits* (*Interim Guidance*) to help the agency resolve a number of pending complaints.[10] In the wake of widespread criticism of the *Interim Guidance,* EPA has promised to issue a revised Title VI guidance in 1999. The revised Guidance will likely have major impact on how the EPA addresses Title VI complaints.

Title VI

Because they have been unsuccessful so far in winning environmental discrimination claims under the Equal Protection Clause, environmental justice advocates are now filing most challenges under Title VI. No Title VI action challenging a recipient agency's approval of a permit for a polluting or disposal facility has yet reached a final decision, but there are several pending administrative complaints before EPA.

The Basic Structure of Title VI

Under Title VI, federal agencies and departments may not provide funding to programs that discriminate on the basis of race.[11] Section 602 of the statute requires every federal agency or department to promulgate regulations that specify how the agency will determine whether grant applicants or recipients are engaging in racially discriminatory practices, and also provide a process for investigating and reviewing complaints of racial discrimination filed with the agency.[12] In 1964, a presidential task force working in conjunction with the Department of Justice, which had helped draft the language of Title VI, issued model Title VI enforcement regulations mandating that recipients of federal funds not use "'criteria or methods of administration which have the *effect* of subjecting individuals to discrimination,'"[13] and shortly thereafter "every Cabinet department and about forty agencies adopted Title VI regulations prohibiting disparate-impact discrimination."[14]

Title VI applies where federal funding is given to an intermediary nonfederal entity that distributes this funding to ultimate beneficiaries, but does not apply to federal programs such as Social Security that pay benefits directly to individual beneficiaries.[15] A typical intermediary grant recipient is a state agency that in turn provides funding to a wide range of beneficiaries, including individuals, local or state governments, nonprofit organizations, or private industry.[16] Title VI applies to recipients as long as they are in a position to accept or reject the funding.[17] While a state may refuse federal funding, if it chooses to accept such funding, it may not invoke its Eleventh Amendment immunity to bar Title VI immunity in cases in which a state is a defendant as long as the state accepts any federal funding.[18] If any program of a state or local government agency receives any federal assistance, Title VI governs the entire agency.[19]

The EPA's Title VI Regulations

EPA's Disparate Impact Regulations

The EPA currently provides several billion dollars of federal funding under 44 different programs to about 1,500 recipients, including virtually all state or regional siting or permitting agencies, and, accordingly, Title VI clearly applies to these agencies.[20] Many local water supply or solid waste programs, however, receive no federal funding and are exempt from Title VI's jurisdiction.[21]

From 1970 to 1973, recipients of EPA funding were governed by the Title VI regulations adopted by the agency or department that had been responsible for the program before President Nixon created the EPA in 1970.[22] In 1973, the EPA adopted its own Title VI regulations, which prohibited a recipient from engaging in actions having discriminatory effects.[23] In 1981, the agency proposed to amend these regulations to express the same discriminatory effects standard "in simple language that preserves their original intent."[24] In 1984, the EPA promulgated amended regulations reiterating its historic policy of forbidding recipients from creating disparate impacts: "A recipient [of federal funds] shall not use criteria or methods of administration which have the effect of subjecting individuals to discrimination because of their race, color, [or] national origin."[25] In addition, EPA's regulations forbid a recipient to choose a site or locate a facility where it will have discriminatory effects.[26] Furthermore, EPA regulations mandate that state recipients maintain Title VI compliance programs addressing both discrimination by the state and any beneficiaries of state-administered funds.[27] Other federal agencies that may be involved in siting risky facilities have similar disparate impact regulations.[28]

EPA's Historical Failure to Enforce Title VI

Despite the broad antidiscriminatory language in the agency's Title VI regulations, from the early 1970s until 1993 the EPA avoided enforcing the statute against state or local recipient agencies because the agency argued that terminating grants to a discriminating recipient under Title VI would undermine its primary goal of providing financial assistance to state and local agencies to reduce pollution.[29] The EPA maintained this approach even though other federal agencies enforced Title VI.[30]

The Clinton Administration Use of Title VI to Promote Environmental Justice

In 1993, however, the newly elected Clinton administration announced that the EPA would enforce Title VI against recipients that engage in discrimination.[31] In 1994, the presidential memorandum accompanying Executive Order 12,898 required federal agencies providing funding to programs affecting human health or the environment to ensure that their grant recipients comply with Title VI, although the directive is not judicially enforceable and does not alter the standard of proof under the statute.[32] (The Executive Order is the subject of Chapter 4 of this book.)

In 1994, the EPA created an Office of Civil Rights to handle Title VI issues.[33] Between September 1993 and July 1998, 58 environmental justice complaints were filed with the agency, including 50 challenging state or local permit decisions.[34] As of July 1998, the EPA had rejected 31 of these complaints, was investigating 15, and was still considering the remaining 12 for investigation.[35]

The Office of Civil Rights has not had enough staff to respond to the increased number of complaints filed in recent years, and, as a result, the agency's Title VI investigations have sometimes remained unresolved for years.[36] However, in the recent *Select Steel* decision, which is discussed on pages 48–50 of this chapter, the EPA was able to make an expeditious decision.[37]

The EPA has taken steps to investigate Title VI complaints more efficiently. For example, in December 1997, the EPA added a new civil rights legal division within the agency's Office of General Counsel to deal exclusively with Title VI issues.[38] The centerpiece of the EPA's efforts to improve its Title VI investigations, however, is its controversial *Interim Guidance for Title VI*, which is discussed on pages 40–45 of this chapter.[39]

Administrative Complaints Under Title VI

Under EPA's Title VI regulations, there are both significant benefits and limitations to filing an administrative complaint.

Filing an Administrative Complaint

To file an administrative complaint with the EPA, a complainant need only file a simple letter alleging that a recipient is engaging in discriminatory practices. Accordingly, a lawyer is not essential to file a complaint.[40]

An administrative complaint must be filed within 180 days of the alleged discriminatory actions, but a complaint alleging a continuing violation is timely if the last incident occurred within 180 days.[41] Complainants can ask for a waiver of the 180-day time limit for good cause, but EPA is usually not receptive to waiver requests.[42] The Interim Guidance, however, explains that EPA will be more receptive to a "good cause" waiver request if the complaint was delayed because the complainants were exhausting the recipient's administrative remedies and the complaint is filed within a reasonable time, such as 60 days after the conclusion of the recipient's administrative appeal process.[43] If a complaint is filed before a recipient has completed the permit process, EPA will notify the recipient about the allegations and retain the complaint until the permit is issued.[44]

Within 20 days of receiving a complaint, the EPA will conduct a preliminary investigation to determine whether the complaint states a valid claim, and, if it does not, the agency will reject the complaint or refer it to another agency.[45] If the EPA accepts the complaint for investigation, the agency first attempts to resolve the matter informally.[46] If informal mediation fails, the EPA will then investigate the allegations.[47] In appropriate cases, EPA may seek comment from the recipient, permittee, or complainant on preliminary data analyses before making an initial finding about the presence of disparate impacts.[48]

EPA's Authority to Punish Discriminatory Recipients

If the EPA's investigation reveals no violations, then the agency will dismiss the complaint and notify the recipient and complainant,[49] who has very limited rights to challenge a dismissal, as discussed below. If the EPA makes a formal determination of noncompliance, the recipient may, within 30 days, request an opportunity for a hearing before an administrative law judge (ALJ) to contest the finding, and the recipient may appeal the ALJ's decision to the EPA Administrator.[50] The Administrator may deny, suspend, or terminate agency funding only to the particular program or the part of it in which the agency has found discrimination, but must wait 30 days after making a full report about such a termination decision to the House and Senate committees with legislative jurisdiction over the program at issue.[51] A recipient may seek judicial review of a termination decision.[52] Normally, a federal agency will first encourage a recipient to modify its behavior to comply with Title VI before revoking funding.[53]

The EPA may also use "any other means authorized by law to get compliance, including a referral to the Department of Justice."[54] Because the agency has never completed a Title VI investigation, the EPA has never invoked this "other means" authority.[55] The Department of Justice has authority to bring "appropriate" proceedings against a grant recipient accused of discriminatory practices, but there is no case law regarding the scope of this authority.[56]

Drawbacks of Title VI Administrative Complaints

COMPLAINANT'S LACK OF PARTICIPATION AND DIRECT REMEDIES. There are major drawbacks to relying on a Title VI administrative complaint.[57] First, a complainant has no formal right to participate in the administrative process.[58] Indeed, if possible, the EPA seeks to keep the complainant's identity confidential unless there is a complaint of employment discrimination.[59] In addition, there are no clear time limits for a response from the EPA, and filing an administrative complaint does not toll the statute of limitations for filing a Title VI suit.[60] The main remedy the agency may impose against a discriminatory recipient is termination of the grantee's funding,[61] but, as the EPA's record before the Clinton administration demonstrates, the agency may be reluctant to withdraw funding that supports important antipollution programs despite evidence of discriminatory practices. Furthermore, the agency cannot provide any damages to the complainant.[62]

COMPLAINANT'S INABILITY TO CHALLENGE AN ADVERSE AGENCY DECISION. Finally, a complainant has very limited or no opportunity to challenge an adverse administrative decision by a federal agency through judicial review under either Title VI or the Administrative Procedure Act (APA).[63] In 1979, in *Cannon v. University of Chicago,* the Supreme Court suggested that Title VI generally does not allow private suits against the federal government.[64] A Title VI suit might be permissible if the plaintiff charges the funding agency itself with discrimination, or with encouraging a recipient's discrimination,[65] but most courts would probably reject any Title VI suit against a federal agency.[66]

Under the APA, a plaintiff may not sue a funding agency providing a grant to a discriminatory recipient if the remedies against the recipient are adequate.[67] Furthermore, courts traditionally defer to an agency's prosecutorial discretion in deciding not to enforce a statute against a possible violator,[68] including Title VI recipients.[69] If an agency willfully refuses to enforce Title VI, a court might possibly allow a suit under the statute or the APA.[70]

Title VI Litigation: Suing the Recipient

There are a number of advantages to suing a funding recipient directly rather than filing an administrative complaint. In the administrative procedures of the EPA and other federal agencies, the complainant has no direct role in the agency's administrative investigation, and judicial review is limited to the record developed by the agency.[71] By contrast, a lawsuit allows a plaintiff to use discovery procedures to conduct her own investigation, to present witnesses and evidence, and to cross-examine a defendant's witnesses.[72] A court trial may serve as an effective political education and mobilizing mechanism in the affected community.[73] Furthermore, an administrative agency may only terminate a recipient's funding, usually after allowing the recipient the opportunity to end its discriminatory practices, but a court may award prospective equitable relief to a plaintiff.[74] Under Title VI, plaintiffs are entitled to lawyers' fees for a successful lawsuit, but not for filing an administrative complaint even if the funding agency finds a violation against the recipient.[75]

Standing

There has been controversy about the standing requirements for plaintiffs suing a funding recipient under Title VI. Some courts have required that plaintiffs prove they are intended beneficiaries under the federally funded program,[76] or at least that the plaintiffs demonstrate that the discriminatory practices of the recipient harm both them and the intended beneficiaries.[77] Even if the intended beneficiary doctrine was arguably a requirement for standing under the original 1964 Civil Rights Act, the Civil Rights Restoration Act of 1987 or evolving standing doctrine has abolished that barrier.[78]

The 1987 Act clearly repudiated *Grove City College v. Bell*,[79] a 1984 Supreme Court decision that had applied the intended beneficiary doctrine to Title IX of the Civil Rights Act by holding that federal funds received by a subunit of an educational institution did not subject the entire institution to the nondiscriminatory demands of the statute. Under *Grove City*'s intended beneficiary test, if a subunit did not receive federal funds, then the presumption was that participants in its activities were not the intended beneficiaries of the federal aid at issue. Because the language of Title IX was expressly modeled after that of Title VI and because the Supreme Court has frequently relied on constructions of one statute in interpreting the other, *Grove City* restricted standing in Title VI cases to intended beneficiaries.[80]

The 1987 Act rejected *Grove City* by broadly defining the term "institution-wide" basis to include "all of the operations" of the recipient.[81] Accordingly, the *Interim Guidance* states that if any program of a state or local government agency receives federal assistance, Title VI governs the entire agency.[82] In light of the 1987 Act's legislative history explicitly stating an intention to overrule *Grove City* and because any plaintiff suing a subunit that does not receive federal funding could not be an intended beneficiary of federal funding, the Restoration Act clearly intended to eliminate the intended beneficiary doctrine under Titles VI and IX.[83]

Despite the 1987 Act, some courts continue to cite earlier decisions and apply the intended beneficiary doctrine to deny standing to plaintiffs filing Title VI actions.[84] However, in *Bryant v. New Jersey Dept. of Transp.*, the district court vacated its prior decision applying the doctrine and held that the Supreme Court's decision in *National Credit Union Administration v. First National Bank & Trust Co.* had relaxed the standing requirements of Title VI by effectively overruling precedent that made being an intended beneficiary of the challenged program an element of the zone-of-interests test for standing.[85]

Nevertheless, if some courts wrongly apply the intended beneficiary doctrine to Title VI plaintiffs, many environmental justice plaintiffs will be unaffected because they will be suing a subunit of a state or local environmental agency that receives federal funding. Furthermore, most of the EPA's funding to state grantees is explicitly intended to benefit all the residents of the jurisdiction, and, accordingly, every citizen of the state or locality arguably meets the intended beneficiary standard.[86] In theory, a state might attempt to avoid Title VI's antidiscrimination requirements by creating a special purpose agency that does not receive any federal funding to issue a particular type of permit, but such a blatant approach could constitute evidence of intentional discrimination in violation of the Equal Protection Clause and possibly other federal civil rights statutes.

Disparate Impacts or Discriminatory Intent

The Supreme Court has required proof of intentional discrimination under Section 601 of Title VI, but has also held that an agency implementing regulations under Section 602 may reach disparate impact discrimination. In *Lau v. Nichols,* the Supreme Court had held that, under the Department of Health, Education and Welfare's Title VI regulations, a plaintiff could use evidence of disparate impacts to prove a violation because "[d]iscrimination is barred which has that effect even though no purposeful design is present."[87] In *Regents of California v. Bakke,* however, the Supreme Court cast some doubts on whether *Lau*'s effects test remained good law by observing that Title VI is coextensive with the Equal Protection Clause, which requires proof of intentional discrimination.[88]

In *Guardians Ass'n v. Civil Service Commission,*[89] seven members of the Supreme Court agreed that proof of discriminatory intent is required by the statute in Section 601.[90] On the other hand, five members of the Court concluded that Section 602 of Title VI permits federal agencies to promulgate regulations that prohibit disparate impact discrimination.[91]

Private Rights of Action

Courts have divided about when a regulatory statute that does not expressly create a private right of action may do so implicitly.[92] The Supreme Court has recognized a private right of action under Section 601 of Title VI, but few plaintiffs have filed such suits in light of that section's requirement of proving intentional discrimination.[93] A number of federal courts of appeals have implied or stated in dicta that Title VI's Section 602 discriminatory effects regulations can be enforced by a private right of action.[94] On June 8, 1998, the Supreme Court in *Seif v. Chester Residents Concerned for Quality Living* granted Pennsylvania's petition for a writ of certiorari to review the Third Circuit's holding that there are private rights of action under Section 602, but on August 17, 1998, the Court dismissed the case as moot and vacated the Third Circuit's decision.[95]

The Judicial Development of Private Rights of Action

In *Cort v. Ash,*[96] the Supreme Court adopted a four-factor test for implying private rights of action:

1. Does the statute intend to provide special benefits or status to the plaintiff?
2. Is there implicit or explicit evidence that Congress intended to create or deny this remedy?
3. Is such a remedy consistent with the underlying purposes of the legislative scheme? and
4. Is the cause of action traditionally relegated to state law, and in an area where a federal cause of action would intrude on important state concerns?

Cannon v. University of Chicago: Recognizing a Private Right of Action Under Titles IX and VI

In *Cannon v. University of Chicago,* the Supreme Court concluded that all four *Cort* factors supported the implication of a private right of action for individuals to sue in federal court educational institutions receiving federal funds under Section 901(a) of Title IX of the 1972 Education Act Amendments, which prohibits discrimination in educational institutions that receive federal funds.[97] The Court established a private remedy even though the funding agency had established administrative procedures allowing individuals to file a complaint requesting that the agency terminate funding to the recipient.[98] The Court emphasized that the agency in charge of administering Title IX strongly favored creating a private right of action because of its limited enforcement resources.

Because Title IX and Title VI contain the same language and identical procedures for terminating funding, the Supreme Court in *Cannon* used Title VI's regulations, case law, and legislative history as a major factor in inferring that Congress had intended to create a private right of action in Title IX. Accordingly, while *Cannon* did not explicitly hold that there is an implied right of action under Title VI, courts have followed *Cannon* by establishing a private right of action under Section 601 of Title VI.[99] *Cannon* did not address whether there also are private rights of action under administrative regulations promulgated by a federal agency to enforce either Title VI or IX.

In his dissenting opinion in *Cannon,* Justice Powell argued that the Court should abandon *Cort*'s four-part test because it inappropriately gives the judiciary too much discretion to legislate new private rights of action and contended that courts should instead focus exclusively on whether Congress intended to create private remedy.[100] In subsequent cases, the Supreme Court has placed a greater burden on the plaintiff to demonstrate that Congress intended to create a private right of action.[101]

Did Guardians Recognize a Private Right of Action Under Title VI Regulations?

In *Alexander v. Choate,* the Supreme Court suggested in dicta that *Guardians* had recognized an implied private right of action for disparate impacts under Section 602 of Title VI.[102] In *Chester Residents Concerned for Quality Living v. Seif,* the Third Circuit observed that five members of the *Guardians* Court had "implicit[ly] approved" a private claim of action for disparate impact discrimination under Title VI's Section 602 implementing regulations, but concluded that the Supreme Court had never explicitly held that such a private remedy exists.[103]

Chester: Private Rights of Action Under Section 602

In *Chester,* plaintiffs alleged that the Pennsylvania Department of Environmental Protection's (PADEP) approval of a permit to allow a private company to build a waste treatment facility in an area with a 65 percent minority population placed a disparate burden on African Americans in Chester. Since 1987, the defendant had approved five waste facilities with a total capacity of over 2,000,000 tons per year in the predominantly minority city of Chester, but only two small facilities with a waste capacity of 700 tons each in predominantly white areas of Delaware County. The district court refused to recognize a private right of action under Title VI's Section 602 regulations, arguing that private rights of action under Title VI are limited to acts of intentional discrimination under Section 601, and suggested that Section 602's sole purpose is to establish an administrative enforcement scheme.[104]

The Third Circuit reversed and held that a private right of action does exist under EPA's Title VI regulations, and implied that plaintiffs do not need to exhaust their administrative remedies before filing suit in federal court. First, the Third Circuit agreed with an amicus brief filed with that court in which the United States argued that the implication of a private right of action under Section 602 and its implementing regulations is consistent with Title VI's legislative intent because Congress acknowledged the existence of such a right when it amended Title VI in enacting the Civil Rights Restoration Act of 1987.[105] The Third Circuit rejected PADEP's argument that the legislative history of the 1987 amendments was not relevant or binding, and found "some indication in the legislative history, here uncontroverted, of an intent to create a private right of action, in satisfaction of the *Cort* factors."[106] However, the Third Circuit's reliance on the 1987 Act to find congressional intent to create a private right of action arguably fails to meet the more demanding standard of proof applied by the Supreme Court in many cases since *Cannon*.[107]

Second, the Third Circuit rejected PADEP's argument that creating a private right of action would interfere with EPA's administrative complaint process and funding termination procedures.[108] The United States in its amicus brief had strongly argued that its Title VI regulations do not preclude a private right of action, will not interfere with the agency's enforcement program, and that this remedy, in fact, will advance the statute's purposes in light of the agency's limited resources.[109] The Third Circuit concluded that a private lawsuit is not inconsistent with the legislative scheme in Section 602 because a suit provides the recipient with similar notice as the filing of an administrative complaint, and the court may not award relief without conducting an extensive trial that accomplishes many of the same functions as an administrative investigation. In addition, the Third Circuit also observed that a private party may not request that a court terminate funding to a discriminatory recipient, and, accordingly, a private suit would not interfere with a federal agency's decision to terminate funding to a discriminatory recipient.

Third, the Third Circuit agreed with the United States that creating a private right of action under Section 602 would advance the statute's dual purposes of preventing recipient discrimination and protecting individual rights identified in *Cannon* by deputizing private attorneys general to enforce Section 602 and its implementing regulations.[110] The United States had acknowledged in its amicus brief that it lacked the resources to achieve adequate enforcement.[111] Accordingly, the Third Circuit found that a private right of action under Section 602 would advance Title VI's dual purposes.

SUPREME COURT GRANTS CERTIORARI, BUT THEN DISMISSES THE CASE AS MOOT AND VACATES THE THIRD CIRCUIT'S DECISION. On June 8, 1998, the Supreme Court granted the PADEP's petition for a writ of certiorari to review the Third Circuit's holding that there are private rights of action under Section 602 against recipients violating discriminatory effects regulations.[112] As it had argued unsuccessfully in the Third Circuit, PADEP maintained in its petition for writ of certiorari that the legislative history of the 1987 Act was insufficient to establish congressional intent to create a private right of action under Section 602, and that such a private remedy would interfere with the EPA's administrative complaint process.[113]

In addition, the Court granted the Washington Legal Foundation's request to file an amicus brief arguing that EPA does not have authority under Title VI to address discriminatory effects, but only intentional discrimination.[114] The Foundation argued that any statements in *Guardians* or *Alexander* suggesting that agencies may issue discriminatory effects regulations under Section 602 were mere dicta. Both the Foundation and PADEP contended that the Court in *United States v. Fordice*[115] had stated that Title VI does not extend beyond the intentional discrimination standard in the Fourteenth Amendment, and, accordingly, that the EPA's discriminatory effects regulations are invalid. If EPA's discriminatory effects regulations are void, there can be no private rights of action under them.

On July 29, 1998, Chester Residents Concerned for Quality Living (CRCQL) filed a motion to dismiss the case as moot because PADEP had revoked the underlying permit in the case, and the permit applicant, Soil Remediation Services, had abandoned efforts to locate in Chester.[116] A few days later, the Commonwealth of Pennsylvania filed a brief in opposition arguing that the case remain justiciable despite the revocation of the permit because the plaintiffs' complaint originally also contended that PADEP's permit review process was discriminatory.[117] In the alternative, Pennsylvania contended that if the Court dismissed the case as moot, the Court should also vacate the Third Circuit's decision to prevent the case from being cited as precedent in the future.

On August 17, 1998, the Supreme Court granted the CRCQL's petition to dismiss the case as moot, but also approved Pennsylvania's request that the Court vacate the Third Circuit's decision.[118] The Court apparently concluded that the revocation of the underlying permit and Soil Remediation Services's decision not to pursue a facility in Chester made the case moot, and did not believe that the broader issue of whether PADEP's permitting process is discriminatory made the case justiciable in the absence of a concrete dispute. If a case becomes moot after the Supreme Court grants certiorari, the Court's established practice is to reverse or vacate the judgment below and remand with a direction to dismiss, unless the petitioner has voluntarily made the case moot by, for instance, entering into a settlement.[119]

The Court's decision to dismiss the *Chester* case and vacate the Third Circuit's decision established no binding legal precedent for the future, but prevents potential plaintiffs from citing the Third Circuit's decision as precedent. On the other hand, civil rights proponents avoided the possibility of a reversal by the Supreme Court on the merits. Both sides agreed that the Supreme Court will ultimately have to decide the important question of whether there are private rights of action under Section 602.[120]

Title VI Remedies

Title VI plaintiffs who prove discriminatory effects discrimination are probably limited to prospective relief. Prevailing Title VI plaintiffs are also entitled to reasonable lawyers' fees.[121]

Justice White's opinion in *Guardians* claimed that a majority of the Court had held that, in Title VI actions, compensatory relief is available only to plaintiffs who prove intentional discrimination, and that a discriminatory effects violation of Section 602's implementing regulations warrants only prospective relief. Some commentators have questioned, however, whether Justice O'Connor's opinion clearly provided the crucial fifth vote for limiting relief to plaintiffs who demonstrate disparate impacts despite her view that even Section 602 requires proof of intentional discrimination.[122] In *Franklin v. Gwinnett County Public Schools,* the Court possibly clarified *Guardians* by holding that damages are available in a Title IX case for intentional violations of Title IX, although not for unintentional violations.[123] While proving an intentional violation of a civil rights statute is arguably less demanding than proving intentional discrimination, some lower courts have read *Gwinnett* narrowly as simply reaffirming *Guardians,* and have allowed compensatory damages only for acts of intentional discrimination.[124]

A recent Title IX case suggests that the Supreme Court will limit Title VI plaintiffs who prove discriminatory effects discrimination to prospective relief. In *Gebser v. Lago Vista Independent School District,* the Court—in a five-to-four decision—held that a student who is a victim of sexual harassment in an educational institution receiving federal funds may not recover monetary damages in an implied right of action suit under Title IX unless a school district has actual notice of the harassment and is deliberately indifferent to the teacher's conduct.[125] In addition, the failure of a school board to comply with Department of Education guidelines requiring recipients to adopt a grievance procedure did not constitute discrimination under Title IX, and the violation of administrative requirements does not justify a damages remedy.

The majority stated that, in cases of implied rights of action, the Supreme Court has latitude to determine the scope of the remedy to fit a statute's structure and purpose, and that monetary damages were inappropriate under Title IX where a school district lacked actual notice of a teacher's sexual harassment, and was not deliberately indifferent to that conduct. Unlike Title VII, which is primarily concerned with compensating victims of discrimination, Justice O'Connor's majority opinion read *Cannon* to suggest that the central purpose of Title IX is "protecting" individuals from discrimination, and, accordingly, that injunctive or equitable relief is appropriate in a private action rather than a damages remedy. Because Titles IX and VI are so similar, her reading of *Cannon* has significant implications for limiting Title VI remedies to injunctive or equitable relief.

The majority favorably discussed Justice White's *Guardians* opinion, which concluded that relief in a Title VI action alleging unintentional discrimination should be prospective only because in such cases a grantee may not be aware that it is discriminating and Congress probably did not want a recipient to pay damages for unintentional discrimination. In addition, Title IX's administrative scheme, as well as the parallel Title VI administrative processes, operate on the assumption of actual notice to the funding recipient to obtain voluntary compliance to avoid discrimination in the future. Justice O'Connor presumed that a central purpose of such notice is to secure voluntary compliance before it becomes necessary for the federal agency to cut off or divert funds that serve beneficial purposes. She repeated Justice White's concern in *Guardians* that a damages remedy might dissuade a state or local agency from accepting federal aid or that damages could possibly exceed the amount of federal funding, and, therefore, a damages remedy could deprive the recipient of the benefit of the federal subsidy. Her discussion of *Guardians* strongly suggests that the Supreme Court would reject a damages remedy in a Title VI case proving only disparate impacts.

In dissent, Justice Stevens argued that the majority had inappropriately relied on Title IX's administrative enforcement scheme to limit the availability of a damages remedy, and was overly concerned about the impact of a damages remedy on the willingness of recipients to accept federal grants when recipients could insure themselves against liability.

In light of *Gebser,* the Supreme Court as currently constituted is unlikely to allow monetary damages in a Title VI case alleging unintentional discrimination unless a recipient agency was aware of discrimination by subordinate officials and deliberately did nothing to stop that discrimination. In most cases alleging environmental disparities, prospective relief will be adequate to veto or relocate a proposed facility and prevent harm to complainants. In addition, because Title VI prohibits discrimination in programs or activities, plaintiffs may seek institutional remedies that require a recipient to alter its siting or permitting practices to address environmental equity concerns—not just in one case, but in the future.[126] The issue of retroactive relief might possibly arise if plaintiffs sought compensatory damages for depreciation of their property while the siting proposal was pending.[127]

Burden of Proof

There is no Title VI case law concerning when an environmental siting or permitting decision might cause unjustified discriminatory effects constituting a violation of the statute. There are numerous Title VI decisions based on alleged discriminatory siting of highways,[128] provision of municipal services,[129] the closing or relocation of health care facilities,[130] or the location of buildings[131] or public housing in minority neighborhoods[132] that provide possible analogies for environmental justice challenges. In addition, federal courts have frequently followed Title VII as a model, but there are questions about whether and to what extent limitations or affirmative defenses found only in Title VII ought to apply to Title VI.[133]

Establishing a Prima Facie Case of Disparate Impacts

Title VI does not specify exactly how much evidence a plaintiff must introduce to establish a prima facie case of disparate impacts, but courts have often been fairly lenient in allowing a plaintiff to prove a prima facie case.[134] Plaintiffs must initially demonstrate by a preponderance of the evidence that the defendant's facially neutral actions have a significant disproportionate adverse impact upon persons of a particular race, color, or national origin protected by the statute, and then courts may rely on that evidence to infer that these practices caused those impacts.[135] To establish a prima facie case, a plaintiff must demonstrate that a specific group of minorities experience disproportionate impacts compared to a relevant comparison group, such as qualified job applicants in a particular labor market or other suitable locations for a facility.[136] While a plaintiff should attempt to present as sophisticated and specific a statistical demonstration of disparity as possible, both Title VII and VI courts have sometimes allowed relatively simple statistical evidence to establish a prima facie case of disproportionate impacts.[137]

Title VII defendants often attempt to settle a case once a plaintiff has established a prima facie case and has shifted the burden to the defendant to show legitimate, nondiscriminatory reasons.[138] In many cases, it may be cheaper for a defendant to settle a case once a plaintiff establishes a prima facie case of discrimination even if a defendant believes that it has valid grounds to justify a siting or employment decision.

Defendant's Burden of Proof

After the plaintiff establishes a prima facie case, the burdens of both production and persuasion shift to the defendant either to disprove the validity of the plaintiff's prima facie case or to demonstrate affirmatively "evidence of a legitimate, nondiscriminatory reason for its action," or, in other words, a legitimate reason of business or educational necessity for its actions causing a disparate impact.[139] In 1989, the Supreme Court in *Wards Cove Packing v. Atonio* held that after a plaintiff in a Title VII case establishes a prima facie case, the burden of going forward shifts to the defendant, but that the ultimate burden of persuasion remains with the plaintiffs.[140] In the 1991 Civil Rights Act, however, Congress rejected this portion of *Wards Cove* and placed the burden of persuasion in Title VII cases on the defendant to "demonstrate that the challenged practice is job related for the position in question and consistent with business necessity" or "that a specific employment practice does not cause the disparate impact."[141] Because they have previously relied on Title VII's standards of production and proof in Title VI cases, courts are likely to adopt the 1991 Act's burden of proof for Title VI.[142]

Appropriate Justifications for Disparate Impacts

In Title VII cases, courts have often concluded that business practices having disparate impacts are justified if a defendant can show that its decision to adopt the practice was motivated by significant cost savings, efficiency, or safety considerations rather than discriminatory animus.[143]

Even though the EPA's Title VI regulations appear to prohibit any discriminatory effects, courts have generally interpreted Title VI implementing regulations to prohibit *unjustified* disparate impacts.[144] Accordingly, courts in Title VI cases are likely to allow defendants to present justifications for their siting decisions similar to the business necessity justifications used in Title VII cases.[145] Title VI cases suggest that defendants may be able to justify disparate impacts through safety or efficiency justifications, significant cost savings, or the unavailability of physically suitable alternative sites.[146]

Plaintiff's Demonstration of Alternative Sites

In Title VII cases, if the defendant meets its burden of production and persuasion by demonstrating a legitimate nondiscriminatory business or educational justification for its actions, the ultimate burden of persuasion shifts to the plaintiff, who must either prove that the defendant's justification is a pretext, or that the defendant has failed to adopt an "alternative employment practice" that would cause less disparate impact and still meet its legitimate goals.[147] Under Title VI, a plaintiff must prove either that the defendant's justification is a pretext for discrimination or that the defendant failed to adopt a less discriminatory alternative practice or location.[148] Some Title VI and VII cases have required a plaintiff to prove that a less discriminatory alternative is "equally effective,"[149] but others have used the possibly different standard that a plaintiff must show that a less discriminatory alternative is "comparably effective."[150]

To prove that a defendant failed to adopt a less discriminatory alternative, a Title VI plaintiff should present a specific alternative to the defendant's plan that would cause less discriminatory impact, but still satisfy the defendant's legitimate business objectives, including cost and safety considerations.[151] Courts may be reluctant to consider siting alternatives that require substantial modification of the defendant's plans such as not building a facility at all, or building the facility in an area outside the siting board's jurisdiction.[152]

Administrative Complaints and EPA's Interim Guidance for Investigating Title VI Administrative Complaints Challenging Permits

In February 1998, the EPA issued an *Interim Guidance for Investigating Title VI Administrative Complaints Challenging Permits* to help the agency's Office of Civil Rights evaluate Title VI complaints.[153] However, because of substantial public criticism of the *Interim Guidance,* the agency has promised to issue a revised Title VI guidance in 1999.[154] The EPA has assigned two separate committees to recommend changes to the *Interim Guidance,* and will also take into consideration written and oral comments from a wide variety of interest groups.[155]

The public response to the *Interim Guidance* has generally been critical, although less so among environmentalists and civil rights advocates. During a 90-day public comment period, a diverse range of groups and individuals filed about 100 comments with EPA, many of which criticized the *Interim Guidance* for failing to clarify crucial terms, especially the definition of "disparate impacts."[156] State and local regulators, including the Environmental Council of the States, representing 49 states and the District of Columbia, the U.S. Conference of Mayors, the Western Governors' Association, and many industry groups have called on EPA to withdraw the *Interim Guidance* on the grounds that it is unclear, places too heavy a burden on recipients, and will discourage economic development in poor and minority areas.[157] For instance, in July 1998, several mayors who are members of the U.S. Conference of Mayors met with EPA Administrator Carol Browner to discuss their concerns that EPA's environmental justice policies could undermine economic redevelopment efforts in minority areas.[158] On the other hand, many environmentalists, civil rights activists, and members of the Congressional Black Caucus have cautiously defended the *Interim Guidance.*[159]

Because of intense public criticism, several EPA officials, including Administrator Carol Browner and Ann E. Goode, director of the agency's Office of Civil Rights, have acknowledged that the agency should have consulted with a wider range of interested parties before issuing the *Interim Guidance* in February 1998 and have promised to issue a revised Guidance in 1999.[160] In March 1998, EPA created a Title VI advisory committee, which is part of the agency's National Advisory Council for Environmental Policy and Technology, to counsel the agency on revising the Guidance and also to suggest how the agency should evaluate whether a state or locality has an effective Title VI compliance program.[161] Unfortunately, the advisory group has divided over a number of important issues and may be unable to achieve consensus.[162] Additionally, in October 1998, EPA's Science Advisory Board (SAB) made several recommendations about improving the agency's methodology for determining whether the issuance of a permit causes a disproportionate impact on minorities.[163]

In October 1998, President Clinton reluctantly signed an appropriations bill that included a rider sponsored by Republican members of Congress that places a moratorium on the EPA accepting new Title VI complaints until the agency issues a final guidance on Title VI.[164] The legislation does not affect the agency's 15 continuing Title VI investigations.[165] Opponents of the *Interim Guidance* argue that the moratorium is a congressional admonition to EPA to embrace a more flexible Title VI policy that allows economic development in minority communities.[166] However, environmental justice advocates suggest that the moratorium will have only a minor impact because the EPA did not have the resources to conduct new investigations and was going to delay assessing new cases until it issues a revised Title VI policy.[167]

The Text of the *Interim Guidance*

Permit Modifications and Renewals

The *Interim Guidance* applies to permit modifications as well as new or renewed permits, but EPA stated that it is likely to dismiss claims of discriminatory effect challenging minor permit modifications that are merely administrative, "neutral," or reduce environmental impacts, and focus on permit modifications that involve net increases. In the context of permit modifications, which the agency carefully distinguished from permit *renewals,* a complaint must show that the modification itself causes adverse impacts.

The *Interim Guidance* states that "permit renewals should be treated as if they were new facility permits, since permit renewal is, by definition, an occasion to review the overall operations of a permitted facility and make any necessary changes."[168] Many regulators and industry officials strongly disagree with the agency's policy of reviewing permit renewals on the same basis as applications for new facilities, even if the facility is continuing at the same level of operations and pollution as it has for many years before.[169] Environmental statutes and regulations frequently apply more lenient standards to existing facilities because, among other reasons, it is more politically and economically difficult to shut down an existing facility that provides jobs and that the surrounding community has often grown to accept than to block the siting of a new facility. (See Chapter 15, *infra*.) The *Interim Guidance* does suggest that the EPA will usually weigh the proven benefits of an existing facility more highly than the unproven advantages of a proposed facility, but this vague assurance does not appear to have addressed the qualms of many industry and regulatory officials.

Defining "Disparate Impacts"

The *Interim Guidance* states that the agency will not use a single methodology for evaluating disparate impacts, but will use several techniques to analyze the "totality of circumstances" in each case. Until further notice, EPA will consider only impacts recognized by the recipient's permitting program, but the agency may also consider the cumulative burden of surrounding facilities even if the recipient's authority to regulate them is unclear because "Title VI is a Federal cross-cutting statute that imposes independent, nondiscrimination requirements on recipients of Federal funds. As such, Title VI, separate from and in addition to the strictures of state and local law, both authorizes and requires recipients to manage their programs in a way that avoids discriminatory cumulative burdens and distributional patterns."[170]

The agency set forth a five-step process for evaluating whether a recipient's approval or renewal of a permit will create disparate impacts:

1. identifying the affected population, especially those in close proximity to the facility;
2. determining the demographics of the affected population through mapping technology such as geographic information systems (GIS);
3. determining the universe(s) of facilities and total affected population(s), especially the cumulative pollution burden of neighboring facilities;
4. conducting a disparate impact analysis both by examining the racial or ethnic composition within the affected population and by comparing that composition to nonaffected populations in other relevant areas; and
5. determining the significance of the disparity through the use of standard statistical methods.

The *Interim Guidance* does not explain how the EPA will define "affected population," or the significance of any "disparate impacts."[171]

Under step three, EPA is more likely to investigate and to find disparate impacts if a proposed facility will be located in a minority or ethnic community that already has several polluting facilities and currently suffers from a disproportionate amount of pollution.[172] In "rare instances," EPA might find that a single permit causes enough impacts or is so unique to support a disparate impact claim. If EPA believes that the number of relevant facilities already in the area is larger or smaller than alleged in the complaint, EPA will notify the complainant and recipient, and offer the complainant the opportunity to amend its complaint.[173]

Mitigation, Justification, and Less Discriminatory Alternatives

If EPA determines that the challenged permit has disparate impacts, the recipient agency that awarded the permit must either:

1. rebut EPA's findings;
2. propose a plan for mitigating the disparate impact; or
3. provide a substantial, legitimate justification for why the benefits of the facility are sufficient to outweigh the cost of the disparate impacts.

EPA encourages mitigation as a way for recipients to avoid the "draconian" penalty of funding termination and because it will often be difficult for recipients to justify disparate impacts without requiring the permittee to mitigate any impacts.[174] According to the *Interim Guidance,* in some cases "it may be possible for the recipient to mitigate public health and environmental considerations sufficiently to address the disparate impact."[175] EPA states that recipients should consult with agency officials about when mitigation will be sufficient. If it is not possible to mitigate impacts sufficiently, a mitigation plan may include "'supplemental mitigation projects'" that are outside the scope of issues usually considered during the recipient's permitting process to compensate the affected community.

If the recipient has failed to rebut a preliminary finding of noncompliance and cannot adequately mitigate any disparate impacts, then the recipient must justify its decision to issue the permit despite the disparate impact by explaining how the permit will advance "substantial, legitimate interests of the recipient," and, indirectly, the permittee. While acceptable justifications will depend on the facts of each case, EPA stated that "merely demonstrating that the permit complies with applicable environmental regulations will not ordinarily be considered a substantial, legitimate justification."[176] In evaluating the proffered justification, EPA will consider the state or local government's interest in approving the project, the seriousness of the disparate impacts, whether the permit involves a renewal of an existing facility "with demonstrated benefits" or a new project with "more speculative benefits," and whether the project will provide employment or other benefits to the particular community that is the subject of the Title VI complaint.[177]

The *Interim Guidance* states that "a justification offered will not be considered acceptable if it is shown that a less discriminatory alternative exists."[178] If a less discriminatory alternative exists that is "equally effective in meeting the needs addressed by the challenged" proposal, the *Interim Guidance* requires the recipient to approve the alternative.[179] The recipient must examine whether mitigation measures will serve as "less discriminatory alternatives" by "including additional permit conditions that would lessen or eliminate the demonstrated adverse disparate impacts."

Criticisms of the *Interim Guidance*

Substantive Criticisms

There is widespread agreement among industry, government, and environmental justice organizations that the *Interim Guidance* fails to provide clear definitions of many crucial issues such as what constitutes a "disparate impact." State and local officials generally believe that uncertainty about how the EPA will apply the Guidance makes it more difficult to site projects in minority areas because industry will not risk the long delays that are likely to occur if a Title VI complaint is filed.[180] On the other hand, some members of the Congressional Black Caucus and environmental justice advocates have argued that the *Interim Guidance* violates Title VI by allowing EPA to accept almost any justification for a project.[181] The substantive controversies about Title VI are unlikely to be resolved until the EPA promulgates a revised Guidance.

Procedural Criticisms

Critics of the *Interim Guidance* have argued that it was improper for EPA to issue such an important policy as a guidance document because the APA's notice-and-comment rulemaking requirements apply to what is essentially a "legislative rule"[182] establishing new policy rather than a mere "interpretive" document[183] interpreting an existing policy.[184] By issuing the document as a "guidance" rather than a "rule," EPA avoided having to perform a cost-benefit analysis, to consider its impact on small businesses, to allow Congress an opportunity to veto the rule, to evaluate whether it is an unfunded mandate, or to submit the proposed rule to the Office of Management and Budget for review.[185] Unfortunately, the line between substantive legislative rules and informal interpretive rules is often hazy.[186] The EPA accepted public comments for 90 days, but did not publish the *Interim Guidance* as a proposed rule in the *Federal Register*.[187] Critics argue that the *Interim Guidance* is a legislative rule requiring notice-and-comment rulemaking in the *Federal Register* because it imposes time limits and rules for the adjudication of Title VI complaints that go beyond EPA's existing regulations or alter state permit rules, which often require permit challenges to be filed in a shorter period than the 180 days allowed under EPA's Title VI regulations.[188]

In February 1999, a newspaper reported that the congressional General Accounting Office's (GAO) general counsel has drafted a legal opinion concluding that the EPA should have promulgated the *Interim Guidance* as a rule because it clearly changed existing regulations.[189] Under the Regulatory Flexibility Act, as amended by the Small Business Regulatory Enforcement Fairness Act of 1996 (SBREFA), and the Unfunded Mandates Reform Act of 1995, the agency arguably should have submitted the *Interim Guidance* to Congress for its review before it took effect and should have justified its reasons for not performing the cost-benefit analysis usually required under those statutes.[190]

Courts will likely have to address whether it was proper for the EPA to issue the *Interim Guidance* as an interpretive document instead of as an APA rule, and whether the agency's provision for public comment satisfies the APA's notice-and-public comment requirements.[191] Furthermore, courts may have to address whether EPA violated the Regulatory Flexibility Act and Unfunded Mandates Act by not submitting the *Interim Guidance* to Congress for review or performing a cost-benefit analysis.

Opponents of the *Interim Guidance* also argue that it violates the APA because it does not protect the due process rights of the permit applicant because only the recipient has the right to participate in the Title VI process.[192] The permittee and recipient's interests in the outcome clearly may be different, and procedural due process arguably requires protection of the permittee's property interest.[193] On the other hand, because EPA itself is not the permitting authority, the agency may not have any obligation to provide due process to the permittee, but rather it may be the state permitting agency that has an obligation to provide due process to the permit applicant, including when a state permitting agency decides to modify a permit to resolve a Title VI complaint.[194]

Recent Title VI Cases

Shintech

During most of 1997 and 1998, public attention focused on a single Title VI complaint involving Shintech's proposed $700 million plastics facility in St. James Parish, Louisiana. In May 1997, the Tulane environmental law clinic filed Title VI petitions on behalf of several citizens' groups challenging the Louisiana Department of Environmental Quality's (LDEQ) approval of the Shintech project.[195] EPA officials announced that the agency would likely use the Shintech complaint as a test case to make the first public decision on the merits about how to apply Title VI to state permitting actions.[196] Because of the case's complexity and controversy over how to apply the *Interim Guidance,* however, the EPA repeatedly delayed making a decision on the merits of the Title VI claim.[197] Finally, Shintech withdrew its proposal and decided to build a smaller plant elsewhere.

The Shintech proposal was controversial because it promised to create a significant number of jobs, but also would have added pollution to an already heavily polluted area with a substantial minority population. St. James Parish, Louisiana, has a substantial minority population and is located in the middle of a heavily industrialized area already so polluted that many people call it "Cancer Alley."[198] In 1996, eight chemical plants and one sugar refinery in St. James Parish released 17.6 million pounds of pollutants to the air, water, and land.[199] In 1995, the average St. James Parish resident was exposed to 360 pounds of toxic air pollutant releases, but the average Louisiana resident was exposed to only 21 pounds.[200] The proposed Shintech facility would have annually emitted over 600,000 pounds of air pollutants, including 143,000 pounds of vinyl chloride, and 3.6 million gallons of wastewater, but Shintech officials argued that their plant would meet all legal requirements and emit no odor.[201]

Shintech argued that it chose the site from among 30 potential sites because the location in St. James Parish offered the best access to raw materials, including salt, water, natural gas, and ethylene; rail and water transportation; and 2,400 acres of land that provides a protective buffer zone from neighboring residents. Louisiana Governor Mike Foster and many other leading state politicians supported building the facility because Shintech would have employed 2,000 temporary construction workers, 165 permanent employees, and 90 permanent contract employees.

On the other hand, the fact that a substantial percentage of the population near the proposed plant was poor and minority raised serious questions about whether the Shintech facility would have created significant disparate impacts affecting these populations. For instance, 95 percent of the 300 people living within one mile of the proposed plant were black and 49 percent of the households had incomes of less than $15,000.[202] In a 50-square-mile area surrounding the facility site, 80 percent of the 4,500 residents were black, and 49 percent of the households earned less than $15,000 a year.

The Shintech case became a major political controversy. Environmental justice advocates strongly encouraged EPA to veto the proposed facility because of the cumulative burden of adding even one more plant to the already significant health risks in the area.[203] Business interests and many Louisiana politicians, however, argued that rejection of the permit would cost jobs and make it much more difficult to build any industrial facilities in minority areas in the future.[204]

Unfortunately, the disagreements between environmentalists and business interests over Shintech often became heated. The Tulane environmental law clinic donated thousands of hours to assist the Shintech complainants, but the clinic's involvement led Governor Foster to denounce the law students involved with the clinic as "outlaws."[205] The Louisiana Supreme Court issued an order amending its rules for student participation in trial work that severely restricts the ability of Louisiana law school clinics to represent environmental justice groups in the future unless a majority of the members of a client organization meet stringent indigency requirements and the client is not affiliated with a national organization.[206] (See Chapter 11, *infra,* for further discussion of this controversy.)

The minority community in St. James Parish and nationwide divided about whether the proposed facility's economic benefits outweighed the health benefits.[207] The Louisiana NAACP initially opposed the plant, but the St. James chapter supported its construction.[208] The U.S. Chamber of Commerce and the Black Chamber of Commerce began working together for the first time to repeal the EPA's environmental justice program on the grounds that the agency's policies will prevent investment in minority communities.[209] On the other hand, nearly all members of the Congressional Black Caucus, including Louisiana's only African American congressperson, William Jefferson, urged EPA to veto the Shintech permit.[210]

In September 1997, the EPA issued a preliminary decision that did not directly address the environmental equity issues raised about LDEQ's approval of the permit application, but the agency for the first time vetoed a state's issuance of a permit under Title V of the Clean Air Act based on the failure of the LDEQ permit to regulate all potential sources of air pollution.[211] While her decision avoided ruling on the pending Title VI complaints against LDEQ, EPA Administrator Carol Browner stated that the agency's Office of Civil Rights had created a special task force to investigate whether the siting process was biased against minorities, and, accordingly, suggested that the agency believed that environmental justice was a legitimate basis to review the permit.[212] Proponents of the Shintech facility argued that Administrator Browner used the threat of funding termination to pressure the LDEQ to reopen the permits to address any possible environmental justice issues.[213] In 1997–98, EPA had provided about 9 million dollars for LDEQ's air and water programs out of a total budget of $111.4 million.[214] Shintech then submitted a revised air permit application to the LDEQ, which EPA intended to review separately from the Title VI complaint.[215]

From September 1997 through September 1998, the EPA made several promises to resolve the Title VI issues in the Shintech case, but kept on delaying its decision.[216] In early 1998, EPA released an 87-page draft report that examined census and Toxic Release Inventory (TRI) data to determine the impact of the facility on minority residents of St. James Parish, but the agency delayed issuing a final report because it was uncertain about the data and its methodology for evaluating disparate impacts.[217] The EPA appeared to be unwilling to reach a final decision on the Title VI complaint in Shintech until after the agency issued a revised Title VI guidance in 1999.[218]

In September 1998, Shintech abandoned its plans to build a large plastics factory in Convent, Louisiana, and substituted a proposal for a smaller facility in Plaquemine, a community with a lower minority population.[219] EPA Administrator Carol Browner tried to place a positive spin on this change by praising Shintech for planning to involve elected officials and community groups before seeking a permit for the facility in Plaquemine.[220] While Browner implied that industry could still build new facilities if they addressed environmental justice issues before applying for a permit, EPA's delays in resolving the Title VI complaint clearly played a role in convincing Shintech to abandon its original proposal.

On the whole, the Shintech case was a victory for environmentalists even though the EPA never decided the merits of the case. Because delays usually increase construction costs, environmentalists would have a powerful weapon against industry if a typical Title VI complaint, usually resulting in a lengthy EPA investigation, substantially delayed final approval for a project. Accordingly, EPA's cautious and time-consuming approach to the Shintech case worked against industry's interests.

There may be still more fallout from the Shintech case. The EPA is considering whether to launch a comprehensive review of whether the LDEQ systematically discriminates against racial minorities, especially African Americans.[221] However, in 1997, the EPA considered consolidating complaints in Louisiana, as well as Texas and California, but never conducted such a review.[222]

Select Steel

On August 17, 1998, the EPA accepted for investigation a Title VI complaint filed on June 9, 1998, by Father Phil Schmitter and Sister Joanne Chiaverini of the St. Francis Prayer Center challenging Select Steel Corp.'s proposal to build a $175 million steel mini-mill in Flint, Michigan.[223] The complaint alleged that the Michigan Department of

Environmental Quality's (MDEQ) issuance of a Clean Air Act's Prevention of Significant Deterioration (PSD)[224] permit would cause discriminatory impacts against minority residents of Flint and that the MDEQ had conducted the permitting process in a discriminatory manner. However, on October 30, 1998, the EPA dismissed the complaint because the agency concluded that the proposal would not have an adverse impact on minority residents, was in compliance with the Act, and that state officials had provided adequate opportunities for public participation.[225]

The EPA's speedy resolution of the Select Steel complaint was in marked contrast to its hesitant approach to the Shintech case. In her letter dismissing the complaint, Ann E. Goode, the director of EPA's Office of Civil Rights, explicitly stated that the agency had conducted the investigation "expeditiously" to address state agencies' and applicants' need for "certainty," while at the same time thoroughly investigating the Complainant's civil rights concerns.[226] Select Steel had threatened to relocate the plant and its 200 jobs to Ohio if the agency took too long to make a decision.[227] Michigan Governor John Engler and other state officials placed heavy pressure on the agency for a speedy resolution of the Title VI complaint.[228] Conversely, the complainant had sought to delay the agency's decision because it believed that the EPA was bending to political pressure in rendering a quick decision.[229] The EPA stated that it was able to reach a fast but thorough decision because Michigan officials had quickly provided the agency with complete records on the original state permit decision.[230] Select Steel was a procedural victory for industry and state officials to the extent it demonstrated that the EPA could make an expeditious decision about a Title VI complaint, at least where state officials strongly pushed for a fast resolution.

On the merits, the EPA emphasized that the Select Steel permit complied with the National Ambient Air Quality Standards (NAAQS) for both ozone and lead.[231] The NAAQS is a health-based standard that the agency sets "at a level presumptively sufficient to protect public health and allows for an adequate margin of safety for the population within the area." Accordingly, the EPA found that "no affected population" could suffer "'adverse' impacts within the meaning of Title VI" from the emissions that Select Steel proposed. The EPA also noted that MDEQ had examined information about the actual lead levels in children living near the proposed plant and found no clear evidence that these levels were already high. The agency also agreed with MDEQ's conclusion that the plant met state standards for air toxics, and that the facility need not monitor dioxin emissions because the EPA has not yet set standards for such monitoring. Finally, the agency rejected the complaint's contention that the public participation process was discriminatory. The agency found that MDEQ had complied with and even exceeded state notice and public hearing requirements.

The *Select Steel* decision suggests that the EPA will not usually find Title VI violations against recipients that meet applicable health-based standards. Ann E. Goode, director of EPA's Office of Civil Rights, later explained her decision by stating the agency considers current regulatory standards to be protective of all people unless the complaint or investigation provides information to the contrary.[232] Furthermore, in a November 1998 meeting with several state officials, EPA Administrator Carol Browner and Goode stated that the agency will review only issues that the permitting authority has authority over, such as ambient air quality standards, but will no longer consider issues that the state or local agency has no control over, such as loss of property values or traffic changes indirectly caused by the granting of a permit.[233]

However, environmentalists are highly critical of *Select Steel*'s apparent position that compliance with the NAAQS necessarily establishes compliance with Title VI because disproportionate impacts against minorities are possible even if a facility meets safety standards for the population as a whole.[234] In the *Interim Guidance,* the agency had stated that "merely demonstrating that the permit complies with applicable environmental regulations will not ordinarily be considered a substantial, legitimate justification."[235]

Professor Richard Lazarus, a member of EPA's Title VI Implementation Advisory Committee, suggests that *Select Steel* provides a limited Title VI safe harbor for recipients if a permit complies with appropriate health-based standards. On the other hand, he maintains that a permit's compliance with either technology-based or performance-based standards that do not specify at what level pollution will cause adverse health effects will not necessarily defeat a Title VI claim.[236] Until EPA revises its Title VI guidance, it is uncertain to what extent a permit's compliance with existing regulatory standards is sufficient to defeat a Title VI complaint.

While pleased with their victory in *Select Steel,* Michigan officials remain concerned that the EPA will not resolve other Title VI complaints as quickly.[237] For example, the EPA has not yet decided a Title VI complaint filed in 1994 challenging the proposed Genesee Power Station, an incinerator that would be located immediately adjacent to an African American community in a heavily polluted area near Flint, Michigan.[238]

Conclusion

Title VI, which prohibits recipients of federal aid from discriminating against protected minority groups, potentially offers the most powerful weapon for environmental justice advocates to challenge state or local permitting decisions that allegedly have disparate impacts against minority groups. Under EPA's Title VI regulations, as well as those of other federal agencies that review siting decisions, citizens may file an administrative complaint alleging that a recipient's actions have caused discriminatory disparate impacts. Additionally, despite the Supreme Court's dismissal and vacatur of the *Chester* case, courts will eventually have to address whether agency regulations promulgated pursuant to Section 602 of Title VI create private rights of action allowing plaintiffs to file a disparate impact suit in the federal courts.

However, Title VI does not provide clear answers about when siting or permitting decisions are discriminatory. In February 1998, the EPA issued the *Interim Guidance* to provide some direction to its Title VI process, but it offers only vague definitions of crucial terms such as "disparate impact," "affected population," "cumulative burden," "mitigation," or "justification."

A wide range of state and local officials fear that uncertainty about how the EPA will apply the *Interim Guidance* could lead industry to refrain from siting projects in minority neighborhoods to avoid Title VI complaints and the possibility that the EPA might find discrimination. While the EPA never decided the Shintech complaint on the merits, the agency's laborious handling of that investigation legitimately raised concerns that the Title VI process might delay projects for years. Conversely, environmental justice advocates argue that the *Interim Guidance* already contains too many loopholes for recipients to use mitigation measures or a project's economic benefits to justify a project that causes significant adverse disparate impacts against minority groups.

The future of the EPA's Title VI program will remain uncertain until it issues a revised Title VI Guidance. However, the recent *Select Steel* decision offers possible insights into how the agency may implement the Title VI program. The agency went out of its way to reach an expeditious decision to address Michigan's concerns that a long Title VI investigation would lead the company to relocate the projected 200 jobs to Ohio. Furthermore, *Select Steel* suggests that the EPA will usually find no adverse effects under Title VI if a permit complies with applicable health-based standards. Whether the EPA will apply the same deference if a permit complies with technology-based or performance-based standards remains uncertain.

In the middle of 1999, the agency plans to issue a draft revision of its Title VI Guidance.[239] During the fiscal year 2000, which begins October 1, 1999, the agency is likely to issue a separate draft Guidance suggesting how state and local agencies can avoid such complaints.[240] Unlike the *Interim Guidance,* which took effect in interim form before the agency accepted any public comments, the EPA plans to issue both Guidances as draft documents and take public comments on them before issuing final versions.[241] However, the agency has so far rejected strong arguments that its Title VI policies must be issued as a formal rule rather than as an internal Guidance document.[242]

The EPA's revised Title VI Guidance will probably resolve some issues, but the agency will likely continue to face difficult issues in developing a policy that balances the protection of minority groups with reasonable opportunities for economic development. There are strong disagreements among various interest groups about how deferentially the EPA should treat the decisions of recipient state or local agencies, about defining what are significant health risks, and balancing the economic benefits of projects with their risks. Title VI cases are a microcosm of the complex issues that the environmental justice movement raises in general.

Notes

* The author thanks Michael Gerrard, Editor, for his assistance on this chapter, Adria Nobles for her fine research assistance, and law librarians Cynthia Aninao and Rick Goheen for obtaining several important references.

1. Civil Rights Act of 1964, Pub. L. No. 88-352, §§ 601–605, 78 Stat. 241, 252–53, 42 U.S.C. § 2000d.

2. "No Person in the United States shall, on the ground of race, color, or national origin, be excluded from participation in, be denied the benefits of, or be subjected to discrimination under any program or activity receiving Federal financial assistance." 42 U.S.C. § 2000d.

3. *See* Chapter 1 *supra*.

4. Each Federal department and agency which is empowered to extend Federal financial assistance to any program or activity, by way of grant, loan, or contract other than a contract of insurance or guaranty, is authorized and directed to effectuate the provisions of section 2000d of this title with respect to such program or activity by issuing rules, regulations, or orders of general applicability which shall be consistent with the achievement of the objectives of the statute authorizing the financial assistance in connection with which the action is taken.

   42 U.S.C. § 2000d-1.

5. 463 U.S. 582 (1983).

6. *See* Paul K. Sonn, Note, *Fighting Minority Underrepresentation in Publicly Funded Construction Projects After* Croson: *A Title VI Litigation Strategy*, 101 YALE L.J. 1577, 1581 n.25 (1992) (listing Title VI regulations for several federal agencies).

7. *See* 40 C.F.R. § 7.35(b) (prohibiting use of discriminatory program criteria), (c) (prohibiting location of facility that has discriminatory effect).

8. *See* Bradford C. Mank, *Is There a Private Right of Action Under EPA's Title VI Regulations?*, 24 COLUM. J. ENVTL. L. 1 (1999) [hereinafter Mank, *Private Right*].

9. *See infra* notes 114–18 and accompanying text.

10. *See* EPA, INTERIM GUIDANCE FOR INVESTIGATING TITLE VI ADMINISTRATIVE COMPLAINTS CHALLENGING PERMITS (Feb. 1998); Cheryl Hogue, *EPA Issues Guidance for Investigating Claims that State, Local Permits Are Discriminatory,* 66 U.S. LAW WEEK (Legal News), at 2504 (Feb. 24, 1998) [hereinafter Hogue, *EPA Issues*].

11. Section 601 of the statute provides that "[n]o person in the United States shall, on the ground of race, color, or national origin, be excluded from participation in, be denied the benefits of, or be subjected to discrimination under any program or activity receiving Federal financial assistance." Civil Rights Act of 1964, Pub. L. No. 88-352, §§ 601-605, 78 Stat. 241, 252–53, 42 U.S.C. § 2000d (1988).

12. *See* 42 U.S.C. § 2000d-1 (1988).

13. Guardians Ass'n v. Civil Service Commission, 463 U.S. 582, 618 (1983) (Marshall, J.) (quoting 45 C.F.R. § 80.3(b)(2) (1964).

14. *Guardians,* 463 U.S. at 592 n.13 (White, J.); *see* Sidney D. Watson, *Reinvigorating Title VI: Defending Health Care Discrimination—It Shouldn't Be So Easy,* 58 FORDHAM L. REV. 939, 947–48 (1990) (discussing how task force helped agencies develop similar disparate impact regulations under Title VI).

15. *See* Soberal-Perez v. Heckler, 717 F.2d 36, 38-39 (2d Cir. 1983); James H. Colopy, Note, *The Road Less Traveled: Pursuing Environmental Justice Through Title VI of the Civil Rights Act of 1964,* 13 STAN. ENVTL. L.J. 125, 154 (1994).

16. *See* Colopy, *supra* note 15, at 154.

17. *See* United States Dep't of Transp. v. Paralyzed Veterans of Am., 477 U.S. 597, 606 (1986); Terence J. Centner et al., *Environmental Justice and Toxic Releases: Establishing Evidence of Discriminatory Effect Based on Race and Not Income,* 3 WIS. ENVTL. L.J. 119, 135–36 (1996).

18. *See* 42 U.S.C. § 2000d-7 (1988); Bryant v. New Jersey Dept. of Transp., 1998 WL 337271 (D. N.J. 1998); Colopy, *supra* note 15, at 154–55.

19. *See infra* notes 78–85 and accompanying text.

20. *See* U.S. COMMISSION ON CIVIL RIGHTS, FEDERAL TITLE VI ENFORCEMENT TO ENSURE NONDISCRIMINATION IN FEDERALLY ASSISTED PROGRAMS 415 (June 1996); Brief for United States as Amicus Curiae at 5, Chester Residents Concerned for Quality Living v. Seif, 132 F.3d 925 (3d Cir. 1997) (No. 97-1125) [hereinafter U.S. Amicus Brief]; Richard J. Lazarus, *Pursuing "Environmental Justice": The Distributional Effects of Environmental Protection,* 87 NW. U L. REV. 787, 835–36 (1993) (citing U.S. EPA, A PRELIMINARY ANALYSIS OF THE PUBLIC COSTS OF ENVIRONMENTAL REGULATION: 1981–2000, at 9 (1988)) (reporting in 1986 the federal government provided 46 percent of the funding for state air pollution programs, 33 percent of the funding for state water pollution programs, and 40 percent of the funding for state hazardous waste programs); Colopy, *supra* note 15, at 129, 154–55.

21. *See* Colopy, *supra* note 15, at 173.

22. *See* 37 Fed. Reg. 11,072 (1972); U.S. Amicus Brief, *supra* note 20, at 5. In 1970, President Nixon established the EPA by consolidating several environmental programs and functions scattered in various government agencies and departments. *See* Bradford C. Mank, *Environmental Protection Agency's Project XL and Other Regulatory Reform Initiatives: The Need for Legislative Authorization,* 25 ECOLOGY L. Q. 1, 38–39 (1998).

23. *See* 38 Fed. Reg. 17,968, 17,969 (1973) (providing a recipient may not "directly or indirectly, utilize criteria or methods of administration which have

or may have the effect of subjecting a person to discrimination because of race, color, or national origin").

24. *See* 46 Fed. Reg. 2,306 (1981).

25. *See* 49 Fed. Reg. 1,661 (1984) (codified at 40 C.F.R. § 7.35(b)).

26. 40 C.F.R. § 7.35(c) (prohibiting location of facility that has discriminatory effect).

27. *See* 28 C.F.R. § 42.410.

28. *See, e.g.*, Nuclear Regulatory Commission, 10 C.F.R. § 4.12(c); Department of Energy, 10 C.F.R. § 1040.13(d); Department of Defense, 32 C.F.R. § 195.4(b)(1)(iii); Secretary of Transportation, 49 C.F.R. § 21.5(b)(3); and Federal Highway Administration, 23 C.F.R. § 200.5(f), 23 C.F.R Pt. 21, App. C (a)(2)(vi).

29. *See* Michael Fisher, *Environmental Racism Claims Brought Under Title VI of the Civil Rights Act*, 25 ENVTL. L. 285, 313–14 (1995); Don Willoh & Tom Collins, *Environmental Justice and TSD Siting Policies: Title VI is the Plaintiffs' Newest and Best Weapon, but Will It Succeed in Missouri*, 3 MO. ENVTL. L. & POL'Y REV. 78, 78–79 (1996); Colopy, *supra* note 15, at 180–88.

30. *See* North Carolina Dep't of Transp. v. Crest St. Council, 479 U.S. 6, 9 (1986).

31. *See* Fisher, *supra* note 29, at 314–15; Willoh & Collins, *supra* note 29, at 79.

32. *See* Presidential Memorandum Accompanying Executive Order 1289, 30 WEEKLY COMP. PRES. DOC. 279, 280 (Feb. 11, 1994); Chapter 4 *infra*.

33. *See* Natalie M. Hammer, *Title VI as a Means of Achieving Environmental Justice*, 16 N. ILL. U. L. REV. 693, 711 (1996).

34. Prepared Testimony of Ann E. Goode, Director of Civil Rights, U.S. EPA, Before the Oversight and Investigations Subcommittee of the House of Representatives Commerce Committee, FEDERAL NEWS SERVICE, Aug. 6, 1998; Paul Connolly, *Environmental Justice: Mayors RAP EPA at Meeting with Browner for Failure to Consult on* Interim Guidance, 29 ENV'T REP. (BNA) 658 (July 24, 1998); Cheryl Hogue, *Environmental Justice: Permits Cited in Civil Rights Complaints Have Remained Valid, EPA Official Says*, 152 DAILY ENV'T REP. (BNA) A-9 (Aug. 7, 1998) [hereinafter Hogue, *Permits Have Remained Valid*].

35. Connolly, *supra* note 34, at 658.

36. *See* Julie Domike & Arthur W. Ray, *EPA, Courts Focus on Title VI Issues in Locating Industrial Plants in Low-Income Areas*, NAT'L L.J., Dec. 1, 1997, at C1; Hammer, *supra* note 34, at 712–13; Hogue, *Permits Have Remained Valid*, *supra* note 35, at A-9; *infra* note 227 (discussing Genesee Power Station Title VI complaint that has remained pending for over four years).

37. *See infra* notes 226–230.

38. ENVTL. POL'Y ALERT (Dec. 31, 1997), at 31.

39. *See* EPA, INTERIM GUIDANCE, *supra* note 10.

40. *See* 40 C.F.R. § 7.120; Luke W. Cole, *Civil Rights, Environmental Justice and the EPA: A Brief History of Administrative Complaints Under Title VI of the Civil Rights Act of 1964*, 9 J. ENVTL. L. & LITIG. 309, 314–15, 319 (1994); Hammer, *supra* note 34, at 710–11.

41. *See* 40 C.F.R. § 7.120(b)(2); Cole, *supra* note 40, at 315–16.

42. Cole, *supra* note 40, at 315 n.18.

43. *See* EPA, INTERIM GUIDANCE, *supra* note 10 (explaining that EPA might waive 180-day time limit for "good cause" if complaint was delayed because the complainants were exhausting the recipient's administrative remedies).

44. EPA, INTERIM GUIDANCE, *supra* note 10; Terry L. Schnell & Kathleen J. Davies, *The Increased Significance of Environmental Justice in Facility Siting, Permitting,* 29 ENV'T REP. (BNA) 528, 530 (July 3, 1998).

45. *See* 40 C.F.R. § 7.120(d)(1).

46. *See* 40 C.F.R. § 7.120(d)(1), (2); Cole, *supra* note 40, at 316–17; Domike & Ray, *supra* note 36, at C1.

47. *See* 40 C.F.R. § 7.115(a) (authorizing EPA's Office of Civil Rights to conduct compliance reviews, including the request of information and on-site reviews); Domike & Ray, *supra* note 36, at C1.

48. *See* EPA, INTERIM GUIDANCE, *supra* note 10.

49. *See* 40 C.F.R. § 7.120(g).

50. *See* 40 C.F.R. § 7.130(b)(1)-(3); Cole, *supra* note 40, at 317–18; Colopy, *supra* note 15, at 129, 155. If the Administrator of the EPA recipient reviews the Administrative Law Judge's determination, all parties may file written statements. 40 C.F.R. § 7.130(b)(3)(ii).

51. *See* 40 C.F.R. § 7.130(b)(3)(iii), (4); 42 U.S.C. § 2000d-1; Cole, *supra* note 40, at 317–18; Colopy, *supra* note 15, at 129, 155.

52. 42 U.S.C. § 2000d-2.

53. *See* Washington Legal Foundation v. Alexander, 984 F.2d 483, 484 (D.C. Cir. 1993); Colopy, *supra* note 15, at 155.

54. *See* 40 C.F.R. § 7.130(a); Domike & Ray, *supra* note 36, at C1.

55. *See* Domike & Ray, *supra* note 36, at C1.

56. *See* 28 C.F.R. § 42.108(a); Colopy, *supra* note 15, at 155 n.134.

57. *See* Cole, *supra* note 40, at 321-24; Bradford C. Mank, *Environmental Justice and Title VI: Making Recipient Agencies Justify Their Siting Decisions,* 73 TUL. L. REV. 787 (1999); Mank, *Private Right, supra* note 8.

58. Cannon v. University of Chicago 441 U.S. 677, 706 n.41 (1979); Cole, *supra* note 40, at 321; Fisher, *supra* note 29, at 316; Mank, *Environmental Justice & Title VI, supra* note 57.

59. *See* 40 C.F.R. § 7.120(e).

60. *See* Cole, *supra* note 40, at 321–22; Hammer, *supra* note 33, at 711. The statute of limitations for Title VI and other civil rights causes of action is the applicable state personal injury statute of limitations. *See* Rozar v. Mullis, 85 F.3d 556 (11th Cir. 1996); Hammer, *supra* note 33, at 711 n.176.

61. *See* 40 C.F.R. § 7.130; Fisher, *supra* note 29, at 316; Colopy, *supra* note 15, at 178–80.

62. *See* 40 C.F.R. § 7.130(a); Hammer, *supra* note 33, at 711.

63. *See* Fisher, *supra* note 29, at 317 n.158; Mank, *Environmental Justice & Title VI, supra* note 57; Mank, *Private Right, supra* note 8; Colopy, *supra* note 15, at 168–69.

64. 441 U.S. 677, 715 (1979); Fisher, *supra* note 29, at 317 n.158.

65. *See* Women's Equity League v. Cavazos, 906 F.2d 742, 750 (D.C. Cir. 1990); Fisher, *supra* note 29, at 317 n.158; Colopy, *supra* note 15, at 169.

66. *See* Fisher, *supra* note 29, at 317 n.158.

67. *See Women's Equity Action League,* 906 F.2d at 748 ("Council for the Blind [v. Regan, 709 F.2d 1521 (D.C. Cir. 1983,] thus confirmed that 'if other remedies are adequate, federal courts will not oversee the overseer.'" (citing Coker v. Sullivan, 902 F.2d 84, 89 (D.C. Cir. 1990))); Fisher, *supra* note 29, at 317 n.158; Colopy, *supra* note 15, at 169.

68. *See* Heckler v. Chaney, 470 U.S. 821, 832 (1985); Colopy, *supra* note 15, at 170.

69. *See* Washington Legal Found. v. Alexander, 984 F.2d 483, 486–88 (D.C. Cir. 1993); Salvador v. Bennett, 800 F.2d 97, 99 (7th Cir. 1986); Fisher, *supra* note 29, at 317 n.158; Colopy, *supra* note 15, at 170.

70. *See* Adams v. Richardson, 480 F.2d 1159, 1162–64 (D.C. Cir. 1973) (Under APA, court enjoins HEW to enforce agency's prior determination that several recipient states operated racially discriminatory higher education systems) (en banc) (per curiam); Colopy, *supra* note 15, at 170.

71. *See* Cole, *supra* note 40, at 323; Colopy, *supra* note 15, at 167; Mank, *Private Right, supra* note 8.

72. *See* Colopy, *supra* note 15, at 167; Mank, *Private Right, supra* note 8.

73. *See* Cole, *supra* note 40, at 323; Mank, *Private Right, supra* note 8.

74. *See* Colopy, *supra* note 15, at 167.

75. *See* North Carolina Dep't of Transp. v. Crest St. Council, 479 U.S. 6, 12–16 (1986).

76. *See* Allen v. City of Chicago, 828 F. Supp. 543, 565 (N.D. Ill. 1993); Vakharia v. Swedish Covenant Hosp., 824 F. Supp. 769, 777-78 (N.D. Ill. 1993); Scelsa v. City Univ. of N.Y., 806 F. Supp. 1126, 1140 (S.D.N.Y. 1992); Coalition of Bedford-Stuyvesant Block v. Cuomo, 651 F. Supp. 1202, 1208 n.2 (E.D.N.Y. 1987); Wrenn v. Kansas, 561 F. Supp. 1216, 1221 (D. Kan. 1983).

77. *See Coalition of Bedford-Stuyvesant, supra* note 76, at 1208 n.2.

78. *See* Civil Rights Restoration Act of 1987, Pub. L. No. 100- 259, 102 Stat. 28 (1988) (codified at 42 U.S.C. § 2000d-4a) (overruling Grove City College v. Bell, 465 U.S. 555 (1984)); Fisher, *supra* note 29, at 318; Colopy, *supra* note 15, at 175; Sonn, *supra* note 6, at 1590-91.

79. 465 U.S. 555 (1984).

80. *See* United States v. Alabama, 828 F.2d 1532, 1548 (11th Cir. 1987) (per curiam), *cert. denied,* 487 U.S. 1210 (1988); Fisher, *supra* note 29, at 318.

81. *See* Civil Rights Restoration Act of 1987, §§ 2(2), 6, 20 U.S.C. § 1687(2)(A), 2000d-4a; Fisher, *supra* note 29, at 318.

82. EPA, INTERIM GUIDANCE, *supra* note 10; *see also* Civil Rights Restoration Act of 1987, 42 U.S.C. § 2000d-4a (overruling Grove City College v. Bell, 465 U.S. 555 (1984)); United States v. Louisiana, 692 F. Supp. 642, 652 (E.D. La. 1988); Fisher, *supra* note 29, at 318; Colopy, *supra* note 15, at 154–55 n.130, 175 nn.235–37; Sonn, *supra* note 6, at 1590–91.

83. *See* 42 U.S.C. § 2000d-4a (overruling Grove City College v. Bell, 465 U.S. 555 (1984)); Fisher, *supra* note 29, at 318; Colopy, *supra* note 15, at 175; Sonn, *supra* note 6, at 1590–91.

84. *See* Hodges v. Public Bldg. Comm'n, 864 F. Supp. 1493, 1506, 1509–10 (N.D. Ill. 1994); Allen v. City of Chicago, 828 F. Supp. 543, 565 (N.D. Ill. 1993); Vakharia v. Swedish Covenant Hosp., 824 F. Supp. 769, 777–78 (N.D. Ill. 1993); Scelsa v. City Univ. of N.Y., 806 F. Supp. 1126, 1140 (S.D.N.Y. 1992); Fisher, *supra* note 29, at 319.

85. 998 F. Supp. 438 (D. N.J. 1998) (reinstating Title VI claim that had been dismissed for lack of standing because National Credit Union Administration v. First National Bank & Trust Co., 118 S. Ct. 918 (1998) revised zone-of-interest

standing test and abolished intended beneficiary doctrine), *vacating*, 987 F. Supp. 343 (D. N.J. 1998) (holding Civil Rights Restoration Act of 1987 did not abolish intended beneficiary doctrine).

86. *See* Fisher, *supra* note 29, at 319.

87. *See* Lau v. Nichols, 414 U.S. 563, 568 (1974) (citing 45 C.F.R. 80.3(b)(2)); Lazarus, *supra* note 20, at 834–35.

88. *See* 438 U.S. 265, 318–19 (1978) (opinion of Powell); Colopy, *supra* note 15, at 158.

89. 463 U.S. 582, 584 n.2 (1983).

90. *See Guardians*, 463 U.S. at 610–11 (Powell, J., concurring in judgment, joined by Burger, C.J. & Rehnquist, J.); *id.* at 615 (O'Connor, J. concurring in judgment); *id.* at 642–45 (Stevens, dissenting, joined by Brennan & Blackmun, JJ.); Colopy, *supra* note 15, at 159. Justices White and Marshall each argued in dissent that showing disparate impacts was sufficient to prove a violation under Section 601. *See id.* 463 U.S. at 584 & n.2, 589–93 (White, J.); *id.* at 615, 623 (Marshall, J., dissenting).

91. "The threshold issue before the Court is whether the private plaintiffs in this case need to prove discriminatory intent to establish a violation of Title VI . . . and administrative implementing regulations promulgated thereunder. I conclude, as do four other Justices, in separate opinions, the Court of Appeals erred in requiring proof of discriminatory intent." *Guardians*, 463 U.S. at 584 (White, J., delivering judgment of the Court) (citations and footnotes omitted); *see Guardians*, 463 U.S. at 584 & n.2 (White, J., delivering judgment of the Court); *id.* at 642–45 (Stevens, J., joined by Brennan & Blackmun, JJ.); *id.* at 623 (Marshall, J.); Alexander v. Choate, 469 U.S. 287, 293 (1985) (Section 504 Rehabilitation Act of 1973 case unanimously interpreting *Guardians* to authorize agencies to issue Title VI regulations defining what constitutes impermissible disparate impacts discrimination); Lazarus, *supra* note 20, at 835; Colopy, *supra* note 15, at 159.

92. *See generally* J.I. Case Co. v. Borak, 377 U.S. 426 (1964) (holding that section 27 of the Securities Exchange Act of 1934 (SEC Act) created an implied right of action for alleged violations of section 14(a) of the Act because these types of suits would further its statutory purposes, including the protection of investors from false and misleading statements in proxy statements); RICHARD J. PIERCE ET AL., ADMINISTRATIVE LAW AND PROCESS 329–30 (2d ed. 1992); Susan J. Stabile, *The Role of Congressional Intent in Determining the Existence of Implied Rights of Action*, 71 NOTRE DAME L. REV. 861 (1996); Richard B. Stewart & Cass R. Sunstein, *Public Programs and Private Rights*, 95 HARV. L. REV. 1193 (1982).

93. *See supra* note 91 and *infra* notes 97–99 and accompanying text.

94. *See, e.g.*, Villanueva v. Carere, 85 F.3d 481, 486 (10th Cir. 1996) (implying private right of action exists under Title VI's Implementing Regulations); New York Urban League v. New York, 71 F.3d 1031, 1036 (2d Cir. 1995) (same); City of Chicago v. Lindley, 66 F.3d 819, 828–29 (7th Cir. 1995) (same); Elston v. Talladega County Bd. of Educ., 997 F.2d 1394, 1406–07 (11th Cir. 1993) (same); Larry P. v. Riles, 793 F.2d 969, 981–82 (9th Cir. 1984) (same); United States v. Lulac, 793 F.2d 636, 648 (5th Cir. 1986) (same); *see also* Buchanan v. City of Bolivar, 99 F.3d 1352, 1356 n.5 (6th Cir. 1995) (dictum); Latinos Unidos de Chelsea en Accion v. Secretary of HUD, 799 F.2d 774, 785 n.20 (1st Cir. 1986) (dictum).

95. *See infra* notes 113–18 and accompanying text.

96. 422 U.S. 66 (1975).

97. 441 U.S. 677 (1979); 20 U.S.C. § 1681.

98. 20 U.S.C. §§ 1681–82.

99. *See* Guardians Ass'n v. Civil Service Commission, 463 U.S. 582, 594 (1983) (White, J., announcing judgment of Court); *Cannon*, 441 U.S. at 694–703; Neighborhood Action Coalition v. City of Canton, 882 F.2d 1012, 1015 (6th Cir. 1989); Mabry v. State Bd. of Community Colleges & Occupational Educ., 813 F.2d 311, 317 (10th Cir. 1987), *cert. den.*, 484 U.S. 849 (1987); Colopy, *supra* note 15, at 156–57 nn.140–41.

100. *See generally Cannon*, 441 U.S. at 730–49 (Powell, J., dissenting).

101. *See, e.g.*, Central Bank v. First Interstate Bank, 511 U.S. 164, 178–80 (1994) (if statute does not explicitly create a private right of action, court examines whether Congress that passed the 1934 Exchange Act would have viewed the implication question); Suter v. Artist M., 503 U.S. 347, 363 (1992) (*Cort* places the burden on plaintiff to demonstrate Congress's intent to make a private remedy available); Karahalios v. National Federation of Federal Employees, Local 1263, 489 U.S. 527 (1989) (courts should focus on congressional intent in deciding whether to imply a private cause of action); Thompson v. Thompson, 484 U.S. 174, 179 (1988) (four factors in *Cort* are guides to congressional intent); Mank, *Private Right, supra* note 8; Stabile, *supra* note 92, at 868–71 (arguing Supreme Court beginning in 1979 began shifting away from four-factor *Cort* test to "an exclusive reliance on legislative intent").

102. 469 U.S. 287, 294 (1985) (footnote omitted).

103. *See* Chester Residents Concerned for Quality Living v. Seif, 132 F.2d 925, 930 (3d Cir. 1997), *vacated* 119 S. Ct. 22 (1998); *see generally Guardians*, 463 U.S. at 584 & n.2, 591–95 (White, J., delivering judgment of the Court); *id.* at 635–39 (Stevens, J., joined by Brennan & Blackmun, JJ.); and *id.* at 625–26, 634 (Marshall, J.); Mank, *Private Right, supra* note 8.

104. 944 F. Supp. 413 (E.D. Pa. 1996), *rev'd*, 132 F.2d 925 (3d Cir. 1997), *vacated* 119 S. Ct. 22 (1998); Mank, *Private Right, supra* note 8.

105. *Chester*, 132 F.3d at 934–35, *vacated* 119 S. Ct. 22 (1998); U.S. Amicus Brief, *supra* note 20, at 19–23; Civil Rights Restoration Act of 1987, Pub. L. No. 100-259, 102 Stat. 28 (1988); Mank, *Private Right, supra* note 8.

106. *See* Chester Residents Concerned for Quality Living v. Seif, 132 F.2d 925, 934-35 (3d Cir. 1997), *vacated* 119 S. Ct. 22 (1998); Mank, *Private Right, supra* note 8.

107. *See* Suter v. Artist M., 503 U.S. 347, 363 (1992) (*Cort* places the burden on plaintiff to demonstrate Congress' intent to make a private remedy available); Mank, *Private Right, supra* note 8.

108. *See* Chester Residents Concerned for Quality Living v. Seif, 132 F.2d 925, 934–35 (3d Cir. 1997), *vacated* 119 S. Ct. 22 (1998); 42 U.S.C. § 2000d-1; Mank, *Private Right, supra* note 8.

109. *See* Chester Residents Concerned for Quality Living v. Seif, 132 F.2d 925, 934–35 (3d Cir. 1997), *vacated* 119 S. Ct. 22 (1998); U.S. Amicus Brief, *supra* note 20, at 12–13; Mank, *Private Right, supra* note 8.

110. *See Cannon*, 441 U.S. at 704; Chester Residents Concerned for Quality Living v. Seif, 132 F.2d 925, 936 (3d Cir. 1997), *vacated* 119 S. Ct. 22 (1998); Mank, *Private Right, supra* note 8.

111. *See* U.S. Amicus Brief, *supra* note 20, at 12–13; Chester Residents Concerned for Quality Living v. Seif, 132 F.2d 925, 936 (3d Cir. 1997), *vacated* 119 S. Ct. 22 (1998), Mank, *Private Right, supra* note 8.

112. Seif v. Chester Residents Concerned for Quality Living, No. 97-1620 (U.S.), 118 S. Ct. 2296 (1998); Mank, *Private Right, supra* note 8.

113. Petition for Writ of Certiorari, Seif v. Chester Residents Concerned for Quality Living (U.S. 1998) (No. 97-1620), 118 S. Ct. 2296 (1998); Mank, *Private Right, supra* note 8.

114. Seif v. Chester Residents Concerned for Quality Living, No. 97-1620 (U.S.), 118 S. Ct. 2296 (1998); Motion for Leave to File Brief and Brief *Amicus Curiae* of the Washington Legal Foundation in Support of Petitioners, Seif v. Chester Residents Concerned for Quality Living (U.S. 1998) (No. 97-1620), 118 S. Ct. 2296 (1998) [hereinafter Foundation Amicus Brief]. On August 7, 1998, the United States Chamber of Commerce and National Black Chamber of Commerce also filed an amicus brief arguing that Title VI is limited to intentional discrimination. Brief of *Amicus Curiae* of Chamber of Commerce of the United States of America, National Black Chamber of Commerce, Inc. and Pennsylvania Chamber of Business and Industry in Support of Petitioners, Seif v. Chester Residents Concerned for Quality Living (U.S. 1998) (No. 97-1620), 118 S. Ct. 2296 (1998); Mank, *Private Right, supra* note 8.

115. 505 U.S. 717, 732 n.7 (1992).

116. *See* Suggestion of Mootness, Chester Residents Concerned for Quality Living, Seif v. Chester Residents Concerned for Quality Living (U.S. 1998) (No. 97-1620); *see also* Megan Defendis, *Pa. Unit Drops Lawsuit,* WASTE NEWS, Aug. 10, 1998, at 1; Mank, *Private Right, supra* note 8; Peyton Sturges, *Environmental Justice: High Court Dismisses Challenge, Vacates Third Circuit Civil Rights Decision,* 160 DAILY ENV'T REP. (BNA), Aug. 19, 1998, at AA-1.

117. *See* Opposition to Suggestion of Mootness, and, In the Alternative, Motion to Vacate, Commonwealth of Pennsylvania, Seif v. Chester Residents Concerned for Quality Living (U.S. 1998) (No. 97-1620); *see also* Megan Defendis, *Pa. Unit Drops Lawsuit,* WASTE NEWS, Aug. 10, 1998, at 1; Mank, *Private Right, supra* note 8; Peyton Sturges, *Environmental Justice: High Court Dismisses Challenge, Vacates Third Circuit Civil Rights Decision,* 160 DAILY ENV'T REP. (BNA), Aug. 19, 1998, at AA-1.

118. Seif v. Chester Residents Concerned for Quality Living, 119 S. Ct. 22 (1998); Mank, *Private Right, supra* note 8.

119. *See* U.S. Bancorp Mortgage Company v. Bonner Mall Partnership, 513 U.S. 18 (1994) (Supreme Court normally vacates moot cases, but not if petitioner voluntarily makes case moot through settlement); United States v. Munsingwear, Inc., 340 U.S. 36, 39 (1950) (Supreme Court normally vacates moot cases); Mank, *Private Right, supra* note 8.

120. *See* Sturges, *supra* note 117, at AA-1; Mank, *Private Right, supra* note 8. On June 3, 1998, in *Sandoval v. Hagan,* the District Court for the Middle District of Alabama agreed with the Third Circuit that a private right of action exists under Section 602. 7 F. Supp. 2d 1234, 1251–65 (M.D. 1998); Mank, *Private Right, supra* note 8.

121. *See* Civil Rights Attorney's Fees Awards Act of 1976, 42 U.S.C. § 1988(b). Because the Awards statute does not clearly waive sovereign immunity, plaintiffs cannot recover fees against the federal government.

122. *See Guardians,* 463 U.S. at 593–603, 607 n.27, 612 (White, J., announcing judgment of the court, joined by Rehnquist, J. in discussion of remedies); *id.* at 612 & n.1 (O'Connor, J. concurring in judgment) ("Because I conclude that the decision below should be affirmed on the ground that petitioners have failed to prove intentional discrimination, I have no occasion to address the question whether there is a private cause of action under Title VI for damages relief"); *but see* Vicki Been, *Environmental Justice and Equity Issues, in* 4 PATRICK J. ROHAN, ZONING AND LAND USE CONTROLS (Matthew Bender), at § 25D.04[3], at 101–02 (arguing Justice O'Connor never clearly provided fifth vote in *Guardians* for limiting remedies to plaintiffs alleging discriminatory effects); Watson, *supra* note 14, at 953 (same).

123. 503 U.S. 60, 74–76 (1992); Fisher, *supra* note 29, at 329.

124. *See* Cantuillo Independent School District v. Leija, 101 F.3d 393, 397 (5th Cir. 1996); Tyler v. City of Manhattan, 849 F. Supp. 1442, 1444–45 (D. Kan. 1994), *aff'd on other grounds,* 118 F.3d 1400 (10th Cir. 1997).

125. Justice O'Connor wrote the majority opinion, which Chief Justice Rehnquist, Justices Scalia, Kennedy, and Thomas joined. 118 S. Ct. 1989 (1998). Justice Stevens filed a dissenting opinion joined by Justices Souter, Ginsburg, and Breyer. Justice Ginsburg filed a dissenting opinion joined by Souter and Breyer.

126. *See* Fisher, *supra* note 29, at 329.

127. *See* Been, *supra* note 122, at § 25D.04[3][h], 102.

128. *See, e.g.,* Bryant v. New Jersey Dept. of Transp., 998 F. Supp. 438 (D. N.J. 1998) (holding plaintiffs have standing under Title VI, but not ruling on merits whether defendant discriminated in locating federally funded highway); Coalition of Concerned Citizens Against I-670 v. Damian, 608 F. Supp. 110, 127 (S.D. Ohio 1984).

129. *See, e.g.,* Dowdell v. Apopka, 511 F. Supp. 1375, 1383 (M.D. Fla. 1981), *aff'd,* 698 F.2d 1181, 1186 (11th Cir. 1983).

130. *See, e.g.,* NAACP v. Medical Ctr., Inc., 657 F.2d 1322, 1334 (3d Cir. 1981) (en banc); Bryan v. Koch, 627 F.2d 612, 618-19 (2d Cir. 1980); *see generally* Watson, *supra* note 14.

131. *See, e.g.,* Houston v. City of Cocoa, 2 Fair Hous.-Fair Lending (P-H) Para. 625 (M.D. Fla., Dec. 22, 1989) (challenge to location of condominiums in minority neighborhoods survives motion to dismiss before being settled).

132. *See, e.g.,* Jaimes v. Toledo Metro Hous. Auth., 758 F.2d 1086 (6th Cir. 1985); Project B.A.S.I.C. v. Kemp, 776 F. Supp. 637 (D. R.I. 1991).

133. *See* Larry P. v. Riles, 793 F.2d 969, 982 n.9 (9th Cir. 1984); Georgia State Conference of Branches of NAACP v. Georgia, 775 F.2d 1403, 1417 (11th Cir. 1985); Been, *supra* note 122, at § 25D.04[3][g][i], 89 n.89; Fisher, *supra* note 29, at 320; Watson, *supra* note 14, at 971–73.

134. *See* Mank, *Environmental Justice & Title VI, supra* note 57.

135. *See* Elston v. Talladega County Bd. of Educ., 997 F.2d 1394, 1407 (11th Cir. 1993) (to establish that a practice has a disproportionate effect, a plaintiff must show that there is a "causal link between the defendant's challenged practice and the disparate impact identified," or, in other words, that the same degree of disparate impact would not exist but for the challenged practice); NAACP v. Medical Ctr., Inc., 657 F.2d 1322, 1332–34 (3d Cir. 1981) (en banc);

Scelsa v. City Univ. of N.Y., 806 F. Supp. 1126, 1141 (S.D.N.Y. 1992); Coalition of Concerned Citizens Against I-670 v. Damian, 608 F. Supp. 110, 127 (S.D. Ohio 1984); Centner, *supra* note 17, at 138–39; Mank, *Environmental Justice & Title VI, supra* note 57; Watson, *supra* note 14, at 958; Colopy, *supra* note 15, at 161.

136. *See* Been, *supra* note 122, at § 25D.04[3][g][i], 90–92; Mank, *Environmental Justice & Title VI, supra* note 57.

137. Watson v. Fort Worth Bank & Trust, 487 U.S. 977, 994–95 (1988) (Title VII case suggesting no "rigid mathematical" threshold is essential to establish a prima facie case (plurality opinion)); Larry P. v. Riles, 793 F.2d 969, 982 n.9 (9th Cir. 1984) (Title VI case); Georgia State Conference of Branches of NAACP v. Georgia, 775 F.2d 1403, 1417 (11th Cir. 1985) (Title VI case); Coalition of Concerned Citizens Against I-670 v. Damian, 608 F. Supp. 110, 127 (S.D. Ohio 1984) (Title VI case); Been, *supra* note 122, at § 25D.04[3][g][i], 89–91.

138. *See* Hammer, *supra* note 33, at 708–09; Lazarus, *supra* note 20, at 838.

139. *See* United States v. Lulac, 793 F.2d 636, 649 (5th Cir. 1986) (In Title VI cases, defendant has burden of production in showing business or educational necessity); NAACP v. Medical Ctr., Inc., 657 F.2d 1322, 1333–34 (3d Cir. 1981) (en banc) (same); Centner, *supra* note 17, at 139; Susan S. Grover, *The Business Necessity Defense in Disparate Impact Discrimination Cases,* 30 GA. L. REV. 387, 394 (1996); Mank, *Environmental Justice & Title VI, supra* note 57.

140. 490 U.S. 642 (1989).

141. *See* Civil Rights Act of 1991, Pub. L. No. 102-166, § 105(a), 105 Stat. 1071, 1074-75 (codified at 42 U.S.C. §§ 2000e-2(k)(1)(A)(i), (B)(ii)); 42 U.S.C. § 2000e(m); Bradley v. Pizzaco of Neb., 7 F.3d 795, 797–99 (8th Cir. 1993) (Title VII case holding 1991 Act places burden of persuasion regarding business necessity on defendant); Fitzpatrick v. City of Atlanta, 2 F.3d 1112, 1117 & n.5 (11th Cir. 1993) (same); Been, *supra* note 122, at § 25D.04[3][g], 87–88 n.85; Fisher, *supra* note 29, at 321; Colopy, *supra* note 15, at 163–64.

142. *See* Elston v. Talladega County Bd. of Educ., 997 F.2d 1394, 1407 n. 14 (11th Cir. 1993); Been, *supra* note 122, at § 25D.04[3][g], 87; Fisher, *supra* note 29, at 321; Mank, *Environmental Justice & Title VI, supra* note 57; Colopy, *supra* note 15, at 163–64; Sonn, *supra* note 6, at 1596–97.

143. Wards Cove Packing v. Atonio, 490 U.S. 642, 660 (1989) (*quoting* Watson v. Fort Worth Bank & Trust, 487 U.S. 977, 998 (1988) (plurality opinion)); *see also* New York City Transit Auth. v. Beazer, 440 U.S. 568, 587 n.31 (1979) (In Title VII case, finding safety and cost savings justify disparate impacts); Furnco Constr. Corp. v. Waters, 438 U.S. 567, 570–71 (1978) (In Title VII case, finding safety and cost savings justify disparate impacts); Been, *supra* note 122, at § 25D.04[3][g][ii][A], 92–93; Mark S. Brodin, *Costs, Profits, and Equal Opportunity,* 62 NOTRE DAME L. REV. 318, 344–57 (1987) (citing cases); Mank, *Environmental Justice & Title VI, supra* note 57.

144. *See NAACP v. Medical Ctr., Inc.,* 657 at 1334 (stating "challenged practice must not only affect disproportionately, it must do so unnecessarily"); *Concerned Citizens,* 608 F. Supp. at 127 ("[d]efendants are not per se prohibited from locating a highway where it will have differential impacts upon minorities. Rather, Title VI prohibits taking actions with differential impacts without adequate justification"); Fisher, *supra* note 29, at 321; Mank, *Environmental Justice & Title VI, supra* note 57; Sonn, *supra* note 6, at 1597.

145. *See* Elston v. Talladega County Bd. of Educ., 997 F.2d 1394, 1407 n. 14, 1412–13 (11th Cir. 1993); Georgia State Conference of Branches of NAACP v. Georgia, 775 F.2d 1403, 1417-18 (11th Cir. 1985); Been, *supra* note 122, at § 25D.04[3][g], 88 n.87; Centner, *supra* note 17, at 139; Mank, *Environmental Justice & Title VI, supra* note 57; Colopy, *supra* note 15, at 162.

146. *See* Elston v. Talladega County Bd. of Educ., 997 F.2d 1394, 1413 (11th Cir. 1993) (lack of land for expansion at only proposed alternative site); Been, *supra* note 122, at § 25D.04[3][g][ii][A], 92-94 (citing cases); Centner, *supra* note 17, at 140 (lack of suitable alternative sites or lower land costs at the chosen site may be justifications for siting decision); Fisher, *supra* note 29, at 321; Mank, *Environmental Justice & Title VI, supra* note 57.

147. 42 U.S.C. § 2000e-2(k)(1)(A)(i)); Albermale Paper Co. v. Moody, 422 U.S. 405, 425 (1975) ("other test or selection devices, without a similarly undesirable racial effect, would also serve the employer's legitimate interest in 'efficient and trustworthy workmanship'") (quoting McDonnell Douglas Corp v. Green, 411 U.S. 792, 802 (1973)); Been, *supra* note 122, at § 25D.04[3][g], 89 n.88; Mank, *Environmental Justice & Title VI, supra* note 57; Colopy, *supra* note 15, at 164.

148. Elston v. Talladega County Bd. of Educ., 997 F.2d 1394, 1407 (11th Cir. 1993); Been, *supra* note 123, at § 25D.04[3][g], 89 n.88; Mank, *Environmental Justice & Title VI, supra* note 57; Colopy, *supra* note 15, at 162–63.

149. *See* York v. ATT, 95 F.3d 948 (10th Cir. 1996) (Title VII); MacPherson v. University of Montevallo, 922 F.2d 766, 771 (11th Cir. 1991) (quoting Wards Cove Packing v. Atonio, 490 U.S. 642, 661 (1989)) (Title VII); Georgia State Conference of Branches of NAACP v. Georgia, 775 F.2d 1403, 1417 (11th Cir. 1985); Mank, *Environmental Justice & Title VI, supra* note 57.

150. Fitzpatrick v. City of Atlanta, 2 F.3d 1112, 1118-19 (11th Cir. 1992) (Title VII); Elston v. Talladega County Bd. of Educ., 997 F.2d 1394, 1407 (11th Cir. 1993) (Title VI); Mank, *Environmental Justice & Title VI, supra* note 57.

151. *See* Georgia State Conference of Branches of NAACP v. Georgia, 775 F.2d 1403, 1417 (11th Cir. 1985) (stating plaintiff must present "equally effective" alternative sites); Coalition of Concerned Citizens Against I-670 v. Damian, 608 F. Supp. 110, 128 (S.D. Ohio 1984) (concluding plaintiff failed to present specific alternative sites); Been, *supra* note 122, at § 25D.04[3][g][iii], 98–100 (arguing environmental justice plaintiff in Title VI action should be prepared to demonstrate availability of alternative sites); Fisher, *supra* note 29, at 321 (same); Hammer, *supra* note 33, at 708–09 (same); Mank, *Environmental Justice & Title VI, supra* note 57; Colopy, *supra* note 15, at 162–63 (same).

152. *See* Bryan v. Koch, 627 F.2d 612, 619 (2d Cir. 1980); Been, *supra* note 122, at § 25D.04[3][g][iii], 99–100; Mank, *Environmental Justice & Title VI, supra* note 57.

153. *See* EPA, INTERIM GUIDANCE, *supra* note 10; Hogue, *EPA Issues, supra* note 10, at 2504.

154. *See infra* notes 239–241 and accompanying text.

155. *See* Hogue, *Permits Have Remained Valid, supra* note 34, at A-9; *infra* notes 161–63.

156. Cheryl Hogue, *Comments on Title VI Guidance Seek Clearer Definitions, Input from More Parties,* 29 ENV'T REP. (BNA) 234, 234 (May 22, 1998) [hereinafter Hogue, *Comments on Title VI Guidance*].

157. Jeffrey B. Gracer, *Taking Environmental Justice Claims Seriously*, 28 ENVTL. L. REP. (News & Analysis) 10373, 10375 (July 1998); Hogue, *Comments on Title VI Guidance, supra* note 156, at 234–35; *Environmental Council of States Resolution on EPA Interim Guidance for Investigating Permit Challenges Approved March 26*, 1998, 59 DAILY ENV'T REP. (BNA) E-1 (March 27, 1998); *U.S. Conference on Mayors Calls on EPA to Suspend Guidance on Civil Rights*, 29 ENV'T REP. (BNA) 469, 469 (June 26, 1998); *Environmental Justice: Western Governors' Association Joins Call for EPA to Withdraw Civil Rights Guidance*, 129 DAILY ENV'T REP. (BNA) A-2 (July 7, 1998).

158. *See* Prepared Testimony of Ann E. Goode, *supra* note 34; Connolly, *supra* note 34, at 658; Hogue, *Permits Have Remained Valid*, *supra* note 34, at A-9.

159. *See* Angela M. Baggetta, *Environmental Justice: Black Caucus, EPA to Meet on Shintech; Dispute May Be Test Case on Title VI Suits*, 139 DAILY ENV'T REP. (BNA), July 21, 1998, at A-1; Luke W. Cole & Richard Moore, *Attacks on EPA Unfair*, USA TODAY, July 20, 1998, at 14A.

160. *See* Prepared Testimony of Ann E. Goode, *supra* note 34; Connolly, *supra* note 34, at 658; Hogue, *Permits Have Remained Valid*, *supra* note 34, at A-9.

161. Cheryl Hogue, *Hansen Suggests 'Template' to Guide States, Localities on Title VI Compliance*, 29 ENV'T REP. (BNA) 232, 232 (May 22, 1998); *Environmental Justice: Agency Relying on Advisory Committee to Face State Title VI Guidance Concerns*, 28 ENV'T REP. (BNA) 2690, 2690 (April 17, 1998); *New EPA Advisory Committee to Address Rights Concerns on State, Local Permitting*, 28 ENV'T REP. (BNA) 2441 (March 20, 1998).

162. *See Environmental Justice Panel Ponders Disputes, Consensus Unlikely*, ENVTL. POL'Y ALERT, Jan. 27, 1999, at 33–34.

163. *See* Cheryl Hogue, *SAB Recommends Steps for EPA in Analyses of Disproportionate Impacts*, 29 ENV'T REP. (BNA) 1310, 1310–11 (Oct. 30, 1998); *see also* Science Advisory Board, Notification of Public Advisory Committee Meetings, 63 Fed. Reg. 43394 (1998); QUESTIONS FOR THE SCIENCE ADVISORY BOARD ON THE TITLE VI RELATIVE BURDEN ANALYSES AND CUMULATIVE OUTDOOR AIR TOXICS CONCENTRATIONS AND EXPOSURE METHODOLOGY <http:www.epa.gov/science1/fsabreq5.htm>.

164. *See* Appropriations Act for Departments of Veterans Affairs and Housing and Urban Development and Independent Agencies for Fiscal Year Ending September 30, 1999, Pub. L. No. 105-276 (H.R. 4194), 112 Stat. 2461, 105th Cong. tit. III (1998); Cindy Skrzycki, *The Regulators: With EPA as Judge-Up Against the Environmental Justice System*, WASHINGTON POST, Oct. 23, 1998, at F1; Bill Walsh, *Law Puts EPA Bias Rules on Hold: Industry Targets Racism Probes*, NEW ORLEANS TIME-PICAYUNE, Oct. 23, 1998, at A8.

165. *See* Skrzycki, *supra* note 164, at F1; Walsh, *supra* note 164, at A8.

166. *See id.*

167. *See id.*

168. INTERIM GUIDANCE, *supra* note 10, at 8.

169. Roy S. Belden, *EPA Releases* Interim Guidance *for Investigating Title VI Environmental Justice Complaints Challenging Permits*, 2 ABA SECTION OF NATURAL RESOURCES, ENERGY, AND ENVTL. LAW, AIR QUALITY NEWSLETTER, No. 2, at 7 (April 1998); Gracer, *supra* note 157, at 10374–75.

170. INTERIM GUIDANCE, *supra* note 10, at 9 n.12.

171. *See* Belden, *supra* note 169, at 8; Gracer, *supra* note 157, at 10375.

172. INTERIM GUIDANCE, *supra* note 10; Schnell & Davies, *supra* note 44, at 530.

173. *Id.*

174. Mank, *Environmental Justice & Title VI, supra* note 57 (arguing EPA should require effective mitigation measures to justify project that would otherwise violate Title VI).

175. INTERIM GUIDANCE, *supra* note 10, at 11.

176. *Id.*, at 12.

177. *Id.*

178. *Id.*

179. *But see* Mank, *Environmental Justice & Title VI, supra* note 57 (arguing EPA should revise standard that recipient must adopt less discriminatory alternative that is "equally effective" and instead require recipients to implement any less discriminatory alternative that is "comparably effective").

180. *See* Belden, *supra* note 169, at 8; Gracer, *supra* note 157, at 10375; Hogue, *Comments on Title VI Guidance, supra* note 156, at 234 (reporting public commenters have criticized Guidance for failing to define terms "disparate impact," "mitigation," or "alternative" facility); David Mastio, *Green Monster,* 50 NATIONAL REVIEW, No. 12, July 6, 1998, at 22 (arguing Guidance fails to define terms "disparate impact" or "impacted community").

181. Baggetta, *supra* note 159, at A-1; Mank, *Environmental Justice & Title VI, supra* note 57 (arguing EPA should place the burden on recipients to justify their permit decisions in a Title VI complaint, but that EPA must give some deference to recipient policy choices).

182. The APA requires agencies to use notice-and-comment rulemaking to issue new "legislative rules" or modify existing substantive rules that are judicially binding. 5 U.S.C. § 553(c); Nat'l Wildlife Found. v. Adamkus, 936 F. Supp. 435, 444 (W.D. Mich. 1996).

183. An agency's interpretation of an existing policy or issuance of a general policy statement that is not judicially binding, however, does not necessarily trigger either the APA's notice-and-comment rulemaking provisions, or require new statutory authority. *See generally* 5 U.S.C. 553(b) (exempting "interpretive rules" and "general policy statement" from notice-and-comment rulemaking); Shalala v. Guernsey Memorial Hospital, 514 U.S. 87, 99 (1995) ("interpretive rules" are exempt from notice-and-comment rulemaking because they are not legally binding); PIERCE ET AL., *supra* note 92, at 285–89.

184. John Chambers, *The Supreme Court has agreed to take up an issue that has stymied regulators and judges: waste disposal facilities planned for construction in minority areas,* NAT. L. J., June 22, 1998, at B6; Hogue, *Comments on Title VI Guidance, supra* note 156, at 236–37.

185. *See* Mastio, *Green Monster, supra* note 170, at 22.

186. Nat'l Medical Enterprises v. Shalala, 43 F.3d 691, 697 (D.C. Cir. 1995).

187. Belden, *supra* note 168, at 8; Chambers, *supra* note 184, at B6; Hogue, *Comments on Title VI Guidance, supra* note 156, at 236–37.

188. Chambers, *supra* note 184, at B6; Hogue, *Comments on Title VI Guidance, supra* note 156, at 236–37; *EPA Civil Rights Policy Lacks Recognition of State Permit Processes, Attorneys Say,* 29 ENV'T REP. (BNA) 183 (May 15, 1998).

189. Letter from Robert P. Murphy, General Counsel, GAO, to Representative David MacIntosh, GAO Legal Opinion B-281575 (January 20, 1999). *See*

David Mastio, *Report: Pollution policy faulty: EPA environmental justice guideline could face overhaul*, DETROIT NEWS, Feb. 5, 1999; David Mastio, *GAO: EPA wrong on enviro policy*, Gannett News Service, Feb. 4, 1999, 1999 WL 6961706.

190. David Mastio, *GAO: EPA wrong on enviro policy*, *supra* note 189; *see generally* Unfunded Mandates Reform Act of 1995, Pub. L. No. 104-4, 109 Stat. 48 (1995) (codified in scattered sections of 2 U.S.C.); Regulatory Flexibility Act, as amended by the Small Business Regulatory Enforcement Fairness Act of 1996 (SBREFA), Pub. L. No. 104-121, §§ 201–253, 110 Stat. 847, 857–74 (1996) (codified at 5 U.S.C. §§ 601–612 and scattered sections of 15 & 28 U.S.C.).

191. *See generally* Chambers, *supra* note 184, at B6; Hogue, *Comments on Title VI Guidance*, *supra* note 156, at 236–37.

192. Chambers, *supra* note 184, at B6.

193. Chambers, *supra* note 184, at B6.

194. Chambers, *supra* note 184, at B6.

195. Schnell & Davies, *supra* note 44, at 530.

196. Baggetta, *supra* note 159, at A-1.

197. Baggetta, *supra* note 159, at A-1; *EPA bungling leaves 'environmental justice' elusive*, USA TODAY, July 20, 1998, at 14A.

198. The term "cancer alley" refers to the approximately eighty-five mile industrial corridor from Baton Rouge to New Orleans, Louisiana, which contains numerous petrochemical facilities and a large minority population. *See* Omar Saleem, *Overcoming Environmental Discrimination: The Need for a Disparate Impact Test and Improved Notice Requirements in Facility Siting Decisions*, 19 COLUM. J. ENVTL. L. 211, 230 n.80 (1994) (discussing high level of pollution and substantial minority population in St. James Parish, Louisiana); *but see* CHRISTOPHER FOREMAN, THE PROMISE AND PERIL OF ENVIRONMENTAL JUSTICE 75–76 (1998)(observing that there are high levels of pollution and substantial minority populations in the so-called "cancer alley" area between New Orleans and Baton Rouge, Louisiana, but arguing that a recent study did not find elevated cancer rates in that area).

199. Mark Schleifstein, *Shintech Is Biding Its Time*, NEW ORLEANS TIMES-PICAYUNE, Aug. 2, 1998, at A15.

200. Laura Litvan, *Fighting Racism: EPA's New Role*, INVESTOR'S BUSINESS DAILY, March 25, 1998, at A1.

201. Dennis Cauchon, *Racial, Economic Divide in Louisiana*, USA TODAY, Sept. 9, 1997, at 3A; Schleifstein, *Shintech Is Biding Its Time*, *supra* note 199, at A15. There is some disagreement about exactly how much pollution the plant would release, depending in part on differing definitions. Shintech has claimed that it will only emit 192,000 pounds of air pollution per year. Margaret Kriz, *The Color of Poison*, NAT'L J., July 11, 1998. Greenpeace, however claims the facility will release more than 600,000 pounds of toxic air pollutants, and 8 million gallons of waste water. *Opposition to Shintech Vinyls Plant Growing*, CHEMICAL MARKET REPORTER, May 18, 1998, at 4.

202. Mark Schleifstein, *Foster, Clinics Face Off on Rules: Legal Debate Goes Beyond Shintech*, NEW ORLEANS TIMES-PICAYUNE, Aug. 2, 1998, at A15.

203. Bruce Alpert, NEW ORLEANS TIMES-PICAYUNE, June 15, 1998, at A1 (1998 WL 6278360) (reporting Senators Carol Moseley-Braun and Paul Wellstone and Representative John Conyers have sent letters to EPA opposing construction of

Shintech plant); *Opposition to Shintech Vinyls Plant Growing*, CHEMICAL MARKET REPORTER, May 18, 1998, at 4 (same).

204. Henry Payne, *Green Nonsense, Black Losses*, THE WEEKLY STANDARD, Aug. 3, 1998, at 25.

205. Joe Gyan, Jr., *Demonstrators Assault Ruling*, THE ADVOCATE (Baton Rouge, La.), June 27, 1998, at 1B–2B.

206. La. S. Ct. Rule XX, Limited Participation of Law Students in Trial Work, as amended by La. Orders 98-25 & 98-28 (La. S. Ct. 1998) (effective July 1, 1998); Mark Ballard, *La. High Court Reins in Legal Clinic*, NAT'L. L. J., July 6, 1998, at A11; Alan Chadwick & Debbie Elliott, *Morning Edition*, (National Public Radio, July 30, 1998), 1998 WL 3308203 (transcript of radio news program); Joe Gyan, Jr., *Law Clinic Ruling Softened*, THE ADVOCATE (Baton Rouge, La.), July 2, 1998, at 1A; Oliver A. Houck, NEW ORLEANS TIME-PICAYUNE, June 25, 1998, at B7 (Houck is a professor at Tulane Law School); *Court's Ruling Unjust to Ordinary Citizens*, Eamon M. Kelly, *A Power Play Against Environmental Justice*, June 25, 1998, at B6 (Kelly is president of Tulane University).

207. *See Shintech debate continues*, Associated Press Political Service, July 17, 1998 (1998 WL 7430299).

208. Schnell & Davies, *supra* note 44, at 530.

209. Donna Porstner, *Chambers align to fight against 'environmental justice' policy*, WASHINGTON TIMES, July 20, 1998, at D17. On August 7, 1998, the United States Chamber of Commerce and National Black Chamber of Commerce filed a joint amicus brief arguing that Title VI is limited to intentional discrimination. *See supra* note 114.

210. David Mastio, *Black Caucus backs EPA rule: Enforce environmental justice guidelines, urges Conyers-led coalition*, DETROIT NEWS, July 17, 1998, at A4; John McQuaid, *Congressional Black Caucus Wants EPA to Block Shintech*, NEW ORLEANS TIME- PICAYUNE, July 17, 1998, at A2 (1998 WL 6283634).

211. *See In re Shintech Inc.*, Petition on Permit Nos. 2466-VO, 2467-VO, 2468-VO (EPA, Sept. 10, 1997); 42 U.S.C. § 7661d(b)(2); Domike & Ray, *supra* note 36, at C1.

212. *See* Belden, *supra* note 169, at 6–7; Stephen C. Jones & Anoop G. Shroof, *Balancing Growth and the Environment; Environmental Justice Concerns Delay Industrial Expansion*, 13 ENVTL. COMPLIANCE & LITIG. STRATEGY, No. 5, at 1 (Oct. 1997).

213. Chambers, *supra* note 184, at B6.

214. Bob Anderson, *Groups Target DEQ on Shintech Permits*, THE ADVOCATE (Baton Rouge, La.), July 17, 1997, at 20A.

215. *See* Andrea Foster, *Shintech Ruling Awaits Review*, 260 CHEMICAL WEEK, No. 28, July 22, 1998, at 56; Susan Hansen, *Backlash on the Bayou*, AM. LAWYER, January/February 1998, at 52, 57.

216.*See generally* Baggetta, *supra* note 159, at A-1.

217. Vicki Ferstel, *Data for EPA's Shintech Decision Confusing at Best*, THE ADVOCATE (Baton Rouge, La.), July 2, 1998, at 1B.

218. Baggetta, *supra* note 159, at A-1.

219. *See* Mark Schleifstein, *Shintech Taking Its Plant Upriver*, NEW ORLEANS TIMES-PICAYUNE, Sept. 18, 1998, at A1; Traci Watson, *La. Town Successful in Stopping Plastics Plant*, USA TODAY, Sept. 18, 1998, at 7A; James Worsham, *Business Loses First Round in Environmental Justice Fight*, NATION'S BUSINESS, Nov. 1, 1998.

220. *See* Worsham, *supra* note 219.

221. *See EPA Moving Toward Statewide Environmental Equity Review in Louisiana*, ENVTL. POL'Y ALERT, Dec. 30, 1998, at 3.

222. *See EPA Moving Toward Statewide Environmental Equity Review in Louisiana*, *supra* note 221, at 3.

223. *See* Letter from Ann E. Goode, Director, EPA's Office of Civil Rights, Re: EPA File No. 5R-98-R5 (Select Steel Complaint) to St. Francis Prayer Center [Complainant] and Michigan Department of Environmental Quality [Recipient] (Oct. 30, 1998) (dismissing Title VI complaint against Michigan Department of Environmental Quality) [hereinafter Letter from Ann E. Goode, *Select Steel* decision].

224. *See generally* 42 U.S.C. §§ 7470–7492.

225. *See* Letter from Ann E. Goode, *Select Steel* decision, *supra* note 223; Paul Connolly, *Environmental Justice: EPA Dismisses Michigan Complaint; State Officials Still Wary of New Policy*, 211 DAILY ENV'T REP. (BNA) AA-1 (Nov. 2, 1998) [hereinafter Connolly, *EPA Dismisses Michigan Complaint*]; *EPA Rejects Select Steel Environmental Justice Complaint*, ENVTL. POL'Y ALERT, Nov. 4, 1998, at 5. The Complainants had also filed a PSD petition under 40 C.F.R. § 124.19 with EPA's Environmental Appeals Board, but the Board summarily rejected the petition. *In re: Select Steel Corporation of America*, Permit No. 579-97, Docket No. PSD 98-21, Sep. 10, 1998; Gerald H. Yamada, *Federal Rights Act Doesn't Authorize "Environmental Justice,"* 9 WASHINGTON LEGAL FOUNDATION, LEGAL OPINION LETTER, No. 2, Jan. 8, 1999.

226. *See* Letter from Ann E. Goode, *Select Steel* decision, *supra* note 224, at 2; Paul Connolly, *EPA Dismisses Michigan Complaint*, *supra* note 225, at AA-1 (Nov. 2, 1998).

227. *See* Connolly, *supra* note 225, at AA-1.

228. *See* Connolly, *supra* note 225, at AA-1.

229. *See EPA Rejects Select Steel Environmental Justice Complaint*, ENVTL. POL'Y ALERT, Nov. 4, 1998, at 5.

230. *See* Letter from Ann E. Goode, *Select Steel* decision, *supra* note 223; Connolly, *supra* note 225, at AA-1.

231. *See* Letter from Ann E. Goode, *Select Steel* decision, *supra* note 223, at 3–4.

232. *See* Cheryl Hogue, *Draft Revision of Guidance for Processing Civil Rights Complaints Expected Mid-1999*, 29 ENV'T REP. (BNA) 1807 (Jan 15, 1999).

233. *See* Cheryl Hogue, *Environmental Justice: Michigan DEQ Chief Says EPA Narrowing Issues Considered in Title VI Complaints*, 225 DAILY ENV'T REP. (BNA) A-1 (Nov. 23, 1998); *EPA Will Limit Scope of Environmental Justice Investigations*, ENVTL. POL'Y ALERT, Dec. 2, 1998; *EPA's Browner Pledges Not to Go Beyond States in Title VI Rulings*, SOLID WASTE REPORT, Dec. 3, 1998.

234. *See, e.g.* Letter from Jerome Balter, Public Interest Center of Philadelphia, to Ann E. Goode, Director of EPA Office of Civil Rights, Nov. 12, 1998.

235. *See* INTERIM GUIDANCE, *supra* note 10, at 12.

236. *See* Hogue, *Draft Revision of Guidance for Processing Civil Rights Complaints Expected Mid-1999*, *supra* note 232, at 1807.

237. *See* Connolly, *supra* note 225, at AA-1; *EPA Turns Away Title VI Challenge to Michigan Steel-Recycling Plant*, SOLID WASTE REPORT, Nov. 12, 1998.

238. *See* EPA File No. 1R-94-R5; Paul Connolly, *Environmental Justice: Michigan Regulators Claim Victory in Ruling Ending Injunction on Issuance of Air Permits*, 29 ENV'T REP. (BNA) 1548 (Dec. 4, 1998). In 1997 a Michigan trial court judge issued an injunction prohibiting the state from issuing new air permits in Genesee County until the state developed procedures to protect the public health, but the Michigan Court of Appeals held the trial court was without authority to issue an injunction sua sponte based on a claim that was neither pleaded nor litigated by the parties. NAACP-Flint Chapter v. Governor of Michigan, Michigan Court of Appeals (Unpublished Nov. 24, 1998) (No. 205264, Genesee Cir. Court LC No. 95-038228 CV); Connolly, *supra*, at 1548.

239. *See* Hogue, *Draft Revision of Guidance for Processing Civil Rights Complaints Expected Mid-1999*, *supra* note 232, at 1807.

240. *Id.*

241. *Id.*

242. *See EPA Defends Environmental Justice Policy, Process to Bliley*, ENVTL. POL'Y ALERT, Dec. 30, 1998, at 30-31 (reporting Ann E. Goode, Director of EPA's Office of Civil Rights, declined Congressman Bliley's suggestion to reformulate the *Interim Guidance* as a rule); *supra* notes 182–191.

CHAPTER 3

Other Civil Rights Titles

COLIN CRAWFORD

Introduction

In 1995, the late Ralph Santiago Abascal, co-counsel in one of the most celebrated environmental justice (EJ) victories of the 1990s,[1] lamented that "reported environmental justice cases that have raised civil rights claims have been litigated under the wrong theories."[2] Abascal regretted that these cases were litigated under the "difficult" legal theory of Fourteenth Amendment equal protection[3] while, he insisted, the civil rights claims more likely to achieve victory included, inter alia, those under the Fair Housing Act (FHA), also known as Title VIII of the Civil Rights Act of 1968.[4] Indeed, he went on to suggest that Title VIII is the civil rights "statute with perhaps the broadest reach" in EJ cases.[5] Subsequently, numerous commentators have endorsed Abascal's suggestion, although some others have doubted that FHA claims in EJ cases are likely to prove any less difficult to litigate than Fourteenth Amendment claims.[6] This chapter, therefore, will explore the potential usefulness of an FHA claim in the context of an EJ challenge to an undesirable or noxious land use, assuming that noxious use demonstrably limits housing opportunities for people of color. In addition, the chapter will explore the possible relevance of related claims as a tool to challenge allegedly discriminatory siting and land use practices. In particular, it will examine Section 1982 of the Civil Rights Act of 1866,[7] which guarantees all citizens the same rights with respect to real and personal property transactions.

At the outset, it bears emphasizing that, as of this writing, no reported cases have successfully advanced Title VIII or Section 1982 claims in support of an EJ case, despite the exhortations of Abascal and others. Furthermore, a review of the case law suggests that, although the federal fair housing and equal property protection laws are potentially powerful tools in EJ lawsuits, EJ plaintiffs who wish to advance FHA or Section 1982 claims should do so only after understanding the differences in coverage between the statutes, and in each instance only when supported by a well-documented factual record.

Before turning to a detailed discussion of both Title VIII and Section 1982, it may be useful to identify briefly the most important concerns regarding possible causes of action under both statutes. First, successful FHA plaintiffs must show that a defendant's actions resulted in the denial of *housing* opportunities to persons covered by the statute—a list that includes but is not limited to people of color.[8] Second, and by contrast, Section 1982 applies not merely to residential realty, but also to personalty and commercial realty—although it protects only racial and ethnic minorities. Third, a Title VIII plaintiff is likely merely to have to show that a defendant's actions had a discriminatory effect, while a Section 1982 claim almost certainly requires the far more difficult showing of discriminatory intent. Finally, and above all, it is essential to keep in mind that neither the FHA nor Section 1982 was designed to be used for general land use challenges.[9] Consequently, in developing a case, prospective EJ plaintiffs using the federal fair housing laws should concentrate on showing damage to their own property and contract rights, rather than generalized assertions about the harms that property in a community may suffer as the result of a noxious or unwanted land use.

Fair Housing Act Claims in Environmental Justice Disputes

Much of the appeal of a Title VIII claim for a prospective plaintiff lies in the fact that Title VIII almost certainly requires only a showing of "discriminatory effect," rather than the much more demanding standard of discriminatory intent. The distinction between effect and intent is discussed elsewhere in this chapter and volume.[10] However, in all of what follows, the discriminatory effect standard that will likely be used in Title VIII actions should be kept in mind.

Three FHA sections are of relevance to the possible EJ plaintiff, and need to be examined in turn. In addition, it is useful to examine other procedural features of the FHA that might be useful in the course of preparing an EJ case.

42 U.S.C. § 3604(a)

Section 3604(a) makes it unlawful:

> To refuse to sell or rent after the making of a bona fide offer, or to refuse to negotiate for the sale or rental of, or otherwise make unavailable or deny, a dwelling to any person because of race, color, religion, sex, familial status, or national origin.[11]

Because Section 3604(a) refers to selling or renting, on its face it appears to have little application to municipal authorities or private enterprises uninvolved in the direct provision of housing.[12] Since these parties—such as a private developer of a waste facility or an agency responsible for environmental permitting—are the most likely defendants in an EJ action, Section 3604(a) might at first blush appear to have limited applicability for the prospective EJ plaintiff. In a relevant case interpreting the potential scope of Section 3604(a), however, the Seventh Circuit observed that "although Section 3604(a) applies principally to the sale or rental of dwellings, courts have construed the phrase 'otherwise make unavailable or deny' in subsection (a) to encompass mortgage 'redlining,' insurance redlining, racial steering, exclusionary zoning decisions, and other actions by individuals or governmental units which directly affect the availability of housing to minorities."[13] For the prospective EJ litigant, the central question raised by this dictum is simple: what "other actions by individuals or governmental units" can be found that directly affect housing availability for people of color?

Unfortunately, the reported case law does not provide a clear answer to that question. In *Southend,* plaintiffs, a coalition of community action groups in East St. Louis, Illinois, complained that the defendant county had purchased large numbers of properties in African American neighborhoods by tax deed and allowed them to deteriorate, adversely affecting conditions and property values in surrounding neighborhoods. The court determined that "[t]his claim is quite different from most of the practices that courts have deemed actions having a direct impact on the ability of potential homebuyers or renters to locate in a particular area, and to indirectly related actions arising from efforts to secure housing."[14] The *Southend* plaintiffs did not allege that defendant's actions had "hindered [them] in an effort to acquire a dwelling, but rather that the County's conduct toward certain properties damaged their own property." Section 3604(a), the court emphasized, "is designed to ensure that no one is denied the right to live where they choose for discriminatory reasons, but it does not protect the intangible interests in the already-owned property raised by the plaintiffs allegations." The court concluded that the county's actions did not affect the "availability of housing" under Section 3604(a), and rejected plaintiff's claim.[15]

With respect to Section 3604(a), *Southend*'s lesson for potential EJ litigants appears to be that the section should be pleaded only if a strong connection can be established between the challenged activity and a showing that the activity will result in the *unavailability* or denial of housing to prospective buyers who are members of a protected class under the FHA.[16] Moreover, in evaluating the possible success of bringing an action under Section 3604(a), potential EJ litigants should recognize that courts may be disinclined to recognize such claims unless the plaintiff's factual case is extremely well documented.[17] That is, an EJ litigant would need to produce evidence demonstrating that the siting or expansion of a noxious or undesirable land use would have the effect of limiting the future quantity of housing available to people of color.[18] Importantly, such a land use must constitute "a direct and immediate affect on a person's ability to obtain housing" and not merely amount to "normal economic competition."[19]

The distinction between restrictions on the availability of housing and normal economic competition was explored in *Michigan Protection and Advocacy Services v. Babin*. In *Babin*, plaintiffs alleged that their effort to buy a home for use by a group of mentally disabled individuals was thwarted by neighbors who purchased the house specifically to prohibit its group use. The Sixth Circuit declined to find that such activity constituted a Section 3604(a) violation because it amounted to normal economic competition.[20]

After *Babin*, the phrase "otherwise make unavailable or deny" may require something more than mere competition; it may instead demand a showing of some "direct and intermediate interference with the effort to obtain housing."[21] Under *Babin* and subsequent cases, then, the purchase of land for a noxious use that might otherwise be used for housing by a protected class would not constitute a Section 3604(a) violation. However, an earlier Seventh Circuit opinion held, on similar facts, that neighbors motivated by racial discrimination would violate Section 3604(a).[22] More recently, a federal district court rejected *Babin*'s economic competition defense as "plainly wrong."[23]

Moreover, even if a court agreed with *Babin*'s economic competition logic, if a plaintiff could demonstrate that the siting of a noxious use would limit future efforts to obtain housing, *Babin* and its followers might be used successfully in support of an EJ case. An ideal EJ plaintiff wishing to use Section 3604(a), therefore, might be a developer or neighboring landowner with a present plan to build housing *but for* the location of an unwanted land use.

Reported cases considering Section 3604(a) claims evidence several instances where plaintiffs proceeded with inadequate factual records. For instance, in *Clifton Terrace Associates*,[24] plaintiffs complained that defendant elevator manufacturer's nonperformance of maintenance constituted a Section 3604(a) violation. Rejecting the Section 3604(a) claim, the United States Court of Appeals for the District of Columbia Circuit demonstrated impatience with a plaintiff who had not signed a maintenance contract with defendant for nearly a decade, and had otherwise not demonstrated a willingness to conduct business with defendant in a fair and open manner.[25] Similarly, a New York City federal district court's refusal to find that the siting of homeless shelters in people-of-color neighborhoods constituted Title VIII violations appears to have been directed in large measure by the conclusion that the trial record simply did not support a finding that racial and ethnic minority neighborhoods would receive a disproportionate number of such shelters.[26] Furthermore, the plaintiffs in that case appear to have erred by suggesting that the siting of shelters would make the neighborhood a less appealing and potentially more dangerous place, and affect access to public education. Instead, the court suggested, plaintiffs ought to have concentrated on making a factual showing that sitings would discriminate with respect to housing availability.[27] Thus, a Section 3604(a) claim might be advanced in the context of an EJ dispute as long as plaintiffs are potential property owners or renters whose access to housing has been or will soon be adversely affected as a direct consequence of defendant's actions.[28]

In addition, courts have not uniformly interpreted the scope of Section 3604(a) and the other important FHA provisions discussed in this chapter. The likelihood of successfully advancing a Section 3604(a) claim may vary significantly depending on the judge. As noted above, in the most frequently cited cases, courts have been reluctant to entertain Section 3604(a) claims of the sort that might be advanced by EJ litigants. Yet in other potentially relevant FHA cases, courts have been persuaded by litigants who stress the statute's broad remedial purposes not only to further the goal of "fair housing," but also to promote housing integration.[29] For instance, in *Jackson v. Okaloosa County*,[30] the Eleventh Circuit held that a Section 3604(a) violation might occur if a housing project was located in a racially segregated area. The court explained that this would hinder the goal of available integrated housing, in contravention of the FHA's purpose.[31] By extension, then, if the siting of a noxious land use "would result in greater segregation in the community by discouraging whites from living in the neighborhood, Section 3604(a) might apply, despite the already-owned property exclusion."[32] This may also be true if the challenged undesirable land use had the effect of making housing unavailable by forcing members of a protected class to leave an area.[33]

It is important to note that potential EJ litigants looking to Section 3604(a) should take special care in selecting possible defendants. What is clear is that persons whose business is directly connected with the provision of housing are included within the reach of Section 3604(a),[34] as are municipal zoning and housing authorities.[35] What is less clear is whether private parties who are not directly involved in real estate sales and rentals are within the reach of Section 3604(a).

On a plain meaning reading of the statutory language, there is no reason to suppose that private parties not engaged directly in the real estate market (as providers of property sales or rentals, or real estate financing) are not covered by this section of the FHA. On the one hand, given the broad remedial purpose of the statute, any party is arguably reachable by Section 3604(a). On the other hand, however, it is difficult to find a case of a private defendant who has been sued successfully under Section 3604(a), where that defendant is neither a governmental authority nor in a business specifically related to housing.[36] Again, however, this failure may not have as much to do with the private character of the defendant as with the failures of plaintiffs to establish properly a strong factual record in support of their Section 3604(a) claims.[37]

Finally, prospective EJ litigants should not overlook activities constituting discriminatory conduct, as determined by the Department of Housing and Urban Development. Indeed, federal regulations suggest several possible grounds that might constitute discriminatory housing practices in the context of an EJ lawsuit.[38] Consider the following provision:

> It shall be unlawful, because of race, color, religion, sex, handicap, familial status, or national origin, *to restrict or attempt to restrict* the choices of a person by word or conduct in connection with seeking, negotiating for, buying or renting a dwelling *so as to perpetuate, or tend to perpetuate* segregated housing patterns, *or to discourage or obstruct choices in a community, neighborhood or development*.[39]

It is possible to imagine a scenario in which this regulation might be used advantageously by an EJ plaintiff. Suppose, for example, that a people-of-color community already hosted multiple undesirable land uses, such as two solid waste dumps, several oil refineries, and a bus transfer station. Suppose further that a sewage treatment plant was proposed for the community and that, upon announcement of the siting of the sewage treatment facility, a low-income housing developer is unable to obtain funding for a residential housing complex in the community. If the housing developer could demonstrate that the reason she could not obtain funding was based upon the increasing saturation of the community with undesirable land uses, she might successfully argue that the proponents of the treatment plant had attempted to restrict the housing rights of people of color to discourage or obstruct housing choices in the community.

Other regulations suggest further possible grounds for complaint. For instance, if a real estate agent discourages a prospective buyer or renter from "inspecting, purchasing or renting a dwelling . . . because of the race, color, religion, sex, handicap, familial status, or national origin of persons in a neighborhood or community" or if that agent discourages a prospective buyer or renter "by exaggerating drawbacks or failing to inform [that prospective buyer or renter] of desirable features of a dwelling or of a community, neighborhood, or development," an FHA violation will have occurred.[40] In the EJ context, it is possible to imagine a situation (provable by the use of testers[41]) where, for example, an agent discouraged a prospective white buyer from buying or renting in an area with noxious land uses that also was predominantly occupied by people of color. This is to suggest that the presence of noxious uses could be used by real estate professionals or landlords as a means of promoting a segregative purpose without using racially or ethnically explicit language, and that such actions might violate the FHA.

In short, then, the advocate for prospective EJ litigants should take great care not only to examine the statutory language and relevant case law for this and other provisions, but should also comb applicable regulations in building a sustainable case.

42 U.S.C. § 3604(b)

The FHA section that presents the greatest likelihood of success for EJ plaintiffs is 42 U.S.C. § 3604(b).[42] Section 3604(b) makes it unlawful:

> To discriminate against any person in the terms, conditions, or privileges of sale or rental of a dwelling, or in the provision of service or facilities in connection therewith, because of race, color, religion, sex, familial status, or national origin.

Two phrases in this section need to be understood by the potential EJ claimant. Both phrases have occasioned considerable disagreement among federal courts about the section's meaning, and, thus, their interpretation could affect the successful advancement of an EJ claim under Section 3604(b).

The first dispute concerns the importance to the section of the words "sale or rental." It has been argued that the words "sale or rental" necessarily modify the phrase "of a dwelling," as opposed to a broader reading of this language, which would imply any discrimination in connection with the terms, conditions, and privileges "of a dwelling" to be covered by Section 3604(b). The principal case to address this issue, *Laramore v. Illinois Sports Facilities Authority*,[43] adopted the narrower reading. In part, this debate about the section's scope may derive from the fact that the bulk of Section 3604(b) litigation involves discrimination in the provision of rental housing both prior to and following rental.[44] Yet for prospective EJ litigants, the narrower reading is clearly a less-than-optimal result, since it considerably restricts the section's reach.

It therefore bears mentioning that the *Southend* court allowed that owners and renters of already-acquired property could bring actions under Section 3604(b) to protect their "intangible" interests. This is significant inasmuch as the *Southend* plaintiffs were not alleging that the defendant county was impeding the immediate sale or rental of their dwellings, but rather that defendant's failure to maintain properties it had acquired by tax deed decreased the value of plaintiffs' property.[45] This portion of *Southend* thus supports reading Section 3604(b) to mean that the words "sale or rental" do not merely modify the phrase "of a dwelling," but may include all "terms, conditions, [and] privileges" of ownership or tenancy. At best, then, it is fair to say that while a conservative reading of Section 3604(b) will limit litigants to actions affecting a dwelling's sale or rental, that is not the inevitable reading of the section.

Given these possible readings of the statute, it is perhaps useful to try to imagine a few examples of circumstances that might present themselves in an EJ context in which a Section 3604(b) claim might be advanced. For instance, an African American landowner in a predominantly African American neighborhood who sought to sell her property might claim that a proposed incinerator or waste disposal and storage facility would diminish her property values and thus discriminate against her "in the terms, conditions, or privileges of sale." Thus, even under the more conservative reading of the statutory language, the claimed discrimination would concern the "sale or rental of a dwelling." Even if this landowner were not trying to sell, however, she might successfully advance a more expansive reading of the statutory language and claim that the undesirable facility adversely affected her "intangible" interests under *Southend*. Moreover, such a claim need not be limited to property owners. For example, an Asian American plaintiff residing as a tenant in a dwelling adjoining a proposed or existing noxious use might also claim that the activity amounted to discrimination against him in the "terms, conditions, or privileges" of the dwelling's rental. Again, such a claim would satisfy either the more conservative or the more expansive reading of Section 3604(b). Similarly, a Latino American landowner or tenant might successfully apply Section 3604(b) to a situation where hazardous or noxious materials were transported through his neighborhood, particularly if the traffic caused by a transport route was heavy, or if there were continual odors released during transport. Although such a claim would be most secure if it could be shown that the transport discriminated against *potential* racial or ethnic minority buyers or renters, the more expansive reading could be used by *current* owners or renters whose "intangible" interests were thereby harmed.[46]

The second phrase subject to disputed interpretation in the federal courts, which is of even greater potential consequence for the EJ litigant, is "services or facilities." The touchstone case for understanding this phrase is, once again, *Southend*. In *Southend,* the court rejected plaintiffs' contention that the defendant county's holding of tax deeds was a "service or facility" under Section 3604(b). In widely quoted dicta, the court observed that "subsection [3604(b)] applies to services generally provided by governmental units such as police and fire protection or garbage collection; the County decisions regarding how to administer properties it holds by tax deeds are distinct from these types of services."[47] The *Southend* court, in turn, based this conclusion on another case, *Mackey v. Nationwide Insurance Co.*[48] In *Mackey,* an African American former agent of defendant, an insurance company, charged, inter alia, that defendant's redlining practices harmed blacks' civil rights by refusing to underwrite property in largely African American neighborhoods. But the *Mackey* court rejected plaintiff's contention "that hazard insurance is a service in connection with a dwelling," concluding as follows:

> . . . surely that is a strained interpretation of the word. It encompasses such things as garbage collection and other services of the kind usually provided by municipalities. The hazard insurance industry is in the business of providing hazard insurance for householders, but what the industry does cannot reasonably be described as the provision of a service in connection with dwellings.
>
> For these reasons, we conclude that Mackey's claims are not within the Fair Housing Act.[49]

The dicta in these two cases are problematic as much for what they leave out as for what they include. The *Mackey* court, for instance, only indicated that the word service "encompasses" certain municipal tasks. This is quite a different thing from delineating the precise coverage of the phrase "services or facilities." For possible EJ plaintiffs, this interpretation raises at least two further questions. The first concerns whether a governmental entity's normal regulatory activities—including, for example, the issuance of permits to site locally undesirable, noxious land uses—are services "of the kind usually provided by municipalities." Second, the *Southend* dicta suggests that "service or facility" only applies to municipal defendants. However, such a reading is clearly inconsistent with judicial interpretation of the section's applicability to the prevention of discrimination in the provision of housing services by *any* party.[50] Thus, EJ litigants who wish to advance Section 3604(b) claims should contest this *Southend* dicta and its widespread reception by other federal courts.

Another relevant reference for possible EJ litigants are HUD regulations interpreting Section 3604(b). Although the regulations do not resolve the issue of what constitutes a "service or facility," they do give examples broader than those considered in *Southend*: "[t]he HUD regulations interpreting Section 3604(b) give a number of examples of practices that would violate the rights of current residents. . . . Among the services and facilities that would be covered by this regulation are recreation facilities, parking privileges, and cleaning and janitorial services."[51] To the extent that courts after *Southend* have addressed the issue of what constitutes a Section 3604(b) service or facility, it is therefore odd to note their extreme caution in sticking very closely to the specific categories of "service or facility" mentioned in *Southend*."[52] Clearly, the phrase's coverage is much broader.

Moreover, other courts have issued opinions suggesting the possible usefulness of Section 3604(b) for EJ litigants. In *Oak Ridge,* for instance, a Wisconsin federal district court noted that usual municipal services include routine regulatory actions like permit issuance. In that case, the defendant county refused an operating permit for a drug and alcohol rehabilitation facility. Citing *Southend,* the court refused to render summary judgment or dismiss for failure to state a claim, noting that exclusionary zoning was covered by the FHA.[53] This opinion bodes well for potential EJ litigants, since the exercise of permitting authority is often a key area of contention.[54] Thus, a Section 3604(b) claim might have been advanced successfully in a much-scrutinized EJ case like *Bean*.[55] In *Bean,* the Texas Department of Health permitted the location of a solid waste disposal facility near homes and churches in a largely African American neighborhood that, plaintiffs claimed, was already disproportionately burdened with such facilities. In dicta, the *Bean* court observed that "[i]t simply does not make sense to put a solid waste site so close to a high school, particularly one with no air-conditioning. Nor does it make sense to put the land site so close to a residential neighborhood."[56]

Although *Bean* was dismissed because plaintiffs could not demonstrate discriminatory intent, they might have won under Section 3604(b) if they could have shown racial discrimination in the exercise of the "service" of waste disposal permit issuance that limited or adversely affected housing opportunities.

It would be hasty, however, to assume that *Oak Ridge* resolves the issue of whether permit issuance amounts to a "usual" municipal service for purposes of Section 3604(b). Another federal district court has taken the opposite view, refusing to extend the reach of Section 3604(b) to the selective enforcement of ordinances, housing codes, and fire and zoning regulations.[57] As with many FHA cases, however, the plaintiff in that case may not have survived summary judgment largely because he failed to establish a solid factual record in support of his claim.[58]

In sum, potential EJ litigants must recognize that courts disagree as to what kinds of services or facilities are covered by Section 3604(b).[59]

A thornier question arises when one tries to determine if parties other than housing providers or governmental authorities can provide services or facilities under the statute. At least one federal district court has taken the position that a defendant who was neither a housing provider nor a municipality was not within the reach of Section 3604(b).[60] However, in *National Assn. for the Advancement of Colored People v. American Family Mutual Ins. Co.*, a more recent case, the Seventh Circuit explicitly rejected such a limited view. Even more important for the prospective EJ litigant, *American Family* repudiated the narrow interpretation of Section 3604(b) by both the *Mackey* and *Southend* courts. Although the Seventh Circuit did not resolve the question of who can be sued under Section 3604(b), in dicta it usefully observed that the statutory language is not limited to state and local governments, adding that in the absence of clear congressional direction there is no reason to limit the language. The Seventh Circuit further noted that the Fourth Circuit's refusal in *Mackey* to extend Section 3604(b) to insurers—on the grounds that they were not directly involved in the sale or rental of a dwelling—had been superseded by subsequent case law and administrative action interpreting the FHA.[61] The Sixth Circuit has endorsed this view, similarly rejecting the narrow *Mackey* holding.[62]

These rulings are clearly important to potential EJ claimants because they invite a broad reading of the Section 3604(b) language[63] and thus may permit lawsuits targeted at nonmunicipal defendants who are neither landlords nor directly involved in real estate sales or rentals.[64] As long as a party's actions have the effect of discriminating "in the provision of services or facilities in connection" with a dwelling, the Sixth and Seventh Circuits' opinions suggest, a plaintiff has a potential claim under Section 3604(b).[65]

Despite its promise, EJ litigants who wish to appeal to Section 3604(b) clearly should do so with caution. The more a challenged action or noxious use affects either the quantity or quality of housing available to persons protected by the statute—or has a segregative impact[66]—the more likely the claim is to succeed. But it is also true that a potential litigant should only advance this claim cognizant that courts have not agreed on the interpretation of these provisions.[67]

42 U.S.C. § 3617

In addition to Sections 3604(a) and (b), prospective EJ litigants would do well to keep Section 3617 in mind when preparing FHA claims.[68] Section 3617 provides as follows:

> It shall be unlawful to coerce, intimidate, threaten, or interfere with any person in the exercise or enjoyment of, or on account of his having exercised or enjoyed, or on account of his having aided or encouraged any other person in the exercise or enjoyment of, any right granted or protected by . . . [inter alia] Section 3604 of this title.[69]

Surprisingly, Section 3617 has largely been neglected by commentators who have examined the FHA with an eye to potential EJ challenges. Section 3617 may have considerable utility for the EJ litigant, however, and for several reasons. First, the potential reach of the section is quite broad. For instance, some courts have allowed Section 3617 to be pleaded even in the absence of a valid claim under, inter alia, Section 3604.[70]

Plaintiffs should be forewarned that some courts may construe Section 3617's anti-intimidation language quite literally, looking for actual physical acts of intimidation or coercion.[71] However, this is not necessarily the sole interpretation of Section 3617. In *Babin,* the Sixth Circuit declined to read the section narrowly, indicating that proof of violence or coercion was not required to sustain a cause of action under the section.[72] Once again, as is often the case in FHA litigation, the possibility for widely divergent readings of the statutory language is not only possible but likely.

Second, Section 3617 is of potentially enormous value to EJ litigants because it creates a cause of action for "interference" with the exercise of FHA rights. The section thus can be used by providers of housing and housing services to reach actions that contribute to violations of Section 3604. For instance, in *People Helpers,* a city's refusal to help housing developers construct integrated developments was found to constitute a Section 3617 violation.[73] Similarly, in *City of Parma*, an Ohio federal district court found violations of both Sections 3604(a) and 3617. Section 3617 violations occurred, the court held, by virtue of the passage of local ordinances that interfered with the rights of low-income housing developers to help create housing opportunities for African Americans.[74]

In the EJ context, it is conceivable that a Section 3617 claim could be applied in a situation where, for instance, a permit for an undesirable land use or rezoning of an area to allow for the siting of undesirable land uses interfered with efforts to provide a racial and ethnic minority neighborhood with adequate housing opportunities.[75] However, *People Helpers* and *City of Parma* suggest that any such interference must be more than merely prospective. That is, potential EJ plaintiffs would need to demonstrate that actual efforts to create housing opportunities had been interfered with in fact, and not just that they might be denied as a result of the claimed environmental injustice.

Third, because Section 3617 reaches acts associated with the denial of housing opportunities and not the actual denial of those opportunities under Section 3604, at least one case suggests that Section 3617 may help preserve a plaintiff's FHA claims. In *Mackey*, a federal appeals court overturned a district court's rejection of plaintiff's Section 3604 claim as time-barred. Yet because the plaintiff had alleged sufficient facts to establish the possibility of a pattern or practice of discrimination under Section 3617, the appellate court held, "by indirection, he . . . properly raised the issue of the application of [Section 3604]."[76]

Fourth, and perhaps most important, Section 3617 is advantageous for the prospective EJ plaintiff because it has been held to apply to housing providers *and others*.[77] Of particular interest in this connection is that portion of the section protecting those who aid or encourage others in the pursuit of their FHA rights. Conceivably, the section could thus be used, for example, by activists opposing a noxious or undesirable land use and seeking concurrently to ensure expanded—and integrated—housing opportunities for people of color. For example, suppose a community group was opposing the proposed siting of a low-level radioactive waste dump and also working concurrently to develop low-income housing in a predominantly Latino American neighborhood. If the prospective dumper then filed a so-called SLAPP suit [78] against the community group, the community group in turn might have grounds successfully to advance a Section 3617 claim.

Section 3617 therefore offers one means to reach defendants other than housing providers and governmental entities. For instance, if the proponent of a refinery or commercial waste facility was shown to have impeded the efforts of third parties to secure fair housing for others, the proponent of the undesirable use might be reachable under Section 3617. Similarly, neighbors who advocated the siting of a noxious use and thereby interfered with efforts to increase housing opportunities for people of color could be reachable under Section 3617.

Other FHA Concerns

Who Can Bring Suit

The FHA does not specify who can bring suit. Rather, it proscribes certain discriminatory actions in the provision of housing. "Obviously, a minority homeseeker who is the direct victim of a discriminatory housing practice condemned by Title VIII is entitled to sue the person who carried out this discrimination. In addition, however, many other categories of plaintiffs and defendants have been held to be proper parties in Title VIII litigation.[79] "Upon timely application" to the Attorney General (AG), the AG may intervene in the action, if he or she determines it to be a case of "general public importance."[80] In addition, the AG may initiate a claim upon his or her own initiative when it is possible that "any person or group of persons is engaged in a pattern or practice of resistance" to the rights guaranteed by the FHA.[81] In addition, private parties may intervene in any such suit brought by the AG, "[u]pon timely application."[82]

The Secretary of Housing and Urban Development (Secretary) also has administrative and legal enforcement authority under the FHA. The matter may be heard either before an administrative law judge or in a civil action.[83] Private parties may file complaints with the Secretary, requesting the Secretary's action. However, in the EJ context it is extremely important to note that any "[c]omplaints involving zoning disputes are referred to the Justice Department for litigation, and [the Department of Housing and Urban Development] may also direct prompt Justice Department litigation in any case where interim relief such as an injunction is called for to protect the rights of the complainant."[84] Since many EJ disputes are likely to involve zoning or the exercise of other municipal permitting authority, many potential EJ claimants will therefore not have the option of pursuing administrative action. In fact, the Department of Housing and Urban Development has received at least four complaints alleging Title VIII violations in connection with broader EJ struggles. The Department's Office of Fair Housing and Equal Opportunity has assigned a staff member to oversee these complaints and coordinate the federal response, since they are usually filed in conjunction with Title VI actions.[85]

Statutes of Limitations

The statute of limitations for exercising the FHA's private right of action is two years, such period not to include any period during which an FHA administrative proceeding was pending.[86] To bring a claim to the Secretary's attention, a party must file a complaint no later than one year after an alleged discriminatory housing practice has occurred or terminated.[87]

Proof Required[88]

In contrast to Fourteenth Amendment equal protection claims, a principal attraction of the FHA for those who may wish to advance discriminatory siting claims is that the FHA may not require the "difficult" proof of discriminatory intent. Proof of "discriminatory effect" is almost certainly sufficient to make a prima facie case of a Title VIII violation.[89] Furthermore, it seems fair to conclude that this is the applicable FHA standard of proof.[90] To quote the Ninth Circuit, for purposes of the prima facie case, "[d]iscriminatory effect means that 'the conduct of the defendant actually or predictably results in racial discrimination. . . . The plaintiff need make no showing whatsoever that the action resulting in racial discrimination . . . was racially motivated."[91] As a general matter, discriminatory effect is demonstrated by the use of statistical surveys and comparative demographics.[92] Prospective EJ plaintiffs would therefore do well to refer to longitudinal studies of disproportionate siting impacts in preparing their claims.[93]

Moreover, unlike Title VI, a major advantage of Title VIII is that potential defendants need not receive federal funding. Subject to the limitations on potential defendants discussed earlier in this chapter ("42 U.S.C. §§ 3604(a) and (b)" and "42 U.S.C. § 3617," pages 74–82), Title VIII fair housing claims may be brought against the full range of private and public defendants.[94]

Nonetheless, it bears noting that, as with so many Title VIII issues, courts have not uniformly understood the meaning of the term "discriminatory effect." At least two separate tests have emerged. In the Second, Third, and Eighth Circuits, proof of discriminatory effect alone is sufficient to establish a claim under the FHA.[95] By contrast, in the Fourth and Seventh Circuits, a showing of discriminatory effect requires consideration of four factors:

1. the strength of the plaintiff's showing of discriminatory effect;
2. whether there was some evidence of discriminatory intent;
3. what the defendant's interest was in taking the action complained of; and
4. whether the plaintiff sought to compel the defendant affirmatively to provide housing for minorities or merely to restrain

> the defendant from interfering with individual property owners who wish to provide such housing.[96]

It is unnecessary in the Fourth and Seventh Circuits to make "strong showings" about each of these factors,[97] and, at least in the Seventh Circuit, the showing of some evidence of discriminatory intent "is the least important of the four factors, . . . and the required showing under it is modest. The plaintiffs' evidence need only give 'some indication—which might be suggestive rather than conclusive—of discriminatory intent.'"[98] Thus, even if the more exacting test of the Fourth and Seventh Circuits is applied, an EJ plaintiff wishing to plead a Section 3604 claim should be free of the "difficult" burden of proving discriminatory intent.

Section 1982 Claims in Environmental Justice Disputes

Section 2 of the Civil Rights Act of 1866, 42 U.S.C. § 1982, provides that

> [a]ll citizens of the United States shall have the same right, in every State and Territory, as is enjoyed by white citizens thereof to inherit, purchase, lease, sell, hold, and convey real and personal property.

Section 1982 is narrower than Title VIII in the sense that it applies only to racial or ethnic discrimination.[99] Moreover, it "may not bar every single racially based practice that violates Title VIII."[100] However, Section 1982 is broader than Title VIII in two respects of potential use to the prospective EJ litigant. First, Section 1982 reaches personal as well as real property. Second, Section 1982 applies to nonresidential real estate.[101]

It is easy to imagine circumstances under which Section 1982's applicability to personalty and commercial realty could benefit potential EJ plaintiffs. For example, Section 1982 thus might be used on behalf of a people-of-color community—residents and business owners—disproportionately affected by airborne contaminants from noxious sources that settle upon real and personal property inherited, purchased, leased, sold, held, or conveyed by a community's inhabitants.[102] If the community could demonstrate that the sources of such pollution were located in or near their community rather than in or near a white community, they might prevail on a theory that an environmental injustice was covered by Section 1982.

Furthermore, it should be noted that, for purposes of Section 1982 actions, potential plaintiffs need not be persons whose property rights have been denied to them as title holders. For example, in *U.S. v. Brown*, the Sixth Circuit affirmed that persons whose rights under Section 1982 have been denied need not be actual title holders so long as they have expectations of *using* the affected property in ways also enjoyed by whites under similar circumstances.[103] For an EJ litigant, such a holding could prove useful if, for instance, a proposed noxious use would adversely affect buildings such as churches, schools, and community centers (providing, perhaps, that plaintiffs had roles in the financial support of such entities).

Despite these advantageous features of Section 1982, however, by contrast to Title VIII, Section 1982 presents considerable roadblocks. Section 1982 has limited value because of its more restricted standing requirements[104] and because plaintiff is required to prove "that the defendant was motivated at least in part by intentional discrimination."[105]

Nonetheless, Section 1982 cases suggest that plaintiffs' 1982 claims will succeed if they are members of a racial or ethnic minority who have been intentionally discriminated against in their efforts to secure contract or property rights.[106] The United States Supreme Court underscored the importance of such a showing in *City of Memphis v. Greene*.[107] *Greene* concerned the closing of a street at the request of white property owners. The closing resulted in the diversion of traffic around an overwhelmingly African American neighborhood, physically separating it from a predominantly white neighborhood. In *Greene*, the Court explained that "the threshold inquiry under Section 1982 must focus on the relationship between the street closing and the property interests of the respondents."[108] Thus, if the contested municipal action benefitted whites but was denied to blacks, or depreciated the value of black homes, or "severely restricted access to black homes," preventing African Americans from using their property, a Section 1982 violation would be found to occur.[109] Under *Greene*, as Professor Been notes, "a siting that lowered neighboring property values, or that restricted 'access' to neighboring homes by making them unsafe would come within the purview of Section 1982."[110]

Several additional cases indicate that Section 1982 could prove a powerful tool in EJ controversies. The Eleventh Circuit allowed a Section 1982 claim to proceed in a case claiming that the selection of locations for public housing projects intentionally aimed to perpetuate segregated housing patterns.[111] Under this ruling, an EJ plaintiff might successfully oppose an unwanted land use if he or she could demonstrate that the use was designed to perpetuate segregated housing. In yet another case, recognizing the "broad" and "liberal interpretation" of Section 1982 applied by the United States Supreme

Court, a federal district court refused to dismiss a Section 1982 claim based on the assertion that mortgage redlining led to the rejection of an African American's second mortgage application, thereby impairing his property rights.[112] In still another promising case for potential EJ litigants, a federal district court refused to dismiss a Section 1982 claim based on objections from African American residents that municipal redevelopment plans would destroy historically African American neighborhoods.[113]

The key to winning such a case seems to be proof of a direct connection between the allegedly discriminatory action and the alleged injury to property or contract rights. Thus, the closing of a city street in *Greene* was not found to constitute a direct interference with property rights, although the Court noted that a street closing involving "a severe restriction on the access to property" would constitute a Section 1982 violation.[114] Similarly a city's provision of municipal services to whites that it did not provide to blacks was deemed impermissible and so might be conduct violating Section 1982.[115]

Notwithstanding the promise of Section 1982 for the prospective EJ plaintiff, as suggested by the cases referred to above, the statute also presents potentially significant hurdles. First, it appears likely that courts will continue to apply an intent standard to Section 1982 claims.[116] This is problematic since intent, it will be remembered, proved to be an overwhelming obstacle in the EJ Equal Protection cases.[117] Second, the range of potential plaintiffs is even narrower than in Section 3604 cases. For example, the Fourth Circuit has held that an African American insurance agent whose business was restricted because of his former employer's redlining practices had no standing to sue under Section 1982.[118] Although a Section 1982 plaintiff need not be a member of a protected class to assert the statute on behalf of that class,[119] courts will not permit claims from plaintiffs who have not, as a result of the alleged racial discrimination, suffered a clear injury themselves.[120] This places Section 1982 standing questions in sharp distinction to comparable FHA standing inquiries, making it far less likely that, by comparison to Title VIII, a party can successfully claim an "indirect" injury under Section 1982.[121] The lesson of such cases for EJ litigants is simple and straightforward: effort should be made to identify plaintiffs who have or will have suffered a deprivation of some contractual or property right as the result of a noxious or other undesirable land use.

In sum, Section 1982 could be a useful tool for prospective EJ litigants, particularly when a plaintiff of color has suffered harms to personalty or commercial realty that are not covered by Title VIII. However, because Section 1982 remains even less tested in the EJ context than Section 3604 of the FHA, and given the likelihood that courts will apply a discriminatory intent standard, the claim should not be advanced without a frank recognition of its potential limitations.

Conclusion

The late Ralph Santiago Abascal's belief that Title VIII and related claims might offer success in EJ disputes remains as tantalizing—and untested—as when he aired it in 1995. What is clear is that when EJ controversies touch issues of housing availability, plaintiffs should proceed only when they have a fully developed factual record at their disposal. Otherwise, the decisions in *Southend* and subsequent cases suggest that plaintiffs will not succeed. That being said, the federal fair housing and equal property protection laws are powerful statutes that have consistently been given broad interpretation to promote the still-unmet goals of fair racially and ethnically integrated housing and equal property rights. EJ controversies commonly involve threats to present housing and housing opportunities (and other property uses) that may be made available to people of color. Therefore, EJ advocates should seriously study Title VIII and, to a lesser extent, Section 1982, for possible causes of action in support of their claims.

Notes

* Associate Professor, Thomas Jefferson School of Law, San Diego. Professors James A. Kushner, Florence Wagman Roisman, and Robert G. Schwemm provided extremely helpful comments on an earlier draft of this chapter. Most of their suggested changes and additions have been incorporated into this chapter. For their considerable contributions, I am grateful to them all.

1. *See, e.g.,* El Pueblo para el Agua y Aire Limpio v. County of Kings, 22 ENVTL. L. REP. (Envtl. L. Inst.) 20,357 (Cal. App. Dep't Super. Ct. 1991).

2. Ralph Santiago Abascal, *Tools for Combating Environmental Injustice in the 'Hood: Title VIII of the Civil Rights Act of 1968,* 29 CLEARINGHOUSE REVIEW 345 (1995). The text of the Fair Housing Act appears at 42 U.S.C. §§ 3601–3631 (1998).

Ralph Santiago Abascal was one of the most distinguished legal aid attorneys of his generation. In 1995, he became the fourth recipient of the American Bar Association's Thurgood Marshall Award—one of many such recognitions for his unselfish legal work. For 28 years, Abascal worked out of California Rural Legal Assistance Foundation, championing the rights of a wide variety of largely disenfranchised populations, including the poor, the elderly, farmworkers, immigrants, welfare recipients and students. Abascal was a master in his use of litigation—and was especially skilled at statutory interpretation—to secure the rights of those populations. This chapter is dedicated to his memory and in memory of his work.

3. Difficult because Fourteenth Amendment claims require proof of discriminatory intent. *See* Chapter 1, "Equal Protection," *supra* pages 3–22.

4. It is worth noting that in a federal action related to the state action cited in *El Pueblo, supra* note 1, plaintiffs included a Fair Housing Act claim that was never adjudicated because the state case was decided in plaintiffs' favor. El Pueblo para el Aire y Agua Limpio v. Chemical Waste Mgmt., Inc., No. C-91-2083 (E.D. Cal. filed July 8, 1991), complaint at 28.

This chapter does not, of course, begin to explore the nuances of FHA law and litigation. For comprehensive treatment on FHA litigation, *see* ROBERT G. SCHWEMM, HOUSING DISCRIMINATION: LAW AND LITIGATION (Clark Boardman 1990 & 1997 Supp.) [hereinafter SCHWEMM, HOUSING DISCRIMINATION]. The other most useful, standard reference work on the subject is JAMES A. KUSHNER, FAIR HOUSING: DISCRIMINATION IN REAL ESTATE, COMMUNITY DEVELOPMENT AND REVITALIZATION (McGraw Hill 2d ed. 1995 & West Supp. 1998) [hereinafter KUSHNER]. Still useful, if dated, perspectives on FHA jurisprudence can be found in Florence Wagman Roisman & Philip Tegeler, *Improving and Expanding Housing Opportunities for Poor People of Color: Recent Developments in Federal and State Courts,* 24 CLEARINGHOUSE REVIEW 312 (1990); THE FAIR HOUSING ACT AFTER TWENTY YEARS (Robert G. Schwemm ed., Yale Law School 1989).

5. Abascal, *supra* note 2. Abascal's suggestion is implicitly endorsed in the dicta of recent FHA case law. *See, e.g.,* Comer v. Kemp, 37 F.3d 775, 789 (2nd Cir. 1994) (allowing FHA claims by wide range of defendants because of law's broad remedial purpose); Michigan Protection & Advocacy Serv., Inc. v. Babin, 18 F.3d 337, 344 (6th Cir. 1994) ("Congress intended [FHA] Section 3604 to reach a broad range of activities that have the effect of denying housing opportunities to a member of a protected class. . . . When Congress amended [FHA] . . . in 1988, it intended . . . to reach not only actors who were directly involved in the real estate business, but also actors who directly affect the availability of housing, such as state or local governments") (citing H.R. Rep. No. 711, 100th Cong., 2d Sess. 22 (1988), reprinted in 1988 U.S.C.C.A.N. 2173, 2183). However, while encouraging, dicta in these cases go to the statute's basic remedial purpose and do not resolve the specific applicability of the FHA claims that may be available to EJ plaintiffs, as discussed below.

Comer is an especially interesting opinion for potential EJ plaintiffs because of the breadth of the FHA claims of the plaintiffs—low-income racial minority residents of Buffalo, New York. These claims included a charge that Buffalo's "suburban preference" policy for residential housing discriminated against them. *Comer, supra* at 780. A similar policy with respect to the siting of noxious uses might be supported with *Comer.* Unfortunately for prospective EJ litigants, however, *Comer* did not resolve these issues; the decision largely concerns procedural issues.

6. Supporters of the idea that Title VIII might be useful in EJ cases include Alice L. Brown & Kevin Lyskowski, *Environmental Justice Litigation: Environmental Justice and Title VIII of the Civil Rights Act of 1968 (The Fair Housing Act),* 14 VA. ENVTL. L.J. 741 (1995); Luke W. Cole, *Environmental Justice Litigation: Another Stone in David's Sling,* 21 FORDHAM URB. L.J. 523, 525 (1994); Eileen Gauna, *The Environmental Justice Misfit: Public Participation and the Paradigm Paradox,* 17 STAN. ENVTL. L.J. 3, 15 n.35 (1998); Richard J. Lazarus, *Pursuing "Environmental Justice":*

the Distributional Effects of Environmental Protection, 87 Nw. U. L. Rev. 787, 839 (1993); Rodolfo Mata, *Hazardous Waste Facilities and Environmental Equity: a Proposed Siting Model,* 13 Va. Envtl. L.J. 375, 419 (1994); Omar Saleem, *Overcoming Environmental Discrimination: The Need for a Disparate Impact Test and Improved Notice Requirements in Facility Siting Decisions,* 19 Colum. J. Envtl. L. 211, 229 (1994); Reynold Siemens, *Environmental Justice: the New Wave,* 14 Va. Envtl. L.J. 567, 568 (1995). *See also* Jon C. Dubin, *From Junkyards to Gentrification: Explicating a Right to Protective Zoning in Low-Income Communities of Color,* 77 Minn. L. Rev. 739, 782–83 (1993); Michael Allan Wolf, *Fruits of the "Impenetrable Jungle": Navigating the Boundary Between Land-Use Planning and Environmental Law,* 50 Wash. U. J. Urb. & Contemp. L. 5, 40 (1996). *But see* Vicki Been, *Environmental Justice and Equity Issues,* in Zoning and Land Use Controls, sec. 25D.05 (Patrick Rohan ed., Matthew Bender 1995); Daniel Kevin, *"Environmental Racism" and Locally Undesirable Land Uses: a Critique of Environmental Justice Theories and Remedies,* 8 Vill. Envtl. L.J. 121, 155 (1997).

7. 42 U.S.C. § 1982 (1998). In Jones v. Alfred H. Meyer Co., 392 U.S. 409, 416–17 (1968), the United States Supreme Court held that Section 1982 creates a distinct remedy from Title VIII for racial discrimination in housing. However, advocates should be careful to understand the different coverage of the two laws. *See* Schwemm, Housing Discrimination, *supra* note 4, at sec. 27.2; Kushner, *supra* note 4, at secs. 1.02 & 3.07. For comprehensive treatment on Section 1982 litigation, *see* Schwemm, Housing Discrimination, *supra* note 4, at ch. 2.

8. In all of what follows, it should be remembered that since 1988, the FHA also covers discrimination for persons with disabilities. *See infra* note 11.

9. *See, e.g.,* discussion of the *Bedford-Stuyvesant* case, *infra* note 26 and accompanying text.

10. See *infra* notes 88 through 98 and accompanying text on the discriminatory effect standard; *supra* note 4 and Chapter 1, "Equal Protection," pages 3–22, on discriminatory intent.

11. The 1988 Amendments to the FHA added handicap discrimination to the list of persons protected by the statute. 42 U.S.C. § 3604(f). The language of Section 3604(f) closely tracks that of Section 3604(a), including the key phrase "otherwise make unavailable or deny." Thus, the discussion in this chapter of Section 3604(a) would also apply to discrimination in EJ controversies involving handicapped persons. *See also* Kushner, *supra* note 4, at sec. 2.09; Schwemm, Housing Discrimination, *supra* note 4, at secs. 11.5(3)(a) and 13.2.

"Handicap" is defined in Title VIII, in relevant part, as "a physical or mental impairment which substantially limits one or more of such person's major life activities." 42 U.S.C. § 3602(h) (1). Courts have found, applying this definition, that a wide range of conditions can constitute a handicap. *See, e.g.,* Anast v. Commonwealth Apartments, 956 F. Supp. 792 (N.D. Ill. 1997) (mental illness); United States v. Massachusetts Indus. Fin. Agency, 910 F. Supp. 21 (1996) (emotionally disturbed adolescents); Support Ministeries for Persons with AIDS, Inc. v. Village of Waterford, 808 F. Supp. 120 (N.D.N.Y. 1992) (homeless persons with HIV); Oxford House, Inc. v. Township of Cherry Hill, 799 F. Supp. 450 (D.N.J. 1992) (persons dealing with alcoholism and drug addiction although not currently drinking or using drugs); Association of Relatives and Friends of AIDS Patients v. Administración de Reglamentos y Permisos, 740 F. Supp. 95 (D. Puerto Rico

1990) (people with AIDS); and K Care, Inc. v. Town of Lac du Flambeau, 510 N.W.2d 697 (Wis. 1993) (elderly infirm). Handicap discrimination thus could easily be part of an EJ lawsuit under Title VIII, if the noxious or unwanted use resulted in the deprivation of housing opportunities to or had a segregative effect on handicapped persons.

12. It is worth stressing, however, that municipal authorities and private enterprises directly involved in the provision of housing are without question covered by the section. *See, e.g.*, Metropolitan Housing Development Corp. v. Village of Arlington Heights, 558 F.2d 1283, 1288–90 (7th Cir. 1977), *cert. denied* 434 U.S. 1025, 54 L. Ed. 2d 772, 98 S. Ct. 752 (1978) (Title VIII violation found where a zoning decision had discriminatory effect). The harder question is what it means not merely to discriminate in housing sales or rentals, but what is meant by the phrase "otherwise make unavailable or deny." For a detailed discussion of this phrase, see SCHWEMM, HOUSING DISCRIMINATION, *supra* note 4 at sec. 13.4. The meaning of this phrase is central to the *Southend* case. *See infra* notes 13–15 and accompanying text.

13. Southend Neighborhood Improvement Ass'n v. County of St. Clair, 743 F.2d 1207, 1209 (7th Cir. 1984) (citing Halet v. Wend Investment Co., 672 F.2d 1305 (9th Cir. 1982) (discriminatory rental decisions). On what might constitute "other actions," *See also* United States v. City of Parma, Ohio, 494 F. Supp. 1049 (N.D. Ohio 1980), *aff'd in part, rev'd in part,* 661 F.2d 562 (6th Cir. 1981), *cert. denied,* 456 U.S. 926, 102 S. Ct. 1972, 72 L. Ed. 2d 441 (1982) (various actions by city including rejection of public and low-income housing and adoption of restrictive land use ordinances); Marable v. H. Walker & Associates, 644 F.2d 390 (5th Cir. 1981), *appeal after remand,* 704 F.2d 1219 (11th Cir. 1983) (unequal application of rental criteria by landlord); United States v. Mitchell, 580 F.2d 789 (5th Cir. 1978) (racial steering); United States v. City of Black Jack, Mo., 508 F.2d 1179 (8th Cir. 1974), *cert. denied,* 422 U.S. 1042 (1975) (adoption of restrictive zoning law).

This portion of the *Southend* decision is cited, for example, in Oak Ridge Care Center, Inc., v. Racine County, Wisconsin, 896 F. Supp. 867, 872 (E.D. Wis. 1995) (contesting denial of operating permit for rehabilitation treatment facility); Campbell v. City of Berwyn, 815 F. Supp. 1138, 1143 (N.D. Ill. 1993) (denial of police protection to existing residents who had been subjected to racial harassment does not amount to a Section 3604(a) violation); Clifton Terrace Associates, Ltd. v. United Technologies Corp., 728 F. Supp. 24, 29 (D.D.C. 1990) (failure to service elevator does not constitute a violation of, inter alia, Section 3604(a)) *aff'd* 929 F. 2d 714 (D.C.Cir. 1991); and Laramore v. Illinois Sports Facilities Auth., 722 F. Supp. 443, 452 n. 5 (N.D. Ill. 1989) (challenging construction of baseball park in racial minority neighborhood).

Leading cases interpreting Title VIII in the context of a land use dispute include Huntington Branch, NAACP v. Town of Huntington, 844 F.2d 926 (2d Cir. 1988); *review declined in part and judgment aff'd sub nom.* Town of Huntington v. Huntington Branch, N.A.A.C.P., 488 U.S. 15 (1988) (successful application of discriminatory effects test against government defendant's exclusionary zoning decisions); *Arlington Heights, supra* note 12; Resident Advisory Board v. Rizzo, 564 F.2d 126 (3d Cir. 1977), *cert. denied* 435 U.S. 908 (1978) (under Section 3604(a) rejecting municipal restrictions on subsidized housing projects).

Luke Cole, a lawyer with the Center on Race, Poverty and the Environment at California Rural Legal Assistance Foundation and a colleague of the late Ralph Santiago Abascal, unsuccessfully raised Title VIII claims in a siting case before a Kern County, California, Superior Court. In retrospect, in light of *Laramore* and similar cases, Cole observed, "Judges don't like to extend Title VIII to cover siting decisions, particularly in conservative rural counties." (Personal communication with author, Jan. 29, 1999.) As emphasized throughout this chapter, therefore, advocates contemplating Title VIII claims should proceed with extreme care.

14. *Southend, supra* note 13 at 1210.

15. *Id.* Ralph Santiago Abascal suggested that "availability" of housing means any action affecting the *quantity* of housing. Abascal, *supra* note 2, at 358. However, Professor James Kushner, one of the nation's leading experts on Title VIII law and litigation, explains that "it is not such an economic analysis—more like proximate cause effect on *specific* housing opportunities." (Written comments on file with author).

16. McDiarmid v. Economy Fire and Casualty Co., 604 F. Supp. 105, 107–108 (S.D. Ohio 1984) (insurance redlining covered by Title VIII because it affects the availability of housing).

17. Professor Vicki Been is especially skeptical about the possible success of such a claim. *See* Been, *supra* note 6, at sec. 25D.05[1][a] (citing *Southend* and other cases where Section 3604(a) claims were disallowed because the plaintiffs were not prospective buyers and renters, and because private, non–real estate-related businesses are not typical Section 3604(a) defendants).

18. In this connection, the longitudinal studies conducted by Professor Been could prove especially useful. Vicki Been with Francis Gupta, *Coming to the Nuisance or Going to the Barrios? A Longitudinal Analysis of Environmental Justice Claims*, 24 Ecology L.Q. 1 (1997); Vicki Been, *Locally Undesirable Land Uses in Minority Neighborhoods: Disproportionate Siting or Market Dynamics?* 103 Yale L.J. 1383 (1994). *See generally* Chapter 12, "Evidentiary Issues," *infra*, pages 397–428.

19. Nationwide Mut. Ins. Co. v. Cisneros, 52 F.3d 1351, 1360 (6th Cir. 1995) *cert denied*, 516 U.S. 1140 (1996).

20. *Babin, supra* note 5, at 344–45.

21. *Nationwide, supra* note 19 (discussing *Babin*).

22. Phillips v. Hunter Trails Community Ass'n, 685 F.2d 184, 187–90 (7th Cir. 1982).

23. United States v. Hughes, 849 F. Supp. 685, 686 (D. Neb. 1994). *See also* Schwemm, Housing Discrimination, *supra* note 4, at sec. 20.2(2) n.36.5 and accompanying text.

24. *See Clifton Terrace, supra* note 13.

25. *Id.* at 29–30.

26. Coalition of Bedford-Stuyvesant Block Association, Inc. v. Cuomo, 651 F. Supp. 1202, 1210 (E.D.N.Y. 1987).

27. *Id.* at 1208 & n.2 (E.D.N.Y. 1987) ("To state a cause of action under 42 U.S.C. §§ 3601 et seq. (The Fair Housing Act), whose primary purpose is to proscribe discrimination in the sale, rental, financing or brokerage of private housing, . . . the illegal action must have a discriminatory effect on the availability of housing. . . . In this case plaintiff has not made a showing of such effects. Instead,

plaintiff asserts that defendants' concentration of homeless shelters endangers the health and access to public education of minority host communities. This kind of alleged discrimination is clearly outside the purview of the Fair Housing Act." (citations omitted).); *but cf.* Been, *supra* note 6, at sec. 25D.05[1][a][i].

28. Prospective plaintiffs therefore would do well to scrutinize the FHA's standing requirements carefully. The statute itself is exceptionally vague about standing. The best places to begin with such an analysis, therefore, are KUSHNER, *supra* note 4, at secs. 8.10–8.14; SCHWEMM, HOUSING DISCRIMINATION, *supra* note 4, at sec. 12.2.

29. *See. e.g.,* Trafficante v. Metropolitan Life Ins. Co., 409 U.S. 205, 211–12 (1972); South Suburban Housing Center v. Greater South Suburban Board of Realtors, 935 F.2d 868, 882 (7th Cir. 1991) *cert. denied,* 502 U.S. 1074 (1992); United States v. Hughes Memorial Home, 396 F. Supp. 544, 548 (W.D. Va. 1975). *See also* Havens Realty Corp. v. Coleman, 455 U.S. 363, 380 (1982); City of Edmonds v. Oxford House, Inc., 514 U.S. 725, 731 (1995) Cabrera v. Jakabovitz, 24 F.3d 372, 388 (2d Cir. 1994) (both cases reaffirming *Trafficante*'s broad reading of Title VIII); *Huntington, supra* note 13; and *Arlington Heights, supra* note 12. On the importance of reading Title VIII broadly to effectuate its purposes, *see also* KUSHNER, *supra* note 4, at sec. 1.05 ("Title VIII is to be accorded a generous construction in order to foster 'truly integrated and balanced living patterns.'"(quoting *Trafficante*)); SCHWEMM, HOUSING DISCRIMINATION, *supra* note 4, at sec. 7.2. Schwemm observes, *id.* at sec. 7.2(1) that "the [United States Supreme] Court's unanimous decision in *Trafficante* is still the most important source of judicial guidance for divining the congressional intent underlying the Fair Housing Act."

30. 21 F.3d 1532 (11th Cir. 1994).

31. *Id.* at 1543–44.

32. Been, *supra* note 6 at sec. 25D.05[1][a][i] & n.17. Been further notes that "[t]he *Southend* reasoning also might not bar a Sec. 3604(a) claim regarding the harm a siting does its neighbors if the neighbors could prove that the siting had the intent or effect of driving people of color from the community." *Id.* (positively evaluating Tinsley v. Kemp, 750 F. Supp. 1001 (W.D. Mo. 1990), which involved the alleged tolerance of Kansas City housing officials for the deterioration and '*de facto* demolition' of a housing project, for "the narrow proposition that actions which force or encourage people of color to leave a neighborhood may violate Section 3604(a) may provide authority for collapsing *Southend*'s distinction between housing availability and habitability in some cases"). Professor Been's comment about *Tinsley* may open a useful window for EJ advocates, although the proposition she mentions is arguably anything but narrow.

33. *See, e.g.,* Avery v. City of Chicago, 501 F. Supp. 1 (N.D. Ill. 1978) (plaintiffs-residents, mostly low-income racial minorities in racially-integrated housing district alleged developers were trying to force them from district). *See also* Been, *supra* note 6, at § 25D.05[1], note 20. Actions by municipal authorities that forces the people who can move out of an area by allowing undesirable land uses have been characterized as "expulsive zoning practices" that "have been and continue to be instrumental influences on both the creation and perpetuation of racial segregation." Abascal, *supra* note 2, at 353 (quoting Yale Rabin, *Expulsive Zoning: The Inequitable Legacy of* Euclid, *in* ZONING AND THE AMERICAN DREAM 101

(Charles Harr & Jerome Kayden eds., 1989).) In the EJ context, the question of whether the siting of undesirable land uses targets poorer communities or creates them is much disputed. *See, e.g.*, Vicki Been with Francis Gupta, *supra* note 18.

34. Including real estate professionals and mortgage lenders. *See, e.g.*, Cartwright v. American Savings & Loan Ass'n, 880 F.2d 912 (7th Cir. 1989) (finding mortgage redlining actionable under Section 3604(a)); SCHWEMM, HOUSING DISCRIMINATION, *supra* note 4 at sec. 13.4(4); KUSHNER, *supra* note 4 at secs. 5.02–5.21.

35. *See, e.g.*, Gautreaux v. Pierce, 690 F.2d 616 (7th Cir. 1982); Huntington, *supra* note 13; and United States v. City of Parma, 494 F. Supp. 1049 (N.D. Ohio, 1980), *aff'd in part, rev'd in part,* 661 F.2d 562, 571–72 (6th Cir. 1981), *cert. denied,* 456 U.S. 926 (1982).

Federal agencies may be reachable under 42 U.S.C. § 3608. State agency defendants may also be possible, although, as Professor Schwemm notes, in neither case has the possibility of suing these defendants been definitively decided. SCHWEMM, HOUSING DISCRIMINATION, *supra* note 4, at secs. 12.3(4) (c–d).

36. See cases cited in Been, *supra* note 6, at § 25D.05[1], notes 28–30 (concluding after a review of cases that "the courts would be unlikely to read Section 3604(a) to reach private defendants siting waste facilities"). Despite Professor Been's skepticism, it is possible to imagine that other kinds of undesirable environmental activities might be reached under Section 3604(a), such as a manufacturer who disposes of hazardous (or some other regulated) substance in violation of federal or state law. Similarly, violators of hazardous materials transportation regulations that resulted in the making unavailable or denial of housing to people of color might be defendants against whom a Section 3604(a) claim could successfully be brought.

37. *See, e.g., Clifton Terrace, supra* note 13.

38. *See, e.g.,* 24 C.F.R. §§ 100.50–100.304 (1988). These sections are understood to help flesh out the meaning of the phrase "otherwise make unavailable or deny" in Section 3604(a). *See* SCHWEMM, HOUSING DISCRIMINATION, *supra* note 4, at sec. 13.4(5).

39. 24 C.F.R. § 100.70(a) (emphasis added).

40. These provisions appear in 24 C.F.R. §§ 100.70(c) (1) and (2).

41. *See* KUSHNER, *supra* note 4, at secs. 3.08, 8.12, and *passim;* SCHWEMM, HOUSING DISCRIMINATION, *supra* note 4, at sec. 12.2(4).

42. *But cf.* Been, *supra* note 6, at sec. 25D.05[1] ("The existing case law accordingly does not give much reason to believe that Section 3604(b) will be useful in challenging discriminatory sitings of noxious [locally undesirable land uses, or] LULUs"). Professor Been may, however, be unnecessarily pessimistic in light of a case like *American Family Mutual, infra* note 61 and accompanying text. Indeed, Professor Florence Wagman Roisman, a leading expert on FHA litigation, strenuously disagrees with Been, noting that "the cases haven't been brought." (Written comments on file with author.)

43. *Laramore, supra* note 13 at 452 ("The Court agrees with defendants that plaintiffs' allegations do not state a claim within the purview of Section 3604(b). The scope of Section 3604(b) depends on whether the language 'in connection with' refers to the 'sale or rental of a dwelling' or more broadly to a 'dwelling.'

The Court finds that the most natural reading of the statute is the narrower reading." (*citing Southend, supra* note 13, at 1210)).

44. Whereby, for example, a landlord proposes charging different rents to racial or ethnic minority applicants, or tells them that a vacant apartment has "already been rented." *See* KUSHNER, *supra* note 4, at sec. 3.16, and compare *id.* at sec. 3.17 (refusal to sell cases); SCHWEMM, HOUSING DISCRIMINATION, *supra* note 4, at secs. 14.1–14.3. As Schwemm notes, *id.* at sec. 14.1, "[m]ost of the cases applying Section 3604(b)'s prohibition against discriminatory terms, conditions, and privileges in housing transactions fall into two categories: (1) those dealing with discrimination in the proposed terms of a sale or rental before the transaction is consummated (and that may block the transaction altogether); and (2) those dealing with discriminatory services to tenants and others after they have become residents of the defendant's housing".

45. *Southend, supra* note 13, at 1210.

46. An example of a situation in which such a Section 3604(b) argument might have been advanced is the protracted dispute over the siting of a substantial urban sewage treatment plant next to the predominantly African American and Latino American neighborhood of West Harlem in New York City. For a history of that struggle, in which the odors from the treatment plant and their health consequences were an issue, *see* Vernice D. Miller, *Planning, Power and Politics: A Case Study of the Land Use and Siting History of the North River Water Pollution Control Plant,* 21 FORDHAM URB. L.J. 707 (1994).

47. *Southend, supra* note 13, at 1210 (*citing* Mackey v. Nationwide Insurance Cos., 724 F.2d 419, 423–24 (4th Cir. 1984)). *See also Campbell, supra* note 13, at 1143; *Clifton Terrace, supra* note 13, at 452; *Laramore, supra* note 13, at 452; Puglisi v. Underhill Park Taxpayer Assoc., 947 F. Supp. 673, 695 (S.D.N.Y. 1996).

48. *Southend, supra* note 13, at 1210.

49. *Mackey, supra* note 48, at 425. *But see McDiarmid, supra* note 16 at 106–07 (despite *Mackey,* affirming that mortgage financing, insurance redlining, and similar financial activities are within the ambit of Section 3604's antidiscrimination provisions, in keeping with the Sixth Circuit's desire to paint "with a broad brush when sketching the parameters of Title VIII").

50. *See, e.g.,* City of Chicago v. Matchmaker Real Estate Sales Center, Inc., 982 F.2d 1086 (7th Cir. 1992), *cert. denied sub nom.* Ernst v. Leadership Council for Metro. Open Communs., 508 U.S. 972, 113 S. Ct. 2961, 125 L. Ed. 2d 662 (1993) (liability of individual real estate agents); U.S. v. Balistrieri, 981 F.2d 916, *cert. denied,* 501 U.S 812, 114 S. Ct. 58, 126 L. Ed. 28 (1993) (liability of private apartment house owner); Davis v. Mansards, 597 F. Supp. 334 (D.C. Ind. 1984) (liability of rental agents, apartment manager, apartment management corporation, and nonprofit corporation).

51. SCHWEMM, HOUSING DISCRIMINATION, *supra* note 4, at sec. 14.3. *See especially id.,* n. 26–27 (*citing,* inter alia, 24 C.F.R. § 100.65(b)(4) and HUD pmbl. I, 53 Fed. Reg. 45,001 (Nov. 7, 1988).

Importantly, in response to Presidential Executive Order 12,898, discussed *infra* at Chapter 4, page 122, HUD has acknowledged that, to be truly fair and equal, housing opportunities must exist in environmentally clean communities:

> We, at HUD, are committed to creating communities of opportunity. However, **real** opportunity—economic, educational, social—is less tangi-

> ble for those Americans who are trapped in run-down, isolated public housing which is contaminated with lead, for those families who live in inner-city neighborhoods on or adjacent to industrial waste sites, and for those families who subsist in border communities that lack basic housing and infrastructure. HUD is helping to change those intolerable conditions—to change the way society thinks about urban policy and environmental issues.

In particular, former HUD Secretary Henry G. Cisneros identified brownfield redevelopment and "regenerating" strong urban communities as two areas in which the agency could serve EJ goals. U.S. DEP'T OF HOUS. & URB. DEV., ACHIEVING ENVIRONMENTAL JUSTICE: A DRAFT DEPARTMENTAL STRATEGY 1–2 (Jan. 6, 1995). Furthermore, HUD avowed that it "will not sway from the basic principle that low-income families and minority families should have equal access to healthy, thriving living environments." In the process of reorienting its mission, the Clinton administration's HUD promised that a "complete" agency "overhaul presents a good avenue for environmental justice considerations to be integrated into the core mission of the 'new' HUD." *Id.* at 4. As of the date of this article, HUD continues to view EJ initiatives pursuant to Executive Order 12,898 as a "[b]asic component" of the responsibilities of HUD's Office of Fair Housing and Equal Opportunity. *See* HUD's website at <http://www.hud.gov/sec8.html#c>.

52. For example, in *Campbell,* the court did not dismiss the 3604(b) claim because the police protection that had been taken away from the African American plaintiff who had moved into an overwhelmingly white neighborhood was one of the services specifically enumerated in *Southend. Campbell, supra* note 13, at 1143–44.

53. *Southend, supra* note 13, at 874.

54. In the EJ context, the best-known examples are Bean v. Southwestern Waste Management Corp., 482 F. Supp. 673, 678 (S.D. Tex. 1979), *aff'd without opinion,* 782 F.2d 1038 (5th Cir. 1986); East Bibb Twiggs Neighborhood Association v. Macon-Bibb County Planning and Zoning Commission, 706 F. Supp. 880 (N.D. Ga. 1989), *aff'd* 896 F.2d 1264 (11th Cir. 1989); R.I.S.E., Inc. v. Kay, 768 F. Supp. 1144 (E.D. Va. 1991), *aff'd* 977 F.2d 573 (4th Cir. 1992). See Chapter 1, "Equal Protection," *supra* pages 3–22.

55. *See Bean, supra* note 54.

56. *Id.* at 679–80.

57. *Puglisi, supra* note 47, at 695. The *Puglisi* court concluded that these actions were reachable under Section 3604(a) but not 3604(b).

58. Plaintiff Puglisi alleged that his neighbors had formed an organization dedicated in part to keeping him from renting to African Americans. However, plaintiff was unable to document his claims to the court's satisfaction. Litigation revealed, for example, that some members of defendant class were landlords who rented to African Americans. *See, e.g., id.* at 698–99. Plaintiff Puglisi may have also erred in failing to bring the appropriate FHA cause of action. Specifically, he may have done better to raise a claim under Section 3617, which is discussed, *infra,* in the section of this chapter entitled 42 U.S.C. § 3617 (pages 80–82).

The sloppiness in pleading by FHA litigants is a strikingly recurrent theme in the reported case law. For example, in Edwards v. Johnston Cty. Health Dep't, 885 F. 2d 1215 (4th Cir. 1989), the court evidenced irritation at the fact that the plaintiff raised the Section 3604(b) claim only on appeal, and therefore declined to consider the claim that inspection of migrant housing was a "service" for purposes of the section.

59. One commentator has advanced the view that uneven provision of municipal services is within the reach of Section 3604(b). Dubin, *supra* note 6, at 784. *See also* KUSHNER, *supra* note 4, at sec. 6.11.

60. *Clifton Terrace, supra* note 13, at 30 ("Read in context, [Section 3604(b)] is directed at housing providers, such as owners and landlords. Case law supports this reading of the Act."(citations omitted)).

61. 978 F.2d 287, 301 (7th Cir. 1992), *cert. denied,* 508 U.S. 907, 124 L. Ed. 2d 247, 113 S. Ct. 2335 (1993) ("Events have bypassed Mackey. . . . Section 3604 applies to discriminatory denials of insurance, and discriminatory pricing, that effectively preclude ownership of housing because of the race of the applicant").

62. *Nationwide, supra* note 19, at 1357–58 (affirming that denials of property insurance constitute violations of Sections 3604(a) and (b)). *But see* Kennedy, J., dissenting in *Nationwide, id.,* and arguing to adopt *Mackey*'s bar to insurance coverage.

63. On the requirement to read the FHA's provisions broadly to effect the statutory purpose, see *supra* note 29.

64. Instead of direct involvement in sale or rental, some courts suggest that the test is whether a party is "integrally involved in the sale or financing of real estate." Steptoe v. Beverly Area Planning Ass'n, 674 F. Supp. 1313, 1320 (N.D. Ill. 1987); United States v. Massachusetts Indus. Fin. Agency, 910 F. Supp. 21 (D. Mass.1996) (quoting *Steptoe*); Devereux Foundation, Inc. v. O'Donnell, 1990 U.S. Dist. LEXIS 368, 1990 WL 2796, at *6 (E.D. Pa. Jan. 12, 1990) (quoting *Steptoe*). In these cases, "integral involvement" referred to some financing activity that had the power effectively to permit or deny someone access to housing. *See also, e.g., McDiarmid, supra* note 16, at 107.

65. Indeed, because Section 3604(b) is a coverage section and neither an exception nor a limitation section, this is arguably the correct reading of the statutory language. Exemptions to statutory coverage (and citations to the relevant statutory sections) are discussed in KUSHNER, *supra* note 4, at sec. 3.17; SCHWEMM, *supra* note 4, at sec. 9.3. *But see* Been, *supra* note 6, at sec. 25D.05[1][b] (while reading N.A.A.C.P. v. American Family. Mut. Ins. Co. as an example of a case where the court "deferred to HUD's interpreting regulations in some circumstances," concluding nonetheless that "even the regulations are unlikely to help much in environmental justice controversies. HUD's explanation for interpreting Section 3604(b) to reach municipal services is that the FHA should be interpreted to cover 'discrimination in the provision of those services and facilities which are prerequisites to obtaining dwellings.' The 'service' of regulating the siting of noxious facilities deemed sufficiently safe to warrant operating permits is not a 'prerequisite' to obtaining dwellings except in the most strained and attenuated sense."(citations omitted).)

66. Ending segregated housing patterns is a major goal of the FHA. *See* SCHWEMM, HOUSING DISCRIMINATION, *supra* note 4, at sec. 2.3.

67. Academic commentators have shown no greater consistency in this respect than have the courts. See *supra* notes 6, 32–33, and 36 and accompanying text.

68. On Section 3617, *see generally* SCHWEMM, HOUSING DISCRIMINATION, *supra* note 4, at ch. 20.

69. 42 U.S.C. § 3617. Section 3617 is routinely pleaded with Sections 3604(a) and (b). *See. e.g.*, Campbell, *supra* note 13, at 1144 ("Since discrimination in the provision of police protection is prohibited by Section 3604(b) of the Fair Housing Act, plaintiffs state a valid claim under Section 3617" and therefore court rejected defendant's motion to dismiss); *Southend, supra* note 13, at 1210, n.4. *See also Puglisi, supra* note 47, at 706.

70. *Puglisi, supra* note 47, at 696. *Contrast* SCHWEMM, HOUSING DISCRIMINATION, *supra* note 4, at sec. 13.4(3)(a) n.93: "Because the exclusionary zoning suits accuse a municipality of interfering with another's effort to provide housing opportunities for those classes of persons protected by Title VIII, the defendant's actions may violate the noninterference provisions of Section 3617 as well as Section 3604(a). . . . While a Section 3617 claim may also be appropriate, no case has yet held that an exclusionary zoning decision violates Section 3617 without also violating Section 3604(a). . . ."(citations omitted) In short, courts are—as with so much in FHA litigation—divided about whether Section 3617 can be pleaded independently of any other substantive Title VII provision.

71. *Clifton Terrace, supra* note 13, at 29 (". . . the intimidation or coercion with the exercise of fair housing rights contemplated by Section 3617 is far more direct, intentional, and indeed different in kind from that alleged herein").

72. However, the *Babin* court also found that the efforts of neighbors to buy a house to take it off the market was not an act that fell within the scope of Section 3617. *Babin, supra* note 5, at 346–48.

73. People Helpers Foundation, Inc. v. City of Richmond, 781 F. Supp 1132 (E.D. Va. 1992), 789 F. Supp.725 (E.D. Va. 1992) and 12 F.3d 1321 (4th Cir. 1993) (setting aside injunctive and monetary relief on appeal).

74. *City of Parma, supra* note 13, at 1100.

75. The *City of Parma* court was clear that such activities can amount to the required showing of a discriminatory "pattern or practice" under the FHA: ". . . failures to act may also constitute violations of the Fair Housing Act. . . . The existence of a discriminatory policy, statute or ordinance is itself a discriminatory pattern or practice. . . . Additionally, the failure to eliminate a policy which prevents fair housing violates the Act." *City of Parma, supra* note 13, at 1094 (citations omitted). On FHA "pattern or practice" litigation, see KUSHNER, *supra* note 4, at sec. 8.30, and SCHWEMM, HOUSING DISCRIMINATION, *supra* note 4, at sec. 26.2.

75. *Mackey, supra* note 47, at 423 n.4. As noted *supra* note 62 and accompanying text, however, *Mackey*'s holding has been called into question on other grounds by the *American Family* case, although *American Family* did not question the portion of *Mackey* discussed here.

77. *See, e.g.*, Ohana v. 180 Prospect Park Realty Corp., 996 F. Supp. 238 (E.D.N.Y 1988) (Section 3617 claim against, inter alia, neighbors who harrassed new tenants on the basis of religion and ethnicity held to withstand a 12(b)(6) motion); *Puglisi, supra* note 47, at 696.

78. Strategic lawsuits against public participation (SLAPP) are retaliatory devices by which proponents of development projects seek to silence community critics. *See* GEORGE W. PRING & PENELOPE CANAN, SLAPPS: GETTING SUED FOR SPEAKING OUT (1996). *See also* Chapter 7, "Public Participation," *infra* pages 185–229.

79. SCHWEMM, HOUSING DISCRIMINATION, *supra* note 4, at sec. 12.2. SCHWEMM, *id.* at ch. 2 gives a detailed discussion of the issue of standing in FHA litigation *See also* KUSHNER, *supra* note 4, at sec. 8.10.

80. 42 U.S.C. § 3613(e).

81. *Id.* § 3614(a).

82. *Id.* § 3614(e).

83. *Id.* §§ 3612(a), (b), and (o).

84. KUSHNER, *supra* note 4, at sec. 8.29 (*citing,* inter alia, 24 C.F.R. § 103.510).

85. As of July 20, 1999, the cases were as follows, according to Sue Scanlon, the HUD official charged with overseeing environmental justice matters:

(1) Honor, Simmons & Joseph v. St. James Parish, Louisiana et al., Case No. 07-97-0007-8 (alleged FHA violations of FHA charging that proposed siting of plastics plant had result of discriminating against African Americans in the conditions or terms or sale or rental of real property);

(2) Gardens Neighborhood Association v. City of Austin, Texas, Claim No. 06-98-0015-X (Title VIII complaint alleging discrimination as a result of proposed siting of waste facility);

(3) Black Citizens Task Force v. City of Austin, Texas, Case No. [unavailable at publication date] (Title VIII complaint filed against city by African American residents claiming discriminatory housing practices due to failure to remediate high lead levels in predominantly black Rosewood Park neighborhood); and

(4) Morrow and Harrison v. City of Natchitoches, Louisiana, Case No. 06-98-0354-8 (Title VIII claim claimed that use of zoning and land use codes discriminated on the basis of race and threatened environmental safety and health of racial minority populations.)

As of March 1, 1999, the first two cases remained open and under active consideration; the *Black Citizens Task Force* complaint awaited a decision on jurisdiction. The *Morrow* complaint was withdrawn when the city denied a developer's request for a building permit. (Correspondence on file with author.)

86. *Id.* § 3613(a)(1)(A-B).

87. *Id.* § 3610(a).

88. For a thorough treatment of this subject in housing litigation, see KUSHNER, *supra* note 4, at ch. 3; SCHWEMM, HOUSING DISCRIMINATION, *supra* note 4, at ch. 10. Schwemm notes that "[t]his issue has not been finally resolved, but there is a strong consensus among the lower courts that the Fair Housing Act does include a discriminatory effect standard." *Id.* at sec. 10.4(1).

89. Keith v. Volpe, 858 F. 2d 467, 482 (9th Cir. 1988); *Huntington, supra* note 13; *Arlington Heights, supra* note 12. However, it must be emphasized that the United States Supreme Court has not issued a definitive ruling on this issue. The conclusion about the appropriateness of applying a discriminatory effects standard in Title VIII jurisprudence depends upon a reading of a Title VII case, Griggs v. Duke Power Co., 401 U.S. 424 (1971), in which the Court applied a discriminatory effects standard in the fair employment practices context. In light of the fact that Title VIII is to be broadly construed to achieve the goal of fair housing, lower courts have therefore generally applied the discriminatory effects standard. It can be said that this is a "cleaner" standard than the disparate

impact standard used in Title VI actions, since the Court held (somewhat illogically) in Guardians Ass'n v. Civil Serv. Comm'n of New York City, 463 U.S. 582, 584 n.2, 608 n.1 (1983), that Title VI requires proof of discriminatory intent but that a claim under regulations promulgated pursuant to Title VI may be based on discriminatory impact. *See* KUSHNER, *supra* note 4, at sec. 3.02; SCHWEMM, HOUSING DISCRIMINATION, *supra* note 4, at sec. 10.4.

90. *See, e.g.,* Casa Marie v. Superior Court of Puerto Rico, 988 F.2d 252, 270 (1st Cir. 1993) (Title VIII claims in connection with housing for disabled elderly); Atkins v. Robinson, 545 F. Supp. 852, 880 (E.D. Va. 1982) (despite no showing of racially discriminatory effect, defendant county Board of Supervisors violated Sections 3604 and 3617 when it disallowed construction of housing that would have benefitted ill-housed African Americans); *Avery, supra* note 33, at 7; *Coalition of Bedford-Stuyvesant, supra* note 26, at 1208; Fox v. United States Dep't of Hous. & Urb. Dev., 468 F. Supp. 907, 915 (E.D. Pa. 1979) ("Of all the civil rights claims alleged, the Fair Housing Act one is the easiest to prove, for plaintiffs need not show under that Act that defendants' discriminatory acts were done intentionally" (citations omitted)). *But see* SCHWEMM, HOUSING DISCRIMINATION, *supra* note 4, at sec. 10.2 ("[I]ntentional discrimination (disparate treatment) claims account for most of the litigation under Title VIII"). *Contrast* SCHWEMM, *id.,* at sec. 10.4 ("The issue has not yet been finally resolved, but there is a strong consensus among the lower courts that the Fair Housing Act does include a discriminatory effects standard") (citations omitted).

91. *Keith, supra* note 89 (*quoting, in turn, Black Jack, supra* note 13, at 1184–85).

92. *See, e.g.,* Hispanics United of DuPage Cty. v. Village of Addison, Ill., 988 F. Supp. 1130, 1154 (N.D. Ill. 1997); *Keith, supra* note 89, at 483–85; *Huntington, supra* note 13, at 937–39.

93. *See, e.g., supra* note 18. This is only, of course, one possible kind of evidence. *See* SCHWEMM, HOUSING DISCRIMINATION, *supra* note 4, at sec. 10.4(2)(b) (in the disparate impact type of discriminatory effects case observing that "[t]he key to proving a disparate impact claim is statistical evidence showing that the defendant's policy or practice has a greater impact on protected class members than others. The statistical evidence should generally focus on the relative impact of the defendant's policy or practice on the local population, but nationwide statistics may also be used in exceptional circumstances."(citations omitted)).

94. *See supra* notes 33–35 and accompanying text.

95. *See, e.g., Huntington, supra* note 13, at 934.

96. *Keith, supra* note 89, at 482–83.

97. *Id. See also Arlington Heights, supra* note 12, at 1291. *See also Huntington, supra* note 13, at 935–36 (suggesting that in *Arlington Heights* the Seventh Circuit confused the required prima facie case with the ultimate decision on the merits, for which it is appropriate to use the four-part test).

98. *Hispanics United, supra* note 92, at 1157 (*citing* Phillips v. Hunter Trails Community Ass'n, 685 F.2d 184, 190 (7th Cir. 1982)). It should further be mentioned that despite widespread recognition of the discriminatory effects standard, some courts appear to cling to a notion that a more exacting, intent-based standard should be applied. *See, e.g., Campbell, supra* note 13, at 1143 (suggesting that the discriminatory "impact" standard might be available to racial minority plaintiffs only); *Edwards, supra* note 58, at 1223 ("absence of discriminatory intent

is not necessarily fatal to a Title VIII discrimination claim"); *Jackson, supra* note 30, at 1543 (allowing plaintiffs' Section 3604 claim to proceed because they showed discriminatory effect).

The various tests that courts may use in determining discriminatory effect are usefully discussed in Roisman & Tegeler, *supra* note 4, at 315–19.

99. Indeed, "[v]irtually every phrase in Section 1982 is important to a proper understanding of the statute's coverage. For example, the protection afforded by Section 1982 extends only to 'citizens of the United States,' and not to all persons who reside or seek to reside here." Schwemm, HOUSING DISCRIMINATION, *supra* note 4, at sec. 27.3(1).

100. SCHWEMM, HOUSING DISCRIMINATION, *supra* note 4, at sec. 27.3(2)(a). *See also* KUSHNER, *supra* note 4, at sec. 1.02.

101. *Jones, supra* note 7, at 416; *but see* Lazarus, *supra* note 6, at 842 (citing authority questioning the scope of Section 1982). For a detailed discussion of Section 1982—and especially of the interrelation of Section 1982 and Title VIII—see SCHWEMM, HOUSING DISCRIMINATION, *supra* note 4, at ch. 27. Schwemm suggests that the 1988 Amendments to the FHA make Section 1982 claims less attractive than before because the 1988 Amendments "removed Title VIII's cap on punitive damages and brought Title VIII's attorney's fees provisions in line with the fees law in Section 1982 cases. . . ." *Id.* sec. 27.2. On the 1988 Amendments, see James A. Kushner, *The Fair Housing Amendments Act of 1988: The Second Generation of Fair Housing,* 42 VAND. L. REV. 1071 (1989).

The definition of what constitutes and how an individual might effectively be denied access to property for Section 1982 purposes is potentially quite broad. *See, e.g.,* Wright v. The Salisbury Club, Ltd., 632 F.2d 309, 314 (4th Cir. 1980) (finding that a private club membership denied to African American applicants was "property" for purposes of Section 1982); *Campbell, supra* note 13, at 1143 n.2 (allowing plaintiff's Section 1982 claim to proceed because denial of police protection could subject them to racial discrimination and thus deprive them of right to hold personalty).

102. This would be to rely upon claims, for example, that people of color communities have suffered discrimination by virtue of the concentration of air-polluting activities. *See, e.g.,* Adam Nossiter, *Asthma Common and on Rise in Crowded South Bronx,* N.Y. TIMES, Sept. 5, 1995, at A1, col. 1 (exploring possible connection between high asthma rates and incinerator emissions); Hugh Hamilton, *Uptown Eco-Blues: Environmental Woes in Harlem,* THE CITY SUN, (June 5–11, 1991), at A5-A7 (asthma and particulates).

103. U.S. v. Brown, 49 F.3d 1162, 1165–66 (6th Cir. 1995) (drive-by synagogue shooting denied rights of Jewish congregants to observe their religion, even though synagogue's title was held by a corporation and not by the harmed individuals), *cert. denied,* 516 U.S. 942 (1995). *See also* Tillman v. Wheaton-Haven, 410 U.S. 431 (1973) (right to join swim club on the basis of residency, as provided in organization's by-laws, cannot be applied in a racially discriminatory fashion); Olzman v. Lake Hills Swim Club, Inc., 495 F.2d 1333 (2d Cir. 1974) (holding, on facts similar to *Tillman,* that "[w]hile the condition of being a guest is not normally considered a 'property' right one can 'hold,' there is authority and justification for considering it such under Section 1982" *Id.* at 1339.

104. *See* SCHWEMM, HOUSING DISCRIMINATION, *supra* note 4, at sec. 27.4.

105. *Id.* sec. 27.5. Schwemm notes, however, that the Supreme Court has not foreclosed the possibility that a discriminatory effects standard may apply in Section 1982 cases.

106. *See, e.g., Southend, supra* note 13, at 1212–13 (disallowing a Section 1982 claim because plaintiffs did not demonstrate how their contract and property rights had been infringed upon).

107. 451 U.S. 100 (1981).

108. *Id.* at 123.

109. Under vigorous dissent from Justice Marshall, the *Greene* Court found that no such violation occurred. *Id.*

110. Been, *supra* note 6, at sec. 25D.05[2]. One federal appellate court decision suggests that *Greene* requires a showing of real damages, rather than an anticipated loss. In Terry Properties, Inc. v. Standard Oil Co., 799 F.2d 1523, 1536 (11th Cir. 1986), plaintiffs'—African American property developers—advanced a Section 1982 violation when a road closing would create minor inconvenience in accessing one of their development sites. Under *Greene,* the claim was disallowed because they had not demonstrated substantial damages.

111. *Jackson, supra* note 30, at 1542.

112. Evans v. First Federal Savings Bank of Indiana, 669 F. Supp. 915, 919–20 (N.D. Ind. 1987). Importantly, however, the *Evans* court did not reach the question of whether discriminatory intent was shown in this case. *See also Mackey, supra* note 47, at 422.

113. Houston v. City of Cocoa, 2 Fair Hous.-Fair Lending (P-H) para. 15,625 (M.D. Fla., Dec. 22, 1989); *see also* Brown & Lyskowski, *supra* note 6, at 756 n.109.

114. *Greene, supra* note 107, at 123–24. In support of this distinction, the Court approvingly cited another road-access case, Jennings v. Patterson, 488 F.2d 436 (5th Cir. 1974). In *Southend,* the Seventh Circuit supported the *Greene* reasoning when it held that the connection between the defendant's alleged failure to maintain properties it had acquired by tax deed and the value of plaintiff's dwellings was "too remote to support a claim of discrimination." *Southend, supra* note 13, at 1211. Yet the *Southend* court further observed that the defendant-county's maintenance failures might have amounted to a Section 1982 violation if plaintiffs had been able to show that the County thereby "affirmatively altered the character of [plaintiffs'] communities in a manner that worsened their perceived plight" amounting to "discriminatory damage to their contract and property rights." *Id.* at 1212.

115. Hawkins v. Town of Shaw, Mississippi, 437 F.2d 1286 (5th Cir. 1971), *aff'd on rehearing en banc,* 461 F.2d 1171 (5th Cir. 1972).

116. *See, e.g., Clifton Terrace, supra* note 13, at 32 ("It is well established that in order to prevail under Section 1981, a plaintiff must allege and prove purposeful discrimination. . . . The parties both agree that these same standards should govern claims under Section 1982") (citations omitted); *Avery, supra* note 33, at 6; *Jackson, supra* note 30, at 1543. *See also* Lazarus, *supra* note 6, at 841 n.253 (noting that the intent question under Section 1982 remains "unsettled"). *See generally* Been, *supra* note 6, at sec. 25D.05[2]; Kelly M. Colquette & Elizabeth A.H. Robertson, *Environmental Racism: The Causes, Consequences, and Commendations,* 5 TUL.

ENVTL. L.J. 153, 198–99 (1991); Dubin, *supra* note 6, at 796 n.274. *But see Atkins, supra* note 90 (even *partially* discriminatory purpose enough to sustain a Section 1982 claim).

117. See Chapter 1, "Equal Protection," *supra* pages 3–22.

118. *Mackey, supra* note 47, at 422 ("There is no impediment to actions by those blacks who were denied property insurance because of the alleged discriminatory practice. Denying standing to Mackey does not insulate [defendant] Nationwide from legal accountability for any deprivation of Section 1981 and Section 1982 rights it may have committed."(citations omitted)).

119. Sullivan v. Little Hunting Park Inc., 396 U.S. 229 (1969) (white man who leased house and accompanying park membership rights allowed to sue for racial discrimination under Section 1982 because lease resulted in his losing park membership as well as rejection of potential black lessee).

120. *See, e.g., Puglisi, supra* note 47, at 686–87 (white landlord has standing under Section 1982 where alleged personal harm resulting from alleged discrimination).

121. For example, the Supreme Court rejected claims of white homeowners under Section 1982 who asserted that their town's exclusionary zoning practices deprived them of the opportunity to live in a racially-integrated neighborhood, a claim that the Court allowed under Title VIII. Warth v. Seldin, 422 U.S. 490 (1975) (contrasting *Trafficante, supra* note 29, at 208, where the Court affirmed that a party merely had to be "aggrieved" to have standing).

CHAPTER 4

Executive Order 12,898

BRADFORD C. MANK

On February 11, 1994, President Clinton recognized the significance of environmental equity issues by issuing Executive Order 12,898 (the Order), which requires all federal agencies to collect data about the health and environmental impact of their actions on minority groups and low-income populations and develop policies to achieve environmental justice "[t]o the greatest extent practicable and permitted by law."[1] At the same time he promulgated the Order, President Clinton also issued an accompanying memorandum that identified certain provisions of existing law that agencies can use to achieve the environmental justice goals in the Order.[2] The Order both symbolizes our nation's commitment to environmental justice and requires federal agencies to take a number of practical steps to avoid discriminatory actions and achieve greater equity.

Origins

President Clinton's decision to issue the Order in 1994 was in part a policy decision to address the important social issue of environmental justice, but it was also a political judgment reflecting the growth of a powerful grassroots environmental justice movement and lobbying by civil rights groups who supported him during his 1992 election campaign. In October 1991, more than 650 grassroots environmental justice advocates had assembled at the First National People of Color Environmental Leadership Summit in Washington, D.C., to adopt a program calling for the end of environmental inequities, and, most important, demonstrated that a broad political movement existed that was determined to address these issues.[3] Furthermore, civil rights groups and the Congressional Black Caucus strongly supported President Clinton's 1992 election campaign, and, as a result, he was favorably disposed toward addressing their concerns about environmental justice.[4]

Clinton's running mate for vice president, Al Gore, was even more committed to environmental justice issues. While he served in the Senate, Gore had sponsored the Environmental Justice Act of 1992, which reflected his interest in environmental equity issues and would have restricted siting of new polluting facilities in the 100 counties or "other appropriate geographic unit[s]" with the greatest amount of toxic chemicals.[5]

Soon after Clinton's November 1992 victory, environmental activists submitted an Environmental Justice Transition Paper proposing several policy initiatives to the president-elect's Environmental Transition Team.[6] In his 1993 Earth Day speech, President Clinton promised to address environmental equity issues.[7] President Clinton's decision in early 1993 to appoint Carol Browner, a protegée of Vice President Gore and head of Florida's environmental agency, as administrator of EPA was favorable to environmental justice advocates because she made environmental justice issues one of the EPA's top priorities.[8]

Both grassroots environmental organizations, which have created a Washington Office on Environmental Justice to lobby more effectively, and national public interest groups have continued to play an important role in pushing EPA to implement its environmental justice goals.[9] The success of Republicans, who are generally more likely to favor business interests than environmental activists, in capturing both Houses of Congress in both the 1994 and 1996 elections has slowed efforts to enact environmental justice legislation, but the Black and Hispanic Caucuses as well as other politicians have continued to raise these issues in Congress and the national media.[10]

President Clinton's Executive Order 12,898

Executive Order 12,898

Section 1-101 of the Executive Order directs each federal agency to "make achieving environmental justice part of its mission by identifying and addressing, as appropriate, disproportionately high and adverse human health or environmental effects of its programs, policies, and activities on minority populations and low-income populations. . . ."

Section 1-102 created a federal Interagency Working Group on Environmental Justice (Working Group), which is chaired by the administrator of EPA, with the mission of providing guidance to federal agencies on setting criteria for what constitutes "disproportionately high and adverse human health or environmental effects on minority populations and low-income populations."[11] The Working Group established eight task forces with representatives from all participating agencies to address environmental justice issues, with two agencies responsible for chairing each task force, and to develop interagency model projects.[12]

Section 1-103 required each federal agency to develop, by February 11, 1995,[13] an agency-wide environmental justice strategy "that identifies and addresses disproportionately high and adverse human health or environmental effects of its programs, policies, and activities on minority populations and low-income populations." The environmental justice strategy must identify programs, policies, processes, and actions that should be revised to:

1. promote enforcement of all health and environmental statutes in areas with minority populations and low-income populations;
2. enhance public participation;
3. improve research and data collection related to the health and environment of minority populations and low-income populations; and
4. catalog differential patterns of consumption of natural resources among minority populations and low-income populations.

The Working Group assisted federal agencies in developing an environmental justice strategy under Section 1-103. On January 20, 1995, the Working Group sponsored an Interagency Public Meeting on Environmental Justice at Clark Atlanta University in Atlanta, Georgia, which ten agencies, National Environmental Justice Advisory Council (NEJAC) committees and subcommittees and 350 people attended, to discuss changes in the agencies' draft environmental justice strategies.[14]

Section 2-2 of the Order sets a nonbinding goal that each federal agency will carry out its programs, policies, and actions that substantially affect human health or the environment in a way that assures that the agency does not exclude persons or groups from their benefits because of their race, color, or national origin.

Section 3-3 establishes important new research and data analysis requirements. Section 3-301 requires agencies conducting environmental or human health research to include, "whenever practicable and appropriate," diverse segments of the population, which may encompass segments at high risk from environmental hazards, minority populations, low-income populations and workers who may be exposed to substantial environmental hazards. In addition, environmental or human health research should attempt to address, "whenever practicable and appropriate," multiple and cumulative exposures. Furthermore, agencies should enhance participation by minority populations and low-income populations in the development and design of research strategies.

Section 3-302 directs agencies "to the extent permitted by existing law, including the Privacy Act," to collect and disseminate information assessing whether their programs, policies, and activities have disproportionately high and adverse human health or environmental effects on minority populations and low-income populations. In particular, when an agency reviews a permit application or takes other legal actions concerning a facility or site that is expected to have a substantial environmental, human health, or economic effect on neighboring populations, the agency should examine the population demographics in the surrounding area. Furthermore, agencies should collect demographic data for areas surrounding federal facilities that are governed by the reporting requirements under the Emergency Planning and Community Right-to-Know Act in Executive Order 12,856, and that are likely to have a substantial environmental, human health, or economic effect on neighboring populations. To reduce the burden of these data collection requirements, agencies may share information or rely on Census Bureau data.

To protect populations that consume more fish or wildlife than the "average" American, Section 4-4 requires agencies, "whenever practicable and appropriate," to investigate and communicate information on the consumption patterns of populations that primarily rely on fish or wildlife for subsistence.

Section 5-5 seeks to promote public participation in environmental decision making and public access to health or environmental information by encouraging agencies to ensure that their public documents, notices, and hearings relating to human health or the environment "are concise, understandable, and readily accessible to the public." In particular, Section 5-5(b) grants agencies the discretionary authority to translate "crucial public documents, notices, and hearings relating to human health or the environment for limited English speaking populations."

Section 6-609 states that the Order was not intended to create a right of judicial review against the United States,[15] but, as discussed below, agencies and judges have sought to fulfill the spirit of the Order by using their discretionary authority under various environmental statutes to achieve the Order's environmental justice goals.

Accompanying Memorandum

The presidential memorandum accompanying the Order requires that:

1. federal agencies providing funding to programs affecting human health or the environment ensure that their grant recipients comply with Title VI of the Civil Rights Act of 1964;[16]
2. all federal agencies address environmental impacts on minority groups and low-income populations and assure the participation of these groups when an agency assesses environmental impacts under the National Environmental Policy Act (NEPA);[17] and
3. that the EPA use its review authority under Section 309 of the Clean Air Act to require that federal agencies analyze environmental impacts on minority groups and low-income populations when they prepare NEPA documents.[18]

If a NEPA assessment promises to carry out or analyzes mitigation measures, agencies should, "whenever feasible," address any significant and adverse environmental effects of the proposed federal actions on minority communities and low-income communities. In addition, the memorandum directs each federal agency to insure that the public, including minority communities and low-income communities, has adequate access to public information relating to human health or environmental planning, regulations, and enforcement "when required under the Freedom of Information Act, 5 U.S.C. § 552, the Sunshine Act, 5 U.S.C. § 552b, and the Emergency Planning and Community Right-to-Know Act, 42 U.S.C. § 11044." Like the Order, the presidential memorandum states that it does not create any enforceable judicial rights.[19]

EPA's Environmental Justice Strategy

Even before President Clinton issued the Order in 1994, EPA Administrator Carol Browner had made environmental justice an important agency priority.[20] In a five-year strategic plan issued in 1994, she pledged to integrate environmental justice concerns fully and consistently into the agency's policies, programs, and activities.[21] The promulgation of the Order hastened EPA efforts to address environmental justice issues. In 1994, EPA issued an Environmental Justice Annual Report that enumerated programs and regional projects that were planned or under way consistent with the Order.[22]

EPA's New Environmental Justice Offices

Both before and after President Clinton issued the Order, EPA established or reorganized several internal offices to address environmental justice issues. During the Bush administration, in 1990, then-EPA Administrator William K. Reilly established the EPA Environmental Equity Workgroup,[23] and in 1992, an Office of Environmental Equity (now the Office of Environmental Justice) to respond to the growing environmental justice movement.[24]

The Office of Environmental Justice provides assistance to other EPA departments and coordinates a large number of activities within the agency.[25] For instance, the Office of Environmental Justice leads the agency's community grant program, which provided $3 million to over 150 grant recipients in fiscal year 1996, and the Community-University Partnership Grants Program, which awarded seven grants of $300,000 each to universities that form partnerships with disadvantaged communities.[26] In fiscal year 1998, the Office of Environmental Justice expected to award $500,000 under the State and Tribal Environmental Justice Grants Program.[27] In addition, the Office of Environmental Justice has provided grants to Historically Black Colleges and Universities (HBCUs), Hispanic Serving Institutions (HSIs), and Tribal Colleges to encourage culturally diverse students to consider environmental careers, to implement environmental courses and curricula, to promote source reduction strategies, and to help minority communities plan economic development projects that will reduce local pollution.[28] In fiscal year 1998, the Office of Environmental Justice expected to award $3.5 million to local governments to establish pilot programs for its enhanced Environmental Monitoring for Public Access and Community Tracking (EMPACT) Grants Program.[29]

On September 30, 1993, EPA in accordance with the requirements of the Federal Advisory Committee Act[30] formed the National Environmental Justice Advisory Council (NEJAC), which is comprised of 25 (originally 23) members and seven (originally four) sub-committees with five to ten additional members each, representing a wide range of backgrounds and interests.[31] The NEJAC provides advice to the agency through the Office of Environmental Justice on matters related to environmental justice, including its environmental justice agenda, the Environmental Justice Strategic Plan, the Environmental Justice Annual Report, and other agency issues.[32] Between 1994 and 1998, NEJAC sponsored more than a dozen national meetings in different areas of the country on environmental justice issues in which many communities and leaders of the environmental justice movement have participated.[33] NEJAC has issued reports based on these public dialogues. For instance, in December 1995, NEJAC's Enforcement Subcommittee issued a report to EPA's Office of Enforcement and Compliance Assurance (OECA) that addressed a series of issues, and cosponsored with OECA a roundtable on these issues during

October 1996 in San Antonio, Texas.[34] As discussed below, in 1995, NEJAC and EPA cosponsored a series of public hearings on the agency's Brownfields Initiative; and NEJAC in 1996 issued a report on those public dialogues.[35] Furthermore, NEJAC's Public Participation and Accountability Subcommittee has held several formal meetings and issued a Model Plan for Public Participation.[36]

EPA used its leadership role in the Working Group to develop several interagency environmental justice projects. For instance, EPA worked with the Department of Housing and Urban Development (HUD) and other agencies to address the issue of lead poisoning residents of public housing.[37]

In 1994, EPA created a new organizational structure to integrate environmental justice into agency work.[38] This process established the Environmental Justice Steering Committee and Policy Workgroup to develop, help implement, and monitor EPA's environmental justice activities.[39] The Steering Committee acts as a senior management "board of directors" to guide environmental justice at EPA.[40] The Policy Workgroup, made up of senior-level staff, develops, implements, and reviews environmental justice policy.[41] In addition, each office or region has appointed an environmental justice coordinator.[42] The Office of Environmental Justice advises the Steering Committee, Policy Workgroup, and all environmental justice coordinators. In addition, the EPA National Goals Project has held a series of public meetings around the country to identify major environmental priorities, including environmental justice issues.[43]

EPA avoided enforcing Title VI against its grant recipients until 1993, but in 1994 the agency created an Office of Civil Rights to address its Title VI responsibilities.[44] In December 1997, EPA added a new civil rights legal division within the agency's Office of General Counsel to deal exclusively with Title VI issues.[45]

Each of EPA's ten regions have appointed environmental justice coordinators and taken various steps to promote environmental justice.[46] For instance, in 1994 Region I quickly implemented an action plan to triple its inspections of industrial facilities to find more violations and, thereby, protect those at greatest risk from pollution, primarily low-income and minority communities.[47]

EPA's Environmental Justice Strategy

On April 3, 1995, the EPA issued its final environmental justice strategy (the EPA strategy).[48] The EPA strategy has the following five environmental justice mission topics:

1. Public Participation, Accountability, Partnerships, Outreach, and Communication with Stakeholders;

2. Health and Environmental Research;
3. Data Collection, Analysis, and Stakeholder Access to Public Information;
4. American Indian and Indigenous Environmental Protection; and
5. Enforcement, Compliance Assurance, and Regulatory Reviews.

The EPA strategy also contains a final section describing a number of model projects.

Public Participation

The EPA strategy promised to make special efforts to encourage early and active public participation by low-income and minority communities, and to form partnerships with them to achieve environmental justice goals. EPA stated it would work with NEJAC early in the decision-making process to encourage community participation and partnerships. The Office of Solid Waste and Emergency Response (OSWER) promised to make special efforts to encourage "early and ongoing public participation in permitting and siting decisions," and active participation in the EPA's efforts "to develop methodologies for defining cumulative risk from multiple sources."[49]

EPA committed to enhance its outreach and educational programs to improve its communication with all stakeholders, especially those living in low-income and minority communities. For example, EPA would work with "academic institutions, including HBCUs [Historically Black Colleges and Universities], HSIs [Hispanic Serving Institutions], and Tribal Colleges, and other local environmental justice groups to develop an educational program that provides affected communities with information on environmental protection. . . ." In addition, EPA would work with such academic institutions to develop an educational program that provides affected communities with information on how various environmental statutes and regulations affect them and their rights to participate when agencies make decisions.

EPA stated it would assure that the general public could understand and would have easy access to agency documents and notices related to human health or the environment. Whenever possible and appropriate, EPA promised to publish public notices for EPA public meetings in languages other than English, in local and minority-oriented newspapers, and through electronic media, including radio and television. EPA also stated it would develop a network of translators to assist in conducting public meetings. In addition, EPA agreed to examine its current technical assistance programs for minority and low-income communities, and pledged to develop grant programs for and provide technical assistance to small businesses, community-based organizations, and tribal governments so they can participate more effectively in environmental decisions.

EPA vowed to strengthen management accountability for environmental justice activities by developing a system for monitoring and evaluating program improvements resulting from the integration of environmental justice into existing and future agency programs. The agency contended that environmental justice principles were already integrated into many of the Agency's programs.

Health and Environmental Research

EPA stated that its primary environmental justice objectives for its health and environmental research are to improve society's scientific knowledge about environmental health risks, and to develop pollution prevention strategies for risk reduction. EPA pledged to support environmental justice research through competitive grants to researchers examining environmental justice questions. In addition, EPA stated it would increase both its intergovernmental and its nongovernmental partnerships, all the better to address cross-disciplinary projects in affected communities.

EPA's strategy committed the agency to evaluate the current state of knowledge in exposure and cumulative risk fields, and then to identify data gaps and research needs. EPA stated it would focus on major pollution sources of high environmental risks in communities, and support pollution prevention research to reduce risk from those sources.

EPA promised to work with minority communities and low-income communities under study to incorporate, to the extent practicable, their concerns and comments in EPA research design, data analysis, implementation, and information dissemination. EPA recognized that future agency research needs to include diverse exposed populations in its epidemiological and clinical studies, especially those population segments at high exposure.

In coordination with other federal agencies, EPA stated it would design and conduct environmental and human health research needed to support its environmental justice programs, especially information on fish or wildlife subsistence consumption patterns, and on the human health risks and effects associated with the consumption of pollutant-bearing fish or wildlife. EPA promised to develop educational programs to communicate the risks of those consumption patterns to the relevant population groups. Furthermore, EPA made a commitment to review its policies to make sure the agency in the future takes into account such differential consumption and exposure patterns when it assesses the risk of pollution to all relevant population groups.

Data Collection, Analysis, and Stakeholder Access to Public Information

EPA stated it would work in partnership with affected communities and stakeholders to improve its information systems so the agency can identify and address disproportionately high and adverse human health or environmental effects on minority populations and low-income populations. EPA promised to conduct an inventory of the agency's major data systems to identify and then to eliminate any data gaps. EPA stated it would develop better databases to identify major facilities or sites posing potentially significant risks on the surrounding populations. Furthermore, EPA will promote the use of Geographical Information Systems (GIS) to enhance identification of disproportionately affected communities. In addition, EPA will collect, analyze, and disseminate data that will compare environmental and human health risks to populations identified by race, national origin, or income. EPA will work with public health departments and other federal agencies to improve its environmental health and exposure databases.

Moreover, EPA promised to modify and upgrade its information systems to encourage two-way communication between the agency and community information users. EPA also pledged to produce educational materials to assist the public in understanding agency data.

Native American, Tribal, and Indigenous Issues

EPA agreed to work with federally recognized tribal governments, indigenous organizations, affected native populations, and NEJAC to address environmental justice issues that are unique to these communities, and to improve tribal health and environmental conditions. EPA stated that its research and other activities involving tribal and indigenous environments and communities will take into account the cultural use of natural resources.

Enforcement

The presidential memorandum issued with the Order emphasized that existing laws provided federal agencies with the authority to address many environmental hazards in minority communities and low-income communities. EPA stated it would collaborate with state and local officials to develop "clear expectations" about Title VI, including when the agency reviews state permit decisions made as part of federally delegated program activities.[50] Furthermore, EPA stated that it would consider environmental justice issues when it used its Section 309 authority to review and comment on other federal agencies' proposals and actions under NEPA.

EPA pledged to use its enforcement discretion to focus on environmental justice issues, particularly where it identifies violations in communities disproportionately impacted by environmental problems. For instance, the agency promised to encourage EPA regional and state officials to approve supplemental environmental projects,[51] which promote pollution prevention or remedy environmental damage to reduce long-term exposures within an affected community.

In addition, EPA promised to consider environmental justice issues whenever it engages in the regulatory process. Furthermore, a intra-agency work group on grants and environmental justice would examine options for incorporating environmental justice into EPA's grant programs to reach minority populations and low-income populations adequately.

EPA also committed to examine jurisdictional hurdles that might pose obstacles to achieving environmental justice. EPA will work with other federal agencies and state, tribal, and local governments to address environmental problems involving jurisdictional disputes or gaps in environmental laws. In addition, EPA will work with Canada and Mexico to address cross-border pollution.

Model Projects

In its recommendations to EPA, the NEJAC strongly supported the use of model or pilot projects to address environmental justice concerns. In the EPA strategy, the agency reported it had launched a major "brownfields" initiative to encourage cleanup and revitalization of contaminated former industrial or commercial facilities, and pledged to establish approximately 50 demonstration projects. EPA committed to a partnership with the Departments of Housing and Urban Development (HUD), Labor, Energy (DOE) and Commerce's Energy Development Agency to promote job training, economic development, and community empowerment at local brownfields sites. In addition, the NEJAC Waste and the OSWER Facility Siting Subcommittees cosponsored a series of public forums to ensure that environmental justice concerns are fully incorporated into economic redevelopment and revitalization projects, and issued a report on those public dialogues.[52] OSWER and the Regions also promised to examine the creation of public/private partnerships to address environmental justice concerns.

In addition, OSWER initiated pilot projects in partnership with the Department of Health and Human Services (HHS) to respond to health concerns of communities living near hazardous waste sites. The two agencies collaborated to establish a Superfund Medical

Assistance Work Group and the Medical Assistance Plan to deal with the health care needs of heavily polluted communities.

EPA's Implementation

In April 1996, the Office of Environmental Justice issued an Environmental Justice Implementation Plan, which discussed the EPA's success in implementing the five major mission areas in the agency's strategy.[53] Whenever possible, EPA tried to quantify its success in meeting the strategy's goals. For example, EPA claimed that 50 percent of stakeholders surveyed reported that the agency's efforts to enhance public participation had improved.

Since 1995, EPA has tried to implement the goals in its Environmental Justice Strategy, but the agency has encountered several formidable problems in evaluating the health risks of proposed projects to minority communities and in balancing those risks against their economic benefits. To better address environmental risks for both minorities and the general population, EPA is increasingly evaluating cumulative and multiple sources of pollution.[54] Yet such cumulative risk assessments raise complex questions at the frontiers of scientific knowledge.[55] To promote economic development in largely minority inner-city areas, EPA has implemented several brownfield initiatives, including 226 brownfield pilot projects.[56] However, a wide range of elected officials and industry leaders have questioned whether the EPA's Title VI policies for preventing disproportionate impacts against minority groups will undermine economic development in minority areas.[57] EPA has found that it is difficult to create environmental justice strategies that satisfy all stakeholders, including environmental activists, industry, and state and local governments.

Other Agencies' Environmental Justice Strategies

Besides the EPA, the following departments or agencies have published final environmental justice strategies: Agriculture; Commerce; Defense (DOD); DOE; HHS; HUD; Interior (DOI); Justice (DOJ); Labor; National Aeronautics and Space Administration (NASA); Nuclear Regulatory Commission (NRC); and Transportation (DOT).[58] The DOT has promulgated final regulations implementing its strategy.[59] Because many of these strategies contain the same goals for improving agency communication with and public participation by disadvantaged groups, developing better health research and data collection programs to examine diverse population groups, and implementing programs to reduce risks to and discrimination against minorities and low-income populations, this chapter will focus on the larger agencies and more important policy initiatives. In

1996, all of the agencies that had promulgated environmental justice strategies, except the Department of Labor, issued reports to the president, through Carol Browner, chair of the Working Group, about their success in implementing their strategies, which the agencies generally claimed were proceeding well.[60]

Department of Transportation Final Order

On June 29, 1995, in its final environmental justice strategy, the Department of Transportation announced that it was proposing a separate order to ensure that DOT would apply the elements of its strategy in all its programs, policies, and actions.[61] Because DOT's final environmental justice strategy left open many issues until the Department issued its final order,[62] a discussion of the final order is more useful than examining the strategy itself.

In 1997, DOT issued a final order that requires agency employees to avoid disproportionate effects on minority populations and low-income populations by:

1. identifying and evaluating the environmental, health, social, and economic effects of DOT activities;
2. proposing measures to avoid or mitigate disproportionate effects;
3. considering alternatives that avoid or minimize any disproportionate impacts; and
4. seeking input from affected minority and low-income populations in considering alternatives.[63]

In determining whether a mitigation measure or an alternative is "practicable," DOT officials should evaluate the social, economic, and environmental costs and impacts of avoiding or mitigating the adverse effects. Under the final DOT order, officials may undertake actions that will have a disproportionately high and adverse effect on populations protected by Title VI only if:

1. there is "a substantial need for the program" and
2. alternatives that would reduce risks to protected populations would either cause other impacts that are more severe, or involve increased costs of "extraordinary magnitude."

On April 3, 1998, the Coast Guard, which is part of the DOT, proposed an environmental justice strategy to comply with the Order and the DOT order.[64] The Coast Guard environmental justice strategy promised greater public outreach, internal training in environmental justice issues, and a management implementation plan.

Department of Defense Environmental Justice Strategy

On March 24, 1995, the Department of Defense published its final environmental justice strategy.[65] To achieve its first goal, implementation, DOD designated the Office of the Deputy Undersecretary of Defense for Environmental Security to implement the strategy. DOD also established a DOD-wide Committee on Environmental Justice to develop, implement, and monitor DOD's environmental justice activities. DOD stated it would evaluate its progress toward implementing the Order on an annual basis, using the framework of the Defense Environmental Quality Annual Report to Congress to collect information and report progress.

The DOD strategy recommended several specific ways to evaluate its progress in implementing the Order. DOD pledged to establish an accountability system for identifying and monitoring environmental justice activities. DOD departments will hold periodic reviews and self-audits to determine whether their activities result in disproportionate health or environmental impacts on minority and low-income populations living near an installation.

To achieve its second goal of improving human health and environmental data collection, analysis and research, DOD's main strategy to implement the Order is simply to comply with NEPA to assess the effects proposed actions may have on minority and low-income populations. As part of their NEPA duties, DOD installations will collect and analyze data on the socioeconomic makeup of the populations that may be affected by proposed actions, as well as on any risks to human health or the environment posed by the proposed action. DOD promised it would revise and reissue DOD guidelines on implementing NEPA to ensure that environmental justice considerations are documented in the NEPA process. For instance, if an installation or activity is located in areas where populations rely on fish or wildlife for subsistence, DOD will consider, during the NEPA process or the development of an integrated natural resource management plan, the cumulative exposures and risks related to different patterns of consumption of fish or wildlife. Both the Department of the Army and the Department of the Air Force have proposed rules modifying their NEPA policies to follow the Order.[66] Only the Air Force proposal specifically addresses how its department will address environmental justice issues, by requiring it to make "special efforts" to reach low-income and minority populations if an action will affect such communities.[67]

Furthermore, DOD promised to improve its implementation of NEPA by spending more time and effort to identify minority and low-income populations. Each DOD installation will strengthen its community relations plan as a way to understand the socioeconomic makeup of the populations in and around their operations. Installations will combine data gathered from interviews with members of the local community with information gathered from various databases. DOD will also work with other agencies and local governments to develop new information.

In addition, when each installation periodically updates its master plan, that installation will evaluate whether there are any adverse health or physical environmental impacts from its operations or activities on any minority or low-income populations. Furthermore, DOD installations will, prior to applying for a variance from any local environmental requirements, evaluate each request to determine if such a variance will have a disproportionately high or adverse human health and environmental effect on minority and low-income populations.

Both to foster research about and to protect minorities and low-income populations from environmental hazards, the DOD strategy announced that the Department had commenced a program to post multilingual signs warning of potential environmental hazards in areas adjacent to cleanup sites, especially about the risks associated with consumption of fish or wildlife. The Navy has taken the lead in communicating to the public about possible risks of consuming fish and wildlife on property undergoing environmental cleanup. For example, one Navy program posts signs along the shoreline of Hunters Point Naval Shipyard in San Francisco, California, in four languages: English, Spanish, Vietnamese, and Chinese. In particular, the signs warn against the consumption of shellfish taken from the waters in the area, as well as cautioning against potential environmental hazards in the area. DOD pledged to broaden its efforts to post environmental warning signs in English as well as in other languages appropriate for the community in which the signs will be posted.

In addition, to protect minorities and low-income populations from potential harms, DOD committed to review and amend, as appropriate, all policy documents addressing procedures for the sale and disposal of surplus and off-specification DOD materials and supplies. DOD stated that its review would focus on the provision of safeguards, including verification of buyer responsibility, to prevent such material from having adverse human health or environmental consequences on minority and low-income populations.

The DOD strategy's third goal is to foster public participation and outreach. DOD primarily uses Restoration Advisory Boards (RABs) to expand public involvement in cleanup decisions at military bases. When an installation needs to remediate environmental harms, DOD creates a RAB that includes a diverse group of community members as well as military officers. Beyond providing recommendations on cleanup activities, each RAB acts as a liaison between the community and the base.

The DOD strategy promised to improve public participation by revising community relation plans, publishing more information in nontraditional media sources used heavily by minorities and low-income populations, and translating important documents and signs into languages other than English, where appropriate.

The DOD strategy's fourth goal is to achieve compliance with Title VI's nondiscrimination provisions. In addition, to address the protection of Native American cultural and natural resources, in November 1990 DOD had already created the Legacy Resources Management Program to advise the Department on how to balance the intensive use of its lands for military training and testing with the protection of natural and cultural resources. The Legacy Program seeks to promote partnerships with Native American tribal governments to collaborate on projects that foster a sensitivity to, and an appreciation for, indigenous natural and cultural resources.

Department of Energy Environmental Justice Strategy

In April 1995, the Department of Energy (DOE) released its environmental justice strategy.[68] On April 14, 1994, Secretary of Energy Hazel R. O'Leary designated a secretarial officer as DOE's Environmental Justice Champion; established a steering committee comprised of four secretarial officers, including the Champion; and created a DOE-wide working group on environmental justice. DOE's Executive Director for Environmental Justice has the responsibility for coordinating the strategy and monitoring its implementation.

Identify DOE Actions That Have Disproportionate Impacts

The first goal of the DOE strategy is to identify agency actions that may have disproportionate impacts on minority and low-income populations by using published data and information from GIS technology. DOE's strategy emphasizes the use of mitigation and pollution prevention to reduce or to avoid such impacts. DOE promised to work with local communities, including minority and low-income community liaisons, to identify mitigation options to address any disproportionately high and adverse human health or environmental effects. In particular, DOE's Office of Civilian Radioactive Waste Management promised to improve its communication with minority and low-income populations to address options for the mitigation of impacts from its or civilian radioactive waste activities.

Public Participation

DOE's strategy devotes the most space to its second goal, enhancing public participation in its operations, planning, and decision making.

DOE promised to review and clarify existing agency public participation plans and guidance documents to encourage public participation and to reduce environmental risks. DOE pledged to give especially high priority to improving public participation and addressing environmental justice issues when the agency deals with activities involving hazardous waste operations, waste recycling, pollution prevention, waste minimization, and the treatment, storage, and disposal of hazardous, radioactive, and mixed waste.

Some of DOE's public participation strategies will improve public participation by all possibly affected populations. DOE pledged to develop information for public distribution describing, in nontechnical terms, the projects and policies of specific program activities. DOE's strategy emphasized the importance of surveying potentially affected populations in specific communities located near agency facilities to assess whether these communities perceive that agency activities and related risks are inequitable. DOE stated it would hold focused educational meetings, including programs at minority educational institutions, to enhance meaningful dialogue with stakeholders regarding issues and problems, and to assist them in understanding significant technical issues. DOE stated it would improve its Pre-notification Analysis Support System spatial database to provide information about the Department's fuel and waste shipping routes, to alert potentially affected communities about possible negative impacts, and to communicate with these communities about alternative routes or solutions.

In addition, DOE promised to insure that minority and low-income populations are appropriately represented in public participation processes. DOE pledged to publish information about the opportunities for participation by minority and low-income populations in its decision-making processes in a wide variety of traditional and nontraditional media sources. DOE committed to insure that its citizens advisory groups and site-specific advisory boards reflect the communities they represent. DOE will even create liaison committees in communities where no active community groups exist. DOE promised to provide appropriate technical assistance to selected community groups unable to participate effectively, because of their lack of adequate resources.

Moreover, DOE pledged to improve its NEPA implementation by communicating better the results of its environmental analyses and impact statements to minority and low-income communities. During NEPA compliance activities, such as public scoping activities for the development of environmental impact statements, DOE promised to conduct outreach activities to minority and low-income populations and Native American tribes by encouraging their participation in the development of NEPA documents through public education and media outreach, through innovative advertising, including local public service radio and television advertisements, and advertising in minority publications. For example, DOE might conduct informal workshops to bring program experts into contact with interested public entities. DOE might use techniques such as video presentations, posters, handouts, and simulations to foster dialogue with potentially affected communities. In addition, DOE would seek to facilitate public participation in the NEPA public scoping process by improving access to information and providing translations of pertinent public documents in languages other than English, where feasible and appropriate.

DOE pledged to improve its NEPA process to identify any disproportionately high and adverse impacts on low-income and minority populations. DOE stated it would examine during the NEPA process demographics and socioeconomic factors, multiple contamination sources, multiple exposure possibilities, unique risk scenarios, and unique use of fish and wildlife by specific communities for subsistence consumption or for religious observances. Especially during the NEPA process, DOE promised to work with local communities, including minority and low-income community liaisons, to identify mitigation options to address any disproportionately high and adverse human health or environmental effects.

Furthermore, the DOE's public participation process emphasizes heightening of the sensitivity of agency personnel and contractors about principles of environmental justice. DOE will explore developing environmental justice workshops to train senior management, document preparers, staff, and public participation facilitators. DOE might also produce a videotape to discuss environmental justice issues. Furthermore, DOE could encourage agency staff and contractors to achieve environmental justice goals by requiring them to consider pollution prevention activities. DOE might achieve its pollution prevention goals through staff and contractor training, by establishing multimedia outreach and awareness programs, by creating partnerships with stakeholders and industry to promote pollution prevention, and through improved local community emergency planning and emergency response capabilities. DOE will seek to insure that environmental justice principles are integrated into all significant departmental reviews and program manager meetings.

Improved Research

The third goal of the DOE environmental justice strategy is to improve its research and data collection methodologies relating to human health and the environment. Many of DOE's strategies for assuring more diverse representation in epidemiological and clinical studies are similar to those of EPA and other agencies. DOE's research agenda does include special issues involving worker and transportation safety because of the agency's significant use of radioactive materials. DOE has a Worker Exposure Surveillance Program designed to collect information on rates and risks of disease and other adverse health outcomes among radioactive workers. DOE's strategy promised to expand medical surveillance where appropriate, to examine whether there are disproportionate racial or ethnic impacts in the workplace, and to improve the tracking of exposed mobile or transient workers.

DOE Implementation

The fourth and final goal of the DOE strategy is to implement environmental justice principles in agency operations. DOE promised to develop criteria for measuring the progress of each senior manager in developing and achieving agency environmental justice strategies. An unusual aspect of DOE's implementation plan is to include academic institutions, including minority educational and research institutions, in assisting the DOE to achieve the goals of its environmental justice strategies.

Department of Justice Environmental Justice Strategy

On January 9, 1995, Attorney General Janet Reno issued a Department of Justice Guidance Concerning Environmental Justice.[69] The Guidance designated the Office of the Associate Attorney General responsible for coordinating the Department's handling of environmental justice matters. The Guidance stated that environmental justice matters involving American Indian issues should be referred to the Environment and Natural Resources Division's environmental justice coordinator so that these matters can be properly coordinated with the Department of the Interior. Finally, the Guidance declared that the Department's compliance with the Guidance was not subject to judicial review.

The DOJ Guidance noted that "the mere presence of environmental hazards in a particular community does not in and of itself mean that an environmental justice problem is addressable in litigation." Instead, a DOJ lawyer must evaluate each environmental justice issue on "a case-by-case basis." The Guidance suggested that DOJ lawyers consider whether a particular situation involves:

a. disproportionate health or environmental effects;
b. certain groups that suffer disproportionate risks or exposure to environmental hazards, or have been disproportionately

harmed by the effects of past underenforcement of state or federal health or environmental laws; or

c. certain groups that "have been denied an equal opportunity for meaningful involvement, as provided by law, in governmental decision making relating to the distribution of environmental benefits or burdens."

The Guidance provided examples where DOJ had become involved in environmental justice litigation. For instance, the Environment and Natural Resources Division had investigated a complaint alleging that an oil spill harmed fish that form part of the subsistence diet of certain Native Americans. The Civil Rights Division was investigating allegations that the New York Department of Environmental Conservation, a recipient of federal funds, violated Title VI of the Civil Rights Act of 1964 by approving the siting of a landfill adjacent to a minority community. To support the Order's policies and goals, the Guidance encouraged DOJ lawyers to consider filing amicus curiae briefs in cases that raise environmental justice issues, and to invite client agencies to recommend that DOJ file such briefs.

The Guidance observed that traditional litigation strategies were not always the most effective means to achieve environmental justice goals. Instead, the Guidance urged DOJ lawyers to consider "alternative dispute resolution or remedial solutions intended to directly benefit affected communities." In addition, the Guidance stated that the DOJ's Community Relations Service is "specifically tasked to prevent and resolve community conflicts arising from actions, policies, and practices perceived to be discriminatory on the basis of race, color, or national origin."

HUD Strategy

On March 24, 1995, HUD published its environmental justice strategy, which emphasized four initiatives to reduce environmental inequities relating to housing and community development:

1. using empowerment zones and enterprise communities to create healthy communities;
2. reducing childhood lead poisoning;
3. revitalizing impoverished urban areas through brownfields redevelopment initiatives in partnership with EPA; and
4. improving health and housing conditions in rural Colonias along the United States-Mexico border.[70]

The HUD strategy also discussed options for implementing the Department's environmental justice program by integrating it into existing HUD policies and practices.

Department of Commerce

The Department of Commerce's strategy committed the Department to work with EPA, HUD, and other agencies to foster brownfields projects and economic development in distressed urban and rural communities.[71] The National Oceanic and Atmospheric Administration, which is a unit within the Department of Commerce, pledged to conduct fisheries research on environmental risks to minority and low-income populations, including both subsistence and commercial fishing activities.

Department of the Interior

Because the DOI manages large tracts of land inhabited by or adjacent to Native American communities, including Alaskan Natives, much of its strategy is concerned with addressing their health and economic concerns, as well as preserving their cultural and natural resources.[72] In addition, DOI operates several national parks in urban areas, and its strategy is committed to improving the access of disadvantaged inner-city residents to these urban parks.

Health and Human Services

The HHS strategy is based on six initiatives: the first and most important initiative is to form partnerships with the public; second, to supply public education and training for residents and workers in affected communities; third, to provide health services in some cases to disadvantaged groups; fourth, to improve its data collection and analysis about diverse groups, especially minority and low-income populations; fifth, to conduct health research programs in partnership with minority and low-income communities; and sixth, to foster interagency coordination.[73] HHS agencies participating in these environmental justice programs include: the Agency for Toxic Substances and Disease Registry (ATSDR); Centers for Disease Control and Prevention (CDC); National Institute of Occupational Safety and Health (NIOSH); National Center for Environmental Health (NCEH); National Institutes of Health (NIH); Indian Health Service (IHS); and National Institute of Environmental Health Sciences (NIEHS).

Judicial Construction

Courts, administrative law judges, and agencies have uniformly interpreted Section 6-609 to preclude independent judicial review based on the Order. EPA's Environmental Appeals Board, the NRC, and the DOI Board of Land Appeals, however, have recognized that agencies may and should seek to fulfill the spirit of the Order to the extent that underlying substantive statutes give an agency discretion to consider disproportionate impacts on minorities or low-income populations during a siting or permitting process. However, if federal agencies begin to reject or modify permits because of environmental justice considerations, industry or state permitting officials may challenge such decisions; the Order cannot have effect unless Congress provides statutory authorization or the agency adopts new regulations incorporating environmental justice principles through notice-and-comment rulemaking as set forth in the Administrative Procedure Act (APA).[74]

Federal Courts

Only one federal court has reached the merits of whether there is a direct cause of action under the Order,[75] or whether the Order expands an agency's responsibilities under NEPA. In *New River Valley Greens v. U.S. Dept of Trans.*,[76] plaintiffs sought to enjoin construction of a portion of a highway in rural Virginia pending completion of a supplemental environmental impact statement (SEIS). They alleged that DOT's conclusory statement that the project would have no impact on low-income and minority populations violated NEPA and required preparation of an SEIS. The district court interpreted the plaintiffs' argument to be premised on the view that the Order required defendants to consider disproportionate impacts on minorities or low-income populations, and, if the defendants found that such impacts existed, then NEPA would require preparation of an SEIS. Because the defendants had provided no information supporting their conclusion that the project would have no impact on low-income and minority populations, plaintiffs argued that the defendants had a duty at least to examine this issue to "make a reasoned determination" whether it was necessary to supplement the EIS.[77]

The district court first concluded that the plaintiffs' claim that the defendants violated the Order by failing to monitor project impacts on low-income and minority populations must fail "[b]ecause the Order denies private rights of action. . . ." Second, the district court rejected the plaintiffs' attempt to use NEPA to incorporate the Order indirectly, or to use the Order to expand NEPA. Because the final EIS (FEIS) was written before President Clinton had issued the Order, the district court held that NEPA did not then require defendants to consider disproportionate impacts on minorities or low-income populations. The defendants, however, had written an addendum to the FEIS after President Clinton had issued the Order. Again, "[b]ecause the Order denies private rights of action . . . ," the district court held "plaintiffs may not use the courts to enforce the Order's commands." Accordingly, even if one assumed arguendo that the defendants had failed to follow the Order when they wrote the addendum, "the plaintiffs have no standing to enforce compliance."

In light of Section 6-609's clear language, there is no private right of action under the Order. The district court in *New River Valley Greens,* however, may have been too quick to dismiss the idea that the Order may indirectly expand NEPA.[78] In *Vermont Yankee Nuclear Power Corp. v. Natural Resources Defense Council, Inc.,* the Supreme Court recognized that the sufficiency of an agency's consideration of issues under NEPA "is an evolving one, requiring the agency to explore more or fewer alternatives as they become better known and understood."[79] While the Order does not directly expand the scope of NEPA, there is a strong argument that there is a much stronger presumption after the Order that agencies must address disproportionate impacts on minorities or low-income populations as part of the normal NEPA process. Indeed, several agency environmental strategies have expanded the relevant agency's responsibilities under NEPA to include an assessment of whether a project is likely to cause disproportionate impacts on minorities or low-income populations. Accordingly, even if there was not a clear duty to do so when they wrote the FEIS, there is a stronger argument that defendants should have examined disproportionate impacts on minorities or low-income populations when they wrote the addendum, and that the defendants had a duty to consider such impacts in determining whether it is necessary to prepare an SEIS. The district court's analysis of Section 6-609 was correct, but the court did not adequately consider whether the Order indirectly expands the definition of the issues a reasonable agency should consider under NEPA.

EPA's Environmental Appeals Board

While Article III courts are likely to remain reluctant to enforce the Order because of Section 6-609's limitations on judicial review, administrative law judges in the EPA, NRC, and DOI have required their agencies to comply with the Order. In 1992, EPA established a three-judge environmental appeals board as the final agency decision maker in administrative appeals, including challenges to various types of permits issued by the agency.[80] The appeals board's decisions are final within the agency and cannot be appealed to the administrator, although the board may on its own initiative, in exceptional circumstances, refer a matter to the administrator.[81]

The EPA appeals board has recognized that the Order does not provide an independent basis for judicial review or change a statute's substantive requirements, but has concluded that some environmental statutes give EPA the discretionary authority to implement the Order's goals. Furthermore, the board has held that EPA has a duty under the Order to use such discretionary authority whenever possible to advance the agency's environmental justice goals.

In re Chemical Waste Management of Indiana,[82] the appeals board concluded that, in light of Section 6-609's explicit rejection of any right to judicial review, "the Executive Order does not purport to, and does not have the effect of, changing the substantive requirements for issuance of a permit under RCRA and its implementing regulations." Under 40 C.F.R. § 124.19(a), however, the appeals board may review any condition of a permit decision or the permit decision in its entirety. Accordingly, the board can review EPA's efforts to implement the Order in the course of determining the validity or appropriateness of the permit decision at issue. The board held "that there are areas where the Region has discretion to act within the constraints of the RCRA regulations and, in such areas, as a matter of policy, the Region should exercise that discretion to implement the Executive Order to the greatest extent practicable."

The board agreed with the agency that under RCRA and its implementing regulations, "there is no legal basis for rejecting a RCRA permit application based solely upon alleged social or economic impacts upon the community."[83] Accordingly, the board observed that "if a permit applicant meets the requirements of RCRA and its implementing regulations, the Agency must issue the permit, regardless of the racial or socioeconomic composition of the surrounding community and regardless of the economic effect of the facility on the surrounding community."

Yet the board also concluded that the RCRA permitting scheme provided the EPA with significant discretion in two areas to pursue the Executive Order's environmental justice goals. First, EPA may in its discretion provide for other opportunities for public involvement beyond those required under 40 C.F.R. Part 124's existing regulations, and, the board held that the agency had a duty to exercise that discretion in light of the Order. If the operation of a proposed facility may have a disproportionate impact on a minority or low-income population in the affected community, "the Region should, as a matter of policy, exercise its discretion to assure early and ongoing opportunities for public involvement in the permitting process."

Second, the board observed that the EPA has significant discretion to implement the Order under the omnibus clause in Section 3005(c)(3) of RCRA.[84] Under the omnibus clause, if the operation of a facility would have an adverse impact on the health or environment of the surrounding community, the agency may be required to include additional permit terms or conditions to ensure that such impacts do not occur. Furthermore, if a facility poses unavoidable, significant health and environmental risks to neighboring populations, the EPA has the duty to impose additional permit conditions to protect public health or the environment. If the operation of a facility poses a significant threat to the health or environment of a low-income or minority community, "the omnibus clause would require the Region to include in the permit whatever terms and conditions are necessary to prevent such impacts. This would be true even without a finding of disparate impact."

The board concluded that the omnibus clause in Section 3005(c)(3) does not prevent EPA from examining allegations that operation of a facility would have a disproportionately adverse effect on the health or environment of low-income or minority populations, but rather requires the agency to address such impacts. If a commenter submits at least a "superficially plausible claim" that operation of a proposed facility will have a disproportionate impact on a minority or low-income population in an affected community, EPA "should, as a matter of policy, exercise its discretion under Section 3005(c)(3) to include within its health and environmental impacts assessment an analysis focusing particularly on the minority or low-income community whose health or environment is alleged to be threatened by the facility." By conducting such an analysis, EPA "may implement the Executive Order within the constraints of RCRA and its implementing regulations."

The board, however, rejected the specific challenges raised by the petitioners in the case. The board rejected the claim that the EPA had inappropriately used a one-mile radius from the facility to determine which populations would be most affected. The Board deferred to the EPA's "highly technical judgment" in defining the scope of the demographic study. The board concluded that the petitioners had failed to meet the "heavy burden" of demonstrating either that EPA erred in concluding that the permit would be protective of populations living within one mile of the facility, or that, even if it were protective of those living closest to the facility, the permit would not protect the health or environment of persons living at a farther distance from the facility.

The board has rejected several challenges under the Order where petitioners have failed to allege specific procedural or factual deficiencies with the EPA's review of a permit. *In re EcoElectrica,*[85] the board concluded that the Order was not violated in any respect where the petitioners provided no specific evidence demonstrating that the proposed facility would have a disproportionately high and adverse human health or environmental impact on a low-income or minority population.[86] *In re Envotech*,[87] the board concluded that EPA properly implemented the Order by ensuring the participation of the community in the permitting process, and by conducting an analysis of any impact of the proposed wells on the minority and low-income segments of the community in which the wells are located. In recognition of the significant public interest in these permits, the Region convened a two-day informal hearing to ensure that the views of the communities surrounding the sites were received and considered, invited elected officials, environmental groups, and the general public, issued press releases, and contacted the media in an effort to disseminate information regarding the permits as widely as possible. The Region's demographic analysis of a two-mile area surrounding the sites had shown that the proposed wells would have virtually no impact on minority or low-income populations. The board rejected petitioner's assertion that the two-mile area in which the Region conducted its demographic analysis was too small because the petitioners provided no evidence that the permit would not protect the drinking water sources of populations within two miles of the well sites, or that citizens at a distance farther than two miles would not be protected.

Similarly, in *Puerto Rico Electric Power Authority (Cambalache Combustion Turbine Project)*,[88] board held that the petitioners failed to produce any evidence that EPA Region II's permit review did not comply with the Order. Region II had taken steps to promote public participation in the permitting process, and had conducted a comprehensive environmental justice analysis based on an examination of information from three databases in the Region's Geographic Information Library to find that the project would not cause disproportionate impacts. Petitioners argued that the Region should have conducted epidemiological studies, but did not explain how this failure violated the Order. The board observed that Section 3-301 encourages agencies to conduct epidemiological research, but does not require such research as part of a permit review process. Accordingly, the board concluded that the Region did not violate the Order by failing to conduct an epidemiological study. The petitioners failed to present even a facial argument to support its contention that the GIS data were flawed, and, therefore, the board dismissed that claim.

Likewise, *In re Ash Grove Cement Company*,[89] the board rejected the petitioner's contention that the failure of EPA Region VII to use quantitative risk assessment to evaluate risks to Native American populations in northern Oklahoma violated the Order. The Region had examined demographic data showing very low percentages of minorities and average per capita income in both the immediate and surrounding areas of the proposed facility, and concluded that there was no evidence of disproportionate impacts on either minorities or low-income persons. In light of the Region's conclusions and the unsubstantiated assertions of the petitioners about disproportionate impacts, the board concluded that the petitioners failed to produce any evidence demonstrating whether a quantitative risk estimate might disclose any disproportionate impacts to minority or low-income populations.

Nuclear Regulatory Commission

The Nuclear Regulatory Commission (NRC) approved Louisiana Energy Services' application to build a $855 million uranium-enrichment facility in the middle of two historically black communities in Claiborne Parish in northern Louisiana. Before giving final approval of the permit, the NRC's staff had prepared a final EIS (FEIS) that examined the environmental impacts of the proposal and some alternatives. A group of local citizens challenged the permit by appealing to the Atomic Safety and Licensing Board (ASLB), which included three NRC administrative law judges.

Like EPA's appeals board, the ASLB read the plain language in Section 6-609 of the Order to preclude a private right of action or remedy based on an agency's alleged violations of the Order. The absence of a private right of action, however, did not eliminate any possible judicial review of the NRC's compliance with the Order. While the Order does not apply to independent regulatory agencies, the ASLB found that the NRC had voluntarily adopted the Order, and, accordingly, was bound by the Order. "The NRC is obligated, therefore, to carry out the Executive Order in good faith in implementing its programs, policies, and activities that substantially affect human health or the environment." The ASLB concluded that the Order is a "procedural directive to the head of each executive department and agency" to use NEPA and other statutes within its jurisdiction to achieve the Order's environmental justice goals.[90]

Because the applicant's siting process had eliminated alternative sites with lower minority populations and resulted in the selection of a site whose population was 97 percent African American, the ASLB "concluded that a thorough Staff investigation of the [Claiborne Enrichment Center] site selection process is essential to determine whether racial discrimination played a role in that process, thereby ensuring compliance with the nondiscrimination directive contained in Executive Order 12,898." Furthermore, the ASLB found that the NRC's FEIS violated NEPA because the NRC staff had inadequately considered the impacts of the project on property values in the minority communities of Forest Grove and Center Springs, of relocating a road running between the two communities, and had failed to consider ways to mitigate these impacts.

On appeal, the NRC Commission affirmed the portion of the ASLB's ruling that the FEIS had inadequately evaluated the disparate impacts of the project on property values and relocating the road, and that the FEIS must consider ways to mitigate these impacts.[91] The commissioners, however, reversed the portion of the ASLB's decision mandating a more complete inquiry into the racial motives of the applicant, and possibly state or local officials as well, in the siting process because such a "free-ranging inquiry" into their subjective racial intent to discriminate would go beyond the requirements of the Order, NEPA, or Council on Environmental Quality's guidelines for implementing NEPA, which, the commissioners argued, all focus on the extent of objective impacts rather than the applicant's or drafters' subjective motives.

According to the majority of the commissioners, NEPA requires consideration of a proposed project's social and environmental impacts, but is not "a tool for addressing problems of racial discrimination." As support for its interpretation of NEPA, the commissioners cited the Council on Environmental Quality's 1996 draft "Guidance for Considering Environmental Justice Under NEPA," which encourages agencies to examine a project's impacts on minorities and low-income populations, "but neither states nor implies that if adverse impacts are found, an investigation into possible racial bias is the appropriate next step."[92] Furthermore, the commissioners argued that *Chemical Waste Management of Indiana* and other EPA decisions had concluded that the Order creates no new rights, but simply encourages agencies to use existing legal authority to achieve environmental justice goals. The commissioners argued that it was inappropriate under NEPA for the NRC to engage in a broad-ranging inquiry into whether racial animus had biased the siting process because "NEPA is not a civil rights law calling for full scale racial discrimination litigation in NRC licensing proceedings." In addition, the commissioners concluded that, even if NEPA had allowed inquiry into racial bias in the siting process, the ASLB's decision violated fundamental procedural fairness because the petitioners had failed to provide adequate notice of their claims of racial bias, and the ASLB had failed to establish standards for proving such allegations. Chairman Shirley Ann Jackson disagreed with some aspects of the commission's reversal. She preferred that the staff further investigate the siting process without focusing on alleged intentional racial discrimination to determine whether the applicant had applied the siting criteria reasonably and equitably.

Nevertheless, the commissioners declared that the NRC was committed to the Order's environmental justice goals and that the NRC would fulfill the spirit of the Order by using NEPA to give "particularly close scrutiny" to "adverse impacts that fall on minority and impoverished citizens" living near the proposed site. By affirming the ASLB's conclusion that the FEIS had failed to consider adequately the economic and road relocation impacts of the project, as well as requiring the NRC to consider how to mitigate such impacts, the commissioners appeared to believe they had done enough to satisfy the spirit of the Order while at the same time limiting the NEPA process to an evaluation of physical and social impacts rather than an inquiry into whether the applicant, state or local officials, or the NRC itself were biased against minorities.

On April 30, 1998, the NRC granted Louisiana Energy Services' request to withdraw its application and terminated the proceeding.[93] The commissioners specifically vacated all unreviewed ASLB rulings, observing this was standard NRC policy and did not suggest any opinion on their validity. The commissioners rejected the petitioners' request for vacating all commission and ASLB decisions in favor of the applicant, and giving res judicata effect to all decisions in favor of the petitioners. While they did not convince the NRC to read the Order or NEPA as broadly as they would have preferred, the petitioners achieved their goal of stopping the project.

Department of the Interior

In *Antonio J. Baca*, the DOI board of land appeals, constituting two DOI administrative law judges, observed that while the Order is not judicially enforceable by any member of the public against the DOI's Bureau of Land Management (BLM), "it is still proper to inquire whether [BLM complied with the Order], since the Order binds BLM."[94] The State Director of BLM in New Mexico had concluded that the proposed land exchange would have no adverse environmental impacts on anyone, and, accordingly, could not disproportionately harm a minority population. Because the petitioner failed to provide any evidence of adverse impacts, the board of land appeals concluded that BLM did not violate the Order.

Do Agencies Have Authority to Follow the Order?

There is an argument that agencies may not use the Order to modify existing policies unless Congress provides statutory authorization or the agency follows APA procedures. First, executive orders have no binding legal effect outside the executive branch unless authorized by statute, and no statute specifically empowered President Clinton to issue the Order.[95] Second, the APA requires agencies to use notice-and-comment rulemaking to issue new "legislative rules" or modify existing substantive rules that are judicially binding.[96] Arguably, if an agency modifies its permitting processes or other legal procedures affecting states or private citizens to follow the Order's principles, the agency must issue new regulations through notice-and-comment rulemaking or Congress must enact empowering legislation.[97]

On the other hand, an agency's interpretation of an existing policy or issuance of a general policy statement that is not judicially binding does not necessarily trigger either the APA's notice-and-comment rulemaking provisions, or require new statutory authority.[98] Unfortunately, the line between substantive legislative rules and interpretive rules is often hazy.[99] Thus, a crucial question is: To what extent has an agency modified its substantive policies as the result of the Order? The NRC's unwillingness to go as far as the ASLB in applying environmental justice principles is more defensible as the interpretation of the NRC's existing NEPA policies than the ASLB's more far-reaching investigation would have been. *Chemical Waste of Indiana* relied on the EPA's existing discretion under RCRA's omnibus clause and public participation requirements to implement the Order. Accordingly, there is a plausible counter-argument that the EPA, NRC, and DOI have simply interpreted existing policy in light of the Order rather than used the Order to establish new policy that requires either new statutory authority or notice-and-comment rulemaking.

Conclusion

The Order and the accompanying memorandum have already had a major impact on how agencies integrate environmental justice issues into their activities. All of the major federal agencies have adopted environmental justice strategies that commit them to greater public participation by and improved communications with minorities and low-income populations, enhanced research and data collection into whether disparate impacts exists, protection of tribal and subsistence cultural and natural resources, and improved enforcement and implementation of these policies. Most agencies have pledged to strengthen their NEPA investigations and reports to identify impacts on minorities and low-income populations better, to consider alternatives that have lesser impacts on disadvantaged populations, or to mitigate such impacts.

The accompanying memorandum requires federal agencies to make sure that their grant recipients comply with Title VI. Furthermore, the memorandum requires all federal agencies to consider adverse impacts on minorities and low-income populations when an agency assesses environmental impacts under NEPA, to consider how any mitigation measures will affect such populations, and to encourage the participation of these groups when the agency requests public comment on its NEPA documents. Finally, EPA must use its review authority under Section 309 of the Clean Air Act to make sure other federal agencies address such impacts in their NEPA documents. The memorandum strengthens the Order's goal of integrating environmental justice into all agency programs and agency reviews of state or local recipients.

While Section 6-609 of the Order clearly precludes a private right of action, EPA, NRC, and DOI administrative law judges have concluded that their agencies are required to implement the Order to the extent possible under existing environmental statutes, and, in particular, when the agencies review permit applications or decisions by state regulators under federally delegated programs. In the future, permit applicants and state or local regulators will have to spend more time evaluating environmental justice issues during siting or permitting processes, including greater consideration of alternative sites or mitigative measures. The use of the Order to expand permit review to include environmental justice issues, however, may raise challenges contending that federal agencies must seek new statutory authority or use agency notice-and-comment rulemaking before they may invoke environmental justice principles to reject or modify a permit application.

The Order and its environmental justice principles are likely to have an even greater influence in the future. On December 5, 1997, Sylvia Lowrance, EPA deputy assistant administrator for enforcement, issued a memorandum strongly encouraging the agency to strengthen its environmental justice efforts.[100] For example, EPA's Clean Air Act Advisory Committee has agreed to establish a workgroup to examine the impact of emissions trading on minorities and low-income groups.[101] The challenge of fulfilling the Order's goals remains unfinished.

Notes

* The author thanks Michael Gerrard, General Editor, for his assistance on this chapter, and Adria Nobles for her fine research assistance.

1. Exec. Order No. 12,898, Federal Actions to Address Environmental Justice in Minority Populations and Low-Income Populations, 59 Fed. Reg. 7629 (1994), 3 C.F.R. § 859, *reprinted in* 42 U.S.C. § 4321.

2. Presidential Memorandum Accompanying Executive Order 12,898, 30 WEEKLY COMP. PRES. DOC. 279, 280 (Feb. 11, 1994).

3. *See* Charles Lee, *Beyond Toxic Wastes and Race, in* CONFRONTING ENVIRONMENTAL RACISM: VOICES FROM THE GRASSROOTS 51–52 (Robert D. Bullard ed., 1993); Clarice E. Gaylord & Geraldine W. Twitty, *Protecting Endangered Communities,* 21 FORD. URB. L.J. 771, 779 (1994); Olga L. Moya, *Adopting an Environmental Justice Ethic,* 5 DICK. J. ENVTL. L. & POL'Y 215, 216–20 (1996).

4. Willie A. Gunn, *From the Landfill to the Other Side of the Tracks: Developing Empowerment Strategies to Alleviate Environmental Injustice,* 22 OHIO N. U. L. REV. 1227, 1252–56 (1996).

5. *See* S. 2806, 102d Cong., 2d Sess., § 9 (1992); Bradford C. Mank, *Environmental Justice and Discriminatory Siting: Risk-Based Representation and Equitable Compensation,* 56 OHIO ST. L.J. 329, 353–55 (1995) (discussing Environmental Justice Act of 1992).

6. Deeohn Ferris, *New Public Policy Tools in the Grassroots Movement: The Washington Office on Environmental Justice,* 14 VA. ENVTL. L.J. 711, 712 (1995)

7. Ferris, *supra* note 6, at 712.

8. *See* EPA, Office of Environmental Justice, Environmental Justice 1994 Annual Report, EPA/200-R-95-003 (April 1995), at 3; Ferris, *supra* note 6, at 712–13; Gunn, *supra* note 4, at 1252; Marianne Lavelle, *Clinton Pushes on Race and Environment,* NAT'L L.J., Dec. 6, 1993, at 1; Anne K. No, Comment, *Environmental Justice: Concentration on Education and Public Participation as an Alternative Solution to Legislation,* 20 WM. & MARY ENVTL. L. & POL'Y REV. 373, 387 (1996).

9. Ferris, *supra* note 6, at 715–20; Gaylord & Twitty, *supra* note 3, at 779; Moya, *supra* note 3, at 219–20.

10. Ferris, *supra* note 6, at 713–14.

11. The Working Group includes the heads of the following executive agencies and offices, or their designees:

(a) Department of Defense;
(b) Department of Health and Human Services;
(c) Department of Housing and Urban Development;
(d) Department of Labor;
(e) Department of Agriculture;
(f) Department of Transportation;
(g) Department of Justice;
(h) Department of the Interior;
(i) Department of Commerce;
(j) Department of Energy;
(k) Environmental Protection Agency;
(l) Office of Management and Budget;
(m) Office of Science and Technology Policy;
(n) Office of the Deputy Assistant to the President for Environmental Policy;
(o) Office of the Assistant to the President for Domestic Policy;
(p) National Economic Council;
(q) Council of Economic Advisers; and
(r) such other Government officials as the President may designate. Executive Order 12,898, *supra* note 2, at § 1-102; *see also* §§ 1-103, 3-301, 3-302; Gunn, *supra* note 5, at 1252–56.

12. The task forces include:

(1) Research and Health;
(2) Outreach;
(3) Data;
(4) Enforcement and Compliance;
(5) Implementation;
(6) Native American;
(7) Guidance; and
(8) Interagency Projects. EPA, 1994 Annual Report, *supra* note 9, at 1–2.

13. On February 1, 1995, President Clinton issued Executive Order 12,948, which amended Executive Order 12,898 by extending the deadline in Section 1-103(e) to March 24, 1995. 60 Fed. Reg. 6381 (1995).

14. *See* EPA, 1994 Annual Report, *supra* note 8, at 5; EPA, Interagency Working Group on Environmental Justice, Notification of National Interagency Public Meeting on Environmental Justice, 60 Fed. Reg. 109 (1995); EPA Office of Environmental Justice, Interagency Working Group Fact Sheet.

15. This order is intended only to improve the internal management of the executive branch and is not intended to, nor does it create any right, benefit, or trust responsibility, substantive or procedural, enforceable at law or equity by a party against the United States, its agencies, its officers, or any person. This order shall not be construed to create any right to judicial review involving the compliance or noncompliance of the United States, its agencies, its officers, or any other person with this order.

Executive Order 12,898, 59 Fed. Reg. 7629 (1994), at § 6-609; Gunn, *supra* note 4, at 1252 n.166, 1256, 1286 n.424.

16. *See* Chapter 2, "Title VI."

17. *See* U.S. EPA, Office of Federal Activities, Final Guidance for Incorporating Environmental Justice Concerns in EPA's NEPA Compliance Analysis (1998). *See* Chapter 9 *infra*.

18. In 1995, EPA distributed a draft guidance for consideration of environmental justice issues when the agency reviews NEPA actions by other agencies under Section 309 of the Clean Air Act. U.S. EPA, Office of Federal Activities, Draft Guidance for Consideration of Environmental Justice in Clean Air Act 309 Reviews (July 19, 1995).

19. This memorandum is intended only to improve the internal management of the Executive Branch and is not intended to nor does it create, any right, benefit, or trust responsibility, substantive or procedural, enforceable at law or equity by a party against the United States, its agencies, its officers, or any person.

Presidential Memorandum Accompanying Executive Order 12,898, 30 WEEKLY COMP. PRES. DOC. 279, 280 (Feb. 11, 1994).

20. *See* Gunn, *supra* note 5, at 1252; Marianne Lavelle, *Clinton Pushes on Race and Environment*, NAT'L L.J., Dec. 6, 1993, at 1; No, *supra* note 8, at 387.

21. *See* OFFICE OF THE ADMIN'R, U.S. ENVTL. PROTECTION AGENCY, PUB. NO. EPA200-2-94-001, THE NEW GENERATION OF ENVIRONMENTAL PROTECTION: A SUMMARY OF EPA'S FIVE-YEAR STRATEGIC PLAN 6 (1994); No, *supra* note 8, at 387.

22. EPA, 1994 Annual Report, *supra* note 8.

23. 1 ENVTL. EQUITY WORKGROUP, OFFICE OF POLICY, PLANNING, AND EVALUATION, U.S. EPA, ENVIRONMENTAL EQUITY: REDUCING RISK FOR ALL COMMUNITIES, WORKGROUP REPORT TO THE ADMINISTRATOR 2 (June 1992).

24. *See* EPA, 1994 Annual Report, *supra* note 8, at 3; James H. Colopy, Note, *The Road Less Traveled: Pursuing Environmental Justice Through Title VI of the Civil Rights Act of 1964*, 13 STAN. ENVTL. L.J. 125, 185–86 (1994).

25. EPA, Office of Environmental Justice, Environmental Fact Sheet, EPA-300-F-96-002 (April 1996).

26. EPA, Office of Enforcement and Compliance Assurance (OECA), Environmental Justice Fact Sheet: Small Grants Program (October 1996); EPA Envi-

ronmental Fact Sheet, *supra* note 25; EPA, Office of Environmental Justice and Office of Civil Rights Solicitation, Environmental Justice Community/University Partnership Grants Program, 60 Fed. Reg. 14,281 (1995).

27. STEJ Grants Program Request for Applications Guidance FY 1998, 63 Fed. Reg. 13,666 (1998); Prepared Testimony of Ann E. Goode, Director of Civil Rights, U.S. EPA, Before the Oversight and Investigations Subcommittee of the House of Representatives Commerce Committee, Federal News Service, Aug. 6, 1998.

28. EPA, 1994 Annual Report, *supra* note 8, at 11–13.

29. *See* <http://es.epa.gov/oeca/oej/empact.html>.

30. 5 U.S.C. § 1988, Apps. I, II 9(c).

31. The subcommittees include:

(1) Waste and Facility Siting;
(2) Enforcement;
(3) Health and Research;
(4) Public Participation and Accountability;
(5) Air and Water;
(6) International; and
(7) Indigenous Peoples.

See National Environmental Justice Advisory Council (NEJAC) Home Page, <http://www.epa.gov/oeca/oej/NEJAC>; Charter of National Environmental Justice Advisory Council (NEJAC) (EPA re-approved NEJAC charter on July 31, 1997) <http://www.prcemi.com/nejac/charter.html>; EPA, 1994 Annual Report, *supra* note 8, at 4–5; EPA Environmental Fact Sheet, *supra* note 25; Moya, *supra* note 3, at 250.

32. EPA Environmental Fact Sheet, *supra* note 25.

33. *See* National Environmental Justice Advisory Council (NEJAC) Home Page <http://www.epa.gov/oeca/oej/NEJAC>.

34. NEJAC Enforcement Subcommittee, Achieving Environmental Protection: Compliance, Enforcement and Environmental Justice 39 (Dec. 1995) (report to EPA's Office of Enforcement and Compliance Assurance).

35. Environmental Justice, Urban Revitalization, and Brownfields: The Search for Authentic Signs of Hope, EPA 500-R-96-002 (1996); *see infra* notes and accompanying text.

36. National Environmental Justice Advisory Council (NEJAC) Public Participation and Accountability Subcommittee, <http://www.epa.gov/oeca/oej/NEJAC>.

37. *See infra* note 70 and accompanying text.

38. EPA 1994 Annual Report, *supra* note 8, at 3.

39. EPA Environmental Fact Sheet, *supra* note 26; EPA 1994 Annual Report, *supra* note 8, at 3.

40. EPA Environmental Fact Sheet, *supra* note 26; EPA 1994 Annual Report, *supra* note 8, at 3.

41. EPA Environmental Fact Sheet, *supra* note 26; EPA 1994 Annual Report, *supra* note 8, at 3.

42. EPA Environmental Fact Sheet, *supra* note 26; EPA 1994 Annual Report, *supra* note 8, at 3.

43. EPA Environmental Fact Sheet, *supra* note 26.

44. *See* Chapter 2 *supra*.

45. ENVIRONMENTAL POLICY ALERT (Dec. 31, 1997), at 31.

46. *See generally* EPA 1994 Annual Report, *supra* note 8, at 40–51.

47. In the News, 24 ENVTL. L. REP. (News & Analysis) 10,420–21 (July 1994).

48. *See* OFFICE OF ENVTL. JUSTICE, U.S. ENVTL. PROTECTION AGENCY, PUB. NO. EPA-200-R-95-002, ENVIRONMENTAL JUSTICE STRATEGY: EXECUTIVE ORDER 12,898 (1995) [hereinafter EPA STRATEGY].

49. *See generally* OSWER Environmental Justice Action Agenda, EPA540/R-95/023 (May 1995); Integration of Environmental Justice into OSWER Policy, Guidance, and Regulatory Development, OSWER Directive No. 9200.3-17 (September 21, 1994).

50. *See* EPA, Interim Guidance for Investigating Title VI Administrative Complaints Challenging Permits (Feb. 1998).

51. EPA, Final Supplemental Environmental Projects Policy, 63 Fed. Reg. 24,796 (1998).

52. Environmental Justice, Urban Revitalization, and Brownfields: The Search for Authentic Signs of Hope, EPA 500-R-96-002 (1996).

53. OFFICE OF ENVIRONMENTAL JUSTICE, EPA, ENVIRONMENTAL JUSTICE IMPLEMENTATION PLAN, EPA 300-R-96-004 (April 1996).

54. *See* U.S. EPA, Science Policy Council, Guidance on Cumulative Risk Assessment. Part 1. Planning and Scoping (July 3, 1997), <http://www.epa.gov/swerops/bf/html-dfoc/cumrisk2.htm>.

55. *Compare* Vicki Ferstel, *Scholar Urges More Debate*, BATON ROUGE ADVOCATE, Jan. 6, 1999, at 1B-2B (reporting Christopher H. Foreman, senior fellow at Brookings Institution, argues there is no proof different pollutants interact to create multiple, cumulative and synergistic risk) *with* Robert R. Kuehn, *The Environmental Justice Implications of Quantitative Risk Assessment*, 1996 U. ILL. L. REV. 103, 117–23, 151–153 (arguing EPA should devote more resources to cumulative and multiple risk assessments).

56. *See* Carol Browner, Administrator of EPA, Speech at Brownfields 98 Conference, Los Angeles, California, Nov. 16, 1998.

57. *See* Chapter 2, *supra*.

58. Agriculture, 200-R-95-900; Commerce, 200-R-95-908; Defense (DOD), 200-R-95-901; Energy (DOE), 200-R-95-902; Health and Human Services (HHS), 200-R-95-903; Housing and Urban Development (HUD), 200-R-95-904; Interior, 200-R-95-905; Justice (DOJ), 200-R-95-906; Labor, 200-R-95-909; National Aeronautics and Space Administration (NASA), 200-R-95-910; Nuclear Regulatory Commission (NRC), 200-R-95-907; and Transportation (DOT), 200-R-95-911, 60 Fed. Reg. 33,896. *See* Interagency Working Group on Environmental Justice: Notification of Availability of Final Federal Agency Environmental Justice Strategies, 60 Fed. Reg. 30,871 (1995); No, *supra* note 8, at 375 n.8.

59. *See, e.g.*, Dept. of Transportation, 62 Fed. Reg. 18,377 (1997).

60. The following agencies issued implementation reports in 1996: Agriculture; Commerce; Defense; Energy; EPA; HUD; Interior; Justice; HHS; DOT; NASA; and NRC. The 1996 Federal Agencies Environmental Justice Implementation Reports (July 1996).

61. Department of Transportation, Final Environmental Justice Strategy, 60 Fed. Reg. 33,896 (1995).

62. DOT Strategy, 60 Fed. Reg. at 33,897–98.

63. Department of Transportation, Department of Transportation (DOT) Order to Address Environmental Justice in Minority Populations and Low-Income Populations, 62 Fed. Reg. 18,377, 18,378 (1997).

64. Coast Guard Environmental Justice Strategy, 63 Fed. Reg. 16,609 (1998).

65. Department of Defense, Strategy on Environmental Justice, 200-R-95-901 (March 24, 1995) [hereinafter DOD Strategy].

66. *See, e.g.*, Dept. of Air Force, 62 Fed. Reg. 67,305, 67,312–13, 67,315 (1997) (32 C.F.R. Parts 989.18(b),.19(c)(3),.33.,.36 (attachment A2.2.8)) (proposed rule) (modifying NEPA policies to address environmental justice issues); Dept. of Army, 61 Fed. Reg. 37,865 (1996) (proposed rule).

67. *See, e.g.*, Dept. of Air Force, 62 Fed. Reg. 67,305, 67,312–13 (1997) (32 C.F.R. Parts 989.18(b),.19(c)(3)) (proposed rule).

68. Department of Energy Environmental Justice Strategy, 200-R-95-902 (April 1995) [hereinafter DOE Strategy].

69. Department of Justice Guidance Concerning Environmental Justice, 200-R-95-906 [hereinafter DOJ Strategy].

70. Housing and Urban Development, Achieving Environmental Justice—A Departmental Strategy, 200-R-95-904 (1995) [hereinafter HUD Strategy].

71. Dept. of Commerce, Environmental Justice Strategy, 200-R-95-908 (1995).

72. Dept. of Interior, Environmental Justice Strategy, 200-R-95-905 (1995).

73. Health and Human Services, Environmental Justice Strategy, 200-R-95-903 (1995).

74. Gregg T. Schultz, *Activist Agencies Lack Authority to Impose Environmental Justice,* 12 LEGAL BACKGROUNDER (Washington Legal Foundation), No. 43, at 1–4 (Dec. 5, 1997) (arguing EPA and NRC decisions using Order to modify agency policy are wrongly decided in light of requirement that Congress adopt statute or agency follows APA's notice-and-comment rulemaking procedures).

75. In *Mt. Lookout-Mt. Nebo Property Association v. Federal Energy Regulatory Commission,* the Fourth Circuit refused to consider an environmental justice claim under Executive Order 12,898 because the petitioners had never raised the issue before the Federal Energy Regulatory Commission and advanced it for the first time on appeal. 1998 WL 211618 (4th Cir. May 1, 1998) (citing 16 U.S.C. § 8251(b), which prohibits party from raising issues on appeal not brought before Federal Energy Regulatory Commission unless there are reasonable grounds for doing so).

76. No. 95-1203-R, 1996 U.S. Dist. LEXIS 16547 (W.D. Va. 1996), *aff'd,* 129 F.3d 1260, 1997 WL 712887 (4th Cir. 1997).

77. *Id.* at 16–17 (*quoting* Warm Springs Dam Task Force v. Gribble, 621 F.2d 1017, 1024 (9th Cir. 1980)).

78. *See* Chapter 9 *infra.*

79. 435 U.S. 519, 552–53 (1978).

80. 40 C.F.R. § 1.25(e); 57 Fed. Reg. 5320 (1992).

81. Nancy B. Firestone, *Practice Before the EPA,* ENVIRONMENTAL LAW PRACTICE GUIDE (Michael B. Gerrard ed., 1997), § 11A.03[5][a], 56.

82. *In re Chemical Waste Management of Indiana,* RCRA Appeal Nos. 95-2 & 95-3, 6 E.A.D. 66, 1995 W.L. 395962 (E.P.A.) 1, 1995 LEXIS 25 (U.S. EPA, Environmental Appeals Bd., June 29, 1995).

83. *Id.* at 73 (quoting EPA Region's Response to Petition at 11).

84. 42 U.S.C. § 6925(c)(3).

85. 1997 WL 160751 1 (E.P.A.), 1997 EPA App. LEXIS 5 (U.S. EPA, Environmental Appeals Bd., April 8, 1997).

86. *In re EcoElectrica,* 1997 WL 160751 at 10.

87. 6 E.A.D. 260, 1996 WL 66307 (E.P.A.) 1, 1996 EPA App,. LEXIS 4 (U.S. EPA, Environmental Appeals Bd., Feb. 15, 1996).

88. PSD Appeal No. 95-2, 6 E.A.D. 253, 1995 EPA App. LEXIS 38, 1995 WL 794466 (U.S. EPA, Environmental Appeals Bd., Dec. 11, 1995).

89. RCRA Appeal Nos. 96-4 & 96-5, 1997 WL 732000 (E.P.A.) 1, 28 ELR 40732 (U.S. EPA, Environmental Appeals Bd., Nov. 14, 1997).

90. In the Matter of Louisiana Energy Services, L.P. (Claiborne Enrichment Center), Docket No. 70-3070-ML, 45 N.R.C. 367, 1997 WL 458771 (N.R.C.), 1997 NRC LEXIS 20 (Atomic Safety and Licensing Board May 1, 1997), *aff'd in part, rev'd in part,* 1998 NRC LEXIS 7 (Nuclear Regulatory Commission April 3, 1998).

91. In the Matter of Louisiana Energy Services, L.P. (Claiborne Enrichment Center), No. 70-3070-ML, 1998 NRC LEXIS 7 (Nuclear Regulatory Commission April 3, 1998). The Commission also affirmed the Board's conclusion that the FEIS had failed to discuss the benefits of not building the project. The Commission also reversed the Board's conclusion that the FEIS had inappropriately considered secondary benefits such as jobs and taxes. *See* Chapter 9 *infra.*

92. *See generally* Chapter 9.

93. In the Matter of Louisiana Energy Services, L.P. (Claiborne Enrichment Center), No. 70-3070-ML, Nuclear Regulatory Commission (April 30, 1998), 1998 NRC LEXIS 13.

94. 144 IBLA 35; 1998 IBLA LEXIS 70 (Interior Bd. of Land Appeals, April 30, 1998).

95. Schultz, *supra* note 74, at 2; *see* Chrysler Corp. v. Brown, 441 U.S. 281, 304 (1979) (holding executive order must be authorized by statute to have binding effect); Meyer v. Bush, 981 F.2d 1288, 1296 n.8 (D.C. Cir. 1992) (executive orders that are explicitly limited to internal management of executive branch have no "legal significance").

96. 5 U.S.C. § 553(c); Nat'l Wildlife Found. v. Adamkus, 936 F. Supp. 435, 444 (W.D. Mich. 1996).

97. Schultz, *supra* note 74, at 2–3; Nat'l Medical Enterprises v. Shalala, 43 F.3d 691, 697 (D.C. Cir. 1995) (substantive rules require notice-and-comment promulgation).

98. *See generally* 5 U.S.C. 553(b) (exempting "interpretive rules" and "general policy statement" from notice-and-comment rulemaking); Shalala v. Guernsey Memorial Hospital, 514 U.S. 87, 99 (1995) ("interpretive rules" are exempt from notice-and-comment rulemaking because they are not legally binding); *Nat'l Medical Enterprises v. Shalala,* 43 F.3d at 697; RICHARD PIERCE ET AL., ADMINISTRATIVE LAW AND PROCESS 285–89 (2d ed. 1992).

99. *Nat'l Medical Enterprises v. Shalala,* 43 F.3d at 697.

100. Terry L. Schnell & Kathleen J. Davies, *The Increased Significance of Environmental Justice in Facility Siting, Permitting,* 29 ENV'T REP. (BNA) 528, 529–30 (July 3, 1998).

101. Schnell & Davies, *supra* note 100, at 529–30.

CHAPTER 5

State Environmental Justice Programs and Related Authorities

CHUCK D. BARLOW

Introduction

Although the innovative use of existing state law designed for other purposes may prove effective in addressing an environmental justice question, few state environmental regulators can point to statutes, regulations, or programs specifically designed for that purpose. Indeed, very few state statutes, constitutions, or regulatory codes include provisions written for the purpose of providing equity in environmental permitting and enforcement. Most state environmental agencies are in the process of developing programs to assess environmental justice claims both as a part of the permitting process and in the enforcement of environmental regulation of existing facilities. States are developing policies against the constantly shifting backdrop of EPA's Title VI Guidance.[1] Many states also are engaging in environmental justice program development in the hope that the operation of adequate state programs will obviate the need for an increased EPA involvement in state permitting and enforcement decisions.[2]

An Overview of State Environmental Justice Programs

The following chart provides a quick overview of the status of state environmental justice programs:

Environmental Justice Policies
State Survey

State	Yes	No	Other
Alabama		✓	
Alaska		✓	
Arizona			Under Development
Arkansas		✓	
California		✓	
Colorado			Incorporated in Performance Partnership Agreement with EPA
Connecticut	✓		
Delaware			Incorporated in Performance Partnership Agreement with EPA
Florida		✓	
Georgia		✓	
Hawaii		✓	
Idaho		✓	
Illinois		✓	
Indiana		✓	
Iowa		✓	
Kansas		✓	
Kentucky		✓	
Louisiana	✓		
Maine		✓	
Maryland			Under Development
Massachusetts		✓	
Michigan		✓	
Minnesota		✓	
Mississippi			Under Development
Missouri		✓	
Montana		✓	
Nebraska		✓	
Nevada		✓	
New Hampshire	✓		
New Jersey			Under Development

State	Yes	No	Other
New Mexico		✓	
New York		✓	
North Carolina		✓	
North Dakota		✓	
Ohio		✓	
Oklahoma	✓		
Oregon			Under Development
Pennsylvania		✓	
Rhode Island		✓	
South Carolina		✓	
South Dakota			Incorporated into Performance Partnership Agreement with EPA
Tennessee		✓	
Texas	✓		
Utah			Incorporated into Performance Partnership Agreement with EPA
Vermont		✓	
Virginia		✓	
Washington		✓	
West Virginia		✓	
Wisconsin		✓	
Wyoming		✓	

State Environmental Justice Programs: Analysis

The following section provides additional information on the status of adopted state programs or other state resources impacting environmental justice decisions:

Arizona

Arizona has not adopted a formal policy regarding environmental justice complaints, but the state currently is drafting a policy. Arizona has implemented a policy of providing notice of major permit actions to environmental justice communities. Ariz. Rev. Stat. Ann. § 49-111 requires the Arizona Department of Environmental Quality to provide notification of major permit applications to counties, cities, and towns that may be impacted by a permitting decision. As part of its Public Notification Policy for A.R.S. § 49-111, the agency has instructed its Air Quality, Water Quality, Hazardous Waste, and Solid Waste Divisions to "proactively support the Environmental Justice program and when deemed necessary by ADEQ management, notify the environmental justice population affected within thirty-one (31) days of receipt of permit applications."

Arkansas

Arkansas has not adopted an environmental justice policy; however, the state is considering the formation of an environmental justice advisory committee pursuant to a 1993 anticoncentration statute discussed below.

Colorado

Colorado has not adopted an environmental justice policy, but the state environmental agency has incorporated environmental justice precepts into its Performance Partnership Agreement with USEPA Region VIII. Specific projects outlined in the PPA include an environmental justice initiative in one neighborhood of Durango and the compilation of a comprehensive community profile of the northeastern section of the Denver metropolitan area, described as the most heavily industrialized area of the state.[3]

Connecticut

Connecticut is among the states that have adopted a formal environmental justice policy, entitled the "Connecticut Department of Environmental Protection Environmental Equity Policy." The policy's chief aim is to enhance the awareness of environmental equity issues both within the public and within the Department itself. The policy commits the Department to six positive steps:

1. Reviewing Department activities in light of impacts to "racial and ethnic minority groups and lower income residents";
2. Enhancing public environmental education programs available to environmental justice communities and encouraging diverse participation on the Department's permitting, advisory, and regulatory panels;
3. Heightening the awareness of environmental equity issues within Department staff;
4. Coordination with other agencies on environmental equity issues;
5. Diversification of Department staff; and
6. Employment of a staff member responsible for the Department's implementation of environmental equity measures.

The Department's environmental equity programs are centered in the Office of Urban and Community Ecology.

Delaware

Delaware has established a work group within the Delaware Department of Natural Resources and Environmental Control to study environmental justice issues. The Department also has included statements regarding environmental justice in its Performance Partnership Agreement with USEPA Region III. The Department PPA for 1997–98 states:

> EPA and DNREC agree that equity must result from the fair treatment of people of all races, income, and cultures with respect to the development, implementation, and enforcement of environmental laws, regulations, and policies. This implies that no person or group of people should shoulder a disproportionate share of negative environmental impacts resulting from the execution of environmental programs.[4]

Georgia

Georgia has not developed an environmental justice policy document, but the state has created a position of Outreach Coordinator to act as a clearinghouse for environmental justice matters.

Louisiana

Although Louisiana has not adopted a formal environmental justice policy, the state has been the focus of a great deal of environmental justice controversy and scrutiny. The Shintec facility permitting process in St. James Parish, the Grand Bois Oil Field waste site in LaForge Parish, and the proposed Louisiana Energy Services uranium enrichment facility near Homer have been the subject of environmental justice lawsuits or administrative proceedings. USEPA Region VI also has become very involved in the Shintec facility environmental justice issues.

Louisiana has not adopted an environmental equity policy, but the state's legislature has created an environmental equity team charged with the task of developing environmental justice statutes,[5] and the state environmental agency has created an environmental equity coordinator's position. The statute instructs the Department to "examine and study the relationship between the emission of the air pollutants and the discharge of wastes by facilities located in or near residential areas."[6] The study will determine "any correlations that may exist between the emissions and discharges and residential areas." A report on the study was to be delivered to the Louisiana Legislature by February 1, 1998; however, the environmental justice study required by this statute has not been funded to date.

Certain environmental controversies in Louisiana are discussed in Chapter 11, "Access to the Courts."

Maryland

In 1997 the Maryland Legislature adopted Md. Ann. Code art. 41, § 18-315, which created an advisory council on environmental justice. The advisory council is instructed to examine environmental justice matters and to make recommendations to the governor and the general assembly. The report is due to be filed to the governor and the general assembly by January 1, 1999.

The advisory council has developed a fact sheet that states that the council's goals are: "to involve affected communities and enhance public participation; increase efforts to integrate public health and planning for revitalization of affected communities, increase awareness and sensitivity of State and local officials to environmental justice issues; assess the impact of State policies, programs and activities on affected communities; and encourage public/private partnerships to address environmental justice issues."

Mississippi

Mississippi has not adopted an environmental justice policy; however, in 1994, the Mississippi Legislature directed the Mississippi Department of Environmental Quality to prepare a comparative risk assessment "that will include consideration of environmental risks to the health and welfare of the citizens of Mississippi and to the environment."[7] In preparing this report, the Mississippi Department of Environmental Quality created and involved a public advisory committee consisting of thirty-two organizations from business, local governments, environmental equity communities, state institutions of higher learning, health agencies and agriculture. The report, completed in February 1997, includes a chapter on environmental equity, which makes specific recommendations to the Department, as follows:

1. DEQ should provide for public comment by developing criteria that provide all segments of a community with an opportunity to participate in the public comment process.
2. DEQ should provide appropriate public education to communities during the initial phase of the permitting process.

3. DEQ should provide information to the general public, local governments, and the corporate and small business community by preparing a document which will give information on how to inform and involve communities during the permitting process for a proposed manufacturing or waste disposal facility. The information should include suggestions regarding
   a. public participation strategies,
   b. a study of projected local employment opportunities, and
   c. the DEQ permit application process.
4. DEQ should work closely with—and at least annually meet with—all appropriate state and federal agencies (e.g., HUD, Mississippi State Department of Health, Department of Education, Department of Economic and Community Development, etc.) to coordinate programs, initiatives, and strategies for those issue areas that involve shared responsibility or environmental impacts (e.g., lead, radon, indoor air pollution, etc.)
5. DEQ should, in its hazardous and solid waste permit application process, make the submittal of a company's financial disclosure information and past compliance record a priority in order to provide the public with complete and current information.
6. DEQ should identify a staff person in the Environmental Resource Center to serve as the focal point for responding to environmental equity issues. In addition, the Center should assure consistency, due process, and equal protection within DEQ by providing internal training, internal monitoring/investigations, outreach activities, and other responsibilities as designated by the Executive Director.
7. DEQ should collect spatial data (latitude and longitude) on the locations of facilities.
8. Within five years, DEQ should develop a plan to integrate environmental equity activities into a Community-Industry Relations Program which will provide information and assistance to both industries and communities in addressing and resolving issues of common concern.[8]

New Hampshire

The New Hampshire Department of Environmental Services created an environmental equity policy in September 1994. The policy includes a policy statement and five specific steps of implementation strategy. The policy states that "the Department's overall approach in implementing this policy is to incorporate equity considerations—in context with other key factors such as environmental risks—into every applicable decision or action."[9] The implementation strategy focuses on environmental equity education within the Department and for the public, the development of written guidance for assuring environmental equity in permitting, enforcement and remedial design decisions, and the inclusion of environmental equity goals in the Department's work plans, grant applications, and strategic plan.

New Jersey

New Jersey is in the process of developing a detailed environmental justice program. The advisory group, assembled from grassroots organizations, industry, and government to formulate the policy, began its meetings in May 1998.

New York

Although New York has not adopted a specific environmental justice policy or program, the state has created an advisory group to make recommendations on the issue.

Oklahoma

The Oklahoma Department of Environmental Quality has adopted an environmental justice provision in its Administrative Procedures Manual. The manual refers to Title VI as the basis for the environmental justice concept. The policy states: "Everyone, regardless of race or ethnicity should get equal environmental protection from the DEQ" in the provision of services, permitting, and enforcement.[10] This administrative procedure was adopted on December 1, 1995.

Oregon

On August 1, 1997, Oregon Governor John Kitzhaber issued Executive Order EO-97-16 in response to the Oregon Environmental Equity Citizen Advisory Committee Report of 1994. That report advised the creation of an Environmental Justice Advisory Board to which state agencies with environmental responsibilities would report regarding the agencies' efforts to increase the participation of minority and low-income citizens in the environmental permitting process. The Executive Order creates the Advisory Board and authorizes its operation through July 1999. The Executive Order directs state agencies to report to the Board and the Governor annually. Governor Kitzhaber also has issued Executive Order EO-96-30 (May 22, 1996), which requires Oregon state agencies to develop methods of communication and participation with the nine Native American tribes in the state regarding governmental activities.

Pennsylvania

Although Pennsylvania has not adopted a specific environmental justice policy or program, the state has created an advisory group to make recommendations on the issue.

South Dakota

South Dakota has included a set of one-year goals and a five-year goal regarding environmental justice in its performance partnership agreement with USEPA Region VIII. The PPA statements focus on South Dakota's future participation in EPA-sponsored environmental justice training, further dialogue with EPA regarding a South Dakota program, and the appointment of a staff-level environmental justice contact for South Dakota. The PPA's five-year goal states: "In five years, all staff and managers will have a good understanding of Environmental Justice concepts and incorporate those concepts into environmental protection programs; there will be increased citizen involvement in state environmental programs, including those involving rural issues."[11] This PPA is effective for fiscal years 1998–2002.

Texas

Texas has developed two programs that impact environmental justice activities in the state. The Texas Natural Resource Conservation Commission has established an Environmental Equity Office to act as a clearinghouse for complaints and for citizen information on TNRCC activities. The program emphasizes public participation in commission decision making and the management of environmental equity concerns "in an environmentally sensitive manner, consistent with sustainable economic development."[12] Additionally, citizens can obtain legal assistance with environmental equity concerns from within the commission. In 1988 the Texas Legislature created the Office of Public Interest Counsel for the purpose of ensuring "that the commission promotes the public's interest and is responsive to environmental and citizens' concerns including environmental quality and consumer protection."[13] The Office of Public Interest Counsel is a party to all matters before the commission and is charged with the duty of representing the "public interest" in those proceedings, but the Office is not authorized to appeal decisions of the commission.[14] The Office aids citizens in developing the administrative record in commission decisions and "attempts to develop evidence on environmental, public or consumer-related issues of concern to the general public or issues and concerns that may affect the citizens of Texas."[15]

Utah

Utah has not developed a formal environmental justice program. A general environmental justice policy statement is included in Utah's Performance Partnership Agreement with USEPA Region VIII.

Virginia

Virginia has established a Joint Legislative Review Commission on the Impact of Waste Management on Minority and Low Income Communities. This Commission issued a report, designated House Document No. 33, in 1995. The report states:

> While the study found no evidence of an intent to discriminate against minorities, the analysis revealed that in some cases siting and monitoring practices have had a disproportionate impact on minority communities.[16]

The preface to the report adds:

> [T]he report found that solid waste sites in minority communities received fewer inspections and had especially long periods of non-compliance compared to those facilities in white communities. . . . The report includes recommendations intended to improve community involvement in the siting process, DEQ's central office oversight program, and the agency's inspection and enforcement activities.[17]

Partially in response to environmental justice issues, the Virginia General Assembly enacted provisions in the mid-1990s insuring greater public participation in permitting decisions.[18]

State Statutes and Constitutional Provisions

Environmental justice advocates have presented claims based on state statutes and constitutional provisions that require nondiscriminatory action on the part of the state without specific application to environmental permitting or enforcement. Advocates base these claims on state provisions that guarantee equal protection or due process in the mold of the Fifth and Fourteenth Amendments to the United States Constitution,[19] and on state declarations demonstrating an intent to protect the environment and human health.[20]

State Constitutional Provisions

A recent commenter gives an example of the variety found in state constitutional declaratory language regarding the environmental responsibility of the state and its citizens:

Policy statements also vary in length and specificity. At one end of the spectrum is Illinois' brief declaration:

> The public policy of the State and the duty of each person is to provide and maintain a healthful environmental for the benefit of this and future generations.

At the other end of the spectrum is the detailed North Carolina declaration:

> It shall be the policy of this State to conserve and protect its lands and waters for the benefit of all its citizenry, and to this end it shall be a proper function of the State of North Carolina and its political subdivisions to acquire and preserve park, recreation, and scenic areas, to control and limit the pollution of our air and water, to control excessive noise, and in every other appropriate way to preserve as a part of the common heritage of this State its forests, wetlands, estuaries, beaches, historical sites, openlands, and places of beauty.[21]

States also have included similar declaratory provisions in their statutes. For example, a Mississippi enactment states: "It is the intent of the Legislature to provide protection for the public health and safety and the environment for the citizens of Mississippi."[22] To date, environmental justice advocates have found little pragmatic application of these constitutional and statutory statements in environmental permitting and compliance issues. The Mississippi statue demonstrates one reason—the practical limitations of such broad declaratory language in the face of harsh day-to-day economic development concerns. The Mississippi statue continues:

> In providing for such protection, the legislature recognizes that environmental rules and regulations should have an identifiable scientific basis and should be adopted after consideration of the costs to the regulated community of implementing the rule or regulation. It is further the intent of the Legislature that environmental rules and regulations be developed which are protective of the environment and can be implemented on a least-cost basis and in a least-intrusive manner.[23]

Use of Other State Provisions

To date, the most developed use of state provisions not aimed directly at environmental justice concerns to address environmental justice claims has occurred in Michigan.[24] In *NAACP-Flint Chapter v. Michigan Dept. of Envt'l Quality*,[25] plaintiffs argued that the state violated its civil rights statute,[26] the Michigan Environmental Protection

Act,[27] and Article IV, Section 51 of the Michigan Constitution[28] in issuing permits for the Genesee Power Station. In the court's words, the plaintiffs argued that "a facially neutral [Clean Air Act permitting] process, not necessitated by a legitimate, non-discriminatory reason that has a disparate impact on African-Americans violates the Elliot-Larson Civil Rights Act."[29] The court, however, enjoined the permit for lack of cumulative impact assessment rather than on grounds of the alleged disparate impact. The court determined that the Michigan DEQ should have conducted a comprehensive risk analysis prior to permitting, regardless of the race of citizens living in the area.[30] The claim of disparate impact was, in fact, denied.[31] At the same time, the court found Michigan DEQ's reliance on national ambient air quality standards and Clean Air Act permitting procedures insufficient to "protect the health, safety and welfare of all the citizens in Michigan in circumstances such as are before this Court," primarily, circumstances adding emission to an already heavily industrialized area.[32] In particular, the permit issuance violated the Michigan Clean Air Act and the Michigan Constitution.[33]

The Michigan Court of Appeals vacated the trial court's injunction, holding that the plaintiffs never sought injunctive relief through their state constitutional claims or under the Michigan Environmental Protection Act. Thus, the trial court lacked the authority to issue an injunction sua sponte.[34] The court of appeals also affirmed the lower court's dismissal of the plaintiffs' Michigan Civil Rights Act claim. The court reasoned that plaintiffs' allegation that Michigan failed to consider "racial cumulative effects" in issuing the power station's air permit failed to state a legal claim under Section 302 of the Act, which bars denial of the "full and equal enjoyment of the goods, services, privileges, advantages, or accommodations of a place of public accommodation or public service."[35] Finally, the court affirmed the denial of plaintiffs' equal protection claims because the plaintiffs failed to adduce evidence of intentional discrimination, an essential element of claims brought under either the state or federal equal protection clause.[36]

Another type of statute not born of the environmental justice movement but sympathetic with it are anticoncentration statutes. The timing of many of these statutes, and their concern only with the siting of solid and hazardous waste management facilities, identifies them more as the result of conflict between the federally imposed hazardous waste capacity planning process and strident local "not in my backyard" sentiment[37] rather than as an attempt at equity in facility siting. The statutes generally prohibit the siting of more than one facility in a given area, such as a county, or within a radius of another facility. A listing of current state statutes follows:[38]

Alabama

Ala. Code § 22-30-5.1 requires legislative approval of the construction of any commercial hazardous waste treatment facility in the state and prohibits the construction of more than one facility within the same county. In evaluating a proposed facility location, the legislative committee is to consider, among other items, the "social and economic impacts of the proposed facility on the affected community, including changes in property values, community perception, and other costs" as well as the "impact of the proposed facility on public safety and provisions made to minimize the risk to public health and safety."[39]

Arkansas

The Arkansas statute is more descriptive than most in stating its reason and purpose:

> National trends indicate a tendency to concentrate high impact solid waste disposal facilities in lower-income or minority communities. Such facilities may place an onus on the host community without any reciprocal benefits to local residents. The purpose of this subchapter is to prevent communities from becoming involuntary hosts to a proliferation of high impact solid waste management facilities.

The subchapter continues in Ark. Code § 8-6-1504 to create a rebuttable presumption against the issuance of a permit for most types of solid or hazardous waste management facilities if the new facility would be located within twelve miles of an existing facility. The determination of whether the presumption is rebutted by benefits to the community is left to the "affected local and regional authorities."[40]

Georgia

After determining that "an excessive concentration of solid waste facilities in any one community can adversely affect the health, safety, well-being, and environment of that community and impose an onus on the community without any reciprocal benefits," Georgia adopted a two-tier system of buffer zones for "solid waste handling facilities," which include both hazardous and nonhazardous waste storage, disposal, or transportation facilities.[41] Permits may not be issued for a facility if three or more solid waste handling facilities exist within a two-mile radius of the proposed facility.[42] The facilities to be counted do not include captive private facilities that handle waste generated only by the owner of the facility.[43]

Georgia statutes also include permit restrictions for municipal solid waste disposal facilities proposed to be located within one-half mile of a neighboring city or county.[44] To gain a permit, the facility must obtain the approval of the neighboring city or county or demonstrate that no reasonable alternative to the proposed site exists.[45] Similarly, no privately owned solid waste handling facility may be permitted if the proposed location is within two miles of a neighboring county without the approval of that county. Exemptions exist for energy recovery and recycling facilities.[46]

Kentucky

Kentucky's anticoncentration statute is very similar to Alabama's.[47] Kentucky requires that a regional waste management facility obtain a "certificate of environmental safety and public necessity" prior to construction. In considering issuance of a certificate, the state considers, inter alia, the "social and economic impacts of the proposed facility on the affected community including changes in property values, community perception and other psychic costs,"[48] as well as public safety factors.[49] The addition of "psychic costs" to the formula may open the door for the mandatory consideration of environmental justice concerns.

Mississippi

Miss. Code Ann. § 17-17-151(4) (Supp. 1998) states: "Based on the needs of the State of Mississippi, it is the intent of the Legislature that there shall not be a proliferation of unnecessary facilities in any one (1) county of the state." Within the context of that statute, "facilities" includes only commercial hazardous waste management facilities.[50]

New York

New York has adopted an elaborate site selection process for siting new hazardous waste management facilities. The statute establishing this process calls for "an equitable geographic distribution of facilities."[51] The state regulations under this process mandate consideration of such factors as the population density near the facility, proposed transport routes, and proximity to historical or cultural resources.[52]

North Carolina

North Carolina requires that either a city or a county government "consider alternative sites and socioeconomic and demographic data" prior to approving a proposed new nonhazardous waste landfill site.[53] The socioeconomic data to be considered includes census data and other data submitted to the governmental authority during a required public hearing.[54]

Notes

* Chief, Legal Division, Mississippi Department of Environmental Quality. LL.M., Northwestern School of Law of Lewis & Clark College; J.D., Mississippi College School of Law; M.A., University of Virginia. The comments and opinions expressed in this chapter are solely those of the author and do not necessarily reflect the opinion of the Mississippi Department of Environmental Quality. The author wishes to thank Kelly Riley, a student at the Mississippi College School of Law and MDEQ summer associate, for excellent research assistance.

1. *See* Chapters 2 and 4 *supra*.

2. *See* June 22, 1998 letter from the Environmental Council of the States to EPA Administrator Browner (signed by thirty-four state environmental agency directors) (available at <www.sso.org/ecos/ejletter.htm>).

3. Colorado Environmental Performance Partnership Agreement for FY 1998, 1999, and 2000 (December 4, 1997) at 4, 21–22.

4. Environmental Partnership Agreement Between Delaware Department of Natural Resources and Environmental Control and US Environmental Protection Agency, Region III for Federal Fiscal Years 1997 and 1998 (as amended October 8, 1997).

5. La. Stat. § 2011.2 (1997).

6. *Id.*

7. Miss. Code Ann. § 49-2-31 (1) (Supp. 1998).

8. Comparative Environmental Risks in Mississippi at 39–40 (Mississippi Department of Environmental Quality, February 1997).

9. New Hampshire Department of Environmental Services Environmental Equity Policy (September 30, 1994).

10. *Subject: Environmental Justice*, Oklahoma Department of Environmental Quality Administrative Procedures Manual (December 1, 1995).

11. Environmental Partnership Agreement Between South Dakota Department of the Environment and Natural Resources and US Environmental Protection Agency, Region VIII for Federal Fiscal Years 1998–2002, § 2.11.

12. Texas Natural Resource Conservation Commission, Public Participation in Permitting at 19 (Rev. 1998). *See also Texas Partners for Environmental Justice*, Natural Outlook (Tex. Nat. Resource Consv. Comm'n.), Winter 1998, at 1.

13. Tex. Water Code Ann. § 5.271 (West 1988).

14. *Id.* §§ 5.273, 5.275.

15. Texas Natural Resource Conservation Commission, Public Participation in Permitting at 16 (Rev. 1998).

16. House Document No. 33 at 1.

17. *Id.*

18. *See* Va. Code Ann. §§ 10.1-1408.1 (requiring local government public hearings prior to solid waste management facility siting; increasing pre-permit application public notice for landfill and transfer station permits; requiring that local government applicants must form a citizen advisory group); 10.1-1307.01

(increasing public prior notice of proposed air emission permits); 62.1-44.15:4 (requiring DEQ to notify local governments of applications for new or modified discharges within the jurisdiction and to notify riparian landowners of new or modified discharge permits).

19. *See* Robert F. Williams, *Equality Guarantees in State Constitutional Law,* 63 TEXAS L. REV. 1195 (1985) (listing state constitutional equality provisions with historical categorization and discussion).

20. *See generally* Carolyn Graham & Jennifer B. Grills, *Environmental Justice: A Survey of Federal and State Responses,* 8 VILL. ENVTL. L.J. 237, n.83 (1997) (discussing New York and Pennsylvania proposed legislation).

21. Robert A. McLaren, *Comment, Environmental Protection Based on State Constitutional Law: A Call for Reinterpretation,* 12 U. HAW. L. REV. 123, 129–30 nn.25–30 (1990) (listing forty-two state constitutional provisions generically declaring citizens' rights to a healthy environment or the state's responsibility in protecting the environment).

22. 1994 MISS. LAWS ch. 598, § 1.

23. 1994 MISS. LAWS ch. 598, § 1 (1)–(2).

24. *See* Terry L. Schnell & Kathleen J. Davies, *The Increased Significance of Environmental Justice in Facility Siting, Permitting,* DAILY ENV'T REP. (BNA) No. 132 (July 10, 1998).

25. Case No. 95-38228-CV (Genesee County Circuit Ct., May 29, 1997).

26. MICH. COMP. LAWS § 37.2101.

27. MICH. COMP. LAWS § 324.1901.

28. MICH. CONST. art. IV, § 51 states: "The public health and general welfare of the people of the state are hereby declared to be matters of primary public concern. The legislature shall pass suitable laws for the protection and promotion of the public health."

29. *Supra* note 26, at 29.

30. *Id.* at 33.

31. *Id.* at 37.

32. *Id.* at 38.

33. MICH. COMP. LAWS § 324.5510 provides that the Department of Environmental Quality may deny or revoke a permit if installation of the source "presents or may present an imminent and substantial endangerment to human health, safety, or welfare, or the environment." The court held that "[u]nless the M.D.E.Q. performs a Risk Assessment to determine the impact of the plant in the surrounding area, at least within a five mile radius, it cannot conclude that the plant does not violate this provision and must therefore refuse to grant a permit." *Supra* note 26, at 42–43.

34. *NAACP-Flint Chapter v. Governor of Michigan,* No. 205264, Op. at 3 (Mich. Ct. App., Nov. 24, 1998).

35. *Id.* at 5 (*quoting* MICH. COMP. LAWS § 37.2302).

36. *Id.* at 7 (*citing* Harrille v. State Plumbing and Heating, Inc., 218 Mich. App. 302, 553 NW2d 377 (1996), People v. Ford, 417 Mich. 66, 103, 331 NW2d 878 (1982)).

37. *See* 42 U.S.C. § 9604(c)(3), CERCLA § 109(c)(3), which made the receipt of federal superfund dollars conditioned on the state's submittal of a "capacity assurance plan" detailing the state's plan to meet its hazardous waste treatment,

storage, and disposal needs over the next twenty-year period. This provision, designed to assure that sufficient hazardous waste capacity was constructed nationwide, has been eviscerated by EPA's determination that sufficient nationwide capacity already exists through 2018. No further capacity assurance plan submittals are required by the states. *See* Memorandum from Michael Petruska, Associate Director, Hazardous Waste Minimization and Management Division, Office of Solid Waste, USEPA to RCRA Docket (Apr. 24, 1998).

38. New York City has adopted a detailed method of siting city public facilities to avoid the concentration of locally unwanted land uses within neighborhoods of the city. The regulations apply general criteria to all city facilities and specialized criteria to certain operations such as transportation and waste management facilities. Criteria for the Location of City Facilities (New York City Planning Commission, Dec. 3, 1990) ("Criteria"); *see* N.Y.C. Charter § 203(a) (1989) (requiring adoption of siting regulations). In evaluating waste management facility siting, the sponsoring city agency is required to "take into consideration the number and proximity of existing city and non-city facilities, situated within approximately a one-half mile radius of the proposed site, which have similar environmental impacts." Criteria § 6.4; *see* William Valetta, *Siting Public Facilities on a Fair Share Basis in New York City,* 25 URB. LAW 1, 16–17 (1993).

39. ALA. CODE ANN. § 22-30-5.1(d)(1), (5).

40. ARK. CODE ANN. § 8-6-1503.

41. GA. CODE ANN. §§ 12-8-25.4(a); *see* 12-8-22 (definitions), 12-8-24 (permitting requirements).

42. GA. CODE ANN. § 12-8-25.4(b).

43. *Id.*

44. GA. CODE ANN. § 12-8-25(3).

45. *Id.*

46. GA. CODE ANN. § 12-8-25(a)(2).

47. KY. REV. STAT. ANN. § 224.46-830(2).

48. *Id.*

49. *Id.* § 224.46-830(2)(e).

50. That term is defined in MISS. CODE ANN. § 17-17-3(c) (Rev. 1995) as a facility that handles hazardous waste from more that one generator for a fee.

51. N.Y. ENV'TL. CONSERV. LAW § 27-1102(f) (1997).

52. N.Y. COMP. CODES R. & REGS. tit. 6, § 361.7(b) (1998).

53. N.C. GEN. STAT. § 160A-325(a); 153A-136(c).

54. N.C. GEN. STAT. § 160A-325(a)(4); 153A-136(c)(4).

CHAPTER 6

Native American Law

JUDITH V. ROYSTER

Environmental justice issues in Indian country often take on a character special to Native American tribes.[1] Although Indian communities share many of the environmental burdens and concerns of other communities of color, Indian tribes are unique among those communities because of their governmental status. The environmental concerns of Indian communities have been amply documented elsewhere,[2] and consequently this chapter will focus on the governmental authority of Indian tribes to manage environmental matters within their jurisdiction.

Indian tribes connect to their lands not only on economic and emotional levels, but also on the levels of culture, religion, and sovereignty. Environmental degradation may, for example, affect land that is sacred to tribes, or pose a threat to the entire territory in which the tribe as government operates. And for Native American tribes, land is not fungible. Most tribes today occupy reservations carved out of their aboriginal territory, lands that the tribes occupied before white contact. The reservations are "place": a homeland, a source of physical subsistence and spiritual sustenance.[3] The loss of the place may impact the identity and destiny of the tribe itself.[4]

Moreover, environmental degradation may impact tribal cultures in special ways because of the limited size of the territory or the subsistence or religious practices of the tribes. Oil pollution may irreparably damage the only source of drinking water on a reservation,[5] or a radioactive spill may contaminate the primary source of drinking and stock water in an arid land.[6] Pollution of fisheries has a far greater effect on Indian communities that historically depend upon the fish for their main food source than it does on the population at large,[7] and the impacts of federal laws protecting species may disproportionately affect tribes that use the species in religious ceremonies.[8]

Because of the often disparate severity of environmental harm in Indian country, Indian tribes increasingly are exploring their governmental authority in environmental matters. Tribes are asserting rights to environmental decision making—under principles of inherent tribal sovereignty, under federal statutes, and pursuant to their treaties with the United States—so that the determinations of whether, when, and how to develop tribal lands and resources are consistent with the tribe's economic and environmental values.[9]

Tribes as Governments: The Concept of Tribal Sovereignty

The Federal-Tribal Relationship

Indian tribes are sovereign governments, exercising powers of self-government over both their citizens and their territories.[10] Tribal sovereignty preexisted the United States Constitution, and is not derived from the federal government or the states.

> Perhaps the most basic principle of all Indian law, supported by a host of decisions . . . is the principle that *those powers which are lawfully vested in an Indian tribe are not, in general, delegated powers granted by express acts of Congress, but rather inherent powers of a limited sovereignty which has never been extinguished*.[11]

Nonetheless, Native American tribes do not have the full sovereignty accorded to nation-states at international law. Instead, tribes are "domestic dependent nations," subject to the authority and jurisdiction of the federal government.[12] Until the 1880s, the exercise of this overarching federal authority was largely confined to regulating the relations between the tribes and foreign nations, the United States, and its citizens.[13] Beginning with the Major Crimes Act of 1885,[14] however, Congress began to assert the power of direct control over internal tribal relations. Today, the Court maintains that congressional power over Indian tribes is plenary, reaching even to "the power of complete defeasance" of tribal self-government.[15]

Congress thus *may* alter tribal sovereign powers, if it chooses to do so. However, federal courts should interpret both treaties and acts of Congress to the benefit of the Indian tribes. Under the Indian law canons of construction, federal statutes should be liberally construed in favor of Indian tribes and all ambiguities should be resolved in the tribes' favor. Accordingly, federal courts generally require either express language or clear expression of congressional intent before they will read statutes to abrogate Indian rights.[16]

Moreover, congressional authority over Native American tribes is offset by the federal trust obligation.[17] Commonly traced to Chief Justice John Marshall's guardian-ward analogy for federal-tribal relations,[18] the trust doctrine likely evolved out of the protectorate status of tribes allied with the stronger United States. Although the trust doctrine was invoked as a source and justification of federal plenary power at the turn of the century,[19] by the 1970s the doctrine was instead a source of federal obligations to the Indian tribes. Today, Congress has the responsibility to protect Indian lands, funds, and resources that are held "in trust" by the federal government for the tribes or individual Indians. That trust obligation is not constitutionally based and therefore is not enforceable against the plenary power of Congress,[20] although congressional action may be reviewed under relevant constitutional provisions.[21] The trust relationship can, however, give rise to enforceable rights and duties on the part of the federal agencies charged with carrying out the federal trust responsibility.[22]

The relationship between the federal government and the Indian tribes has undergone frequent and often dramatic changes over the years.[23] For much of the nineteenth century, federal Indian policy focused on the separation of tribes and white citizens, from the removal of Indian tribes west of the Mississippi in the early decades to the establishment of reservations throughout the mid- to late 1800s. By the mid-1880s, however, federal policy changed markedly. The breakup of the reservations, the destruction of the tribes, and the assimilation of the Indians became the paramount federal concern for a half-century. In the early 1930s, responding to the horrors of the assimilation years, Congress embarked on a short-lived policy of promoting tribal reorganization and self-government. Within a decade, however, policy shifted back to assimilation, this time by "terminating" federal recognition of tribes and liquidating tribal assets. During the 1960s, the termination policy was repudiated, and by 1970 the federal government embarked on the current federal Indian policy of promoting tribal self-determination and ensuring a "government-to-government relationship" between the federal government and the tribes.[24]

Indian Country and Land Tenure Patterns

With few exceptions, tribal governmental authority extends only within the boundaries of Indian country. Indian country is defined by federal law as including:

> (a) all land within the limits of any Indian reservation under the jurisdiction of the United States government, notwithstanding the issuance of any patents, and including rights-of-way running through the reservation, (b) all dependent Indian communities . . . and (c) all Indian allotments, the Indian titles to which have not been extinguished, including rights-of-way running through the same.[25]

Although this definition is contained in the federal criminal code, the Supreme Court has provided that it applies to issues of civil as well as criminal jurisdiction.[26] Moreover, the Court has held that Indian country encompasses all lands set aside for tribal use under federal protection, even if those lands do not fit neatly into one of the formalistic statutory categories. Thus, for example, lands held in trust for an Indian tribe are Indian country even if the lands do not constitute a "formal" reservation.[27]

Within Indian country, there is a variety of land tenure patterns that impact tribal governmental rights. When most reservations were created, virtually the entire land base was held in trust for the governing tribe. That is, fee title was in the United States while the Indian tribe was the beneficial communal owner. Trust status extends as well to the natural resources such as minerals, timber, fossils, and certain water rights.[28] Lands and resources that are held in trust may not be alienated or encumbered without the consent of the federal government; moreover, trust lands and Indian activities on those lands are free of state taxation and, generally, of state regulation without congressional consent.[29]

In the mid-1880s, as the cornerstone of the drive to assimilate the Indians, the federal government instituted a policy of allotment of reservation lands. Under the General Allotment Act of 1887,[30] Congress authorized the allotment of communal trust lands to individual Indians in plots of 80 to 160 acres. Allottees received trust patents, under which the land was to be held in trust for the individual owner for 25 years. At the end of the statutory period, the allottee would receive a patent in fee, and the land would be freely alienable and subject to encumbrance and taxation.[31] Once tribal lands were allotted, the Secretary of the Interior was authorized to open the "surplus" lands to settlement.

Although many of the reservations in the Southwest escaped allotment, the allotment process was instituted on 118 reservations, and 44 of those had their surplus lands opened to settlement.[32] By the time Congress ended the allotment policy in 1934,[33] vast numbers of allottees had lost their fee-patented lands to speculators or to sheriffs' auctions for nonpayment of taxes. Two thirds of the lands allotted, some 27 million acres, passed into non-Indian ownership by 1934; another 60 million acres were lost under the surplus lands program.[34]

The allotment policy forever altered land tenure within Indian country. Primarily as a result of the allotment years, many Indian reservations today are a checkerboard of ownership patterns. Virtually all reservations still contain tribal trust lands, and any given reservation may also include individual trust lands, fee lands owned by the tribes or their members, and nonmember fee lands that may be owned by individuals, states and their political subdivisions, or the federal government. In general today, the term "fee lands" refers to nonmember-owned lands within reservations, although it may also include certain state highways that are the jurisdictional equivalent of fee lands.[35] The term "Indian lands," by contrast, refers to all lands owned or held in trust for the governing tribe or its members. Nonetheless, *all lands* within Indian reservation borders, however owned, are Indian country.

Tribal Governmental Authority

Tribal governmental authority may stem from any of three sources: inherent tribal sovereignty, treaties and agreements with the United States, and congressional delegation.

First, Native American tribes retain the inherent authority of any sovereign to act, unless that authority has been limited by treaty, by federal statute, or by the common law doctrine of "implicit divestiture."[36] The notion of implicit divestiture of tribal sovereign powers affects tribal authority over nonmembers of the governing tribes, but does not limit tribes' sovereignty over their citizens.

Subject to certain congressional limitations,[37] Indian tribes have full governmental authority over their members and over Indian lands within Indian country.[38] States, on the other hand, have no authority over tribal members or Indian lands absent congressional delegation or "exceptional circumstances." The only exceptional circumstance ever recognized has been state regulation of migratory fish to ensure preservation of the species.[39]

Tribal authority over nonmembers is more limited. Although tribes freely exercise governmental powers over nonmembers on Indian lands,[40] tribes may not assert authority over nonmembers' activities on fee lands unless those activities implicate one of two exceptions created in the case of *Montana v. United States*.[41] The first exception provides that "[a] tribe may regulate, through taxation, licensing, or other means, the activities of nonmembers who enter consensual relationships with the tribe or its members, through commercial dealing, contracts, leases, or other arrangements."[42] The second states that "[a] tribe may also retain inherent power to exercise civil authority over the conduct of non-Indians on fee lands within its reservation when that conduct threatens or has some direct effect on the political integrity, the economic security, or the health or welfare of the tribe."[43] Recently, the Supreme Court has held that the second *Montana* exception requires an impact on "'the right of reservation Indians to make their own laws and be ruled by them.'"[44]

The second source of tribal authority derives from treaties or agreements signed with the United States. Within Indian country, tribes retain sovereign rights not ceded; tribes need not preserve those rights expressly in their treaties.[45] Nonetheless, treaties or agreements with Indian tribes may recognize or affirm tribal sovereign powers, serving as a textual source that supplements, but does not supplant, inherent tribal authority. Treaties and agreements may also reserve certain tribal rights on lands outside reservation borders that were ceded to the federal government. Many tribes reserved rights to hunt, fish, and gather on ceded lands that remain viable today.[46]

The third source of tribal authority is the ability to carry out powers delegated by the federal government. Because Indian tribes are governments exercising powers of sovereign authority within their territories, Congress may delegate governmental powers to the tribes.[47] Congressional delegation to Indian tribes is valid even if inherent tribal sovereignty would not necessarily support the precise or total authority delegated.[48]

Tribal Environmental Authority

Environmental authority within Indian country is traceable to two primary and interrelated sources: the inherent authority of Indian tribes to govern their territories and the federal environmental statutes, most of which treat tribes as states.

As governments, Native American tribes may assert environmental authority through direct tribal regulation and enforcement, to the limits of inherent tribal authority.[49] Tribes may, for example, enact tribal environmental codes and permit requirements, and enforce those provisions through agency actions and judicial proceedings in tribal court. Most tribes, however, prefer to seek primacy to implement and administer the programs of the federal environmental statutes within their borders, at least in part because of the availability of limited federal financial assistance.[50] For example, of the 77 tribes that sought primacy for one or more programs under the Clean Water Act (CWA) by 1994, 76 did so for the Section 106 grants program.[51]

Under the principle of cooperative federalism, the federal environmental acts generally establish programs and set uniform minimum standards applicable nationwide, and the states may seek primacy to implement and administer the federal programs within their borders. These federal statutes apply within Indian country, and empower the U.S. Environmental Protection Agency (EPA) to promulgate regulations for implementation in tribal territories.[52] Most of the federal environmental statutes also provide expressly that Indian tribes may be treated as states (TAS) for purposes of assuming primacy.[53] Under the statutory schemes, then, both tribes and states may potentially assert the right to implement the environmental programs within Indian country.

The EPA takes the position that environmental authority in Indian country should not be checkerboarded, that sound environmental management requires one government to have regulatory authority over the whole of Indian country. Thus the EPA will grant primacy in Indian country only to that government—state or tribe—that can demonstrate its authority to regulate pollution sources throughout the tribal territory.[54] In the absence of a grant of primacy either to the tribe or to the state government, the EPA will implement and enforce the federal laws in Indian country.[55]

A state seeking primacy in Indian country must demonstrate either a congressional delegation of jurisdiction or authority to regulate under principles of federal Indian law.[56] The federal environmental laws themselves do not serve as a delegation of authority to the states,[57] and no state has been able to point to any other congressional delegation of environmental authority in Indian country. Under principles of federal Indian law, state authority over Indian lands within Indian country is extremely limited: states generally have no inherent regulatory authority over Indian lands.[58] As a result, no state has been able to demonstrate authority over Indian lands, and without that jurisdiction, a state cannot meet the EPA's requirement of showing authority over pollution sources throughout Indian country. No state, consequently, has taken primacy within Indian country.

Most of the federal environmental statutes treat tribes as states. Unlike states, however, tribes must be certified for TAS by meeting certain statutory requirements. Although these requirements vary somewhat from statute to statute, they generally include federally recognized status, a governmental structure, jurisdiction to operate the federal program, and reasonable capability to carry out the program.[59] A tribe that meets the statutory criteria may be granted TAS if the environmental statute delegates authority to the tribe or, if it does not, the tribe can demonstrate its inherent authority to implement the federal program throughout its Indian country.

Tribal Authority over Air Resources: Federal Delegation

The EPA has interpreted the Clean Air Act (CAA) as taking "a territorial view of tribal jurisdiction."[60] Under that view, the CAA operates as a delegation of federal authority to tribes to administer programs with respect to all air resources within the tribe's reservation.[61] The EPA's interpretation is based on the language of the CAA, which authorizes the EPA to grant TAS if "the functions to be exercised by the Indian tribe pertain to the management and protection of air resources within the exterior boundaries of the reservation or other areas within the tribe's jurisdiction,"[62] and on the legislative history, which described the CAA as "an express delegation" to Indian tribes.[63] Because the CAA is a congressional delegation to tribes, Indian tribes seeking TAS with respect to air resources within the exterior boundaries of their reservations are not required to demonstrate jurisdiction over reservation lands; tribes seeking TAS with respect to "other areas within the tribe's jurisdiction," however, must establish their jurisdiction over those areas under principles of federal Indian law.[64]

Tribal Authority over Water Resources: Inherent Rights

The showing of jurisdiction that tribes must make under the CAA for non-reservation lands is similar to the showing tribes must make for TAS status under such environmental statutes as the Clean Water Act and Safe Drinking Water Act (the Water Acts). Because the EPA has determined that the Water Acts do not delegate federal program authority to Indian tribes,[65] a tribe seeking TAS must demonstrate its inherent governmental authority to regulate.

Indian tribes possess inherent authority to regulate pollution sources on Indian lands within their territories.[66] However, tribes are generally divested of regulatory authority over nonmember fee lands, at least in areas of Indian country that have been broadly opened up to public use, unless the tribe can demonstrate that nonmember activities on those lands meet one of the *Montana* tests: a consensual relationship with the tribe or its members, or direct impacts on core tribal governmental functions.[67] In the environmental context, the more important of these is the exception for tribal regulation when nonmembers' conduct impacts such governmental interests as health and welfare.

The EPA has determined that "the activities regulated under the various environmental statutes generally have serious and substantial impacts on human health and welfare," and therefore that the federal environmental statutes represent Congress's determination that activities affecting the environment have significant direct effects on health and welfare.[68] As a consequence, the EPA considers that Indian tribes will ordinarily be able to make the required showing of "serious and substantial" impacts on tribal environments that the EPA demands to accord tribes primacy for the programs contained in the federal environmental statutes.[69] In *Montana v. U.S. Environmental Protection Agency*, the Ninth Circuit held that the EPA's approach was consistent with the *Montana* line of Supreme Court cases, and therefore that the agency's regulations for granting TAS status under the Clean Water Act were valid.[70]

Tribal authority to regulate activities on nonmember fee lands generally requires a specific factual showing of impacts, although tribes are not required to wait until pollution occurs before asserting their right to regulate.[71] Where Native American tribes have met their burden of demonstrating actual or potential impacts on tribal health and welfare from pollution sources on fee lands, their authority to regulate has been affirmed.[72] In cases where tribes have not met that burden, their inherent authority does not extend to nonmember fee lands.[73]

Tribes that take primacy under TAS provisions have essentially the same rights and obligations with respect to those programs as states that take primacy, including the right to promulgate standards and regulations that are more stringent than federal minimum standards.[74] Not all provisions of the environmental laws apply to tribes: statutory deadlines for states are often inapplicable, as are provisions requiring a demonstration of criminal enforcement authority.[75] Nonetheless, tribes with TAS exercise their environmental program authority throughout their territories.

For example, tribes with primacy for the water quality standards (WQS) program of the CWA will promulgate WQS for all waters within the borders of the tribe's Indian country.[76] Tribal WQS may be used to protect unique tribal values and uses for water resources, such as the "primary contact ceremonial use" standard established by the Isleta Pueblo.[77] Once tribal WQS are approved by the EPA, any discharge permit issued under the CWA's National Pollutant Discharge Elimination System (NPDES)[78] program for a point source within the tribe's territory must include conditions to ensure compliance with the tribe's WQS.[79] Although no tribe has yet sought primacy for the NPDES program,[80] the EPA will issue NPDES permits within Indian country unless and until a tribe does so.[81] A tribe that has adopted WQS, however, can exercise substantial control over the federal permits.[82] Any tribe that receives TAS for setting WQS is also treated as a state for purposes of Section 401 of the CWA,[83] under which the tribe may review federally issued permits within its territory for compliance with tribal WQS.[84] Pursuant to Section 401, a tribe may certify the federally permitted activity, certify it with conditions, or refuse certification if the tribe determines that the activity would result in a violation of its WQS. If the tribe refuses certification, the EPA cannot issue the permit. Moreover, any NPDES permit issued for a point source upstream of the tribe's territory, whether the permit is issued by the EPA or the state pursuant to a delegated NPDES program, must include conditions to ensure compliance with the downstream tribe's WQS.[85]

Tribal Authority over Waste Management

If a federal statute does not contain a TAS provision, but treats tribes only as municipalities, the EPA may not grant primacy to Indian tribes.[86] Among the major federal environmental laws, only the Resource Conservation and Recovery Act (RCRA) does not treat tribes as states, defining tribes instead as municipalities for purposes of the act.[87] Because RCRA authorizes "states" to develop landfill permit programs, the D.C. Circuit struck down an EPA rule that would have authorized tribes to issue solid-waste landfill permits within their reservations.[88] Nonetheless, the court noted that tribes retain their inherent authority to regulate landfills through such mechanisms as environmental codes, agency enforcement, and tribal court actions, as well as the ability to seek a site-specific waiver of the applicable federal standards from the EPA.[89]

Remediation and Recovery for Environmental Damage

Indian tribes are entitled to treatment as states for most purposes of the Comprehensive Environmental Response, Compensation, and Liability Act (CERCLA).[90] Tribes are treated as states, without the need to apply for TAS certification, for purposes of notification of releases, consultation on remedial actions, access to information, roles and responsibilities under the National Contingency Plan, and submittal of priorities for remedial action, although tribes are not entitled to the state prerogative of having at least one facility on the National Priorities List for remedial action. Moreover, tribes are authorized, on the same basis as states, to enter into contracts or cooperative agreements with the federal government to carry out removal or other remedial actions.[91] Similar to other federal environmental laws, CERCLA exempts tribes from certain financial burdens and time limitations that are placed on states.[92]

In addition, both CERCLA and the Oil Pollution Act (OPA) authorize Indian tribes to act as trustees for purposes of natural resources damages actions.[93] Both statutes provide that liability shall be to an Indian tribe for damage to natural resources "belonging to, managed by, controlled by, or appertaining to" the tribe. Lands and natural resources held by or in trust for an Indian tribe or its members should constitute resources "belonging to" or "managed by" the tribe, but tribes are expressly authorized to serve as trustees for resources beyond those that they own. Tribes should also be able to assert trusteeship over fee lands within their reservations if the tribes may regulate environmental activities on those lands because of the effects on tribal health and welfare.[94] Where tribes can regulate fee lands, those lands and the associated resources should be considered "managed by" or "controlled by" the tribe. Finally, many tribes exercise off-reservation rights to hunt, fish, and gather under their treaties and agreements with the United States.[95] Tribes may be able to serve as trustees for damage to these resources on the grounds that treaty-reserved resources "appertain" to the tribes.

Federal Environmental Laws as Limits on Tribal Authority

Although the federal environmental laws hold substantial promise for tribes seeking to assert decision-making power over environmental matters within Indian country, the statutes also have been interpreted in ways that place potentially significant limits on tribal governmental authority. Federal statutes may, for example, regulate tribal governmental activity or preempt tribal authority.

Limitation and Abrogation of Tribal Rights

Native American tribes are "persons" under most of the federal environmental statutes,[96] and thus may be regulated by those laws as any other person. For example, tribes are subject to the prohibition on open dumping of solid wastes and to citizen suits in federal court for violation of environmental requirements.[97] Several courts have held that the citizen suit provisions of the federal statutes abrogate tribal sovereign immunity from suit,[98] although Indian tribes generally enjoy sovereign immunity absent express tribal or congressional waiver.[99] Moreover, because federal jurisdiction over citizen suits is exclusive, tribal courts have been divested of jurisdiction to hear citizen suits under the environmental statutes.[100]

Certain aspects of tribal environmental authority may have been abrogated or preempted by statute. Some federal statutes preempt tribal (and state) authority to regulate in a manner inconsistent with the statute. For example, the Hazardous Materials Transportation Act (HMTA) prohibits any tribal or state regulation of the transport of hazardous materials that is not "substantively the same" as federal regulations.[101] Thus a tribal statute imposing permit fees and substantial notice requirements on shipments of nuclear materials was held preempted under the HMTA.[102] Similarly, tribes that take primacy under the federal environmental statutes, like states with primacy, may not regulate less stringently than the federal minimum requirements, although the right of tribes, like states, to regulate more stringently is preserved in the federal laws.[103]

Environmental Impact Assessment

The National Environmental Policy Act (NEPA), which requires the preparation of an environmental impact statement (EIS) for "major Federal actions significantly affecting the quality of the human environment,"[104] applies to federal actions in Indian country.[105] Leases of trust lands, including activities with the potential for environmental harm, such as landfill development, mining, grazing, and timber harvesting, typically require the approval of the Secretary of the Interior.[106] The Secretary's approval constitutes major federal action for purposes of NEPA,[107] and federal approval of a lease without compliance with NEPA renders the lease invalid as long as the objection is timely raised.[108]

Pursuant to NEPA, the Bureau of Indian Affairs (BIA) within the Department of the Interior has designated certain types of federally approved activities on trust lands that will normally require the preparation of an EIS and certain types of activities that are categorical exclusions from the EIS process.[109] Any federally approved activity that does not fall into either category requires the preparation of an environmental assessment (EA), which will result either in a finding of no significant impact on the environment (FONSI) or in the preparation of a more detailed EIS.[110] The BIA is responsible for the preparation of any EIS for proposed development on Indian lands.[111]

NEPA can present a dilemma for tribes seeking development of their lands. On the one hand, the NEPA process can provide tribes with increased information prior to entering into leases and agreements, allowing tribes to choose on an environmentally informed basis whether to proceed with development activities. On the other hand, to the extent that an EIS must consider the adverse environmental consequences of tribal lands development on communities and resources outside Indian country, it introduces non-Indian considerations into the federal approval process. Moreover, neighboring non-Indian interests as well as tribal members may delay or potentially even block projects on tribal lands by bringing a challenge in federal court to the adequacy of an EIS or to the BIA's determination that no EIS is required because an EA supports a FONSI.[112]

In addition to the procedural consideration mandated by NEPA, regulations implementing the leasing statutes for tribal lands may specify substantive consideration of environmental values. For example, the Secretary of the Interior must determine that a proposed mineral agreement "does not have adverse cultural, social, or environmental impacts sufficient to outweigh its expected benefits to the Indian mineral owners."[113]

Treaty Rights as a Source of Environmental Protection

Most Indian tribes have treaties or agreements with the United States. Any reservation set aside by a treaty or treaty-substitute carries with it an implied reserved right to water. Moreover, many tribes expressly reserved in their treaties the right to use resources that the tribes depended upon for their livelihood and subsistence. In some areas of the country, tribes generally reserved the rights to hunt, fish, and gather throughout the territories they ceded to the United States in exchange for reservations. In the Pacific Northwest, the fishery-dependent tribes more specifically reserved the right to take fish at their traditional fishing grounds or sites, whether located within or outside their reservations. Both types of reserved rights—the implied right to water and the express right to take resources—may give tribes an additional avenue of environmental protection.

Under the *Winters* doctrine of reserved water rights, Native American tribes with reservations have an implied right to sufficient water to fulfill the purposes for which their reservations were created.[114] For tribes to take advantage of their water rights, however, the water must be of a quality that makes it usable for the purpose for which it was intended.[115]

For example, one purpose for which all reservations were created was agricultural, and Indian tribes therefore are entitled to water for irrigation and related purposes.[116] If the water provided to the reservation is so degraded by upstream practices that it cannot be used for irrigation, however, the upstream uses may be enjoined to ensure an adequate water quality for the tribe. For example, upstream non-Indian irrigation practices that rendered water too saline to support traditional salt-sensitive crops on the downstream reservation were enjoined pending negotiations between the tribe and the irrigators.[117]

In addition, fishery-dependent tribes generally have a reserved right to sufficient water to maintain the fishery resource,[118] which includes not only the fish but the conditions essential to their survival. Thus, a tribe with a reserved water right for fisheries purposes should be entitled to enough water to maintain optimum conditions for fish survival. One tribe, for example, was awarded enough water to maintain an instream temperature of 68 degrees or less to avoid depletion degradation by warming the waters beyond the tolerance of the native species.[119]

Fishery tribes may also have a broader right to habitat protection under their express treaty rights to take fish at traditional fishing places.[120] Courts have, for example, halted the construction of dams that would destroy fishing rights,[121] and ordered the release of reservoir water necessary to preserve salmon nests.[122] Fishery tribes may thus have a dual argument—both their reserved water rights and their reserved fishing rights—for the protection of minimum stream flows to preserve the fish and their habitat. Moreover, although the right to habitat protection has been developed in the context of the Pacific Northwest fishing tribes, the same environmental rights should accrue to other tribes that reserved the right to take off-reservation resources. For example, the Chippewa tribes of the western Great Lakes should have as great a right to protection of their off-reservation wild rice areas as the Northwest tribes do for the fisheries.

Despite some success in claiming a right to habitat protection, fishery tribes have not fared well when claiming damages for environmental harm to the fisheries. Yakima Indians asserting harm to the salmon resource from effluent discharges at the Hanford Nuclear Reservation were unable to prove either causation or economic damages.[123] In addition, a federal district court denied damages to the Nez Perce Tribe, which alleged that the Hells Canyon dam complex reduced the numbers of salmon returning to spawn and inundated tribal fishing grounds.[124] The court determined that the tribe had no property right in the fish, and ruled that the tribe could assert a right to habitat protection only if it could show that the dams constituted "part of a pattern of discrimination against Indian treaty fish runs."[125] Subsequently, the Nez Perce Tribe settled the lawsuit for $16.5 million in exchange for a promise to support the relicensing of the Hells Canyon Dam complex in 2003.[126]

Tribal Interests in Sacred Sites and Cultural Property

Tribal cultures and religions are often intimately tied to the land, to specific areas and places that are sacred to the tribes. Because of the way in which reservations were generally created, sacred sites and other properties of cultural importance may be located outside tribal territorial borders, frequently on federal lands. Although these sacred areas may have been taken unconstitutionally, only once has Congress returned a sacred place to a tribe.[127] Other tribes, notably the Sioux in their quest for the Black Hills, have spent decades in an unavailing attempt to secure the return of their lands.[128]

The First Amendment and Sacred Sites

The First Amendment offers virtually no protection to Indian tribes concerned about the degradation of their sacred sites located on federal lands. In *Lyng v. Northwest Indian Cemetery Protective Association*, for example, the Supreme Court upheld the government's decision to build a road through a national forest area that was sacred to three tribes. Although the Court found that the road "will have severe adverse effects on the practice of [the tribes'] religion," it held that the government's action did not constitute an unconstitutional burden on that religious practice.[129]

The *Lyng* Court stated that its decision should not "discourage" the federal government from accommodating tribal religious practices,[130] but the government's attempts at accommodation have generally either been unenforceable or attacked by non-Indians as violations of the Establishment Clause. For example, the American Indian Religious Freedom Act (AIRFA) asserts "the policy of the United States to protect and preserve" tribal freedom of religion, specifically including access to sacred sites.[131] Nonetheless, the Court in *Lyng* determined that AIRFA was nothing more than a general statement of policy without "so much as a hint" that it created a cause of action.[132] More recently, President Clinton issued Executive Order 13,007—Indian Sacred Sites, mandating federal land agencies to accommodate tribal access to and use of sacred sites, and to avoid adverse impacts on the physical integrity of sacred sites.[133] Executive Order 13,007, however, like all executive orders, does not create a cause of action and is not enforceable by the tribes.[134]

A number of federal agencies with management responsibilities for federal lands, however, have attempted to accommodate Indian rights in federal lands, including the protection of religious practices and sacred sites. Several of the agencies have issued policy statements and agency guidelines calling for consultation with tribes and cooperation and accommodation in agency decision making and implementation.[135] Moreover, and more generally, Executive Order 13,084 requires federal agencies to respect tribal rights and establish procedures for tribal input on federal regulatory policies "on matters that significantly or uniquely affect their communities."[136]

Agency attempts to protect tribal sacred sites on federal lands, however, run the risk of violating the Establishment Clause. In *Bear Lodge Multiple Use Association v. Babbitt*, for example, the court held that the National Park Service (NPS) could not refuse to issue commercial climbing licenses at Devils Tower National Monument during the month of June to protect tribal religious use of the Monument, because the regulation unconstitutionally coerced support for one religion.[137] The court determined, however, that the NPS could request climbers to voluntarily refrain from climbing during the month of June, and subsequently dismissed a lawsuit challenging the "voluntary climbing ban" on Establishment Clause grounds.[138]

Thus, tribes have essentially no enforceable religious rights against federal actions that harm sacred places, but agencies that actively seek to protect sacred sites may run afoul of the Establishment Clause. Federal agencies may not prohibit public access to sacred sites on public lands, even on a temporary basis, but must confine their actions to public education and requests for voluntary public compliance.

Historic and Cultural Preservation Statutes

Three statutes form the federal framework for the protection of places and objects of religious, cultural, or historical importance to Indian tribes.[139] Where the First Amendment and federal policy statements fail tribes, these laws—particularly the National Historic Preservation Act (NHPA)—may offer some protection for sacred sites. All three statutes, in addition, provide some protections for cultural property.

The NHPA establishes the National Register of Historic Places (National Register). Properties "of traditional religious and cultural importance" to tribes may be eligible for inclusion on the National Register,[140] and sacred sites may thus be listed if they are of sufficient historic importance. A listing does not in itself protect a sacred site, however, as demonstrated by the fact that the area at issue in *Lyng* was a traditional cultural and religious property listed on the National Register.[141]

Section 106 of the NHPA requires a consultation process for any "undertaking" by or licensed by a federal agency that may have an effect on "any district, site, building, structure, or object" that is in, or is eligible to be included in, the National Register.[142] The consultation process is largely managed by state historic preservation officers (SHPOs), and includes the agency, the Advisory Council on Historic Preservation, and other interested persons.[143] The 1992 amendments to the NHPA provide that tribes have a right to participate in the consultation process whenever a federal undertaking may affect a property of "traditional religious and cultural importance" to the tribe,[144] although this statutory right has not yet been implemented through amendments to the regulations. Under the current regulations, tribes are involved in the consultation process in two roles: first, if a federal undertaking will affect Indian lands, the tribe is a "consulting party" and must concur in any agreement; and second, if an undertaking will affect properties of historic value to an Indian tribe that are located on non-Indian lands, the tribe is invited to participate as an "interested person."[145] In the course of the Section 106 process, federal agencies must make reasonable efforts to identify historic properties, including the obligation to investigate in cases where tribal traditions demand secrecy regarding religious sites.[146] A failure to consult as required by Section 106 may result in an injunction against the federal undertaking.[147]

The SHPOs are responsible for evaluating properties for historic significance, nominating properties for inclusion in the National Register, and designing steps to protect historic properties.[148] A tribe may assume the functions of an SHPO with respect to tribal lands, defined in the NHPA as all lands within the exterior boundaries of a reservation and all dependent Indian communities,[149] if the tribe designates a preservation official and provides a preservation plan that is approved by the Secretary of the Interior.[150] A tribal plan must allow a nonmember who owns land in fee within the tribal territory to request the SHPO to share preservation responsibilities with the tribal official for that land.[151] Once a tribal preservation plan has been approved, the tribe may also enter into contracts or cooperative agreements to assist the Secretary in such functions as identification, preservation, and maintenance of historic properties.[152] Alternatively, a tribe may enter into an agreement to review undertakings on tribal land under tribal historic preservation regulations, without the necessity for a tribe to develop a tribal historic preservation plan.[153]

The second statute in the federal framework is the Archaeological Resources Protection Act (ARPA) of 1979.[154] ARPA focuses on protecting archaeological resources and sites on federal public lands and Indian lands, although it has been held to extend to objects recovered from sites on private land as well.[155] Archaeological activities on federal and Indian lands require a permit.[156] Before a permit will issue, however, an Indian tribe must be notified if the excavation or removal of archaeological resources "may result in harm to, or destruction of, any religious or cultural site" of the tribe.[157] An excavation or removal permit for tribal lands requires the consent of the tribe, and a permit for allotted lands requires the consent of the Indian landowner and the tribe.[158] Moreover, an Indian tribe need not obtain a permit to excavate archaeological resources on its trust lands; nor need a tribal member obtain a permit if the tribe has enacted laws regulating the excavation of archaeological resources.[159]

The third statute is the Native American Graves Protection and Repatriation Act (NAGPRA) of 1990.[160] NAGPRA provides for Indian ownership and control of cultural items taken from or discovered on federal or tribal lands after the effective date of the Act.[161] Human remains and associated funerary objects belong first to lineal descendants. For other funerary, sacred, or cultural objects—and for those human remains and associated funerary objects where the lineal descendants cannot be identified—ownership and control vests in the tribe on whose land the objects were discovered or that has the closest cultural affiliation with the objects or that aboriginally occupied the land. Excavation and removal of cultural items from federal or tribal lands is prohibited unless the items are excavated and removed pursuant to a federal permit: permits for excavations on federal lands require prior consultation with the culturally affiliated tribe, and permits for excavations within reservation boundaries require the consent of the tribe.[162]

NAGPRA further directs all federal agencies and museums to inventory Native American human remains and cultural items, and provide or make available to tribes the information assembled.[163] At the request of a lineal descendant or the tribe, human remains and cultural objects are to be "expeditiously returned" by the agency or museum.[164]

Conclusion

In environmental matters, Indian tribes acting as governments face both tremendous opportunities and enormous obstacles. Perhaps the most significant obstacle to tribes' assertions of their environmental rights is money. Despite the recent success of some tribal casinos, most Indian reservations remain among the poorest communities in the nation. Tribes have neither the economic base nor the monetary resources to undertake major environmental protection programs, generally from scratch, without substantial federal financial assistance. Although the federal government has offered limited funding for tribes,[165] the lack of money has been identified as the "key problem" in a study of tribal actions to protect reservation water quality.[166] As one scholar has noted, "[w]hatever else environmental justice means[] in Indian country," it must include sufficient funding for tribes to develop effective environmental programs designed to serve tribal needs and protect tribal values.[167]

Notes

1. The two collective nouns for the indigenous peoples of what is now the United States, "Indian" and "Native American," will be used interchangeably in this chapter.

2. *See, e.g.*, JIM SCHWAB, DEEPER SHADES OF GREEN: THE RISE OF BLUE-COLLAR AND MINORITY ENVIRONMENTALISM IN AMERICA 321–82 (Sierra Club Books 1994); Dean B. Suagee, *Turtle's War Party: An Indian Allegory on Environmental Justice*, 9

J. ENVT'L L. & LITIG. 461 (1994) [hereinafter Suagee, *Turtle's War Party*]; Scott Morrison & LeAnne Howe, *The Sewage of Foreigners*, 39 FED. BAR NEWS & J. 370 (1992).

3. *See* Frank Pommersheim, *The Reservation as Place: A South Dakota Essay*, 34 S.D. L. REV. 246 (1989).

4. *See* Mario Gonzalez, *The Black Hills: Why the Black Hills are Sacred to Lakota*, INDIAN COUNTRY TODAY, Feb. 29–Mar. 4, 1996, at A6.

5. *See* Consent Decree and Final Judgment Among the United States of America and the Sac and Fox Nation and Tenneco Oil Co., No. CIV-96-017-C (W.D. Okla) (entered June 2, 1997), discussed in Judith V. Royster, *Oil and Water in the Indian Country*, 37 NAT. RESOURCES J. 457, 476–79 (1997).

6. *See* Lise Young, *What Price Progress? Uranium Production on Indian Lands in the San Juan Basin*, 9 AM. INDIAN L. REV. 1, 21–22 (1981).

7. *See* Marcia Coyle, *A Way of Life Is Threatened*, NAT'L L.J., Sept. 21, 1992, at S9.

8. *See, e.g.*, United States v. Jim, 888 F. Supp. 1058 (D. Or. 1995); United States v. Lundquist, 932 F. Supp. 1237 (D. Or. 1996).

9. *See, e.g.*, Rebecca Tsosie, *Tribal Environmental Policy in an Era of Self-Determination: The Role of Ethics, Economics and Traditional Ecological Knowledge*, 21 VT. L. REV. 225 (1996). For a case study of one tribe's decision to locate a solid waste landfill on its reservation, *see* DAN MCGOVERN, THE CAMPO INDIAN LANDFILL WAR: THE FIGHT FOR GOLD IN CALIFORNIA'S GARBAGE (University of Oklahoma Press 1995); *see also* Kevin Gover & Jana L. Walker, *Escaping Environmental Paternalism: One Tribe's Approach to Developing a Commercial Waste Disposal Project in Indian Country*, 63 U. COLO. L. REV. 933 (1992).

10. *See* United States v. Mazurie, 419 U.S. 544, 557 (1975).

11. FELIX S. COHEN, HANDBOOK OF FEDERAL INDIAN LAW 122 (U.S. Gov't Printing Office 1941).

12. Cherokee Nation v. Georgia, 30 U.S. (5 Pet.) 1, 17 (1831).

13. *See* Johnson v. M'Intosh, 21 U.S. (8 Wheat.) 543 (1823); Cherokee Nation v. Georgia, 30 U.S. (5 Pet.) 1 (1831).

14. 18 U.S.C. § 1153.

15. United States v. Wheeler, 435 U.S. 313, 323 (1978).

16. *See* FELIX S. COHEN'S HANDBOOK OF FEDERAL INDIAN LAW 224 (Rennard Strickland, ed., Michie Co. 1982).

17. *See generally* Mary Christina Wood, *Indian Land and the Promise of Native Sovereignty: The Trust Doctrine Revisited*, 1994 UTAH L. REV. 1471; Mary Christina Wood, *Protecting the Attributes of Native Sovereignty: A New Trust Paradigm for Federal Actions Affecting Tribal Lands and Resources*, 1995 UTAH L. REV. 109.

18. Cherokee Nation v. Georgia, 30 U.S. (5 Pet.) 1, 17 (1831).

19. *See* Lone Wolf v. Hitchcock, 187 U.S. 553 (1903).

20. *See* Nell Jessup Newton, *Federal Power Over Indians: Its Sources, Scope, and Limitations*, 132 U. PA. L. REV. 195, 231 (1984).

21. *See* United States v. Sioux Nation, 448 U.S. 371 (1980) (takings clause); Morton v. Mancari, 417 U.S. 535 (1974) (equal protection clause).

22. *See, e.g.*, United States v. Mitchell, 463 U.S. 206 (1983); United States v. Brown, 86 F.3d 1554 (Fed. Cir. 1996). *See generally* Nell Jessup Newton, *Indian Claims in the Courts of the Conqueror*, 41 AM. U.L. REV. 753 (1992).

23. *See generally* ROBERT N. CLINTON, NELL JESSUP NEWTON & MONROE E. PRICE, AMERICAN INDIAN LAW: CASES AND MATERIALS 137–164 (Michie Co., 3d ed. 1991); WILLIAM C. CANBY, JR., AMERICAN INDIAN LAW IN A NUTSHELL 10–32 (West Publishing Co., 3d ed. 1998).

24. *See* Special Message to the Congress on Indian Affairs, PUB. PAPERS 564 (1970) (President Nixon); Statement on Indian Policy, 1 PUB. PAPERS 96, 99 (1983) (President Reagan); Statement Reaffirming the Government-to-Government Relationship Between the Federal Government and Indian Tribal Governments, PUB. PAPERS 662 (1991) (President Bush); Memorandum of Government-to-Government Relations with Native American Tribal Governments, 59 Fed. Reg. 22,951 (1994) (President Clinton). *See also, e.g.,* Indian Self-Determination and Education Assistance Act of 1975, 25 U.S.C. § 450a(b); Tribal Self-Governance Demonstration Project Act of 1991, Pub. L. No. 102-84, 105 Stat. 1278 (amending provisions of the Indian Self-Determination Act, 25 U.S.C. §§ 450–450n).

25. 18 U.S.C. § 1151.

26. DeCoteau v. District County Court, 420 U.S. 425, 427 n.2 (1975); Alaska v. Native Village of Venetie Tribal Gov't, 118 S. Ct. 948, 952 (1998).

27. *See* Oklahoma Tax Comm'n v. Sac and Fox Nation, 508 U.S. 114, 123, 128 (1993).

28. *See* United States v. Shoshone Tribe of Indians, 304 U.S. 111 (1938). *See also* Black Hills Institute of Geological Research v. South Dakota School of Mines & Technology, 12 F.3d 737 (8th Cir. 1993), *cert. denied,* 513 U.S. 810 (1994). Water, because of its importance in the arid western regions, is treated differently from other natural resources. *See infra* pages 167–168.

29. *See, e.g.,* 25 U.S.C. § 177; Worcester v. Georgia, 31 U.S. (6 Pet.) 515 (1832); Oklahoma Tax Commission v. Chickasaw Nation, 515 U.S. 450 (1995).

30. 24 Stat. 388 (1887) (codified in part at 25 U.S.C. §§ 331–381).

31. *See* County of Yakima v. Yakima Indian Nation, 502 U.S. 251 (1992).

32. 1 AMERICAN INDIAN POLICY REVIEW COMMISSION, FINAL REPORT 309 (1977). *See generally* Judith V. Royster, *The Legacy of Allotment,* 27 ARIZ. ST. L.J. 1, 7–14 (1995).

33. Indian Reorganization Act of 1934, ch. 576, 48 Stat. 984 (codified as amended at 25 U.S.C. §§ 461–495).

34. COHEN'S HANDBOOK, *supra* note 16, at 138.

35. *See* Strate v. A-1 Contractors, 520 U.S. 438, 456 (1997).

36. Oliphant v. Suquamish Indian Tribe, 435 U.S. 191, 208–10 (1978); Montana v. United States, 450 U.S. 544, 565 (1981). For critiques of the implicit divestiture doctrine, see generally N. Bruce Duthu, *Implicit Divestiture of Tribal Powers: Locating Legitimate Sources of Authority in Indian Country,* 19 AM. INDIAN L. REV. 353 (1994); David H. Getches, *Conquering the Cultural Frontier: The New Subjectivism of the Supreme Court in Indian Law,* 84 CAL. L. REV. 1573 (1996).

37. *See, e.g.,* Indian Civil Rights Act of 1968, 25 U.S.C. § 1302.

38. *Montana,* 450 U.S. at 557; *see also* Brendale v. Yakima Indian Nation, 492 U.S. 408, 445 (Stevens, J.) and 460 (Blackmun, J.) (1989).

39. New Mexico v. Mescalero Apache Tribe, 462 U.S. 324, 331–32 & n.25 (1983); Puyallup Tribe, Inc. v. Washington Game Dep't, 433 U.S. 165, 176–77 (1977).

40. *Montana,* 450 U.S. at 557; *Mescalero Apache Tribe,* 462 U.S. 324; Merrion v. Jicarilla Apache Tribe, 455 U.S. 130 (1982).

41. 450 U.S. at 565–66. *See also* Strate v. A-1 Contractors, 520 U.S. 438, 456 (1997).

42. 450 U.S. at 565.

43. *Id.* at 566.

44. *Strate,* 520 U.S. at 458 (quoting Williams v. Lee, 358 U.S. 217, 220 (1959)).

45. United States v. Winans, 198 U.S. 371, 381 (1905).

46. *See, e.g., Winans,* 198 U.S. 371; Minnesota v. Mille Lacs Band of Chippewa Indians, 119 S. Ct. 1187 (1999).

47. *Montana,* 450 U.S. at 564.

48. United States v. Mazurie, 419 U.S. 544, 557 (1975).

49. *See* Backcountry Against Dumps v. Environmental Protection Agency, 100 F.3d 147, 151 (D.C. Cir. 1996); Governing Council of Pinoleville Indian Community v. Mendocino County, 684 F. Supp. 1042 (N.D. Cal. 1988).

50. *See, e.g.,* Clean Water Act §§ 106 (grants to states) & 518(e) (tribes as states), 33 U.S.C. §§ 1256, 1377(e).

51. GOVER, STETSON & WILLIAMS, P.C., SURVEY OF TRIBAL ACTIONS TO PROTECT WATER QUALITY AND THE IMPLEMENTATION OF THE CLEAN WATER ACT 54 (National Indian Policy Center 1994) [hereinafter WATER QUALITY SURVEY].

52. Phillips Petroleum Co. v. U.S. Environmental Protection Agency, 803 F.2d 545, 552–56 (10th Cir. 1986).

53. *See, e.g.,* Clean Water Act (CWA) § 518, 33 U.S.C. § 1377(e); Safe Drinking Water Act (SDWA) § 1451, 42 U.S.C. § 300j-11(b)(1); Clean Air Act (CAA) § 301(d), 42 U.S.C. § 7601(d); Comprehensive Environmental Response, Compensation, and Liability Act (CERCLA) § 126, 42 U.S.C. § 9626. *See generally* Judith V. Royster & Rory SnowArrow Fausett, *Control of the Reservation Environment: Tribal Primacy, Federal Delegation, and the Limits of State Intrusion,* 64 WASH. L. REV. 581 (1989); David F. Coursen, *Tribes as States: Indian Tribal Authority to Regulate and Enforce Federal Environmental Laws and Regulations,* 23 ENVT'L L. REP. (ENVT'L L. INST.) 10,579 (1993).

54. U.S. Envt'l Protection Agency, *Federal, Tribal and State Roles in the Protection and Regulation of Reservation Environments* 3 (1991) [hereinafter *EPA Concept Paper*].

55. Washington Dep't of Ecology v. U.S. Environmental Protection Agency, 752 F.2d 1465, 1472 (9th Cir. 1985); *EPA Concept Paper, supra* note 54, at 3–4; 40 C.F.R. § 71.4(b) (CAA operating permits program).

56. *See, e.g.,* 45 Fed. Reg. 33,066, 33,378 (1980); U.S. Envt'l Protection Agency, *Administration of Environmental Programs on Indian Lands: EPA Indian Work Group Discussion Paper* 9 (1983).

57. *See Washington Dep't of Ecology,* 752 F.2d at 1467–68.

58. *Id.* at 1470.

59. *See* statutes cited *supra* note 53. *See also* 40 C.F.R. § 49.6 (CAA); § 131.8 (CWA); § 142.72 (SDWA public water system program); § 145.52 (SDWA underground injection control program).

60. *See* 63 Fed. Reg. 7254 (1998).

61. *Id.*

62. CAA § 301(d)(2)(B), 42 U.S.C. § 7601(d)(2)(B); *see also* 40 C.F.R. § 49.6(c).

63. S. Rep. No. 228, 101st Cong., 1st Sess. 79 (1989).

64. 63 Fed. Reg. at 7255; 40 C.F.R. § 49.7(a)(3).

65. 56 Fed. Reg. 64,876, 64,880 (1991).

66. *See* Montana v. United States, 450 U.S. 544, 505 (1981).

67. *Id.* at 565–66; *see also* South Dakota v. Bourland, 508 U.S. 679, 695 (1993); Strate v. A-1 Contractors, 520 U.S. 438, 456 (1997).

68. 56 Fed. Reg. 64,876, 64,878 (1991) (specifically referencing the Clean Water Act).

69. 56 Fed. Reg. at 64,877.

70. 137 F.3d 1135, 1140–41 (9th Cir. 1998), *cert. denied,* 119 S. Ct. 275 (1998).

71. Montana v. EPA, 941 F. Supp. 945, 958 (D. Mont. 1996), *aff'd,* Montana v. U.S. EPA, 137 F.3d 1135.

72. *See, e.g.,* Montana v. U.S. EPA, 137 F.3d 1135; Governing Council of Pinoleville Indian Community v. Mendocino County, 684 F. Supp. 1042 (N.D. Cal. 1988).

73. Yankton Sioux Tribe v. Southern Missouri Waste Management Dist., 890 F. Supp. 878, 888 (D.S.D. 1995), *aff'd,* 99 F.3d 1439 (8th Cir. 1996), *rev'd on other grounds sub nom.* South Dakota v. Yankton Sioux Tribe, 522 U.S. 329 (1998).

74. City of Albuquerque v. Browner, 97 F.3d 415, 423 (10th Cir. 1996), *cert. denied,* 118 S. Ct. 410 (1997); *see also* 40 C.F.R. § 49.1(b).

75. *See, e.g.,* 40 C.F.R. § 49.4 (provisions of the CAA for which it is inappropriate to treat tribes as states). As a matter of federal law, Indian tribes may not exercise criminal jurisdiction over non-Indians. Oliphant v. Suquamish Indian Tribe, 435 U.S. 191 (1978).

76. Montana v. U.S. EPA, 137 F.3d 1135; *City of Albuquerque,* 97 F.3d 415. For more detailed examinations of tribal WQS, see James M. Grijalva, *Tribal Governmental Regulation of Non-Indian Polluters of Reservation Waters,* 71 N.D. L. REV. 433 (1995); Denise D. Fort, *State and Tribal Water Quality Standards Under the Clean Water Act: A Case Study,* 35 NAT. RESOURCES J. 771 (1995).

77. *City of Albuquerque,* 97 F.3d at 428–29.

78. CWA § 402, 33 U.S.C. § 1342.

79. *See* 40 C.F.R. § 122.4(d).

80. *See* WATER QUALITY SURVEY, *supra* note 51, at 55.

81. *See EPA Concept Paper, supra* note 54, at 3–4.

82. Section 401 certification is triggered not only by a NPDES permit, but also by a dredge and fill permit from the Army Corps of Engineers pursuant to § 404 of the CWA, 33 U.S.C. § 1344, and by a hydroelectric project license from the Federal Energy Regulatory Commission. *See* PUD No. 1 of Jefferson County v. Washington Dep't of Ecology, 511 U.S. 700, 709, 711 (1994). However, one court has ruled that a federal permit for activities that result only in nonpoint sources of water pollution, such as cattle grazing on federal lands, is not subject to § 401 certification. *See* Oregon Natural Desert Ass'n v. Dombeck, 172 F.3d 1092 (9th Cir. 1998).

83. 40 C.F.R. § 131.4(c).

84. 33 U.S.C. § 1341. *See generally* Debra L. Donahue, *The Untapped Power of Clean Water Act Section 401,* 23 ECOLOGY L.Q. 201 (1996).

85. *City of Albuquerque,* 97 F.3d at 423–24 (relying in part on 40 C.F.R. § 122.4(d)) (federal permits); CWA § 402(b)(5), 33 U.S.C. § 1342(b)(5) (state permits); 40 C.F.R. § 123.44 (EPA review of state permits).

86. Backcountry Against Dumps v. Environmental Protection Agency, 100 F.3d 147 (D.C. Cir. 1996). *But see* Nance v. Environmental Protection Agency, 645 F.2d 701 (9th Cir. 1981), *cert. denied sub nom.* Crow Tribe of Indians v. Environmental Protection Agency, 454 U.S. 1081 (1981).

87. RCRA § 1004(13), 42 U.S.C. § 6903(13).

88. *Backcountry Against Dumps,* 100 F.3d at 150–51.

89. *Id.* at 151–52.

90. 42 U.S.C. § 9626(a). *See generally* Richard A. Du Bey & James M. Grijalva, *Closing the Circle: Tribal Implementation of the Superfund Program in the Reservation Environment,* 9 J. NAT. RESOURCES & ENVT'L L. 279 (1993-94).

91. 42 U.S.C. § 9604(d)(1)(A).

92. *Id.* §§ 9604(c)(3), 9626(d).

93. *Id.* § 9607(f)(1) (CERCLA); 33 U.S.C. § 2706(a)(3) (OPA). *See generally* Rachel Jacobson & Peter Monson, *Natural Resources Damages: Tribes as Trustees,* 5TH ANNUAL CONF. ON NAT. RESOURCES MGT. AND ENVT'L ENFORCEMENT ON INDIAN LANDS (ABA SONREEL 1993).

94. *See supra* notes 64–71.

95. *See infra* pages 169–170.

96. Generally the definition of "person" includes a municipality, and the definition of "municipality" includes an Indian tribe. *See* CWA § 502, 33 U.S.C. § 1362(4)–(5); SDWA § 1401, 40 U.S.C. § 300f(10), (12); RCRA § 1004, 42 U.S.C. § 6903(13), (15). *But see* CAA § 302, 42 U.S.C. § 7602(e)–(f).

97. Blue Legs v. U.S. Bureau of Indian Affairs, 867 F.2d 1095, 1097–98 (8th Cir. 1989).

98. *Id.* at 1096–97; Backcountry Against Dumps v. Environmental Protection Agency, 100 F.3d 147, 152 (D.C. Cir. 1996); Atlantic States Legal Foundation v. Salt River Pima-Maricopa Indian Community, 827 F. Supp. 608, 609–10 (D. Ariz. 1993); Public Serv. Co. v. Shoshone-Bannock Tribes, 30 F.3d 1203, 1206–07 (9th Cir. 1994).

99. Kiowa Tribe of Oklahoma v. Manufacturing Technologies, Inc., 523 U.S. 751 (1998). *See* James M. Grijalva, *Environmental Citizen Suits in Indian Country, in* 8TH ANNUAL CONF. ON ENV'T & DEV. IN INDIAN COUNTRY (ABA SONREEL 1996) (arguing that tribal sovereign immunity should not be abrogated under citizen suit provisions).

100. *Blue Legs,* 827 F.2d at 1097–98. *But see* Davis v. Sun Oil Co., 148 F.3d 606, 612 (6th Cir. 1998), *cert. denied,* 119 S. Ct. 543 (1998) (federal jurisdiction over citizen suits under RCRA is not exclusive but concurrent with state court).

101. 49 U.S.C. § 1804(a)(5).

102. Northern States Power Co. v. Prairie Island Mdewakanton Sioux Indian Community, 991 F.2d 458 (8th Cir. 1993).

103. *See* City of Albuquerque v. Browner, 97 F.3d 415, 423 (10th Cir. 1996), *cert. denied,* 118 S. Ct. 410 (1997).

104. 42 U.S.C. § 4332(C) (1988). *See generally* Chapter 9, *infra.*

105. *See generally* Dean B. Suagee, *The Application of the National Environmental Policy Act to "Development" in Indian Country,* 16 AM. INDIAN L. REV. 377 (1991).

106. 25 U.S.C. § 177. *See also* Indian Mineral Leasing Act, 25 U.S.C. § 396a; Indian Mineral Development Act, 25 U.S.C. § 2102(a); 25 U.S.C. § 406(a) (timber

sales); American Indian Agricultural Resources Management Act of 1993, 25 U.S.C. § 3715(a).

107. Davis v. Morton, 469 F.2d 593, 597 (10th Cir. 1972). Moreover, federal regulations governing development of tribal lands often specifically mandate compliance with NEPA. *See, e.g.,* 25 C.F.R. §§ 163.34 (forest management), 225.24(a) (mineral development).

108. Sangre de Cristo Development Co., Inc. v. United States, 932 F.2d 891 (10th Cir. 1991), *cert. denied,* 503 U.S. 1004 (1992); Jicarilla Apache Tribe v. Andrus, 687 F.2d 1324, 1337–40 (10th Cir. 1982).

109. *See* 61 Fed. Reg. 67,845, 67,847–48 (1996) (codified at 516 DM 6, App. 4).

110. *See* 40 C.F.R. §§ 1501.4.

111. *See* Cady v. Morton, 527 F.2d 786, 790 (9th Cir. 1975); Manygoats v. Kleppe, 558 F.2d 556, 559 (10th Cir. 1977); County of San Diego v. Babbitt, 847 F. Supp. 768 (S.D. Cal. 1994), *aff'd w/o opinion,* 61 F.3d 909 (9th Cir. 1995) (full text available at 1995 WL 438180, 1995 U.S. App. LEXIS 20727).

112. *See, e.g., County of San Diego,* 847 F. Supp. 768.

113. 25 C.F.R. § 225.22(c)(2) (1994).

114. Winters v. United States, 207 U.S. 564 (1908). *See generally* Judith V. Royster, *A Primer on Indian Water Rights,* 30 TULSA L.J. 61 (1994); 4 WATERS AND WATER RIGHTS ch. 37 (Robert E. Beck ed., Michie Co. 1996).

115. *See generally* Judith V. Royster, *Water Quality and the Winters Doctrine,* 107 WATER RESOURCES UPDATE 50 (1997); Margaret S. Treuer, *An Indian Right to Water Undiminished in Quality,* 7 HAMLINE L. REV. 347 (1984).

116. *See* Arizona v. California, 373 U.S. 546, 600–01 (1963).

117. *See* United States v. Gila Valley Irrigation Dist., 920 F. Supp. 1444 (D. Ariz. 1996), *aff'd,* 117 F.3d 425 (9th Cir. 1997).

118. *See* Colville Confederated Tribes v. Walton, 647 F.2d 42, 48 (9th Cir. 1981), *cert. denied,* 454 U.S. 1092 (1981).

119. *See* United States v. Anderson, 6 Indian L. Rep. F-129 (E.D. Wash. 1979).

120. *See* United States v. Washington, 506 F. Supp. 187, 203 (W.D. Wash. 1980), *vacated,* 759 F.2d 1253 (9th Cir. 1985), *cert. denied,* 474 U.S. 994 (1985). The Ninth Circuit vacated the habitat protection ruling on the ground that no factual dispute was before the court. 759 F.2d at 1357. *See generally* Michael C. Blumm & Brett M. Swift, *The Indian Treaty Piscary Profit and Habitat Protection in the Pacific Northwest: A Property Rights Approach,* 69 U. COLO. L. REV. 407 (1998); Martin H. Belsky, *Indian Fishing Rights: A Lost Opportunity for Ecosystem Management,* 12 J. LAND USE & ENVT'L L. 45 (1996).

121. Confederated Tribes of the Umatilla Indian Reservation v. Alexander, 440 F. Supp. 553, 556 (D. Or. 1977).

122. Kittatas Reclamation Dist. v. Sunnyside Valley Irr. Dist., 763 F.2d 1032 (9th Cir. 1985), *cert. denied,* 474 U.S. 1032 (1985).

123. *In re Hanford Nuclear Reservation Litigation,* 894 F. Supp. 1436 (E.D. Wash. 1995).

124. Nez Perce Tribe v. Idaho Power Co., 847 F. Supp. 791 (D. Idaho 1994).

125. *Id.* at 809.

126. *Nez Perce Settle Salmon Lawsuit,* INDIAN COUNTRY TODAY, May 12–19, 1997, at B1.

127. Act of Dec. 15, 1970, Pub. L. 91-550, 84 Stat. 1437. *See generally* R.C. GORDON-MCCUTCHAN, THE TAOS INDIANS AND THE BATTLE FOR BLUE LAKE (1995).

128. United States v. Sioux Nation, 448 U.S. 371 (1980). *See also* Nell Jessup Newton, *Indian Claims in the Courts of the Conqueror,* 41 AMER. U.L. REV. 753, 764–65 (1992); David Melmer, *Chairmen Divided Over Docket 74-A,* INDIAN COUNTRY TODAY, June 18–25, 1996, at A2.

129. 485 U.S. 439, 447–53 (1988). *See also* Wilson v. Block, 708 F.2d 735 (D.C. Cir. 1983), *cert. denied,* 464 U.S. 1056 (1984); Badoni v. Higginson, 638 F.2d 172 (10th Cir. 1980), *cert. denied,* 452 U.S. 954 (1981).

130. 485 U.S. at 454.

131. 42 U.S.C. § 1996.

132. 485 U.S. at 455.

133. 32 WEEKLY COMP. PRES. DOC. 942 (May 24, 1996), § 1.

134. *Id.* § 4.

135. *See* U.S. DEP'T OF AGRICULTURE, FOREST SERVICE NATIONAL RESOURCE BOOK ON AMERICAN INDIAN AND ALASKA NATIVE RELATIONS (1997); U.S. Nat'l Park Service, Native American Relationships Management Policy, 52 Fed. Reg. 35,674 (1987).

136. 63 Fed. Reg. 27,655 (1998).

137. No. 96-CV-063-D (D. Wyo. June 8, 1996). *See also* Badoni v. Higginson, 638 F.2d 172, 179 (10th Cir. 1980).

138. Bear Lodge Multiple Use Ass'n v. Babbitt, 2 F. Supp. 2d 1448 (D. Wyo. 1998).

139. *See generally* Dean B. Suagee & Karen J. Funk, *Cultural Resources Conservation in Indian Country,* 7 NAT. RESOURCES & ENV'T 30 (Spring 1993).

140. 16 U.S.C. § 470a(d)(6)(A). *See generally* Dean B. Suagee, *Tribal Voices in Historic Preservation: Sacred Landscapes, Cross-Cultural Bridges, and Common Ground,* 21 VT. L. REV. 145 (1996).

141. *See id.* at 172–73.

142. 16 U.S.C. § 470f.

143. *See id.* § 470a(b)(3).

144. *Id.* § 470a(d)(6).

145. 36 C.F.R. § 800.1(c)(2)(iii). *See also* Attakai v. United States, 746 F. Supp. 1395, 1408–09 (D. Ariz. 1990).

146. Pueblo of Sandia v. United States, 50 F.3d 856 (10th Cir. 1995).

147. *Attakai,* 746 F. Supp. at 1409.

148. 16 U.S.C. § 470a(b)(3).

149. *Id.* § 470w(14).

150. *Id.* § 470a(d)(2).

151. *Id.*

152. *Id.* § 470a(d)(4).

153. *Id.* § 470a(d)(5).

154. 16 U.S.C. §§ 470aa–470mm.

155. *See* United States v. Gerber, 999 F.2d 1112 (7th Cir. 1993).

156. 16 U.S.C. § 470cc(a).

157. *Id.* § 470cc(c).

158. *Id.* § 470cc(g)(2); 43 C.F.R. §§ 7.35(a)–(b), 7.8(a)(5).

159. 16 U.S.C. § 470cc(g)(1).

160. 25 U.S.C. §§ 3001–3013.

161. *Id.* § 3002.

162. *Id.* § 3002(c); 43 C.F.R. §§ 10.3–10.5. The permits required by NAGPRA are issued pursuant to ARPA. *See* 43 C.F.R. § 10.3(b)(1).

163. *Id.* §§ 3003–3004.

164. *Id.* § 3005.

165. *See, e.g.,* Indian Environmental General Assistance Program Act of 1992, as amended, 42 U.S.C. § 4368b; Indian Environmental Regulatory Enhancement Act of 1990, 42 U.S.C. § 2991b(d).

166. *See* WATER QUALITY SURVEY, *supra* note 51, at 66–68.

167. Suagee, *Turtle's War Party, supra* note 2, at 492.

PART II

Legal Procedures

CHAPTER 7

Public Participation

SHEILA FOSTER

Introduction

The environmental movement, and environmental decision making generally, have been criticized for their historic failure to include minority voices and concerns.[1] Leading environmental justice advocates have urged traditional environmental organizations to include minority and low-income individuals, and their concerns, in those organizations. Increasingly, policy makers and government agencies are heeding the calls for more inclusive decision making by proposing reforms that ensure input from affected communities in policy and adjudicative decisions. President Clinton's Executive Order on Environmental Justice, for instance, requests that each federal agency take steps to ensure that there is adequate and effective communication between decision makers and affected minority and low-income communities.[2]

Most federal and state environmental statutes mandate some form of public participation. Over the past 30 years, Congress has included public participation provisions in a number of environmental laws.[3] These provisions generally have several features in common: public input during the environmental decision-making process, a requirement that agencies respond to that public input, and provisions allowing lawsuits by the public (known as "citizens' suits") to enforce the law.[4] Many agencies have adopted extensive regulations to implement the citizen participation mandates of these statutes.[5]

Not all public participation laws are the same. Federal and state permitting laws vary from the bare-bones public notice and comment requirement, to local citizen advisory committees, to the intricate impact review processes contained in the National Environmental Policy Act (NEPA) and its state counterparts. Depending upon the mechanisms for citizen input in the decision-making process, the process can be an exercise in democratic deliberation with the proposed host community, an aggregation of pluralistic viewpoints on the proposed siting, or a vehicle for exclusion of citizens most affected by the proposed land use.[6] Not surprisingly, commentators have been advocating, and tracking, the recent move away from "announce and defend" decision making—characterized by the notice-and-comment approach—toward a more deliberative or collaborative process in environmental decision making.[7] This shift is evident in the rise of citizen advisory boards, both in the siting and cleanup process, as well as technical assistance to support those efforts.

Regardless of the formal mechanisms for public participation, low-income communities and communities of color face a number of obstacles in effectuating that participation.[8] Undoubtedly, information, education, and an understanding of risk communication are necessary for members of the public to discuss issues with experts and bureaucrats.[9] Moreover, low-income and communities of color often enter the decision-making process with fewer resources than communities that are less disadvantaged. These communities have less time, less information, and less specialized knowledge concerning the legal, technical, and economic issues involved.[10] Lack of early, direct, significant citizen participation decreases the legitimacy of agency action for many affected communities.[11]

This chapter will focus on citizen participation in federal and state permitting statutes. Legal challenges based on permitting laws is where most lawyers practicing environmental justice law have been, and can be, most effective.[12] Public participation under NEPA and its state equivalents, mini-NEPAs, are also covered in this chapter. Cleanup and remediation of hazardous waste sites, under Superfund and Brownfields legislation, also mandate public participation. This chapter, though, will not discuss public participation in those actions, as they are thoroughly treated elsewhere.[13]

Public protest over a proposed land use may provoke a response from parties who view such protest as disruptive to their development plans. One response to the increasing voices of citizens in environmental decision-making processes, particularly on the grassroots level, was a wave of lawsuits against public participation. Strategic Lawsuits Against Public Participation (SLAPPs) are not particular to environmental decision-making processes, nor are they a new form of litigation. Rather, "SLAPP" is just the new *name* given to a "breed" of lawsuits that have been taking place on American soil for hundreds of years.[14] The practice of bringing SLAPPs, however, has been "reborn" with the political activism of the 1960s and 1970s, grew and multiplied in the 1980s, and continues to be a "major threat" to involved citizens in the 1990s.[15] Courts and legislatures, as discussed below, have become increasingly intolerant of SLAPPs. As such, the legal landscape in which such actions take place is shifting toward the eradication of SLAPPs. This phenomenon is discussed in the latter part of this chapter.

Public Participation Under Federal Permitting Regulations

Procedures for issuance of most environmental permits are contained in Volume 40 of the Code of Federal Regulations, Part 124. This part covers permit issuance, modification, revocation and termination under numerous statutes. Included under the purview of this regulation are permits issued pursuant to the Resource Conservation and Recovery Act (RCRA), Safe Drinking Water Act (SDWA), Clean Water Act (CWA), and Clean Air Act (CAA). Specifically, it covers all RCRA, Underground Injection Control (UIC), Prevention of Significant Deterioration (PSD), and National Pollutant Discharge Elimination System (NPDES) permits.[16] Part 124 also includes expanded public participation provisions that are unique to RCRA permits.

Mandatory Notice and Written Comment

Once a permit applicant submits the application, and the permitting agency deems it complete, the agency prepares either a draft permit or notice of intent to deny the permit.[17] There is no public involvement at this stage of the process. The agency and the applicant are normally the only parties involved in the drafting of the permit, if one is issued. Once a draft permit is issued, however, the agency must give notice to the public by printing the notice in a local newspaper, broadcasting it over a local radio station, and send a copy to a mailing list, relevant agencies, and applicable state and local governments.

The permitting agency must also prepare a fact sheet if the proposed facility or activity is "major" or is the "subject of widespread public interest or raises major issues."[18] The fact sheet includes the principal facts and the "significant factual, legal, methodological and policy questions considered in preparing the draft permit,"[19] as well as a description of the procedures for reaching a final decision on the draft permit.[20] A more abbreviated statement of basis must be prepared for less significant facilities, describing how the agency determined the conditions of the permit.[21] The draft permit and fact sheet must be made available to the public.[22] Anyone may submit written comments on the draft permit. Commenting, however, may be difficult, given that permits are usually written in very technical and legal language—detailing emission and technology standards, for instance—making them incomprehensible to the average layperson.

Public Hearings

Conditional/Discretionary Hearings

Anyone may request a public hearing during the public comment period.[23] The request must be in writing and must state the nature of the issues proposed to be raised at the hearing. If so requested, the permitting agency must hold a public hearing on an RCRA permit, if made within 45 days of public notice of the draft permit.[24] Whenever possible, the agency must schedule the hearing at a location convenient to the nearest population center to the proposed facility. For other permits issued under the regulations, the permitting agency need only hold a hearing if it finds that, on the basis of requests, there is a "significant degree of public interest in a draft permit."[25] Otherwise, a permitting agency may hold a public hearing at its discretion whenever, for instance, "such a hearing might clarify one or more issues involved in the permit decision."[26]

Hearing Procedures

If the EPA is the permitting agency, the EPA Regional Administrator must designate a Presiding Officer for the hearing who is responsible for its schedule and orderly conduct.[27] The hearing is a legislative type of hearing in which the permitting authority explains its justification for the terms and conditions of the permit, after which the applicant may make a statement; interested members of the public may also make statements (written or oral) and ask questions. A tape recording or written transcript of the meeting is also available to the public.

If the permitting agency is the EPA, the Regional Administrator has the discretion to conduct the permit review under a "panel procedure" instead of the notice, comment, and hearing process discussed above.[28] The panel is presided over by either an Administrative Law Judge, appointed by the Chief Administrative Law Judge, or a lawyer employed by the agency.[29] A panel of EPA experts also evaluates the permit at the hearing. This is more like an adjudicative hearing—including summoning and cross-examining of witnesses and filing briefs.[30] Participants may also submit written questions to the Presiding Officer specifically directed to any person appearing or testifying in the hearing. The Presiding Officer, after consultation with the panel, and in his sole discretion, may ask the submitted questions.[31] The decision by the panel is appealable to the Environmental Appeals Board, and, upon its final decision, subject to judicial review.[32]

Responsiveness to Public Comments

At close of the comment period, the permitting agency reviews and evaluates all comments and determines if, in light of the feedback, it should modify the draft permit.[33] The agency then issues or denies the final permit. The agency must send a notice of decision to both the facility owner and any persons who submitted public comments or requested notice of the final permit decision. The agency must also prepare a written response to comments, including a summary of all significant comments submitted and an explanation of how those comments are addressed in the final permit decision.[34]

If EPA is the permitting authority, "any interested person" who filed comments or participated in the public hearing may challenge issuance or denial of permit or any of its terms and conditions.[35] Only objections made during the public comment period, including at the hearing, are preserved for appeal before the Environmental Appeals Board.[36] Judicial challenges to the hearing process become ripe only when a final permit decision is made and agency appeal procedures are exhausted.[37] However, since administrative bodies typically make de novo determinations, and courts review merely to see if the agencies have been arbitrary and capricious, and followed the proper procedures, administrative hearings are the preferable forum for raising technical objections to permits.

The Adequacy of Public Participation in Federal Permitting Processes

Despite criticism of the "announce and defend" approach to public participation embodied by formal notice and comment requirements,[38] courts have not been responsive to complaints that a permitting process that follows such a process is not a "meaningful opportunity" for public participation. For instance, in *Alabama ex rel. Siegelman v. United States Environmental Protection Agency,* a federal appeals court rejected the argument that the EPA failed to provide a meaningful opportunity for public participation by:

1. making it difficult for members of the public to obtain information about the permit application;
2. failing to provide such information in a form understandable to the public; and
3. failing to conduct more than a "pro forma" public information meeting on the day of the public hearing.[39]

In rejecting the complaint that citizens did not have a meaningful opportunity for public comment, the *Siegelman* court relied on the fact that EPA made available copies of relevant documents at the local public library, at the county probate judges' office, and at the state agency's trailer located near the facility. EPA also made available to anyone who requested it a 17-page fact sheet, which provided a detailed description of the draft permit and of procedures governing public comments. Though EPA held a public question-and-answer session on the same day as the public hearing, the court opined that there was adequate time afterward for written comments to be filed. The court also found significant the fact that though EPA was required to leave the comment period open for only 45 days, it allowed 68 days. EPA received 145 comments and 78 oral statements.

For some permits, EPA itself has recognized some of the shortcomings of its long-standing permit decision-making processes. As explained below, recent regulatory changes now provide for more extensive public participation in the permitting of waste facilities under RCRA.

Additional Public Participation Provisions for RCRA Permits

In 1995, the EPA adopted regulations that significantly expanded public participation opportunities under RCRA in permitting hazardous waste facilities.[40] EPA adopted the new regulations in direct response to many "stakeholder" concerns that the old RCRA permitting process did not involve the public at an early stage in the process, did not provide adequate information, and did not provide an equitable opportunity to participate.[41] The EPA anticipates that these regulations will provide an opportunity for the public to participate earlier in the permitting process, give the public increased access to facility and permitting information, and help people become involved in the permitting process and increase understanding of hazardous waste management facilities.[42] The EPA believes that the 1995 regulations "present significant opportunities to be responsive to environmental justice concerns in the context of public involvement" and will "provide all communities with a greater voice in decision making and a stronger opportunity to influence permit decisions early in the process."[43]

Pre-Application Meeting

The 1995 regulations require a prospective applicant to hold an informal public meeting *before* submitting an application for an RCRA permit.[44] This meeting is held "to solicit questions from the community and inform the community of proposed hazardous waste management activities." This meeting, according to the EPA, "will provide a chance for the community to interact with and provide input to a facility owner or operator before the owner or operator submits a permit application." [45] Most important, the EPA hopes that the pre-application meeting will be the "opening of a dialogue between the permit applicant and the community."[46]

In its *RCRA Public Participation Manual,* the EPA suggests that applicants not concern themselves with "technical aspects" of the permit application in extensive detail at the pre-application stage; such technical matters are more suited to the draft permit stage. The applicant should, however, make a "good faith effort" to provide the public with sufficient information about the proposed facility operations and enough information to understand the potential impacts on human health and the environment.[47] By providing this information, and learning about the public concerns up front, the applicant "may be able to prevent misunderstanding from escalating into community opposition." Moreover, the public will have a "clear and open" opportunity to interact and communicate with the applicant.[48]

Indeed, the EPA envisions, in many cases, an informal meeting atmosphere where the applicant and the public each share their concerns and start to build a "framework" for a "solid" working relationship. Toward this end, the rule allows "flexibility" in the type of meeting held by the permit applicant. It can hold an "availability session" or an "open house" in place of a "traditional" meeting. As long as the meeting adheres to the "spirit" of the regulation, the EPA will not "preclude applicants from tailoring meeting styles to fit particular situations."[49] However, given the informality of this type of meeting, the EPA cautions the public that "not all aspects" of the permit application will be clear at this stage, in part because the facilities are being encouraged to meet with the public before making all final decisions on their permit applications.[50]

The regulations also require the applicant to provide clear notice that will reach as many members of the public as possible, and encourage as many people as possible to attend the meeting. The applicant must provide notice of the meeting in three ways:

- advertise the meeting in the newspaper;
- through a broadcast announcement (say, by radio or television); and
- on a visible and accessible sign posted at or near the property.[51]

The EPA encourages applicants to go beyond the "minimum requirements" in the regulations when providing notice of the pre-application meeting.[52] EPA also encourages the permit applicant to hold the meeting at a time and place that is convenient to the particular community and that has suitable access for all persons.[53] The applicant must also post a sign-in sheet, or similar mechanism, to allow participants to volunteer their names and addresses for inclusion on the facility mailing list.[54] Additionally, there may be instances where more than one meeting is necessary at the pre-application stage—for instance, where there is a long lapse of time between the meeting and the submittal of the application.[55]

The permitting agency does not have to attend the pre-application meeting; but if it does, the facility owner *must* conduct the meeting.[56] However, nothing in the regulations "preclude" state agencies and permit applicants from "working together to combine state siting meetings with pre-application meetings." Indeed, the EPA encourages them to do so, provided that the combined meeting fulfills the requirements of the pre-application meeting.[57] In either case, the applicant must include copies of comments or written materials that it receives at the meeting, along with a list of attendees and their addresses, with its application sent to the permitting agency.

Application Notice

The 1995 regulations direct the permitting agency to mail a notice to interested people when the facility submits its application, including those on the facility mailing list and appropriate units of state and local government.[58] The notice will tell members of the public where they can examine the application at the same time that the agency reviews it. The permitting agency must place the permit application and any supporting documents in a location "accessible to the public in the vicinity of the facility or at the permitting agency's office." The agency must also issue notice of the application in a daily or weekly major local newspaper as well as broadcasting it over local radio stations, or any other method "reasonably calculated" to give actual notice of the permit.[59]

Information Repository

EPA points out in its ruling that RCRA permits can be the subject of intense debate; and, when permits raise a lot of public interest, the public's demand for information increases.[60] The 1995 regulations give the EPA the authority to require a facility owner or operator to set up an information repository at any time during the permitting process or the permit life.[61] EPA anticipates that agencies will use this authority only in those permitting cases that raise much public interest, or in other cases where the public needs more access to information.[62] However, the regulations leave it up to the agency to assess the need for such repository, on a case-by-case basis, according to a variety of factors.[63] The repository will hold all information and documents that the permitting agency decides are necessary to fulfill the purposes for which the repository was established. The repository should be located and maintained at a site chosen by the facility, unless the EPA found the site not suitable.[64]

EPA Encourages, But Does Not Require, Facility Owners to Ensure "Equal Opportunity" for Public Participation

Notably, EPA chose not to implement requirements, proposed by environmental justice advocates, that facility owners "make all reasonable efforts to ensure equal opportunity for the public to participate in the permitting process." The proposed rule language defined "reasonable efforts" as including the use of multilingual fact sheets and interpreters at meetings and hearings, when the "affected community contains a significant non-English speaking population." The EPA decided not to include the "equal opportunity" requirement in response to concerns expressed by many commentators. The Agency agreed with the commentators who expressed concern that the language in the proposed "equal opportunity" requirement was ambiguous, making compliance difficult to evaluate and enforce, and could engender disputes and litigation without advancing the objectives of the requirement.[65]

In rejecting this language, the EPA instead reaffirmed that it is "committed to the principles of equitable public participation and equal treatment of all people under our environmental statutes and regulations" and that the amendments "will enhance the RCRA public participation process for all citizens." The agency concluded that while it continues to promote equitable public participation, it will instead "address the objectives of [the proposed requirement] in guidance rather than through regulatory language." As such, the EPA urged all permitting agencies, permit holders, and applicants, to "follow the spirit" of the rejected requirement and "use all reasonable means to ensure that all segments of the population have an equal opportunity to participate in the permitting process and have equal access to information in the process."[66] Reasonable means may include, but are not limited to, multilingual notices and fact sheets, as well as translators, in areas where the affected community contains significant numbers of people who do not speak English as a first language. In addition, the Agency recommends that "facilities make efforts to tailor public participation activities to fit the diversity, character, and culture of the affected community."[67]

Additional activities that permitting agencies can undertake, but which aren't required in the regulations, include:

- holding informal public meetings prior to a public hearing;
- providing a telephone hotline or voicemail recordings to supplement public notices; and

- providing a news release when issuing the draft permit or intent to deny.[68]

The Effect of President Clinton's Executive Order on Public Participation in Federal Permitting Processes

In his Executive Order on Environmental Justice, President Clinton called on federal agencies to "translate crucial public documents, notice, and hearings," whenever practicable and appropriate, for "limited English-speaking populations." Additionally, agencies must work to ensure that "public documents, notices, and hearings" are "concise, understandable, and readily accessible to the public."[69] No federal agency has made President Clinton's recommendations a mandate in permitting processes. However, as mentioned above, the EPA does urge agencies to follow these and other recommendations in the RCRA permitting process. Similarly, the EPA's Environmental Appeals Board (EAB) has made clear that agencies have the discretion to implement President Clinton's recommendations in other permitting processes.[70]

In at least two appeals, the EAB has answered environmental justice challenges to federal permitting processes by opining that federal administrators have the discretionary authority to implement the mandates of President Clinton's Executive Order by providing other opportunities for public involvement beyond those required. The two cases involved challenges to RCRA and UIC system permits under 40 C.F.R. pt. 124. In both cases, the EAB took note that the EPA's strategy for implementing the Executive Order expressly calls for "early and ongoing public participation in permitting and siting decisions."[71] While the EAB did not specify what those expanded opportunities might entail, it made clear that when a region has a basis to believe that operation of a proposed facility may have a disproportionate impact on a minority or low-income segment of the affected community, the region "should, as a matter of policy, exercise its discretion to assure" early and ongoing public participation opportunities.[72]

Technical Assistance Grants

The EPA also provides for technical assistance to communities participating in cleanup and other decisions. The best-known technical assistance program is the CERCLA, or "Superfund," technical assistance grant (TAG) program, which provides for grants of up to $50,000 to residents near Superfund sites who need a technical adviser to review and explain EPA procedures at the site.[73] Under the TAG program, the EPA gives the grant to a community group, which then contracts with a technical advisor for the needed assistance. The grant period is currently three years, although the EPA is considering eliminating the time period for contracting and allowing community groups to negotiate longer budgets.[74] Currently, community groups must contribute the equivalent of 20 percent of the grant to pay for administrative costs, although the EPA is considering allowing the groups to use part of the TAG grant to pay these costs.[75] The EPA has awarded few grants under the TAG program, and has come under some criticism over the difficulty of obtaining these grants.[76]

Recently, the EPA has offered technical assistance grants of up to $25,000 per project as part of its pilot Project XL, which promotes innovative permits and alternative compliance strategies in regulatory programs.[77] Unlike the CERCLA TAG program, the EPA does not give the grant directly to community groups. Rather, it pays a technical advisor to work on a specific assistance activity for a group of community stakeholders involved in negotiating a Project XL agreement with a project sponsor. An individual stakeholder may not obtain technical assistance under Project XL. However, only the direct participating stakeholder group may seek such assistance, and only after exploring the use of local resources.

NEPA/SEPA Process

State laws based on NEPA[78] provide for some of the most extensive public participation opportunities in environmental decision-making processes.[79] Sixteen states plus the District of Columbia and Puerto Rico have impact review processes modeled after NEPA; these laws are often referred to as State Environmental Policy Acts (SEPAs).[80] The scope and impact review requirements of both NEPA and it state counterparts, SEPAs, are discussed in Chapter 9, "Impact Assessment," pages 256–306. This section will only address the extent of public participation under these statutes.

Both NEPA and most SEPAs require public involvement at virtually every step of the impact review process. These statutes complement, rather than replace, other procedures for public participation in state permitting laws. The EPA and the White House Council on Environmental Quality recently published guidelines, pursuant to the Executive Order, outlining public participation requirements under NEPA that address environmental justice concerns.[81]

Overview of Public Participation in the NEPA/SEPA Process

NEPA requires an environmental impact statement (EIS) for federal actions that "will significantly affect the quality of the human environment"[82] Most SEPAs similarly have a "significantly affect" threshold before requiring an EIS.[83] For the most part, SEPAs adhere to the public participation process set out in NEPA, with some minor deviations. For this reason, this section will not analyze corresponding SEPAs requirements in any detail, except where they may significantly differ from, or elaborate on, the NEPA process.

The Threshold Determination Stage—EA and FONSI documents

In an early step under NEPA, and most SEPAs, the lead agency must decide whether to prepare an EIS.[84] An Environmental Assessment (EA), a public document, provides information from which an agency determines if an EIS is required.[85] The inquiry in an EA focuses on whether the possible proposed action may have a significant impact on the human environment. If the answer is yes, the agency prepares an EIS. If the answer is no, the agency makes a finding of no significant impact (FONSI).[86]

Generally, an agency is not mandated to consult with the public in preparing an EA or in issuing a FONSI.[87] The EA and FONSI documents themselves, however, are available to the public for review and become important when a party challenges in court a decision not to prepare an EIS.[88] Under certain "limited" circumstances, federal regulations recommend a 30-day public review period between the issuance of a FONSI and the final decision not to prepare an EIS.[89] Nevertheless, while some federal agencies—such as the Department of Energy, the Department of the Army, and the U.S. Forest Service—provide for a public comment period on EAs,[90] many do not. On the other hand, many SEPAs do require such a public comment period.[91]

Scoping the EIS

If the agency determines that an EIS is required, it usually must commence a process called "scoping," in which the agency holds a meeting to identify the range of issues for consideration in the EIS.[92] The agency must arrange the scoping meeting, if one is held, so that it takes place "early" in the EIS process, with public notice, and is "open" to members of the public and other agencies.[93] The scoping process requires the agency to seek actively the participation of other agencies and the public. Scoping comments can occur both in writing and through public meetings held by the agency.

Preparing and Commenting on the EIS

Following scoping, the agency prepares a draft EIS, detailing the potential effects of the project. The agency then distributes the draft EIS to the public for written comments,[94] with a minimum time of 45 days to respond.[95] The agency must then send a copy of the draft EIS to any member of the public who requests it[96] and "affirmatively solicits comments from those persons or organizations who may be interested or affected."[97] Public hearings on the EIS, however, are discretionary. The agency may hold public hearings "whenever appropriate" or according to established criteria. In determining the appropriateness of holding a public hearing, agencies generally must consider whether there is "substantial environmental controversy concerning the proposed action or substantial interest in holding the hearing."[98] In some states, however, agencies are explicitly encouraged or required to hold public hearings.[99]

After receiving comments from the public and other agencies, the agency then revises the draft EIS to produce a final EIS. The final EIS must include and respond to "responsible" opposing viewpoints.[100] Thirty days after distribution of the final EIS, the agency must issue a "record of decision" (ROD).[101] The ROD should state the agency's decision, identify the alternatives considered, specify the environmentally preferable alternatives, discuss factors that the agency balanced in making its decision, and indicate whether all practical means of avoiding or minimizing environmental harm were incorporated into the decision.[102] The ROD must also be made available for public comment.[103]

The Future of Public Participation Under NEPA/SEPAs

In General

Even when an EIS is prepared, and opportunities for public participation are plentiful, there are still limits to the participatory and deliberative nature of the NEPA/SEPA process. As the Council for Environmental Quality recently reported as part of its review of the first 25 years of NEPA, many communities feel that the process is often triggered too late to be fully effective. Agency and private sector planning processes begin long before the NEPA or SEPA process. By the time the EIS process is started, some alternatives and strategic choices are foreclosed.[104] CEQ found widespread agreement that although NEPA has improved public information and input into the environmental decision-making processes, the desired level of public involvement is not always achieved. Indeed, some communities view the EIS process as "largely a one-way communication track that does not use their input effectively."[105]

The study also made clear that some states, citizen groups, and businesses believe that certain EAs are prepared to avoid public involvement. As CEQ notes, the preparation of an EA, rather than an EIS, is the most common source of conflict and litigation under NEPA. CEQ understands that "avoiding an opportunity for public comment on draft EAs and FONSIs can create mistrust and add costs and time as projects are delayed by ensuing controversy and legal challenges" and that "when agencies do not seek interagency and public review of an EA, a fundamental opportunity is lost to build trust with the neighboring community."[106]

The study concludes that creating a true partnership with the community involves more than holding a hearing and making documents available. Public involvement takes effort and time.[107] CEQ recognizes that more guidance is needed to increase public involvement in the EA process, including improving mechanisms for public comment, and agency incorporation of these comments. In the future, CEQ may consider suggesting alternatives to public hearings such as roundtables, workshops, and informal dialogues in the EA process. It noted that some agencies have used scoping in the EA process, and discovered that not only does it build trust in the community, but it often identifies potential impacts and mitigation strategies earlier (thus saving time and money).

CEQ also suggested the need to produce NEPA documents that are easy to read and understand as a way of facilitating agency and public input into decisions.[108] For instance, it opined, an EA should not be written as a scientific paper for peer review. Instead, EISs and EAs should address the general public and emphasize points important to the decision-making process. CEQ also suggests that technical documents be placed in an appendix, and earlier coordination be conducted with other federal, state, local, and tribal agencies and the public to narrow issues and make use of existing information.

Judicial Enforcement of NEPA/SEPA Procedural Requirements in the Environmental Justice Context: The Kettleman City Case

While agencies have recently begun to recognize the limits of public participation in the implementation of NEPA, at least one state court has recognized substantial limitations in communities that are vulnerable and disenfranchised. In 1991, a groundbreaking environmental justice case brought under California's SEPA enhanced the right of communities to have access to key documents in the decision-making process. In *El Pueblo para el Aire y Agua Limpio,* a low-income minority community brought a successful suit challenging a state agency's failure to comply with the SEPA's public participation provisions because the EIS was available only in English and should have been translated into Spanish.[109]

The dispute in *El Pueblo* involved the siting of a hazardous waste incinerator in Kettleman City, California, which is 95 percent Latino, with a 40 percent monolingual Spanish-speaking population. When the permitting agency, Kings County, provided the community with the required documents—the hearing notices, public testimony, and three versions of the EIR—it had not translated them into Spanish. Moreover, the EIR was difficult to read in English due to its highly technical language and employment of obscure scientific terms.[110]

In response to eighty-one written requests for translation of notices and the draft EIS, the County Planning Commission informed the community that "it is the policy of Kings County to publish environmental documents in English."[111] At the only public hearing on the proposed facility, the Planning Commission refused to provide translation or allow private interpreters for Spanish-speaking attendees.[112] Nor were Spanish statements translated for English speakers in the audience, except for the Commissioners, who could listen through earphones to their own interpreter.[113]

After the Planning Commission approved the permit, a group of Kettleman City residents brought a lawsuit under, among other statutes, California's Environmental Quality Act (CEQA), its SEPA, to invalidate the permit and enjoin construction of the incinerator. The residents argued that the failure to translate crucial documents and meetings had effectively excluded many citizens from exercising their statutory right to participate in the decision-making process. They also alleged that the EIS was inaccessible even in English, having been written in "highly technical language, incomprehensible to the average Kings County resident."[114] The California Superior Court agreed, ruling that "meaningful involvement in the CEQA process was effectively precluded by the absence of Spanish translation."[115]

Federal Agencies' Environmental Justice NEPA Guidance

The Kettleman City case undoubtedly influenced President Clinton's Executive Order, particularly its recommendation that crucial documents be translated into a community's language. As also discussed in Chapter 4, "Executive Order 12,898," pages 103–139 of this volume, federal agencies are following the recommendations contained in the Executive Order in setting new policies designed to provide meaningful public involvement for minority and low-income communities in the NEPA process.

CEQ, for instance, recommends early and meaningful public participation when decisions potentially impact vulnerable communities—low-income, minority, and tribal populations.[116] In particular, CEQ recognizes that vulnerable communities may require "adaptive" or "innovative" approaches to overcome "linguistic, institutional, cultural, economic, historical, or other potential barriers" to effective participation in environmental decision-making processes. These barriers, for instance, may range from an agency's failure to provide "translations of documents" to the scheduling of meetings at times and in places that are "not convenient to working families." As such, CEQ lists, but does not recommend or encourage, a number of innovative strategies that an agency can use for effective public participation. Among them are: translation of major documents, provision of translators at meetings, use of periodic newsletters or summaries to provide updates on the NEPA process, use of different meeting sizes or formats, variations on the type and number of media used, circulation or creation of specialized materials that reflect concerns and sensitivities of particular populations (such as information about risks specific to subsistence consumers of fish, vegetation, or wildlife), use of locations and facilities that are convenient and accessible to the community, and assistance to hearing-impaired or sight-impaired persons.

EPA's NEPA guidance similarly suggests ways to encourage and facilitate more active participation by low-income communities and minority communities, particularly when the screening analysis indicates there may be a disproportionately high and adverse effect on the host community.[117] EPA recognizes that to establish trust with "all types of stakeholders," interaction with the affected community should:

1. encourage active community participation;
2. recognize community knowledge; and
3. utilize cross-cultural formats and exchanges.

Specifically, EPA suggests careful identification of target audiences and aggressive community outreach beyond the traditional forms. Once community leaders and stakeholders have been identified (through various methods) and a dialogue established, EPA recommends that a mailing list should be assembled for information dissemination and formal public meeting announcements. Where appropriate, EPA recommends that accessible information repositories be established and technical documents contain a summary written to the lay public and translated into the "dominant language of the affected community." Additional mechanisms suggested include: allowing for public review of RODs, government-to-government consultation with tribal governments, community advisory boards for the development of NEPA documents, community consultants, and technical assistance to affected communities to enhance understanding of proposed action, technical documents, and full range of potential alternatives and mitigation measures.[118]

Public Participation Under State Permitting Laws

Though state laws cover permitting processes for a variety of land uses, full coverage would be impossible in this limited space. As such, this section will focus on state laws in the hazardous waste permitting context as a model for state laws covering the permitting of other types of land uses. Citizen participation under state hazardous waste permitting statutes largely mirrors the federal permitting rules discussed above. There is, however, some variation in the requirements for notice and comment and hearing procedures. Some states also offer community advisory boards, providing earlier and more substantive opportunities for public participation.

Overview of State Permitting Processes

The federal RCRA comprehensively regulates solid and hazardous wastes from "cradle to grave"—from waste creation through disposal—but essentially delegates[119] responsibilities for locating and permitting waste processing facilities to state environmental agencies.[120] There are two main ways states regulate or take part in waste facility siting: the *passive* and *active* approaches.

Most states take a *passive* or *ad hoc* approach to siting, allowing private companies to initiate the process by seeking a permit to construct and/or operate a facility at a specific location.[121] After the prospective waste facility developer initiates the process by choosing a potential site location, it applies for permits from the state environmental agency. The agency evaluates the application, then approves or rejects the permit application according to whether or not the applicant has met all the legal criteria for receiving a permit. Special siting boards, or site review boards, often make the initial, and sometimes final, decision regarding the suitability of the site.[122] A couple of states leave the decision to local control—that is, an applicant must obtain approval from the county or municipality where the site is proposed.[123] One state allows, upon submittal of a petition by county voters, for the ultimate permit decision to be made by referendum.[124]

Far fewer states take an *active* or *"advance site designation"* approach, whereby the state siting committee initiates the siting process by identifying suitable sites around the state for future waste facilities.[125] The state then solicits private sector proposals for developing facilities on those sites or simply maintains the inventory of sites until project proposals are submitted by developers.[126] The sites designated by the committee need not be exclusive. In one state, developers may propose alternative or additional sites designations other than those chosen by the siting board.[127]

Given the predominance of states following the passive approach to permitting, the remainder of this part of Chapter 7 will focus primarily on those states. Nevertheless, public participation is an integral part of the site designation approach as well. A siting board chosen by, usually, the governor of the state solicits public input for possible sites for inclusion in the state siting plan.[128] Before a siting plan for the state has been adopted, or before a particular site is approved, the decision maker gives notice and seeks comment from the public in much the same manner in states following the passive approach to siting.[129] Hence, there is some degree of overlap between the public participation mechanisms employed in both approaches to siting waste facilities.

Mandatory Notice and Comment

At a minimum, an applicant or agency must provide notice to the public and provide a reasonable period to receive written comments by the public on the proposed waste facility permit or a proposed waste plan. Public notice is typically provided for in state statutes by newspaper publication prior to a public hearing and, less often, by broadcast on local radio stations. Many states additionally provide for special notice and comment procedures for local officials and property owners near the site.[130]

Despite basic notice and comment requirement, however, many host communities do not receive adequate notice of proposed facilities. In communities where literacy levels are low, it is unlikely that many citizens will become aware of or read the official notice.[131] In some communities, notices are put in a minuscule space at the back of the local newspaper, eluding notice by average readers of the newspaper.[132] In many Latino communities, notices in English may be overlooked due to language barriers.

Fortunately, permitting laws and policies are beginning to address obstacles to participation by many communities by requiring, for instance, that public notices be of a size large enough to attract public attention,[133] that key government documents be translated into the community's language,[134] and that supporting permit documents be written in plain language and limit use of technical terms.[135]

What Must Be Noticed

Adequate notice greatly depends upon when notice is given to the community in the permitting process, as well as what the community is provided notice *about.* Exactly what must be noticed varies from state to state, and can make a huge difference in the ability of an affected community to obtain meaningful and early involvement in the decision-making process. The earlier the opportunity for public input, the more participatory and fair the process will seem to the affected community.

The earliest a community may receive notice is in the pre-application phase of the process. Some states require the applicant to publish notice of its intent to apply for a permit before filing a permit application.[136] Most states, however, require public notice only upon filing an application.[137] Still other states only require published notice when the decision maker has made a preliminary decision on the permit or issued a draft permit.[138] If the requirement is only to notice a preliminary permit decision or a draft permit, the public enters the decision-making process virtually in its last stages. Technical review of the application by an environmental agency would have already occurred, largely out of public view. During this period of review, "there is often considerable informal communication between the applicant's representatives and the agency's personnel" whereby "discussion of permit terms takes place, as well as some negotiation over them."[139] As such, public response is likely to be reactive to a decision many will see as a having been made without consideration of the public's concerns.

Information Repository

In some states, an "information repository," theoretically accessible to the public, and intended to provide the public with documents relating to a permit, is required or permitted in the agency's discretion.[140] While in theory providing the public access to documents, many of these information repositories are in practice inaccessible to the public: they may be in cities far away from the host community (such as in the state capital) or in a local library with limited and inconvenient hours. On the other hand, many communities that are opposed to proposed waste facilities do have dedicated individuals who will go to the repositories (even if they are inconvenient) and mine them for useful information. Unfortunately, many residents in target communities may not even be aware that the information repositories exist and thus are unable to take advantage of them even if they are convenient. Where the community is aware of information repositories, documents should ideally be translated into the community's language and written in language that is accessible to relatively educated people.

Public Hearings

Along with formal notice and written comments, most states allow for, or require, a public hearing on the proposed permit. Public hearings provide an opportunity for the community to come out in force and express itself to the decision makers, face to face. It is not uncommon for concerned residents to fill, or overflow, public meetings on permit applications, sending a clear message to the decision makers that any action taken without consideration of community concerns would be a mistake. Public hearings also provide an opportunity for industry, local officials, and local businesses to express their support or opposition to the facility.

Type of Hearing

As with the notice requirement, the earlier the opportunity for public input, the greater the opportunity for a community to attempt to influence the decision maker. The earliest opportunity for public input is at the pre-application stage. A handful of states require that before a company applies for a waste permit, it has to send a letter of intent to the local agency and hold a public hearing.[141] The purpose of the pre-application hearing is to explain the project and the permitting process—the public can hear about the project for the first time, and can often ask questions of agency officials. The pre-application hearing also gives the company involved a chance to evaluate potential opposition to the facility. If there is overwhelming opposition, a company may reconsider or modify the project.

Most states do not require a pre-application hearing. Most states either mandate a public hearing on the permit application itself[142] or allow such a hearing at the decision makers' discretion.[143] Under the latter provisions, a public hearing is only held when the decision maker determines that there is "significant public interest," or a hearing is otherwise deemed "appropriate" or in the public interest. These determinations are sometimes left entirely to an administrator's discretion, subject (of course) to judicial review. Often, however, such determinations are guided by specific criteria set out in agency regulations. In some communities, many residents are not even aware of the public hearing and find out about the proposed development only after the permit is issued, and hence feel excluded from the decision-making process.[144]

Hearing Procedures

As with federal permitting processes, most permitting hearings, if held, are legislative types of hearings. At the hearing, permitting agency officials explain the justification for the permit and interested members of the public comment have an opportunity to present their views, with perhaps a limited question-and-answer period. Few states provide for an adjudicative hearing with an administrative judge or hearing officer, which would include an opportunity to examine witnesses and demand documents.[145] Many states also require the agency to consider the public comments received at the hearing and be responsive to those comments in their final decision.

Nevertheless, public meetings can be frustrating and trying exercises that fall far short of the level of participation that some communities and environmental justice advocates desire. Public hearings that simply allot a certain amount of time to hear testimony by the public do not foster substantive opportunities for dialogue between decision makers and those most affected by a proposed project or development. As one commentator explains, "although in all proceedings there is a potential for dialogue, the 'step up to the microphone and have your say in less than fifteen minutes' approach of many [public] meetings resembles more of a crude preference tally rather than meaningful deliberation," and—more often than not—"the commentator has her say and sits down without any indication that the decision maker has seriously considered the position."[146] Public hearings may be a good opportunity for decision makers to hear the views of the affected community and perhaps engage in brief question-and-answer sessions; however, they are a poor forum for "extensive development of information, a shared baseline of understanding, and the development of a consensus," necessary for a truly deliberative decision-making process.[147]

Citizen Advisory Boards

Increasingly, environmental decision-making processes involve consultation with local advisory committees, intended to provide different constituencies in affected communities with more meaningful and representative public participation than public notice and comment procedures.[148] In the permitting process for waste facilities, only a few states mandate such committees.[149] Where provided for, advisory committees are usually active only for the time period for which a specific permit is under consideration. Such committees often complement, rather than replace, other public participation mechanisms in the siting process such as review and comment procedures and public hearings.

Generally, state laws aim for a diverse membership on advisory committees, including representatives of the proposed host community, affected business and industries, environmental and other public interest groups. Members are generally appointed by either the chief executive officer (typically the mayor), or legislative body (for example, the city or county council), of the host community. The committee is generally appointed from the filing of the notice of intent to file application or notice of application, allowing for early public involvement in the process. Part of the charge of such committees is to promote public education, information, and participation in the permitting process.

In addition, site-specific advisory committees are typically directed to assess the social, environmental, and economic impact on the proposed facility and report their findings to the entity responsible for making the final permit decision. They often have access to the relevant permit application and supporting documents. Some states give technical assistance to local review committees, usually in the form of grants for hiring consultants, lawyers, and other necessary personnel.[150] The committee may hire technical and legal consultants to assist in this process, help develop permit conditions and requirements, and review information for issuance of special zoning permits; in some situations, a committee's request for such technical expertise may be denied or subverted by the decision-making body.[151] A few states provide for a direct negotiation process between the developer and the proposed local advisory committee.[152]

Site-specific advisory committees are an improvement on the public participation process in that they offer more opportunities for a qualitatively deliberative process—one that creates an opportunity for lay and technical people to work together, have a dialogue, and reach consensus.[153] However, because these committees are advisory only, it is not clear how much weight their analysis is given in the final decision. The decision makers are, to be sure, counseled to consider the recommendations of the advisory committee; but, in the end, they retain the discretion to dismiss or discount its recommendations in the final decision. Representation can be an issue as well, given the difficulty of identifying diffuse and unorganized interests in a community.[154] Advisory committee members are often not chosen by the populace, but are instead appointed by local officials who normally support incoming waste facilities touting economic benefits. As a result, community groups likely to oppose additional waste facilities may easily be left out of the deliberative process. If this happens, local advisory groups may even serve to limit public participation, "functioning as a gatekeeper and filters, and as a fifth, or even sixth, branch of government."[155]

The Adequacy of Public Participation in State Permitting Processes

In a recent challenge to an air pollution (PSD) permit under Michigan law, one court has called into question the adequacy of basic notice-and-comment public participation required in most permitting processes. The EPA, in contrast, has rejected a challenge to those same permitting processes, involving a different facility, ruling that the notice-and-comment procedures were not discriminatory.

The Genesee Power Case

The first case, *Genesee Power,* arises out of a challenge to a permit issued to the Genesee Power Station, a steam-electric generation plant fired by wood waste, by the Air Pollution Control Commission (Commission) of the Michigan Department of Environmental Quality (MDEQ). African Americans comprise the majority of the population living within three miles of the Genesee Power Station.[156] Many residents in the community opposed the permit because it would allow significant levels of lead in an already environmentally burdened community.

Among other bases, the community challenged issuance of the permit on the basis that opportunities for public participation were "inadequate." The public comment period for the permit lasted 42 days, beyond the required 30 days. Two separate public hearings were held, although none is required unless the permit issuer determines that there is strong public interest, in which case only one hearing is required. Nevertheless, community members asserted that they were made to sit for hours during the second public hearing while the committee conducted other business; and, among other things, the Commission members talked and laughed while opponents stated their objections. According to the community group, the decision makers delivered a revised draft permit to the group that afternoon, leaving no time for review by the public. When the group finally got a chance to testify, the decision makers talked, laughed, and paid little attention, the group alleged. Moreover, the hearing took place over an hour from the proposed site, forcing concerned residents to rent a bus. The MDEQ did not contradict these allegations.

An EAB disagreed with the challengers, ruling that the community did have a "meaningful opportunity" to air views during the course of the permitting process. The EAB ruled that, while insensitive—and it would have been better to reschedule the meeting—the Commission's behavior was not so serious that the Commission should be required to go through the whole process again. An important factor was the fact that there was a public hearing prior to the one at issue, in which members of the public were allowed to make their views known. Moreover, the EAB noted, the final draft permit reflected changes based on comments received at the first hearing and during the public comment period.[157]

The Michigan Circuit Court (in an unpublished opinion), however, disagreed with the EAB's assessment. Basing its decision in part on the Michigan Constitution, the Circuit Court issued an injunction prohibiting the State of Michigan from granting any more permits until it has reformed its system of environmental protection—including the requirement that the state perform risk assessments and reform its public hearing process, which the court found was not "meaningful."[158] The court found specifically that "the opportunity to make public comment without the power to apply political pressure on the decision makers does not constitute a situation where people who are affected have a real voice in the decision."[159] Another problem that attracted the court's attention was the fact that the local zoning board (Genesee Township) that authorized the initial siting was in a different jurisdiction from the community that would suffer the primary impact. The court opined that this resulted in denial of an adequate avenue for "cities and other governmental units . . . to have a meaningful and knowledgeable opportunity to have its concerns and those of its residents considered in the siting process involving plants that are located in another jurisdiction, but which pollute adjoining governmental units."[160] The state appealed the injunction imposed on it by the Circuit Court. On November 24, 1998, the Michigan Court of Appeals, in an unpublished opinion, overturned the injunction.

The appellate court ruled that the Circuit Court judge exceeded his authority when issuing the injunction because the lawsuit did not contend the permitting process violated the state constitution.[161]

The Select Steel Case

The second case, *Select Steel,* arises out of a challenge to MDEQ's issuance of a CAA PSD permit to the Select Steel Corporation for a proposed steel recycling mini-mill in Genesee Township.[162] The challenge was brought pursuant to Title VI of the Civil Rights Act of 1964 and EPA's implementing regulations.[163] The challengers, co-directors of the St. Francis Prayer Center in Flint, alleged that the permit would lead to a discriminatory impact on minority residents and that the permitting process was conducted in a discriminatory manner.

In particular, with respect to the permitting process, the challengers alleged that the permit was "hastily sped through" by MDEQ to avoid permitting requirements—that is, conducting a risk assessment, providing opportunity for public comment on risk assessment, and allowing meaningful opportunity for all affected parties to participate in the permit process—imposed by the state trial court in the *Genesee Power* case. The challengers also alleged that:

1. the manner of publication of the permit hearing notice, in newspapers, was insufficient to inform the predominantly minority community because few community members have access to newspapers;
2. the MDEQ failed to provide individual notice of the hearing to more members of the community; and
3. the location of the public hearing made it difficult for minority members of the community to attend.

The EPA rejected the allegation of a discriminatory permitting process, holding that MDEQ had satisfied EPA's regulatory requirements for issuing PSD permits (in 40 C.F.R. pt. 124). Concerning the allegation of a "hastily sped through" process, the EPA found that the five months between receipt of the complete permit application and permit approval is "actually slower than the average time of one and a half months for the past twenty-six PSD permits approved by MDEQ." Hence, the public participation process was not compromised by the pace of the process. Regarding the other allegations, EPA found that:

1. MDEQ's publication of the permit hearing notice in three local newspapers went beyond the EPA's PSD permitting regulations, which require notice of a public hearing to be published in a newspaper within the affected area;
2. the mailing list, which consisted of the challengers and nine other individuals in the community who expressed interest in the permit, was adequate to inform the community about the public hearing, in part because the challengers "took it upon themselves to contact other members of the community"; and
3. MDEQ's selection of a public high school located within a predominantly white area, and two miles from the proposed Select Steel site, for the permit hearing, as opposed to an elementary school located in a predominantly minority area, was not erroneous.

The EPA found that MDEQ had explored other possible locations and chose the high school, among other reasons, "because of its ability to accommodate the expected number of citizens and its close proximity to the proposed site." EPA also found that the high school is accessible by the general public via Genesee County public transportation.

Importantly, the EPA closed its opinion in the *Select Steel* case with a caveat about the need for earlier public participation in the permitting process. The EPA "believes that many of the issues raised in the context of Title VI administrative complaints could be better addressed through early involvement of affected communities in the permitting process." Earlier public consultation, the EPA continued, "will better ensure that communities are fairly and equitably treated with respect to the quality of their environment and public health, while providing State and local decision makers and businesses the certainty they deserve."

"SLAPPs": Getting Sued for Speaking Out

The opposition of citizen groups to various development projects, including waste facility development, has sparked a backlash by private developers: the Strategic Lawsuit Against Public Participation

(SLAPP). The paradigm SLAPP suit is brought by a project applicant or developer against individuals or groups who have opposed the project. SLAPPs are typically filed in response to a citizen filing public interest litigation, engaging in formal government appeals, reporting violations of law, testifying at public hearings, submitting various written communications, and as a result of demonstrating or boycotting.[164] The issue most likely to initiate a SLAPP is one involving real estate development and/or land use.[165] The targets of SLAPPs are often "concerned citizens."[166] Of the organizations sued, the largest category is public interest groups, particularly those that focus on environmental and civil rights.[167]

What distinguishes a SLAPP suit from "everyday retaliatory lawsuits" is the "single element" of "reaction to political action."[168] According to the most prominent observers of SLAPPs, one can identify such a lawsuit by one primary and three secondary criteria. First and foremost, the lawsuit will usually "involve communications made to influence a governmental action or outcome." Once that initial threshold has been met, a SLAPP can be identified by the presence of:

a) a civil complaint or counterclaim;
b) filed against nongovernmental individuals or organizations (NGOs); and
c) on a substantive issue of some public interest or social significance.[169]

Some prime examples of a SLAPP include:

- testifying against a real estate development at a zoning hearing;[170]
- campaigning for or against a ballot issue;[171]
- collecting signatures on a petition;[172] and
- reporting violations or filing complaints with a government agency—for example, about environmental, health, safety, consumer, civil rights, or employment issues.[173]

SLAPP defendants, usually citizen groups and citizens, increasingly have filed so-called "SLAPP-back" suits either by way of counterclaim or in separate litigation.[174] Additionally, there is one constitutional defense, based on the Petition Clause, which more often than not allows the defenders of a SLAPP to fight back effectively. As such, the vast majority of SLAPPs are successfully defended and ultimately dismissed.[175] Moreover, the landscape of SLAPP litigation has become increasingly unfavorable to plaintiffs who bring SLAPPs, due to recent legislation that recognizes the antidemocratic nature of such lawsuits.

SLAPP Suits and Claims

Typical Claims

The typical SLAPP claims made by developers against organizations or citizens are based in tort and constitutional theories. Such claims include: defamation, interference with business relations (for example, interference with contract, or economic advantage-expectation), process violations (malicious prosecution, judicial or administrative abuse of process), conspiracy, and constitutional/civil rights violations.[176] The proof of these alleged violations often lies in the representations that citizens have made to elected boards or regulatory agencies. The damage claimed by developers is the injury that results from an individual or organization protesting or petitioning the government.

Typical of a SLAPP claim is the *Sierra Club. v Butz* lawsuit.[177] In 1965, the U.S. Forest Service optioned for logging a virgin 3,500-acre area near what was to become the Salmon-Trinity Alps Wilderness in the far northwest corner of California. The contract was awarded to the Humboldt Fire Company, but the company did not begin logging immediately. Five years later, in 1970, the Sierra Club began petitioning the Forest Service, alleging that the proposed logging was "illegal" and requesting that the tract of land be preserved. The government denied the request, and, in 1972, the Sierra Club filed a challenge in federal court to overturn the government's decision. Three days later Humboldt filed a counterclaim demanding an injunction, and seeking actual and punitive damages against the Sierra Club. Humboldt claimed to have been driven into bankruptcy and charged "interference with contract" because the Sierra Club "orally and by letter and by administrative appeal proceedings and by the complaint herein, engaged in a calculated course of conduct to induce the Forest Service . . . to refuse to continue the performance of its said contract." The court ultimately dismissed the developer's claims on the basis of the First Amendment provision "guaranteeing the right of the people to petition the government for a redress of grievances."[178]

Judicial Treatment

Most courts look askance at SLAPPs, and the vast majority of such cases are ultimately dismissed.[179] The Petition Clause defense is raised as the defense in the majority of SLAPP cases, and the invocation of the defense, according to one commentator, "almost doubled targets' chances of winning."[180] The right to petition the government has entitled citizens to near-immunity from lawsuits when they petition public officials. As the U.S. Supreme Court said in *City of Columbia v. Omni Outdoor Advertising, Inc.*, "[the Petition Clause shields efforts] to influence public officials regardless of intent or purpose" except when it is "not genuinely aimed at procuring favorable government action."[181] Raising the Petition Clause defense, rather than just Free Speech or nonconstitutional defenses, enables targets to "retransform" the "legalistic dispute back into the political dispute, in the court's mind."[182]

Citizen Responses: SLAPPback Suits and Claims

Increasingly, the subjects of SLAPPs are aggressively responding to assaults on their right to public participation by filing "SLAPPbacks." "SLAPPbacks" are filed either as independent lawsuits or counterclaims in the SLAPP suit. The SLAPPback can be based on many theories, including some of the same claims made in the SLAPP. In a sense, the SLAPPbacks "recycle" the SLAPP filers' original charges. Malicious prosecution and abuse of process head the list of SLAPPback allegations, followed by defamation, interference with business, conspiracy, and other familiar complaints.[183] SLAPPbacks, however, succeed where typical SLAPPs usually fail.[184]

Typical of a SLAPPback lawsuit or counterclaim is the *Shell v. Leonardini* case.[185] In *Leonardini,* Shell sued a consumer advocate and union lawyer for reporting to a state health agency that there were cancer-causing substances in a Shell product used in home plumbing. Leonardini responded with a dismissal motion charging constitutional rights violations. Shell first "pressed its lawsuit and then, in a turnabout, voluntarily dismissed it, claiming that a codefendant's settlement was vindication."[186] Leonardini filed a SLAPPback charging malicious prosecution to violate Leonardini's constitutional rights.

At trial, Leonardini argued that Shell's suit was groundless and designed to keep Leonardini from testifying to the government against its product.[187] Shell responded with the "standard" SLAPPback defense strategy—they denied the suit had anything to do with constitutional rights and portrayed their initial suit as an ordinary defamation action based on Leonardini's circulation of false, incomplete, and misleading statements concerning Shell's product.[188] Shell's tactics failed. The Superior Court awarded Leonardini $175,000 in actual damages for intimidation, $22,000 in lawyers' fees, and $5,000,000 in punitive damages.[189]

Legislative Responses

Nine states have adopted modern anti-SLAPP statutes.[190] Four other states are considering passing anti-SLAPP legislation.[191] The statutes and bills fall into two general categories: those that provide for immunity from SLAPP lawsuits and those that create a special motion to dismiss or strike the SLAPP claim or lawsuit. Many states also provide for lawyers' fees from SLAPP filers and, under certain circumstances, SLAPPback lawsuits.[192]

Defining the SLAPP

The anti-SLAPP statutes vary in their definitions of a SLAPP suit. The common element, however, is that the challenged action or statement pertains to an issue that the public agency or body has under consideration.[193] Some statutes define a SLAPP as a lawsuit or claim brought against a party's exercise of its rights of petition or free speech. Such challenged action must involve any written or oral statement made either on an issue before a legislative, executive, or judicial body or any other governmental proceeding and/or in connection with an issue of public concern.[194] A SLAPP in other states is a "good faith" communication to a government agency, usually consisting of a complaint regarding a matter "reasonably of concern" to that agency.[195]

Other states define a SLAPP suit or claim more narrowly, as that brought by a public applicant or permittee against one challenging an application or permit.[196] In other words, such statutes only apply to those SLAPP filers who have "applied for or obtained a permit, zoning change, lease, license, certificate or other entitlement for use or permission to act from any government body" or persons affiliated with them.[197] Such definitions similarly limit targets to those who "report on, comment on, rule on, challenge or oppose such application or permission."[198] This means that such statutes cover only about half of all SLAPPs.[199]

Immunities

The broadest anti-SLAPP statutes grant complete or conditional immunity from liability to SLAPP targets and their communications to public agencies. Washington's statute is the paradigmatic broad immunity statute. The statute provides immunity from civil liability on claims brought against a person who in "good faith" communicates a complaint or information to an agency" regarding "any matter reasonably of concern to that agency."[200] At least one court of appeal equated "good faith" to mean the absence of malice. As such, a SLAPP plaintiff must provide clear and convincing evidence that the defendant "knew of the falsity of the communication or acted with reckless disregard of its falsity" to get around the broad immunity given to defendants.[201] Moreover, the statute authorizes the agency receiving the complaint or attorney general to intervene and defend against a SLAPP suit.[202] If the agency or attorney general prevails, it may recover reasonable lawyers' fees incurred in defense of the suit.[203]

Rhode Island, on the other hand, grants only conditional immunity from SLAPP lawsuits or claims. The Rhode Island statute provides that a court shall stay all discovery proceedings where a party against whom a SLAPP has been brought files a motion asserting the immunity established by the statute.[204] However, the statute does include a "sham" exception to otherwise broad immunity. That is, the immunity provided for in the statute does not apply where the party's "petition or free speech" is "not genuinely aimed at procuring favorable government action, result or outcome, regardless of ultimate motive or purpose."[205] The petition or free speech will be deemed a sham, the statute goes on to explicate, if it is both "objectively baseless"—no reasonable person could realistically expect success in procuring the government action, result, or outcome—and is "subjectively baseless"—it is actually an attempt to use the governmental process itself for its own direct effects.[206] However, the mere allegation that the SLAPP target has engaged in tortious conduct is not enough to avoid the immunity granted by the statute.[207]

Special Motion Practices

Many anti-SLAPP statutes provide a special procedure to test the sufficiency of the allegations against the SLAPP target. These statutes give a type of immunity by providing for a special motion to dismiss the action unless the plaintiff can show that the action of the SLAPP targets are not immunized from liability.[208] While there have been challenges to the constitutionality of these statutes—based on the claim that they deny SLAPP filers due process by requiring them to litigate without the benefit of discovery and deny them a jury trial—most courts have rejected such challenges outright.[209]

New York's statute is a good example of the type of procedural safeguards provided by special anti-SLAPP motions. The New York "Citizen Participation Act" requires a dismissal or summary judgment motion be given a quick hearing, shifts the burden of proof to the SLAPP filer, and places a fairly heavy burden (strict scrutiny standard) on the SLAPP filer's proof by requiring dismissal "unless the [SLAPP filer] demonstrates that the [SLAPP] has a substantial basis in law or is supported by a substantial argument for an extension, modification or reversal of existing law."[210] Even if the case is not dismissed under this standard, the SLAPP filer may not recover monetary damages or lawyers' fees without proving by "clear and convincing evidence" that the target's petitioning was done with actual malice—"knowledge of its falsity or with reckless disregard of whether it was false."[211] However, this provision is bilateral, requiring the SLAPP target to prove actual malice to recover damages from the SLAPP filer.

California has established a slightly different type of motion practice—the "special motion to strike."[212] This procedure requires the SLAPP filer to marshall facts sufficient to show the viability of the action before filing a SLAPP suit.[213] In considering the special motion, the court reviews pleadings as well as supporting and opposing affidavits that state the facts upon which the lawsuit or claim is based.[214] To overcome the motion, the SLAPP filer must establish that "there is a probability that [the SLAPP filer] will prevail on the claim."[215] The statute also provides that all discovery proceedings will be stayed upon the filing of the notice of motion to strike, although the court may, upon good cause shown, order that specified discovery shall be conducted.[216]

Notes

* Associate Professor of Law, Rutgers University-Camden. Many thanks to Moze Cowper for expert research assistance. This chapter was made possible by a grant from Rutgers School of Law.

1. Nearly a decade ago, a letter from over 100 community leaders of color to eight national environmental organizations accused the organizations of racist and exclusionary hiring practices, as well as policy positions inimical to environmental justice. *See* Phillip Shabecoff, *Environmental Groups Told They Are Racists in Hiring*, N.Y. TIMES, February 1, 1990, at A20; Nonny De La Pena with Susan Davis, *The Greens Are White: And Minorities Want In*, NEWSWEEK, Oct. 15, 1990, at 34.

2. Exec. Order No. 12,898, 3 C.F.R. § 859 (1995). *See generally* Chapter 4, *supra*.

3. *See, e.g.*, National Environmental Policy Act, 42 U.S.C. §§ 4332(C), 4368; Comprehensive Environmental Response, Compensation and Liability Act, 42 U.S.C. §§ 9617, 9659; Emergency Planning and Community Right-to-Know Act, 42 U.S.C. §§ 11,044, 11,046; Clean Water Act, 33 U.S.C. §§ 1365, 1344(o), 1342(j); Federal Insecticide, Fungicide, And Rodenticide Act, 7 U.S.C § 136; Resource Conservation and Recovery Act, 42 U.S.C § 6974; Toxic Substances Control Act, 15 U.S.C.A. §§ 2619–2620; Coastal Zone Management Act, 16 U.S.C. §§ 1457, 1458(b); Surface Mining Control and Reclamation Act, 30 U.S.C. § 1270.

4. *See generally supra* note 3. Citizen suit provisions appear in, among others, the Clean Air Act, 42 U.S.C. § 7604; Clean Water Act, 33 U.S.C § 1910; Endangered Species Act of 1973, 16 U.S.C. § 1540(g); Resource Conservation and Recovery Act, 42 U.S.C. § 6972; Safe Drinking Water Act, 42 U.S.C. § 300J-8; Toxic Substances Control Act, 15 U.S.C. § 2619; Comprehensive Environmental Response, Compensation, and Liability Act of 1980, 42 U.S.C. § 9659; Emergency Planning and Community Right-to-Know Act, 42 U.S.C. § 11,046. Some environmental statutes do not contain citizen suit provisions—such as the Federal Insecticide, Fungicide and Rodenticide Act (FIFRA), 7 U.S.C. § 136. *See also* Eileen Gauna, *Federal Environmental Citizen Provisions: Obstacles and Incentives on the Road to Environmental Justice*, 22 ECOLOGY L.Q. 1 (1995).

5. *See, e.g.*, 40 C.F.R. § 124.1–.66 (1998) (adopting public participation regulations for permits under the Resource Conservation and Recovery Act, the Clean Water Act, the Safe Drinking Act, and the Clean Air Act).

6. *See, e.g.* Eileen Gauna, *The Environmental Justice Misfit: Public Participation and the Paradigm Paradox*, 17 STAN. ENVTL. L.J. 3, 17–31 (1998) (describing these various approaches); *see also* Jonathan Poisner, *A Civic Republican Perspective on the National Environmental Policy Act's Process for Citizen Participation*, 26 ENVTL. L. 53 (1996).

7. Eileen Gay Jones, *Risky Assessments: Uncertainties in Science and the Human Dimensions of Environmental Decision making*, 22 WM. & MARY ENVTL. L. & POL'Y REV. 1, 24–27 (1997) (discussing how "announce and defend" decision making framework codified in the Administrative Procedure Act is replicated in substantive environmental law); *see also* Jody Freeman, *Collaborative Governance in the Administrative State*, 45 U.C.L.A. L. REV. 1, 14–19 (1997); *but see* Jim Rossi, *Participation Run Amok: The Costs of Mass Participation for Deliberative Agency Decisionmaking*, 92 NW. U. L. Rev. 173 (1998) (arguing that excessive public participation impedes agency deliberation).

8. *See generally* Sheila Foster, *Justice from the Ground Up: Distributive Inequities, Grassroots Resistance, and the Transformative Politics of the Environmental Justice Movement*, 86 CAL. L. REV. 775 (1998) (recounting some of these difficulties by a low-income, minority community in Chester, Pennsylvania).

9. Jones, *supra* note 7, at 41–42 (arguing that "education provides the skills to debate with experts, a basis for criticizing personal habits relevant to the quality of the environment, and facilitates dialogue necessary to reach agreement among decision makers").

10. Gauna, *supra* note 6, at 14.

11. Luke W. Cole, *Macho Law Brains, Public Citizens, and Grassroots Activists: Three Models of Environmental Advocacy*, 14 VA. ENVTL. L.J. 687, 697–701 (1995) (relating view of community activists).

12. Luke W. Cole, *Environmental Justice Litigation: Another Stone in David's Sling*, 21 FORDHAM URB. L.J. 523 (1994).

13. Bradford C. Mank, *Public Participation in the Cleanup and Redevelopment Process*, in I BROWNFIELDS LAW AND PRACTICE: THE CLEANUP AND REDEVELOPMENT OF CONTAMINATED LAND, ch. 31 (Michael B. Gerrard ed., Matthew Bender 1998). *See also* Chapter 17, "Redeveloping Old Facilities," *infra* pages 561–584.

14. GEORGE W. PRING & PENELOPE CANAN, SLAPPS: GETTING SUED FOR SPEAKING OUT 3 (1996) [hereinafter PRING & CANAN] (noting that a form of SLAPP appeared as early as the Revolution when numerous citizens were sued for speaking out against corrupt government officials and citing *Harris v. Huntington*, 2 Tyl. 129 (Vt. 1802)).

15. *Id.*

16. Part 124 does not cover RCRA and UIC "emergency permits" and RCRA "permits by rule." 40 C.F.R. § 124.1 (a). Part 124 also does not apply to PSD permits issued by a State approved to operate a PSD permit program. *Id.* § 124.1 (e).

17. 40 C.F.R. § 124.10.

18. 40 C.F.R. § 124.8.

19. ENVIRONMENTAL PROTECTION AGENCY, RCRA PUBLIC PARTICIPATION MANUAL, ch. 3, at 18, found at <http://www.epa.gov/OSWRCRA/hazwaste/permit/pubpart/manual.htm>.

20. These procedures include beginning and ending dates of public comment period, procedures for requesting a hearing, nature of hearing, and any other procedures by which the public may participate in the final decision. 40 C.F.R. § 124.8 (b).

21. 40 C.F.R. § 124.7.

22. 40 C.F.R. § 124.11.

23. *Id.*

24. 40 C.F.R. § 124.12 (a)(3).

25. 40 C.F.R. § 124.12 (a)(1).

26. 40 C.F.R. § 124.12 (a)(2).

27. 40 C.F.R. § 124.12 (b)–(d).

28. 40 C.F.R. § 124.12.

29. 40 C.F.R. § 124.119.

30. 40 C.F.R. § 124.120–.123.

31. 40 C.F.R. § 124.120.

32. 40 C.F.R. § 124.124–.127.

33. 40 C.F.R. §§ 124.15–.17.

34. 40 C.F.R. § 124.17.

35. 40 C.F.R. § 124.19.

36. 40 C.F.R. § 124.13. A person must petition the Regional Administrator within 30 days of the permit issuance or denial. The petition must identify the issues raised and demonstrate that they were raised during the public comment period. The administrator either grants or denies the petition for review. If review is granted, it is argued on briefs. 40 C.F.R. § 124.19.

37. 40 C.F.R. § 124.19 (f)(1).

38. *See, e.g.* Jones, *supra* note 7, at 24–26 ("Environmental decision making literature indicates there is a pivotal period for public input, after which public participation will not seriously affect substantive decision making. . . . When the public has not participated meaningfully in the proceedings (both in an informal and formal sense) leading to the pivotal decision, or series of pivotal decisions, then the decision rests on a weakened form of political legitimacy and stability.").

39. 911 F.2d 499 (11th Cir. 1990).

40. 40 C.F.R. §§ 124.31–.33.

41. RCRA Expanded Public Participation, 60 Fed. Reg. 63,417–63,434 (December 11, 1995), Number 237, Rules and Regulations [hereinafter RCRA Expanded Public Participation]. Taken from the Federal Register Online via GPO Access <wais.access.gpo.gov>.

42. *Id.* at page 63,419.

43. *Id.* at page 63,420. Elaborating on this, the EPA stated:

> "Prior to the promulgation of today's rule, the permitting process did not formally involve the public until the permitting agency issued a draft permit or an intent to deny a permit. In many cases, communities around RCRA facilities felt that the draft permit stage was too late to enter the process, that the facility and the permitting agency had already made all the major decisions by that point, and any comments the public offered would have no real effect. Insufficient opportunity for communities to become involved in environmental decision making is a contributing factor to environmental justice concerns. The provisions in today's rule will address many of these concerns by expanding public participation and

> access to permitting information. EPA continues to see public participation as an important activity that empowers communities to become actively involved in local waste management activities. The Agency believes that this rulemaking is an important step in empowering all communities, including communities of color and low-income communities."

Id.

44. 40 C.F.R. § 124.31.

45. RCRA Expanded Public Participation, *supra,* note 41 at 63,419.

46. RCRA PUBLIC PARTICIPATION MANUAL, *supra,* note 19, ch. 3, at 4.

47. *Id.* at 5. The EPA advises that applicants address such issues as: what type of facility the company will operate; the location of the facility; the general processes involved and the types of wastes to be generated and managed; and the extent to which minimization and pollution prevention may supplement or replace waste treatment needs. The discussions should also include the transportation routes to be used by waste transporters and planned procedures and equipment for preventing or responding to accidents or releases. *Id.*

48. *Id.*

49. RCRA PUBLIC PARTICIPATION MANUAL, *supra,* note 19, ch. 3, at 4.

50. RCRA PUBLIC PARTICIPATION MANUAL, *supra,* note 19, ch. 3, at 8.

51. 40 C.F.R. § 124.31.

52. RCRA PUBLIC PARTICIPATION MANUAL, *supra,* note 19, ch. 3, at 11.

53. RCRA PUBLIC PARTICIPATION MANUAL, *supra,* note 19, ch. 3, at 8–9.

54. 40 C.F.R. § 124.31(b)

55. RCRA PUBLIC PARTICIPATION MANUAL, *supra,* note 19, ch. 3, at 8.

56. RCRA PUBLIC PARTICIPATION MANUAL, *supra,* note 19, ch. 3, at 7.

57. *Id.* If the meetings are combined, the facility must conduct the part of the meeting dedicated to the RCRA permit.

58. 40 C.F.R. § 124.32.

59. 40 C.F.R. §§ 124.32, 124.10.

60. RCRA Expanded Public Participation, *supra,* note 41, at 63,419.

61. 40 C.F.R. § 124.33.

62. RCRA Expanded Public Participation, *supra,* note 41, at 63,419.

63. Such as:

- the level of public interest;
- the type of facility;
- the presence of an existing repository; and
- the proximity of to the nearest copy of the administrative record.

40 C.F.R. § 124.33(b).

64. The 1995 amendments also require combustion facilities (in other words, incinerators and other facilities that burn hazardous wastes) to notify the public before they hold a trial burn.

65. Specifically, some commentators asked the Agency to define many of the terms in the proposed section, including "all reasonable efforts," "significant," "non-English speaking," and "affected community." The commentators were concerned about the disputes, controversy, and litigation that could arise from these undefined terms. RCRA Expanded Public Participation, *supra,* note 41 at 63,420.

66. *Id.*

67. RCRA Public Participation Manual, *supra*, note 19, at 2. The EPA further explains that "[w]hen communicating with a community, participants in the permitting process should take into account the particular pathways and methods of information transfer that are used by that community." *Id.*

68. *Id.* at 20.

69. Exec. Order No. 12,898, 3 C.F.R. § 859 (1995).

70. *In re Chemical Waste Management of Indiana, Inc.*, RCRA Appeal Nos. 95-2 and 95-3, 1995 EPA App. LEXIS 25, 6 E.A.D. 66, 73–75 (E.A.B. June 29, 1995) (RCRA permit); *In re Envotech, L.P. Milan, MI*, UIC Appeal Nos. 95-2 through 95-37, 1996 EPA App.. LEXIS 4, 6 E.A.D. 260, 280–281 (E.A.B. Feb. 15, 1996) (UIC permit).

71. *Id.* (quoting EPA memorandum entitled Environmental Justice Strategy: Exec. Order 12,898, EPA/200-R-95-002, at 8, Apr., 1995).

72. *In re Chemical Waste Management of Indiana, Inc., supra* note 70; *In re Envotech, L.P. Milan, MI, supra* note 70.

73. The grants are available to any group or individual affected by a release or threatened release at any abandoned hazardous waste facility that is listed on the National Priorities List under the National Contingency Plan. 42 U.S.C. § 9617(e); 40 C.F.R. §§ 35.4000–4130.

74. *As EPA Eyes Changes to TAG Program Citizens Complain NCP Reforms May Hurt Technical Assistance Program*, Envtl. Pol'y Alert, Aug. 12, 1998, at 10.

75. *Id.*

76. *See* GAO, EPA's Superfund Tag Program: Grants Benefit Citizens But Administrative Barriers Remain (Nov. 1992); Deeohn Ferris, *Communities of Color and Hazardous Waste Cleanup: Expanding Public Participation in the Federal Superfund Program*, 21 Fordham L.J. 671, 679 (1994); Mank, *supra* note 13, at 31–17.

77. 62 Fed. Reg. 19,872, 19,881 (1997); *see also* Bradford Mank, *The EPA's Regulatory Reform Initiatives: The Need for Legislative Authorization*, 24 Ecology L.Q. 1 (1998).

78. 42 U.S.C. §§ 4321–70 (1994).

79. The best use of SEPAs in the environmental justice context is expertly set out in Peter Reich, *Greening the Ghetto: A Theory of Environmental Race Discrimination*, 41 Univ. Kan. L. Rev. 271, 305–13 (1992). For more on state mini-NEPA laws, *see generally* Nicholas A. Robinson, *SEQRA's Siblings: Precedents from Little NEPAs in the Sister States*, 46 Alb. L. Rev. 1155 (1982); Jeffrey T. Renz, *The Coming of Age of State Environmental Policy Acts*, 5 Pub. Land L. Rev. 31 (1984); Stephen M. Johnson, *NEPA and SEPAs in the Quest for Environmental Justice*, 30 Loy. L.A. L. Rev. 565 (1997).

80. *See* Alaska Stat. § 38.50.130 (Michie 1997); Cal. Pub. Res. Code §§ 20000–21177 (West 1997); Conn. Gen. Stat. Ann. §§ 22a-1a to -1h (West 1997); D.C. Code Ann. §§ 6-981 to -990 (1997); Ga. Code Ann. §§ 12-16-1 to 12-16-8 (1997); Haw. Rev. Stat. §§ 343-1 to -8 (Michie 1997); Ind. Code Ann. §§ 13-12-4-1 to -4-10 (Burns 1998); Md. Code Ann. Nat. Res. I, §§ 1-301 to -305 (Michie 1997); Mass. Gen. Laws Ann. ch. 30, §§ 61-62H (West 1998); Minn. Stat. Ann. §§ 116D.01 to -.07 (West 1997); Mont. Code Ann. §§ 75-1-101 to -324 (1997); N.Y. Envtl. Conserv. Law §§ 8-0101 to -0117 (1998); N.C. Gen. Stat. §§ 113A-1 to -13 (1997); P.R. Laws Ann. tit. X §§ 1121–1142 (1992); S.D. Codified Laws §§ 34A-9-1 to -13 (Michie 1997); Va. Code Ann. § 10.1-1188 to -1192 (Michie 1997); Wash. Rev. Code Ann. §§ 43.21C.010 to -.910 (West 1997); Wis. Stat. Ann. § 1.11 (West 1997).

81. U.S. Environmental Protection Agency, INTERIM FINAL GUIDANCE FOR INCORPORATING ENVIRONMENTAL JUSTICE CONCERNS IN NEPA COMPLIANCE ANALYSIS (Sept. 30, 1997), found at <http://es.epa.gov/oeca/ofa/ejepa.html>.

82. 42 U.S.C.A. § 4332(2)(C); *see* 40 C.F.R. pts. 1501–08 (1993).

83. *See* Chapter 9, "Impact Assessment," pages 256–306.

84. Under NEPA, each agency is required to develop a classification system that includes three types of agency actions:

1) actions that normally require an EIS;
2) actions that normally require an Environmental Assessment (EA), but not necessarily an EIS; and
3) actions that normally do not require either an EA or EIS.

40 C.F.R. § 1507.3(b). If an agency determines that the 3rd category applies, the regulations require no further work under NEPA. 40 C.F.R. § 1508.4.

85. 40 C.F.R. § 1508.9(a)(1).

86. 40 C.F.R. § 1508.13.

87. 40 C.F.R. § 1501.4. *See also* Richland Park Homeowners Ass'n v. Pierce, 671 F.2d 935, 943 (5th Cir. 1982) (no obligation for public input at this stage); Como-Falcon Community Coalition, Inc. v. United States Dep't of Labor, 609 F.2d 342, 345 (8th Cir. 1979) (same), *cert. denied*, 446 U.S. 936 (1980).

88. 40 C.F.R. § 1501.4 (e)(1).

89. The 30-day public review period is appropriate where: 1) the proposed action is, or is closely similar to, one that normally requires the preparation of a EIS under an agency's procedures; or 2) the nature of the proposed action is one without precedent. 40 C.F.R. § 1501.4(e)(2). *See also* CONN. GEN. STAT. § 22a-1d (the agency preparing an evaluation of or finding of no significant impact must hold a public hearing on the evaluation or finding *if* 25 persons or an association having not less than 25 persons requests such a hearing within 10 days of publication of the notice); MON. ENVIR. HEALTH & SAF. REGS. 17.4.610 (2)–(4) (public review on EA normally not required; however, where an action is one that normally requires an EIS, but effects that otherwise might be deemed significant are mitigated in the project proposal or by controls imposed by the agency, public involvement must include the opportunity for public comment, a public meeting or hearing, and adequate notice).

90. Council on Environmental Quality, Executive Office of the President, THE NATIONAL ENVIRONMENTAL POLICY ACT: A STUDY OF ITS EFFECTIVENESS AFTER TWENTY-FIVE YEARS, January 1997, at 19, found at <http://ceq.eh.doe.gov/nepa/nepanet.htm>.

91. *See, e.g.*, 14 CAL. CODE REGS. tit. X, § 15,073 (Barclays 1998) (agency shall provide a public review period of not less than 30 days for a "proposed negative declaration" or "mitigated negative declaration"); HAW. REV. STAT. § 343–5(c) (public review and comment period of 30 days must be made available for EAs that find no significant impact (FONSI); 1 N.C. ADMIN. CODE tit. X, r.25.0506 (August 1997) (public review comment for period of 30 days).

92. 40 C.F.R. § 1501.7. *But see* 6 N.Y. CODE RULES & REGS. tit. X, § 617.8 (1998) (scoping is not required, but may be initiated by the lead agency or project sponsor.); 1 N.C. ADMIN. CODE tit. X, § 25.0602 (August 1997) (an agency may choose to request advice from the general public and other agencies on what alternatives and issues should be addressed in the EIS).

93. 40 C.F.R. § 1501.7.

94. 40 C.F.R. § 1502.19.

95. 40 C.F.R. § 1506.10(c).

96. 40 C.F.R. § 1502.19(c).

97. 40 C.F.R. § 1503.1(a)(4).

98. 40 C.F.R. § 1506.6(c); *see also* GA. CODE ANN. § 12-16-5 (agency must hold public hearing if it receives requests in writing from at least 100 state residents within the 30 days of publication of notice); 6 N.Y. COMP. CODE RULES & REGS. tit. X, § 617.9(a)(4) (1998) (in determining whether or not to hold a hearing, the lead agency will consider:

- the degree of interest in the action shown by the public or involved agencies;
- whether substantive or significant adverse environmental impacts have been identified;
- the adequacy of the mitigation measures and alternatives proposed; and the extent to which a public hearing can aid the agency decision-making processes by providing a forum for; or
- an efficient mechanism for the collection of, public comment);

1 N.C. ADMIN. CODE tit. X, r.25.0604 (August 1997) (agency may hold a public hearing where significant public interest is expressed in the proposed activity and where such a hearing would be helpful in increasing public awareness, clarifying the issues, and gathering additional public comment).

99. *See, e.g.*, MASS. REGS. CODE tit. X, § 11.08 (West 1998) (agency encouraged to hold public hearings, informal workshops, or public meetings); MINN. R. 4410.2100(10) (informational meeting should be held); WIS. STAT. § 1.11(2)(d) (West 1997) (every proposal other than for legislation shall receive a public hearing before a final decision is made).

100. 40 C.F.R. § 1502.9(b).

101. 40 C.F.R. §§ 1505.2, 1506.10(b)(2).

102. 40 C.F.R. § 1505.2.

103. COUNCIL ON ENVIRONMENTAL QUALITY, FORTY MOST ASKED QUESTIONS CONCERNING CEO'S NATIONAL ENVIRONMENTAL POLICY ACT REGULATIONS, Question 34, 46 Fed. Reg. 18,026, 18,036 (1981) (stating that ROD must be made available for public comment).

104. COUNCIL ON ENVIRONMENTAL QUALITY, EXECUTIVE OFFICE OF THE PRESIDENT, THE NATIONAL ENVIRONMENTAL POLICY ACT: A STUDY OF ITS EFFECTIVENESS AFTER TWENTY-FIVE YEARS, Jan. 1997, 11 at <http://ceq.eh.doe.gov/nepa/nepanet.htm>.

105. *Id.*

106. *Id.* at 18.

107. *Id.* at 18.

108. *Id.* at 29.

109. *El Pueblo para el Aire y Agua Limpio v. County of Kings,* Civ. 366,045, Ruling on Submitted Matter (Sacramento Super. Ct., Dec. 30, 1991), found in 22 ENVTL. L. REP. 20,357.

110. Nine of the terms used in the EIR could not be located in a Webster's unabridged dictionary. *See* Reich, *supra* note 79, at 308. (*citing* Petitioner's Second Amended Petition, at 24–27, *El Pueblo* (No. 366045) *supra* note 109).

111. *Id.* at 309 (*citing* Petitioner's Memorandum of Points and Authorities in Support of Petition for Peremptory Writ of Mandate, 24).

112. *Id.* (*citing* Petitioner's Memorandum of Points and Authorities in Support of Petition for Peremptory Writ of Mandate, at 31–37).

113. *Id.* at 309, n.223 (*citing* Second Amended Petition, at 19).

114. *Id.* at 310 (*citing* Second Amended Petition, at 27).

115. *El Pueblo,* No. 366,045, *slip op.,* at 10. For more on this lawsuit, and the surrounding controversy, see Luke W. Cole, *The Struggle of Kettleman City: Lessons for the Movement,* 5 MD. J. CONTEMP. LEGAL ISSUES 67 (1993–94); Luke W. Cole, *Empowerment as the Means to Environmental Protection: The Need for Environmental Poverty Law,* 19 ECOLOGY L. Q. 619, 674–79 (1992).

116. COUNCIL ON ENVIRONMENTAL QUALITY, ENVIRONMENTAL JUSTICE: GUIDANCE UNDER THE NATIONAL ENVIRONMENTAL POLICY ACT Dec. 10, 1997, at 12–13 <http://ceq.eh.doe.gov/nepa/nepanet.htm>.

117. EPA INTERIM FINAL GUIDANCE FOR INCORPORATING ENVIRONMENTAL JUSTICE CONCERNS IN EPA'S NEPA COMPLIANCE ANALYSIS, Sept. 30, 1997, at sec. 4.2, <http://es.epa.gov/oeca/ofa/ejepa.html>.

118. *See also* U.S. GENERAL SERVICES ADMINISTRATION, PUBLIC BUILDINGS SERVICE, ENVIRONMENTAL JUSTICE AND NEPA, Fact Sheet, NEPA Call-In (February 1998) (making similar recommendations), <http://www.gsa.gov/pbs/pt/call-in/factshet/0298b/02_98_3.htm>.

119. Some may question whether EPA actually has "delegated" its responsibility for managing waste to the states. As one commentator notes, state authority to administer and enforce federal requirements is not a result of "delegation" as that practice is understood in administrative law. Rather, "the federal government suspends its authority to operate its own programs once it approves state programs." Jody Freeman, *Collaborative Governance in the Administrative State,* 45 U.C.L.A. L. J. 1, 15, n.36 (1997).

120. RCRA allows states to establish solid and hazardous waste programs that are more restrictive than the federal minimum. 42 U.S.C. § 6902 (b), 6929. RCRA explicitly acknowledges that "the collection of solid wastes should continue to be primarily the function of State, regional and local agencies." *Id.* § 1002(a)(4). *See also* Celeste P. Duffy, *State Hazardous Waste Facility Siting: Easing the Process Through Local Cooperation and Preemption,* 11 B.C. ENVTL. AFF. L. REV. 755, 757–58, 766–67 (1984); Rodolfo Mata, *Hazardous Waste Facilities and Environmental Equity: A Proposed Siting Model,* 13 VA. ENVTL. L.J. 375, 395–400 (1994).

121. *See, e.g.,* ANDREW SZASZ, ECOPOPULISM: TOXIC WASTE AND THE MOVEMENT FOR ENVIRONMENTAL JUSTICE 183 n.26 (1994) (describing as "passive" approach); Duffy, *supra* note 120 at 766–69 (describing as "ad hoc" approach); *See also* Rachel D. Godsil, *Remedying Environmental Racism,* 90 MICH. L. REV. 394, 403–04 (1991) (describing as "super review" approach); *see also* MICHAEL B. GERRARD, WHOSE BACKYARD, WHOSE RISK: FEAR AND FAIRNESS IN TOXIC AND NUCLEAR WASTE SITING (M.I.T. 1994) (describing and assessing federal and state siting processes).

122. These boards are generally made up of technical experts (geologists, chemical engineers, toxicologists), representatives from industry, state and local public representatives. CONN. GEN. STAT. § 16-50J (1997); IOWA ADMIN. CODE r.150.7 (1997); KY. REV. STAT. ANN. § 224.46-820 (1996); 38 ME. REV. STAT. tit. X,

§ 2152 (1997); MICH. COMP. LAWS § 324.11117 (1998); N.H. REV. STAT. ANN. § 147-A:4 (1997); N.Y. ENVTL. CONSERV. LAW § 27-1113 (1998); OHIO REV. CODE ANN. § 3734.05 (1997); W.VA. CODE ANN., § 22C-5-4 (1997). Some states allow technical assistance to such boards to carry out their duties. *See, e.g.,* MICH. COMP. LAWS § 324.11118 (1998) (providing for application fee from developer to be used by the site review board).

123. COLO. REV. STAT. § 25-25-201, 202 (1997); FLA. STAT. ANN. § 403.723 (1997).

124. W.VA. CODE ANN. § 22C-6-3 (1997).

125. SZASZ, *supra* note 121, at 183; Duffy, *supra* note 120, at 769. Most of the site designation programs were adopted in the 1980s at a time when there was a perceived need for many new hazardous waste disposal facilities. These programs largely failed. The demand for such facilities has greatly declined, and few if any of these programs are still operative for hazardous waste facilities (though they are still common for solid waste facilities). *See* GERRARD, *supra* note 121.

126. *See, e.g.,* IDAHO CODE § 39-5806 (1997); MD. CODE ANN. ENVIR. § 7-410, 411 (1997); N.J. STAT. ANN. §§ 13:1E-54, 59 (1997), UTAH CODE ANN. § 19-6-205 (1997).

127. *See, e.g.,* N.J. ADMIN. CODE tit. X, § 1:26G-15.6 (1998).

128. *See* UTAH CODE ANN. § 19-6-205.

129. *See* UTAH CODE ANN. § 19-6-205 (1997); MD. CODE ANN., ENVIR. § 7-406 (1997).

130. *See, e.g.,* ALA. CODE ANN. § 22-30-12 (1997) (local governing bodies); COLO. REV. STAT. § 25-15-202 (1997) (county commissioners and governing body of any county or municipality within 20 miles of proposed facility); CONN. GEN. STAT. § 22a-119 (1998) (governor and chief elected official of county); FLA. STAT. ch. 403.722 (1997) (each city and county within one mile of facility); GA. CODE ANN. § 12-8-66 (1997); ILL. COMP. STAT. ANN. § 5/39 (1997) (property owners within subject area and within 250 feet in each direction of lot line; and notice general assembly from legislative district where facility located); IOWA CODE § 455B.443 (1997) (city council and board of supervisors of each city and county in which facility is located); 38 ME. REV. STAT. ANN., § 1319-R (1997) (municipal officers); 25 PA. CODE § 271.141 (1997) (property owners); 10 MONT. ENVTL. HEALTH & SAFETY REGS. § 25-8.010 (1996) (adjoining property owners and local representatives); N.H. REV. STAT. ANN. § 147-A:4 (1997) (governing board of municipality); N.Y. ENVTL. CONSERV. LAW § 27-1105 (1998) (property owners of record within 300 feet of facility). Some states also allow individuals to personally request placement on a mailing list. *See, e.g.,* MONT. ENVTL. HEALTH & SAFETY REGS. § 17.54.907 (1995); 20 N.M. ADMIN. CODE, § 4.1.IX.901 (1998). Pursuant to such a request, the state will personally notify the individual of a proposal to construct a facility in the community. 40 C.F.R. § 124.10 (RCRA permits).

131. Omar Saleem, *Overcoming Environmental Discrimination: The Need for a Disparate Impact Test and Improved Notice Requirements in Facility Siting Decisions,* 19 COLUM. J. ENVTL. L. 211, 240–41 (1994).

132. *See, e.g.,* Foster, *supra* note 8, at 815 (recounting this incident in Chester, Pennsylvania); Cole, *supra* note 115 (recounting that public notice may have escaped the community due to publication of such notice in a small box in the classified ads in the newspaper of "general circulation").

133. *See, e.g.*, TEX. HEALTH & SAFETY CODE ANN. § 361.0791 (1998) (requiring published notice be no smaller than 96.8 square centimeters or 15 square inches with the shortest dimension at least 7.6 centimeters or 3 inches).

134. *See, e.g.*, Exec. Order No. 12,898, *supra* note 69, § 5-5; COUNCIL ON ENVIRONMENTAL QUALITY, ENVIRONMENTAL JUSTICE: GUIDANCE UNDER THE NATIONAL ENVIRONMENTAL POLICY ACT, *supra* note 116, at 12–13.

135. *See, e.g.*, Exec. Order No. 12,898, *supra* note 69, § 5-5; H.B. 518, 90th Leg., 1st Sess. § 15 (Ill. 1997).

136. *See, e.g.*, CAL. PUB. RES. CODE § 25199.7 (1997); IOWA ADMIN. CODE r.150.3 (1997); MASS. ANN. LAWS ch. X, § 21D-7 (1998); MICH. COMP. LAWS ANN. § 11,118 (1998); NEB. REV. STAT. § 81-1521.09 (1997); N.D. ADMIN. CODE § 33-24-07-25 (1998); N.J. ADMIN. CODE tit. X, 1:26G-15.6 (1998); VT. STAT. ANN. tit. X, § 6606A (1997); VA. CODE ANN. § 10.1-1437 (1997); WASH. ADMIN. CODE §§ 173-303-281 & 173-303-902 (1997). RCRA also requires pre-application notice and meeting. 40 C.F.R. § 124.31.

137. ALA. CODE § 22-30-12 (1997); COLO. REV. STAT. § 25-15-202 (1997); CONN. GEN. STAT. § 22A-119 (1998); 7 DEL. CODE ANN. tit. X, § 6004 (1997); FLA. STAT. ch. 403.722 & 723 (1997); GA. ANN. CODE § 12-8-66 (1997); IDAHO CODE § 39-5814 (1997); 415 ILL. COMP. STAT. ANN. 5/39.2 (1997); IND. CODE ANN. 13-22-10-14 (1998); KAN. STAT. ANN. § 65-3433 (1997); KY. REV. STAT. ANN. § 224.46-825 (1996); LA. REV. STAT. ANN. § 30:2199 (1998); 38 ME. REV. STAT. ANN. tit. X, § 1319-R (1997); MINN. R. 7001.0660 (1997); 10 MO. CODE REGS. ANN. tit. X, § 25-8.010 (1996); N.H. REV. STAT. ANN. § 147-A:4 (1997); N.Y. ENVTL. CONSERV. LAW § 27-1105 (1998); OHIO ADMIN. CODE § 3745-50-40 (1998); ORE. REV. STAT. § 466.125 (1996); 25 PA. CODE § 269.124 (1997); TENN. COMP. R. & REGS. tit. X, ch. 1200-1-14.02 (1997); WIS. STAT. § 289.25 (1997); WYO. STAT. ANN. § 35-11-502 (1997).

138. *See, e.g.*, MONT. ENVT. HEALTH & SAFETY REGS. § 17.54.903 (1995) (draft permit); N.M. ADMIN. CODE tit. X, § 4.1.IX.901 (1998) (draft permit); W. VA. CODE § 22-18-10 (1997). In some of these states, however, other opportunities are given for public participation. *See, e.g.*, R.I. GEN. LAWS § 23-19.7-6 (1997) (permit notice, but local advisory committee).

139. DANIEL P. SELMI & KENNETH A. MANASTER, STATE ENVIRONMENTAL LAW, § 8.03[2][c], at 8-30 (West Group, 1997).

140. *See, e.g.*, PA. CODE § 269.142 (1997); TENN. COMP. R. & REGS. tit. X, ch. 1200-1-14-.02 (1997); UTAH ADMIN. CODE § R315-3-38.3 (1997).

141. *See, e.g.*, CAL. PUB. RES. CODE § 25199.7 (1997); NEB. REV. STAT. § 81-1521.11 (1997); N.J. ADMIN. CODE tit. X, § 1:26G-15.6 (1998); N.D. ADMIN. CODE § 33-24-07-25 (1998); VA. CODE ANN. § 10.1-1439 (1997). RCRA also requires pre-application meeting. 40 C.F.R. § 124.31.

142. *See, e.g.*, ARK. CODE ANN. § 8-7-217 (1997); CAL. HEALTH & SAFETY CODE § 20-6.5-25199.7 (1997); COLO. REV. STAT. § 25-15-202 (1997); CONN. GEN. STAT. § 22A-119 (1998); IDAHO CODE § 39-5814 (1997); ILL. COMP. STAT. ANN. 5/39.2 (1997); IOWA CODE § 455B.452 (1997); KY. REV. STAT. ANN. § 224.46-825 (1996); ME. REV. STAT. ANN. tit. X, § 1319-R (1997); MD. CODE ANN. ENVIR. § 7-406 (1997); MASS. ANN. LAWS ch. X, § 21D-8 (1998); MICH. COMP. LAWS ANN. § 324.11120 (1998); MISS. CODE ANN. § 17-18-19 (1997); N.H. REV. STAT. ANN. § 147-A:4 (1997); OHIO REV. CODE ANN. § 3734 (1997); ORE. REV. STAT. § 466.130 (1996); 25 PA. CODE § 269.13 (1997); TENN. COMP. R. & REGS. tit. X, § 1200-1-14-.02 (1997); TEX. HEALTH

& SAFETY CODE ANN. § 361.0791 (1998); 10 VT. STAT. ANN. tit. X, § 6606A (1997); VA. CODE ANN. § 10.1-1444 (1997); W. VA. CODE § 22C-5-4 (1997).

143. *See, e.g.*, ALA. CODE § 22-30-12 (1997); DEL. CODE ANN. tit. X, § 6004 (1997); GA. CODE ANN. § 12-8-66 (1997); HAW. REV. STAT. § 342J-5 (1997); IND. STAT. ANN. § 13-5-3-3 (1998); LA. REV. STAT. ANN. § 30:2018 (1997); MINN. R. 7001.0670 (1997); 10 MO. CODE REGS. ANN. tit. X, § 25-8.010 (1996); MONT. ENVTL. HEALTH & SAFETY REGS. 17.54.909 (1997); NEB. REV. STAT. § 81-1521.20 (1997); 20 N.M. ADMIN. CODE tit. X, § 4.1.IX.901 (1998); N.D. ADMIN. CODE § 33-24-07-08 (1998); WASH. ADMIN. CODE § 173-303-840 (1997); WIS. STAT. § 289.26 & .37 (1997); WYO. STAT. ANN. § 35-11-502 (1997). However, even though a public hearing on the application may be discretionary, some states also require a pre-application hearing or have a local advisory committee to facilitate public involvement. *See, e.g.*, IND. ADMIN. CODE. tit. X, r.3.1-13-10 & 12 (1998); NEB. REV. STAT. § 1521.09 (1997); WASH. ADMIN. CODE § 173-303-282 (1997); WIS. STAT. § 289.33 (1997).

144. *See, e.g.*, Marke Jaffe, *A Local Victory in Pollution War*, PHILA. INQUIRER, Dec. 31, 1997, at 1 (noting that the proposed plant "had received its permits by the time the community found out about it, and efforts to rescind them were unsuccessful").

145. *See, e.g.*, N.Y. ENVTL. CONSERV. LAW § 27-1105(3); (1998) N.J. ADMIN. CODE tit. X, § 1:26-15.6.

146. Gauna, *supra* note 6, at 65.

147. John S. Applegate, *Beyond the Usual Suspects: The Use of Citizens Advisory Boards in Environmental Decision Making*, 73 IND. L.J. 903, 910 (1998).

148. *See generally* Applegate, *supra*, note 147.

149. *See, e.g.*, CAL. HEALTH & SAFETY CODE § 20-6.5-25199.7 (1997); CONN. GEN. STAT. 22A-127 (1998); MASS. ANN. LAWS ch. X, § 21D-5 (1998); MISS. CODE ANN. § 17-18-35 (1997); NEB. REV. STAT. § 1521.09-.11 (1997); N.H. REV. STAT. ANN. § 147-C:4 (1997); N.Y. ENVTL. CONSERV. LAW. § 27-1113 (1998); N.C. GEN. STAT. § 130B-19 (1997); ORE. REV. STAT. § 466.050 (1996); R.I. GEN. LAWS § 23-19.7-4 (1997); VA. CODE ANN. § 10-1-1437 (1997); WASH. ADMIN. CODE § 173-303-902 (1997).

150. *See, e.g.*, CAL. HEALTH & SAFETY CODE § 20-6.5-25199.7 (1997) (providing for grant to assist local assessment committee); CONN. GEN. STAT. § 22A-127 (applicant fee available to local project review committee for technical and professional assistance) (1998); MASS. ANN. LAWS ch. X, § 21D-11 (1998) (providing for technical assistance grants at the request of the local assessment committee); N.C. GEN. STAT. § 130B-20 (1997) (providing for local advisory committee to apply for a portion of the developer's application fee); R.I. GEN. LAWS § 23-19.7-7 (1997) (providing for compensation to local assessment committee for, among other things, hiring expert witnesses); VA. CODE ANN. § 10-1-1438 (1997) (providing for funds to local advisory committee to hire consultants for technical assistance); WASH. ADMIN. CODE § 173-303-902 (1997) (providing for citizen proponents negotiation grant).

151. *See, e.g.*, Luke W. Cole, *The Theory and Reality of Community-Based Environmental Decision Making: The Failure of California's Tanner Act and Its Implications for Environmental Justice*, 25 ECOLOGY L.Q. 733, 745–47 (1999).

152. MISS. CODE ANN. § 17-18-35 (1997); N.Y. ENVTL. CONSERV. LAW. § 27-1113 (1998); ORE. ADMIN. R. § 340-120-020 (1996); R.I. GEN. LAWS § 23-19.7-6 (1997);

WASH. ADMIN. CODE § 173-303-902 (1997) (providing for "citizens proponents negotiation" process).

153. Applegate, *supra*, note 147, at 921.

154.. *Id. See also* Cole, *The Theory and Reality of Community-Based Environmental Decision Making, supra* note 151.

155. Jones, *supra*, note 7, at 60.

156. The following account is taken from two opinions in the case of the Genesee Power Plant in Flint, Michigan, one from the U.S. Environmental Protection Agency Appeals Board, *In re Genesee Power Station Ltd. Partnership,* 1993 WL 484880 (E.P.A. at 7) (Oct. 22, 1993), and another from a state court suit, NAACP v. Engler, Genesee County Circuit Court, unpublished opinion, Case 95-38228-CV (May 29, 1997).

157. *In re Genesee Power Station Ltd. Partnership,* 1993 WL 484880 (E.P.A. at 7) (Oct. 22, 1993)

158. NAACP v. Engler, Case No. 95-38228-CV, Genesee County Circuit Court, at 43, May 29, 1997.

159. *Id.* at 14.

160. *Id.* at 43.

161. *See generally* Mary Greczyn, *Michigan Court Allows Permit,* WASTE NEWS, Dec. 7, 1998, 1998 WL 8229771.

162. *See Letter from EPA's Office of Civil Rights re Select Steel,* October 30, 1998. This letter can be found at <http://www.epa.gov/reg5oopa/steelcvr.htm>.

163. 42 U.S.C. §§ 2000d–2000d-4 (1994). (Title VI); 40 C.F.R. pt. 7 (regulations). There are obvious benefits to suing under the regulations, as opposed to the statute itself. The United States Supreme Court has ruled that a violation of the statute requires proof of discriminatory intent, whereas proof of discriminatory effect suffices to establish liability when the suit is brought to enforce regulations issued pursuant to the statute. *See* Guardians Ass'n v. Civil Service Comm'n of New York, 463 U.S. 582, 591–93 (1983). *See also* Chapter 2, "Title VI," *supra* pages 23–68.

164. *See* ALI-ABA Course of Study, *SLAPPs: Strategic Lawsuits Against Public Participation in Government,* at C935 ALI-ABA 1, 9 (1994).

165. *Id.* at 10. Other issues, in descending order, likely to initiate a SLAPP are: criticism of public officials, environmental protection, civil/human rights, neighborhood problems, and consumer issues. *Id.*

166. *Id.* Others that are frequently the targets of SLAPPs, in descending order, are: citizens representing organizations, citizens acting on their own vested economic/property interests, or citizens dealing with family matters. *Id.*

167. *Id.* These are followed by civic organizations (neighborhood groups/good government leagues), membership/property groups (homeowner associations, unions), political groups, and business-industry/professional groups. *Id.*

168. PRING & CANAN, *supra* note 14, at 8.

169. *Id.* at 8–9.

170. Gorman Towers, Inc. v. Bogoslavsky, 626 F.2d 607 (8th Cir. 1980).

171. Maple Properties v. Harris, No. C299570 (Super. Ct., Los Angeles County, Cal., Apr. 24, 1980), *rev'd and remanded sub. nom.* Okun v. Superior Court, 29 Cal. 3d 442, 629 P.2d 1369, 175 Cal. Rptr. 157 (1981), *cert. denied,* 454 U.S. 1099 (1981), *dism. on remand* (Super. Ct., Los Angeles County, Cal., 1984), *aff'd,* 158 Cal. App. 3d 997, 205 Cal. Rptr. 532 (1984), *cert. denied,* 105 S. Ct. 1758 (1985).

172. Westfield Partners, Ltd. v. Hogan, 740 F. Supp. 523 (N.D. Ill. 1990).

173. Webb v. Fury, 282 S.E.2d 28 (W.Va. 1981); Leonardini v. Shell Oil Co., 216 Cal. App.3d 547, 264 Cal. Rptr. 883 (1989), *cert. denied,* 111 S. Ct. 293 (1990); Story v. Shelter Bay Co., 52 Wash. App. 334, 760 P.2d 368 (1988); Streif v. Bovinette, 88 Ill. App. 3d 1079, 411 N.E.2d 341 (1980).

174. *See* ALI-ABA Course of Study, *SLAPPs: Strategic Lawsuits Against Public Participation in Government, supra* note 164, at 17.

175. *Id.* at 12.

176. *See* ALI-ABA Course of Study, *SLAPPs: Strategic Lawsuits Against Public Participation in Government, supra* note 164, at 12. (1994). *See, e.g.,* SRW Associates v. Bellport Beach Property Owners, No. 24211/84 (Sup. Ct., Suffolk County, N.Y., *filed* Oct. 26, 1984); 129 A.D.2d 328, 517 N.Y.S. 2d 741 (*dismissed* July 13, 1987); Webb v. Fury, 282 S.E. 2d 28 (W.Va. 1981).

177. 349 F. Supp. 934 (N.D. Cal. 1972).

178. 349 F. Supp. at 936.

179. *See* ALI-ABA Course of Study, *SLAPPs: Strategic Lawsuits Against Public Participation in Government, supra* note 164, at 12.

180. *See id.* at 12. *See, e.g.,* SRW Associates v. Bellport Beach Property Owners, 129 A.D.2d 328, 517 N.Y.S. 2d 741 (*dismissed* July 13, 1987); Webb v. Fury, 282 S.E. 2d 28 (W.Va. 1981).

181. 499 U.S. 365, 380, 111 S. Ct. 1344 (1991).

182. *See* ALI-ABA Course of Study, *SLAPPs: Strategic Lawsuits Against Public Participation in Government, supra* note 164, at 12.

183. *See* PRING & CANAN, *supra* note 14, at 169; *See generally* ALI-ABA Course of Study, *SLAPPs: Strategic Lawsuits Against Public Participation in Government, supra* note 164, at 17.

184. *See* PRING & CANAN, SLAPPs, *supra* note 14, at 173.

185. 216 Cal. App. 3d 547, 566, 264 Cal. Rptr. 883, 894 (1989).

186. *See* PRING & CANAN, *supra* note 14, at 170.

187. 264 Cal. Rptr. 883, 901.

188. *Id.* at 898.

189. *See also* Martin L. Haines, *SLAPPing Back,* N.J. L.J., Sept. 21, 1998 (noting the largest verdict in a SLAPPback case: $86.5 million against an infectious waste disposal company that SLAPPed a critic of its incinerator operation).

190. CAL. CIV. PROC. CODE § 425.16 (1992); N.Y. C.P. L.R., 3211, 3212 (1986); N.Y. CIV. RIGHTS LAW § 70-a (1992), 76-a (1993); R.I. GEN. LAWS § 9-33-1, 9-33-2 (1993); WASH. REV. CODE ANN. § 4.24.500–.520 (1989); MASS. ANN. LAWS ch. 231, § 59H (1995); NEV. REV. STAT. § 41.637–.660 (1997); MINN. STAT. ANN. § 554 (1994); DEL. CODE ANN. tit. 10, § 8136–38 (1992); NEB. REV. STAT. § 25-21,241–46 (1994).

191. *See* 1997 TENN. S.B. 396, 1997 TENN. H.B. 2129 (bills provide for immunity from liability, lawyers' fees and damages, and government intervention on behalf of moving party); 1997 PA. H.B. 1868, 1997 PA. H.B. 394, 1997 PA. S.B. 987, 1997 PA. H.B. 1744 (bills provide for immunity, lawyers' fees, and intervention of a government agency); 1997 FL. H.B. 3549, 1997 FL. S.B. 272, 1999 FL. S.B. 18 (bills provide motion for summary judgment procedure, suspension of discovery process, damages for moving party, lawyers' fees and costs); 1998 N.J. A.B. 1788, 1998 N.J. A.B. 1194, 1998 N.J. S.B. 745 (bills provide for prompt motion to dismiss, stay of discovery, and lawyers' fees and costs).

192. N.Y. CIV. RIGHTS LAW § 76-a (1992) (SLAPPback plaintiffs need prove only that the filer lacked a "substantial basis" for suing and had the "purpose of harassing, intimidating" the plaintiff); WASH. REV. CODE ANN. § 4.24.510 (1989) (reasonable lawyers' fees and costs to prevailing defense party); CAL. CIV. PROC. CODE § 425.16 (c) (1992) (lawyers' fees and costs to party prevailing on special motion to strike); MINN. STAT. ANN. §§ 554.0 (1994) (lawyers' fees and costs to party prevailing on his motions to dismiss), 554.04 (SLAPP defendant may recover actual or punitive damages where the SLAPP was brought for purpose of harassment, to interfere with the defendant's exercise of protected constitutional rights, or otherwise wrongfully injured the SLAPP defendant), and 549.20 (punitive damages); DEL. CODE ANN. tit. X, § 8136 (1992) (recovery of lawyers' fees and costs) and 8138 (recovery of compensatory damages where a SLAPP defendant can prove that the suit was "commenced or continued without a substantial basis in fact or law" and punitive damages where the defendant can prove that the suit was commenced for the purpose of "harassing, intimidating, punishing, or otherwise maliciously inhibiting the free exercise of speech, petition or association rights"); NEB. REV. STAT. § 25-21,243 (1994) (lawyers' fees and costs may be recovered where the action was "without a substantial basis in fact and law and could not be supported by a substantial argument for the extension, modification, or reversal of existing law"; also allows for compensatory damages where the action was commenced or continued for the purpose of "harassing, intimidating, punishing, or otherwise maliciously inhibiting the free exercise of petition, speech or association rights").

193. SELMI & MANASTER, *supra* note 139, § 11.12[3][a], at 11-111.

194. R.I. GEN. Laws § 9-33-2 (e) (1993); MASS. ANN. LAWS ch. 231, § 59H (1995); CAL. CIV. PROC. CODE § 425.16 (e) (1992).

195. WASH. REV. CODE ANN. § 4.24.510 (1989); NEV. REV. STAT. § 41.637 (1997).

196. N.Y. CIV. RIGHTS LAW § 76-a (1); DEL. CODE ANN. § 8136 (a); NEB. REV. STAT. § 25-21,242.

197. *See supra* note 196.

198. N.Y. CIV. RIGHTS LAW § 76-a (1).

199. *See* PRING & CANAN, *supra* note 14, at 192.

200. WASH REV. CODE ANN. § 4.24.510 (1989).

201. Gilman v. MacDonald, 74 Wash. App. 733, 875 P.2d 697, 700 (1994).

202. WASH. REV. CODE ANN. § 4.24.520 (1989).

203. *Id.* § 4.24.510 (1989).

204. R.I. GEN. LAWS § 9-33-2 (1993).

205. *Id.*

206. *Id.*

207. *See* Hometown Properties, Inc. v. Fleming, 680 A.2d 56, 64 (R.I. 1996).

208. NEV. REV. STAT. § 41.637 (1997) (special motion to dismiss); MINN. STAT. ANN. § 554.02 (1994) (discovery suspended and responding party has burden of proof or persuasion on motion to dismiss); MASS. ANN. LAWS ch. 231, § 59H (1995) (court suspends discovery process until a ruling is made on a motion to dismiss); CAL. CIV. PROC. CODE § 425.16 (1992) (discovery stayed during motion to strike); DEL. CODE ANN. § 8137 (1992) (motion to dismiss and summary judgement); NEB. REV. STAT. §§ 25-21,245 and 25-21,246 (1994) (setting out similar requirements for motion to dismiss and motion for summary judgment); N.Y.

C.P. L.R. §§ 3211(g)–3211(h) (requirements for motion to dismiss and summary judgment).

209. *See* Dixon v. Superior Court, 30 Cal. App. 4th 733, 36 Cal. Rptr. 2d 687, 697 (1994) (rejecting argument that statute deprives litigants right to jury trial on the ground that there was no question of fact to be decided by the trial court); Hometown Properties, Inc. v. Fleming, 680 A.2d 56, 60 (R.I. 1996) (rejecting constitutional challenges); *but see Opinion of the Justices (SLAPP Suit Procedure)* 641 A.2d 1012, 1015 (N.H. 1994) (ruling that such legislation unconstitutionally deprives plaintiffs of their right to jury trial under the New Hampshire constitution).

210. N.Y. C.P. L.R. §§ 3211(g)–3211(h).

211. N.Y. CIV. RIGHTS LAW § 70-a(1)(a) (1992).

212. CAL. CIV. PROC. CODE § 425.16 (1992).

213. *See* Ludwig v. Superior Court, 37 Cal. App. 4th 8, 43 Cal. Rptr. 2d 350, 356 (1995).

214. *Id.*

215. CAL. CIV. PROC. CODE § 425.16(b) (1992).

216. *Id.* at § 425.16(g).

CHAPTER 8

Access to Information

BERNARD A. WEINTRAUB

Introduction: Access to Information in the Environmental Justice Context

Access to relevant information plays a central role in creating and resolving controversies, including environmental controversies, in the United States. Because environmental and other quality-of-life laws often rely on citizen enforcement to supplement underfunded governmental agencies, such enforcement could not occur without public access to information regarding the compliance behavior of a regulated entity. Furthermore, as any person experienced in litigation can attest, access to potent information can help persuade a trier of fact to find in one side's favor or can change significantly the value of a claim. Access to such information, therefore, can shift the relative strengths of the parties' positions and make settling the controversy more or less desirable than had been the situation before the information in question came into play. In short, access to information can improve one's ability to create, understand, or settle an environmental controversy.

In the environmental justice context, access to information about environmental matters is of extraordinary importance. This is so because community members alleging environmental injustices often have less access to relevant information than the targets of their allegations. In fact, some environmental justice advocates have claimed that systematic inequality in the distribution of information about environmental matters is a symptom of environmental injustice. Certain proposals to counter environmental injustices include the reallocation of resources in a manner that assures more equitable access to relevant information about environmental matters.

This chapter describes different sources of publicly available information that may be of use in environmental justice controversies. Such information can concern, for example, a regulated entity's compliance with environmental law, its involvement in site contamination and/or remediation, its environmental management policies and practices, and its specific projects that might have an adverse environmental impact.[1] While the primary source of most information discussed in this chapter is a regulated entity (which may be the target of a particular allegation of environmental injustice) that is required to disclose the information in question to the government, the information is made available to the public in most cases by governmental agencies.

It should be noted that this chapter will not address two traditional sources of information relevant to environmental justice controversies. First, as numerous anecdotes and experience generally suggest, the members of the community adversely affected by a threat to environmental justice often have information and insights regarding the source of that threat that the source itself either is unwilling to provide to the public or, in some cases, does not know. However, because this source of information is not institutionalized and because seeking and obtaining information from community members frequently must be undertaken in an informal, community-specific manner, it is left to the party seeking useful information to devise a method of accessing and extracting it. Second, because numerous other texts are better suited to provide an outline and discussion of the relevant procedures, discovery of information in the context of litigation will not be treated here.[2]

Electronic Databases

Large caches of data are available on electronic databases that are increasingly accessible via the Internet. The number of databases accessible to the public is large and growing. Only a few of the more noteworthy ones are mentioned in this chapter.

The information contained in electronic databases is collected in many ways. It often is difficult to ascertain and scrutinize the manner of such collection from the database itself. Therefore, it is difficult to judge the quality and comprehensiveness of the information provided. It is prudent to be skeptical of all information gathered from electronic databases.

Government Databases

Various governmental agencies have established databases that may provide useful information to the public. Many of these databases are available both directly (for the price of a computer telephone connection) by contacting the relevant originating agency or any associated Internet web site and indirectly (often for a surcharge) through database information providers such as LEXIS/NEXIS and WESTLAW. Most databases may be searched with reference to one or more variables that are database-specific. Many databases also may be searched for "key words," which may be any word or words that identify characteristics of interest to the user (for example, "copper," "particulate," "transfer site," or "violation").

The United States Environmental Protection Agency (EPA) and many state agencies have established publicly available databases providing information regarding various aspects of the agency's environmental activities. Examples of EPA databases that may be of interest to those involved with an environmental justice controversy, which are available from for-profit access providers such as LEXIS/NEXIS (by searching the ENVIRON library and SITES file) or directly from the agency via the Internet by contacting the EPA's Envirofacts database at <http://www.epa.gov/enviro/index_java.html>, include:

- Potentially Responsible Parties Superfund Enforcement Tracking System (PRP)
- RCRA Corrective Action Records (CORRACTS)
- Toxic Chemical Release Inventory (TRIS)[3]
- Leaking Underground Storage Tanks Site Records (LUST)

The United States Securities and Exchange Commission provides access to information regarding publicly traded companies, such as environmental and financial disclosures required by federal law, at <http://ftp.sec.gov/edaux/formlynx.htm>. The Department of Commerce also provides census information that may be useful to those seeking more information regarding the demographic profile of specific locations, at <http://www.census.gov>.

Of related interest is the One Stop Reporting Program, which was initiated in 1995 by the EPA to:

1. improve state and federal regulatory management by promoting cross-media approaches to solving environmental problems;
2. improve public access to environmental information; and
3. simplify reporting burdens by taking advantage of new technologies.

To further these goals, the Program attempts to build EPA/state partnerships in data management to establish an efficient, national environmental data management system that serves and is accessible by regulators, the public, and the regulated community. The One Stop Reporting Program provides information, guidance, and grant money to states to help foster state-level, cross-media environmental databases and information-access templates. States that already have received grants from and joined the One Stop Reporting Program (as of May 1998) are: Arizona, Florida, Georgia, Indiana, Maryland, Massachusetts, Minnesota, Mississippi, Missouri, New Hampshire, New Jersey, New Mexico, New York, Oklahoma, Oregon, Pennsylvania, Texas, Utah, Washington, West Virginia, and Wisconsin. EPA has stated its goal to have all 50 states join the Program by the year 2003. The One Stop Program can be accessed via the Internet at <http://www.epa.gov/ooaujeag/onestop/index.html>.

Internet

The Internet has been a great benefit to those seeking information relating to environmental justice topics. Not only do many grassroots environmental justice organizations have Internet web sites that provide valuable (and not-so-valuable) information, including case studies and "lessons learned" discussions, but many environmental justice web sites have been established primarily to be a resource in an environmental justice controversy.

While there are many environmental justice links, the web sites at <www.halcyon.com/ccej/EJlinks> and <www.ecok.edu/~polsci/envrjust/ejlinks/ejlinks.html> provide useful access points. These web sites provide links to sources, bibliographies, organizations, governmental web sites, international web sites, academic web sites, and web sites categorized by case studies, health effects, and "solutions." These web sites as well as other similar web sites, also can provide links to publicly available information organized by a Geographic Information Systems (GIS) database. See "Geographic Information Systems Mapping," pages 235–237.

A few interesting new web sites have come online in the recent past. These include the following four EPA web sites and one web site established by a national environmental organization.

Envirofacts <www.epa.gov/enviro.index.html> has been established by EPA. Updated monthly, the Envirofacts database contains cross-media (for example, Superfund status, hazardous waste issues, drinking water violations, water pollution discharges, toxic and air releases) information on individual facilities. A user of Envirofacts can search selected or all linked databases, by facility name, location,

Standard Industrial Classification (SIC) code number or any other data elements. The database in some instances includes a link to allow the user to access the web site of a specific facility. EPA plans to expand this database to include more information and compliance and enforcement information.

In the summer of 1998, EPA opened a web site that permits users to search a wide range of agency databases by ZIP code or county at <www.epa.gov/ceis>. The web page is administered by EPA's Center for Environmental Information and Statistics and includes links to information on health effects of pollutants. The web site includes more than 100 EPA reports related to environmental quality in select states, communities, counties, ZIP codes, EPA regions, and the nation overall, and also includes maps showing environmental data in graphic form.

EPA's Sector Facility Indexing Project (the SFIP) can be located at <www.epa.gov/oeca/sfi>. The SFIP provides facility-specific information across media, but does not provide information on the company that is responsible for the facility. Initiated on May 1, 1998, the database provides comprehensive information on a facility-specific basis for 653 facilities in five sectors: automobile assembly, pulp manufacturing, petroleum refining, iron and steel production, and smelting and refining of nonferrous metals (aluminum, copper, lead and zinc). Information provided includes information on past inspections and enforcement actions, facility size, Toxic Release Inventory (TRI) information, and some data about surrounding communities. EPA plans to expand the database to include other sectors.

In December 1998, EPA initiated a web site at <www.epa.gov/oppecumm> that allows any user to access, by state or county, concentrations of hazardous air pollutants (HAPs) regulated under the Clean Air Act.[4]

The Environmental Defense Fund (EDF) recently established the Chemical Scorecard at <www.scorecard.org>. The Chemical Scorecard, which combines information from more than 150 databases and provides summary data on 50 states, 2,000 counties, 5,000 ZIP codes and 17,000 facilities, provides the public with information about chemical releases from industrial sources. Users who enter a ZIP code are provided with a list of TRI reporters in that ZIP code. Also provided are maps indicating the location of the reporting facilities. Going one step beyond just providing information, the Chemical Scorecard ranks chemicals on the severity of the health risks created by exposure to those chemicals and ranks each facility in terms of the EDF-determined health risks posed. The Chemical Scorecard provides users with the ability to send a free fax to the facility expressing concerns about emissions.

Examples of web sites of potential use in an environmental justice controversy, other than those listed in this chapter, include:

- EcoNet's Environmental Racism/Environmental Justice Resources <http://www.igc.apc.org/envjustice>
- Environmental and Occupational Health Resources Guide, The Environmental and Occupational Health Sciences Institute (EOHSI) <http://www.eohsi.rutgers.edu/newPublic/ascii/guide1.html>
- Environmental Inequality Bibliography <http://www.cruzio.com/~meuser/ejwww.html>
- (EPA) Office of Solid Waste and Emergency Response Environmental Justice Publications <http://www.epa.gov/swerosps/ej/ejpub.htm>
- Executive Order: Federal Actions to address environmental justice in minority populations and low-income populations <http://www.fs.fed.us/land/envjust.html>
- Summary of the Environmental Justice Movement <http://es.inel.gov/program/initiative/justice/ej-ovrvw.html>
- University of Michigan Environmental Justice Database <http://www.msue.msu.edu/msue/imp/modej/masterej.html>

Popular Media and Scholarly Journals

Information of potential use in an environmental justice controversy is also provided by the popular media and/or scholarly journals. For years, newspapers, magazines, radio stations, and television stations have made copies of articles and transcripts available for public dissemination. While little of this information was available electronically in the past, increasingly the information is available via computer. Many of these sources have their own web sites. For-profit database access providers such as LEXIS/NEXIS and WESTLAW provide the ability to search numerous media sources simultaneously, including many sources that do not provide electronic access themselves.

Geographic Information Systems Mapping

A Geographic Information System (GIS) can be used to link geographically coded databases to maps of a given area. Thus, if the information contained in a database can be coded to a map, by selecting desired coordinates and variables a user of a GIS will be treated to a visual representation of the geographic distribution of the variables within the selected coordinates. Such computer maps provide graphic information that heretofore had never been correlated in one place. For example, if programmed to do so, a GIS can display all tax lots within the selected area that are:

(a) within neighborhoods where the average family income is below the federal poverty level;
(b) within one quarter of a mile of a known leaking underground storage tank; and
(c) that have buildings on them that are at least 40 years old.

Or, as another example, a GIS may be able to show all public schools that are within two blocks of manufacturing plants that use toxic chemicals where spills of those chemicals have occurred during selected years.

Proponents of GIS imaging claim that the correlations depicted on GIS maps may provide visual proof of environmental injustice. Regardless of the probity of any given GIS map, such maps are powerful tools for visualizing and understanding the distribution of various benefits and burdens, including environmental ones, borne by communities.

A GIS database can include any variable that can be represented on a map. The quality of a given GIS program is correlated to the quality of the databases on which the mapping is based. While an enormous amount of information is available for geographic representation, the information varies dramatically in quality. Some information is updated frequently; some is not. However, with respect to environmental justice information, where it is not always obvious which sets of data will indicate a pattern that can be claimed to prove unjust distribution of environmental burdens and/or benefits, a general rule is that the more varied and more comprehensive the databases (representing various relevant variables) gathered in one GIS database, the better. Generally, the information contained in a GIS database that is useful in the environmental justice context includes, at least, demographic (for instance, census, socioeconomic) information, land use information, and relevant environmental databases (for example, TRI information, proximity to National Priorities List and state-listed sites, proximity to regulated facilities). GIS allows database information to be mapped at various levels, including tax lots, city blocks, counties, ZIP codes, or any other useful level of specificity. In many GIS databases, the information is coded for more than one mapping level.

GIS databases are costly to initiate and maintain. Not every area is served by a GIS database system, and many GIS databases that do exist are inaccessible because they are maintained by private entities or by public sector entities that are not set up for public distribution of information. However, as a public service, some community-based organizations and governmental agencies that have GIS information provide onsite access to the technology, and in many instances GIS databases relating to the distribution of environmental impacts serving a given area may be accessed through Internet links (search for "GIS" or "pollution maps"). Some private enterprises have GIS capabilities that can be accessed for a fee.

Freedom of Information Laws

In 1966, Congress enacted the federal Freedom of Information Act[5] (FOIA). FOIA initially established the "right to know" (RTK) doctrine, whereby citizens employing the procedures promulgated under FOIA enjoy a presumption of access to information held by the federal government. This establishes that the federal agency from which information is requested has the burden of justifying denial of the request based on an exemption permitting nondisclosure. Since 1966, many states have enacted parallel statutes, effectively providing public access similar to that provided under FOIA to information held by state and local governmental agencies.

FOIA and its state counterparts are essential tools for those seeking information related to an environmental justice controversy. Entities regulated by environmental laws are required under numerous statutes to disclose specified information to various regulating authorities. Under these freedom of information (FOI) statutes, nonconfidential information disclosed to the government must be disclosed to any person who makes a proper request.

A partial limitation on the usefulness of the FOI statutes is that despite any required response time set forth in the statute or implementing regulations, FOI requests may take months or even years before being answered. The FOI statutes typically provide for administrative appeals that may be invoked to help catalyze the process when an agency response has been unsatisfactory, but litigation to enforce FOI requirements often is of limited use because those who would rely on FOI statutes often do not have the resources (especially in light of the uncertain value or quantity of the information in question) or the time to support the effort.

Moreover, even when time is not the issue, agency personnel can be less than ideally responsive. For better or worse, the FOI statutes rely on perennially overburdened governmental agency personnel who often are not enthusiastic about providing the reams of information requested. Because the FOI statutes usually provide agencies with various exemptions that exclude certain information from disclosure in response to an FOI request, unresponsive agency personnel have added flexibility by which to formulate their response to

FOI requests. While some of the interpretations of permissible exemptions relied upon by agency personnel for refusing to disclose information would not stand a court challenge, as stated above, requestors of information under FOI statutes often do not have the resources or time to use the applicable FOI law to its fullest.

The Federal FOIA in Particular

Generally, FOIA requires a federal agency to publish and otherwise make available information about the agency's organizational description, its operational procedures, its rules and regulations, its substantive rules of general applicability, and other information potentially of relevance or interest to the public.[6] Most important, however, FOIA provides that, except with respect to records already made publicly available:

> "Each agency, upon any request for records which . . . reasonably describes such records and . . . is made in accordance with published rules stating the time, place, fees (if any), and procedures to be followed, shall make the records promptly available to any person."[7]

Note that the information requested must be supplied to "any person." The statute was designed to relieve agency personnel of any need to review or even to contemplate the motivation of the request, and such information need not be included in the FOIA request unless there otherwise is reason to include it. It generally is understood that any information contained in any medium that is controlled by the agency in question and that may be reproduced is a covered "record" for the purposes of FOIA.

Covered agencies are required to disclose every record that is responsive to a FOIA request, with the exception of those that are deemed to be exempt or excluded. Under Section (b) of FOIA, a federal agency may claim an exemption under any of nine categories:

1. classified as secret or confidential under the Executive Order on Security Classification[8];
2. related solely to the internal personnel rules and practices of the agency in question;
3. explicitly restricted disclosure under other laws;
4. relating to trade secrets and commercial or financial information obtained from a person and privileged or confidential;
5. internal agency memoranda or letters that would not be available by law to a party other than an agency in litigation with the agency;
6. personal and medical files or similar files;

7. records compiled for law enforcement purposes;
8. records related to the regulation of financial institutions; and
9. geological and geophysical information concerning wells.

Under the Freedom of Information Reform Act of 1986, instead of simply being exempted from FOIA, certain information originally contained in exemption category number (7) above has become officially excluded from FOIA. This change in status allows an agency to refuse to respond to an FOIA request when the mere acknowledgment of the existence of the requested record could produce seriously adverse consequences to law enforcement activities. The information that now is fully excluded from FOIA is:

(a) information about a criminal investigation where there is reason to believe that the subject of the investigation is not aware of the investigation and disclosure of the requested records could reasonably be expected to interfere with the enforcement;
(b) informant records kept by a criminal law enforcement agency; and
(c) classified records kept by the Federal Bureau of Investigation regarding intelligence, counterintelligence or international terrorism.

With respect to information falling into these categories, an agency need not formally respond to the request even to convey that the requested information is exempt from disclosure, as is necessary in the case of exempt information.

As required, each federal agency has adopted rules to implement FOIA. These rules cover technical matters regarding the required form of the FOIA request (including pertinent fee schedules for processing information and information about mandatory and discretionary fee waivers), agency review and response time frames, and appeal of FOIA requests. The regulations implementing FOIA for some agencies of interest are ratified at:

- 10 C.F.R. part 1004 (Department of Energy);
- 32 C.F.R. part 518 (Department of Defense, Army Corps of Engineers);
- 40 C.F.R. part 2 (EPA); and
- 43 C.F.R. part 2, subpart A and B (Department of the Interior).

As a general matter, it is relatively easy to make an FOIA request. An FOIA request should be made in a brief letter outlining or listing in as much detail as possible the exact information being requested of the agency. The broader the request, the greater the burden will be on the agency to respond, and the more time the agency will take to respond. The request letter should make clear that the request is being made under FOIA and should recite the requestor's name, address, and daytime telephone number. If no copying costs should be incurred without the requestor's consent, or if copying costs in excess of a stated amount should not be incurred without the requestor's consent, it should be made clear that the official responding to the FOIA request should call the requestor to ascertain any such consent. A lawyer's assistance with the submittal of a FOIA request, while useful in certain situations, is not necessary. FOIA request letters should be sent to as many agencies or offices within agencies that may have relevant information as necessary; different agencies or even offices within agencies may have different response rates, methods of responding to the request, and, perhaps, even different philosophies with respect to which documents must be provided in response to a FOIA request. Perhaps most important, make sure that the request letter is sent to the proper person (that is, the Freedom of Information officer) at the agency. The United States Government Manual, an annually updated reference located in many public libraries and via the Internet at <http://www.gpo.ucop.edu/search/govman.html>, is a good source for the names and addresses of FOIA offices.

FOIA provides that a dissatisfied requestor may appeal an agency's allegedly improper response. Reasons for making an administrative appeal often concern failure to meet required or promised time frames and denial of certain records. As most agency FOIA implementation regulations do not specify a particular format for preparing an FOIA administrative appeal, a succinct letter to the head of the relevant federal agency will usually suffice. Such a letter should attach copies of the initial FOIA request and any agency denials. An agency head is required to respond to an administrative appeal within 20 business days of the receipt of the appeal letter,[9] subject to a ten-day extension. EPA has promulgated specific regulations regarding administrative appeals.[10] Denial of administrative appeals may be appealed either to the United States District Court either in the district where the requestor resides or in the district where the requested documents are located, or to the United States District Court for the District of Columbia.[11]

Additional information regarding FOIA may be obtained via the Internet at <http://www.usdoj.gov/foia/handbook.htm>.

State-Level Freedom of Information Statutes

Many states have enacted FOI statutes substantially parallel to the federal statute.[12] These statutes, for the most part, require disclosure of agency records to any person and provide for certain exemptions—more or less parallel with the federal exemptions—to this requirement. Unless a given state or municipality requires otherwise, the procedures set forth above with respect to the federal law for submitting an FOIA request may be used for making a request under a state FOI law.

While the general outlines of the state FOI laws parallel the federal law, it is prudent to review the relevant law of the state in question as the state FOI laws may vary with respect to certain administrative and interpretative aspects of the law. In particular, municipal implementation of a state FOI law often varies widely from municipality to municipality. Some state FOI laws provide that only a state resident may make requests under the statute.[13]

Open Meeting Laws

In 1976, President Ford signed into law the Government in the Sunshine Act.[14] The Sunshine Act generally requires that meetings of government agencies be open to the public, the underlying principle being that the government should conduct the public's business under full public scrutiny. Every state has enacted a parallel statute, often referred to as a state's "open meeting law," requiring that official meetings generally be open to the public. While these state statutes often have significant exceptions that are susceptible to broad interpretation by the regulated government agencies, the statutes may be successfully invoked as a method of gaining access to important meetings that have been closed to public scrutiny.

Chemical Exposure Right-to-Know Laws

While the term "right-to-know" originally was associated with FOIA and the general right of access to governmental information, since the mid-1980s the term has also been associated with the idea that information about potential exposure to hazardous substances should be readily available to those who might be so exposed. This idea most clearly has been expressed in two federal laws: the Occupational Safety and Health Act of 1970 (the OSH Act)[15] and the Emergency Planning and Community Right-to-Know Act (EPCRA).[16] While the information that must be reported to the applicable federal agencies under these Acts is accessible via FOIA request, the mandate of these statutes is to disseminate this information actively and, therefore, the information for the most part is more easily accessible than through a FOIA request. For example, most of the information described in this section is readily available on publicly available governmental electronic databases via the Internet.

Employee Exposure to Hazardous Chemicals in the Workplace

Under the OSH Act, as modified in 1985, all employees working in industries where they might be exposed to certain hazardous chemicals have the right to know about the presence and potential for exposure to those chemicals. While states may adopt their own employee RTK programs, unless these programs are at least as comprehensive as the federal program and have been approved by the Occupational Safety and Health Administration (OSHA), the federal program governs the relevant reporting requirements.

Under the OSH Act, employers are required to inform their employees about hazardous chemicals to which they might be exposed during routine operations or during foreseeable nonroutine circumstances. While this requirement must be fulfilled in numerous ways (including requirements for the labeling of chemicals and the provision of chemical use training programs), the principal way is by providing access to a Material Safety Data Sheet (an MSDS) for each covered chemical to each employee who risks exposure.[17]

MSDSs are prepared by the manufacturer or importer of covered chemicals. At a minimum, each MSDS must provide basic information identifying covered chemicals, essential information about the chemical's physical properties, information about physical and/or health hazards associated with the chemical (including medical conditions that the chemical may aggravate), exposure limits, and precautions for safe handling, spill cleanup, and proper first aid procedures. Each MSDS also must provide the name, address, and telephone number of a designated person to provide additional information and emergency handling procedures.

The MSDS reporting requirement is imposed on three types of chemicals:

1. chemicals that pose a health hazard because they have been shown to cause acute or chronic health effects;
2. chemicals that pose a physical hazard because they are explosive, combustible, flammable, unstable or water-reactive; and
3. mixtures of two or more chemicals that pose physical or health hazards.[18]

Certain chemicals are exempted from the reporting requirements, including:

(a) hazardous wastes, as defined by the Resource Conservation and Recovery Act[19], that are subject to EPA regulation;
(b) hazardous substances, as defined by the Comprehensive Environmental Response, Compensation and Liability Act[20]

(CERCLA), when the hazardous substance is the focus of a remedial or removal action in accordance with EPA regulations;

(c) certain specified products, such as tobacco, drugs, cosmetics, and alcoholic beverages; and

(d) certain products that release only trace amounts of otherwise included chemicals, such as adhesive tape, stainless steel, and automobile tires.[21]

OSHA is responsible for enforcement of the OSH Act. The OSH Act authorizes OSHA to enter into and inspect specified workplaces without prior warning.[22] If an inspection indicates a failure to comply with the OSH Act, OSHA may issue a citation describing the violation, indicating the steps for abatement of the violation and a timeframe for so abating, and penalties. OSHA-issued citations may be appealed to any United States Court of Appeals for the circuit in which the violation is alleged to have occurred or where the employer has its principal office, or in the Court of Appeals for the District of Columbia Circuit.[23]

Many companies will make available to the public the MSDSs kept on file at a regulated facility. Information about OSHA inspections and citations are available by FOIA request directed to OSHA (which may be contacted via Internet at <http://www.osha.gov>).

The Emergency Planning and Community Right-to-Know Act (EPCRA)

In part as a response to the disastrous 1984 leak of methyl isocyanate from a pesticide manufacturing facility in Bhopal, India, which caused serious injury or death to over 50,000 local residents, CERCLA was amended in 1986 to foster protection from the dangers of accidental exposure to hazardous chemicals. Title III of the Superfund Amendments and Reauthorization Act of 1986, also known as EPCRA, is a free-standing environmental statute. EPCRA is administered by EPA, which, together with at least 11 other agencies, writes and disseminates technical guidance documents to help local communities and companies fulfill their EPCRA responsibilities.

EPCRA was primarily designed to further two goals:

1. to provide citizens with information regarding toxic chemicals present in their communities and thereby to empower communities to force businesses to be accountable for the safe handling of these chemicals; and
2. to establish reporting, notification, and planning requirements that would aid state and local governments, and, ultimately, communities, in preparing for an emergency caused

by the accidental release of specified "extremely hazardous substances."

To meet these goals, Congress established two programs. One establishes a community-based planning process, overseen by state officials, that attempts to ready the community in question for a local toxic emergency. The second program establishes a regulatory scheme whereby owners or operators of covered facilities must provide information to designated government authorities and the public regarding toxic chemicals stored and used by the facility as well as information regarding any releases of toxic chemicals from the facility.

The governmental agencies that gather the information reported under EPCRA generally are required to make that information available to the public. As discussed in the sections entitled "Electronic Databases" (pages 231–237) and "Federal Community Right-to-Know Law" (pages 245–251, especially pages 247–249), one method increasingly being used by the government to meet this goal is by making the information available on electronic databases, and especially by providing access to these databases over the Internet.

While ambitious, EPCRA has been criticized as being implemented unevenly and providing information of dramatically disparate quality. Much of this criticism is part of a larger concern relating to EPCRA, which is that because the federal government provides little direct funding for EPCRA programs, the quality of the actual administration of EPCRA on the state and local level often reflects budgetary constraints.[24]

Aspects of these programs that may result in publicly-accessible information that may be of use in an environmental justice controversy are summarized below.

Emergency Planning and the Information Accessible Therefrom

Under EPCRA, the governor of each state or territory must designate a State Emergency Response Commission (a SERC) composed of people with expertise in relevant aspects of emergency response planning.[25] A SERC oversees and provides guidance to Local Emergency Planning Committees (LEPCs), which are composed of local community members, appointed by the SERC, who meet certain qualifications with respect to diversity, expertise, and representativeness. In most cases, the SERC (and/or a specific LEPC) can be located by contacting the relevant state emergency response officials or emergency response officials at a local fire or police department.

The foremost responsibilities of each SERC are to oversee the development and implementation of local emergency response plans (ERPs) and to develop, maintain, and publicize a method for making information available to the public about potential toxic accidents and emergency planning. To these ends, some SERCs have established publicly accessible databases. Each SERC also designates emergency planning districts, the emergency planning for each of which is to be undertaken by a LEPC. The extremely hazardous substances (EHSs) that give rise to the required response actions are specified in the federal Community Right-to-Know Law, as set forth in the section entitled "Federal Community Right-to-Know Law" (pages 245–250).

Each LEPC is responsible to develop and implement an ERP and to disseminate information regarding emergency responsiveness. To meet these objectives, the LEPC must hold public meetings and hearings to discuss emergency planning, review existing emergency response plans, identify and assess facilities and transportation routes of importance with respect to emergency planning, evaluate the capabilities of local police, fire and other relevant local agencies, draft an ERP, disseminate the draft ERP to the public, develop procedures to respond to requests for information, educate the public regarding the ERP and emergency planning in general, and recommend a final ERP. Reviewing the effectiveness of the ERP is to be an ongoing program.

The information amassed by the SERC and by LEPCs with respect to the presence of specific EHSs comes directly from the facilities that store, utilize, and, in some cases, release such chemicals into the environment. For the most part, this information is provided to the SERC and LEPC primarily via reporting under the federal reporting requirements of EPCRA (as set forth in the next section). Furthermore, as it is part of the responsibility of each LEPC to provide information to the public—upon request and at its own initiative—with respect to hazards in the relevant community, LEPCs potentially are sources of information with respect to certain hazards. "The Right-to-Know Network," a free nonprofit network that provides various EPCRA information via Internet at <www.rtk.net>, provides links to SERC and LEPC web sites in 21 states. EPCRA provides that citizens may sue the governor and/or the SERC to enforce failure of those parties to provide public access to the information amassed under EPCRA.[26]

Federal Community Right-to-Know Law

Under EPCRA, owners and operators of covered facilities must disclose certain information to specified authorities under two sets of provisions:

1. those relating to hazardous chemical inventory reporting; and
2. those relating to toxic chemical release inventory reporting.

FEDERAL HAZARDOUS CHEMICAL INVENTORY REPORTING (EPCRA SECTIONS 311 AND 312). An owner or operator of a facility that is required to make available an MSDS under the OSH Act[27] must also make certain information known to the applicable LEPC, the SERC, and the local fire department pursuant to EPCRA Sections 311 and 312. Specifically, such an owner or operator must provide required information regarding the presence and amounts of each hazardous chemical listed on an MSDS at a facility if the chemical in question is present in a quantity above a specified threshold amount. EPA exempts certain hazardous chemicals from EPCRA Section 311 and 312 reporting,[28] including:

- Any food, food additive, color additive, drug, or cosmetic regulated by the federal Food and Drug Administration;
- Any substance present as a solid in any manufactured item to the extent exposure to the substance does not occur under normal conditions of use;
- Any substance to the extent it is used for personal, family, or household purposes, or is present in the same form (for instance, packaging) and concentration as a product packaged for distribution and use by the general public;
- Any substance to the extent it is used in a research laboratory, hospital, or other medical facility under the direct supervision of a technically qualified individual;
- Any substance to the extent it is used in routine agricultural operations or as a fertilizer held for sale by a retailer to the ultimate customer.

Reporting requirements under EPCRA Sections 311 and 312 is triggered whenever a hazardous chemical is present at a covered facility at any one time in an amount equal to or greater than 10,000 pounds (4,540 kilograms). Reporting is required for extremely hazardous substances (EHSs)—those hazardous chemicals listed at 40 C.F.R. Section 370.20(b)—present at a covered facility at any one time in an amount equal to or greater than 500 pounds (227 kilograms) or the designated threshold planning quantity (TPQ),[29] whichever is lower.

If the EPCRA Sections 311 and 312 reporting requirements are triggered, the owner or operator must submit two types of information to the designated authorities:

- Under EPCRA Section 311, an MSDS must be submitted to the designated public authorities for each relevant hazardous chemical or a list of hazardous chemicals for which an MSDS is required, such list to include certain information about each such hazardous chemical.[30]

- Under EPCRA Section 312, an emergency and hazardous chemical inventory form (a Tier I form) reflecting each relevant hazardous chemical present at the facility during the preceding calendar year must be submitted prior to March 1 of each year. A Tier I form contains information identifying:
  (1) the facility;
  (2) the name, address and telephone number of the owner or operator;
  (3) the name and telephone number of an emergency contact;
  (4) estimates of the maximum amount of each category of chemical at any time during the previous year;
  (5) estimates of the ranges of average daily amounts of chemicals in each category; and
  (6) the general locations of the chemicals in each category. A Tier II form, which provides more detailed information than does the Tier I form, may be submitted in lieu of the Tier I form. Owners and operators must submit a Tier II form within 30 days of being requested to do so by the LEPC, the SERC, or the local fire department with jurisdiction over the facility

If EPA approves a "trade secret" petition, a regulated entity may withhold information regarding the identity of the specific hazardous chemical (including the chemical name and other identifying characteristics) when making submissions under EPCRA Sections 311, 312, and 313.[31] Only the chemical's identity, however, may be withheld as a trade secret; all other information submitted under EPCRA is available to the public.

Besides being subject to disclosure under the relevant FOI statutes, any person may obtain an MSDS and Tier II information with respect to a covered facility by submitting a written request to the appropriate LEPC.[32]

TOXIC CHEMICAL RELEASE INVENTORY REPORTING (EPCRA SECTION 313). If EPCRA Section 313 reporting requirements are triggered, the owner or operator of a covered facility must submit an annual report (a Form R) to EPA and designated state officials. The information that must be contained on a Form R includes data regarding:

- the facility;
- the toxic chemical manufactured, processed, or used;
- off-site transfers and on-site waste treatment; and
- source reduction and recycling activities with respect to the toxic chemical in question, as required under Section 6607 of the Pollution Prevention Act of 1990.[33]

Perhaps of most importance, EPCRA Section 313 requires reporting on Form R of intentional as well as accidental releases of toxic chemicals, including:

- discharges to streams or other waters;
- fugitive or nonpoint air emissions;
- stack or point emissions; and
- transfers of wastes to off-site locations, including publicly owned treatment works.

Each annual Form R must be submitted on or before July 1 of the year after the applicable year.

EPA and other government agencies use the information collected from the Form Rs to create the annual Toxic Release Inventory (TRI). The designated recipients of the EPCRA Section 313 data are required to make the information readily available to the public; to facilitate this, many states maintain electronic databases of EPCRA Section 313 information submitted for public inspection. Each year, the TRI is widely disseminated (for example, in addition to the database locations described on pages 232–235, the TRI and information thereabout may be accessed at <www.epa.gov/enviro/html/tris/tris_overview.html> and <www.rtk.net>). Because the TRI provides solid statistics in an otherwise unreported arena, the TRI data is used to shape policy and to inform the public about trends in chemical releases.

The TRI has become one of the most important sources of environmental release information for activists, politicians, and other people concerned with human exposure to dangerous chemicals. For example, in a recent report based on a review of all 1995 Form Rs, the U.S. Public Interest Research Group found that 41 million people in the United States live near facilities that handle toxic chemicals disclosed by the TRI.[34] Even some representatives from the chemical industry have admitted that citizen enforcement and the sheer power and volume of TRI data published and widely broadcast on a single day each spring have resulted in industry cost savings and efficiencies that not only have saved the industry and consumers money, but have made competitive advantages for those companies that incorporated changes.[35] Moreover, while the reasons for reported reductions in annual releases do not always reflect a reduction in a facility's reliance in a specific toxic chemical, there is little dispute that the TRI has resulted in considerable real reductions in the quantity of covered chemicals entering the environment.[36] And because TRI information can be easily correlated to demographic or geographic information, the information has been particularly valuable in environmental justice controversies.[37]

Facilities potentially covered by EPCRA Section 313 are those that:

1. manufacture, process, or otherwise use any of the over 500 toxic chemicals listed pursuant to 40 C.F.R. § 372.65 above threshold amounts during the previous year;
2. have 10 or more employees; and
3. are described by SIC code numbers 20 through 39.[38]

Currently some 24,000 facilities are subject to EPCRA Section 313 reporting. Recently, various facilities that had previously been exempted from the scope of EPCRA Section 313 reporting, including mining operations, petroleum storage facilities, electrical utilities, and chemical wholesalers, were included as covered facilities for the first time.

The reporting thresholds for toxic chemicals subject to EPCRA Section 313 relate to the activities of the reporting facility. With respect to facilities that "manufactured" or "processed" toxic chemicals during a year that is covered by EPCRA Section 313, the relevant threshold amount for the 1989 reporting year and thereafter is 25,000 pounds of the chemical manufactured or processed. With respect to facilities that "otherwise used" toxic chemicals during a covered year, the threshold amount generally is 10,000 pounds.

There are several exemptions from the EPCRA Section 313 reporting requirements.[39]

Each person subject to EPCRA Section 313 reporting must retain certain information, including a copy of each Form R submitted and all supporting materials and documentation, at the subject facility for a period of 3 years from the date that a Form R is submitted.

ENFORCEMENT OF EPCRA SECTIONS 311, 312, AND 313. EPA has enforced EPCRA with increasing aggressiveness in recent years. In 1997, the agency brought approximately 300 enforcement actions against alleged EPCRA violations and assessed penalties for those violations at more than $15 million.

While EPA may impose both civil and criminal penalties under EPCRA, the Agency may enforce EPCRA Sections 311, 312, and 313 only through civil penalties. EPA may assess civil penalties of up to $10,000 for each violation of EPCRA Section 311, each day of violation constituting a separate violation. EPA may assess civil penalties of up to $25,000 for each violation of EPCRA Section 312 or Section 313, each day of violation again constituting a separate violation. EPA may assess these penalties and seek to collect them through administrative order or through a civil action in federal court, or both.

State and local governments may also bring civil suits against parties for failure to comply with EPCRA Section 311 or Section 312. Furthermore, unless the Administrator of EPA has already initiated an enforcement action, under EPCRA's citizen suit provision "any person," including state and local governments, may bring a civil action against an EPCRA-covered party for violation of EPCRA Section 311, Section 312 or Section 313. However, no citizen action may be initiated until 60 days after the citizen has given notice of the alleged violation to the Administrator, the state, and the alleged violator.

Other Laws That Promote Public Access to Exposure Information Regarding Dangerous Chemicals

RTK laws have been enacted in other contexts than those covered by the OSH Act and EPCRA. While these laws vary in scope and enforcement parameters, like the original federal laws their underlying premise is that the requirement to make exposure information available to the public will result in the public demand for decreased exposure to the covered chemicals, the voluntary reduction in chemical use, or both.

For example, under the 1996 amendments to the Safe Drinking Water Act, EPA recently finalized a rule requiring approximately 55,000 water systems serving about 240 million people in the United States to provide "consumer confidence" reports to the water users.[40] These reports will inform consumers whether the drinking water meets federal health standards, where the water comes from, and the likely source of any contaminants found in the water.

One example of a state-initiated RTK law is California's Safe Drinking Water and Toxic Enforcement Act, commonly known as Proposition 65, passed by voter referendum in 1986.[41] Proposition 65 prohibits any person "in the course of doing business" from "knowingly and intentionally exposing any individual to a chemical known to the state to cause cancer or reproductive toxicity without first giving clear and reasonable warning to such individual." Therefore, every business entity that might cause the prohibited exposure must label its products or processes as carcinogenic or a threat to healthy childbearing. Failure to label regulated products and processes properly subjects the responsible parties to fines of up to $2,500 per violation. Proposition 65 is enforceable by any person who sends an "intend-to-sue" notice to the alleged violator, the California Attorney General (who may join any Proposition 65 suit), the relevant district attorney, and the local city attorney. Because citizen enforcers may be awarded up to 25 percent of all civil penalties awarded, Proposition 65 has operated like a traditional RTK law: a cottage industry of citizen enforcers has asserted numerous claims leading, in the large majority of cases, to pretrial settlements.

A second example of a nonfederal law enacted to empower citizen access to information is a local law enacted in Passaic County, New Jersey, on September 8, 1998.[42] The local law establishes a process by which residents living near an industrial facility, as well as employees of the facility, can petition the county health officer to form a Neighborhood Hazard Prevention Advisory Committee. Such committees must include a facility manager, neighbors of the facility, employees, and a municipal representative. Under certain circumstances, representatives of these committees must be permitted access to inspect facilities to make recommendations to the facility's management with respect to reducing health and environmental hazards.

Required Corporate Disclosure Under Securities and Exchange Commission Regulations

In the wake of the 1929 stock market crash, Congress enacted laws to ensure that those who invest in publicly traded securities would have access to information material to an informed investment decision. Specifically, companies that publicly trade regulated securities (for instance, stock) are required by federal law to disclose to the United States Securities and Exchange Commission (the SEC) specified information relating to various aspects of their businesses, including information regarding known environmental conditions. Generally, the information submitted to the SEC is public and, in the case of many SEC disclosure statements, is accessible via FOIA request, commercially available databases such as LEXIS/NEXIS and WESTLAW, and the Internet at <http://ftp.sec.gov/edaux/formlynx.htm>. Reviewing disclosure statements may provide general information about a company's environmental conditions (that is, environmental conditions that the company believes may or will have a significant financial impact on the company). Because the disclosure statement is drafted by the company, based on the company's interpretation of the relevant environmental conditions, the information contained in SEC disclosures statements tends to be vague and generalized.

The disclosures required by Congress must be made by covered companies at least annually on SEC Form 10-K, but also may be required in other contexts, such as in an initial public offering of covered securities.

While specified information must be reported, the SEC does not require companies to disclose their general environmental management policies. If a company does make a disclosure concerning its general environmental management policies, however, the disclosure must be accurate and not misleading. As a general matter, failure to comply with SEC environmental disclosure requirements may result in judicial and administrative proceedings, including, in unusual circumstances, criminal prosecution.

The disclosure requirements for covered companies are set forth on SEC Regulation S-K.[43]

- Item 101 of Regulation S-K requires disclosure of a comprehensive description of the business of the reporting company, including material effects of environmental compliance or other liabilities with federal, state and local laws on its capital expenditures, earnings, and competitive position.[44] Generally, a fact is "material" if a substantial likelihood exists that a reasonable investor would have viewed its disclosure as having significantly altered the information available to the public to make an informed investment decision. While most commentators acknowledge that materiality only can be truly be determined after a fact-specific inquiry, the SEC has articulated rules of thumb for the determination of materiality: the disclosed information implicating a liability of "above 10%—material; 5–10%—may be material; under 5%—usually not material."[45] The SEC has not clarified what should be measured by these percentages: gross profits, stockholders' equity, net income, or some other measurement of a company's health.
- Item 103 of Regulation S-K requires disclosure of any material pending or contemplated judicial or administrative proceedings.[46] Such proceedings include those that are material to the business or financial condition of the company in question, those that may result in damages or costs to the company in excess of 10 percent of the company's current consolidated assets, and those in which the government is a party (unless potential sanctions are reasonably expected to be less than $100,000). It is not clear what events must have occurred before it can be determined that a judicial or administrative proceeding is contemplated. In the end, many decisions regarding the disclosure of liabilities are business decisions based on the unique facts of the situation
- Item 303 of Regulation S-K, "Management's discussion and analysis of financial condition and results of operations," requires discussion of the effect of environmental risk on historic and future operating results, liquidity or financial condition, including any discernible trends with respect to such effects.[47] Information about such trends should be reported when the company determines that the trends are reasonably likely to occur and the trend, if it occurs, will have a material effect on the company's financial condition or results of operations

Many of the matters that may have to be disclosed under SEC Regulation S-K relate to contingent liabilities: those financial liabilities that were incurred by past behavior but may not be paid out until the future. It is inherently difficult to account for contingent liabilities. Financial Accounting Standards Board (FASB)[48] Statement of Financial Accounting Standards No. 5 (FASB Statement 5) specifically defines a contingency as "an existing condition, situation, or set of circumstances involving uncertainty as to possible loss to an enterprise that will ultimately be resolved when one or more future events occur or fail to occur. Resolution of the uncertainty may confirm the impairment of an asset or the incurrence of a liability."[49] SEC's general approach to accounting for contingent liabilities is that estimated future costs of the contingency should be reflected on the financial statements associated with the period in which the contingent liability occurred. Specifically, FASB Statement 5 requires that a contingent liability be expressed on a company's financial statement when information available prior to the issuance of the financial statement in question indicates that it is "probable" that an asset has been impaired or a liability has been incurred, and the amount of loss can be "reasonably estimated." If the company determines that a contingent liability meets these criteria, the company must report the estimated value of that loss as a charge against income.

The value of a contingent liability, because the contingency has yet to be realized, is difficult to estimate. Staff Accounting Bulletin Number 92 (SAB 92) formalizes the SEC's position with respect to the proper method of estimating and accounting for a company's contingent environmental liabilities. Generally, SAB 92 provides that disclosure should be sufficiently specific to enable a reader of the financial statement to understand the contingencies and uncertainties affecting the company and disclosure also should be sufficiently comprehensive to provide the investor with complete information regarding the full scope of environmental contingencies that the company faces.

Notes

1. The role of environmental impact assessment laws in the context of environmental justice controversies is explored in Chapter 9, "Impact Assessment."

2. *See, e.g.*, JAMES L. UNDERWOOD, A GUIDE TO FEDERAL DISCOVERY RULES, ALI-ABA COMM. ON CONTINUING PROF. EDUC., (2nd ed., 1985); WILLIAM W. SCHWARZER, & LYNN H. PASAHOW, CIVIL DISCOVERY: A GUIDE TO EFFICIENT PRACTICE (Prentice Hall Law & Business, 1989.

3. For more information on this and related databases, see pages 247–249.

4. 42 U.S.C. § 7401–7671q.

5. 5 U.S.C. § 552.

6. *See* 5 U.S.C. §§ 552(a)(1) and 552(a)(2).

7. 5 U.S.C. § 552(a)(3).

8. *See* 3 C.F.R. pt. 166 (Exec. Order No. 12,356).

9. 5 U.S.C. § 552(a)(6)(A)(ii).

10. *See* 40 C.F.R. §§ 2.114-2.117.

11. 5 U.S.C. § 552(a)(4)(B).

12. *See* FRANKLIN & BOUCHARD, GUIDEBOOK TO THE FREEDOM OF INFORMATION AND PRIVACY ACTS STATE STATUTES app. AL-1.

13. *See, e.g.*, Pennsylvania Right-to-Know Act, 65 P.S. § 66.1–66.4.

14. 5 U.S.C. § 552b.

15. 29 U.S.C. § 651–678.

16. 42 U.S.C. § 11001–11050.

17. 29 C.F.R. § 1910.1200(g)(8).

18. 29 C.F.R. § 1910.1200(c).

19. 42 U.S.C. § 6901–6992k.

20. 42 U.S.C. § 9601–9675.

21. *See* 29 C.F.R. § 1910.1200(b)(6).

21. 29 C.F.R. § 657(a).

22. OSH Act § 8(a).

23. OSH Act § 11(a).

24. *See* UNITED STATES GENERAL ACCOUNTING OFFICE, TOXIC CHEMICALS: EPA's TOXIC RELEASE INVENTORY IS USEFUL BUT CAN BE APPROVED (1991); Rebecca S. Weeks, *The Bumpy Road to Community Preparedness: The Emergency Planning and Community Right-to-Know Act*, 4 ENVTL. LAW., 827, 827–89.

25. 42 U.S.C. § 11001.

26. 42 U.S.C. § 11046(a).

27. *See* "Employee Exposure to the Hazardous Chemicals in the Workplace," pages 242–243.

28. *See* 40 C.F.R. § 370.2; 29 C.F.R. § 1910.1200(b)(6).

29. *See* 40 C.F.R. pt. 355.

30. 40 C.F.R. § 370.21(d).

31. 42 U.S.C. § 11042(a).

32. 40 C.F.R. § 370.30.

33. 42 U.S.C. § 13101–13109.

34. U.S. PUBLIC INTEREST RESEARCH GROUP, *Too Close to Home: A Report on Chemical Accident Risks in the United States*, (July 22, 1998).

35. *See* Bruce Selcraig, *What You Don't Know Can Hurt You*, SIERRA, Jan./Feb. 1997, at 40.

36. *See, e.g.*, Thomas E. Natan & Catherine G. Miller, *Are Toxic Release Inventory Reductions Real?*, 32 ENVTL. SCI. & TECH. 368 (1998).

37. In addition to the electronic databases listed in this chapter that, by design, provide various correlations that may be of interest in environmental justice controversies, many studies that purport to provide evidence of environmental discrimination seek to correlate TRI information with demographic and geographic information. *See, e.g.*, Susan A. Perlin et al., *Distribution of Industrial Air Emissions by Income and Race in the United States: An Approach Using the Toxic Release Inventory*, 29 ENVTL. SCI. & TECH. 69–80 (1995).

38. 40 C.F.R. § 372.22.

39. 40 C.F.R. § 372.38.

40. *See Clinton Unveils "Right-to-Know" Rule Requiring Disclosure of Water Quality,* BNA DAILY ENV'T REP., Aug. 12, 1998, at AA-1. Apparently, the rule, which will be promulgated under 40 C.F.R. pts. 141 & 142, will be published in the Federal Register in December 1998. The rule and information about it can be accessed via the Internet at <http://www.epa.gov/safewater>.

41. CAL. HEALTH & SAFETY CODE 25249.7–25249.13.

42. *See Local Law Will Allow Facility Inspections by Neighborhood Residents, Groups Say,* BNA ENV'T REP., 29, Sept. 18, 1998, at 1007; Maia Davis, *Chemical Plants May Face Added Scrutiny; Wary Neighbors Can Inspect Them,* BERGEN RECORD, Sept. 9, 1998, at L2.

43. SEC Regulation S-K is codified at 17 C.F.R. pt. 229.

44. *See* 17 C.F.R. § 229.101.

45. Remarks of Richard Y. Roberts, Commissioner, United States SEC, Overview of Environmental Liability Disclosure Requirements, Recent Developments and Materiality, American Bar Association 1993 Annual Meeting, Toxic & Hazardous Substances Committee Program, New York, Aug. 9, 1993.

46. *See* 17 C.F.R. § 229.103.

47. *See* 17 C.F.R. § 229.303.

48. The positions taken by the SEC with respect to GAAP is formalized through statements issued by FASB, often in the form of so-called Staff Accounting Bulletins.

49. 58 Fed. Reg. 32,844 (1993).

CHAPTER 9

Impact Assessment

SHEILA FOSTER

Introduction

Environmental laws may be one cause of the inequitable distribution of environmental hazards, particularly toxic waste sites.[1] However, environmental laws may also be a cure. Environmental review requirements, embodied in statutes such as the National Environmental Policy Act[2] (NEPA), and its state equivalents, provide one mechanism for assessing the impact of a proposed land use on a vulnerable, or already overburdened, community. Other federal and state statutes provide for similar impact assessment before siting, particularly, a hazardous waste facility. Perhaps the most significant federal policy/law to date addressing distributional impacts of federal actions is President Clinton's 1994 Executive Order on Environmental Justice.[3] This order directs each federal agency to identify and address "disproportionately high and adverse human health or environmental effects of its programs, policies and activities on minority populations and low-income populations."[4] The implementation of this Order, in turn, is strengthening existing environmental review procedures.

Some state laws go further than their federal equivalents. For instance, "mini-NEPAs" in numerous states provide for more extensive environmental impact review than NEPA itself. Some state hazardous waste laws also go further than their federal equivalent, the Resource Conservation and Recovery Act (RCRA), in their consideration of factors assessing the suitability of a proposed facility in a host community. Aside from the technical and environmental assessment criteria—proximity to wetlands, geology of site, impact on groundwater, and impact on health—states are increasingly mandating consideration of a proposed facility's socioeconomic impacts on a host community, or mandating a more equitable distribution of facilities throughout the state. The adoption of such "soft criteria" reflects the fact that environmental risk assessment and management are becoming as much social and political assessments as technical. How much consideration is actually given to these socioeconomic impacts on the state level, however, is not clear. Often there is no guidance about the weight decision makers should, or can, give to these factors in the environmental assessment process. Nevertheless, the proliferation of these types of laws indicates an increased focus on environmental impacts in minority and low-income communities, and a movement toward more equitable distribution of environmental hazards.

Socioeconomic Impact Assessment Under the National Environmental Policy Act

NEPA is the primary mechanism for consideration of social or economic impacts pertaining to actions either undertaken by federal agencies or with substantial federal participation. Social and economic impacts encompass a broad array of concerns. The Interorganizational Committee on Guidelines and Principles for Social Impact Assessment defines "social impacts" as "consequences to human populations of any public or private actions that alter the ways in which people live, work, play, relate to one another, organize to meet their needs and generally cope as members of society."[5] Social impacts thus may include effects on population characteristics, community and institutional structures, political and social resources, individual and family changes, and community resources. Economic impacts may encompass such variables as job creation or loss, strains on city services, favorable or adverse impacts on property value, and impacts on the local tax base.[6]

NEPA requires an environmental impact review for major federal actions with a significant impact on the human environment. In this review, decision makers are required to document and consider a range of possible impacts—ecological, aesthetic, historic, cultural, economic, social, or health, whether direct, indirect, or cumulative.[7] However, as discussed below, NEPA's primary concern is with impacts on the natural, or physical, environment. As such, socioeconomic impacts are considered only when they are connected to and/or interrelated with physical environmental impacts.

Below is an overview of the types of actions subject to NEPA and the consideration of socioeconomic impacts at three crucial phases in the NEPA process—the "threshold determination" stage, the environmental impact statement (EIS) "preparation" stage, and the judicial review of the "adequacy" of the EIS stage. This section also gives an overview of federal agency policies regarding the implementation of NEPA in the environmental justice context. The Council on Environmental Quality (CEQ) implements NEPA and provides guidelines for federal agencies on when and how to prepare an impact statement.[8] CEQ recently published guidelines on how better to incorporate environmental justice concerns into NEPA implementation. These guidelines were prompted by Clinton's Executive Order, which specifically directs federal agencies to analyze the various environmental impacts of its actions, including effects on minority and low-income communities, when such analysis is required by NEPA. Many federal agencies, such as the EPA, are following CEQ's guidance and have issued new policies on using NEPA as a tool to identify and address disproportionate impacts in minority and low-income communities of color.

Actions Subject to NEPA

Major Federal Actions

NEPA requires an EIS for all "major" federal actions that will have a "significant effect" on the quality of the "human" environment.[9] The first step under NEPA is to determine whether a proposed action falls within NEPA's purview—a "major federal action."

CEQ defines federal actions, and inactions (failure to act),[10] as those that are "potentially subject to federal control and responsibility."[11] Federal actions include those that are entirely or partly financed, assisted, conducted, regulated, or approved by federal agencies.[12] Federal actions subject to NEPA tend to fall into one of the following categories:

1. adoption of an official policy—including interpretations and alterations of a policy, treaties, and international agreements;
2. adoption of formal plans upon which future agency actions will be based—including those that guide or prescribe alternative uses of federal resources;
3. adoption of programs—including a group of concerted actions to implement a specific policy or plan, systematic and connected agency decisions allocating agency resources to implement a specific statutory program or executive directive; and
4. approval of specific projects—including those approved by permit or other regulatory decision, federal, and federally assisted projects.[13]

Ministerial, or nondiscretionary, actions do not constitute a federal action sufficient to trigger NEPA.[14]

An issue of whether an action is sufficiently "federal" may come up if there is only small or marginal federal participation in the project. This is referred to as the "small handle problem." For instance, federal approval of a small part of an otherwise nonfederal project may not be enough to convert that project into a federal action subject to NEPA.[15] Similarly, marginal federal control and responsibility over a project will not convert an otherwise nonfederal project into a federal action.[16] Although NEPA usually applies when a federal agency provides federal financial assistance for an activity or project implemented by a nonfederal entity, there may not be a sufficient nexus between the federal money and the activity or project, or between federal control and the project, to consider the activity or project a federal action.[17] A recent NEPA-based challenge by environmental justice advocates to enjoin the sale of a former bus depot, from which proceeds were to go toward the construction of a state-of-the-art bus facility, failed because of lack of a sufficient federal nexus.[18] The environmental group's claim that the federal defendants violated NEPA by refusing to conduct an environmental review before entering into the transaction failed because the federal agency involved, through partially funding the project, had no control over the decision making in the project.[19]

An analysis of whether an impact is "major" often overlaps with the determination of whether an action "significantly" affects the environment. CEQ regulations do not differentiate between the two inquiries, providing that "'[m]ajor' reinforces but does not have a meaning independent of 'significantly'."[20] Many courts concur, and have adopted a unitary standard to assess both of these determinations, whereby any significant action is automatically deemed to be major.[21] Other courts have adopted a dual standard, requiring an action to be both "major" and "significant."[22] Nevertheless, the determination of what federal actions are "major" is generally made on a case-by-case basis, taking into account the magnitude and size of the action, as well as the extent of federal involvement in the project.[23] That is, a large project with substantial impacts will likely be classified as major, while a small and limited project with minimal environmental impact will most likely be classified as minor.[24]

Notable Exemptions from NEPA

Many EPA actions are notably exempt from NEPA, either by way of statutory exemptions or common law doctrine. Perhaps the most important exemption, for environmental justice purposes, is the so-called "functional equivalence" doctrine created by federal courts. This doctrine holds that the agency does not have to comply with

NEPA where the environmental assessment, and public participation procedures, provided in a regulation or legislation are the functional equivalent of those provided by NEPA. The functional equivalent doctrine has not been applied outside of exempting EPA.[25]

A federal court first applied the "functional equivalence" doctrine to exempt the EPA from complying with NEPA when it promulgated new source performance standards under the Clean Air Act.[26] Most notably for environmental justice purposes, the federal permitting of solid and hazardous waste facilities under the Resource Recovery and Conservation Act (RCRA) is exempt from NEPA under the "functional equivalent" doctrine.[27] Courts subsequently have created other exemptions for EPA, under the functional equivalence doctrine, for various actions taken under other environmental laws such as the Federal Insecticide, Fungicide and Rodenticide Act (FIFRA),[28] the Safe Drinking Water Act (SDWA),[29] and the Toxic Substances Control Act (TSCA).[30]

Congress has also provided EPA with certain exemptions from NEPA, either full or partial.[31] For instance, Section 511(c) of the Clean Water Act exempts the EPA from compliance with NEPA except for issuance of permits for new sources of water pollution and providing grants to municipalities to build sewage treatment plants.[32] Congress has also explicitly exempted the EPA from all actions under the Clean Air Act.[33]

Consideration of Socioeconomic Impacts at the Threshold Determination Stage

Assuming that NEPA applies to a proposed federal action, the agency must then decide whether to prepare an EIS. The threshold determination at this stage is whether a proposed action is likely to "significantly affect the quality of the human environment."[34] In making this threshold determination, the agency responsible for the action must prepare an "environmental assessment" (EA) in which it assesses the significance of the impact on the environment.[35] If the agency determines that the action will cause a significant impact on the environment, the lead agency must prepare an EIS. If the agency finds the action will not cause such impact, the agency may proceed with the action, issuing a Finding of No Significant Impact (FONSI) in which it presents the reasons why an action will not have a significant impact on the human environment.[36]

Range of Impacts Can Trigger EIS Requirement

Broad regulatory definitions anticipate that a range of impacts will be considered in determining whether an action "significantly affects the quality of the human environment," and hence require an EIS.

CEQ regulations define "significance" by the context and intensity of an action's impact.[37] Whether an action is significant will vary with the setting of the proposed action depending on the affected region, interests, and locality.[38] The significance determination may also be affected by the intensity, or severity, of the proposed action's impact. The regulations list a number of factors to be considered when evaluating the severity of an impact. These factors include:

- effects on public health and safety;
- the unique characteristics of the geographic area;
- the degree to which the effects are "likely to be highly controversial";[39]
- the degree to which the effects are "highly uncertain or involve unique or unknown risks";
- the cumulative effect of the action when considered with other actions; and
- whether the action threatens a violation of a federal, state, or local environmental law.[40]

The effects of an action need not be adverse to be found "significant"; both adverse and beneficial effects are considered "significant" per CEQ regulations.[41] An action may have a significant effect if it causes an impact, beneficial or harmful, on any one of a broad range of aspects of the environment—streams, plant life, wildlife habitats, fish and wildlife, and the soil and air—even if other elements of the environment are not affected.[42]

Similarly, the type of "effects" that must be significant are broad as well, according to regulatory definitions. "Effects," which are synonymous with "impacts," may include ecological, aesthetic, historic, cultural, economic, social, or health effects.[43] However, as discussed below, these impacts are not always enough to require preparation of EIS, even when they are significant. Both indirect and cumulative effects of an action may require preparation of an EIS.[44]

Indirect effects triggering NEPA include effects that may change land patterns, population growth, or ecosystem development.[45] Indirect effects, though they can be "later in time or farther removed in distance," must be reasonably foreseeable to require an EIS.[46] Effects having a "cumulative impact" are those that result from "the incremental impact of the [proposed] action when added to other past, present, and reasonably foreseeable future actions" undertaken by another public or private entity. Cumulative impacts can result from "individually minor but collectively significant actions taking place over a period of time."[47] An effect thus may be significant "if it is related to other actions with individually insignificant" impacts, but "it is reasonable to anticipate a cumulatively significant impact on the environment."[48] In a recent report, CEQ makes clear that cumulative impacts can result from "single or multiple" actions and may result in "additive" or "interactive" effects.[49]

Socioeconomic Impacts Must Have Sufficiently Close Connection to Physical Changes in the Environment to Trigger EIS Process

Socioeconomic effects *alone* do not trigger the EIS process. Even though NEPA speaks of the impact of proposed actions on the "human" environment, its primary concern is with significant impacts on the natural and physical environment. CEQ regulations define the "human environment" as including not only "the natural and physical environment," but the relationship of the people with that environment.[50] In accordance with this broad definition, early cases held that agencies must consider the effects on "urban environments"—such as the contribution to urban decay and blight—and the "quality of life for city residents"—such as the risk of crime and effect on traffic patterns—in their determination of "significance."[51]

Subsequent cases and the CEQ regulations make clear, however, that NEPA is triggered only when impacts on the physical environment are the primary effects stemming from the federal action. CEQ states plainly that "economic or social effects are not intended by themselves to require preparation of an environmental impact statement."[52] Social and economic effects that are not physical in nature must have a nexus—a clear causal relationship—to the impact on the physical environment resulting from the major federal action.[53] The urban environment cases are arguably in accord with this nexus requirement to the extent that the socioeconomic effects in those cases were related to physical effects on the urban environment.[54]

Consideration of Socioeconomic Impacts at the EIS Preparation and Adequacy Stage

Agencies Have Responsibility, and Considerable Discretion, to Collect and Include a Range of Impacts in the EIS

After an agency determines that an EIS is required, and before it drafts the EIS, it must determine its scope. This process is called "scoping" and must be done early in the EIS preparation process.[55] During scoping, an agency identifies the range of issues for consideration in the EIS, as well as their relative significance to the impact analysis. Scoping narrows the EIS analysis, in part, by eliminating issues that are either not significant or that have been, or will be, discussed as part of other environmental reviews. Scoping is also the point at which other environmental requirements applicable to the proposed action are identified and the structure and process of the EIS report are discussed with all participants. The scoping process requires the agency to actively seek the participation of other agencies and the public. Scoping comments can be submitted both in writing and through public meetings held by the agency.

Following scoping, the agency prepares a draft EIS. After a draft EIS is prepared, the agency then distributes the EIS to appropriate agencies and the public. The agency must "affirmatively solicit comments from those persons or organizations who may be interested or affected."[56] The agency must also establish criteria to determine when to hold public hearings or meetings to receive oral input. The agency must hold a hearing or meeting when, among other things, there is "substantial environmental controversy concerning the proposed action or substantial interest in holding the hearing."[57]

The scoping and comments on a draft EIS are key moments for public input on the impact, including socioeconomic impact, of the proposed action.[58] At scoping meetings, and public hearings, agency officials can hear from the public the types of impacts they might experience from the proposed action. "No one better knows how truck traffic down a main street will affect a community than those neighbors who live on that street."[59] Though the EIS is often an impenetrable, technical document, some affected citizens have found innovative ways to parse through the document and comment on its findings.[60] For instance, with technical consultants, some groups have used the EIS in a study-group fashion. Members take different chapters of the EIS and analyze them with a technical consultant, learn as much as possible about a particular topic (for instance, air pollution, traffic impacts, waste management projections), and compare what they learn with the information found in the EIS.[61] Scoping and public hearings on the EIS are also an opportunity for the public to participate in the development of a reasonable array of alternatives and mitigation measures, as well as to present opportunities for socioeconomic impact analysis.[62]

An agency must consider and respond to comments—including those about perceived environmental or socioeconomic impacts—received from the public in the final EIS. Ultimately, however, an agency has the ultimate discretion to determine whether an asserted impact is environmentally significant.[63] If the agency does find significant environmental impacts, the EIS must include a "full and fair discussion" of such impacts.[64]

Analysis of Socioeconomic Impact in the EIS Required Only When Interrelated with Natural/Physical Environmental Effects

NEPA requires that the EIS analyze the direct and indirect environmental consequences of a proposed action, as well as any "alternatives" to that action, and "mitigation" measures, when preparing an

EIS.[65] The EIS may also include a cost-benefit analysis if it is relevant to the choice among environmentally different alternatives, including consideration of factors "not related to environmental quality" but "likely to be relevant and important to a decision."[66] This cost-benefit analysis often calls for some sort of weighing of the environmental costs against the economic, technical, or other public benefits of a proposal.[67] Agencies must also evaluate the cumulative environmental impacts of a proposed action[68] and impacts on "urban quality, historic and cultural resources, and the design of the built environment."[69]

CEQ makes clear, however, that socioeconomic impacts will only be discussed in the impact statement when "economic or social and natural or physical environmental effects are interrelated."[70] This requirement is consistent with the case law discussed above requiring that socioeconomic impacts be causally related to physical effects on the environment to trigger an EIS. When there is such a relationship, as discussed in the NRC case below, the disparate impact on minority and low-income communities should be thoroughly analyzed in the EIS.[71]

NEPA Is a Purely Procedural Statute and Has No Automatic Effect on Decision-Making Outcomes

Even if NEPA applies and an environmental impact statement is required, and completed, the EIS's conclusions may not determine the outcome of the ultimate decision. When an agency reaches a decision on an action for which an EIS was prepared, a public record of decision (ROD) must be prepared that provides information on the alternatives considered, mitigation measures, and other factors considered in the decision-making process.[72] However, the degree to which the alternatives and mitigation measures are actually followed is totally within the agency's discretion. There is no statutory or judicial mandate that an agency follow the least environmentally onerous course. Nevertheless, the information disclosed as part of the NEPA process can affect official or public opinion in a way that significantly affects outcomes.

NEPA is an "essentially procedural" guarantee,[73] and does not establish any substantive environmental standards nor mandate particular outcomes.[74] That is, a court cannot order an agency, on the basis of its conclusion that an impact statement is inadequate, to reject or modify a proposed action.[75] In fact, the Supreme Court has made clear that, for instance, the inclusion of mitigation measures does not impose a "substantive duty to mitigate."[76] The agency does not have to follow the best environmentally sound path or alternative recommended in the document.

The EIS serves two main purposes: to ensure that agencies *consider* environmental impacts, and to ensure that they *disclose* the relevant information to the public.[77] Courts will, and do, review the EIS for its adequacy in discussing the types of impacts required by NEPA, as well as alternatives to the action and mitigation of the anticipated environmental effects. A plaintiff can thus challenge an EIS on "procedural" grounds to determine if it adequately considers all possible impacts, alternatives, and mitigation strategies.[78] If the EIS is not adequate, a court can only order the preparation of an impact statement that meets the requirements of the statute.[79] However, courts normally give considerable deference to agency decisions, including agency decisions not to prepare an EIS and the adequacy of an EIS.[80] As such, judicial challenges to the adequacy of EISs are usually unsuccessful.

One caveat to the above is that information disclosed in the EIS process may ultimately influence the outcome of a proposed project. An agency may become less inclined to follow through with a proposed action, or more inclined to require substantial modifications to the project, if significant impacts will result from the action. If the public believes that the proposed project will cause significant impacts, the project will quickly become controversial. The degree of controversy may either sway an agency's stance toward the project or affect the developer's willingness to through with the project. The Louisiana Energy Services case, discussed below, is one example of a developer's unwillingness to go through with a project after an extended EIS process documenting significant impacts on the affected communities. Last, the EIS analysis may potentially influence future public and private decisions.

The Impact of President Clinton's Environmental Justice Executive Order on Consideration of Socioeconomic Impacts Under NEPA

In his Executive Order (EO) and accompanying Memorandum, President Clinton directed all federal agencies to document "disproportionately high and adverse human health or environmental effects" of its actions on minority and low-income populations.[81] Specifically, with regard to NEPA, the EO requires each federal agency to analyze all environmental effects, including "human health, economic and social effects" of federal actions when such analysis is required by NEPA.[82] The EO specifically requires that, "whenever practicable and appropriate," environmental human health analyses should "identify multiple and cumulative exposures." The EO also calls for mitigation measures, analyzed in an environmental assessment or environmental impact statement, to address "significant and adverse" environmental effects of the federal action on minority communities and low-income communities where feasible.

There is nothing in the EO that changes the causal nexus required between the physical environmental and socioeconomic impacts flowing from a major federal action. However, recent decisions and agency guidance make clear that the EO has substantially bolstered the treatment of such impacts in the NEPA process. As courts and agencies respond to the EO, more attention and focus are directed toward the discernment and consideration of socioeconomic impacts on minority communities.

The Effect of the EO on Agency Compliance with NEPA: CEQ's Guidance

The Interagency Working Group (IWG), created by the EO to implement its requirements, and composed of the heads of federal agencies, has developed guidance on key terms in the Executive Order.[83] Following this guidance on key terms, the CEQ has provided guidance for all federal agencies toward incorporating environmental justice considerations in their NEPA process.[84] The CEQ Guidance sets the stage for how federal agencies will incorporate disproportionate social and economic impacts on minority and low-income communities into their NEPA obligations. At the outset, CEQ advises that agencies recognize "that the question of whether agency action raises environmental justice issues is highly sensitive to the history or circumstances of a particular community or population, the particular type of environmental or health impact, and the nature of the proposed action itself."

While CEQ disavows any "standard formula" for identifying and addressing environmental justice issues, it establishes six general principles to guide agencies in their NEPA compliance. For impact assessment purposes, it is important to understand three of these principles. First, agencies should consider the composition of the affected area to determine whether vulnerable populations (minority, low-income, Indian tribes) are present in the area affected by the proposed action, and, if so, whether there may be disproportionately high and adverse human health and environmental effects on those populations. Second, agencies should consider available public health and industry data concerning the potential for multiple or cumulative exposure to human health or environmental hazards in the affected population and historical patterns of exposure to environmental hazards. Third, agencies should recognize the interrelated cultural, social, occupational, historical, or economic factors that may amplify the physical environmental effects of the proposed agency action—such as physical sensitivity of the community or population to particular impacts, the effect of any disruption on the community structure associated with the proposed action, and the nature and degree of impact on the physical and social structure of the community.

CEQ's principles, however, come with an important caveat. The Presidential Executive Order, CEQ emphasizes, does not "change the prevailing legal thresholds and statutory interpretations under NEPA and existing case law."[85] CEQ makes clear that social or economic effects do not trigger the requirement for an EIS absent a relationship to "significant" impacts on the physical environment. However, agency consideration of impacts on vulnerable communities may lead to the identification of disproportionately high health or environmental impacts that are significant and "that otherwise would be overlooked." CEQ also makes clear that the identification of disproportionately high and adverse human health and environmental effects on vulnerable communities does not preclude a proposed agency action from going forward, nor compel a conclusion that the proposed action is environmentally unsatisfactory. Such identification should instead "heighten agency attention to alternatives, mitigation strategies, monitoring needs, and preferences expressed by the affected community or population."

Federal Agencies' Guidelines on Implementing NEPA in the Environmental Justice Context

EPA and the General Services Administration (GSA) have followed CEQ's guidance and developed specific guidelines for considering environmental justice criteria in implementing NEPA.[86] EPA has, by far, the most extensive guidance on incorporating environmental justice concerns in NEPA analyses. The agencies' guidance will be discussed as they relate to the data collection, socioeconomic analysis, and mitigation/alternatives analysis in the NEPA process. Since much of both EPA's and GSA's guidances follow, or adopt, CEQ's recommendations, this section will further explicate CEQ's recommendations.

Establishing the Affected Environment: Data Collection

CEQ recommends that agencies first determine whether a proposed action is likely to have an impact on low-income or minority populations, or on Indian tribes. Toward this end, CEQ recommends the use of easily accessible census data.[87] This census data will allow agencies to identify the composition of the "potentially affected population." Additionally, agencies should determine whether other federal, tribal, state, and local health, environmental, and economic agencies have useful demographic information to assist in determining whether the proposed action is likely to have a disproportionate impact on the potentially affected population.

Both EPA's and GSA's guidance documents generally concur with CEQ's data collection and environmental assessment strategy.[88] However, EPA and GSA go further in their recommendations. In addition to identifying the proportion of the population of individual census tracts that are composed of minority individuals, EPA suggests that its analysts also attempt to identify whether "high concentration 'pockets' of minority populations are evidenced in specific geographic areas."[89] EPA cautions that traditional census-based population tract data may miss high "pockets" of minority or low-income communities. Census data have proven unreliable in some cases, "in part because the level of aggregation may not offer a fine enough mesh to identify the existence of [minority and/or low-income populations]."[90] As such, and because census data rely on self-reporting, these data are not always "consistent" and are "prone to undercounting" minority and low-income populations "due to a perceived reluctance for certain populations to divulge information."[91] EPA thus recommends that census data be supplemented with data from other sources—such as local agencies; locality-specific questions, interviews, and research; outreach to community groups; geographical information system (GIS), or other mapping systems.[92]

The GSA Guidance shares EPA's concern about masking "pockets" of minority and low-income populations, as well as the need to use "site visits, interviews, [GIS] databases, and other sources to supplement documentary research findings."[93] The GSA also recommends that, in determining whether particular communities may be affected, its analysts must consider "both residents and people who use the affected area." While in some cases these two groups of people will be the same population, sometimes they differ. For instance, it gives an example of a community where residents of the downtown commercial area might be predominantly Latino, but the area might contain small businesses like grocery stores that are heavily used by members of a Southeast Asian community who reside elsewhere. While census data may identify people who *live* in the area, it will not identify those who *use* the affected area. To identify the latter group, "discussions with local sources of expertise and the community itself" will be necessary.[94]

Assessing the Impact on Vulnerable Populations: The Role of Culture

In determining whether a disproportionate impact exists, CEQ indicates that additional demographic analysis may be necessary due to specific cultural factors.[95] That is, agencies "should recognize" that impacts on vulnerable populations—minority and/or low-income populations, and Indian tribes—"may be different from impacts on the general population due to a community's distinct cultural practices." As such, an agency should also gather data on "different patterns of living, such as subsistence fish, vegetation, or wildlife consumption and the use of well water in rural communities" where relevant to the disproportionate impact analysis. Where Indian tribes may be affected, agencies must also consider "pertinent treaty, statutory, or executive order rights and consult with tribal governments in a manner consistent with the government-to-government relationship."

EPA's Guidance gives two illuminating examples of how cultural practices might affect disproportionate impact analysis.[96] For instance, a portion of an area's total population may be disproportionately affected if the construction of a new treatment plant will discharge into a river or stream used by subsistence anglers. A local Native American community may be disproportionately impacted if a proposed project affects on- or off-reservation tribal resources (for example, treaty-protected resources, cultural resources, and sacred sites), thus implicating the federal trust responsibility to tribes. EPA thus recommends that its NEPA analytical teams identify both the "presence of distinct minority communities" residing within and in close proximity to the proposed project, as well as those "minority groups which utilize or are dependent upon natural resources that could be potentially affected by the proposed action."

Socioeconomic Impact Analysis in the EA and EIS Process

CEQ recommends that agencies clearly and concisely state in the EIS or EA any disproportionately high and adverse human health or environmental impacts on minority and/or low-income communities and Indian tribes.[97] It also recommends that even when no EIS or EA is prepared—either because an exemption applies or when an agency claims that another environmental statute establishes the "functional equivalent" of an EIS or EA—agencies should "augment their procedures as appropriate to ensure that the otherwise applicable process or procedure for a federal action addresses environmental justice concerns.[98]

EPA is more specific in its guidance regarding the extent of socioeconomic discussions in EISs and EAs. EPA also directs its analysts to analyze social and economic impacts, including the unique cultural aspects of populations, in EISs and EAs. Though it is bound by current law—the rule, for instance, that economic or social effects alone do not trigger an EIS—EPA nevertheless attempts to get the most out of socioeconomic analysis in the NEPA process. As a matter of policy, the EPA "will consider interrelated social and economic impacts in EAs." However, "the initial step in the analysis of potential effects is to assess whether there indeed will be potential physical or natural environmental effects."[99] Where "grey areas" exist in the determination of whether the natural or physical effects will be "significant," EPA encourages further analysis. In such cases, the EA should include an analysis of interrelated social and economic effects, and an "EIS-like scoping process" should begin where there may be disproportionately high and adverse effects on vulnerable populations.[100] The EA should "include socioeconomic analyses scaled according to the severity of the impacts."[101]

Even if an EIS is not required, EPA expresses hope that environmental justice concerns "should sensitize EPA NEPA analysts to the need to focus" their analyses which may demonstrate that potential impacts that are not significant in the NEPA context "are particularly disproportionate or particularly severe on minority and/or low-income communities." Where such impacts exist, regardless of whether an EIS is prepared, they should "trigger the serious consideration of alternatives and mitigation actions in coordination with extensive community outreach."[102]

If an EIS is required, EPA recommends that the scoping notices should "include a description of the results of the environmental justice screening analysis."[103] If the analyst concludes that there is a potential for disproportionately high and adverse effects, the analyst should:

- ensure that the EIS scoping process raises environmental justice concerns;
- provide sufficient data and information to evaluate these potential effects;
- conduct public outreach strategies; and
- specifically ask the public to suggest alternatives and mitigation measures aimed at reducing or avoiding disproportionately high and adverse effects.

The analyst should also design "comparative socioeconomic, environmental and health analyses of all reasonable alternatives and mitigation measures" that are "tailored and/or scaled" to evaluate the impacts to the affected population.

Cumulative and Indirect Impact Analysis

Often minority and/or low-income communities are exposed to multiple environmental hazards, through various pathways. Hence, a major issue for impact analysis in these communities is the cumulative effects of such exposure.[104] CEQ recently issued a separate report on cumulative impact analysis, pointing out the centrality of cumulative impact analysis to the NEPA process, and providing tools for performing cumulative impact assessment and analysis.[105] The report notes that federal agencies routinely address the direct and, to a lesser extent, the indirect effects of a proposed action on the environment. However, there is insufficient attention to cumulative effects analysis, partly due to the increased use of EAs rather than EISs in the NEPA process.[106] CEQ does recognize that "analyzing cumulative effects is more challenging" due to the difficulty of "defining the geographic (spatial) and time (temporal) boundaries."[107] Nevertheless, CEQ believes that "adequate consideration" of cumulative effects requires that EAs more fully address those effects.

EPA's Environmental Justice Guidance builds on CEQ's stance on cumulative effects.[108] EPA analysts "must" consider the cumulative effects on a vulnerable community by addressing "the full range of consequences of a proposed action" as well as "other environmental stresses which may be affecting the community." In particular, EPA analysts are directed to place "special emphasis" on other sources of environmental stress within the region, including those that have "historically existed," those that "currently exist," and those that are "projected for the future."[109] For instance, the EPA notes, when considering a project that will have a permitted discharge to surrounding surface waters, "it may be of concern to populations who rely on subsistence living patterns" (for instance, fishing) and "already receive public water through lead service lines." As such, the EPA must take into account the cumulative effects associated with both the discharges and the lead service lines. Analysts should also look at a community's dependence on "natural resources for its economic base" (for example, tourism and cash crops), as well as "cultural values" that the community may place on a "natural resource at risk." The analyst should thus consider the cumulative impacts from the "perspective of these specific resources or ecosystems which are vital" to the communities of interest.

Similarly, EPA encourages particularized attention to indirect effects of an action on minority and low-income communities.[110] EPA calls special attention to indirect effects such as increased air pollution, lower housing values, and reduced access to fishing/farming locations resulting from increased urbanization around a new facility due to increased employment or transportation system upgrades. Indirect impacts, such as loss of a sacred site and/or other natural resources may also result from government actions. Actions that result in business failure (and associated unemployment), erosion of tax bases, and reduced public services may be exacerbated in low-income and minority communities due to an inability to relocate, the need to travel long distances to find alternative means of employment, or a failure to attract new industry or commerce.

The Effect of the EO on Agency Adjudication Under NEPA: The Louisiana Energy Services Case

Recent agency decisions confirm that the Presidential EO, and CEQ's Guidance, are having a demonstrable effect on NEPA's implementation vis-a-vis minority and low-income communities. For instance, relying in part on the EO, the EPA recently revoked air permits issued by the State of Louisiana to the Shintech Corporation for a multimillion-dollar chemical plant proposed in a community that is over 80 percent African American. In part, the decision was based on a failure by Louisiana to ensure that "minority and low-income communities [would] not be disproportionately subjected to environmental hazards."[111]

Another recent published decision, the *Louisiana Energy Services* case, involving a proposed uranium facility in Louisiana, is quite significant in terms of its explication of what implementation of President Clinton's Executive Order in the NEPA context requires. The developer twice lost before the Nuclear Regulatory Commission on the adequacy of its EIS for the project. Eventually, after the second decision, the developer terminated the project.[112]

The NRC Licensing Board Decision

On May 1, 1997, the Atomic Safety and Licensing Board (Board) of the Nuclear Regulatory Commission (NRC) found deficient an EIS for a license to construct and operate a privately owned uranium enrichment facility immediately adjacent to the mostly poor and African American communities of Forest Grove and Center Springs, Louisiana.[113] As a result, the three-judge Board panel rejected the license of the Louisiana Energy Services (LES) to build and operate the plant. A local citizens group, Citizens Against Nuclear Trash (CANT), had charged the company with environmental racism and contested the permit to operate the plant. The group's claims were grounded in NEPA. CANT contended that the agency's EIS inadequately considered the negative economic and social impacts of closing a central road connecting the two African American communities to make way for the plant. Further, the group claimed that the siting process itself was racially discriminatory. Relying on the EO, the Board required a more thorough disparate impact analysis by the agency than perhaps otherwise would have been required absent the EO. It also directed a thorough investigation of potential racial discrimination in the siting process, which culminated in the choice of the host location for the facility.

The Background

The facility was to be sited in Claiborne Parish, Louisiana, which is immediately adjacent to and between the unincorporated communities of Center Springs and Forest Grove. African Americans make up over 97 percent of the population in the two surrounding communities of Forest Grove and Center Springs. The 1990 census statistics demonstrate that the residents of Forest Grove and Center Springs are part of a population that is among the poorest and most disadvantaged in the United States. African Americans make up 46 percent of the population in the community where the facility was to be located, Claiborne Parish, Louisiana. Over 58 percent of Claiborne Parish's African American population live below the poverty level, as compared to 30 percent of its total population. Per capita income of the black population of Claiborne Parish is only 36 percent of the white population, compared to the national average of 55 percent.

Construction of the facility would necessitate the closing and relocation of a road, Parish Road 39, that is a vital and frequently used pedestrian link between the two surrounding African American communities. Aside from Parish Road 39 and another road, State Road 9, the roads in Center Springs or Forest Grove are either unpaved or poorly maintained. The two community churches, which share a single minister, are one mile apart, with the land on which the facility would be located lying between them. The Board noted that there are no stores, schools, medical clinics, or businesses in Center Springs or Forest Grove. The citizens group, CANT, contended that the road closing would have caused hardships to families who use the road, residents who carpool to work, school transportation, sports-related activities that involve children living in both communities, and church services that are divided between the two communities.

The EIS's Treatment of Evidence of Racial Bias in the Site Selection Process

The citizens group also contended that the siting process was racially discriminatory and hence followed a national pattern of siting such facilities in minority communities. This charge was based largely on the research and expert testimony of Dr. Robert D. Bullard, the prominent academic who pioneered work on environmental racism.[114] Professor Bullard presented evidence that, in his view, demonstrated that racial considerations were a factor in the site selection process. According to Bullard's statistical analysis, the levels of poverty and of African Americans in the local population rose dramatically at each progressively narrower stage of the company's site selection process until they culminated in the selection of a site with a local population that is extremely poor and 97 percent African American. Based on his assessment of the applicant's testimony of the site selection process, Bullard also concluded that the race-neutral siting criteria—including the criteria of low population and siting the facility five miles from institutions such as schools, hospitals, and nursing homes—operated in conjunction with the current racial segregation and the resulting inferior infrastructure (lack of adequate schools, road paving, water supply, and other conditions) in a manner that ensured that the final selection would be a poor community of color.

The applicant, through its witnesses, denied that the site selection process was racially biased or based on racial considerations. The NRC staff's EIS mirrored this general denial. Responding to many comments on the draft environmental impact statement, which alleged that the applicant deliberately chose the site because of its demographic makeup, the staff responded that the site selection process was "reasonable" and "appears to be based solely on business and technical considerations." Moreover, the staff found "no specific evidence that racial considerations were a factor" in the process. It based this assessment both on the fact that none of the commenters cited any specific evidence to support the charge of racism in the site selection process and from a review of information about the site selection process contained in the applicant's environmental assessment report. The staff's findings on this issue further suggested that the Board approach the issue by "looking at the question whether the selection process was overtly racist."

The Board found that Bullard's evidence was more than sufficient to raise a reasonable inference that racial considerations played some part in the site selection process and that additional inquiry was warranted. Moreover, the Board opined that Bullard's evidence had not been persuasively rebutted. The Board further opined that the NRC staff failed to comply with the EO by limiting its review of the siting process in the EIS to a "facial" and "cursory" review of the description of that process (as it appeared in the applicant's environmental report). Instead, only a "thorough and in-depth investigation" of the process would "insure compliance" with the Presidential nondiscrimination directive contained in the EO.[115] As such, it ordered the staff to "lift some rocks and look under them" because racial discrimination is "rarely, if ever, admitted," is "often rationalized under some other seemingly racially neutral guise, making it difficult to ferret out," and "direct evidence of racial discrimination is rarely found." If racial discrimination were "so easily detected," the board opined, racial discrimination "would not be such a persistent and enduring problem in American society."

The EIS's Treatment of Disparate Socioeconomic Impacts

The citizens group, CANT, also contended, among other things, that the EIS failed to address the impacts of closing and/or relocation of Parish Road 39 on the surrounding African American communities.[116] The EIS indicated that the road relocation would add approximately one mile of distance between the Forest Grove Church and the Center Springs Church, which are the centers of the respective African American communities. It also indicates that the two communities would be "inconvenienced" by the road relocation due to the increased driving time between the communities. The NRC staff concluded in the EIS that the impacts associated with the road relocation would be "very small and would not impose unacceptable risks to the local community" and that "there will not be a disproportionate adverse impact on minority or low-income populations."

The citizens group challenged the EIS's assessment of the impact from relocating the road on the two African American communities. Specifically, it asserted that the disproportionate impacts would result from the fact that the road was a "vital and regularly used pedestrian link" between the two communities. Census Bureau evidence bolstered this assertion, indicating that over 31 percent of African American households in the Claiborne Parish area have no motor vehicles. The evidence was undisputed. The EIS had not discussed the road's status as a pedestrian link and the impacts of the relocation on those who must walk the distance between the communities on this road. The Board opined that while adding .38 mile to the distance between the Forest Grove and Center Springs communities may be a mere "inconvenience" to those who drive, as the staff suggests, it amounts to a more significant impact for those who must regularly "make the trip on foot" and who may be "old, ill or otherwise infirm." Since the staff had not considered the impacts of the road relocation upon residents who walk, the Board concluded that the EIS must be revised to discuss those impacts.

Last, the citizens group challenged the EIS's assessment of property value impacts in the two African American communities, Forest Grove and Center Springs. The EIS noted that there might be "changes in property values (some positive, some negative)" and that any impacts on property values "would be distributed throughout the region and are not expected to disproportionately or adversely impact Forest Grove or Center Springs." Moreover, the applicant indicated in its environmental assessment report that property values might be enhanced by the facility's presence, due to the "location of business ventures supporting [the facility's] operations" (for example, food service, equipment vendors). The applicant also pointed to other areas around the country where property values had increased after the siting of similar facilities. Ultimately, these seemingly upper-middle-class communities, where property values had increased, were incomparable to the disadvantaged minority communities of Forest Grove and Center Springs.

The Board found the EIS's consideration of property impacts deficient. The Board agreed with the citizens group that the staff needed to conduct a more focused analysis of property value impacts, taking into account the demographics of the people in communities hosting facilities.[117] The Board found "reasonable" and "persuasive" Dr. Bullard's testimony challenging the staff's failure to assess the impacts of the facility on the African American communities at issue, asserting that when facilities like the one at issue are placed in the midst of poor, minority communities, the facility has negative impacts on property values in the immediate area of the facility. Because the EIS did not consider the racial makeup of the homes surrounding the site when it analyzed the impacts from the facility on property values, the Board concluded that "the staff apparently has not considered the economic impact on property values on siting the [facility] in the midst of these neighboring minority communities." As such, the Board found that "exploration of this matter would likely be another circumstance that merits scrutiny" under the President's EO. The staff was thus ordered to consider these impacts and factor them into its weighing of the costs and benefits of the facility and in its environmental justice determination.

The Nuclear Regulatory Commission Decision

On appeal, a three-commissioner panel of the NRC upheld the aspect of the decision regarding the treatment of disparate socioeconomic impacts, but overturned the board's order to investigate racial discrimination in the siting process.[118]

The EIS Must Consider Disparate Socioeconomic Impacts When Related to Physical Impacts

The NRC agreed that staff had failed to consider adequately the disparate impact of the road closure and relocation on the pedestrian mobility of the surrounding poor African American communities. The NRC accepted the contention that the two impoverished African American communities would be disparately impacted by the relocation of the road. It agreed that the evidence established that residents of the African American communities rely heavily on the existing road and that its closing would result in larger impacts on these communities than was reflected in the EIS. Since the socioeconomic impacts on these communities were related to the physical impacts of the proposed facility—they "may be fairly said to be within the impacts of closing the existing road"—the NRC ruled that EIS should consider them more thoroughly.

The NRC also ruled that the EIS failed to analyze adequately adverse property values impacts on the African American communities. The EIS gave a cursory analysis of the issue, stating only that "some negative" impact on property values would occur, without explanation or analysis. The NRC rejected the developer's argument that property values in the two communities might actually increase, as had property adjacent to other nuclear plants sited by the developer. The NRC pointed out that the sites of the two nuclear power plants offered as examples by the developer "could not be more different in terms of demographics from the [impoverished African American communities in this case]." The "allegedly analogous" nuclear power plants lie adjacent to prestigious resort communities, whereas the two African American communities impacted in the present case "are inhabited by some of the most economically disadvantaged people in the United States." Thus, factors that might increase the value of property near some nuclear facilities, such as "increased demand for homes by migrating employees," the NRC opined, simply "do not apply to [the two African American communities in the present case] because new employees probably would choose to live in communities with more amenities." Moreover, since Forest Grove and Center Springs "receive almost no [Claiborne Parish] services, their property values would not necessarily benefit from the influx of new tax money into [Claiborne Parish] from the [facility]."

NEPA Is Not a Tool to Address Racial Bias in the Siting Process

The NRC decision also illustrates that there are limits to the type of analysis required by EIS, even with the EO. The Commission refused to force the investigation of the site selection process that led to the choice of the facility site, to permit a determination of whether "the selection process was tainted with racial bias." The Commission reasoned that though NEPA does force agencies to consider social and economic impacts ancillary to physical environmental impacts, it is not a tool for addressing problems of racial discrimination. Relying on CEQ's *Guidance for Considering Environmental Justice Under NEPA,* NRC acknowledged that though CEQ calls for a close NEPA examination of a proposed project's impacts on vulnerable communities, CEQ neither "states nor implies that if adverse impacts are found, an investigation into possible racial bias is the next possible step." Moreover, the NRC noted that an inquiry into a license applicant's supposed discriminatory motives or acts would be far removed from NEPA's core interest—"the physical environment, the world around us, so to speak." As such, the NRC held, NEPA "is not a civil rights law calling for full scale racial discrimination litigation in NRC licensing procedures."

Impact Assessment Under Other Federal Laws

Other federal laws also allow consideration of disproportionate socioeconomic impacts. A pair of decisions by the Environmental Protection Agency makes clear that there are important opportunities to implement President Clinton's Executive Order in federal statutes other than NEPA—most particularly permitting statutes. These decisions also indicate that there are substantial limitations to considering environmental justice concerns in permitting processes as well. The EO does not change existing law, as these opinions note, but merely allows implementation of the EO's mandates consistent with existing law.

Other federal statutes also provide for impact assessment of social and/or economic considerations.[119] Of these statutes, the National Historic Preservation Act is worth mention for its emphasis on historic resources, and for a recent ruling which resulted in a successful negotiated settlement that protected a historic black neighborhood in Florida from redevelopment into luxury residences and office buildings.[120]

Impact Assessment Under Federal Environmental Statutes: Permits Under the Resource Conservation and Recovery Act, the Safe Drinking Water Act, and the Clean Air Act

Impact Assessment Under RCRA

Courts and regulators assume that the environmental review process imbedded in RCRA is the "functional equivalent" of NEPA's process.[121] This assumption is probably technically correct in that the EPA "considers fully, with the assistance of meaningful public comment, environmental issues involved in the permitting of hazardous waste management facilities." RCRA, like many federal permitting statues, conditions issuance of a permit on the environmental impact of a proposed facility—taking into consideration the facility's proximity to surface and groundwaters, floodplains, wetlands, and surrounding land uses.[122] However, there are clear disadvantages to minority and low-income populations when RCRA, but not NEPA, is used to assess the environmental impacts of a project. Unlike NEPA, RCRA does not require the government to collect or consider information about the socioeconomic impacts of its actions or the indirect effects of those actions, even when related to physical environmental impacts. RCRA also does not require the government to consider alternatives to issuing a permit, or to consider mitigation measures to address social and economic impacts that will be caused if the agency issues the permit. However, the functional equivalence doctrine probably has little remaining effect on the bulk of waste permits, as EPA has delegated the task of RCRA permitting to most states. As such, either the state permitting process, or the state equivalent of NEPA, may allow for socioeconomic impact analysis.

Nevertheless, President Clinton's Executive Order appears to have strengthened and expanded impact assessment under RCRA. An EPA Environmental Appeals Board (Board) has recently held that the Agency may, in its discretion, focus its health and environmental assessment under RCRA specifically on a vulnerable community, as a means of implementing the President's Executive Order.[123] In *In re Chemical Waste,* the Board relied on RCRA's omnibus clause, which counsels that "each permit" contain "such terms and conditions" as the administrator or state "determines necessary to protect human health and environment."[124] Pursuant to this clause, if the operation of a facility would have an adverse impact on the health or environment of a surrounding community, regardless of its demographics, the Agency would be required to include permit terms or conditions that would ensure that such impacts do not occur. Moreover, if the nature of the facility and its proximity to the community would make it impossible to craft a set of permit terms that would protect the health and environment of such populations, the Agency would have the authority to deny the permit.[125] The Board reasoned that there is nothing in the omnibus clause that prevents the Agency from taking a more refined look at its health and environment impacts assessment, in light of allegations that operation of the facility would have a disproportionately adverse effect on the health or environment of vulnerable populations. Thus, the Board concluded, when a "superficially plausible" claim of disproportionate impact is alleged, the Agency should "as a matter of policy" exercise its discretion under the omnibus clause to include a health and environmental impact assessment "focusing particularly on" the vulnerable community.

As with impact assessments under NEPA, the scope of an impact assessment of a minority or low-income community under RCRA is limited. The EPA Board in *Chemical Waste* emphasized that the Agency does not have the discretion to "redress impacts that are unrelated or only tenuously related to human health and the environment," such as disproportionate impacts on the economic well-being of a minority or low-income community. It thus follows that the Agency could not reject a RCRA permit "based solely upon alleged social or economic impacts upon the community," if unrelated to health and environmental impacts. The Board concluded that "[i]f a permit applicant meets the requirements of RCRA and its implementing regulations," the permitting Agency "must" issue the permit, "regardless of the racial or socioeconomic composition of the surrounding community" and "regardless of the economic effect of the facility on the surrounding community."

Moreover, the Board held that the Agency has considerable discretion in determining the scope of a demographic study intended to measure whether there would be a disproportionate impact on a vulnerable community. The Board opined that "the proper scope of the demographic study to consider such impacts is an issue calling for a highly technical judgment as to the probable dispersion of pollutants through various media into the surrounding community." That sort of judgment, in the Board's mind, is "precisely the kind of issue that the [Agency], with its technical expertise and experience, is best suited to decide." The Board gave great deference to the Agency in the face of a challenge to the Agency's decision to restrict the focus of its study to communities within a one-mile radius of the facility.[126]

Impact Assessment Under the Safe Drinking Water Act

The President's Executive Order can also be implemented in a similar way under the Safe Drinking Water Act (SDWA) and its Underground Injection Control (UIC) regulations. In *In re Envotech,* the EPA Appeals Board mirrored its ruling in *Chemical Waste* and held that the UIC regulatory omnibus authority also gave the Agency authority to impose special permit conditions to prevent drinking water sources from being endangered by underground injection.[127] As such, the Board reasoned, nothing in the UIC omnibus authority prevents the Agency from performing a disparate impact analysis when there is an allegation that the drinking water of minority or low-income communities may be particularly threatened by a proposed underground injection well. The Board thus held that when a commenter submits a "superficially plausible claim" that a proposed underground injection well will "disproportionately impact the drinking water" of a vulnerable community in which the well is located, the Agency should "as a matter of policy" exercise its discretion "to include within its assessment of the proposed well an analysis focusing particularly" on the vulnerable community whose drinking water is affected.

However, like the RCRA omnibus clause, there are limitations to what types of impacts the Agency can address pursuant to the UIC omnibus clause. The omnibus clause speaks only of protection of drinking water. As such, an impact assessment, and any permit modifications, should only focus on identifying and addressing disproportionate impacts to a vulnerable community's drinking water. The Agency could not redress impacts "unrelated to the protection of underground sources or drinking water, such as alleged negative economic impacts on the community, diminution in property values, or alleged proliferation of local undesirable land uses."

Impact Assessment Under the Clean Air Act

In two recent decisions, the Environmental Appeals Board has addressed environmental justice issues in the context of permits issued pursuant to the Clean Air Act. Similar to its implementation of the President's Order in the RCRA and SDWA context, the Board has held that EPA has considerable discretion to perform a disparate impact analysis when there is an allegation that a minority or low-income population may be disproportionately affected by a particular facility. In both cases, *In re Puerto Rico Electric Power Authority*[128] and *In re EcoElectrica*,[129] the Board gave considerable deference to the disparate impact analysis conducted by EPA in the face of claims that such analysis was deficient. In *In re Puerto Rico*, an EPA region had undertaken a disparate impact analysis as part of its issuance of a final prevention of significant deterioration (PSD) permit and approval to construct a power plant pursuant to the Clean Air Act. As part of that disparate impact analysis, EPA concluded that the facility would "cause no disproportionate adverse health impacts to lower-income populations." The challenger argued that EPA erred in not performing an epidemiology study, in violation of the President's Order, despite the testimony at the public hearing concerning the treatment of various respiratory diseases that may be exacerbated by the facility. The Board deemed the census and GIS analysis performed by EPA enough to support the finding of no disparate impact, even in the absence of an epidemiology study. The challengers failed, the Board concluded, to make even a facial demonstration that EPA's methods or conclusions were wrong.

In *In re EcoElectrica*, the Board upheld a similar disparate impact analysis performed by an EPA region in response to a challenged PSD permit. There, the challenger asserted that EPA's discretionary decision not to require "multisource modeling"—an analysis of the combined impact from existing facilities in the vicinity—was an example of environmental injustice. Because the challenger's reference to environmental justice was "entirely unexplained," the Board felt at a loss to ascertain "the specific basis" for the contention that additional modeling, or additional information gathering, should have been required for reasons of environmental justice. Nevertheless, the Board reviewed EPA's analysis performed to identify any disproportionate impact of the permit decision upon a low-income community. In its disparate impact analysis, EPA assembled per capita income data from the Census Bureau, and source location data from the Toxics Release Inventory and the region's own Permit Compliance System. EPA concluded that the proposed facility would not have a disproportionately high impact on lower-income communities.[130] Hence, the Board declined to review the permit decision on the ground of environmental justice, given the absence of the challenger to dispute the procedures employed in the disparate impact analysis and an explanation of why additional data would reveal such an impact.

The National Historic Preservation Act

NEPA, as described below, requires federal decision makers to assess, among other things, the historic impacts of proposed projects. Another very important source of historic impact assessment in vulnerable communities is the National Historic Preservation Act of 1966 (NHPA).[131] If a federal, federally assisted, or federally licensed project could potentially affect a landmark listed on, or eligible for, the National Register, a "Section 106 review" must be conducted before the project can begin.[132] Under Section 106, the federal or state agency undertaking the project must "take into account" its effects on the host community's historic resources, prior to the approval of the expenditure of funds or the issuance of a license. If a government fails to conduct Section 106 reviews where appropriate, it could be enjoined from carrying out federally assisted activities and possibly be ordered to reimburse federal funds already expended on those activities.[133] As in the *City of Cocoa* case, described below, this review may result in a negotiation process that leads to cooperative efforts between the lead agency and a vulnerable community, which balances a city's need for economic development with a community's desire to maintain historic resources.[134]

An Overview of Section 106 Review

The Section 106 review begins with the agency determining whether the proposed project could result in changes in the character or use of historic properties—defined as properties that are included on, or meet the criteria of, the National Register of Historic Places (National Register).[135] Based on the nature of the undertaking and the area of potential effects, the agency then identifies the historic properties that the proposed project may affect. Depending on what is already known of the area, the agency reviews background information, consults with the State Historic Preservation Officer (SHPO) and others, such as the Tribal Historic Preservation Officer (THPO), and conducts additional studies including field surveys. Districts, sites, buildings, structures, and objects listed in the National Register are considered. Section 106 review gives equal consideration to properties that have already been included in the National Register as well as those that are eligible for inclusion.

If historic properties are found, the agency then assesses what effect its undertaking will have on them.[136] The agency again works with the SHPO, and considers the views of others. The agency makes its assessment based on criteria found in the Council's regulations, and can make one of three determinations:

- "no effect": the undertaking will not affect historic properties;
- "no adverse effect": the undertaking will affect one or more historic properties, but the effect will not be harmful; or
- "adverse effect": the undertaking will harm one or more historic properties.[137]

If the Section 106 review determines that the project would have an adverse effect on a historic property, the government must afford the federal Advisory Council on Historic Preservation a reasonable opportunity to comment on the project.[138] In addition to the Advisory Council, which oversees and administers the process, the agency in charge of the process will also consult the SHPO and the THPO.[139] Others who may be consulted, under various circumstances, include local governments, Indian tribes, permit or license applicants, property owners, other members of the public, and the Council.[140] Consultation is designed to result in a Memorandum of Agreement (MOA), which outlines agreed-upon measures that the agency will take to reduce, avoid, or mitigate the adverse effect.[141] If an MOA is executed, the agency proceeds with its undertaking under the terms of the MOA. In the absence of an MOA, the agency head must take into account the Council's written comments in deciding whether and how to proceed.[142]

Houston v. City of Cocoa

In *Houston v. City of Cocoa*,[143] plaintiffs from a historic black neighborhood challenged a municipal redevelopment plan that would replace much of the neighborhood character with large office complexes and luxury residential buildings. The City of Cocoa was established in the 1880s, with many blacks among the first settlers. Over time, the black and white communities sprang up separately, with white settlers building their homes and stores on the shoreline of the Indian River and blacks building their homes and businesses several blocks west, on the other side of the Florida East Coast railroad tracks. Many of the homes built by the first black settlers are still standing in the neighborhood, as are many of the businesses. In 1940, the City of Cocoa adopted its first zoning ordinance which zoned the entire

African American residential neighborhood for commercial uses. In the ensuing decades, the neighborhood became occupied by heavy commercial enterprises such as auto body shops, junkyards, a paint factory, and, eventually, a major utility company. However, despite the proliferation of commercial uses, the "essentially residential character of the neighborhood . . . as well as its function as the center of the black community in Cocoa persisted."[144] The neighborhood retained a relatively high proportion of owner-occupied low-income housing, as well as its churches.

In 1981, the City of Cocoa adopted a Redevelopment Plan (Plan), which was to be funded by a Community Development Block Grant administered by the U.S. Department of Housing and Urban Development. The historic African American neighborhood of the city was designated as the "core" of the redevelopment area and identified as Project 12. A diagram of Project 12 illustrated that all of the "core" area homes were to be replaced with townhouses, shopping centers, professional offices, and a city park. The Plan anticipated relocating all of the residents to other suitable housing, as the new housing was clearly not affordable to any of the existing residents. Virtually all of the residents living in the "core" area were African Americans, and severe poverty characterized the neighborhood: 76 percent of the residents earned less than $5,000 per year.[145]

The Plan did not materialize right away. Instead, the city "redlined" the neighborhood by stopping public funds for housing improvements in the redevelopment area until the Plan was adopted. Simultaneously, the city used block grant funds to begin to develop the infrastructure for the Plan—adding parking lots and repaving streets. In 1988, the city rezoned the historic African American neighborhood for high-density residential and "core commercial" uses. In addition, minimum lot size requirements were tripled, rendering most existing lots nonconforming. The ordinance "specifically referred to the [Plan] and stated its intention to implement the Core Area Redevelopment element of that plan."[146]

The rezoning action prompted eight long-standing residents of the neighborhood to bring the lawsuit on behalf of themselves and a class of African American residents in the "core" redevelopment area. They alleged, among other things, that the city had violated the NHPA by failing to identify historic properties within the African American neighborhood, failing to assess the effects of the proposed redevelopment on the structures within the neighborhood that are eligible for inclusion on the National Register, and failing to consult with the State Historic Preservation Office and Advisory Committee on Historic Properties regarding such effects. Although the city had performed a survey to identify National Register–eligible properties, it failed to identify any such properties within the historic African American neighborhood. The U.S. District Court, Middle District of Florida, upheld these allegations against the city's motion to dismiss on the ground that plaintiffs had alleged facts to show that some of the properties within the African American neighborhood could be eligible for inclusion on the National Register.

Shortly after the denial of the city's motion to dismiss the complaint, the parties reached a negotiated settlement of all the plaintiff's claims. Under the settlement terms, the city appropriated $675,000 of future grant money and redevelopment funds for single-family housing rehabilitation in the African American neighborhood. Money was also earmarked to fund a not-for-profit community center and low-income housing. The neighborhood was rezoned for low-density, small-lot residential uses, thus bringing the area in conformity with zoning laws. Existing wholesale commercial uses were grandfathered, allowing for the peaceful coexistence of residents and businesses, and for voluntary conversions of businesses to residential uses. However, once a piece of land is converted from a commercial to a residential use, the right to future commercial use is terminated—the business cannot thereafter return to a commercial use. Finally, the city designated a portion of the neighborhood as a local historic district, "in recognition of the historic structures remaining and the role that the neighborhood played in the history of the black community in Cocoa."[147]

Impact Assessment Under State Laws

Sixteen states plus the District of Columbia and Puerto Rico have so-called "mini-NEPAs."[148] Some of these State Environmental Policy Acts (SEPAs) are modeled directly after, and very similar in their requirements to, NEPA.[149] The scope and strength of other SEPAs vary widely, however. For instance, while some states allow socioeconomic factors to be taken into account, as discussed below, many others do not.[150] States like California, New York, and Washington go beyond NEPA, particularly in their treatment of socioeconomic effects. Additionally, a number of states have a lower threshold for determining whether an EIS must be prepared, requiring an EIS where an action "may" or "[may] potentially" affect the environment.[151]

Some states require an environmental impact assessment statement for every governmental action, local and statewide, while others only require one for select agencies and actions.[152] Some states, for instance, specifically allow permits for hazardous waste facilities subject to the EIS requirement.[153] Others explicitly exempt waste facility permits, or permits and licenses generally.[154] One state makes the EIS process completely optional, not requiring an EIS for any action.[155] Some SEPAs, unlike NEPA, attempt to affect substantive decision making by imposing an obligation that the decision maker either follow the least environmentally onerous alternative, or justify not doing so on the basis of other factors.[156]

States without SEPAs, and some states with SEPAs, may take into account socioeconomic factors in their hazardous or solid waste siting process. Like RCRA, most states condition the issuance of a permit on technical factors—for example, compliance with various environmental regulations and requirements—and environmental impacts—such as proximity to surface waters, groundwater, floodplains, wetlands, and surrounding land uses. While many states simply adopt the permit requirements set out in RCRA, many others go beyond those minimal requirements.

Socioeconomic Impact Assessment Under SEPAs

Like NEPA, most SEPAs provide that social and economic impacts alone will not trigger an EIS. Instead, such impacts must form a causal nexus with the physical environment, or be so interrelated with the physical environment to be considered a part of physical environmental changes.[157] In some states, a project's "significant effects" on the environment, necessary to trigger an EIS, can include social and economic impacts unrelated to physical effects.[158] However, these states are clearly in the minority.

Once an EIS is triggered, a number of states require or permit the EIS to analyze social and economic impacts.[159] However, some states also limit discussion of socioeconomic impacts in an EIS to tracing out physical effects of the proposed project.[160]

The California regulation provides some examples of how socioeconomic and physical effects might be interrelated, and how socioeconomic impacts could render an otherwise minor physical change "significant." For instance, if a project would cause overcrowding of a public facility and the overcrowding causes an adverse effect on people, the overcrowding would be regarded as a significant environmental effect.[161] Likewise, if the construction of a new freeway or rail line divides an existing community, the construction would be the physical change, but the social effect on the community would be the basis for determining that the effect would be significant.[162] As an additional example, if the construction of a road and the resulting increase in noise in an area disturbed existing religious practices in the area, the disturbance of the religious practices could be used to determine that the construction and use of the road and the resulting noise would be significant effects on the environment.

The religious practices would need to be analyzed only to the extent that they would show that the increase in traffic and noise would conflict with the religious practices.[163]

Washington's SEPA, for instance, does not specify "socioeconomic" in the statute itself, because "the term does not have a uniform meaning and has caused a great deal of uncertainty."[164] However, the SEPA does indicate that areas of urban environmental concern specified in the statute must be considered, as should all significant impacts on both the "natural" and "built" environment. Discussion of significant impacts must include the cost of and effects on public services, such as utilities, roads, and fire and police protection, that may result from a proposal. EISs shall also discuss significant environmental impacts upon land and shoreline use, which includes housing, physical blight, and significant impacts of projected population on environmental resources. EISs should also incorporate, where appropriate, urban quality and historic and cultural resources. The Washington Supreme Court, toward this end, has held that an EIS improperly ignored the probability that a suburban shopping center would cause job losses and social decay by drawing customers away from a city's main business district.[165] An EIS may also include whether housing is low, middle, or high income.[166] However, one Washington court has held that it is not erroneous to decline to consider devaluation of surrounding property in an EIS.[167]

New York considers some social and economic impacts physical impacts in and of themselves. Environmental impacts, under New York's SEPA, can be found in an action's effects on land use, as well as its effects on population patterns and community character.[168] For instance, the New York Court of Appeals has held that gentrification—the displacing of low-income Asian American residents and businesses by a high-rise luxury development—must be considered in determining whether an EIS was required.[169] The gentrification would essentially alter the traditionally Asian American area's character, as well as affecting population patterns in the community. Because "environment" is defined in the statute as "community" or neighborhood "character," it therefore encompassed gentrification.

Socioeconomic Impact Assessment in Hazardous or Solid Waste Siting Processes

Many types of siting process reforms have been enacted at the state level. One of the most common aspects of these reforms is their effort to control or influence the distribution of hazardous waste facilities. In this sense, these reforms get right at the heart of the empirical evidence illustrating disproportionate distribution of waste facilities in minority and low-income communities. Another prominent reform directs decision makers to incorporate "soft" criteria in the decision-making process, requiring an assessment of the social and economic impacts of the facility on the community. Thus, in addition to the technical and environmental assessment, decision makers can also take into account the impact of the facility on property values, cumulative health risks, population density, governmental services, and historical and cultural resources.

Distributional Limitations

There are weak and strong versions of statutory constraints on the distribution of waste sites. Stronger versions of such constraints prohibit placing a waste facility where others exist.[170] Or, for instance, legislation may require the state to prepare hazardous waste management plans that provide for a "reasonable geographic distribution" of waste facilities.[171] These constraints do not, however, prohibit other types of developments, aside from waste facilities, from being placed in communities already hosting potentially hazardous facilities. Weaker versions of distributional constraints merely express an aspiration for distributional equity, or direct the decision maker to "consider" the equitable distribution of sites along with other factors.[172]

Other statutes that seek to influence the distribution of waste facilities fall in between the strong and weak versions. For instance, some states create a rebuttable presumption against placing a waste facility where others exist.[173] Depending upon the type of showing that can rebut the presumption, the distributional constraint may be weaker or stronger. The rebuttable presumption in Arkansas, for example, borders more on the weak end of distributional constraints since it can be easily rebutted with evidence that, among other things, "no other suitable site for such a facility is available within the regional solid waste management district because of the restraints of geology or any other factors listed [in the environmental assessment criteria]."[174] The presumption may also be rebutted if "incentives have prompted the host community to accept the siting of the facility."[175] Although this presumption ostensibly preserves community choice in the siting process, allowing the presumption to be rebutted by evidence of incentives may be problematic. Proffers of increased employment opportunities and host fees are often subject to the charge of environmental blackmail, as it is precisely the poorest communities that will have the greatest incentives to site such a facility.[176] Without technical support from the state agency or an assurance that technical experts have consulted with the community about the potential social and economic benefits and costs of the proposed facility, the community's choice may remain under a cloud of suspicion.[177]

Social and Economic Considerations in the Siting Process—"Soft Criteria"
The most common reform in waste-siting processes is the adoption of "soft" criteria, as opposed to the technical criteria that dominate siting decisions. Soft criteria counsel decision makers to consider the socioeconomic status of the host community, community perceptions, psychic costs, the potential for change in property values, and the cumulative health risks presented from other environmental sources in the host community.[178] Soft criteria by definition, however, lack the weight and force of technical criteria that normally drive the decision-making process. More often than not, there is no statutory guidance for the weight decision makers can, or should, give these factors in the permitting process.[179] Administrators retain considerable discretion, allowing for the possibility that these criteria will be overridden, or ignored, in the final decision.

Notes

*Associate Professor of Law, Rutgers University–Camden. Many thanks to Moze Cowper for expert research assistance. This chapter was made possible by a research grant from Rutgers School of Law–Camden.

1. Sheila Foster, *Justice from the Ground Up: Distributive Inequities, Grassroots Resistance and the Transformative Politics of the Environmental Justice Movement*, 86 CAL. L. REV. 775, 798–802 (1998) [hereinafter Foster, *Justice from the Ground Up*].

2. 42 U.S.C. §§ 4321–4345.

3. Exec. Order. No. 12,898, 3 C.F.R. § 859 (1995).

4. *Id.* at 3 C.F.R. § 1-101. The Order further requires all federal agencies to develop a strategy that identifies the distributional implications of existing programs and improve the distributional fairness of those programs. *Id.* The Order also mandates that federal agencies gather information regarding demographic consequences of their decisions; § 1-103(a).

5. INTERORGANIZATIONAL COMMITTEE ON GUIDELINES AND PRINCIPLES FOR SOCIAL IMPACT ASSESSMENT, GUIDELINES AND PRINCIPLES FOR SOCIAL IMPACT ASSESSMENT, Washington, D.C., U.S. Department of Commerce, National Oceanic and Atmospheric Administration, National Marine Fisheries Service (NOAA Technical Memorandum NMFS-F/SPO-16) (1994).

6. *See* U.S. GENERAL SERVICES ADMINISTRATION, PUBLIC BUILDINGS SERVICES, NEPA DESK GUIDE, INTERIM GUIDANCE, September 1997.

7. 40 C.F.R. § 1508.8 (listing broad range of effects to consider under NEPA).

8. Section 202 of NEPA established the CEQ "to appraise programs and activities of the Federal Government in the light of the policy set forth in [NEPA]"; 42 U.S.C. 4342 (1994). CEQ regulations implement NEPA and provide guidance to federal agencies administering NEPA; 40 C.F.R. §§ 1500–1508.

9. 42 U.S.C. § 4332(2)(C).

10. CEQ includes a federal official or agency's "failure to act" as a potential "federal action" where the failure to act "is reviewable by courts or administrative tribunals under the Administrative Procedure Act or other applicable law." 40 C.F.R. § 1508.18. However, federal courts have consistently required an "overt act" to satisfy the "action" requirement, rejecting claims that an impact statement was required when a federal agency had the authority to act but did not act. *See, e.g.*, Defenders of Wildlife v. Andrus, 627 F.2d 1238, 1244 (D.C. Cir. 1980); Aircraft Owners & Pilots Ass'n v. Hinson, 102 F.3d 1421 (7th Cir. 1996); Minnesota Pesticide Info. & Educ., Inc. v. Espy, 29 F.3d 442 (8th Cir. 1994).

11. 40 C.F.R. § 1508.18.

12. 40 C.F.R. § 1508.18(a). Federal actions do not include funding assistance solely in the form of general revenue sharing funds, distributed under the State and Local Fiscal Assistance Act of 1972, 31 U.S.C. 1221 with no Federal agency control over the subsequent use of such funds. *Id.* Such actions also do not include bringing judicial or administrative civil or criminal enforcement actions. *Id.*

13. 40 C.F.R. § 1508.18(b).

14. State of South Dakota v. Andrus, 614 F.2d 1190 (8th Cir. 1980).

15. *See e.g.*, Winnebago Tribe of Nebraska v. Ray, 621 F.2d 269 (8th Cir), *cert. denied*, 449 U.S. 836 (1980) (federal permit for crossing a navigable waterway did not turn an otherwise private project to construct a power transmission line into a federal action); Save the Bay, Inc. v. United States Corps of Engineers, 610 F.2d 322 (5th Cir.), *cert. denied*, 449 U.S. 963 (1980) (federal pollution discharge permit for a private sewage treatment plant did not turn project into a federal action); *but see* Colorado River Indian Tribes v. Marsh, 605 F. Supp. 1425 (C.D. Cal. 1985) (EIS required on 150-acre private development project where it required a federal permit to reinforce a river bank). *See also* DANIEL R. MANDELKER, NEPA LAW AND LITIGATION, § 8.04[2] (2nd ed. 1997).

16. *See, e.g.*, Marbled Murrelet v. Babbitt, 111 F.3d 1447 (9th Cir. 1996) (federal advisory activity not enough); *But see* Citizens Awareness Network v. Nuclear Regulatory Comm'n, 59 F.3d 284 (1st Cir. 1995) (decommissioning of private nuclear power plant held subject to federal regulation). *See also* MANDELKER, NEPA LAW AND LITIGATION, *supra* note 15, § 8.04[2].

17. *See, e.g.*, Macht v. Skinner, 916 F.2d 13, 20 (D.C. Cir. 1990) (federal funding for a preliminary study not enough; absent some indication that the "federal government has discretion over substantial portions of the project, NEPA . . . provides no basis for enjoining [the project]"); Village of Los Ranchos de Albuquerque v. Barnhart, 906 F.2d 1477 (10th Cir. 1990) (expectation of federal funding not enough), *cert. denied* 498 U.S. 1109 (1991); Enos v. Marsh, 769 F.2d 1363 (9th Cir. 1985) (no nexus between state-funded and federally funded project); Atlanta Coalition on the Transp. Crisis v. Atlanta Reg. Comm'n, 599 F.2d 1333, 1344 (in determining whether an action constitutes a "major federal action" under NEPA, "courts have looked to the nature and scope of the federal action being undertaken and have considered the usefulness to the federal decision-making process of the information an impact statement would provide both in determining whether an impact statement is required at all . . . and in deciding what kind of statement need be prepared") (5th Cir. 1979). *See also* MANDELKER, NEPA LAW AND LITIGATION, *supra* note 15, § 8.04[3].

18. South Bronx Coalition for Clean Air v. Conroy, 1998 WL 575173 (S.D.N.Y. 1998).

19. *Id.* (The Federal Transit Administration "is statutorily prohibited from regulating the operational decisions of mass transit systems and its role in this case was limited to providing funds for the purchase and construction of the [bus depot] and concurring in [the state agency's] proposal to apply the proceeds of the sale to the Coliseum project (which is not the subject of this lawsuit)").

20. 40 C.F.R. § 1508.18.

21. *See, e.g.,* Minnesota Public Interest Research Group v. Butz (I), 498 F.2d 1314 (8th Cir. 1974).

22. *See e.g.,* National Ass'n for the Advancement of Colored People v. Wilmington Medical Center, Inc., 584 F.2d 619 (3d. Cir. 1978).

23. MANDELKER, NEPA LAW AND LITIGATION, *supra* note 15, § 8.06[3].

24. *Id.* Mandelker gives some telling examples of projects classified as both major and minor. Those classified as major include:

1. a $14 million bridge with 60 percent federal funding, Monroe County Conservation Council, Inc. v. Volpe, 472 F.2d 693 (2d Cir. 1972);
2. the conversion of a large federally subsidized housing project with a major change in use, Jones v. United States Dep't of Housing & Urban Development, 390 F. Supp. 579 (E.D. La. 1974);
3. a 66-mile water channel project costing $1.5 million with $706,000 of federal funding, Natural Resources Defense Council, Inc. v. Grant, 341 F. Supp. 356 (E.D. N.C. 1972).

Id.

Those classified as minor include:

1. a replacement bridge, Sierra Club v. Hassell, 636 F.2d 1095 (5th Cir. 1981);
2. retrofitting 20,000 railway cars to meet federal safety regulations, Association of American Railroads v. Adams, 485 F. Supp. 1077 (D.D.C. 1978);
3. minor traffic improvements, Julis v. City of Cedar Rapids, Iowa, 349 F. Supp. 88 (N.D. Iowa 1972);
4. federally subsidized housing projects under agency regulations requiring a minimum "threshold" project size before an impact statement is required, United Neighbors Civic Ass'n of Jamaica, Inc. v. Pierce, 563 F. Supp. 200 (E.D. N.Y. 1983).

Id.

25. *See, e.g.,* Texas Comm. on Natural Resources v. Bergland, 573 F.2d 201 (5th Cir.), *cert. denied,* 439 U.S. 966 (1978) (noting that the exemption had generally been limited to environmental agencies and refusing to apply it to the Forest Service and its actions under the National Forest Management Act).

26. Portland Cement Ass'n v. Ruckelshaus, 486 F.2d 375 (D.C. Cir. 1973), *cert. denied,* 417 U.S. 921, *rehearing denied,* 423 U.S. 1092. Subsequent legislation provided an exemption for all actions under the Clean Air Act. *See infra* note 33.

27. *Alabama ex rel.* Siegelman v. EPA, 911 F.2d 499 (11th Cir. 1990) (holding that NEPA does not apply to EPA's procedure for permitting hazardous waste landfills authorized by RCRA); *see also* 40 C.F.R. 124.9(b)(6) (1995) (providing

that the agency does not have to prepare an EIS when it issues or approves a hazardous waste permit, regardless of impact the permitted facility will have on the environment).

28. Environmental Defense Fund v. Environmental Protection Agency, 489 F.2d 1247, 1256 (D.C. Cir. 1973) (EPA order canceling the registration of DDT under FIFRA held to be the functional equivalent of the EIS process).

29. *See, e.g.*, Western Nebraska Resources Council v. Environmental Protection Agency, 943 F.2d 867 (8th Cir. 1991).

30. Twitty v. State of North Carolina, 527 F. Supp. 778 (E.D. N.C. 1981).

31. *See* MANDELKER, NEPA LAW AND LITIGATION, *supra* note 15, § 5.03[1].

32. 33 U.S.C. § 1371(c)(1).

33. Energy Supply and Environmental Coordination Act of 1974, 15 U.S.C. § 793 (c)(1) (providing that "no action taken under the Clean Air Act shall be deemed a major federal action significantly affecting the quality of the human environment within the meaning of the National Environmental Policy Act").

34. 42 U.S.C. § 4332(c).

35. Most government actions reviewed under NEPA are reviewed under EAs, not EISs. CEQ notes that since CEQ regulations were promulgated, "all signs point to a significant increase in EAs and a decrease in EISs." The annual number of draft, revised, supplemental, and final EISs prepared has declined from approximately 2,000 in 1973 to 608 in 1995, averaging 508 annually between 1990–1995. By 1993, a CEQ survey of federal agencies estimated that about 50,000 EAs were being prepared annually. That same survey found that five federal agencies—the U.S. Forest Service, the Bureau of Land Management, the Department of Housing and Urban Development, the U.S. Army Corps of Engineers, and the Federal Highway Administration—produce more than 80 percent of EAs. Moreover, while some agencies—-such as the Department of Energy, Department of Army, and the U.S. Forest Service—provide for a public comment period on EAs, many do not. COUNCIL ON ENVIRONMENTAL QUALITY, EXECUTIVE OFFICE OF THE PRESIDENT, THE NATIONAL ENVIRONMENTAL POLICY ACT: A STUDY OF ITS EFFECTIVENESS AFTER TWENTY-FIVE YEARS, January 1997, at 19, found at <http://ceq.eh.doe.gov/nepa/nepanet.htm>.

36. 40 C.F.R. § 1508.13. Both the EA and FONSI documents are available to the public and become important when a party challenges in court a decision not to prepare an EIS. 40 C.F.R. § 1501.4 (e)(1). Under certain circumstances CEQ Regulations recommend a 30-day delay between the issuance of a FONSI and the final decision not to prepare an EIS. 40 C.F.R. § 1501.4(e)(2) (setting forth the circumstances).

37. 40 C.F.R. § 1508.27.

38. 40 C.F.R. § 1508.27.

39. One court has said that the term "controversial" refers to those situations "where a substantial dispute exists as to the size, nature or effect of the major federal action rather than to the existence of opposition to a use, the effect of which is relatively undisputed. Hanly v. Kleindienst (Hanly II), 471 F.2d 823, (2d Cir. 1972) at 830; *see also* Rucker v. Willis, 484 F.2d 158, 163 (4th Cir. 1973).

40. 40 C.F.R. § 1508.27.

41. *But see* Hanly v. Kleindienst (II), 471 F.2d 823, 830–831 (2d Cir. 1972), *cert. denied*, 412 U.S. 908 (1973) (describing a slightly different test for "significance": effects may be "significant" if the proposed action might cause "adverse

environmental effects in excess of those created by existing uses in the area" or quantitatively increase the existing adverse environmental effects in the affected area, thus having a cumulative effect).

42. Bargan v. Department of Defense, 623 F. Supp. 290 (D. Nev. 1985).

43. 40 C.F.R. § 1508.8.

44. *See, e.g.*, State of North Dakota v. Andrus, 483 F. Supp. 255 (D. N.D. 1980) (following regulation on indirect impacts); Manatee County v. Gorsuch, 554 F. Supp. 778 (M.D. Fla. 1982) (cumulative impacts).

45. 40 C.F.R. §§ 1502.16(b), 1508.8(b), 1508.9.

46. 40 C.F.R. § 1508.8(b).

47. 40 C.F.R. §§ 1508.8(b), 1508.7.

48. 40 C.F.R. § 1508.27.

49. COUNCIL ON ENVIRONMENTAL QUALITY, EXECUTIVE OFFICE OF THE PRESIDENT, CONSIDERING CUMULATIVE EFFECTS UNDER THE NATIONAL ENVIRONMENTAL POLICY ACT (1997), found at <http://ceq.eh.doe.gov/nepa/nepanet.htm>. "Interactive" effects, it explains, may be either "countervailing"—where the net adverse cumulative effect is less than the sum of individual effects, or "synergistic"—where the net adverse cumulative effect is greater than the sum of the individual effects. *Id.* at 9.

50. 40 C.F.R. § 1508.14.

51. Hanly v. Mitchell (I), 460 F.2d 640 (2d Cir. 1972); Hanly v. Kleindienst (II), 471 F.2d 823, 830–831 (2d Cir. 1972), *cert. denied*, 412 U.S. 908 (1973); City of Rochester v. United States Postal Service, 541 F.2d 967 (2d Cir. 1976).

52. 40 C.F.R. § 1509.14; Image of Greater San Antonio v. Brown, 570 F.2d 517 (5th Cir. 1978).

53. Metropolitan Edison Co. v. People Against Nuclear Energy, 460 U.S. 766, 773 (1983) (to determine if a particular effect must be considered, must look at the relationship between the effect and the change in the physical environment caused by the major federal action issue).

54. *See* MANDELKER, NEPA LAW AND LITIGATION, *supra* note 15, § 8.07[6].

55. 40 C.F.R. § 1501.7. Scoping begins when the agency publishes, in the Federal Register, its intent to prepare an EIS. 40 C.F.R. § 1508.22.

56. 40 C.F.R. § 1503.1(a).

57. 40 C.F.R. § 1506.6(c).

58. *See* COUNCIL ON ENVIRONMENTAL QUALITY, MEMORANDUM FOR GENERAL COUNSELS, NEPA LIAISONS AND PARTICIPANTS IN SCOPING (April 30, 1981), found at <http://ceq.eh.doe.gov/nepa/regs/scope/scoping.htm>.

59. Luke Cole, *Macho Law Brains, Public Citizens, and Grassroots Activists: Three Models of Environmental Advocacy*, 14 VA. ENVT'L L. J. 687, 695 (1995).

60. *Id.* at 696.

61. *Id.*

62. More on NEPA's public participation requirements can be found in Chapter 7.

63. 40 C.F.R. §§ 1503.4, 1502.1, 1502.2.

64. 40 C.F.R. § 1502.1.

65. 42 U.S.C. § 4332(2)(C); 40 C.F.R. § 1502.16. Agencies are to consider "reasonable alternatives not within the jurisdiction of the lead agency" and the "no-action" alternative. 40 C.F.R. § 1502.14.

66. 40 C.F.R. § 1502.23.

67. Idaho by and Through Idaho Public Utils. Comm'n v. ICC, 35 F.3d 585, 595 (D.C. Cir. 1994); Calvert Cliffs' Coordinating Comm., Inc. V. AEC, 449 F.2d 1109 (D.C. Cir. 1971).

68. COUNCIL ON ENVIRONMENTAL QUALITY, CONSIDERING CUMULATIVE EFFECTS UNDER THE NATIONAL ENVIRONMENTAL POLICY ACT (1997), found at <http://ceq.eh.doe.gov/nepa/nepanet.htm>.

69. 40 C.F.R. § 1502.16(g).

70. 40 C.F.R. § 1509.14.

71. At least one court has held, however, that NEPA does not require an "environmental justice" analysis—presumably meaning an analysis of "disparate impact" on minority communities. *See Citizens Concerned About Jet Noise, Inc. v. Dalton,* 1999 WL 322635 (E.D. Va.).

72. 40 C.F.R. § 1505.2.

73. VERMONT YANKEE NUCLEAR POWER CORP. v. NATURAL RESOURCES DEFENSE COUNCIL, 435 U.S. 519, 558 (1978).

74. *See, e.g.,* Robertson v. Methow Valley Citizens Council, 490 U.S. 332, 349–53 (1989); Marsh v. Oregon Natural Resources Council, 490 U.S. 360, 371 (1989). NEPA merely prohibits "uninformed—rather than unwise—agency action." *Methow Valley,* 490 U.S. at 350–51.

75. MANDELKER, NEPA LAW AND LITIGATION, *supra* note 15, § 10.01, page 10-3.

76. Robertson v. Methow Valley Citizens Council, 490 U.S. 332, 352 (1989).

77. *Methow Valley,* 490 U.S. at 349; Strycker's Bay Neighborhood Council, Inc. v. Karlen, 444 U.S. 223, 227–28 (1979) ("once an agency has made a decision subject to NEPA's procedural requirements, the only role for a court is to insure that the agency has considered the environmental consequences").

78. *See* MANDELKER, NEPA LAW AND LITIGATION, *supra* note 15, § 10.05, for judicial review standards.

79. *See* MANDELKER, NEPA LAW AND LITIGATION, *supra* note 15, § 4.10[2][i].

80. Marsh v. Oregon Natural Resources Council, 490 U.S. 360, 371 (1989) (applying "arbitrary and capricious" standard to agency's decision not to prepare a supplemental impact statement); Dubois v. U.S. Dep't of Agric., 102 F.3d 1273 (1st Cir. 1996) (arbitrary and capricious standard in context of review of adequacy of impact statement). However, a higher standard of review, "reasonableness," may apply to the threshold issue of NEPA's applicability—whether the action is a "major federal action." *See* Goos v. Interstate Commerce Comm'n, 911 F.2d 1283 (8th Cir. 1990). *See* MANDELKER, NEPA LAW AND LITIGATION, *supra* note 15, §§ 7.04[2], 8.02[4], 10.05 for judicial standards of review.

81. The Executive Order is the subject of Chapter 4 of this volume.

82. PRESIDENT WILLIAM J. CLINTON, MEMORANDUM ON ENVIRONMENTAL JUSTICE (February 11, 1994).

83. INTERAGENCY WORKING GROUP ON ENVIRONMENTAL JUSTICE, DRAFT GUIDANCE FOR FEDERAL AGENCIES ON KEY TERMS IN EXECUTIVE ORDER 12,898 (August 8, 1995).

84. COUNCIL ON ENVIRONMENTAL QUALITY, ENVIRONMENTAL JUSTICE GUIDANCE UNDER THE NATIONAL ENVIRONMENTAL POLICY ACT, December 10, 1997, found at <http://ceq.eh.doe.gov/nepa/nepanet.htm>.

85. *Id.* at 9.

86. *See, e.g.,* UNITED STATES ENVIRONMENTAL PROTECTION AGENCY, INTERIM FINAL GUIDANCE FOR INCORPORATING ENVIRONMENTAL JUSTICE CONCERNS IN EPA'S

NEPA COMPLIANCE ANALYSIS (September 30, 1997), found at <http://es.epa.gov/oeca/ofa/ejepa.html>; UNITED STATES GENERAL SERVICES ADMINISTRATION, NEPA DESK GUIDE, INTERIM GUIDANCE (September 1997), found at <http://www.gsa.gov/pbs/pt/call-in/erl/deskref/toc.htm>. Other agencies have adopted environmental justice strategies, but have not given specific guidance on incorporating environmental justice issues in their implementation of NEPA. *See, e.g.*, UNITED STATES DEPARTMENT OF DEFENSE, STRATEGY ON ENVIRONMENTAL JUSTICE, March 24, 1995; UNITED STATES DEPARTMENT OF ENERGY, ENVIRONMENTAL JUSTICE STRATEGY (April 1995); UNITED STATES DEPARTMENT OF JUSTICE, GUIDANCE CONCERNING ENVIRONMENTAL JUSTICE (February 16, 1994); UNITED STATES NUCLEAR REGULATORY COMMISSION, ENVIRONMENTAL JUSTICE STRATEGY (March 1995); UNITED STATES DEPARTMENT OF TRANSPORTATION, OFFICE OF THE SECRETARY, FINAL ENVIRONMENTAL JUSTICE STRATEGY (June 29, 1995); UNITED STATES DEPARTMENT OF TRANSPORTATION, COAST GUARD ENVIRONMENTAL JUSTICE STRATEGY (April 3, 1998).

87. CEQ GUIDANCE, at 13–14.

88. *See* EPA GUIDANCE, *supra* note 86, §§ 2.1.1, 2.1.2, 3.2.1; GSA GUIDANCE, *supra* note 85, Chapter 9.

89. EPA GUIDANCE, *supra* note 86, § 2.1.1; *see also* § 2.1.2.

90. EPA GUIDANCE, *supra* note 86, § 3.2.1.

91. *Id.* EPA additionally cautions using census data particularly in areas of "high Hispanic or Native American" populations due to the "possibility of distortion of population breakdowns." *Id.* at 2.1.1.

92. EPA GUIDANCE, *supra* note 86, §§ 2.1.2, 3.2.1.

93. GSA GUIDANCE, *supra* note 86, § 9.2.3.

94. GENERAL SERVICES ADMINISTRATION, FACT SHEET, ENVIRONMENTAL JUSTICE AND NEPA, ENVIRONMENTAL JUSTICE AND ENVIRONMENTAL IMPACT ASSESSMENTS (February 1998) hereinafter GSA FACT SHEET, found at <http://www.gsa.gov/pbs/pt/call-in/factsheet/0298b/02_98_3.htm>.

95. CEQ GUIDANCE, *supra* note 87, at 14.

96. EPA GUIDANCE, *supra* note 86, § 2.1.1.

97. CEQ GUIDANCE, at 14; *see also* GSA FACT SHEET *supra* note 93 ("In the analysis performed for an EA or EIS[, the impacts] should be considered in detail, and the distribution of environmental and health effects within the affected community should be considered").

98. *Id.* at 16.

99. EPA GUIDANCE, *supra* note 86, § 3.1.

100. *Id.*

101. *Id.*

102. EPA GUIDANCE, *supra* note 86, § 3.21; *see also* GSA FACT SHEET, *supra* note 93 (even where the socioeconomic impact is not related to the changes in the physical environment, "it would be appropriate to include measures to mitigate socioeconomic impacts in the FONSI . . . and to include measures to ensure that mitigation was completed").

103. EPA GUIDANCE, *supra* note 86, § 3.2.3.2.

104. *See, e.g.*, Dominique R. Shelton, *Environmental Justice and Cumulative Impact Analysis*, 7 ENV'TL LAW NEWS 25–29 (Winter 1998) (discussing issue under California's mini-NEPA). One area in which this issue is quickly developing is in the area of toxics, where low-income and minority communities are increasingly

concerned about the presences of "hot spots"—dense toxic air emissions—in their communities. *See, e.g.*, Shipra Bansal & Scott Kuhn, *Stopping an Unfair Trade: Environmental Justice, Pollution Trading, and Cumulative Impacts in Los Angeles*, 7 ENVT'L LAW NEWS 16–24 (Spring 1998).

105. COUNCIL ON ENVIRONMENTAL QUALITY, EXECUTIVE OFFICE OF THE PRESIDENT, CONSIDERING CUMULATIVE EFFECTS UNDER THE NATIONAL ENVIRONMENTAL POLICY ACT, *supra* note 49.

106. It notes that while EAs tend to be the more cost-effective way to determine whether potentially significant effects are likely and whether a project can mitigate those effects, EAs tend to "underestimate the cumulative effects of their projects." *Id.* at 4.

107. If the boundaries are defined too broadly, CEQ acknowledges, "the analysis becomes unwieldy." On the other hand, if the boundaries are defined too narrowly, "significant issues may be missed" and "decision makers will be incompletely informed about the consequences of their actions." *Id.* at v.

108. *See* EPA GUIDANCE, *supra* note 86, § 2.2.2.

109. To determine future actions, the EPA recommends that EPA analysts "go beyond the number of projects that are funded in the area, and predict which of the actions in the early planning stage have realistic potential to move forward." In doing so, EPA analysts should consult both with local government planning agencies in the region and with "private land-owners and organizations" willing to disclose their future land use plans.

110. *Id.* § 2.2.2.

111. Dominique R. Shelton, *Environmental Justice and Cumulative Impact Analysis*, 7 ENV'TL LAW NEWS, 27 (1998) (quoting letter from Carol M. Browner, EPA Administrator, to J. Dale Givens 1 (September 10, 1997)). See also "EPA Objection to Airport Plan May Raise Environmental Justice Profile," Environmental Policy Alert, May 5, 1999 (reporting EPA's Objection to a Federal Aviation Administration airport expansion plan in Boston in part due to concerns about the environmental impact of the expansion on minority communities).

112. For a different view of the Shintech and Louisiana Services cases, *see* Henry Payne, *Green Redlining: How Rules Against "Environmental Racism" Hurt Poor Minorities Most of All*, REASON (October 1998), found at <http://www.reason.com/9810/fe.payne.html>.

113. *See In re Louisiana Energy Services* (Special Nuclear Material License) *(Claiborne Enrichment Center)*, U.S. Nuclear Regulatory Commission Atomic Safety and Licensing Board, Docket No. 70-3070-ML (May 1, 1997).

114. *See, e.g.*, ROBERT BULLARD, DUMPING IN DIXIE: RACE, CLASS AND ENVIRONMENTAL QUALITY (Westview Press 1990); ROBERT BULLARD, CONFRONTING ENVIRONMENTAL RACISM: VOICES FROM THE GRASSROOTS (South End Press 1993); ROBERT BULLARD, UNEQUAL PROTECTION: ENVIRONMENTAL JUSTICE AND COMMUNITIES OF COLOR (Sierra Club Books 1994).

115. The Board stressed the "nondiscrimination component" of the EO, which requires that "the NRC conduct its licensing activities in a manner" that "ensures" that those activities do not have the "effect of subjecting any person or populations to discrimination because of their race or color" (*citing* 3 C.F.R. at 861).

116. The Board questioned the NRC's staff assessment that the road would simply be relocated, and instead found that it was a distinct possibility that the

road could be closed. As such, the Board found the EIS deficient in that it did not analyze the impacts on the communities of Forest Grove and Center Springs on closing Parish Road 39. However, the Board found this defect was remedied at the hearing when the applicant indicated, for the first time, that it would relocate the road, if necessary. The Board took that as a "concession" by the applicant that "the impacts of closing the road are sufficiently detrimental to the communities of Forest Grove and Center Springs that those impacts must be addressed by road relocation." Accordingly, the Board made the relocation of the road a condition of any construction permit or operating license authorization.

117. The applicant conceded that it had no knowledge of whether any of the communities experiencing enhanced property values after the siting of nuclear facilities were African American communities.

118. *In re Louisiana Energy Services (Claiborne Enrichment Center),* Docket No. 70-3070-ML (April 3, 1998).

119. *See, e.g.,* Federal Highway Act, 23 U.S.C. § 109(h) (requiring Department of Transportation to "promulgate guidelines designed to assure that possible adverse economic, social and environmental effects relating to any proposed [highway] project on any Federal-aid system have been fully considered in developing such project").

120. *See also* Department of Transportation Act, Section 4(f), 49 U.S.C.A. § 303(c) (West 1997) (provides that the Secretary of Transportation may approve a transportation program or project requiring the use of historic properties only if 1) there is no "prudent" or "feasible" alternative to using the site and 2) the program or project includes all possible planning to minimize the harm to the historic site resulting from the proposed use).

121. Alabama ex rel. Siegelman v. EPA, 911 F.2d 499 (11th Cir. 1990) (holding that NEPA does not apply to EPA's procedure for permitting hazardous waste landfills authorized by RCRA). *See also* 40 C.F.R. 124.9(b)(6) (1995) (providing that the agency does not have to prepare an EIS when it issues or approves a hazardous waste permit, regardless of impact the permitted facility will have on the environment).

122. 40 C.F.R. § 264.18.

123. *See In re Chemical Waste Management of Indiana, Inc.,* RCRA Appeal Nos. 95-2 & 95-3, 6 E.A.D. 66 (June 29, 1995).

124. *Id.* (*citing* 42 U.S.C. § 6925(c)(3)).

125. *Id.* (*citing In re Marine Shale Processors, Inc.,* RCRA Appeal No. 94-12, at 48, n.64 (E.A.B., Mar. 17, 1995).

126. *Id.* (noting that the "procedural rules governing appeals of permitting decisions place a heavy burden on petitioners who seek Board review of such technical decisions" and that petitioners failed to meet that burden in this case).

127. *In re Envotech, L.P. Milan, Michigan,* UIC Appeal Nos. 95-2 through 95-37, 6 E.A.D. 260 (February 15, 1996) (relying on omnibus authority contained in 40 C.F.R. § 144.52(a)(9)).

128. *In re Puerto Rico Elec. Power Auth. (Cambalanche Combustion Turbine Project),* PSD Appeal No. 95-2, 1995 EPA App. Lexis 1, 4–10, 6 E.A.D. 253, 255–58 (Dec. 11, 1995) (order denying review).

129. *In re EcoElectrica, L.P.,* PSD Appeals Nos. 96-8 and 96-13, 1997 EPA App. LEXIS 5, 27–32 (April 8, 1997).

130. Specifically, the region determined that the maximum emission impacts from the proposed facility would occur primarily in areas of higher median income households than the surrounding lower-income areas. The region also emphasized that the "modeled maximum emission impacts from this project are insignificant and well below [national ambient air quality standards] and the project therefore could have insignificant impacts on the surrounding communities." *In re EcoElectrica, L.P., supra* note 129, at 30.

131. Some states also have historic preservation or antiquities protections.

132. 16 U.S.C.A. § 470f (West Supp. 1997); Protection of Historic Properties, 36 C.F.R. § 800 (1986). *See also* 42 U.S.C.A. § 5304(g) (West Supp. 1997); Housing and Urban Development, 24 C.F.R. § 5810 (1995) (community development block grant projects).

133. *See* Ely v. Velde, 497 F.2d 252 (4th Cir. 1974); Hall County Historical Soc'y v. Georgia Dep't of Transp., 447 F. Supp. 741 (N.D. Ga. 1978).

134. For a general discussion of consideration of historic sites of significance to minority and low-income populations, see Ned Kaufman, *Heritage and the Cultural Politics of Preservation*, PLACES, Winter 1998, at 58. *See also* Kemba Johnson, *Landmarks Omission: Historic Preservation in the City's Black Neighborhoods Is a Struggle Against Snobbery—and Local Leaders Bent on Development*, CITY LIMITS, Sept./Oct. 1998, at 19.

135. The criteria for eligibility of properties for inclusion on the National Register is set forth in 36 C.F.R. § 60.4.

136. 36 C.F.R. § 800.5(a)–(d).

137. 36 C.F.R. 800.5, 800.9.

138. 36 C.F.R. § 800.5(e).

139. The SHPO is a state official appointed by the governor of each state or territory to participate in the federal program, to administer federal matching funds for preservation activities, and to assist in carrying out federal historic preservation policy on behalf of the state. In 1992, Congress adopted amendments to the National Historic Preservation Act that allow federally recognized Indian tribes to assume any or all of the functions of an SHPO. Among other functions, the THPO may identify and maintain inventories of culturally significant properties, nominate properties to national and tribal registers of historic places, conduct Section 106 reviews of federal agency projects on tribal lands, and conduct educational programs on the importance of preserving historic properties.

140. 36 C.F.R. § 800.1(b).

141. 36 C.F.R. § 800.6.

142. Section 106 regulations also provide several alternative means of complying with Section 106. Chief among such alternatives is that a local or state government may execute a programmatic agreement (PA). In a PA, an agency, the Council, and other parties agree on a process for considering historic properties with respect to an entire agency program. 36 C.F.R. § 800.13. Other alternatives include: counterpart procedures developed by an agency and approved by the Council; an agreement between the Council and a State, which substitutes a state review system for the standard Section 106 review process; and an agreement between the Council and a tribe, which substitutes use of tribal regulations for those of the Council on tribal land. *See* 36 C.F.R. § 800.7.

143. No. 89-82-CIV-ORL-19 (M.D. Fla. Dec. 22, 1989); *see also* Karl S. Coplan, *Protecting Minority Communities with Environmental, Civil Rights Claims*, N.Y.L.J. (Aug. 20, 1991) [hereinafter Coplan], at 1 (discussing case); Judith E. Koons, *Fair Housing and Community Empowerment: Where the Roof Meets Redemption*, 4 GEO. J. ON FIGHTING POVERTY 77 (1996) (detailed history of the litigation, the surrounding events, and the city) [hereinafter Koons].

144. Coplan, *supra* note 143, at 2.

145. Koons, *supra* note 143, at 83 (1996) (citing 1980 U.S. census data).

146. Coplan, *supra* note 143, at 2.

147. *Id.* at 4.

148. *See* ALASKA STAT. § 38.50.130 (Michie 1997); CAL. PUB. RES. CODE §§ 20000–21177 (West 1997); CONN. GEN. STAT. ANN. §§ 22a-1a to -1h (West 1997); D.C. CODE ANN. §§ 6-981 to -990 (1997); GA. CODE ANN. §§ 12-16-1 to 12-16-8 (1997); HAW. REV. STAT. §§ 343-1 to -8 (1997); IND. CODE ANN. §§ 13-12-4-1 to 4-10 (Burns 1998); MD. NAT. RES. CODE ANN. §§ 1-301 to 305 (1997); MASS. GEN. LAWS ANN. ch. 30, §§ 61–62h (West 1998); MINN. STAT. ANN. §§ 116d.01 to .07 (1997); MONT. CODE ANN. §§ 75-1-101 to -324 (1997); N.Y. ENVTL. CONSERV. LAW §§ 8-0101 to -0117 (1998); N.C. GEN. STAT. §§ 113a-1 to -13 (1997); P.R. LAWS ANN. tit. §§ 1121–1142 (1992); S.D. CODIFIED LAWS §§ 34a-9-1 to -13 (1997); VA. CODE ANN. §§ 10.1-1188 to 1192 (1997); WASH. REV. CODE ANN. §§ 43.21c.010 to .910 (West 1997); WIS. STAT. ANN. § 1.11 (West 1997).

149. *See, e.g.*, Indiana State Hwy. Comm'n v. Ziliak, 428 N.E.2d 275 (Ind. App. 1981), *rehearing denied*, 431 N.E.2d 842 (Ind. App. 1982) (mirrors NEPA also verbatim, and thus is subject to the same interpretation); IND. CODE ANN. §§ 13-12-4-1 to -4-10; P.R. LAWS ANN. tit. §§ 1121–1142; VA. CODE ANN. §§ 10.1-1188 to 1192; WIS. STAT. ANN. § 1.11 (EIS should substantially follow the guidance issued by the United States Council on Environmental Quality).

150. CONN. GEN. STAT. ANN. § 22a-1c (significant effects defined as those that could have a "major impact on the state's land, water, air, historic landmarks . . . , existing housing, or other environmental resources, or could serve short term to the disadvantage of long term environmental goals"); D.C. CODE ANN. § 6-982 (3) ("Environment" means "physical conditions"); GA. CODE ANN. § 12-16-3 (requires significant adverse impact on "natural environment," including air, land, water, plants, animals, historical sites or buildings, or cultural resources); MASS. GEN. LAWS ANN. § 61 (preparation of EIS for impacts on the "natural" environment).

151. N.Y. ENVTL. CONSERV. LAW § 8-0109 ("may have a significant effect on the environment"); CAL. PUB. RES. CODE § 21100 ("may have a significant effect"); MINN. STAT. ANN. § 116D.04 ("where there is a potential for significant environmental effects"); CONN. GEN. STAT. ANN. § 22a-1b ("may significantly affect the environment").

152. *See, e.g.*, CAL. PUB. RES. CODE § 21100 (requires impact report for discretionary, but not for ministerial projects); GA. CODE ANN. § 12-16-3 (applies to "land-disturbing activity" and sale of state land); MD. NAT. RES. CODE ANN. § 1-301 (applies to requests for legislative appropriations or other legislative actions that will alter the quality of the air, land, or water resources); N.Y. ENVTL. CONSERV. LAW § 8-0105 (defining "agency" to include any state or local agency);

WASH. REV. CODE ANN. § 43.21C.030 (includes "all branches of government of this State, including state agencies, municipal public corporations, and counties"); VA. CODE ANN. § 10.1.1008 (covers "all state agencies, boards, authorities and commissions or any branch of the state government"); WIS. STAT. ANN. § 1.11 (applies to "all agencies of the state").

153. *See, e.g.*, CAL. PUB. RES. CODE § 21151.1(a)(2)(3); MASS. REGS. CODE § 11.25. *See also* MASS. GEN. LAWS ANN. § 21D-9 (developer of hazardous waste facility must submit state EIS and social and economic appendix for each site under consideration).

154. IND. CODE ANN. § 13-12-4-8 (environmental impact statement not required for issuance of "license or permit" by "any state agency"); WIS. STAT. ANN. § 1.11 (2) (EIS not required for license because a license determination does not constitute a major state action); *but see* WIS. STAT. ANN. § 291.27 (EIS is required for a new solid or hazardous waste disposal facility if the area committed to it exceeds 80 acres and the total volume intended for disposal under the plan exceeds one million cubic yards).

155. S.D. CODIFIED LAWS § 34A-9-4 (all agencies "may" prepare . . . an environmental impact statement or any major action they propose or approve which may have a significant effect on the environment").

156. MINN. STAT. ANN. § 116D.04 ("No state action significantly affecting the quality of the environment shall be allowed . . . where such action . . . has caused or is likely to cause pollution, impairment, or destruction of the air, water, land or other natural resources . . . so long as there is a feasible and prudent alternative consistent with the reasonable requirements of the public health, safety, and welfare and the state's paramount concern for the protection of its air, water, land and other natural resources from pollution, impairment or destruction. Economic considerations alone shall not justify such Conduct)"; N.Y. ENVTL. CONSERV. LAW § 8-0109 ("Agencies shall use all practicable means to realize the policies and goals set forth in this article, and shall not act and choose alternatives which, consistent with social, economic and other essential considerations, to the maximum extent practicable, minimize or avoid adverse environmental effects, including effects revealed in the environmental impact statement process"); CAL. PUB. RES. CODE § 21061.1, CAL. CODE REGS. § 15021 (provides that agencies "should not approve projects as proposed if there are feasible alternatives or mitigation measures available that would substantially lessen any significant effects that the project would have on the environment"; "feasible" defined as "capable of being accomplished in a successful manner in a reasonable period of time, taking into account economic, environmental, social and technological factors").

157. *California*: CAL. PUB. RES. CODE § 21100(d) ("significant effect on the environment" means "substantial, or potentially substantial, adverse changes in physical conditions"); § 21151(b) (significant effect means an effect that has a "substantial or potentially substantial, adverse changes in physical conditions"); § 21082.2(c) (evidence of "social or economic impacts which do not contribute to, or are not caused by, physical impacts on the environment" are not enough to trigger the EIS requirement); CAL. CODE REGS. § 15064(f) (economic or social changes may be used, however, to determine that a physical change will have a significant effect on the environment. For instance, where a physical change is

caused by economic or social effects of a project, the physical change may be regarded as a significant effect in the same manner as any other physical change resulting from the project. Alternatively, economic and social effects of a physical change may be used to determine that the physical change is a significant effect on the environment.).

Montana: MONT. ENVTL. & HEALTH SAFETY REGS. § 17.4.603 (12) ("human environment includes, but is not limited to biological, physical, social, economic, cultural, and aesthetic factors that interrelate to form the environment;" economic and social impacts do not by themselves require an EIS).

New York: N.Y. ENVTL. CONSERV. LAW § 8-0105(6) ("environment" means the *physical conditions* that will be affected by a proposed action, including land, air, water, minerals, flora, fauna, noise, and objects of historic or aesthetic significance; existing patterns of population concentration, distribution, or growth; and existing community or neighborhood character); see also Chinese Staff and Workers Ass'n v. City of New York, 68 N.Y.2d 359, 509 N.Y.S.2d 499, 502 N.E.2d 176 (1986) (potential displacement of local residents and businesses was effect on population patterns and neighborhood character that city was required to consider in determining whether requirement for environmental impact statement was triggered); *but see* Wilder v. New York State Urban Development Corp., 154 A.D.2d 261, 546 N.Y.S.2d 95, *appeal denied* 75 N.Y.2d 709, 555 N.Y.S.2d 692, 554 N.E.2d 1280 (1989) (economic impact of redevelopment project was not "physical condition" requiring environmental impact statement).

South Dakota: S.D. CODIFIED LAWS § 34A-9-1 (provision identical to that of New York).

Wisconsin: Wisconsin's Environmental Decade Inc., v. Wisconsin Dept. of Natural Resources, 340 N.W.2d 722 (1983) (socioeconomic injuries alleged by parties seeking environmental impact study did not have a direct causal relationship to minor changes in the physical environment and hence did not trigger the EIS requirement).

158. HAW. REV. STAT. § 343-2 (significant effects include those adverse to "economic and social welfare"); MD. NAT. RES. CODE ANN. § 1-301(b) ("environmental effects" can be natural as well as socioeconomic and historic).

159. CONN. GEN. STAT. ANN. § 22a-1b (EIS should include, among other things, "an analysis of the short term and long term economic, social and environmental costs and benefits of the proposed action"); HAW. REV. STAT. § 343-2 (significant effects include those adverse to "economic and social welfare"); Molakia Homesteaders Cooperative Ass'n v. Cobb, 629 P.2d 1134 (Haw. 1981) (this section definitely contemplates a consideration of the secondary and nonphysical effects of a proposal prior to governmental approval thereof, and the effects to be studied include the socioeconomic consequences of a proposed action, as well as its direct physical impact); MINN. STAT. ANN. § 116D.04(2a) (EIS shall analyze economic, employment, and sociological effects that cannot be avoided should the action be implemented); MONT. ENVTL. & HEALTH SAFETY REGS. § 17.4.609 (EIS must contain an analysis of, among other things, an evaluation of the impacts, including cumulative and secondary impacts, on the human population in the area to be affected by the proposed action. This evaluation may take the form of an environmental checklist and/or, as appropriate, a narrative containing more detailed analysis of topics and impacts that are potentially

significant, including, where appropriate, social structures and mores; cultural uniqueness and diversity; access to and quality of recreational and wilderness activities; local and state tax base and tax revenues; agricultural or industrial production; human health; quantity and distribution of employment; distribution and density of population and housing; demands for government services; industrial and commercial activity; locally adopted environmental plans and goals; and other appropriate social and economic circumstances.)

160. *California:* CAL. CODE REGS. § 15131(a) (EIS may only analyze socioeconomic effects in no greater detail than necessary to trace their relationship to physical environmental changes, or to demonstrate the significance of physical changes caused by the project; an EIS thus "may trace a chain of cause and effect from a proposed decision on a project through anticipated economic or social changes resulting from the project to physical changes caused in turn by the economic or social changes").

Montana: MONT. ENVTL. & HEALTH SAFETY REGS. § 17.4.603 (whenever an EIS is prepared, economic and social impacts and their relationship to biological, physical, cultural, and aesthetic impacts must be discussed).

Wisconsin: Save Downtown Committee, Inc. v. Wisconsin Dep't of Natural Resources, 340 N.W.2d 722 (Wisc. 1983) (socioeconomic effects need not be considered).

161. CAL. CODE REGS. § 15064(f).

162. CAL. CODE REGS. § 15131(b).

163. CAL. CODE REGS. § 15131(b).

164. WASH. ADMIN. CODE § 197-11-448(2).

165. *See also* Barrie v. Kitsap County, 613 P.2d 1148 (Wash. 1980).

166. Examples of information that is not required to be discussed in the EIS are: methods of financing proposals, economic competition, profits and personal income and wages, and social policy analysis (such as fiscal welfare policies and nonconstruction aspects of education and communications). WASH. ADMIN. CODE § 197-11-448(3).

167. SEAPC v. Cammack II Orchards, 49 Wash. App. 609, 744 P.2d 1101, 1106 (1987).

168. MICHAEL B. GERRARD ET AL., ENVIRONMENTAL IMPACT REVIEW IN NEW YORK, § 5.12 [10] (Matthew Bender 1998 Supp.).

169. Chinese Staff and Workers Ass'n v. City of New York, 68 N.Y.2d 359, 509 N.Y.S.2d 499, 502 N.E.2d 176 (1986).

170. *See, e.g.,* GA. CODE ANN. § 12-8-25.4 (1996) (prohibiting the permitting of any solid waste handling facility within an area that already includes all or a portion of three or more landfills in a two-mile radius); ALA. CODE ANN. § 22-30-5.1(c) (1997) (provides that "there shall be no more than one commercial hazardous waste treatment facility or disposal site" situated within "any one county of the state"); WIS. STAT. ANN. § 289.29(2)(a) (1997) ("the department may not issue a favorable determination of feasibility for a solid waste disposal facility in a 3rd class city if two or more approved facilities that are solid waste disposal facilities are in operation within the city in which the solid waste disposal facility is proposed to be located").

171. *See, e.g.,* IDAHO CODE ANN. § 39-5806(2)(a) (1997) (State Hazardous Waste Management Committee must prepare a hazardous waste siting manage-

ment plan that, among other things, provides for a "reasonable geographic distribution of hazardous waste facilities" and publish plan for public comment); MICH. COMP. LAWS ANN. § 324.11110 (1998) (Department of Environmental Protection must prepare and update hazardous waste management plan that, among other things, plans for a "reasonable geographic distribution" of treatment, storage, and disposal facilities to meet future and existing needs); N.Y. ENVTL. CONSERV. LAW § 27-1102(2)(f) (similar provision).

172. *See, e.g.*, MD. CODE ANN. ENVIR. § 7-402(b)(9) (hazardous waste facilities shall be located subject to, among other things, "due consideration for the equitable distribution of sites," including consideration of these subdivisions that presently have sites, to avoid to the extent feasible certifying sites disproportionately in any one subdivision); N.C. GEN. STAT. § 160A-325(a) (governing board of a city shall consider alternative sites and socioeconomic and demographic data; "socioeconomic and demographic data" means the most recent socioeconomic and demographic data compiled by the United States Bureau of the Census and any additional socioeconomic and demographic data submitted at the public hearing).

173. *See, e.g.*, ARK. CODE ANN. § 8-6-1504 (1997) (creates a rebuttable presumption against permitting a "high impact solid waste management facility" within twelve miles of any existing "high impact solid waste management facility"); *see also* H.B. 1195, 61st Leg., 2d Sess. (Colo. 1998) (creating identical presumption).

174. ARK. CODE ANN. § 8-6-1504(b).

175. *Id.* Such incentives could include, without limitation: increased employment opportunities, reasonable host fees not to exceed the prevailing state average, contributions by the facility to the community infrastructure, compensation to adjacent individual landowners for any assessed decrease in property values, or subsidization of community services.

176. *See* Robert Bullard, *Environmental Blackmail in Minority Communities, in RACE AND THE* INCIDENCE OF ENVIRONMENTAL HAZARDS 83–84 (Bunyan Bryant & Paul Mohai eds., 1992) (explaining that minority communities are often vulnerable to economic inducements and may minimize their opposition to sitings whose risks might outweigh their benefits because these communities are beset by rising unemployment, extreme poverty, a shrinking tax base, and decaying business infrastructure).

177. Foster, *Justice from the Ground Up*, *supra* note 1, at 830.

178. *See, e.g.*, *Alabama*: Requires selection committee to consider and include in its written report the "social and economic impacts of the proposed facility on the affected community, including changes in property values, community perception and other costs." ALA. CODE ANN. § 22-30-5.1(d) (1997).

Connecticut: In determining whether to issue a hazardous waste certificate of "public safety and necessity," the siting council must consider the impact of the proposed facility on the municipality and affected geographic area in terms of "public health, safety and welfare." The siting council must also specifically consider the adverse economic impacts of the facility during construction and operation, the population density of the proposed location, and its proximity to residential areas and schools. CONN. GEN. STAT. ANN. § 22a-122(b) (1998).

Illinois: Case law allows other discretionary criteria not listed in statute. Southwest Energy Corp. v. Illinois Pollution Control Bd., 275 Ill. App. 3d 211, 655 N.E.2d 304 (4th Dist. 1995) (although the 9 statutory criteria must be satisfied before local siting approval can be granted, these are not the only factors to be considered; thus, a local governing body may find the applicant had met the statutory criteria and properly deny the application based upon "legislative-type considerations"). Examples of criteria that courts have held were properly taken into consideration are whether the proposed facility was located to minimize incompatibility with the character of the surrounding area and the effect on the value of surrounding property. Fairview Area Citizens Taskforce v. Pollution Control Bd., 198 Ill. App. 3d 541, 555 N.E.2d 1178 (3 Dist. 1990) (approved permit in part because local siting approval board believed the landfill would provide an economic benefit to community); and whether the proposed landfill presents a potential health hazard to the surrounding community. McHenry County Landfill, Inc. v. EPA, 154 Ill. App. 3d 89, 506 N.E.2d 372 (2 Dist. 1987).

Indiana: Decision maker must hold an adjudicatory hearing to review and evaluate the impact of the proposed facility on the county and municipality. IND. CODE ANN. § 13-22-10-18(a) (1998). In making this evaluation, the authority shall consider the environmental and social impacts, including predictable adverse effects on public health, population density, and safety, as well as scenic, historic, cultural, and recreational values. Must also consider the "concerns and objections raised by the public." *Id.* § 13-33-10-18(b).

Iowa: Decision maker must consider, among other things: "impact of the proposed facility on the area in which it is located," "land uses and density of population in areas near the facility," and "density of population in areas adjacent to probable transportation routes to facility." IOWA CODE § 455B.448(1) (1997). The decision maker must also consider "the public health, environmental, social and economic advantages, disadvantages, and risks associated with alternative methods of meeting the established need [of facility]." IOWA ADMIN. CODE § 150.8(2) (1997).

Kentucky: Siting Board must consider "social and economic impacts of the proposed facility" on the "affected community" including "changes in property values, community perception and other psychic costs." KY. REV. STAT. ANN. § 224.46-830(2)(a) (1996).

Louisiana: Decision maker must assess the impact of the location of the facility on the citizens in the surrounding area, on the local infrastructure, and on the environment. The assessment report shall include a determination of whether or not the facility poses undue health risks because of potential human exposure. LA. STAT. REV. § 2178(A) (1998). A facility or proposed facility may be deemed to pose undue health risks for the following nonexclusive reasons: proximity to various land uses including schools, public buildings, and residential areas; the number and density of existing hazardous waste disposal facilities, solid waste disposal facilities, and inactive and abandoned hazardous waste sites in the area; the number and density of existing industrial facilities that discharge hazardous or toxic substances into the air or water; the existence of any community health problem that may be aggravated by the operation of a commercial hazardous waste disposal facility. *Id.* § 2178(B)(2)(b). The Secretary's report regarding the siting area of the proposed facility shall include a determination of whether or not the siting of the facility in the area may reasonably be determined to preclude the economic development of the area by businesses or industries because of undue risk associated with establishing such operations of such entities adjacent to said facility. *Id.* § 2178(B)(2)(c).

Michigan: Directs state agency to propose criteria for determining acceptable locations for these facilities. The criteria shall include a consideration of a location's geology, geography, demography, and waste generation patterns, along with environmental factors, public health factors, and other relevant characteristics as determined by the department. MICH. COMP. LAWS ANN. § 324.11110 (1998). Directs siting review board, in determining the suitability of a particular facility, among other things: public health and safety, scenic/historical/cultural/recreational value, and the "concerns and objections submitted by the public." *Id.* § 324.11120.

Mississippi: Site selection criteria must be based on consideration of, among other things, socioeconomic factors, including, but not limited to, impact on local land use, property values, and governmental services. MISS. CODE ANN. § 17-18-15 (1997).

Minnesota: In evaluating and selecting sites for stabilization and containment facilities, the office shall consider at least the following factors:

(a) economic feasibility, including proximity to concentrations of generators of the types of hazardous wastes likely to be proposed and permitted for stabilization and containment;
(b) intrinsic suitability of the sites;
(c) federal and state pollution control and environmental protection rules;
(d) the risk and effect for local residents, units of government, and the local public health, safety, and welfare, including such dangers as an accidental release of wastes during transportation to a facility or at a facility, water, air, and land pollution; and fire or explosion;
(e) the consistency of a facility with, and its effect on, existing and planned local land use and development; local laws, ordinances, and permits; and local public facilities and services;
(f) the adverse effects of a facility at the site on agriculture and natural resources and opportunities to mitigate or eliminate such adverse effects by stipulations, conditions, and requirements respecting the design and operation of a disposal facility at the proposed site.

MINN. STAT. ANN. § 115A.20.

Nevada: Applicant must submit information concerning, among other things:

(a) the effect of the proposed facility on the public health, safety and welfare in the geographic area and any municipality near its proposed location (including the effect of facility on scenic/historic/recreational areas);
(b) the density of the population in the proximity of the proposed location for the facility;
(c) the public benefits of the proposed facility;

(d) whether any other available site or method for the management of hazardous waste would be less detrimental to the public health or safety or to the quality of the environment.

NEV. ADMIN. CODE § 444.8458 (1998).

New Jersey: Applicant for new hazardous waste facility must submit an impact statement, which assesses facility's effect on demography of area (existing population totals and describing present and projected future population and trends for the area within which the facility will be located) and property values within the immediate neighborhood with respect to median sales prices and recent (1–2 year) trends. The descriptions must include such factors as zoning changes, development patterns, and development approvals that can affect property values. The description of property values in the immediate area of the facility shall be sufficiently detailed to allow assessment of the effect construction and operation of the facility may have on such values. N.J. ADMIN. CODE § 7:26G-12.2(g)(3)(ii)(4) (1998).

Tennessee: The owner or operator of a proposed new commercial facility must submit a report documenting the results of a study evaluating the economic impacts the proposed facility would have on the local community and surrounding communities and demonstrating how any adverse economic impacts will be minimized. The economic impact shall be projected based on the following factors assessed over the period beginning with the initiation of construction and extending through the expected operating life of the facility or, for disposal facilities, through the post-closure care period: effects on property values; tax revenue to be generated and/or other direct compensation to the community; effects on employment (for instance, increases or decreases in job opportunities and/or personal incomes); increases in public expenditures for services such as police protection, fire and emergency response, sewers, water, electricity, roads, or schools; decreases in hazardous waste management costs to local, state, or regional generators; and attractiveness to existing or potential industrial neighbors. TENN. ENVTL. HEALTH & SAFETY REGS. § 1200-1-14-.03(3)(q) (1997).

179. *But see* H.B. 518, 90th Leg., 1st Sess. § 15 (Ill. 1997) (bill instructs local permitting authority to "give great weight to the community impact statement when making a final decision regarding the issuance of a permit").

CHAPTER 10

Risk Assessment, Susceptible Subpopulations, and Environmental Justice

CARL F. CRANOR

Introduction

As laws have been enacted to protect citizens from environmental health harms, it has become necessary to identify the substances that cause or pose risks of causing such harms. The step in regulatory procedures at which risks to persons is addressed is called "risk assessment." Risk assessment is the use of a factual base utilizing human studies, animal studies, chemical structure-activity relationships, a variety of short-term tests and appropriate exposure information "to define the health effects of exposure of individuals or populations to hazardous materials and situations."[1] Although it was not utilized to a great extent until the early 1970s in environmental regulation and not fully developed for that purpose until the early 1980s, risk assessment has become central to a regulatory process that seeks to protect citizens from carcinogens, reproductive toxins, neurotoxins, and various other pollutants. Most agencies now utilize risk assessment in some form to help guide their decision making about the risks to health from environmental pollutants.[2] And, its use in regulation received considerable political reinforcement from the 104th and subsequent Congresses.[3]

Simultaneous with the increasing importance of risk assessment in regulation, citizen groups, the National Academy of Sciences, and ultimately the regulatory agencies recognized that some citizens and some groups were not well protected by environmental health laws.[4]

These concerns led to a quasi-political movement for "environmental justice" or "environmental equity"[5] and to a Presidential Order[6] and agency initiatives for environmental justice.[7] A principle underlying environmental justice is that every person, even the most susceptible, has a right to protection from invasion of his or her interests by environmental toxicants.[8] However, risk assessment as a guide to decision making for environmental health protections and environmental justice as a goal do not rest easily together. At a minimum there is tension between the two; at the extreme they appear to be and to represent parts of quite different approaches to protecting human health from environmental insults. Since it seems that for now and into the foreseeable future agencies and decision makers are likely to rely heavily on risk assessments to guide their decisions, they must address some of the implicit and explicit tensions between risk assessment and environmental equity even to approximate environmental justice.

In what follows, after considering some preliminary issues, I discuss the legal authorities providing protections for susceptible subpopulations, summarize the extent to which agencies rely upon risk assessment for regulation, address how risk assessment might incorporate risks to susceptible subpopulations as well as its limitations for these purposes, and, finally, consider how risk assessments have been reviewed on appeal.

Preliminary Issues

There are a variety of legal and/or procedural contexts in which environmental health regulation may occur where risk assessment is likely to be utilized and its results may have an impact on susceptible subpopulations or on minority or low-income communities. Risk assessments are typically utilized in setting ambient environmental health exposures, in the registration of pesticides, in permitting the manufacture of new products that use toxic substances, and in governing the reduction or concentration levels of such substances. They also have a role in siting new waste disposal and hazardous waste facilities and in guiding cleanup levels for sites contaminated by hazardous substances and environmental assessments of brownfield sites (abandoned or underutilized commercial and industrial properties[9]). Finally, they are used implicitly or explicitly in the private tort law in determining whether someone who allegedly has been exposed to potentially toxic substances has been harmed by the exposure (and thus deserves some compensation for any injuries suffered).

Risk assessment has been one lightning rod of regulatory disputes.[10] "[S]parseness and uncertainty of the scientific knowledge of the health hazards addressed"[11] plagued early risk assessments and remains a constant.[12] These issues led in turn to concerns about the extent to which various generic risks and harms have been identified and properly assessed. Potential victims of pollution may be concerned that risk assessments either fail to identify risks to which they are exposed or fail fully to indicate the seriousness of the risks. Regulated firms or industries tend to be concerned that risk assessments wrongly identify risks as present when they are not or overestimate risks and protect too much. Nonetheless, risk assessment has become more accepted, routinized, utilized, and ultimately embedded in agencies, as they and some of the stakeholders, especially risk producers, appear relatively comfortable with identifying and assessing the risks to persons.[13]

Recently, however, a "second generation" of more subtle concerns has arisen as the environmental health movement matured—that some individuals and some communities have not been fully acknowledged and protected by legislation, regulations and risk assessments. These issues have been brought to attention by the environmental justice movement and a change in presidential administrations. If at first the concerns about risk assessment were simply to identify and assess risks to some generic person, typically the seventy-kilogram (white?) male, the new issues are more complex and more difficult: what are the risks to those who differ from the generic person—for example, women, fetuses, children, and the elderly, as well as minority and low-income individuals? What are the risks to heavily impacted communities? It is the second generation of concerns about risk assessment that are the object of this chapter.

There is no question, however, that such subpopulations of the citizenry should be addressed in both risk assessment and regulations. One of the basic ideas for such protections has been in the tort law for more than one hundred years: if individuals' fundamental legal interests have been invaded, then they have legal standing to be protected from harm even if they happen to be particularly vulnerable or fragile, or have unusual temporary or permanent susceptibilities to disease or injury.[14] The underlying moral consideration seems to be that *everyone* has *equal* standing to be protected from harm even though some have eggshell skulls, some are pregnant, or some have predispositions to disease or to "loss of hair from fright."[15] An analogous principle seems appropriate in regulatory law, which typically has a much more prospective orientation.[16] If all in the community have equal moral standing to be protected or all have a right to environmental health protections, we should not in principle discriminate between the healthy and the especially susceptible in the population.[17]

There are narrower and broader conceptions of environmental equity. The narrower view, which has provided much of the motivation and much of the quasi-legal or legal authority for environmental justice, concerns equal protection for minority and low-income communities and is expressed in President Clinton's Executive Order 12,898 of February 11, 1994:

> [t]o the greatest extent practicable and permitted by law . . . each Federal agency shall make achieving environmental justice part of its mission by identifying and addressing, as appropriate, disproportionately high and adverse human health or environmental effects of its programs, policies and activities on minority populations and low-income populations in the United States. . . . [18]

The concerns to protect both minority and low-income *communities* are several. First, there is a normative view—every person, even the most vulnerable or the most highly exposed, is entitled to protection from invasions of his or her interests by environmental toxicants. Second, this is supplemented with at least two important factual premises: that both minority and low-income communities tend to be much more exposed than others to environmental pollutants and that the individuals within those communities may be more susceptible to environmental insults. Moreover, some argue that it is no accident that these communities are more highly exposed.[19]

A broader conception of environmental justice aims to provide protections for all who are particularly vulnerable as a result of greater susceptibility, greater exposure, or both, whether or not they live in heavily impacted communities. Such a conception would provide protection to those *individuals* who may not be part of a particularly vulnerable organized *community* but who have intrinsic susceptibilities to disease (for example, genetic, metabolic, or gender-based vulnerabilities), acquired susceptibilities to disease (as those resulting from asthma or diabetes), or greater exposures. The broader idea underlies the environmental justice movement, since its advocates have emphasized from the beginning that *everyone* is entitled to environmental health protections.[20] Both the broader and narrower notions of environmental justice are included in what follows.

Different subpopulations have susceptibility to diseases resulting from *intrinsic* or *acquired factors*. *Intrinsic factors* are "inherent, fixed characteristics in an individual or population at a point in time."[21] These include susceptibilities resulting from persons' genetic makeup (for instance, a biologic tendency to eliminate toxins from one's body slower than others), gender (for instance, pregnant women), age (for example, fetuses, children, and the elderly), and ethnicity or race (such as enzyme deficiencies that may make some populations more vulnerable to ozone or nitrogen oxide) or genetic differences (such as sickle-cell anemia, which increases susceptibility to carbon monoxide).[22] For example, "the very young and the elderly are more vulnerable to the effects of some air pollutants, including aeroallergens (e.g. pollens), microorganisms (e.g. bacteria and viruses) and pesticides (e.g. organophosphates). Pregnant women and particularly their fetuses are an especially sensitive group due to physiologic changes during pregnancy, and may be more susceptible to pollutants such as carbon monoxide and pesticides that are cholinesterase inhibitors."[23] Genetic differences may result in alleles that "promote adverse effects from exposures or by the absence of alleles that provide protection (e.g. resistance) from environmentally induced disease."[24] Genetic factors may even affect susceptibility to particular chemicals.[25] There is some evidence "showing differences in genetically determined traits among certain ethnic and racial groups . . . [but] . . . [i]n most cases, it is likely that the variability within a particular ethnic or racial group is greater than the variability between any two groups."[26]

Acquired susceptibility factors include *quality of life* and *lifestyle factors. Quality of life factors* are such things as access to health care (inadequate access to health care delays recognition, diagnosis, and treatment of environmentally induced diseases or leads to a poorer health status, which increases vulnerability to diseases), pre-existing diseases or injuries (such as asthma or diabetes, which increase susceptibility to the adverse effects of exposure), psychosocial factors (for instance, stress resulting from "unemployment, underemployment, poverty, inadequate living and working conditions and language problems, reduces host resistance to adverse health effects"[27]), and exposure to environmental agents. Quality of life factors often "develop from the realities of being poor and disadvantaged, and are factors over which those in the lower socioeconomic strata have little or no control."[28] *Lifestyle factors* are those "over which people nominally exercise control; however, personal decisions about lifestyle are strongly influenced by [socioeconomic status]."[29] These include such things as "nutrition [for example, inadequate diet may impair host defense mechanisms and systems], fitness, alcohol and tobacco use, illicit drug use and sexual behavior."[30] While evidence appears to be limited on these effects, "there is little doubt that acquired susceptibility factors can have a profound impact on both exposures to environmental pollutants and vulnerability to related adverse health effects."[31]

Intrinsic and acquired susceptibility factors may characterize anyone anywhere, but both link the broader conception of environmental justice to the narrower. Minorities and low-income individuals statistically tend to have additional acquired susceptibility factors because of their quality of life and lifestyle. Moreover, since developing fetuses, infants, and children are among the more susceptible groups, and since minority and low-income communities tend to have a greater percentage of children, this is an additional reason for concern.[32]

Minority and low-income communities also typically have greater exposures, because of the communities in which they live, and, thus, face the double whammy of greater susceptibility and greater exposure.[33] People in such communities may be subject to both cumulative and multiple exposures.[34] As a result, any unusual *individual* susceptibilities may be potentiated by increased exposures and stresses to which people in such *communities* are subject. It is, thus, appropriate for minority and low-income communities to be singled out for special consideration. Moreover, historical decisions and community policies may have led to such "differential and negative impact[s]" on such communities.[35]

However, even if we agree in principle that susceptible subpopulations should be protected by environmental health laws, how well do current laws protect them?

Leading Legal Authorities Providing Environmental Health Protections

Legal authorities that address issues of susceptible subpopulations and minority and low-income communities include statutes that explicitly address such issues, those that implicitly address them, and finally, those that do not, but that may be applicable in certain circumstances. Consider these in reverse order.

Unreasonable Risk Statutes

There are statutes that on their face neither explicitly nor implicitly address environmental justice for individuals or for communities, but may require attention to such issues in particular circumstances. Several statutes require an agency to issue regulations so that there are no "unreasonable risks" to human health or the environment.[36] In particular circumstances, such statutes might provide substantial protections for these groups. For example, if there were few communities in which copper or other kinds of metal smelters were located and the communities tended were composed largely of working-class people or people of color, such statutes might require legal protections because pollutants posed risks to enough people that there could be a finding of "unreasonable risks to human health." In addition, if substances tend to accumulate in the human body and pose risks to an especially susceptible subpopulation (for example, infants and children), these might pose "unreasonable risks to human health." What makes the risks "unreasonable" are either large enough numbers of highly susceptible or highly exposed individuals (for instance, infants or the elderly), or even a small number of heavily impacted communities.

However, even if such statutes might provide protections for susceptible subpopulations in some circumstances, if the circumstances do not exist, these groups are not likely to be well-protected by unreasonable risk statutes. Whether a risk is "unreasonable" or not is a function of statutory interpretation and typically requires a balancing test similar to the tort law's "Learned Hand" test:[37] "the regulation may issue if the severity of the injury that may result from the product, factored by the likelihood of the injury, offsets the harm the regulation itself imposes upon manufacturers and consumers."[38] If the chances are low that susceptible individuals may be harmed, but most others are protected, and if the costs are relatively high for protecting those who are susceptible, an unreasonable risk statute may not protect those who are most vulnerable.

Statutes Protecting the Public Health

A second group of statutes requires an agency to protect the general public from exposure to toxic substances or to protect the public health. Such statutes might be open to either a nondistributive or a distributive interpretation. A statute protecting the public health might protect the public health generically, but not require that *each* person or that the most susceptible persons be protected. It might also have a more distributional interpretation requiring that each member of the public be protected. Since such statutes in most cases require protections with an "adequate" or "ample" margin of safety, it is arguable that the agency should be concerned about *all* members of the public. These two points at least suggest that everyone in the public is entitled to such protections, but nothing in the language guarantees such protections or guarantees, as some statutes do, that *no* individual suffer material impairment of health, for example.

The Federal Clean Water Act

The federal Clean Water Act (CWA) makes it illegal to discharge pollutants into the water except in compliance with the law, which typically requires a National Pollutant Discharge Elimination System permit (NPDES) issued by the EPA or the states. These permits cover conventional and toxic pollutants; only the latter are considered here. The CWA prohibits the "discharge of toxic pollutants in toxic amounts. . . ."[39] The CWA originally envisioned regulating ambient levels of pollutants in water, using so-called "effluent based standards"[40] that would protect fish, shellfish, and wildlife as well as protecting human recreation in and on the water[41] "with an ample margin of safety."[42] Statutory requirements for toxic substances, however, were difficult to meet (only six toxic pollutants were regulated in six years).[43] A suit by environmentalists resulted in a consent degree in which EPA agreed to list 65 toxic pollutants in 21 "primary" industries[44] and agreed to regulate them in accordance with technology-based "effluent limitations."[45] This utilizes technological devices, typically the "best available technology" (BAT), to limit the amount of pollutants that can be discharged from a particular point source, such as a pipe.[46] Permits for a facility must contain a list of pollutants to be regulated and specify permissible amounts of each pollutant, monitoring requirements, and any special conditions the permit writers think should be required.[47] The Act also requires states "to develop water quality standards," which are criteria specifying the maximum concentration of substances in a stream designated for a certain use (for example, restricting concentrations of cyanide in a fishery).[48] Finally, if effluent limitations will not sufficiently protect a stream, Section 302 authorizes "'water quality related effluent limitations'" more stringent than BAT.[49]

Under CWA, EPA is also authorized to issue water quality criteria for all pollutants. These are not legally binding, but may be used as goals to improve the quality of water courses.[50] A major risk assessment activity of EPA in the late 1970s was to do the risk assessments utilized in criteria documents.[51] NPDES permit writers may require permittees to adhere to more stringent pollution standards than those imposed by toxic effluent limitations in accordance with the water quality criteria documents.[52]

The Clean Air Act

The Clean Air Act (CAA) authorizes regulations for primary ambient air quality standards concerning the public health and secondary ambient air quality standards concerning the public welfare.[53] Primary ambient air quality standards shall allow for "an adequate margin of safety" and be "requisite to protect the public health."[54] These generally concern such pollutants as ozone, nitrogen oxide, and carbon monoxide.

The CAA, in addition, requires regulation of "hazardous air pollutants," substances that "may reasonably be anticipated to result in an increase in mortality or an increase in serious irreversible, or incapacitating reversible, illness."[55] The 1990 amendments to this Act require the EPA to set standards for a list of hazardous air pollutants based upon the maximum achievable control technology (MACT), which standards should achieve "the maximum degree of reduction in emissions of . . . the pollutants."[56] If the technology-based controls do not adequately protect the public health, the agency must set "residual risk standards that protect *public health with an ample margin of safety*."[57] The agency must set a residual-risk standard if the MACT emission standard leaves a lifetime cancer risk *for the most exposed person* of greater than one in a million.[58]

The 1990 amendments also specifically called on the EPA to have the National Academy of Sciences review the risk assessment methodology for estimating and describing carcinogenic potency of hazardous air pollutants and in particular to estimate the effect of carcinogens on "hypothetical and actual maximally exposed individuals . . ."[59] The resulting report called attention to shortcomings in risk assessments concerning variability in susceptibility and highly exposed individuals, helping to provide a factual basis for the environmental justice movement.[60]

The Safe Drinking Water Act

The Safe Drinking Water Act (SDWA) aims to ensure that the suppliers of drinking water, mainly public water agencies, provide drinking water sufficiently safe to ingest. The Act authorizes EPA to set health-based "maximum contaminant level goals" (MCLGs) "at the level at which no known or anticipated adverse effects on the health of persons occur and which allows an adequate margin of safety."[61] It then envisions setting legally enforceable drinking water standards, called "national primary drinking water regulation" for each contaminant for which a maximum contaminant level goal is established.[62] These should "specify a maximum contaminant level for such contaminant which is as close to the maximum contaminant level goal as is feasible."[63] In setting these standards "the administrator shall use—(i) the best available, peer-reviewed science and supporting studies conducted in accordance with sound and objective scientific practices; and (ii) data collected by accepted methods or best available methods (if the reliability of the method and the nature of the decision justifies use of the data)."[64]

While this statutory language may appear not to concern itself with the health effects for individual persons as some other laws do, it does require:

a) that there be no known or anticipated adverse effects on persons; and
b) that the standards established in the MCLGs be set with an ample margin of safety.

Thus, there appears to be an individual, distributive effect from this requirement that protects all persons, even those who are most susceptible and those most exposed to pollutants in drinking water. In addition, the requirement to use the "best available, peer-reviewed science and supporting studies"[65] to justify the regulations in setting

MCLGs arguably requires the use of studies addressing highly susceptible individuals because of intrinsic or acquired susceptibility factors as well as highly exposed individuals in minority or low-income communities (if this should be the case). The SDWA permits the agency to take costs into account in setting the National Primary Drinking Water Standards. This modifies what the legally enforceable drinking water standard will be.

The Resource Conservation and Recovery Act

The Resource Conservation and Recovery Act (RCRA) is intended to ensure that hazardous waste is properly handled, that hazardous wastes are not openly dumped on land, and that such wastes are managed in "a manner which protects human health and the environment."[66] Under RCRA, the EPA is required to issue regulations to the owners and operators of hazardous waste facilities to guide the storage, disposal, and treatment of hazardous waste in ways that are "necessary to protect human health and the environment."[67] Substances classified as hazardous[68] or listed as such[69] must then be handled in accordance with certain specific procedures issued by EPA. The idea behind this legislation and its attendant regulations is that if the hazardous wastes are "properly" handled from cradle to grave, they will not "escape into the environment—that 'proper handling' will prevent escape."[70] Violations of requirements of the law are subject to civil penalties,[71] and knowing violation of any of several requirements of the statute or its regulations—for instance, transport of hazardous waste to a facility that does not have a RCRA permit, or falsification of records—is subject to criminal penalties including fines and imprisonment.[72] Anyone who commits an act subject to criminal penalties and who also knowingly places another person in "imminent danger of death or serious bodily injury" is subject to more severe criminal penalties.[73] The judgment of imminent endangerment appears to be a qualitative judgment, not one requiring a risk assessment. Finally, other provisions of RCRA address the siting of disposal waste facilities (addressed in Chapter 14, "Stopping and Building New Facilities," pages 465–489).

The Comprehensive Environmental Response, Compensation and Liability Act

The remediation of toxic waste spills, waste dumps, and contaminated industrial facilities is authorized by the Comprehensive Environmental Response, Compensation and Liability Act of 1980 (CERCLA) as amended by the Superfund Amendments and Reauthorization Act of 1986 (SARA).[74] (See also Chapter 16, "Cleaning Up Abandoned or Inactive Contaminated Sites," pages 522–560.) Superfund statutes address both emergency and nonemergency sites. Serious hazardous waste sites are "placed on the National Priorities List through a process that assigns numerical values to various indicators of danger and potential for harm to health and the environment."[75] The Administrator of the Agency for Toxic Substances and Disease Registry "shall perform a health assessment for each facility on the national Priorities List established under" CERCLA[76] and "may perform health assessments" where individuals have been exposed to hazardous substances.[77]

For sites targeted for cleanup, a combined remedial investigation and feasibility study is then done, after "which the EPA regional administrator selects the remedial option which appears to best satisfy the broad . . . statutory requirements for cleanup."[78] Remedies are then selected in accordance with general statutory guidance[79] that receives further specifications in nine regulatory criteria,[80] two of which pertain to risk assessment: "(A) Overall protection of human health and the environment . . . whether they can adequately protect human health and the environment, in both the short- and long-term, from unacceptable risks posed by hazardous substances, pollutants or contaminants present at the site . . . ,"[81] and "(B) . . . whether they attain applicable or relevant and appropriate requirements under federal environmental laws and state environmental or facility siting laws. . . ."[82] These requirements incorporate by reference other statutes, including the maximum contaminant levels goals of SDWA[83] and water quality criteria established under the authority of CWA,[84] thus subjecting cleanups to their statutory authorities, their regulations and their risk assessment requirements. The first two criteria—protection of human health and the environment, and conformity with other federal and state laws—appear to be viewed as necessary conditions to be satisfied under Superfund provisions with the other seven considerations to be addressed only if the first two are satisfied. However, other language seems to contravene this, including cost provisions that might override the environmental health protections, and some commentators are concerned that the cost considerations may come to dominate the structure of priorities.[85]

Finally, for Superfund cleanups the EPA is currently evaluating the use of an "additional 10-fold safety factor in Superfund risk assessments to protect infants and children. . . ."[86] The agency must weigh the protection of susceptible subpopulations against the possibility of making cleanups more expensive. While use of such a safety factor is not required by law, the agency is considering it as part of any overall agency initiative adequately to protect children's health.

Legislation Protecting Individual Persons

In contrast to the statutes just considered, some statutes either explicitly aim at protecting each individual or implicitly achieve this by their requirements. The Occupational Safety and Health Act and the Delaney Clause of the Food, Drug and Cosmetic Act exemplify these characteristics.

The Occupational Safety and Health Act

The Occupational Safety and Health Act (OSH Act) requires the Secretary of Labor when issuing a health standard to assure "to the extent feasible, on the basis of the best available evidence, that *no employee* will suffer material impairment of health or functional capacity even if such employee has regular exposure to the hazard dealt with by such standard for the period of his working life [normally considered to be 45 years]."[87] Such statutory language referring to individuals appears to require attention in regulation to highly exposed or very susceptible individuals in the workforce, since the statutory requirement has not been satisfied, at least in principle, if there are some employees who would suffer material impairment of health or functional capacity even after the standard was implemented. A federal appellate court has held that the Occupational Safety and Health Administration (OSHA) may take susceptibilities resulting from lifestyle into account (for instance, employees' smoking) in setting its proposed exposure levels.[88]

The health protective goals of the OSH Act, however, are attenuated by "feasibility" considerations in particular cases, given the technological difficulties or economic costs of providing the protections. The OSH Act requires regulations to protect employees from material impairment of health or functional capacity "to the extent feasible" where this includes both technological and economic feasibility. How effective the OSH Act is in protecting highly exposed or highly susceptible individuals is not clear, since in many cases the residual risk after stricter regulations are imposed could be quite high in the workplace.

Finally, OSHA initially explicitly stated that "quantitative risk assessments would be used only to set priorities . . . ," and for carcinogens, once substances were identified as carcinogens, "it would then set an exposure standard based only on feasibility."[89] However, since the Supreme Court's decision in the *Benzene* case,[90] the agency has utilized risk assessments to guide judgments about "significant risks" to workers and the feasibility of setting lower exposure standards that would protect them.[91] Subsequent to the *Benzene* decision, OSHA has utilized risk assessment in regulations (discussed below).[92]

The Food, Drug and Cosmetic Act

The Delaney Clause of the Food, Drug and Cosmetic Act (FDCA) also arguably protects individual persons against exposures to carcinogens even though its language is not quite as explicit as the language of the OSH Act. The Delaney Clause applies to food additives, direct and indirect; drugs fed to animals; and color additives.[93] The FDCA requires the safe use of these substances and provides "that no additive shall be deemed to be safe if it is found to induce cancer when ingested by man or animal, or if it is found, after tests which are appropriate for the evaluation of the safety of food additives, to induce cancer in man or animal . . ."[94] The premise of the Delaney Clause is that "no dose of a carcinogenic chemical could be shown to be safe, and that any dose posed *some* risk of cancer."[95] While it is barely conceivable that such tests might miss cancer risks to persons who are most vulnerable to cancer, this seems unlikely. Moreover, this is quite a health-protective statute, since it requires no balancing between potential harms to persons and the costs of regulating the substance in question. "[I]f appropriate evidence [human or animal] indicates that a food additive is carcinogenic, FDA may not consider it safe and must prohibit its use. . . ."[96] The FDA must engage in risk assessment for purposes of the Delaney Clause only to the extent of identifying a hazard as carcinogenic. Despite the protective nature of this statute, there are a number of ways of avoiding the Delaney Clause even if it is facially applicable to the substance in question.[97]

Portions of the general provisions of FDCA concerning food adulteration also protect sensitive subpopulations. Section 402(a)(1) declares food "adulterated" if it contains "added" substances that "may render it injurious to health," or if it contains any substances, whether or not added, that would "ordinarily render it injurious to health."[98] The first standard applies to substances added during the processing of food while the second applies also to natural contaminants. The first is also more stringent in allowing the agency to establish the risk of harm with a lower probability, and it permits consideration of sensitive subpopulations, while the second does not.[99]

The Food and Drug Administration was the first federal agency to use risk assessment to guide its regulations of potentially toxic substances. It originally published guidelines for testing the toxicity of food and color additives in 1955 with revisions and updates in 1959 and 1970. It officially began using quantitative risk assessments in the 1970s for some categories of additives.[100]

Legislation Specifically Concerned with Susceptible Subpopulations

The Food Quality Protection Act of 1996 amended both the Federal Insecticide, Fungicide and Rodenticide Act and the Food, Drug and Cosmetic Act.[101] It eliminated the Food, Drug and Cosmetic Act's Delaney Clause for determining the safety of pesticide residues in processed foods and replaced it with a standard requiring a "reasonable certainty that no harm would result from aggregate exposure to the pesticide chemical residue, including all anticipated dietary exposures and all other exposures for which there is reliable information."[102] The lifetime risk posed by nonthreshold effects is "appropriately assessed by quantitative risk assessment. . . ."[103] One of its main aims is to protect children from the possible toxic effects of pesticides in foods. This Congressional action appears to have resulted, *inter alia,* from a National Academy of Sciences report challenging EPA's criteria setting safe tolerances for foods that would affect children and infants.[104] Tolerance levels for pesticide residues are to be set for both substances acting by means of "threshold" mechanisms (there is "a level of exposure to the residue at which the residue will not cause or contribute to a known or anticipated harm to human health") and "nonthreshold" mechanisms (there is no "level of exposure to the residue at which the residue will not cause or contribute to a known or anticipated harm to human health").[105]

The Act requires "that there is [be] reasonable certainty that no harm will result to infants and children from *aggregate* exposure to the pesticide chemical residue, [and that the agency] publish a specific determination regarding the safety of the residue for *infants and children.*"[106] For carcinogens, consumers must face "no more than a negligible risk—described in the legislative history as 1 in 1 million lifetime risk. For pesticides causing threshold-limited effects, EPA is expected to apply a 100-fold margin of safety."[107]

This law specifically addresses a particularly susceptible subpopulation—infants and children—and addresses both concerns about cumulative or aggregative exposures to potentially toxic pesticides. Thus, it arguably requires the EPA to address not only the effects of pesticide residues in processed foods for children of all social and economic classes, but also any aggregate exposures to pesticide residues to children in minority or low-income communities, should those be greater than for nonminority and higher-income children. When there is increased exposure, an "additional tenfold margin of safety for the pesticide chemical residue *and other sources of exposure* shall be applied for infants and children to take into account potential pre- and post-natal toxicity and completeness of the data with respect to exposure and toxicity to infants and children."[108] Thus, "if EPA finds that infants or children will be significantly exposed to a pesticide, it is directed to apply an additional safety factor of 10 (thus a factor of 1000) in establishing the [Acceptable Daily Intake of a food]."[109] In principle, it could be quite far-reaching as applied, for instance, to the children of farm workers or perhaps the children of employees in pesticide manufacturing plants (both of whom might have dietary and other exposures to pesticides).

Executive Branch Initiatives

A final strategy for protecting susceptible subpopulations rests not on statutes, but on executive branch initiatives. One initiative mandates that federal agencies take minority and low-income communities into account in their actions and a second one, perhaps in conjunction with the Food Quality Protection Act, aims in particular to protect children from the effects of environmental hazards.

Executive Order 12,898 directs each federal agency "to the greatest extent practicable and permitted by law" to "make achieving environmental justice part of its mission by identifying and addressing, as appropriate, disproportionately high and adverse human health or environmental effects of its programs, policies and activities on minority populations and low-income populations in the United States. . . ."[110] This order directs EPA to convene an interagency working group on environmental justice that includes some eighteen agencies and to develop agencywide strategies on environmental justice, and then directs each agency to "conduct its programs, policies and activities that substantially affect human health or the environment" in a manner that does not exclude participation in, deny the benefits of, or subject persons to discrimination in programs of environmental justice.[111] Moreover, environmental health research in such agencies must include attention to diverse segments of the population in scientific studies, take into account multiple and cumulative exposures to persons, and give minority and low-income populations opportunity to comment on research strategies for such communities.[112] Consistent with other laws, the Order directs that the collection and analysis of information assessing and comparing environmental and human health risks borne by populations be identified by race, national origin, or income and make it available to the public.[113] Finally, the Order does not "create any right to judicial review involving the compliance or noncompliance of the United States, its agencies, its officers, or any other person with this order."[114] Agencies affected by this order have developed implementation of it in agency documents.[115]

While this order is explicitly aimed at the internal management of the executive branch and its agencies, thus appearing not to create legal requirements, it can do so.[116] Many agencies have adopted strategies under the order that may affect their licensing, siting, and data requirements.[117] Such requirements can be substantial.[118] For example, a small steel plant to be located in Flint, Michigan, that would have burned wood waste has been denied an air pollution permit until impacted communities have been consulted and until a local risk assessment, taking into account the effects of pollution on heavily impacted minority and low-income communities, has been completed.[119] Even though the EPA had done a risk assessment on lead at its national offices, trying to take into account susceptible subpopulations, when the mill was proposed to be near a community already heavily impacted by lead, a state court judge found under provisions of state law that the national risk assessment for lead was an inadequate basis for estimating risks to local and heavily impacted populations.[120]

An executive branch initiative to protect children from health hazards is clearly evident from implementation of the Food Quality Protection Act of 1996. However, it appears to be broader than merely implementing that statute. The EPA is creating "two national children's health research centers at U.S. medical or academic institutions . . ." and "a new office of Children's Health Protection . . . to coordinate agency activities."[121] This initiative has also been manifested in agency consideration of additional safety factors to protect children for guiding toxic waste cleanups.[122]

However, even if susceptible subpopulations are, in principle, protected to varying degrees by environmental health laws, this cannot be effectively accomplished if these subpopulations are not taken into account in risk assessment. This, however, may be easier said than done, as critics of risk assessment have argued.[123]

Risk Assessment

An Overview of Risk Assessment

For estimating harms or risks of harm under the authority of most of the above statutes, regulatory agencies utilize *quantified* risk assessments. At its most general, risk assessment "entails the evaluation of scientific information on the hazardous properties of environmental agents and on the extent of human exposure to those agents. The product of the evaluation is a statement regarding the probability [expressed quantitatively or qualitatively] that populations so exposed will be harmed, and to what degree."[124] Comparative risk assessment seeks to rank environmental agents or activities by the extent of their adverse effects or seriousness.[125]

Risk assessment is typically divided into hazard identification, dose-response assessment, exposure assessment, and an overall risk characterization.

Hazard Identification

Hazard identification is a qualitative assessment of whether a substance poses a hazard to human health and, in particular, "whether exposure to an agent can cause an increase in the incidence of a health condition . . ."[126]—for instance, cancer or a birth defect. Typically this is a yes/no decision, relying largely on a qualitative assessment of the evidence concerning the toxicity of a substance,[127] but since it typically relies upon epidemiological or animal studies, it also includes substantial quantitative data and information.[128] Hazard identification might result in a correct decision to identify a substance as toxic when it is toxic or to identify a substance as nontoxic when it is nontoxic. This step might also result in mistakes: wrongly identifying a substance as toxic when it is not, a "false positive," or wrongly identifying a substance as non-toxic when it is toxic, a "false negative."[129]

Dose-Response Assessment

Dose-response or potency assessments utilize scientific data, theories, and policy considerations—typically animal bioassays, human epidemiological studies, and inferences from them—to characterize quantitatively "the relation between the dose of an agent administered or received and the incidence of an adverse health effect in exposed populations and [to estimate] the incidence of the effect as a function of human exposure to the agent."[130] Such assessments might either over- or underestimate the true risk in question, although in the present state of knowledge, it may be difficult to determine when either occurs.

Well-conducted epidemiological studies with sufficient sample size and sufficient statistical power to detect health effects of concern provide the best evidence that a substance is toxic and of the relationship between dose received and effect observed. A number of factors are germane to evaluating the quality of epidemiological studies:

> strength of association, level of statistical significance, information on dose-response relationships, biological plausibility, temporal relationships, confounding factors and bias, accuracy of exposure and cause-of-death classifications, adequacy of follow-up, and whether sufficient time has elapsed to allow for latent effects.[131]

Failure to attend to some of these issues may result in studies or their interpretations that will result in false negatives or underregulation, while failure to attend to others will result in false positives or overregulation. If studies are not "statistically significant," they might suggest an association between exposure and disease when there is none.[132] If the relative risk detected by a study (the strength of association) is too small, this raises the question of whether the risk revealed by the study is real or of sufficient magnitude to warrant concern.[133] The presence of confounding factors may wrongly suggest an adverse effect when there is none, but a too-demanding search to ferret out confounders may paralyze actions to address adverse effects.[134] Epidemiological studies that are of insufficient duration may fail to detect an existing relative risk since the latency of the disease might be longer than the study.[135] Similarly, epidemiological studies that are based on too small a sample may be inadequate to detect a relative risk of concern even if it exists.[136] Studies that lack sufficient statistical power[137] to detect relatively small relative risks may mistakenly leave toxic substances undetected.[138]

Several other considerations render epidemiological studies problematic for detecting and assessing risks. Diseases with long latency periods, such as cancer, may frustrate discovery.[139] Few toxic substances leave a unique "fingerprint" of their presence, thus making the identification of disease etiology difficult.[140] Finally, and most seriously, however, because it is difficult and expensive to conduct epidemiological studies, few substances have been subjected to them.[141]

Because of the above problems, agencies have tended to utilize animal studies to try to estimate risks of concern. Animal studies are faster and cheaper than human studies. Moral considerations preclude waiting for "evidence of harm in exposed people when risks can be established relatively quickly by animal experimentation."[142] Human and animal molecular, cellular, tissue, and organ functions as well as metabolic processes are thought to be similar.[143] For carcinogens, the development of tumors in various species of animals in most cases is believed to resemble that in humans. These similarities form much of the basis for predictive and regulatory toxicology.[144] Animal studies are not always fully predictive of effects in humans, however. Occasionally, effects have been seen in humans where a similar response has not been seen in animal studies,[145] but such cases tend to be exceptions rather than the rule.[146] Conversely, adverse effects of chemical agents may have been seen in animals, but not (or not yet) seen in humans.[147] In such circumstances, however, regulatory scientists and researchers have developed procedures to evaluate animal data and its relevance to humans.[148]

In an animal study, there are usually two, sometimes three groups of about 50 animals each that are compared with a control group:

1. an experimental group fed the maximum tolerated dose (MTD) of a toxic substance, "a dose as high as possible without shortening the animals lives from noncarcinogenic toxic effects;"[149]
2. an experimental group fed one-half the MTD; and
3. sometimes an experimental group fed one-fourth the MTD.

If the tumor results in the experimental groups differ statistically from the results in the control group, tumor data from each of the experimental groups become fixed data points on a graph. To estimate low-dose responses in animals, risk assessors fit a mathematical model through the experimental data points to determine a dose-response curve. Choice of the appropriate model is fraught with uncertainty and, thus, with controversy.

Since rats and mice are mammals but not human, estimating human risks on the basis of rodent studies involves extrapolating from the effects at high doses of substances fed to experimental animals (to have large enough effects in the small samples of animals to produce statistically significant results) to low-dose effects in them and then extrapolating from rodents to humans. These steps and others[150] introduce uncertainty and, as a result, controversy because of inference gaps from established data in animals to estimating risks to humans.[151] The gaps arise because there are insufficient data points to enable researchers to find a unique curve to fit the data, and insufficient understanding of the biological mechanisms involved (for instance, of cancer) or the relationships between biological effects in one species compared to another to settle the scientific questions at issue.[152] Mathematical models or other generalizations typically used to fill the gaps can result in dose-response estimates that differ substantially from one another.[153] Thus, critics charge that high doses fed to animals may result in toxic effects that are not pertinent to humans exposed to low doses, while advocates note that animal studies are routinely relied upon in toxicology. Moreover, the use of models and policy considerations to fill inference gaps in estimating risks to human beings invites controversy. Such disagreements provide grounds for one side or the other in a regulatory controversy to raise questions on judicial appeal (discussed below). Nonetheless, there is a substantial consensus for continuing the use of inference guidelines or default options to bridge the gaps in scientific knowledge and experimental data.[154]

All of the above issues affect the estimation of risks to a generic person such as a seventy-kilogram male, but generic estimates may fail to account for toxic effects to quite different persons such as infants, children, pregnant women, those suffering from pre-existing diseases, or those in quite different exposure circumstances who might be more heavily exposed than is assumed in a generic dose-response analysis. I return to both below.

Exposure Assessment

Exposure assessment uses scientific data and theories concerning the environmental fate of pollutants, together with information about the population that is likely to be affected, to estimate human exposure to toxic substances when they are released into the environment.[155] Once risk assessors have estimated the potency of a substance, the next step is to indicate the concentration of the substance that will reach human beings through the environment—via soil, air, water, or food. This might be known through direct measurement (a less common practice), or through estimates provided by environmental fate models. It is difficult enough to provide accurate exposure information in occupational settings, but even more difficult to provide such information for environmental exposures.[156] Risk assessors might use emission rates from pollution sources combined with transport and environmental degradation models to estimate the concentration of a substance reaching persons.

Such models can introduce additional uncertainties.[157] These can be further complicated by the use of biological (pharmacokinetic) models to estimate how much of a substance that reaches a person is likely to be absorbed into the body and to reach target organs (this could also be part of dose-response assessment). Exposure estimates are complicated by variations in diet, personal habits, other exposures to the same substance, exposures to mixtures of substances, and other factors.

While even early discussions of risk assessment noted the need to take into account the different exposures and vulnerabilities of the "very young and very old people and persons with impaired health,"[158] they may not have received much attention until the advent of the environmental justice movement and EPA's initiative on the health effects on children.

Risk Characterization

Finally, risk assessors utilize dose-response assessments, exposure assessments, and any other information available to them to provide an overall characterization of the risks to persons and an "estimate of the public health problem."[159] This step "involves no additional scientific knowledge or concepts. However, the exercise of judgment in the aggregation of population groups with varied sensitivity and different exposure may affect the estimate."[160] Any problems and uncertainties affecting either dose-response or exposure assessment will also influence an overall risk characterization. In fact, because of this problem, agencies and the National Research Council suggest that risk assessors explicitly acknowledge uncertainties in risk characterization as well as in other steps of the risk assessment process.[161]

Prima Facie Tension Between Risk Assessment and Environmental Justice Strategies

In considering the use of risk assessment to help address issues of environmental justice, it is important to note a tension between the two approaches to similar problems. While some, but not all, of these problems can be resolved, this leaves risk assessment as an imperfect tool to address such concerns.

The overall strategies and aims of environmental justice emphasize intervention with processes, activities, and institutions that tend to pollute human populations and the environment and to change them to reduce or eliminate the problems. Underlying environmental justice is a view that every person has the right to be free from exposure to toxic substances, much like the ideal behind the criminal or civil law more generally: that is, a right to be free from invasions of their legitimate interests. Moreover, the environmental justice movement aims to prevent threats from pollution before they materialize into harm, as well as considering whether such risks are necessary in the community. In addition, environmental justice is concerned with a just distribution of benefits and burdens in society and especially with a just distribution between social classes and between racial groups, which its advocates argue has been overlooked, ignored, or worse, deliberately contravened up to this time.[162] Finally, environmental justice advocates have sought to "empower those persons subjected to involuntary risks and to give them a major role in the process of assessing and managing the risks in their communities."[163] In addition, commentators have noted that political empowerment itself will be relatively ineffective unless the participation is active and involved from the beginning and the affected communities have technical and other resources comparable to the risk producers, to participate effectively.[164]

By contrast, risk assessors, recognizing that toxic substances are harmful, seek to identify which substances are hazards, how potent they are, what exposures people are subjected to, and how much of a threat they constitute. Risk assessments tend to focus on "how much insult a person or the environment can bear rather than suggesting the means to eliminate the trauma [and] resources . . . are directed toward arguments over precise levels of acceptable risk from these pollutants and shifted away from issues relating to the prevention of the risk, the necessity of the risk and the distribution of the risk."[165] Thus, the scope of the issues considered in risk assessment tends to be much narrower than the scope of issues addressed by the environmental justice advocates.

Moreover, risk assessment tends to transform disputes, which as often as not are about values, ways of life, or policies, into narrower scientific disputes that will be inaccessible to many citizens and that will distort the debate from their points of view.[166] Thus, the public conception of risks and their acceptability depend upon a variety of features not captured by quantified procedures.[167] Risk assessment appears to be "woefully inadequate in characterizing the many aspects of risk that the public deems important."[168] It also tends to "squeeze out" nonquantifiable factors that are pertinent to judging the acceptability of risks and to managing them, such as the distributions of risks from pollutants and the benefits and burdens of environmental protection.[169] When considerable uncertainty is present in our risk judgments, they may be as much as or more about our values and what we consider important as they are about the probabilities of the harms in question.[170] If quantified risk assessment cannot measure effects or there is not appropriate data available or it is not in a form that can be appreciated, it will be biased against persons on that side of the argument.[171]

In addition, a major component of the environmental justice movement is procedural equity. As its advocates and others have noted, all persons substantially affected by a governmental action should have "the right to participate as equal partners at every level of decision making including needs assessment, planning, implementation, enforcement and evaluation."[172] Communities' having substantial and meaningful participation in all levels of planning for, deciding upon, and implementing, say, siting decisions, is a way in which both the values and self-protective concerns of the affected communities can be taken into account. Participation helps to ensure that these are recognized.

Finally, risk assessment is often used in conjunction with cost-benefit analysis to estimate the extent to which it is worth reducing the risks in question. Since a cost-benefit analysis of a toxic pollution problem typically does not support protecting all persons (because the marginal costs will be too high), cost-benefit analysis is incompatible with the goals of environmental justice. Cost-benefit analysis and its philosophic ancestor, utilitarianism, compared with environmental justice are simply two different and incompatible views for addressing the problems of guiding exposures to toxic substances.

Despite these differences in overall aim and in strategy, there are some ways in which risk assessors can take into account considerations of highly susceptible subpopulations, as well as minority and low-income communities, and some procedural considerations that can address issues of environmental justice. How successfully such concerns can be incorporated into a more sophisticated risk assessment remains to be seen (see "Incorporating Environmental Justice Concerns into Risk Assessment," pages 332–333).

Shortcomings of Risk Assessment in Addressing Risks to Susceptible Subpopulations

In addition to the generic concerns noted in the presentation of different steps in a risk assessment, critics have posed a number of particular objections to risk assessments. Risks to susceptible subpopulations are most likely to be missed in dose-response and exposure assessments, but some arguably could be missed in hazard identification as well.

The generic problem in dose-response assessments is that the human population of concern may be quite varied in its susceptibility to environmental insults. Recent research suggests that individual variability could range from a factor of 10 up to more than 1000, depending upon the aspect of biology in question.[173] Insufficient attention to this will underestimate risks. However, typically dose-response models utilizing either experimental animal studies or human epidemiological studies have not taken these variations into account. Extrapolations from high-dose responses in genetically quite similar animals to low-dose responses in animals and then to low-dose responses (or even lower-dose responses) in humans may ignore the possibly wide variations in human populations that result from genetic makeup, age, sex, ethnicity, and so on, as well as from acquired factors typically not characteristic of experimental animals. Risk assessments based upon animal studies try to account for variability by extrapolating from the most sensitive sex and species of experimental animal, but since the test animals are bred to "minimize genetic variability," this may not be adequate.[174] In addition, risk assessors have also tried to account for human variability by utilizing various safety factors.[175] Whether safety factors result in overestimation or underestimation of risks awaits considerable study.

Epidemiological studies have tended to be done on workers because they are easier to study than the general population, are subject to greater exposures that are more likely to produce effects that relatively insensitive epidemiological studies can detect, and have exposure data that is comparatively easier (but often not easy) to estimate. However, workers typically exhibit a "healthy worker effect";[176] they tend to be healthier than the general population because those who are not healthy do not stay in the workforce or in difficult or comparatively risky jobs. Thus, when results from worker studies are extrapolated to the general population either the hazard identifications or dose-response assessments that are based upon them may underestimate the hazard or the extent of the environmental health risks.[177] Moreover, this is not merely a theoretical or speculative point. The National Academy of Sciences reported that "[i]nterindividual variability is not generally considered in EPA's cancer risk assessments . . . [although it does consider, on a limited basis, variability in] noncarcinogenic effects such as asthmatic responses to sulfur dioxide exposure."[178]

Exposures may be underestimated because of multiple or cumulative exposures, because of increased exposures in particular communities, and because of synergistic or additive effects from pollutants.

First, risk assessments tend to be done on a substance-by-substance basis. To the extent that susceptible (or even average) individuals are exposed to multiple or cumulative exposures,[179] such assessments may underestimate the risks in question. However, the total risk for a person is an aggregate of many individual risks. A person exposed to 100 risks, each posing a one in one million lifetime risk of premature death, has a one in ten thousand risk of premature death. Second, either multiple or cumulative exposures may have additive, synergistic, or antagonistic effects.[180] The EPA typically assumes that risks are additive, but should they turn out to be synergistic (as perhaps as many as 5 percent may be[181]), this policy will result in an underestimation of risks to those exposed. EPA's assumption of additivity will overestimate the antagonistic risks. Third, however, in fact many risk assessments tend to lack adequate exposure data and appropriate models for assessing cumulative and synergistic effects.[182] Fourth, persons are often exposed to mixtures of substances. These are so poorly understood, it is difficult to estimate risks from mixtures.

The above difficulties exist for any risk assessment, even for risks affecting the seventy-kilogram white male. They are even worse for especially susceptible individuals, and they pose particular problems for individuals in minority and low-income communities. Such communities tend to be closer to sources of pollution and toxic waste dumps, to be subject to greater amounts of air contaminants, and to be subjected to higher exposures from lead.[183] Moreover, individuals in subsistence communities may rely to a greater extent than those in other communities on fish in their diets, and if the fish are contaminated, this may have an adverse effect on them.[184]

Problems with dose-response and exposure assessment will affect the final stage in risk assessment, risk characterization. However, risk assessments are frequently criticized as being too conservative, because, the argument goes, since most risk assessments are based upon the most sensitive animal species, upon extrapolation models that aim not to underestimate the risks projected to the general population, and (often) upon unrealistically high exposure estimates, they are surely overestimating the risk, perhaps by several orders of magnitude. While this argument is offered by persons on one side of the debate, they may not have attended to the variety of ways that risk assessments can underestimate risks to sensitive subpopulations or heavily impacted communities. Where the truth lies is difficult to know, since risk assessments are fraught with so many uncertainties, lack of adequate data, and lack of appropriately validated theoretical models for extrapolating risks. It is easy to show quantitatively that risk assessments *may* overestimate risks; it is currently less easy to show how much they may be underestimating risks because of variations in susceptibility and exposure.

There has been a tendency to focus on cancer as the endpoint of concern in most risk assessments, probably on the view that carcinogens have no safe level,[185] but this may or may not be the case as scientists learn more about the variety of ways in which different cancers develop and as they learn more about reproductive toxicants or endocrine disrupters.[186] Other biological endpoints may be more sensitive to toxicological insults.

The Promise of Risk Assessment for Environmental Health Protection

Despite the concerns expressed above, there are arguments that quantified risk assessment can reveal information that results in greater and appropriate protections for minority and low-income populations. While environmental justice is well supported by considerations of justice, this tends to be a vague idea, one not providing very precise guidance in practical issues. Limited guidance is especially a concern if this increases the politicization of the issues; indeed, one author argues that this "*is counterproductive from the perspectives of both society as a whole and even the specific groups whose interests it tries to champion.*"[187] With limited resources to address such problems, society will ultimately have to choose which risks to address first and which may be addressed later. Environmental justice seems to leave the choice of strategies to the political system, but this has failed minority and low-income communities to date, because success depends upon political organization and influence, which is typically absent for them.[188] Moreover, the reduction of minority and low-income exposure to lead (and accompanying pollutants) was a direct consequence of risk assessments showing the benefits to children and other people and the environment that resulted from eliminating the lead in gasoline.[189] Thus, it is claimed, a risk-based approach resulted in a faster phasedown of lead in the environment (protecting some five million children from adverse effects) than had it been left to the political process, which had largely stalled by 1983–84.[190] By contrast, a court-ordered regulation of airborne radionucleotides occurring about the same time would have saved less than one cancer case per year, yet an environmental justice rights–based approach has difficulty distinguishing between and among such cases, since in each case someone's rights are violated.[191]

In spite of the success of a risk-based approach in the case of lead, we have seen risk assessments suffer from a number of shortcomings that in their current state make them relatively insensitive tools to address issues concerning susceptible subpopulations. These need to be understood and addressed so that risk assessment can serve better to identify the risks to these individuals and communities.

Incorporating Environmental Justice Concerns into Risk Assessment

Some environmental justice concerns can be incorporated into risk assessment. First, there needs to be much better exposure information, including information about baseline risks (to address distributions of environmental risk exposure), demographic information, and environmental impacts on minority and low-income communities.[192] Second, risk assessors should reduce reliance on generalized exposure and susceptibility estimates, and attend much more to differences in the distributions of risk in communities and across communities.[193] This would include, for example, "systematic, ongoing collection of exposure-related, health-related and susceptibility-related information in economically disadvantaged populations . . ."[194] and the study of susceptible groups, including children.[195] Third, underlying these recommendations is a need for greater research into differences in susceptibility from intrinsic and acquired susceptibility factors, into exposure data, and into the effects of mixtures and multiple exposures on individuals (all difficult topics).

While it is important to gather and use such information, there is a danger in such an agenda. There may be a temptation on the part of agencies and certainly on the part of those who are subject to regulation to treat lack of information in these areas as indicating no basis of concern. But without data susceptible subpopulations may be unprotected. And, there is little incentive for some of the parties to the disputes to do the studies. Another temptation is that a more extensive research agenda will make regulation even slower than it is at present.[196] Such temptations need to be dealt with on policy grounds. For example, if preliminary information indicates, as some of the research suggests, that individual variability in susceptibility is much greater than the normal assumption of a ten-fold variation, then risk assessors should incorporate default assumptions into their risk assessments to provide for what is *presumed* to be a greater variation in susceptibility than has been allowed for to date.[197]

Short of the detailed research needed, agencies can address some of these problems by considering various options similar to the shifting of burdens of proof: for example, by "a reasonable worst case as an incentive for the private sector to fill important data gaps,"[198] by "imposing the burden of demonstrating safety on the private sector,"[199] or by "reversing some of the usual burdens of proof that exist in science and in post-market regulatory statutes [requiring risk assessments and scientific information]."[200] Two related reasons support these strategies. For one thing, too much scientific analysis can produce regulatory paralysis, and there may be little information gained as a result of the additional analysis. The data are important, if they can be readily provided. However, if they cannot, then policy reasons to adopt default assumptions until the data are provided or policy reasons to reverse the burdens of proof on particular issues will help ensure the population is protected and that risk assessments are done in a more timely manner.[201] More significantly, expediting risk assessments is important, because if susceptible persons or impacted communities are currently subjected to unacceptable risks, the risks continue until the assessments are complete and the risks are reduced through regulation.[202]

Finally, agencies should also address and remedy some of the procedural shortcomings of risk assessment, the process of decision making, which at present tends to exclude impacted communities, their values and input, and their conception of the problem. Agencies and others doing the required risk assessments need to tend much more to procedural equity between parties and Executive Order 12,898 specifics.[203]

The above recommendations will improve risk assessment compared with current practices for addressing environmental justice problems, but they do not remove all the tensions or solve all the problems.

Judicial Review of Risk Assessment

With risk assessment the focus of much criticism of regulation, it is not surprising that there has been considerable judicial attention on risk assessments as part of judicial review of regulations. I review below some leading judicial decisions in which the main focus of review is the agency's risk assessment.

OSHA Risk Assessments

OSHA risk assessments are considered first, since it is arguable that the Fifth Circuit's and Supreme Court's review of OSHA's benzene regulation has been particularly influential in setting the tone of, if not formally, the precedents for other reviews of agency regulations and their attendant risk assessments.

In 1978 the Occupational Safety and Health Administration issued a regulation reducing the ambient exposure of benzene in the workplace from 10 ppm to 1 ppm.[204] Industry and unions both appealed aspects of the standard, which appeal was ultimately heard in the Supreme Court (the *Benzene* Case).[205] Reviewing the regulation, the Court held that the agency must show that employees face a "significant health risk of material impairment of health" at existing exposure levels and that it must establish this by a preponderance of the evidence.[206] While the plurality noted that the significant risk requirement was not a "mathematical straitjacket" (but at the same time giving mathematical examples of significant risks) and that OSHA need not have scientific certainty about such a risk before regulating, its interpretation of the substantial evidence standard of review suggested that OSHA should rely on quantified data.[207] However, "OSHA is not required to support its finding . . . with anything approaching scientific certainty."[208] Moreover, the agency was given "leeway where its findings must be made on the frontiers of scientific knowledge."[209] Finally, the court noted as long as agency findings "are supported by a body of reputable scientific thought, the Agency is free to use conservative assumptions in interpreting the data with respect to carcinogens, and risk error on the side of overprotection rather than underprotection."[210]

Following up the *Benzene* Case in *ASARCO, Inc. v. OSHA*,[211] the Ninth Circuit Court of Appeals reviewed maximum permissible exposure levels of airborne arsenic against industry challenge. The court upheld OSHA's inferences from the risk data, deferring to the agency on feasibility findings and on its choice of risk assessment models. In particular, even though there is contradictory evidence in the record, "the possibility of drawing two inconsistent conclusions from the evidence does not prevent an administrative agency's finding from being supported by substantial evidence."[212] And, the court held that "we 'give OSHA some leeway where its finding must be made on the frontiers of scientific knowledge.' "[213] Where petitioners challenge OSHA's methodology, this would "require [the court] to evaluate conflicting inferences drawn from comparable or identical evidence. In such a case we must defer to OSHA."[214] And the court upheld OSHA's choice of extrapolation models, finding that they were supported by the "best available evidence," and not adopted by administrative fiat.[215]

In *Public Citizen Health Research Group v. Tyson*,[216] the D.C. Circuit reviewed OSHA's ethylene oxide (EtO) regulation, which was issued in the face of inconclusive epidemiological evidence but with evidence that EtO causes cancer in laboratory animals.[217] Industry petitioners challenged many aspects of OSHA's risk assessment. The court upheld OSHA's risk assessment of ethylene oxide and its specific regulatory level.[218] Importantly, the court held that "when the evidence can be reasonably interpreted as supporting the need for regulation, we must affirm the agency's conclusion, despite the fact that the same evidence is susceptible of another interpretation."[219] Moreover, the "agency must be given leeway when regulatory subject matter is not subject to strict proof one way or the other . . . [for otherwise] strict proof would fatally cripple all of OSHA's regulatory efforts and run counter to the legislative branch's express delegation of hybrid rulemaking power to OSHA."[220]

The significance of this for risk assessments attempting to address environmental justice issues is that, while evidence may be conflicting about whether subpopulations are more susceptible or some are more exposed, it appears that if the agency can draw reasonable conclusions about effects on susceptible subpopulations, it would be upheld, even if reasonable persons might "draw the opposite conclusions"[221] or find that the "same evidence is susceptible of another interpretation."[222] By contrast, if an agency drew the opposite conclusion in the face of conflicting evidence that subpopulations were *not* more susceptible or *not* more highly exposed, it would be upheld on that inference from the risk data as well.

The District of Columbia Court of Appeals in *Building and Constr. Trades Dept., AFL-CIO v. Brock*,[223] reviewing OSHA's revised standards governing workers' exposure to asbestos, upheld regulations against industry challenge on two of three major issues—on technical and policy decisions concerning exposure duration and on OSHA's technical risk assessment assumptions including use of the linearized high-dose to low-dose extrapolation model and use of "conservative assumptions in interpreting the data with respect to carcinogens, risking error on the side of overprotections."[224] The court could not find substantial evidence in the record for several other of the agency's conclusions.[225]

That court recognizes the authority of the OSH Act to protect employees from workplace exposures resulting in part from employees' acquired susceptibility factors, such as smoking. The court, deciding against industry challenge that employers are required by the regulation to "bear part of the burden imposed by employees' decisions to smoke," notes that "we do not think that at this stage of American history smokers can be regarded as so far beyond the pale as to *require* OSHA to disregard them in computing the risks of asbestos."[226] Thus, according to this court even acquired susceptibilities are entitled to protection under the OSH Act's requirement that "*no employee* suffer material impairment of health or function capacity" (emphasis added).

In 1989 OSHA issued an Air Contaminants Standard, which was a set of permissible exposure limits for 428 toxic substances.[227] The Eleventh Circuit Court of Appeals in *AFL-CIO v. OSHA*[228] struck down the Air Contaminants regulation because risk assessments had not been properly done on all the substances. OSHA "failed to establish that existing exposure levels in the workplace present a significant risk of material health impairment or that the new standards eliminate or substantially lessen the risk."[229] While not opposing such a "generic" rulemaking,[230] the court did hold that "the PEL for each substance must be able to stand independently, i.e., that each permanent exposure level (PEL) must be supported by substantial evidence in the record considered as a whole and accompanied by adequate explanation."[231] While it found that OSHA did justify that there was "material impairment of health or functional capacity,"[232] the court also found that the agency "has a responsibility to quantify or explain, at least to some reasonable degree, the risk posed by *each* toxic substance regulated.[233] Thus, even though its "deference to the agency is at a peak for its choices among scientific predictions, we must still look for *some* articulation of reasons for those choices."[234] In particular, "mere conclusory statements . . . are simply inadequate to support a finding of significant risk of material health impairment."[235] OSHA has a duty to explain the method by which risks are determined[236] and may use assumptions in utilizing safety factors but only to the extent that they have some basis in "reputable scientific evidence."[237]

The Consumer Product Safety Commission

While the Consumer Product Safety Commission (CPSC) has not been a major player in regulating toxic substances (it has limited resources and, since the *Gulf South* decision, discussed below, has labored under a heavy statutory burden), one review of risk assessment did come from the Fifth Circuit; this circuit's views may pose substantial barriers to agencies' carrying out their regulatory mandates. On the other side of the issue, the court's assessment of the regulations discussed in *Gulf South* may be sufficiently anomalous that it represents less of a barrier than it might seem initially.

On another risk assessment issue, in 1982 the CPSC issued a regulation to reduce exposure to formaldehyde in residences and schools.[238] The Commission found that urea-formaldehyde Foam Insulation (UFFI) "presents an unreasonable risk of injury from irritation and cancer. . . ."[239] Subjecting this regulation to review under the "substantial evidence test" and under a statute that requires the agency to find that the toxic substance poses an "unreasonable risk" of harm, the Fifth Circuit held, inter alia, that the risk assessments the Commission performed did not justify by substantial evidence in the record that "UFFI poses an unreasonable risk of cancer. . . ."[240] There were several specific shortcomings. The exposure data did not result from a controlled random study, and thus did not adequately represent an "average" home.[241] The sample for the epidemiological studies was too small to identify the risk in question and the studies were inconclusive (a point that the Commission readily recognized).[242] The Commission relied upon only one animal study for setting its standard, and that study was so small that it had a large margin of error. The court's comments on this point, however, were much more controversial.[243] Finally, contrary to most other courts, the Fifth Circuit, in what it called the Commission's most controversial assumption, objected to the use of a linear no-threshold extrapolation model.[244]

As we have seen above, most courts have not tended to micromanage choices of scientific models or science policy choices as does the Fifth Circuit in objecting to the use of a linearized multistage no-threshold model. Clearly, other courts reviewing OSHA regulations under the substantial evidence standard of review have been deferential to the agency's choices in estimating risks to employees, as long as its choices were reasonable based upon substantial evidence in the record.[245]

The Environmental Protection Agency

In 1989 the EPA issued a final rule under Section 6 of the Toxic Substances Control Act (TSCA) "to prohibit the future manufacture, importation, processing and distribution of asbestos in almost all products."[246] This rule, subject to the substantial evidence test standard of review, was reviewed by the Fifth Circuit Court of Appeals and invalidated and remanded to the agency for further consideration.[247]

The court noted that the agency, in utilizing "analogous exposure" data after the close of hearings to calculate the expected benefits of certain product bans, "deprived the petitioners of the notice that they required in order to present their own evidence . . ." on various issues.[248] Moreover, the court held that EPA "presented insufficient evidence to justify its asbestos ban . . . on two grounds: the failure of the EPA to consider all necessary evidence and its failure to give adequate weight to statutory language requiring it to promulgate *the least burdensome,* reasonable regulation required to protect the environment adequately."[249] TSCA requires the agency to consider a variety of regulatory remedies and to choose the "least burdensome" alternative. EPA rejected various intermediate alternatives and failed to calculate the risk levels "for intermediate levels of regulation."[250] The court was also concerned about some of the methodology utilized by the agency in making various risk calculations concerning the costs and benefits of some of the options it did consider, and whether it had a "reasonable basis" for its regulations.[251] Finally, as a general consideration, the court ruled that any TSCA rulemaking must be designed to prevent "unreasonable" risks,[252] which it held involves a balancing test familiar from tort law.[253] Thus, the agency not only must balance the severity of injuries prevented against the costs of preventing them (there must be a reasonable relationship between the two),[254] but the agency must also engage in a *comparative risk analysis* of injuries prevented by the ban compared with injuries resulting from substitute products.[255] The agency is not required to seek out and test "all possible substitutes, . . . [but] when an interested party comes forward with credible evidence that the planned substitutes present a significant, or even greater toxic risk than the substance in question, the agency must make a formal finding on the record that its proposed action still is both reasonable and warranted under TSCA."[256]

Two features of this opinion are of interest. First, the court was constrained by clear language of TSCA, which requires that the agency consider the "least burdensome" regulation. Second, the court appears to mandate a qualified comparative risk judgment, such that the agency must not only consider the risks and costs of reducing them under the regulation in question, but also the risks the regulation might pose from substitute products (for instance, greater deaths from brakes not made from asbestos), provided that this is raised by an interested party. A comparative risk analysis test could be quite far-reaching, and even speculative, both greatly complicating agency regulatory activities under Section 6 of TSCA and greatly slowing the pace of regulation.

In 1992 the EPA issued a report on the health effects of passive smoking and lung cancer and other disorders[257] under the authority of the Radon Gas and Indoor Air Quality Research Act of 1986.[258] The district court for the middle district of North Carolina reviewed this report in *Flue-Cured Tobacco Co-Op. Stabil. v. U.S. EPA.*[259] That court held, inter alia,

1. that the risk assessment EPA performed on passive smoking was not prohibited by the Radon Gas and Indoor Air Quality Research Act or by TSCA, but
2. that EPA's Science Advisory Board and its subcommittee was not the appropriate representative advisory group required by the Act, which defect required vacating EPA's risk assessment.

Moreover, the court discussed at length some of the shortcomings of the risk assessment.[260] The court found problems with the bioplausibility of the claim that environmental tobacco smoke (ETS) was a class A carcinogen (instead of being classified in some other category), holding that had the agency been "confronted by a representative committee that voiced industry concerns, EPA would likely have had to resolve these issues in the record . . . [which] it is not clear [it] could have."[261] It was also concerned about EPA's selection of epidemiological studies that helped form the basis of its risk assessment—some were excluded from a meta-analysis, some were included, but the court was not persuaded by EPA's explanation and noted that had it utilized the kind of advisory committee contemplated by the Act, it would have had a better record on these issues.[262] Additional concerns were that EPA changed its typical level confidence interval from .95 to .90, without persuasive reason to the court; that it based its conclusion that ETS was a class A carcinogen on a relatively "weak" relative risk of 1.19 (in contrast to findings in other cases);[263] that EPA did not appropriately make its reasons known for its decisions and findings;[264] and that had EPA not analyzed the epidemiology in the problematic ways the court found, it might not have concluded that ETS was a class A carcinogen.[265]

Other Judicial/Legal Actions on Risk Assessment

In *NAACP v. Engler*,[266] a Michigan Circuit Court held that the policies of the Michigan Department of Environmental Quality (MDEQ) did "not protect the health, safety and welfare of all the citizens in Michigan . . ." in issuing a permit for a 35-megawatt wood-waste fired steel mill. It also found that Michigan violated the Michigan Clean Air Act by not performing a risk assessment to determine the effects of pollutants added to the air and surrounding area.[267] Finally, the court found that the MDEQ failed to provide a "meaningful avenue for cities and other governmental units to have a meaningful and knowledgeable opportunity to express it's [sic] concerns and those of it's [sic] residents considered in the siting process involving plants that are located in another jurisdiction, but which pollute adjoining governmental units."[268] It issued an injunction against MDEQ "preventing it from granting permits to major pollution sources . . . until a Risk Assessment is performed and those interested parties and governmental units that will be impacted based upon the Risk Assessment Study are notified and given a opportunity to be heard before the [MDEQ]."[269] Both plaintiffs and defendants appealed. The Michigan Court of Appeals held, inter alia, "that the trial court had no authority to issue the injunction *sua sponte*."[270] Since the plaintiffs did not request, plead, or argue for an injunction that the permitting process violated the state constitution and the Natural Resources and Environmental Protection Act, this violated principles of due process "because the defending party has been given no notice of the need to defend against the claim."[271] Because the Court of Appeals vacated the injunction, the underlying issues concerning the adequacy of the risk assessment were not addressed.[272]

In May 1997 the Atomic Safety and Licensing Board, basing its decision on environmental justice, Executive Order 12,898, and the

National Environmental Policy Act, denied Louisiana Energy Services a Nuclear Regulatory Commission construction permit and operating license to enrich uranium at a proposed plant near Homer, Louisiana.[273] The agency found that the Nuclear Regulatory Commission (NRC) staff, while appropriately assessing physical impacts, had not found inadequate staff treatment of road relocation and economic impacts on impoverished local communities.[274] The full NRC reviewed this decision, agreeing in part and disagreeing in part. It did not find that "racial considerations" affected siting,[275] but did find that the siting of the plants had "disparate impacts" on the low-income minority communities, and remanded the report for further proceedings on these issues.[276]

Generic Lessons

Some generic lessons can be drawn about judicial review of risk assessments from the above discussion of agency regulations. First, courts are constrained by the statute in question (for example, TSCA Section 6), or by leading judicial decisions (the *Benzene* case with its "significant risk" requirement).

Second, most judicial reviews of regulations considered above have been subject to the more stringent substantial evidence test of court review because of the statutes in question. These are more likely to be challenged because petitioners have a greater chance of success than when challenging regulations reviewed under the "arbitrary and capricious" standard of review. Nonetheless, even subjecting agency regulations to the substantial evidence standard of review, most of the courts have granted the agencies considerable deference for their scientific procedures as long as there has been sufficient evidence in the record and sufficient explanation for the action, even though different inferences might have been drawn from the same data and theories and even though courts themselves sometimes suggest that they might have drawn different conclusions. The deference shown such agency actions is not as great, of course, as that shown agencies under the arbitrary and capricious test.

Third, courts tend not to micromanage choice of risk assessment models and inferences vis-a-vis risks, as long as there are scientific or policy bases for the choices and they are explained. The notable exception to this is the decision of the Fifth Circuit Court of Appeals in *Gulf South Insulation v. CPSC,* which judicially ruled against a linearized, no-threshold model for extrapolating from high-dose health effects to low-dose health effects. That court appears virtually alone in its micromanaging of risk assessment. However, for agencies to receive court deference under the substantial evidence review, they must have in the record "sufficient" evidence to support their inferences, rulings, choices, and ultimate regulations, and they must appropriately explain what they were doing in making decisions (a shortcoming of OSHA's air toxics generic ruling). In particular, at least under the OSH Act, OSHA must consider the risks from each substance and address them on their own merits.

Finally, even for risk assessments under the OSH Act, it is not clear how much quantification of risk is necessary in light of judicial review of the air toxics standard. As long as the agency has addressed each substance posing a risk and has some "appropriate" explanation for its judgment that a risk is "significant" and should be reduced, this might be enough.

What does judicial review of risk assessments suggest for risk assessments that incorporate environmental justice concerns? It appears that agencies may permissibly incorporate considerations of the effects of pollution on susceptible subpopulations and impacted communities. That they can do this seems clear from the deference courts grant agencies to review the scientific evidence and draw inferences from it as long as they have appropriate "sufficient" evidence for their inferences. Thus, it seems clear that agencies can take some initiative to protect these subpopulations, provided they have appropriate data and policies to support their regulations (even for regulations subject to the substantial evidence standard of review). Agency regulations that aim to protect susceptible subpopulations and that are subject to the arbitrary and capricious standard of review are even more likely to withstand judicial scrutiny. Of course, courts can also defer to agencies ignoring susceptible populations except where some legal authority requires them to be addressed (for example, the Food Quality Protection Act).

While agencies can consider evidence of the effects of pollutants on susceptible subpopulations in their risk assessments, the agencies may face greater difficulties in fully protecting vulnerable subpopulations, at least under statutes that have "feasibility" requirements or that require the "least burdensome regulations," because both of these are likely to attenuate the achievement of health protective goals that may seem required as a result of the risk assessment.

Under what circumstances might agencies or private parties be required to consider the effects of pollutants on susceptible subpopulations? Clearly, EPA is required to consider the effects of regulating pesticide residues in processed foods on infants and children under the provisions of the Food Quality Protection Act. It is also arguable, under a few statutes that require that agencies act on the "best available scientific evidence," that an agency might be remiss in failing to consider scientific evidence showing that susceptible subpopulations were at greater risk. At present, this remains an open question.

Notes

1. NATIONAL RESEARCH COUNCIL, RISK ASSESSMENT IN THE FEDERAL GOVERNMENT: MANAGING THE PROCESS 3 (1983) [hereinafter NATIONAL RESEARCH COUNCIL, RISK ASSESSMENT IN THE FEDERAL GOVERNMENT].

2. *See* U.S. CONGRESS, OFFICE OF TECHNOLOGY ASSESSMENT, IDENTIFYING AND REGULATING CARCINOGENS (1987) [hereinafter OTA, IDENTIFYING AND REGULATING CARCINOGENS] for a general discussion of risk assessment in the federal agencies concerning carcinogens and its use in regulation.

3. H.R. 9, 104th Cong., 1st Sess. Sec 80 (1995); H.R. 1022, 104th Cong., 1st Sess. (1995). See also Linda-Jo Schierow, CONGRESSIONAL RESEARCH SERV., RISK AND COST-BENEFIT: COMPARISON OF PROVISIONS IN THE 104TH CONGRESS (1995).

4. NATIONAL RESEARCH COUNCIL, PESTICIDES IN THE DIETS OF INFANTS AND CHILDREN (1993); COMMITTEE ON RISK ASSESSMENT OF HAZARDOUS AIR POLLUTANTS, NATIONAL RESEARCH COUNCIL, SCIENCE AND JUDGMENT IN RISK ASSESSMENT (1994) [hereinafter NATIONAL RESEARCH COUNCIL, SCIENCE AND JUDGMENT IN RISK ASSESSMENT].

5. Robert D. Bullard, *The Threat of Environmental Racism,* 7 NATL. RESOURCES & ENV'T 24 (1993) [hereinafter Bullard, *The Threat of Environmental Racism*).

6. Exec. Order No. 12,898, 3 C.F.R. § 859 (1995), *reprinted in* 42 U.S.C.A. § 4321 (West 1994) ("Federal Actions to Address Environmental Justice in Minority Populations and Low-Income Populations").

7. OFFICE OF SOLID WASTE & EMERGENCY RESPONSE ENVTL. JUSTICE TASK FORCE, U.S. ENVTL. PROTECTION AGENCY, DRAFT FINAL REPORT (1994); NATIONAL INST. OF ENVTL HEALTH SCIENCE, SYMPOSIUM ON HEALTH RESEARCH AND NEEDS TO ENSURE ENVIRONMENTAL JUSTICE; EXECUTIVE SUMMARY OF RECOMMENDATIONS (1994); OFFICE OF ENVTL. JUSTICE, U.S. ENVTL. PROTECTION AGENCY, ENVIRONMENTAL JUSTICE STRATEGY; U.S. DEP'T OF ENERGY, U.S. DEP'T OF ENERGY ENVTL. JUSTICE STRATEGY, EXECUTIVE ORDER 12,898 (1995).

8. Bullard, *The Threat of Environmental Racism, supra* note 5.

9. John M. Sagnelli, *Draft Guide Proposed on Sustainable Brownfields,* NATIONAL LAW JOURNAL B8 (Mar. 16, 1998).

10. NATIONAL RESEARCH COUNCIL, RISK ASSESSMENT IN THE FEDERAL GOVERNMENT, *supra* note 1, at 5 (Dissatisfaction with the actions of federal regulatory agencies is often expressed as criticism of the conduct and administration of the risk assessment process. *Id.* at 5). Other concerns have been statutory interpretations and procedural issues. See also *infra* text and notes at 207–274.

11. *Id.* at 6.

12. NATIONAL RESEARCH COUNCIL, SCIENCE AND JUDGMENT IN RISK ASSESSMENT, *supra* note 5, at 1–3.

13. OTA, IDENTIFYING AND REGULATING CARCINOGENS, *supra* note 2, at 23–75.

14. The tort law principle is well-expressed by Prosser.

> It is as if a magic circle were drawn about the person, and one who breaks it, even by so much as a cut on the finger, becomes liable for all resulting harm to the person although it may be death. The defendant is held liable when the defendant's negligence operates upon a concealed physical condition, such as pregnancy, or a latent disease, or susceptibility to disease [psychotic tendencies, neurotic predisposition, predisposition to amnesia, ruptured disc, delirium tremens], to produce consequences

> which the defendant could not reasonably anticipate. The defendant is held liable for unusual results of personal injuries which are regarded as unforeseeable, such as tuberculosis, paralysis, pneumonia, heart or kidney disease, blood poisoning, cancer or the loss of hair from fright. . . . One of the illustrations which runs through the English cases is that of the plaintiff with the 'eggshell skull,' who suffers death where a normal person would have had only a bump on the head. . . ."

W. PAGE KEETON ET AL., PROSSER AND KEETON ON TORTS 291–92 (1984). The defendant is, however, liable "only for the extent to which the defendant's conduct has resulted in an aggravation of the pre-existing condition, and not for the condition as it was. . . ." (*Id.* at 291–92).

15. *Ominsky v. Chas. Weinhagen & Co.*, 113 Minn. 422, 129 N.W. 845–846 (1911).

16. Elsewhere I have suggested that the following principle is appropriate for the preventive goals of the regulatory law: "[I]f the healthy are entitled to preventive measures to protect them from invasion of their interests, others who might be much less healthy and more vulnerable are entitled to the same protections." Carl F. Cranor, *Eggshell Skulls and Loss of Hair from Fright: Some Moral and Legal Principles that Protect Susceptible Subpopulations*, 4 ENV'TL TOXICOL. & PHARMACOL. 239–45 (1998) [hereinafter Cranor, *Eggshell Skulls*]. The argument for this may be stronger than one by analogy. Regulatory laws may be seen as complementing the tort law and as seeking to prevent injuries from occurring which would be incompensable in torts: for instance, death. Thus, if the tort law seeks to protect even especially susceptible persons from harm from toxic substances, since ex post compensation will not achieve this aim, various regulatory laws should address it. (I owe this point to Gregory Keating and Ed McCaffery of the University of Southern California School of Law.)

17. As I argued elsewhere, "[S]uppose we did *not* seek to protect everyone from harm, and did *not* protect from harm those who, through no fault of their own, were much more susceptible to disease caused by the actions of others than the rest of the population. Do we want to suggest that the most susceptible people in the community do not have sufficient moral standing to warrant protection, or that their standing to be protected is not equal to the healthy among us? Such implications seem unacceptable. Those with particular susceptibilities not only would not have protections provided to the healthy; through no fault of their own they would lack the full range of opportunities open to others with similar abilities and motivations.

"Thus, my conclusion is that both the particularly susceptible and the healthy have equal moral standing to be protected from the actions of the rest of us in the community and that some provision has to be made for the most vulnerable members of the moral community." (*Id.* at 245.)

18. Exec. Order No. 12,898, 3 C.F.R. 859 (1995). See Chapter 4 *supra*.

19. Bullard, *The Threat of Environmental Racism*, *supra* note 5.

20. *See* Robert D. Bullard, *Unequal Environmental Protection: Incorporating Environmental Justice in Decision Making*, *in* WORST THINGS FIRST? (Adam M. Finkel & Dominic Golding eds., 1994) 237 [hereinafter Bullard, *Unequal Environmental Protection*] (arguing that, while communities of people of color and low-income communities have received less environmental protection and bear

greater health and environmental burdens, the principle that justifies protection for the people of these communities is *"the right of all individuals to be protected from environmental degradation"* (at 243, emphasis in original).

21. Ken Sexton, *Sociodemographic Aspects of Human Susceptibility to Toxic Chemicals: Do Class and Race Matter for Realistic Risk Assessment?* 4 ENV'TL TOXICOL. & PHARMACOL. 261, at 265 (1997) [hereinafter Sexton, *Do Class and Race Matter?*].

22. *Id.*

23. *Id.*

24. *Id.*

25. *Id.*

26. *Id.*

27. *Id.* at 266.

28. *Id.*

29. *Id.*

30. *Id.*

31. *Id.* (citing Sexton et al., *Environmental Justice: The Central Role of Research in Establishing a Credible Scientific Foundation for Informed Decision Making,* 9 TOXICOL. IND. HEALTH 685–727 (1993); K. Sexton et al., *Air Pollution Health Risks: Do Class and Race Matter?* 9 TOXICOL. IND. HEALTH 843–78 (1993); and J. A. Grassman, *Obtaining Information About Susceptibility from the Epidemiological Literature,* 111 TOXICOL. 253–70 (1996)).

32. Robert R. Kuehn, *The Environmental Justice Implications of Quantitative Risk Assessment,* 1996 U. ILL. L. REV. 124 (1996) [hereinafter Kuehn, *Environmental Justice*] (citing Richard Rios et al., *Susceptibility to Environmental Pollutants Among Minorities,* 9 TOXICOL. IND. HEALTH 797, 798–803 (1993)) and Brian D. Israel, *An Environmental Justice Critique of Risk Assessment,* 3 N.Y.U. ENVT'L L. J. 469, 508 (1994).

33. Bullard, *Unequal Environmental Protection, supra* note 20 (citing a host of studies addressing these points and arguing that:

> Low-income communities and communities of color continue to bear greater health and environmental burdens, while the more affluent and white communities receive the bulk of the benefits . . .
>
> Both race and class have been found to be related to the distribution of air pollution . . . location of municipal landfills and incinerators . . . , lead poisoning in children . . . , and contaminated fish consumption . . . (at 239–40)).

Presidential Executive Order 12,898 specifically identifies "disproportionately high and adverse human health or environmental effects of its programs, policies and activities on minority populations and low-income populations. . . ." (Exec. Order No. 12,898, 3 C.F.R. 859 (1995)). Very recent evidence appears to confirm these concerns. (National Research Council, Toward Environmental Justice: Research, Education, and Health Policy (1999).)

34. "Multiple exposures occur when a person is exposed to a combination of two or more different chemicals or pollutants, while cumulative exposures result when an individual is exposed to one or more chemicals or pollutants from different media or over time." Kuehn, *Environmental Justice, supra* note 32, at 117 (citing INTERAGENCY ENVT'L JUSTICE COMM., SUMMARY REPORT TO THE SUBCOMM. ON MULTIPLE AND CUMULATIVE EXPOSURES (Draft) 2 (Nov. 8, 1994)).

35. Bullard, *Unequal Environmental Protection, supra* note 20 at 240–41. Should such differential and negative impacts have clear adverse effects, policies that have led to them might be appropriate targets for compensatory justice claims.

36. These include, inter alia, the Consumer Product Safety Act (standards "shall be reasonably necessary to prevent or reduce an unreasonable risk of injury associated with such product" (15 U.S.C. § 2056(b) (1995)); the Toxic Substances Control Act (the statute aims "to regulate chemical substances and mixtures which present an unreasonable risk of injury to health or the environment," but not so as to create "unnecessary economic barriers to technological innovation" (15 U.S.C. § 2601(b)(2) and (b)(3) (1995)); the Federal Insecticide, Fungicide and Rodenticide Act (pesticides must perform their intended functions without "any unreasonable risk to man or the environment, taking into account the economic, social and environmental costs and benefits of the use of any pesticide" (7 U.S.C. § 136(bb) (1995)); and the Federal Hazardous Substances Act (an article presents a hazard if it "presents an unreasonable risk of personal injury or illness" (15 U.S.C. § 1261(s)(1995)).

37. The amount of care placed on an actor required to avoid a risk is "the resultant of three factors: the likelihood that his conduct will injure others, taken with the seriousness of the injury if it happens and balanced against the interest which he must sacrifice to avoid that risk" (Conway v. O'Brien, 111 F.2d 611 (2d Cir. 1940)).

38. Corrosion Proof Fittings v. EPA, 947 F.2d 1201, 1222 (5th Cir. 1991), quoting Forester v. CPSC, 559 F.2d 774, 789 (D.C. Cir. 1977) (interpreting the Federal Hazardous Substances Act).

39. 33 U.S.C. § 1251(a) (1995).

40. 33 U.S.C. § 1317(a)(2) (1995).

41. 33 U.S.C. § 1251(a)(2) (1995).

42. 33 U.S.C. § 1317(1)(4) (1995).

43. OTA, IDENTIFYING AND REGULATING CARCINOGENS, *supra* note 2, at 109 (citing K. Hall, Jr., *The Evolution and Implementation of EPA's Regulatory Program to Control the Discharge of Toxic Pollutants to the Nation's Waters,* 10 NAT. RESOURCES LAW. 507 (1977)).

44. NRDC v. Train, 8 Env't. Rep. Cas. (BNA) 2120 (D.D.C. Cir. 1976), *as modified sub. nom.,* NRDC v. Costle, 12 Env't. Rep. Cas. (BNA) 1833 (D.D.C. 1979).

45. 33 U.S.C. § 1311(b)(1)(A)(1995).

46. *Id.*

47. OTA, IDENTIFYING AND REGULATING CARCINOGENS, *supra* note 2, at 211.

48. J.M. Gaba, *Regulation of Toxic Pollutants Under the Clean Water Act: NPDES Toxic Control Strategies* 50 J. AIR L. & COM. 761, 768–69 (1985).

49. *Id.* at 769–70. Since this section requires that "that the cost of achieving the restrictions is greater than the environmental benefits . . ." it has not been used (*Id.* at 770).

50. These documents "present information on protecting human health and aquatic organisms (fish, shellfish, plants, etc.)." They protect against both non-carcinogenic and carcinogenic substances and are based upon consumption of drinking water and aquatic organisms. The recommended criterion for protecting human health from exposure to carcinogens is zero. "The published criteria

include the concentrations of the chemical in water that corresponded to calculated lifetime cancer risks of 10^{-5}, 10^{-6}, and 10^{-7}" (*Id.* at 111).

51. *Id.* at 212.

52. *Id.* at 212.

53. 42 U.S.C. § 7409(a) and 7409(b) (1995).

54. 42 U.S.C. § 7409(b)(1) (1995).

55. 42 U.S.C. § 7412(a)(2) (1995)

56. 42 U.S.C. § 7412(d)(2) (1995).

57. 42 U.S.C. § 7412(f)(2)(A) (1995) Moreover, even more stringent regulations can be set, taking costs and other considerations into account, if they are needed to prevent an "adverse environmental effect." *Id.*

58. 42 U.S.C. § 7412(f)(2)(A) (1995) (emphasis added).

59. 42 U.S.C. § 7412(o)(2) (1995).

60. NATIONAL RESEARCH COUNCIL, SCIENCE AND JUDGMENT IN RISK ASSESSMENT, *supra* note 4, at 188–243.

61. 42 U.S.C. § 300g-1(4)(A) (1995).

62. 42 U.S.C. § 300g-1(a) (1995).

63. 42 U.S.C. § 300g-1(4)(A) (1995).

64. 42 U.S.C. § 300g-1(3)(A) (1995).

65. 42 U.S.C. § 300g-1(3)(A) (1995).

66. 42 U.S.C. § 6902(a) (1995).

67. 42 U.S.C. § 6924(a) (1995).

68. 40 C.F.R. 261.24, 261.30 (1997).

69. EPA published three lists of waste subject to RCRA regulation: hazardous waste from nonspecific sources (40 C.F.R. § 261.31) (1997); hazardous waste from specific sources (40 C.F.R. § 261.32) (1997); and discarded commercial chemical products, off specification species, and containers and spill residues thereof (40 C.F.R. § 261.33) (1997).

70. OTA, IDENTIFYING AND REGULATING CARCINOGENS, *supra* note 2, at 219.

71. 42 U.S.C. § 6928(a) (1995).

72. 42 U.S.C. § 6928(d) (1995).

73. 42 U.S.C. § 6928(e) (1995).

74. 42 U.S.C. § 9601–75 (1995).

75. THOMAS W. CHURCH & ROBERT T. NAKAMURA, CLEANING UP THE MESS: IMPLEMENTATION STRATEGIES IN SUPERFUND (1993) at 5.

76. 42 U.S.C. § 9604(i)(6)(A) (1995).

77. 42 U.S.C. § 9604(i)(6)(B) (1995).

78. CHURCH & NAKAMURA, *supra* note 75, at 7.

79. 42 U.S.C. § 9621(a) (1995).

80. 40 C.F.R. § 300.430(e)(9)(iii)(A-I).

81. 40 C.F.R. § 300.430(e)(9)(iii)(A).

82. 42 U.S.C. § 9621(d)(2), (d)(4) (1995) and 40 C.F.R. § 300.430(e)(9)(iii)(B).

83. 42 U.S.C. §§ 300f–300j-26(1995).

84. 33 U.S.C. §§ 1251–1387 (1995).

85. 40 C.F.R. § 300.430(a)(a)(iii) (Engineering controls, for instance, containment, or deed restrictions may be used when it is not "practicable" to meet goals of protecting health and the environment); Donald A. Brown, *What Is Wrong with the 1990 National Contingency Plan?* 20 ELR 10,371 (1990) ("[A] close examination of other sections of the recent NCP leads to the conclusion that EPA considers

cost at virtually every step of the remediation selection process." *Id.* at 10,373), and noting that engineering controls (55 Fed. Reg. at 8732) and classification of groundwater (55 Fed. Reg. at 8732) may attenuate achievement of health and environmental protection goals. *Id.* at 10,374–75.

86. "EPA Eyes Application of Children's Safety Factor to Superfund Cleanups," SUPERFUND REPORT 10, July 22, 1998.

87. 29 U.S.C. § 655(b)(5) (emphasis added).

88. Building and Constr. Trades Dept., AFL-CIO v. Brock, 838 F.2d 1258, 1265 (D.C. Cir. 1988).

89. OTA, IDENTIFYING AND REGULATING CARCINOGENS, *supra* note 2, at 35.

90. Industrial Union Dept., AFL-CIO v. American Petroleum Institute, 448 U.S. 607 (1980).

91. *Id.*

92. See "OSHA Risk Assessments," pages 333–336.

93. Until the passage of the Food Quality Protection Act of 1996, it also applied to pesticide residues in processed foods, but this provision has since been eliminated.

94. 21 U.S.C. § 348(c)(3)(a) (Supp. II, 1997).

95. Richard A. Merrill, *Food Safety Regulation: Reforming the Delaney Clause,* 18 ANN. REV. PUBLIC HEALTH 313, 322 (1997). In addition, "Delaney proponents also accepted, of course, the premise that any substance found to induce cancer in animals had the potential to cause cancer in humans, and the law embodied this animal-to-man extrapolation" (*Id.* at 322, n.7).

96. OTA, IDENTIFYING AND REGULATING CARCINOGENS, *supra* note 2, at 203).

97. Merrill, *supra* note 95, at 223–31.

98. 21 U.S.C. § 342(a)(1) (Supp. II, 1997).

99. Richard A. Merrill & Michael Schewel, *FDA Regulation of Environmental Contaminants of Food,* 8 VA. L. REV. 1357, 1372 (1980).

100. OTA, IDENTIFYING AND REGULATING CARCINOGENS, *supra* note 2, at 29–30.

101. 7 U.S.C. § 136 (Supp. II, 1997).

102. 21 U.S.C. § 408(a)(2)(A)(ii) (Supp. II, 1997).

103. 21 U.S.C. § 408(a)(2)(B)(i) (Supp. II, 1997).

104. NATIONAL RESEARCH COUNCIL, PESTICIDES IN THE DIETS OF INFANTS AND CHILDREN (1983) and Merrill, *Food Safety Regulation, supra* note 95, at 332.

105. 21 U.S.C. § 408(a)(2)(B)(i) (Supp. II, 1997).

106. *Id.* (emphasis added).

107. Merrill, *supra* note 95, at 332–33; 21 U.S.C. § 346(b)(2)(C) (Supp. II, 1997).

108. 21 U.S.C. § 346(a)(2)(C) (Supp. II, 1997) (emphasis added).

109. Merrill, *supra* note 95, at 332–33.

110. Exec. Order No. 12,898, 3 C.F.R. § 859 (1995).

111. *Id.* at 861.

112. *Id.*

113. *Id.*

114. *Id.* at 863.

115. *Supra* note 7.

116. However, see the Nuclear Regulatory Commission, Commission Decision—Louisiana Energy Services (Docket No. 70-3070-ML) (located at the NRC web site <http://www.nrc.gov/OPA/reports/lesdocs.htm>) (noting that the

Executive Order "by its own terms creates no new rights or remedies," but rather "underscore[s] certain provision[s] of existing law that can help ensure that all communities and persons across this Nation live in a safe and healthful environment" (emphasis in original)).

117. 60 Fed. Reg. 30,871 (June 12, 1995).

118. For some discussion of this, see Chapter 4 of this volume, "Executive Order 12,898."

119. NAACP v. Engler 45, Case No. 95-38228-CV (Circuit Court for the County of Genesee, May 29, 1997).

120. *Id.*

121. "Children's Health to Be New Focus for EPA, Research, Says Browner," 31 ENVT'L SCI. & TECHNOL./NEWS 174 (1997).

122. *EPA Eyes Application of Children's Safety Factor to Superfund Cleanups,* SUPERFUND REPORT 10 (July 22, 1998).

123. Kuehn, *Environmental Justice, supra* note 32, at 105 (1996).

124. NATIONAL RESEARCH COUNCIL, SCIENCE AND JUDGMENT IN RISK ASSESSMENT, *supra* note 4, at 26.

125. *Id.* For some issues concerning comparative risk assessments, see WORST THINGS FIRST?, *supra* note 20.

126. NATIONAL RESEARCH COUNCIL, SCIENCE AND JUDGMENT IN RISK ASSESSMENT, *supra* note 4, at 26.

127. *Id.*

128. *Id.* and NATIONAL RESEARCH COUNCIL, RISK ASSESSMENT IN THE FEDERAL GOVERNMENT, *supra* note 1, at 20–23.

129. CARL F. CRANOR, REGULATING TOXIC SUBSTANCES: A PHILOSOPHY OF SCIENCE AND THE LAW 14–15 (1993) [hereinafter CRANOR, REGULATING TOXIC SUBSTANCES].

130. *Id.*

131. OTA, IDENTIFYING AND REGULATING CARCINOGENS, *supra* note 2, at 45. For a classic discussion of many of these factors, see Austin Bradford Hill, *The Environment and Disease: Association or Causation?*, 58 PROCEEDINGS OF THE ROYAL SOCIETY OF MEDICINE 295, 299 (1965), *reprinted in* EVOLUTION OF EPIDEMIOLOGIC IDEAS: ANNOTATED READINGS ON CONCEPTS AND METHODS 15, 19 (Sander Greenland ed., 1987).

132. The concern with statistical significance is that studies must have less than a certain low probability, typically below .05, that a statistical association between exposure to a toxic substance and a disease is not the result of random chance. If a study fails to satisfy the designated level of statistical significance, this tends to undermine its acceptability in the scientific community (although there is some movement away from strict adherence to such rules).

133. Tort law courts frequently insist on a relative risk of at least two (in order, it is claimed, to satisfy tort law burdens of proof), but if a study is large enough and enough people are affected by an exposure, lower relative risks may be of concern. On the first point, see, for example, Daubert v. Merrell Dow Pharm., Inc., 43 F.3d 1311, 1320–21 (9th Cir. 1995), *on remand from* 509 U.S. 579 (1993). On the second point, see Carl F. Cranor et al., "Judicial Boundary Drawing and the Need for Context-Sensitive Science in Toxic Torts After *Daubert v. Merrell Dow Pharmaceuticals, Inc.*," 16 VA. ENV'TL L. J. 2 (1996).

134. *Compare* H. J. Eysenck, *Were We Really Wrong?*, 133 AM. J. EPIDEMIOLOGY 429, 432 (1991) *with* Sander Greenland, *Invited Commentary: Science Versus Public Health Action: Those Who Were Wrong Are Still Wrong*, 133 AM. J. EPIDEMIOLOGY 435 (1991).

135. Manolis Kogevinas & Paolo Boffetta, 48 BRIT. J. INDUS. MED. 575–76 (1991) (letter to editor criticizing a study by O. Wong, *A Cohort Mortality Study and a Case Control Study of Workers Potentially Exposed to Styrene in Reinforced Plastics and Composite Industry*, 47 BRIT. J. INDUS. MED. 753–62 (1990), for having too short a follow-up—seven years—even though the author had a large sample population to study).

136. CRANOR, REGULATING TOXIC SUBSTANCES, *supra* note 129, at 34–38.

137. Statistical power is a probability measure of being able to detect an adverse health effect when in fact it exists. KENNETH J. ROTHMAN, MODERN EPIDEMIOLOGY 79 (1986).

138. CRANOR, REGULATING TOXIC SUBSTANCES, *supra* note 129, at 34–38.

139. L. Tomatis, *Environmental Cancer Risk Factors: A Review*, 27 ACTA ONCOLOGICA 465–72 (1988).

140. Occasionally a substance leaves a trace behind (for instance, asbestos fibers) or is so rare it can more easily be detected (for instance, as was the case with the carcinogen diethylstilbestrol). On the latter, see Sindell v. Abbott Laboratories et al., 26 Cal. 3d 588, 607 P.2d 924 (1980).

141. For example, in 1988 researchers comparing epidemiological with animal bioassay estimates of cancer potency considered epidemiological results for only 23 chemicals. B.C. Allen, K.S. Crump, & A.M. Shipp, *Correlations Between Carcinogenic Potency of Chemicals in Animals and Humans*, RISK ANALYSIS 531–44 (1988).

142. David P. Rall, Testimony in United States Dept. of Labor, OSHA 45 *Fed. Reg. Identification, Classification, and Regulation of Potential Occupational Carcinogens* 5002, 5190 (1980) [hereinafter U.S. Dept. of Labor, OSHA].

143. David P. Rall, *The Role of Laboratory Animal Studies in Estimating Carcinogenic Risks for Man*, CARCINOGENIC RISKS: STRATEGIES FOR INTERVENTION 179 (International Agency for Research on Cancer, Lyon, France, 1979) and David P. Rall et al., *Alternatives to Using Human Experience in Assessing Health Risks*, 8 ANN. REV. PUBLIC HEALTH 355, 356 (1987).

144. Ping Kwong Chan & A. Wallace Hayes, *Principles and Methods for Acute Toxicity and Eye Irritancy*, *in* PRINCIPLES AND METHODS OF TOXICOLOGY 169, 206–12 (A. Wallace Hayes ed., 1989); A.T. Mosberg & A. Wallace Hayes, *Subchronic Toxicity Testing*, *in* PRINCIPLES AND METHODS OF TOXICOLOGY, *supra* at 221, 226–31; *see also* JOHN J. COHRSSEN & VINCENT T. COVELLO, UNITED STATES COUNCIL ON ENVIRONMENTAL QUALITY, RISK ANALYSIS: A GUIDE TO PRINCIPLES AND METHODS FOR ANALYZING HEALTH AND ENVIRONMENTAL RISKS 38 (1989) [hereinafter COHRRSEN & COVELLO].

145. For example, fenclozic acid, a potential anti-inflammatory drug, was seen to cause acute cholestatic jaundice in humans even though studies on a series of other species failed to produce similar toxic effects. *See* Shayne C. Gad, *Model Selection and Scaling*, *in* ANIMAL MODELS IN TOXICOLOGY (Shayne C. Gad & Christopher P. Chengelis eds., 1992), 813, 818–19. These differences are sometimes widely publicized by special interest groups, giving the public the mis-

taken impression that the results seen in experimental animals have little value for predicting adverse effects in humans. *See* ANIMAL MODELS IN TOXICOLOGY (Shayne C. Gad & Christopher P. Chengelis eds., 1992) at 2.

146. *See* FILOV ET AL., QUANTITATIVE TOXICOLOGY at 18–20 (1979); Chengelis & Gad, *id.* at 1–20.

147. *See* J. Huff, *Chemicals and Cancer in Humans: First Evidence in Experimental Animals,* 100 ENVTL. HEALTH PERSP. 201 (1993); International Agency for Research on Cancer, *Ethylene Oxide, in* 60 IARC MONOGRAPHS ON THE EVALUATION OF CARCINOGENIC RISKS TO HUMANS 73, 139 (1994).

148. *See* COHRRSEN & COVELLO, *supra* note 144, at 49–50; International Agency for Research on Cancer, *Preamble, in* 63 IARC MONOGRAPHS ON THE EVALUATION OF CARCINOGENIC RISKS TO HUMANS 9, 17–19 (1995).

149. OTA, IDENTIFYING AND REGULATING CARCINOGENS, *supra* note 2, at 39.

150. These include the relative weighting of positive and negative animal studies for the same substance, whether benign and malignant tumors should be weighted equally as evidence for carcinogenicity in animals (and thus in humans), whether and how data from two or more nonhuman species should be combined, and so on. (NATIONAL RESEARCH COUNCIL, RISK ASSESSMENT IN THE FEDERAL GOVERNMENT, *supra* note 1, at 29–33).

151. Different high-dose to low-dose extrapolation models can introduce risk estimates that differ by several orders of magnitude. The use of different rodent to human extrapolation models might result in differences in risk estimates that vary by a factor of six to thirty-five, depending upon the method used. U.S. Dept. of Labor, OSHA, *supra* note 142, at 5190.

152. NATIONAL RESEARCH COUNCIL, RISK ASSESSMENT IN THE FEDERAL GOVERNMENT, *supra* note 1, at 28–33.

153. Such models introduce uncertainties because surrogates for the proper quantities (if they have even been identified) are used, because some possibly appropriate variables may be excluded, or because the proper model for representing and quantifying the data is not known. Adam M. Finkel, CONFRONTING UNCERTAINTY IN RISK MANAGEMENT: A REPORT 12–15 (1990). Uncertainties can be introduced because of the inherent variability in biological response between individuals, the concern of environmental justice advocates.

154. NATIONAL RESEARCH COUNCIL, RISK ASSESSMENT IN THE FEDERAL GOVERNMENT, *supra* note 1, at 69–72; NATIONAL RESEARCH COUNCIL, SCIENCE AND JUDGMENT IN RISK ASSESSMENT, *supra* note 4, at 85–105.

155. NATIONAL RESEARCH COUNCIL, RISK ASSESSMENT IN THE FEDERAL GOVERNMENT, *supra* note 1, at 27–28; NATIONAL RESEARCH COUNCIL, SCIENCE AND JUDGMENT IN RISK ASSESSMENT, *supra* note 4, at 26–27.

156. NATIONAL RESEARCH COUNCIL, RISK ASSESSMENT IN THE FEDERAL GOVERNMENT, *supra* note 1, at 27.

157. As I noted elsewhere, "models for predicting the transport of ethyl benzene from leaking gasoline tanks [in soil] differ by as much as a factor of 1500, and there appears no easy way to validate the correct model for making such assessments." While the "theoretical models for predicting the environmental fate of substances such as benzene, xylene, toluene, and ethyl benzene are reasonably well understood at least in laboratory settings, applying the models

under actual field conditions could produce substantial differences in the estimates of the risks. The differences in this case are for the most part due not to a failure of theoretical understanding of the environmental fate of substances under controlled conditions, for this seems to be reasonably well understood. Instead there is typically insufficiently detailed site-specific information about the behavior of substances in the soil, ground water, or air. Additional on-site field research could remove some of these uncertainties (this is not true for many of the uncertainties connected with toxicological risk assessment). But it is time-consuming, probably expensive, and of limited value since the results could vary by individual substance, type of soil, underlying impermeable stratum, ground water properties, and other factors specific to the location." CRANOR, REGULATING TOXIC SUBSTANCES, *supra* note 129, at 20.

158. NATIONAL RESEARCH COUNCIL, RISK ASSESSMENT IN THE FEDERAL GOVERNMENT, *supra* note 1, at 28.

159. *Id.*

160. *Id.*

161. NATIONAL RESEARCH COUNCIL, SCIENCE AND JUDGMENT IN RISK ASSESSMENT, *supra* note 4, at 184–85.

162. Environmental justice "emphasizes prevention and intervention . . . adopts the public health approach of seeking to prevent the threat before it occurs and of remedying problems that already exist . . . [and] . . . the distribution of societal benefits and burdens and the justifications for action that result in harm are as important as the science-based characterization of environmental hazards." Kuehn, *Environmental Justice, supra* note 32, at 167. *See also* Bullard, *Unequal Environmental Protection, supra* note 20, at 237.

163. Kuehn, *Environmental Justice, supra* note 32, at 160. For further discussion of these issues, see Chapter 7 of this volume.

164. *Id.* at 163.

165. *Id.* at 167.

166. *Id.* at 171.

167. *Id.*; Clayton P. Gillette & James E. Krier, *Risk, Courts and Agencies,* 138 U. PA. L. REV. 1027, 1073 (1990); Peter Sandman, *Risk Communication: Facing Public Outrage,* EPA J., Nov. 1987, at 21; Paul Slovic, *Perception of Risk,* 236 SCI. 280, 283 (1987); MICHAEL B. GERRARD, WHOSE BACKYARD, WHOSE RISK: FEAR AND FAIRNESS IN TOXIC AND NUCLEAR WASTE SITING, 99–113 (MIT Press, 1994).

168. Kuehn, *Environmental Justice, supra* note 32, at 126.

169. *Id.* at 127–28.

170. *Id.* at 127; CRANOR, REGULATING TOXIC SUBSTANCES, *supra* note 129, at 152–75.

171. *Id.* at 126.

172. THE FIRST PEOPLE OF COLOR ENVIRONMENTAL LEADERSHIP SUMMIT, PRINCIPLES OF ENVIRONMENTAL JUSTICE, ¶ 7 (Oct. 27, 1991). *See also* JOHN RAWLS, A THEORY OF JUSTICE 221–34 (1971) (arguing as part of a principle of justice for a limited principle of participation in matters that affect the lives of citizens; his arguments may be more widely applicable than he suggests (thus, suggesting broader forms of argument), restricting his arguments as he does to the right to vote). For further discussion of these issues, see Chapter 7, "Public Participation."

173. For discussion of these issues, see Dale Hattis, *Variability in Susceptibility: How Big, How Often, for What Responses to What Agents?* J. TOXICOL. & ENVTL. PHARMACOL. 195 (1997); D. Hattis & K. Barlow, *Human Interindividual Variability in Cancer Risks: Technical and Management Challenges,* 2 HEALTH AND ECOLOGICAL RISK ASSESSMENT 194 (1996); Federica Perera, *Molecular Epidemiology: Insights into Cancer Susceptibility, Risk Assessment, and Prevention,* 88 J. NATL. CANCER INST. 496 (1996); S. Venitt, *Mechanisms of Carcinogenesis and Individual Susceptibility to Cancer,* 40 CLIN. CHEM. 1421 (1994).

174. Kuehn, *Environmental Justice, supra* note 32, at 123 (*citing* NATIONAL RESEARCH COUNCIL, RISK ASSESSMENT IN THE FEDERAL GOVERNMENT, *supra* note 1, at 20–23; and COHRSSEN & COVELLO, *supra* note 144, 27–48 (1989)).

175. NATIONAL RESEARCH COUNCIL, RISK ASSESSMENT IN THE FEDERAL GOVERNMENT, *supra* note 1, at 28.

176. Kuehn, *Environmental Justice, supra* note 32, at 123.

177. *Id.* at 125.

178. NATIONAL RESEARCH COUNCIL, SCIENCE AND JUDGMENT IN RISK ASSESSMENT, *supra* note 4, at 11.

179. Kuehn, *Environmental Justice, supra* note 32 at 117.

180. The total risk posed by exposure to the risks of each of several substances is additive if the lifetime risk from exposure to one substance is added to the lifetime risk of exposure to another substance. For example, if smoking increases the risk of contracting cancer by a factor of five, and exposure to asbestos increases the risk by a factor of ten, an additive effect would increase the risk of cancer by a factor of 15. A synergistic effect occurs when the total risk posed by exposure to the individual risks of each of several substances is greater than an additive function of the individual risks (for example, synergism between smoking and exposure to asbestos might result in a combined risk of 50, not 15). An antagonistic effect results when the total risk posed by exposure to the risks of each of several substances is less than an additive function of the individual risks. Kuehn, *Environmental Justice, supra* note 32, at 119–20.

181. *Id.* at 120 (citing Barbara D. Beck et al., *The Use of Toxicology in the Regulatory Process, in* PRINCIPLES AND METHODS OF TOXICOLOGY 19, 28 (A. Wallace Hayes ed., 1994)).

182. ENVIRONMENTAL EQUITY WORK GROUP, U.S. ENVTL. PROTECTION AGENCY, ENVIRONMENTAL EQUITY: REDUCING RISK FOR ALL COMMUNITIES, SUPPORTING DOCUMENT 35–36 (1992) [hereinafter ENVIRONMENTAL EQUITY REPORT].

183. Kuehn, *Environmental Justice, supra* note 32, at 118–19; ENVIRONMENTAL EQUITY REPORT, *supra* note 182, at 12.

184. ENVIRONMENTAL EQUITY REPORT, *supra* note 182, at 12.

185. It was assumed that carcinogens acted directly on DNA and thus did not have threshold effects in individuals. Moreover, even if there were individual threshold effects, no single threshold would be applicable to a population. NATIONAL RESEARCH COUNCIL, RISK ASSESSMENT IN THE FEDERAL GOVERNMENT, *supra* note 1, at 25. *See also* Merrill, *supra* note 95, at 322.

186. *Id.* at 127; Marla Cone, *River Pollution Study Finds Hormonal Defects in Fish,* L.A. TIMES, Sept. 22, 1998, at A1 (reporting reproductive health effects in fish at "normal," not highly concentrated, levels of pollution).

187. Albert L. Nichols, *Risk-Based Priorities and Environmental Justice, in* WORST THINGS FIRST?, *supra* note 20, at 267 (emphasis in original).

188. *Id.* at 268.

189. *Id.* at 270.

190. *Id.*

191. *Id.* at 271. (Of course, it is arguable from the environmental justice perspective that a wider group of rights violations be addressed first.)

192. Kuehn, *Environmental Justice, supra* note 32, at 151; Sexton, *Do Class and Race Matter?, supra* note 21, at 267.

193. Kuehn, *Environmental Justice,* at 151–53; Sexton, *Do Class and Race Matter?, supra* note 21, at 267. The EPA Science Advisory Board's Integrated Human Exposure Committee recently gave general approval (with some recommendations for refinement) to three different computer-based local exposure models for judging whether there has been disparate exposure impact on local populations. U.S. ENVIRONMENTAL PROTECTION AGENCY, Science Advisory Board, Review of Disproportionate Impact Methodologies, EPA-SAB-IHEC-99-XXX, located at EPA web site (last modified October 15, 1998) <http://www.epa.gov/science1/disp.htm>.

194. Sexton, *Do Class and Race Matter?, supra* note 21, at 267.

195. Site-specific exposure information can be particularly important in assessing children's exposure through the soil because of their typical "hand-to-mouth activity." Barbara D. Beck, *Sensitive Subpopulations from an Exposure Standpoint, in* TRENDS IN RISK AND REMEDIATION (Gradient Corporation).

196. OTA, IDENTIFYING AND REGULATING CARCINOGENS, *supra* note 2, at 18–21 (documenting agency response to identified carcinogens). Sara M. Hoover et al., *Improving the Regulation of Carcinogens by Expediting Cancer Potency Estimation,* 15 RISK ANALYSIS 267 (1995); Carl F. Cranor, *The Social Benefits of Expedited Risk Assessment,* 15 RISK ANALYSIS 353 (1995).

197. Cranor, *Eggshell Skulls, supra* note 16, at 244; Carl F. Cranor, *Learning from Law for Regulatory Science,* 14 LAW AND PHILOSOPHY 115 (1995).

198. Kuehn, *Environmental Justice, supra* note 32, at 154.

199. Sexton, *Do Class and Race Matter?, supra* note 21, at 267.

200. Cranor, *Eggshell Skulls, supra* note 16, at 244.

201. *Id.* at 244.

202. Cranor, *The Social Benefits of Expedited Risk Assessment, supra* note 196.

203. Kuehn, *Environmental Justice, supra* note 32, at 160–66.

204. 43 Fed. Reg. 5918–70 (1978).

205. Industrial Union Dept., AFL-CIO v. American Petroleum Institute, 448 U.S. 607 (1980).

206. 448 U.S. 607 at 642–44, 653.

207. The substantial evidence standard of review is generally considered more rigorous than the "arbitrary and capricious" standard normally applied to informal rulemaking. *See* Universal Camera Corp. v. National Labor Rel. Bd., 340 U.S. 474, 488 (1951) and Motor Vehicle Mfrs. Assn. v. State Farm Mut., 463 U.S. 29, 43 (1982). Moreover, as one court puts it, the substantial evidence test "'afford[s] a considerably more generous judicial review [to petitioners] than the arbitrary and capricious test' . . . and 'imposes a considerable burden on the agency and limits its discretion in arriving at a factual predicate.'" Corrosion Proof Fittings v. EPA, 947 F.2d 1201 at 1214 (5th Cir. 1991).

208. 448 U.S. at 656.

209. *Id.*

210. *Id.*

211. 746 F.2d 483 (9th Cir. 1984).

212. *Id.* at 490 (*quoting* American Textile Mfrs. Inst. v. Donovan, 452 U.S. 490 at 523).

213. *Id.* at 490 (*quoting* Industrial Union Dept. AFL-CIO v. American Petroleum Institute, 448 U.S. 607 at 656 (1980).

214. *Id.* at 491.

215. *Id.* at 493.

216. 796 F.2d 1479 (D.C. Cir. 1986).

217. *Id.* at 1489.

218. *Id.* at 1503.

219. *Id.* at 1495; *see also* "A reasonable person could draw from this evidence the conclusion that exposure to EtO presents a risk of cancer. Thus, the substantial evidence test is met. Even if a reasonable person could also draw the opposite conclusions, we must uphold the agency's findings." *Id.* at 1489.

220. *Id.* at 1499.

221. *Id.* at 1489.

222. *Id.* at 1495.

223. 838 F.2d 1258 (D.C. Cir. 1988).

224. *Id.* at 1264–67.

225. *Id.* at 1262 (concerning a categorical ban of the spraying of asbestos-containing products, its decision not to adopt a lower PEL for certain major industrial subgroups, some smoking-related regulations, and some suggested safety measures).

226. *Id.* at 1265.

227. Air Contaminants Standard, 54 Fed. Reg. 2332 (1989) (codified at 29 C.F.R. § 1910.1000).

228. 965 F.2d 962 (11th Cir. 1992).

229. *Id.* at 980.

230. *Id.* at 971.

231. *Id.* at 972.

232. *Id.* at 972–73.

233. *Id.* at 975 (OSHA merely provided a conclusory statement that the new PEL will reduce the "significant" risk of material health effects shown to be caused by that substance without any explanation of how the agency determined that the risk was significant).

234. *Id.* at 976 (*quoting* International Union v. Pendergrass, 878 F.2d 389, 392 (D.C. Cir. 1989)).

235. *Id.* at 976.

236. *Id.* at 978.

237. *Id.* at 979.

238. 47 Fed. Reg. 14,366 (1982).

239. Gulf S. Insul. v. Consumer Product Safety Commission, 701 F.2d 1137, 1139 (5th Cir. 1983).

240. *Id.* at 1147.

241. *Id.* at 1143–45.

242. *Id.* at 1145–46.

243. *Id.* at 1146 (for example, had two fewer rats, or 20 more, developed carcinomas, the risk predicted by [the risk extrapolation model] would be altered drastically. [One hundred and three out of 240 rats contracted nasal cancer.]). As the Office of Technology Assessment noted, however, "This is very close to saying that if the victim of the gunshot wound had not died, the defendant wouldn't be guilty of murder." (OTA, IDENTIFYING AND REGULATING CARCINOGENS, *supra* note 2,208).

244. *Id.* at 1147, n.19.

245. See specifically the reasoning in ASARCO, Inc. v. OSHA, and Building and Constr. Trades Dept., AFL-CIO v. Brock, 838 F.2d 1258 (D.C. Cir. 1988).

246. 54 Fed. Reg. 29,460 (1989).

247. Corrosion Proof Fittings v. EPA, 947 F.2d 1201, 1207 (5th Cir. 1991).

248. *Id.* at 1229–30 (the agency should not "hold critical analysis in reserve and then use it to justify its regulation despite the lack of public comment on the validity of its basis;" *id.* at 1212).

249. *Id.* at 1215 (emphasis added).

250. *Id.* at 1217.

251. *Id.* at 1218–21.

252. *Id.* at 1222.

253. "The regulation may issue if the severity of the injury that may result from the product, factored by the likelihood of the injury, offsets the harm the regulation itself imposes upon manufacturers and consumers." *Id.* at 1222 (*quoting* Forester v. CPSC, 559 F.2d 774, 789 (D.C. Cir. 1977) *and following* Aqua Slide'NDive v. CPSC, 569 F.2d 831, 839 (5th Cir. 1978)).

254. *Id.* at 1223.

255. *Id.* at 1224 (concerning the specific ban of friction products (nonasbestos brakes may be less safe than asbestos brakes)), at 1226–27 (concerning asbestos-cement pipe products (polyvinyl chloride pipe substitutes carry cancer risks of their own)).

256. *Id.* at 1230.

257. U.S. ENVIRONMENTAL PROTECTION AGENCY, RESPIRATORY HEALTH EFFECTS OF PASSIVE SMOKING, LUNG CANCER AND OTHER DISORDERS, EPA/600/6-90/00F, December 1992.

258. Public Law No. 99-499, 100 Stat. 1758-60 (1986), codified at 42 U.S.C. § 7401 (1994).

259. 1998 WL 403334 (M.D.N.C).

260. *Id.* at 13–32.

261. *Id.* at 23.

262. *Id.* at 23–26 (it had a concern that EPA "cherry-picked" its data, that it excluded nearly "half of the available studies," and that its selective use of studies "conflicts with Radon Research Act"; *id.* at 26).

263. *Id.* at 27.

264. *Id.* at 28.

265. *Id.* at 29.

266. Case No. 95-38228-CV (May 29, 1997).

267. *Id.* at 42.

268. *Id.* at 43.

269. *Id.* at 45.

270. NAACP v. Engler (Case No. 205264, Mich. Ct. App., November 24, 1998) at 2.

271. *Id.* at 4.

272. *Id.*

273. Nuclear Regulatory Commission, Atomic Safety and Licensing Board (Docket No. 70-3070-ML, May 1, 1997) (located at the NRC web site <http://www.nrc.gov/OPA/reports/lesfnl.htm>) at Section IV. *See also* Stan Milan, *Enviro-Bias Is Hot Topic in Facility Siting*, NAT'L L. J. (Jun. 23, 1997) at B8.

274. *Id.* (Sections III.B and III.C, respectively).

275. Nuclear Regulatory Commission, Commission Decision—Louisiana Energy Services (Docket No. 70-3070-ML, April 3, 1998) (located at the NRC web site <http://www.nrc.gov/OPA/reports/lesdocs.htm>) (recognizing that Executive Order No. 12,898 "creates no new rights or remedies," and noting that an inquiry into racial discrimination goes "well beyond what NEPA [requires]" and beyond what the Council on Environmental Quality requires by way of licensing requirements ((5s)(a)(2))).

276. *Id.* (finding that the EIS "did not consider the interference with pedestrian traffic between [two low-income minority communities] ((5)(b)(i)) and adverse effects on property values in those communities ((5)(b)(ii)))."

CHAPTER 11

Access to the Courts

ELLEN P. CHAPNICK

This chapter discusses the basic requirements for bringing an environmental justice conflict into court. The first part considers the law of standing and shows that environmental justice's focus on specific injuries suffered by people in low-income and minority communities, rather than defendants' bad acts, may be useful, given the Supreme Court's recent decisions limiting standing in environmental law cases. The second part discusses the availability of lawyers' fees. The third part presents an overview of the expert not-for-profit organizations that may be available to help environmental justice litigants and their counsel.

Standing

Overview of Constitutional and Prudential Requirements

In environmental justice cases, as elsewhere, the doctrine of standing addresses "whether a party has a sufficient stake in an otherwise justiciable controversy to obtain judicial resolution of that controversy."[1] In actions commenced under federal law, the sufficiency of a party's stake is limited both by the Constitution and by prudentially imposed requirements.[2] Actions brought under state statutes may be subject to different standing criteria, as not all state constitutions have a "case or controversy" requirement. This section reviews the requirements of standing for actions commenced under federal environmental law.[3]

Four decisions by the U.S. Supreme Court in the 1990s provide the bedrock for both the constitutional and prudential inquiries.[4] Three of the cases denied standing[5] and the fourth granted standing to businesspeople who asserted economic, not environmental, interests.[6] The implications of these decisions for parties in environmental justice cases are far from clear. However, it is certain that plaintiffs bear the burden of proving standing at all phases of the litigation.

Constitutional Limitations

The federal constitutional limitations on standing derive from the "case or controversy" requirement of Article III. *Lujan II* established that three elements must be met as an irreducible constitutional minimum. First, plaintiff must have suffered an "injury in fact," which the Court defines as an invasion of a legally protected interest that is both (a) concrete and particularized, affecting plaintiff in a personal and individual way; and (b) actual or imminent, not conjectural or hypothetical.[7] Second, a causal connection must exist between the injury and the conduct complained of, such that the injury is "fairly traceable" to the challenged action of defendant.[8] Third, it must be likely that a court ruling in plaintiff's favor will redress the injury.[9] These requirements are discussed in greater depth below.

The practical effect of *Lujan II*, the first Supreme Court case to consider standing under a citizen suit provision, was to clarify that Congress could not statutorily create a right of action in persons who have not met the constitutional requirement of injury in fact by conferring upon such persons the right to enforce environmental laws, as private attorneys general.[10] In traditional citizen suits brought under the environmental regulatory statutes, the focus has been on whether a defendant violated permit or statutory provisions, or whether an administrative agency acted consistently with the governing statute. By focusing on allegations about the harm or imminent harm that specific plaintiffs and/or their communities will suffer as a result of defendants' violations, environmental justice citizen suits may avoid the injury-in-fact problems that beset plaintiffs who assert standing in traditional cases.

Prudential Limitations

With regard to prudential standing doctrine, judicially imposed limitations on standing are "founded in concern about the proper—and properly limited—role of the courts in a democratic society."[11] Examples of such prudential restrictions include a proscription against individual assertion of "generalized grievances" and a limitation on third-party standing. Unlike the constitutional requirements of standing, which may not be abrogated or modified by Congress or by the courts, nor waived by the parties, prudentially imposed limitations on standing may be modified or overcome by Congress.[12]

In *Bennett,* the Court confirmed that Congress could abrogate, or expand, the prudentially created "zone of interests" test in promulgating citizen suit provisions, such as that in the Endangered Species Act (ESA),[13] which provides that "*any person* may commence a civil suit."[14] The zone-of-interests is part of a two-prong test required to establish standing to bring an action under the Administrative Procedures Act (APA).[15] In addition to asserting an injury in fact, "a plaintiff's grievance must arguably fall within the zone-of-interests protected or regulated by the statutory provision or constitutional guarantee invoked in the action."[16] It had traditionally been invoked to deny standing under citizen suit provisions of environmental statutes to plaintiffs advancing economic, rather than environmental, interests.

Noting the broad language of the ESA's citizen suit provision, the Court concluded that there is no "textual basis" for saying that "expansion of standing requirements applies to environmentalists alone."[17] The Court specifically noted that business claims are within the ESA's zone-of-interests because "economic consequences are an explicit concern of the Act"[18] as evidenced by its provisions that each agency must "use the best scientific and commercial data available" and be sure that the benefits of its action outweigh the benefits of any reasonable and prudent alternatives. In the wake of the *Bennett* decision, plaintiffs asserting economic interests may have a right of action under those environmental statutes that feature similarly worded citizen suit provisions.[19]

More contentious, however, is the question of whether plaintiffs asserting purely economic rights have standing to sue under the National Environmental Policy Act[20] (NEPA), because APA-based suits under NEPA carry a more stringent standing requirement than do statutes worded like the ESA. Two recent decisions have split on this issue.[21] The Eighth Circuit in *Dombeck* held that economic interests are within the zone-of-interests that NEPA seeks to regulate or protect.[22] The Southern District of Texas reached a contrary result in *Hurd,* declining to interpret *Bennett* as overturning sub silentio pre-*Bennett* decisions, which consistently held that economic interests fall outside the sphere of interests governed by NEPA.[23]

Constitutional Requirements of Standing for Citizen Suits Under the Traditional Federal Environmental Statutes

Elements of standing must be established by the party invoking federal jurisdiction, and each element must be supported to the same extent required by any other matter on which plaintiff bears the burden of proof. Where plaintiff is the object of a challenged government action (or foregone action), there is generally little question that the elements of standing have been satisfied. However, where plaintiff's asserted claim arises from the government's allegedly unlawful regulation (or lack of regulation) of another party, standing is ordinarily "substantially more difficult" to establish.[24]

Requirement of "Injury in Fact"

Lujan I relied on the two-prong injury-in-fact and zone-of-interests test established in *Data Processing* to reassert the Court's insistence that the injury-in-fact standing requirement be taken seriously and that it cannot be abrogated by statute. However, Congress is afforded some latitude even in the area of constitutional standing doctrine, to the extent that the types of "injury in fact" can be statutorily defined. For instance, under the CAA, plaintiff may allege an injury arising from violation of an emission standard or limitation provided by the CAA,[25] while a constitutionally sufficient injury under EPCRA arises only from the narrowly defined set of violations provided in that statute.[26]

For an injury to meet the "concrete and particularized" standard, it must affect plaintiff in a personal and individual way.[27] For instance, an injury that is specific to the injured party's transferable or terminable position, and that would cease to harm that party upon the transfer or termination of such position, is not sufficiently "concrete and particularized" to confer standing.[28] Moreover, in a representational standing context, an allegation that defendant's conduct conflicts with the mission of the organization seeking judicial relief is too abstract to satisfy the "concrete and particularized" standard.[29]

In *Lujan II*, plaintiffs' vague and undefined intentions to return "someday" to visit the areas where development projects allegedly threatened the continued existence of certain endangered species were held to be insufficient to satisfy the requirement that an injury be "actual or imminent."[30] Even accepting as fact plaintiffs' contentions that they would one day return to observe the animals in question, the Court held that an imminent injury could not be found absent a more specific description of concrete travel plans.[31] A district court, after discussion of *Lujan*, found that plaintiffs had standing to assert a claim of injury under RCRA, where plaintiffs had used the allegedly polluted river for boating in the past, lived ten to fifteen miles from its shores, and alleged that they would return if the river were cleaned up and no longer posed a serious health risk.[32]

The *Lujan II* Court suggested that to establish a sufficiently concrete and particularized injury in fact, plaintiff must demonstrate both that the alleged harm will occur to a particular geographic area and that plaintiff has a relationship to the allegedly threatened area.[33]

Declining to extend this principle beyond these limits, the *Lujan II* Court forcefully rejected an "ecosystem nexus," on the ground that such a standard would confer citizen standing on anyone using any part of a contiguous ecosystem that may be adversely affected by defendant's actions.[34] The Court further rejected "animal nexus" and "vocational nexus" tests, which would have conferred standing upon those with a personal or professional interest in the ecosystem in question, regardless of the geographic location of such persons.[35] However, in accord with the geographic nexus standard, persons living or otherwise situated in close proximity to an activity that is allegedly harmful to health or the environment are generally found to have sustained an injury sufficient to support citizen suit standing.[36]

In the wake of *Lujan II*, several circuit courts have suggested that even absent an observable impact of pollution, an interest in the affected area may alone be sufficient to establish standing under the citizen suit provision of the Clean Water Act (CWA).[37] Similarly, proof that the nature of a defendant's CWA violation could be harmful to a waterway was found to negate the need for proof that defendant's own emissions had a quantifiable impact.[38]

The Third Circuit recently refused to construe broadly the CWA's standing requirements and vacated a $2.6 million judgment.[39] The court refused to deem sufficient plaintiff's showing that defendant violated its permit limits, and that plaintiff's members use the waters at issue and had reduced their recreational activities because of defendant's pollution. The court instead imposed a new stringent standard that required plaintiffs to prove that defendant's violations resulted in actual harm or posed an imminent threat to them.[40] Invoking the prudential bar on generalized grievances, the court struck down plaintiff's contention that its knowledge of defendant's pollution constituted a judicially cognizable injury in fact, because knowledge of defendant's CWA violation caused its members no special injury that distinguished them from members of the public at large.[41]

Procedural defects also may be insufficient to create the private injury necessary for standing, even where the defect deprives plaintiffs of statutorily created rights. At least one circuit court has held that defendant's flagrant failure to provide the public comment period mandated by CERCLA does not alone create a constitutionally sufficient injury.[42]

Requirement of Causation

The requirement that an injury be "fairly traceable" to the challenged behavior of the defendant examines whether it is "substantially probable" that the defendant, rather than a third party, has caused or will cause the plaintiff's particularized injury.[43]

Establishment of a causal nexus between defendant's challenged activity (or lack of activity) and plaintiff's injury does not require the equivalent of tort causation. Plaintiff need not satisfy a "but-for" test of causation by showing to a scientific certainty that defendant's effluent alone caused the precise harm suffered by plaintiff.[44] Instead, plaintiff must show that a defendant discharges a pollutant that causes or contributes to the types of injuries alleged by plaintiff.[45] Plaintiff's location, a considerable distance from defendant's challenged activity, may result in a finding that plaintiff's injuries were not "fairly traceable" to that activity, absent evidence of an injury attributable to defendant. Traditionally, plaintiffs have had standing to assert CWA claims if they showed that defendant violated its discharge permit and that defendant's discharge affects or has the potential to affect waters in which plaintiffs or their members have a legally protected interest. In at least one circuit, this no longer is sufficient. The Fourth Circuit recently dismissed a CWA action because plaintiffs had not provided evidence of "an observable negative impact on the waterways" such as a toxicity test.[46] Plaintiffs had shown that the distance between the source of the alleged pollution and the water used by at least one of plaintiff's members was as little as four miles downstream and others were less than 16.5 miles away, and that the members suffered specific, personal lost uses due to the alleged pollution. The dissenting opinion noted that the decision departs from all other circuits by "refusing to consider the claims of a citizen living within the known discharge range of a polluting industrial facility."[47] An example of causation sufficient to establish that plaintiff's injuries are fairly traceable to a U.S. government action is the necessity of federal funds to the continuance of the challenged project.[48]

Requirement of "Redressability"

The redressability requirement of standing analysis has two lines of inquiry: whether "the line of causation between the illegal conduct and [alleged] injuries is too attenuated . . . [and whether] the prospect of obtaining relief from the injury as a result of a favorable ruling [is] too speculative."[49]

The Supreme Court's recent decision in *Citizens for a Better Environment v. Steel Co. of Chicago*[50] applied this doctrine to deny standing to a plaintiff who sued for wholly past violations of EPCRA because the civil penalties sought could not redress its injuries, but rather were payable to the U.S. Treasury. Plaintiff's generalized vindication or gratification in seeing justice faithfully executed will not suffice to support standing. There, the defendant argued that its compliance with EPCRA requirements, after receiving notice of its violation, redressed plaintiff's injury such that plaintiff no longer had a live "case or controversy" and lost its standing to sue. The Court agreed, reasoning that because plaintiff's "psychic satisfaction" would fail to redress a cognizable Article III injury, it cannot be an acceptable Article III remedy, and that relief that does not remedy the injury suffered cannot confer jurisdiction.[51] Moreover, interest in pursuing an award of lawyers' fees is insufficient to create a case or controversy where none exists on the merits of the underlying action.[52]

The Court noted that an action for deterrence of future violations of EPCRA may be cognizable as remedial, where threatened injury is one of the gravamen of the complaint.[53] Absent such a pleading of continuing or foreseeable future violations that can be remedied by the court, however, a generalized interest in deterrence will not support standing.[54] Similarly, a district court has held that there is no standing to complain about injuries suffered in the past under RCRA because those injuries cannot be redressed and Section 7002 creates a cause of action only for present and imminent harms.[55]

In *Friends of the Earth v. Laidlaw*,[56] the Fourth Circuit relied on the redressability test of *CBE* to vacate the district court's assessment of a $405,800 fine against defendant for hundreds of permit violations, because the penalty was payable to the U.S. Treasury, not the environmental groups that brought the action under the CWA's citizen suit provision.[57] The Court of Appeals held that plaintiffs lost standing and the case became moot when plaintiffs appealed the insufficiency of the fine but not the district court's denial of declaratory and injunctive relief.[58] The Fourth Circuit further instructed the district court to dismiss the entire action, without any consideration of lawyers' fees, because plaintiffs had failed to obtain relief on the merits.[59]

The doctrine does not require plaintiff in an action alleging failure of defendant to follow proper procedures to demonstrate that it would have benefitted under the ultimate outcome, if defendant had followed the proper procedures.

Statutory Requirements for Standing

Citizen Suit Provisions of Traditional Federal Environmental Statutes

Congress has long recognized the value and necessity of private enforcement of environmental laws. For this reason, citizen suit enforcement provisions, which confer upon individuals and organizations the right to act as private attorneys general to compel enforcement of federal law, have been a standard feature of environmental statutes since the 1970 Clean Air Act. Such provisions permit private parties to file civil actions to remedy statutory violations or to compel the performance of nondiscretionary federal agency actions mandated by the statutes. However, since the inception of citizen suits, these provisions have included limitations on the range of potential plaintiffs and imposed other procedural requirements that restrict access to the courts for private plaintiffs. For example, most citizen suit provisions mandate a 60-day notice period to allow the agency to begin enforcement proceedings. Most also prohibit the commencement of citizen suits where an agency is diligently prosecuting the violation. Although marked similarities inhere among the various citizen suit provisions of environmental statutes, several significant differences have developed.

WHO MAY SUE UNDER ENVIRONMENTAL CITIZEN SUIT PROVISIONS. The CWA citizen suit provision is unique among the federal environmental statutes in its authorization of "any *citizen*" to commence a civil action on her own behalf.[60] "Citizen" is defined as a person whose interest is or may be adversely affected by the challenged action or lack of action.[61] The other statutes confer upon "any *person*" the right to bring suit.[62] "Person" is in turn defined by CERCLA,[63] RCRA,[64] CAA,[65] and EPCRA[66] to include corporations, associations, and governmental entities. It should be noted, however, that although the citizen suit provisions of many environmental statutes extend the right to sue to governmental agencies, such agencies do not automatically have standing to bring actions that would frustrate the purposes of the statutes.[67]

WHAT CONSTITUTES AN INJURY UNDER ENVIRONMENTAL CITIZEN SUIT PROVISIONS. The citizen suit provisions of CERCLA,[68] RCRA,[69] CAA,[70] CWA,[71] and TSCA[72] permit plaintiff to bring an action for any injury arising from defendant's violation of any standard or requirement of the relevant Act's substantive provisions. In contrast, a citizen suit may be brought under EPCRA only for injuries arising from a set of narrowly defined violations of the Act.[73] Because a primary purpose of the Act is to provide for the production and public dissemination of information, failure to timely file reports mandated by the statute can be the basis for an action to redress an injury stemming from the resulting lack of information.[74]

PROSECUTION FOR PAST VIOLATIONS. The CAA expressly provides for the maintenance of a citizen suit against a defendant who is alleged to have violated the Act's standards repeatedly as well as a defendant who currently is violating the statute.[75]

The language of the CWA citizen suit provision does not explicitly address the issue of whether an action may be brought to remedy wholly past violations. However, the Supreme Court has interpreted the statute's facial ambiguity to require that plaintiffs allege either a continuing violation or a reasonable likelihood that a past polluter would continue to pollute in the future.[76] As the provision does not require that defendant "be in violation," but only that it be "alleged to be in violation," plaintiffs need not prove their allegations of noncompliance before jurisdiction attaches. Rather, a good faith allegation of defendant's violation will suffice.[77] An allegation or finding that defendant has repeatedly violated the provisions of the Act in the past may not satisfy the "likelihood of future violations" standard.[78]

The remedies available in a CWA citizen suit may depend on whether the violations are ongoing. A district court recently held that citizen plaintiffs may seek civil monetary penalties in an action under the CWA where they also seek injunctive relief for alleged ongoing violations of the Act.[79] The court distinguished *CBE* and *Laidlaw,* which were interpreted as suggesting that plaintiffs in citizen suits do not have standing to seek civil penalties against alleged violators of environmental statutes, by noting that both involved actions only limited to past violations.

The question of whether RCRA's citizen suit provision applied to past transgressions was resolved in 1996, when the Supreme Court held that Congress had not intended to authorize citizen suits for wholly past violations of that Act.[80] In *Meghrig,* the Court rejected a private cause of action to recover costs of cleaning up toxic waste, which did not continue to pose a danger to health or the environment, because it failed to satisfy RCRA's requirement of a showing of imminent and substantial endangerment to health or the environment.

The applicability of EPCRA's citizen suit provision to purely historic violations recently was before the Supreme Court but was not clearly decided.[81] The Court's holding that plaintiffs' failure to allege a redressable injury was a constitutional jurisdictional defect included, but was not controlled by, discussion of the inadequacy of plaintiffs' claim for injunctive relief because they had alleged only past harms.[82]

THE SIXTY-DAY NOTICE REQUIREMENT. No suit may be brought pursuant to the citizen suit provisions of CERCLA,[83] RCRA,[84] CAA,[85] CWA,[86] TSCA,[87] and EPCRA[88] prior to sixty days after a plaintiff has given notice of the alleged violation to the appropriate individuals or entities. Strict compliance with these notice prerequisites is required. In *Hallstrom v. Tillamook County,*[89] the Supreme Court held that the sixty-day notice requirement in RCRA's citizen suit provision, which is functionally identical to those of the other citizen suit provisions, is a mandatory condition precedent to the commencement of a citizen action.[90] When a citizen suit plaintiff has failed to comply with the notice requirement, the courts must dismiss plaintiff's claim for lack of subject matter jurisdiction.[91] Failure to satisfy the notice requirements of CERCLA and RCRA prior to filing the initial complaint required dismissal of claims under those statutes, even when notice was provided well in advance of filing the amended complaint. However, dismissal was without prejudice to refile the action after compliance with the notice provisions.[92]

STANDING TO SUE UNDER THE NATIONAL ENVIRONMENTAL POLICY ACT. While the citizen suit provisions of traditional federal environmental statutes are valuable weapons in challenging the effects of projects that have already been completed, they are often ill-suited to contesting proposed projects. Plaintiffs therefore often turn to the National Environmental Policy Act of 1969 (NEPA)[93] when there is sufficient federal involvement in the challenged project. NEPA does not include provisions for private actions.[94] Standing for a citizen suit under NEPA most often is found in the general review provision of the APA,[95] which provides a cause of action for "persons adversely affected" by an agency action. Federal agencies attempting to assert NEPA claims must overcome a presumption that this language reflects congressional intent that such private interests be litigated by private parties.[96]

In addition to satisfying the constitutional prerequisites set forth in Article III, a plaintiff invoking judicial review of an agency's actions under NEPA pursuant to Section 702 of the APA must:

1. identify some agency action affecting it in the specified manner; and
2. show that it suffered a "legal wrong" as a result of the agency's action, or was adversely affected or aggrieved within the meaning of the relevant statute.

With regard to the first statutory requirement, the challenged agency action must be a "final action."[97] An allegation of injury that results from an incomplete or nonfinal agency action is insufficient to confer standing for judicial review. In determining whether an agency action is final, the Supreme Court has noted that "the core question asks whether the agency has completed its decisionmaking process, and whether the result of that process is one that will directly affect the parties."[98] In answering this inquiry, a court may consider whether the action's impact is "sufficiently direct and immediate," and whether it has a "direct effect on . . . day-to-day business."[99]

The doctrine of exhaustion of administrative remedies, whereby a party is not entitled to judicial relief for a supposed or threatened harm until the prescribed administrative remedy has been exhausted, is well established in the jurisprudence of administrative law.[100] This requirement serves the dual purpose of promoting agency autonomy and preventing a flood of potential litigants seeking judicial intervention before a final agency determination has been made.[101] Application of the doctrine, however, is a matter of judicial discretion,[102] and courts have traditionally been sparing in their application of this doctrine to claims brought under NEPA.[103]

The "legal wrong" required by the second statutory requirement for standing to sue under the APA for violations of NEPA is defined as "the invasion of a legally protected right."[104] Thus, plaintiffs must plead a legal right that was violated by the final agency action. To be "adversely affected or aggrieved . . . within the meaning of the relevant statute," plaintiff must establish that the injury in fact complained of falls within the zone-of-interests sought to be protected by the statutory provision whose violation forms the legal basis of the claim.[105]

In invoking judicial review under the APA for violation of NEPA, environmental interest groups typically raise one of two claims of injury in fact to support standing.[106] First, where the challenge is derivative, a group generally alleges that its members will suffer harm to their environmental, recreational, and aesthetic interests.[107] Alternatively, an interest group alleges injury to its own interests, such as the impairment of its ability to pursue its central educational or political purpose as a result of the agency's denial of the interest group's right to statutorily mandated information.[108]

With reference to the specific applicability of the test for standing under the APA to aesthetic or environmental injury claims under NEPA, the Supreme Court has consistently recognized that recreational, environmental, and aesthetic injury satisfies the injury-in-fact (adversely affected or aggrieved) test.[109] Moreover, such injury clearly falls within the zone-of-interests that NEPA was intended to protect.[110] The Court has further indicated that in some circumstances, a plaintiff bringing suit under a statute conferring a procedural right may have standing even absent the traditional Article III requirements of redressability and immediacy where an agency's violation of that right has impaired a "separate concrete interest" specific to plaintiff.[111] These circumstances are narrowly defined.[112] Standard Article III requirements will apply in the majority of cases, particularly where the procedural right violated does not inflict an injury that is both discrete and particular to that plaintiff, and where the challenged site is not in very close proximity to the plaintiff.

In raising claims under NEPA through the APA, interest group plaintiffs generally allege that the lack of information resulting from the agency's failure to comply with NEPA impedes their ability to carry out their primary function of educating the public and lobbying Congress on environmental issues.[113] Although such claims have been heard, the validity of informational injury as an injury in fact sufficient to confer standing remains unclear. Some critics of the informational injury approach have argued that these claims should be barred pursuant to the prudential prohibition of generalized grievances, because plaintiffs cannot distinguish their benefit from judicial relief from those of the public at large.

Representational Standing

The constitutional tests to determine when an organization has standing to sue on behalf of its members are significant to environmental justice law because community organizations, civil rights groups, and/or local and national environmental organizations often are plaintiffs. Using the principles of *Warth,* the U.S. Supreme Court formulated a three-prong test to determine when groups can sue in a representational capacity:

1. at least one of the organization's members must have standing to sue in his or her own right;
2. the interests that the organization seeks to protect must be germane to the organization's purpose; and
3. the lawsuit must not require the individual participation of organization members to assert the claim or obtain relief.[114]

This formula still constitutes the representational standing doctrine.[115]

Until 1996, the Court consistently defended the test on both constitutional and prudential grounds, explaining that judicial policy favors organizational standing because an association may have a pre-existing reservoir of expertise and capital, which works to the benefit of both courts and plaintiffs and because a single action on behalf of all members promotes judicial economy.[116]

However, the Court has since specified that while the first two prongs of the test are Article III requirements, the third is prudential in nature and may be abrogated by Congress.[117] The *Lujan II* Court's requirements for standing are satisfied, therefore, when an organization suing in a representative capacity includes at least one member with standing to assert the claim individually,[118] and the organization's purpose guarantees that it has a stake in the resolution of the dispute such that it is a natural adversary to the defendant.[119] Representational standing on certain RCRA claims was denied where none of the named members could show that they would be affected by the alleged threat to drinking-water fields, even though representational standing existed on other claims because they could show an imminent threat arising from related pollution of a river.[120]

The *Hunt* test's requirement of "indicia of membership" does not mandate formal membership, but rather is interpreted to permit standing where the organization has a clearly articulated membership structure, and purported members have elected its governing body and financed its activities.[121]

Phase at Which Standing Defect May Be Raised

Standing is a jurisdictional requirement that remains subject to review at all phases of litigation. If plaintiffs lack standing, the case is moot and may not constitutionally be maintained or continued no matter how far it has progressed.[122] A defect in standing may be raised, either by the parties or by the court, whenever it becomes apparent.[123] Although general factual allegations of injury suffice to support standing at the pleading stage, as the case proceeds through summary judgment motions and later phases of litigation, facts alleged to support standing must, if controverted, be proven with the same manner and degree of evidence required of any other matter on which plaintiff bears the burden of proof.[124]

Generally, then, proof that a dispute was alive at the time an action was commenced is not enough to dispose of the standing question; rather, the parties must continue to have a personal stake in the outcome of the action.[125] Where a defendant claims that its voluntary action has mooted the controversy, defendant bears the burden of proving that it is "absolutely clear that the allegedly wrongful behavior could not be expected to recur."[126] However, where defendant's actions mooting the suit were undertaken involuntarily under threat of enforcement action, the burden shifts to plaintiff to prove that the claim is not moot due to a reasonable expectation that the wrong will be repeated.[127]

The Third Circuit's decision in *PIRG v. Magnesium Elektron Inc.*[128] is striking because the Court of Appeals vacated a judgment on review in the penalty phase of the case. The court had previously upheld the trial court's pretrial finding that plaintiffs had citizen standing to sue for noncompliance with the Clean Water Act. After the trial, the Third Circuit revisited the standing issue sua sponte and vacated the judgment for lack of standing due to the "extraordinary circumstances" of the trial court's determination that the defendant's repeated violations of the CWA did not actually amount to an injury to plaintiffs.[129]

After *Magnesium* and *Laidlaw,* plaintiffs clearly must ensure that standing elements are properly preserved throughout the entire course of litigation. When viewed in conjunction with several other significant environmental citizen suit cases of the 1990s, *Magnesium* and *Laidlaw* appear to reflect a trend toward more stringent limits on standing in such cases.

CHECKLIST OF STANDING REQUIREMENTS.[130] After the Supreme Court's decisions throughout the 1990s, plaintiffs' standing to sustain an environmental justice action is likely to be one of the hard-fought issues in many cases. Counsel should make sure that named plaintiffs meet the constitutional and statutory requirements from the outset of the litigation until it concludes. Resources expended by plaintiffs and defendants on challenges to standing and the attendant discovery can be considerable.

CONSTITUTIONAL REQUIREMENTS.

- Plaintiff must suffer an "injury in fact" to a legally protected interest, which is both concrete and particularized, and current or imminent. (pages 360–61)
- The injury must be "fairly traceable" to the challenged actions of defendants. (pages 361–62)
- A court ruling in plaintiff's favor must be likely to redress the injury. (pages 362–63)

REQUIREMENTS FOR CITIZEN SUITS UNDER THE TRADITIONAL ENVIRONMENTAL STATUTES.

- Plaintiff must assert an injury arising from defendant's violation of a standard or requirement set forth in the statute that is actionable under the citizen suit provision of the statute. (page 364)
- Suit may be brought to remedy past violations under some statutes, but most others require a current violation, a continuing violation, or a reasonable likelihood of future violation. (pages 364–65)
- Plaintiff cannot file suit until sixty days after notice of the alleged violation was given to the appropriate individuals or entities. (pages 365–66)

REQUIREMENTS FOR SUITS UNDER THE NATIONAL ENVIRONMENTAL POLICY ACT, USING THE ADMINISTRATIVE PROCEDURES ACT (PAGES 366–68).

- There must be a "final" action by the agency that affected plaintiff, and plaintiff must have exhausted its administrative remedy.
- Plaintiff must suffer a "legal wrong" as a result of the agency's action or be adversely affected or aggrieved within the meaning of the statute.
- Plaintiff's injury in fact must fall within the zone-of-interests sought to be protected by the statutory provision whose violation forms the legal basis of the claim.
- The injury may be environmental, recreational, or aesthetic.

REPRESENTATIONAL STANDING (PAGES 368–69). An organizational plaintiff must:

- Include at least one member who has standing to bring the action on his or her own behalf.

- Seek to protect interests that are germane to the organization's purpose.
- In some circumstances, the organization must not need the individual participation of its members to assert the claim or obtain relief.

BURDEN OF PROOF (PAGE 369).

- Plaintiff bears the burden to prove a personal stake in the outcome of the litigation at all phases of the action.
- Allegations of injury, causation, and remedy that meet the constitutional and statutory prerequisites should be sufficient to withstand a motion to dismiss.
- Plaintiffs must provide evidence of the facts alleged to support standing to rebut defendant's arguments on a motion for summary judgment.

Lawyers' Fees

In suits filed by low-income communities and communities of color, the ability to recover lawyers' fees is very helpful in assuring that these communities have meaningful access to the courts.[131]

Lawyers' Fees in Federal Court Cases

Common Law Precedent

The American Rule is that absent a statutory fee-shifting provision, the prevailing litigant is not entitled to collect lawyers' fees from the loser.[132] However, there are three important exceptions to the rule. First, the common fund exception allows lawyers to collect fees when a common fund is created by the litigation for the benefit of a class of individuals.[133] Second, the court may assess lawyers' fees as part of a punishment for "willful disobedience of a court order."[134] Finally, a court may impose lawyers' fees when the losing party has "acted in bad faith, vexatiously, wantonly or for oppressive reasons."[135]

Fees in Citizen Suit Cases

Congress has inserted citizen suit provisions that provide for an award of lawyers' fees into most major environmental statutes. Most of these fee-shifting provisions allow the award of reasonable lawyers' and expert witness fees to the "prevailing or substantially prevailing party"[136] where appropriate. In *Ruckelshaus v. Sierra Club*,[137] the Supreme Court ruled that the CAA provision allowing the award of lawyers' fees where "appropriate" requires that plaintiffs achieve some degree of success on the merits. The Court thereby brought that Act in line with the fee-shifting provisions in other federal environmental statutes and harmonized fee-shifting provisions in environmental statutes with those in other federal statutes.[138]

PREVAILING OR PARTIALLY PREVAILING PARTY STANDARD. To be a "prevailing party" under fee-shifting statutes, a claimant must succeed on "any significant issue in the litigation which achieves some of the benefit the parties sought in bringing the suit."[139] The claimant must succeed on at least one "substantial" claim.[140] A party may qualify as a prevailing party by obtaining a favorable settlement or consent decree[141] or where the lawsuit was a "material factor" or catalyst that prompted defendant to take action favorable to plaintiff, which moots the lawsuit.[142] The court usually will not award fees for success on procedural, evidentiary, or preliminary matters.[143] The Fourth Circuit recently instructed the district court to dismiss a CWA citizen action without any consideration of lawyers' fees because the $405,800 fine assessed against defendant as a result of the action was payable to the U.S. Treasury, not plaintiff.[144]

TIMING. A claim for lawyers' fees must be made within fourteen days after the entry of judgment on the merits, unless a statute provides for a different period or the court by order specifies another time.[145]

MEASURING THE "LODESTAR" AMOUNT. The methodology for determining the appropriate lawyers' fee award to a successful plaintiff is well established. The court must calculate a "lodestar" amount by determining the hours reasonably expended by counsel on the litigation and multiplying them by a reasonable hourly rate for each lawyer who worked on the case.[146] Determining what constitutes reasonable hours and rates can be more difficult.

A lawyer may be compensated for time spent on activities reasonably related to achieving relief on claimant's actions, including administrative hearings,[147] some prelitigation activities,[148] travel time,[149] appellate work,[150] post-judgment enforcement hours,[151] and time spent getting the fee award.[152] Claimed lawyers' fees may be reduced when a court determines that the hours claimed were excessive for a particular task or proceeding,[153] that a partner handled work more appropriate for an associate[154] or that a lawyer handled work more appropriate for a nonprofessional,[155] that the hours claimed were nonproductive time,[156] or that work performed by lawyers was duplicative.[157] Lawyers seeking a fee award should keep a contemporaneously recorded time log of the hours for which compensation may be sought.[158] District court judges also have the discretion to reduce claimed hours by a fixed percentage in fee disputes.[159]

The "reasonable rate" usually is the average rate typically charged in the community where the action was filed, not that in which the claimant's lawyer practices.[160] Comparison of a lawyer's usual billing rate with the rate claimed in the petition also may be an important factor in determining reasonableness and the prevailing community rate.[161] Courts can consider a variety of factors including the lawyer's level of skill, expertise in the subject matter, and reputation as well as the undesirability of the case.[162] A few circuits have found that a lawyer's actual billing rate can be determinative, regardless of the prevailing community rate.[163] Fees may not be inflated by multipliers based on contingency,[164] risk of nonpayment factors, or quality of representation, if the rate claimed is both reasonable for that particular lawyer and compensates counsel for fees lost by litigating the case without providing a windfall.[165] Paralegals, clerks, and other support staff are treated as expense items and billed at the prevailing market rate.[166]

Especially important for the lawyer involved in an environmental justice case, lawyers who lack an actual billing rate, such as those in not-for-profit or public interest organizations, can collect the same fee award as a private lawyer with similar expertise and experience.[167]

Courts may reduce fee awards to claimants who are only partially successful, by subtracting hours attributed to unsuccessful claims. However, in *Hensley v. Eckerhart*, the Supreme Court stated that "where a lawsuit consists of related claims, a plaintiff should not have his attorney's fee reduced simply because the district court did not adopt each contention raised. But where the plaintiff has achieved only limited success, the district court should award only that amount of fees that is reasonable in relation to the results obtained."[168] Determining the reasonableness of a full award of lawyers' fees in cases where success is less than absolute has been left largely to the discretion of the district courts.[169]

DELAY IN RECEIPT OF FEES. The courts are authorized to adjust the fee award to account for the delay between when legal services are performed and the date fees are awarded. The Supreme Court has ruled that, unless fees are sought from the government, "an appropriate adjustment for the delay in payment, whether by the application of current rather than historic hourly rates or otherwise, is within the contemplation of" the federal fee-shifting provisions.[170] However, with the exception of Title VII cases, in which Congress has provided a statutory "no-interest" waiver,[171] compensation for delay in receiving the fee awarded is unavailable against the federal government.[172]

INTERVENERS. One area that bears watching is the status of interveners in environmental suits. A California federal district court recently awarded lawyers' fees to the Sierra Club, which intervened in a case involving enforcement of the Clean Water Act. The court determined that the statutory language allowing the award of fees to "any prevailing or substantially prevailing party" covers interveners. The court also awarded the Sierra Club lawyers' fee expenses for Congressional lobbying expenses related to the litigation.[173]

Equal Access to Justice Act

The Equal Access to Justice Act (EAJA) waives the sovereign immunity of the United States so that it is liable for an award of lawyers' fees, expert witness fees, and other costs in certain specified situations.[174] The statute contains two separate fee-shifting provisions:

- Section 2412(b) makes the government liable for fees under the same common law or statutory rules as private parties;[175]
- Section 2412(d) allows an award of lawyers' fees against the government when the government's position is not substantially justified.[176]

SECTION 2412(B). EAJA Section 2412(b) makes the United States liable for lawyers' fees and expenses "to the same extent that any other party would be liable under the common law or under the terms of any statute which specifically provides for such an award."[177] This puts the United States on equal footing with private parties both in terms of common law fee-shifting awards[178] and statutory fee-shifting awards. The provision renders all statutes that allow an award of lawyers' fees against nonfederal parties applicable to the federal government. Courts have interpreted the provision to apply to federal, not state, fee-shifting statutes.[179]

Section 2412(b) has been held to encompass the Civil Rights Attorney's Fees Awards Act.[180] Passed in reaction to the Supreme Court's *Alyeska* decision, the Act authorizes the court to award lawyers' fees to the prevailing party in a civil rights action, except in cases where it would be unjust.[181] EAJA's coverage of the Act has been somewhat limited by the courts.[182] For example, 42 U.S.C. § 1983 makes parties liable for violations of statutory and constitutional rights under the color of state law. For a party to collect an award of fees against the federal government using the EAJA, the government must have acted under the color of state law within the meaning of Section 1983. This requires the somewhat rarely found occurrence of federal officials conspiring or acting in concert with state officials.[183] The presence of a cooperative federal-state operation is not enough.[184] The court must find some sort of "symbiotic" relationship between the federal and state government.[185]

SECTION 2412(D). Section 2412(d) creates a new basis for the award of fees to a qualified prevailing party in civil actions (other than torts) against the federal government, beyond common law and statutorily created provisions.[186] For example, Section 2412(d) has been one of the primary methods of recovering lawyers' fees against the government under NEPA, which does not contain a fee-shifting provision.[187]

Section 2412(d) requires the court to award lawyers' fees to the prevailing party "unless the court finds that the position of the United States was substantially justified or that special circumstances make an award unjust."[188] The Supreme Court has interpreted the "substantially justified" requirement to mean justified well enough to satisfy a reasonable person, or having a "reasonable basis in law and fact."[189] This analysis can focus on the alleged government wrongdoing giving rise to the lawsuit or the government's litigation position.[190]

Fee awards under Section 2412(d) are calculated with the traditional "lodestar" method, but a $125 per hour cap (with a 1981 base year cost of living adjustment) is imposed on the hourly rate.[191] Most courts apply historic rates for work performed,[192] rather than current rates.[193] The EAJA permits a fee enhancement above the $125 per hour cap for a "special factor, such as the limited availability of qualified attorneys for the proceedings involved."[194]

The Supreme Court, in *Pierce v. Underwood,* severely limited the scope of these special factors[195] and interpreted the "limited availability of qualified attorneys" special factor as requiring a three-step analysis. First, the lawyer must have "some distinctive or specialized skill" such as specialized practice area or knowledge of foreign laws or language.[196] Second, the skill must be necessary for litigating the case.[197] Third, the party must prove that lawyers with such qualifications can only be obtained at rates above the cap.[198] The circuits remain split on what constitutes a sufficiently specialized practice area, with the Ninth Circuit sometimes taking a more liberal stance (notably in environmental cases),[199] and the Fifth Circuit adopting a more rigorous standard.[200] Section 2412(d) also will not support an award to individuals with a net worth of $2 million[201] or organizations with a net worth of $7 million[202] (excluding tax-exempt organizations and cooperative agricultural organizations)[203] and more than 500 employees.[204]

Participation Fee Provisions

Some statutes have provisions authorizing federal agencies acting as tribunals or rule-making bodies to pay legal expenses for individuals or groups participating in administrative proceedings as a method for encouraging public participation.[205] Through this process, the agency is exposed to a broad array of views, including those of low-income individuals, small businesses, consumers, community members, and others who would otherwise be effectively excluded by their lack of legal representation. Requirements vary across statutes, but may include "the significance of the proceedings, the financial hardship of the represented party, the need for representation of all interests, the value of the contribution to the decision-making process, and the limited appropriations available to make such payments."[206] The Toxic Substances Control Act[207] and the Surface Mining Control and Reclamation Act[208] include such a provision.

Recovering Fees Under State Law

Some states have carved out a large exception to the American Rule, adopting a private attorney general theory. The theory allows an award when the action enforces an important public right that affects the public interest.[209] It requires that a significant benefit be conferred on the general public or a large class of persons, that the necessity and financial burden of private enforcement are such as to make the award appropriate, and that such fees should not in the interest of justice be paid out of the recovery, if any.[210]

In California[211] and New York,[212] the legislature adopted a private attorney general statute. In other states, such as Idaho[213] and Wisconsin,[214] it has been judicially fashioned. Most state courts, however, have adopted the Supreme Court's logic in *Alyeska*,[215] rejecting any new, nonstatutory fee-shifting theories. These include Alabama,[216] Connecticut,[217] Illinois,[218] Massachusetts,[219] Oregon,[220] Pennsylvania,[221] Rhode Island,[222] South Dakota,[223] and Washington.[224]

Most state courts have been reluctant to move beyond *Alyeska* without statutory authority. Michigan, for example, does not allow the collection of lawyers' fees except as expressly allowed by statute.[225] In fact, even where the Michigan Environmental Protection Act specifically stated that "[c]osts may be apportioned to the parties if the interests of justice require,"[226] state courts have held that costs do not mean lawyers' fees.[227]

Sources of Legal Representation

In addition to private counsel who rely on lawyers' fees to support themselves, or who take cases on a pro bono basis, low-income individuals and communities can draw upon not-for-profit organizations for representation in environmental justice matters. These organizations also often form co-counsel relationships with or provide expertise to private lawyers. While these organizations all do some environmental justice litigation, to varying degrees many regard environmental justice issues as primarily political in nature, requiring complex strategies for an effective resolution. Most, therefore, take a multifaceted approach to the problems (including environmental and health concerns) of at-risk communities and to expansion of traditional notions of environmental law. They place differing emphases on, among other things, litigation, administrative hearings, legislative processes, mass and community education, politics, and organizing.

The groups use overlapping strategies that result from different starting points, definitions of environmental justice, client bases, and organizational cultures. In a situation of severely limited resources, it is useful to understand the differences among them. (It should be noted at the outset that any attempt at taxonomy risks overgeneralization and oversimplification.) The organizations fit into three rough categories:

1. national, which includes traditional environmental organizations and civil rights organizations;
2. local, which includes legal services organizations and community-based environmental organizations; and
3. law schools.

A resource guide is provided at the end of this chapter to facilitate contacting organizations of interest.

National Organizations

Traditional Environmental Organizations

In 1988 the head of the Sierra Club Defense Fund said "litigation is the most important thing the environmental movement has done in 15 years."[228] Most of the environmental groups that dominate the national scene today began in the 1960s and 1970s to provide legal and scientific expertise on environmental matters.[229] Their focus was on requiring corporate polluters to comply with the law and strengthening the law by forcing the federal governmental to adopt and enforce better statutes and regulations.[230] Although they may have used membership drives as fund-raising devices, their members had little to no say about what matters were accepted or how they were pursued.[231] Decisions were made by staffs of lawyers, scientists, and other experts. The organizations themselves often served as plaintiffs, under the liberal representational standing requirements of the 1970s and 1980s.[232]

Several of these groups added concerns about urban environmental issues to their agendas after the 1978 "Urban Environment Conference" in Detroit, Michigan. The conference, which was co-convened by the Sierra Club and the Urban League, was an effort by civil rights activists to educate environmental organizations about the health issues facing central city residents, in part as a result of their inadequate consideration in the development of environmental statutes such as the CAA and the CWA.[233] Eventually, some of the traditional environmental groups, most notably the Natural Resources Defense Council (NRDC), the Sierra Club Legal Defense Fund (recently renamed the Earth Justice Legal Defense Fund), and the Environmental Defense Fund (EDF) began to participate in environmental justice efforts on the national level and to support specific grassroots efforts.

Reflecting their origins and their structures, the traditional environmental organizations today typically engage in long-term battles with long and wide-ranging consequences. They choose their issues based on concerns of sustainable development, ecosystem management, and overall pollution reduction, rather than solely on the immediate health or economic development needs of particular communities. Not being tied to specific communities, or often even specific regions, they enjoy great flexibility in selecting environmental justice issues according to their own priorities and law reform interests.

Because the traditional environmental groups helped to create the current body of environmental laws and regulations and often have more access to current lawmakers than do civil rights and community-based organizations, they often regard lobbying and legislation as more effective tools in the pursuit of environmental justice than do others, who are generally suspicious of laws, which they see as imposed on marginal communities, and of legal-political processes, from which they feel excluded. Traditional environmental organizations, therefore, often focus their efforts on proper implementation of the legal and regulatory system already in place, rather than extensive systemwide reform of the legal structure. With some exceptions, political empowerment of persons of color and low-income persons in specific communities is rarely their goal.[234]

Most of these organizations focus primarily on the national level, or on local issues with broad implications. They deploy legal expertise, scientific research, and other sophisticated resources in impact litigation, widespread public education, and legislative and rulemaking efforts. They also can be effective at attracting media interest and public support, sometimes through nationwide consumer boycotts.

Civil Rights Organizations

Civil rights organizations consider themselves the pioneers of environmental justice. A 1979 Texas civil rights case often is cited as the forerunner of environmental justice litigation. On behalf of the residents of Houston's Northwood Manor, Linda McKeever Bullard asserted that the City of Houston and Browning Ferris Industries had violated the Equal Protection Clause of the Fourteenth Amendment when they sited an unwanted waste facility in that mostly African American community.[235] The court rejected her legal theory and refused to enjoin the permit for the garbage dump.[236] While the insistence of the federal courts on a showing of specific discriminatory intent has rendered the Equal Protection Clause ineffective as a basis for relief in environmental justice cases,[237] *Bean v. Southwestern Waste Management Corp.* was successful in adding a civil rights dimension to environmental justice lawyering.

Concomitantly, civil rights legal organizations, such as the NAACP Legal Defense and Education Fund, the Center for Constitutional Rights, and the Lawyers Committee for Civil Rights, have taken up issues previously overlooked. They are particularly engaged when siting or development will have a disparate impact on the health of a minority community, and they are interested in obtaining compliance by regulatory agencies and municipalities with laws requiring meaningful public information and participation. Efforts are made through public pressure, negotiation, and, where necessary, litigation. The national civil rights organizations also can provide links between isolated communities by assisting in the creation of coalitions of multiple neighborhood-based groups.[238]

Legal Services Organizations

As part of the "war on poverty," Congress created the Legal Services Corporation (LSC) in 1974[239] to fund community-based civil legal services offices that were to represent welfare recipients and other low-income people. Legal services offices typically represented their clients on housing, labor, education, health, and other concrete issues. As part of this daily fare, legal services offices from the outset brought suits on behalf of farmworkers to ban dangerous pesticides and stop strip mining on behalf of rural communities in Kentucky, and used lead paint contamination as a defense against eviction for nonpayment of rent.[240] Environmental law and ordinary statutory and common law, not civil rights laws, provide the legal basis for most of these actions.

Legal Services has been under attack almost from the outset. Funding of LSC was drastically cut during the Reagan administration and by Congress in the 1990s. Although there always were restrictions on what LSC-funded offices could do,[241] in 1996, Congress expanded these limitations considerably.[242] These law offices no longer can represent their clients, among other things, by "influencing the issuance of any regulation by any federal, state or local agency,"[243] or by "influencing any part of any agency adjudicatory proceeding, if the proceeding concerns the formulation or modification of any policy of general applicability,"[244] or by participating in a class action suit.[245] Obviously, compliance with these restrictions bars these legal services offices from many of the traditional activities used by proponents of environmental justice, including but not limited to some forms of impact litigation.[246]

Some legal services offices have decided to reject LSC funds to avoid the restrictions. Others accept LSC funds and comply with the restrictions by raising environmental justice issues only in individual cases and educating client communities about their rights to a healthy environment. Some have formed legally separate entities with separate personnel and facilities that do not receive LSC money to perform restricted work,[247] including environmental justice representation and legal assistance for community economic development, which many see as integral to the sustainable development required for true economic justice.[248] Both LSC-funded legal services offices and unrestricted providers also have formed alliances with local not-for-profit organizations that have a substantial environmental justice component.

Local environmental justice advocacy organizations must rely on nongovernmental sources for substitutional or supplemental material support for litigation. The main sources are the multistate Interest on Lawyers' Trust Account (IOLTA) system, the private bar, and law schools.[249]

IOLTA, a federally authorized program, was initiated in 1983 and has provided over $100 million annually to providers of legal services to low-income persons and communities. IOLTAs are pooled interest-bearing lawyer fiduciary accounts containing client funds, which are typically too small in amount or will be held for too short a time to generate sufficient interest income to justify placement in a separate account.[250] IOLTA funds have been dwindling during the past several years due to falling interest rates and rising bank service charges. They also have been challenged as an unconstitutional taking of private property. In a five-to-four decision, the Supreme Court applied the "interest follows principal rule" to hold that client funds in IOLTAs are the clients' private property for purposes of the Fifth Amendment Takings Clause.[251] The Court remanded the questions of whether IOLTA funds have been "taken" by the state and the amount of "just compensation," if any, due plaintiffs.[252]

Many legal service providers, LSC-funded and others, form partnerships with private law firms. Particular cases may be referred to a pro bono program at a private firm or co-counseled by both the organization and the firm. Private firms may cover the costs of expert witnesses and other expenses in connection with their pro bono work. However, large corporate firms, which perform the majority of the pro bono work done in large cities, often are reluctant to get involved in environmental justice cases because of client conflicts and/or issue conflicts with their clients. Similarly, a few of the grants given by these firms to fund post-graduate, summer, and part-time work by law students exclude environmental law and environmental justice from the scope of permissible work.

Even with IOLTA funding and bar initiatives, resources for environmental justice litigation by local legal services providers are very limited. They cannot compete with the funds, experts, and other assets that are readily available to their opponents. In approaching environmental justice issues, these organizations, therefore, face a three-pronged deficiency: lack of access to lawyers, to political levers, and to the tools essential for affirmative community development. While they would like to take a systematic approach to achievement of their objectives, too often they are required to engage in triage. Wherever possible, scarce resources are devoted to systemic problems plaguing affected communities. For example, lead paint will be addressed in the arena of environmental justice because of its toxicity, but also as a matter of housing, healthcare, and education.

Large case litigation, including class actions, often is a tool of last resort due to the organizations' belief that litigation is a distraction from the community's efforts, takes much too long, and rarely is worth the requisite time and expense. Instead, they provide a wide variety of legal services including, among other things:

1. individual representation of clients in civil matters that raise environmental justice issues;
2. legal assistance and representation in administrative hearings on siting decisions, environmental impact statements, and other issues;
3. legal education of communities, legal advocates, and future trainers; and
4. transactional work such as negotiation of conditions to siting permits or empowerment zone tax credits for brownfields redevelopment.

In addition to traditional legal representation and assistance, local organizations also frequently provide legal expertise and technical support to community organizing and such political activities as protests and demonstrations, participation in public hearings, campaigning for state and local governmental candidates, door-to-door organizing, voter registration efforts, formation of issue-specific coalitions with purely environmental organizations, and organized imposition of directed economic pressure.

Law Schools

Law school clinics can provide legal services to low-income and otherwise underrepresented individuals and communities while fulfilling their educational mission of educating students to become able practitioners. In live-client clinics, students confront the often messy real problems of real clients by assuming the lawyer role and representing them under the critical eye of a professor-supervisor. The clinics also can serve the law school's research mission by exploring innovative substantive, procedural, and policy solutions to social justice issues. Clinics that have a substantial focus on environmental justice can provide important resources to lawyers, communities, and individuals.[253]

Over twenty-five law schools offer their students experiential learning in environmental law. Most are within this chapter's description of a law school clinic.[254] Others are either externships[255] or seminars that require a paper responsive to a problem posed by a local organization or other "client."[256] Only about seven of these law school programs have significant environmental justice components.[257] Discussion of some of the leading clinics will demonstrate their diversity.

The Tulane Environmental Law Clinic has been so effective at representing some of the state's poorest residents that industry opponents have mobilized the Louisiana Supreme Court and governor to shut it down.[258] Staffed by a professor, three law fellows, and a citizen liaison, the clinic assists individuals and citizen groups with environmental problems in administrative hearings, community education forums, and litigation in federal and state courts. Issues that the clinic has addressed include hazardous wastes, toxic air emissions, scenic river regulations, and rules for managing toxic releases from pesticides.

The clinic has recently drawn national attention to its support of the largely African American Convent, Louisiana, community that opposed issuance of a permit to Shintech Corp. to open a new plastics plant in an area already suffering from substantial petrochemical plant emissions. The Shintech permitting proceeding was selected by the U.S. EPA to be the arena in which it fleshed out its *Interim Guidelines for Investigating Title VI Administrative Complaints* (put on hold due to congressional objections). Shintech subsequently withdrew its permit application pending approval of another site. The clinic's efforts to provide legal services not otherwise available in Louisiana have been challenged by amendments to the Law Student Practice Rule that authorizes law students to appear in court and do other work, which otherwise would constitute the "unauthorized practice of law."[259]

The Environmental Law and Justice Clinic is part of extensive offerings in environmental law at Golden Gate. The clinic provides legal services and education to San Francisco Bay area residents, community groups, and public interest organizations—particularly communities of color and low income. The clinic is staffed by two professor co-directors, a staff lawyer, and a graduate fellow. It works with outside counsel on large or protracted cases and with a team of multidisciplinary professionals who serve as expert consultants. A joint effort by the Golden Gate and Boalt Hall clinics helped defeat the siting of a third power plant in Bayview-Hunters Point, a Southeast San Francisco community that was saturated with toxic waste and hazardous industries.[260]

Georgetown's Institute for Public Representation provides legal representation to unrepresented groups and interests before administrative agencies, courts, and other decision-making bodies. Environmental law is one component of the Institute (others are communications law and policy, and civil rights). The Institute recently broadened its focus on inner city quality of life problems by adding cases that will expose students to traditional environmental/natural resources law. Projects include representing a tribe in southern Virginia that wants to block a drinking water reservoir, assisting citizens in a D.C. suburb in efforts to expand a bridge heavily used by commuters, and working with communities concerned with waste industry and trash transfer facilities.

Rutgers has a large, multifaceted environmental law clinical program that sometimes represents or co-counsels with NRDC, EDF, or other environmental legal organizations on behalf of communities and environmental organizations in New Jersey. The clinic's environmental justice component is part of a program that also includes affordable housing and economic development,[261] and more traditional environmental issues under CWA, RCRA, and other state and federal statutes. In addition to the clinic director, four staff lawyers and a staff scientist supervise the clinic's students. Their work includes large case litigation, administrative proceedings, and policy at the state and national levels. The clinic's clients include the Hackensack Riverkeeper, the Baykeeper, citizens in Newark's Iron Bound district who successfully opposed the location of a sludge treatment plant in their midst, and a community group in Trenton that is fighting the paving over of the only accessible part of the river in town.

The Environmental Justice Clinic at Thurgood Marshall Law School represents or assists about 25 communities in Texas and neighboring states. The clinic's project director, staff attorney, and law students provide a range of legal services including representation at administrative hearings and in federal and state court proceedings. The clinic networks with other public interest groups and research facilities to achieve a multidisciplinary approach to problem solving for low-income and minority communities.

Law schools also are preparing students to engage in environmental justice controversies through lecture courses and seminars. For example, at SUNY Buffalo, environmental law classes focus on the problems of rural communities and include discussions of environmental justice concerns, which it explicitly defines to include class as well as race. Buffalo's Environment and Society Institute is creating a set of web-based materials that address questions of environmental justice, starting with Native American losses of natural resource rights and running through issues such as Love Canal. Environmental law is incorporated in Maryland's Legal Theory and Practice Program, which uses practice experience to teach first- and second-year students to understand and critique legal doctrine. Students represent minority and low-income communities and groups on various matters including environmental justice, in two courses: Legal Theory and Practice: Civil Procedure; and Legal Theory and Practice: Complex Litigation/Environmental Justice.

Resource Directory

There are numerous resources available to lawyers and groups who seek assistance with environmental justice matters. A few of them are listed here.[262]

Legal organizations that do environmental justice work often can provide manuals, pamphlets, briefs, and other publications in addition to legal services. There are two excellent guides to these organizations:

Directory of Pro Bono Legal Service Providers for Environmental Justice, ABA Section of Litigation and Section of Natural Resources, Energy and Environmental Law (in cooperation with the Center on Race, Poverty and the Environment—California Rural Legal Assistance Foundation and the National Conference of Black Lawyers)—a national listing of more than 180 providers, including not-for-profit organizations, law firms, lawyers, Legal Services offices, law school clinics, and others who have pledged not to charge a fee for services to individuals and communities. Available through the ABA Service Center, American Bar Association, 750 N. Lake Shore Drive, Chicago, IL 60611, telephone 800-285-2221. Orders should include the title and its product code (359-7001). $15.00, plus $3.95 shipping and handling.

The People of Color Environmental Groups Directory (1994), created by Robert Bullard—includes a directory of over 300 groups that represent people of color, environmental justice resource groups, and legal resource groups in the United States, Canada, and Mexico. (An updated version of the directory may be forthcoming.) Available through Charles Steward Mott Foundation, 1200 Mott Foundation Building, Flint, MI 45802-11851; 810-766-1766 (publications hotline). The directory also is available on the Internet, at <http://www.igc.org/envjustice>, with a search feature that allows research by a state, city, or keyword.

ONLINE LEGAL RESEARCH. **Ejlinks** (<http://www.halcyon.com/ccej/ejlinks>) provides a comprehensive list of environmental justice sites including information about policy, law education, and demographics.

Westlaw (ENV-TP) and **LEXIS** (ENVIRN) both have databases that cover only environmentally-related legal journals and periodicals. (Note: A search restricted to these databases can miss pertinent materials.)

Congressional Quarterly Washington Alert is a database for federal and state statutes and legislative materials. (Note: Available through Westlaw and LEXIS, but stand-alone version is easier to use.)

Course readers prepared for environmental justice classes at law schools and elsewhere are available at the Environmental Justice Resource Center on the Clark Atlanta University web page, <http://www.ejrc.cau.edu>.

LegalTrac, a CD-ROM version of the *Current Law Index,* indexes over 800 legal journals, periodicals, and newspapers issued since 1980.

Notes

* The author is grateful for the assistance of Columbia Law School students Sean Arian, Laura Carrier, Melissa Epstein, and Arin Greenwood.

1. Sierra Club v. Morton, 405 U.S. 727 (1972).
2. Warth v. Seldin, 422 U.S. 490 (1975). The Supreme Court recently noted that statutory standing may properly be treated before Article III standing. Ortiz v. Fibreboard Corp., __ U.S. __, 119 S. Ct. 2295, 2307 (1999).
3. Standing for suits brought under Title VI and other civil rights provisions is discussed in Chapters 2 and 3.
4. Lujan v. National Wildlife Federation, 497 U.S. 871 (1990) *(Lujan I)*; Lujan v. Defenders of Wildlife, 504 U.S. 555 (1992) (*Lujan II*); Bennett v. Spear, 520 U.S. 154 (1997) *(Bennett)*; and Steel Company v. Citizens for a Better Environment (*CBE*), 523 U.S. 83 (1998).
5. *Lujan I, Lujan II,* and *CBE.*
6. *Bennett.*
7. *Lujan II,* 504 U.S. at 560.
8. *Lujan II,* 504 U.S. at 560.
9. *Lujan II,* 504 U.S. at 560.
10. *Lujan II,* 504 U.S. at 566.
11. *Warth,* 422 U.S. at 498.
12. *Bennett,* 520 U.S. 154.
13. 16 U.S.C. § 1540(g).
14. *Bennett,* 520 U.S. at 156 (emphasis added).
15. Association of Data Processing Service Organizations Inc. v. Camp, 397 U.S. 150 (1970) (*Data Processing).*
16. *Bennett,* 520 U.S. at 163.

17. *Bennett,* 520 U.S. at 156.

18. *Bennett,* 520 U.S. at 177.

19. These include the Clean Air Act, 42 U.S.C. § 604(a) (CAA); the Resource Conservation and Recovery Act, 42 U.S.C. § 6972 (RCRA); the Comprehensive Environmental Response, Compensation and Liability Act, 42 U.S.C. § 9659 (CERCLA); Emergency Planning and Community Right-to-Know Act, 42 U.S.C. § 11,046(a)(1) (EPCRA); the Toxic Substances Control Act, 15 U.S.C. § 2619 (TSCA); and the Safe Drinking Water Act, 42 U.S.C. § 300j-8 (SDWA).

20. 42 U.S.C. § 4321.

21. *Compare* Friends of the Boundary Waters Wilderness v. Dombeck, 164 F.3d 1115 (8th Cir. 1999) *(Dombeck), with* Hurd Urban Development v. Federal Highway Administration, 33 F. Supp. 2d 570 (S.D. Tex. 1998) (*Hurd*).

22. *Dombeck,* 164 F.3d 1115.

23. *Hurd,* 337 Supp. 2d at 573–74.

24. *Lujan II,* 504 U.S. 555.

25. 42 U.S.C. § 7604(a).

26. 42 U.S.C. § 11,046(a)(1).

27. *Lujan II,* 504 U.S. at 560 n.1.

28. *Raines v. Byrd,* 521 U.S. 811 (1997) (injury that runs with political office of member of Congress and not with member personally does not support standing).

29. National Treasury Employees Union v. U.S., 101 F.3d 1423, 1429 (D.C. Cir. 1996).

30. *Lujan II,* 504 U.S. at 564. *See also* Louisiana Envt'l Action Network v. Browner, 87 F.3d 1379 (D.C. Cir. 1996) (standing denied in CAA case challenging an EPA rule before the state's program was implemented even though plaintiffs asserted that they would be injured by breathing the potentially more polluted air that could be caused by the rule's enforcement gap).

31. *Lujan II,* 504 U.S. at 564.

32. Citizens for a Better Environment v. Caterpillar Inc., 30 F. Supp. 2d 1053 (C.D. Ill. 1998) (*Caterpillar).*

33. *See Lujan II,* 504 U.S. at 563, 571.

34. *Id.* at 571.

35. *Id.* at 565–67.

36. *Id.* at 571.

37. 33 U.S.C. § 1365; *see* DuBoise v. U.S. Dept. of Agriculture, 102 F.3d 1273 (1st Cir.), *cert. denied,* 117 S. Ct. 2510 (1997); Sierra Club, Lone Star Chapter v. Cedar Point Oil Co., 73 F.3d 546 (5th Cir.), *cert. denied,* 117 S. Ct. 57 (1996).

38. NRDC v. Texaco Refining and Marketing Co. Inc., 2 F.3d 493 (3d Cir. 1993).

39. PIRG v. Magnesium Elektron, Inc., 123 F.3d 111 (3d Cir. 1997).

40. *Magnesium,* 123 F.3d at 121. The court distinguished from its earlier decision in *Texaco Refining* by noting that there, plaintiffs had alleged environmental injury to the water itself.

41. *Magnesium,* 123 F.3d at 120–21.

42. U.S. v. AVX Corp., 962 F.2d 108, 119 (1st Cir. 1992).

43. Florida Audubon Society v. Bentsen, 94 F.3d 658, 663, *citing Warth,* 422 U.S. at 504.

44. PIRG v. Powell Duffryn Terminals, Inc., 913 F.2d 64, 72 (3d Cir. 1990), *cert. denied,* 498 U.S. 1109 (1991) (liability found based upon numerous violations

of permit, some of which involved toxic substances and many of which included pollutants known to harm marine life).

45. NRDC v. Watkins, 954 F.2d 974, 980 (4th Cir. 1992); *PIRG,* 913 F.3d at 72.

46. Friends of the Earth, Inc. v. Gaston Copper Recycling Corp., 179 F.3d 107 (4th Cir. 1999).

47. *Id.* at __.

48. Township of Belleville v. Federal Transit Administration, 30 F. Supp. 782 (D.N.J. 1998) (holding that plaintiff had met the causation element of Article III standing sufficient to link the agency action to its alleged injury where a project was unlikely to go forward without the grant of federal funds and that the funds were contingent upon an agency's Finding of No Significant Impact determination). However, plaintiff's claim must assert that the injury results from the agency's action or nonaction and not that of third parties. Duquesne Light Co. v. EPA, 166 F.3d 609, 612 (1999) (no standing to sue EPA where EPA lacks authority to disallow the state plan that caused plaintiff's injuries because the injuries are not "traceable" to defendant and a favorable ruling could not redress the harm).

49. Allen v. Wright, 468 U.S. 737, 752 (1984).

50. *CBE,* 523 U.S. 83, 118 S. Ct. 1003 (1998).

51. *CBE,* 523 U.S. 83, 118 S. Ct. at 1019.

52. *CBE,* 523 U.S. 83, 118 S. Ct. at 1019. Defendant's motion for attorney's fees and expenses similarly was dismissed for lack of subject matter jurisdiction. CBE v. The Steel Co., __ F. Supp. __, 1999 WL 412439 (N.D. Ill., June 9, 1999).

53. *CBE,* 523 U.S. 83, 118 S. Ct. at 1019–20.

54. *CBE,* 523 U.S. 83, 118 S. Ct. at 1019–20.

55. *Caterpillar,* 30 F. Supp. 2d at 1053.

56. 149 F.3d 303, 307 (4th Cir. 1998), *cert. granted,* 119 S. Ct. 1111 (1999); 119 S. Ct. 2390 (deferring consideration of mootness to hearing on the merits).

57. The court assumed for purposes of the appeal that plaintiffs had standing to initiate the action and had proven a continuous injury in fact. 149 F.3d at 306 n.3.

58. 149 F.3d at 306–07.

59. 149 F.3d at 307 n.5.

60. 33 U.S.C. § 1365 (emphasis added).

61. 33 U.S.C. § 1365.

62. CERCLA, 42 U.S.C. § 9659(a); RCRA, 42 U.S.C. § 6972(a); CAA, 42 U.S.C. § 7604(a); EPCRA, 42 U.S.C. § 11,046(a)(1); TSCA, 15 U.S.C. § 2619(a); SDWA, 42 U.S.C. § 300j-8(a).

63. 42 U.S.C. § 9601(21).

64. 42 U.S.C. § 6903(15).

65. 42 U.S.C. § 7602(2)(e).

66. 42 U.S.C. § 11,049(7).

67. Director, Office of Workers' Comp. v. Newport News, 514 U.S. 122, 132 (1995). (Director of the Office of Workers' Compensation Programs lacks standing to seek judicial review of Benefits Review Board decisions because claimants are the aggrieved parties, not Director.)

68. 42 U.S.C. § 9659.

69. 42 U.S.C. § 6972.

70. 42 U.S.C. § 7604.

71. 33 U.S.C. § 1365.

72. 15 U.S.C. § 2619.

73. 42 U.S.C. § 11,046.

74. *See* Atlantic States Legal Foundation, Inc. v. Buffalo Envelope, 823 F. Supp. 1065 (W.D.N.Y. 1993).

75. 42 U.S.C.A. § 7604.

76. Gwaltney v. Chesapeake Bay Foundation, Inc., 484 U.S. 49, 50 (1987).

77. *Gwaltney,* 484 U.S. at 50.

78. *See* Russian River Watershed Protection Committee v. City of Santa Rosa, 142 F.3d 1136 (9th Cir. 1998).

79. Natural Resources Defense Council v. Southwest Marine, Inc., 28 F. Supp. 2d 584 (S.D. Cal. 1998).

80. Meghrig v. KFC Western, Inc., 516 U.S. 479 (1996).

81. *CBE,* 523 U.S. 83, 118 S. Ct. 1003.

82. *CBE,* 523 U.S. 83, 118 S. Ct. at 1019–20; *see* discussion on pages 362–363 of this chapter, "Requirement of 'Redressability?' "

83. CERCLA requires that notice be given to the President, to the state in which the alleged violation has occurred, and to the party who has allegedly perpetrated the violation. 42 U.S.C. § 9659.

84. RCRA requires that notice be given to the Administrator. 42 U.S.C. § 6972.

85. CAA requires that such notice be given to the Administrator, to the state in which the alleged violation has occurred, and to the alleged violator. 42 U.S.C. § 7604.

86. CWA requires that notice be given to the Administrator, to the state in which the alleged violation has occurred, and to the alleged violator. 33 U.S.C. § 1365.

87. TSCA requires that notice be given to the Administrator and to the alleged violator. 15 U.S.C. § 2619.

88. EPCRA requires that notice be given to the Administrator, to the state in which the alleged violation has occurred, and to the alleged violator. 42 U.S.C. § 11,046.

89. 493 U.S. 20 (1989).

90. *Id.* at 33.

91. *Id.* at 31, 33.

92. West Dallas Coalition for Environmental Justice v. U.S., 198 WL 892122 (N.D. Tex., December 14, 1998). On defendant's motion for reconsideration, the district court refused to dismiss plaintiff's claims under the APA and the Fifth Amendment of the U.S. Constitution alleging that the EPA's failure to clean up hazardous waste sites constituted environmental racism, because they did not challenge an ongoing EPA removal action and, therefore, were not barred by CERCLA § 113(h). West Dallas Coalition for Environmental Justice v. U.S., 199 WL 102810 (N.D. Tex., Feb. 22, 1999).

93. 42 U.S.C. § 4321.

94. *See, e.g., Lujan I,* 497 U.S. at 872.

95. 5 U.S.C. §§ 702–04. The purpose of the APA is to set forth the procedures by which federal agencies are accountable to the public and their action subject to review by the courts. *See* Franklin v. Massachusetts, 505 U.S. 788, 796 (1992).

96. *See Newport News,* 514 U.S. at 132.

97. 5 U.S.C. § 704 (agency action made reviewable by statute and *final agency action* for which there is no other adequate remedy in a court is subject to

judicial review) (emphasis added); *see also Lujan I,* 497 U.S. at 882 (1990); Wyoming v. Outdoor Council v. U.S. Forest Service, 163 F.3d 43 (D.C. Cir. 1999) ("Wyoming") (plaintiff lacks standing to sue for violation when agency has not yet issued lease to drill for oil and gas but has standing to assert claim that agency had violated its own procedures when those procedures are completed).

98. *Franklin,* 505 U.S. at 797 (1992).

99. *Franklin,* 505 U.S. at 796–97, *quoting* Abbott Laboratories v. Gardner, 387 U.S. 136, 152 (1967).

100. *See, e.g.,* McKart v. U.S., 395 U.S. 185, 192–93 (1969).

101. *See* Susannah T. French, *Judicial Review of the Administrative Record in NEPA Litigation,* 81 CAL. L. REV. 929 (1993).

102. *See* BERNARD SCHWARTZ, ADMINISTRATIVE LAW § 8.37 (3d ed. 1991).

103. *Southwest Alaska Conservation Council,* 697 F.2d 1305, 1309 (9th Cir. 1983) (exhaustion not required where irreparable injury will result unless immediate judicial review is permitted; exceptions to exhaustion doctrine have been made in NEPA cases where drawbacks of application outweigh advantages in a particular case); California v. Bergland, 483 F. Supp. 465, 473 (E.D.C.A. 1980), *aff'd in part and rev'd in part (on other grounds),* 690 F.2d 753 (9th Cir. 1982) (failure to exhaust is "disfavored remedy" in NEPA cases), *citing* City of Suffolk v. Sec'y of Interior, 562 F.2d 1368, 1385 (2d Cir. 1977), *cert. denied,* 434 U.S. 1064 (1978). *But see* Amigos Bravos v. Molycorp, Inc., 1998 WL 792159 (10th Cir., Nov. 13, 1998) (court lacks jurisdiction because plaintiffs failed to pursue FWPCA claims during the permit renewal process).

104. Pennsylvania R. Co. v. Dillon, 335 F.2d 292, 294 (D.C. Cir. 1964), *cert. denied,* 379 U.S. 945 (1964).

105. 5 U.S.C. § 702; *Lujan I,* 497 U.S. at 883. The recognition in *Bennett* of Congress's power to abrogate the prudentially created zone-of-interests requirement by conferring standing upon, for example, "any person" meeting the Article III minimum elements is not applicable here, because the *Lujan I* Court interpreted the "within the meaning of a relevant statute" language of Section 702 as a legislative creation of a zone-of-interests test under the APA.

106. *See, e.g.,* Bucklin, *The Importance of Standing: The Need to Prioritize Standing Review Under the National Environmental Policy Act of 1969,* 3 J.L. & POL'Y 289, 306–07 (1994).

107. *Id.* at 306.

108. *Id.* at 307.

109. *Lujan II,* 504 U.S. at 562–63 (holding aesthetic injury to be "undeniably a cognizable interest for purpose of standing"); *Morton,* 405 U.S. at 734 (recognizing environmental and aesthetic injury as a sufficient basis for standing).

110. *Lujan I,* 497 U.S. at 886 ("We have no doubt that 'recreational use and aesthetic enjoyment' are among the sorts of interests [NEPA was] specifically designed to protect").

111. *Lujan II,* 504 U.S. at 573 n.7 ("The person who has been accorded a procedural right to protect his concrete interests can assert that right without meeting all the normal standards for redressability and immediacy").

112. *Lujan II,* 504 U.S. at 573 n.7 (for example, "one living adjacent to the site for proposed construction of a federally licensed dam has standing to challenge the licensing agency's failure to prepare an environmental impact statement, even though he cannot establish with any certainty that the statement will cause

the license to be withheld or altered, and even though the dam will not be completed for many years").

113. *See, e.g.*, Public Citizen v. U.S. Trade Representative, 782 F. Supp. 139, 141 (D.C. Cir. 1992) (*Public Citizen I*), *aff'd* 970 F.2d 916 (D.C. Cir. 1992); Foundation on Economic Trends v. Lyng, 943 F.2d 79, 83–85 (D.C. Cir. 1991).

114. Hunt v. Washington State Apple Advertising Comm'n, 432 U.S. 333, 343 (1977) (a Commerce Clause case where a memberless commission sought to represent individuals who had "all the indicia of membership").

115. Louisiana Environmental Action Network v. EPA, 172 F.3d 65 (D.C Cir. 1999) (representational standing exists where organization's RCRA claim asserts that EPA rule will increase risk of harm to members living near the landfill site and standing is not defeated by internal conflict of interest with the suit, as long as there is no violation of internal decision-making procedures); *see, e.g.*, Presidio Golf Club v. National Park Service, 155 F.3d 1153, 1159 (9th Cir. 1998).

116. UAW v. Brock, 477 U.S. 274, 289 (1986).

117. Local 751 v. Brown Group, Inc., 517 U.S. 544 (1996) (union had standing to sue on behalf of its members).

118. *Local 751*, 517 U.S. at 555.

119. *Local 751*, 517 U.S. at 555–56.

120. *Caterpillar*, 30 F. Supp. 2d at 1053.

121. *Hunt*, 432 U.S. at 344–45; Friends of the Earth v. Chevron Chemical Co., 129 F.3d 826, 829 (5th Cir. 1997).

122. NOW v. Scheidler, 510 U.S. 249, 255 (1994); *Laidlaw*, 149 F.3d at 306.

123. *AVX*, 962 F.2d at 116 (1st Cir. 1992).

124. *Lujan II*, 504 U.S. at 561–62.

125. *See* Lewis v. Continental Bank Corp., 894 U.S. 472, 477–78 (1990); Comfort Lake v. Dresel Contracting, Inc., 138 F.3d 351, 354 (8th Cir. 1998).

126. *Comfort Lake*, 138 F.3d at 354, *quoting* U.S. v. Concentrated Phosphate Export Ass'n, 393 U.S. 199, 203 (1968).

127. *Comfort Lake*, 138 F.3d at 354.

128. 123 F.3d 111 (3d Cir. 1997). *See also* discussion of *Laidlaw* in this chapter, page 390.

129. *Id.*

130. Parenthetical references are to the page numbers in this chapter that discuss the annotated requirement.

131. *See* Chapter 7, "Public Participation," for discussion of lawyers' fees in connection with SLAPP suits.

132. Alyeska Pipeline v. Wilderness Society, 421 U.S. 240, 257–59 (1975).

133. *Id.* at 257.

134. *Id.* at 258.

135. *Id.* at 258–259.

136. CWA, 33 U.S.C. § 1365(d); TSCA, 15 U.S.C. § 2618(d); SDWA, 42 U.S.C. § 300j-8(d); Noise Control Act, 42 U.S.C. § 4911(d); Energy Policy and Control Act, 42 U.S.C. § 6305(d); RCRA, 42 U.S.C. § 6972(e); CERCLA, 42 U.S.C. § 9659(f).

137. 463 U.S. 680 (1983).

138. *See, e.g.*, City of Burlington v. Dague, 505 U.S. 557 (1992); Texas State Teachers Association v. Garland Independent School District, 489 U.S. 782 (1989); Hensley v. Eckerhart, 461 U.S. 424 (1983).

139. *Texas State Teachers Association*, 489 U.S. at 792 (1989).

140. Reel v. Arkansas, 672 F.2d 693 (8th Cir. 1982).

141. Maher v. Gagne, 448 U.S. 122, 129 (1980).

142. *See, e.g.*, Kasza v. Browner, 133 F.3d 1159, 1175 (9th Cir. 1998); Beard v. Teska, 31 F.3d 942, 951–52 (10th Cir. 1994); LaRouche v. Kezer, 20 F.3d 68, 72 n.4 (2d Cir. 1994). Oregon Environmental Council v. Kunzman, 817 F.2d 484, 497 (9th Cir. 1987); Lampher v. Zagel, 755 F.2d 99, 104 (7th Cir. 1985).

143. Hanrahan v. Hampton, 446 U.S. 754, 758–9 (1980).

144. *Laidlaw*, 149 F.3d at 307. *See* discussion *supra.*

145. FED. R. CIV. P. 54(d)(2)(B).

146. *City of Burlington*, 505 U.S. at 557, 559–61; Blanchard v. Bergeron, 489 U.S. 87, 94 (1989).

147. Sullivan v. Hudson, 490 U.S. 877, 887–90 (1989).

148. Webb v. Board of Education of Dyer County, 471 U.S. 234, 243 (1985).

149. Perotti v. Seiter, 935 F.2d 761, 764 (6th Cir. 1991).

150. Hutto v. Finney, 437 U.S. 678, 693–700 (1978).

151. Pennsylvania v. Delaware Valley Citizens' Council for Clean Air, 478 U.S. 546, 559 (1986).

152. Commissioner, Immigration and Naturalization Service v. Jean, 496 U.S. 154, 161–62 (1990).

153. Grendel's Den, Inc. v. Larkin, 749 F.2d 945, 952–55 (1st Cir. 1984).

154. Kronfeld v. Transworld Airlines, Inc., 129 F.R.D. 598, 602–03 (S.D.N.Y. 1990).

155. New Mexico Citizens for Clean Air v. Espanola Mercantile Company, Inc., 72 F.3d 830, 835 (10th Cir. 1996).

156. Copeland v. Marshall, 641 F.2d 880, 902–03 (D.C. Cir. 1980).

157. *New Mexico Citizens for Clean Air*, 72 F.3d at 835; Action on Smoking and Health v. Civil Aeronautics Board, 724 F.2d 211, 222 (D.C. Cir. 1984).

158. *Webb*, 471 U.S. at 238 n.6.

159. *See, e.g.* New York Association for Retarded Children v. Carey, 711 F.2d 1136, 1146 (2d Cir. 1983).

160. Luciano v. Osten Corp., 109 F.3d 111, 115 (2d Cir. 1997); Sierra Club v. United States Army Corps of Engineers, 776 F.2d 383, 392 (2d Cir. 1985).

161. McCann v. Coughlin, 698 F.2d 112, 130 (2d Cir. 1983); National Association of Concerned Veterans v. Secretary of Defense, 675 F.2d 1319, 1326 (D.C. Cir. 1982).

162. Blum v. Stenson, 465 U.S. 886, 896 n.11 (1984); Hensley v. Eckerhart, 461 U.S. at 430–31 (1983); Johnson v. Georgia Highway Express, Inc., 488 F.2d 714 (5th Cir. 1974); Gregory Sisk, *A Primer on Awards of Attorneys' Fees Against the Federal Government, Arizona State Law Journal*, 25 ARIZ. ST. L.J. 733, 753–54 (1993).

163. Gusman v. Unisys Corp., 986 F.2d 1146, 1149–51 (7th Cir. 1993); Scales v. J.C. Bradford & Co., 925 F.2d 901, 909–10 (6th Cir. 1991); Shakopee Mdewakanton Sioux Community v. City of Prior Lake, 771 F.2d 1153, 1160 (8th Cir. 1985).

164. *City of Burlington*, 505 U.S. at 557.

165. *Delaware Valley*, 478 U.S. 546.

166. Missouri v. Jenkins, 491 U.S. 274, 274–75 (1989).

167. Blum v. Stevens, 465 U.S. 886 (1984).

168. Hensley v. Eckerhart, 461 U.S. at 440.

169. *See, e.g.*, Grant v. Martinez, 973 F.2d 96, 101 (2d Cir. 1992).

170. *Jenkins*, 491 U.S. at 284.

171. 42 U.S.C. § 2000e-5(k).

172. Library of Congress v. Shaw, 478 U.S. 310, 322–23 (1986).

173. U.S. v. City of San Diego, 18 F. Supp. 2d 1090 (S.D. Cal. 1998).

174. 28 U.S.C. § 2412.

175. 28 U.S.C. § 2412(b).

176. 28 U.S.C. § 2412(d).

177. 28 U.S.C. § 2412(b).

178. *See* discussion, *supra,* "Common Law Precedent."

179. Anderson v. United States, 127 F.3d 1190 (9th Cir. 1997); Olson v. Norman, 830 F.2d 811, 822 (8th Cir. 1987); Joe v. United States, 772 F.2d 1535, 1537 (11th Cir. 1985).

180. 42 U.S.C. § 1988(b).

181. Hensley v. Eckerhart, 461 U.S. 424, 429 (1983).

182. Unification Church v. INS, 762 F.2d 1077, 1079–81 (D.C. Cir. 1985); Lauritzen v. Lehman, 736 F.2d 550, 552–59 (9th Cir. 1984).

183. Strickland v. Shalala, 123 F.3d 863, 866 (6th Cir. 1997); Cabrera v. Martin, 973 F.2d 735, 742 (9th Cir. 1992); Kali v. Bowen, 854 F.2d 329, 331 (9th Cir. 1988); Olson v. Norman, 830 F.2d 811, 821 (8th Cir. 1987).

184. *Olson,* 830 F.2d at 821.

185. *Cabrera,* 973 F.2d at 742–43.

186. 28 U.S.C. § 2412(d)(1)(A).

187. *See, e.g.,* City of Carmel v. U.S. Dep't of Transportation, 123 F.3d 1142 (9th Cir. 1997); Louisiana v. Lee, 853 F.2d 1219 (5th Cir. 1988); Sierra Club v. Secretary of the Army, 820 F.2d 513 (1st Cir. 1987); Sierra Club v. U.S. Army Corp of Engineers, 776 F.2d 383 (2d Cir. 1985).

188. 28 U.S.C. § 2412(d)(1)(A) (1996).

189. Pierce v. Underwood, 487 U.S. 552, 565 (1988).

190. Commissioner, Immigration and Naturalization Service v. Jean, 496 U.S. 154 (1990).

191. 28 U.S.C. § 2412(d)(2)(A) (1996); *see* Griffen v. Apfel, 197 WL 766886 (N.D. Ill. 1997).

192. A few courts have held that it may be proper to charge current, rather than historical rates. *See, e.g.,* Garcia v. Schweiker, 829 F.2d 396, 402 (3d Cir. 1987).

193. Marcus v. Shalala, 17 F.3d 1033 (7th Cir. 1994); Perales v. Casillas, 950 F.2d 1066, 1074–77 (5th Cir. 1992); Chiu v. United States, 948 F.2d 711, 719–22 (Fed. Cir. 1991).

194. 28 U.S.C. § 2412(d)(2)(A) (1996).

195. They do not include "the novelty and difficulty of issues," "the undesirability of the case," "the work and ability of counsel," or "the result obtained." 487 U.S. 552, 573 (1988).

196. *Underwood,* 487 U.S. at 572.

197. *Id.*

198. *Id.*

199. National Wildlife Federation v. Federal Energy Regulatory Commission, 870 F.2d 542, 547 (9th Cir. 1989).

200. Perales v. Casillas, 950 F.2d 1066 (5th Cir. 1992).

201. 28 U.S.C. § 2412(d)(2)(B)(i) (1996). *See* Kuhns v. Board of Governors of Fed. Reserve Sys., 930 F.2d 39, 40–42 (D.C. Cir. 1991) (discussing the calculation of an individual's net worth for determination of eligibility under the EAJA).

202. *See* National Association of Manufacturers v. Dep't of Labor, 159 F.3d 597 (D.C. Cir. 1998); Texas Food Indus. Ass'n v. United States Dep't of Agric., 81 F.3d 578, 581 (5th Cir. 1996); Love v. Reilly, 924 F.2d 1492, 1494 (9th Cir. 1991). *But see* National Truck Equip. Ass'n v. National Highway Traffic Safety Admin., 972 F.2d 669 (6th Cir. 1992) (narrow definition of eligible organizations).

203. 28 U.S.C. § 2412(d)(2)(B)(ii). For a full discussion of Congress's intent in determining which organizations would be available for fees, *see National Association of Manufacturers*, 159 F.3d 597.

204. *Id;* Sisk, *supra* note 162, at 798.

205. Sisk, *supra* note 154, at 797–99.

206. *Id.* at 798.

207. 15 U.S.C. § 2605(c)(4)(A), (B).

208. 30 U.S.C. § 1275(e).

209. *See, e.g.*, Serrano v. Priest, 569 P.2d 1303 (Cal. 1977).

210. *See, e.g.* California Private Attorney General Act, CAL. CIV. PROC. CODE, § 1021.5.

211. CAL. CIV. PROC. CODE, § 1021.5.

212. CPLR 8601, which resembles the EAJA more than it does the usual private attorney general provision.

213. Hellar v. Cenarrusa, 682 P.2d 524 (Idaho 1984).

214. Watkins v. Labor & Industry Review Comm'n, 345 N.W.2d 482 (Wis. 1984).

215. *Alyeska*, 421 U.S. at 270–71.

216. Shelby County Comm'n v. Smith, 372 So.2d 1092, 1096–97 (Ala. 1979).

217. Doe v. Heintz, 526 A.2d 1318 (Conn. 1987).

218. Hamer v. Kirk, 356 N.E.2d 524 (Ill. 1976).

219. Pearson v. Board of Health, 525 N.E.2d 400, 403 (Mass. 1988).

220. Cook v. Employment Div., 649 P.2d 594 (Or. 1982).

221. Jones v. Muir, 515 A.2d 855 (Pa. 1986).

222. Providence Journal Co. v. Mason, 359 A.2d 682 (R.I. 1976).

223. Van Emmerik v. Montana Dakota Utils. Co., 332 N.W.2d 279, 284 (S.D. 1983).

224. Blue Sky Advocates v. State, 727 P.2d 644 (Wash. 1986).

225. Platte Lake Improvement Ass'n v. Department of Natural Resources, 554 N.W.2d 342 (Mich. App. 1996).

226. MICH. COMP. LAWS ANN. § 324.1703(3) (West 1997).

227. *See Platte Lake*, 554 N.W.2d 342.

228. Rick Sutherland *quoted in* Tom Turner, *The Legal Eagles*, 10 AMICUS J. 25, 27 (1988).

229. Ann E. Carlson, *Standing for the Environment*, 45 UCLA L. REV. 931, 932 (1998).

230. Carlson, *supra* note 229, at 932–33.

231. Roger Allan Stone, *The Mass Plaintiff: Public Interest Law, Direct Mail Fundraising and the Donor/Client*, 25 COLUM. J.L. & SOC. PROBS. 197, 236 (1992).

232. Carlson, *supra* note 229, at 961–62; Stone, *supra* note 231, at 233–35.

233. Gerald Torres, *Environmental Justice: The Legal Meaning of a Social Movement*, 15 J.L. & COM. 597, 599–600 (1996).

234. A. Dan Tarlock, *City Versus Countryside: Environmental Equity in Context*, 21 FORDHAM URB. L.J. 461, 462, 470–72 (1994); Richard J. Lazarus, *Pursuing*

"Environmental Justice": The Distributional Effects of Environmental Protection, 87 NW. U. L. REV. 787 (1993); Luke W. Cole, *Empowerment as the Key to Environmental Protection: The Need for Environmental Poverty Law*, 19 ECOLOGY L.Q. 619 (1992).

235. Bean v. Southwestern Waste Management Corp., 482 F. Supp. 673 (S.D. Tex. 1979). *See* ROBERT D. BULLARD, DUMPING IN DIXIE: RACE, CLASS AND ENVIRONMENTAL QUALITY 53 (1990) and Chapter 1 *supra*.

236. *Bean*, 482 F. Supp. at 680.

237. *See* Chapter 1 *supra*.

238. For further information, *see* Alice L. Brown & Kevin Lyskowski, *Environmental Justice and Title VIII of the Civil Rights Act of 1968 (The Fair Housing Act)*, 14 VA. ENVT'L. L.J. 741 (1995).

239. Legal Services Corporation Act, 42 U.S.C. § 2996.

240. *See* Luke Cole, *Environmental Justice Litigation: Another Stone in David's Sling*, 21 FORDHAM URB. L.J. 523, 527 (1994); Rivkin, *Doing Environmental Justice in Appalachia: Lawyers at the Grassroots and the Aspiration of Social Change*, 96 W. VA. L. REV. 1109 (1994). This section relies, in part, on conversations with and written materials provided by Marlen Bodden, The Legal Aid Society of New York; Matthew Chachère, staff lawyer at the Northern Manhattan Improvement Corp. and counsel to the New York City Coalition to End Lead Poisoning; Ed Copeland and Sam Sue, who are respectively the General Counsel and former environmental justice lawyer at New York Lawyers for the Public Interest; Mathy V. Stanislaus, co-chair, Minority Environmental Lawyers Assn., Inc. and member, National Environmental Justice Advisory Council–Waste and Facility Siting Subcommittee; and others who preferred to speak without attribution.

241. Notably, legal assistance could not be provided in desegregation cases. 42 U.S.C. § 2996f(b)(9).

242. Omnibus Consolidated Rescissions and Appropriations Act of 1996, Pub. L. No. 104-134, §§ 504, 508, 110 Stat. 1321, 1321-50 to -57, 1321-57 to -58 (1996) (Budget Act). Congress reenacted these restrictions in the Omnibus Consolidated Appropriations Act, 1997, Pub. L. No. 104-208, § 502(a), 110 Stat. 3009, 3009-59 to -60 (1996) and again in 1998, Pub. L. No. 105-119, 111 Stat. 2440, 2440-2510.

243. *See id.* at § 504(a)(3).

244. *See id.* at § 504(a)(3).

245. *See id.* at § 504(a)(7).

246. The Supreme Court has decided not to review the Ninth Circuit's determination that these restrictions are constitutional. Legal Aid Society of Hawaii v. Legal Services Corporation, 145 F.3d 1017 (9th Cir. 1998), *cert. denied*, 119 S. Ct. (1998).

247. The restrictions originally extended to organizations that did not receive LSC funds but were "interrelated" with a recipient of LSC funds as determined by a "control" test. However, LSC revised the regulations governing the relationships between LSC funded entities and others in response to a ruling by the District Court for the District of Hawaii that these restrictions were an unconstitutional deprivation of First Amendment rights. *Legal Aid Society of Hawaii*, 145 F.3d at 1023.

248. *See, e.g.*, Godsil and Freeman, *Jobs, Trees and Autonomy: The Convergence of the Environmental Justice Movement and Community Economic Development*, 5 MD. J. CONTEMP. LEGAL ISSUES 25 (1993/94).

249. Foundation support for litigation, including environmental justice cases, is very limited. *See* Stone *supra* note 229, 212–14.

250. In some states, the program is also referred to as the Interest on Lawyers' Accounts (IOLA). Each state administers its IOLTA program according to its individual rules.

251. Phillips v. Washington Legal Foundation, 524 U.S. 156, 118 S. Ct. 1925 (1998).

252. 118 S. Ct. at 1934.

253. *See generally* Babcock, *Environmental Justice Clinics: Visible Models of Justice,* 14 STAN. ENVT'L. L.J. 3 (1995); *but see* Luke W. Cole, *Forward: A Jeremiad on Environmental Justice and the Law,* 14 STAN. ENVT'L. L.J. ix, xv–xvi (1995) (questioning whether pedagogical goals conflict with good environmental justice practice).

254. University of Baltimore; University of California, Berkeley (Boalt Hall) (suspended due to lack of funds); University of California, Los Angeles (UCLA); University of Colorado, Boulder; University of Denver College of Law; Emory University, Atlanta, Georgia; University of Florida College of Law, Gainesville, Florida; Georgetown University Law Center, District of Columbia; Golden Gate University, San Francisco, California; Northwestern School of Law at Lewis and Clark, Portland, Oregon; University of Michigan, Ann Arbor; Nova Southeastern University, Fort Lauderdale, Florida; University of Oregon, Eugene; Pace University School of Law, White Plains, New York; Rutgers–The State University of New Jersey, Newark, New Jersey; Stanford University, Palo Alto, California; Thurgood Marshall School of Law at Texas Southern University, Houston; Tulane University, New Orleans, Louisiana; Valparaiso University, Valparaiso, Pennsylvania; Vermont Law School, South Royalton, Vermont; Widener University, Harrisburg, Pennsylvania, and Wilmington, Delaware; William and Mary School of Law, Springfield, Virginia; and Yale University, New Haven, Connecticut. (List is based upon e-mail exchanges [November–December 1998] with Professor Robert Kuehn, who administers an e-mail listserve for the directors of law school environmental law clinics and [fall 1998] with the directors of some of the clinics as well as a conference of environmental clinic directors [January 1999]). Other schools are seriously exploring starting a clinic, including Chicago-Kent College of Law, Illinois; Columbia Law School, New York; University of Nevada at Las Vegas; Washington University School of Law, St. Louis, Missouri. (Based upon 1998–99 conversations and e-mail exchanges with professors and administrators involved in these efforts.)

255. University of California, San Francisco (Hastings) has an externship originated by Ralph Abscal and continued by Luke Cole of CRLA; Cleveland–Marshall College of Law, Ohio; New York University School of Law offers externships at the NRDC and the UN.

256. Cleveland–Marshall College of Law, Ohio; University of Maryland School of Law, Baltimore; Northwestern School of Law, Chicago, Illinois; Thomas Cooley Law School, San Diego, California; University of Tennessee College of Law.

257. University of Baltimore, University of California–Berkeley (suspended), Georgetown, Golden Gate, University of Maryland, Rutgers–Newark, Thurgood Marshall, and Tulane. Vermont Law School expects to start an environmental clinic to serve Indians in 1999. The University of Maryland intends to open an Environmental Justice Legal Resources Center, which will provide legal

education in local communities and access to experts necessary for environmental advocacy, in the fall of 1999.

258. *See, e.g.*, Marcia Coyle, *Governor v. Students in $700 M Plant Case,* NAT'L L.J., September 8, 1997; *CBS Evening News* (Oct. 19, 1998); Schmitt, *Louisiana Shackles Law School Clinics,* WALL STREET JOURNAL, Oct. 29, 1998, at Section B, page 1, col. 3.

259. Supreme Court of Louisiana Resolution amending Rule XX, Limited Participation of Law Students in Trial Work, issued June 17, 1998, and amended June 30, 1998, to be effective as of July 1, 1998. Rule XX and the amendments apply to faculty, staff, and students in all of the clinics at Louisiana law schools. After the court denied requests that the new rule be suspended to allow for public input, students, professors, and environmental and civic groups brought an action to enjoin the amendments in federal court. They alleged that the changes violated their First Amendment rights to free association, free speech, and, by extension, academic freedom. The action was dismissed in late July 1990.

260. *See* Schwartz, *Environmental Racism: Using Legal and Social Means to Achieve Environmental Justice,* 12 J. ENVTL. L. & LITIG. 409, 422–429 (1997).

261. Similarly, the University of Baltimore's Community Development Clinic, which represents community groups in "blighted neighborhoods," may address environmental issues in the course of the representations.

262. *See* Shanklin, *Pathfinder: Environmental Justice,* 24 ECOLOGY L.Q. 333 (1997), an excellent compendium of resources (including, inter alia, online sources, CD-ROMs, books, periodicals, videos, and organizations) and research tips. Accessing the Pathfinder online is a particularly useful interactive experience.

CHAPTER 12

Evidentiary Issues: Proving Intent and Effect and Defining the Affected Community

KENNETH J. WARREN

Introduction

The central concern of environmental justice is whether governmental decisions in the environmental arena discriminate against minority or low-income populations.[1] From the vantage point of environmental justice advocates, discrimination occurs not only when an action is taken with an intent to burden members of a minority or low-income community, but also when an action produces a disproportionate adverse effect, even if undertaken with nondiscriminatory motives. Regardless of whether one is a decision maker seeking to act in a fair and racially neutral manner, or a litigant in an environmental justice claim, it is crucial to define the community that a governmental decision potentially impacts. Most commonly, the community is defined spatially by specifying geographic boundaries in proximity to the source or potential source of an environmental hazard.

At first look, it would not seem difficult to define the impacted community. Political boundaries or well-recognized "neighborhoods" provide readily discernable units whose demographics may be compared with those of populations residing outside these boundaries. Unfortunately, upon closer examination, comparing populations residing in geographic units defined by political boundaries may reveal little about the populations actually impacted by a governmental decision. The extent or reach of the burdens of a governmental decision may be difficult to define and rarely coincides precisely with political subdivisions. Moreover, once the actual area of impact is delineated, the fit between geographic boundaries by which available data have been gathered and published and the geographic extent of impact is often inexact. These limitations require persons examining the potential discriminatory effects of an environmental decision to make simplifying assumptions that are subject to challenge.

The delineation of a community's geographic boundaries and the choice of which source of demographic data to use to characterize the population within these boundaries may determine whether one finds a discriminatory impact to exist. Researchers have defined communities and gathered data utilizing political boundaries (for instance, municipality or county), census block, block groups and tracts, zip code areas, concentric circles measuring distance from a facility, and population surveys. This chapter will show that no geographic unit is intrinsically better than another. Rather, the appropriate choice of geographic unit depends upon the fit between the available or obtainable data and the area that the government decision impacts.

Four additional factors are important to an appropriate analysis. First, the question being analyzed must be carefully stated. For example, the selection of an appropriate geographic unit may be influenced by whether one is examining the extent of impacts of a particular facility, or looking at the total impacts of all facilities existing and planned. Second, the extent to which a community should be defined based on racial, ethnic, social, or political ties or common health concerns independent of the particular decision at issue must be resolved. For example, some or all members of a minority community may oppose the siting of a waste facility in their neighborhood even if there is no risk posed to certain of those members. Whether an environmental justice analysis should consider "community" members who are not at risk as nonetheless within the affected community is a controversial decision.

Third, the specific effects to be examined must be closely identified. For example, persons exposed to air emissions from a facility and those exposed to groundwater contaminants from the same facility may constitute distinct populations. Significantly, courts or governmental decision makers do not always find all effects that community members consider detrimental to be cognizable, even though they may be important factors in a political or social debate. Finally, once the affected population is identified, the comparison group must be selected. Defining the group with which the minority or low-income neighborhood is to be compared may affect the outcome of the analysis as much as the initial decision of how to define the minority or low-income community itself.

This chapter concludes that an environmental justice analysis should first identify the geographic area impacted by the governmental action. Thereafter, the appropriate unit of demographic data to be utilized is the one that most closely corresponds to the population actually affected by the government decision in question. The inquiry thus focuses on the "fit" between the available data and the actual area of impact.

Although the area of physical impact may not correspond to preexisting political or neighborhood boundaries, these boundaries should not be ignored in the analysis. Communities defined by common ethnicity, social ties, health conditions, or other factors may have unique susceptibilities or common cultural practices that, if closely examined, would demonstrate that they are in fact impacted. For example, neighborhood members relying on crops grown in community gardens may all be affected by emissions depositing hazardous substances on those gardens. Moreover, where community members perceive any detriment to a portion of their social community as an insult to them, decision makers may choose to consider the broader community's views, even if not legally mandated to do so. Finally, the comparison or "control" group should be established only after defining the affected population to ensure it represents only populations not affected by the decision at issue.

Proving or Disproving Discriminatory Intent

The foundations for environmental justice claims are the Due Process and the Equal Protection clauses of the United States Constitution, which render unlawful government actions that discriminate intentionally on the basis of race. Section 601 of Title VI of the Civil Rights Act of 1964 implements this constitutional mandate by providing:

> No person in the United States shall, on the ground of race, color, or national origin, be excluded from participation in, be denied the benefits of, or be subjected to discrimination under any program or activity receiving federal financial assistance.

42 U.S.C. § 2000(d). *See* Chapter 2 *supra* pages 23–68. Courts have interpreted Title VI to prohibit intentional discrimination on ground of race, color, or national origin.[2]

Court decisions under other civil rights statutes prohibiting actions motivated by an intent to discriminate against a protected class may provide guidance in evaluating environmental justice claims under Title VI. In *McDonnell Douglas Corp. v. Green*,[3] the U.S.

Supreme Court reviewed a claim by a black employee brought under Title VII of the Civil Rights Act of 1964, 42 U.S.C. § 2000e *et seq*. The employee alleged that he had been discharged, and then not rehired, because of his race. The Supreme Court established a three-step analysis for evaluating the claim. Plaintiff bore the initial burden of establishing a prima facie case of racial discrimination by showing that he was a member of a protected group, that he applied for and was qualified for a job for which the employer was seeking applicants, that despite his qualifications he was rejected, and that subsequently the employer continued to seek applicants. Once plaintiff met his initial burden, the burden of production shifted to the employer to articulate a legitimate, nondiscriminatory reason for the employee's rejection. If the employee produces such evidence, the employee must then demonstrate that the employer's stated reason was a pretext. The employee bears the ultimate burden of demonstrating that he has been the victim of intentional discrimination.[4]

McDonnell Douglas's analytical framework has been applied outside the Title VII arena. For example, claims under the Americans with Disabilities Act (ADA), 42 U.S.C. § 1201 *et seq*. and 42 U.S.C. §§ 1981 and 1983, and the Age Discrimination in Employment Act (ADEA), 29 U.S.C. § 621 *et seq*., have all been adjudicated pursuant to the tripartite burden shifting framework of *McDonnell Douglas*.[5]

Although *McDonnell Douglas* does not require an individual who has been subjected to intentional discrimination because of race or other prohibited classification to demonstrate that other members of the same group have suffered similar discrimination, such proof may bolster plaintiff's case. For example, in *Bazemore v. Friday*,[6] the Court (in a concurrence by Brennan, J., in which all justices joined) noted that expert statistical regression evidence to show that blacks were paid less than similarly situated whites was relevant to demonstrating a pattern or practice of racial discrimination under Section 707(a) of the Civil Rights Act of 1964.[7] Likewise, in *Coward, supra*, a regression analysis was found to be an appropriate technique to account for disparities in pay between African American and white employees. The *Coward* court nonetheless excluded the particular analysis proffered because it omitted major factors such as the type of work performed.

Courts have applied the burden-shifting mechanism developed in Title VII cases to claims brought under Title VI.[8] Under this framework, plaintiffs pursuing environmental justice claims under Title VI must demonstrate a prima facie case of discrimination by proving plaintiff's status as a member of a protected class, the existence of an environmental hazard resulting from a governmental decision, plaintiff's exposure to the hazard as a result of the decision, and the availability of alternatives (for instance, other potential sites for a facility) that would not have caused the impact on plaintiff's class. The government agency is then required to come forward with a legitimate, nondiscriminatory purpose for its action. If the government agency produces the requisite evidence, plaintiff must then show that the stated reason was a pretext. Evidence that the action may produce a disproportionate adverse effect on a protected class is relevant to showing pretext. In this context, plaintiff will ordinarily proffer statistical evidence comparing the demographics of the affected community with the demographics of the communities that might have been affected had an alternative governmental decision been made. Indeed, regardless of whether or not a court will follow the *McDonnell Douglas* presumptions, the evidence on each of these factors is nonetheless relevant to an examination of discriminatory intent.

Just as evidence of discriminatory impact is used under the civil rights statutes as one indicator of discriminatory intent, so too has such evidence been considered in claims brought under the Equal Protection Clause. In the rare case, evidence of discriminatory impact may alone constitute sufficient proof of discriminatory intent.[9] Ordinarily, however, impact is only one of many factors to be considered.[10] Under either scenario, however, impact is a relevant consideration and, therefore, the analyses under the discriminatory intent and discriminatory effect standards at a minimum overlap. Accordingly, the definition of the affected "community" is important under both legal standards.

Discriminatory intent, however, will seldom if ever be proven in environmental challenges because racially neutral considerations are usually determinative.[11] For example, a site for a hazardous waste facility is often selected on the basis of proximity to transportation, the geology of the site, the cost of land, and other facially neutral factors. Indeed, in no known environmental justice case has a plaintiff succeeded in proving actual discriminatory intent. Thus, challenges to environmental decision making usually involve allegations that a contemplated government action will produce a discriminatory impact.

Proving or Disproving Discriminatory Effect

Unlike proof of discriminatory intent, proof of discriminatory effect requires demonstration of harm to an impacted group, not simply an impacted individual. The gravamen of the environmental justice analysis is that a minority group is disproportionately burdened. An assessment of an environmental justice disparate impact claim requires identification of the types of impacts occurring, the geographical extent of the impacted area, and the minority composition of the area's residents.

Over the past several years, an executive order and new regulations have brought discriminatory impact claims to the fore. As discussed in Chapter 4, "Executive Order 12,898" (pages 103–39), Federal Actions to Address Environmental Justice in Minority Populations and Low-Income Populations directs federal agencies to ensure that federal actions affecting human health or the environment do not produce discriminatory effects on minority groups defined by race, color, national origin, or income. EPA has similarly required recipients of its funds to avoid actions with discriminatory effects on minority populations.[12] The Supreme Court has upheld the authority of agencies to promulgate regulations incorporating a discriminatory effect standard.[13]

Because discriminatory intent cases consider the existence or absence of discriminatory impact as one of several indicators of whether a discriminatory motive exists, it is not surprising that courts look to the framework of such cases even when the "discriminatory effect" legal standard is to be applied. In *South Bronx Coalition for Clean Air, Inc. v. Conroy,*[14] an environmental justice case challenging the expansion of a waste transfer facility in a minority community, the court enunciated the legal standards governing the case in language typical of cases under Title VI and Title VII of the Civil Rights Act of 1964. The court stated:

> To establish liability under the Title VI regulations disparate impact scheme, a plaintiff must first demonstrate by a preponderance of the evidence that a facially neutral practice has a disproportionate adverse effect on a group protected by Title VI. If the plaintiff makes such a *prima facie* showing, the defendant then must prove that there exists a substantial legitimate justification for the challenged practice in order to avoid liability. If the defendant carries this rebuttal burden, the plaintiff will still prevail if able to show that there exists a comparably effective alternative practice which would result in less disproportionality, or that the defendant's proffered justification is a pretext for discrimination.[15]

The decision of the *South Bronx* court to follow the framework of the Title VII cases when evaluating discriminatory impact under Title VI is consistent with the practice of other courts. For example, in *N.A.A.C.P. v. Medical Center, Inc.,*[16] a Title VI challenge to the planned relocation and reorganization of a medical center, the Court of Appeals for the Third Circuit stressed that "uniformity in the procedural aspects of impact and intent cases is highly desirable." The Third Circuit followed the Title VII framework.[17] The most significant difference in the formulations of Title VII and Title VI cases is the ability of the plaintiff in Title VI discriminatory impact cases to rebut the defendant's justification by proffering evidence of an equally effective alternative that would result in less disproportionality. Demonstrating alternatives (for example, in a siting case showing the existence of suitable alternative locations) will ordinarily be much easier than showing that defendant's reasons were pretexts. It is significant, however, that courts evaluating discriminatory impact claims under Title VI's regulations consider defendant's justifications and examine the existence or absence of alternatives rather than absolutely prohibiting all governmental actions that produce disparate adverse effects.

Although EPA's regulations prohibit governmental actions that produce discriminatory effects, they do not specify the methodology to be used to determine whether a particular action may produce a disproportionate impact. In particular, the regulations do not provide rules for defining the impacted community or selecting sources of demographic information pertinent to that community. EPA has, however, provided some assistance in its guidance documents. To provide a mechanism for citizen enforcement of its regulations in the controversial area of permitting decisions, EPA issued interim guidelines for investigating Title VI complaints regarding permitting decisions.[18] The Interim Guidance directs EPA's Office of Civil Rights (OCR) to investigate whether the challenged permit has a disparate impact on racial or ethnic populations. If a discriminatory impact is found, the permittee is given the opportunity to rebut the finding, to propose a plan for mitigating the disparate impact, or to justify the disparate impact.

EPA recognizes that to prove that an action has produced a disparate impact, the demographic profile of the impacted minority or low-income population must be compared with the demographics of the unaffected areas. Unfortunately, the Interim Guidance pays scant attention to defining the boundaries of the impacted population. The Interim Guidance states that the demographic profile of the impacted population will be determined by OCR on a case-by-case basis. Where more precise information is unavailable, proximity to a facility will be utilized as a "reasonable indicator of where impacts are concentrated." The relevant distance, however, is unspecified. Demographic mapping technology, discussed further in "Research Using Radial Distances from the Source," pages 418–19, is then to be used to determine the demographics of the population residing at a given distance from the facility.

To the extent, as advocated in this chapter, that the proper approach is to define the impacted community by the geographic boundaries of the impacted area, the Interim Guidance does offer some assistance in performing the first step in the analysis—selecting the impacts to be considered. The Interim Guidance expressly identifies the relevant impacts as those cognizable under the permitting program at issue. Even here, however, uncertainties remain. Will EPA consider the cumulative effects of multiple sources of contaminants and multiple routes of exposure? Should the existing health and other characteristics of the affected population be ascertained and considered, or is the environmental inquiry restricted to those effects that the governmental action at issue may cause? Curiously, after specifying that the analysis should focus on the impacts cognizable under the regulatory program, the Interim Guidance then embraces proximity as the governing measure even though, as discussed further below, proximity and impact may not go hand-in-hand. The Interim Guidance should have directed the regulators to determine the populations at risk and then employ the unit of measure that best fits the area actually impacted.

EPA is not as blind to the problems of identifying the appropriate community as the Interim Guidance might suggest. EPA's Final Guidance for Incorporating Environmental Justice Concerns in EPA's NEPA Compliance Analyses (April 1998)[19] advocates a more fact-sensitive approach. This Guidance (also discussed in Chapter 9, "Impact Assessment," pages 256–306) is intended for EPA's internal use in circumstances when EPA's own actions trigger the procedural requirements of the National Environmental Policy Act of 1969[20] (for example, when EPA issues construction grants or permits for new sources).

The Guidance notes that although the term "affected area" is undefined, the focus is on the "area which the proposed project will or may have an effect on."[21] The Guidance also appropriately cautions that data units such as census tracts that in certain cases approximate the demographics of an impacted area may, in other cases, not provide a complete picture of the affected population. A census tract–based analysis, in EPA's view, may not always be appropriate, as it may miss pockets of minority or low-income communities, or be influenced by possible distortions in census population breakdowns.[22]

In addition, a minority population, even if constituting only a small portion of the affected population, may as a result of cultural practices experience disproportionately high adverse effects (for example, subsistence anglers using a stream or tribal members concerned over a sacred site). Thus, under the Guidance, the impacts of agency action must be clearly specified and the customs as well as geographic location of minority community members analyzed. This approach recognizes, at least to some extent, that social and economic ties among community members may increase the likelihood that all members of a social or economic community may be affected by a government activity. The Guidance constitutes a thoughtful general approach that recognizes the complexities of the community definition. The devil is in the details, to which we now turn.

Defining the Concepts of Minority and Low Income

To determine whether the effects of an environmental decision fall disproportionately upon minority or low-income populations, it is necessary to define the attributes that classify a person as "minority" or "low-income." As with other terms in environmental justice analysis, the definition of these categories can be elusive.

Because data gathered by the United States Bureau of the Census often constitute the statistical foundation for examining the environmental justice implications of government decisions, use of the relevant terms in the decennial census constitutes an appropriate starting point. The census establishes separate categories for race and ethnicity and creates numerous subcategories for each racial or ethnic group. Some of the subcategories are based on country of origin (for example, for Asians, Pacific Islanders, and Hispanics), while the Native Americans category is subdivided into tribes.[23] Despite this somewhat inconsistent classification methodology, the decennial census remains the most widely used source of data to characterize populations based on race or ethnicity.

The census classifies people based upon their own designations in survey responses. It thus reflects people's views of the racial and ethnic group with which they identify rather than a scientific or objective categorization. Zimmerman notes that other methods of classification might include blood quantum or physical features.[24] Aside from their unpalatable historical precedents, each of these measures would require development of a scale since these characteristics are not dichotomous variables.[25] Zimmerman further reports the difficulties of obtaining accurate demographic information. In a study of infants who died within a year of birth, race and ethnicity designations on birth certificates and those on death certificates for the same individuals have shown inconsistencies.[26] Inconsistencies in definitions of race and ethnicity are likewise reflected in the variations in measurement and interpretation of health statistics.[27]

Low-income populations are generally defined in relation to poverty thresholds. For example, EPA's NEPA Guidance recommends identifying low-income populations by reference to the annual statistical poverty thresholds from the Bureau of the Census' Current Population Reports, Series P-60 on Income and Poverty.[28] EPA also recommends considering state and regional low-income and poverty definitions. Moreover, EPA cautions that even where community median household income exceeds the poverty line, conditions generally associated with low-income communities may be present (for example, limited access to health care, inadequate infrastructure, and subsistence living) that trigger environmental justice concerns.[29] Thus, while on its face low-income may be more susceptible to quantification than data on race or ethnicity, low income may include more than the literal meaning of the term would suggest. Indeed, some environmental justice advocates would focus the environmental justice inquiry principally on community "stressors" such as poor health as reflected in morbidity and mortality data rather than strictly on race, ethnicity, or income.[30] Although EPA, particularly in its NEPA Guidance, has recognized the relevance of these "stressors" to environmental justice evaluations, in the absence of specific statutory or regulatory authority for viewing them as independent factors, to date they have been subsumed under an examination of race, ethnicity, and income.

Defining the Affected Community

Judicial Decisions Examining Environmental Justice

Courts adjudicating environmental justice claims must confront several complex issues. First, should a community be defined by preexisting social, political, or economic ties, the area of impact of the regulated activity, or some combination? Second, what "impacts" are cognizable? Finally, what data units are most appropriate to use?

For the most part, courts employ a more limited definition of the impacted "community" than is at times utilized when environmental justice claims are debated in the political arena or resolved by exercise of agency discretion. Although persons with social, economic, religious, or political ties may for many purposes constitute a community, and indeed people may be part of different communities for different activities, to date courts have rarely interceded in governmental decision making unless the proposed or effectuated government action causes—or has the potential to cause—a direct, adverse discriminatory impact such as personal injury, property damage, or unequal distribution of government benefits. Those whose injuries are limited to psychological or social impacts will likely be considered outside the affected area, even if they consider themselves to be part of the same community as persons who are damaged in more traditional ways. Conversely, those with few social ties may be defined as "community" members if only because they suffer similar damages.

Courts have diverged to a greater extent on the issue of what data units to employ. Several courts have failed to examine rigorously the fit of the proffered data with the "community" defined by the area of impact. Other courts have better understood the need for close examination of the methodology employed. We now turn to some examples of how courts have defined the relevant community.

In *The South Bronx Coalition for Clean Air, Inc. v. Conroy,*[31] discussed above, groups located in the South Bronx section of New York City claimed that the Long Island Rail Road's agreements restricting the handling and transportation of solid waste on Long Island and the simultaneous expansion of a waste transfer facility at the Harlem River Yard in the South Bronx discriminated against minority residents of the South Bronx. Plaintiffs initially claimed that these decisions were part of a deliberate policy to protect white Long Island residents at the expense of minority residents of the South Bronx, but failed to produce evidence of any such intent. Nevertheless, because of the existence of agency regulations prohibiting governmental actions with a discriminatory impact, the court looked to whether a disparate impact could be shown.

Plaintiffs contended that their community experienced rates of asthma among the highest in the country. They did not, however, attempt to define the boundaries of the community by specific evidence of the distribution of existing asthma cases nor by the geographic extent of potential new or aggravated asthma cases that may be caused by the proposed facility expansion. Instead, emphasizing existing political and neighborhood boundaries, plaintiffs requested the court to take "judicial notice that the South Bronx is poor and minority, while much of Long Island is mostly middle class and white."[32] Essentially, plaintiffs contended that an existing minority community with substandard health conditions should not be subjected to further burden from a new facility.

The court rejected plaintiffs' attempts to define the community by political boundaries or pre-existing health conditions. Rather, the court found legally relevant only the specific health effects that the challenged decision might cause. The court stated:

> The plaintiff's duty to show that a practice has a disproportionate effect by definition requires the plaintiff to demonstrate a causal link between the defendant's challenged practice and the disparate impact identified. Thus, the plaintiff cannot make out a *prima facie* disparate impact claim if the evidence tends to show that even had the defendant not engaged in the challenged practice, the same disparate impact would nonetheless have existed.[33]

By focusing on existing health conditions and requesting the court to take judicial notice of the racial composition of the South Bronx, two factors that might be critically important in a political or regulatory setting, in the court's view plaintiffs had missed the mark. The court required plaintiffs to show the impacts from the regulated activity at issue, not merely the pre-existing health conditions. The court dismissed plaintiffs' complaint because plaintiffs failed to present evidence comparing the South Bronx and Long Island with regard to racial and ethnic composition, volume of waste transferred or generated, costs of waste haulage, environmental effects of waste haulage, or health effects of waste haulage. In the court's view, proof of discriminatory impact required use of appropriate statistical measures to define the impacted community and demonstrate that it had or would suffer disproportionately from the regulated activity at issue.

One of the earliest environmental justice cases, *Bean v. Southwestern Waste Management Corp.*,[34] also illustrates plaintiffs' burden to prove that the regulated activity at issue caused, or would likely cause, discriminatory effects on a specified community. In *Bean*, plaintiffs challenged the decision of the Texas Department of Health to grant a permit to operate a solid waste facility in Houston, Texas. The plaintiffs sought to meet their burden of proving discriminatory intent through statistical evidence that government agencies had disproportionately sited waste facilities in minority areas. Plaintiffs defined the community in broad terms without specific evidence of the harms the facilities caused or the area impacted.

Plaintiffs noted that if Houston were viewed in halves or quadrants, a disproportionate percentage of waste facilities are located in minority areas. Without proof of harms or area of impact, however, the court had no reason to prefer plaintiffs' definition of community over any other. The court chose, perhaps because of the ease of acquiring and utilizing census data, to focus upon the census tract in which the facility was located. Census tract data painted a very different picture than the data grouped by quadrant. The court noted that minority census tracts (that is, census tracts with a minority population greater than the citywide average) had a slightly smaller percentage of solid waste sites than one would proportionately expect.[35]

The court tacitly recognized the limitations of the census tract approach. On the one hand, the census tract area may be larger than the impacted community. The court noted: "It may be that more particularized data would show that even those sites approved in predominately Anglo census tracts were actually located in minority neighborhoods, but the data available here do not show that."[36] Similarly, census tracts may underestimate the size of the affected area. Limited by the discriminatory intent standard governing cases before promulgation of the current regulations, the court stated: "Without some proof that the sites affect an area much larger than the census tract in which they are in, it is very hard to conclude that the placing of a site in the target area evidences purposeful racial discrimination." *Id.* at 678. By failing to identify the area that the siting decision impacted, plaintiffs lost the battle, and thus the war, over the appropriate geographic unit to employ.

In *East Bibb Twiggs Neighborhood Association v. Macon-Bibb County Planning & Zoning Comm'n*,[37] a case also decided under the then-applicable discriminatory intent standard, the court found that plaintiffs had shown a discriminatory impact on a community defined by political boundaries. Plaintiffs challenged the siting of a private landfill in a census tract containing a majority black population. The court noted that the only other approved landfill was located in a census tract containing a majority white population. This existing landfill, however, was located within a county commission district whose black residents comprised approximately 70 percent of the total population. Thus, understanding the area of impact—census tract, county, or other area—would be critical to the outcome. Without much analysis, however, the court concluded that "the Commission's decision to approve the landfill for location in census tract no. 133.02 does of necessity impact to a somewhat larger degree upon the majority population therein." Nevertheless, in the absence of additional evidence of discriminatory intent, the court concluded that the Commission's decision "fails to establish a clear pattern of racially motivated decisions."[38]

The *East Bibb* court's suggestion that discriminatory impact had been shown through a focus on county commission districts is in contrast to the *Bean* court's unwillingness to look beyond census tract boundaries to the "quadrants" that plaintiffs advocated. Perhaps because the *East Bibb* court found the discriminatory impact data to be, alone or in combination with other facts, insufficient to establish discriminatory intent, it did not analyze the unit of analysis more closely. Had it done so, perhaps it would have looked to the geographic extent of the impacts to determine whether the census tract, the county commission district, or some other unit best fit the area of harm.

R.I.S.E., Inc. v. Kay[39] presents the most disciplined analysis of community definition in an environmental justice opinion. In *R.I.S.E.*, residents brought a claim under the Equal Protection Clause challenging the development of a regional landfill in their community. The plaintiffs identified five potential harms from the facility:

1. increased noise, dust, or odor;
2. decline in property values;
3. interference with worship activities;
4. enhanced need for major road improvements; and
5. blighting of an historic church and community.

The court focused on whether these impacts fell disproportionately on minorities.[40]

The court found that the population within one-half mile of the proposed landfill was 64 percent black (39 individuals). Of the population along the impacted roads, twenty-one of the twenty-six families were black. Three other landfills had been sited in the county, all of which were located in 90 percent–100 percent black areas defined in terms of distance from the site (the court used varying measures ranging from one-half mile to two miles). A fourth landfill straddling two counties was located in a predominantly white area.

Based upon the enumeration of harms, the identification of the affected community and the selection of the demographic data best reflecting the population affected by each of the alleged harms, the court concluded that "the placement of landfills in King and Queen County from 1969 to the present has had a disproportionate impact on black residents."[41] Like the *East Bibb* court, however, the *R.I.S.E.* court concluded that when evidence of other factors relevant to a determination of discriminatory intent was considered, discriminatory intent had not been shown.

R.I.S.E. presents an example of a flexible or multifaceted approach to defining community, with consideration given to direct areas of impact (for instance, families along the roads), potential areas of impact delineated by proximity to the site (at varying distances), and political boundaries (counties). It is noteworthy for its specification of the harms considered, and its flexible identification of the affected population based on the particular harm examined. The ultimate conclusion that, despite the existence of an disparate impact, discriminatory intent was not proven illustrates the importance of the new discriminatory impact standard to the environmental justice debate.

R.I.S.E.'s multifaceted approach invites further attention to the inquiry about how the community should be defined and data selected. We turn next to the question of how social scientists have defined community.

Definitions of Affected Community Utilized in Environmental Justice Studies

Although the few judicial decisions in the environmental arena have focused primarily on geographic areas of impact rather than preexisting social relationships within neighborhoods, environmental justice proponents often claim to speak for communities suffering from substandard health or other adverse conditions, not simply the population likely impacted directly by the government decision under review.

Because communities exist independently of the actual or potential effects of a governmental decision under scrutiny, one approach to environmental justice could be to analyze whether the effects of a governmental decision fall disproportionately on the population of a community defined independently of the decision at issue. This approach would trigger a multifaceted analysis of the ties that bind people into a social unit.

One commentator, John J. Fahsbender, has surveyed the social science literature to discern the various approaches of social scientists to community definition.[42] Fahsbender notes that the neighborhood can be defined sociologically by the perceptions or patches of common life of the residents interacting within a physical space.[43] In addition, political boundaries can be utilized to differentiate among neighborhoods. These boundaries may be established by existing political demarcations or use of major physical features such as roadways and railroad tracks.[44] Neighborhoods can also be defined by statistical areas for which the Bureau of the Census maintains data. In particular, "census tracts are designed to constitute homogeneous units with shared population characteristics, economic status and living conditions."[45] Finally, Fahsbender notes that economists have addressed the geographic extent of a neighborhood by examining the economic effects of an undesirable land use, particularly as it may affect housing prices.[46] This approach, however, is not instructive since ordinarily, for ease of analysis, economists will utilize "statistical neighborhoods": that is, multiple and varying units based upon the boundaries utilized by whoever compiled the statistics.[47] Nevertheless, it highlights the need either to tailor any analysis to the units on which data has been gathered or to obtain new data more accurately reflecting the geographic area considered.

How social scientists and other researchers have applied these varying definitions of community, and how they have selected and utilized available statistics and demographic information, may be instructive to those prosecuting or defending an environmental justice claim.

One of the first studies of environmental justice examined whether solid waste sites in Houston, Texas, were disproportionately located in the black community.[48] Dr. Bullard found that African Americans comprised only 28 percent of Houston's population, but that six of the city's eight municipal incinerators and fifteen of its seventeen landfills were located in predominantly black areas. Based upon this evidence, Dr. Bullard concluded that facility-siting decisions in Houston disproportionately affected minorities. The Bullard study was designed as expert evidence to be used in the *Bean* proceeding discussed above. While apparently based on census tract data from various years, the study does not specify the source of the data used,[49] and thus its methodology and evidentiary reliability are not easily determined.

Subsequent studies are ordinarily classified by the geographic unit selected for analysis. The studies also demonstrate that the unit selected may affect the outcome of the analysis.

Countywide Analysis

Political units may constitute appropriate geographic boundaries if the minority populations are evenly distributed throughout each unit. A study conducted in South Carolina using a series of different spatial scales found a negative association on the county level between percentage of black and low-income populations and the number of hazardous waste facilities.[50] Waste facilities were identified through databases of hazardous waste treatment, storage, and disposal facilities (TSDs), Toxic Release Inventory (TRI) sites, and sites on the National Priority List or Comprehensive Environmental Response, Compensation, and Liability Information System (CERCLIS) for eventual remediation.

The use of data from large geographic units presents a risk that pockets of minorities residing close to a facility will be overlooked. Cutter, et al. tested the extent of the aggregation error[51] in their countywide analysis by examining the data for smaller geographic units such as census tracts. When the community was defined by the geographic extent of the census tract in which the facilities were located, the negative correlation between race, income, and the number of facilities disappeared. The authors attributed the difference in results between counties and smaller units on the heterogeneity of South Carolina's counties; that is, minority and low-income populations were not uniformly distributed throughout the county studied. The study reported that the social indicators best able to differentiate the populations surrounding the facilities from the comparison population were not racial factors, but rather percentage of residents employed in labor occupations, percentage of residents with college degrees, and percentage employed in manufacturing occupations.

ZIP Code Area Analysis

Two of the principal studies analyzing environmental justice claims on a nationwide basis have utilized ZIP code areas to define the potentially affected populations. In 1983, the General Accounting Office (GAO) issued a report analyzing ZIP code level population data for areas surrounding four hazardous waste landfills located in the Southeast (EPA Region IV).[52] The GAO utilized census data reported by ZIP code areas to derive demographic information concerning populations residing within designated ZIP codes. ZIP code areas surrounding three of the four facilities studied contained 52 percent, 66 percent, and 90 percent African Americans. African Americans comprised no more than 30 percent of the populations of the states in which the landfills were located. Based upon these statistics, the researchers concluded that African Americans in the Southeast bore a disproportionate burden of hazardous waste facilities. The GAO report also found that the regions hosting hazardous waste facilities were disproportionately poor.

The Commission for Racial Justice, United Church of Christ (UCC) conducted the most frequently cited empirical study on environmental justice.[53] The UCC performed a national study comparing the demographic profiles of communities with commercial hazardous waste treatment, storage, and disposal facilities (TSDFs) to those without TSDFs.[54] Like the GAO, the UCC chose to utilize ZIP codes to define the communities in which the TSDFs had been located.

The UCC analyzed three population parameters of the community selected—percentage of minority population, mean household income, and mean value of owner-occupied housing. The researchers selected the first of these parameters to determine whether TSDFs were disproportionately located in minority communities. The other two parameters were designed to permit the same analysis with respect to the economic status of the community residents.

The UCC found that the percentage of minorities in communities hosting one hazardous waste facility was twice that of communities with no facilities. Additionally, the percentage of minority residents of areas with more than one TSDF was three times greater than that of communities without such facilities. These findings led the UCC to conclude that minority communities were disproportionately burdened with hazardous waste facilities. The UCC also found that socioeconomic status correlated with the location of hazardous waste facilities, but was less predictive of facility location than race.

In 1994, the UCC in conjunction with the Center for Policy Alternatives and the National Association for the Advancement of Colored People examined how the composition of communities hosting hazardous waste sites had changed from the date of the 1987 report.[55] According to the 1994 report, between 1980 and 1993 the percentage of minority residents living in ZIP code areas with hazardous waste facilities had increased from 25 percent to almost 31 percent. The data further revealed that racial minorities were 47 percent more likely than whites to live near a TSDF. The study concluded that increased awareness of environmental justice issues had not inured to the benefit of minority and low-income communities.

Rather, "the racial gap between communities with commercial toxic wastes sites and those without has grown significantly."[56]

One drawback of setting community boundaries using ZIP codes is that the population residing in the same ZIP code as the TSDF may not be coextensive with the population actually affected by the facility. Because some facilities were located near the boundary of a ZIP code area, residents located in a neighboring ZIP code area may have suffered greater risks or harms from the facility. This is particularly true where the cross-boundary population is in the direction that a potential air emission or effluent plume is likely to move. In addition, the geographic and population size of ZIP code areas varies significantly, reducing the usefulness of a ZIP code analysis for comparison purposes. Thus, the unverified assumptions underlying the GAO and UCC studies left open the possibility that use of a different geographic unit to define the affected population might produce a different statistical result.

Census Tract Level of Analysis

The availability of a broad range of data, including race and income, through responses to surveys conducted by the United States Bureau of the Census on a census tract, block group, and block level has led certain researchers to utilize census areas to define the relevant population. Responses to surveys that the Bureau of the Census conducts each decade provide a widely utilized data base of race, income, and other characteristics of the populations. The Bureau of the Census reports the data by political units, by ZIP code, and by statistical units of varying size including census tracts, block groups, and blocks. Census tracts and their components are relatively small geographical units that can be consolidated or grouped to fit the area that the facility impacts.

Analysis by census tracts has several advantages over analysis utilizing ZIP code areas. Census tracts vary less in population size than do ZIP code areas, thereby decreasing the need for standardization or other weighting techniques to make the data between units comparable. Additionally, because the geographic boundaries of census tracts are defined in part by community members, census tracts more closely resemble homogeneous neighborhoods than do ZIP code areas, which are defined largely for the convenience of the Postal Service.

In 1994, researchers at the Social and Demographic Research Institute of the University of Massachusetts (SADRI) utilized census data to challenge the findings of the UCC report.[57] SADRI focused upon the demographics of the populations residing in the same census tract as the TSDF rather than the same ZIP code area. The SADRI reasoned that in the absence of evidence of the aerial distribution of harm from a TSDF, it was appropriate to begin with the smallest available units. SADRI found no statistically significant differences in the racial composition of census tracts with hazardous waste facilities compared to those without. The disagreement between these findings and those of the UCC study appeared to be explained by the SADRI's focus on census tracts rather than ZIP code areas as the UCC had done.

To test the validity of this explanation, the SADRI study examined how the demographics varied with the size of the methodological unit employed. SADRI aggregated census tract data to construct an area comprised of all census tracts with at least 50 percent of their areas falling within a 2.5-mile radius of the center of the census tract hosting each facility. The data revealed that the percentage of minority and low-income residents was significantly higher than in surrounding tracts and increased with distance from the facility.[58] Thus, the choice of data based on the smaller census tract rather than the larger ZIP code area appeared to influence the result. The SADRI did not, however, have information concerning the impact from the facilities that might counsel in favor of using one unit or another.[59]

The SADRI study has been the subject of intense criticism. For example, in an article comparing the methodologies employed in the SADRI study and the UCC study, Paul Mohai has found several advantages in the UCC approach.[60] Mohai noted that census tracts are not inherently better than larger units unless they are appropriately aggregated to approximate the areas impacted by the environmentally hazardous and locally undesirable land use. If a unit is too large, it may include minorities unaffected by the facility, thereby inflating the alleged concentration of minorities. Alternatively, a unit that exceeds the boundaries of the area actually impacted may include numerous nonminorities unaffected by the facility, thereby diluting the concentration of minorities. If the unit utilized is too small, the analysis may underestimate the affected minority population by excluding from the affected community certain impacted minority members. The risk of census tract boundaries circumscribing too limited an area is particularly significant in cities where, because of high concentrations of populations, census tracts become smaller in geographic size.

Mohai's analysis of the SADRI data surprisingly found that the difference in results between the UCC and SADRI study was not, as the SADRI study suggested, principally caused by the difference in the unit of analysis (that is, ZIP code data versus census tract data), but rather was better explained by the difference in the comparison population utilized in the two studies. The UCC study compared the demographics of the population residing in the same ZIP code area as the facility with the demographics of the population of all ZIP codes without a waste facility. The SADRI study, in contrast, eliminated, for purposes of its comparison, all population tracts outside of Census Bureau–defined "standard metropolitan statistical areas" regardless of whether these tracts contained a hazardous waste facility. The SADRI also did not include in its comparison group tracts in standard metropolitan statistical areas if those tracts had no facility.

The SADRI excluded certain tracts on the basis of the availability of census data[61] and their conclusion that those tracts were unsuitable to host a facility.[62] To be sure, comparison with only "suitable" communities (that is, communities in which the siting of a waste facility was legally and technically feasible) would better reveal the significance of minority concentration and income upon the site selection process than would a comparison to all areas. Nevertheless, the accuracy of the SADRI study depends in part on whether the sites excluded from the comparison group on the basis that they were unsuitable hosts for a TSDF facility could not in fact serve as hosts. Mohai notes, however, that many areas excluded from the SADRI comparison group could in fact host a waste facility.[63] By excluding these census tracts, the SADRI increased the percentage of minorities in the comparison population to 23 percent from the 12 percent minority population utilized in the UCC study. In Mohai's view, the higher minority population in the SADRI comparison group may have served to reduce improperly the disparity in minority population between the host and comparison groups.[64]

Mohai concludes that the SADRI study and the UCC study actually analyzed different questions. Because the SADRI study excluded sites outside of metropolitan areas and sites within metropolitan areas without TSDFs, the SADRI examined only whether, in metropolitan areas already containing TSDFs, additional TSDFs were most likely to be placed in minority or low-income communities. The UCC, on the other hand, principally examined the initial choice of location for a hazardous waste facility. Thus, the results of these studies may not conflict but may address different issues.

The 1996 Cutter, Holm & Clark study discussed above lends support for the conclusion that differences in the methodological unit utilized may alter the result. The study initially performed a countywide analysis. Utilizing this unit, the study concluded that a disproportionate number of hazardous waste facilities were located in counties comprised mostly of white, middle-income residents, not minority or low-income residents. The authors then shifted to census tract data to focus more narrowly on portions of the South Carolina counties previously examined. At the census tract level, the authors found no association between race and the siting of hazardous waste facilities. However, a slight correlation was found between low-median household income and the location of hazardous waste facilities: the median income for census tracts containing a TSDF was 5 percent lower than that of tracts without a facility.

One of the questions unresolved in the various studies discussed above was whether disparities in waste facility siting reflected the initial placement of waste facilities in minority communities or whether the siting of a hazardous waste facility caused an increase in the percentage of minority and low-income residents in the years following the facility's commencement of operation.[65] EPA funded a study to resolve that question (the Been study).[66] The Been study utilized census tracts as its unit of analysis because of the availability of historic as well as current data from the Bureau of the Census on a census tract level, expense considerations, and the fact that census tracts are delineated by local committees to reflect neighborhoods.[67]

The Been study concluded that facilities that began operating between 1970 and 1990 were not placed in areas that were disproportionately African American or poor. They were, however, disproportionately sited in Hispanic communities.[68] The Been study further found little evidence that siting was followed by substantial changes in the socioeconomic status or the racial or ethic composition of the host community.[69] The study acknowledged that areas currently surrounding TSDFs are disproportionately populated by African Americans and Hispanics. In light of the finding that siting decisions between 1970 and 1990 did not reflect this disparity, the authors suggested that disparate pre-1970 siting decisions may continue to be reflected in current disparities.[70]

The Been study's conclusions concerning the absence of discriminatory siting decisions on a nationwide basis since 1970 may have policy implications for addressing environmental justice concerns. To the extent that equality of results is a goal of environmental justice advocates, this may be achievable only by undoing the effects of siting decisions made long in the past rather than focusing principally on current decisions. This study does not, however, refute the possibility that any particular siting decision might produce a disproportionate impact upon a community. Accordingly, while as a general matter the Been study suggests that past 1970 siting decisions are not producing unfair results, it offers little guidance how a challenge to an individual siting decision should be adjudicated. Moreover, while because of its national scope, the Been study researchers felt constrained to rely on census tract data, more limited inquiries directed to a particular facility may have greater flexibility in defining the community and obtaining data.

Research Using Radial Distances from the Source

More recent studies have attempted to define the impacted community by including all residents within a given radius of a facility in the affected population. In 1992, Mohai & Bryant published a report that evaluated the distribution of sixteen hazardous waste facilities in three counties surrounding Detroit.[71] The study found the racial composition of residents within one mile of a TSDF to be 48 percent black. That number declined to 39 percent for the one-mile to 1.5-mile range and to 18 percent for the population living more than 1.5 miles from a facility.

Significantly, rather than relying on census data, the researchers conducted a probability sample survey of residents to determine demographic data. They then mapped the location of residents and the distance of the residents from the facilities. This technique avoided the inaccuracies inherent in fitting boundaries utilized for statistical reports with the actual demographics of the area of concern.

In 1995, the GAO published a study employing radial distances from nonhazardous municipal landfills.[72] The GAO study found that racial minorities and low-income residents were not overrepresented in the areas surrounding such facilities. More specifically, for 73 percent of metropolitan landfills and 63 percent of nonmetropolitan landfills, the percentage of minorities residing outside a one-mile radius of the facility but within the county was higher than the percentage of the minorities living within one mile of the facility. In addition, for 54 percent of the metropolitan landfills and 52 percent of the nonmetropolitan landfills, median household incomes were higher for those people living within one mile of the facility than for the residents of the remainder of the county. The authors emphasized that the conclusions of this study are limited in scope to nonhazardous waste facilities.

Modern computerized databases in combination with Government Information System (GIS) software enable users to specify and map the geographic area at a specified geographic radius from a facility.[73] One advantage of the GIS approach over other approaches is that it allows the population to be measured by distance from the facility itself rather than from the central point in a ZIP code area or census tract area. The latter technique may result in some residents being included in the targeted population who actually reside more than the specified distance from the facility while other residents at less than the specified distance or at greater risk are not included.

Although the mapping process can be done accurately, and the census tract data can be integrated, the problem of reconciling the prescribed geographic area with the available census tract data remains. To correspond to the area designated, census data units may have to be intersected and only a portion of the units used. Researchers employing this technique generally assume that populations are homogeneously distributed in the intersected unit. As one researcher has pointed out, this assumption may be particularly inappropriate when assessing minority or low-income populations since these subgroups tend to be concentrated in discrete areas rather than equally distributed throughout a census tract.[74]

The use of GIS accentuates one fundamental methodological concern—defining the distance from the facility that will be utilized. With the more simplistic technique of using a ZIP code area or a census tract in which the host facility is located, researchers often simply assume that the chosen unit represents the appropriate geographic area. Even in those instances, however, more sophisticated research techniques will call for the aggregation of ZIP code or census tract areas to the extent that the impact goes beyond a single tract or area. With GIS, the problem cannot be sidestepped at all. The researcher needs to select one or multiple distances from the facility to utilize in the analysis. This brings us to the evidentiary issues intrinsic to proving or disproving the existence and extent of impacts from the facility and their disproportionate effect.

Evidentiary Issues

Determining the Impact from the Facility

In examining whether a governmental decision such as issuance of a permit for the siting of a facility will adversely impact a minority or low-income population, it is important to assess and specify what the impacts may be and the geographic extent of the population impacted. The impacts from a facility may be varied, and thus evidence employing a single geographic unit of analysis may in many instances not suffice to characterize the potential problem fully.[75]

Potential health impacts are frequently a principal concern of community residents faced with the siting of a hazardous waste facility or the enforcement of environmental laws within their community. These in turn depend upon potential emissions from the facility including the toxicity of the chemicals emitted, the routes of exposure to the community (for instance, air, water), the quantity and concentration of chemicals potentially released, and the opportunities for community members to come into contact with those chemicals.[76] These types of issues are generally evaluated by toxicologists and other scientists trained to perform risk assessments.

Although whether a formal risk assessment process is warranted when analyzing environmental justice claims can be debated, the methodologies utilized in the risk assessment process may provide a foundation for introducing evidence on risk. In its Final Guidance for Incorporating Environmental Justice Concerns in EPA's NEPA Compliance Analyses (April 1998), EPA has recognized the applicability of risk assessment techniques to environmental justice evaluations. EPA notes that "risk assessments should be conducted to determine exposure pathways and potential effects."[77]

Indeed, the methodology for defining a population affected by emissions from a facility for environmental justice purposes is similar to defining the population in need of medical monitoring for purposes of a tort claim seeking medical monitoring relief.[78] To succeed in a medical monitoring claim, plaintiff must demonstrate, among other things, that he or she has been exposed to levels of a hazardous substance above background levels and that a prescribed medical monitoring regime different from that normally recommended for the population as a whole is reasonably necessary.[79] Similarly, in an environmental justice claim, EPA is of the view that, to be "adverse," an exposure to a regulated pollutant must exceed existing health-based standards.[80] In the absence of a health-based standard, a risk-based standard may be used.[81] Thus, evidence of the magnitude of exposure or potential exposure and the risk posed by such exposure may be required elements of plaintiff's claim. The use of risk assessments in the environmental justice context is discussed in Chapter 10, "Risk Assessment, Susceptible Subpopulations, and Environmental Justice," pages 307–356.

Identifying the populations potentially injured[82] by a governmental decision requires evidence of the substances emitted and their toxicities, concentrations, and routes of exposure. For example, the effects of a toxic chemical release to the air will require knowledge of exposure-related issues such as the chemical's concentration, the timing and magnitude of the release, wind patterns, and other factors, as well as toxicity issues such as any known dose-response relationship. Releases to surface or groundwater will affect populations differently depending upon the concentration and timing of the releases, the dilution of those releases, and the uses to which water resources are put (for example, whether the releases affect drinking water, recreational streams, or subsistence fishing grounds). Where a facility produces both air and water emissions, different populations may be affected by each.

Although defining the geographic area in which human health impacts may be suffered is itself complicated, to the extent that a broad range of risks is cognizable the analysis is further confounded by the existence of other potential detriments.[83] For example, ecological receptors as well as humans may suffer from facility emissions.

An ecological risk assessment may be the best way of determining these impacts. Harms from trucks and other modes of transportation (whether by emissions, spills, noise, or otherwise) may be a further injury that the community suffers. The location of truck routes, however, may not correspond with the areas impacted by other emissions. In addition, property values may be affected based upon community perception in ways different from the distribution of actual risk.[84] Finally, demographic data may not be easily obtainable for the geographic area delineated. In light of these complexities, it would seem impossible to reduce the selection of the geographic unit to an exact science. Because the distribution of risks ascertained through risk assessment techniques or otherwise will not always be fully ascertainable or correspond with any particular unit of analysis, the choice of methodologies among those attempting to prove or disprove risk or impact and the appropriateness of any particular definition of community will vary on a case-by-case basis. The court is likely to find that the geographic unit that best "fits" the affected population is in that instance the appropriate unit to use.

Use of Social Science Methodologies

From an evidentiary standpoint, the existence of established social science methodologies may enable a party in the context of a judicial proceeding to offer expert evidence founded on any of these approaches. Under Fed. R. Evid. 702 and the U.S. Supreme Court's opinion in *Daubert v. Merrell Dow Pharmaceuticals, Inc.*,[85] expert evidence following scientifically valid methodologies passes the reliability prong of the admissibility analysis. The Supreme Court has applied *Daubert*'s test to expert testimony that is not scientifically based.[86] It is likely that adherence to established social science methodologies will be deemed reliable.

Daubert also requires the expert testimony to be sufficiently tied to the facts of a case. *Id.* at 591. This consideration, described as one of "fit," requires a valid connection between the proffered testimony and the issue to be determined. Challenges to evidence in an environmental justice case are likely to focus on the element of "fit" at least as much as on the reliability of the methodology. Although sociological, political, or statistical boundaries may define a community for various purposes, they may not correspond well to the inquiry under the current state of the law. For example, while members of a sociological community may experience or perceive a psychological injury from an environmental decision, absent a risk of physical, economic, or perhaps aesthetic harm to a person or his/her environment, the impact may not be a legally cognizable harm. Similarly, such individual may not have standing to sue because he or she has suffered no injury in fact or any remedy would not redress a harm to such person. *See, e.g., Steel Company v. Citizens for a Better Environment*, 118 S. Ct. 1003 (1998); *Lujan v. Defenders of Wildlife*, 504 U.S. 555, 560 (1992). To the extent social scientists have defined various "neighborhoods" for purposes different from the court's inquiry, their fit with the relevant inquiry, and hence their admissibility, are in doubt.[87]

Use of Statistical Measures

The complexity of defining the community and comparison group, obtaining the necessary data, and then selecting and properly applying appropriate statistical measures is likely to engender admissibility battles. In the Title VII context, statistical evidence to prove or disprove discrimination has routinely been proffered and challenged.

For example, in *Forehand v. Florida State Hospital at Chattahoochee*,[88] black state hospital workers claimed that they had suffered discrimination in job promotion because of their race. Both plaintiffs and defendants proffered statistical comparisons utilizing different definitions of the qualified labor market. The court examined the utilized populations carefully, holding that the labor market to which those in plaintiff's desired job position are compared should reflect the pool of workers from which promotion to that position are granted, not a pool containing workers ineligible for that position or excluding workers who are eligible. The court also recognized that if the eligible pool had been skewed by other discriminatory practices, a different analysis might be required.[89]

Similarly, in *Bazemore, supra*, the Supreme Court reviewed a statistical regression analysis used as part of the plaintiff's evidence of discriminatory intent. Defendant objected to the admissibility of the analysis on the grounds that certain variables had been omitted. The Court (per Brennan, J., concurring with all members joining) noted that the failure to include variables will ordinarily affect the regression analysis's probativeness, not its admissibility.[90] The Court further suggested that the standard for admissibility may be relaxed where the analysis is proffered as only one of many pieces of evidence. The Court noted that plaintiff need only prove its case by a preponderance of the evidence, not scientific certainty.

As noted above, *Daubert*[91] establishes as a threshold test of scientific reliability for the admissibility of expert scientific opinion. Courts have yet to resolve, in light of *Daubert*, what threshold test governs the admissibility of statistical evidence in a civil rights case. Compare *Coward, supra* note 5 (excluding evidence that the court deemed unreliable because of omitting variables) with *Bevan, supra* note 5 (allowing statistical charts to be used as circumstantial evidence of pretext even where such evidence would not be competent to show intentional discrimination).

As the cases discussed in "Judicial Decisions Examining Environmental Justice," pages 406–10, illustrate, in the environmental justice arena the few judicial decisions to date have employed relatively simplistic comparisons. For example, in *Bean, supra* note 34 the court for the most part simply recited the percentage of minorities residing in the census tracts in which the facilities were located. For purposes of a citywide comparison, the court defined "minority census tracts" as those with a percentage of minority residents greater than the minority population of Houston as a whole.

Researchers conducting nationwide studies have used far more sophisticated techniques. For example, the Been study employed multivariate techniques to isolate the importance of variables, such as race and class, that are highly correlated with each other.[92] It is likely that environmental justice cases will consist in part of battles of statistical experts who may disagree over the appropriate statistical tests, the delineation of the impacted community, and the appropriate demographic data to use.

Notes

The author thanks Felicity E. Rowe, a student at the University of Pennsylvania School of Law, for her assistance in the preparation of this chapter.

1. The term "government" is used throughout this chapter as a shorthand for federal, state, and local governmental units and recipients of federal funds.

2. *See, e.g.*, Alexander v. Choate, 469 U.S. 287, 293 (1985). *See* Chapter 2 *supra*.

3. 411 U.S. 792 (1973).

4. *See* St. Mary's Honor Center v. Hicks, 509 U.S. 502, 508 (1993).

5. *See, e.g.*, Coward v. ADT Security Systems, Inc., 140 F. 3d 271 (D.C. Cir. 1998) (§ 1981 claim for intentional wage discrimination); Annis v. County of Westchester, 136 F.3d 239 (2d Cir. 1998) (§ 1983 claim); Stratton v. Department for the Aging, 132 F.3d 869 (2d Cir. 1997) (ADEA claim); Bevan v. Honeywell, Inc., 118 F.3d 603 (8th Cir. 1997) (ADEA claim); Olson v. General Electric Astrospace, 101 F.3d 947 (3d Cir. 1996) (ADA claim).

6. 478 U.S. 385 (1986).

7. 42 U.S.C. § 2000e-6(a).

8. *See, e.g.*, Elston v. Talladega County Board of Education, 997 F.2d 1394, 1407 (11th Cir. 1993) (following Title VII precedent despite acknowledging the applicability of the discriminatory effects standard under agency regulations implementing Title VI). *See also* discussion in "Proving or Disproving Discriminatory Effect," pages 401–405.

9. *See, e.g.*, Yick Wo v. Hopkins, 118 U.S. 356 (1886).

10. *See, e.g.*, Village of Arlington Heights v. Metropolitan Housing Development Corp., 429 U.S. 252 (1977).

11. *See, e.g.*, Chester Residents for Quality Living v. Seif, 132 F.3d 925 (3d Cir. 1997), *vacated*, 119 S. Ct. 22 (1998), in which plaintiffs declined an opportunity to amend their complaint to allege that the Pennsylvania Department of Environmental Protection's decision to approve the siting of a waste facility in the predominantly black community of Chester was racially motivated.

12. 40 C.F.R. §§ 7.80(a) and 7.35(b), promulgated under section 602 of Title VI of the Civil Rights Act of 1964, 42 U.S.C. § 2000d-1.

13. Alexander v. Choate, *supra* note 2, at 292–94 (1985).

14. 20 F. Supp. 2d 565 (S.D.N.Y. 1998).

15. *Id.* at 572 quoting *Elston,* supra note 8, at 1407.

16. 657 F.2d 1322, 336 (3d Cir. 1981) (en banc).

17. *See also* Georgia State Conf. of Branches of NAACP v. State of Georgia, 775 F.2d 1403 (11th Cir. 1985) (following *Medical Center*); *Elston, supra* note 8; Young by and through Young v. Montgomery County, 922 F. Supp. 544, 549–50 (M.D. Ala. 1996).

18. EPA, INTERIM GUIDANCE FOR INVESTIGATING TITLE VI ADMINISTRATIVE COMPLAINTS CHALLENGING PERMITS, <http://es.epa.gov/oeca/oej/titlevi.html> [hereinafter EPA, INTERIM GUIDANCE].

19. <http://es.epa.gov/oeca/ofa/ejepa.html>.

20. 42 U.S.C. § 4321 to § 4370(c).

21. EPA NEPA GUIDANCE, *supra* note 19 § 2.i.

22. *Id.*

23. For a discussion of the varying use of racial and ethnic classifications, see Rae Zimmerman, *Issues of Classification in Environmental Equity: How We Manage Is How We Measure*, 21 FORDHAM URB. L.J. 633, 635–644 (1994).

24. *Id.* at 639.

25. *Id.*

26. *Id.* at 640–41, citing Robert A. Hahn et al., *Inconsistencies in Coding of Race and Ethnicity Between Birth and Death in U.S. Infants*, 267 JAMA 259 (1992).

27. *Id.* at 643–44.

28. EPA, NEPA GUIDANCE, *supra* note 19 § 2.1.2.

29. *Id.*

30. For example, the Public Interest Law Center of Philadelphia, which prosecuted the *Chester Residents* case, *supra* note 11, on behalf of the plaintiffs has proposed to EPA's Environmental Justice Implementation Advisory Committee an environmental justice protocol that focuses upon whether the existing public health of residents of an affected area is substandard based upon government health department records.

31. 20 F. Supp. 2d 565 (S.D.N.Y. 1998).

32. *Id.* at 573 (*citing* Plaintiffs' Reply Memorandum of Law).

33. *Id.*, quoting *Elston, supra* note 8, at 1407 (citation omitted). The Environmental Appeals Board has likewise limited the proper scope of a demographic study to the geographic area in which pollutants were disbursed. See, e.g., In re Environmental Disposal Systems, Inc., 1998 EPA App. LEXIS 105 (October 15, 1998) rejecting challenge to EPA Region 5's use of a two-mile radius from pro-

posed injection wells). The board has, however, upheld consideration of a broad range of potential effects. *Id.*

34. 482 F. Supp. 673 (S.D. Tex. 1979), *aff'd without op.*, 782 F.2d 1038 (5th Cir. 1986).

35. *Id.* at 679.

36. *Id.* at 677.

37. 706 F. Supp. 880 (M.D. Ga. 1989).

38. *Id.* at 885 (footnote omitted).

39. 768 F. Supp. 1144 (E.D. Va. 1991), *aff'd without opinion*, 977 F.2d 573 (4th Cir. 1992).

40. Plaintiff *R.I.S.E.* was an organization consisting of black and white members, none of whom initially challenged the siting on grounds of disparate impact. The focus of the case changed to an environmental justice claim when that claim appeared more likely to succeed. The *R.I.S.E.* court's analysis is supportive of those advocating consideration of a wide range of potential harms.

41. *Id.* at 1149.

42. John J. Fahsbender, *An Analytical Approach to Defining the Affected Neighborhood in the Environmental Justice Context*, 5 N.Y.U. ENVTL. L.J. 120 (1996).

43. *Id.* at 127.

44. *Id.* at 128.

45. *Id.* at 131, *citing* BUREAU OF THE CENSUS, 1990 CENSUS OF POPULATION AND HOUSING, TECHNICAL DOCUMENTATION, SUMMARY Tape File 3, Appendix A, A.5 (May 1992).

46. *Id.* at 137.

47. *Id.*

48. R. Bullard, *Solid Waste Sites and the Houston Black Community*, 53 SOC. INQUIRY 273–88 (1983).

49. For a discussion of the possible sources of Bullard's data, and their possible deficiencies, see Vicki Been, *Locally Undesirable Land Uses in Minority Neighborhoods: Disproportionate Siting or Market Dynamics?*, 103 YALE L.J. 1383, 1396 n.50 & 1400–04 (1994). Been further notes that Bullard may have analyzed only some of the landfill sites in the geographic area selected, thereby diminishing the accuracy of his findings. *Id.* at n.69.

50. S. L. Cutter, et al., *The Role of Geographic Scale in Monitoring Environmental Justice*, RISK ANALYSIS 16, 517–26 (1996).

51. The use of large geographic units creates "aggregation" errors by grouping neighborhoods with high minority composition together with neighborhoods of low minority composition.

52. GENERAL ACCOUNTING OFFICE, SITING OF HAZARDOUS WASTE LANDFILLS AND THEIR CORRELATION WITH RACIAL AND ECONOMIC STATUS OF SURROUNDING COMMUNITIES (Washington, D.C.: U.S. Government Printing Office, 1983).

53. UNITED CHURCH OF CHRIST COMMISSION FOR RACIAL JUSTICE AND PUBLIC DATA ACCESS, INC., TOXIC WASTES AND RACE IN THE UNITED STATES: A NATIONAL REPORT ON THE RACIAL AND SOCIOECONOMIC CHARACTERISTICS OF COMMUNITIES WITH HAZARDOUS WASTE SITES (New York, NY: United Church of Christ Commission for Racial Justice, 1987).

54. The UCC report did not include among the TSDFs, analyzed Superfund sites, certain closed facilities, or on-site, noncommercial hazardous waste facilities.

55. Benjamin Goldman & L. Fitton, TOXIC WASTE AND RACE REVISITED: AN UPDATE OF THE 1987 REPORT ON THE RACIAL AND SOCIOECONOMIC CHARACTERISTICS OF COMMUNITIES WITH HAZARDOUS WASTE SITES (New York, NY: United Church of Christ Commission for Racial Justice, 1994).

56. *Id.* at Executive Summary (unpaginated).

57. D. L. Anderton et al., *Hazardous Waste Facilities: Environmental Equity Issues in Metropolitan Areas,* 18 EVALUATION REV. 123–40 (1994) [hereinafter SADRI].

58. *Id.* at 131–33.

59. The SADRI study also found that as compared to tracts with no TSDFs, census tracts hosting TSDFs contained a lower percentage of employed males but a higher percentage employed in industrial firms as compared to tracts with no TSDF. This suggests that TSDFs are disproportionately located in certain industrial areas.

60. Paul Mohai, *The Demographics of Dumping Revisited: Examining the Impact of Alternate Methodologies in Environmental Justice Research,* 14 VA. ENVTL. L.J. 615 (1995).

61. SADRI, *supra* note 57, at 128.

62. Mohai, *supra* note 60, at 624, *citing* Anderson et al., *Environmental Equity: Evaluating TSDF Siting over the Past Two Decades,* WASTE AGE, Jul. 1994 at 83.

63. Mohai, *supra* note 60, at 625.

64. The 1994 UCC update, *supra* note 55, also emphasized that SADRI's exclusion of certain geographic areas from the comparison group inflated the percentage of minorities in the control group. The 1994 update further noted that SADRI's failure to consider Asians and Native Americans and the failure to examine the significance of possible white enclaves within census tracts further undermines the SADRI's conclusions. *Id.* at 14–15.

65. As discussed above, the UCC study suggested that hazardous waste facilities were disproportionately located in minority communities. The 1994 follow-up to that study, also discussed above, found that the disparities in minority composition had increased since the initial research was performed.

66. V. Been & F. Gupta, *Coming to the Nuisance or Going to the Barrios? A Longitudinal Analysis of Environmental Justice Claims,* 24 ECOLOGY L. Q. 1 (1997) [hereinafter Been study].

67. *Id.* at 11. The Been study also noted the need to control for differences in density, a shortcoming of the SADRI study. *Id.* at 33.

68. *Id.* at 8.

69. *Id.* at 9.

70. *Id.* at 32.

71. Paul Mohai & Bunyan Bryant, *Environmental Racism: Reviewing the Evidence, in* RACE AND THE INCIDENCE OF ENVIRONMENTAL HAZARDS 163–76 (B. Bryant & P. Mohai eds., Boulder, Colo.: Westview, 1992).

72. General Accounting Office, HAZARDOUS AND NONHAZARDOUS WASTE: DEMOGRAPHICS OF PEOPLE LIVING NEAR WASTE FACILITIES (Washington, D.C.: U.S. Government Printing Office, 1995).

73. GIS Systems such as ARCINFO and Landview II can create maps utilizing digitized geographic boundary files such as the Census Bureau's TIGER/Line '92 files to display locational information. This technology allows

various information, such as proposed facility locations, and demographic information such as income level, ethnicity, race, and population density to be displayed on a single map. Digitized information from EPA or other government agencies can likewise be included on the map. EPA is currently utilizing this technique in several of its offices.

74. *See* Rae Zimmerman, *supra* note 23.

75. *See* Mohai, *supra* note 60, at 638–41. Mohai notes the advantages of assessing the presence of multiple environmental hazards in communities rather than examining the distribution of hazards one by one in isolation. This approach is consistent with the recommendations of the PRESIDENTIAL/CONGRESSIONAL COMMISSION ON RISK ASSESSMENT AND RISK MANAGEMENT, RISK ASSESSMENT AND RISK MANAGEMENT IN REGULATORY DECISION MAKING (1997). *See also* Been study, *supra* note 66, at 12 ("A better unit of analysis would be one based on the actual distribution of the risks of the facility, which would further depend upon the types of substances the facility handled, wind patterns, the hydrology and geology of the site, and transportation routes to the facility, among other factors"); *R.I.S.E.*, *supra* note 39 (utilizing varying definitions of the impacted area).

76. *See* Cutter et al., *supra* note 50, at 525 (suggesting that focusing on potential exposures to hazardous substances from facilities and not simply the presence or absence of the facility in the community constitutes the most important consideration for environmental justice research).

77. EPA NEPA GUIDANCE, *supra* note 19, § 5.2.

78. *See, e.g.*, Redland Soccer Club, Inc. v. Department of the Army, 548 Pa. 178, 696 A.2d 137 (1997).

79. *Id.*

80. *See* INVESTIGATIVE REPORT FOR TITLE VI ADMINISTRATIVE COMPLAINT FILE No. 5R-98-R5 (Select Steel Complaint).

81. *Id.*

82. As discussed above, not all social or economic injuries are ordinarily legally cognizable. EPA has recognized this concept by providing in the NEPA context that economic or social effects alone do not trigger an environmental impact statement. 40 C.F.R. § 1508.14. EPA notes, however, that it may be appropriate to take social or economic impacts into account in the risk management or remedy stage if other factors have exceeded the threshold for environmental justice concerns. Environmental justice advocates contend that Title VI allows consideration of a broad range of impacts.

83. For a discussion of the spectrum of views on defining the scope of cognizable impacts, see Report of the Title VI Implementation Advisory Committee (March 1, 1999) at 55–56.

84. Environmental decisions such as the issuance of a permit to operate a waste facility may have property devaluation or other "blighting" economic effects. While social ties and other bonds among community members may play a role in defining the extent of economic harm, the boundaries of economic harm may not be coextensive with the social neighborhood. *See also* Michael B. Gerrard, *Territoriality, Risk Perception, and Counterproductive Legal Structures: The Case of Waste Facility Siting*, 27 ENVT'L. L. 1017 (1997).

85. 509 U.S. 579 (1993).

86. Kumho Tire Co. Ltd. v. Carmichael, 119 S. Ct. 1167 (1999).

87. Proponents of utilizing a definition of community based upon a community's self-perception or social cohesion may gain support from cases outside the environmental justice arena. *See, e.g.*, King v. Harris, 464 F. Supp. 827 (E.D. N.Y. 1979), *aff'd sub nom.* King v. Faymor Devel. Co., 614 F.2d 1288 (2d Cir. 1979), *vacated and remanded*, 446 U.S. 905 (1980) (challenging the Department of Housing and Urban Development's decision to site a public housing project in a racially integrated neighborhood). In a case like *King*, however, the community's self-perception may define the extent and nature of the effect of the project on racial integration: that is, perceptions influence who will relocate in reaction to the siting decision. To date, in analyzing environmental justice claims that allege adverse impacts on health or ecology, courts have not focused on residents' perceptions of the injury but rather on more objective measurements. The extent to which a court finds a community's self-perception to be relevant to the legally cognizable harms at issue may influence the court's willingness to define a community by criteria related to those perceptions.

88. 89 F.3d 1562, 1571–75 (11th Cir. 1996).

89. *Id.* at 1574.

90. 478 U.S. at 400.

91. 509 U.S. 579 (1993).

92. Been study, *supra* note 66, at 33–34.

CHAPTER 13

Issues of Legal Ethics in Environmental Justice Matters

IRMA S. RUSSELL

Introduction

This chapter considers questions of legal ethics and morality that lawyers encounter in representing industrial clients, individuals, and public interest groups in environmental justice matters.[1] Like risk management tools, its purpose is to assist lawyers in anticipating and analyzing difficult ethical issues. Such proactive analysis is intended to help lawyers make reasoned decisions when they face ethical issues in the demanding context of the practice of law.

Environmental justice matters present a blend of legal ethics, policy, morality, and public interest concerns that go to the heart of the lawyer's role in the law. In the area of standing, for example, the interests of the named plaintiffs in an environmental justice action may diverge from the interests of the overall class or group. What are the lawyer's obligations when the defendant offers the named plaintiffs a lump sum settlement to drop the suit (and thereby defeat standing)? Is it ethical for the lawyer to set up meetings to educate and solicit residents as plaintiffs for an environmental justice case? May the lawyer for a corporate defendant disclose environmental problems that she discovers while working on an environmental justice case? What should a lawyer do when she becomes convinced that her client's position, though colorable, is morally or legally wrong? Is it appropriate for defendant companies in a geographic area or industry group to create a joint defense group, gaining the right to the privilege of confidentiality for intragroup communications? May a defendant's lawyer ethically threaten the plaintiffs with a Strategic Lawsuit Against Public Participation (SLAPP suit)?

This chapter explores these and other ethical questions, primarily by examining the American Bar Association (ABA) Model Rules of Professional Conduct (Model Rules or ABA Model Rules), the ABA Model Code of Professional Responsibility (Model Code), the American Law Institute's Restatement of the Law Governing Lawyers, and related decisional law. The current statement of the rules of ethics according to the ABA is provided in the Model Rules of Professional Conduct, adopted in 1983 by the association and subsequently passed as law in approximately 80 percent of United States jurisdictions.[2] The Model Rules superseded the ABA Model Code, which the association had adopted in 1969.[3] Nevertheless, approximately 20 percent of the jurisdictions have retained the Model Code as the basis for their rules of ethics.[4] An ABA commission, The Ethics 2000 Commission, is currently studying and revising the Model Rules of Professional Conduct. The commission recently proposed changes to some of the Rules, including Model Rule 1.6 on confidentiality, Rule 4.2 on contacts with represented persons, and Rule 1.7 on conflicts of interest. The commission's work is an example of the continual study and evaluation necessary to ensure that the rules of ethics of the profession evolve as the practice of law in society changes.

In considering questions of legal ethics, the primary focus of a lawyer's analysis should be the rules of his or her jurisdiction. Each jurisdiction establishes the ethical rules related to the practice of law in that jurisdiction, drawing on varying statements of ethical principles such as the Model Rules, the Model Code, or the ALI Restatement.

The Model Rules acknowledge that the framework they construct does not always exhaust the moral and ethical questions presented in the practice of law. Indeed, the Model Rules suggest that the lawyer refer to his or her conscience. The Preamble to the Model Rules states that ethical "issues must be resolved through the exercise of sensitive professional and moral judgment guided by the basic principles underlying the Rules."[5] Likewise, Rule 2.1 acknowledges the role of morality in the lawyer's role as advisor, authorizing the lawyer to "refer not only to law but to other considerations such as moral, economic, social and political factors" in advising clients.[6] In line with this guidance, this chapter considers general ethical precepts outside the text of the Rules.[7]

The second part of this chapter examines the lawyer-client relationship, exploring issues relating to client identification, duration of representation, solicitation, and settlement. The next part notes the fundamental responsibilities of lawyers to their clients, the institutions of justice and third parties, including the lawyer's duty of truthfulness and candor. The fourth section deals with conflicts that can arise in representation, including joint representation, former client conflicts, and conflicts relating to former government lawyers. The fifth part surveys problems surrounding the duty of confidentiality in environmental justice matters, including the possibility that substantive law[8] may trump the lawyer's duty of confidentiality in some situations. It also considers the lawyer's duty of confidentiality when a lawyer withdraws from representation. The sixth part considers the use of the media and nonlawyer professionals in environmental justice proceedings. And the last part describes one controversial adjunct action, SLAPP suits, and considers whether such suits are an abuse of process.

The Lawyer-Client Relationship

Client Status

It is axiomatic that the duties of the lawyer spring from the lawyer-client relationship. The lawyer's responsibilities toward an individual or entity exist because that person or entity is properly classified as a client. Thus, a threshold issue in many ethics questions is whether a particular party has the status of a client. Client status is a matter of state common law, although legislatures could also control the issue by statute. The Scope section of the Rules acknowledges this fact: "for purposes of determining the lawyer's authority and responsibility, principles of substantive law external to these Rules determine whether a client-lawyer relationship exists."[9] Thus, in disputed matters, the court decides whether an individual is a client of a particular lawyer, applying the substantive law of the jurisdiction.

Ordinarily, a lawyer and client will enter an express agreement concerning legal services. The best practice is for the lawyer and clients to enter a written agreement, making clear the fact and scope of the representation, specifying the duties of each party, and resolving potential ambiguities.[10] Some jurisdictions require a written agreement for certain types of representation. In any case, a written agreement is preferable because it provides certainty about the representation.

Even when the lawyer and client do not enter a written or express oral agreement, a contractual relationship of lawyer-client may arise. A party may present evidence of the conduct of the parties that arguably gave rise to the relationship to establish the lawyer-client relationship.[11] Courts address this issue on a case-by-case basis rather than relying on categorical rules. Neither payment of a fee nor a written agreement is necessary to establish the existence of a lawyer-client relationship.[12] For example, in *Procanik v. Cillo*,[13] the court held that, despite the absence of a written agreement of employment, the relationship of lawyer and client existed because the client manifested reliance "on the lawyer in his professional capacity."[14] By contrast, in *State v. Hansen*,[15] the Supreme Court of Washington held that a phone conversation between a defendant and a lawyer did not create a lawyer-client relationship although the caller was seeking legal advice.[16]

The issue of who is a client can present difficulties in environmental justice cases. For example, when a lawyer files an environmental justice complaint, does the lawyer represent the full group of people adversely affected by the action complained of or only the named plaintiffs? Should the named plaintiffs be seen as the primary client and the group as the derivative client?[17] For example, an action seeking an injunction or other protective restrictions on construction of a hazardous waste facility presents an indivisible claim of the entire group. By contrast, existing conditions or past harms may create individual claims for many potential plaintiffs that these parties decide to group together for purposes of litigation or other action.[18]

The written representation agreement or retention agreement should clearly answer the question of who is the client for purposes of the representation. A detailed joint representation agreement may prevent later disputes relating to who may set the objectives of the representation and direct the lawyer's efforts. Although the lawyer may have personal inclinations about whether he or she represents the group or individuals in the group, the lawyer's representation must comport with the agreement. A related issue may arise in bellwether actions when the group chooses representative plaintiffs with the assistance of the lawyer. A bellwether trial is one intended to resolve claims or issues common to a large number of claimants.[19] The purpose of such a trial is to establish causation or liability or to resolve other issues common to the group.[20] But these benefits cannot be achieved if the named plaintiffs are not representative of the group.[21]

Solicitation of Clients

State regulations and ethical rules speak to the issue of lawyer solicitation of clients, setting guidelines, and limits on solicitation. Such controls are constrained by First Amendment protection afforded commercial speech. State regulations controlling lawyer advertising often require that lawyers retain copies of advertisements they publish for a specified period of time.[22] Some states require more, mandating that lawyers file copies of ads with the state disciplinary authorities.[23] Model Rule 7.1 prohibits false or misleading communications concerning lawyer services. Model Rule 7.2 makes clear that lawyers may advertise their services through a broad range of media.

> [A] lawyer may advertise services through public media, such as a telephone directory, legal directory, newspaper or other periodical, outdoor advertising, radio or television, or through written or recorded communication.[24]

Model Rule 7.3 prohibits many instances of direct contacts with potential clients. The Rule may make contacting prospective clients who are the subject of adverse disproportionate impact of hazardous waste more difficult by its statement that a lawyer "shall not by in-person or live telephone contact solicit professional employment from a prospective client."[25] Rule 7.3 prohibits such contact only when the profit motive is present and no prior relationship exists between the lawyer and the prospective client. That is, the rule applies only when "a significant motive for the lawyer's [contact] is the lawyer's pecuniary gain."[26] Contacts made by lawyers to offer pro bono services to potential environmental justice plaintiffs do not appear to violate the rule.

Supreme Court decisions on commercial speech relating to legal services protect the right of lawyers to advertise and to initiate contact with prospective clients.[27] In *Shapero v. Kentucky Bar Association*, the United States Supreme Court validated the practice of sending direct mailings to potential clients.[28] The *Shapero* holding did not address the issue of in-person solicitation and did not overrule the case of *Ohralik v. Ohio State Bar Ass'n*,[29] in which the Supreme Court disapproved in-person solicitation. In *Ohralik* the Court upheld an indefinite suspension of an Ohio lawyer who solicited accident victims by in-person visits.[30] Justice Marshall described the lawyer's actions in the case as "classic examples of 'ambulance chasing.'"[31] The Supreme Court again addressed the issue of solicitation in *Florida Bar v. Went For It, Inc*,[32] validating a Florida Bar restriction on written communication by lawyers to victims of accidents for 30 days after the accident or disaster. Applying an intermediate scrutiny test, the Supreme Court held that the bar restrictions passed First Amendment scrutiny based on the Bar's showing of its substantial interests in protecting injured Floridians from intrusive lawyer conduct and, additionally, in preventing the erosion of public confidence in the legal profession.

A lawyer who speaks at an organizational meeting of residents in an area subject to disproportionate impacts of environmental hazards seems different in kind from the sort of overreaching in the *Ohralik* and *Went for It* cases. Nevertheless, environmental lawyers should contact potential clients initially by mail rather than in person to avoid the argument that they are soliciting clients improperly. When an existing client requests that the lawyer talk with a neighbor, the client can set up a meeting and ask the lawyer to attend. Such a meeting does not appear to violate the rule against client solicitation since the lawyer is acting pursuant to a client's request.

The Organizational Client

Model Rule 1.13 deals with the lawyer's relations with corporations and unincorporated entities, mandating that the lawyer act for the organization rather than for its constituents.[33] The Rule does not anticipate loosely defined groups such as some organized to lodge a complaint with EPA's Office of Civil Rights (OCR). Thus, the issue of client identity is not easily isolated. The lawyer who represents a group in an environmental justice action may face difficult questions of who commands primary allegiance—the group or the named individuals. As suggested earlier, the lawyer's affiliation with the group should be made clear in a detailed joint representation agreement. This agreement should specify not only the existence and scope of the representation but also the governance structure of the group and the methods for achieving agreement on important issues such as settlement. The lawyer, organization, and the individuals represented individually are the parties to this agreement. In some cases it may also be advisable for the environmental justice group to form a nonprofit corporation and seek tax-exempt status from the Internal Revenue Service. Fund-raising for the group may be enhanced when supporters are able to deduct their contributions to the organization.

When an organization is a client, the Model Rules assume that the lawyer will have contact with the membership through the officers of the organization. Rule 1.4, Comment 3 notes that "ordinarily, the lawyer should address communications to the appropriate officials of the organization." An environmental justice group that wants to maintain a high degree of group control may include provisions in its by-laws to ensure group involvement or consensus. For example, a group might indicate that officers must transmit information to all group members and that officers are not authorized to settle a group claim[34] absent approval by a majority (or even higher percentage) of the group's members.

A different type of problem may arise for the lawyer representing a corporate client. Rule 1.13 makes clear that the lawyer's duty runs to the corporate entity rather than to individuals in the company. For example, Rule 1.13 requires that a lawyer for an organization take action to protect the organization when the lawyer learns that someone associated with the organization intends to violate a law or a legal obligation to the organization. What action the lawyer should take depends on the lawyer's assessment of the seriousness of the situation. The rule indicates several avenues that the lawyer may explore in response to such a situation, including "asking reconsideration" of an issue, advising the client to seek "a separate legal opinion," and "referring the matter to higher authority in the organization."[35] Whether a lawyer should take action because of an administrative violation depends not only on the nature of the violation but also on potential consequences to the organization.[36] If a plant is in violation of a law such as a discharge permit, the lawyer may have a duty to bring the violation to the attention of authorities higher in the corporation than those who know about the problem. The rule states that the lawyer should refer the issue to the "highest authority that can act on behalf of the organization" when "warranted by the seriousness of the matter,"[37] leaving the question of whether a particular problem warrants this action for case-by-case determination by lawyers and disciplinary boards.[38] Other corporate employees who interact with the lawyer at the "working level" may view this step of reporting to higher authorities in a negative light. They may see the decision as going "over the head" of the in-house counsel who originally retained the lawyer or as evidence of disloyalty to them or to the corporation. Nevertheless, the lawyer has an obligation under Rule 1.13 to communicate the problem to a person with authority to act to remedy the violation and a corollary obligation to inform constituents (that is, employers, officers, and directors of the corporation) of the lawyer's role and the client's identity when the interests of the organization and its constituents are adverse.[39]

Duration of Representation

A separate problem for lawyers representing groups with environmental justice claims relates to the duration of the representation and the duty of diligent representation while the representation continues. When a claim is delayed for months (or years), the group's consensus may falter or fail, making it unclear whether the group wishes to continue to pursue its complaint. Rule 1.3 imposes the duty of diligence on lawyers. A comment to the rule notes the lawyer's responsibility to resolve questions about whether the representation continues.[40] The lawyer must keep in touch with the group and continue to represent the group actively until the relationship is clearly terminated. Thus, the lawyer must take the initiative to clarify the existence or termination of the representation.

When the representation is not pro bono and the client fails to make payments for legal services as agreed, the lawyer may want to terminate the representation. This potential problem should be addressed in the representation agreement. In the case of representation for compensation, the agreement should state the obligation and timing of payment for legal services and the point in time at which termination will occur if the client fails to pay.[41] The best practice in the event of nonpayment is for the lawyer to write the client to give reasonable warning that termination is imminent.[42] This notice should indicate the date upon which the representation will terminate if the client fails to remit payment and should reference the provision of the representation agreement that provides for such a result. After the stated time, the lawyer should write again to declare the representation terminated.

Abiding by Client's Objectives

Subject to some exceptions such as the right or duty to withdraw, Model Rule 1.2 requires that lawyers "abide by a client's decisions concerning the objectives of representation."[43] The rule also expressly requires that lawyers abide by "a client's decision whether to accept an offer of settlement."[44] This requirement can be a source of disputes in cases such as mass toxic torts that involve numerous plaintiffs with potentially varying objectives and interests.[45] The problem may be less pronounced in the typical environmental justice case seeking injunctive relief rather than damages. In such matters there is usually little potential for differential treatment of plaintiffs and, thus, less conflict will arise. Nevertheless, some of the problems inherent in mass tort settlements may also be present in environmental justice actions. Individuals may disagree regarding whether accommodations offered by an industrial source are sufficiently protective. After all, whenever a large group of people is involved in legal action, the potential for disagreement exists. While the rules do not dictate a path for the lawyer whose clients disagree on a settlement, environmental justice groups may choose to resolve such conflicts prospectively by setting the rules for settlement or all group decision making.

Foundational Ethical Principles of Representation

The lawyer owes duties to the client and the institutions of justice and, in a more limited way, to third parties affected by his or her representation. The lawyer's primary duty of loyalty to the client is well-known. It includes the obligation of diligence and competence in pursuing the client's claims and serving the client's interests. Its prominence is demonstrated by its premier place in the Model Rules: Rule 1.1 states the duty of competence.[46] Inherent in this duty is the requirement that the lawyer spend the requisite time and attention needed to serve client interests.[47]

The lawyer's duty to clients is limited by duties to nonclients and the institutions of justice. Candor and truthfulness are the subject of several Model Rules.[48] Decisional law also sets a standard of truthfulness for lawyers. Moreover, tort law requires that lawyers refrain from making false statements and that they disclose material facts in some circumstances. For example, the lawyer's duty of truthfulness includes the obligation to use due care in providing information to nonclients who will rely on the information.[49] Lawyers and their clients must respond truthfully to discovery requests such as deposition questions or interrogatories.[50] When a party to a transaction seeks information (such as the environmental condition of property to be conveyed), a half-truth as well as a misrepresentation provides a basis for rescission of the contract by a party who relies on the misleading statement.[51] If a lawyer passes on information that he or she knows is false, the lawyer (as well as the client) can be held liable for third-party injuries caused by the misrepresentation. Providing incomplete or misleading information relating to discharges of a particular facility may violate statutory or common law and result in sanctions or damages.[52]

Conflicts

Model Rule 1.7 sets forth the ABA's standard regarding current representation of clients. Two distinct types of conflicts should be noted in this context:

1. where the lawyer has been asked to represent two different clients in two different matters (the simultaneous representation situation); and
2. where the lawyer represents several parties in the same litigation (the multiple representation situation).

While Model Rule 1.7 is the standard for determining the appropriateness of both kinds of representations, these two situations raise different kinds of problems and will be discussed here separately.

The Model Code and Model Rules present a similar structure. The processes of Model Rules and the Model Code conflict rules are substantially similar apart from the standard of the lawyer's judgment.[53] The Model Code permits representation despite the existence of representation of another party with differing interests when "it is obvious that [the lawyer] can adequately represent the interest of each [client]."[54] Model Rule 1.7 allows potentially adverse multiple representation when "the lawyer reasonably believes the representation will not adversely affect the relationship with the other client."[55] Informed client consent to the representation is a requirement under either approach.[56]

Model Rule 1.7 limits representation in two situations:

1. when the representation "will be directly adverse" to the other (existing) client; and
2. when the representation "may be materially limited by the lawyer's responsibilities to another client or to a third person, or by the lawyer's own interests."[57]

In either case, the representation does not violate the rule when two curative elements are present:

1. the clients consent to the representation after consultation; and
2. the lawyer has a reasonable belief that the representation will not adversely affect the client.[58]

As a practical matter, in cases of direct conflict it seems likely that the additional representation will create problems for the original client.

In addition to the objective elements of "directly adverse" and "materially limited" representation, Rule 1.7 adds the subjective element of the lawyer's belief regarding the effect of the representation, creating a possible defense even when the representation is objectively adverse. While the rule stops short of a clear prohibition (leaving room for lawyer judgment and defense), it seems unlikely that a lawyer will accept joint representation in questionable circumstances. Likewise, it seems unlikely that a lawyer would accept representation in questionable circumstances or form a reasonable belief that such joint representation would not have an adverse effect.

Rule 1.7 qualifies client consent with the phrase "after consultation."[59] The Terminology section of the Model Rules defines "consultation" as "communication of information reasonably sufficient to permit the client to appreciate the significance of the matter in question."[60] A reasonable reading of "consultation" in the context of adverse representation seems to require that the lawyer provide the client with information necessary to understand the suggested arrangement and its risks. The cautious lawyer will insure a meaningful consultation by fully disclosing actual and potential conflicts.[61] A comment to the rule makes clear that when confidentiality concerns prevent a lawyer from revealing relevant information to the potential client, the lawyer must not undertake the additional representation.[62]

Assessment of the possibility of future conflicts in environmental matters can be difficult. If a substantial conflict develops during the representation, the lawyer must withdraw from representing both clients.[63] The opposing party may move for disqualification of the lawyer if he or she refuses to withdraw from the case.[64]

Conflicts Relating to Simultaneous Representation

A lawyer who is asked to represent a party whose interests may be in conflict with an existing client should also consult Rule 1.7.[65] The fact that the representations are unrelated—the parties are not in direct opposition in any legal action—does not determine this issue.

As the above discussion indicates, line drawing is necessary in such situations. The rule acknowledges the possibility of appropriate representation of two parties despite the fact that the interests of the two are adverse in some general sense, such as competing economic interests. A comment to the rule explains the situation in which representation could go forward:

> [A] lawyer ordinarily may not act as advocate against a person the lawyer represents in some other matter, even if it is wholly unrelated. On the other hand, simultaneous representation in unrelated matters of clients whose interests are *only generally adverse,* such as competing economic enterprises, does not require consent of the respective clients.[66]

The comment makes clear that the Model Rules do not recognize a conflict when clients are "only generally adverse" to each other. It also makes clear the general principle that lawyers will not ordinarily enter representation that will directly oppose a client. Suppose current client A is in the same business as potential client B. Does the fact of ordinary competition between these parties make it inappropriate for a lawyer to represent the two in separate matters? What if the conflict is not between Corporation A and Corporation B, but between A and Corporation B's sister corporation, C?

Model Rule 1.7 requires the lawyer to accomplish four tasks before deciding to accept proffered employment by a new client. After noting the existence of a potential conflict (the first step), the lawyer must take the (second) step of gathering information about the proffered employment and determining personally whether the representation will adversely affect the current client.[67] Third, assuming that the lawyer determines that the representation will not adversely affect the client, the lawyer will consult with the current client and the potential client regarding the potential representation. Of course, the disclosures made in pursuit of this decision must preserve the confidentiality of each of the clients. Finally, if the representation is to go forward, the lawyer must obtain the waiver and consent of each of the clients after the consultation.

The situation of potential conflict between a new client and a sister corporation of the current client seems to formulate a situation of a remote conflict that may not prevent the lawyer from forming a reasonable belief that both representations can be accomplished without adverse effect on either. Of course, the particulars of the case could render even this apparently benign conflict objectionable if the new representation could compromise the loyalty of the lawyer to the existing client.

Conflicts Relating to Current Clients—Multiple Representation

Multiple representation of parties in environmental matters is common.[68] Lawyers and environmental justice clients (whether plaintiffs or defendants) may seek joint representation in environmental justice matters as a way of decreasing costs and of sharing information. Moreover, in some cases, joint representation may equalize the bargaining power of the parties and even "increase the likelihood that parties can reach an equitable settlement" with the Environmental Protection Agency.[69]

People who complain individually to companies about environmental problems sometimes receive less attention than those who join together and take collective action. Industrial facilities may dismiss the complaints of individuals, classifying those who complain as cranks or troublemakers. Indeed, this fact is one underlying reason for the recently expanded[70] Office of Civil Rights (OCR) in the EPA.[71] By taking collective legal action—either through the OCR or other legal avenues—individuals signal that they raise serious concerns that cannot be ignored. Once individuals have formed a group to oppose a work practice or the siting of hazardous waste, joint legal representation may be useful for coordinating legal strategies and pooling resources.

Collective action can increase the power and bargaining position of either party in a controversy. Opponents to environmental justice claims may also benefit from joint representation, and some companies in a geographic area or industry group have created joint defense groups. This move allows the companies to share information and to claim the right to the privilege of confidentiality for intragroup communications. This sort of collective action raises troubling issues from the perspective of environmental justice advocates because it enhances the power of the corporate opponent. On the other hand, corporate entities accused of environmental justice offenses may not necessarily see themselves as dominant in the dispute. Moreover, they may regard collective action with other corporations as crucial to an effective legal defense.

The fact that joint representation is necessary to capture the attention of an opponent does not mean that it is easy or without risks. While there are good reasons for joint representation of both plaintiffs and defendants in environmental justice cases, lawyers who represent more than one party in a case may face conflict problems.[72]

Positional or Issue Conflicts

Lawyers should be mindful of the balance of interests in relation to the conflict problem of positional or issue conflicts that can arise even when a lawyer is representing different companies in entirely different cases. The question presented here is whether a lawyer can ethically take differing positions on behalf of clients on some issue of law. For example, one client might seek a ruling that a substance is a RCRA hazardous waste, and another client of the lawyer might want to establish that the substance is not hazardous. Is such a situation prohibited by Model Rule 1.7? If it is, could the lawyer ethically represent the two clients in different jurisdictions?

A comment to Model Rule 1.7 presents the ABA's analysis of issue conflicts:

> A lawyer may represent parties having antagonistic positions on a legal question that has arisen in different cases, unless representation of either client would be adversely affected. Thus, it is ordinarily not improper to assert such positions in cases pending in different trial courts, but it may be improper to do so in cases pending at the same time in an appellate court.[73]

This statement expresses the extent of the guidance of the Model Rules on this problem and suggests that the representation is generally acceptable despite positional conflicts at the trial court level. Bars and boards of professional responsibility have now begun to address this issue.[74] Recent scholarship elucidates some of the hard issues presented when representation results in issue conflicts.[75] An ABA opinion suggests that issue conflicts may often be impermissible, and draws the trial versus appellate representation distinction into question.[76] ABA Opinion 93-377 (1993) states that a firm should not accept representation that would result in an issue conflict in the same jurisdiction except when each client gives informed consent to the representation and neither case is likely to lead to a precedent harmful to the other client.

Conflict Problems Relating to Settlement Offers

As other sections of this chapter suggest, disagreements between environmental justice plaintiffs on the desirability of a settlement proposal may raise difficult conflict issues. For example, when a lawyer represents several environmental justice plaintiffs, some of those represented may wish to accept a settlement despite the fact that others are dissatisfied with the offer. Model Rule 1.8 offers guidance, albeit no easy answers:

> (g) A lawyer who represents two or more clients shall not participate in making an aggregate settlement of the claims of or against the clients . . . unless each client consents after consultation, including disclosure of the existence and nature of all the claims or pleas involved and of the participation of each person in the settlement.[77]

Rule 1.8(g) relates only to settlements that resolve aggregate or shared claims of the clients. It does not prohibit a settlement when the claims of other clients are not resolved by the settlement. Moreover, the provision does not purport to deal with settlements of a single claim such as that of an environmental justice claimant group. When the claim is one for injunctive relief against a future harm, such as the siting of a hazardous waste facility, the settlement is unitary (on behalf of one entity) rather than aggregate. When a unitary group claim is the subject of settlement, Rule 1.8 is not applicable. It would be unreasonable to read the provision to mean that each individual represented as part of an organization has the power to veto a settlement. In the unlikely event that a group intended to vest such veto power in individual members, it could include a by-law provision expressly allowing settlement only upon unanimous approval. If, on the other hand, the group has formed to seek damages for individual harms suffered by each member of the group, each plaintiff has a separate claim that can be settled with other claims or pursued separately.

Conflicts Relating to Former Clients

Subsequent representation of another client may present a conflict of interest because of the lawyer's prior representation.[78] Model Rule 1.9 deals with conflicts based on prior representation, employing a test similar to that of Rule 1.7 to protect the former client. It states:

> A lawyer who has formerly represented a client in a matter shall not thereafter represent another person in the same or a substantially related matter in which that person's interests are materially adverse to the interests of the former client unless the former client consents after consultation.[79]

The rule prohibits subsequent representation of another whose interests are "materially adverse" to the former client. Likewise, prior representation by a lawyer's former firm disqualifies the lawyer from subsequent representation of a person whose interests are "materially adverse," when the lawyer knows confidential information about the former client "that is material to the matter" of representation. Finally, the Rule prohibits use or disclosure of confidential information about the former client.[80]

Similarly, the Restatement of the Law Governing Lawyers states that a lawyer continues to owe some duties to former clients, noting that the lawyer must avoid conflicts of interest with regard to the interests of both current and former clients.[81] Unless both clients consent to the representation, a lawyer may not represent a new client with "interests materially adverse" to a former client in a related matter. She or he may not serve as a representative in an unrelated matter if there is a "substantial risk" that the representation would "require the lawyer to make use of confidential information of the former client."[82] The Restatement also expressly notes that the former client injured by a lawyer's breach of the duty not to create conflicts has the right to malpractice damages.[83]

Conflicts Based on Prior Government Work

A significant number of lawyers who have worked for governmental agencies (including EPA) leave government service for work in the private sector, often representing industrial clients.[84] Model Rule 1.11 prohibits a lawyer from representing a private client "in a matter in which the lawyer participated personally and substantially as a public officer or employee" unless the lawyer consults with and obtains the consent of the agency involved.[85] To comply with Rule 1.11, a lawyer who has worked for the government and intends to represent an industrial client in an environmental justice matter must obtain the consent of the agency that formerly employed him. The same duty applies to the government lawyer who leaves the employ of the government and intends to represent environmental justice complainants though such representation is less common. Additionally, agency regulations often bar a departing lawyer from representing a party he had substantial contact with for a set period of time.[86]

The Duty of Confidentiality

The Rule and Exceptions

The duty of confidentiality, regarded by many as the central ethical rule of the profession,[87] is broader than the evidentiary privilege against lawyer testimony about a client.[88] Model Rule 1.6 prohibits lawyers from revealing information relating to a client. It provides:

> (a) A lawyer shall not reveal information relating to representation of a client unless the client consents after consultation,

> except for disclosures that are impliedly authorized in order to carry out the representation, and except as stated in paragraph (b).[89]

Subsection (b) sets forth the exceptions to this general prohibition:

> (b) A lawyer may reveal such information to the extent the lawyer reasonably believes necessary: (1) to prevent the client from committing a criminal act that the lawyer believes is likely to result in imminent death or substantial bodily harm; or (2) to establish a claim or defense on behalf of the lawyer in a controversy between the lawyer and the client, to establish a defense to a criminal charge or civil claim against the lawyer based upon conduct in which the client was involved, or to respond to allegations in any proceeding concerning the lawyer's representation of the client.[90]

The exceptions empower lawyers to disclose information in two situations:

1. to prevent the client from committing a crime that is likely to result in "imminent death or substantial bodily harm"; and
2. to protect lawyer interests.[91]

Significant debate exists about the appropriate scope of lawyer disclosure. In 1991, the ABA Committee on Ethics proposed amending Rule 1.6.[92] The Proposed Restatement (Third) of the Law—The Law Governing Lawyers—rejects the categorical approach of the Model Rules,[93] and scholars argue that the disclosure of client information is sometimes justified in circumstances not included in the rule.[94] Most states have tempered the force of the rule. Of the approximately 40 jurisdictions that adopted the Model Rules, only six retained Model Rule 1.6 in the form endorsed by the ABA.[95] Some states adopted a standard of mandatory disclosure rather than the permissive disclosure of Rule 1.6.[96] Others allow disclosure of information without regard to whether the harm suffered will be substantial.[97] Accordingly, the rule on confidentiality provides a dramatic example of the need for lawyers to review carefully the rules of their respective jurisdictions.

In relation to the first exception, suppose an environmental lawyer learns that protestors plan to sabotage a plant with explosives or that a facility operator intends to put protestors at physical risk. May the lawyer reveal such information? Clearly these actions create a risk of physical harm. It may be difficult, however, for the lawyer to determine whether the actions are crimes. The lawyer's decision is made more difficult by the wide range of state rules. Based on the same fact pattern, some states require disclosure, while others allow or forbid disclosure.[98] This diversity heightens the importance of the choice of law question.[99]

Confidentiality and Positive Law

Lawyers should assess relevant laws prior to complying with production requests and should seek protective orders from a court when disclosure laws seem to compromise client interests unfairly. Of course, a court may find that the client has a duty to disclose information despite the effect on the client's interests. The Preamble and Comments to the Model Rules note the lawyer's duty to comply with positive law (substantive statutory and common law).[100] The Preamble to the Model Rules states: "A lawyer should keep in confidence information relating to representation of a client except so far as disclosure is required or permitted by the Rules of Professional Conduct or other law." Additionally, Comment 20 to Rule 1.6 notes the priority of positive law: "In addition to these provisions, a lawyer may be obligated or permitted by other provisions of law to give information about a client." The environmental lawyer must be familiar with federal and state statutes relating to environmental hazards.[101] Examples of laws that require disclosure of information abound in the environmental context.[102] Thus, a client may have a duty to disclose information that it considers confidential.[103]

Whether the lawyer is permitted or required to report the condition to authorities depends primarily on the substantive law rather than the rules of professional ethics of his jurisdiction. The separate issue of lawyer liability can create a "catch-22" situation in which no option is risk-free for the lawyer. Tort law may impose a duty on anyone, including a lawyer, to act to prevent harm in cases of clear and dramatic peril.[104] Some courts have imposed a duty to warn despite the absence of a relationship with the person endangered. In the well-known Tarasoff case, the California Supreme Court recognized a cause of action against a psychologist despite the duty of confidentiality when a patient revealed he intended to kill a third party, reasoning that "the public policy favoring protection of the confidential character of patient-psychotherapist communications must yield . . . to avert danger to others. The protective privilege ends where the public peril begins."[105] The fact that lawyers lack the training that mental health professionals receive in evaluating the mental intent of clients argues against imposition of such a duty on lawyers. This distinction seems to protect lawyers in all but the most extreme cases.[106]

In defining their duty as well as that of clients, lawyers should consult positive law, recognizing that constitutionally sound law may trump ethics statements. For example, constraints such as public records laws have the power to require lawyers for public agencies to reveal confidential information obtained in an environmental justice case. Similarly, laws requiring that doctors or lawyers disclose child abuse or the existence of an unauthorized nuclear stockpile may require a disclosure that would otherwise violate the duty of confidentiality.

The lawyer may reveal client information without client consent only in the rare cases described above of future dangerous crimes and lawyer self-defense. Thus, we can easily give at least a partial answer to the introductory question of the lawyer's options when convinced that the client's position is wrong. If the jurisdiction adopts Model Rule 1.6 without variation, the lawyer must *not* disclose confidential client information based on the clash of views unless the client is planning to commit a crime of the type described in Rule 1.6. The fact of a lawyer's disagreement with a client's goals or intent is an insufficient basis for disclosing confidential client information—whether the disclosure would be to an opponent or to anyone else. The possibility of withdrawal presents a separate, interesting question.

Confidentiality and the Right to Withdraw from Representation

Model Rule 1.16 requires that a lawyer withdraw from the representation when it involves a "violation of the rules of professional conduct or other law" or in the obvious cases of discharge or impairment of the lawyer's ability to do his job.[107] Additionally, Rule 1.16 permits a lawyer to withdraw when the withdrawal "can be accomplished without materially adverse effect on the interests of the client" except when a tribunal orders the lawyer to continue representation.[108] Model Rule 1.16 also allows withdrawal in six stated situations despite the fact that materially adverse effects may accrue to the client.[109] These include some open-ended tests that may address the hypothetical of the lawyer who believes her client is in the wrong. The rule allows withdrawal when the client "has used the lawyer's services to perpetrate a crime or fraud,"[110] when the client "persists in a course of action involving the lawyer's services that the lawyer reasonably believes is criminal or fraudulent,"[111] or when the client's objective is, in the lawyer's view, "repugnant or imprudent."[112] An additional catch-all provision allows the lawyer to withdraw for "good cause."[113] The lawyer's belief that the client is wrong posed in the introduction may constitute good cause or signal "repugnant or imprudent"[114] conduct allowing discretionary withdrawal.

Rule 1.16 provides a broad range for discretionary withdrawal based on strong differences of views regarding the client's objectives, provided the tribunal hearing a matter does not order the lawyer to continue representation. Although the Rule makes no mention of seeking the approval of the court or other tribunals for withdrawal, it acknowledges that a court may refuse to allow a lawyer to withdraw from a matter (ordinarily a matter in litigation), and most states provide for such controls by courts. Subsection (c) to the Rule states: "When ordered to do so by a tribunal, a lawyer shall continue representation notwithstanding good cause for terminating the representation."[115] The comment to the Rule makes clear that the lawyer should seek court approval for withdrawing when the lawyer has been appointed to the case. It states:

> When a lawyer has been appointed to represent a client, withdrawal ordinarily requires approval of the appointing authority. See also Rule 6.2. Difficulty may be encountered if withdrawal is based on the client's demand that the lawyer engage in unprofessional conduct.[116]

Lawyers often seek permission before withdrawing from a matter pending before a tribunal, and court rules typically prohibit lawyers from withdrawing from litigated cases without the consent of the court.[117] This procedure comports with the Rule since the tribunal has the power to require the lawyer to continue the representation.

Clearly, the lawyer has significantly greater discretion to withdraw under Rule 1.16 than to disclose information under Rule 1.6.[118] The standard set by Rule 1.16 can be met despite the fact that the lawyer is not allowed to reveal the source of the disagreement with the client. In the provision allowing withdrawal, the Rule does not specify the nature of the client's criminal or fraudulent conduct that provides a basis for withdrawal, leaving the possible inference that any crime or fraud will suffice as long as it somehow involves the lawyer's representation.[119] By contrast, only criminal conduct that is likely to result in "imminent death or substantial bodily harm" qualifies for permissive disclosure.[120] If the client agrees that his or her interests will not be impaired by withdrawal, there seems little reason to require continued representation.

Confidentiality and Prospective Clients

The duty of confidentiality may apply to prospective clients even when they do not retain the lawyer's services. Gaining confidential information about an adverse prospective client can carry high costs. The Scope section of the Model Rules states:

> Most of the duties flowing from the client-lawyer relationship attach only after the client has requested the lawyer to render legal services and the lawyer has agreed to do so. But there are

> some duties, such as that of confidentiality under Rule 1.6, that may attach when the lawyer agrees to consider whether a client-lawyer relationship shall be established.[121]

Learning information about a matter from an adverse prospective client carries the risk that it may disqualify the lawyer from representing other clients.[122] Indeed, nothing in the rule exempts disqualification from cases for existing clients.

It may seem unlikely that a manufacturing or industrial party would interview or seek to retain a lawyer who represents environmental justice clients, or vice versa. Nevertheless, exceptions to this intuition exist. Moreover, mix-ups and setups[123] sometimes do occur, making it advisable for lawyers to run a conflicts check before conferring with a prospective client or learning any information about the case. The conflicts check should include the identity of the parties involved, the location of the project or contamination, and the nature of the matter in which representation is sought.

The Lawyer's Obligations Relating to the Use of Consultants and the Media

The lawyer's role in serving the ends of a client is not limited to representing the client in court or administrative proceedings. Often lawyers use methods for resolving disputes outside the traditional juridical or administrative system. Lawyers act as negotiators and advisors to clients on a wide range of interests, including environmental compliance. Similarly, lawyers often properly act outside the traditional advocacy system to further the interests of clients.

Working with Consultants

In environmental matters generally, lawyers often need to coordinate the work of the case among a variety of professionals and disciplines such as biologists, geologists, and toxicologists.[124] Consultants and the scientific evidence they gather and explain are crucial to environmental justice. Model Rule 5.3 creates an obligation on lawyers to take steps to assure that the conduct of nonlawyer associates is compatible with the rules of professional conduct applicable to lawyers. Although the Model Rules are not directly applicable to nonlawyers, Rule 5.3 imposes on lawyers a duty to assure that ethical standards of the legal profession are heeded by professionals who work with lawyers.

A separate issue relating to consultants may arise when a lawyer needs to communicate with the professionals employed by opponents. For example, environmental justice plaintiffs may need to learn the state of contamination of a site or the effects of various options for remediation. A lawyer who communicates with representatives of an opposing party should be careful not to violate Rule 4.2, the "no-contact" provision. This rule, entitled Communication with Person Represented by Counsel, states as follows:

> In representing a client, a lawyer shall not communicate about the subject of the representation with a person the lawyer knows to be represented by another lawyer in the matter, unless the lawyer has the consent of the other lawyer or is authorized by law to do so.[125]

When an organization is represented, the Rule prohibits the lawyer from contacting persons (1) with managerial responsibility (2) whose act or omission may be imputed to the organization or (3) whose statement may constitute an admission of the organization.[126] Thus, the Rule can present a significant bar in some cases.[127] Lawyers should consult the rules of their jurisdictions for variations regarding communication with employees or exemployees of adverse parties.

Of course, the fact that a lawyer may ethically contact an individual does not obligate the individual contacted to provide information or even to talk with the lawyer.[128] Rule 4.2 is a one-way street in that it does not prohibit represented parties from contacting opposing counsel. The no-contact rule simply prohibits lawyers from contacting parties who are represented by other lawyers. Additionally, a comment to the Rule recognizes that a special need may exist to communicate with government lawyers or officials.[129]

When matters are under dispute, the no-contact rule can be waived by an agreement. If parties and their lawyers expressly indicate that their representatives are allowed to communicate with each other and the parties on stated matters, Rule 4.2 provides no obstacle to such communications. Such an approach is likely to have undesirable side effects, however. For example, such a contract provision could unintentionally waive the confidentiality of client information.

Use of the Media

Model Rule 3.6, entitled Trial Publicity, sets forth guidelines and limits on the information lawyers share with the media in relation to matters under investigation or litigation. It makes clear the certain obligation of the lawyer not to prejudice the client's case by any extrajudicial statement and includes a detailed list of the types of information it deems nonprejudicial.[130] The use of the media in today's world goes beyond statements relating to cases in litigation, however. The lawyer who makes use of the media in pursuit of client objectives should scrutinize his motives as well as the potential for adverse effects on the client.[131]

SLAPP Suits

In recent years, a significant amount of news coverage and legal scholarship has discussed the phenomenon of SLAPP suits.[132] SLAPP stands for Strategic Lawsuit Against Public Participation[133] and refers to actions instituted for the purpose of punishing a person who seeks redress for wrongs in a public forum.[134] What follows is a discussion of SLAPP suits from the perspective of legal ethics; other aspects of SLAPP suits are discussed in Chapter 7.

Whether a suit is undertaken for a proper purpose or for the purpose of discouraging individuals from exercising their public participation rights hinges on the motivation of the person bringing the suit. In litigation and disciplinary hearings, one cannot assume that a suit is brought in bad faith or for improper purposes.

Courts have denounced strongly the use of the judicial process for the purpose of silencing individuals for exercising their legal rights.[135] Several states (including California, Delaware, Georgia, Minnesota, Nevada, New York, Rhode Island, and Washington) have passed legislation aimed at protecting citizens from SLAPP suits.[136] Scholars have debated whether such suits are unethical per se and whether they amount to malicious prosecution.[137]

Model Rule 3.1, entitled Meritorious Claims and Contentions, states:

> A lawyer shall not bring or defend a proceeding, or assert or controvert an issue therein, unless there is a basis for doing so that is not frivolous, which includes a good faith argument for an extension, modification or reversal of existing law.[138]

While this text casts the rule in terms of a minimum basis for filing an action, a comment to Rule 3.1 provides a gloss on the meaning of a "frivolous" action. According to the comment, an action is frivolous:

> . . . if the client desires to have the action taken primarily for the purpose of harassing or maliciously injuring a person *or* if the lawyer is unable either to make a good faith argument on the merits of the action taken or to support the action taken by a good faith argument for an extension, modification or reversal of existing law.[139]

A SLAPP suit, by definition, has the purpose of discouraging legal action. Such a purpose seems squarely within the described intent of "harassing or maliciously injuring a person," and, thus, should be seen as a nonmeritorious claim. The fact that a lawyer can make an argument for the action does not make it a "good faith argument." By using the disjunction "or," the comment suggests that the malicious purpose is independently sufficient to take an action outside the definition of "meritorious claim." Moreover, history and common sense counsel that a suit brought for improper purposes is ethically indefensible.[140]

While a lawyer may not always know a client's motivation for instituting proceedings, the lawyer may know or have good evidence of the client's motivation in some cases. Statements such as "X will pay for his stand," or "It's time to go after X," give an indication that the suit constitutes retaliation. A lawyer who brings an action when he or she has such knowledge is misusing the legal process. Whether a suit is undertaken for a proper purpose or for the purpose of discouraging individuals from exercising their public participation rights hinges on the motivation of the person bringing the suit. In litigation and disciplinary hearings, one cannot assume that a suit is brought in bad faith or for improper purposes.

Conclusion

All lawyers are subject to the ethics rules of their jurisdictions. The numerous prescriptive laws applicable to the environmental area make it necessary for lawyers to be familiar with and research federal and state statutes relevant to particular hazards as well as the rules of ethics applicable to their conduct. Lawyers should consult the rules regularly in relation to questions occurring in practice and strive to develop knowledge of the precepts laid out in the rules and the practical wisdom to apply them.

Notes

The author thanks all colleagues who discussed the issues raised here and extends special thanks to Ernest Lidge III, and Edward Brewer for their thoughtful comments on earlier drafts of this chapter. She thanks Caroline Critchfield Hunter for her research assistance.

1. Other authors in this book have defined and described the term "environmental justice." It refers to claims that minority or low-income communities bear a disproportionate share of pollution.

2. Tennessee, Vermont, and Virginia are in the process of considering adoption of the Model Rules. *See generally* A. Jeffry Taylor, *Work in Progress: The Vermont Rules of Professional Conduct,* 20 VT. L. REV. 901 (1996); *Proposed Model Rules of Professional Conduct,* VA. LAW., Mar. 1997, Tennessee Proposed Rules, November 1, 1997, 957 S.W.2d Ct.R-37 (1997).

3. The Code, in turn, had superseded the ABA Canons of Professional Ethics, the first statement of the rules of legal ethics which the ABA had adopted in 1908.

4. For this reason, this chapter refers to the Code in the present tense rather than the past tense.

5. MODEL RULES OF PROFESSIONAL CONDUCT, Preamble, [hereinafter "MODEL RULES,"] para. 8 (1994).

6. MODEL RULE 2.1. *In re Marriage of Foran*, 834 P.2d 1081, n.14 (Wash. Ct. App. 1992) (noting a lawyer representing either party to a prenuptial may consider moral and social factors; an unenforceable, unfair contract does not promote marital tranquility); Friedman v. Comm'r of Pub. Safety, 473 N.W.2d 828, 834 (determining that if the underlying goal of DWI laws is to deter drinking and driving and promote sobriety, a lawyer can play a crucial role, citing MINN. R. PROF. CONDUCT 2.1).

7. The Scope section to the ABA Rules notes that the Rules "do not exhaust the moral and ethical considerations that should inform a lawyer, for no worthwhile human activity can be completely defined by rules." *See* MODEL RULES, Scope, para. 2 (1996).

8. Substantive law is also referred to as "positive law."

9. MODEL RULES, Scope, para. 2; *see also* MODEL RULE 1.16(a)(1) (prohibiting representations that "will result in violation of . . . law").

10. *See* MODEL RULE 1.2, comment para. 4 & 5.

11. *See* Debra A. Saunders & Richard S. Humphrey, *The Thickening Briar Patch of Legal Malpractice*, 46 R.I. BR. J. 9 (April 1998).

12. *See, e.g.*, Westinghouse Electric Corp. v. Kerr-McGee Corp., 580 F.2d 1311 (7th Cir.1978); *see also* Tormo v. Tormark, 398 F. Supp. 1159 (D.N.J. 1975) (imposing attorney-client relationship duties upon a lawyer who gave legal advice and counsel without expectation of payment).

13. 502 A.2d 94, 100 (finding in a medical malpractice action an attorney-client relationship existed due to the party's conduct despite the absence of a written agreement).

14. *Id.* at 99.

15. *See* State v. Hansen, 862 P.2d 117, 118–19 (Wash. 1993).

16. The court also held that the remarks of the defendant were not protected because they related to a future crime. *Id.*

17. The distinctions between primary and derivative clients is stated in THE RESTATEMENT OF THE LAW GOVERNING LAWYERS, § 1.3:108.

18. *See generally* Deborah L. Rhode, *Class Conflicts in Class Actions*, 34 STAN. L. REV. 1183 (1982).

19. The term bellwether is derived from the ancient practice of belling a wether (a male sheep) selected to lead his flock. The ultimate success of the wether selected to wear the bell was determined by whether the flock had confidence that the wether would not lead them astray, and so it is in the mass tort context. The notion that the trial of some members of a large group of claimants may provide a basis for enhancing prospects of settlement or for resolving common issues or claims is a sound one that has achieved general acceptance by both bench and bar. References to bellwether trials have long been included in the MANUAL

FOR COMPLEX LITIGATION. *See* MANUAL FOR COMPLEX LITIGATION § 33.27–.28 (3d ed. 1995).

In re Chevron U.S.A., Inc., 109 F.3d 1016, 1019 (5th Cir. 1997).

20. If a representative group of claimants are tried to verdict, the results of such trials can be beneficial for litigants who desire to settle such claims by providing information on the value of the cases as reflected by the jury verdicts. Common issues or even general liability may also be resolved in a bellwether context in appropriate cases.

In re Chevron U.S.A., Inc., 109 F.3d 1016, 1019 (5th Cir. 1997) (granting defendant's request for mandamus and holding that the trial had no preclusive effect on the ground that the trial court's method of selecting "bellwether" cases for trial failed to represent adequately the core claims of all plaintiffs).

21. *See* CHARLES ALAN WRIGHT ET AL., FEDERAL PRACTICE AND PROCEDURE, FEDERAL RULES OF CIVIL PROCEDURE § 1782, p. 23); *see also* James W. Elrod, Comment, *The Use of Federal Class Actions in Mass Toxic Pollution Torts*, 56 TENN. L. REV. 243 (1988) (arguing that pollution cases should be tried under Rule 23).

22. MODEL RULE 7.2 states that "[a] copy or recording of an advertisement or communication shall be kept for two years after its last dissemination along with a record of when and where it was used." MODEL RULE 7.2 (b). Many states that have adopted this approach have modified the time period for which the lawyer must keep the ad. *See e.g.*, IN ST RPC Rule 7.1(e) (requiring advertisement be kept for six years); CT R RPC Rule 7.2(b) (requiring advertisement be kept for three years); NY ST CPR DR 2-101(F) (requiring lawyers to retain broadly disseminated ads and to file individualized contacts such as letters with the state disciplinary committee).

23. *See, e.g.*, FL ST BAR Rule 4-7.5(b) (mandating a copy of advertisement be "filed with the standing committee on advertising for evaluation of compliance with these rules . . . either prior to or concurrently with the lawyer's first dissemination of the advertisement"); TX ST RPC Rule 7.07(a) (requiring filing with the Lawyer Advertisement and Solicitation Review Committee of the State Bar of Texas); NM R RPC Rule 16-707 (requiring filing a copy of advertisement with the legal advertising committee).

24. MODEL RULE 7.2. The MODEL CODE provision differs significantly. Compare MODEL RULE 7.2 and DR 2-101.

25. MODEL RULE 7.3(a). The rule also limits the prohibition to cases in which "the lawyer has no family or prior professional relationship" with the person contacted. *Id.*

26. *Id.*

27. *See* Shapero v. Kentucky Bar Ass'n, 486 U.S. 466, (1988) (holding state violates U.S. Constitution by prohibiting lawyers from sending truthful letters to potential clients known to face particular legal problems); Bates v. State Bar of Arizona, 433 U.S. 350 (1977) (holding that a state ethics rule that prohibited lawyers from advertising violated First Amendment); *see also* Vincent R. Johnson, *Solicitation of Law Firm Clients by Departing Partners and Associates: Tort, Fiduciary, and Disciplinary Liability*, 50 U. PITT. L. REV. 1 (1988); John T. Ballantine, Jr., *After Shapero v. Kentucky Bar Association, Much Remains Unresolved About the Allowable Limits of Restrictions on Attorney Advertising*, 61 U. COLO. L. REV. 115 (1990).

28. 486 U.S. 466 (1988).

29. 436 U.S. 447 (1978).

30. *Id.*

31. *Id.* at 469.

32. 515 U.S. 618 (1995).

33. *See* MODEL RULE 1.13(d).

34. "Group claim" in this context means a non-divisible claim advanced by a group of individuals such as a petition to EPA's Office of Civil Rights seeking denial of a permit or other prospectively protective action. *See* note 18 and accompanying text.

35. MODEL RULE 1.13 (b)(1)–(3).

36. *Id.*

37. MODEL RULE 1.13(b)(3).

38. The current position of the OTS [Office of Thrift Savings] seems to be that, while the attorney may have a duty to report misconduct to the directors of a financial institution, this duty does not extend to reporting to the regulators absent special circumstances. However, the regulators have argued that MODEL RULE 1.13 requires the lawyer to attempt to change the offending conduct by talking to the perpetrator, and disclosing the problem up the chain of command to the directors, if necessary, to remedy the misconduct. Both the RTC and the OTS have taken the position that a lawyer's failure to inform the directors of misdeeds that are occurring may be the basis for lawyer liability.

Brian W. Smith & M. Lindsay Childress, *Avoiding Lawyer Liability in the Wake of Kaye, Scholer,* 8 ST. JOHN'S J. LEGAL COMMENT. 392 (1993).

39. *See* MODEL RULE 1.13 (a) & (d).

40. *See* MODEL RULE 1.3, comment 3; *see also* Neville v. Vingelli, 826 P.2d 1196 (Ariz. Ct. App. 1991) (imposing duty on lawyer to inform lenders that he was not representing borrower, notwithstanding that lenders initiated transaction); *In re Halprin,* 798 P.2d 80 (Mont. 1990) (disbarring lawyer for failing to act with reasonable diligence and failing to give notice of termination).

41. *Compare* MODEL RULE 1.16 and MODEL CODE DR 2-110(A).

42. *See* MODEL RULE 1.16(b)(4).

43. MODEL RULE 1.2.

44. *Id.*; *see* Lord v. Money Masters, Inc., 435 S.E.2d 247 (Ga. 1993).

45. For a full treatment of the complexities and ethical problems raised in settlement of mass tort actions, see Carrie Menkel-Meadow, *Ethics and the Settlements of Mass Torts: When the Rules Meet the Road,* 80 CORNELL L. REV. 1159 (1995) (arguing that the MODEL RULES do not contemplate either lawyer-client relations of mass torts and do not provide adequate guidance for mass tort settlements).

46. MODEL RULE 1.1 states: "A lawyer shall provide competent representation to a client. Competent representation requires legal knowledge, skill, thoroughness and preparation reasonably necessary for the representation."

47. The MODEL CODE recognized this duty. *See, e.g.,* DR 6-101(A)(3) (forbidding neglect); DR 6-101(A)(2) (requiring adequate preparation).

48. These include MODEL RULE 2.3, "Evaluation for Use by Third Persons," MODEL RULE 3.3, "Candor toward the Tribunal;" and MODEL RULE 4.1, "Truthfulness in Statements to Others." Rule 8.4 defines misconduct to include engaging in conduct that involves "dishonesty, fraud, deceit or misrepresentation," that

"is prejudicial to the administration of justice," or that seeks to "influence improperly a government agency or official." The comment to Rule 2.3 acknowledges that a lawyer may owe duties to nonclients. It also notes that these duties spring from law other than the MODEL RULES. "When the evaluation is intended for the information or use of a third person, a legal duty to that person may or may not arise. That legal question is beyond the scope of this Rule." MODEL RULE 2.3 com. 4.

49. *See* Eisenberg v. Gagnon, 766 F.2d 770 (3d Cir. 1985), *cert. denied*, 474 U.S. 946 (1985).

50. FED. R. CIV. P. 26(e) & 26(g).

51. Many states allow avoidance of a contract to purchase property before conveyance when a seller fails to disclose contamination. *See, e.g.*, IDAHO CODE §§ 55-2515, 55-2517 (1994 & Supp. 1997) (providing for rescission); IND. CODE §§ 24-4.6-2-10, 24-4.6-2-13 (1996) (requiring seller disclosure to buyer before acceptance and allowing buyer to nullify contract within two business days of receipt of disclosure); MICH. COMP. LAWS §§ 565.954, 565.964 (1997) (allowing termination by written notice).

52. For example, the Clean Water Act requires owners or operators of a facility discharging pollutants to record and report information about discharges into the waters of the United States. *See* Clean Water Act §§ 308(a), 502(14), 33 U.S.C. §§ 1318(a), 1362(14) (1994). Similarly, the Clean Air Act requires owners or operators of a source of acid deposition to monitor and report emissions to the state permitting authority. See Clean Air Act §§ 412(a), 502, 42 U.S.C. SS 7651k(a), 7661a (1994); 42 U.S.C. §§ 6991a, 6991b (1994); 42 U.S.C. § 9603 (1980). *See also* 42 U.S.C. § 7413(c)(2) (classifying knowing failure to make required reports or keep records of compliance required by the Clean Air Act as a felony).

53. Compare MODEL RULE 1.7 and DR 5-101.

54. MODEL CODE DR 5-105(C).

55. MODEL RULE 1.7.

56. *See* MODEL RULE 1.7(a); MODEL CODE DR 5-105(C).

57. MODEL RULE 1.7.

58. The Rule varies slightly the description of the lawyer's belief in each of the two circumstances. In the "directly adverse" case, the rule focuses on the relationship of the lawyer and the original client. It does not prohibit representation if the lawyer "reasonably believes the representation will not adversely affect the *relationship* with the other client." Rule 1.7(a)(1) (emphasis added). In the "materially limited" case, the rule focuses the test on the representation rather than the relationship. It does not prohibit representation if the lawyer "reasonably believes the *representation* will not be adversely affected" by the conflict. MODEL RULE 1.7(b).

59. MODEL RULE 1.7(a)(2).

60. Terminology para. 2.

61. *See* Patrick E. Donovan, *Serving Multiple Masters: Confronting the Conflicting Interests That Arise in Superfund Disputes,* 17 B.C. ENVTL. AFF. L. REV. 371, 377 (1990).

62. > [T]here may be circumstances where it is impossible to make the disclosure necessary to obtain consent. For example, when the lawyer represents different clients in related matters and one of the clients refuses to

> consent to the disclosure necessary to permit the other client to make an informed decision, the lawyer cannot properly ask the latter to consent.

MODEL RULE 1.7, Comment.

63. *See* MODEL RULE 1.16(c)(1).

64. *In* Brennan's, Inc. v. Brennan's Restaurants, Inc., 590 F.2d 168 (5th Cir. 1979) (applying the CODE OF PROFESSIONAL RESPONSIBILITY, Canon 4, EC4-4, EC4-5), the Court of Appeals for the Fifth Circuit held that a lawyer was properly barred from representing a corporate defendant on the ground of conflict of interest when the lawyer had represented both plaintiff and defendant on earlier matters substantially related to the action).

65. For an attorney, the danger is that he will be tempted, perhaps unconsciously, to favor the interests of a particularly important client over the adverse or potentially adverse interests of a less favored client. The lawyer's conflicting loyalties might lead him to recommend, for example, that the less favored client appears as a co-defendant or that the former unnecessarily concede a point in a negotiation with the latter.

Developments—Conflicts of Interest, 94 HARV. L. REV. 1244, 1296 (1981).

66. MODEL RULE 1.7, comment 3 (emphasis added).

67. The Rule varies slightly the description of the lawyer's belief in each of the two circumstances. In the "directly adverse" case, the rule focuses on the relationship of the lawyer and the original client. It does not prohibit representation if the lawyer "reasonably believes the representation will not adversely affect the *relationship* with the other client." MODEL RULE 1.7(a)(1) (emphasis added). In the case "materially limited" representation, the rule focuses the test on the representation rather than the relationship. MODEL RULE 1.7(b).

68. For a full treatment of conflicts at Superfund sites, see Andrew Kenefick et al., *Assessing Conflicts of Interest at Multiparty Superfund Sites: From First Involvement to Litigation*, 4 ENVTL. L. 721 (1998).

69. Donovan, *supra* note 61, at 403.

70. While the Office of Civil Rights at the EPA has existed for some time (at least since 1975), EPA has recently expanded its role to include processing complaints filed under Title VI of the Civil Rights Act. The Office of Civil Rights at the EPA "has traditionally been almost exclusively concerned with personnel issues." Richard J. Lazarus, *Pursuing "Environmental Justice": The Distributional Effects of Environmental Protection*, 87 NW. U. L. REV. 787 (1993). "[The] EPA has also explored its role in achieving environmental justice by forming the Environmental Equity Workgroup ("the Workgroup"). A Workgroup report recommended that EPA raise the priority assigned to the environmental justice movement." Mariaea Ramirez Fisher, *On the Road from Environmental Racism to Environmental Justice*, 5 VILL. ENVTL. L.J. 475–76 (1994).

71. "[The] EPA has also explored its role in achieving environmental justice by forming the Environmental Equity Workgroup ("the Workgroup"). A Workgroup report recommended that EPA raise the priority assigned to the environmental justice movement." Ramirez Fisher, *supra* note 70, at 475–76.

72. Large firms involved in environmental practice have identified conflict of interest problems as their greatest fear. Donovan, *supra* note 61, at 372. *See also* Marla B. Rubin, *The Problems Get Tougher*, THE RECORDER, Sept. 1992, at 16.

73. MODEL RULE 1.7, Comment 9.

74. Calif. Standing Comm. on Professional Responsibility and Conduct, Op. 1989-108 (undated); Phila. (Pa.) Bar Ass'n, Professional Guidance Comm., Op. 89-27 (1990).

75. For a comprehensive exploration of the problems that can arise as a result of issue conflicts and a suggested rule to regulate the area, see John Dzienkowski, *Positional Conflicts of Interest,* 71 TEX. L. REV. 457 (1993) (suggesting changes in the Model Rules to clarify lawyer responsibility relating to positional conflicts). *See also* Norman W. Spaulding, *The Prophet and the Bureaucrat: Positional Conflicts in Service Pro Bono Publico,* 50 STAN. L. REV. 1395 (1998).

76. ABA Comm. on Ethics and Professional Responsibility, Op. 93-377 (1993).

77. MODEL RULE 1.8(g).

78. *See* T.C. Theater v. Warner Bros. Pictures, 113 F. Supp. 265 (S.D. N.Y. 1953) (granting motion to disqualify lawyer from representing a party when he had represented the opponent in a related action).

79. MODEL RULE 1.9.

80. A lawyer who has formerly represented a client in a matter or whose present or former firm has formerly represented a client in a matter shall not thereafter:

(1) use information relating to the representation to the disadvantage of the former client except as Rule 1.6 or Rule 3.3 would permit or require with respect to a client, or when the information has become generally known; or

(2) reveal information relating to the representation except as Rule 1.6 or Rule 3.3 would permit or require with respect to a client.

MODEL RULE 1.9(c).

81. THE RESTATEMENT OF THE LAW GOVERNING LAWYERS, § 213.

82. *Id.*

83. *Id.*

84. This phenomenon is referred to as the revolving door syndrome. *See Developments—Conflicts of Interest, supra* note 65, at 1248.

85. MODEL RULE 1.11.

86. 5 C.F.R. § 2641.201 (1998) (prohibiting senior employee from seeking to influence an employee of a department or agency in which he was employed for one year following his departure).

87. *See generally* Robert P. Lawry, *The Central Moral Tradition of Lawyering,* 19 HOFSTRA L. REV. 311 (1990).

88. The recent decision of the United States Supreme Court in the Vincent Foster case underscores the importance of the duty by upholding the privilege even when information about the client is sought after the death of the client. *See* Swidler & Berlin v. United States, 118 S. Ct. 2081 (1998) (holding that attorney-client privilege survives the death of the client because the privilege is broader than Fifth Amendment's protection against self-incrimination).

89. MODEL RULE 1.6.

90. *Id.*

91. Interestingly, the exception for dangerous crimes is stated more narrowly than the lawyer self-defense exception, allowing disclosure only in the rare circumstance of a reasonable belief that disclosure is "necessary to prevent

the client from committing a criminal act that the lawyer believes is likely to result in imminent death or substantial bodily harm." MODEL RULE 1.6(b)(1). By contrast, Rule 1.6(b)(2) states a liberal disclosure rule, allowing a lawyer to reveal information about the client to protect his or her own interests. *See* MODEL RULES OF PROFESSIONAL CONDUCT Rule 1.6.(b)(2).

92. *See* Geoffrey C. Hazard, Jr., *Lawyers and Client Fraud: They Still Don't Get It,* 6 GEO. J. LEGAL ETHICS 701, 720–21 (1993).

93. *See* RESTATEMENT OF THE LAW (THIRD): THE LAW GOVERNING LAWYERS §§ 112–117A (March 29, 1996).

94. *See* Geoffrey C. Hazard, Jr., *Rectification of Client Fraud: Death and Revival of a Professional Norm,* 33 EMORY L.J. 271, 285 (1984) (advocating recognition of an exception "in practice" for disclosure of a client's fraud); Monroe H. Freedman, *The Lifesaving Exception to Confidentiality: Restating Law Without the Was, the Will Be, or the Ought to Be,* 29 LOY. L.A. L. REV. 1631, 1636 (1996) (suggesting an exception to allow lawyers to reveal client information when such disclosure protects third parties).

95. *See* ALA. RULES OF PROF'L CONDUCT Rule 1.6 (1996); DEL. RULES OF PROF'L CONDUCT Rule 1.6 (1997); LA. RULES OF PROF'L CONDUCT Rule 1.6 (1997); MO. RULES OF PROF'L CONDUCT Rule 1.6 (1997); MONT. RULES OF PROF'L CONDUCT Rule 1.6 (1997); R.I. RULES OF PROF'L CONDUCT Rule 1.6 (1996) (adding words "but is not obligated" to modify "may. . . reveal").

96. *See, e.g.,* ARIZ. RULES OF PROF'L CONDUCT Rule 1.6(b) (1997); CONN. RULES OF PROF'L CONDUCT Rule 1.6(b) (1997); FLA. RULES OF PROF'L CONDUCT Rule 4-1.6(b) (1997); HAW. RULES OF PROF'L CONDUCT Rule 1.6(b) (1997); ILL. RULES OF PROF'L CONDUCT Rule 1.6(b) (Supp. 1997); NEV. RULES OF PROF'L CONDUCT Rule 156 (1997); N.J. RULES OF PROF'L CONDUCT Rule 1.6(b) (1997); N.D. RULES OF PROF'L CONDUCT Rule 1.6 (1997). For a full list of the states in this category, see Irma S. Russell, *Unreasonable Risk: Model Rule 1.6, Environmental Hazards, and Positive Law,* 55 WASH. & LEE L. REV. 117, 172–75 (1998).

97. Russell, *supra* note 96, at 175.

98. *Id.*

99. MODEL RULE 8.5(b) and the law of conflicts govern questions of jurisdiction.

100. MODEL RULES, Preamble, para. 8 (1994). While both the MODEL RULES and the MODEL CODE set up a general prohibition against disclosure of client information and limited exceptions, the MODEL CODE more clearly bows to the imperative of substantive law, allowing disclosures of future crimes and of any information "required by law." DR 4-101(C)(2).

101. *See, e.g.,* 42 U.S.C. §§ 6991a, 6991b (1994); 42 U.S.C. § 9603 (1980); 42 U.S.C. § 7413(c)(2) (classifying knowing failure to make required reports or keep records of compliance as a felony).

102. *See, e.g.,* CERCLA § 103(a), 42 U.S.C. § 9603(a) (1994) (requiring person in charge of vessel or facility to report release of hazardous substance as soon as he or she has knowledge of quantities of substances released); Pollution Prevention Act of 1990 (PPA) § 6607(b)(1), (3), (7), 42 U.S.C. § 13106(b)(1), (3), (7) (1994) (requiring annual report of chemicals discharged into environment); Clean Water Act §§ 308(a), 502(14), 33 U.S.C. §§ 1318(a), 1362(14) (1994); Clean Air Act §§ 412(a), 502, 42 U.S.C. §§ 7651k(a), 7661a (1994).

103. [R]equiring a lawyer to disclose . . . information can only become an issue if the client has a right not to disclose. In litigation, the client generally has that right, which derives from protections such as the privilege against self-incrimination and the adversary's burden of proof, and the lawyer may not unilaterally disclose client confidences.

Stuart M. Gerson, *When Lawyers Must Disclose,* CHICAGO DAILY L. BULL., Apr. 10, 1992, at 6.

104. The existence of a duty is something that a court may find after the fact in a cause of action to determine whether the lawyer should have acted to prevent harm. In other words, the fact that no relationship exists between the lawyer and the third party may not categorically protect the lawyer from an action by the third party or representatives of the third party. *See* Tarasoff v. Regents of the Univ. of Cal., 551 P.2d 334, (Cal. 1976) (concluding that health care professionals have duty to warn nonclients of threats of violence made by patient); *see also* Freedman, *supra* note 94; Russell, *supra* note 96, at 172–75 (1998).

105. *Id.* at 442.

106. *See* Hawkins v. King County, 602 P.2d 361, 363, 365 (Wash. Ct. App. 1979) (rejecting client's claim against lawyer but recognizing common law duty to warn third parties that "must be permissive" except when "client has formed a firm intention to inflict serious personal injuries on an unknowing third person"); State v. Hansen, 862 P.2d 117, 118–19 (Wash. 1993) (reasoning arguendo that lawyer may have duty to reveal client threats against judge); *see also* Jeffrey P. Kerrane, *Will Tarasoff Liability Be Extended to Attorneys in Light of New California Evidence Code Section 956.5?*, 35 SANTA CLARA L. REV. 825, 830–33 (1995); John R. Murphy III, *In the Wake of Tarasoff: Mediation and the Duty to Disclose,* 35 CATH. U. L. REV. 209, 213–18 (1985).

107. MODEL RULE 1.16(a).

108. MODEL RULE 1.16(b), (c).

109. MODEL RULE 1.16(b).

110. MODEL RULE 1.16(b)(2).

> Subparagraphs 1.16(b)(1) and (b)(2), like DR 2-110(C)(1)(b) and (c) of the predecessor Model Code, permit a lawyer to withdraw when the client pursues an action that the lawyer reasonably believes is criminal or fraudulent, or when the client has used the lawyer's services to perpetrate a crime or fraud. *See e.g.,* Matza v. Matza, 610 A.2d 702 (Conn. 1992) (lawyer's allegations that client engaged in fraud in connection with dissolution of marriage proceedings justified lawyer's withdrawal, notwithstanding adverse effects on client's interests).

MODEL RULES OF PROFESSIONAL CONDUCT Rule 1.16(b) Legal Background. *See also* Matza v. Matza, 610 A.2d 702 (Conn. 1992) (lawyer acted appropriately in withdrawing when client engaged in fraud).

111. MODEL RULE 1.16(b)(1).

112. MODEL RULE 1.16(b)(3); *see also* James P. Hemmer, *Resignation of Corporate Counsel: Fulfillment or Abdication of Duty,* 39 HASTINGS L.J. 641 (1988).

113. MODEL RULE 1.16(b)(6). Lasser v. Nassau Community College, 457 N.Y.S.2d 343 (App. Div. 1983) (approving the withdrawal of a lawyer who was required to consult with another lawyer (who represented his client on a related matter) on all actions regarding the case).

114. MODEL RULE 1.16(b)(3).

115. MODEL RULE 1.16(c).

116. MODEL RULE 1.16, Comment 3.

117. *See, e.g.*, New York Civil Practice Law and Rules 321(b), DR 2-110, [22 N.Y. C.R.R. 1200.15]; *see also* Lawrence J. Fox & Jeanine M. Kasulis, *Firing Clients*, LITIGATION, (1995).

118. *See* MODEL RULE 1.6, Comment ¶ 15–17.

119. Rule 1.16 states two separate grounds for withdrawal based on crimes or frauds: "(1) the client persists in a course of action involving the lawyer's services that the lawyer reasonably believes is criminal or fraudulent," and "(2) the client has used the lawyer's services to perpetrate a crime or fraud." Each of these turns on use of the lawyer in the crime or fraud. *See* MODEL RULE 1.16(b)(1)–(2).

120. MODEL RULE 1.6.

121. MODEL RULES, Scope, ¶ 3.; *see* ABA Comm. on Ethics and Professional Responsibility, Formal Op. 90-358 (1990) (duty of confidentiality attaches in favor of prospective client).

122. *See* Bridge Products, Inc., v. Quantum Chemical Corp., 1990 U.S. Dist. Lexis 5019; 20 ELR 20940 (D. N. D. Ill. 1990) (granting motion to disqualify Sidley & Austin from representing a new client based on confidential information a partner of the firm learned in earlier consultations with the client's opponent).

123. The writer knows of instances in which a party consulted a lawyer ostensibly to consider retaining the lawyer but with the actual purpose of preventing an opponent from later hiring that lawyer.

124. J. Berton Fisher & William R. Keffer, *Selection, Use and Management of Experts in Environmental Legal Practice*, 33 TULSA L.J. 1003–1017 (1998).

125. MODEL RULE 4.2.

126. *See* MODEL RULE 4.2, Comment 4.

127. *See, e.g.*, Frey v. Department of Health and Human Services, 106 F.R.D. 32 (E.D. N.Y. 1985) (applying the Model Code counterpart, DR 7-104, to hold that only agency personnel that are alter ego of agency are within rule's prohibition against communication); State Bar of Montana Ethics Committee Opinion 940430 (1994) (allowing lawyer to interview agency personnel except for those with managerial responsibility).

128. Some lawyers counsel their clients to advise employees and agents to refuse to talk with lawyers—whether or not the employees come within the three-part test noted above. *See* MODEL RULE 3.4(f).

129. "Communications authorized by law include, for example, the right of a party to a controversy with a government agency to speak with government officials about the matter." MODEL RULE 4.2, Comment 1. Similarly, the Rule does not prevent a lawyer from seeking information from an agency via a Freedom of Information Act (FOIA) request. *See* Fusco v. Albany, 509 N.Y.S.2d 763 (1986).

130. (b) Notwithstanding paragraph (a), a lawyer may state:

(1) the claim, offense or defense involved and, except when prohibited by law, the identity of the persons involved;

(2) information contained in a public record;

(3) that an investigation of a matter is in progress;

(4) the scheduling or result of any step in litigation;

(5) a request for assistance in obtaining evidence and information necessary thereto;
(6) a warning of danger concerning the behavior of a person involved, when there is reason to believe that there exists the likelihood of substantial harm to an individual or to the public interest; and
(7) in a criminal case, in addition to subparagraphs (1) through (6):
(i) the identity, residence, occupation and family status of the accused;
(ii) if the accused has not been apprehended, information necessary to aid in apprehension of that person;
(iii) the fact, time and place of arrest; and
(iv) the identity of investigating and arresting officers or agencies and the length of the investigation.

MODEL RULE 3.6(b).

131. Jennifer L. Johnson, *Empowerment Lawyering: the Role of Trial Publicity in Environmental Justice,* 23 B.C. ENVTL. AFF. L. REV. 567 (1996).

132. *See* Phillip S. Berry, *SLAPP: Strategic Lawsuits Against Public Participation in Government the "Environmental" SLAPP* C935 ALI-ABA 61 (Aug. 19, 1994); Jennifer E. Sills, *SLAPP (Strategic Lawsuits Against Public Participation): How Can the Legal System Eliminate Their Appeal?* 25 CONN. L. REV. 547 (1993); John C. Barker, *Common-Law and Statutory Solutions to the Problem of SLAPP,* 6 LOY. L.A. L. REV. 395 (1993).

133. The acronym was coined by George W. Pring and Penelope Canan. *See* 47 SMU L. REV. 95, n.4.

134. *See* George W. Pring & Penelope Canan, *Strategic Lawsuits Against Public Participation ("SLAPP"): An Introduction for Bench, Bar and Bystanders,* 12 BRIDGEPORT L. REV. 937 (1993); George (Rock) Pring & Penelope A. Canan, *SLAPP: An Overview of the Practice,* C935 ALI-ABA 1 (Cosponsored by the University of Denver College of Law's Political Litigation Project and California Continuing Education of the Bar) (Aug. 19, 1994). Similar techniques include retaliation for environmental claims, proceedings to impose sanctions against attorneys, and political maneuvers to silence opponents. *Id.* Carl Tobias, *Environmental Litigation and Rule 11,* 33 WM. & MARY L. REV. 429 (1992) (noting the use of Rule 11 actions to discourage lawyers and the parties they represent from "commencing, or zealously pursuing, legitimate actions").

135. "[T]he wholly lawful exercise, by citizens in a community, of the right to petition their local government to follow a certain course of action . . . should be vigorously protected and should not expose individuals to suit by persons unhappy with the results of such petitioning." Westfield Partners, Ltd. v. Hogan, 740 F. Supp. 523 (N.D. Ill. 1990) (dismissing complaint of conspiracy by real estate developer against landowners who had successfully petitioned against development), quoted in Chad Baruch, *"If I Had a Hammer": Defending SLAPP Suits in Texas,* 3 TEX. WESLEYAN L. REV. 55 (1996).

136. *See* Yvette Mendez, *"SLAPP" Attack: Has Public Concern Gone South in Massachusetts?,* 42-MAR BBJ 6, 21 (1998); Susan D. Hargus, *Civil Practice Act: Prohibit a Civil Litigant from Interposing a Claim for an Improper Purpose Such As to Suppress a Person's Right of Free Speech or Right to Petition Government; Provide for a*

Motion to Strike or Dismiss That May Be Interposed by a Civil Defendant Whose Rights as Above Are Infringed by Such a Claim; Include Statements Made in Furtherance of the Right of Free Speech or Right to Petition Government in Connection with an Issue of Public Interest as Privileged Communications That May Not Be Used as a Basis for a Libel or Slander Tort Claim, 13 GA. ST. U. L. REV. 23 (1996); Edward W. McBride, Jr., *The Empire State SLAPP Back: New York's Legislative Response to SLAPP Suits*, 17 VT. L. REV. 925 (1990).

137. Marnie Stetson, *Reforming SLAPP Reform: New York's Anti-SLAPP Statute*, 70 N.Y.U. L. REV. 1324 (1995).

138. MODEL RULE 3.1.

139. MODEL RULE 3.1, Comment, ¶ 2 (emphasis added).

140. James W. Harper, *Attorneys as State Actors: A State Action Model and Argument for Holding SLAPP-plaintiffs' Attorneys Liable under 42 U.S.C. § 1983*, 21 HASTINGS CONST. L.Q. 405 (1994). Historically, ethical rules have prohibited a lawyer from filing a suit solely or merely to harass or to delay an action. *See* MODEL CODE DR 7-102(A)(1) (1980); *see also* Walker v. City of Bogalusa, La., 168 F.3d 237 (5th Cir. 1999) (upholding sanction against attorney for pursuing a meritless suit alleging racial discrimination by city officials who failed to evacuate African American community following an explosion); John C. Barker, *Common-Law and Statutory Solutions to the Problem of SLAPP*, 26 LOY. L.A. L. REV. 395, 417 (1993) (stating "lawyer must have probable cause to bring the suit, and the suit must have some substantial purpose other than harassment or delay").

PART III

Legal Objectives

CHAPTER 14

Stopping and Building New Facilities

MICHAEL B. GERRARD

Introduction

A central claim of the environmental justice movement has been that hazardous facilities are disproportionately located in minority and low-income communities, and a focus of the movement's activities has been to prevent new facilities from being built. Likewise, since the emergence of this movement, a major challenge for project sponsors who wish to build facilities that they believe are environmentally and socially responsible has been to navigate the increasingly difficult waters of project approvals.

Environmental justice advocates often point, as the birth of their movement, to a demonstration in 1982 against the construction of a facility for the disposal of 32,000 cubic yards of PCB-contaminated dirt in the mostly African American community of Afton, North Carolina. Some 414 demonstrators were arrested.[1] Among the protesters was the District of Columbia's delegate to the House of Representatives, Walter E. Fauntroy, who then asked the U.S. General Accounting Office to study siting in the region of EPA that covers the southeastern states. The resulting 1983 report, *Siting of Hazardous Waste Landfills and Their Correlation with Racial and Economic Status of Surrounding Communities,* concluded that blacks comprised the majority of those living near three of the four off-site hazardous waste landfills in this region. Four years later the Commission for Racial Justice of the United Church of Christ published its landmark study, *Toxic Wastes and Race in the United States*, which concluded that the location of active and inactive hazardous waste disposal facilities was heavily correlated with the racial composition of surrounding communities (even more than with income).

Numerous subsequent studies have reviewed siting patterns.[2] Some of these studies have reached the same conclusions as the United Church of Christ report;[3] others have argued that that report and its progeny suffer from serious methodological flaws.[4] The availability, reliability, and use of evidence of disproportionate siting and impacts are the subject of Chapter 12, pages 397–428.

Most of the scholarly and political attention has focused on the siting of new hazardous waste disposal facilities. (The distinction between operating disposal facilities, and places where waste was left behind after factories shut down, has often been lost.) In the late 1980s and early 1990s, when the central premises of the environmental justice movement were being formed, there was also a perceived shortage in hazardous waste disposal capacity and many new hazardous waste disposal facilities were proposed. Beginning around 1992, however, that shortage largely seemed to evaporate, and most of the pending proposals for new disposal facilities were abandoned.[5] Thus there were few battles over hazardous waste disposal facilities left to fight.

Much of the battleground (in the field, though not so much in academia) shifted to the siting of industrial plants, spawned by the strong economy of the late 1990s. These fights (such as several protracted fights over proposed petrochemical plants in Louisiana) were harder for opponents, because industrial plants tend to create far more jobs than waste disposal facilities, and thus garner much greater political support, and also because (as will be seen below) certain highly restrictive laws apply to hazardous waste disposal but not to operating facilities.

This chapter concerns the legal tools available to those seeking to stop the construction of new facilities, as well as the countermeasures available to project proponents. It begins by discussing legal issues in the decision whether the facility should be built at all. It then covers challenges to the decision about where to site the facility, followed by challenges to the permits required for these projects. Finally, the chapter ends with a discussion about the negotiation of compensation packages for communities that are willing (or forced) to accept a facility.

Challenging the Need for the Facility

Proposals for major new facilities do not spring out of nothingness; they emerge from processes that determine that the facilities are needed. Thus opponents would do well to challenge, if they can, the process that leads to the determination of need, and the need itself.

The method of determining need varies considerably depending on the type of project, and there are too many types of projects to list them all. These are some examples:

Hazardous waste disposal—In 1986, Congress amended the Comprehensive Environmental Response, Compensation and Liability Act (CERCLA) to require that each state determine how much hazardous waste disposal capacity it needed, and to adopt a plan for providing that capacity (either on its own or in conjunction with other states).[6] Every state completed this plan by 1991. However, with the sharp downturn in hazardous waste generation in the early 1990s, this effort became largely obsolete, and EPA essentially abandoned it in 1997.[7] Disposal capacity shortages still exist for certain specialized waste streams in some parts of the country, but on a national level and in almost every state there is no ongoing process for determining need for hazardous waste disposal capacity.

Low-level radioactive waste (LLRW)—Congress determined, in enacting the Low Level Radioactive Waste Act of 1980, that numerous new LLRW disposal facilities were needed, and it directed the states (acting alone or in compacts with other states) to develop capacity.[8] As noted below, this process has had few tangible results, and (despite dire warnings of zero nationwide capacity) there are now three operating facilities that accept civilian LLRW (one each in South Carolina, Utah, and Washington).

Solid waste—In contrast to the languid pace at which hazardous waste and LLRW facilities are being built, there is currently a great deal of activity in building solid waste disposal facilities. Stringent new environmental regulations that require the closure of many old disposal facilities, and the opening of state borders to solid waste from other states, spawned by a number of decisions under the Commerce Clause,[9] have led to a scramble to build large, low-cost landfills. There is no official national program to identify solid waste disposal needs. Some states require the preparation of solid waste management plans, providing a useful forum for discussion concerning the substitution of waste reduction and recycling for new disposal capacity.

Highways—The Federal Highway Administration undertakes a complex planning process to determine the need for major transportation investments such as highways and bridges. This process is carried out in conjunction with the states and cities and typically takes years, if not decades, and offers multiple opportunities for public input.[10]

Airports—Determination of the need for a new airport is primarily a state responsibility. Most states have statutes requiring anyone who desires to build or expand an airport to obtain a state certificate of need. The Federal Aviation Administration influences the process by its allocation of federal funds for airport development and improvement.[11]

Electric generating plants—Almost every state has a public service commission that is responsible for deciding whether new electric generating plants can be built. Most of these commissions require that electric utilities obtain a "certificate of public convenience and necessity" before building new plants or major transmission lines. This system has been cast into turmoil by the deregulation of the electric utility industry, which began in 1978 with the Public Utility Regulatory Practices Act,[12] and continued with the Energy Policy Act of 1992.[13] Third-party electric producers have been entering the market at an accelerated pace; most states require these new producers to obtain certificates, but some states are considering dropping that requirement.[14] Thus, the opportunities for public involvement in deciding the need for these facilities may diminish.

Manufacturing plants—The need for a new manufacturing facility is entirely a matter for its corporate sponsor, perhaps in conjunction with its bankers, large customers, and other private entities. There is typically no role for governmental or public input in the need determination.

Where there are formal public processes for determining need, the timing typically works out in a way to preclude much community involvement. Transportation projects like highways are necessarily site-specific (or at least corridor-specific), so neighbors of contemplated projects will usually know, and have reason to be concerned, about the ongoing planning process. Waste disposal projects, on the other hand, are not so geographically specific, and thus while the need determination process is underway, particular locations have usually not been identified. By the time sites are announced and communities are alerted, the need process is usually long past. Ideally, national or statewide groups would participate in the need process and argue, where appropriate, that waste minimization, recycling, energy conservation, and other techniques provide a superior alternative to construction of a new facility. However, few such groups have the resources to participate widely in these processes.

Nonetheless, it may still be worthwhile for a targeted community to raise the issue of need long after the formal need determination process has concluded. The moral authority for building an unpopular project—that society needs this electricity, or this waste disposal capacity—can be undercut by serious questions about whether the need is really present. Moreover, certain construction permits—especially the Section 404 dredge and fill permits, and the Section 4(f) parkland destruction permits, both of which are discussed below—involve a need determination.

None of this is to say that there should always be a reflexive decision to oppose a project. Blocking a hazardous waste disposal facility will have certain salutary environmental impacts—it protects the particular site, and it may so restrict the availability of disposal facilities that it could raise the price of waste disposal, thereby creating an economic disincentive to generate waste. On the other hand, blocking such a disposal facility may have negative impacts as well: it could perpetuate the operation of old, substandard, poorly sited disposal facilities (which may well be located in minority or low-income communities);[15] it could prolong the extended and possibly unsafe storage of hazardous wastes that are awaiting permanent disposal; it could cause the facility to be relocated to another location (possibly in another state or country) where the environmental impacts might be just as bad, or possibly much worse.[16] Little of this is likely to concern organizations based in the communities where the unwanted facilities are proposed, but it should be of interest to groups with broader geographic or policy concerns.

Challenging the Siting Process

Once the need for a facility has been established, the next step is to decide where to put it. This decision is very important from an environmental justice perspective. There has been relatively little concern that decisions *whether* to build facilities have been made in a discriminatory manner,[17] but there have been persistent charges that choices of *where* to build have been made in a way that disadvantages minority and low-income communities.

As with the need issue, the methods for selecting sites depend on the nature of the project:

Hazardous waste—The federal government has at various times considered establishing a nationwide program for siting hazardous waste disposal facilities; but it has never adopted one, leaving the task to the states.[18] Most of the states adopted formal siting processes in the 1970s; no two are the same, but they typically involve siting commissions, technical siting criteria, and formalized public participation.[19] However, not a single hazardous waste landfill or incinerator has ever been sited pursuant to these processes (though some treatment plants and transfer stations have gotten through). There is so much opportunity for public opposition to delay or halt these procedures that no project has ever successfully run the gauntlet. With only two exceptions (one in Colorado, the other in Texas), all the permitted hazardous waste landfills in operation in the United States today were sited before the enactment of the Resource Conservation and Recovery Act in 1976, and both of those were advanced by private companies outside the siting system.

LLRW—The story here is about the same as it is with hazardous waste. Numerous states developed formal siting processes, and several sites have been tentatively designated after multistep processes that involved progressively winnowing down sites to exclude those with any of various physical, economic, or social shortcomings.[20] Every one of these sites was met with ferocious opposition at the local or state level. Most of the sites have been formally abandoned; as of this writing, none of them is near final permitting. One LLRW site was developed in Utah by a private company outside the formal site selection process, and another is now being pursued by a private company in Texas.

Solid waste—Site selection for solid waste facilities (landfills, incinerators, and transfer stations) is typically done at the county or the municipal level. Many counties and some cities have developed formal multistep processes that resemble those that have been used (and have invariably failed) for hazardous waste and LLRW facilities, except that some of these county solid waste siting processes have succeeded, in large part because solid waste facilities tend to engender less public opposition.[21]

Transportation facilities—Highways and transit lines, more than almost any other kind of facility, are geography-specific. The need determination process is closely tied to the site selection process, because transportation networks tend to be built to accommodate travel between particular origins and destinations. State transportation officials, acting under federal guidance, use a multistep process that narrows down the route from a broad corridor to a more and more specific band until the final route is selected.

Airports—Airports require so much land that there are seldom a large number of available sites near cities. Many states require that airport master plans be developed as part of the decision where to place new airports. Because airports serve regional needs, conflicts frequently arise between the often unwilling host municipality (which bears the brunt of adverse environmental impacts) and the rest of the region.[22]

Electric generating plants—Most of the states adopted power plant siting legislation in the 1970s in the face of then-expanding demand for electricity. These state laws run a gamut from some that merely call for nonbinding studies of available sites, to others that provide "one-stop shopping" with all necessary permits being subject to one consolidated proceeding and (in some instances) state preemption of local zoning powers.[23] In at least one instance, environmental justice has been an explicit subject of administrative adjudication in such a proceeding.[24]

Manufacturing plants—The same autonomy that corporations enjoy in deciding whether to build new factories also applies where they build them. However, state and local governments are often so eager for new industry to locate within their borders that they provide assistance in finding sites, sometimes going as far as to condemn land in the place selected by the companies, to make up for the companies' lack of eminent domain power.[25]

One lesson of the above brief catalog of siting procedures is that the multistep processes involved in siting LLRW facilities, highways, and certain other types of facilities are extremely vulnerable to public opposition. Citizens who organize early, and especially those who have persuaded their municipalities to finance opposition work, have frequently been able to block proposed facilities.

One prominent example of a multistep siting process that ran afoul of environmental justice concerns was a proposed $855 million uranium enrichment facility (to make fuel for nuclear power plants) in Louisiana. The proposal was announced in 1989 by Louisiana Energy Services, a consortium of five energy companies. The chosen site was in Clairborne Parish, five miles from the town of Homer. The 442-acre site is immediately between two unincorporated communities, Forest Grove (population 150) and Center Springs (population 100). Citizens Against Nuclear Trash (CANT) intervened in the proceedings of the Atomic Safety and Licensing Board (ASLB) of the Nuclear Regulatory Commission (NRC). After several years of hearings, the ASLB concluded that the facility met all applicable environmental, health, safety, and financial requirements. Then the ASLB took up CANT's environmental justice claims.

The ASLB issued its ruling on May 1, 1997.[26] It decided that CANT's principal witness, Dr. Robert D. Bullard, a sociology professor at Clark Atlanta University and a leading environmental justice advocate, had established that, while support from the community was purportedly one of the principal site selection criteria, the communities of Forest Grove and Center Springs (unlike the more distant town of Homer) were not informed of the siting decision until it was too late for the residents to affect the siting process.

Dr. Bullard analyzed the applicant's multistep siting process, which had begun with an analysis of 78 potential sites. As these sites were progressively winnowed down, those remaining at each stage had a larger percentage of black population within a one-mile radius, until the site finally selected had the highest percent black population—97 percent—of all 78 sites. "This statistical evidence very strongly suggests that racial considerations played a part in the site selection process," the ASLB declared. "It does not, of course, rule out all possibility that race played no part in the selection process. Nonetheless, the Intervenor's statistical evidence clearly indicates that the probability of this being the case is unlikely."

The ASLB directed the NRC staff to go back and thoroughly investigate the siting process. The board said that CANT's evidence "is more than sufficient to raise a reasonable inference that racial considerations played some part in the site selection process," but that a "finding that the selection process was tainted by racial bias is far too serious a determination, with potentially long-lasting consequences, to render without the benefit of a thorough and professional Staff investigation aided by whatever outside experts as may be necessary."

The ASLB said that if Staff comes back and concludes that racial considerations played no role at all in the site selection process, the application can proceed, but then an additional question will have to be faced: whether the facility will disproportionately affect minority populations.

The applicant appealed, and in April 1998 the full NRC reversed the portion of the ASLB's decision that required a more thorough inquiry into possible racial discrimination in siting, but called for further study about the actual effects that the facility would have on the neighboring communities.[27] In April 1998 the applicant, apparently discouraged by the extensive permitting delays, withdrew its application and cancelled its plans to build the plant.[28]

Challenging Permits

Introduction

When the objective is to prevent the construction of a new facility, experience shows that the legal tactic with the highest probability of success is to try to prevent the developer from obtaining or keeping its environmental permits. The environmental justice theories discussed elsewhere in this book must still be regarded as experimental, with a small handful of successes to date. Challenges to permits, on the other hand, have a long history of successes for plaintiffs. Environmental justice claims may be very good devices for mobilizing popular and political support for an opposition campaign, but they are less likely than permit challenges to win in administrative tribunals and in court. Correspondingly, developers who do not pay scrupulous attention to the permit process, ensuring that they have identified all required permits and satisfied the criteria for obtaining them, are at risk.

Thus one of the first things the lawyer for any side of a siting controversy should do is identify each and every permit and approval the project will require. The applicant's counsel will begin this process immediately upon being retained. As for the opponents' counsel, the best initial source is usually the environmental impact statement (EIS) for the project, if one has already been prepared; it will almost always identify these permits. Otherwise, Freedom of Information Act searches of the relevant government files (see Chapter 8, "Access to Information") may unearth correspondence concerning required permits. The inquiry should not end there, however, because it has happened more than once that all parties—the applicant and the government—have simply overlooked a permit requirement, and that opponents were able to make great use of that error. The principal kinds of permits are listed below, but this is by no means comprehensive. Serious legal research is often required to identify the required state and local permits, in particular, because the requirements for them are often embodied in regulations that are unavailable on the Internet, LEXIS, and Westlaw and may only be found in specialized libraries. Many important guidance documents are not published at all and can only be obtained from regulators or from active practitioners.

Once all the permits have been enumerated, counsel should identify the substantive criteria that must be met to obtain each permit. This will help determine what facts must be developed to mount a successful challenge or defense. The factual issues that can lead to permit denial are often much different from the issues that are of initial concern to the community. A classic example of this difference arose with Westway, a proposed interstate highway in New York City along the west side of Manhattan on the Hudson River shore. Between 1972, when the highway was first proposed, and about 1980, the opponents and their lawyers (including the author of this chapter) focused on the road's impacts on traffic and air pollution, and the alternative of using the available federal funds for mass transit. Beginning around 1980, however, the legal focus shifted to the impact that the landfill for the highway would have on the striped bass of the Hudson River. The courts eventually determined that the project's EIS had inadequately studied these aquatic impacts, and that led to the abandonment of the project.[29]

In the same way, the issues that are most successful in fighting waste disposal facilities are often different from those that initially capture the neighbors' attention. The issue on which most landfill applications turn, for example, is the hydrogeology of the site. On the other hand, traffic, noise, and odors from site operations, though of major concern to neighbors, are rarely a basis for defeating a project.

As will now be shown, permit requirements tend to fall into several categories: site-based; technology-based; and applicant-based.

Site-Based Permit Requirements

The most powerful permit rules from the opponents' perspective—that is, those most likely to kill a project outright—are those based on the site itself, especially its ecological qualities. Thus, most of these rules are of greater importance in a rural setting than in an urban setting, where the natural environment has probably already been degraded.

These are some of the most important permits:

Wetlands—Federal and state governments, and many municipalities, heavily regulate work in wetlands (which were called swamps, marshes, bogs, and the like in a less enlightened day). The definition of what is a "wetland" varies between one level of government and another, and depends on highly technical aspects of soils and vegetation that must be interpreted by a specialist, usually a botanist. Certain areas may be federal wetlands but not state wetlands, or vice versa, and several projects have foundered on ignorance of the difference. Some places may be "wetlands" even if they do not look especially wet, so (outside of deserts) it is usually worthwhile to determine whether any piece of ground is a wetland under any program. At the federal level, wetlands permits are issued under Section 404 of the Clean Water Act (CWA)[30] by the Army Corps of Engineers (Corps) in accordance with EPA guidelines[31] and with the Corps' "public interest review" procedures.[32] The EPA guidelines prohibit the issuance of Section 404 permits "if there is a practicable alternative to the proposed discharge which would have less adverse impact on the aquatic ecosystem, so long as the alternative does not have other significant adverse environmental consequences."[33] Certain kinds of work in wetlands do not require individual permits, but are instead covered by blanket authorizations called "nationwide permits."[34] A prerequisite to a Corps wetlands permit is the issuance by the state of a certification that the project will not contravene water quality standards.[35]

Waterways—Work such as rechanneling, filling, and sinking of piles in rivers and streams, as well as on the coasts of oceans and lakes, is heavily regulated. As with wetlands, the definitions of protected waters and regulated work will vary between the federal government and the states. The federal programs are administered by the Corps of Engineers, primarily under Section 10 of the CWA,[36] and generally cover only navigable waters, though that term is broadly defined.[37] These rules may be especially important when a project requires pipes or cables to be buried under a waterway. At common law, the public trust doctrine also may inhibit construction in waterways.[38]

Parkland—Official parklands enjoy special protections under the law. Some state constitutions require parklands to be preserved in perpetuity unless the state legislature specifically authorizes their conversion for another purpose.[39] An important federal statute, Section 4(f) of the Department of Transportation Act, prohibits any federal transportation project "which requires the use of any publicly owned land from a public park, recreation area, or wildlife and waterfowl refuge . . . or any land from an historic site . . . unless . . . there is no feasible and prudent alternative to the use of such land."[40] This covers activities of all units of the Department of Transportation, including the Federal Highway Administration, the Federal Transit Administration, the Federal Aviation Administration, and the U.S. Coast Guard (which must grant permits for many kinds of bridges).

Historic areas—Historic buildings and districts are protected by the federal and state governments and by many cities. Each level of government may have its own registries of historic properties. At the federal level, the National Historic Preservation Act (NHPA) provides that before a federal agency undertakes or allows any project that may adversely affect a property that is on, or has been declared eligible for, the National Registry of Historic Places (National Registry), the state historic preservation officer (SHPO) must be consulted, and if the SHPO does not concur, the Advisory Council on Historic Preservation must be consulted.[41] The NHPA does not affect projects that have no federal involvement. Adverse effects can include visual impacts even if the historic property is not physically touched. Some cities have historic preservation ordinances that are much more vigorous than the NHPA, requiring (and making it difficult to obtain) local permits before city-designated buildings can be altered or demolished. Historic preservation laws are discussed in Chapter 9, "Impact Assessment," pages 256–306.

Endangered species habitat—The Endangered Species Act, like the NHPA, regulates only projects that have federal involvement. It prohibits federal projects that would jeopardize the continued existence of an endangered species or destroy or adversely modify the habitat of such species.[42] Most states restrict their regulation in this area to prohibiting the killing of or traffic in individual endangered animals, but some also regulate habitat destruction.

Floodplains—Acting under the encouragement of the National Flood Insurance Program, many municipalities have enacted land use controls that restrict development within floodplains.[43]

Contaminated sites—At the opposite end of the scale from natural areas are sites that have been so used, or abused, by humankind that they are contaminated with hazardous substances. Construction of projects on contaminated lands involves several important federal and state laws, which are discussed in Chapters 16 and 17.

Zoning—Most urban and suburban areas, and some rural areas, are subject to local zoning. An important threshold question concerning any construction project that might be subject to environmental justice controversy is whether the local zoning for such a project has been preempted by the federal or state governments. The Atomic

Energy Act preempts most forms of state and local control over nuclear facilities,[44] though states may enter into agreements with the Nuclear Regulatory Commission to implement certain federal requirements within their borders.[45] Pursuant to the Telecommunications Act of 1996, the Federal Communications Commission has adopted regulations preempting many local controls over cellular towers.[46] There is limited federal preemption over state regulation of hazardous waste disposal facilities.[47] Some states have also preempted municipalities from regulating certain kinds of facilities, such as landfills;[48] each state's laws must be checked on this subject. (While states in the United States are sovereign entities, municipalities are not; they derive their powers from state law.) Where there is no preemption, municipalities in most states have considerable discretion to regulate land uses within their borders, and some towns have used their zoning authority to keep out unwanted facilities.[49] A very few municipalities—most notably New York City—have adopted "fair share" rules as part of their zoning codes designed to prevent the overaccumulation of unwanted facilities in particular neighborhoods.[50] It should be cautioned, however, that some courts will strike down zoning ordinances that are written or applied unreasonably, and a municipality's chances of surviving a challenge to its zoning actions will greatly increase if the municipality develops a written record that establishes the factual basis for its actions.[51]

Technology-Based Permit Requirements

The types of permits listed above focus on the location of a particular facility. Those listed below focus instead on the facility's technologies, functions, and emissions.

RCRA/Hazardous Waste—The federal Resource Conservation and Recovery Act (RCRA) tightly regulates the construction and operation of "TSD" facilities—facilities for the treatment, storage, or disposal of hazardous wastes.[52] This encompasses hazardous waste landfills, incinerators, land impoundments, and many other kinds of units. EPA's regulations contain considerable detail on how these facilities must be built and run.[53] EPA regulations also dictate minimum standards for public participation in TSD facility siting.[54] RCRA allows EPA to delegate most of its implementation to the states, and most states have received this delegation and operate the RCRA program, subject to oversight by the EPA regional offices. Thus, applications for TSD facilities are primarily processed by the states rather than EPA. For the most part, states are free to impose regulations that are more, but not less, stringent than EPA's.

RCRA/Solid Waste—In 1991, EPA, acting under the authority of RCRA, promulgated regulations governing the location, design, operation, and closure of new municipal waste landfills.[55] Many of the states have been delegated the authority to implement these regulations. Virtually every state also has its own environmental regulations for the siting, construction, and operation of solid waste facilities.

Toxic Substances Control Act (TSCA)—The handling and disposal of polychlorinated biphenyls (PCBs) is regulated under TSCA[56] rather than RCRA. EPA has regulations on the siting and operation of PCB disposal facilities.[57] Unlike RCRA, TSCA cannot be delegated to the states, so all facilities that dispose of PCBs require EPA permits.

Clean Air Act (CAA)—The CAA[58] is the longest and most elaborate statute in all of environmental law, and several full-length books analyze and describe it.[59] Several provisions are particularly important in the environmental justice context:

- the regulation of significant new sources of air pollution, such as industrial plants and incinerators, in areas that do not comply with air quality standards;[60]
- the prevention of significant deterioration rules, which govern new facilities in areas that currently have clean air;[61]
- the Title V program, only now being implemented, which requires all sources of air pollution to have unified permits, and subjects them to detailed monitoring and reporting requirements;[62]
- the rules governing the emissions of methane and other gases from municipal solid waste landfills;[63] and
- the transportation planning provisions that (often operating in conjunction with related provisions of the Intermodal Surface Transportation Efficiency Act) require assessment of, and efforts to reduce, the effect that highways and other transportation facilities have on air pollution.[64]

An emerging environmental justice issue is the use of emissions offsets and trading—the tool, allowed in some circumstances by the Clean Air Act, whereby one facility can emit more air pollution than would otherwise be allowed if it arranges for another facility to reduce its emissions. No clear framework has emerged for dealing with the disparate impacts that can arise under this system, especially where the two involved facilities are in different communities.[65]

Clean Water Act (CWA)—The CWA requires that permits be obtained for all point sources of water pollution (such as from pipes and drains) into waters of the United States,[66] and that those discharging indirectly into the waters via municipal sewage systems also receive permission to do so.[67] Thus, virtually every industrial facility in the United States requires a CWA permit. Implementation of the CWA can be, and in most cases has been, delegated to the states.

Environmental Review Requirements

The National Environmental Policy Act[68] (NEPA) and its rough equivalents in about half the states are a procedural overlay on top of the permit requirements. They do not impose substantive standards, but they require full study and disclosure of impacts, and thus often reveal the applicability of permit requirements and influence the outcome of permit applications. These rules are the subject of Chapter 9, "Impact Assessment," pages 256–306.

Applicant-Based Permit Requirements

Several federal agencies and states have adopted "bad actor" rules designed to prevent individuals or companies with histories of repeated and serious environmental violations from obtaining permits to operate new facilities.[69] These rules provide opponents with a good opportunity to press their objections to unsavory facility operators. For example, in 1998 the California Department of Toxic Substances Control denied a permit to Broco Environmental Inc. for a waste storage and transfer facility because of the company's poor compliance history.[70]

Civil Rights Claims

Legal theories are emerging for challenging environmental permits on civil rights grounds, including suits under the Equal Protection Clause of the U.S. Constitution, Titles VI and VII of the Civil Rights Act of 1964, and various state civil rights laws. These theories are discussed in detail in Chapters 1–5 of this book, and thus will not be covered further here.

Common Law and Constitutional Tools

A few common law and constitutional theories may be available to prevent the construction of new facilities. The "anticipatory nuisance" theory applies to proposed facilities that, if built, would cause injury. Though this theory is not widely accepted, a few courts have used it to enjoin projects.[71] Two states—Georgia and Alabama—have codified this doctrine and make it available where the plaintiff can prove that the injury is "reasonably certain" to occur.[72]

Using takings theories, a few courts have granted monetary compensation to property owners whose land was reduced in value because of proposed hazardous use in neighboring property.[73]

State statutory and constitutional theories are discussed in Chapter 5, "State Environmental Justice Programs and Related Authorities," pages 140–56.

Procedural Issues

Siting controversies tend to proceed in three stages: pre-application, permitting, and litigation. The edges of these stages sometimes blur into each other, but it is useful to consider them in that order.

Pre-Application

The earlier it is in the process, the more vulnerable a project is to defeat and the more susceptible it is to change. At the beginning, the potential sponsor needs to assess the viability of the contemplated project, which includes its chances of ultimately securing government approval. The sponsor also must prepare conceptual drawings and, for private projects, begin to think about how to assemble financing. Additionally, sponsors start the process of gathering political support.

At this early stage, a little bit of community opposition can go a long way. If the sponsor has several different options for where to site the project, protests in one community and silence in another may point to the path of least resistance. If it is the sort of project that a community might accept if it were modified in certain ways, at this preliminary stage modifications are often rather easy, before heavy investments have been made in design and engineering.

Public notice of proposed projects is rarely required before a formal application is filed, and in many places not before the application is ready for public hearings. Local governments (especially their planning departments, in towns large enough to have them) usually know about contemplated projects at an early stage. Communities that are not well represented in local government—and traditionally this has included many low-income and minority communities—often do not learn of proposals until the earliest, most vulnerable stage has passed. The importance of keeping one's ears open to the earliest rumblings of development planning cannot be overstated. Where such rumblings are detected, informal conversations with local officials may yield much useful information; the freedom of information laws (discussed in Chapter 8, "Access to Information," pages 230–55) can also be employed.

It is also at this early stage that project sponsors select their strategy for dealing with neighboring communities. For projects that will obviously be controversial, such as waste disposal sites, the traditional approach has been called "decide-announce-defend." There is no public word of the project until the sponsor has decided to build it. More enlightened sponsors are coming to the realization, however, that it is often better to consult with the community at an earlier stage and to address its concerns before making a firm decision on proceeding.[74]

Another decision that must be made early in the process is whether to prepare a full environmental impact statement (EIS). As discussed above and in Chapter 9, EISs are required under NEPA for major federal actions significantly affecting the environment, and about half the states have comparable laws for state and local actions. The decision whether to require an EIS rests with the governmental lead agency, but the project sponsor is often influential in this decision. As a legal matter, it is usually safer to prepare an EIS than not to, because courts are far more likely to overturn a project's approvals because no EIS has been prepared than because there was a poor EIS.[75] Communities that are concerned about projects definitely want a detailed EIS, both because that can delay the project and because it will reveal much information that can be useful in the later stages of the project controversy. For project sponsors, there is a great premium on candor in preparing EISs; just as high officials have been known to get into much more trouble for lying about improper activities than for the activities themselves, projects have foundered because the EISs concealed important information that, if revealed, would not necessarily have led to denial of the needed permits. A classic instance of this is the already-discussed Westway project, which was defeated in court because the EIS concealed its impacts on the fish of the Hudson River.

Permitting

Once the applications and EIS (if any) have been filed, the permitting agencies must decide whether to accept them as complete. Sometimes project opponents can informally argue that the documents are incomplete and must be revised. Once the documents are declared complete, they are made publicly available, and there is usually an opportunity for a public hearing and the submission of written comments.

As discussed in greater detail in Chapter 7 ("Public Participation," pages 185–229), some federal and state agencies provide the opportunity for adjudicatory hearings for certain kinds of applications. These are trial-like proceedings before administrative law judges (ALJs), at which the applicant's representatives and experts must testify under oath and are subject to cross-examination. Where these hearings are available, they are by far the best opportunity that citizens will ever have to probe and challenge the technical basis for project proposals. In most jurisdictions, the ALJs undertake de novo review of the evidence.

It is essential for project opponents to retain qualified experts to assist them in the adjudicatory hearings. Care must be taken in selecting experts, in terms of their area of expertise as well as their independence. There are no generic all-purpose environmental experts; some are specialists in hydrogeology, others in air pollution modelling, and so on. The key issues in the case must be identified before the experts can be selected. In some disciplines, it is very difficult to find experts, at least in the same state, who do not customarily work for the industry that is seeking the permit being challenged. (This is a particular problem in finding traffic engineers to help in antihighway cases.) Sympathetic professors at local universities are often available to help at much lower fees than those charged by consulting firms. If that is not possible, it is often necessary to go to another region to find an independent expert.

Litigation

Challenges to proposed projects are usually ripe for challenge in court when permits have been formally issued. Communities often wish to begin litigation earlier as a way to stress the seriousness of their opposition and in the hopes of swiftly derailing the project. This approach is usually counterproductive. Such premature lawsuits are almost always unsuccessful, and the defeats are often demoralizing (not to mention fruitlessly expensive) for the communities or their pro bono counsel. The odds of success are diminished not only by the actions' prematurity, but also because they are necessarily brought before the project opponents have the full set of facts that will enable them to mount the most effective challenge. There is even the danger that the court will issue a ruling that is damaging to later challenges by preliminarily finding the site or the project to be generally suitable.

Moreover, the technical decisions of expert administrative agencies enjoy a presumption of soundness, and will not be overturned unless the court finds that they were arbitrary and capricious—a very difficult standard. Thus, adjudicatory hearings before administrative agencies are a much better forum for technical issues. On the other hand, courts are usually the best place to argue that the administrative agency followed the wrong procedures, or interpreted the laws or regulations incorrectly.

Defensive Measures

Government agencies and project proponents have found a number of arguments and tactics to be especially useful in defending against challenges to proposed projects, including:

Standing—The federal and many state courts are becoming increasingly receptive to arguments that environmental plaintiffs lack standing to sue, usually on the grounds that the plaintiffs are not directly affected by the challenged action or would not directly benefit from a favorable outcome. This issue is discussed in greater detail in Chapter 11, "Access to the Courts," pages 357–96.

Exhaustion of administrative remedies—Substantive (as opposed to procedural) arguments can usually not be made in court unless they were first raised at the administrative level. This doctrine has been used to defeat legal challenges to projects that had already received their permits.[76]

Standard of review—Defendants typically stress the considerable deference that is accorded expert agencies.

Statute of limitations—Some states provide extremely short statutes of limitations (as short as 30 days in some instances) for challenges to administrative decisions. Missing a statute of limitations is fatal, regardless of the merits of the case.[77]

Discovery—Especially, but not exclusively, when the challenge is accompanied by some kind of toxic tort action, defendants attempt to secure significant and expensive discovery against the plaintiffs.

Marginalization—Where the applicants can point to a substantial history of consultation with the affected communities, some of whom came to accept the project (perhaps after concessions were made), applicants may be able to paint the remaining opponents as the disgruntled few. This theoretically has little legal import, but it can influence how some judges see the case overall.

Bonds—If the plaintiffs seek a preliminary injunction against the construction of a project, the defendants will invariably request (and sometimes be granted) a ruling that the plaintiffs post a very large bond, often in amounts far exceeding what communities are able to raise.

Where the plaintiffs overcome these defenses and tactics, litigation can be very effective in delaying projects, even in the absence of an injunction. This is especially true for projects that rely on private financing or bond issues, since pending litigation severely chills a developer's ability to raise money. More than a few projects have been delayed so long that the market or other impetus for the project evaporated, leading to withdrawal of the proposal.

Negotiating About Facilities

Sometimes communities conclude that they may be willing to accept a project if it is modified in certain ways, or if they receive certain community benefits or compensation. This is more likely to occur where the facility creates inconveniences (such as traffic delays) or poses aesthetic problems (such as unsightliness and noise) than where there is concern that the facility will cause adverse health effects. Some things are negotiable, but health (and especially the health of one's children) is not.

Where a community agrees to negotiate, it is sending a strong signal that its response to the project is not "absolutely not" but rather "maybe if." Thus, serious consultations within the community are advisable before sending this signal.

Where there is room for talking, one question is the format for these discussions. The talks, if successful, will result in a formal written document. It is essential that each side be represented by counsel who can make sure that these documents accurately reflect the parties' mutual understandings.

A large literature has developed on the use of mediation in resolving environmental disputes.[78] Mediation tends to be most useful where the issues are especially complex; where there are many different interests represented at the table, so it is not just a two-party controversy; and where (as often arises in siting disputes) personal antagonisms have arisen, impeding direct dialog.

It sometimes occurs that the great bulk of the community is in agreement on a settlement, but a small group dissents. The community and its leadership (as well as the government and the developer) will then have to decide whether that small group will be able to muster the organization and resources to torpedo the agreement, either politically or in court. Where everyone in a large community seems to agree on a settlement, but the government or developer requires certainty, one device sometimes used is to file a class action lawsuit against the project, naming as the plaintiff class all members of the entire community, and immediately settling that lawsuit with a document that embodies the agreement; if the class is certified by the court and no one has opted out of the class, everyone is bound by the settlement.

In negotiating agreements, communities should never underestimate their own power. A well-organized, well-represented community may be the most serious threat to a project that is worth hundreds of millions or billions of dollars, and the community may well have enough leverage to extract significant concessions.[79]

These are some of the concessions that are sometimes granted in agreements:[80]

- Caps on facility capacity and operations;
- Limitations on future expansion;
- Appointment of a community advisory board that will have access to facility operating information and meet periodically with plant management;
- Appointment of a technical advisor (selected by and accountable to the community, but paid with company money) to monitor operations;
- Mandatory suspension of plant operations if predetermined limits (such as effluent levels) are exceeded;
- Contingent mitigation measures (for instance, sound barriers) that are installed if set limits are exceeded;
- Offers to purchase the homes nearest the facility;
- Property value guarantees, so that neighbors who later sell their homes will be paid the difference in the value of those homes with and without the facility's presence;
- Enhancements to the community's emergency response capabilities (such as purchase of additional ambulances and fire trucks);
- Commitments to hire local workers and procure products and services locally;
- Procurement of insurance and trust funds to ensure fulfillment of commitments and compensation for mishaps.

Enforcement mechanisms are an important element of these agreements. It is especially important that the commitments be binding on the future owners of facilities. The agreements should be written into the plant's permits. Sometimes the agreements are prepared in the form of covenants, for the benefit of the municipality or an established community organization, that are recorded with the deed and run with the land.

It is a matter of particular sensitivity when the negotiation concerns cash payments to the municipality or neighbors. For waste disposal facilities in particular, a frequent method is a set fee per ton of waste. Some communities have accepted a flat fee of $1 per ton; this is likely to be far lower than what is achievable. Negotiators should determine the likely tipping fee (the amount the facility will charge its customers to dispose of their waste) and consider what would be a reasonable percentage of that.

One common use of the money received is to offset local taxes. Indeed, a number of communities have zero property taxes thanks to funds received from local facilities. Care should be taken, however, lest this make the town so dependent on the continued operations of the facility that there will seem to be no options if the plant does indeed turn out to pose health threats.

If cash payments to neighbors are contemplated, serious thought should be given to the timing of those payments, because today's neighbors may move away, leaving future generations to live next to an undesirable facility without compensation.

Notes

1. ROBERT D. BULLARD, DUMPING IN DIXIE 35–38 (Boulder, Colo.: Westview Press 1990).

2. Many of these studies are analyzed in U.S. General Accounting Office, Doc. GAO/RCED-95-84, HAZARDOUS AND NONHAZARDOUS WASTE: DEMOGRAPHICS OF PEOPLE LIVING NEAR WASTE FACILITIES (June 1995).

3. *E.g.*, BENJAMIN GOLDMAN & L. FITTON, TOXIC WASTE AND RACE REVISITED: AN UPDATE OF THE 1987 REPORT ON THE RACIAL AND SOCIOECONOMIC CHARACTERISTICS OF COMMUNITIES WITH HAZARDOUS WASTE SITES (Center for Policy Alternatives, NAACP, and United Church of Christ Commission for Racial Justice, 1994); Paul Mohai & Bunyan Bryant, *Environmental Racism: Reviewing the Evidence, in* RACE AND THE INCIDENCE OF ENVIRONMENTAL HAZARDS 163–76 (Bunyan Bryant & Paul Mohai eds., 1992).

4. *E.g.*, CHRISTOPHER H. FOREMAN, JR., THE PROMISE AND PERIL OF ENVIRONMENTAL JUSTICE (Brookings 1998); Vicki Been, *Locally Undesirable Land Uses in Minority Neighborhoods: Disproportionate Siting or Market Dynamics?* 103 YALE L.J. 1406 (1994); Douglas L. Anderton, *Hazardous Waste Facilities: "Environmental Equity" Issues in Metropolitan Areas,* 18 EVALUATION REV., Apr. 1994, at 123.

5. This shift in the hazardous waste disposal market is discussed in MICHAEL B. GERRARD, WHOSE BACKYARD, WHOSE RISK: FEAR AND FAIRNESS IN TOXIC AND NUCLEAR WASTE SITING 10–11 (MIT 1994) [hereinafter WHOSE BACKYARD, WHOSE RISK].

6. 42 U.S.C. § 9604(c)(9).

7. EPA, CERCLA 104(c)(9) Capacity Assurance Planning: National Capacity Assessment Report, 62 Fed. Reg. 2156 (Jan. 15, 1997).

8. Pub. L. 96-573, 94 Stat. 3347 (codified at 42 U.S.C. § 2021b–2021d).

9. *E.g.*, C & A Carbone, Inc. v. Town of Clarkstown, 511 U.S. 383 (1994); City of Philadelphia v. New Jersey, 437 U.S. 617 (1978).

10. *See* 23 U.S.C. § 134; A. Reitze, Jr., *Improving Transportation-Related Air Quality Under the Clean Air Act's Conformity Requirements and the Intermodal Surface Transportation Efficiency Act of 1991,* 3 ENVTL. LAW. 631 (1997).

11. Airport and Airway Improvement Act of 1982 and the Airport and Airway Safety and Capacity Expansion Act of 1987 (codified at 49 U.S.C. § 2103).

12. 16 U.S.C. §§ 2601–45.

13. 16 U.S.C. §§ 796(22)–(25), 824(j)–(l).

14. *See* STEVEN FERRY, LAW OF INDEPENDENT POWER (1998).

15. *See* Chapter 15, "Controlling Existing Facilities," *infra*.

16. *See* Michael B. Gerrard, *The Victims of NIMBY,* 21 FORDHAM URB. L.J. 495 (1994).

17. *But see* R. W. Lake & L. Disch, *Structural Constraints and Pluralist Contradictions in Hazardous Waste Regulation,* 24 ENV'T PLAN. A 663 (1992).

18. Note that EPA has published a brochure suggesting that hazardous waste facilities should not be sited in environmentally sensitive locations such as floodplains, wetlands, earthquake zones, karst soils, unstable terrain, or near hospitals or schools. EPA, Doc. EPA530-K-97-003, SENSITIVE ENVIRONMENTS AND THE SITING OF HAZARDOUS WASTE MANAGEMENT FACILITIES, May 1997.

19. BARRY G. RABE, *BEYOND NIMBY: HAZARDOUS WASTE SITING IN CANADA AND THE UNITED STATES* (Brookings 1994); Richard N.L. Andrews, *Hazardous Waste Facility Siting: State Approaches, in* DIMENSIONS OF HAZARDOUS WASTE POLITICS AND POLICY 117 (Charles E. Davis and James P. Lester eds., 1988).

20. *See* MARY R. ENGLISH, SITING LOW-LEVEL RADIOACTIVE WASTE DISPOSAL FACILITIES: THE PUBLIC POLICY DILEMMA (Quorum 1992).

21. For a discussion of the reasons for this difference in public reaction, see WHOSE BACKYARD, WHOSE RISK, *supra* note 5, at 99–113.

22. *See* Troy J. Cole, Comment, *Zoning Control of Airport Expansion by Host Cities and the Battle over Dallas/Fort Worth International Airport,* 59 J. AIR L. & COM. 193 (1993).

23. *See* JOHN V. WINTER & DAVID A. CONNER, POWER PLANT SITING (Van Nostrand Reinhold, 1978); Dennis W. Ducsik, *Citizen Participation in Power Plant Siting: Aladdin's Lamp or Pandora's Box?, in* RESOLVING LOCATIONAL CONFLICT (Robert W. Lake ed., Rutgers 1987).

24. That instance concerned a proposed plant in San Francisco that was ultimately abandoned after extensive hearings. *See* Laura H. Kosloff & Emilio E. Veranini III, The Hunters Point Cogeneration Project: Environmental Justice and Power Plant Siting, presentation to Air & Waste Management Association conference, Toronto, Ontario, June 8–13, 1997; Alan Ramo, *Hunters Point: Energy Development Meets Environmental Justice,* 5 ENVT'L L. NEWS, Spring 1996, at 28; Clifford Rechtschaffen, *Fighting Back Against a Power Plant: Some Lessons From the Legal and Organizing Efforts of the Bayview-Hunters Point Community,* 3 HASTINGS WEST-NORTHWEST J. ENVT'L L. & POL'Y 407 (1996).

25. *E.g.,* Poletown Neighborhood Council v. City of Detroit, 304 N.W.2d 455 (Mich. 1981).

26. U.S. Nuclear Regulatory Commission, Atomic Safety and Licensing Board, In the Matter of ASLBP No. 91-641-02-ML, Louisiana Energy Services L.P. (Special Nuclear Material License) (Clairborne Enrichment Center), May 1, 1997 (available on the Internet, <http://www.nrc.gov/NRC/ASLEP/lesj9.html>).

27. U.S. Nuclear Regulatory Commission, In the Matter of ASLBP No. 91-641-02-ML, Louisiana Energy Services L.P. (Special Nuclear Material License) (Clairborne Enrichment Center), 1998 NRC Lexis 7 (April 3, 1998) (available on the Internet, <http://www.nrc.gov/OPA/reports/lesorder.htm>).

28. *Nuclear Power: Plug Pulled on Enrichment Plant,* ENGINEERING NEWS-RECORD, May 4, 1998, at 17.

29. *See* Sierra Club v. U.S. Army Corps of Engineers, 772 F.2d 1043 (2d Cir. 1985).

30. 33 U.S.C. § 1344. *But see* Resource Investments, Inc. v. U.S. Army Corps of Engineers, 151 F.3d 1162 (9th Cir. 1998) (construction of a municipal solid waste landfill in a wetland is subject to solid waste permitting programs but not to regulation by Corps under Section 404).

31. 40 C.F.R. pt. 230.
32. 33 C.F.R. § 320.4.
33. 40 C.F.R. § 230.10(a).
34. 33 U.S.C. § 1344(e); 33 C.F.R. pt. 330; 61 Fed. Reg. 65,874 (Dec. 13, 1996).
35. 33 U.S.C. § 1341(a).
36. 33 U.S.C. § 403.
37. 33 C.F.R. § 329.4.
38. Phillips Petroleum Co. v. Mississippi, 484 U.S. 469 (1988); Illinois Central Railroad Co. v. Illinois, 146 U.S. 387 (1892).
39. *See, e.g.*, Ackerman v. Steisel, 480 N.Y.S.2d 556 (App. Div. 1984).
40. 49 U.S.C. § 303; *similarly*, 23 U.S.C. § 138, 49 C.F.R. § 1653(f), 23 C.F.R. § 771.135. *See also* Citizens to Preserve Overton Park, Inc. v. Volpe, 401 U.S. 402 (1971).
41. 16 U.S.C. § 470(f); 36 C.F.R. §§ 800.3–800.9.
42. 16 U.S.C. § 1536(a)(2). *See* Tennessee Valley Auth. v. Hill, 437 U.S. 153 (1978).
43. *See* 42 U.S.C. §§ 4001 to 4128; DeMeo & Merriam, *Flood Damage Protection: Impact of the National Flood Insurance Program*, 11 ZONING & PLAN. L. REP. 65 (1988).
44. Pennsylvania v. General Public Utilities Corp., 710 F.2d 117 (3d Cir. 1983); Northern States Power Co. v. Minnesota, 447 F.2d 1143 (8th Cir. 1971), *aff'd*, 405 U.S. 1035 (1972).
45. 42 U.S.C. § 2021; 10 C.F.R. pt. 150.
46. 47 C.F.R. § 1.1307(e).
47. 40 C.F.R. § 271.4(b); Ensco, Inc. v. Dumas, 807 F.2d 743 (8th Cir. 1986). *See* Patrick O'Hara, Comment, *The N.I.M.B.Y. Syndrome Meets the Preemption Doctrine: Federal Preemption of State and Local Restrictions on the Siting of Hazardous Waste Disposal Facilities*, 53 LA. L. REV. 229 (1992).
48. Neil R. Shortlidge & S. Mark White, *The Use of Zoning and Other Local Controls for Siting Solid and Hazardous Waste Facilities*, 7 NAT. RESOURCES & ENV'T 3 (Winter 1993).
49. *Cf. Ex Parte William Fred Horn*, 718 So.2d 694 (Ala. 1998) (awarding fees to citizens' lawyer who played major role in persuading city to condemn property to prevent it from being used as a solid waste transfer facility).
50. New York City Charter § 203(a).
51. *See* Village of Hempstead v. SRA Realty Corp., 617 N.Y.S.2d 794 (N.Y.A.D. 1994).
52. 42 U.S.C. §§ 6924–6925.
53. 40 C.F.R. pt. 264.
54. 40 C.F.R. §§ 124.31–.33. *See also* Chapter 7, "Public Participation," *supra*.
55. 40 C.F.R. pt. 258. *See* Kathleen Farrelly, *The New Federal Standards for Municipal Solid Waste Landfills: Adding Fuel to the Regulatory Fire*, 3 VILL. ENVTL. L.J. 383 (1992).
56. 15 U.S.C. § 2605(e).
57. 40 C.F.R. pt. 761.
58. 42 U.S.C. §§ 7401 et seq.
59. *E.g.*, THE CLEAN AIR ACT HANDBOOK (Robert J. Martineau, Jr. & David P. Novello eds., American Bar Association 1998).
60. 40 C.F.R. §§ 51.160–166.

61. 40 C.F.R. § 52.20. State issuance of a prevention of significant deterioration permit for a proposed manufacturing plant was remanded for fuller discussion of the environmental justice implications of the plant. *In re Knauf Fiber Glass,* GmbH, PSD Appeal Nos. 98-3 through 98-20, EPA Environmental Appeals Board, November 30, 1998.

62. 42 U.S.C. §§ 7661–7661f.

63. 40 C.F.R. §§ 60.30c–60.36c, 60.750–60.759.

64. 42 U.S.C. §§ 7408(e), 7506.

65. *See* Dawn Somerville Zalfa, Comment, *Air Pollution Trading Programs Under the Clean Air Act: Compliance or Civil Rights Contravention?* 20 WHITTIER L. REV. 485 (1998); Eileen Guana, *Major Sources of Criteria Pollutants in Nonattainment Areas: Balancing the Goals of Clean Air, Environmental Justice, and Industrial Development,* 3 HASTINGS WEST-NORTHWEST J. ENVT'L L. 379 (1995).

66. 33 U.S.C. § 1342.

67. 40 C.F.R. pt. 403.

68. 42 U.S.C. §§ 4321–4370d.

69. *See* Melissa Jean Horne, *Bad Actor Statutes: An Environmental Trojan Horse?*, 48 VAND. L. REV. 771 (1995); James M. Strock & Brian A. Runkel, *Environmental Bad Actors and Federal Disqualification,* 15 HARV. ENVT'L L. REV. 529 (1991).

70. *California: State Rejects Permit for Waste Facility Based on Company Compliance History,* BNA DAILY ENV. REP., May 8, 1998, at A-1. Similarly, *Air Pollution: Florida Permit Denied Based on History of Company Chief's Violations, Florida Says,* BNA Daily Env. Rep., June 29, 1999, at A-4.

71. Sharp v. 251st Street Landfill, Inc., 810 P.2d 1270 (Okla. 1991), *overruled on other grounds,* Dulaney v. Oklahoma State Dep't of Health, 868 P.2d 676 (Okla. 1992); Village of Wilsonville v. SCA Services, Inc., 396 N.E.2d 552 (Ill. App. Ct. 1979), *aff'd,* 426 N.E.2d 824 (Ill. 1981); Fink v. Bd. of Trustees of S. Ill. Univ., 218 N.E.2d 240 (Ill. App. Ct. 1966). *See* Serena M. Williams, *The Anticipatory Nuisance Doctrine: One Common Law Theory for Use in Environmental Justice Cases,* 19 WM. & MARY ENVTL. L. & POL'Y 223 (1995); Charles J. Doane, Comment, *Beyond Fear: Articulating a Modern Doctrine in Anticipatory Nuisance for Enjoining Improbable Threats of Catastrophic Harm,* 17 B.C. ENVTL. AFF. L. REV. 441 (1990).

72. ALA. CODE § 6-5-125; GA. CODE ANN. § 41-2-4.

73. *E.g.,* City of Santa Fe v. Komis, 114 N.M. 659, 845 P.2d 753 (1992) (landowner awarded damages because highway through his property would carry nuclear waste, diminishing value of land due to fear of the waste); Texas Elec. Serv. Co. v. Nelon, 546 S.W.2d 864 (Tex. Civ. App. 1977) (allowing recovery for fear of owner of land adjacent to railroad through which nuclear wastes were transported); Heddin v. Delhi Gas Pipeline Co., 522 S.W.2d 886 (Tex. 1975) (damages awarded to landowner who feared that pipeline on adjoining land would explode). *See also* Michael B. Gerrard, *Groundwater Contamination as a 'Taking,'* N.Y. L.J., July 23, 1999, at 3.

74. *See* Michael B. Gerrard, *Building Environmentally Just Projects,* N. Y. ENVTL. LAW., May 1996, at 1.

75. For a statistical analysis of this phenomenon in one state, see MICHAEL B. GERRARD ET AL., ENVIRONMENTAL IMPACT REVIEW IN NEW YORK § 7.04[4] (Matthew Bender, 1998 Supp.).

76. *E.g.*, Greenpeace v. Waste Technologies Industries, 9 F.3d 1174 (6th Cir. 1993) (dismissing challenge to proposed hazardous waste incinerator in East Liverpool, Ohio, where objections to alleged dioxin emissions had not been raised during permit proceedings). *See also* BENJAMIN DAVY, ESSENTIAL INJUSTICE: WHEN LEGAL INSTITUTIONS CANNOT RESOLVE ENVIRONMENTAL AND LAND USE DISPUTES 89–172 (Springer-Verlag/Wien 1997) (account of East Liverpool controversy).

77. *See* Rozar v. Mullis, 85 F.3d 556 (11th Cir. 1996); Aiello v. Browning-Ferris, Inc., 24 ENVTL. L. REP. 20771, 1993 WL 463701 (N.D. Cal. 1993).

78. This literature is collected in David L. Markell, Pamela R. Esterman & Robin E. Rosenberg, *Alternative Dispute Resolution, Chapter 11C in* ENVIRONMENTAL LAW PRACTICE GUIDE (Michael B. Gerrard ed., Matthew Bender & Co. 1998).

79. *E.g.*, Thomas A. V. Cassel & Terence P. Walmsley, *Environmental Justice in Hazardous Waste Siting: An Empowered Community of Color Sites a Waste-to-Energy Facility*, J. ENVTL. L. & PRAC., May/June 1995, at 48. *See also* M. V. Rajeev Gowda & Doug Easterling, *Nuclear Waste and Native America: The MRS Siting Exercise*, 9 RISK—HEALTH, SAFETY & ENV'T 229 (1998).

80. *See also* NEW YORK STATE LEG. COMM'N ON SOLID WASTE MANAGEMENT, *WHAT'S IN IT FOR US: A SUMMARY OF HOST COMMUNITY BENEFITS AND POLICIES* (January 1998) (also includes samples of host agreements); Howard Kunreuther & Doug Easterling, *The Role of Compensation in Siting Hazardous Facilities*, 15 J. POL'Y ANALYSIS & MGMNT. 601 (1996); Vicki Been, *Compensated Siting Proposals: Is It Time to Pay Attention?*, 21 FORDHAM URB. L.J. 787 (1994).

CHAPTER 15

Controlling Existing Facilities

HEIDI GOROVITZ ROBERTSON

Existing Facilities as Sources of Environmental Inequity

Although there is considerable debate about whether newer polluting facilities are being sited discriminatorily or disproportionately in low-income or minority communities, there is little debate that the longer a polluting facility has been around, the more likely it is that the community around it is low-income, minority, or both. Therefore, environmental justice advocates seek to curtail pollution from older existing facilities, just as they try to influence the siting decisions that would place newer facilities in low-income and minority communities.

This chapter first will address the environmental grandfather clauses that allow older, existing facilities to pollute more heavily than newer facilities of the same type. It will discuss allegations of unequal government enforcement as a driver of environmental inequity. It will then address the statutory, administrative, and common law methods citizens might use to control existing facilities that degrade the environment in low-income and minority communities. Finally, it will briefly address methods for controlling existing facilities that are available only to government entities.

Grandfather Clauses in the Environmental Laws

Sociologists, lawyers, scientists, and the general public have discovered that hazardous waste–generating facilities, hazardous waste landfills, hazardous waste incinerators, and other major sources of pollution and environmental risk are sited disproportionately in low-income communities. Studies have also shown that of the low-income neighborhoods chosen as sites for polluting facilities, the neighborhoods of Hispanics and African Americans are chosen most frequently. This point, however, is somewhat controversial and has been vigorously debated. (See Chapter 12 for a discussion of the evidentiary issues regarding discriminatory siting.) Regardless whether the siting decision was discriminatory, the fact that low-income, minority communities ultimately host a disproportionate number of polluting facilities suggests that they also bear a disproportionate burden of the environmental risk that accompanies those facilities.

Of critical importance for these low-income and minority communities, then, is the environmental compliance and enforcement status of the facilities they host. Unfortunately, there are significant inequalities inherent in the environmental laws partly due to "environmental grandfather clauses"—environmental law provisions that treat older facilities differently from newer facilities. Specifically, they exempt existing polluting facilities from the more stringent environmental standards applicable to new facilities.[1] One example of environmental grandfather clauses lies in the interim status provisions of the Resource Conservation and Recovery Act (RCRA), through which older facilities may operate without complying with the tough permit standards applicable to new facilities.[2] In effect, RCRA's interim status provisions subject facilities that existed prior to November 19, 1980 to less stringent standards than those built thereafter.

Another example of environmental grandfather clauses lies in a comparison of the new source performance standards and prevention of significant deterioration program in the Clean Air Act (CAA).[3] In these provisions, the Act makes a clear, formal distinction between existing and new sources of air pollution and requires more stringent performance standards for "new sources." Although all sources of air pollution are subject to ambient air quality regulation through source-specific emission limitations, new sources are subject to more stringent pollution control technologies and permitting requirements than are required for existing facilities.[4] Like the two-tiered regulatory system in RCRA, the similar system in the CAA allows older polluting facilities to emit air pollutants in greater amounts than would be permitted of new facilities.

Finally, in addition to the numerous statutory grandfather clauses, principles of land use and zoning law may constitute environmental grandfather clauses when they allow prior nonconforming uses to operate in areas where new uses of the same type would not be allowed. In addition to the examples of grandfather clauses in the federal environmental laws and common law, grandfather clauses exist in state law as well.[5]

With the protection of grandfather clauses, older facilities, often located in low-income, minority communities, emit significantly more pollution than the newer, more modern facilities subject to the most stringent regulation. A recent study by the U.S. Public Interest Research Group Education Fund found that grandfathered power plants emit 4 to 10 times more pollution than their newer counterparts. The group's report indicates that elimination of the grandfather clauses applicable to the 559 dirtiest plants would eliminate 69 percent of the NO_X and 77 percent of the SO_2 released into the air each year by electric utilities.[6]

Most troubling, however, is that environmental grandfather clauses make it difficult to reduce the environmental and health risks presented by the many polluting facilities already located in low-income, minority communities. By allowing older facilities to operate under less stringent environmental regulation, environmental grandfather clauses substantially hamper the opportunities of communities located near existing facilities to improve environmental quality in their neighborhoods.

Unequal Enforcement

In addition to the grandfather clauses that allow older, existing facilities to operate at less stringent standards of regulation, some studies, including an influential *National Law Journal* report, have shown a substantial disparity between the federal government's diligence in enforcement and cleanup in minority communities and nonminority communities.[7] Specifically, the studies allege that the penalties government officials impose on violators of environmental regulations are higher when the violations occur in largely nonminority communities than they are for similar violations in minority neighborhoods. The *National Law Journal* report found that under RCRA, penalties were 500 percent higher in white communities than in minority communities.[8] The report alleges that penalties under all of the major federal environmental laws combined were 46 percent higher in white communities than in minority communities.[9]

In addition, the *National Law Journal* report claimed that cleanups are slower in minority communities: abandoned waste sites take 20 percent longer to be added to the Superfund cleanup program in minority areas than in white areas.[10] Finally, there is evidence that in minority areas, EPA allows less permanent forms of treatment, such as containment, rather than actual cleanup of contamination.[11] Both U.S. EPA and its regional offices have contradicted the results of these controversial studies.[12]

To improve its tracking of allegedly unequal or discriminatory enforcement, EPA recently merged its enforcement and demographic data.[13] The merged data set will include information on facility emissions, violations and permitting, as well as demographic information for certain parts of the country. This will allow the agency to create targeted enforcement areas. It will also allow the agency to provide better, more useful information to communities. With better information, communities can be better prepared and more involved in local facilities' compliance and permit renewal processes.

Statutory Tools for Citizens to Use in Controlling Existing Facilities

This section will describe provisions in the federal environmental laws that citizens can use to help control pollution from existing facilities. It will do so by describing the citizen suit provisions in the Clean Water Act (CWA), CAA, and RCRA. This section will then address lawsuits against the government for failure to enforce environmental laws. Finally, this section will address some state and local legislative initiatives for controlling existing facilities.

The citizen suit provisions of the Comprehensive Environmental Response, Compensation and Liability Act (CERCLA) and the corrective action provisions of RCRA will be discussed in Chapter 16, "Cleaning Up Abandoned or Inactive Contaminated Sites," pages 522–60. Civil rights lawsuits are discussed in Chapters 2 and 3, pages 23–102. The Emergency Planning and Community Right-to-Know Act (EPCRA) is discussed in Chapter 8, "Access to Information," pages 230–55. These topics therefore are omitted here.

Citizen Suit Provisions—Forcing Polluting Facilities to Comply with Environmental Laws

In the major federal environmental laws, Congress has charged U.S. EPA with enforcement responsibility. EPA, however, is chronically underfunded and understaffed and cannot, therefore, carry out its stated duties to the extent the law requires. In certain circumstances, the environmental laws allow citizens to bring private enforcement actions against violators, as private attorneys general, to require regulated parties to comply with the laws.[14] The environmental laws also provide opportunities for citizens to sue EPA for failing to discharge mandatory enforcement obligations.[15]

As private attorneys general, citizens sue violators on behalf of the community at large, rather than to vindicate personal harm. Typically, therefore, the provisions provide for injunctive relief, but not damages. This means that a citizen may achieve an order directing a polluter to comply with the law. The citizen cannot receive money, however, to compensate for the violation or punish the violator. The major environmental laws' citizen suit provisions do provide for recovery of lawyers' fees.[16]

In addition to the limitation on remedies, there are technical and procedural limitations on private enforcement actions. Generally, citizens may bring a lawsuit for enforcement of an environmental law only after sufficient notice, generally 60 days, to the violator, the state, and U.S. EPA.[17] The citizen may then proceed only if a government agency is not already diligently prosecuting an action against the violator.[18] Generally, citizens may also sue states and municipalities to the extent permitted by the 11th amendment to the U.S. Constitution.[19]

One serious problem with citizen suits is that it is difficult for citizens to determine whether a violation is taking place. This is because, in addition to the statutory and regulatory requirements, many legal requirements are included in a facility's permits, which are difficult to locate and decipher. Other enforceable requirements include court orders and administrative orders, which, like permits, are difficult to find and understand. Unless the discharger is required to report on its compliance with regulatory requirements (as occurs with discharge monitoring reports under the CWA), determining facility compliance is also very difficult.

Citizen Suits Under the CWA

The CWA provides citizens opportunities to sue alleged violators of the act.[20] As compared to the other environmental laws, CWA violations are easy to detect and prosecute. Citizen suits under the CWA, therefore, make up a disproportionately large percentage of citizen suits brought under the major environmental laws.[21] Citizen suits are easier under the CWA, in part, because it is realistically possible for citizens to get information about the requirements that apply to a facility and whether the facility is meeting those requirements.

For example, the CWA requires any facility discharging a regulated pollutant into a body of water from a discrete conveyance to obtain a permit under the National Pollutant Discharge Elimination System (NPDES) program.[22] NPDES permits require facilities to limit the amount of specific pollutants in their effluent, to test the effluent regularly, and to report to the permitting agency the actual concentrations of the regulated pollutants in their effluent. Citizens may review a facility's NPDES permit and compare it to the discharge monitoring reports also required of existing facilities.[23] If there is a violation, citizens should be able to establish that fact at a summary judgment phase of a case by submitting the documents showing discharges beyond the permit limitations.

Most citizen suits under the CWA are settled for less than the penalties that would theoretically be due to an enforcing agency for the violations at issue. And although the act prohibits citizens from recovering damages, it allows citizens to deposit funds acquired through an enforcement suit either with the U.S. Treasury or to a special fund for environmental mitigation projects.[24] The court administering the settlement must approve plans for dispersal of damage money and mitigation projects.

Some argue that because citizens in low-income minority communities may not have experience to create and manage environmental mitigation projects, these communities may not see the incentive of these projects as a reward for pursuing a CWA enforcement action.[25]

One impediment to citizen suits under the CWA is that citizens cannot sue under the act if EPA or the state is "diligently pursuing a civil or criminal action."[26] Another potential impediment to successful CWA citizen suits is that courts have held that such suits cannot stand for "wholly past violations." [27] The Supreme Court found that the applicable language of the CWA citizen suit provision is entirely in the present tense, which indicated a "prospective orientation" of the provision.[28] Once a citizen has filed a 60-day notice of intent to sue, a facility can correct the violation, which will then become inactionable under the citizen suit provision as a "wholly past violation."

Citizen Suits Under the CAA

Under the CAA, citizens may sue violators of emission standards or limitations.[29] However, the terms "standards and limitations" apply not only to concentrations of emitted air pollutants, but also to things that cannot easily be measured, like design and work practices, and operation and maintenance requirements. They are therefore difficult to identify.

The largest sources of air pollution, excluding mobile sources, are categorized under a complicated scheme of definitions that consider the age, size, and type of the facility, in addition to the status of its location with respect to air quality. However, most smaller, nonmobile sources of air pollution actually are regulated, not under a uniform, federal system, but through state implementation plans. States design their implementation plans to enable them to attain federal standards for concentrations of specific pollutants in the ambient air. Methods vary according to how states have chosen to achieve or maintain compliance with the national ambient air quality standards. States sometimes implement their plans by operating state air permit programs. It is therefore difficult for citizens to discover and quantify violations of the CAA.

For existing facilities, those not subject to new source review, it is difficult to determine federally enforceable requirements. Instead, citizens could review the applicable state implementation plan to determine whether a source's emissions are limited, or if the industry belongs to a regulated source category. Citizens must then determine whether the requirements contained in the plan are enforceable standards or limitations under the CAA. Because these standards often are vague or difficult to apply, this can be a formidable, frustrating task. In addition, what may appear to be a clear standard will not apply in some cases to the facility at issue due to negotiations and compromises made during the permit process. Even where citizens can determine what standards apply under an applicable state implementation plan, they will have difficulty collecting information to prove a violation.

Under current law, it is difficult to identify the nature and source of air pollution and to determine whether specific activities or pollution constitutes a violation of the federal CAA. In addition, it is difficult to prove that a violation of a "standard or limitation" has occurred. For all of these reasons, citizens face an uphill battle using the citizen suit provisions of the CAA to control existing facilities.

Although well-funded national environmental groups may have the resources to bring citizen suits under the current implementation of the CAA, even then they are expensive and unlikely to succeed. However, enforcement suits should become easier and perhaps more successful with full implementation of Clean Air Act Title V. Title V, which was added to the CAA with the Clean Air Act Amendments of 1990, requires a comprehensive permitting program for sources of air pollution, with reports that will resemble CAA discharge monitoring reports. Under Title V, states were required to submit permit programs for EPA review and approval by November 15, 1993.[30] Once EPA has approved a state program, or substituted its own for an inadequate one, facilities subject to permit requirements have one year to submit a complete permit application.[31] Permits issued under this program should more clearly define the CAA standards and limitations, federal requirements regarding monitoring, testing methods, record keeping, and reporting. They should also clearly separate requirements that would not be subject to federal citizen suit enforcement, called "state only" requirements, from the enforceable federal requirements.[32]

Finally, there are some problems with bringing CAA citizen suits that will not be solved by Title V implementation. States can exempt air pollution sources that do not meet the CAA definition of a "major source" from the Title V program until U.S. EPA finishes writing a rule explaining how to incorporate them into the Title V permit program.[33] Also, in locations where air pollution comes from a variety of small sources regulated under the act's New Source Performance Standards rather than Title V, it will be difficult for citizens to get the information that will be available to them regarding Title V sources. Citizens will be left trying to figure out the current complicated system of standards and regulations and will not have at their disposal the clearer Title V permit conditions.

Citizen Suits Under RCRA

RCRA, which regulates the treatment, storage, and disposal of solid and hazardous wastes, provides for two types of citizen suits against existing facilities. First, citizens may sue to enforce any RCRA "permit, standard, regulation, condition, requirement, prohibition or order."[34] Second, citizens may sue any person who is contributing, or has contributed "to the handling, storage, treatment, transportation, or disposal of solid or hazardous waste in a manner that presents an imminent or substantial endangerment to health or to the environment."[35]

RCRA ENFORCEMENT SUITS. The RCRA enforcement suit provisions allow citizens to enforce any RCRA "permit, standard, regulation, condition, requirement, prohibition or order." To gather evidence to support a claim of violation, citizens may review a facility's permit to operate and prosecute an enforcement action if there are violations of permit conditions. It is difficult, however, to prove RCRA violations from the documents the statute requires facilities to submit to EPA. Citizens often can get better information regarding the compliance status of a facility by requesting the facility's inspection reports from the state or U.S. EPA. Citizens can do this by filing a request under the federal Freedom of Information Act or a state equivalent. These reports often refer explicitly to actionable violations.

In addition, citizens cannot proceed under RCRA's citizen suit provisions if EPA is in the process of bringing a civil or criminal action.[36] Because the language of the statute allows actions against any person "in violation" of RCRA, citizens also cannot prosecute for "wholly past violations."[37] Once a citizen files a 60-day notice of intent to sue, often a facility will correct the violation. As such, although the violation becomes nonactionable under the citizen suit provisions as a "wholly past violation," the citizen may have achieved the fundamental goal of correcting the violation.

Citizens bringing an enforcement suit under RCRA can obtain an injunction ordering the regulated party to comply with a RCRA requirement, but cannot gain a private monetary reward.[38] Citizens also cannot monitor the contaminated site, as that function belongs to EPA.[39]

RCRA IMMINENT HAZARD SUITS. Congress amended RCRA in 1984 to allow citizens to sue any person who is contributing (or has contributed) to the handling of solid or hazardous waste in a manner that presents an imminent and substantial endangerment to health or the environment.[40] As such, citizen suits are not barred under this provision with respect to "wholly past violations."[41] This provision is particularly useful because it does not require citizens to identify specific violations and may be used to remedy hazards to land, water, or air.

As with RCRA enforcement provisions, the imminent hazard provisions do not allow citizens to sue if an agency is diligently prosecuting actions. For this kind of citizen suit, the statute includes prosecution under CERCLA as well as RCRA. It also prohibits lawsuits when the agency is engaging in a removal action, has incurred costs to initiate a Remedial Investigation-Feasibility Study, or has obtained a court order or administrative order under CERCLA.[42]

Also, unlike the standard 60-day notice provisions found elsewhere in environmental citizen suit provisions, RCRA's imminent hazard provisions require notice to the violator, the state, and U.S. EPA, followed by a 90-day waiting period before a citizen may sue. However, the 90-day waiting period does not apply if the hazard at issue pertains to a violation of hazardous waste provisions.[43] Finally, despite dangers to human health and the environment, if a facility is operating within the scope of its permit, a suit will not stand under this provision.[44]

Even assuming a citizen can satisfy the procedural requirements of RCRA's imminent hazard citizen suit provisions, there still remain the substantive requirements. Citizens must prove:

1. "that the conditions at the site present an imminent and substantial endangerment to health or the environment";
2. "that the endangerment stems from the handling, storage, treatment, transportation, or disposal of a solid or hazardous waste"; and
3. that "the defendant has contributed or is contributing to such handling, storage, treatment, transportation or disposal."[45]

Generally, citizen plaintiffs do not have to prove an emergency or irreparable injury,[46] nor do they need to sustain actual harm to succeed in an imminent hazard case. If a release of a hazardous waste has occurred and presents a risk of exposure from which harm eventually will occur,[47] a plaintiff can succeed under this provision.

Although RCRA authorizes citizen suits to minimize dangers to human health and the environment caused by imminent and substantial endangerment, the U.S. Supreme Court has held that citizens cannot recover the cost of cleanups that do not pose a current or future danger. As such, if the danger has been alleviated, an imminent hazard suit will not stand.[48]

False Claims Act

Another option for citizens to act as private attorneys general to control existing facilities lies in the False Claims Act. The act, originally enacted in 1863 and amended in 1986, allows citizens to sue anyone who claims money or property from the U.S. government if that claim is false and knowingly presented.[49] As such, citizens can sue contractors doing business with the government when those contractors fail to comply with the environmental laws despite contract provisions attesting to environmental compliance.[50] The act allows for penalties of $5,000 to $10,000 for each violation of the act, which can mean for each false invoice. In addition, the act allows citizens, suing on behalf of the government, to receive from 15 to 30 percent of the proceeds of the action.

For environmental justice advocates seeking to control existing facilities, the False Claims Act is not ideal. For example, it does not provide for injunctions stopping the activity that violates an environmental law. Regardless, it does have several advantages. It is a source of funding, and if claims are plentiful and successful, they could encourage government contractors to be more careful in their environmental compliance. A False Claims Act claim can pressure a facility to achieve compliance if the facility has federal contracts that require compliance with environmental permits.

Lawsuits Against the Government for Nonenforcement

Although the 11th amendment to the U.S. Constitution appears to prohibit the federal courts from hearing citizen suits against states,[51] many of the federal environmental laws specifically allow citizens to sue government agencies for failure to perform a nondiscretionary duty to enforce the laws.[52] The environmental laws allow citizens to bring these lawsuits "to the extent permitted by the 11th amendment to the constitution."[53] To date, courts have allowed citizens to sue state officials under the environmental citizen suit provisions for violating federal laws,[54] but recent U.S. Supreme Court cases indicate that the Court is tightening up on 11th amendment restrictions.[55]

Regardless, courts generally have deferred to agencies in such lawsuits by finding most enforcement actions discretionary.[56] The U.S. Supreme Court has said that "an agency's decision not to take enforcement action should be presumed immune from judicial review"[57] because the agency may decide whether a violation has occurred, how to use its resources, and whether an enforcement action best serves its policies.[58] Although citizens may sometimes be able to use judicial proceedings to force an agency to make a decision regarding a facility's compliance with the statute, or with respect to a specific violation, it is difficult for citizens to challenge the content of those decisions.[59]

Specifically, the CWA includes provisions stating that if the administrator of EPA finds a person in violation of the act, she shall:

1. issue an order;
2. bring a civil action; or
3. notify the alleged violator, and if the violator does not take appropriate action, commence an appropriate enforcement action.[60]

This means that if the administrator finds a violation, she must issue an order or commence a civil action. Most courts have held, however, that because the EPA administrator must find a violation before the statute requires her to take additional enforcement action, there is no mandatory, nondiscretionary duty to investigate every citizen complaint of alleged violation.[61] This same analysis applies to the CAA citizen suit provisions.

In addition to the dubious lawsuits to force agency action under the federal environmental laws, citizens could sue similarly under state environmental laws. Citizens could also bring mandamus actions to compel performance of a nondiscretionary "ministerial" act by a public official. Once again, the chances of success in such lawsuits are seldom bright.

Statutory Tools Available to Government Entities for Controlling Existing Facilities

Civil Enforcement

Other options for controlling existing facilities lie in the civil enforcement provisions of the major federal environmental laws. Every major federal environmental law includes a range of civil enforcement options available to the applicable government agency, usually EPA. Generally, the statutes provide opportunities for the imposition of civil penalties, ranging from $10,000 to $50,000 per violation and per day of violation. They also include opportunities for civil action leading to injunction or other forms of judicial control. According to EPA policy, the agency calculates penalties by evaluating the gravity of the violation and the economic benefit derived from it.[62] Once EPA has determined a base penalty, the agency may raise or lower it based on its evaluation of:

1. the degree of willfulness and/or negligence of the violation;
2. the degree of cooperation of the violator;

3. the violator's compliance history; and
4. other factors unique to the violation.

Clean Air Act

The CAA allows EPA to impose civil administrative penalties of up to $25,000 per day of violation for violating any implementation plan requirement, or any other CAA requirement, or for failure to comply with new source requirements.[63] For these administrative penalties, EPA may not impose a total penalty greater than $200,000 and the agency must initiate administrative action leading to the penalty within 12 months of the violation.[64] These requirements may be waived, however, when EPA and the Department of Justice agree to waive them.

The Clean Air Act Amendments of 1990 added a new form of administrative enforcement, the "field citation" program.[65] Under this program, EPA inspectors can issue traffic-type tickets for fines up to $5,000 per day per violation. Violators may elect to pay the fine, or request a hearing.

Finally, the act includes authority for EPA to pay a "bounty" of up to $10,000 to any person who furnishes information leading to a civil penalty or criminal conviction.[66]

Clean Water Act

In addition to issuing orders requiring compliance, under the CWA, EPA may issue administrative orders imposing penalties for violations of the act, including permit violations. The act divides penalties into two classes. Class I penalties may not exceed $10,000 per violation, with a minimum of $25,000. For Class I penalties, EPA must provide the violator with notice of the penalty and an opportunity to request an informal hearing.[67] Class II penalties may not exceed $10,000 per day per violation, and may not exceed $25,000. For Class II penalties, EPA must provide notice and an opportunity for a full adjudicatory hearing, as opposed to an informal hearing.[68]

In addition to administrative orders and penalties, EPA may bring action in U.S. district courts seeking civil penalties for violations of the act. The agency may impose civil penalties without a showing of negligence or fault on the part of the defendant, and may assess up to $125,000 in penalties per day for each violation.[69] In addition to civil penalties, EPA may litigate to obtain an injunction.[70]

Criminal Enforcement

In addition to citizen suit provisions, the major federal environmental laws have criminal enforcement options.[71] Of course, with criminal enforcement, a government entity, usually the Department of Justice, must prosecute the violator.

As many environmental crimes are committed by a person working for a corporation, it is important to note that corporate liability for environmental crimes may derive from the conduct of persons employed by the corporation, under the legal doctrine of respondeat superior, or by the conduct of their subsidiary or predecessor corporations.[72] Some argue that criminal prosecution of corporate violators is especially important to enforcement of the environmental laws because:

1. the harms posed by environmental crimes may be as significant as those posed by other crimes;
2. the corporate environmental criminal may be as morally culpable as other criminals; and
3. without criminal sanctions, corporate environmental criminals may view environmental civil sanctions merely as a cost of doing business, which they can pass on to consumers.

Prosecution for environmental crimes is an especially useful tool for controlling existing facilities because of the stigma a corporation can suffer upon conviction.[73]

State and Local Initiatives

The federal permit and enforcement laws discussed above generally are paralleled by similar state laws. Therefore, much of the information discussed above regarding methods for controlling existing facilities using federal statutory tools also applies at the state level. Also, state laws offer several additional tools for controlling existing facilities not offered at the federal level.

Environmental Benefit Program

An example of state initiatives, New York state's Environmental Benefits Program takes money New York City owes to New York state for State Pollutant Discharge Elimination System permit violations and makes it available to low-income and minority communities to establish environmental study and action programs.[74] Although this does not directly control pollution from existing facilities, it helps provide communities with the tools and resources to bring appropriate citizen suits.

In a recent settlement of an RCRA citizen suit, New York State agreed to pay $1.3 million to operate two environmental education centers in a low-income neighborhood in Albany. The settlement followed a lawsuit against the state regarding pollution from a state-operated trash incinerator. Nearby soils were contaminated by lead and other materials released by the plant. In addition to the payments for environmental programs, the state decommissioned the incinerator and converted it to a natural gas steam plant. So here, citizen action led to monetary and environmental benefits in addition to the conversion of an existing facility.

State Statutory Provisions

Some states have citizen suit provisions within their own environmental laws that groups could use as an addition or alternative to the federal provisions. In addition, some states allow citizens to participate in the enforcement of state environmental laws. In those states, citizens can intervene in lawsuits brought by the state to ensure that the concerns of local citizens are recognized by the court.[75]

Informer Rewards

Some federal and state statutes include provisions that award money to citizens who provide information leading to the arrest and conviction of criminal violators of environmental laws.[76] These rewards can provide an incentive for citizens to get involved in environmental enforcement and play a role in the environmental health of their communities. They can also help earn funding for subsequent efforts on behalf of the environment. Informer rewards are also good for the state because they:

1. reward citizens for turning in violators of environmental laws;
2. discourage state agency officials from being lax with violators; and
3. aid the protection of the state's citizens, health, and the environment.[77]

Administrative Tools for Controlling Existing Facilities

In addition to statutory tools for controlling existing facilities, there are several tools available through the administrative process. Those tools include, for example, participation in the original permitting process, participation in the permit renewal process, and involvement in negotiations for settlements and consent decrees. In addition, federal and state agencies' ability to interpret regulations also provides a tool for controlling existing facilities.[78]

The Permitting Process

The process through which polluting facilities must obtain and renew permits to construct, operate, and install can provide numerous additional opportunities for controlling the permitted facilities.

In addition to suing under the environmental citizen suit provisions, citizens can work within the administrative process to control existing polluting facilities by participating in the process by which these facilities obtain, modify, and renew the required permits. These opportunities allow citizens, administrative agencies, environmental groups, and the regulated community to provide input into the standards that will apply to individual polluting facilities.

Permits play a critical role in establishing the "law" that applies to existing polluting facilities and to their specific discharges or emissions. As such, to the extent that one can influence the permitting process, one can play a role in controlling existing facilities. For example, when a facility seeks to have a permit renewed or modified, opportunities arise for the public to participate and voice concerns about the compliance status of the facility.

In addition, permits often incorporate by reference the operating manuals and other documents relevant to the operation of the facility. Most permits require the regulated party to inform the permitting agency of violations of the permit requirements. These documents can provide information to help establish a permit violation that could be the subject of a lawsuit.

A recent decision by the Texas Supreme Court supported the ability of citizen groups to participate in the permitting process in their efforts to control existing facilities. West Dallas Coalition for Environmental Justice attempted to participate in a contested case hearing as part of a facility's permit renewal proceedings. The facility challenged the group's standing to challenge the permit renewal. The Texas Supreme Court declined to review an appellate court decision that upheld an earlier decision that one must only show "that they will potentially suffer harm or have a 'justiciable interest' related to the proceedings" to have standing to challenge a permit.[79] This decision confirms that citizens and citizen groups can help control existing facilities by participating in the permit process.

In fact, a recent decision in the 10th Circuit confirmed that if citizens fail to pursue their claims during the permit process, they may be barred from pursuing them later under a citizen suit provision.[80] In this case, a citizen group failed to challenge a facility's NPDES permit during the permit renewal process and the court dismissed their subsequent citizen suit due to lack of subject matter jurisdiction.[81]

Agencies can control existing facilities by amending permits to make more stringent the rules that apply to those facilities, or by refusing to renew permits. Courts support this. For example, a Pennsylvania court recently held that a local environmental agency abused its discretion by allowing a company to renew a permit to operate a municipal waste transfer station. The agency should not have allowed the permit renewal because the facility operator failed to comply with a regulation requiring it to exercise its rights under the permit within a certain amount of time.[82]

In another example of an agency controlling an existing facility, a hazardous waste plant's noncompliance with state environmental laws caused the California Department of Toxic Substances Control to refuse to renew the plant's long-term operating permit.[83] As such, the state regulators prevented the facility from continuing to accept, treat, and transfer hazardous waste. The facility was located in a residential area and was held up as an environmental justice issue.

Directly connected to the environmental justice issue, U.S. EPA Region V is considering reviewing the RCRA permit of a facility specifically on the grounds that it is causing disparate adverse impact on the nearby minority community. One interesting point about this action is that although the facility is located within the boundaries of a largely nonminority city, it is across the street from another, overwhelmingly low- to middle-income, minority community. The issue is particularly pressing in this instance because EPA recently issued a guidance prohibiting states from granting discriminatory permits.[84] Failure to review this situation, and deny the permit if discriminatory, would put EPA in a difficult position with respect to the states when EPA is implementing its policy to punish states for doing the very same thing.

Corrective Action Orders

Under RCRA, EPA can issue administrative orders requiring an existing facility to comply with the law. Most significantly, EPA can issue compliance orders under RCRA Section 3008(h). As a practical matter, because most states have authority delegated by U.S. EPA to implement the RCRA permit program, the applicable state agency would issue a compliance order. Specifically, if EPA or the applicable state agency determines that a hazardous waste has been released into the environment from a facility, it may issue an order requiring "corrective action" or other action necessary to protect human health or the environment.[85] The range of responses EPA might order include measures to determine the extent of the pollution, temporary cleanup actions, or long-range remediation efforts.

Compliance orders similar to those available under RCRA are also available in other environmental law statutes: for example, the CWA[86] and the CAA.[87]

Settlements and Consent Devices

Especially with regard to lawsuits brought by EPA against potentially responsible parties under CERCLA, negotiations leading toward settlement and consent devices offer opportunities to reduce pollution suffered by low-income and minority communities. Because many Superfund sites are located in low-income minority communities, agreements with respect to their cleanup are tools for controlling existing polluting facilities. Because all federal consent decrees are subject to public comment before courts will approve them,[88] citizens have an opportunity to see and comment on an arrangement before it becomes final.

Common Law Tools for Controlling Existing Facilities

Although there are many statutory claims available for environmental plaintiffs to use to control existing facilities, none is perfect and all involve gathering or deciphering some manner of technical information or documents. In contrast, common law actions such as nuisance, negligence, trespass, and strict liability for abnormally dangerous activities provide useful, possibly more user-friendly, options. Some have described the legal theory behind both common law nuisance and trespass actions as "You dumped it, it hurt me or my property, and you should pay."[89]

Also, common law actions may be available when statutory enforcement actions are barred, such as when a facility is operating within legal limits. For example, holding a valid permit to operate in a particular manner may be a defense to a statutory cause of action, but it is not a defense to a nuisance claim and does not bar the nuisance action.[90] In addition, statutory claims are subject to notice provisions that delay the commencement of lawsuits. Common law causes of action are not subject to such waiting periods. Finally, unlike the statutory enforcement provisions, common law actions can yield both injunctive and monetary relief.

Nuisance

Nuisance actions allow citizens to sue for unlawful interference with their use and enjoyment of their property due to activities taking place entirely outside their property.[91] They present attractive alternatives or additions to statutory enforcement actions, in part because the legal theories behind them and methods of proof that support them are simple. A plaintiff must prove "that the pollution . . . 'looks bad, smells bad, and does bad things' . . . without getting mired in the scientific underpinnings" of a statutory enforcement action.[92]

Private Nuisance

Private nuisance is a nontrespassory unreasonable interference with the plaintiff's use and enjoyment of his or her property.[93] This is the most popular common law approach to redressing environmental harms. Examples of environmental harms that might constitute a private nuisance include: noise pollution, dust, smoke, and odors.[94] Any environmental contaminants that invade a plaintiff's property through air, land, or water may constitute a nuisance.

To state a claim for a private nuisance, the plaintiff must show that the alleged perpetrator of the nuisance intended to do the activity that constitutes a nuisance.[95] The plaintiff must also show that a substantial and unreasonable interference with the plaintiff's use and enjoyment of his or her property resulted from the activity.[96] Therefore, an interference that is either minor or of short duration will not constitute a nuisance. Courts determine whether an interference is substantial by evaluating the activity according to the senses of the normal person in the community.

The unreasonableness requirement does not mean that the activity itself is an inherently unreasonable one, just that the burden it imposes on the plaintiff is unreasonable. In fact, it must cause actual physical discomfort and annoyance to a person of ordinary sensibilities.[97]

Once the plaintiff has established these two elements, the plaintiff is entitled to a remedy. This is true even if the perpetrator of the nuisance is using all due care conducting the complained-of activity. In general, a nuisance action will stand if the plaintiff's use and enjoyment of his or her property is unreasonably burdened. Once the plaintiff has established these elements, the burden shifts to the defendant to show that the activity was reasonable or that the interference with the plaintiff's property was minimal.[98]

Public Nuisance

Public nuisance is an unreasonable interference with the right of, or a threat to, the general public.[99] Examples of public nuisance include keeping diseased animals, storing explosives in the midst of a city, or obstructing a public highway.[100] Statutes usually define public nuisances, and suits against the perpetrators of public nuisances usually are brought by governmental entities. Although public nuisance actions normally are civil actions, they may also be prosecuted criminally. A private individual may bring a cause of action for public nuisance only if that plaintiff has suffered an injury that is different in kind from the injuries suffered by the general public.[101]

If a public nuisance claim is strong enough, it may provide citizens with power to force polluters to pay for damages in enforcement actions brought under federal laws.[102] What makes public nuisance claims particularly interesting for controlling existing facilities is that courts and private citizens have power to use nuisance law to fill the enforcement gaps left by the environmental laws. In some instances, it may be important to combine common law actions, especially nuisance, with enforcement actions under the federal environmental laws.[103] In certain circumstances, federal or state laws may preempt or limit relief from a public nuisance cause of action.[104] However, stating a claim under a federal or state law does not necessarily bar public nuisance claim.[105]

One limitation of public nuisance actions is that, although private parties may use them against those responsible for contamination, courts have indicated that state common law nuisance claims may not be used to challenge ongoing Superfund cleanups.[106]

Trespass

To recover under a theory of common law trespass, a plaintiff must show:

- an invasion affecting an interest in the exclusive possession of the plaintiff's property;
- an intentional doing of the act that constitutes the invasion;
- reasonable forseeability that the act could result in an invasion of the plaintiff's property; and
- damage to the person or property.[107]

So, if pollution from an existing facility is deposited on a plaintiff's property and causes damage, a plaintiff may seek monetary damages under a trespass theory. Trespass can be particularly useful for situations where hazardous waste leaked from one property to another or contaminates groundwater. Courts also will often allow recovery for plaintiffs who have suffered chemical-related injuries, and trespass can be a viable theory of liability.[108]

If there is an invasion with only minimal harm to a person or property, trespass has occurred but damages will be nominal. Finally, because trespass has an intent requirement, a plaintiff could seek to recover punitive damages from the defendant responsible for the invading pollution.[109]

Negligence

To succeed in a negligence action, a plaintiff must show:

1. a legal duty to conform to a certain standard of conduct to protect others;
2. failure to conform to that standard;
3. causal connection between the conduct and a resulting injury; and
4. loss or damage to the interests of another.[110]

Plaintiffs must attempt to mitigate damages in negligence cases, so monetary rewards are reduced if the plaintiff did not try to reduce the damages caused by the plaintiff's actions. Further, a plaintiff can receive punitive damages if a defendant's actions were particularly reckless, malicious, "wanton or willful."[111]

Strict Liability

When an activity is particularly hazardous, the person who engages in it may be strictly liable for the damages it causes.[112] For such activities, the defendant will be liable for harm regardless of the level of care he or she used to prevent it. In the case of existing facilities, improper storage of hazardous materials may qualify as an "ultrahazardous" or "abnormally dangerous" activity for which the defendant may be strictly liable.[113]

Constitutional Limitations on Our Ability to Control Existing Facilities

Use Restrictions: Commerce Clause (Article I, Section 8)

Families living near waste disposal facilities are particularly interested in limiting the amount and type of waste a site may accept. In fact, such facilities and other sources of contamination near people's homes have made those homes, "rather than a place to escape to, . . . a place that residents could not escape from."[114] In addition, residents tend to fear waste coming to their neighborhood from out of state more than they fear waste generated nearby.[115] As such, there is great pressure from citizens to exclude out-of-state waste from local facilities. States and municipalities have responded by trying to set rules regarding what a facility may accept in terms of waste, especially from out of state.

However, the U.S. Supreme Court has said that the Commerce Clause[116] prohibits states and municipalities from excluding or discriminating against out-of-state waste.[117] The Court has held that attempts to control the amount and/or nature of out-of-state waste constitute impermissible discrimination against interstate commerce. States and municipalities may not discriminate among transactions on the basis of their interstate nature. Courts find laws or regulations that discriminate against interstate commerce virtually per se invalid. As such, the Commerce Clause has prevented states and municipalities from enacting certain controls on existing facilities.[118]

There is an exception, however, to the rule prohibiting states from excluding out-of-state waste. When a state participates in an existing waste disposal market as if it were a private actor, it may regulate more freely.[119] To be a private actor, states usually must operate a state-owned landfill site. In such circumstances, states may set policies for their own disposal facilities that may otherwise amount to discrimination against out-of-state waste. Although the

Supreme Court generally accepts the market participant exception, it is not a viable option for states with significant solid waste problems. This is because, to protect oneself from out-of-state waste, it is not sufficient to prohibit out-of-state waste at the state's own landfill. The state would also need to prohibit it at private landfills within the state. In doing so, the state would fall outside the market participant exemption and thus run afoul of the Commerce Clause.[120]

Sovereign Immunity: The Problem of Federal Facilities

Many of the existing facilities that benefit from environmental grandfather clauses by virtue of their age are owned and operated by the federal government. Studies have shown that federal facilities fail to comply with environmental laws to a greater extent, perhaps twice as much, as other facilities.[121]

In addition to having poor compliance records, federal facilities get some protection from Congress in the form of limitations on citizen suits and remedies. The doctrine of sovereign immunity provides additional protection from prosecution.

In some cases, even where Congress seems to have waived immunity and allowed the government to be sued, courts have interpreted the waiver so narrowly as not to allow recovery. For example, the state of Ohio sued the U.S. Dept. of Energy for violations of the CWA and RCRA arising from a uranium processing plant the DOE operated in Ohio.[122] The Supreme Court held that Congress had not waived sovereign immunity with respect to the CWA's and RCRA's citizen suit and federal facilities provisions and refused to hold the federal facility responsible for punitive civil penalties. Some argue that by refusing to allow citizens to sue federal facilities for civil penalties, the courts have removed the teeth from pollution control laws with respect to federal facilities.[123]

The Federal Facility Compliance Act of 1992 (FFCA),[124] which amended RCRA, has effectively reversed the *Ohio* case on the punitive civil penalties issue. The FFCA clarifies that states can assess civil penalties against federal facilities for RCRA violations. In addition, they can issue administrative orders to compel federal agencies to comply with RCRA's requirements. The FFCA does not authorize civil actions by EPA against other federal agencies, thereby avoiding potential constitutional problems. Also, the FFCA did not address reasoning in the *Ohio* case that called into question the sovereign immunity waivers in the CAA and CERCLA. Some argue, therefore, that Congress should extend the scope of the FFCA to include these and other federal environmental laws.[125] As such, sovereign immunity and the courts' limitations on interpreting waivers of sovereign immunity present an impediment to controlling pollution and encouraging cleanup of existing facilities owned and/or operated by the federal government.

Pollution Prevention

Traditionally, methods for controlling pollution from existing facilities have focused on managing facilities' discharges and releases of pollutants into the environment. As such, rather than reducing the amount of a pollutant produced, the laws encouraged protection of one part of the environment by changing pollutants in it to another form. For example, pollutants removed from wastewater often are converted into sludge, another form of pollution. Though the pollutant has not disappeared, it is now regulated as either hazardous or solid waste sludge under RCRA.[126]

Rather then merely changing the medium in which pollutants appear, the pollution prevention model focuses on reducing the amount of pollution industry generates overall. As such, pollution prevention would reduce the amount of pollution generated by existing facilities, many of which are located in low-income and minority neighborhoods. In addition, many believe that pollution prevention is, in the long term, more cost-effective than "end of the pipe" regulation.

Methods for achieving pollution reduction include source reduction, waste minimization, and toxics use reduction. Facilities can achieve source reduction in several ways, including process changes, changing the materials used in production, changing the product itself, improving plant operations and/or maintenance, and employing closed loop or in-process recycling.[127] Although environmental groups have long encouraged pollution prevention, it was not, until recently, a part of EPA's agenda. Pollution prevention was one of the "guiding principles" in EPA's 1994, Five-Year Strategic Plan.[128] EPA now has an active Office of Pollution Prevention and Toxics, charged with overseeing the implementation of the Pollution Prevention Act of 1990.[129]

The Pollution Prevention Act of 1990

Although EPA had drafted a pollution prevention bill in the late 1980s, Congress adopted a more limited Pollution Prevention Act in 1990.[130] In the Act, Congress found that:

1. The United States produces an enormous amount of pollution every year;
2. controlling this pollution requires the expenditure of billions of dollars annually;

3. significant opportunities exist to reduce or prevent pollution at the source in a cost-effective manner;
4. source reduction is "fundamentally different and more desirable than waste management and pollution control"; and
5. the existing environmental regulatory scheme diverts attention from source reduction opportunities to treatment and disposal, creating a need to encourage source reduction activities.[131]

Congress further set forth priorities that:

- pollution should be prevented or reduced at the source whenever feasible;
- pollution that cannot be prevented should be recycled in an environmentally safe manner, whenever feasible;
- pollution that cannot be prevented or recycled should be treated in an environmentally safe manner whenever feasible; and
- disposal or other release into the environment should be employed only as a last resort and should be conducted in an environmentally safe manner.[132]

In addition to setting forth these findings and priorities regarding pollution prevention, the Act required EPA to create and publish a pollution prevention strategy, which the agency did in 1991.[133] The Act's only direct impact on industry thus far, however, is an expansion of the annual reporting requirements already existing under EPCRA.

Specifically, the Act requires owners or operators of facilities subject to the emissions reporting requirements in EPCRA's toxic release inventory program to include with their annual filing a toxic chemical source reduction and recycling report for the preceding calendar year.[134] This report must cover each toxic chemical that EPCRA requires the facility to report on the annual toxic chemical release form. It must include for each toxic chemical:

1. the quantity of the chemical entering the waste stream prior to recycling, treatment or disposal, and the percentage change from the previous year; and the recycling process used;
2. the amount of the chemical recycled; the percentage change from the previous year; and the recycling process used;
3. the amount of the chemical that is treated during the year and the percentage change from the previous year;
4. the source reduction practices used for the chemical;
5. how much the company expects to dispose of or recycle for the next two years;

6. a comparison of the amount of production compared to the previous year;
7. how the company identified the source reduction opportunities (e.g. through employee recommendations, outside audits, etc.)[135]

Companies failing to submit these reports are subject to the sanctions applicable under the toxic release inventory program, up to $25,000 per day in penalties.[136]

In addition, the Act requires EPA to promote pollution prevention. The agency has begun to do so through its pollution prevention program and by pressuring companies to include pollution prevention plans in permits and settlements.[137] According to a General Accounting Office report, however, EPA has not been particularly successful at establishing a pollution prevention ethic or encouraging companies to reduce pollution voluntarily.[138] The Act also creates an information clearinghouse and grants program intended to create incentives for states to encourage facilities to create and implement source reduction techniques.[139]

Although the Pollution Prevention Act does not require regulated industries to reduce pollution, it creates and strongly suggests a hierarchy for handing pollution problems. It suggests, first, that pollution be prevented or reduced at the source. Second, if pollution cannot be prevented, it should be recycled in an environmentally safe manner. If it cannot be prevented or recycled, it should be treated in an environmentally safe manner. Only as a last resort should pollution be disposed of or released into the environment. When it must be released, it should be done in an environmentally safe manner.[140]

The Act has been criticized for its failure to require reduction or prevention of specific pollutants in specific ways or amounts.[141] It has also been criticized for its limited scope—applying only to facilities in industries covered under the toxic release inventory program.[142] Although the Act does not require facilities to reduce the amounts of their releases, the additional reporting requirements may help focus public attention on pollution prevention and enhance public pressure to reduce releases.

Pollution Prevention in the Other Major Federal Environmental Laws

Pollution prevention, although relatively new on EPA's radar, is not a new concept. Several of the other major federal environmental laws contain similar provisions that EPA could use in the future to advance a pollution prevention agenda.

Pollution Prevention in RCRA

The 1984 Hazardous and Solid Waste Amendments to RCRA reflect Congress's developing policy of minimizing the generation of hazardous waste. Specifically, the Act states that it is national policy that "whenever feasible, generation of hazardous waste is to be reduced or eliminated as expeditiously as possible."[143] In support of that policy, generators of hazardous waste must certify that they have a "program in place to reduce the volume or quantity and toxicity of [their] waste to the degree determined by the generator to be economically practicable."[144] Although EPA does not vigorously enforce this provision, it has served as a forerunner to EPA's more recent efforts in pollution prevention. Also, the provision's presence provides an opportunity for EPA to enforce in the future.

Another RCRA provision that plays a role in pollution prevention is the biennial reporting requirement.[145] A generator of hazardous waste must submit a report biennially to EPA (or to the state agency if it is authorized to administer the RCRA program) describing its waste reduction efforts.[146] Although this noncoercive effort to encourage waste minimization has not been very effective, EPA historically has not taken advantage of its enforcement authority with respect to the certification and biennial reporting requirements. Should EPA choose to step up enforcement in these areas, it could apply its civil and criminal enforcement options.[147]

Pollution Prevention Under the Clean Water Act

Like the other major federal environmental laws, the CWA sets forth primarily an "end of the pipe" regulatory system. However, some argue that there are pollution prevention aspects of and opportunities in the act.[148]

First, the Act provides an opportunity to incorporate pollution prevention into EPA's regulation of effluent discharges.[149] For example, in EPA's proposed rule for the Oil and Gas Extraction Subcategory, the agency cited the Pollution Prevention Act and incorporated pollution prevention technologies into the regulation.[150]

Second, EPA has included pollution prevention in its storm water regulations. Each facility covered by a general storm water permit must submit a "site-specific storm water pollution prevention plan."[151] Finally, because the storm water pollution prevention plan is required under the general permit, it is enforceable as a permit condition. Facilities therefore must implement the plans created in satisfaction of the permit requirement.[152]

Pollution Prevention Under the Clean Air Act

Congress and EPA have sought to promote pollution prevention in their respective enactment and implementation of the CAA. Specifically, Section 112 allows companies an additional six years to meet Maximum Achievable Control Technology (MACT) standards if they participate in the Early Reduction Program and reduce their emissions of hazardous air pollutants by 90 percent.[153] This effort has not been successful because few companies have participated in the Early Reduction Program due to the difficulty of establishing base year emissions levels and to EPA's delay in proposing MACT standards.[154]

Notes

1. *See generally* Heidi G. Robertson, *If Your Grandfather Could Pollute, So Can You: Environmental Grandfather Clauses and Their Role in Environmental Inequity,* 45 CATH. U. L. REV. 131 (1995).

2. RCRA § 3005(e), 42 U.S.C. 6925(e) (1998). *See* General Motors Corp. v. Dept. of Natural Resources, 472 N.W.2d 49, 50 (Mich. 1991) in which the Michigan Court of Appeals stated that "[i]nterim status is merely a statutorily conferred grandfather provision which allows a facility to continue operations until a permit is issued.

The Resource Conservation and Recovery Act of 1976, 42 U.S.C. § 6901-92(k) (1976) was amended by the Hazardous and Solid Waste Amendments of 1984, P.L. 98-616, 98 Stat. 3221 (1984), which made major modifications to the solid waste section of RCRA, Subtitle D.

3. Standards of Performance for new stationary sources, 42 U.S.C. § 7411, and Prevention of Significant Deterioration of Air Quality, 42 U.S.C. §§ 7470–7479.

4. F. William Brownell, THE CLEAN AIR ACT, *in* THE ENVIRONMENTAL LAW HANDBOOK, Government Institutes, Inc., 1993.

5. One example of grandfathering in state law is in New York's State Environmental Quality Review Act (SEQRA). SEQRA allows an action undertaken or approved prior to the statute's effective date not to comply with SEQRA. N.Y. ENVTL CONSERV. LAW, § 8-0111.5(a) (McKinney's). *See also* Maine's Hazardous Waste Septage and Solid Waste Management Act, 33 M.R.S.A § 1308, which allows facilities in existence on October 3, 1973 to continue to operate without complying with the law's provisions on location, establishment, and construction of solid waste disposal facilities. Note, however, that this law does not exempt such facilities, even those in existence on October 3, 1973, from complying with regulations regarding alteration or operation. Department of Environmental Protection v. Emerson, 563 A.2d 762, 764–68 (Maine 1989). *See also* Florida Administrative Code § 62-701.330(1), and New York State's air pollution regulations, 6 N.Y.C.R.R. § 201.6(r), (y).

6. Lethal Loophole, U.S. Public Interest Research Group (June 1998).

7. Marianne Lavelle & Marcia Coyle, *Unequal Protection: The Racial Divide in Environmental Law,* NAT'L L.J., Sept. 21, 1992, S1–S12. *See also* Rae Zimmerman, *Social Equity and Environmental Risk,* 13 RISK ANALYSIS 649 (1993) (finding that with respect to inactive hazardous waste disposal sites on the NPL, communities with relatively higher percentages of racial minority populations have fewer cleanup plans (as evidenced by signed Records of Decision) than other commu-

nities with NPL sites); CLEAN SITES, HAZARDOUS WASTE SITES AND THE RURAL POOR: A PRELIMINARY ASSESSMENT (1990) [hereinafter CLEAN SITES] (finding that hazardous waste sites in rural counties were more likely to be cleaned up than in other counties, but failing to address any racial variable in the analysis) *But see* John A. Hird, *Environmental Policy and Equity: The Case of Superfund,* 12 J. POL'Y ANALYSIS & MGMT. 323, 337 (1993) (finding no relationship between the speed with which sites are cleaned up and the host county's socioeconomic characteristics); U.S. EPA REGION 9 WASTE COMPLIANCE STUDY—FINAL DRAFT (1994) (finding "no causal relationship between the percentage minority and the penalty amount assessed").

8. Lavelle & Coyle, *supra* note 7, at S4.

9. *But see Georgia: State Report Looks at Waste Site Fines, Finds No Discrimination in Minority Areas,* 24 ENV'T REP. (BNA) No. 6, at 284 (June 11, 1993).

10. Lavelle & Coyle, *supra* note 7, at S2, S6.

11. Lavelle & Coyle, *supra* note 7, at S2, S6. *See also* CLEAN SITES, *supra* note 7.

12. *See* U.S. EPA, *Responses by the Environmental Protection Agency to Questions by the United States Commission on Civil Rights on Environmental Equity and Civil Rights Enforcement, reprinted in* LOUISIANA ADVISORY COMM. TO THE U.S. COMMISSION ON CIVIL RIGHTS, THE BATTLE FOR ENVIRONMENTAL JUSTICE IN LOUISIANA . . . GOVERNMENT, INDUSTRY AND THE PEOPLE, 82, 89 (1993); U.S. EPA, REGION 9 EPA WASTE COMPLIANCE STUDY—FINAL DRAFT, *passim* (1994).

13. *Enforcement: EPA Expands Environmental Justice Focus, Merging Demographics, Enforcement Data,* CHEM. REG. REP. June 17, 1994.

14. Note, however, that several recent federal decisions have imposed significant restrictions on the ability of citizens and citizen groups to obtain standing to sue in citizen suits. See Chapter 11 for a discussion of these cases.

15. *See infra* "Lawsuits Against the Government for Nonenforcement," pages 499–500. For more detailed information on the citizen suit provisions in the federal environmental laws and their role in the environmental justice movement, *see* Eileen Gauna, *Federal Environmental Citizen Provisions: Obstacles and Incentives on the Road to Environmental Justice,* 22 ECOLOGY L.Q. 1 (1995).

16. 42 U.S.C. § 1364(d) (1998) (Clean Water Act); 42 U.S.C. § 7604(d) (1998) (Clean Air Act); 42 U.S.C. § 6972(e) (1998) (RCRA).

17. 42 U.S.C. § 6972(b)(1)(A) (1998) (RCRA) (The 60-day notice provision, however, does not apply for hazardous waste facility violations.) 33 U.S.C. § 1365 (b)(1)(A) (1998) (Clean Water Act).

18. 33 U.S.C. § 1365 (b)(1)(B) (1998) (Clean Water Act), 42 U.S.C. § 6972(b)(1)B) (1998) (RCRA).

19. 33 U.S.C. § 1365(a)(1) (1998) (Clean Water Act), 42 U.S.C. § 6972(a)(1)(A) and (b) (1998) (RCRA).

20. 33 U.S.C. § 1365 (1998).

21. *See* Gauna, *supra* note 15, at 46, *citing* BUREAU OF NATIONAL AFFAIRS, ENVIRONMENTAL CITIZEN SUITS: CONFRONTING THE CORPORATION 10–11 (1988); Adeeb Fadil, *Citizen Suits Against Polluters: Picking Up the Pace,* 9 HARV. ENVTL. L. REV. 23, 35–53 (1985).

22. 33 U.S.C. §§ 1311(a), 1342(a) (1998).

23. 33 U.S.C. § 1318 (1998).

24. Gauna, *supra* note 15, at 47.

25. Gauna, *supra* note 15, at 48.

26. 42 U.S.C. § 1365(b)(1)(B) (1998). *See* Citizens for a Better Environment-California v. Union Oil Co., 83 F.3d 1111 (9th Cir. 1996), Knee Deep Cattle Company, Inc. v. Bindana Investments Co., 94 F.3d 514 (9th Cir. 1996). However, citizens can join EPA's or the state's lawsuit. Also, the statute's bar on lawsuits may not apply if the state or EPA is suing for past violations. 42 U.S.C. § 1365(b)(1)(B) (1998).

27. Gwaltney of Smithfield v. Chesapeake Bay Foundation, Inc., 484 U.S. 49 (1987). *See also* Steel Company v. Citizens for a Better Environment, 118 S. Ct. 1003 (1998) (reaffirming Gwaltney by holding that citizen suits will not stand under the EPCRA when past violations have been corrected).

28. Gwaltney, *supra* note 27, 484 U.S. at 57.

29. 42 U.S.C. § 7604(a)(1) (1998).

30. 42 U.S.C. § 7661a(d) (Supp. V 1993).

31. 42 U.S.C. § 7661b(a)(2) (Supp. V 1993).

32. 40 C.F.R. pt. 70 (1998).

33. 40 C.F.R. § 70.3(b) (1998).

34. 42 U.S.C. § 6972(a)(1)(A) (1998).

35. 42 U.S.C. § 6972(a)(1)(B) (1998).

36. 42 U.S.C. § 6972(b)(1)(B) (1998).

37. 42 U.S.C. § 6972(a)(1)(A) (1998). Lutz v. Chromatex, Inc., 718 F. Supp. 413 (M.D. Pa. 1989).

38. Environmental Defense Fund, Inc. v. Lamphier, 714 F.2d 331 (4th Cir. 1983), Walls v. Waste Resource Corp., 761 F.2d 311 (6th Cir. 1985).

39. Lamphier, 714 F.2d at 337 n.4.

40. Pub. L. No. 98-616, 98 Stat. 3269 (1984) 42 U.S.C. § 6972(a)(1)(B) (1988 ed. & Supp. V).

41. 42 U.S.C. § 6972(a)(1)(B) (1998).

42. 42 U.S.C. § 6972(a)(2)(B) (1998).

43. 42 U.S.C. § 6972(b)(2)(A) (1998).

44. Gauna, *supra* note 15, at 66, *citing* Greenpeace, Inc. v. Waste Technologies Indus., 9 F.3d 1174 (6th Cir. 1993).

45. Gauna, *supra* note 15, at 66, *citing* United States v. Bliss, 667 F. Supp. 1289 (E.D. Mo. 1987).

46. Gauna, *supra* note 15, at 67, *citing* Waste Industries, Inc. v. North Carolina Dept. of Human Resources, 734 F.2d 159, 165 (4th Cir. 1984).

47. Gauna, *supra* note 15, at 67, *citing* United States v. Ottati & Goss, Inc., 630 F. Supp. 1361 (D.N.H. 1985).

48. Meghrig v. KFC Western, Inc., 116 S. Ct. 1251, 1254 (1996). This case is discussed in detail in Chapter 16, *infra*.

49. 31 U.S.C. §§ 3729–33 (1988 & Supp. V 1993).

50. United States *ex rel.* Fallon v. Accudyne Corp., 880 F. Supp. 636 (W.D. Wis. 1995). *See* Michael B. Gerrard and Deborah Goldberg, *Update on False Claims Act Suits*, Toxics Law Reporter (BNA), Mar. 20, 1998.

51. The 11th Amendment provides that "the judicial power of the United States shall not be construed to extend to any suit in law or equity, commenced or prosecuted against one of the United States by Citizens of another State, or by Citizens or Subjects of any Foreign State." U.S. Const. amend. XI. *See also* Hans v. Louisiana, 134 U.S. 1 (1890) (interpreting the 11th amendment to prohibit suits by all persons against a state in federal court).

52. 15 U.S.C. § 2619 (1998) (Toxic Substances Control Act), 33 U.S.C. § 1365(a)(2) (1998) (Clean Water Act), 42 U.S.C. § 6972(a)(1)(C) (1998) (RCRA), 42 U.S.C. § 7604(a)(2) (1988 & Supp. IV 1992) (Clean Air Act), 42 U.S.C. § 9659(a)(2) (1998) (CERCLA), 42 U.S.C. § 11,046(a)(1)(B) (1998) (Emergency Planning and Community Right–to-Know Act). In addition, the Administrative Procedure Act gives authority to the federal courts to "compel agency action unlawfully withheld or unreasonably delayed." 5 U.S.C. § 706(1) (1998).

53. 15 U.S.C. § 2619 (a)(1) (1998) (Toxic Substances Control Act); 33 U.S.C. 1365(a)(1) (1998) (Clean Water Act); 7604(a)(1) (Clean Air Act); 42 U.S.C. § 6972(a)(1)(A) and (B) (1998) (RCRA); 42 U.S.C. § 9659(a)(1) (1998) (CERCLA).

54. *Ex Parte Young*, 209 U.S. 123 (1908); Natural Resources Defense Council v. California Dept. of Transp., 96 F.3d 420 (9th Cir. 1996); Strahan v. Coxe, 939 F. Supp. 963 (D. Mass. 1996).

55. *See* Idaho v. Coeur d'Alene Tribe of Idaho, 117 S. Ct. 2028 (1997). *See also* Seminole Tribe of Florida v. Florida, 116 S. Ct. 114 (1996).

56. Gauna, *supra* note 15, at 70, *citing* Robert Glicksman & Christopher H. Schroeder, *EPA and the Courts: Twenty Years of Law and Politics*, 54 L. & CONTEMP. PROBS. 249 (1991). *See* Heckler v. Chaney, 470 U.S. 821 (1985); Massachusetts Public Interest Research Group, Inc. v. U.S. Nuclear Regulatory Commission, 852 F.2d 9 (1st Cir. 1988); Dubois v. Thomas, 820 F.2d 943 (8th Cir. 1987).

57. Heckler v. Chaney, 470 U.S. at 832.

58. Heckler v. Chaney, 470 U.S. 821 at 831. *See also* Robert R. Kuehn, *Remedying the Unequal Enforcement of Environmental Laws*, 9 ST. JOHN'S J. LEGAL COMMENT 625, 648 (1994). Although in a case decided under a labor statute, not an environmental law, the U.S. Supreme Court has found that an agency has a nondiscretionary duty to take enforcement action. Dunlop v. Bachowski, 421 U.S. 560, 566–68 (1975).

59. Gauna, *supra* note 15, at 71.

60. Kuehn, *supra* note 58, at 649, *citing* 33 U.S.C. §§ 1319(a)(1) and (3) (1988).

61. Kuehn, *supra* note 58, at 650.

62. 42 U.S.C. § 7413(e) (1998); U.S. EPA, A FRAMEWORK FOR STATUTE-SPECIFIC APPROACHES TO PENALTY ASSESSMENTS: IMPLEMENTING EPA'S POLICY ON CIVIL PENALTIES (Feb. 16, 1984).

63. 42 U.S.C. § 7413(d)(1) (1998), Clean Air Act, § 113(d)(1) (1998).

64. 42 U.S.C. § 7413(d)(1)(1998).

65. 42 U.S.C. § 7413(d)(3)(1998); Field Citation Program, 59 Fed. Reg. 22776 (1994) (to be codified at 40 C.F.R. pt. 59 (proposed Apr. 15, 1994)).

66. 42 U.S.C. § 7413(f) (1998).

67. 33 U.S.C. § 1319(g)(2)(A) (1998).

68. 33 U.S.C. § 1319(g)(2)(B) (1998).

69. 33 U.S.C. § 1319(d) (1998).

70. 33 U.S.C. § 1319(b) (1998).

71. 42 U.S.C. §§ 6901–6992 (k) (1998) (RCRA), 15 U.S.C. §§ 2601–92 (1998) (TSCA), 7 U.S.C. § 136 (1998) (FIFRA), 42 U.S.C. §§ 9601–75 (1998) (CERCLA), 42 U.S.C. §§ 7401–7671 (1998) (Clean Air Act), 33 U.S.C. §§ 1251–1387 (1998) (Clean Water Act), 33 U.S.C. § 407 (1998) (Rivers and Harbors Act), 42 U.S.C. §§ 300-f to 300-j-26 (1998) (SDWA), 16 U.S.C. § 1531 (1998) (ESA). For a comprehensive discussion of environmental crimes, see Note, *Environmental Crimes*, 35 AMER. CRIM. L. REV. 597 (1998).

72. V. S. Khanna, *Corporate Criminal Liability: What Purpose Does It Serve?*, 109 HARV. L. REV. 1477, 1489 (1996).

73. Richard J. Lazarus, *Assimilating Environmental Protection into Legal Rules and the Problem with Environmental Crime*, 27 LOY. L.A. L. REV. 867, 880 (1994).

74. Nancy E. Anderson, *Notes from the Frontline*, 21 FORDHAM URB. L.J. 757 (1994).

75. *See, e.g.*, Pennsylvania's Solid Waste Management Act, 53 PA. CONST. STAT. § 4000.1710.

76. 42 U.S.C. § 9609(d) (1998) (CERCLA); 33 U.S.C. § 411 (1998) (Rivers and Harbors Act; 31 U.S.C. §§ 3729–33 (1988 & Supp. V. 1993) (False Claims Act); N.J. STAT. ANN. 13:1E-9.2(1989).

77. Melissa Thorme, *Local to Global: Citizen's Legal Rights and Remedies Relating to Toxic Waste Dumps*, 5 TUL. ENVTL. L.J. 101, 132 (1991).

78. For example, because state and federal agencies have reinterpreted portions of the CAA, companies that plan to modify existing industrial facilities may now face lengthy permit reviews. Specifically, the recent interpretations may cause companies to trigger the CAA new source requirements when they make what used to be a minor modification or repair to their facility. This is because the EPA has changed the way it calculates net emissions increases. *Air Pollution: New Interpretations of NSR Provisions Have Significant Implications, Attorneys Say*, 121 BUREAU OF NATIONAL AFFAIRS (BNA) DAILY ENV'T REP., A-1, 1999.

79. Heat Energy Advanced Technology, Inc. v. West Dallas Coalition for Environmental Justice, 962 S.W.2d 288 (Tex. App. 1998) (NO. 03-97-00382-CV), *writ denied* (Aug 25, 1998).

80. Amigos Bravos v. Molycorp, Inc., No. 97-2327 (10th Cir., Nov. 13, 1998).

81. *Id.*

82. Tri-State Transfer Co., Inc. v. Dep't of Environmental Protection Tinicum Township, 722 A.2d 1129 (Pa. Commw. Ct. 1999).

83. *California: Hazardous Waste Plant Faces Shutdown After Permit Denial*, 156 BUREAU OF NATIONAL AFFAIRS (BNA) DAILY ENV'T REP., A-6, 1998. (Regulators issued a final decision Aug. 7, 1998, denying Statewide Environmental Services (SES) the permit it needs to continue accepting, treating, and transferring toxic wastes due to noncompliance with California environmental laws.).

84. See Chapter 2, "Title VI," for further discussion of this EPA Guidance.

85. 42 U.S.C. § 6928(h)(1) (1998).

86. 42 U.S.C. § 1319(a) (1998).

87. 42 U.S.C. § 7413(d) (1998).

88. U.S. Department of Justice Statements of Policy, Consent Judgments in Actions to Enjoin Discharges of Pollutants, 28 C.F.R. § 50.7 (1998).

89. Langrock, *Class Action Litigation*, 25 TRIAL, Oct. 1989, at 48.

90. Illinois v. City of Milwaukee, 406 U.S. 91 (1972).

91. W. PAGE KEETON ET. AL., PROSSER AND KEETON ON THE LAW OF TORTS § 87 (5th ed. 1984).

92. Langrock, *Class Action Litigation*, 25 TRIAL, Oct. 1989, at 47. *See also* Prosser, *supra* note 91, at § 87.

93. Prosser, *supra* note 91, at § 87. *See also* Restatement of Torts (Second) § 821D.

94. *Id.*

95. Prosser, *supra* note 91, at § 87.

96. Prosser, *supra* note 91, at § 88.

97. Prosser, *supra* note 91, at § 88. *See also* Goeke v. National Farms, Inc., 512 N.W.2d 626 (Neb.1994), *citing* Restatement of the Law of Torts (Second) § 822.

98. Prosser, *supra* note 91, at § 88A.

99. Prosser, *supra* note 91, at § 90. *See also* Restatement of the Law of Torts (Second) § 821(B).

100. Restatement of the Law of Torts (Second) § 821(B), comment b.

101. Restatement of the Law of Torts (Second) § 821(B), comment h.

102. David R. Hodas, *Private Actions for Public Nuisance: Common Citizen Suits for Relief from Environmental Harm*, 16 ECOLOGY L.Q. 883, 887 (1989).

103. U.S. v. Ottati & Goss, 630 F. Supp. 1361 (D.N.H. 1985) (combining a RCRA § 7002 claim with common law nuisance).

104. *Id.*

105. Environmental Defense Fund v. Lamphier, 714 F.2d 331 (4th Cir. 1983).

106. Arrest the Incinerator Remediation (A.I.R.) Inc. v. OHM Remediation Services Corp., No. 4:CV-98-0398 M.D. Pa., 4/14/98, *citing* Clinton County Commissioners v. EPA, 116 F.3d 1018 (3d Cir. 1997). *See also* Chapter 16, *infra*.

107. Restatement of Torts (Second) § 214; *see also* Prosser, *supra* note 91, at § 13.

108. Thorme, *supra* note 77, at 117.

109. Thorme, *supra* note 77, at 117.

110. Prosser, *supra* note 91, at § 30.

111. Prosser, *supra* note 91, at § 34.

112. Restatement of the Law of Torts (Second) § 524.

113. Crawford v. National Lead Co., 784 F. Supp. 439 (S.D. Ohio 1989).

114. MICHAEL R. EDELSTEIN, CONTAMINATED COMMUNITIES: THE SOCIAL AND PSYCHOLOGICAL IMPACTS OF RESIDENTIAL TOXIC EXPOSURE 64 (1988).

115. *Id.*

116. U.S. CONST. art. 1, § 8, cl. 3.

117. Fort Gratiot Sanitary Landfill, Inc. v. Michigan Dept. of Natural Resources, 112 S. Ct. 2019 (1992), Chemical Waste Management v. Hunt, 112 S. Ct. 2009 (1992); C and A Carbone, Inc. v. Town of Clarkstown, 511 U.S. 383 (1994).

118. *Id.*

119. *See* Barker Bros. Waste, Inc. v. Dyer Cnty Legislative Body, 923 F. Supp. 1042 (W.D. Tenn. 1996); South Central Timber Dev. v. Wunnicke, 467 U.S. 82 (1984); White v. Massachusetts Council of Constr. Employers, Inc., 460 U.S. 204 (1983).

120. Paul E. McGreal, *The Flawed Economics of the Dormant Commerce Clause*, 39 WM. & MARY L. REV. 1191 (1998).

121. Nelson D. Cary, Note, *A Primer on Federal Facility Compliance with Environmental Laws: Where Do We Go from Here?*, 50 WASH. & LEE L. REV. 801 (1993). Randall S. Abate & Carolyn H. Cogswell, *Sovereign Immunity and Citizen Enforcement of Federal Environmental Laws: A Proposal for a New Synthesis*, 15 VA. ENVTL. L.J. 1, 8 (1995).

122. U.S. Dept. of Energy v. Ohio, 503 U.S. 607 (1992). Some argue that the Sixth Circuit decision in this case would have made better law. It held that when Congress enacts a clear waiver of its sovereign immunity, courts should not thwart Congressional intent by interpreting the waiver in an unduly restrictive manner. 904 F. 2d 1058, 1060 (6th Cir. 1990).

123. Abate & Cogswell, *supra* note 121.

124. Pub. L. No. 102-386, 106 Stat. 1505 (1992).

125. Nelson D. Carey, Note, *A Primer on Federal Facility Compliance with Environmental Laws: Where Do We Go From Here?* 50 WASH. & LEE L. REV. 801 (1993).

126. Bert Black & David H. Hollander, Jr., *Forced Volunteerism: The New Regulatory Push to Prevent Pollution*, CHEM. REG. REP., Jan. 22, 1993.

127. Black & Hollander, *supra* note 126.

128. David L. Markell, *Regulatory Reform at the State Department of Conservation*, 1 ALB. L. ENVTL OUTLOOK 8 (1995), *citing* U.S. EPA, PUB. NO. 200-B-94-002, *The New Generation of Environmental Protection: EPA's Five-Year Strategic Plan* 2 (1994).

129. EPA established this office pursuant to 42 U.S.C. § 12,103(a).

130. 42 U.S.C. §§ 13,101–09 (1998).

131. David L. Markell, *Pollution Prevention, Chapter 18A* in ENVIRONMENTAL LAW PRACTICE GUIDE (Michael B. Gerrard ed., 1995), *citing* 42 U.S.C. § 13,101(a).

132. 42 U.S.C. § 13,101(b) (1998).

133. 56 Fed. Reg. 7849 (Feb. 26, 1991).

134. 42 U.S.C. § 13,106(a) (1998).

135. Markell, *supra* note 131, at 18A-14, *citing* 42 U.S.C. § 13,106(b).

136. Markell, *supra* note 131, at 18A-15, *citing* 42 U.S.C. § 13,106(c).

137. Black & Hollander, *supra* note 126.

138. Markell, *supra* note 131, at 18A-20, *citing* U.S. General Accounting Office, GAO/OCG-95-1, Implementation of National Performance Review's Recommendations 9 (1994).

139. 42 U.S.C. § 13,104 (1998).

140. 42 U.S.C. §§ 13,101–09 (1998). *See also* POLLUTION PREVENTION 1997: A NATIONAL PROGRESS REPORT, U.S. EPA OFFICE OF POLLUTION PREVENTION AND TOXICS (1997).

141. Markell, *supra* note 131, at 18A-20.

142. The Toxic Release Inventory program only applies to companies within the Standard Industrial Classification (SIC) codes 20 through 39, which employ 10 or more full-time employees and use more than a certain amount of specific chemicals. *Id.*, *citing* 42 U.S.C. § 11,023(h).

143. 42 U.S.C. § 6902(b) (1998).

144. Black & Hollander, *supra* note 126. 42 U.S.C. § 6922(b) (1997).

145. Markell, *supra* note 131, at 18A-33.

146. 42 U.S.C. § 6922(a)(6)(A)–(D) (1998).

147. 42 U.S.C. § 6928 (1998).

148. For additional pollution approaches relevant to the Clean Water Act, see Markell, *supra* note 131, at 18A-44.

149. Markell, *supra* note 131, at 18A-40, *citing* Brothers & Hauser, *The HON Rule Evolution: An Analysis of the Difficulties of Incorporating Pollution Prevention into Regulations*, 1 ENV'T MANAGER 14, 15 (Mar. 1995).

150. Markell, *supra* note 131, at 18A-40, *citing* 60 Fed. Reg. 9428 (1995).

151. Markell, *supra* note 131, at 18A-40, *citing* 23 Env't Rep. (BNA) 1371 (Sept. 11, 1992); 57 Fed. Reg. 41,242, 41,307 (Sept. 9, 1992).

152. 57 Fed. Reg. 41,315 (Sept. 9, 1992); 33 U.S.C. § 1319 (1998).

153. Markell, *supra* note 131, at 18A-45, *citing* 42 U.S.C. § 7412(I)(5).

154. Markell, *supra* note 131, at 18A-46, *citing* U.S. Gen. Accounting Office, GAO/RCED-94-207, TOXIC SUBSTANCES: STATUS OF EPA'S EFFORTS TO REDUCE TOXIC RELEASES 8 (1994).

CHAPTER 16

Cleaning Up Abandoned or Inactive Contaminated Sites

LARRY SCHNAPF

Environmental justice lawsuits are usually brought to block the approval of a new waste disposal business or to impose stricter environmental standards on ongoing industrial facilities. However, there are a number of federal and state environmental statutes that community groups can use to compel the cleanup of inactive or abandoned industrial properties. This chapter will discuss the framework of those statutes and how they may be used to force cleanups of contaminated properties.

Comprehensive Environmental Response, Compensation and Liability Act (CERCLA)[1]

Under CERCLA, environmental authorities can undertake a cleanup of contaminated sites and seek reimbursement from potentially responsible parties (PRPs) or order PRPs to clean up sites. In addition, private persons and PRPs who incur cleanup costs can seek reimbursement from other PRPs. CERCLA also created a fund known as "Superfund" that may be used to finance cleanups performed by the government. While citizen groups or community organizations have limited ability to compel cleanups by PRPs, they can bring a contaminated site to the attention of government authorities who can compel cleanups and also participate in the selection of the cleanup remedy for a contaminated site.

Overview of CERCLA Liability Framework

CERCLA imposes strict liability on four classes of PRPs for the cleanup of releases or threatened releases of hazardous substances. These PRPs include:

- the present or former owners of facilities or vessels (for example, tanks) where the release or threatened release occurs (owners);
- present and former operators of a facility or vessel (operators);
- persons who arranged for the disposal, treatment, or transportation of hazardous substances (generators); and
- persons who accepted hazardous substances for transportation to a waste disposal site (transporters).[2]

Liability can be imposed on current owners or operators even where they were not responsible for the contamination.

To establish CERCLA liability, a plaintiff must demonstrate that there has been:

1. a release or threatened release
2. of hazardous substances
3. from a facility
4. that caused the incurrence of response costs and
5. the defendant falls within one of the categories of PRPs identified by the statute.

EPA Information Gathering Authority

CERCLA Section 104 authorizes the federal Environmental Protection Agency (EPA) to perform an investigation or cleanup of a site where a release or threatened release of hazardous substances has occurred or is suspected to occur. Before any enforcement or cleanup action may be taken under CERCLA, the EPA must determine if there has been a release or threatened release of hazardous substances. Under Section 104(e),[3] the EPA has broad investigatory powers to inspect sites where there may be releases or threatened release, to obtain information about the materials at the site, to determine the nature of the release, to evaluate the ability of the facility's owner to pay for a cleanup, and to copy records or documents.[4] As part of this process, the EPA typically requires PRPs to complete detailed and lengthy questionnaires about the generation and disposal of hazardous substances. The information obtained is generally available to the public unless the PRP demonstrates that disclosure would divulge information protected as a trade secret under 18 U.S.C. Section 1905 and also meets certain requirements, such as confirming that steps have been taken to protect the confidentiality of such information.[5]

Types of Response Actions That May Be Conducted Under CERCLA

CERCLA authorizes the EPA to investigate and clean up releases of hazardous substances or to allow private parties to take such actions. The process of responding to releases of hazardous substances is known as a "Response Action." The EPA has established the National Oil and Hazardous Substances Contingency Plan (NCP), which contains procedures that must be followed in responding to oil spills and releases of hazardous substances.[6] The EPA has also compiled a list of those sites that it believes pose the greatest danger. These sites are placed on the National Priorities List (NPL), also known as the Superfund List, which is published as Appendix B to the NCP.[7]

The NCP defines two types of response actions: removal actions and remedial actions. These response actions have their own procedures for conducting investigatory and cleanup activities. Community groups need to be aware of these different procedures to assure that they have an adequate opportunity to participate in the development and selection of the cleanup.

Removal Actions

Removal actions are interim or short-term measures that are designed to contain or stabilize releases of hazardous substances but not to eliminate all of the contamination at a site. Removal actions are intended to be used when a prompt response is necessary to minimize the immediate effects of a release of hazardous substances.[8] The NCP describes circumstances when removal actions may be appropriate. These include situations in which there is:

- actual or potential exposure to nearby human populations, animals, or the food chain;
- actual or potential contamination of drinking water supplies or sensitive ecosystems;
- hazardous substances in drums or barrels;
- threat of fire and explosion; and
- highly contaminated soils at or near the surface.

The NCP contains a nonexclusive list of nine actions that may be considered removal actions. These include:

- posting of warning signs or taking other site security measures;
- drainage controls to reduce migration of hazardous substances or pollutants or contaminants;

- stabilization of berms, dikes, or impoundments or drainage or closing of lagoons;
- using chemicals and other materials to retard the spread of the release or to mitigate its effects;
- excavation, consolidation, capping, or removal of highly contaminated soils;
- removal of drums, barrels, tanks, or other bulk containers that contain or may contain hazardous substances; and
- providing alternative water supply where necessary to prevent exposure to contaminated household water.[9]

Removal actions are generally performed by the EPA using the Superfund. However, state agencies may conduct a Superfund-financed removal action if the state enters into a site-specific cooperative agreement (CA) provided that the negotiation of the CA does not unduly delay the implementation of an emergency or time-critical response activity.[10] If the identity of the PRPs for a particular site is known, the EPA or a state agency may give the PRPs an opportunity to perform the removal action.

CERCLA imposes certain limitations on Superfund-financed removal actions. Such removal actions may not exceed $2 million in cost and may not continue for more than 12 months. When these limits are reached, the removal action must be terminated unless the agency performing the removal action determines that:

1. there is an immediate risk to public health or the environment;
2. a continued response is appropriate and consistent with the remedial action to be taken; and
3. the continued response shall, to the extent practicable, contribute to the efficiency of the anticipated remedial action.[11]

While Superfund-financed removal actions may be performed on non-NPL sites, the EPA has generally limited fund-financed removal actions to sites that are listed or proposed to be listed on the NPL. As a result, the exemption from the time and money limits will rarely be used for a site that is not likely to be placed on the NPL.[12] Thus, if a community is located in a state which does not have sufficient funding to perform removal actions, the community group should try to convince the EPA to perform the removal action, order PRPs to perform the removal action, or begin the process of evaluating the site for possible inclusion on the NPL.

Prior to initiating a removal action, the EPA or state agency that has been designated to be in charge of the removal action must prepare an engineering evaluation/cost analysis (EE/CA) that evaluates the removal alternatives. The lead agency is required to select a spokesperson to inform the community of actions taken, respond to inquiries, and provide information about the release.[13] For removal actions when on-site activity will commence in less than six months, the EPA or state agency must publish a notice of the existence of the administrative action in a local newspaper of general circulation within 60 days after commencing on-site activities, provide for a 30-day public comment period thereafter, and prepare written responses to "significant comments."[14] Where the agency will have at least six months to plan the removal action, the notice must be published when the EE/CA is approved and followed by a 30-day public comment period.[15] When the removal action will take longer than 120 days, the lead agency is required to conduct interviews with local officials, residents, public interest groups, or other affected parties by the end of the 120-day period to solicit their concerns and information needs, and to determine how they would like to be involved in the process.[16] The lead agency is also required to develop a community relations plan (CRP) and establish a local information repository, which is often located at a nearby public library.

Remedial Actions

A Remedial Action consists of long-term work designed to permanently eliminate the risk posed by the release or threatened release of hazardous substances.[17] Examples of remedial activities include soil excavation, groundwater treatment, offsite disposal of contaminated materials, and permanent relocation of residents and businesses affected by hazardous substances.

The NCP contains comprehensive procedures for characterizing sites as well as for identifying, evaluating, and implementing remedial actions. The NCP organizes the remedial action selection process into a number of distinct phases, which will be discussed in the section entitled "Site Remediation Process," pages 531–34.

In addition to these remedy selection requirements, the NCP also contains further procedural restrictions on Superfund-financed cleanups. For example, Superfund-financed remedial actions may be performed only on NPL sites.[18] States are required to share 50 percent of the cost of Superfund-financed response actions when the site was owned by the state or political subdivision at the time of the disposal.[19] For all other Superfund-financed remedial actions performed at nonfederal facilities, a state must contribute 10 percent of the cost of the remedial action and pay for 100 percent of the oversight or post-remedial operation and maintenance costs.[20]

A removal action may be conducted in conjunction with the performance of a remedial action. This will usually occur during the early stage when a distinct source of contamination is discovered that could pose an immediate threat to human health or the environment. These actions are sometimes informally called interim remedial measures (IRMs). Because removal actions are often performed by personnel different from those performing the remedial actions, it is important to ensure that site information is exchanged between the work groups to prevent duplicative or even counterproductive work.

Another important distinction between removal and remedial actions is that there are fewer procedural requirements that a government agency or private party must meet before selecting a removal action. The party performing the removal action only has to perform an engineering evaluation/cost analysis (EE/CA), which is much more streamlined and less costly than the remedial investigation/feasibility study (RI/FS) required for a remedial action (described in the next section).[21] Moreover, a removal action does not require the same level of public participation that the NCP requires for remedial actions.[22]

CERCLA Site Identification, Ranking, and Remediation Process

The EPA is directed under Section 105 to identify those sites that require priority cleanups.[23] The various sites are ranked according to the relative risks they present to human health or the environment. Those sites that pose the greatest danger are placed on the NPL.

Site Identification Process

There are three ways that a site may be listed on the NPL. The principal method is by investigating and evaluating the danger posed by the release using the Hazardous Ranking System (HRS), which is attached to the NCP as Appendix A.[24] The HRS is a scoring system that is used to assess the relative threat associated with actual or potential releases of hazardous substances.

Sites that do not score high enough on the HRS may also be placed on the NPL if either a state where the site is located designates that site as the top-priority site in that state presenting the greatest danger to the public health or the environment.[25] Finally, a site may be added to the NPL if the Agency for Toxic Substances and Disease Registry (ATSDR) issues a "public health advisory" recommending that individuals be isolated from the release of hazardous substances, the EPA determines that the release poses a significant threat to the public, and that a remedial action will be more cost-effective than removal action.[26]

When the EPA first learns that a release of hazardous substances may have occurred at a facility, the release and the facility may be recorded in the CERCLA Information System (CERCLIS), which is a database that EPA has developed to inventory and manage sites where releases of hazardous substances are known to have occurred. Inclusion of a site in CERCLIS does not represent a finding of liability or a determination that a response action is necessary. Indeed, only between 2 and 7 percent of the sites listed in CERCLIS have eventually been placed on the NPL.[27]

To determine if a site should be placed on the NPL using the HRS, the EPA will first take the site through a two-stage site assessment. The first step is a preliminary assessment (PA), which consists of an office review of the existing information on the site and possibly a visual observation of the site. The second step is a site investigation (SI), where more detailed information is collected, including soil and groundwater sampling.[28] Nearly half of the CERCLIS sites that are evaluated are eliminated from further consideration after the PA. It is also possible that the EPA may determine during the PA/SI that a removal action may be necessary.

If the EPA determines that a site does not require further investigation, a "No Further Response Action Planned" (NFRAP) designation will be placed in CERCLIS for that site, which means that no additional actions will be taken by the federal government under CERCLA unless additional information becomes available that suggests more investigatory steps are warranted at the site.[29] It is important to understand that NFRAP designation does not necessarily mean a hazard does not exist, but simply that the EPA does not plan to take any action based on the available information.[30] An NFRAP determination does not preclude a state from initiating enforcement action under its own environmental laws. Indeed, a small percentage of NFRAP sites do eventually become active CERCLIS sites after the EPA notifies states of an NFRAP decision.

Under Section 105 of CERCLA, any person who is or may be affected by a release of a hazardous substance, pollutant or contaminant may petition the EPA to conduct a PA of a site that has not yet been placed on the NPL.[31] Section 104 of CERCLA requires the EPA to conduct the PA within 12 months of the request or provide an explanation why a PA is not appropriate. Individuals may also request that the ATSDR conduct a preliminary health assessment on a non-NPL site where there is information that individuals have been exposed to hazardous substances and the probable cause of the exposure is a release of hazardous substances.[32] If a petition is submitted and a preliminary health assessment is not initiated, the ATSDR is required to provide an explanation why health assessment was not appropriate.[33] The purposes of the preliminary health assessments are to determine if steps are necessary to reduce the exposure and whether additional information is required. For example, the ATSDR may determine, on the basis of the health assessment, that a pilot study may be appropriate to determine the desirability of performing a full-scale epidemiological study.[34] Where the preliminary health assessment indicates that there is a potential significant risk to human health, the ATSDR must consider if the establishment of a registry of exposed persons would be useful.[35] When the ATSDR determines, based on the preceding studies, that the exposure to hazardous substances poses a significant increased risk of adverse health effects in humans and that the exposure is the result of a release, the ATSDR shall initiate a health surveillance program.[36] If a preliminary health assessment or other study contains a finding that the exposure presents a significant risk to human health, the EPA is required to take response actions to reduce the exposure and eliminate or substantially mitigate the significant risk to human health.[37] Such actions may include but are not limited to providing alternative water supplies as well as permanent or temporary relocation of individuals.[38]

Site Ranking Process

The information gathered during the PA/SI will be evaluated by EPA under the HRS. The states have the primary responsibility for identifying sites, computing HRS scores, and submitting candidate sites to the EPA regional offices. The EPA will then review the proposals, develop a final score, and propose adding the suitable sites through notice and comment rulemaking.

Under the HRS, the EPA examines migration pathways (groundwater, surface water, air, soil exposure), which are the ways that hazardous substances may come into contact with humans or the environment. Each pathway is assigned a pathway score using a mathematical formula. The pathway scores are then combined using another mathematical formula to obtain an aggregate site score that ranges from 0 to 100. The HRS evaluates the magnitude of harm that the site may pose to human health or the environment and not the feasibility or scope of a cleanup.[39] Those sites that score 28.50 or greater are eligible for listing on the NPL.

The EPA considers the risk reductions that are achieved by removal actions, provided the removal actions are performed prior to the SI. Once the SI is performed, the site conditions will be essentially "frozen" for scoring purposes. Thus, if after the SI a removal action is performed that eliminates a large quantity of hazardous substances, the site will be scored by the HRS as if the hazardous substances were still present.[40] The EPA believes that this policy will encourage PRPs to perform rapid removal actions. However, the HRS will not consider the effects of pre-SI removal actions, such as providing alternative water supplies that do not reduce the quantity of waste volume at the site.[41]

If a site receives a HRS score of 28.5 or more, the EPA will place the site on the NPL using the process required under the Administrative Procedures Act for promulgating regulations. The NPL must be revised annually. The procedure that the EPA usually follows is that it will first propose placing a group of sites on the NPL. This notice of proposed inclusion on the NPL will be published in the Federal Register. Then, after a public comment period, the EPA will issue a final rule in the Federal Register formally adding sites to the NPL. Listing of a site on the NPL may be challenged only in the Court of Appeals for the District of Columbia. Petitions challenging the listing of a site must be filed within 90 days of the final notice to list the site on the NPL.[42] Approximately 1,300 sites have been included or proposed for inclusion on the NPL.

The EPA will defer listing a site on the NPL or may delete from that list a site that may be remediated under the federal Resource Conservation and Recovery Act (RCRA).[43] However, the EPA may decline to defer a site if the RCRA corrective action may not apply to all of the contamination at a site.[44] In addition, the EPA has chosen not to list contaminated facilities licensed by the Nuclear Regulatory Commission (NRC) because the NRC has the authority to clean up releases from those facilities.[45] Current EPA policy is also to defer cleanup of abandoned mine sites to the Department of Interior's (DOI) Abandoned Mine Lands (AML) program, which is administered under the Surface Mining Control and Reclamation Act (SMCRA).[46] Under the AML, the DOI may evaluate coal and noncoal mine areas, make remedy decisions, and perform actual cleanups. However, AML trust funds cannot be used to finance cleanups if responsible parties are located. In addition, noncoal sites may not be addressed in a state using AML funds until cleanup of coal sites has been completed. Likewise, the EPA will defer cleanups to the Department of Energy (DOE) under the Uranium Mill Tailings Radiation Control Act (UMTRCA) for inactive uranium mill sites.[47] Facilities that are owned or operated by the federal government, such as military installations, may also be added to a special federal section of the NPL.[48]

An NPL listing is not, by itself, a determination of CERCLA liability, nor does it require site owners or operators to undertake response actions. Moreover, the EPA may undertake a removal action and pursue enforcement actions against PRPs even when the site is not on the NPL. However, Superfund-financed remedial actions may not be undertaken unless the site is on the NPL.[49] Although the NPL sites are listed according to their HRS scores, response actions do not have to be implemented in the same order as a site's ranking. Private parties may pursue cost recovery and contribution actions even for non-NPL sites.

Site Remediation Process

The remedial action selection process has several phases. It begins with a "Remedial Investigation" (RI), which involves a complete technical assessment of the site, including characterizing the hydrology, identifying the source and extent of the contamination, and identifying the pathways the contamination may follow. The RI also evaluates the health risks posed by the site and identifies the "applicable or relevant and appropriate requirements" (ARARs), which are state and federal laws or regulations that must be used to establish cleanup levels for the site.[50]

Once the RI is completed, the next phase is the "Feasibility Study" (FS), which identifies and evaluates alternatives for decontaminating the site. Often, because of the site complexities, the RI and/or FS will address only a portion of the site contamination, such as groundwater, or a geographic area of the site. These distinct areas are known as operable units. A study evaluating the remedy for an operable unit is an Operable Unit Feasibility Study (OUFS).

The FS must develop at least four types of remedial alternatives:

- an alternative that attains ARARs;
- an alternative that exceeds those standards;
- a "no-action" alternative; and
- an alternative that does not meet ARARs but reduces the threat and adequately protects public health and the environment.[51]

Often, the FS will contain a dozen cleanup options. The list of remedial alternatives is then narrowed or screened by evaluating the following nine statutory criteria:

1. degree of protection of human health and the environment;
2. compliance with ARARs;
3. long-term effectiveness;
4. permanence;
5. reduction of toxicity, mobility, or volume through treatment;
6. short-term effectiveness;
7. implementability;
8. cost; and
9. state and community acceptance.[52]

The nine statutory criteria are not equally weighted. Instead, they are categorized into three groups: threshold, primary balancing, and modifying. The first two criteria are the minimum threshold requirements that a remedy must meet. Criteria 3–8 above are the balancing criteria whereby the EPA (or state agency if the state has been given the authority to make a particular remedy selection) evaluates these factors and balances the tradeoffs. Finally, state and community acceptance is factored into the remedy selection process.[53]

A problem with this approach is that community input cannot be evaluated until after the public comment period has expired and a "preferred remedy" has already been selected. When the EPA revised the NCP in 1990, citizen advocates argued that community acceptance should play a more significant role and that the public should be given the ability to participate earlier during the RI/FS.[54] However, the EPA replied that the procedures it established accomplished that goal since the EPA was required to consult with the state during the RI/FS and the lead agency was responsible for developing a CRP.[55] Nevertheless, because the public usually does not become involved in the remedy selection process until after the RI/FS has been completed, there may be considerable institutional momentum in favor of the "preferred remedy" by the time of the public comment period.

After the RI/FS is completed, the EPA will propose the selected remedy for the entire site or just an operable unit in the draft Record of Decision (ROD).[56] The ROD must summarize the site conditions, the threat posed, and the remedy selected. In addition, it must describe the relative weaknesses and strengths of the remedial alternatives and offer a clear justification for the final remedy that is selected. In particular, the EPA must demonstrate that the selected remedy demonstrates cost-effectiveness, protects human health and the environment, attains the specified cleanup levels, and utilizes permanent solutions to the maximum extent practicable. If the selected remedy does not satisfy the preference for permanent solutions, the agency must explain why it did not select an alternative that would have reduced the toxicity, mobility, or volume of waste. The EPA must identify the ARARs for the site, or the health-based standards that must be met in the absence of ARARs. Furthermore, the ROD must detail which ARARs will not be met and justify waivers for those ARARs.[57]

The ROD is only released to the state where the site is located. To inform the public and the PRPs about the proposed remedy, the EPA will issue a proposed remedial action plan (PRAP) in the Federal Register. The EPA will hold public meetings where the affected community can respond to the proposed cleanup. The EPA will review the public comments and issue a final ROD that responds to the public comments and selects one of the remedial alternatives.

During the public comment period, citizen groups can question the adequacy of ATSDR health assessments or use the health assessments to challenge the proposed remedy. This may be accomplished by submitting comments to the EPA that the agency is required to address. The EPA is also required to try to receive concurrence of state environmental officials for remedy selection.[58] A state may ask the EPA to enhance or expand a remedy, and the EPA may agree to incorporate the changes in the remedy if it finds the changes are necessary and appropriate. If the EPA finds the changes are not necessary but will not interfere with the selected remedy, the EPA may incorporate the changes.[59] Where the remedial action is being performed under Section 106 (discussed on pages 536–37) and the state does not concur with the remedy because the remedy does not conform to an ARAR that has been waived, the state may intervene as a matter of right to have the remedial action conform to the ARAR.[60] Thus, citizen groups can try to apply pressure to the state agencies to have their concerns over the adequacy of the remedy addressed.

To enable meaningful public participation, CERCLA provides that technical assistance grants (TAGs) of up to $50,000 be awarded to citizen groups whose members are affected by releases or threatened releases of hazardous substances at NPL sites.[61] The TAGs are intended to help the community evaluate the risks posed by a site. While the grants may not be used to underwrite citizen suits, the information generated from the grants may be used in subsequent litigation.[62] Only one TAG may be issued per site, but it may be renewed for each phase of the cleanup. Generally, the TAGs are conditioned on the recipients' contributing at least 20 percent of the total costs of the technical assessment. Since this requirement can pose hardships on poorer communities, the EPA may waive both the 20 percent participation and $50,000 ceiling if necessary to facilitate public participation.[63]

After the final ROD has been published, the EPA will authorize drafting of the detailed engineering plans, known as the "remedial design" (RD).[64] If the RD differs significantly from the ROD, the agency responsible for performing or supervising the work must either publish an explanation of significant differences (ESD) or propose an amendment to the ROD if the difference between the ROD and RD fundamentally alters the scope, performance, or cost of the remedy.[65] The ESD or ROD amendment will usually be published before the draft RD is issued.

After the publication of an RD fact sheet and a public comment period, a construction contract will be awarded to perform the "remedial action" (RA), which typically will be implemented in several phases, such as a surface cleanup followed by a groundwater treatment program. The EPA will generally authorize the PRPs to perform the RA if the agency determines that the PRPs may conduct it properly.[66] Where the RI/FS has been performed pursuant to an administrative order or consent decree, PRPs may not undertake remedial work until the remedial action is authorized by the EPA.[67]

After the construction of the remedy has been completed, the final step in the CERCLA remedial process is long-term operation and maintenance (O & M), such as groundwater treating and monitoring.[68] The EPA generally requires the states to pay for all O & M costs but under Section 104, a remedial action is not considered completed and O & M costs do not begin to become the state's responsibility until ten years after the installation or construction of the RA.[69] CERCLA also requires the EPA to review sites every five years if hazardous substances remain on the site to determine whether additional remedial work is required.[70]

Once the construction of the remedy has been completed and the EPA is assured that the remedy is operating properly, the site will be deemed complete even if the concentrations of hazardous substances have not yet been reduced to the levels set forth in the ROD. The EPA may then propose to remove the site from the NPL (delist) by publishing a notice of intent to delist in the Federal Register. Following a public comment period, the EPA may then publish a final delisting notice in the Federal Register.[71] The EPA formerly delayed delisting sites until after the agency completed its five-year review of the site, but it has recently accelerated the delisting process as a response to mounting public frustration over the slow pace of CERCLA cleanups. Sites that have been remediated may be subsequently relisted without having to go through an HRS evaluation if a significant release is subsequently discovered. Such sites are eligible for further Superfund-financed remedial actions if conditions warrant such action.[72]

Recovery of Response Costs by EPA and Private Parties

Section 107 authorizes the government and private parties to recover their costs to investigate or clean up a site where there has been a release or threatened release of hazardous substances (response costs).[73] The government is entitled to recover all of its costs that are "not inconsistent" with the NCP.[74] Courts have generally held that the word "not" means that the government's costs are presumed to be consistent with the NCP unless the defendants can introduce evidence rebutting this presumption.[75] State agencies also enjoy the presumption of consistency, but municipalities and private parties are not entitled to the presumption of consistency.[76]

There are only three statutory defenses to an action brought by the government under Section 107: act of war, act of god, and the third-party defense.[77] The most commonly asserted defense is the third-party defense, but it is extremely limited because the release of hazardous substances must have been *solely* caused by a third party who was not in a contractual relationship with the defendant. Thus, a purchaser cannot use this defense if the contamination was caused by the seller, since the sales and purchaser agreement would qualify as a contractual relationship.[78]

Even if a current owner can get past the "contractual relationship" barrier, there are two additional hurdles it must satisfy before it can successfully assert a third-party defense. The owner would also have to show that it took reasonable precautions against the acts or omissions of third parties, and that it exercised due care regarding the hazardous substances at the property. In other words, if an owner wants to qualify for the third-party defense, the owner could not, for example, allow third parties to dump wastes on its property nor allow previously deposited drums to deteriorate while it owned the property.

Because the third-party defense was largely unavailable to new landowners who did not cause the contamination at a site, Congress enacted the innocent landowner's defense in 1986. This provision states that a purchaser will not be considered to be in a "contractual relationship" and thus will be able to assert the defense if the purchaser could establish that it had no reason to know about the contamination. To establish that it had no reason to know, the purchaser must show that it undertook a reasonably appropriate inquiry into the past uses and practices of the property that was consistent with good commercial and customary practices.[79]

Private plaintiffs may recover only "necessary" response costs that are consistent with the NCP. There is general agreement that private plaintiffs have the burden of establishing consistency with the NCP.[80] However, when the costs are incurred to comply with a consent decree, some courts have ruled that there is a presumption that the response costs were consistent with the NCP.[81] Strict compliance with the NCP is not required as long as the response action taken as a whole is in substantial compliance with the NCP and results in a CERCLA-quality cleanup.[82]

Private plaintiffs may seek to recover their response costs by filing either a CERCLA Section 107 cost recovery action[83] or a CERCLA Section 113 contribution action.[84] Like a government Section 107 cost recovery action, the liability in a private cost recovery action is based on principles of strict and joint liability. In contrast, in contribution actions, courts may apportion liability using "such equitable factors as the court determines are appropriate."[85] Most courts have held that private plaintiffs who are PRPs are limited to filing contribution actions to recover their response costs when the PRP has incurred more than its fair share of the response costs for a site.

It is important to remember that CERCLA Sections 107 and 113 allow only private parties to recover costs associated with the cleanup of releases or threatened releases of hazardous substances. These sections may not be used to recover property damage claims or to pursue personal injury claims.

EPA Authority to Issue Section 106 Administrative Orders

Under CERCLA Section 106, the EPA and certain other federal agencies[86] may issue an administrative order or seek injunctive relief directing PRPs to abate a release of hazardous substances to protect the public health or the environment.[87] To invoke Section 106, the agency must determine that there "may be an imminent and substantial endangerment to the public health or welfare or the environment because of an actual or threatened release of a hazardous substance from a facility."[88] Because Section 106 was modeled after Section 7003 of the RCRA,[89] courts have used the case law that has been developed under Section 7003 to construe Section 106. Thus, the "imminent" requirement of Section 106 has been held not to mandate the existence of immediate harm but simply to note that conditions exist that may lead to harm in the future.[90] Likewise, "substantial" does not require precise proof of harm but only that there is reasonable cause for concern that someone or something may be exposed to a risk of harm if remedial action is not taken.[91] The United States Court of Appeals for the Ninth Circuit recently held that the word "substantial" implies that the release must present more than a "minimal threat" to human health, welfare, or the environment.[92] The term "endangerment" does not require an emergency or actual harm but only that there is a probability of potential harm.[93]

While Section 106 does not specify the parties that may be subject to liability, most courts have held that the classes of persons specified in Section 107 may also be subject to liability under Section 106.[94] Thus, virtually any person connected with an inactive site, including a nonnegligent, offsite generator, may be subject to the provisions of Section 106.[95]

Likewise, while Section 106 does not specify the standard of liability for persons who may be required to abate site conditions, the majority of courts have imposed a strict liability standard under Section 106. Unlike a government cost recovery action under Section 107, many courts have held that PRPs named in a Section 106 order are not limited to the three statutory defenses listed in Section 107(b).[96] As a result, equitable defenses may be raised in a Section 106 action.

A person failing to comply with a Section 106 order may be fined $25,000 per day.[97] In addition, anyone who "without sufficient cause" fails to take remedial or removal action ordered under Section 106 may also be subject to punitive damages of three times the response costs.[98] As a result, Section 106 is a valuable tool to commence cleanups promptly. However, only the EPA or the authorized federal agencies have the right to seek injunctive relief under Section 106. While citizens may not directly seek relief under Section 106, they can try to convince the EPA or the appropriate federal agency to issue a Section

106 order or try to compel the EPA to issue such an order under the citizen suit provisions of Section 310.[99]

Citizen Suits

Like a number of federal environmental statutes, CERCLA allows private citizens to file lawsuits under certain circumstances. In effect, these citizen suit provisions allow citizens to act as private attorneys general. Citizen-plaintiffs have tried to use the citizen suit provision of CERCLA to compel cleanups, to require additional cleanups at sites where response actions have been taken in the past, and to challenge the cleanup remedy selected by EPA on the grounds that the cleanup would expose the community to additional hazards. As will be discussed in the next section, these citizen suits have met with mixed success.

Under Section 310 of CERCLA, a citizen-plaintiff may bring an action alleging that a person is violating a requirement of CERCLA.[100] Since CERCLA is not a regulatory statute that imposes its own standards, what constitutes a violation will vary from site-to-site depending on the particular cleanup standards established for that site. Citizen suits may be brought for violations of administrative consent orders and settlements by PRPs to perform cleanups and interagency agreements involving cleanups at federal facilities.

Citizen suits may also be brought against the EPA or the ATSDR for failing to perform a nondiscretionary duty.[101] Since the EPA is required to take response actions when an ATSDR health assessment finds that a site poses significant risk to public health, a citizen suit may be commenced to compel the EPA to undertake cleanup action, to perform an additional cleanup, or to order PRPs to do a cleanup.

The citizen-plaintiff may commence actions to order the defendant to comply with the applicable CERCLA requirements or order and may also seek civil penalties.[102] In addition, the court may award costs, including lawyers' fees, to a prevailing plaintiff.[103] However, as with Sections 107 and 113, citizens may not file actions under Section 310 for personal injuries or property damage.

Citizen suits must be brought in the judicial district where the alleged violation or endangerment has occurred, although suits against the EPA Administrator must be filed in the District Court for the District of Columbia.[104] A citizen suit alleging violations of CERCLA requirements cannot be commenced until the plaintiff has given 60 days' written notice of the alleged violation to the EPA, the state where the violation has occurred and to the alleged violator.[105] However, the action will be barred if the EPA has commenced and is "diligently prosecuting" a civil or criminal action under CERCLA or RCRA on the requirement for which enforcement is sought.[106] While consent decrees are generally recognized as satisfying diligent prosecutions that would preclude the initiation of a citizen suit, only federal consent decrees and not state consent decrees will bar a citizen suit.[107] Since federal consent decrees often take over 60 days to complete because of the required cooperation between the EPA and the Justice Department, this defense may prove to be of little use to PRPs.

Ban of Judicial Review of Response Actions

Section 113(h) of CERCLA prohibits federal courts from reviewing challenges to removal or remedial actions selected under Section 104 until the remedial work is completed, or challenges to any order issued by the EPA under Section 106.[108] This so-called ban on pre-enforcement review is not really a prohibition but delays the time when a court may hear a challenge to the selection of a remedy. Often, the delay caused by the ban may render a challenge largely academic. Once the EPA seeks to enforce a Section 106 order or brings a Section 107 cost recovery action, courts are free to entertain challenges to the remedy.[109]

The purpose of the pre-enforcement ban was to prevent private parties from filing lawsuits that would delay or slow down the progress of cleanup actions.[110] However, residents near a CERCLA site may be concerned that a proposed cleanup may not be sufficient to eliminate the risk posed by the contaminants or that the implementation of the remedy (such as the operation of an incinerator) might expose them to additional health risks. While Section 113(h)(4) does contain an exemption for citizen suits, such challenges have met with only limited success. As a result, Section 113(h) has prevented community groups from having their challenges heard. This once again reaffirms the importance of community groups becoming involved as early as possible in the remedy selection process.

Some courts have held that the ban on pre-enforcement review does not apply to citizen suits alleging that one phase of a response action violates CERCLA standards.[111] These cases have relied on language in the legislative history of CERCLA that said that "the phrase 'removal and remedial actions' is not intended to preclude judicial review until the total response action is finished if the response action proceeds in distinct and separate phases. . . . Any challenge under this provision to a completed stage of a response action shall not interfere with those stages of the response action which have not yet been completed."[112]

Under this approach, a citizen suit could be brought charging that a phase of a cleanup, such as a surface cleanup, does not meet CERCLA standards even though groundwater remediation remains to be implemented. Likewise, a federal court could review a citizen action challenging a cleanup performed at one portion of a site while additional work is being performed elsewhere at the site.

However, a number of courts have barred reviews of ongoing cleanups.[113] In *Clinton County Commissioners v. EPA,*[114] the plaintiffs sought to enjoin a remedy that required the installation of a mobile incinerator on the grounds that the remedy would cause irreparable injury to residents living near the incinerator. In overruling a prior decision,[115] the Court of Appeals for the Third Circuit ruled that the federal judiciary could not entertain the challenge to the remedy until the remedial action had been completed regardless of the harm that might be caused by the cleanup action.

A similar result was reached in *Concerned Citizens of Agricultural Street Landfill, Inc. v. EPA.*[116] In this case, a residential community, school, and community center had been constructed on a portion of a 95-acre site which had formerly been a municipal landfill. The EPA had removed several feet of contaminated soil years earlier and had determined that no further remedial actions were required for the area where the school was located or for the groundwater. The undeveloped area was to be covered with an additional layer of soil and an impermeable cap. The plaintiffs argued that they could maintain a challenge to the two distinct phases of the cleanup. However, the court rejected this argument on procedural grounds, ruling that their pleadings only sought relief from future action and that the plaintiffs could not amend their pleadings because they had failed to meet the jurisdictional notice requirement.

Courts have strained to find that actions or agreements fall within the scope of the ban on pre-enforcement review. For example, a court held that the performance of a health assessment was a removal action that precluded judicial review.[117] Similarly, a court ruled that an administrative consent order, in which a PRP agreed to perform an RI/FS, did not constitute an "agreement" under Section 122(d)(3) that allowed for judicial review because that section referred to agreements under Section 104(d) and the performance of a RI/FS was covered by Section 104(c). Courts have also used the pre-enforcement review ban to deny requests to compel the ATSDR to undertake a health surveillance program while a response action was being conducted.[118] Likewise, the ban has been held to preclude review of the adequacy of a cleanup commenced under a Section 106 order until the EPA takes action to enforce the order.[119]

Some local governments have tried unsuccessfully to block cleanups on the grounds that the remedy violated local rules or ordinances. For example, in *United States v. City of Denver,*[120] the EPA required a landowner to perform on-site solidification of contaminated soils in an area where the zoning ordinance prohibited the maintenance of hazardous wastes. The City of Denver tried to block the execution of the cleanup order, but the Court of Appeals for the Tenth Circuit ruled that a zoning ordinance that imposed requirements that would be contrary to a remedy chosen under CERCLA Section 104 was pre-empted by CERCLA. Moreover, the court ruled that a zoning ordinance did not fall within the definition of a "state law" for purposes of CERCLA Section 121, which requires cleanups to comply with state laws that are more stringent than federal law.

Another area of confusion over the scope of the pre-enforcement review involves the ability of citizens to challenge cleanups at federal facilities. Section 120 of CERCLA requires federal agencies to perform cleanups at federal facilities. Since Section 113(h) bars review of response actions taken pursuant to Section 104 and 106 orders, some plaintiffs have argued that the ban should not apply to cleanups performed under Section 120. However, most courts that have faced the issue have ruled that Section 120 just provides a road map for conducting cleanups and that the authority to perform cleanups originates in Section 104. Therefore, under this view, the pre-enforcement ban applies to federal facility cleanups as well.[121]

While the pre-enforcement ban applies to actions filed under CERCLA or other federal laws, some courts have construed language in the legislative history of Section 113(h), as allowing citizens to bring nuisance actions under state law.[122] Similarly, some courts have allowed suits brought by states to enforce state cleanup standards that the remedy was required to achieve.[123] Other courts, though, have held that while Section 113(h) preserves state nuisance claims, it prohibits those claims from being used to enjoin an ongoing site cleanup.[124]

In challenging a remedy, the objecting party must demonstrate that the decision was arbitrary and capricious or otherwise not in accordance with the law.[125] Thus, relief may be afforded where the EPA fails to provide the requisite public participation[126] or where the remedy does not meet the statutory cleanup standards.[127] However, the courts have been extremely reluctant to exercise their power of judicial review and have deferred to the technical judgment of the EPA. Courts have refused to consider a pre-enforcement challenge that an RI/FS was not performed in accordance with the National Historic Preservation Act[128] or that the administrative record failed to support the remedy selected by the EPA.[129] Likewise, a court ruled that it did not have jurisdiction to review a modification of ROD.[130] Another court held that it did not have the jurisdiction to review a challenge that a remedy did not comply with state cleanup standards because the placement of the site on the NPL stripped the court of its subject matter jurisdiction.[131]

Judicial review of challenges to the remedy selection of the EPA is limited to the administrative record.[132] This restriction obviates the need for discovery, and the EPA has been able to obtain protective orders prohibiting depositions of EPA employees. The administrative record will include all the materials considered by the agency, including the ROD and RI/FS. As a result, it is essential that community groups submit comments and questions throughout the remedy selection process to document the basis upon which to challenge the remedy. If the record does not support the agency action, the matter may be remanded for further supplementation of the administrative record, but de novo review will not usually be granted. The limitation of judicial review to the administrative record will not apply when the EPA seeks injunctive relief under Section 106. In such instances, the PRPs will be entitled to de novo review, though the review would take place after the cleanup has been completed.[133]

Resource Conservation and Recovery Act

RCRA law establishes standards for the generation, storage, treatment, and disposal of hazardous wastes. Companies that generate hazardous wastes (Generators) generally may not store the hazardous wastes on-site for more than 90 days without obtaining a permit and must prepare manifests for wastes that are shipped off-site for treatment or disposal. Facilities that treat, store, or dispose of hazardous wastes (TSD Facilities) must obtain permits and comply with RCRA design and operating standards.

Unlike CERCLA, the EPA may delegate the authority to administer RCRA to states that have enacted a hazardous waste program that is at least as stringent as RCRA. Facilities located in states that have received delegation must comply with the state RCRA requirements.

One of the advantages of RCRA is that it may be used to compel cleanups of sites contaminated with petroleum that generally cannot be addressed under CERCLA. This is because CERCLA excludes crude oil or any of its refined fractions from the definition of hazardous substances.[134] RCRA not only covers petroleum products but also extends to substances that are not covered by CERCLA because RCRA regulates not only hazardous wastes but may also address contamination caused by solid wastes as well. Under RCRA, solid waste includes any "garbage, refuse . . . and other discarded material, including solid, semi-solid or contained gaseous material resulting from industrial, commercial, mining, and agricultural operations, and from community activities. . . ."[135] Courts have held that petroleum fuel leaking from an underground storage tank is a "discarded material resulting from commercial activity and, therefore, qualifies as a solid waste."[136]

RCRA Authority to Require Testing and Investigations

If the EPA has information that the presence of hazardous waste that is or has been stored, treated, or disposed of at a site or facility, or a release of hazardous waste from such site or facility, may present "a substantial hazard" to human health or the environment, RCRA Section 3013 authorizes the EPA to issue an order requiring the owner or operator of that facility or site to perform monitoring, testing, or analysis that the agency deems is "reasonable" to determine the extent of the hazard.[137] When the threat is posed by a facility or site that is no longer in operation, the EPA may issue the investigation order to the most recent previous owner or operator who could "reasonably be expected" to have actual knowledge about the presence of the hazardous wastes and the potential for release.[138] If the EPA cannot find a previous owner or operator that can conduct the work to the satisfaction of the agency, the EPA may perform the work itself or authorize a state to perform the work.[139] Such sites are often transferred to the CERCLA program. The EPA is not required to provide public participation when issuing orders under Section 3013.

RCRA Imminent Hazard Authority

RCRA Section 7003 authorizes the EPA to take a broad range of action when it has evidence that the past or present handling, storage, treatment, transportation, or disposal of any solid or hazardous waste poses an imminent and substantial endangerment to health or the environment.[140] Congress intended Section 7003 to codify and expand the common law of nuisance.[141] Thus, courts have held that liability under this section is joint and several where the harm is indivisible.[142] This section also imposes strict liability.[143]

The authority under Section 7003 is broader in some respects than the corrective action authority of Section 3008(h) (discussed in the next section), which is limited to releases at TSD facilities. In contrast, Section 7003 allows the EPA to address endangerments resulting from releases of hazardous or solid wastes wherever they occur. However, unlike Section 3008(h), the EPA must show that there is an imminent and substantial endangerment. The test under Section 7003 is the same as that of Section 106 of CERCLA. Thus, the "imminent" requirement of Section 7003 has been held not to mandate the existence of immediate harm but simply that conditions exist that may lead to harm in the future.[144] Likewise, "substantial" does not require precise proof of harm but only that there is reasonable cause for concern that someone or something may be exposed to a risk of harm from a release or threatened release of hazardous substances if remedial action is not taken.[145] The term "endangerment" does not require an emergency or actual harm but only that there is a probability of potential harm.[146]

The EPA is required to provide immediate notice of the imminent and substantial endangerment to local government agencies as well as to ensure that notice of the endangerment be promptly posted at the site where the waste is located.[147] When the EPA decides to issue a covenant not to sue, to forbear from filing suit, or to settle any claim arising out of Section 7003, the agency is required to provide notice, the opportunity for a public meeting in the affected area, and opportunity to comment on the proposed settlement.[148]

RCRA Corrective Action Authority

Generators and TSD facilities may be required to take corrective action to remediate soil and groundwater that is contaminated with hazardous wastes and their constituents. Under Section 3004(u), existing TSD facilities may be required to take corrective action for all releases of hazardous wastes or constituents from solid waste management units (SWMUs) regardless of when the wastes were placed in the TSD facilities and even if those units are now inactive.[149] Thus, if hazardous wastes or even solid wastes were placed, deposed, or placed on a portion of a site that is not now actively used to manage hazardous wastes, the current facility owner or operator could be required to perform corrective action in that former disposal area even where the owner or operator did not use that inactive area.

Under Section 3004(v), TSD Facilities may also be required to take corrective action for contamination beyond the facility boundary when necessary to protect human health and the environment.[150] Finally, Section 3008(h) authorizes the EPA to issue corrective action orders or take other appropriate measures when the agency determines that there is or has been a release of hazardous wastes into the environment from a RCRA-regulated facility.[151]

Corrective actions conducted pursuant to Section 3004 are imposed under the RCRA permit process. Under these permitting procedures, the corrective action requirements of a permit would be available for public review during the permitting process and the public can comment on the provisions during the draft permit stage.[152] In addition, the EPA has issued a RCRA Expanded Public Participation rule that creates more opportunities for public participation than the permitting process. However, this rule is generally effective only in states that have amended their hazardous waste programs to adopt this requirement. All states were required to adopt this rule by July 1, 1997.[153]

Under the RCRA Expanded Public Participation Rule, prospective applicants must advertise and hold informal hearings before submitting an RCRA permit application. The state agency must mail a notice when the permit has been filed informing the public where the application may be examined and require the operator/owner to establish an information repository. The EPA is also encouraging state agencies and RCRA facilities to use "all reasonable means" to ensure equal opportunity for participation and access to information, including, but not limited to, the use of multilingual notices, fact sheets, and translators.[154]

Section 3008(h) corrective action orders are issued outside the permitting process. When the EPA issues a Section 3008(h) order, the recipient has 30 days to request a hearing. While the public will be given the opportunity to comment on the proposed corrective action measure and will receive notice of the agency's final corrective action plan, the public does not have a right to participate in the Section 3008(h) hearing process.[155]

The procedure that the EPA has adopted for conducting corrective action is modeled after the CERCLA remedy selection process. The first phase is the RCRA Facility Assessment (RFA), which is similar to the CERCLA PA/SI. The RFA is designed to uncover evidence of releases of hazardous wastes or constituents. If evidence of releases requiring corrective action is detected, the facility will be required to conduct a RCRA Facility Investigation (RFI), which is equivalent to the CERCLA Remedial Investigation. The RFI evaluates the nature and extent of the releases from regulated hazardous waste management units, SWMUs, and other sources of contamination.

If the RFI reveals excessive contaminant concentration levels, a Corrective Measures Study (CMS) will have to be performed. The CMS is akin to the CERCLA Feasibility Study and is designed to examine remedial alternatives and select a remedial action. After the remedy has been selected, a Corrective Measure Implementation (CMI) must be prepared, which involves the design, construction, implementation, and long-term maintenance of the cleanup. The CMI is similar to the CERCLA Remedial Design and will be deemed complete when the contaminant concentrations meet acceptable levels. As part of its policy of providing meaningful public participation in the corrective action program, the EPA expects that, at a minimum, copies of the RFI and CMS reports should be made available to the public and that the public should be given an opportunity to comment on proposed corrective action remedies.

Citizen Suits

Section 7002 of RCRA allows citizen plaintiffs to bring three types of civil actions.[156] The first type of citizen suit is an action under Section 7002(a)(1)(A) alleging that a person is violating any permit, standard, regulation, condition, requirement, prohibition, or order issued pursuant to RCRA.[157] Under Section 7002(a)(1)(B), a citizen suit may also be commenced against a current and past generator, transporter, or TSD owner or operator who is alleged to have contributed or who is contributing to past or current hazardous waste management practices or hazardous wastes that present an imminent and substantial endangerment to health or the environment.[158] Finally, actions may also be brought against the administrator of the EPA for failing to perform a nondiscretionary duty.[159]

Unlike other federal environmental statutes that preclude citizen suits for wholly past violations, citizen-plaintiffs may maintain suits for past conduct under Section 7002(a)(1)(A) if the past disposal of wastes constituted a continuing violation.[160] However, this section may be of limited use at facilities where hazardous wastes may have been released prior to the enactment of RCRA in 1976 and, thus, no regulatory requirements were in effect.[161] Similarly, suits may be maintained for past conduct and against past owners or operators under Section 7002(a)(1)(B) if the past disposal created a present substantial endangerment.[162] However, plaintiffs may have to link specific wastes causing the imminent and substantial endangerment to specific defendants to be able to obtain relief.[163]

One of the advantages of the RCRA citizen suit provision is that it can be particularly useful to address sites contaminated with petroleum. In contrast, the CERCLA citizen suit authority cannot generally be used to require cleanups of petroleum because that substance is excluded from definition of hazardous substances.[164] Indeed, because RCRA addresses not only hazardous wastes but solid wastes as well, the RCRA citizen suit can be used to address a broad universe of contaminants. Parties seeking to compel cleanups under a RCRA citizen suit may also be eligible for reimbursement of their lawyers' fees.[165]

Elements of a Citizen Suit Action to Compel Cleanup

In order to plead a Section 7002(a)(1)(B) action successfully, the plaintiffs will have to establish that the defendants (1) are contributing or have contributed to the handling, storage, treatment, transportation, or disposal of solid or hazardous wastes that (2) may present an imminent and substantial endangerment to human health or the environment.

Are Contributing or Have Contributed—The first element that a plaintiff must show is that the defendant "contributed to" the imminent and substantial endangerment. Courts have construed this term, which is not defined in RCRA, broadly. Generally, defendants who have engaged in the handling or disposal of solid or hazardous wastes that have caused the present conditions will have to share responsibility for the abatement of those conditions. The key question for plaintiffs is what kind of nexus must be shown between the defendants and the solid waste to establish that the defendant "contributed" to the site conditions.

For owners or operators of facilities, plaintiffs do not have to allege that the defendants had actual control over waste disposal but merely that they had the authority to control the waste disposal activity that has led to the imminent and substantial endangerment.[166] In one case, an owner of land containing a gasoline station who had leased the property to a number of tenants since 1956 was found to have "contributed to" the contamination caused by leaking USTs because it had owned the USTs and received rent tied to the volume of gasoline sales.[167] Indeed, in *Zands v. Nelson*,[168] the court held that if the plaintiff can establish that contamination occurred prior to its ownership or occupancy and all prior owners/operators were joined in the action, then the burden shifted to those defendants to prove that they had not contributed to the present conditions.

Former owners have also been found to be liable under Section 7002. In *Truck Components, Inc v. Beatrice*,[169] a former owner argued it could not be liable under Section 7002(a)(1)(A) because it no longer owned the site and the prospective nature of the injunctive relief sought could not be applied for violations that may have occurred in the past. However, the court ruled that the continuing consequences of wastes disposed of in the past were sufficient to hold the former owner liable as a person "contributing to" a present endangerment.

A narrower application of the phrase "contributed to" was reached in *Triffler v. Hopf*.[170] In that case, the prior owners of property that had contained an abandoned leaking UST were not found to be liable because they had not operated the UST and there was no evidence that the defendants were aware the USTs were leaking. The court said that for the plaintiffs to establish that the former defendant/owners had "contributed to" the contamination, there would have to be a showing that the defendants either:

(i) directly caused the contamination by using the petroleum products;
(ii) knew about the leakage; or
(iii) had reason to know that the USTs were leaking and failed to act.

At first glance, it would appear that RCRA citizen suits might not be limited to CERCLA PRPs but could be brought against a broader range of defendants. However, unlike CERCLA, it would appear that mere status as a former owner or operator may not be enough to impose liability under RCRA Section 7002. The "contributed to" language appearing in Section 7002(a)(1)(B) suggests that a past owner or operator had to do something before it can be found liable.[171]

For transporters and generators, it would appear that their liability is at least as broad as their CERCLA liability. In other words, they would be viewed as having contributed to the imminent and substantial endangerment if they arranged for the disposal of the hazardous or solid wastes causing the present conditions. However, at least one court has held that the kind of involvement required to meet the contributed/contributing requirement is less than "to arrange."[172]

Imminent and Substantial Endangerment—Section 7002(a)(1)(B) authorizes relief when the solid or hazardous waste may present an "imminent and substantial endangerment." This phrase is interpreted in the same fashion as the language appearing in CERCLA Section 106 and RCRA Section 7003. Thus, a citizen suit filed under Section 7002(a)(1)(B) will not have to establish that actual harm will occur immediately but simply allege that there is a risk of threatened harm.[173] As a result, merely showing that an underground storage tank is leaking gasoline or that there are levels of contaminants in the soil or groundwater above applicable cleanup levels may be sufficient to establish an imminent endangerment.[174] However, the presence of asbestos and other contaminants beneath a concrete foundation of a house was held not to present an imminent and substantial endangerment in *Price v. U.S. Navy*.[175]

The nature of the contaminants and how they disperse into the environment may play a role in determining whether an imminent and substantial endangerment exists. For example, in *The Birch Corporation v. Nevada Instrument Holding, Inc.*, the current landowner commenced a RCRA citizen suit to compel the defendant to remediate contaminated groundwater. The plaintiff relied on a letter from the Regional Water Quality Control Board (RWQCB) that gasoline floating on the groundwater "may pose a significant risk to public health/safety unrelated to water pollution at the site. . . ." The letter went on to say utility trenching, well drilling, and other subsurface excavations could increase the risk of explosion and fire. The RWQCB then indicated that it was turning over supervision of the site to the county because the site was determined to be a low priority. The United States Court of Appeals for the Ninth Circuit ruled that contamination did not present an imminent and substantial endangerment. The court relied heavily on the fact that the consultant retained by the plaintiff testified that the contaminant concentrations did not pose a significant risk. Other factors mentioned by the court included statements by plaintiff's consultant that the contamination had stabilized, that the plume or zone of contamination was not likely to migrate, and that the community did not use the groundwater for drinking purposes. Moreover, the consultant proposed that the contamination be allowed to degrade naturally, since this would be as effective as requiring the installation of a groundwater treatment system.[176] Another circuit court also held that the existence of contaminated groundwater may not necessarily constitute an imminent and substantial endangerment where a filtration system eliminated the risk.[177]

Similarly, to establish "substantial endangerment," a plaintiff does not have to present proof of actual harm or present risk assessments that quantify the risk but simply show a threatened or potential harm.[178] It will be enough to show that there is reasonable cause for concern that someone or something may be exposed to a risk of harm by the waste if an abatement action is not taken.[179]

Furthermore, because of the use of the word "may," citizen-plaintiffs are not required to prove that there is an emergency situation for there to be an "imminent and substantial endangerment."[180] Thus, proof that past or present handling or disposal of solid wastes may present an imminent and substantial endangerment is sufficient grounds for relief. In *KFC v. Meghrig*, the United States Supreme Court ruled that to obtain relief, a plaintiff must establish that there was a present imminent and substantial endangerment at the time the complaint was filed even though the impact of the threat may not be felt until later.[181]

Defenses to Liability

Section 7002 does not list any statutory defenses, and the decisions interpreting Section 7002(a)(1)(B) have not discussed the kinds of defenses that might be available to defendants. Presumably, the whole range of common law defenses may be raised for Section 7002(a)(1)(B) defendants. For example, one court seemed implicitly to endorse the intervening, passive landowner defense, or the concept of an innocent landowner's defense but did not require the passive landowner to perform an appropriate commercial inquiry that is required under CERCLA.[182] Thus, the defense may be broader under RCRA than CERCLA.

Procedural Requirements

RCRA citizen suits must be brought in the judicial district where the alleged violation or endangerment has occurred, although suits against the EPA administrator must be filed in the District Court for the District of Columbia.[183] If the suit is brought in a state that has been delegated authority to administer its own state RCRA program in lieu of the federal program, some courts have held that a Section 7002(a)(1)(A) claim must assert violations of the state RCRA program.[184]

There are two different notice periods for filing RCRA citizen suits. Actions alleging violations of permits, standards, regulations, conditions, requirements, prohibitions, or orders cannot be commenced until the plaintiff has given 60 days' written notice of the alleged violation to the EPA, the state where the violation has occurred, and the alleged violator. However, if the action involves a violation of Subtitle C (the section of RCRA addressing hazardous wastes), the action may be brought immediately after notice has been provided.[185] The imminent endangerment citizen suits cannot be commenced until the plaintiff has provided 90 days' written notice of the imminent endangerment to the EPA, the state where the endangerment has occurred, and the alleged violator, although such an action may be brought immediately if it involves a violation of Subtitle C.[186]

A citizen suit alleging violations of conditions, standards, and so on is barred if the EPA or the state "has commenced and is diligently prosecuting a civil or criminal action in a court of the United States, or a State to require compliance with such permit, standard, regulation, condition, requirement, prohibition, or order" for which enforcement is sought.[187]

The diligent prosecution ban does not apply to imminent endangerment suits. However, such suits are barred when any of the following cleanup actions are undertaken to abate the condition creating imminent endangerment:

1. the EPA is diligently prosecuting an action under Section 7003 or Section 106 of CERCLA or the state is diligently prosecuting an equivalent action under state law;
2. the EPA or the state is engaged in a removal action under Section 104 of CERCLA;
3. the EPA or the state has incurred response costs to undertake a Remedial Investigation and Feasibility Study under Section 104 of CERCLA and is diligently proceeding with a remedial action; or
4. the responsible party is conducting a removal action pursuant to a court order or administrative order obtained or issued by the EPA.[188]

Because of this section and the pre-enforcement ban of CERCLA, some citizen suits have been dismissed after a remedy has been selected or a cleanup was underway under CERCLA.[189] However, there is some language in the legislative history of RCRA that the ban on imminent endangerment suits is limited to the scope of the cleanup work being performed.[190] Thus, if only surface cleanup is undertaken at a site, it is possible that a court may allow a citizen suit to proceed that addresses groundwater contamination that is alleged to present an imminent and substantial endangerment.

State Superfund Laws

About 40 states have enacted laws similar to the federal Superfund laws. The mini-Superfunds are generally patterned after the federal law but may differ significantly in terms of the types of hazardous substances regulated, the identity of liable parties, and the defenses available to responsible parties.

For example, one distinction may be the definition of "discharge" or "release." While CERCLA includes the mere abandonment of drums within the definition of release,[191] some states require that the hazardous substance come into contact with the environment.[192] In addition, some states may distinguish a discharge from existing contamination from an old spill. Thus, a New Jersey court declined to allow a property owner to recover costs of remediating groundwater contaminated by an adjacent landfill because the contamination was the result of an old spill and was not a present discharge.[193] Likewise, the gradual migration of hazardous chemicals over a 15–30 year period through soil was held not to constitute a discharge under a New York law because the definition of "discharge" required some active human conduct as opposed to mere seepage over the course of time.[194]

Likewise, the right of citizens to compel cleanups under these state mini-Superfund statutes may vary. Some states have provisions that mirror the CERCLA citizen suit provision. Others may not provide citizens with such opportunities but may allow the public to participate in the remedy selection process. Likewise, many states have also enacted so-called "brownfield" laws that seek to encourage the cleanup and development of abandoned or underutilized industrial properties. Since these brownfield statutes are intended to encourage voluntary cleanups, citizens generally do not have any rights to compel cleanups under these laws. However, these laws do generally provide the public with the opportunity to comment on the proposed remedial plans. Brownfield statutes are discusssed in greater detail in Chapter 17, "Redeveloping Old Facilities," pages 561–84.

Nuisance

Prior to the enactment of CERCLA, RCRA, and the state mini-Superfund laws, parties had to resort to common law actions such as trespass and nuisance to force the cleanup of contaminated properties. These common law actions are difficult to bring because plaintiffs in common law actions have to establish some connection between the defendant and the harm alleged to have been caused. CERCLA, in particular, creates a much lower threshold for plaintiffs because plaintiffs need only establish that a defendant falls within one of the categories of PRPs and does not require proof of fault or causation. Nevertheless, because neither CERCLA nor RCRA creates a federal cause of action for personal injury or property damage, the common law actions are often the only recourse for plaintiffs who have been injured by exposure to hazardous wastes. These actions can be used to enjoin a defendant's activity. Bringing an order to show cause seeking injunctive relief can prove to be a useful device to bring an otherwise recalcitrant opponent to the negotiating table. Finally, common law actions may be joined as state pendant claims to a complaint alleging CERCLA violations since CERCLA does not preempt state claims. Recovery of monetary damages under common law is discussed in Chapter 19, "Assisting Injured Individuals," pages 619–61.

Nuisance is a cause of action is based on the concept that persons are generally free to use their land or personal property in a way they see fit as long as that use does not unreasonably interfere with other persons' private use and enjoyment of their property.[195] There are two distinct types of nuisance actions: private and public. A "private nuisance" involves an unreasonable interference with the private property of another. On the other hand, a "public nuisance" is an unreasonable interference with a right common to the general public. In either cause of action, the interference may be caused by intentional or negligent conduct or as a result of an abnormally dangerous activity.[196]

Nuisance does not require an actual entry onto the land but simply an activity that unreasonably interferes with the use and enjoyment of the land of someone who has a possessory interest in the property. To prevail, the plaintiff must establish that the defendant's interference with the land was substantial and unreasonable.[197] Usually, a plaintiff will be required to show there has been physical damage to the land, tangibles, or personal property located on the land or some economic loss such as diminution in market or rental value of the land to maintain a nuisance action. In the environmental context, soil or water contamination can be the physical damage needed to demonstrate "substantial interference."

In determining whether a particular activity constitutes an unreasonable interference with the use and enjoyment of land, the utility or social benefits of the conduct must be balanced against the gravity of the harm.[198] For a public nuisance, the plaintiff must show that the conduct:

1. significantly interfered with public health, safety, peace, or comfort;
2. is proscribed by a statute, rule, or ordinance; or
3. continues and has a long-lasting effect on the public.[199]

Generally, a private individual will not have standing to assert a public nuisance claim unless the individual can show that it sustained a special injury that is different in kind and magnitude than that suffered by the public.[200] Thus, contamination of a private drinking well will be considered a private nuisance whereas contamination of municipal wells would constitute a public nuisance.[201] In addition, pecuniary losses suffered by a business because of the nuisance would constitute the special damages needed to support a private action for public nuisance.

Some states have created a statutory right of action by providing that violations create a nuisance per se.[202] However, compliance with applicable environmental laws may not be a defense to private nuisance action. Thus, a licensed landfill or facility discharging pollutants pursuant to a NPDES permit may nevertheless still constitute a common law nuisance and be subject to a private nuisance action from adjoining landowners for odors, noise, and discharge of pollutants.[203]

Strict Liability

Many states have adopted the principle of strict liability for abnormally dangerous activities that create an unreasonable risk of harm.[204] Under this doctrine, liability will be imposed even though the defendant did not intentionally or even negligently interfere with a legally protected interest of another. The underlying premise for this doctrine is that the defendant is in the best position to take precautions against injury to others and can pass along any costs of such liability to its customers.

An "abnormally dangerous activity" is one that cannot be eliminated through the use of utmost care.[205] The Second Restatement of Torts lists the following six factors that must be considered by a court in determining whether the activity is abnormally dangerous:

1. the defendant was engaged in an activity that involves a high degree of risk of harm to persons, land, or chattels of another;
2. the likelihood that the resulting harm would be great;
3. an inability to eliminate the risk by the exercise of reasonable care;
4. the extent to which the activity is not a matter of common usage;
5. the inappropriateness of the activity to the place where it is located; and
6. the extent that its value is outweighed by its dangerous attributes.[206]

A number of courts have held that disposal of toxic wastes is an abnormally dangerous activity as a matter of law.[207] One of the leading strict liability cases is *State Department of Environmental Protection v. Ventron.*[208] In *Ventron,* the New Jersey Department of Environmental Protection filed suit against past and present owners and operators of a mercury processing plant to abate mercury contamination in a tidal creek. The New Jersey Supreme Court found that toxic wastes caused a variety of harms, that even with the exercise of reasonable care there was no way to dispose of hazardous wastes safely and that the wastes may also react synergistically to form highly toxic compounds.[209] Because of these considerations, the court concluded that the disposal of toxic wastes was an abnormally dangerous activity and ruled the "law of liability has evolved so that a landowner is strictly liable to others for harm caused by toxic wastes that are stored on his property and flow onto the property of others."[210] Although conceding that businesses involved in the disposal of toxic wastes performed a valuable service to society, the court observed that "the unavoidable risk of harm that is inherent [in disposing toxic wastes] requires that it be carried on at his peril, rather than at the expense of the innocent person who suffers harm as a result of it."[211]

Other courts have followed the lead of the *Ventron* court and have extended strict liability to the storage of hazardous wastes on property.[212] In *Sterling v. Velsicol Chemical Co.,*[213] a commercial hazardous waste disposal company was found strictly liable for discharges of hazardous wastes that had migrated off-site and contaminated the water wells of the plaintiffs. In so holding, the federal district court in Tennessee noted "Velsicol was carrying on an abnormally dangerous activity when it created, implemented, operated and closed its chemical waste burial site. . . . The operation [of the site] by Velsicol makes Velsicol strictly liable to the plaintiffs for all injuries caused thereby."[214] Strict liability has also been imposed for discharges of radium wastes into vacant urban lots[215] and the leakage of PCBs from manufacturing facilities.[216]

Most opinions classifying the handling of hazardous wastes as abnormally dangerous activities involved situations where the wastes leached from the defendants' property to damage the plaintiffs. However, generators who arranged to have hazardous substances disposed at an off-site facility have also been held strictly liable. For example, in *Kenney v. Scientific, Inc.,*[217] residents living next to a hazardous waste landfill filed suit against 625 off-site generators whose waste was deposited at the landfill as well as the transporters who brought the wastes to the site. On the issue that strict liability should be limited to landowners, the court noted that comment (e) to Section 520 of the Second Restatement of Torts specifically allowed the imposition of strict liability when an abnormally dangerous activity was conducted on the land of another.[218] The court reasoned that since the basis for imposing strict liability on hazardous waste activities was the "potential for calamity lurking in abnormally dangerous substances . . . the place where the substance ultimately does its marauding should not serve to dissipate such liability."[219]

In response to the defense that the landfill had been licensed and approved by the state, the court ruled this did not preclude the imposition of strict liability on the generators because the regulations were designed to prevent harm to people residing near the landfill and such a holding would vitiate such protection.[220]

The court also held that generators must be vicariously liable for the acts of independent contractors hired to dispose of hazardous wastes because a "company that creates the Frankenstein monster of abnormally dangerous wastes should not be expected to be relieved of accountability for the depredations of its creature merely because the company entrusts the monster's care to another, even an independent contractor."[221]

Transporters of hazardous waste have been more successful in limiting the application of strict liability. In *Kenney,* the court distinguished between defendants who bring hazardous waste into the world and those who act merely as a conduit for transporting waste.[222] Relying on the comment (e) to Section 519(2) of Second Restatement of Torts, the court held that the liability of a hauler was absolute only for the period it possessed and controlled the waste.[223] However, the court went on to say that transporters could be liable for negligently selecting or delivering wastes to a landfill that the transporter knew of should have known to be dangerous.[224]

In *Yomner v. McKenzie,* a Maryland court found the defendant to be strictly liable for damage to the plaintiff's water wells as a result of a release from underground gasoline storage tanks owned and operated by the defendant.[225] However, a number of courts have ruled that the storage of gasoline is not an abnormally dangerous activity because of its common usage and that the risk of harm can be eliminated through the exercise of reasonable care.[226] The RCRA underground storage tank program standards have been cited by courts as evidence that gasoline can be handled safely.[227]

Notes

1. 42 U.S.C. §§ 9601–9675.
2. 42 U.S.C. § 9607(a)(1).
3. 42 U.S.C. § 9604(e).
4. 42 U.S.C. § 9607(e).
5. 42 U.S.C. § 9607(e)(7).
6. 40 C.F.R. § 300.1.
7. 40 C.F.R. pt. 300, app. B.
8. 55 Fed. Reg. 8696 (Mar. 8, 1990).

9. 40 C.F.R. § 300.415(d).
10. 55 Fed. Reg. 8697 (Mar. 8, 1990).
11. 40 C.F.R. § 300.415(b)(5).
12. 55 Fed. Reg. 8694 (Mar. 8, 1990).
13. 40 C.F.R. § 300.415(m).
14. 40 C.F.R. § 300.415(m)(2).
15. 40 C.F.R. § 300.415(m)(4).
16. 40 C.F.R. § 300.415(m)(3).
17. 42 U.S.C. § 9601(24).
18. 40 C.F.R. § 300.425(b).
19. 40 C.F.R. § 300.510(b).
20. 42 U.S.C. § 9604(c)(6).
21. 40 C.F.R. § 300.415(i).
22. *Compare generally* 40 C.F.R. § 300.415 *with* 40 C.F.R. § 300.430.
23. 42 U.S.C. § 9605(a)(8)(A).
24. 40 C.F.R. pt. 300, app. A.
25. 42 U.S.C. § 9605(a)(8)(B).
26. 40 C.F.R. § 300.425 (c). The ATSDR is required to list the 100 hazardous substances posing the most significant risk at NPL sites and prepare a toxicological profile of each substance. 42 U.S.C. § 9604(i).
27. 55 Fed. Reg. 8692–93 (Mar. 8, 1990).
28. 40 C.F.R. § 300.420.
29. 55 Fed. Reg. 8692 (Mar. 8, 1990).
30. *Id.* at 8692–93.
31. 42 U.S.C. § 9605(d).
32. 42 U.S.C. § 9604(i)(6)(B).
33. *Id.*
34. *Id.* § 9604(i)(7)(A).
35. *Id.* § 9604(i)(8).
36. *Id.* § 9604(i)(9).
37. *Id.* § 9604(i)(10).
38. *Id.*
39. 42 U.S.C. § 9605(a)(8)(A).
40. 55 Fed. Reg. 51,568 (Dec. 14, 1990).
41. *Id.*
42. 42 U.S.C. § 9613(a).
43. 42 U.S.C. §§ 6901–6992k.
44. 53 Fed. Reg. 23,978 (June 24, 1988). There are distinctions between the cleanups that may be required under the RCRA corrective action authority and those required under CERCLA. For example, RCRA does not expressly require public participation in the selection of cleanup actions, health assessments nor require costs to be a factor in determining the scope of the corrective action.
45. 48 Fed. Reg. 40,661 (Sept. 8, 1983).
46. 53 Fed. Reg. 51,415 (Dec. 21, 1988).
47. 52 Fed. Reg. 36,001 (Sept. 24, 1987).
48. 42 U.S.C. § 9620(a).
49. 40 C.F.R. § 300.66(c)(2).
50. 40 C.F.R. § 300.430(e).
51. 40 C.F.R. § 300.430(e)(3).

52. 40 C.F.R. § 300.430(e)(9).
53. 55 Fed. Reg. 8724 (Mar. 8, 1990).
54. *Id.* at 8730.
55. *Id.* at 8847.
56. 40 C.F.R. § 300.430(f).
57. 40 C.F.R. § 300.430(f)(5).
58. 40 C.F.R. § 300.515.
59. 40 C.F.R. § 300.515(f).
60. 42 U.S.C. § 9621(f)(2)(A).
61. 42 U.S.C. § 9617(e).
62. H.R. REP. 99-962, at 3324.
63. *Id.*
64. 40 C.F.R. § 300.435(b).
65. 40 C.F.R. § 300.435(c).
66. 42 U.S.C. § 9622(a).
67. 42 U.S.C. § 9622(e)(6).
68. 40 C.F.R. § 300.435(f).
69. 42 U.S.C. § 9604(c)(6).
70. 42 U.S.C. § 9621(c).
71. 40 C.F.R. § 300.425(e).
72. 40 C.F.R. § 300.425(e)(3).
73. 42 U.S.C. § 9607(a)(4)(A).
74. 40 C.F.R. § 300.
75. U.S. v. Gurley Refining Co., 788 F. Supp. 1473 (E.D. Ark. 1992); Ambrogi v. Gould, 750 F. Supp. 1233 (M.D. Pa. 1990).
76. Town of Bedford v. Raytheon Co., 755 F. Supp. 469 (D. Mass. 1991).
77. 42 U.S.C. § 9607(b).
78. 42 U.S.C. § 9601(35)(A); *see also* SCHNAPF, ENVIRONMENTAL LIABILITY: MANAGING ENVIRONMENTAL RISKS IN CORPORATE/REAL ESTATE TRANSACTIONS AND BROWNFIELD REDEVELOPMENT § 10.07 (LEXIS Publishing, 1998).
79. 42 U.S.C. § 9601(35).
80. Versatile Metals, Inc. v. Union Corp., 693 F. Supp. 1563 (E.D. Pa. 1988).
81. U.S. v. Western Processing Co., No. C89-214M (W.D. Wash., July 31, 1991).
82. 40 C.F.R. § 300.700.
83. 42 U.S.C. § 9607(A)(4)(B).
84. 42 U.S.C. § 9613(f)(1).
85. *Id.*
86. Under Exec. Order 13,016, 61 Fed. Reg. 4587 (1996), the Departments of Interior, Commerce, Agriculture, Defense, and Energy may with the concurrence of the EPA issue orders under Section 106 for sites affecting natural resources under their control, jurisdiction, custody, or trusteeship.
87. 42 U.S.C. § 9606(a).
88. 42 U.S.C. § 9606(a).
89. 42 U.S.C. § 6973.
90. U.S. v. Conservation Chemical Co., 619 F. Supp. 162 (W.D. Mo. 1985).
91. *Id.*

92. A & W Smelter & Refiners, Inc. v. Clinton, 1998 WL 3314170 (9th Cir., June 24, 1998).

93. U.S. v. Conservation Chemical Co., 619 F. Supp. 162 (W.D. Mo. 1985).

94. *See* U.S. v. Outboard Marine Corp., 556 F. Supp. 54 (N.D. Ill. 1982); U.S. v. A & F Materials, Inc., 578 F. Supp. 1249 (S.D. III. 1984); U.S. v. NEPACCO, 579 F. Supp. 823 (W.D. Mo. 1984); U.S. v. Price, 577 F. Supp. 1103 (D. N.J. 1983); U.S. v. Conservation Chemical Co., 589 F. Supp. 59 (W.D. Mo. 1984).

95. United States v. Price, 577 F. Supp. 1103, 1110–13 (D. N.J. 1983).

96. U.S. v. Atlas Minerals and Chemicals, Inc., 797 F. Supp. 411, 416 (E.D. Pa. 1992); U.S. v. Kramer, 757 F. Supp. 397, 425–26 (D. N.J. 1991); U.S. v. Hardage, 116 F.R.D. 460 (W.D. Okla. 1987).

97. 42 U.S.C. § 9607(c)(3).

98. 42 U.S.C. § 9607(c)(3).

99. 42 U.S.C. § 9659.

100. 42 U.S.C. § 9659.

101. 42 U.S.C. § 9659(b)(2).

102. 42 U.S.C. § 9659(c).

103. 42 U.S.C. § 9659(f).

104. *Id.*

105. 42 U.S.C. § 9659(d)(1).

106. 42 U.S.C. § 9659(d)(2).

107. *Id.*

108. 42 U.S.C. § 9613 (h).

109. 42 U.S.C. § 9613 (h).

110. H.R. Rep. No. 99-25(I), at 266 (1985).

111. U.S. v. Princeton Gamma-Tech, Inc., 31 F.3d 138 (3d Cir. 1994); Ehrlich v. Reno, 1994 WL 613698 (E.D. Pa. 1994); Neighborhood Toxic Cleanup Emergency v. EPA, 716 F. Supp. 828 (D. N.J. 1989).

112. H.R. Rep. No. 99-962, at 3317 (1986).

113. U.S. v. Denver, 100 F.3d 1059 (10th Cir. 1996); McClellan Ecological Seepage Situation v. Perry, 47 F.3d 325 (9th Cir. 1995); Razore v. Tulalip Tribes of Washington, 66 F.3d 236 (9th Cir. 1995); U.S. v. NL Industries, 936 F. Supp. 545 (N.D. Ill. 1996).

114. 116 F.3d 1018 (3d Cir. 1997).

115. U.S. v. Princeton Gamma-Tech, Inc., 31 F.3d 138 (3d Cir. 1994).

116. No. 98-0124 (E.D. La. 1998).

117. Environmental Waste Control, Inc. v. ATSDR, 763 F. Supp. 1576 (N.D. Ga. 1991).

118. Hanford Downwinders Coalition, Inc. v. Dowdle, 1995 WL 716871 (9th Cir. 1995).

119. Employers Insurance of Wausau v. Browner, 848 F. Supp. 1369 (N.D. Ill. 1994).

120. 100 F.3d 1059 (10th Cir. 1996).

121. Heart of America Northwest v. Westinghouse Hanford, 820 F. Supp. 1265 (E.D. Wash. 1993); Werlein v. U.S., 746 F. Supp. 887 (D. Minn. 1990).

122. H.R. Rep. No. 99-962, at 3317 (1986).

123. Louisiana v. Reilly, No. 92-274 (W.D. La. 1992).

124. Arrest the Incinerator Remediation, Inc. V. OHM No 4:CV-98-0398 (M.D.Pa. 1998).

125. 42 U.S.C. § 9613(j)(2).

126. 42 U.S.C. § 9613(k).

127. 42 U.S.C. § 9622.

128. Boarhead Corp. v. Erickson, 923 F.2d 1011 (3d Cir. 1991).

129. Cooper Industries v. United States, 775 F. Supp. 1027 (W.D. Mich. 1991).

130. Fairchild Semiconductor Corp. v. EPA, 769 F. Supp. 1553 (N.D. Cal. 1991).

131. U.S. v. Colorado, 33 Env't Rep. Cas. (BNA) 1585 (D. Colo. 1991).

132. 42 U.S.C. § 9613(j).

133. United States v. Hardage, Civ. No. 85-3060 (E.D. Pa. 1987).

134. 42 U.S.C. § 9601(14).

135. 42 U.S.C. § 6903(27).

136. Pantry, Inc. v. Stop-N-Go Foods, Inc., 796 F. Supp. 1171 (S.D. Ill. 1992); 779 F. Supp. 1254 (S.D. Cal. 1991).

137. 42 U.S.C. § 6934(a).

138. *Id.* § 6934(b).

139. *Id.* § 6934(c).

140. 42 U.S.C. § 6973.

141. S. REP. NO. 96-172, 96th Cong., 1st Sess., at 5, *reprinted in* 1980 U.S. CODE CONG. & AD. NEWS 5019, 5023.

142. U.S. v. Valentine, 856 F. Supp. 627 (D. Wyo. 1994).

143. H.R. REP. NO. 198, 98th Cong., 2d Sess., pt. I, at 48 (1983).

144. U.S. v. Conservation Chemical Co., 619 F. Supp. 162 (W.D. Mo. 1985).

145. *Id.*

146. U.S. v. Conservation Chemical Co., 619 F. Supp. 162 (W.D. Mo. 1985).

147. 42 U.S.C. § 6973(c).

148. 42 U.S.C. § 6973(d).

149. 42 U.S.C. § 6924(u).

150. 42 U.S.C. § 6924(v).

151. 42 U.S.C. § 6928(h).

152. *See generally,* 40 C.F.R. § 124, 270.

153. 61 Fed. Reg. 19,454 (1996).

154. *Id.*

155. 53 Fed. Reg. 12,262 (1988).

156. 42 U.S.C. § 6972.

157. 42 U.S.C. § 6972(a)(1)(A).

158. 42 U.S.C. § 6972(a)(1)(B).

159. 42 U.S.C. § 6972(a)(2).

160. Truck Components Inc. v. Beatrice Co., No. 94 C 3228, 1994 U.S. Dist. Lexis 13319 (N.D. Ill. 1994); Gache v. Town of Harrison, 813 F. Supp. 1037 (S.D. N.Y. 1993).

161. Interfaith Community Org. v. Allied Signal, Inc., 928 F. Supp. 1339 (D. N.J. 1996); Pennsylvania Real Estate Trust v. SPS Technologies, Inc., 1995 WL 687003 (E.D. Pa. 1995).

162. Aurora National Bank v. Tri Star Marketing, Inc., 955 F. Supp. 894 (N.D. Ill. 1997); City of Toledo v. Beazer Materials & Services, Inc., 833 F. Supp. 646 (N.D. Ohio 1993).

163. Prisco v. New York, 1996 U.S. Dist. LEXIS 1444 (S.D. N.Y. Feb. 8, 1996).

164. 42 U.S.C. § 9601(14).

165. PMC, Inc. v. Sherwin-Williams Co., No. 93-C-1379, 1997 WL 359977 (N.D. Ill. 1997).

166. Acme Printing Ink Co. v. Menard, 812 F. Supp. 1498 (E.D. Wis. 1992).

167. Bayless Investment & Trading Co. v. Chevron USA, Inc., U.S. Dist. LEXIS 12190 (D. Ariz. 1994).

168. 797 F. Supp. 805 (S.D. Cal. 1992).

169. No. 94 C 3228, 1994 U.S. Dist. LEXIS 13319 (N.D. Ill. 1994).

170. 1994 U.S. Dist. LEXIS 16158 (N.D. Ill. 1994).

171. San Diego Properties v. Exxon Co., 1994 WL 421791 (S.D. Cal. 1994); Petropoulos v. Columbia Gas of Ohio, Inc., 840 F. Supp. 511 (S.D. Ohio 1993).

172. U.S. v. Aceto Agricultural Chemicals Corp., 872 F.2d 1373 (8th Cir. 1989).

173. Dague v. City of Burlington, 935 F.2d 1343 (2d Cir. 1991).

174. Dominick's Finer Foods, Inc. v. Amoco Oil Co., 867 F. Supp. 120 (E.D. Ill. 1993); Petropoulos v. Columbia Gas of Ohio, Inc., 540 F. Supp. 511 (S.D. Ohio 1993); Zands v. Nelson, 797 F. Supp. 805 (S.D. Cal. 1992).

175. 39 F.3d 1011 (9th Cir. 1994).

176. 1998 U.S. App. LEXIS 14923.

177. Leister v. Black & Decker (U.S.), Inc., 117 F.3d 1414 (unpublished table decision) 1123 (4th Cir. 1997).

178. Buggsi, Inc. v. Chevron USA, Inc., 857 F. Supp. 1427 (D.Or. 1994); Lincoln Properties Ltd. v. Higgins, 36 ERC 1228 (E.D. Cal. 1993).

179. U.S. v. Conservation Chemical Co., 619 F. Supp. 162, 193–94 (D.C. Mo. 1985).

180. U.S. v. Waste Industries, 734 F.2d 159 (4th Cir. 1984).

181. 516 U.S. 479, 116 S. Ct. 1251, 134 L.Ed.2d 121 (March 19, 1996).

182. First San Diego Properties v. Exxon Co., 859 F. Supp. 1313 (S.D. Cal. 1994).

183. 42 U.S.C. § 6972(a).

184. AM International, Inc. v. Datacard Corp., 106 F.3d 1342 (7th Cir. 1997); Murray v. Bath Iron Works Corp., 867 F. Supp. 33 (D. Me. 1994).

185. 42 U.S.C. § 6972(b)(1)(A).

186. 42 U.S.C. § 6972(b)(2)(A).

187. 42 U.S.C. § 6972(b)(1)(B).

188. 42 U.S.C. § 6972(b)(2)(B),(C).

189. Clinton County Commissioners v. EPA, 116 F.3d 1018 (3rd Cir. 1997).

190. H.R. CONF. REP. No. 1133 at 118, reprinted in 1984 CODE U.S. CONG. & ADMIN. NEWS at 5689.

191. 42 U.S.C. § 9601(22).

192. N.J.S.A. 58:10-23.11b.

193. Atlantic City Municipal Utilities Authority v. Hunt, 210 N.J. Super. 76, 509 A.2d 225 (App. Div. 1986).

194. State v. Schenectady Chemicals, Inc., 479 N.Y.S.2d 1010 (A.D. 3d Dept. 1984).

195. Restatement (Second) of Torts, 821B and 821D.

196. Restatement (Second) of Torts, 822.

197. PROSSER & KEATON ON TORTS, 88 at 626.

198. *Id.* at 826.

199. *Id.* at 821(B).

200. *Id.* at 821(C). *See also* Philadelphia Electric Co. v. Hercules, Inc., 762 F.2d 303 (3d Cir. 1985).

201. Anderson v. W.R. Grace, 628 F. Supp. 1219 (D. Mass. 1986).

202. CAL. HEALTH & SAFETY CODE § 5410.

203. Village of Wilsonville v. SCA Services, Inc., 426 N.E. 2d 824 (1981).

204. Restatement (Second) of Torts, 519, 520.

205. Restatement (Second) of Torts, 519(1).

206. Restatement (Second) of Torts, 520.

207. Department of Environmental Protection v. Ventron Corp., 94 N.J. 473 (1983); Sterling v. Velsicol Chemical Corp., 647 F. Supp. 303 (W.D. Tenn. 1986); Department of Transportation of the State of New Jersey v. PSC Resources, Inc.; New York v. Schenectady Chemical Co., 103 A.D. 2d 33 (1984); Atlas Chemical Indus. v. Anderson, 514 S.W. 2d 309 (Tex. Civ. App. 1974); Ashland Oil v. Miller Purchasing Co., 678 F.2d 1293 (5th Cir. 1982).

208. 94 N.J. 473, 463 A.2d 893 (1983).

209. 94 N.J. at 492.

210. 94 N.J. at 488.

211. 94 N.J. at 493.

212. Branch v. Western Petroleum, 657 P.2d 267 (Utah 1982); McLane v. Northwest Natural Gas Co., 467 P.2d 635 (Or. 1970); City of Bridgeton v. B.P. Oil, 146 N.J. Super. 169, 369 A.2d 49 (Law. Div. 1976); Cities Service Co. v. Florida, 312 So. 2d. 799 (Fla. Dist. Ct. App. 1975).

213. 647 F. Supp. 303 (W.D. Tenn 1986).

214. 647 F. Supp. at 311.

215. T & E Industries, Inc. v. Safety Light Corp., 123 N.J. 371, 587 A.2d 1249 (1991).

216. Prospect Industries Corp v. Singer Co., 238 N.J. Super. 394, 569 A.2d 908 (Law. Div. 1989).

217. 204 N.J. Super. 228 (Law Div. 1985).

218. 204 N.J. Super. at 248.

219. 204 N.J. Super. at 248.

220. 204 N.J. Super. at 250.

221. *Id.*

222. *Id.* at 261–62.

223. *Id.*

224. *Id.* at 262.

225. 257 A.2d 138 (Md. 1969).

226. Hahn v. Chevron U.S.A., No. 94-54-66 (6th Cir. July 5, 1995); Triffler v. Hopf, 1994 WL 643237 (N.D. Ill. 1994) Dominick's Finer Foods Inc. v. Amoco Oil Co., 1993 WL 524808 (N.D. Ill. 1993); Arlington Forest Associates v. Exxon Corp., 774 F. Supp. 387 (E.D. Va. 1991).

227. T & E Industries, Inc. v. Safety Light Corp., 587 A.2d 1249 (1991).

CHAPTER 17

Redeveloping Old Facilities

ELIZABETH A. STRINGER

Introduction

Many communities have in their midst sites with real or perceived contamination, left as a result of industrial activities. These places often blight neighborhoods, both economically and environmentally. Local residents, as well as municipal governments and real estate developers, aspire for the sites to be cleaned up and redeveloped. These kinds of places are called "brownfields."

The U.S. Environmental Protection Agency (EPA) defines brownfields sites as "abandoned, idled or underutilized industrial and commercial facilities where expansion or redevelopment is complicated by real or perceived environmental contamination."[1] Brownfields are found all over the United States, particularly in urban areas. Minority and low-income communities seem especially likely to be exposed to brownfields and their contamination. Estimates of the number of such sites vary, but there are at least thousands.

Visions of abandoned urban lots can stigmatize communities, since they embody many of the elements commonly associated with the decline of our cities: pollution and garbage, unemployment, poverty, racial isolation, crime, drugs, declining public services, and architectural eyesores.[2] As a result, contamination is not cleaned up, and businesses will decide that it is cheaper and easier to purchase vacant property outside of the blighted urban centers. This, in turn, leads to development of "greenfields"—suburban or exurban sites that have not previously been used for commercial or industrial production. Frequently greenfields are able to be developed without expenditures to remove old industrial structures; they involve little or no cleanup expense; and there will be no delays resulting from environmental investigation and rehabilitation. However, the shift in development from urban brownfields to suburban greenfields often creates its own set of environmental problems—sprawling land use patterns that increase automobile usage, gobble up farmland, forests, wetlands, and open spaces, and can contribute further to unemployment and an underutilized urban infrastructure. Thus, much of the government's interest in brownfields redevelopment and most existing brownfields initiatives focus upon urban brownfields sites, especially those sites located in economically depressed areas.

This chapter discusses legal mechanisms that are available to redevelop brownfields, and the accompanying issues of cleanup standards and public participation.

Redeveloping Contaminated Sites

Legal Procedures Available for Redevelopment

Introduction

As mentioned above, a major obstacle to brownfields redevelopment has been the uncertain, but potentially substantial, liability that may result from acquiring and rehabilitating a brownfields site. If there has been a release of a hazardous substance, the owners and operators of the site may be held jointly and severally liable for the entire cleanup cost. Even if a site is cleaned up in accordance with all applicable federal and state environmental laws, the owner may incur additional costs if further contamination is discovered at a later time. Under federal and state statutes, a former owner may have continuing liability if contamination can be traced to hazardous substances that were disposed of on the property at the time he or she owned it, even if the "disposal" occurred without the owner's knowledge.

Another major impediment to brownfields redevelopment has been uncertain cleanup standards. Potential developers are often unwilling to purchase or rehabilitate contaminated sites where they cannot adequately predict the required level of cleanup, and hence its cost and duration.

A related obstacle has been inadequate or nonexistent financing opportunities. The Comprehensive Environmental Response, Compensation and Liability Act (CERCLA) provides that the "owner and operator" of a contaminated facility may, under certain circumstances, be responsible for the cost of cleaning it up.[3] Banks and other lenders that made loans to the owners of contaminated facilities, and later foreclosed and took over operation as well as ownership, have on occasion been found potentially liable for cleanup under this provision.[4] In one celebrated case, *United States v. Fleet Factors Corp.*, an appellate court panel went as far as to suggest (in dictum) that "[i]t is not necessary for the secured creditor actually to involve itself in the day-to-day operations of the facility in order to be liable . . . Nor is it necessary for the secured creditor to participate in management decisions relating to hazardous waste. Rather, a secured creditor will be liable if its involvement with the management of the facility is sufficiently broad to support the inference that it could affect hazardous waste disposal decisions if it so chose."[5]

Fleet Factors led to an uproar in the financial community. The EPA attempted to negate the judicial decision through regulatory action, but failed.[6] As far as is known, no financial institution was ever actually held liable for the cleanup of hazardous waste under the *Fleet Factors* capacity-to-control test; the several judicial decisions finding banks potentially liable arose in the context of preliminary motions where the actual facts of the banks' involvement had not yet been determined. Nonetheless, concern was sufficiently great that in September 1996, Congress amended CERCLA with the Asset Conservation, Lender Liability and Deposit Insurance Protection Act (the Asset Conservation Act),[7] which creates a safe harbor from CERCLA liability for lenders.

This safe harbor does not extend to current owners or prospective purchasers or developers. Thus, even after the Asset Conservation Act, such parties still desire a legal framework to secure governmental blessing for cleanups. To encourage cleanups, the EPA and many state governments have developed several initiatives and programs that afford some protection from liability, and thereby alleviate some of the concerns typically associated with brownfields redevelopment. Virtually every brownfields cleanup must proceed under one of these mechanisms.

EPA Prospective Purchaser Agreements and Comfort/Status Letters

PROSPECTIVE PURCHASER AGREEMENTS. EPA prospective purchaser agreements (PPAs) can be an effective mechanism for facilitating the cleanup of brownfields sites. They are available whether or not the site is listed, being considered for listing, or not listed on the EPA Superfund list (the National Priorities List).[8] PPAs afford considerable protection from future EPA enforcement actions, as well as from contribution actions and private cost recovery actions from third parties. PPAs may be transferable to third-party developers, and they can be especially helpful when a buyer is seeking financing to redevelop a brownfields site by providing a secured creditor with a certain level of comfort that there will not be future unanticipated cleanup costs.

In 1995 EPA issued new and revised guidelines for PPAs, replacing earlier guidelines issued in 1989 that, in very limited circumstances, authorized EPA to enter into agreements that included EPA's "covenant not to sue" or to seek contribution costs under CERCLA. The 1995 Guidance sets out five criteria that should be met before EPA will consider entering into a prospective purchaser agreement.

First, the Guidance requires that an EPA action at the site "has been taken, is ongoing, or is anticipated to be undertaken by the Agency."[9] However, EPA will not enter into a PPA at a site in the absence of actual or anticipated federal expenditure of funds unless:

1. there is a real possibility of the prospective purchaser incurring CERCLA liability against the federal government; and
2. EPA involvement is necessary to remove the potential liability and facilitate the cleanup and redevelopment of the property.[10]

EPA is more likely to enter into an agreement when there is a high probability of a federal response action at the site, but is unlikely to enter into an agreement where cleanup is being undertaken by a state agency. Another consideration is whether the prospective purchaser has other forms of assurance against liability, such as an indemnification agreement with a private party that has available resources to remediate the property and admits liability.[11]

Second, the 1995 Guidance requires EPA to receive a substantial benefit either in the form of a direct benefit, such as reimbursement for the cleanup, or as a substantial public benefit in combination with a reduced direct benefit to EPA. Public benefits include:

- the creation or retention of jobs;
- the creation of conservation or recreation areas;
- the lessening of environmental risk; or
- the provision of community service, such as the improvement of public transportation and infrastructure.[12]

The third criterion of the 1995 Guidance prohibits the new operator from developing or operating on the property in a manner that exacerbates or contributes to the existing contamination.[13] EPA will not enter into a PPA if it lacks sufficient information to evaluate the impact of a proposed action at the site.[14]

The 1995 Guidance also states that continued operation or new development of the property must not pose health risks to the community and those persons likely to be present at the site.[15] Finally, the Guidance requires that the prospective purchaser be financially viable with regard to the magnitude of cleanup costs.[16] If a prospective purchaser meets all five criteria, EPA will consider entering into a PPA.

After EPA receives "adequate consideration" from the prospective purchaser and consults with the appropriate agency officials, it will enter into a PPA promising that the United States "covenants not to sue or take any other civil or administrative action against the [prospective purchaser] for any and all civil liability for injunctive relief or reimbursement of response costs pursuant to Sections 106 and 107 of CERCLA with respect to existing contamination at the site in question."[17] Prospective purchasers are also protected against contribution actions under CERCLA Section 113(f)(2), 42 U.S.C. Section 9613(f)(2).

EPA's covenant not to sue does *not* extend to:

1. claims based on the prospective purchaser's failure to meet a requirement of the agreement;
2. liability resulting from past or future release of hazardous substances at the site caused by the prospective purchaser or those in privity with the prospective purchaser;
3. liability resulting from the release or threat of release of hazardous substances not within the meaning of "existing contamination" at the site on the effective date of the PPA;
4. criminal liability;
5. liability resulting from exacerbation of existing contamination by a prospective purchaser or those in privity with the prospective purchaser;
6. liability for injury to or the loss of natural resources and the costs of any natural resource damage assessment incurred by federal agencies other than EPA; and
7. liability for any violations of local, state, or federal law or regulations.

Thus, there are some shortcomings to PPAs. Potential liability under state law remains. A cleanup performed pursuant to a PPA may not have followed the procedures necessary to allow the purchaser to bring a CERCLA cost recovery or contribution action against responsible parties, or to secure insurance recovery.

EPA COMFORT/STATUS LETTERS. In 1997, EPA issued another policy that is designed to encourage the redevelopment of brownfields, although it does not protect against potential liability.[18] Under EPA's Comfort/Status Letter policy, the agency may issue a letter to a brownfields developer stating its position with regard to site contamination. The letter provides the developer with a way to assess the probability of incurring CERCLA liability. These letters are issued for informational purposes only, and do not protect a purchaser from potential liability.

EPA's policy allows the various EPA regions to issue letters at their discretion.[19] However, the policy limits issuance of the letters to brownfields that meet certain requirements. First, there must be a realistic perception or probability of incurring CERCLA liability. Second, the letter must facilitate the cleanup and redevelopment of brownfields. Third, there must be no alternative mechanisms available to address the purchaser's concern adequately.[20]

If the contaminated property meets the above requirements, EPA may issue one of the following:

1. a "No Previous Superfund Interest" Letter;
2. a "No Current Superfund Interest" Letter;
3. a "Federal Superfund Interest" Letter; or
4. a "State Action" Letter.

A No Previous Superfund Interest Letter may be issued where a site has had no prior connection to federal activities under CERCLA, including not being listed on EPA's CERCLIS list (an exhaustive list of sites where contamination is suspected but not necessarily confirmed). The No Previous Superfund Interest Letter is intended to inform the prospective purchaser that, to the best of EPA's knowledge, the site has not interacted with the federal CERCLA program.

A No Current Superfund Interest Letter may be issued where a site has been either removed from CERCLIS or deleted from the NPL, or for sites that are situated in close proximity to, but not within, the boundaries of a CERCLIS site. The No Current Superfund Interest Letter is used to inform a potential purchaser that EPA does not plan on taking any, or additional, response actions at the site.

A Federal Superfund Interest Letter may be issued where EPA has responded to the site, or plans on responding, under CERCLA. A site that is listed on the NPL or on the CERCLIS list would fall into this category. The Federal Superfund Interest Letter is issued to explain what type of remediation the Agency has taken with respect to the site, as well as any future anticipated response or enforcement actions by EPA under CERCLA.

Finally, EPA may issue a State Action Letter when the Agency has no knowledge of federal CERCLA involvement or where its role is secondary to that of the state. This type of letter would be provided where a state has the lead role in day-to-day oversight of response actions at the site through a cooperative agreement with EPA, or when the state is performing its own response under a state statute.

Federal Facilities

Although the term "brownfields" is most commonly associated with contamination from commercial or industrial uses of property, the federal government has also caused the contamination of thousands of brownfields.[21] The cleanup of federal facilities must be consistent with CERCLA.[22] As a result, the same concerns of liability that hinder the redevelopment of privately owned brownfields also discourage the rehabilitation of federal sites by private parties. Due to the growing number of contaminated federal facilities being made available for development, especially from military base closures, several programs have been enacted to help facilitate their redevelopment.

In 1992, Congress amended CERCLA with the passage of the Community Environmental Response Facilitation Act (CERFA).[23] CERFA permits federal agencies to transfer "uncontaminated" parcels of federal facilities for redevelopment before the entire facility has been completely cleaned. "Uncontaminated" parcels are defined as those "on which no hazardous substances and no petroleum products or their derivatives were stored for one year or more, known to have been released, or disposed of."[24] In addition, EPA guidance states that some contaminated parcels may be eligible for the "uncontaminated" designation, as long as they do not pose a "threat" to human health or the environment.

In the fiscal year 1997 Defense Authorization Act, Congress further amended CERCLA to allow the transfer of federal property prior to the completion of remedial actions.[25] The amendment permits EPA, with the consent of the state governor, to authorize the deferral of some remedial actions under the property transfer. To qualify, EPA and/or the state governor must conclude that:

1. the property is suitable for the transferee's intended use, and the intended use is consistent with the protection of human health or the environment;
2. the deed or other agreement governing the transfer includes certain response action assurances;
3. the federal agency requesting deferral of the remedial action provided notice by publication of the proposed transfer and an opportunity for public comment; and
4. the deferral and the transfer will not substantially delay any necessary response action at the property.[26]

EPA also has issued guidance for federal agencies to follow when transferring potentially contaminated property.[27] Before a federal agency transfers property on which hazardous substances have been stored for a year or more, the agency must comply with the provisions of CERCLA Section 120(h)(3), and include specific information on the face of the deed, such as:

1. information on the type and quantity of hazardous substances;
2. information on when the storage, release, or disposal occurred;
3. information on any remedial actions taken;
4. a covenant warranting that all remedial action necessary to protect human health and the environment with respect to any such hazardous substance has been taken (although in certain circumstances this requirement may be deferred);
5. a covenant warranting that additional remedial action found to be necessary after the date of the transaction will be conducted by the United States; and
6. a clause granting the United States access to the property in any case in which remedial action or corrective action is found to be necessary after the transfer date.[28]

Such information and warranties are intended to help facilitate the redevelopment of potentially contaminated federal properties by providing the developer with a way to assess the extent of contamination at the site and by protecting the developer against liability for that contamination.

The Department of Defense (DOD) has responsibility for the identification and cleanup of potentially contaminated sites that are currently or were formerly used as military installations. In 1993, President Clinton presented a plan for the economic reuse of military bases that became law as part of the fiscal year 1994 National Defense Authorization Act.[29] The plan offers potential developers a fast track cleanup provision that is intended to avoid delays in the cleanup and reuse of closed defense bases, while still protecting human health and the environment.

The Base Closure Community Redevelopment and Homeless Assistance Act of 1994[30] requires that local or state governments that are affected by base closures designate a Local Redevelopment Authority, comprised of members of the community, to develop a plan for the redevelopment of the base. In addition, DOD may enter into agreements with states and territories under which they are reimbursed for technical services provided in connection with DOD cleanup activities.[31] These programs facilitate the cleanup of contaminated bases by involving the local community in remedial decision making.

The Department of Energy (DOE), unlike DOD, is not under a congressional mandate to dispose of its property; however, DOE undergoes a periodic review of sites to determine when they are no longer needed. Before transfer, contaminated DOE properties are decontaminated by its Office of Environmental Management. Moreover, DOE has specified requirements for entering into agreements to sell property it no longer needs, including contaminated land.

DOE requires that the property to be transferred be "acquired" and not "withdrawn" land.[32] No other parties may hold legal rights to the land, unless rights do not hinder transfer.[33] The property must have been declared excess by DOE because it is not needed for any present or reasonably foreseeable use. The property's redevelopment must not interfere with DOE's remaining site activities. The property must be either in a safe condition, be decontaminated cost-effectively, or be subject to use restrictions to protect against harmful future uses. In addition, prospective purchasers must have been identified or must be likely. Finally, the sale must promote the most beneficial use of the property.[34] If the property meets the above requirements, DOE may transfer it.

State "Little Superfund" Programs

Even though the dreaded federal Superfund statute casts its shadow over all hazardous waste cleanup, most states have enacted their own hazardous waste cleanup laws. State cleanup laws generally address sites where contamination is not so significant that it requires NPL listing. However, the sites still require remediation before being used safely. Accordingly, states have created their own "little superfund" programs. Under these programs, each state provides its own hazardous waste list of contaminated sites. The number of sites on state Superfund lists far outnumber those on the federal NPL.[35]

There is no uniform state Superfund law; each state program differs on the procedures for listing sites, public notice, cleanup standards, and other elements. Nevertheless, the main elements of most state Superfund programs are:

1. procedures for emergency response actions at sites that pose a risk to human health or the environment;
2. financial programs to help pay the cost of administering the state superfund program, as well as the site cleanup;
3. enforcement authority to force responsible parties to conduct site assessments and cleanups;
4. programs to compile lists of sites; and
5. procedures to develop or adopt cleanup standards.

Depending on the particular state program, there can be a number of differences between the state cleanup statute and CERCLA. For example, many state programs have a broader reach than CERCLA, and may include sites that might not fall within CERCLA's definition of regulated substances—such as those contaminated from petroleum products (like gas stations).[36] Some states do not adopt CERCLA's imposition of joint and several liability, though this does not prevent prospective plaintiffs from going to federal court and seeking cost recovery or contribution under CERCLA.[37]

State Property Transfer Acts

Some states have enacted statutes that require certain actions to be undertaken in connection with the transfer of potentially contaminated real property.[38] In a few states, these laws also establish a framework for government-approved cleanup of contaminated properties.[39]

Unlike CERCLA and state Superfund statutes, property transfer provisions are triggered by the occurrence of a business transaction, and not by the release or threatened release of hazardous substances. Property transfer laws were enacted mainly to protect buyers from purchasing contaminated land without their knowledge, and therefore may provide the basis for a site cleanup.

The most sweeping such law is New Jersey's Industrial Site Recovery Act,[40] which requires notice to the state before the transfer of any property that has been used for various specified industrial or commercial purposes. Before the transfer, the site must be investigated and (if impermissible levels of contamination are found) cleaned up, unless the parties enter into a binding agreement with the state to conduct the cleanup after the transfer.

The Connecticut Transfer Act[41] is of similar effect, though it does not require cleanup before transfer.

Delaware, Minnesota, North Carolina, Pennsylvania, and Rhode Island require that certain known contamination be recorded in the property's land records,[42] and Kentucky, Massachusetts, and Nebraska require deed registry only for sites used formally for hazardous waste disposal.[43] Arkansas and Delaware require deed registry for sites that have been remediated pursuant to a state brownfields program.[44]

Written notice of known contamination must be given pursuant to statute or regulation, to potential purchasers in Arizona, California, the District of Columbia, Georgia, Illinois, Indiana, Michigan, Missouri, and West Virginia.[45] In some other states, failure to give such notice may amount to common law fraud.

State Voluntary Cleanup Programs

An increasing number of states have state voluntary cleanup programs that can provide an effective mechanism for the cleanup and redevelopment of brownfields.[46] Such programs facilitate brownfields cleanup and redevelopment in several ways. Generally, these programs allow a developer to volunteer to clean up a site with minimal state oversight. Using specific, numerical cleanup standards or site-specific risk assessment techniques, volunteers must ensure that redevelopment will not threaten the public health, safety, or the environment. Once cleanup is completed in accordance with specified procedures, a volunteer receives protection from state liability. The protection is usually in one of two categories: a covenant not to sue, which relieves the volunteer from future state enforcement action; or a certificate of completion, a no-further-remediation letter, or a no-further-action letter, all of which provide evidence that the site has been cleaned up to state standards.

Despite significant differences in the details, all of the state programs attempt to provide:

1. flexible cleanup standards and procedures;
2. reduced levels of governmental oversight;
3. some finality or closure to the cleanup process;
4. certain liability protection; and
5. financial incentives.

With respect to cleanup levels, many states permit a volunteer to choose among a set of parameters and standards against which cleanup is measured. Common choices include:

1. cleaning up to background levels of contamination;
2. cleaning up to certain state numerical standards;
3. tailoring cleanup standards for the intended use of the property;
4. imposition of engineering and institutional controls to restrict future uses of the property; and
5. cleaning up to site-specific standards, considering exposure levels, nature of contaminants, and actual use of the property.

Among the kinds of financial incentives offered by many state voluntary cleanup programs are low-interest loans, tax increment financing, and tax abatements. Under tax increment financing, the state expends the additional tax monies that are anticipated to be received from the redevelopment of the property for remediation purposes. Tax abatements involve elimination, reduction, or freezing of the amount of the developer's tax obligations. To qualify for the financial incentives, many state programs require that the property be redeveloped for a public purpose.

These state programs, despite their advantages, do have some drawbacks for potential redevelopers. Most state covenants not to sue allow future enforcement actions in certain circumstances, such as when previously unknown contamination is discovered. The liability protections in the state voluntary cleanup programs do not necessarily insulate volunteers from federal enforcement actions for violations of federal law, from private cost recovery actions under CERCLA, or from private tort actions.

Some states limit participation in voluntary cleanup programs (or at least the availability of liability relief) to parties that are not responsible for causing the site's contamination.[47] A majority of states also make certain sites ineligible for the program, such as:

- sites subject to pending state or federal enforcement action;
- sites listed on the National Priorities List;
- sites subject to closure requirements under state solid or hazardous waste laws; and
- hazardous waste treatment, storage, or disposal facilities.

Most state programs require a volunteer to submit a site environmental assessment report and remediation plans as part of the application process. The remediation plans must be approved by the state prior to acceptance in the program. Some states impose an application fee, and others subject applications to public notice and comment.[48] Once an application is approved, the state environmental agency will enter into an agreement with the volunteer. When cleanup is completed in accordance with the approved remediation plan, the state will issue one of the assurances discussed above.

RCRA Corrective Action

The RCRA corrective action program governs the cleanup of hazardous waste treatment, storage, and disposal (TSD) facilities.[49] Under this program, a brownfields developer who plans to redevelop a TSD facility must either remove the hazardous substances present at the site and dispose of them at an approved RCRA facility, or treat and contain them in place.[50]

The corrective action program involves a set of procedures that resemble those under the National Priorities List. Detailed investigations of subsurface conditions must be performed, followed by review of several remedial options and approval of one by EPA or the state after an opportunity for public comment.[51]

EPA encourages brownfields developers to involve the public in the corrective action process. EPA suggests that the site studies be made available for public review and comment, and will consider the level of public participation conducted by a facility owner/operator when determining the acceptability of a voluntary response action.[52]

Underground Storage Tank Cleanups

It is common for brownfields sites to contain old and/or abandoned underground storage tanks (USTs). Most USTs are used to store petroleum products, particularly gasoline and oil. However, USTs also may be used to store other liquids, such as waste oil, solvent, hydraulic fluid, process chemicals, completed product, and hazardous waste. The presence of USTs on a brownfields site can pose a number of potential problems in connection with redevelopment.

For example, a potential brownfields developer should ascertain the location of USTs on the site, since pipes connected with operating tanks can be accidently severed during redevelopment. If a UST is still in use and will continue in use after the brownfield is redeveloped, then the potential site owner must determine whether it meets current standards.[53] If the UST does not meet required standards, then the cost of repair or replacement should be included in the final transaction.

If a UST is not currently in use, the brownfields developer must investigate the history of the tank. It may not be necessary to remove the tank, but certain factors should be evaluated. The developer should determine when the tank was taken out of service, the nature of its former contents, whether the tank integrity was compromised and, if so, whether groundwater or the environment was impacted. The manner of abandonment is also important; a tank that was emptied and abandoned can create an underground void that could pose a danger of collapse.

Many USTs, but not all, are regulated under RCRA's Subtitle I.[54] RCRA regulates USTs only if they contain a "regulated substance" and only if 10 percent or more of its volume is beneath the surface of the ground.[55] Regulated substances include CERCLA hazardous substances (but not hazardous wastes under RCRA Subtitle C) and petroleum and petroleum-based products. Certain other exemptions apply.[56]

USTs that fall within RCRA are subject to a variety of federal and state requirements for closure and cleanup.[57] EPA will delegate to the states the task of administering the RCRA UST program, if the state program is "no less stringent" than the federal program.[58] However, even if a state's program has not received federal approval, each state has its own set of UST regulations that must be followed. All USTs regulated under RCRA and in operation after January 1, 1974, must be registered with designated state agencies.[59] Many states have established UST trust funds to reimburse owners for certain costs associated with the cleanup of petroleum releases.

Generally, a developer that discovers USTs on a site has three options:

1. the USTs can be removed;
2. the USTs can stay in the ground and be permanently sealed; or
3. the USTs can be continued in, or returned to, productive use.

Permanent closure requires that the tanks be emptied, rendered vapor-free, and cleaned out.[60] After cleaning and properly sealing the pipes, the tanks can be removed, or left in the ground and filled with an inert solid material such as sand or cement.[61] Advance notification to EPA or the state agency, as well as the performance of a site assessment, is required before permanently closing a tank.[62] The site assessment is conducted to ensure that the tank did not leak or spill its contents. If a release is detected, the developer must clean up the contamination.

Reuse of a UST requires that the developer make substantial upgrades to the tank, including corrosion protection and the installation of devices to protect against spills and overfills.[63] Another alternative would be "temporary closure" for tanks that are temporarily out of service. Temporary closure requires owners and operators to continue maintenance and release detection if the UST system is not empty. However, temporary closure can only last for 12 months, and then permanent closure is mandated, unless the tank adheres to the requirements for an upgraded UST.[64]

Asbestos Cleanups

Brownfields development often involves demolition or rehabilitation of abandoned structures left on the site. Many older buildings contain asbestos, which was commonly used as insulation from the 1950s to the 1970s.[65] EPA regulates the cleanup of asbestos contaminated facilities, and so do the federal Occupational Safety and Health Administration (OSHA),[66] most states, and some large cities. Thus, a brownfields developer must follow specified legal procedures when rehabilitating or demolishing old structures containing asbestos. A failure to follow requires procedures can result in severe federal and state penalties, including criminal prosecution.

Asbestos can also be found in the soil surrounding older buildings. Under CERCLA, a building that contains asbestos is deemed to be a "consumer product for consumer use" and thus not a "facility."[67] However, asbestos is considered a hazardous substance under CERCLA.[68] Thus, a brownfields developer should be aware that asbestos found in soil is subject to regulation under CERCLA.

Federal law does not require the removal of nonfriable asbestos—that is, asbestos that is not crumbling or otherwise prone to becoming airborne. Whether to remove nonfriable asbestos from a building is a decision left mostly to the site owner. However, federal law requires the remediation of friable asbestos that causes airborne asbestos contamination levels that endanger people who work in a building. In addition, state and local rules may also impose specific requirements for removal.

Nevertheless, purchasers or long-term lessees often require the removal or encapsulation of asbestos before proceeding with a transaction, or a reduction in the purchase price or rent to allow them to perform the asbestos work themselves.

The federal Clean Air Act (CAA) regulates activities that may result in a release of asbestos into the air from demolition or restoration of buildings through its National Emission Standards for Hazardous Air Pollutants (NESHAP) program.[69] The NESHAP demolition and renovation regulations include requirements that vary depending on whether the material is friable or nonfriable. Site owners and operators must investigate the possible location of asbestos prior to commencing any demolition or renovation activity, and, depending on what they find, they may have to notify EPA or another governmental entity before starting the work. Failure to follow specified procedures can result in criminal penalties and large civil fines.[70]

FINANCIAL ASSISTANCE. There are three overall sources of financing for brownfields redevelopment:

1. privately capitalized investment funds;
2. nonprofit organizations; and
3. public financial assistance programs.

Private investment groups can play an important role in brownfields redevelopment through the use of "vulture funds" and real estate investment trusts (REITs). Vulture funds usually form a joint venture with an environmental engineering firm and insurance company who provide their services in exchange for an opportunity to profit from resale. The strategy of the funds is to purchase, remediate, and then quickly resell brownfields properties. REITs are private or publicly traded companies that specialize in the acquisition, improvement, management, and sale of commercial and residential properties.

A few nonprofit organizations also can provide financial assistance to brownfields developers who wish to redevelop properties that have significant public benefits. Some nonprofits purchase options on contaminated property, while others take an equity position on the property, thereby reducing a project's risk ratio (loan-to-value ratio).

The federal government is currently experimenting with a variety of financial incentives to encourage brownfields redevelopment, such as the Brownfields National Partnership Action Agenda. Under the Agenda, the federal government has agreed to invest approximately $300 million in brownfields communities and make an additional $165 million available in the form of loan guarantees.[71] EPA has also established a brownfields economic redevelopment initiative, which includes two financial assistance programs to facilitate the cleanup and reuse of contaminated sites: the Brownfields Assessment Demonstration Pilot Program, and the Brownfields Cleanup Revolving Loan Fund (BCRLF).[72] EPA hopes that these initiatives will help foster cooperation among local governments, community groups, lenders, developers, and investors so that properties can be brought back into productive use. These EPA programs have specific eligibility requirements, and make money available only for a limited range of activities.

The Department of Housing and Urban Development (HUD) also provides incentives for redevelopment. HUD programs include Community Development Block Grants (CDBGs), guaranteed loan funds, and economic revitalization grants. Other agencies with programs that potentially encourage brownfields development include the Small Business Administration and the Economic Development Agency.

Section 198 of the Internal Revenue Code allows business to deduct certain remediation costs.[73] In addition, many state and local governments have established financial assistance and tax incentive programs. Some states have created public or quasi-public agencies that may help finance redevelopment. Further, state and local governments also offer:

1. tax exemptions, credits, and deductions;
2. tax increment financing, which can be used to pay remediation costs and stimulate redevelopment in economically depressed areas;
3. property tax abatements, to attract or retain business and industry; and
4. remediation tax credits, to reduce project costs.[74]

Some states have established trusts to help pay for the cleanup of certain types of remediation, such as UST releases and dry cleaner solvent contamination.[75]

CLEANUP STANDARDS. The remediation process includes a determination of cleanup levels.[76] The question of "how clean is clean?" often depends on the intended use of the property, whether a site is undergoing a voluntary cleanup, or whether the cleanup is required pursuant to CERCLA. Sites that are listed on the NPL must meet all "applicable or relevant and appropriate requirements" (ARARs) in determining a cleanup standard.

The identification of ARARs is determined on a site-specific basis, following the completion of a remedial investigation/feasibility study. "Applicable requirements" are those cleanup standards and other substantive environmental protection requirements, criteria, or limitations adopted or promulgated under federal, state, or local law that directly apply and address remediation or other circumstances at the site. "Relevant and appropriate requirements" are those cleanup standards promulgated under federal, state, or local law that address similar circumstances to those encountered at the CERCLA site.[77] CERCLA cleanups must achieve ARARs and otherwise provide "overall protection of human health and environment."[78] Also included in the remedy selection process are various balancing criteria (such as the permanence of the remedy, its implementability, and its cost) and modifying criteria (state acceptance and community acceptance).[79]

If a developer moves a site through a state voluntary cleanup program or otherwise addresses site contamination through the state's authority, the state will provide specific cleanup standards, often depending on the intended use of the property. Some state programs require preparation of a baseline health risk assessment (HRA). The HRA helps to determine the level of cleanup necessary to ensure long-term protection of human health and the environment. In addition, risk-based corrective action tailors cleanup standards to the risk associated with human and ecological populations.[80]

Institutional controls also can play an important role in the redevelopment of brownfields.[81] These controls are generally inexpensive substitutes for more complicated and costly remediation actions. EPA defines "institutional controls" as measures that "either prohibit certain kinds of site uses, or, at a minimum, notify potential owners or land users of the presence of hazardous substances remaining on site at levels that are not protective for all uses."[82] However, on the federal level, institutional controls may not substitute for active response measures, and they are typically applied where property will be put to industrial or commercial, rather than residential, use.[83]

The most common types of institutional controls are deed notices, deed restrictions, and access restrictions. Deed notice provisions put subsequent purchasers on notice of site contamination,[84] while deed restrictions usually prohibit specific types of use or construction on the property.[85] Access restrictions (such as fences) generally limit exposure of others to the site, and are used to ensure the protection of nearby residents.

Environmental Justice and Brownfields Redevelopment

Public Participation in Brownfields Cleanups

Brownfield redevelopment is of great concern to the affected communities. The level of the cleanup performed, and the nature of the new use of the property, will affect those living nearby for decades to come. Local communities are often concerned that EPA or states will lower cleanup standards in an effort to attract industry to an eroding urban center, which means that brownfields sites located near low-income or minority communities will remain permanently "dirty." Further, where cleanup standards are relaxed, it is not always certain that the benefits of jobs or tax revenues will outweigh the health risks associated with continued contamination.

One way to alleviate community fears about the potential injustices of a redevelopment project and to ensure that decisions reflect community concerns is to involve the public in the cleanup process. The legal mandates for public participation in environmental decision making are the subject of Chapter 7 of this book (see pages 185–229).[86] However, it should be noted here that the degree of required community involvement varies widely depending on the cleanup program involved. At the federal level, the National Contingency Plan (NCP) requires a private party undertaking removal or remedial actions to engage in "community relations," including an opportunity for public notice and comment.[87] In addition, CERCLA Section 122 settlements mandate public participation, but administrative consent orders, prospective purchaser agreements, and status and comfort levels do not. In brownfields programs receiving federal assistance, the degree of citizen participation has varied widely, ranging from intimate involvement in decision making to after-the-fact notification.[88]

State public participation requirements in voluntary cleanup programs also vary considerably. Some states require public notice or remedial actions,[89] some mandate public comment,[90] and a few require public hearings.[91] However, several states do not require public participation in brownfields redevelopment projects at all.[92]

Nevertheless, a developer may always voluntarily meet with the community, either in public sessions, in private meetings, or in any combination.[93] In addition, a developer may consult a community advisory board regarding local concerns about a project. EPA encourages federal agencies to create site-specific citizen advisory boards when making decisions about cleaning up and redeveloping contaminated federal property.[94] Public consultations tend to build mutual trust between communities and developers, and to improve the quality and durability of decisions that are made.

Further, EPA and many states promote brownfields remediation in federal "empowerment zones" or "state enterprise zones."[95] Such zones provide special tax incentives and job training programs to increase the likelihood that local residents will fill an adequate portion of the new jobs created by a brownfields redevelopment project.[96]

Part of the difficulty in determining an appropriate mode of citizen participation in a brownfields project stems from the differing objectives of the parties. To the developer, brownfield redevelopments are generally straightforward real estate projects. Anything that slows down the approval process or imposes restrictions on the nature or scale of development is unwelcome and costly, unless it confers tangible economic benefits of some sort. To neighbors, the fate of a site is often tightly bound to the community's aspirations for its future economic, social, and environmental development. In the community's eyes, a decision made on purely economic grounds will miss many of the most important factors, and represents yet another violation of a community's right to self-determination.[97] Thus, these are ultimately political and social issues, and the legal framework only loosely determines the outer bounds of permissible modes of participation.

Effect of Title VI Guidance

Although the effect of EPA's Title VI Guidance (discussed in Chapter 2, pages 23–68) remains to be seen, many states and developers fear that the policy will actually hinder brownfields redevelopment. Critics of the policy claim that it creates a new layer of requirements that supersede existing environmental mandates. Critics charge that the policy will stall rehabilitation because it will be much more difficult for new facilities on brownfields sites to acquire necessary environmental permits.

In addition, many states are concerned that EPA's policy creates confusion over intergovernmental relations. That is, states are worried that the policy will establish a new type of federal permit system. For example, if a state grants a facility permit and then an environmental justice complaint is filed that claims that the placement of the facility has a disparate impact, states fear this will undermine the state and local role in granting environmental permits.

Critics of EPA's Title VI guidance also fear that the policy will result in delays in the permitting process. Under the policy, complaints may be filed up to 180 days after the issuance of a permit. This casts into doubt the finality of the permits, and may inhibit the availability of financing or the ability to start work on the project until the expiration of this 180-day period and the resolution of any complaints that are filed.

These potential effects have not been realized. EPA officials have stated that there has never been a formal civil rights complaint against a brownfields project (though some have been threatened). An EPA study has concluded that Title VI has not, in fact, impeded brownfields development.[98]

Notes

1. U.S. GENERAL ACCOUNTING OFFICE, SUPERFUND: BARRIERS TO BROWNFIELD REDEVELOPMENT, GAO/RCED-96-125 (Jun. 17, 1996). *See generally* BROWNFIELDS LAW AND PRACTICE: THE CLEANUP AND REDEVELOPMENT OF CONTAMINATED LAND (Michael B. Gerrard ed., Matthew Bender 1998) [hereinafter Gerrard ed., BROWNFIELDS].

2. *See generally* P. Kibel, *The Urban Nexus: Open Space, Brownfields, and Justice,* 25 B.C. ENVTL. AFF. L. REV. 589 (1998); S. Johnson, *The Brownfields Action Agenda: A Model for Future Federal/State Cooperation in the Quest for Environmental Justice?*, 37 SANTA CLARA L. REV. 85 (1996).

3. 42 U.S.C. § 9607(a)(1).

4. United States v. Maryland Bank & Trust Co., 632 F. Supp. 573 (D. Md. 1986).

5. United States v. Fleet Factors Corp., 901 F.2d 1550, 1557–58 (11th Cir. 1990), *cert. denied,* 498 U.S. 1046 (1991).

6. *See* Stephen L. Kass & Michael B. Gerrard, *The Return of Lender Liability,* N.Y.L.J., Feb. 25, 1994, at 3:1.

7. Pub. L. No. 104-208, § 2502, 110 Stat. 3009.

8. 40 C.F.R. Pt. 300, Appendix B. *See* Gerrard ed., BROWNFIELDS, *supra* note 1, at ch. 13. For a discussion of additional mechanisms for cleaning up Superfund sites, see Chapter 16, *supra,* "Cleaning Up Abandoned and Inactive Contaminated Sites," pages 522–60.

9. 60 Fed. Reg. 34,793 (1995).

10. *Id.*

11. *Id.*

12. 60 Fed. Reg. 34,794 (1995).

13. *Id.*

14. *Id.*

15. *Id.*

16. *Id.*

17. 60 Fed. Reg. 37,497 (1995).

18. 62 Fed. Reg. 4624 (1997).

19. *Id.*

20. *Id.*

21. *See* GERRARD ed., BROWNFIELDS, *supra* note 1, at ch. 14.

22. 42 U.S.C. § 9620(a)(2).

23. Pub. L. No. 102-426, 106 Stat. 2176 (1992).

24. 42 U.S.C. § 9620(h)(4)(A).

25. 42 U.S.C. § 9620(h)(4)(A).

26. 42 U.S.C. § 9620 (h)(3)(C)(i)(IV).

27. EPA Memorandum, Transmittal of the Model Comfort Letter Clarifying NPL Listing, Uncontaminated Parcel Identification, and CERCLA Liability Involving Transfers of Federally Owned Property (Aug. 9, 1995).

28. 42 U.S.C. § 9620(h)(3)(A).

29. National Defense Authorization Act for Fiscal Year 1994, Pub. L. No. 103-160, 107 Stat. 1547, § 2903 (1993).

30. Pub. L. No. 103-421, 108 Stat. 4346 (1994), *amended by* Pub. L. No. 104-106, 110 Stat. 186 (1996).

31. *See* DEPARTMENT OF DEFENSE, COMMUNITY GUIDE TO BASE REUSE 19–24 (May 1995).

32. Acquired land was originally purchased by DOE from private owners; withdrawn land is land that has been taken from the Department of Interior's lands in the public domain for use by a federal agency.

33. *See* DOE/EM-0284, RESOURCEFUL REUSE: A GUIDE TO PLANNING FUTURE USES OF DEPARTMENT OF ENERGY SITES (May 1996).

34. *Id.*

35. Gerrard ed., BROWNFIELDS, at. ch. 15. *See also* Chapter 16, "Cleaning Up Abandoned or Inactive Contaminated Sites," pages 522–60, *supra.*

36. For more information on state cleanup standards, see U.S. GOVERNMENT ACCOUNTING OFFICE, SUPERFUND: HOW STATES ESTABLISH AND APPLY ENVIRONMENTAL STANDARDS WHEN CLEANING UP SITES, GAO/RCED-96-70FS (Mar. 20, 1996).

37. State programs that *do* adopt CERCLA's imposition of joint and several liability include: Connecticut, CONN. GEN. STAT. § 22a-443; Delaware, DEL. CODE ANN. tit. 7, § 9105(b); Illinois, 20 ILL. COMP. STAT. § 2305/3(f); Indiana, IND. CODE § 13-7-8.7-8(a); Maine, ME. REV. STAT. ANN. tit. 38, § 1367; Montana, MONT. CODE ANN. § 75-10-715(2); New Hampshire, N.H. REV. STAT. ANN. § 147-B:10.I(d), New Jersey, N.J. REV. STAT. § 58:10-23.11g(c)(1); Pennsylvania, PA. STAT. ANN. tit. 35, § 6020.702(a); and Washington, WASH. REV. CODE § 70.105D.040(2). Those states that *do not* adopt CERCLA's approach of imposing joint and several liability include: Alabama, ALA. CODE § 22-30-A-8(c); Arkansas, ARK. CODE ANN. § 8-7-513(a)(2); California, CAL. HEALTH & SAFETY CODE § 25363; Louisiana, LA. REV. STAT. ANN. § 2276.F; Tennessee, TENN. CODE ANN. §§ 68-46-207(b)(1)(A), 68-46-207(b)(3); Utah, UTAH CODE ANN. § 19-6-316(2)(a)(I); and Wisconsin, WIS. STAT. § 144.422(9)(c).

38. *See e.g.,* CONN. GEN. STAT. § 22a-134b; IND. CODE § 13-25-3-3; IOWA CODE ANN. § 455B.430(1); and N.J. STAT. ANN. § 13:1K-13. For more detail on state property transfer laws, *see* Gerrard ed., BROWNFIELDS, *supra* note 1, at ch. 16.

39. *See, e.g.,* N.J. STAT. ANN. § 13:1K-9.

40. N.J. STAT. ANN. § 13:1K-7.

41. CONN. GEN. STAT. §§ 22a-134–22a-134d.

42. *See* DEL. CODE ANN. tit. 7, §§ 9104(b)(2), 9115(a)(1)–(5); MINN. STAT. § 115B.16(2); N.C. GEN. STAT. § 130A-310.8; PA. STAT. ANN. tit. 35, § 6018.405; and R.I. GEN. LAWS § 5-20.8-2.

43. *See* KY. REV. STAT. ANN. § 224.46-510(1)(a); MASS. GEN. LAWS ch. 21c, § 7; and NEB. ADMIN. R. & REGS. tit. 128, Ch. 14, § 007.

44. *See* ARK. CODE ANN. § 8-7-417 (ERFA), § 8-7-516 (RAFTA); DEL. CODE. ANN. tit. 7, § 9115(b).

45. *See* ARIZ. REV. STAT. ANN. § 33-434.01; CAL. HEALTH & SAFETY CODE § 25359.7; D.C. MUN. REGS. tit. 20, § 4302.3; O.C.G.A. § 12-8-97(b), GA. COMP. R. & REGS. r. 391-3-19-.08(1); 765 ILL. COMP. STAT. § 90/4(a); IND. CODE ANN. § 13-25-3-7; MICH. COMP. LAWS § 324.20116; MO. REV. STAT. § 260.465, MO. CODE REGS. ANN. tit. 10, § 25-10.010(3)(B); and W.VA. CODE § 22-18-21.

46. *See generally* Gerrard ed., BROWNFIELDS, *supra* note 1, at ch. 17. For more detail on individual state voluntary cleanup programs, see Gerrard ed., BROWNFIELDS, *supra* note 1, at vol. 2.

47. In those states that *do* allow parties that caused or contributed to the release of contamination to participate in a VCP, the state will not give such "responsible parties" the same liability protections that are given to other volunteers. *See, e.g.*, COLO. REV. STAT. § 25-16-301 *et seq.*; 415 ILL. COMP. STAT. 5/58.1-58.12; MD. CODE ANN., ENVIR. § 7-501 *et seq.*; MICH. COMP. LAWS § 324.20101 *et seq.*; MINN. STAT. ANN. §§ 115.B.175–115.B.177; N.J. ADMIN. CODE tit. 7, § 26C; PA. STAT. ANN. tit. 35, § 6026.101 *et seq.*; R.I. GEN. LAWS § 23-19.14-1 *et seq.*; and TEX. HEALTH & SAFETY CODE ANN. § 361.601 *et seq.*

48. *See, e.g.*, IND. CODE ANN. § 13-7-8.9-15(b); KY. REV. STAT. ANN. § 224.01-400(18).

49. *See* Gerrard ed., BROWNFIELDS, *supra* note 1, at ch. 18. There are more than 5,000 hazardous waste TSD facilities that require cleanup under RCRA. *See* 61 Fed. Reg. 19,432, 19,440 (1996).

50. 40 C.F.R. § 264.100(b).

51. *See* 55 Fed. Reg. 19,432, 19,447 (proposed May 1, 1996).

52. 55 Fed. Reg. 19,432, 19,454 (proposed May 1, 1996).

53. *See* subtitle I, 42 U.S.C. §§ 6901 *et seq.*; 40 C.F.R. pt. 280.

54. 42 U.S.C. §§ 6901 *et seq.*

55. 42 U.S.C. § 6991(1); 40 C.F.R. § 280.12.

56. *See* 42 U.S.C. §§ 6991(1)(A)-(1), 6991c(a); 40 C.F.R. § 2810.12.

57. *See* Gerrard ed., BROWNFIELDS, *supra* note 1, ch. 18.

58. RCRA § 9004(a); 42 U.S.C. § 6991c(a).

59. RCRA § 9002(a)(1), 42 U.S.C. § 6991a(a)(1). The applicable state agencies are identified in 40 C.F.R. pt. 280, app. II.

60. 40 C.F.R. § 280.71.

61. 40 C.F.R. § 280.71(b).

62. 40 C.F.R. §§ 280.71(a); 280.72.

63. December 28, 1998 was the deadline for compliance with EPA's 1988 UST regulations. Those regulations required all substandard systems installed before December 22, 1988 that were not already protected against corrosion, spills, and overfills, to be upgraded, replaced, or properly closed. *See* 40 C.F.R. pt. 280.

64. 40 C.F.R. § 280.70(a).

65. *See* Gerrard ed., BROWNFIELDS, *supra* note 1, at ch. 19.

66. 29 U.S.C. § 651 *et seq.*

67. *See* Kane v. United States, 15 F.3d 87 (9th Cir. 1994); 42 U.S.C. § 9601; Gerrard ed., BROWNFIELDS, *supra* note 1, at 19-3.

68. 40 C.F.R. pt. 300.

69. CAA § 112, 42 U.S.C. § 7412; 40 C.F.R. pt. 61, subpt. M.

70. CAA § 113(b) & (c).

71. *See* Gerrard ed., BROWNFIELDS, *supra* note 1, at ch. 27.

72. *See* 62 Fed. Reg. 24,915 (May 7, 1997).

73. *See* Gerrard ed., BROWNFIELDS, *supra* note 1, at ch. 30.

74. *See* Gerrard ed., BROWNFIELDS, *supra note* 1, at 27-31, 32.

75. For example, Connecticut has a UST Clean-Up Review Board that oversees a UST Clean-Up Account from which an applicant can request reimbursements and payments for costs, expenses, or other obligations incurred as a result of UST releases. CONN. GEN. STAT. § 22a-449(c), (d). States that have established

dry cleaner solvent trust fund programs include: Florida, Georgia, Kansas, Minnesota, North Carolina, South Carolina, Tennessee, and Wisconsin. *See* Gerrard ed., BROWNFIELDS, *supra* note 1, at vol. 2.

76. *See* Gerrard ed., BROWNFIELDS, *supra* note 1, at ch. 22.

77. *See* Gerrard ed., BROWNFIELDS, *supra* note 1, at 22-9. The key statutory and regulatory references for ARARs are 42 U.S.C. §§ 9621(b), (d), and 40 C.F.R. § 300.430(e).

78. 40 C.F.R. § 300.430(e)(9)(iii)(A).

79. 40 C.F.R. § 300.430(e)(9)(iii)(I).

80. The American Society for Testing and Materials (ASTM) has developed a risk-based corrective action standard framework. *See* Gerrard ed., BROWNFIELDS, *supra* note 1, at 22-15.

81. *See* Gerrard ed., BROWNFIELDS, *supra* note 1, at ch. 24.

82. LAND USE IN THE CERCLA REMEDY SELECTION PROCESS, OSWER Directive No. 9355.7-04.

83. *See* John S. Applegate & Stephen Dycus, *Institutional Controls or Emperor's Clothes? Long-Term Stewardship of the Nuclear Weapons Complex*, 28 ENVT'L L. REP. 10,631 (November 1998); George Wyeth, *Land Use and Cleanups: Beyond the Rhetoric*, 26 ENVT'L L. REP. 10,358 (July 1996); ROBERT HERSH ET AL., LINKING LAND USE AND SUPERFUND CLEANUP: UNCHARTERED TERRITORY (Resources for the Future 1996).

84. *E.g.*, 42 U.S.C. § 9620(h)(3)(A)(i) (CERCLA); 40 C.F.R. § 264.119 (RCRA).

85. Many legal issues arise in the enforcement of deed restrictions. *See* Susan F. French, *Servitudes Reform and the New Restatement of Property: Creation Doctrines and Structural Simplification*, 73 CORNELL L. REV. 928 (1988).

86. *See also* Bradford C. Mank, *Public Participation in the Cleanup and Redevelopment Process*, in BROWNFIELDS LAW AND PRACTICE: THE CLEANUP AND REDEVELOPMENT OF CONTAMINATED LAND, at vol. I, ch. 31 (Michael B. Gerrard ed., Matthew Bender 1998).

87. *See* 40 C.F.R. § 300.415(n)(2)(i)(ii).

88. Center for Energy and Environmental Policy, University of Delaware, *The Brownfields Challenge: A Survey of Environmental Justice and Community Participation Initiatives Among Ten National Brownfield Pilot Projects* (May 1999); Lincoln L. Davies, *Working Toward a Common Goal? Three Case Studies of Brownfields Redevelopment in Environmental Justice Communities*, 18 STANFORD ENVT'L L. J. 285 (1999)

89. *See, e.g.*, ARK. CODE ANN. § 8-7-523(d)(3); CAL. HEALTH & SAFETY CODE § 25398(d)(1); and PA. STAT. ANN. tit. 35, § 6026.302(e) to -.303(h), to name a few.

90. *See, e.g.*, CAL. HEALTH & SAFETY CODE § 25398(d)(1), 25398.7(c)(2); IND. CODE § 13-25-5-11(b); MICH. COMP. LAWS ANN. § 324.20120d(3); and VT. STAT. ANN. tit. 10, § 6615a(h)(5), to name a few.

91. *See, e.g.*, CAL. HEALTH & SAFETY CODE § 25398(d)(2); MASS. REGS. CODE tit. 310, § 40.1404; and PA. STAT. ANN. tit. 35, § 6026.304(o).

92. These states include Colorado, Illinois, Louisiana, Maine, Missouri, New Hampshire, New Jersey, Ohio, and Washington.

93. *See* Michael B. Gerrard, *Building Environmentally Just Projects*, N.Y. ENVTL LAW., May 1996, at 1.

94. *See* Gerrard ed., BROWNFIELDS, *supra* note 1, at 31-13.

95. In 1997, President Clinton signed a tax relief bill that includes a provision giving special tax advantages to brownfields developers who locate in certain low-income areas, including federal empowerment or enterprise zones. *See* H.R. 2014 (1997).

96. The American Society for Testing and Materials is currently developing a standard to streamline brownfields cleanup that calls for community participation in each state of redevelopment. *Guide to Process of Sustainable Brownfields Redevelopment,* E1984 (to be published in early 1999).

97. *See* Rachel D. Godsil & James S. Freeman, *Jobs, Trees and Autonomy: The Convergence of the Environmental Justice Movement and Community Economic Development,* 5 MD. J. CONTEMP. LEGAL ISSUES 25 (1993–94).

98. U.S. Environmental Protection Agency, Office of Solid Waste and Emergency Response, Pub. No. EPA 500-R-99-003, *Brownfields Title VI Case Studies* (June 1999).

CHAPTER 18

Controlling Residential Exposure

BARNETT LAWRENCE

Introduction

The environmental laws enacted since the 1970s have strengthened the protection of the outdoor environment—the air, land, and water. However, much less attention has been given to the indoor environment, where we spend most of our time.[1] Most of the regulations affecting the indoor environment have focused on occupational exposure. Although the U.S. Environmental Protection Agency (EPA) has identified exposure to indoor air pollution as a significant health hazard that may exceed the dangers of outdoor pollution,[2] there is no comprehensive state or federal regulation of residential indoor air quality.[3]

Some federal and state regulations address bits and pieces of the residential environment. However, the most important remedies for residents harmed by exposure to residential contaminants are often state tort law claims. Different remedies may be available for apartment renters, renters living in housing owned or subsidized by the government,[4] house renters, and homeowners. Low-income people are especially vulnerable to certain indoor pollutants, such as lead paint. A number of indoor air problems are associated with older and inadequately maintained buildings, where low-income people are more likely to live.

This chapter presents the legal remedies available to address various sources of residential contamination, including lead paint, asbestos, radon, pesticides, and other indoor air pollutants. The available remedies under statutory and common law may include forcing the responsible party to remediate the contamination, or obtaining some form of compensation, such as damages for personal injuries or property damage.

The chapter concludes with a brief discussion of a particular type of dietary exposure that may have a disproportionate impact on low-income people: consumption of contaminated fish by subsistence fishermen.

Indoor Air Pollution

Sources and Health Hazards

Residential exposure to indoor air pollutants can come from a variety of sources,[5] including:

- lead-based paint;[6]
- asbestos;[7]
- pesticides;[8]
- radon;[9]
- formaldehyde;
- inadequate heating, ventilation, and air conditioning (HVAC) systems;
- biological contaminants, such as bacterial, molds, mildew, viruses, dust mites, cockroaches, and pollen;
- combustion products, such as unvented kerosene and gasoline space heaters, wood and gas stoves, and fireplaces;
- perchloroethylene emissions from dry cleaners;
- household cleaning and maintenance products; and
- paint.

Health effects from exposure to indoor air pollutants depend on the particular pollutant, but can include irritation of the eyes, nose, and throat; headaches; dizziness and fatigue; respiratory diseases; heart disease; cancer; chronic organ damage; and acute toxicity.[10] Health effects often develop only after repeated exposures and can vary substantially from person to person.[11] The precise impacts of some indoor air pollutants at the levels typically found in homes are subject to scientific debate.

Inadequate HVAC systems can intensify indoor air pollution by not bringing in enough outdoor air to dilute emissions from indoor sources and by not carrying indoor pollutants out of the home. Faulty HVAC systems can also sometimes lead to serious problems, such as carbon monoxide poisoning.

Urea-formaldehyde foam insulation (UFFI),[12] carpeting, and certain pressed-wood products can be sources of formaldehyde.[13] Formaldehyde is a respiratory and skin irritant and potential carcinogen. Household products, such as paints, wax, cleaning products, and cosmetics, often contain volatile organic compounds (VOCs). EPA has found that levels of certain common organic pollutants can be two to five times higher inside homes than outside, regardless of whether the homes were located in rural or industrialized areas.

VOC emissions and other fumes from paint can be hazardous to residents during painting operations and for several days after painting.[14] Apartment buildings are especially vulnerable to indoor air quality problems from painting, since vapors can travel through ventilation systems and affect people far from the paint's source. Pregnant women and children are thought to be the most vulnerable to VOCs. Paint fumes can cause eye irritation and short-term central nervous system symptoms such as headaches, nausea, and dizziness.

Another potential source of indoor pollution for some apartment residents is emissions of perchlorethylene (perc) from dry cleaners. High concentrations of perc, particularly in closed, poorly ventilated areas, can cause dizziness, headaches, sleepiness, confusion, nausea, and difficulty in speaking and walking.[15] Studies have linked long-term exposure to perc to cancer, kidney and liver damage, harm to the reproductive system, and possible toxicity to the central nervous system.[16]

Role of Residential Segregation in Exposure

The role that residential exposure plays in exposure to indoor air pollutants varies with the particular pollutant. For example, only residents of apartments located adjacent to dry cleaners are likely to suffer significantly from perc emissions. Formaldehyde emissions were formerly a major problem for residents of certain prefabricated and mobile homes and homes insulated with UFFI. About 500,000 homes still contain UFFI, although it is no longer used in new products. Older homes and homes with inadequately maintained HVAC systems are more likely to have problems with biological contaminants.

Federal Regulation

There is no comprehensive federal program to regulate indoor air quality in private homes.[17] EPA has developed several educational programs.[18] The Occupational Safety and Health Administration (OSHA) regulates worker exposure to indoor air contaminants.[19] Some federal laws affect specific indoor air pollutants, such as asbestos, pesticides, and radon.[20] EPA has issued rules that regulate VOC emissions from various consumer products and paints.[21]

State Regulation

A number of states have their own indoor air quality (IAQ) programs, although most focus on occupational exposure, smoking, or specific substances.[22] State environmental or health departments may have educational programs for indoor air quality. Some state agencies will conduct IAQ consultations with building owners.

Most state and local governments have adopted a building code that applies to residential construction. These codes provide minimum standards for protecting health and safety, and may include ventilation requirements.[23] Housing codes generally hold the owner responsible for maintaining the property and prohibit leasing of rental units that are out of compliance. A few states provide tenants with legal remedies for code violations.[24]

Voluntary Standards

Some professional organizations have issued voluntary standards for indoor air quality. One of the most influential voluntary standards is the ventilation standard issued by the American Society of Heating, Refrigeration, and Air Conditioning Engineers (ASHRAE). The current standard, known as ASHRAE 62-1989, defines acceptable indoor air quality as "air in which there are no known contaminants at harmful concentrations as determined by cognizant authorities and with which a substantial majority (80% or more) of the people exposed do not express dissatisfaction."[25]

Tort Actions

State law tort actions are sometimes the only or best remedy for people harmed by residential exposure to indoor pollutants. Plaintiffs often name multiple defendants in indoor air quality cases, since numerous factors can contribute to indoor pollution and plaintiffs may not know the specific cause of their injuries. Potential defendants include landlords, builders, architects, engineers, general contractors, subcontractors, sellers, and real estate brokers. Suits may also be brought against manufacturers for injuries caused by exposure to manufactured substances in the home.

Plaintiffs in indoor air quality cases have several potential causes of action.[26] Negligence and strict liability are the most common. Other theories of liability include breach of express or implied warranties, misrepresentation or fraud, and trespass or nuisance.[27]

Negligence claims allege that a defendant breached a duty to exercise reasonable care.[28] Tenants may bring negligence claims alleging that landlords breached their general duty to maintain the premises free of defects or breached their duty to warn of latent defects.

Plaintiffs may also assert a negligence per se theory, in which plaintiffs allege that statutory requirements established a standard of conduct breached by the defendant.

In addition to negligence claims, plaintiffs in indoor air quality and other toxic tort cases often assert strict liability claims. These claims relieve plaintiffs of the burden of proving unreasonable conduct by the defendant. To assert a strict liability claim, plaintiffs must assert that the defendant engaged in an usually dangerous activity[29] or that it designed or manufactured a defective product.[30] A product can be defective because of its manufacture or design. For example, a mobile home that does not permit sufficient ventilation could be considered to have a design defect.

Landlords were traditionally immune from tort liability for injuries to tenants resulting from defects in the premises. However, most state courts have recognized an implied warranty of habitability in rental housing. Some states have codified this implied warranty.[31] In those states with a common law or statutory warranty of habitability, tenants can sue for injuries caused by unfit housing. Habitability is generally defined broadly to protect tenants' safety, health, or well-being.[32] Although the scope may vary from state to state, the warranty of habitability generally provides that a landlord implicitly warrants that there are no latent defects in the unit and that the landlord will maintain the unit in habitable condition. Plaintiffs may have to show that the landlord had knowledge of the dangerous condition.

Residents of rental housing that is owned or subsidized by the government may have additional grounds for asserting claims. This housing must comply not only with state statutory and common law requirements, but also with any standards contained in the regulations governing the subsidy program.[33]

Plaintiffs may seek the traditional common law damages of personal injuries, property damage, and economic injury. Personal injuries can include a wide range of temporary and permanent conditions, as well as death. Property damages can be measured by the reduced value of a building or the costs of correcting the indoor air quality problem. Plaintiffs may also seek damages under various novel theories developed in toxic tort litigation, including increased risk of cancer or other disease,[34] medical monitoring, and emotional distress.[35] Tenants may seek rent abatement and repairs from their landlords in some jurisdictions. To succeed with these claims, tenants usually must have notified the landlord of the defective condition and allowed a reasonable amount of time for the landlord to make repairs.

Thousands of suits have been filed involving UFFI. These suits were filed against formaldehyde manufacturers, architects, builders, contractors, building product manufacturers, and real estate agents. Most cases that went to trial resulted in defense verdicts. UFFI has been effectively taken off the markets, and the number of lawsuits has tapered off.[36] In one case, property owners filed a tort suit against the company that installed UFFI. The complaint alleged that noxious fumes from insulation caused allergic reactions and repulsed visitors. The Alaska Supreme Court held that plaintiffs stated claims for breach of warranty, strict products liability, and negligence.[37]

Apartment residents located above or adjacent to dry cleaners may be able to sue their landlords or the dry cleaners for exposure to perchloroethylene. Landlords may be subject to claims for constructive eviction, while dry cleaners may be subject to personal injury claims. In one New York case, two families living in a New York City apartment building withheld rent because of perc emissions from a dry cleaner below their apartments.[38] Air samples taken from the apartments indicated that perc exposure levels were well above levels considered safe by the New York State Department of Health.[39] The court held that the continuous presence of perc fumes in the apartments constituted constructive eviction and a breach of the warranty of habitability. The court awarded the residents a 75 percent rent abatement for the period of exposure.

Litigation Hurdles

Plaintiffs in IAQ cases can face all the barriers common to toxic tort actions.[40] The statute of limitations can sometimes present a challenge because of the long latency periods for some diseases.[41] Proving that the defendant caused the plaintiff's injury can also be difficult. Plaintiffs may have trouble pinpointing the specific substance or condition that caused the injuries, or in establishing that a specific defendant among several potential defendants should be liable.

Many issues are highly technical and at the frontiers of scientific knowledge. The admissibility of scientific evidence can be critical. In *Daubert v. Merrell Dow Pharmaceuticals*,[42] the U.S. Supreme Court clarified the standard for admitting expert testimony under the Federal Rules of Evidence.[43] The Court found that when faced with a proffer of expert scientific testimony, the trial judge must first determine whether the expert is proposing to testify to: 1) scientific knowledge that 2) will assist the trier of fact to understand or determine a fact in issue. This requires the trial judge to make a preliminary assessment of whether the reasoning or methodology underlying the testimony is scientifically valid and whether that reasoning or methodology can properly be applied to the facts in issue.

The Court in *Daubert* set out a list of four nonexclusive factors for determining the admissibility of expert testimony:

1. whether the theory or technique has been or could be tested;

2. whether the theory or technique has been subject to peer review or publication;
3. the known or potential rate of error; and
4. the general acceptance of the technique by the relevant scientific community.

The 4th Circuit recently applied the *Daubert* test to a case in which plaintiffs alleged that they were injured by exposure to fumes from a carpet in their home.[44] Plaintiffs sued the carpet manufacturer and retailer, and alleged that they suffered from nosebleeds, rashes, extreme sweating, chills, sleeplessness, and racing of the heart. Plaintiffs asserted claims for breach of implied warranty of merchantability, breach of express warranty, strict liability, and negligence. Plaintiffs' expert witness performed a test in which she heated a sample of the carpet to 98 degrees Fahrenheit inside a sealed glass container, and then circulated the air from the container into a second room that contained four mice. The expert witness found sensory and pulmonary irritation in the mice, which suggested to the expert that humans could suffer the same symptoms. The 4th Circuit found that plaintiffs' evidence failed to pass the *Daubert* test, since EPA was unable to duplicate the expert's test results, peer reviewers criticized the expert's methodology, and the expert's technique was not generally accepted in the toxicological community.

Multiple Chemical Sensitivity

Some people have alleged that they suffer from a condition called multiple chemical sensitivity (MCS) that causes them to have severe reactions to very low concentrations of chemicals in indoor air. The scientific community is divided over the existence of MCS, and whether its causes are physical, psychological, or both. The theory behind MCS is that various types of chemical exposures may depress a person's immune system so that the exposed person becomes hypersensitive to chemicals and some naturally occurring substances.[45] It may be caused by either an initial acute exposure to a large quantity of a chemical, or by continuing low-level exposures.

Plaintiffs have had very limited success in bringing lawsuits alleging MCS, but they have won some jury awards.[46] In addition, HUD has determined that MCS can constitute a handicap under the Fair Housing Act.[47]

Every federal court that has addressed the issue of the admissibility of expert testimony on MCS under the *Daubert* standard has found that the testimony was too speculative to meet the requirement of scientific knowledge.[48] In one case, a state employee alleged that she contracted MCS as the result of exposure to pesticide sprayed in her office building, but the court excluded her expert testimony on MCS.[49]

Sick Building Syndrome

Sick building syndrome (SBS) describes situations in which building occupants complain of health-related problems that they attribute to the building's indoor environment, but for which no specific causes can be readily identified.[50] Building occupants can develop eye irritation, dizziness, nausea, headaches, rashes, and upper respiratory problems. Potential sources include poorly designed HVAC systems and chemical and biological contaminants. SBS claims have been raised in numerous lawsuits in recent years, mostly involving commercial buildings.[51] Suits have been brought by building owners against building designers and construction companies. Commercial tenants have filed suits against building owners, designers, and construction companies. Individuals have filed personal injury suits against all these parties.[52]

Lead Exposure

Sources and Health Hazards

Exposure to lead, even in small amounts, can be harmful, especially to children and pregnant women. According to the Centers for Disease Control, lead poisoning is one of the most common childhood health problems.[53] Lead exposure can be harmful to children because they absorb a greater portion of the lead to which they are exposed than adults, and their rapidly developing nervous systems are particularly sensitive. Lead exposure in children can cause learning disabilities, lower intelligence, behavioral problems, growth impairment, permanent hearing and visual impairment, and other damage to the brain and nervous system.[54]

Chronic exposure to low levels of lead can cause memory and concentration problems in adults, as well as hypertension, cardiovascular disease, and damage to the male reproductive system. Exposure to lead before or during pregnancy can alter fetal development and cause miscarriages.

There are a number of potential sources of lead exposure. Lead was formerly used in many products, including gasoline, plumbing hardware, solder, pottery, and crystal. Lead can be found in drinking water in homes with lead pipes. Although EPA banned leaded gasoline, the lead that was released into the air from this gasoline can still be found in the ground in some places.[55]

The greatest risk of residential lead exposure, especially for children, is lead-based paint chips or paint dust. Houses built before

1978 may contain lead paint.[56] Children may ingest lead paint particles by eating paint chips or putting fingers coated with paint dust in their mouths.[57]

Role of Residential Segregation in Exposure

Several studies have demonstrated that lead poisoning has a disproportionate impact on African American children and children in low-income families. These children are more likely to live in older housing, which is more likely to have lead paint. One survey found that the incidence of elevated blood levels among African American children between one and two years old was 2.5 times higher than for white children.[58]

Federal Regulation

In response to the recognition of lead's health hazards, the federal government has enacted a number of laws and regulations. EPA phased out the use of lead in gasoline. The Consumer Product Safety Commission banned the use of lead-based paint in residential housing in 1978.[59]

In 1992, Congress enacted the Residential Lead-Based Paint Hazard Reduction Act (commonly called Title X).[60] In 1996, EPA and HUD issued disclosure regulations to implement Title X.[61] Title X requires sellers and lessors of most residential property built before 1978 (called "target housing") to inform purchasers and lessees about any lead paint hazards and give purchasers a 10-day period to conduct an inspection.[62] The law does not require testing for, or removal of, lead paint.

Before a tenant signs a lease or rental agreement, Title X requires the landlord to give the tenant an EPA pamphlet entitled *Protecting Your Family from Lead in Your Home* and inform the tenant of the presence of known lead-based paint. The notice is based on actual knowledge and does not require the landlord to undertake any special studies to obtain that knowledge. The landlord and tenant must sign an EPA-approved disclosure form that states that the landlord informed the tenant about any known lead-based paint hazards.[63]

If a seller or landlord fails to comply with Title X, the sale or lease is still valid. The remedy for a buyer or tenant is to recover civil monetary penalties. HUD and EPA have the primary enforcement authority, and may impose civil fines of up to $10,000 per day.[64] EPA may also pursue criminal sanctions under the Toxic Substances Control Act (TSCA).

Title X also creates a private right of action,[65] which can be brought by any purchaser or tenant for treble damages against any person who knowingly violated the Residential Lead-Based Paint Hazard Reduction Act. Damages could conceivably include reducing the value of the property, paying for injuries caused by lead poisoning, or following through on what the buyer or tenant would have done if disclosure had been provided.[66]

EPA adopted another disclosure regulation in 1998 to implement the pre-renovation education program in TSCA § 406(b).[67] The rule requires building contractors, renovation companies, and certain property management companies who plan to renovate or remodel housing built before 1978 to disclose possible lead-based paint hazards. These companies must distribute the EPA pamphlet on lead-based paint hazards to occupants before renovation or remodeling. The rule took effect on June 1, 1999. EPA estimates that the rule will affect 12 million renovation and remodeling projects annually.[68]

Also in 1998, EPA issued proposed rules under the Residential Lead-Based Paint Hazard Reduction Act to establish criteria for identifying lead-based paint hazards.[69] The rules set numerical hazard levels for lead-contaminated paint, dust, and soil. These regulations will play a critical role in the federal lead-based paint program. Risk assessors will use the standards to determine if lead-based paint hazards exist in pre–1978 housing. Property owners will use the standards to identify conditions that must be disclosed before the lease or sale of target housing. HUD will incorporate the standards into its regulations on lead-based paint control in federally assisted and owned housing. The standards may also be incorporated into local laws, housing codes, and lending and insurance underwriting standards.

Under TSCA, paint, dust, and soil are considered sources of lead that constitute lead-based paint hazards if exposure would result in adverse human health effects. EPA's proposed rule defines hazardous conditions for paint, dust, and soil. The rule provides that lead-based paint is in "poor condition" and therefore a hazard in the following conditions:

1. more than two square feet of deteriorated paint on interior components with large surface areas, such as inside walls, ceilings, floors, and doors;
2. more than 10 square feet of deteriorated paint on exterior components with large surface areas, such as outside walls; or
3. deteriorated paint on more than 10 percent of the total surface area of interior or exterior components with small surface areas, such as window sills, baseboards, soffits, and trim.[70]

Under the proposed rule, dust would be considered a hazard based on average measurements of the loading of lead in dust. Loading is the weight of lead present per unit of surface area. The proposed dust-lead hazard standards are 50 micrograms per square foot or higher for uncarpeted floors and 250 micrograms per square foot or higher for interior window sills. Bare soil on residential property and child-occupied facilities would be hazardous based on the yard-wide average lead concentration. The proposed hazard standard for soil is 2000 parts per million. EPA recommends removing or permanently covering soil containing lead that equals or exceeds this level.

EPA's proposed rule on identification of lead-based paint hazards does not require property owners to take any specific actions once the hazards are identified. EPA recommends that certain abatement actions be taken, and expects that concern about children's health, liability exposure, and other market forces will provide incentives for property owners to take action voluntarily.[71]

State Regulation

Many states and localities have enacted legislation to regulate lead-based paint in residential housing.[72] Some states have enacted consumer protection laws that have been extended to the landlord/tenant relationship.[73] Some states have statutory warranties of habitability that could apply to lead-based paint cases.[74]

Only a few states require the testing of dwellings for lead-based paint before a child becomes ill. Most state and local laws have adopted a "health approach," which consists of testing children for elevated blood levels, treating afflicted children, and then abating the hazard. For example, California's lead legislation focuses primarily on identifying and responding to lead-poisoned children.[75]

The "health approach" has been criticized for focusing on reducing the consequences of lead poisoning, but not its sources. A few states have responded by adopting the "housing approach" to lead regulation.[76] Under this approach, jurisdictions establish systematic programs to test housing and to abate lead-based paint hazards regardless of the presence of a child or the condition of a child's health.

Massachusetts has been one of the leaders in adopting an aggressive "housing approach." The Massachusetts Lead Poisoning Prevention and Control Act requires systematic inspection of housing for lead-based paint, and requires removal of lead-based paint before a child becomes ill.[77] Property owners must abate lead-based paint hazards if a child under six resides or is expected to reside at the premises. The property owner must also pay to relocate a tenant during lead abatement and for any additional rent. A property owner who receives a certification that the premises meets all statutory requirements cannot be held strictly liable for injury or damages caused by lead poisoning, but remains subject to the negligence standard of reasonable care. Property owners who fail to correct lead-based paint hazards after official notification are subject to punitive damages of three times actual damages.

New York City law requires apartment building owners to remove or cover lead-based paint on the interior walls, ceilings, doors, window sills, and moldings of apartments in which a child or children six years of age and under reside.[78] However, the highest court in New York has ruled that the New York City law does not establish a strict liability scheme, but requires a showing that the landlord was negligent.[79] The court held that the law imposes a standard of reasonableness on landlords to determine whether children six years old or under live in their apartments, but does not require them to inspect for the presence of children. To be liable under the New York City law, a landlord must have actual or constructive notice of both the hazardous lead condition and the residency of a child six years old or younger. Where a landlord has notice that a child under the specified age lives in an apartment, the law provides for constructive notice of the hazardous lead condition.

Tort Law

Litigation on behalf of children suffering from lead poisoning is generally brought against the landlord of the residence of the lead-exposed child.[80] Suits have also been brought against property management companies, public housing authorities, cities, lenders,[81] realtors, childcare facilities, and contractors. An especially high number of cases have been brought in northeast states, including Massachusetts, New York, and Maryland. Plaintiffs have obtained a number of large verdicts and settlements against landlords and other defendants. The major remedies available to plaintiffs include rent abatement, repairs, and damages for personal injuries.[82]

Landlords and owners may be subject to liability for lead poisoning under a variety of theories. Many states apply negligence principles, under which landlords must have knowledge of the presence of lead-based paint to be liable.[83] Some courts have accepted negligence per se claims based on violations of state or local lead abatement laws. A few courts have found landlords strictly liable for lead poisoning. Other theories include breach of the implied warranty of habitability, violations of state consumer protection acts,[84] and nuisance. A property owner may be also found liable to buyers or tenants for breach of contract, fraud, or misrepresentation if the owner failed to disclose known lead-based paint hazards.

A key element of most lead-based paint cases is proving that the landlord had notice of a condition that was hazardous to young children.[85] The type of proof varies by jurisdiction, and may depend in part on the local lead paint laws. Plaintiffs must usually prove that the landlord had actual or constructive notice of chipping or peeling lead-based paint, and that a young child lived on the premises.[86] In light of the publicity created by legislation, lawsuits, and media reports, it is becoming increasingly difficult for landlords to claim that they do not know about the hazards of lead-based paint.

Some defendants in lead exposure cases have attempted to compel nonparty relatives of children exposed to lead to submit to IQ and psychological testing.[87] Discovery requests in personal injury litigation have traditionally been directed almost exclusively at the plaintiff. However, defendants in lead exposure cases have attempted to obtain information about the IQ of parents and siblings to show that the plaintiff's condition resulted from genetic factors rather than the defendants' actions.[88]

Asbestos

Sources and Health Hazards

Asbestos is a group of naturally occurring fibrous minerals with high tensile strength, flexibility, and resistance to thermal, chemical, and electrical conditions. It was commonly used in a variety of construction materials for insulation and as a fire retardant. Many uses of asbestos have been banned, but it can still be found in many products in use today. Asbestos is most commonly found today in older homes, in pipe and furnace insulation, asbestos shingles, fire-resistant drywall, textured paints and other coating materials, and floor tiles.[89]

Asbestos-containing material (ACM) in its intact, undamaged state does not generally present health hazards. The danger occurs when the material becomes "friable" and fibers are released and inhaled into the lungs. ACM is considered friable when it can be crushed by hand pressure or the surface is not sealed to prevent small pieces from escaping. Inhalation of airborne particles of ACM can cause lung cancer, mesothelioma (a cancer of the chest and abdominal linings), and asbestosis (an irreversible lung scarring that can be fatal). Symptoms of these diseases do not appear until many years after exposure began, and some diseases can result from only minimal exposure.[90]

The primary threat of asbestos exposure is to workers who worked with asbestos, and to family members who were exposed to asbestos from the workers' clothing. There have been no documented cases of illnesses from exposure to in-place ACM in homes or offices. However, there is potential for exposure if ACM in homes or offices is disturbed, such as during renovation work.[91]

Role of Residential Segregation in Exposure

ACM is more likely to be present in older homes. Buildings constructed from the 1940s through the 1970s often included ACM. To the extent that low-income people are more likely to live in older homes, they would potentially be more subject to asbestos exposure.

EPA recommends that homeowners should hire a professional in the asbestos abatement field when they need to repair an item containing asbestos, remove ACM material such as pipe insulation, or remove damaged ACM.[92] However, homeowners in most localities are not prohibited from repairing or even removing ACM from their homes. Low-income residents may be less likely to hire expensive asbestos abatement companies. By performing the work themselves, these residents are susceptible to asbestos exposure.

Federal Regulation

EPA has banned the use of asbestos in most products manufactured in the U.S.[93] EPA has issued strict regulations for asbestos in schools.[94] OSHA has issued rules governing workplace exposure.[95]

EPA also regulates asbestos under its Clean Air Act (CAA) national emission standard for hazardous air pollutants (NESHAP).[96] The asbestos NESHAP is designed to minimize the release of asbestos fibers during building demolition and renovation operations. The regulations cover any party that owns, leases, operates, controls, or supervises the facility being renovated or demolished, as well as any party that owns, leases, operates, controls, or supervises the demolition or renovation operations. Private remedies are available in CAA citizen suits.

The asbestos NESHAP applies to apartment buildings with more than four dwelling units, but does not cover individual residential buildings with four or fewer dwelling units (the "residential building exemption"), even if they are safety hazards or public nuisances under local law.[97] Multiple small buildings on the same site and under common ownership and control are not exempt if they are demolished or renovated. Residential structures that are demolished as part of a commercial or public project are also not exempt. The asbestos NESHAP requires a building owner to survey for the presence of ACM before renovation or demolition.

State Regulation

A number of states have enacted asbestos legislation. Some states require building owners and operators to disclose the presence of asbestos in buildings. California requires real property owners to disclose the presence of asbestos.[98] New York requires sponsors of cooperative and condominium offerings to prepare an asbestos report.[99] Some states also require the seller in real estate transactions to disclose hazardous substances present on the property.

Tort Claims

A huge number of personal injury lawsuits have been filed, mostly involving occupational exposure.[100] The so-called "asbestos-in-building" cases were the "second wave" of asbestos litigation. In these cases, an owner of a building sues the asbestos manufacturer to recover costs of removing or abating the asbestos hazard.[101]

A "third wave" of asbestos litigation involves those who have been "passively" exposed to asbestos. These cases include suits filed by relatives or other people who lived with individuals who worked with asbestos. These plaintiffs came into contact with asbestos by washing the worker's clothes and cleaning the dust shaken from the clothes. These cases also include school children, teachers, and other school employees who were exposed to asbestos in school buildings.

There have been relatively few cases filed for residential exposure to asbestos. Potential defendants include landlords, home builders, and manufacturers of ACM. The potential for personal injury claims involving in-place ACM is small, since there have been no proven health impacts from in-place ACM. Plaintiffs have had some success in bringing claims for property damages, such as reduced property values and abatement costs.

Personal injury claims are likely to succeed only if asbestos has been disturbed, such as during renovation or repair work. A landlord whose failure to maintain the premises results in the release of asbestos fibers could also be subject to personal injury claims. Tenants may also bring claims for rent abatement and repairs in cases of crumbling asbestos.[102]

Asbestos claims can arise out of real estate transactions. A home buyer can bring misrepresentation or failure to disclose claims against the seller. A home buyer may have a claim against a seller who fails to disclose an asbestos problem of which the seller was or should have been aware.[103]

Pesticides

Sources and Health Hazards

Pesticides were used in about three-quarters of U.S. households in 1996. Eighty percent of most people's exposure to pesticide occurs indoors, and measurable levels of about a dozen pesticides have been found in the air inside homes. Pesticides used in and around the home include products to control insect (insecticides), termites (termiticides), rodents (rodenticides), fungi (fungicides), and microbes (disinfectants).[104]

Chlordane, a commonly used termiticide banned by EPA, could still present a health hazard in homes built before April 1988.[105] Some studies have shown that homes treated 20–30 years ago can have unsafe levels of chlordane in the indoor air. This problem occurs when chlordane underneath a home slowly evaporates and rises through cracks in the foundation or around plumbing pipes.

A 1990 study by the American Association of Poison Control Centers found that about 79,000 children were involved in common household pesticide poisonings or exposures. In households with children under five years old, almost half store at least one pesticide product within reach of children. Indoor pesticide exposure can also result from outdoor spraying that comes into a residence.[106]

A pesticide's active ingredient, as well as some inert ingredients, can be dangerous to human health if not properly applied.[107] Health impacts can include irritation to the eyes, nose, and throat, damage to the central nervous system and kidneys, and cancer. There is some evidence that children may be susceptible to toxicological effects from pesticide exposure even from proper applications.[108]

Role of Residential Segregation in Exposure

Homes built before 1988 are more likely to be contaminated with chlordane. In addition, large apartment buildings can have more persistent pest problems, such as cockroaches, than single-family homes. More frequent pesticide application may be required to control insects in these buildings. To the extent that low-income people are more likely to live in apartment buildings, they may be at a higher risk of exposure to pesticides. Children living on or near farms may be exposed to disproportionately high levels of pesticides.[109]

Federal and State Regulation

The Federal Insecticide, Fungicide, and Rodenticide Act (FIFRA)[110] regulates the production and use of pesticides. EPA regulates indoor exposure by banning or limiting their use and by establishing directions for safe use. Manufacturers must put information on the label about when and how to use the pesticide. EPA has banned the sale and commercial use of certain pesticides called cyclodiene pesticides: chlordane, dieldrin, aldrin, and heptachlor.[111] Many states and local governments have requirements for posting lawns treated with pesticides and for notifying nearby residents about pesticides used.

Tort Actions

Homeowners can file suits against exterminators for negligent application of pesticides. Numerous suits were filed alleging the negligent application of the termiticide chlordane.[112] Apartment residents can file suits against landlords and exterminators for negligent pesticide application. Plaintiffs in these suits often also allege that the defendants should be strictly liable for their injuries.[113]

Another type of suit for pesticide exposure is a state tort claim charging a defendant with inadequate labeling of its pesticide or with failure to warn of the dangers associated with use of the pesticide. Most courts have held that these claims are preempted by FIFRA. Many courts have held that FIFRA preempts failure-to-warn claims based on inadequate labeling in which the warning is designed to protect the consumer or end users.[114] However, some courts have held that state tort claims based on theories of design defect or negligent testing, manufacturing, and formulation are not preempted.[115]

Radon

Sources and Health Hazards

Radon gas, which enters buildings through the foundations and basements, has become well known as a potential hazard in single-family homes.[116] However, it can also pose a hazard to some apartment units on the first and second floors. Radon is a gas produced from the radioactive decay of uranium that occurs naturally in rocks and soil.[117] It is colorless and odorless. Radon gas can enter homes through dirt floors, cracks in concrete walls and floors, floor drains, and sumps.

Radon is radioactive, and it can damage cells when inhaled or ingested. The primary health effect associated with exposure to elevated levels of radon is lung cancer. Outside air contains very low levels of radon, but the gas can build up to higher concentrations inside. The northern United States and some areas in southern states tend to have higher indoor air radon concentrations. New England states and some areas in the southwest have higher concentrations of radon in water. Appalachian and Rocky Mountain states and some areas in the Great Plains have higher than average radon in both water and indoor air. Indoor radon concentrations can be reduced by improving a building's ventilation system and sealing areas where the radon is entering the foundation.

Role of Residential Segregation in Exposure

Regulatory efforts for radon have focused mostly on educating single-family homeowners. These efforts may not help house and apartment renters, who may lack legal and financial means to make necessary repairs and may not be in a position to force landlords to make repairs.[118] In affected parts of the country, much rental housing, including single-family homes or apartments on the second floor or below, may be subject to radon contamination.

Federal and State Regulation

Federal and state efforts to address radon have emphasized education over regulation. The programs generally provide basic information about radon and encourage testing in the home. For example, the Indoor Radon Abatement Act of 1988 provided funding for states and aid to homeowners to control radon in schools, homes, and federal buildings.[119]

In 1989, EPA and Centers for Disease Control set an action level for radon at four picocuries per liter of air (pCi/L). Residential indoor air that exceeds that level should be subject to further testing and possible corrective renovation within a few years. EPA recommends corrective action within a few months for levels over 20 pCi/L, and immediate corrective action for levels over 200 pCi/L.[120] In 1994, EPA issued model standards for the control of radon in new residential buildings. These standards require passive control systems to be used in areas of high radon potential.[121]

Most state laws focus on public education and promotion of radon testing. Some states have imposed regulatory requirements, such as requiring disclosure during residential real estate transactions.[122]

Tort Actions

A number of suits have been brought by plaintiffs who owned homes built on uranium mill tailings.[123] Homeowners have filed some cases in which the radon source was not mill tailings.[124]

Tenants may face a number of difficulties in bringing claims alleging that high radon levels violate a warranty of habitability or statutory duty to repair.[125] Courts may be reluctant to find that radon mitigation falls within a landlord's duty, since radon occurs naturally. There have also been some questions about the precise nature of radon's threat and the radon level at which action should be taken.

Drinking Water Contamination

Sources and Health Hazards

Drinking water can be a source of residential exposure to harmful substances, including lead, pesticides, other chemicals, and microbial contaminants.[126] The U.S. drinking water supply is not immune from widespread outbreaks of microbial contamination. Milwaukee's drinking water suffered a major outbreak of an intestinal parasite called cryptosporidium in 1993, during which 370,000 people became ill and 40 died.

Lead is another dangerous drinking water contaminant. Lead can enter drinking water from lead pipes, lead or tin solder on pipe joints, fittings on spouts and faucets, and lead-lined water cooler tanks. The major source today is sloppy lead-soldered joints.[127]

Groundwater is the source of over half of our drinking water. Groundwater can be contaminated by numerous sources, including leaking underground storage tanks, leachate from landfills, and agricultural chemicals.

Radon in household drinking water poses a small risk to public health, according to a National Research Council study.[128] Drinking water that contains radon is much less of a health risk than inhaling radon. The most likely health threat from consuming radon in water, stomach cancer, is very small—about 20 of the 13,000 stomach cancer deaths each year may result from consuming water that contains radon. Much more radon enters houses through soil beneath the home than through water supplies.[129]

Role of Residential Segregation in Exposure

Older homes are more likely to have lead pipes and therefore have lead in their drinking water. People who live in rural areas are more likely to rely on wells for drinking water. These wells can be contaminated by agricultural chemicals, leaking underground storage tanks, landfill leachate, and migration of contaminants from hazardous waste sites.

Federal and State Regulation

The Safe Drinking Water Act[130] governs the safety of public drinking water supplies.[131] EPA has issued regulations under the Act to limit the level of contaminants in drinking water and to protect underground sources.

In 1998, EPA issued a rule that requires water utilities to issue regular reports to their customers on the quality of their drinking water.[132] Water utilities must inform their customers where the drinking water comes from, likely sources of any contaminants, and any potential health effects if the EPA standard for a particular contaminant is violated. Water suppliers are only required to identify contaminants that EPA regulates or requires to be monitored.

California's Proposition 65[133] is the most prominent of the state laws affecting drinking water. The California Supreme Court has held that Proposition 65 should be broadly interpreted to apply to faucets, as well as river and groundwater sources of drinking water. The court held that Proposition 65 applied to faucet manufacturers, who were sued over alleged contamination of drinking water by lead in brass faucets.[134]

Tort Actions

Many toxic tort actions have been filed by residents alleging drinking water contamination from various sources. A landmark decision was *Sterling v. Velsicol Chemical Corp.*[135] In that case, residents whose drinking wells were contaminated by a nearby hazardous waste dump filed a class action against a chemical company. Plaintiffs asserted a number of theories of liability, including strict liability for abnormally dangerous activities, trespass, nuisance, and negligence. The trial court awarded damages for actual injuries, pain and suffering, enhanced susceptibility to future disease, impairment of the immune system, fear of increased risk of disease, and impairment of the quality of life. On appeal, the Sixth Circuit required more demanding proof that plaintiffs' injuries were caused by the contaminated drinking water. The Sixth Circuit allowed recovery for certain types of injuries, including liver cancer, loss of kidney and liver functions, central nervous system disorders, and diminution in property values. It disallowed recovery for other types of injuries, including optic atrophy, neuritis, increased susceptibility to cancer, immune system impairment, learning disorders, post-traumatic stress, and loss of future earning capacity. The court approved in principle recovery for the reasonable fear of increased risk of cancer and other diseases.

Another well-known drinking water contamination case was the Woburn, Massachusetts, water well case.[136] In that case, residents alleged that their exposure to chemicals in their drinking water resulted in leukemia deaths and other injuries. In a ruling that addressed plaintiffs' emotional distress claims, the court held that proof of physical harm manifested by objective symptoms can support a claim for emotional distress flowing from the harm. People who suffered from a variety of physical ailments, such as shortness of breath, fatigue, and headaches, could pursue claims for anxiety over increased susceptibility to disease brought on by the alleged harm to their immune systems. However, they could not recover for anxiety, depression, fear, and frustration linked only to the drinking of contaminated water and not to their physical injuries.

People whose drinking water is contaminated by leaking underground storage tanks (USTs) can pursue tort actions against the tank owner or operator.[137] Plaintiffs can pursue a variety of theories of liability, including negligence, nuisance, and trespass. Although some early cases held defendants strictly liable for leaking USTs, most courts have rejected strict liability claims on the grounds that USTs are very common, are valuable in comparison to the danger they pose, and are not sufficiently dangerous if the owner exercises due care.

Petroleum products that leak from USTs can include a number of contaminants, including benzene, xylene, and toluene. The gasoline additive methyl tertiary butyl ether (MTBE) has received attention in recent years as a potential widespread source of groundwater contamination.

Electromagnetic Fields

Sources and Health Hazards

Electromagnetic fields (EMFs) are produced by both natural and manmade sources.[138] An EMF is the invisible line of force that surrounds any electric device. It consists of an electric field and a magnetic field. Electric fields are produced by the presence of electrical charges, while magnetic fields are produced by the movement of those charges.

Residential exposure to EMFs can come from outside power lines, wiring in the home, electric heat and hot water heaters, electrical appliances, and other electric devices. Natural sources of EMFs include the earth's magnetic field, lightning, and even the human body. The pervasiveness of EMFs makes it difficult to assess their exposure and health impacts.

Numerous studies have been performed, but health impacts of exposure to EMFs are uncertain.[139] Two major recent studies did not find any evidence that exposure to EMFs presents a human health hazard. A 1996 report by the National Research Council concluded that the current body of evidence does not show that EMF exposure presents a human health hazard.[140] A 1997 report from the National Cancer Institute and Children's Cancer Group found little support for the hypothesis that living in houses with high weighted average magnetic field levels or in homes close to electrical transmission or distribution lines is related to childhood leukemia.[141]

However, a 1998 study by the National Institute of Environmental Health Sciences (NIEHS) concluded that extremely low frequency EMFs are possibly carcinogenic to children.[142] NIEHS found the possibility of a slight increase in childhood leukemia risk from power line/residential exposure, but inadequate evidence of any adult cancer risks from residential exposure to extremely low frequency magnetic fields. The panel chairman noted that the risk associated with EMF exposure is probably very small compared to other public health risks, but that additional research should be pursued to reduce uncertainties.

Role of Residential Segregation in Exposure

Housing near electrical lines and transmission equipment is more susceptible to any harmful impacts of EMFs.

Tort Claims

A number of cases were brought in the early 1990s, but with little success for plaintiffs. The success of future suits may depend on restrictions courts place on the use of questionable scientific evidence under the *Daubert* test.[143] The NIEHS study may give plaintiffs a glimmer of hope, but substantial obstacles remain.

In 1998, plaintiffs in a closely watched EMF case withdrew their lawsuit that alleged that EMFs from an electric utility caused their daughter's brain cancer.[144] Plaintiffs decided to drop their suit against the Connecticut Light & Power Company after one of their expert witnesses declined to testify. The expert witness, the head of neurosurgery at the Yale School of Medicine, was slated to testify that EMFs played a role in causing the daughter's brain tumor. Utility lawyers reacted to the withdrawal of the case by stating that such claims are not supported by the present state of the science. Lawyers who have represented plaintiffs in other EMF cases predicted that these cases will resurface as the science continues to develop.

Most EMF suits have been filed against electric utilities. Cases could also conceivably be brought against building owners with electrical transmission equipment on their property and contractors responsible for construction and installation of the equipment.

Possible actions include:

- suits by property owners to recover diminution in market value;[145]
- suits by groups and communities to block proposed new developments, especially power lines; and
- suits by individuals exposed to EMFs seeking compensation for health impacts and emotional distress.[146]

Damages claimed typically include actual physical injury in the form of cancer, fear of developing cancer in the future, and decrease in property value due to the stigma associated with EMFs. Theories of liability include:

- negligence based on failure to warn of the dangers of EMFs;
- trespass or nuisance based on EMFs from high voltage equipment coming onto one's property;
- strict product liability based on the theory that electricity is a product rather than a service and that associated EMFs caused product-related damages; and
- inverse condemnation based on an electric utility's ability to condemn land for the public good in providing electricity.

Dietary Exposure

In addition to exposure from the contaminants in the air and water, people can ingest contaminants directly when they eat. Our diet can be the source of numerous potentially dangerous substances, but this section will discuss one specific source that has received considerable attention in the environmental justice context: consumption of mercury-contaminated fish by subsistence fishermen and their families.

Mercury is a naturally occurring element that can be toxic when consumed by people. It gets into the air and water from natural weathering of the earth's crust, burning of garbage and fuels, and emissions from factories that use mercury. Mercury is concentrated through the food chain in the tissues of fish. Ingestion of mercury can harm the human brain and nervous system. Young children are especially at risk, and the brain and nervous system in developing fetuses can be permanently damaged if pregnant women eat foods containing elevated levels of mercury.

Federal and state agencies have issued numerous advisories in recent years warning people not to eat more than specified amounts of various fish.[147] Some states have issued statewide advisories against fish consumption. Mercury contamination appears to be most widespread in the Midwest.[148]

Families that rely heavily on subsistence fishing could be more likely to suffer adverse health effects from mercury ingestion. However, some studies have indicated that limiting the consumption of fish could do more harm than good by:

- reducing the health benefits from consumption of fish;
- increasing the consumption of alternative foods that have potential health risks; and
- disturbing the lifestyle of subsistence populations.[149]

As the numbers of some fish species have diminished, the federal and state governments have imposed various restrictions on fishing by recreational fishermen. Some of these rules have the unanticipated effect of making it more difficult for poor people to take advantage of a high-quality, low-priced food source.[150]

Notes

1. Most people spend about 90 percent of their time indoors. EPA, REPORT TO CONGRESS ON INDOOR AIR QUALITY (1989). Groups that are more likely to be harmed by indoor air pollution, including infants, the elderly, and the infirm, often spend almost all of their time indoors.

2. EPA AND CONSUMER PRODUCT SAFETY COMMISSION, THE INSIDE STORY: A GUIDE TO INDOOR AIR QUALITY (1997) [hereinafter THE INSIDE STORY] (available at <http://www.epa.gov/iaq/pubs/insidest.html>). The report notes that a "growing body of scientific evidence has indicated that air within homes and other buildings can be more seriously polluted than the outdoor air in even the largest and most industrialized cities."

3. Laws directed primarily at the outdoor environment, such as the Clean Air Act, have an impact on indoor air quality, since pollutants in the outdoor air enter residences. This chapter focuses on indoor sources of indoor air pollutants.

4. For example, tenants of federally owned or -subsidized apartments may have claims against the Department of Housing and Urban Development (HUD). *See, e.g.,* Mann v. Pierce, 803 F.2d 1552 (11th Cir. 1986); Lindley v. Cisneros, 74 F.3d 1076 (11th Cir. 1996) (suits by tenants of housing project owned by HUD for restitution of rent for HUD's failure to maintain premises adequately, including claims of crumbling asbestos from ceiling tiles).

5. This chapter does not address environmental tobacco smoke (secondhand smoke), one of the biggest sources of indoor air pollution.

6. *See infra,* "Lead Exposure," pages 592–97, for more detail on lead-based paint.

7. *See infra,* "Asbestos," pages 597–99, for more detail on asbestos.

8. *See infra,* "Pesticides," pages 599–601, for more detail on pesticides.

9. *See infra,* "Radon," pages 601–02, for more detail on radon.

10. For more information on the health impact of indoor air pollution, see Laurence S. Kirsch & Geraldine E. Edens, *in* ENVIRONMENTAL LAW PRACTICE GUIDE, at ch. 17A (Michael B. Gerrard ed., *Indoor Air Quality,* Matthew Bender & Co., 1999); Arnold W. Reitze, Jr. & Sheryl-Lynn Carof, *The Legal Control of Indoor Air Pollution,* 25 B.C. ENVTL. AFF. L. REV. 247 (1998).

11. *See* THE INSIDE STORY, *supra* note 2. EPA also operates an Indoor Air Quality Information Clearinghouse, which can be reached at (800) 438-4318. EPA has issued two publications designed for building managers. *Building Air Quality Action Plan* (1998) <http://www.epa.gov/iaq/base/actionpl.html> is a refresher tool and checklist for facility managers. *An Office Building Occupant's Guide to Indoor Air Quality* (Oct. 1997) <http://www.epa.gov/iaq/pubs/occupgd.html> is designed to educate building managers on the common sources of IAQ complaints.

12. Some in the scientific community argue that UFFI emits vapors that may, over time, cause cancer. According to the Consumer Product Safety Commission, most outgassing occurs in the first year. After eight years, the level of formaldehyde gas should be no higher than in any other house with the insulation.

13. Since 1985, HUD has allowed only the use of plywood and particle board that conform to specified formaldehyde emission limits in the construction of prefabricated and mobile homes.

14. The Montgomery County, Maryland Department of Environmental Protection has produced a brochure entitled HEALTHY INDOOR PAINTING PRACTICES: A SAFETY GUIDE FOR RESIDENTS, PROPERTY MANAGERS, AND PAINTING CONTRACTORS. The county has received hundreds of requests for the brochure from county residents and from 22 states. *See* Barbara Ruben, *Painting Advice Is Catching On: County's Safety Brochure Is a Hit,* WASHINGTON POST, Oct. 15, 1998, Montgomery Weekly section at 1.

15. NEW YORK CITY DEPARTMENT OF HEALTH, BUREAU OF ENVIRONMENTAL INVESTIGATIONS, PERC Fact Sheet (June 1997).

16. *See* EPA OFFICE OF POLLUTION PREVENTION AND TOXICS, CHEMICAL SUMMARY FOR PERCHLOROETHYLENE (EPA Report No. 749-F-94-020a, Aug. 1994). *See also Dry Cleaners in N.Y. Face New Emission Standards,* N.Y. TIMES, Mar. 20, 1997, at B8:1; *Cleaners' Chemical Has Unsavory Resume,* N.Y. DAILY NEWS, Oct. 7, 1997, at 4:4.

17. *See* Reitze & Carof, *supra* note 10.

18. EPA and the U.S. Department of Agriculture-Cooperative State Research, Education, and Extension Service have developed a national consumer education program to improve the quality of indoor air in homes. The program has produced a brochure called INDOOR AIR HAZARDS EVERY HOMEOWNER SHOULD KNOW ABOUT. *See also* THE INSIDE STORY, *supra* note 2.

19. OSHA has published a proposed rule for indoor air quality in the workplace, but the rule has been delayed by objections from Congress and industry. 59 Fed. Reg. 15,968 (Apr. 5, 1994). OSHA has also issued air contaminant standards for asbestos, lead, and certain chemicals. These air contaminant standards set permissible exposure limits in the workplace. *See, e.g.,* 29 C.F.R. §§ 1910.1000 (various chemicals), 1910.1001 (asbestos). For more information on occupational exposure, see Chapter 20, "Controlling Exposures in the Workplace," pages 662–717.

20. *See* Kirsch & Edens, *supra* note 10, at 17A.03.

21. 40 C.F.R. pt. 59, 63 Fed. Reg. 48,819, 48,848 (Sept. 11, 1998). The consumer products rule sets VOC limits for 24 categories of household products, such as cleaning products, personal care products, and insecticides. The architectural coatings rule applies to various types of paint, including exterior and interior paints. Manufacturers covered by the rule must reformulate their products to comply with the VOC limits within one year.

22. New Jersey regulates the indoor air quality of public employees under its Public Employees Occupational Safety and Health Act. N.J. STAT. ANN. § 34:6A-25. The regulations that implement the act adopt the ASHRAE ventilation standards.

23. *See, e.g.,* CHICAGO MUN. CODE § 13-13-176 et seq., which includes detailed ventilation requirements for new construction. The state of Washington has

adopted a ventilation and indoor air quality code that requires use of radon-resistant construction techniques in new residential construction. WASH. ADMIN. CODE § 51-13-500.

24. *See, e.g.*, MASS. GEN. LAWS ch. 111, §§ 127C, F, L (state sanitary code provides rent escrow, and repair and deduct remedies); OHIO REV. CODE ANN. § 5321.07 (providing rent escrow and injunctive relief generally).

25. ASHRAE 62-1989: Ventilation for Acceptable Indoor Air Quality (1989). *See also* ASHRAE 55-1981: Thermal Environmental Conditions for Human Occupancy (1981); American Conference of Governmental Industrial Hygienists, Threshold Limit Values for Chemical Substances and Physical Agents and Biological Exposure Indices (1993). The Building Officials and Code Administrators (BOCA) has a national building and mechanical code that specifies ventilation requirements.

26. *See* Kirsch & Edens, *supra* note 10, at 17A-50.

27. For a discussion of the theories of liability and damages in toxic tort cases, *see infra* Chapter 19, "Assisting Injured Individuals," pages 619–661. *See also* James D. Pagliaro & Paul J. Greco, *in* ENVIRONMENTAL LAW PRACTICE GUIDE, at ch. 33 (Michael B. Gerrard ed., *Toxic Torts*, Matthew Bender & Co., 1999).

28. Plaintiffs must prove four basic elements in a negligence claim: duty, breach, proximate cause, and damages. *See, e.g.*, Stoney Run Co. v. Prudential-LMI Commercial Insurance Co., 47 F.3d 34 (2d Cir. 1995) (apartment residents killed or injured by inhalation of carbon monoxide emitted into their apartments due to a faulty heating and ventilation system brought negligence action against apartment owners).

29. Restatement (Second) of Torts § 519. *See, e.g.*, Langan v. Valicopters, Inc., 88 Wash. 2d 855, 567 P.2d 218 (1997) (strict liability imposed against aerial pesticide sprayer for damages caused by crop dusting); Sterling v. Velsicol Chem. Corp., 855 F.2d 1188 (6th Cir. 1988) (strict liability imposed in class action to recover personal injuries and property damage incurred by residents who lived near defendant's chemical waste burial site).

30. Restatement (Second) of Torts § 402A. *See, e.g.*, Elmore v. Owens-Illinois, Inc., 673 S.W.2d 434 (Mo. 1984) (plaintiff who contracted asbestosis from prolonged exposure to an asbestos-containing product argued that the manufacturer should be held strictly liable because its product was defective and unreasonably dangerous when sold without an adequate warning; court upheld jury verdict for plaintiff on this theory).

31. *See* Kirsch & Edens, *supra* note 10, at 17A-57.

32. Restatement or Torts (Second), § 63, at 434 (5th ed).

33. *See* Tobie Bernstein, *Radon in Rental Housing: Legal and Policy Strategies for Reducing Health Risks*, 26 ENVTL. L. REP. 10,466 (Sept. 1996) [hereinafter Tobie Bernstein, *Radon in Rental Housing*].

34. The only type of suit in which plaintiffs have had much success in recovering damages for increased risk of disease is cases involving occupational exposure to asbestos. *See* Deidre McDonnell, *Increased Risk of Disease Damages: Proportional Recovery as an Alternative to the All or Nothing System Exemplified by Asbestos Cases*, 24 B.C. ENVTL. AFF. L. REV. 623 (1997).

35. One type of emotional distress often asserted by plaintiffs in toxic tort cases is fear of future disease, which is distinct from a claim for increased risk of

disease. Plaintiffs have not often been successful in asserting these claims. *See, e.g.,* Witchita v. U.S. Gypsum Co., 72 F.3d 1491 (10th Cir. 1996) (tort liability may not be based on fear or a risk of potential future harm). *But see* Potter v. Firestone, 863 P.2d 795 (Cal. Sup. Ct. 1993) (plaintiffs may recover damages for fear of cancer after exposure to toxic substance if fear stems from knowledge, corroborated by medical evidence, that they are more likely than not to develop cancer due to the exposure).

36. *See* Kirsch & Edens, *supra* note 10, at 17A.02[4][c].

37. Shooshanian v. Wagner, 672 P.2d 455 (Alaska 1983).

38. Goldman v. Sears-Robbins, 6/24/98 N.Y.L.J. 26:3 (N.Y. Sup. Ct. N.Y. Co.).

39. State officials testified that apartment dwellers should not be exposed to over 100 micrograms of perc per cubic meter of air. Samples from the apartments found exposure levels of 450 to 8,600 micrograms of perc per cubic meter of air.

40. *See infra* Chapter 19, "Assisting Injured Individuals," pages 619–661. *See also* Pagliaro & Greco, *supra* note 27; Aaron Simon & Nicholas Chiaia, *Good Exposure: How to Know When a Toxic Tort Case Is a Safe Bet,* 6 INDOOR POLLUTION L. REP., Jan. 1993, at 1.

41. The critical distinction is whether the time periods start to run from the date of exposure or from the date of discovery of the injury.

42. 509 U.S. 597 (1993).

43. FED. R. EVID. 702.

44. Ruffin v. Shaw Industries, No. 94-1882 (4th Cir. 1998).

45. FEDERAL JUDICIAL CENTER, REFERENCE MANUAL ON SCIENTIFIC EVIDENCE 73 (1994).

46. *See, e.g.,* Morrison v. Terminix, No. 32,711 (Miss. Cir. Ct. Hinds Co., jury verdict Feb. 12, 1990) ($250,000 award to a family that allegedly developed MCS after an exterminator misapplied the termiticide aldrin in their home). *See also* Kirsch & Edens, *supra* note 10, at 17A.01[1][b].

47. *See* Kirsch & Edens, *supra* note 10, at 17A.09[2][b].

48. *See, e.g.,* Frank v. State of New York, 972 F. Supp. 130 (N.D.N.Y. 1997); Summers v. Missouri Pacific R.R. System, 897 F. Supp. 533 (E.D. Okla. 1995), *aff'd* 132 F.3d 599 (10th Cir. 1997).

49. Coffin v. Orkin Exterminating Co., No. CIV 97-258-B (D. Me. 1998).

50. *See Sick Buildings: A Modern Health Threat,* A.B.A. LITIG. SEC., 2 COURSE MATERIALS, 857–946 (Aug. 4, 1998).

51. *See, e.g.,* Call v. Prudential Insurance Co. of America, No. SWC 90913 (Cal. Super. Ct. Los Angeles Co. filed 1985, settled in 1990) (any party in chain of people associated with the HVAC system or leasing of the building could be strictly liable for injuries caused by sick building syndrome). Sick building syndrome has also affected school buildings. *See Polluted Air in Schools Causes Health Problem, Study Finds,* N.Y. TIMES, Mar. 25, 1993.

52. *See* Gene Heady, *Stuck Inside These Four Walls: Recognition of Sick Building Syndrome Has Laid the Foundation to Raise Toxic Tort Litigation to New Heights,* 26 TEX. TECH. L. REV. 1041 (1995); Thomas Icard & W. Cary Wright, *Sick Building Syndrome and Building-Related Illness Claims: Defining the Practical and Legal Issues,* 14 CONSTRUCTION LAWYER 1 (1994).

53. CENTERS FOR DISEASE CONTROL & PREVENTION, U.S. DEP'T HEALTH & HUM. SERVICES, PREVENTING LEAD POISONING IN YOUNG CHILDREN (1991).

54. *Id. See also* Reitze & Carof, *supra* note 10.

55. EPA has published a 70-page reference guide entitled LEAD IN YOUR HOME: A PARENT'S REFERENCE GUIDE. Copies are available from the National Lead Information Center Clearinghouse at (800) 424-LEAD and on EPA's web page at <http://www.epa.gov/lead>.

56. EPA estimates that 83 percent of privately owned homes built before 1980 (64.4 million homes) contain some lead paint. EPA proposed rule on identification of lead-based paint hazards, 63 Fed. Reg. 30,305 (June 3, 1998).

57. Lead poisoning among children is more likely to occur to malnourished children and children who have a condition called "pica" that compels them to pick up and eat paint particles. *See* John P. Fensler & Leonard A. Bernstein, *Lead Poisoning at Home: New Federal Disclosure Duties,* 26 REAL EST. L.J. 7 (Summer 1997).

58. Debra J. Brody et al., *Blood Lead Levels in the U.S. Population,* 272 JAMA 277 (1994). *See also* Jennifer Wriggins, *Genetics, IQ, Determinism, and Torts: The Example of Discovery in Lead Exposure Litigation,* 77 B.U. L. REV. 1025 (Dec. 1997) (see sources cited in note 20 for other studies demonstrating the disproportionate impact of lead-based paint on poor, minority children).

59. 16 C.F.R. pt. 1303. Paint may contain no more than 0.06 percent (660 parts per million) of lead.

60. 42 U.S.C. §§ 4851–56. (The Residential Lead-Based Paint Hazard Reduction Act is Title X of the Housing and Community Development Act of 1992, Pub. L. 102-550). For more information on the requirements of the Act and its regulations, contact the National Safety Council's National Lead Information Clearinghouse at (800) 424-LEAD, or visit EPA's internet site at <www.epa.gov/lead>.

61. 61 Fed. Reg. 9064 (Mar. 6, 1996). EPA's regulations are at 40 C.F.R. pt. 745. HUD's regulations are at 24 C.F.R. pt. 35. HUD and EPA have concurrent enforcement jurisdiction. *See* Alvin C. Harrell, *Lead Paint Disclosure Requirements for Residential Real Estate,* 51 CONSUMER FIN. L. Q. REP. 380 (Fall 1997).

62. Exclusions from the disclosure requirements for landlord/tenant transactions include: housing built after 1977; housing for the elderly or disabled; zero-bedroom dwellings; and commercial lodging. Owners of rental housing are also excluded from complying with the disclosure rules if they have a determination made that the housing is free of lead-based paint.

63. *See* Fensler & Bernstein, *supra* note 57.

64. EPA issued an interim penalty policy for violations of the disclosure regulations in Feb. 1998. *See* DAILY ENV'T REP. (BNA), Feb. 19, 1998, at A-10. EPA took its first enforcement actions in July 1998. EPA issued four administrative complaints against landlords, a realty firm, and a Naval air station. EPA also issued 22 notices of noncompliance for minor violations to sellers, brokers, agents, and landlords. *See* DAILY ENV'T REP. (BNA), July 30, 1998, at A-7. EPA may waive penalties for companies that voluntarily disclose and correct violations after a self-audit. *See* DAILY ENV'T REP. (BNA), Sept. 23, 1998, at A-2.

65. Section 1018(b)(3), 42 U.S.C. § 4852d(b)(3).

66. See Fensler & Bernstein, *supra* note 57.

67. 63 Fed. Reg. 29,907 (June 1, 1998).

68. In December 1998, EPA issued a proposed rule under TSCA to provide new standards for management and disposal of lead-based paint debris. The reg-

ulations, which would replace existing RCRA regulations, will make abatement of lead-based paint more affordable by allowing disposal in construction and demolition landfills. The regulations would not apply to debris generated by homeowners in their own homes. 63 Fed. Reg. 70,189 (Dec. 18, 1998).

69. 63 Fed. Reg. 30,302 (June 3, 1998). Until EPA issues a final rule, EPA's existing guidance on lead-based paint hazards remains in effect. 60 Fed. Reg. 47,248 (Sept. 11, 1995). EPA hopes to issue a final rule by Jan. 2000.

70. EPA did not propose separate standards for chewable surfaces or friction and impact surfaces, but asked for public comment on these sources.

71. 63 Fed. Reg. at 30,304. Another EPA regulation establishes training and certification requirements for lead-based paint contractors. 61 Fed. Reg. 45,778 (Aug. 29, 1996). The rule is intended to ensure that all lead-based paint inspections, risk assessments, and abatements are performed by trained and certified individuals. The rule allows states to seek authorization from EPA to implement their own training and certification programs.

72. *See* Jennifer Bush, *The Federal Lead Poisoning Prevention Program: Inadequate Guidance for an Expeditious Solution,* 23 B.C. ENVTL. AFF. L. REV. 645 (1996); Jennifer Tiller, *Easing Lead Paint Laws: A Step in the Right Direction,* 18 HARV. ENVTL. L. REV. 265, 268 nn. 23 & 25 (1994) (listing 25 states with lead statutes, including five that require inspection and six with screening programs).

73. *See, e.g.,* Underwood v. Risman, 414 Mass. 96, 605 N.E.2d 832 (Mass. 1993) (discussing the applicability of the Massachusetts unfair trade practices statute to the landlord/tenant relationship in a lead-based paint exposure case); Hardy v. Griffin, 41 Conn. Supp. 283, 569 A.2d 49 (1989) (finding landlord liable under the Connecticut unfair trade practices law where the landlord failed to inform the tenant of the presence of lead paint when the lease was signed).

74. *See supra,* text accompanying notes 31–32.

75. The California Childhood Lead Poisoning Prevention Act established a universal standard of care for screening, case management, and treatment of lead-poisoned children. CAL. HEALTH & SAFETY CODE §§ 105,275–310. Another potential statutory remedy in California is a suit under Proposition 65 against landlords for failure to warn of lead hazards (CAL. HEALTH & SAFETY CODE §§ 25,249.6–.13). *See* Ellen G. Widess & Heidi P. Poppe, *Preventing Childhood Lead Poisoning,* 5 ENVTL. L. NEWS, Spr. 1996.

76. Maryland requires that lead-based paint be removed in all rental housing built before 1950. MD. ANN. CODE §§ 6-804 et seq. Vermont enacted legislation in 1997 requiring annual visual inspections for chipping and peeling paint in pre-1978 rental housing and day care facilities. Notices must be posted at covered premises urging occupants to report deteriorating paint to the owner or managing agent. 18 VT. STAT. ANN. §§ 1751–65. The Illinois Department of Public Health has the authority under the state Lead Poisoning Prevention Act to investigate lead levels in residential dwellings, and to require building owners to remove, replace, or secure lead-containing materials. 410 ILL. COMP. STAT. 45/1 to 45/17.

77. MASS. GEN. LAWS ANN. ch. 111, §§ 190–99. *See also* Bush, *supra* note 72.

78. Local Law 1 of the HOUSING MAINTENANCE CODE OF THE CITY OF NEW YORK ADMIN. CODE § 27-2013(h)(1). *See also* James J. Periconi, *Sick Building Syndrome: A Look at the Legal Issues Surrounding Lead-Based Paint, Asbestos Containing*

Material and Heating, Ventilation and Air Conditioning Systems (presented at the N.Y. State Bar Ass'n Annual Meeting, Jan. 24, 1997).

79. Juarez v. Wavecrest Management Team Ltd., 88 N.Y.2d 628, 672 N.E.2d 135 (N.Y. 1996).

80. Sean F. Mooney, *Insurance Information Institute, Lead Liability* (1995), *reprinted in* 4 MEALEY'S LITIG. REP., LEAD 15, May 3, 1995, at C2.

81. *See* Joseph J. Ortego et al., *Limit Lenders' Lead Paint Liability,* 115 BANKING L. J. 18 (Jan. 1998).

82. For a review of the defendant's perspective, see Thomas F. Segalla, *How to Win Early in Lead Paint Litigation: A Defense Perspective,* 48 FED'N INS. & CORP. COUNS. Q. 381 (1998).

83. The California Supreme Court has ruled that residential landlords are not strictly liable for injuries to occupants caused by latent or unknown defects in the property. However, landlords remain liable for defects in their property under general tort principles, such as negligence and the warranty of habitability. Peterson v. Superior Ct. of Riverside County, 10 Cal. 4th 1185 (1995).

84. *See, e.g.,* Hardy v. Griffin, 41 Conn. Supp. 283, 569 A.2d 49 (Super. 1989) (renting property in which lead-based paint exceeded allowable levels was contrary to public policy and constituted unfair trade practice under Unfair Trade Practices Act).

85. Judy Keenan & Erin K. Hurley, *Get the Lead Out: Proving Notice in Lead Paint Cases,* 34 TRIAL 20 (Mar. 1998).

86. *See, e.g.,* Richwind Joint Venture 4 v. Brunson, 645 A.2d 1147 (Md. 1994) (jury could have found that management received actual notice of peeling paint, and management knew or had reason to know that peeling paint in older houses was lead-based).

87. Wriggins, *supra* note 58.

88. *See, e.g.,* Little v. McIntyre, 672 A.2d 1271 (N.J. Super. Ct. App. Div. 1996) (refusing to order plaintiff's mother to submit to a physical or mental examination); Campbell v. Bonner, No. 92-7771 (D.C. Super. Ct., Jan. 4, 1994) (granting defendant's motions to conduct clinical interviews and intelligence testing of mother and non-party siblings); Salkey v. Mott, 656 N.Y.S.2d 886 (N.Y. App. Div. 1997) (affirming lower court's decision allowing IQ test of plaintiff's mother as within lower court's discretion); Cantres v. Brook Management Corp., No. 15561/91 (N.Y. Sup. Ct. Bronx Co. 1998) (barring disclosure of siblings' academic records, where defendants' claims were based on mere supposition); Pena v. 602 West 137th Street Realty Co., No. 107400/97 (N.Y. Sup. Ct. N.Y. Co. 1998) (ordering mother of lead-exposed child to undergo IQ testing); Andon v. 302–304 Mott Street Associates, No. 123557/93 (N.Y. Sup. Ct. N.Y. Co., June 1, 1998) (ordering mother of lead-exposed child to undergo IQ testing).

89. *See* Anne C. Weisberg, *in Asbestos,* ENVIRONMENTAL LAW PRACTICE GUIDE at ch. 36 (Michael B. Gerrard ed., Matthew Bender & Co.).

90. AMERICAN LUNG ASSOCIATION, ASBESTOS FACT SHEET (1997) <http://www.lungusa.org/air>.

91. The Consumer Product Safety Commission, ALA, and EPA have issued a booklet called ASBESTOS IN YOUR HOME (1997) <http://www.epa.gov/asbestos/ashome.htm#6>. EPA's TSCA Hotline at (202) 554-1404 provides information on EPA's asbestos program and on whether your state has a training and certification program for asbestos removal contractors.

92. EPA REGION 4, ASBESTOS IN THE HOME: A HOMEOWNER'S GUIDE (1996).

93. EPA's asbestos phaseout rule was vacated by the 5th Circuit in 1991. Corrosion Proof Fittings v. EPA, 947 F.2d 1201 (5th Cir. 1991). EPA responded by lifting the ban on eight categories of products and continuing the ban on six categories of products, including all new uses of asbestos. In 1994, EPA banned asbestos-containing flooring felt. 58 Fed. Reg. 58,964 (1993). Asbestos-containing commercial paper, corrugated paper rollboard or specialty paper were banned effective Aug. 26, 1994. 59 Fed. Reg. 33209 (1994) (codified at 40 C.F.R. pt. 763).

94. Asbestos Hazard Emergency Response Act, 15 U.S.C. § 2641.

95. 29 C.F.R. § 1910.1001. OSHA has established a permissible exposure limit of 0.1 fibers per cubic centimeter of air, averaged over an eight-hour day.

96. 40 C.F.R. pt. 61, subpt. M.

97. 60 Fed. Reg. 38,725 (July 28, 1995).

98. CAL. HEALTH & SAFETY CODE §§ 25,915–24.

99. 13 N.Y.C.R.R. §§ 18.7(aa), 20.7(z), 21.7(z).

100. *See* Joseph F. Rice & Nancy Worth Davis, *Judicial Innovation in Asbestos Mass Tort Litigation,* 33 TORT & INS. L.J. 127 (Fall 1997).

101. *See, e.g.,* San Francisco Unified School District v. W.R. Grace & Co., 44 Cal. Rptr. 2d 305 (Cal. Ct. App. 1995) (property owner's cause of action for strict liability or negligence accrues only upon asbestos contamination, not upon owner's discovery of the presence of asbestos in the building); BellSouth Telecommunications v. W.R. Grace & Co., 77 F.3d 603 (1995) (building owner's claim under Connecticut Product Liability Act accrued when its senior managers knew that abatement was necessary and that it had cause of action against defendants for abatements costs).

102. *See, e.g.,* Mann v. Pierce, 803 F.2d 1552 (11th Cir. 1986); Lindley v. Cisneros, 74 F.3d 1076 (11th Cir. 1996) (suits by tenants of housing project owned by HUD for restitution of rent for HUD's failure to maintain premises adequately, including claims of crumbling asbestos from ceiling tiles).

103. *See, e.g.,* Kinsey v. Jones, CV 87-2959 (E.D.N.Y. Jan. 30, 1989) (allowing misrepresentation claims in sale of residence).

104. THE INSIDE STORY, *supra* note 2, at 21.

105. EPA sponsors the National Pesticide Telecommunications Network, which provides information to the general public and the medical, veterinary, and professional communities. It can be reached at (800) 858-PEST.

106. EPA, OFFICE OF PESTICIDE PROGRAMS, CITIZEN'S GUIDE TO PEST CONTROL AND PESTICIDE SAFETY (Sept. 1995).

107. There have been several incidents involving the illegal use of agricultural pesticides in homes. In 1996, thousands of homes in several states were sprayed by unlicensed exterminators using methyl parathion, which is not licensed for indoor use. Over 2,000 people were relocated from their homes, and over 700 homes and businesses required decontamination. *Methyl Parathion Comes Inside,* 105 ENVIRONMENTAL HEALTH PERSPECTIVES 690 (1997).

108. LONG ISLAND NEIGHBORHOOD NETWORK, PESTICIDES & CHILDREN: AVOIDING THE RISKS (1995). This group claims that following pesticide label instructions does not guarantee safety for children.

109. *See* NATURAL RESOURCES DEFENSE COUNCIL, TROUBLE ON THE FARM: GROWING UP WITH PESTICIDES IN AGRICULTURAL COMMUNITIES (Oct. 1998).

110. 7 U.S.C. §§ 136–136y.

111. 60 Fed. Reg. 46,592 (Sept. 7, 1995).

112. *See, e.g.,* Wallace v. Lanier Exterminating Serv., Toxic Chem. Lit. Rep. at 11,464 (Dec. 21, 1989) (Forsyth County Ct., Ga., Dec. 8, 1989) (family awarded $900,000 after negligent application of pesticide caused elevated levels of chlordane and heptachlor in their home).

113. For more information of pesticide litigation, see Searcy, *How to Handle a Pesticide Case,* A GUIDE TO TOXIC TORTS, at ch. 23, (Matthew Bender & Co., 1999).

114. *See, e.g.,* Pappas v. Upjohn Co. 926 F.2d 1019 (11th Cir. 1991). *But see* Etcheverry v. Tri-Ag Service, Inc., No. C024045 (Cal. App. 3d, July 8, 1998) (FIFRA does not bar a state failure-to-warn claim).

115. *See, e.g.,* Reutzel v. Spartan Chemical Co., 903 F. Supp. 1272 (N.D. Iowa 1995).

116. Radon is estimated to contribute to 7,000 to 30,000 lung cancer deaths each year. Smokers have a higher risk of developing radon-induced lung cancer.

117. Radon is produced by the natural decay, in several steps, of uranium-238. Radon is the immediate decay product of radium-226.

118. Tobie Bernstein, *Radon in Rental Housing, supra* note 33.

119. 15 U.S.C. §§ 2661–71.

120. EPA, OFFICE OF RADIATION PROGRAMS, INDOOR RADON AND RADON DECAY PRODUCT MEASUREMENT PROTOCOLS 101 (1989).

121. Model Standards and Techniques for Control of Radon in New Residential Buildings, 59 Fed. Reg. 13,402 (1994).

122. *See., e.g.,* OHIO REV. CODE ANN. § 5302.30; S.D. CODIFIED LAWS ANN. 43-4-44; VA. CODE ANN. § 550,519.

123. *See, e.g.,* Brafford v. Susquehanna Corp., 586 F. Supp. 14 (D. Colo. 1984) (family living in radon-contaminated home entitled to trial against uranium mine operator on whether presence of radon had forcibly evicted them from their home).

124. *See, e.g.,* Nobel v. Marvin E. Kanze, Inc., No. 83-05253 (Pa. Ct. C.P. Montgomery Co., filed Apr. 13, 1983) (homeowner's claim against ventilation contractor who had installed an allegedly defective system that permitted natural radon in the soil to be swept into the home's air supply); Tanner v. Adams, 1993 N.Y. A.D. LEXIS 9846 (presence of radon gas in home, although a health hazard at high levels, was not a defect within meaning of sales contract and thus was not grounds for cancellation of contract); Wilson v. Koval, No. 88-201958 (Wash. Super. Ct. Spokane Co. 1990) (seeking compensation for contract price of home, diminished value of home, and damages for exposure where radon levels were 12-30 pCi/L).

125. Tobie Bernstein, *Radon in Rental Housing, supra* note 33.

126. EPA, OFFICE OF WATER, WATER ON TAP: A CONSUMER'S GUIDE TO THE NATION'S DRINKING WATER (1997).

127. Flushing the water by letting the cold water faucet run for an extra minute can help minimize the amount of lead in drinking water. However, this may not work in high-rise buildings because of the large diameter of water supply pipes.

128. NATIONAL RESEARCH COUNCIL, RISK ASSESSMENT OF RADON IN DRINKING WATER (1998).

129. The report noted that of the estimated 19,000 lung cancer deaths each year from a combination of indoor radon and smoking, about 160 deaths are caused by inhaling radon that is emitted from household water. The report found that efforts to reduce the health risks from radon should focus on removing radon from indoor air. EPA is required to prepare new drinking water standards for radon in drinking water in 1999, based in part on the findings of the National Research Council report.

130. 42 U.S.C. §§ 300f to 300j-26.

131. Several other federal environmental laws impact groundwater, including the Clean Water Act, CERCLA, and RCRA. These laws include citizen suit provisions or private causes of action that could be helpful to plaintiffs in some groundwater contamination cases.

132. 63 Fed. Reg. 44,512 (Aug. 19, 1988). Water systems that serve over 10,000 people must send the reports to their customers by Oct. 1, 1999. Systems that serve over 100,000 people must post the reports on the Internet. Systems serving fewer customers can post the reports in a central location or local newspaper.

133. Safe Drinking Water and Toxic Enforcement Act of 1986, CAL. HEALTH & SAFETY CODE §§ 25,249.6–.13

134. People *ex rel.* Lungren v. Superior Court of the City & County of San Francisco, 926 P.2d 1042, 58 Cal. Rptr. 2d 855 (Cal. 1996).

135. 647 F. Supp. 303 (W.D. Tenn. 1986), *aff'd in part, rev'd in part* 855 F.2d 1188 (6th Cir. 1988).

136. Anderson v. W.R. Grace & Co., 628 F. Supp. 1219 (D. Mass. 1986).

137. *See* Allison Rittenhouse Hayward, *Common Law Remedies and the UST Regulations,* 21 B.C. ENVTL. AFF. L. REV. 619 (1994); Jason M. Basile, *Still No Remedy After All These Years: Plugging the Hole in the Law of Leaking Underground Storage Tanks,* 73 IND. L.J. 675 (Spring 1998) (noting that remedies under CERCLA, RCRA, and state underground storage tank programs are inadequate for victims of leaking underground storage tanks).

138. For more detail on the nature of electric fields, see Michael C. Anibogu, *The Future of Electromagnetic Field Litigation,* 15 Pace ENVTL. L. REV. 517 (1998). EPA has established an EMF Hotline at (800) EMF-2383.

139. *See* Anibogu, *supra* note 138, for a summary of the relevant international and United States studies.

140. NATIONAL RESEARCH COUNCIL, COMMITTEE ON THE POSSIBLE EFFECTS OF ELECTROMAGNETIC FIELDS ON BIOLOGIC SYSTEMS, REPORT ON POSSIBLE HEALTH EFFECTS OF EXPOSURE TO RESIDENTIAL ELECTRIC AND MAGNETIC FIELDS (1996). This study found that "no conclusive and consistent evidence shows that exposure to electric and magnetic fields produces cancer, adverse neurobehavioral effects, and reproductive and developmental effects."

141. National Cancer Institute & Children's Cancer Group, *Residential Exposure to Magnetic Fields and Acute Lymphoblastic Leukemia in Children,* 337 N. ENG. J. MED. 1 (1997). This report was the result of an eight-year, $50 million power line research project.

142. The NIEHS study grew out of the 1992 Energy Policy Act, which established a research program called the EMF Research and Public Information Dis-

semination (RAPID) Program, jointly implemented by NIEHS and the Department of Energy.

143. *See* Anibogu, *supra* note 138 (noting that the *Daubert* case and the available scientific studies will make it difficult, but not impossible, for plaintiffs to prevail in EMF litigation).

144. MICROWAVE NEWS, Nov./Dec. 1998, at 1.

145. *See, e.g.*, San Diego Gas & Electric Co. v. Daley, 205 Cal. App.3d 1334, 253 Cal. Rptr. 144 (1988). In that case, a gas and electric company brought an eminent domain action to acquire a power line easement. The jury awarded compensation for the property condemned and also damages for diminution in the value of the remaining property. During trial, the court admitted evidence relating to the controversy over whether EMFs pose a health hazard. A California Court of Appeal affirmed and found that the trial court properly admitted this evidence.

146. *See* San Diego Gas & Electric Co. v. Superior Court, 55 Cal. Rptr. 2d 724, 920 P.2d 669 (Cal. 1996). In this case, homeowners sued a utility for personal injuries and property damage. Plaintiffs alleged that EMFs had caused them emotional distress, made their home uninhabitable, and destroyed its market value. The court dismissed the suit on the grounds that the California Public Utilities Commission had exclusive jurisdiction over the issues raised by the complaint.

147. For example, the Texas Department of Health issued an advisory on June 10, 1997 recommending that people limit their consumption of king mackerel from the Gulf of Mexico after tests showed elevated mercury levels in the fish.

148. ENVIRONMENTAL WORKING GROUP, EPA REPORTS THAT 1.6 MILLION KIDS, MOMS AT RISK OF MERCURY POISONING, WARNINGS IN 37 STATES AGAINST FRESH-CAUGHT FISH (Dec. 17, 1997).

149. Grace M. Egeland & John P. Middaugh, *Balancing Fish Consumption with Mercury Exposure*, 278 SCIENCE, Dec. 12, 1997, at 1904.

150. *See* Sarah Lyall, *New Rules for Bluefish Give the Poor the Blues*, N.Y. TIMES, Aug. 17, 1991.

CHAPTER 19

Assisting Injured Individuals

ALLAN KANNER

Nature of the Problem

Too many Americans needlessly suffer from having to live, work, or play in unhealthy environments. Many racial minorities and low-income populations suffer above-average exposure to hazardous waste, air and water pollutants, dangerous products, and workplace carcinogens.[1] Although we continue to make progress in solving and preventing health and environmental problems, much remains to be done, especially in minority communities, to ensure that all Americans enjoy certain basic environmental health protections. However, the problem is not simply an environmental one or a racial one, but includes an economic opportunity component as well. This in turn has led to some conflicts between minorities and environmentalists.

Numerous studies point to the extra burden of pollution on minority communities.[2] Low-income and minority communities suffer in terms of physical and psychological health, as well as overall quality of life. The Environmental Protection Agency (EPA) has acknowledged both that polluting industries and hazardous waste dumps are most often located in predominantly poor minority communities, and that such sitings have an adverse impact on the affected people and their community.[3] To the extent that these burdens, in fact, exist in a particular community and have produced real injury, a toxic tort suit might be an appropriate vehicle for redress, or form part of an overall strategy for the affected community.[4] Part of any notion of justice would include just compensation for legitimate injuries wherever they occur.

However, the environmental justice plaintiff often must surmount more hurdles than the typical plaintiff.[5] These hurdles include the added causation problems presented by multiple possible industrial sources ("Cancer Alley" or "Refinery Row"), a history of poor medical care and a lack of medical records, risks associated with more dangerous work and lifestyle factors, and circumstances of the poor that often present as alternative causal factors (for instance, bad diet, infrequent medical attention, smoking), along with the problem of jurors judging others by their different life experiences. These combine to make it more difficult for low-income minorities to prove to a middle-class jury that they have suffered harm as a result of their environmental victimization and thus to prevail in toxic tort litigation.[6]

Moreover, even assuming that these plaintiffs are awarded some compensation, the ultimate solution to problems of environmental justice is generally political or administrative, not judicial. Lawyers always have to be honest with their clients about the realistic goals of toxic tort litigation and vigilant in pursuing a client's goal.[7] While toxic tort litigation can provide important compensation to victims who have been damaged, it can rarely alter the political status quo that has allegedly produced and sustained the complained-of injustice.[8] Indeed, counsel must be cautious not to misrepresent the efficacy of law, or to undercut the political goals of his or her clients inadvertently.[9] Environmental racism involves greater issues beyond the siting of industrial facilities and the disposal of hazardous wastes in or near minority or poor communities and the disproportionate burden carried by those communities in terms of adverse health and environmental impacts.[10] In most cases, facilities will not be moved. This means that residents of these communities will continue to bear an unjust share of the health,[11] economic,[12] and other quality of life risks and burdens[13] associated with pollution. This reality cannot easily be undone and certainly cannot be wholly rectified in the context of a toxic tort lawsuit.[14]

Prior to Litigation

Lawyers involved in these cases on behalf of putative plaintiffs will generally find themselves intimately involved in pre-suit strategy planning with clients. Community groups and individual victims are rarely passive about, or ignorant of, their situation. Greater involvement by counsel in working through the ramifications of different strategies is generally the norm.

One of the most important things counsel can do at an early stage is to assist the clients in assessing their situation. This has two components. First, counsel will need to gather information about the subject environmental situation, often by taking advantage of the self-reporting information available under various laws;[15] and the connection, if any, between that situation (and/or potentially others) and the clients' concrete complaints.[16] Second, counsel will need to make recommendations about how to shape the litigation. For example, people living next door to an ongoing polluting facility may want to stop the problem, rather than initiating a suit for damages. On the other hand, if the plant is generally in compliance with the law, a federal citizen suit may not be possible or desirable, and a nuisance action must be considered.[17] Shooting with a rifle or a series of rifles, instead of a shotgun, enables the advocate to focus the court on the client's core goal quickly and efficiently.[18]

Defense counsel likewise need to focus on the dynamic that gave rise to an environmental justice or community-based lawsuit. Is the issue protection of property values only? Is the concern the timing of a governmental supervised cleanup operation (perhaps, being run by other lawyers for the same client)? Very often the problem that gives rise to litigation is avoidable. Moreover, if litigation is commenced with a shotgun blast of theories of liability and claims for relief, it is important to try to sift through the suit to see if there is a basis for focusing the parties' attention on resolving the underlying problem. This is not to suggest that defense of the entire complaint should in any way be slighted; however, lawyers on both sides of these types of cases tend to avoid problem solving in favor of a frenzy of litigation.[19]

Focusing on the Problem

Introduction

A lawyer should start by evaluating damages, current and prospective. The theories of liability tend to fall into place once the problems warranting compensation or other relief are clearly focused. Most environmental justice cases raise only a limited number of state law toxic tort issues. The "problem" to be rectified is any one or a combination of the following:

1. manifest personal injury;
2. concern about potential future personal injuries (referred to herein as "medical monitoring");
3. concern about property and/or its values;
4. concern about quality of life, including "nuisance," "pain and suffering," or "economical distress";

5. concern about invasions of property rights ("trespass"); and
6. the need to punish the responsible malefactor.

This list does not include "environmental racism" itself. First, this is not a recognized cause of action in tort.[20] Second, abstractions as opposed to concrete items are generally not effective in front of a jury. However, to the extent that an otherwise avoidable harm or risk of harm was imposed due to racism—for instance, moving a tank car with volatile chemicals from an industrial facility to a rail siding in a minority community—this concrete activity will likely weigh heavily in any punitive damage award. Third, liability without compensable and identifiable harm is generally not actionable.[21]

Although it is tempting to sue under any or all of these theories, it is often not good strategy to do so.[22] For example, if neighboring properties are polluted and there is property damage, it does not always make sense to "throw in" a claim for medical monitoring or fear of cancer. If there is no basis for these claims, they should never be added. Even if there were a basis, however, the following need to be considered: the added costs of litigating medical issues where there is no manifest harm; the resulting expanded scope of discovery, including investigation of the clients' lifestyles; and the possible loss of credibility in the eyes of the court or jury by pursuing a de minimis or even frivolous claim.

Personal Injuries and Wrongful Death

The claim for manifest personal injury is probably the most difficult toxic tort claim to establish. First, there is the relative lack of good scientific information in the case of many nonagent-specific products (for example, asbestos and mesothelioma; vinyl chloride and angiosarcoma of the liver). In the post-*Daubert* world, state and federal courts are very focused on the quality of plaintiffs' proof.[23] Indeed, in some cases, companies that have sold relatively untested products or discharged unstudied wastes have been rewarded for their misconduct by being allowed to hide behind a shield of scientific uncertainty. On the other hand, under the Toxic Substances Control Act (TSCA) and the Occupational Safety and Health Administration (OSHA), health effect information must be maintained and could prove valuable to the toxic tort plaintiff. The Agency for Toxic Substances and Disease Registry (ATSDR) and various state agencies are likewise involved in investigating these matters. Second, part of the basis of any medical causation opinion will include information about dose and exposure.[24] Again, much of this information should be on file pursuant to federal reporting requirements.[25]

If such evidence is not publicly available, often it will be sufficient to show the presence of the chemical as sensed by the plaintiff and others, as well as from the immediate adverse impact the dose caused the plaintiff.[26]

The identity of the toxic substances to which the harm is attributed thus may be shown by circumstantial evidence.[27] As noted in *Elam v. Alcolac, Inc.*:[28]

> A person subjected to chronic, long-term chemical exposures is not expected to foster a study group in order to gather evidence to prove liability for a disease not even anticipated. An industrial polluter who refuses to make possible the measurement of the pollution—despite official obligation to that end—cannot complain that the measurement lacks.

Defendants will insist that an association between exposure and reaction is insufficient. They will insist on quantification of dose, and then argue, when appropriate, that the number proven is in some sense safe. Typically, defendants attempt to invoke workplace safety numbers as evidence of a safe threshold.[29]

The major contemporary questions in private toxic tort litigation concerning personal injuries—proving the amount of dose, and laying the foundation for scientific opinion on causation—are nevertheless inextricably tied to substantive notions of responsibility. Although some defendants would rather deal with legal abstractions about the nature of "causation" apart from the facts of the case, plaintiff's counsel must shape his or her case in light of a defendant's actual role in using the nature and quality of available evidence. Thus, if a defendant fails to monitor its uncontrolled toxic releases or fails to test its toxic products for medical risks, plaintiff's counsel must take a position on how this impacts on theories of liability (for instance, duty to test) and the requisite proof (for instance, adverse inference rule needed to prove causation damages).[30] Defendant should not be allowed to profit from the lack of data caused by the avoidance of its responsibilities to the public health. Indeed, in the extreme case where evidence is destroyed or falsified, a cause of action for spoilation or fraud may be properly filed.[31] On the other hand, the defendant with a good story to tell—for example, long-term monitoring program designed to protect against needless exposures—will be hard to beat at trial.

The key to success in manifest personal injury litigation remains expert-proof. The best expert is the local treating physician. The worst situation occurs in which a plaintiff sees a doctor for years without complaining about injuries or relating them to a tortfeasor, and then suddenly the plaintiff comes into court with an out-of-town expert who ties an incredible list of injuries into a local problem. However, many people, especially poor people, do not have a regular doctor or take advantage of available medical care in the same way as the middle class. For example, absent an effective presentation of the circumstances, it is hard for a jury to understand why a plaintiff did not see a doctor after a miscarriage or after a prolonged period of headaches or diarrhea. Very often, the best advice a lawyer can give a client is not to sue on an alleged manifest personal injury until some doctor (in the best scenario, a local one) ties it to the alleged tortfeasor. In many jurisdictions, the statute of limitations will not run based on mere suspicions coupled with a negative medical opinion.[32]

The "standard" categories of compensation for bodily injury do not change in toxic tort cases, and include medical expenses, loss of earning capacity, pain and suffering, and the loss of enjoyment of life. Damages for wrongful death vary somewhat from state to state, but generally are largely based on the expected earning capacity of the decedent. However, the unique circumstances of toxic tort cases have led to some expansion of the traditional damage categories.

Increased Risk of Cancer or Other Future Illness

Tort law for the most part concerns itself with actual and manifest damages.[33] To the extent that the victim of environmental injustice has been hurt, a private tort action is more likely to succeed than in the case of a mere increased risk of harm.[34]

A number of toxic tort plaintiffs have sought to recover for the increased risk that they will develop cancer or some other physical illness in the future because of their exposure to hazardous substances. For the most part, these efforts have been unsuccessful, because damages for speculative risk of future disease are generally not recoverable.[35] Several courts considering this issue have noted the inherent unfairness in awarding damages for the risk of future illness, as those who do not develop the illness will be overcompensated while those who do will be undercompensated.[36] However, where there is some present physical injury and the plaintiff can demonstrate future consequences of the present illness that are reasonably probable or reasonably certain to occur, recovery is generally allowed. The standards for recovery for increased risk have been described as follows:

1. plaintiff must show to a "reasonable certainty" that he or she will develop the disease;[37]
2. plaintiff must show to a "reasonable medical certainty" that he or she will develop the disease;[38] or
3. plaintiff must show that it is "more likely than not" that he or she will develop the disease.[39]

Many defendants argue that these standards all seem to require that plaintiff's risk exceed 50 percent,[40] and some courts seem to prefer a specific numerical percentage or statistic in this situation.[41] However, plaintiffs might want to try to avoid having their experts pinned down to a specific number.[42] In effect, this type of number game distracts from the real issue.[43]

For the environmental justice plaintiff, there is the added burden of defending against the other "risks" extant in his or her life: "Doctor, would you agree that plaintiffs' smoking [or diet, and so on] poses a greater risk of harm?" Further, claims for increased risk often fail because plaintiff cannot show to a reasonable degree of medical certainty that he or she will develop a specific disease.[44] However, claims for medical monitoring, which are discussed later in this chapter, appear to be gaining acceptance as an interim measure of relief for victims with an elevated risk of injury in the future.[45]

Fear of Cancer or Other Illness

Historically, damages for emotional distress were not favored, and were allowed only where the claimed emotional distress was connected with a physical injury upon which recovery was primarily based. Now, however, many courts that will deny a claim for increased risk of developing an illness in the future will recognize a claim for present emotional distress based on a reasonable *fear* of the increased risk of illness.

Fear of future illness claims are generally subject to specific threshold requirements to be compensable. With respect to cancer, typical threshold requirements have included:

- a serious fear of cancer (cancerphobia);
- the fear being caused by exposure to the substance involved; and
- reasonableness of the fear (there is a scientifically valid basis for concluding the risk of contracting cancer is substantial).

In addition, and often most important, some courts still require some present physical injury or at least demonstrable "physical impact" before allowing recovery for fear of a future illness.[46]

Plaintiffs seeking damages for cancerphobia will find support in several previous cases where damages have been awarded for mental anguish resulting from cancerphobia when the plaintiff suffered contemporaneous burns and ulcerations as a result of acute exposure to potentially carcinogenic chemicals and x-rays.[47] Similarly, the publicity given to birth defects at Love Canal could give rise to claims for mental anguish associated with the fear of birth defects in unborn children of pregnant women who have been exposed to toxic chemicals and display some form of physical injury as a result of such exposure.[48] However, there is clearly a point beyond which the possibility of developing cancer or other latent diseases is so remote that it renders parasitic damages for cancerphobia or the fear of developing other latent disease noncompensable as a matter of public policy.[49] Some cases accordingly hold that there must be some physical component to the harm before any damages will be awarded for emotional harm,[50] although the required showing may be minimal.[51] This view appears to be waning in judicial popularity.

Parasitic damages for mental anguish and emotional trauma can be expected to comprise a significant portion of the damage awards in those cases where the plaintiff can prove some form of contemporaneous physical injury as a result of exposure to toxic chemicals released into the environment by the defendant.[52] Given the long latency period for cancer and other diseases commonly associated with toxic chemicals, claims for parasitic damages of mental anguish resulting from the fear of developing cancer and other diseases will most likely be a standard element in the plaintiff's request for damages.

A growing number of courts have dispensed with the physical harm prerequisite altogether.[53] Such decisions generally require that any fear of future disease be reasonable.[54] At minimum it would appear that exposure to the toxic substance must be proven,[55] and the degree of enhanced risk may be relevant to whether such a fear is reasonable.[56]

For example, in *Laxton v. Orkin Exterminating Co.*, a family was exposed to chlordane through contaminated household water but experienced no physical harm or pain. The court held that the jury could find ingesting a carcinogen to be an "injury" sufficient to support an award for mental anguish, even if subsequent medical diagnosis failed to reveal any other physical injury. Where blood tests proved negative, "[t]he period of mental anguish, of course, would be confined to the time between discovery of the ingestion and the negative medial diagnosis or other information that puts to rest the fear of injury."[57]

In re Moorenovich, supra note 53, held that fear of cancer from asbestos was a recoverable element of damages, even though enhanced risk was not. The court also noted that the fear in this case was reasonable, where it derived from the facts that:

1. asbestos is a known carcinogen;
2. the plaintiff had prolonged exposure to the asbestos; and
3. plaintiff's coworkers were dying at a higher than normal rate from asbestos-related cancer.

The Court also noted that if the plaintiff eventually did contract cancer, he would then be able to sue for the disease itself.[58]

In *Potter v. Firestone Tire & Rubber Co.,*[59] an award of compensatory damages for "fear of cancer" (at $200,000 per plaintiff), "psychological damage," and "disruption of lives" was affirmed. Firestone had sent toxic wastes to a Class II landfill that was not permitted to receive them. As a result, toxic chemicals found their way into plaintiffs' drinking water. The court specifically held that where the plaintiffs had shown that they ingested carcinogens (arguably a "physical impact"), there was no requirement they demonstrate a present physical injury in order to recover for fear of cancer.

Medical Monitoring

Toxic tort cases often present nontraditional harms, or situations, where defendants have placed a victim at some indeterminate risk. In the original *In re Three Mile Island Litigation,*[60] everyone knew that the victims had been exposed to some indeterminate amount of radiation (due to negligent post-accident monitoring by defendant), and that this was probably harmful from a medical point of view.[61] Given such a situation, a number of remedial options suggest themselves:

- Sue now for all possible present and future harms;
- Sue now for all present and/or future harms of some degree of likelihood;
- Sue now for all present harms and the increased risk of future harms; or
- Sue now for all present harms and for medical monitoring into the future.

The solution often turns on a recognition that the victims have been placed at an "indeterminate risk" by the tortfeasor either because the tortfeasor failed to study the hazards presented by its chemicals or to monitor/measure the victims' exposure to the same, or both.[62]

It is a well-established principle of tort law that a tortfeasor is liable for medical costs necessitated by a plaintiff's injury. In the late 1970s and early 1980s, plaintiffs began to argue that even when there was no physical injury, the medical costs necessary to make a diagnosis were recoverable.[63] The classic example offered by one court was a motorcycle hitting a pedestrian: Surely the driver is liable for a hospital visit to determine whether the pedestrian is injured.[64] And what if a second or third visit is required to ensure there is no latent injury? Those expenses are covered as well, the courts concluded.

Two tort doctrines have had a significant impact on the development of medical-damage screening damages. First, under the avoidable-consequences rule, courts and commentators recognize that a plaintiff "injured by the tort of another is not entitled to recover damages for any harm that he could have avoided by the use or reasonable effort of expenditure after the commission of the tort."[65] Advocates of medical screening therefore argue that because people exposed to toxic substances are required by the avoidable-consequences rule to undertake medical screening, the tortfeasor should be required to reimburse them for the cost of medical testing.

Second, under the single-recovery rule, a plaintiff must include in a single action all claims against an alleged tortfeasor arising out of the same transactions or occurrence. Under this rule, a plaintiff who sued for an injury and then later developed cancer would be unable to bring a second action to recover for the later-occurring cancer and its attendant medical costs.[66] In jurisdictions in which this rule applies, medical-screening damages are viewed as a way to prevent the development of uncompensable disease.

In *Three Mile Island,* plaintiffs successfully argued that given the medical uncertainty associated with the event, the victim should be allowed to sue immediately for mental anguish arising from the accident and the future medical uncertainty. In addition, plaintiffs successfully argued that medical monitoring of the victim's medical condition should be paid for by the tortfeasor.[67]

Future physical harms are often a very real and serious concern of a population exposed to pollution. Although some lawyers have tried to express these concerns—the idea that one is more likely, but not certain, to suffer injury in the future by virtue of the tortfeasor's conduct—as "fear of cancer" or "increased risk" claims,[68] the trend is toward using the medical monitoring claim to address these concerns. Under the appropriate circumstances, medical monitoring is a means of shifting the cost of reasonably prudent medical intervention to the tortfeasor that has wrongfully imposed a new risk of harm on the plaintiff.[69]

Plaintiffs have been relatively successful in obtaining awards requiring defendants to pay for future medical monitoring to determine if illnesses will develop in the future. Such awards have been justified on the ground that the need for medical monitoring is a present need resulting from the defendants' actions. No present injury or illness is generally required, as long as medical testimony indicates that medical monitoring is reasonably necessary because of the increased risk of future illness.

For example, *In re Paoli RR Yard PCB Litigation,*[70] the Third Circuit[71] (applying Pennsylvania law) stated:

> The future expense of medical monitoring could be a recoverable consequential damage provided that plaintiffs can establish with a reasonable degree of medical certainty that such expenditures

are "reasonably anticipated" to be incurred by reason of their exposure.

The Third Circuit further stated that evidence of the probability of future harm is not necessary, as long as the monitoring is necessitated by the plaintiffs' exposure and the need for early detection and diagnosis of future disease.[72]

In *Amaranda Hess Mirada v. Shell Oil Co.*,[73] the Court held that medical monitoring costs are compensable under California law, following the *Paoli* decision. The court identified five factors bearing on recoverability:

1. the significance and extent of exposure;
2. the relative toxicity of the chemicals;
3. the seriousness of the diseases for which there is an increased risk;
4. the relative increase in chances for developing these diseases; and
5. the clinical value of early detection and diagnosis.

Consistent with the above is the case of *Friends For All Children, Inc. v. Lockheed Aircraft Co.*[74] *Friends for all Children* was brought by Canadian and European parents on behalf of their adopted Vietnamese children who had been orphaned as a result of a plane crash caused by a locking systems malfunction. The plaintiffs claimed the children were entitled to diagnostic examinations to be performed if the cabin depressurization had the potential to cause injuries which could prove irreparable if not detected early. The court noted the recognition of the right to the claim "sever[s] the two principal parts of tort-law—the deterrence of misconduct and the provision of just compensation to victims of wrongdoing."[75] The court found that the need for diagnostic exams was both based on competent medical testimony and caused by the defendant.[76]

In *Ayers v. Township of Jackson*,[77] commonly referred to as "*Ayers I*," the trial court ruled that plaintiffs did not have to show a "reasonable probability" that the feared illnesses would develop. Rather, they only had to show that surveillance would be necessary to "properly diagnose the warning signs of the development of the disease." The New Jersey Supreme Court reversed the Court of Appeals (*Ayers II*), and upheld the trial court's determination (and an $8.2 million dollar award for medical surveillance) that medical surveillance damages should be recognizable in tort.[78] The New Jersey Supreme Court found the trial court's conclusion reasonable that, based on "competent medical testimony was offered to prove that a program of regular medical testing and evaluation was reasonably necessary and consistent with contemporary scientific principles. . . ."[79]

The *Ayers* plaintiffs asserted that surveillance would "permit the earliest possible diagnosis of illnesses, which could lead to improved prospects for cure, prolongation of life, relief of pain, and minimization of disability."[80] Damages to fund medical surveillance were found to be reasonable *even though*, as defendants argued, *the occurrence of the threatened physical injuries was not probable.*

In *City of Northglenn v. Chevron*,[81] Chevron attempted to exclude evidence of plaintiffs' claimed increased risk. Judge Carrigan ruled that Chevron misconstrued the limits of the rule "requiring medical probability as the standard to support a finding of causation." The judge concluded that the plaintiffs would be permitted to introduce expert testimony in support of claims for reasonably probable medical expenses arising from an extended testing program.

In *Merry v. Westinghouse*,[82] the court pointed to three elements of a claim for medical monitoring:

1. exposure to a hazardous substance;
2. the potential for injury; and
3. the need for early detection and treatment.

In *Askey v. Occidental Chemical Corp.*,[83] the court held that to recover for future medical surveillance costs, a plaintiff must "establish with a reasonable degree of medical certainty that such expenditures are 'reasonably anticipated' to be incurred by reason of the exposure." As indicated, *Askey* and a number of other courts have been less receptive to increased risk claims,[84] reasoning that:

1. the mere risk is not a present "injury";[85]
2. a plaintiff should sue when, and if, he contracts the feared disease;[86] and
3. it would be inequitable to award damages on this basis.[87]

In spite of these arguments, a number of courts have held that a plaintiff may recover for the enhanced risk of disease if a sufficient showing has been made.[88] Many of these courts apparently fear that if plaintiff is not awarded damages in one initial action, the "single action rule" may bar him or her from later presenting another claim when the disease finally does appear.[89] For the trial lawyer, pleading damages will be a function of the local single action rule and statute of limitations law.

The problem with medical-screening claims is that they are often highly speculative. As such, some courts have permitted these claims only when the plaintiff proves the existence of a present physical injury.[90] Commentators have said that the "injury is 'proof', a tangible recognition that an event has taken place which becomes a touchstone for further damages."[91] Other courts have completely abandoned the physical injury requirement. Because it is exposure—not physical injury—that necessitates medical screening, recovery may be had without proof of physical injury.[92]

The Utah Supreme Court set forth criteria for obtaining medical-screening damages in *Hansen v. Mountain Fuel Supply Co.*[93] In *Hansen,* the plaintiffs sought, among other things, medical screening, claiming they were exposed to asbestos. The trial court granted summary judgment in favor of the defendants on the ground that the plaintiffs had not suffered a present physical injury and therefore could not recover medical screening damages. The Utah Supreme Court reversed, holding that medical-screening damages may be had without a present physical injury. The court noted, however, that "mere exposure to an allegedly harmful substance . . . is not enough for recovery."[94] The court held that plaintiffs have the burden of meeting an eight-factor test to recover medical-screening costs. These criteria, the court explained, ensured "that only those plaintiffs who need monitoring above and beyond basic medical care will recover costs," and were designed to "prevent unnecessary litigation and unwarranted recoveries."[95]

The criteria established by the *Hansen* court require plaintiffs to prove each of the following elements to recover damages for medical screening:

> (1) exposure (2) to a toxic substance, (3) which exposure was caused by the defendant's negligence, (4) resulting in an increased risk (5) of a serious disease, illness or injury, (6) for which a medical test for early detection exists (7) and for which early detection is beneficial, meaning that a treatment exists that can alter the course of the illness, (8) and which test has been prescribed by a qualified physician according to scientific principles.[96]

Proving exposure is no easy task. For example, the New Jersey Supreme Court explained that medical-screening damages are available only to those who have been directly exposed to a substance. In *Theer v. Phillip Carey Co.,*[97] the Court denied medical screening to a woman who allegedly had secondary exposure to asbestos from washing her husband's clothes. In another 1993 case, a federal court in Pennsylvania denied recovery when the plaintiffs could not prove exposure to a toxic agent but merely submitted an expert affidavit that speculated on possible means of exposure.[98]

A basis of the Utah Supreme Court's decision in *Hansen* was that plaintiffs should recover only for the additional medical screening made necessary by the defendant's conduct. Thus, if the screening is of the kind that the plaintiff should have undergone anyway, the defendant should not be required to pay for it. Some commentators have agreed with this approach.[99]

In *Hansen,* the court described the basic purpose for medical screening: the detection and treatment of disease before it manifests itself clinically. At the same time, the court realized that some diseases are undetectable or untreatable before their clinical manifestation. Thus, there is no test that can detect "the onset of the illness before it would be apparent to the layperson . . . then periodic monitoring is pointless."[100] And if there is no treatment "available that would be more beneficial to the plaintiff if administered before the illness becomes obvious . . . medical monitoring cannot fulfill its purpose."[101]

In requiring that a physician actually prescribe the screening procedure, the *Hansen* court explained that it was "creating a real hurdle for plaintiffs. It would not be enough to show merely that some doctor would prescribe screening, rather, the area of specialty would order for a patient similarly situated."[102] This test therefore establishes that the screening must be "generally accepted in the medical community."[103]

In stressing that defendants should be made to pay only for the additional screening that plaintiffs actually undergo as a result of the defendants' conduct, the court concluded that plaintiffs should not receive individual damage awards for past, present, and future screening. Instead, the court stated, trial courts should consider a court-supervised fund to administer medical-screening payments, or should require defendants to purchase insurance for plaintiffs that would cover the screening. The *Hansen* court, in adopting its rule against lump-sum damage awards for medical-screening claims, relied heavily on the New Jersey Supreme Court's analysis in the 1987 case *Ayers v. Jackson Township.*[104]

Property Values

Property damages recoverable under tort law generally fall within three basic categories:

1. cost of repair;
2. diminution of value; and
3. loss of or unreasonable interference with use and enjoyment.

In general, at common law "permanent" damage is remedied by the diminution in value, and "temporary" damage by the cost of repair, except where repair would not make economic sense or would be greater than the value of the property (although there are exceptions to this exception). Although many states will allow damages for restoration of property even at a considerable expense, public law theories of liability may provide a better vehicle for relief.[105] For example, the remedy under CERCLA is often stipulated to be measured in terms of cost of repair (response costs or cleanup costs), even though this often exceeds the market value of the property.[106]

It is well-settled in many states that the basic measure of damages for injury to real property is ordinarily the so-called "market value measure"—the difference between the market value of the property immediately before and immediately after the injury.[107] However, almost as soon as the general rule was first recognized, courts have acknowledged that this general measure is not written in stone, and that under certain circumstances the broader policy of making sure victims of torts are adequately compensated may require the market value measure to yield to the so-called "remediation measure," under which a plaintiff is entitled to recover the costs of restoring his or her property to its pre-tort condition.

An important case marking this shift in the judicial perspective on the appropriate measure of damages is *Samson Construction Company v. Brunsowankin*,[108] in which the plaintiff's homesite was bulldozed by a construction company. The court stated that the measure of damages for the destruction of fruit trees "was not invariably the market value of the land on which the trees stood before and after the wrong, but under appropriate circumstances may be the value of the trees or the reasonable restoration of the property as it was before the wrong."[109] The court's reasoning recognized that the landowners had a right to enjoy the realty according to their personal preferences.[110] Thus, a landowner could recover for the cost of restoration upon a showing of a personal reason for restoring the premises to the condition that it was in before the wrong. This result parallels in its scope to specific relief to an injured party to his original position, and since this is usually an accepted aim of the law of damages, other courts have agreed that such a measure is an appropriate one.[111]

For example, the shade tree cases illustrate the importance of the use factor in awarding restoration costs. When forest land is damaged, recovery is only based on the diminished value of the land or on the timber value of the trees cut. But, if an ornamental or shade tree is taken from a residential area, it is more appropriate to allow the cost of restoring the area to its original condition by replanting the tree.[112] Numerous cases also focus on the other interests or uses the trees/shrubbery provide to the landowner, such as their aesthetic value,[113] their functional purpose,[114] and the personal reasons of the landowners.[115]

Restoration costs are not only recovered in cases involving damaged or destroyed trees and shrubbery, but also in cases where a landowner's well has been polluted. The courts in these cases have held that the cost of procuring a new well was a proper element to consider in awarding damages.[116] Similarly, courts have granted restoration costs for the cleaning up of polluted streams.[117] The examples below show that "[w]hen property has been damaged by oil or hazardous waste and cost of restoration exceeds the value of the property, diminution in market value is not always a fair and reasonable remedy."[118]

- "To allow a defendant to simply pay for the extent of a neighbor's property which has been damaged may establish a poor precedent. Such a result would allow a property owner to do as he will with his property in order to reap major economic benefit, since any damage to neighboring property can be remedied by the payment of a sum that is relatively nominal when the gain involved is considered."[119]
- *Davey Compressor Co. v. City of Delray Beach*[120] was brought by a city against a company whose manufacturing operations contaminated the city's groundwater supply. The court noted the general rule that damages to property are measured by diminution in the property's value or the cost of repairing or restoring the property to its prior condition. The cost of restoration cannot be used as the measure of damages if that cost is greater than the value of the property in its original condition, the value of the depreciation, or the actual damage. This rule did not apply to this case, according to the Florida Supreme Court, because the reason for limiting recovery (that is, to avoid overcompensation of the injured party) "does not justify limiting the measure of damages to the value of the" city's well field,[121] since damage was to a public entity's water supply.
- *Nischke v. Farmers & Merchants Bank & Trust*[122] is a case by a landowner for negligence against a bank holding a security interest in underground gasoline tanks on the landowner's property. A Wisconsin appeals court held that the general rule that nuisance damages should be the lower of the cost of repair or the diminution in the property's value did not apply in this case because the landowner was compelled to clean up the property because of a legal duty to restore the environment imposed by statute. This entitled the plaintiff to damages in the amount of cleanup costs.[123]

The Restatement (Second) of Torts supports the view of the more recent cases by recognizing that where land is used for "a purpose personal to the owner," the replacement cost is the proper measure even when there is no diminution of value.[124] The Restatement (Second) of Torts Section 929 recognizes, at least in a trespass context, that remediation may, in the appropriate circumstances, be the measure of damages to real property, and, at comment b, states as follows:

> [I]f a ditch is wrongfully dug upon the land of another, the other normally is entitled to damages measured by the expense of filling the ditch, if he wishes it filled. If, however, the cost of replacing the land in its original condition is disproportionate to the diminution in the value of the land caused by the trespass, unless there is a reason personal to the owner for restoring the original condition, damages are measured only by the difference between the value of the land before and after the harm.

Under this Restatement protocol, the first inquiry is whether the use of the property was "personal." If not, then remediation costs may exceed the amount of market value diminution only if that excess is not "disproportionate." Presumably, if the use of the property is "personal," then the plaintiff is entitled to remediation under Section 929 regardless of whether the costs of remediation are "disproportionate" to the diminution in value.

Many courts expressly recognize the importance of these comment b factors, while rejecting the particular analysis contained in comment b:[125]

> We agree that the factors enumerated in Restatement (Second) of Torts § 929 comment b are important in determining whether a case is appropriate for application of "cost of restoration" rather than "diminution of market value" as the measure of damages for tortious injury to land. We conclude, however, that the considerations governing what is an "appropriate case" for departure from the market value standard are not susceptible to reduction to set list and that no formula can be devised that can produce litmus test certainty and yet retain the flexibility to produce fair results in all cases.[126]

Instead of any particular mechanical approach, the court outlined several broad principles to be considered. First, the court rejected the notion that remediation damages ipso facto may not exceed market value damages, noting that it is precisely because the market value measure may not adequately compensate landowners that the remediation measure may come into play.[127] The court then rejected the notion that remediation damages can never exceed the pre-tort market value of the property to be remediated:

> If the damage is reparable, and the costs, although greater than original value, are not wholly unreasonable in relation to that value, and if the evidence demonstrates that payment of market value likely will not adequately compensate the property owner for some personal or other special reason, we conclude that the selection of the cost of restoration as the proper measure of damages would be within the limits of a trial court's discretion.[128]

Finally, the court articulated two cardinal principles that must be kept in mind in making the market value/remediation decision: On the one hand, the award must make the plaintiff whole; on the other hand, it cannot so exceed the goal of full compensation that it constitutes in effect a punishment of the defendant or encourages wasteful remedial expenditures by the plaintiffs.[129]

Quality of Life

Courts have allowed recovery for impairment of the quality of life caused by exposure to toxic substances. This theory is derived from the law of nuisance and may be dependent upon a showing of an interference with a property right.[130]

The Restatement (Second) of Torts[131] sets out three distinct categories of compensation with respect to invasions of an interest in land:

1. the difference between the value of the land before the harm and the value after the harm, or a [plaintiff's] election in an appropriate case, the cost of restoration that has been or may be reasonably incurred;
2. the loss of use of the land; and
3. discomfort and annoyance to him or her as occupant.

While the first two of these components constitute damages for the interference with plaintiff's use and enjoyment of his or her land, the third category compensates the plaintiff for personal losses flowing directly from such an invasion.[132] As such, damages for inconvenience, discomfort, and annoyance constitute "distinct grounds of compensation for which in ordinary cases the person in possession is entitled to recover *in addition* to the harm to his proprietary interests."

In *Ayers,* proof of loss of quality of life focused on the concrete problems faced by residents. Specifically, following testing that revealed the presence of toxic chemicals in the community's wells, the residents were instructed not to drink and to limit exposure to the well water. Water was supplied to the residents first by a container system and then by barrels. The barrels often froze in cold weather and on occasion contained dirt or debris in the water.

The Appellate Division opinion described the inconvenience experienced by one resident:

> One witness, who suffered from arthritis, testified to hauling her water for drinking, cooking and bathing up nine steps because, as she said,
>
> [t]here was no way I could get the water upstairs except by hauling pot after pot out of the containers, . . . which was a consider-

> able amount of hauling every day just to use for drinking and bathing the children and cooking.[133]

As the Appellate Division noted, the lack of running water was an understandable source of tension and friction among members of the plaintiff's households, who for nearly two years were compelled to obtain water in this primitive manner.[134]

The trial court charged the jury that plaintiffs' claim for "quality of life" damages encompassed "inconveniences, aggravation, and unnecessary expenditure of time and effort related to the use of the water hauled to their homes, as well as to other disruption in their lives, including harmony in the family unit."[135] The aggregate jury verdict on this claim was $5,396,940. This represented an average award of slightly over $16,000 for each plaintiff; thus, a family unit consisting of four plaintiffs received an average award of approximately $64,000.[136]

Loss of Use

Interference with use of property is compensable. Moreover, even if the property would not have been used at all absent the damage, recovery is appropriate for loss of use. As one court succinctly stated:

> The theory behind the allowance of damages for loss of use is that it is not the actual use but the right to use that is compensable . . . It is no answer then to say to the victim of the tort; since you have failed to prove that you would have made a net profit from use of the damaged property, you may take nothing. For it is the right to use that marks the value.[137]

This rule is mirrored by the Restatement:

> The owner of the subject matter is entitled to recover as damages for the loss of the value of the use . . . This is true even though the owner in fact has suffered no harm through the deprivation, as when he was not using the subject matter at the time or had a substitute that he used without additional expense to him. . . . [138]

At common law, this view, that one has a right to control use of one's own property, and a right to damages for such loss of control, began with the decisions of British Admiralty Courts in the *Great Holme*[139] and *The Mediana,*[140] both cases concerning damaged ships. These cases "maintained the principle that a plaintiff had an intrinsic right to use his or her property and that injury to that right warranted compensation regardless of the manner in which the property would have been used."[141] American state courts followed these cases, and uniformly applied them to resolve the question of damages for loss of use.[142] Thus, precedent emerged permitting owners to recover value for loss of use without showing a need for or anticipated use of the property.[143] Professor McCormick concludes in his treatise on damages:

> [T]he owner is entitled to compensation for the most advantageous use of his property which was open to him regardless of whether he intended so to use it or whether he intended to waste it or give it away. . . . [144]

The same result obtains under the civil law, with even greater force. The right of ownership confers "on a person direct, immediate, and exclusive authority over a thing. The owner of a thing may use, enjoy, and dispose of it within the limits and under the conditions established by law."[145] The right of use is one of the three integral emoluments of ownership and has a value all its own: It is a "real thing" that may be the subject of a contract, and granted to another.[146] Thus, the right to use and enjoy property has an intrinsic value all of its own, regardless of the value that may be placed on property from the whims of the market.[147]

However, here as in all damage issues, the right to ask a jury for compensation does not alone guarantee that a jury will respond favorably. The circumstances of a particular case are crucial in guiding the lawyers' evaluation.

Stigma Damages

An industrial nuisance or other pollution might well stigmatize neighboring property to devalue it. As one author described, "when given a choice between property with no history of contamination and one with prior environmental problems (even after an effective cleanup program), a knowledgeable and prudent user or investor would choose the property with no *prior environmental* problems."[148] When this is true and provable—recognizing that properties are often already depressed for and because of other reasons—an action for stigma damages may be appropriate.[149] For example, *Criscuola v. Power Authority*[150] involved claims for diminution of the market value of property resulting from a high voltage power line easement acquired by the Power Authority. In an evidentiary ruling, the New York Court of Appeals agreed with the property owners that, when seeking to recover consequential damages for a taking of property where the value of the property is affected by a public fear of danger or health risks resulting from the taking, plaintiffs do not need to prove that the fear is reasonable. However, plaintiffs "must still establish some prevalent perception of a danger emanating from the objectional condition."[151] In proving that there is an adverse impact on the market value of the property, plaintiffs must present "[s]ome credible, tangible evidence that a fear is prevalent."[152] Finally, the diminution in market value must be linked to the fear "in much the same manner that any other adverse market effects are shown," for example, "by proffering evidence that the market value of property across which power lines have been built has been negatively affected in relation to comparable properties across which no power lines have been built."[153] However, there is also considerable jurisprudence that would not allow for the recovery of stigma damages for a party who has not been harmed under theories of either negligence or nuisance.[154]

Punitive Damages

In some states, under appropriate circumstances, punitive damages are available to the pollution victim. To recover punitive damages, a plaintiff must satisfy the trier of fact that the defendant has acted with a heightened degree of fault. This standard has been characterized in some jurisdictions as willful, wanton, and/or reckless. However, the mere possibility of punitive damages does not transform a weak compensatory case into a more viable suit. Many lawyers and clients fail to understand this reality, and learn expensive and wrenching lessons as a result. In addition, the availability of punitives does not mean that litigation should be prosecuted solely to punish a perceived malefactor. Although punishment and deterrence are traditional ends of the tort system, most juries want to see real and substantial damages before they will give significant attentions to awarding punitive damages.

Summary of Damages Issues

The principal objective of compensatory tort damages is to place the injured person in a position as good as the person occupied before he or she was wronged. Unlike contract damages, however, compensatory tort damages are awarded for both readily calculable losses, such as the cost incurred for medical treatments and other "direct" (out-of-pocket) losses, as well as for losses not easily translated into monetary terms, such as pain and suffering, emotional distress, and loss of consortium. The principal limit on compensatory damages is the foreseeability of the harm, as consequences that are remote and would not likely have been foreseen by a reasonable defendant as a potential result of its actions are generally not compensable. In addition to compensatory damages, punitive damages may also be available in tort cases, although in theory limited to situations where the defendant's conduct has been egregious or outrageous.

Toxic Tort Theories of Relief

Introduction

Given the aforementioned types of damages, and assuming that the facts substantiate the client's claim, different theories of liability are appropriate under different circumstances. When public consciousness first began to focus on our toxic problems nationally, it was thought that traditional private law would prove ineffective to clean up and protect the environment and public health.[155] As a result, Congress and the states passed many new environmental laws, such as CERCLA and parts of RCRA. However, lawyers and citizen groups have been successful in using private law remedies to protect and clean up the environment.[156] As a result, private law has been used with increasing frequency, although it often builds on public records and public investigations. Most significantly, private law courts have responded to the unique nature of toxic tort injuries by developing new remedies, such as medical monitoring.[157]

Environmental contamination may be addressed through nuisance, trespass, dangerous condition of public property, negligence, liability for ultrahazardous activity, and public trust doctrines as well as under theories of fraud, waste, breach of implied warranty, and restitution.[158] Additionally, contractual and property relationships may also provide a foundation for environmental suits.[159] Certain federal statutes are also available to provide tort-like relief.[160]

Strict Liability

Where applicable, strict liability is probably the most useful theory of liability in these cases. Since the 1868 case of *Rylands v. Fletcher*,[161] it has been clear that strict liability can be imposed on parties engaged in ultrahazardous activity for profit constituting a non-natural use of land. This is a matter governed by state common law, but the Restatement of Torts has been very influential in the development of this liability theory. Restatement (Second) of Torts Section 519 states the principle as follows:

> One who carries on an abnormally dangerous activity is subject to liability for harm to the person, land or chattels of another resulting from the activity, although he has exercised the utmost care to prevent the harm.

Per Restatement (Second) of Torts Section 520,[162] a balancing of interrelated factors is required to determine whether the doctrine applies, including:

1. the degree of risk involved;
2. the likelihood that the resultant harm will be great;

3. the ability to eliminate the risk through careful conduct;
4. the extent to which the activity is not a matter of the common usage;
5. the appropriateness of conducting the activity at the particular location; and
6. the value of the activity to the community.

In recent years, claims relying on the "abnormally dangerous," "ultrahazardous" theory have been brought against owners of hazardous waste disposal sites, as well as against generators and transporters of hazardous wastes. Most courts have applied strict liability to these parties.[163]

Negligence

Negligence liability is the failure to use due care (the level of care expected of a "reasonable man" under like circumstances). Negligence liability requires the existence of a duty of care, conduct falling short of that duty, proximate cause, and injury. Negligence cases are generally governed by state common law, although some state statutes may also be applicable in particular cases. Negligence may be alleged to recover damages for personal injury or injury to personal property resulting from toxic exposure.[164]

To establish negligence, plaintiffs must prove:

1. that the defendant breached a duty owed plaintiff;
2. the plaintiff's injury; and
3. that that injury proximately resulted from the breach.[165]

Decisions indicate a trend toward relaxing the burden of proof in environmental negligence cases by adoption of evidentiary doctrines such as negligence per se.[166] Negligence per se is frequently used by environmental plaintiffs. Plaintiffs often seek to use a violation of an applicable environmental statute or regulation (for instance, RCRA) as a basis for imposing negligence liability. In some states, a violation of applicable statute or regulation may be held to constitute negligence per se, or at least prima facie evidence of negligence. This is the doctrine by which a court constructs a statute, ordinance, or administrative regulation to set a standard of care.[167]

Trespass

The essence of trespass is a wrongful invasion or encroachment of an interest in property.[168] Although actionable in itself, jury appeal will require a showing of significant harm.[169] However, plaintiff need not prove specific intent to invade but only that defendant acted with knowledge of the substantial certainty of invasion.[170] More important, pleading trespass (as opposed to other theories) will require proof of invasion. If government studies or defendants' own admissions have not established this fact, proof of trespass can be potentially very expensive.

Nuisance

Nuisance is an important theory of relief in toxic tort cases. It provides a vehicle for damages as well as injunctive relief. Plaintiffs must carefully assess whether the nuisance is public or private; and if private, whether it is permanent or not. If public, it is not necessarily actionable by the individual. If permanent, a restoration remedy (as opposed to market value) may not be available.

Nuisance is the intentional use that substantially interferes with the reasonable use, enjoyment, or value of another's property.[171] In some cases, a manufacturer may be held liable for nuisance.[172] Any resulting harms to property or the environment are actionable, as well as offenses to the senses or principles of decency. In effect, nuisance law forces an actor to internalize the external costs associated with its enterprise.[173]

Causation

Causation refers to two distinct issues. First, is this defendant causally related to the liability-creating actions? For example, if a community's drinking supply is polluted by a dumpsite, did this defendant contribute to that site? Second, is there a medical connection between the liability-creating act and the complained-of injuries? For example, did drinking the polluted water cause the victim's cancer?

The goal of some defendants in toxic tort cases is to give inordinate weight to medical causation questions relative to issues of liability and damages, and to convince courts to pre-screen opinions relative to these medical questions. However, concrete internal corporate documentation—old studies or employee records—indicating a knowledge of potential harm should not be excluded or ignored. Indeed, corporate decisions to create and/or ignore the very risk of harm being sued upon, by marketing products that have not been proven safe, should not be excluded.

Defendants have combined this abstract causation defense with attempts either to stay discovery until these causation or "*Lone Pine*"[174] motions are decided, or to create a privilege of "self-critical analysis,"[175] which means that information regarding prior corporate awareness of risk[176] is not even to be available to plaintiffs or the court.[177] Thus, a defendant in possession of information indicating harm, such as an environmental health audit or a secret settlement from another case,[178] might still move for dismissal on the grounds that plaintiff's expert is outside the mainstream of the scientific community, which also has not been privy to this information.[179]

In toxic tort cases alleging personal injuries, polluters also blame diseases on the individual's behavior, lifestyle, and character.[180] Under certain circumstances, it is possible that malnourishment or a hazardous work environment can cause as much, if not more, harm than a toxic pollutant. Poor people and people of different backgrounds from their jurors generally are less likely to fend off this defense tactic successfully, even assuming that they have access to equally competent and able counsel. Similarly, the poor and minorities are less able to fend off allegations of having brought suit to win "something for nothing." Dangerous stereotypes about the poor and people of color are potentially invoked by such arguments about motives and about the lack of "risk avoidance" conduct by the plaintiffs. Counsel have to be sensitive to the fact that there is a continuum of argument, and that one moves rather quickly from one end of legitimate advocacy to improper ad hominem attacks.

Finally, the poor are less likely to have been able to afford to document, and/or to take steps to mitigate health damages. Plaintiffs will be vigorously cross-examined on whether they have seen a doctor about their alleged problems, or whether they have undergone treatment. Both of these omissions will weigh against any toxic tort plaintiff. The problem is more likely one suffered by poor plaintiffs. However, it is not insurmountable. In cases where medical documentation does not exist, the jury may still believe the plaintiff. The likelihood of this occurring, however, turns in part on the jury's ability to relate to, and accept, the plaintiffs' testimony as a predicate to medical testimony, and so is of vital importance to the success of the suit. Similarly, a plaintiff who is seeking a medical monitoring remedy, but in the past has not been able to afford regular medical visits, will be attacked as seeking to use the lawsuit to get "the kind of health insurance we all want." The argument fails if the plaintiff is lucky enough to have health insurance coverage already.

Group Litigation Issues

Class Actions

On one level, environmental justice claims seem well suited for class action treatment, the argument being that the affected group or tribe is victimized because of its shared status relative to the source of the wrong. In such situations, the alleged wrongs arise from a common set of facts (about the pollution), and this commonality outweighs individual damage questions in the calculus of class action certification. Indeed, in certain cases (for example, abatement of a nuisance), the argument for class certification is stronger because the remedy should be unitary so that the defendant is not forced to comply with inconsistent standards or relief.[181]

However, the analysis is not so straightforward. In some cases, there are multiple sources of pollution, and courts are increasingly reluctant to undertake the responsibility of managing "shotgun" complaints in which plaintiffs have not precisely targeted the defendant and the causal process by which that defendant's activities have given rise to the damages plaintiffs are seeking to remedy.[182] Courts are less inclined today than in the past to allow manifest personal injury claims to proceed as a class action. In a series of decisions, courts have turned against certification, especially in cases involving personal injury claims.[183] This seems to be especially true in federal courts when the putative nationwide class action suit is based predominantly on state law.[184] Such claims may, however, be handled in tandem with other loss claims by means of pretrial consolidation or coordination.[185]

Settlements

This trend against class actions raises problems in the context of putative settlements. The Supreme Court has heightened the level of scrutiny applicable to settlement classes.[186] This should only accelerate the current trend of federal courts refusing to act as national mass tort courts.[187]

Before too much is read into any one decision, *Amchem* is not the death knell for nationwide class actions. Instead, the decision focuses attention on whether the claims presented by the putative class pose conflicts within the class to defeat the requirements of predominance and adequacy of representation as construed in *Amchem.* Without a doubt, at least some cases may still be certified and managed as a litigation class, and certain proposed settlement classes may satisfy the requirements of Rule 23 and the principles of *Amchem.*

Conclusion

The quest for justice means that something needs to be done about racism and its effects. The goal of equal treatment before the law, although a fundamental principle of our democracy, is offended by this disproportionality of risk and harms among our communities. Equality in the sense of equal burdens and risks is not being met. Yet, the rectification of inequality is not necessarily at odds with ordered liberty.[188]

No reduction or restriction of other fundamental rights is necessary to remedy much of what is offensive about environmental racism.

There is much that can be accomplished for victims of environmental injustice through a toxic tort suit, if that is their choice. If, indeed, the problem of environmental justice is one of disproportionate *impacts,* then toxic tort litigation may be appropriate where that impact is actionable at law.

However, counsel and client must address and surmount the difficult issues of proof faced by minorities and the poor, including proof of causation, in environmental litigation. The trial process involves both fact-finding and normative judgments. As Professor Keeton has observed:

> Perhaps more than any other branch of the law, the law of torts is a battleground of social theory. Its primary purpose, of course, is to make a fair adjustment of the conflicting claims of the litigating parties. But the twentieth century has brought an increasing realization of the fact that the interest of society in general may be involved in disputes in which the parties are private litigants. The notion of "public policy" involved in private cases is not by any means new to tort law, and doubtless has been with us ever since the troops of the sovereign first intervened in a brawl to keep the peace; but it is only in recent decades that its influence on tort law has been openly considered in judicial decisions, and not merely in commentaries on the law.[189]
>
> * * *
>
> In any society, it is inevitable that these interests come into conflict. In cases of conflict, cultures that we choose to call "primitive" determined who should prevail with sword and club; and there is recent melancholy evidence that the law of the jungle has not yet departed from the affairs of nations. The administration of the law becomes a process of weighing the interests for which the plaintiff demands protection against the defendant's claim to untrammeled freedom in the furtherance of defendant's desires themselves. When the interest of the public is thrown into the scales and allowed to swing the balance for or against the plaintiff, the result is a form of "social engineering." A decision-maker might deliberately seek to use the law as an instrument to promote the "greatest happiness of the greatest number," or instead might give greater emphasis to protecting certain types of interests of individuals as fundamental entitlements central to an integrity of person that the law upholds above all else. This process of weighing the interests is by no means peculiar to the law of torts. . . .[190]

Professor Elliot of Yale goes further in applying this understanding of tort trials to the toxic tort arena:

> [T]oxic tort cases are about redefining our public morality for a new era in which we must confront the troubling truth that we do not fully comprehend the relationships between the things that we have made and our health and well-being. . . . [Toxic tort cases] involve basic controversies over evolving public values; these are fundamental political issues that experts have no greater right to resolve than anyone else in a democratic society.[191]

The problem with the foregoing is keeping bad or prejudicial facts and norms out of the process and leveling the playing field. Certainly, *voir dire*,[192] judicial vigilance, and the advocates' professionalism are important—but imperfect—solutions to prevent contamination of the adjudicatory process by the existence of prejudice against the poor and minorities.

Notes

1. *See, e.g.*, ENVIRONMENTAL PROTECTION AGENCY, ENVIRONMENTAL EQUITY: REDUCING RISK FOR ALL COMMUNITIES (June 1992) [hereinafter ENVIRONMENTAL EQUITY].

2. U.S. GENERAL ACCOUNTING OFFICE, SITING OF HAZARDOUS WASTE LANDFILLS AND THEIR CORRELATION WITH RACIAL AND ECONOMIC STATUS OF SURROUNDING COMMUNITIES (1983) (the GAO study concluded that three out of four commercial hazardous waste sites in the southeastern United States were located in predominantly African American communities); COMMISSION FOR RACIAL JUSTICE, UNITED CHURCH OF CHRIST, TOXIC WASTES AND RACE IN THE UNITED STATES (1987) (three of the five largest commercial hazardous waste landfills in the United States, which account for 40 percent of the total estimated commercial landfill capacity in the nation, were located in predominantly African American or Hispanic communities); JAY M. GOULD, QUALITY OF LIFE IN AMERICAN NEIGHBORHOODS, LEVELS OF AFFLUENCE, TOXIC WASTE, AND CANCER MORTALITY IN RESIDENTIAL ZIP CODE AREAS 29 (Alice Tepper Marlin ed., 1986); Paul Mohai & Bunyan Bryant, *Environmental Racism: Reviewing the Evidence, in* RACE AND THE INCIDENCE OF ENVIRONMENTAL HAZARDS: A TIME FOR DISCOURSE (Bunyan Bryant & Paul Mohai eds., 1992); Robert D. Bullard & Beverly H. Wright, *The Quest for Environmental Equity: Mobilizing the African American Community for Social Change*, 3 SOCIETY AND NATURAL RESOURCES (1990); ENVIRONMENTAL EQUITY, *supra* note 1; *infra* notes 6, 10–13, and 16.

3. ENVIRONMENTAL EQUITY, *supra* note 1 (concluding that racial minority and low-income populations experience higher than average exposures to selected air pollutants, hazardous waste facilities, contaminated fish, and agricultural pesticides in the workplace). This report examined whether there was evidence that racial minorities and low-income communities bore a higher environmental risk than the general population, and considered actions that the EPA might take on any identified disparities.

4. This is not to say that all disproportionate burdens are inescapably racist in origin or practice. It is simply to say that racism exists in some instances, that racism is wrong, and that racism is hard to eliminate because of its deep and pervasive roots. Kelly M. Colquette & Elizabeth A. Robertson, Note, *Environmental Racism: The Causes, Consequences and Commendations,* 5 TUL. ENVTL. L.J. 153 (1991).

5. *See, e.g.,* Allan Kanner, *Environmental Justice, Torts and Causation,* 34 WASHBURN L.J. 505 (1995).

6. *Id.* at 509–10.

7. Elsewhere in this book, various direct environmental justice theories are discussed.

8. *See, e.g.,* YALE LAW SCHOOL CONFERENCE REPORT, EARTH RIGHTS AND RESPONSIBILITIES: HUMAN RIGHTS AND ENVIRONMENTAL PROTECTION 29 (1992) (". . . litigation is one important tool . . . [but] those in pursuit of environmental justice must also seek other means of taking effective action").

9. *See* Luke W. Cole, *Empowerment as the Key to Environmental Protection: The Need for Environmental Poverty Law,* 19 ECOLOGY L.Q. 619 (1992); Richard J. Lazarus, *Pursuing "Environmental Justice": The Distribution Effects of Environmental Protection,* 87 NW. U. L. REV. 787 (1993); Peter L. Reich, *Greening the Ghetto: A Theory of Environmental Race Discrimination,* 41 KAN. L. REV. 271 (1992).

10. *See* Luke W. Cole, *Remedies for Environmental Racism: A View from the Field,* 90 MICH. L. REV. 1991 (1992); R. Colling, *Environmental Equity: A Law and Planning Approach to Environmental Racism,* 11 VA. ENVTL. L.J. 495 (1992); Paul Mohai & Bunyan Bryant, *Environmental Injustice: Weighing Race and Class as Factors in the Distribution of Environmental Hazards,* 63 U. COLO. L. REV. 921 (1992); S. Morrison & L. Howe, *The Sewage of Foreigners: An Examination of the Historical Precedent for Modern Waste Disposal on Indian Lands,* 39 FED. B. NEWS & J. 370 (1992).

11. *See, e.g.,* James M. Melius et al., *Facility Siting and Health Questions: The Burden of Health Risk Uncertainty,* 17 NAT. RES. L. 467 (1984).

12. *See, e.g.,* GERALD E. SMOLEN & GARY MOORE, ECONOMIC EFFECTS OF HAZARDOUS WASTE LANDFILLS ON SURROUNDING REAL ESTATE VALUES IN TOLEDO, OHIO (Ohio State Univ., Center for Real Estate Education & Research, Feb. 1991).

13. *See, e.g.,* MICHAEL R. EDELSTEIN, CONTAMINATED COMMUNITIES: THE SOCIAL AND PSYCHOLOGICAL IMPACTS OF RESIDENTIAL TOXIC EXPOSURE 17–117 (1988).

14. Good client communications are vital. It is important that counsel adequately explain these systemic limitations to clients and other stakeholders at an early stage. By the same token, even if counsel were solicited by a group to bring individual damage cases, counsel's obligations are to the individual client or, in class actions, to the class as a whole. *Infra,* "Settlements," page 644.

15. *See* Chapter 8, "Access to Information," *supra* pages 230–55. Records or reports that a party is required to keep by law may be admissible in some circumstances to establish civil liability. United States v. Ward, 448 U.S. 242 (1980); SPIRG of New Jersey v. Fritzcher, 570 F. Supp. 1528, 1538–40 (D.N.J. 1984), *aff'd,* 759 F.2d 1131 (3d Cir. 1985); Chesapeake Bay Found. v. Bethlehem Steel Corp., 608 F. Supp. 440, 451–53 (D. Md. 1985).

16. ALLAN KANNER, ENVIRONMENTAL & TOXIC TORT TRIALS 3 (Michie, 1997 Supp.) [hereinafter KANNER, ENVIRONMENTAL & TOXIC TORT TRIALS]. Counsel will need to assess litigation and nonlitigation options designed to gather more

information (FOIA, Agency for Toxic Substances and Disease Registry) or to redress some or all of the damages complained of by the client.

17. *See* Chapter 15, "Controlling Existing Facilities," *supra* pages 490–521. On the need to consider a sequenced approach to litigation, see KANNER, ENVIRONMENTAL & TOXIC TORT TRIALS, *supra* note 16, at 21.

18. For our purposes in this section, assume that tort compensation and/or medical monitoring is the goal.

19. On the use of ADR in environmental and toxic tort litigation, see CPR PRACTICE GUIDE ON ADR (1989).

20. *See* Aiello v. Browning-Ferris, Inc., 1993 WL 463701, 24 ELR 20771 (N.D. Cal. 1993) (action under Section 1983 for discriminatory siting).

21. However, by example, where differential standards of care are used as between employees on the one hand, and neighbors or independent contractors on the other, a jury may well conclude in the absence of any contrary proof that racism is the root cause of this differential treatment.

22. On the construction of rules against splitting causes of action, and on the running of statute of limitations or prescriptive periods, see KANNER, ENVIRONMENTAL & TOXIC TORT TRIALS, *supra* note 15 §§ 1.09, 1.11, at 12–13.

23. Daubert v. Merrell Dow Pharmaceuticals, 509 U.S. 579 (1993); General Electric Co. v. Joiner, 1997 WL 764563 (1997).

24. Most toxic tort personal injury cases involve some proof that the client suffered an injurious exposure. Dose refers to how much of the exposure affected the individual. With the possible exception of medical monitoring claims, proof of dose involves an assessment of the various pathways—inhalation, dermal absorption, and ingestion—of exposure, and some quantification of the chemical of concern.

It should be emphasized that measured exposures do not reflect actual absorbed dose, due to the possibility of multiple exposure routes, as well as metabolic considerations. Not all material inhaled or ingested is absorbed. The percentage of absorption depends on a variety of factors often not considered by standards, including particle size and chemical form. For these reasons, standards should be regarded only as guidelines, and exposures should be kept as low as possible by the use of engineering controls and sound work practices.

Causation evidence is also confounded by the fact that the individual's work and home environments contain a variety of potentially hazardous agents capable of adverse health effects if exposures are excessive, additive, or synergistic.

25. On the use of the results of prior litigation, see Parklane Hosiery Co. v. Shore, 439 U.S. 322 (1979) ("offensive use of collateral estoppel without mutuality of estoppel"). For example, the doctrine of administrative preclusion means that plaintiffs will not necessarily have to reprove matters already established in competent administrative proceedings. *See, e.g.*, United States v. Utah Construction Co., 384 U.S. 394, 422 (1966) (when an "administrative agency is acting in a judicial capacity and resolves disputed issues of fact properly before it which the parties have had an adequate opportunity to litigate, the courts have not hesitated to apply *res judicata* to enforce repose"). Given the need to promote economy and efficiency in our civil justice system, this trend includes cases considering issue preclusion in environmental matters, even where one party to the case was

not a party to the administrative proceeding. *See, e.g.*, United States v. Allegan Metal Finishing Co., 696 F. Supp. 275, 293–95 (W.D. Mich. 1988) (administrative *res judicata* in subsequent RCRA suit); Chesapeake Bay Found. v. Bethlehem Steel Corp., 652 F. Supp. 620 (D. Md. 1987) (*res judicata* in CWA litigation). Even a consent decree is treated as a final judgment on the merits and accorded preclusive effect. United States v. Fisher, 864 F.2d 434, 439 (7th Cir. 1988); United States v. Athlone Industries, Inc., 746 F.2d 977, 983 n.5 (3d Cir. 1984); Amalgamated Sugar Co. v. NL Industries, 825 F.2d 634, 639 (2d Cir. 1987).

26. *See, e.g.*, Smith v. Ithaca Corp., 612 F.2d 215, 217–18, 219 (5th Cir. 1980).

27. Roehling v. National Gypsum Company Gold Bond Building Products, 786 F.2d 1225, 1228 (4th Cir. 1986); Drayton v. Jiffee Chem. Corp., 395 F. Supp. 1081, 1087 (N.D. Ohio 1975), *modified and aff'd*, 591 F.2d 352 (6th Cir. 1978).

28. 765 S.W.2d 42, 179–80 (Mo. App. 1988) (footnote omitted).

29. For most toxic substances, there exists a threshold dose below which adverse health effects do not occur; however, for carcinogens, mutagens, and teratogens, these thresholds may not exist. The scientific basis for many current standards must be critically reviewed on a periodic basis, because observed effects (or a lack thereof) have been related to historical or cumulative doses that were estimated retrospectively, using current exposure measurements coupled with knowledge of past controls and process operations. Studies of exposed worker populations, with reliable exposure measurements and comparisons to appropriate control groups, were rare until passage of the Occupational Safety and Health Act of 1970.

Standards generally do not protect the hypersusceptible or hypersensitive individual. Hypersusceptible hosts include infants and elderly, malnourished or poverty-stricken persons, those with pre-existing chronic lung disease or compromised lung defense mechanisms, and those with abnormal immunological, genetic, or metabolic predispositions; also, high risk groups include those with hazardous occupational or avocational exposures. *See* Chapter 10, *supra* pages 307–356.

30. To lessen the burden of plaintiffs and to advance the policies of deterrence for wrongdoers, courts have adopted approaches that shift to defendants the burden of proving they did not cause an injury. For example, the court in Pereira v. Dow Chemical Co., 129 Cal. 3d 685 (1982) held that the burden of identifying which chemical exposure caused which injury rested not on the plaintiff but on the defendants. Thus, once the plaintiff's injury is shown to have been caused by an occurrence or product for which defendants were responsible, even though the particular culpable defendant cannot be identified, the burden can shift to defendants to exculpate themselves.

31. On spoilation, see KANNER, ENVIRONMENTAL & TOXIC TORT TRIALS, *supra* note 16, at 188.

32. Smith v. Ithaca Corp., 612 F.2d 215 (5th Cir 1980).

33. *See generally* SUPERFUND § 301(E) STUDY GROUP, INJURIES AND DAMAGES FROM HAZARDOUS WASTE—ANALYSIS AND IMPROVEMENT OF LEGAL REMEDIES—A REPORT TO CONGRESS IN COMPLIANCE WITH § 301(E) OF THE COMPREHENSIVE ENVIRONMENTAL RESPONSE, COMPENSATION, AND LIABILITY ACT OF 1980, Part 1, at 55–56, 116–17, 196; Comment, *Hazardous Waste Liability and Compensation: Old Solutions, New Solutions, No Solutions*, 14 CONN. L. REV. 301 (1982).

34. *See e.g.*, Allan Kanner, *Emerging Conceptions of Latent Personal Injuries in Toxic Tort Litigation*, 18 RUTGERS L.J. 343 (1987). *But see* Askey v. Occidental Chem. Corp., 102 A.D.2d 130, 477 N.Y.S.2d 242 (App. Div. 1984).

35. KANNER, ENVIRONMENTAL & TOXIC TORT TRIALS, *supra* note 16, at 284–85.

36. *See* Andersen v. W.R. Grace & Co., 628 F. Supp. 1219 (D. Mass. 1986); Sterling v. Velsicol Chemical Corp., 856 F.2d 1188 (6th Cir. 1988) (25 percent–30 percent increase in risk was insufficient to prove a reasonable medical certainty, requiring award for increased risk to be vacated).

37. Stites v. Sundstrand Heat Transfer, Inc., 660 F. Supp. 1516, 1525 (W.D. Mich. 1987); Anderson, 628 F. Supp. at 1231; Bennett v. Mallinckrodt, Inc., 698 S.W.2d 854, 866 (Mo. Ct. App. 1985); Morrissy v. Eli Lilly & Co., 394 N.E.2d 1369, 1377 (Ill. App. 1979).

38. Herber v. Jones-Manville Corp., 785 F.2d at 79, 82 (3d Cir. 1986); Adams v. Johns-Manville Sales Corp., 783 F.2d 589, 591–92 (5th Cir. 1986); Dartez v. Fibreboard Corp., 765 F.2d 456, 466 (5th Cir. 1985) (holding that a worker exposed to asbestos could recover for the increased risk of cancer or mesothelioma only "if he introduces expert testimony establishing that there is a reasonable medical probability that the disease will appear" if the plaintiff could show that he would more probably than not contract the disease, the court was prepared to allow full damages, *id.*; where the expert doctors gave varying estimates (some above 50 percent, some below) the court determined that it was not a "reasonable medical probability"; *id.* at 467).

39. Hagerty v. L&L Marine Services, Inc., 788 F.2d 315, 319 (5th Cir. 1986); *Dartez*, 765 F.2d at 466.

40. Johnson v. Armstrong Cork Co. et al., 645 F. Supp. 764, 769 (W.D. La. 1986).

41. *See Stites*, 660 F. Supp. at 1524; Ayers v. Township of Jackson, 525 A.2d 287 (N.J. 1987) (The New Jersey Supreme Court held that an "enhanced risk" of cancer due to exposure to contaminated well water constituted an "injury" under the N.J. Tort Claims Act, *id.* at 305; even though plaintiff's expert "*could not quantify the extent of the enhanced risk of cancer* . . . the jury could reasonably have inferred from his testimony that the risk, although unquantified, was medically significant," *id.* at 303; due to its speculative nature, however, the court refused to recognize a cause of action for the "unquantified" enhanced risk of disease, declining to rule on whether testing showing a "reasonable probability" would be allowed, *id.* at 308). *See also* Zatz & Sherwood, *Defending Speculative Injury Claims*, 2 TOXIC L. REP. 76, 77–78 (June 17, 1987).

42. *Methods to Counter Courtroom Tactics in Toxic Tort Cases Aired at ATLA Meeting*, 1 TOXIC L. REP. 1002, 1003 (February 11, 1987).

43. *Compare* Don Elliot, *The Future of Toxic Torts: of Chemophobia, Risk as a Compensable Injury and Hybrid Compensation Systems*, 25 HOUS. L. REV. 781 (July 1988) *with* Allan Kanner, *Emerging Conceptions of Latent Personal Injuries in Toxic Tort Litigation*, 18 RUTGERS L.J. 343 (1987).

44. *See, e.g.*, Dartez v. Fibreboard Corp., 765 F.2d 456, 466 (5th Cir. 1985).

45. *See, e.g.*, Ayers v. Township of Jackson, 106 N.J. 557, 525 A.2d 287 (1987); Allan Kanner, *Perspectives on Medical Monitoring*, 2 TUL. ENVTL. L.J. 1 (Spring 1989); Annotation, *Recovery of Damages for Expenses of Medical Monitoring to Detect or Prevent Future Disease or Condition*, 17 A.L.R. 5th 327, 332–48 (Supp. 11–14).

46. *See e.g.,* Eagle-Picher Industries, Inc. v. Cox, 481 So.2d 517 (Fla. App. 3d Dist. 1985).

47. *See* 71 A.L.R. 2d 338 § 5; Lorenac v. Chemirad Corp., 37 N.J. 56, 179 A.2d 401 (1962) (damages for cancerphobia awarded to a cancer researcher who, after being exposed to ethylene amine, developed burns and ulcerations on his hand and feared developing cancer); *and* Ferrara v. Galluchio, 5 N.Y.2d 16, 152 N.W.2d 249, 186 N.Y.S.2d 996 (1958) (patient who developed x-ray burns and was informed of an increased risk of cancer awarded $15,000 in damages for mental anguish associated with ensuing cancerphobia).

48. *See* 145 A.L.R. 1004; Caspermeyer v. Florsheim Shoe Store Co., 313 S.W.2d 198 (Mo. Ct. App. 1958) (pregnant woman who fell into a sidewalk loading chute and was confined to bed for several weeks awarded $3,000 in damages for resulting physical injuries and mental anguish of worry about the health of her unborn child).

49. *See* Howard v. Mt. Sinai Hospital, 63 Wis. 2d 515, 217 N.W.2d 383, *adhered to on reh'g,* 63 Wis. 2d 523A, 219 N.W. 2d 576 (1974) (plaintiff's fear of developing cancer from broken catheter in her shoulder was so remote as to be noncompensable as a matter of public policy).

50. Deleski v. Raymark Industries, 819 F. 2d 377, 380 (3d Cir. 1987); *Adams,* 783 F.2d at 593; *Jackson,* 781 F.2d at 413–14; Villari v. Temmix International, Inc., 663 F. Supp. 727, 734–35 (E.D. Pa. 1987); McAdams v. Eli Lilly Co., 638 F. Supp. 1173, 1178 (N.D. Ill. 1986); Plummer v. Abbott Laboratories, 568 F. Supp. 920, 927 (D.R.I. 1983).

51. *Herber,* 785 F.2d at 85 (infiltration of asbestos into lungs was sufficient impact); *Stites,* 660 F. Supp. at 1526–27.

52. 71 A.L.R. 2d 338.

53. *See In re Moorenovich,* 634 F. Supp. 634, 637 (D. Me. 1986); Ayers, 525 A.2d at 295.

54. *In re Moorenovich,* 634 F. Supp. at 637; Payton v. Abbott Labs, 437 N.E.2d 171, 181 (Mass. 1982).

55. Harper v. Illinois Central Gulf Railroad, 808 F.2d 1139, 1140 (5th Cir. 1987).

56. *Dartez,* 765 F.2d at 468.

57. 639 S.W.2d at 434. *See also* Gale & Goyer, *Recovery for Cancerphobia and Increased Risk of Cancer,* 15 CUMB. L. REV. 734 (1985).

58. 643 F. Supp. at 636, 637. This is the "two disease" rule: One need only sue for present manifest injuries. Limitations on future harms begin to run when and if they manifest.

59. 225 Cal. App. 213, 274 Cal. Rptr. 885 (6th Dist. 1990).

60. 87 F.R.D. 433 (M.D. Pa. 1980).

61. Similarly, in Moore v. Pavex, Inc., 514 A.2d 137 (Pa. Super. 1986), the Pennsylvania Superior Court took judicial notice that exposure to radiation or fallout from a meltdown of a nuclear power plant causes injury to persons and property with which it comes into contact.

62. *See* note 50, *supra.*

63. *See, e.g.,* Morrissy v. Eli Lilly & Co., 76 Ill. App. 3d 753, 394 N.E.2d 1369 (1979).

64. *See* Friends for All Children v. Lockheed Aircraft Corp., 746 F.2d 816, 825 (D.C. Cir. 1984).

65. RESTATEMENT (SECOND) OF TORTS § 918(1) (1977).

66. *See* Note, *Medical Monitoring Funds: The Periodic Payment of Future Medical Surveillance Expenses in Toxic Tort Litigation,* 43 HASTINGS L.J. 661, 669 (1992).

67. Note 65, *supra; accord,* Redland Soccer Club, Inc. v. Dept. of the Army, 696 A.2d 137 (Pa. 1997). However, medical monitoring proof does not necessarily satisfy proof of causation for manifest personal injuries. *See, e.g., In re TMI Litigation Consolidated Proceedings,* 927 F. Supp. 834 (M.D. Pa. 1996) (dismissing all personal injury claims on *Daubert* grounds).

68. *See* "Increased Risk of Cancer or Other Future Illnesses," *supra* pages 624–25.

69. *See, e.g.,* Doe v. City of Stanford, 241 Conn. 692, 699 A.2d 52 (1997); Reed v. Phillip Morris, Inc., No. 96-5070 1997 WL 538921 (D.C. Super. Aug. 18, 1997); Day v. NLO, 851 F. Supp. 869 (S.D. Ohio, 1994). Allan Kanner, *Perspectives on Medical Monitoring,* 2 TUL. ENVTL. L.J., Spring 1989, at 1.

70. 916 F.2d 829, 851 (3d Cir. 1990), *cert. denied,* 499 U.S. 961 (1991).

71. *Citing* Askey v. Occidental Chemical Corp., 102 A.D.2d 130, 477 N.Y.S. 2d 242 (N.Y. App. Div. 1984).

72. The court ruled that the evidentiary burden could be met by proving through competent medical testimony that:

1. Plaintiff was significantly exposed to a proven hazardous substance through the negligent actions of the defendant.
2. As a proximate result of exposure, plaintiff suffers a significantly increased risk of contracting a serious latent disease.
3. That increased risk makes periodic diagnostic medical examinations reasonably necessary.
4. Monitoring and testing procedures exist that make the early detection and treatment of the disease possible and beneficial.

Id. at 852.

73. 1992 Cal. App. LEXIS 537 (Apr. 22, 1992, 5th Dist. Ct. App.).

74. 746 F.2d 816 (D.C. Cir. 1984).

75. *Id.* at 825.

76. *See also* Bourgeois v. A.P. Green Industries, Inc., No. 97-C-3188 (La July 8, 1998).

77. 189 N.J. Super. 561, 461 A.2d 184 (1983).

78. Ayers v. Township of Jackson, 106 N.J. 557, 579 87, 525 A.2d 287, 298–302 (1987), commonly referred to as "*Ayers III.*"

79. *Id.* at 309.

80. *Id.* at 304.

81. No. 81-C-44 (D.C. Colo.).

82. 684 F. Supp. 847, 848 (M.D. Pa. 1988).

83. 477 N.Y.S.2d at 247.

84. *See* "Increased Risk of Cancer or Other Future Illness," pages 624–25.

85. Deleski v. Raymark Indus., 819 F.2d 377, 380–81 (3d Cir. 1987); Plummer v. Abbott Laboratories, 568 F. Supp. 920, 922 (D.R.I. 1983); Bennett v. Mallinckrodt, Inc., 698 S.W.2d 854, 866 (Mo. App. 1985); Askey v. Occidental Chemical Corp., 477 N.Y.S.2d 242, 246 (N.Y. App. Div. 1984).

86. Hagerty v. L & L Marine Servs., 788 F.2d 315, 317 (5th Cir. 1986); Herber v. Johns-Manville Corp., 785 F.2d 79, 82 (3d Cir. 1986); *In re Moorenovich,* 634 F. Supp. 634, 637 (D. Me. 1986).

87. Anderson v. W. R. Grace & Co., 628 F. Supp. 634, 637 (D. Mass. 1986).

88. *Compare* Evers v. Dollinger, 95 N.J. 399 (1984) (Handler, J., concurring) ("medical science does acknowledge the existence of an increased risk . . . sufficient to satisfy the standard of reasonable medical probability that we generally recognize. . . .") *with* Ayers v. Township of Jackson, 106 N.J. 557 (1987) (no compensation for unquantified increased risk).

89. *See, e.g., Hagerty,* 788 F.2d at 320–21; Johnson v. Armstrong Cork Co., 645 F. Supp. 764, 769 (W.D. La. 1986) (on an evidentiary ruling in an asbestos case, the judge held that evidence of the increased risk of cancer was admissible only where the plaintiff could show "that the toxic exposure more probably than not will lead to cancer," *id.* at 769: this means that "[w]here there is no evidence that the increased risk of cancer exceeds 50 percent, there may be no recovery for the increased risk of cancer").

90. *See* Ball v. Joy Mfg. Co., 958 F.2d 36 (4th Cir. 1991); Rittenhouse v. St. Regis Hotel Joint Venture, 565 N.Y.S.2d 365 (Sup. Ct. 1990); *aff'd in pertinent part;* 579 N.Y.S.2d 100 (1st Dept. 1992).

91. Parnell, Curia & Bridges, *Medical Monitoring: A Dangerous Trend, in* FOR THE DEFENSE, at 8 (1992).

92. *See, e.g.,* Cook v. Rockwell Int'l Corp., 755 F. Supp. 1468, 1477 (D. Colo. 1991); Cook v. Rockwell Int'l Corp., 1993 WL 408301 (D. Colo. 1993) (certifying a medical screening class action involving the Rocky Flats weapons production facility).

93. 858 P.2d 970 (Utah 1993).

94. *Id.* at 978.

95. *Id.*

96. *Id.* at 973.

97. 628 A.2d 724, 733 (N.J. 1993).

98. Redland Soccer Club, Inc. v. Department of the Army, 1993 WL 427365 (M.D. Pa., Oct. 19, 1993).

99. *See., e.g.,* McCarter, *Medical Sue-Velliance: A History and Critique of the Medical Monitoring Remedy in Toxic Tort Litigation,* 45 RUTGERS L. REV. 227, 266–67 (1993).

100. *Hansen,* 858 P.2d at 980.

101. *Id.*

102. *Id.*

103. *Id.*

104. 525 A.2d 287 (1993). *In Ayers,* the court stressed that the court-supervised fund concept was superior to lump-sum damage award in three important respects. First, the concept ensures that money is actually used for medical-screening purposes. Second, the fund limits the defendants' liability to costs actually incurred. Third, the fund encourages plaintiffs to receive regular medical screening. The lump-sum payment, in contrast, likely would overcompensate or undercompensate plaintiffs and would tempt them to use the money for something besides medical screening. Accordingly, the *Ayers* court used its equitable powers to create a court-supervised fund to administer medical-screening costs.

105. When cleanup as opposed to tort compensation is the client's goal, public law often provides options that may be available under private law. These public laws work in tandem with the private law; generally, the two coexist as part of our federalist tradition. Indeed, most public environmental laws expressly

preserve in "savings clauses" all private law rights. *See* Allan Kanner, *Tort Law in the Regulatory Age*, 43 WASH. U. J. URB. & CONTEMP. L., 401–24 (1993).

106. To the extent plaintiffs had prevailed on their cleanup claim under RCRA or state law, it is possible that plaintiffs would not have also recovered for diminution in property values. Courts have held that recovery of both cleanup costs and diminution in values constitutes an impermissible double recovery. SUSAN COOKE, THE LAW OF HAZARDOUS WASTE: MANAGEMENT, CLEANUP, LIABILITY AND LITIGATION, § 17.04[2][a] (1994); T&E Industries Inc., v. Safety Light Corp., 587 A.2d 1249, 1263 (N.J. 1991) ("When the property has been decontaminated, it will be restored to full value. [The property owner] will then be able to sell the property at market value").

107. *See, e.g.*, DOBBS ON REMEDIES 310–73 (1973) [hereinafter DOBBS].

108. 147 A.2d 430 (Md. 1958).

109. *Id.* at 437.

110. *Id.* at 437.

111. DOBBS, *supra* note 107, at 316.

112. *See, e.g.*, Leavitt v. Continental Telephone Co. of Maine, 559 A.2d 786, 788 (Me. 1989); Harper v. Morris, 365 S.E.2d 176, 178 (N.C. App. 1988); R&R S Dev. Inc. v. Wilson, 534 So.2d 1008, 1012–13 (Miss. 1988); Otto v. Cornell, 349 N.W.2d 703, 707 (Wis. App. 1984); Benavie v. Baker, 420 N.Y.S.2d 735 (N.Y. A.D.2d 1979).

113. *See, e.g.*, Canton Village Construction, Inc. v. Huntington, 510 A.2d 1377, 1378 (Conn. App. 1986); Kroulik v. Knuppel, 634 P.2d 1027 (Colo. App. 1981); Rector, Etc. v. C.S. McCrossan, 235 N.W.2d 609 (Minn. 1975).

114. *See, e.g.*, Bangert v. Oseola County, 456 N.W.2d 183, 190 (trees were maintained for sentimental and historical reasons, for shade and windbreaks, as well as for environmental and wildlife and special landmark cases); Baker v. Ramirez, 235 Cal. Rptr. 857 (Cal. App. 5th 1987) (orange groves); Gross v. Jackson Township, 476 A.2d 974 (Pa. 1984) (hedges and shrubs provided privacy and natural fence for pets); Rector, Etc. v. C.S. McCrossan, Inc., 235 N.W.2d 609 (trees screened sound and provided privacy, as well as shade and aesthetic value).

115. *See, e.g.*, Heninger v. Dunn, 162 Cal. Rptr. 104, 108–09 (Cal. App. 1980); Bowman v. McFarlin, 615 S.W.2d 383 (Ark. 1981) (plaintiffs brought land because they wanted a wooden setting).

116. *See, e.g.*, Miller v. Cudahy Co., 592 F. Supp. 976 (D. Kan. 1984); *see generally* 76 A.L.R. 4th 629.

117. *See, e.g.*, Freel v. Ozark-Mahoning Co., 208 F. Supp. 93 (D.D.C. of Colo. 1962). *But see* 49 A.L.R. 2d 253 § 4[a] (cases classifying stream pollution as permanent, and thus plaintiffs were awarded damages based on the diminution in value).

118. Mailman's Steam Carpet Cleaning v. Lizotte, 616 N.E.2d 85, 88 (Mass. 1993) (*quoted in* Wm. R. Peterson Oil Co., Inc. v. Chadwick, 1994 WL 260701 (Conn. Super. Ct. 1994)):

> In *Mailman's Steam Carpet Cleaning Corp. v. Lizotte*, the property purchaser sued the seller for breach of seller's warranty that underground gasoline storage tanks had not caused contamination, among other claims. In determining the appropriate measure of damages, the Supreme Judicial Court of Massachusetts held that restoration of the property was an appropriate remedy even though restoration costs exceeded the fair mar-

ket value of the property without contamination. The court noted the principle that damages in a breach of contract action were based on restoring the injured party to the position it would have been in without the breach, as long as the loss followed as a natural consequence of the breach and was within the contemplation of the parties. The seller could reasonably have been aware that it would be liable for cleanup costs as a result of its warranty breached, and that these costs could exceed the fair market value of the property, and the cost of cleanup was not disproportionate to the value of the property, assessing damages in the amount of cleanup costs was appropriate.

119. Barr v. Smith, 631 So.2d 76, 78 (La. App. 2d Cir.), *writ denied*, 637 So.2d 466 (La. 1994).

120. 639 So.2d 595 (Fla. 1994).

121. *Id.* at 596.

122. 522 N.W. 2d 542 (Wis. 1994).

123. *See also* T&E Industries v. Safety Light Corp., 587 A.2d 1249, 1263 (N.J. 1991) (stressing that "when the property has been decontaminated, it will be restored to full value"); *In re Paoli R.R. Yard PCB Litigation,* 811 F. Supp. 1071, 1074, 7 TXLR 731 (E.D. Pa. 1992) (the court emphasized that, under Pennsylvania law, "the cost of remediating harm to property is the exclusive measure of damages where the harm is temporary and remediable").

124. RESTATEMENT (SECOND) OF TORTS § 929 cmt. b (1979).

125. *See, e.g.,* Board of County Comm'rs v. Slovek, 723 F.2d 1303, 1309 (Colo. 1986), 75 A.L.R. Fed. 315.

126. 723 P.2d at 1315–16.

127. 723 P.2d at 1316.

128. *Id.* at 1317.

129. *Id.; see also* Escamilla v. Asarco, 91-CV-5716 (D. Ct. Denver, Apr. 23, 1993):

1. "The award must make the plaintiff whole."
2. "It cannot so exceed the goal of full compensation that it constitutes in effect a punishment . . . or encourages wasteful remedial expenditures by the plaintiff."

130. Sterling v. Veliscol Chemical Corp., 855 F.2d 1188, 1200 (6th Cir. 1988); Ayers v. Township of Jackson, 106 N.J. 557, 525 A.2d 287 (1987); Kornoff v. Kingsburg Cotton Oil Co., 45 Cal. 2d 265, 288 P.2d 507 (1955); Nailor v. C.W. Blakeslee & Sons, 117 Conn. 241, 167 A. 548 (1933); Dixon v. New York Trap Rock Corp., 293 N.Y. 509, 58 N.W.2d 517 (1944); *see also* W. KEETON ET AL., PROSSER AND KEETON ON THE LAW OF TORTS § 89, at 639 (5th ed. 1984) (quoting with approval from Dobbs, *supra* note 107).

131. Section 929 (1977).

132. *See* Kornoff v. Kingsburg Cotton Oil Co., 45 Cal. 2d 265, 273–75, 288 P.2d 507, 512–13 (1955); Miller v. Carnation Co., 39 Colo. App. 1, 4, 564 P.2d 127, 130 (Colo. Ct. App. 1977); Rust v. Guinn, 429 N.E.2d 299, 303–04 (Ind. Ct. App. 1981).

133. Ayers v. Township of Jackson, 493 A.2d 1314, 1319 (N.J. Super. Ct. App. Div. 1985).

134. *Ayers,* 525 A.2d at 293.

135. *Id.*

136. *Id.* at 569–70.

137. Koninklijke Luchtvaan Maatschaapij, N.V. (KLM Royal Dutch Airlines) v. United Technologies Corporation, 610 F.2d 1052 (2d Cir. 1979).

138. RESTATEMENT (SECOND) OF TORTS § 931 cmt. b.

139. 1897 A.C. 596.

140. 1900 A.C. 113.

141. Brownstein, *What's the Use? A Doctrinal and Policy Critique of the Measurement of Loss of Use Damages*, 37 RUTGERS L. REV. 433, 493 (Spring 1985).

142. *Id.*

143. *See e.g.*, Finn v. Witherbee, 126 Cal. App. 2d 45, 47–48, 271 P.2d 606, 609 (1954) ("Whether personal property, unjustly taken, is put to use or placed in storage, its reasonable rental value is just the same. It belongs to its owner and he is entitled to the value of its use"); Ancira-Winton Chevrolet, Inc. v. Wilkerson, 507 S.W.2d 854 (Tex. Civ. App. 1973); Kroger Food Co. v. Singletary, 438 S.W.2d 621, 629 (Tex. Civ. App. 1969). *See also* Cook v. Packard Motor Car Co., 88 Conn. 590, 594, 92 A. 413, 415–16 (1914); Dettmar v. Burns Bros. 111 Misc. 189, 181 NYS 146 (App. Term. 1920) (property owners need not prove actual pecuniary loss to recover loss of use damages).

144. C. MCCORMICK, HANDBOOK ON THE LAW OF DAMAGES § 124 (1935).

145. LA. CIV. CODE, art. 477.

146. LA. CIV. CODE, art. 535, and cmt. (a) thereto.

147. *Cf.* State v. Blair, 285 So.2d 212, 214 (La. 1983).

148. J. MCGEE, REAL ESTATE GUIDE APPRAISAL OF AN ENVIRONMENTALLY CONTAMINATED PROPERTY (1992) (*emphasis in original*).

149. *See, e.g.*, Bixby Ranch Co. v. Spectrol Electronics Corp., No. BC-052566 8 TX L.R. 955 (Sup. Ct. L.A. County 1993) ($826,500 for the diminished property value following after a complete cleanup); DeSario v. Industrial Excess Landfill, Inc., No. 89-570 (Ohio Ct. Common Pleas, Stark County, Dec. 6, 1994) ($6.7 million in property loss to 1713 property owners adjoining a hazardous waste site that could not be cleaned up); *Post-Cleanup Stigma Claims: The Latest Front in the War over Hazardous Waste Cost Recovery*, 9 TXLR 918; *Homeowners near Toxic Dump Win $6.7 Million for "Stigma,"* 95 LWUSA 99 (1/30/95) (*discussing* DeSario v. Industrial Excess Landfill, Inc., No. 89-570 Stark Cty, Ohio 12/6/94), BNA TXLR (12/14/94); Strawn v. Canuso, 638 A.2d 141 (N.J.), 94 LWUSA 29. *See also* Kusum Ketkar, *Hazardous Waste Sites and Property Values in New Jersey*, 24 APPLIED ECON. 647, 653 (1992) (finding presence of a hazardous waste site in a municipality to be negatively correlated with property values in municipality); Janet E. Kohlhase, *The Impact of Toxic Waste Sites on Housing Values*, 30 J. URB. ECON. 1, 11–19 (1991) (finding that prior to public announcement that a site had been placed on the EPA's National Priorities List for cleanup, the site either had no effect or a positive effect on nearby property values, but that after the announcement, the proximity of the site was significantly correlated with lower house values); Gary H. McClelland et al., *The Effect of Risk Beliefs on Property Values: A Case Study of a Hazardous Waste Site*, 10 RISK ANALYSIS 485, 493–494 (1990) (finding a correlation between neighborhoods' assessments of the risk posed by a nearby landfill and property values); R. Gregory Michaels & V. Kerry Smith, *Market Segmentation and Valuing Amenities with Hedonic Models: The Case of Hazardous Waste Sites*, 28 J. URB. ECON. 223 (1990) (finding a statistically significant relationship between a house's distance from a publicized hazardous waste site and its price when data for an

entire city housing market was studied, but finding no such relationship when the data was analyzed by submarkets); GERALD E. SMOLEN & GARY MOORE, ECONOMIC EFFECTS OF HAZARDOUS WASTE LANDFILLS ON SURROUNDING REAL ESTATE VALUES IN TOLEDO, OHIO (Ohio State Univ., Center for Real Estate Education & Research, Feb. 1991) (finding a strong negative relationship between proximity to a toxic water landfill and sales price, for as far as five and three quarter miles from the site). *See also* V. Kerry Smith & William H. Desvousges, *The Value of Avoiding a LULU: Hazardous Waste Disposal Sites,* 68 REV. ECON. STAT. 293, 298 (1986) (using survey of suburban Boston households, rather than hedonic studies, to estimate that distance from a hazardous waste disposal site is valued at $330 to $495 per mile per year).

150. 621 N.E. 2d 1195 (N.Y. 1993).

151. *Id.*

152. *Id.*

153. *Id.*

154. *See, e.g.,* 2000 Watermark Ass'n, Inc. v. Celotex Corp., 784 F.2d 1183 (4th Cir. 1986) (no recovery under negligence on theory that polluted creek that caught fire in the past makes property less valuable where plaintiff's property or person suffered no physical damage); *Berry,* 989 F.2d 822 (5th Cir. 1993), *cert. denied,* 510 U.S. 1117 (1994) (no recovery for damages for reduced market value caused by stigma absent some physical damage to plaintiff's land); McGinnis v. Tennessee Gas Pipeline Co., 25 F.3d 1049 (6th Cir. 1994) (no recovery for alleged loss of property value absent evidence of contamination on property); Miller v. Cudahy Co., 567 F. Supp. 892 (D. Kan. 1983) (no recovery for groundwater contamination by plaintiffs whose property has not been reached by leading edge of contamination; pollution needs to be sole factor depressing land values to be compensable); Adams v. Star Enterprise, 851 F. Supp. 770 (E.D. Va. 1994); Adkins v. Thomas Solvent Co., 440 Mich. 293, 487 N.W.2d 715 (Mich. 1992); Mercer v. Rockwell Int'l, No. 1:87 CV-1060H (W.D. Ky. 9/1/98), 13 BNA TOX. L. REP. No. 15, 471 (9/9/98) (no stigma damages).

155. *See* SUPERFUND SECTION 301(E) STUDY GROUP, INJURIES AND DAMAGES FROM HAZARDOUS WASTE—ANALYSIS AND IMPROVEMENT OF LEGAL REMEDIES, A REPORT TO CONGRESS IN COMPLIANCE WITH SECTION 301(e) OF THE COMPREHENSIVE ENVIRONMENTAL RESPONSE, COMPENSATION, AND LIABILITY ACT OF 1980 (P.L. 96-510), Serial No. 97-12, pts. 1 & 2 printed for the use of the Senate Committee on Environment and Public Works, 97th Cong., 2d Sess. (Sept. 1982); H.R. CONF. REP. 962, 99th Cong., 2nd Sess., 261 (1986). For discussion of the study's recommendations, see Frank Grad, *Remedies for Injuries Caused by Hazardous Waste: The Report and Recommendations of the Superfund 301(e) Study Group,* 14 ELR 10,105 (Mar. 1984); Zazzali & Grad, *Hazardous Waste: New Rights and Remedies?* 14 SETON HALL L. REV., 446 (1983). *But see* Alfred Light, *Federal Preemption, Federal Conscription Under the New Superfund Act,* 38 MERCER L. REV. 643 (1987) (arguing that Congress misread Study Group's recommendations).

156. In International Paper Company v. Ouellette, 402 U.S. 558 (1987), the Court allowed a state nuisance and trespass claim against a polluter that otherwise complied with regulatory discharge requirements.

157. The major limitation of tort law is that it has rarely been used to prevent the event giving rise to the harm or the increased risk. However, in at least one case, the neighbors of a proposed rayon plant successfully sued under an

anticipatory nuisance theory to enjoin the construction of the plant. *See, e.g.*, Carol Strickland, *Seeking a New Route*, HIST. PRESERVATION NEWS, Feb. 1993, at 14 ("a potentially groundbreaking legal case that has implications for future industrial siting challenges"); LOUISIANA ADVISORY COMMITTEE TO THE U.S. COMMISSION ON CIVIL RIGHTS, THE BATTLE FOR ENVIRONMENTAL JUSTICE IN LOUISIANA, Sept. 1993, at 56.

158. *See* SELMI & MASTERSON, STATE ENVIRONMENTAL LAW, Part B, "THE COMMON LAW," § 2.01-4.05; State (N.Y.) v. Shore Realty Corp., 759 F.2d 1032, 1050–52 (2d Cir. 1985) (nuisance). However, no list can be exhaustive. For example, neighbors of a waste landfill were certified as a class under Connecticut's Unfair Trade Practices. Faith Marr et al. v. WMX Technologies, Inc., No. SC 15802 Conn. Sup. Ct. (5/12/98).

159. CERCLA, § 107(e)(i); Mangini v. Aeroject-General Corp., 230 Cal. App. 3d 1125, 281 Cal. Rptr. 827 (1991) (allowing a current owner to sue a former lessee under theories of public and private nuisance).

160. For example, the Radiation Exposure Compensation Act of 1990, Pub. L. 101-426, 104 Stat. 920 (1990) establishes a workers'-compensation–like system for disbursement of benefits to uranium mine workers and other persons who were presumptively exposed to radiation during the early years of the nation's nuclear testing program.

161. L.R. 3 H.L. 330.

162. Over 30 states have approved of either the RESTATEMENT OF TORTS §§ 519 & 520 or Rylands v. Fletcher, *supra* note 161.

163. *See, e.g.*, Sterling v. Velsicol Chemical Corp., 647 F. Supp. 303 (W.D. Tenn. 1986), *rev'd in part, aff'd in part* 855 F.2d 118 (6th Cir. 1988) (operation of chemical waste burial site found ultrahazardous); Chavez v. Southern Pacific Transportation Co., 413 F. Supp. 1203 (E.D. Cal. 1976) (transport of explosives by rail found ultrahazardous); National Steel Service Center, Inc. v. Gibbons, 319 N.W.2d 269 (Iowa 1982) (transport of propane gas by rail deemed ultrahazardous); United States v. Hooker Chemicals & Plastics Corp., 722 F. Supp. 960, 966–67 (W.D.N.Y. 1989) (disposal of hazardous chemicals in Love Canal deemed ultrahazardous); N.J. Dept. of Environmental Protection v. Ventron Corp., 94 N.J. 473, 468 A.2d 150 (1983) (disposal of mercury is ultrahazardous). *But see* Avemco Insurance Co. v. Rooto Corp., 967 F.2d 1105 (6th Cir. 1992).

164. Greyhound v. Blakely, 262 F.2d 401 (9th Cir. 1958); Dillon v. Acme Oil Company, 49 Hunn. 565, 18 N.Y. St. Rep. 477, 2 N.Y.S. 289 (N.Y. Sup. Ct. 1888).

165. *See, e.g.*, Jersey City Redevelopment Authority v. PPG Industries, 655 F. Supp. 1257 (D. N.J. 1987); Driekosen v. Black, Siralls & Bryson, Inc., 64 N.W.2d 88 (Neb. 1954)

166. Branch v. Western Petroleum, Inc., 657 P.2d 267, 276 (Utah 1982).

167. W. Prosser & W.P. Keaton, THE LAW OF TORTS, § 36 (5th ed. 1984), or *res ipsa loquitur*, Reynolds Metals Co. v. Ulurbide, 258 F.2d 321, 329–330 (9th Cir.), *cert. denied*, 358 U.S. 840, 790 Sup. Ct. 66, Lawyer's Edition 2d 76 (1958), and strict liability is applied to the generation, transport, discharge, or disposal of toxic substances into the environment. Mowrer v. Ashland Oil and Ref. Co., 518 F.2d 659, 662 (7th Cir. 1975).

168. *See, e.g.*, Borland v. Sanders Lead Company, Inc., 369 So.2d 523 (Ala. 1979); Martin v. Reynolds Metal Co., 342 P.2d 790 (Or. 1959).

169. Martin v. Amoco Oil Co., 679 N.E.2d 139 (Ind. Ct. App. 1997), *aff'd* 696 N.E.2d 383 (Ind. 1998).

170. RESTATEMENT (SECOND) OF TORTS § 158.

171. *See, e.g.*, RESTATEMENT (SECOND) OF TORTS, § 822; Boomer et al. v. Atlantic Cement Company, 26 N.Y.2d 219, 257 N.E.2d 870, 309 N.Y.S.2d 312 (N.Y. Ct. App. 1970); Madison v. Ducktown Sulfur, Cooper & Iron Co., 83 S.W. 658 (Tenn. 1904). On public nuisance, *see, e.g.*, Spur Industries, Inc. v. Del Webb Development Co., 108 Ariz. 178, 494 P.2d 700 (Az. 1972); Village of Wilsonville v. SCA Services, Inc., 426 N.E.2d 824 (Ill. 1981); Town of Mt. Pleasant v. Van Tassell, 7 Misc. 2d 243 166 N.Y.S.2d 458 (N.Y. Sup. Ct. 1957). The requisite intent has been found in the failure to abate a dangerous condition created by others on one's property. RESTATEMENT SECOND TORTS § 839, cmt. d (1979); New York v. Shore Realty Corp., 759 F.2d 1032 (2d Cir. 1985).

172. *See, e.g.*, City of Bloomington v. Westinghouse Electric Corp., 891 F.2d 611 (7th Cir. 1989).

173. Wright, *The Cost-Internationalization Case for Class Actions*, 21 STAN. L. REV. 383 (1969).

174. The term "Lone Pine" is coined from Lore v. Lone Pine Corp., No. L-00306-85, *slip. op.* (N.J. Sup. Ct. Law Div. 1986), wherein the trial court in a case management order directed the plaintiffs to provide, among other things, expert opinions regarding causation by substances from the landfill. When the plaintiffs failed, the Court dismissed their cases with prejudice. *See* Kinnick v. Schierl, Inc., 541 N.W.2d 803 (Wis. Ct. App. 1994) (citation omitted).

175. *See, e.g.*, Simon v. G.D. Searle & Co., 816 F.2d 397, 400 (8th Cir. 1988).

176. *See, e.g.*, Grimshaw v. Ford Motor Co., 119 Cal. App. 3d 757, 813 (1981) (the Pinto memo).

177. Experience has taught us that the discovery Rules are "not infrequently exploited to the disadvantage of justice." Herbert v. Lando, 441 U.S. 153, 179 (1979) (Powell, J., concurring).

178. This was the case in the asbestos litigation. P. BRODEUR, OUTRAGEOUS MISCONDUCT: THE ASBESTOS INDUSTRY ON TRIAL (1985).

179. The ethical problems with defense counsel filing a motion to dismiss or for summary judgment that counsel knows is contrary to the actual facts—for example, the company has an internal memo to the contrary—has been too little explored and left in the penumbra between the lawyer's role as the client's zealous advocate and the lawyer's role as guardian of the judicial system's integrity.

180. *See, e.g.*, KANNER, ENVIRONMENTAL & TOXIC TORT TRIALS, *supra* note 16 § 10.03, p. 240 ("Another causation problem in proving a plaintiff's case is dealing with the defendant's attempt to attribute the illness at issue to personal factors, such as social history, smoking, genetic predisposition, and so on."); *id.*, § 10.08, p. 243 ("Negative information about a party to a lawsuit generally tends to be more believable and memorable than positive testimony. This is why many defendants sling mud at the plaintiffs.") (footnotes omitted).

181. City of Independence et al. v. Amoco, 95-0019-CV-W-2, *consolidated with* 95-0121-CV-W-2, (W.D. Mo. Order 7/27/98) (certifying a mandatory class for injunctive relief provided in settlement; holding that "[c]ertificaton pursuant to this section [23(b)(1)(A)] is particularly apt in order to effectively clean up the site, protect Amoco from inconsistent orders, and allow settlement of this complex case").

182. *Compare* Ford v. Murphy Oil, U.S.A., Inc., 96-C-2913, 96-C-2917, 96-C-2929 (La. Sup. Ct. 9/9/97) (decertifying a class of "thousands of residents who live near the Ford petrochemical plants and who clam physical and property damages as a result of the continuous emissions combined") *with* Coastal Corp. v. Garza., 13 BNA TOX. L. REP. p. 251 (July 22, 1998) (Texas Sup. Ct. decision 7/13/98) (dismissing appeal of certification of a property damage class action against petrochemical plants in Corpus Christi's Refinery Row).

As indicated elsewhere in certain circumstances, a group may be well advised to pursue informational gathering and/or citizen suit litigation before turning to compensatory litigation. Allan Kanner, *Future Trends in Toxic Tort Litigation,* 20 RUTGERS L.J. 667 (1989); *supra* notes 19–20.

183. *See* Amchem Products, Inc. v. Windsor, 117 S. Ct. 2231 (1997). Over the last few years, several courts of appeal have reversed trial court decisions certifying actions for class treatment, directing district courts to apply the class certification requirements more rigorously. *See, e.g., In re Rhone-Poulenc Rorer, Inc.*, 51 F.3d 1293 (7th Cir. 1995) (issuing writ of mandamus reversing certification of nationwide class action involving personal injury claims on grounds that state common law standards vary materially among the 50 states); *In re American Medical Systems, Inc.*, 75 F.3d 1069 (6th Cir. 1996) (same); Castano v. American Tobacco Co., 84 F.3d 734 (5th Cir. 1996) (same on discretionary appellate review of class certification order; "rigorous analysis" standard).

184. *See* Amchem Products Inc. v. Windsor, 117 S. Ct. 2231, 2250 (1997) (differences in applicable state law mentioned as one reason for overturning nationwide class action settlement); Castano v. American Tobacco Co., 84 F.3d 734, 741 (5th Cir. 1996) ("In a multi-state class action, variations in state law may swamp any common issues and defeat predominance"); *In re American Medical System,* 75 F.3d 1069, 1085 (6th Cir. 1996) (class certification overturned in part because "[t]he district court . . . failed to consider how the law of negligence differs from jurisdiction to jurisdiction"); *In re Rhone-Poulenc Rorer Inc.*, 51 F.3d 1293 (7th Cir. 1995) (nationwide class certification improper because of variations in state law).

185. Class action and complex litigation are relatively specialized fields and should not be undertaken lightly or without adequate preparation. Good sources of information include the MANUAL FOR COMPLEX LITIGATION (3rd ed. 1995) and HERBERT NEWBERG & ALBA CONTE, NEWBRERG ON CLASS ACTIONS (3d ed. 1992).

186. Amchem Products, Inc. v. Windsor, 117 S. Ct. 2231 (1997).

187. By the same token, state courts are likewise responding to these changes, and often filling some of the void by certifying statewide and national mass torts. Many plaintiffs and defendants appear to support this trend. Indeed, "litigation in the federal courts may not always be the most desirable means of handling complex litigation. First, some believe that federal courts should focus their attention and resources on those cases that involve federal interests, which federal courts uniquely are qualified to hear. When substantive state interests are at issue, forcing all the actions regardless of where they were filed into a consolidated federal court action might be thought to raise federalism concerns." *Complex Litigation: Statutory Recommendations and Analysis,* AMERICAN LAW INSTITUTE, 1993, p. 167. Nevertheless, this trend, combined with the efforts of many defendants to remove mass tort cases to federal forums, has produced an explosion of

decisions on federal class action jurisdiction, including issues of jurisdictional amount and fraudulent joinder.

188. Bernard Williams, *The Idea of Equality, in* PHILOSOPHY, POLITICS AND SOCIETY, at 125 (2d series, Laslett & Runciman ed., 1962) (noting that equality in the popular mind is often thought to be the enemy of liberty).

189. W.P. KEETON, PROSSER & KEETON ON TORTS § 3 at 15 (5th ed. 1984); *id.*, § 9 at 42 ("protection according to the usages of decent society, and offensive contacts, or those which are contrary to all good manners . . . [a]t the same time, in a crowded world, a certain amount of personal contact is inevitable, and must be accepted").

190. *Id.* § 3 at 16 (footnotes omitted).

191. Don Elliot, *The Future of Toxic Torts: Of Chemophobia, Risk as a Compensable Injury and Hybrid Compensation Systems*, 25 HOUS. L. REV. 781, 782 (1988) ("In America, lawsuits are morality plays"); *see also*, Laurence Tribe, *Trial by Mathematics: Precision and Ritual in the Legal Process*, 84 HARV. L. REV. 1329, 1351 (1974) (a trial "is also, and no less importantly, a ritual"); Allan Kanner, *Future Trends in Toxic Tort Litigation*, 20 RUTGERS L.J. 669 (1989).

192. *See, e.g.*, KANNER, ENVIRONMENTAL & TOXIC TORT TRIALS, ch. 2 (voir dire).

CHAPTER 20

Controlling Exposures in the Workplace

BARBARA J. OLSHANSKY

More than eighty years have passed since the deaths of over 100 workers in the Triangle Shirt Waist fire in New York City, and public concern about hazardous and inhumane workplace conditions continues to wax and wane. But, in the wake of the deaths of seven workers in a fireworks factory in Osseo, Michigan on December 12, 1998, and the deaths of twenty-five workers in a fire in a poultry processing plant in Hamlet, North Carolina in 1991,[1] few today would dispute that our current system of occupational safety and health protections is inadequate, and its enforcement seriously deficient. Nevertheless, for many years, the most blatant and deplorable safety and health problems in American workplaces have remained unaddressed by those with the authority to encourage or dictate beneficial changes.

Advocates in the environmental justice movement have reinvigorated the discourse on this long-neglected sector of the human environment, and have honed the discussion by demarcating the cardinal issues that demand serious attention:

1. the disproportionately high risk of occupational disease and injury faced by workers of color compared to the risk faced by the general working population;
2. poor access to clinical occupational health services for workers of color;

3. gross underreporting of state and national occupational disease statistics, and the failure to collect such statistics by ethnicity or race; and
4. the total inadequacy of remedies available to those who suffer from workplace injuries and illnesses.[2]

Despite the nation's continuing failure to gather occupational injury and illness statistics by race and ethnicity, the few studies undertaken to date plainly indicate that workers of color and low-wage workers are far more likely than the rest of the population to work in jobs with higher and more frequent exposure to toxic chemicals and greater risks of injury.[3] Workers of color are pushed by various social and economic factors, not the least of which are discriminatory employment practices, into the lowest paying and most hazardous occupations.[4] Moreover, the studies to date show that within these occupations, workers of color are assigned in disproportionate numbers to the most dangerous job classifications.[5] Experts studying occupational health have long postulated that placement in dangerous jobs means that these workers are most likely to be exposed to higher risks of occupational injury and acute illness,[6] and a number of occupational health experts have concluded that there are statistically significant disparities in rates of exposure to occupational hazards among workers of different races.[7]

Given the weakness of substantive occupational health and safety standards,[8] the inadequate enforcement mechanisms, the limited resources allotted for monitoring and enforcement, and the narrow range of legal remedies available to remedy violations of standards, advocates who seek to reduce workplace hazards and assist workers who have already been injured face a difficult task. Perhaps one of the most important tasks in this effort is to ensure greater awareness by workers of the risks they face every day. Access to such information is a key to effective advocacy for the enforcement of existing protections, the provision of fair and adequate remedies for injuries suffered, and the prevention of future harms, exposures, and illnesses. The discussion below sets forth the various means by which critical information regarding workplace risks can be garnered, the statutory requirements regarding the communication of information to workers, the range of substantive standards governing workplace exposures to toxic substances, the mechanisms available to enforce such protections, the means of achieving remedies for injuries and illnesses beyond those provided under state workers' compensation schemes, and some of the limitations inherent in the various facets of this patchy network of legal protections.

The Scope of Substantive Workplace Safety and Health Protections

Enforcing Affirmative Federal Statutory Mandates

The Occupational Safety and Health Act

The Occupational Safety and Health Act (OSH Act)[9] was enacted "to assure so far as possible every working man and woman in the Nation safe and healthful working conditions . . . ,"[10] and remains the primary federal statute intended to address hazards in the workplace. The Act provides two means of protection for workers: it imposes a general duty of care for all covered employers, and it requires employers to comply with specific safety and health rules and standards.

The general duty clause of the Act requires employers to furnish their employees with a working environment "free from recognized hazards."[11] Decisional authority interpreting the scope of this protection makes clear that the Occupational Safety and Health Administration (OSHA), the enforcing agency, has authority to investigate violations of the general duty clause,[12] and that employee complaints alleging violations of this clause are a sufficient basis for OSHA to inspect the workplace even where no specific regulation deals with the alleged harm.[13] Courts have also recognized that even potential hazards may fall within the definition of the term "recognized hazards" and have required employers to remedy such conditions or face a violation.[14] Finally, recent decisions have found that compliance with a specific rule or standard may not excuse an employer from the independent obligations imposed on it under the general duty clause.[15]

The Secretary of Labor is charged with setting and enforcing specific health and safety standards.[16] Safety standards, intended to address workplace conditions that can lead to traumatic injury,[17] are subject to a cost-benefit analysis in which OSHA must show that the requirements imposed produce measurable benefits in mitigating the risk of injury without undermining the economic viability of the regulated industry.[18]

Under Section 6(b)(5) of the Act, OSHA must establish health standards for exposure to toxic substances and physical agents which "most adequately assures, to the extent feasible, on the basis of the best available evidence that no employee will suffer material impairment of health or functional capacity even if such employee has a regular exposure to the hazard . . . for the period of his working life." The agency bears the burden of proving the hazardous nature of a substance as well as showing that the proposed controls are technologically feasible. This provision permits OSHA to adopt the most current and effective measures practicable.[19]

In addition to safety and health standards, OSHA adopts specification and performance standards. Specification standards prescribe the means by which employers are to abate a hazard.[20] Performance standards, by contrast, are goal oriented and merely delineate a broad requirement.[21]

Finally, under Section 6(c) of the Act,[22] OSHA has the authority to issue emergency temporary standards that are effective for six months if it determines that employees are subject to extreme danger from exposure to substances known to be toxic or physically harmful, and an emergency standard is necessary to protect employees from the danger. This procedure has been used infrequently by OSHA in part because of the high standard that must be met to justify the ex parte nature of the process and, in part, because the issuance of such a standard triggers an accelerated rulemaking timetable that the agency has difficulty meeting.

The Occupational Safety and Health Administration may commence the rulemaking process on its own initiative, on the recommendations of other federal agencies, and on the basis of petitions submitted by interested parties.[23] Notice and public comment are required, and interested parties may request a public hearing to discuss the proposed standard.[24] While the Secretary is mandated to publish the final standard within sixty days of the hearing date or the close of the comment period if no hearing is held,[25] in practice this never occurs. Furthermore, the OSH Act permits any person aggrieved by a new or revised standard to file a petition in the appropriate U.S. Court of Appeals seeking review of the standard and a stay pending final determination.[26] The rulemaking process, coupled with the burden of proof placed on the agency in promulgating and justifying standards, has prevented OSHA from keeping up with the increasing proliferation of chemicals used in the work environment.

In addition to direct federal agency control, the OSH Act permits states to exercise jurisdiction over any occupational safety and health issue where no federal standard exists, and to operate an occupational health and safety program comparable in funding, authority, and staffing to the federal program. Twenty-three states and two territories have state plans that have been approved by the Secretary of Labor.[27] Section 18 of the OSH Act requires a state to submit a plan to OSHA if it desires to assume responsibility for the development and enforcement of state standards for which a federal standard has been issued. While some states have tended to adopt the federal standards, others have acted in advance of the federal government to address health concerns more quickly and comprehensively, and have adopted standards that are significantly different from the federal standards.[28]

In addition to mandating the promulgation of safety and health standards, the OSH Act also imposes recordkeeping and monitoring requirements on employers that provide a significant source of information regarding exposures and injuries. Employers covered under the Act are required to make and maintain injury and illness records for each establishment they operate.[29] New recordkeeping rules are issued whenever OSHA adopts a new standard that imposes exposure monitoring requirements and regulates toxic materials or harmful physical agents. Thus, the standards for occupational exposure to asbestos, arsenic, lead, and cotton dust, among others, all require the employer to monitor the workplace for the presence of the regulated substance and determine whether the quantities present exceed the permissible exposure level or other action levels.[30] Employees or their representatives have a statutory right to observe these monitoring activities while they are being done.[31] Further, many of these standards also include medical monitoring provisions and medical recordkeeping requirements.

Although the OSH Act provides workers with the right to complain about workplace conditions, attend OSHA inspections, contest the agency's action with regard to a violation, and refuse to do work that presents an imminent hazard to their safety or health, in reality the protection afforded by these statutory rights is extremely limited given the inadequate resources that the agency has to inspect workplaces and enforce the law.[32]

Employees may present their concerns about workplace hazards to OSHA through either the formal or informal complaint process. Formal complaints must be written, must be signed by an employee or an employee representative,[33] and must describe an imminent danger which threatens harm to an employee.[34] The agency must physically inspect the plant as soon as possible in response to such a complaint. Informal complaints, by contrast, may be filed by anyone, and may be submitted orally or in written form. They need not be signed.[35] OSHA area directors have discretion in responding to informal complaints and may order an inspection or write to the employer and request that it investigate and correct the conditions. The employer is then required to reply to the area director and detail the corrective action taken.

If OSHA determines that an inspection is necessary, the OSH Act requires that employers permit either a representative of the employees, or, if there is no union, an employee selected by the other employees, to accompany the OSHA compliance officer during the inspection of the workplace.[36] The employee representative is entitled to be present during every phase of the inspection, the opening and closing conferences with the employer, and the walkaround. During the inspection, employees may raise other possible violations with the inspector, and any interview is confidential.

Under Section 10(c) of the Act,[37] employees may contest a citation issued to the employer as a result of the inspection. Such a challenge must be filed within 15 working days after the employee representative is notified of the issuance of the citation, and is limited to an attack on the abatement period delineated by OSHA.[38] If a hearing is held, employees have the right to intervene and present evidence but must notify the Occupational Safety and Health Review Commission (OSHRC), an independent adjudicatory agency, of their desire to participate at least ten days prior to the scheduled hearing.[39]

Regardless of their decision to intervene in the hearing, employees are entitled to notification of all proposed settlement agreements. Over 90 percent of all employer contests of violations are resolved by settlement.[40] Employees also have the right to object to a settlement[41] but cannot challenge OSHA's decision to withdraw a citation.[42]

Finally, employees have a protected right to refuse to do work that presents an imminent hazard to their health and safety. The regulation promulgated by OSHA provides that an employee is protected from discipline or discharge if he or she refuses to work when "confronted with a choice between not performing assigned tasks or subjecting himself to serious injury or death arising from the hazardous condition of the workplace."[43] For the refusal to be protected, five conditions must be met:

1. the refusal must be made in good faith because of a perceived danger;
2. the employee must lack a reasonable alternative;
3. the hazard must be one that any reasonable person would assess as creating a real risk of death or serious injury;
4. there must be insufficient time to seek to remedy the hazard through the normal statutory enforcement channels; and
5. the employee must first attempt to get the employer to correct the hazard before resorting to the self-help remedy.[44]

In practice, the refusal right actually provides little protection for workers given the Act's procedure for the resolution of discrimination complaints. Section 11(c)(1)[45] prohibits retaliation against employees for exercising their rights under the Act or for testifying in hearings adjudicating issues arising under the Act. Retaliation includes acts short of discharge, such as suspensions, demotions, and reductions in pay. The agency interprets this section as prohibiting discrimination by anyone, including employment agencies, unions, and individual officers of the company.[46] However, the broad statutory language and the intent to provide protection against all forms of discrimination are significantly undermined by the complaint resolution procedure.[47] Complaints must be filed with the appropriate OSHA Area Director within thirty days of the adverse action.[48]

Employer Defenses

If an employer chooses to contest a civil citation,[49] the appeal is adjudicated by the OSHRC.[50] Initial hearings are held by administrative law judges, and the determination can be appealed to the entire Commission. The OSHRC's findings of fact are binding, but the interpretation of the standards is determined by OSHA. Decisions of the OSHRC represent final administrative orders and can be appealed by either the employer or OSHA to the federal courts of appeals.[51]

An OSHA compliance officer need not prove to himself or herself that a violation of the Act has occurred; the officer may issue a citation if he or she believes that one has occurred.[52] If challenged, for all but the most de minimis offenses, OSHA must prove some degree of employer knowledge of the existence of the violation. For example, courts have noted that for both serious[53] and nonserious[54] violations, OSHA must show that the employer knew or reasonably should have known of the existence of the dangerous condition.[55]

Penalties under OSHA are keyed to the type of violation. A serious violation is found when there is a substantial risk of serious physical harm,[56] defined as an "impairment of the body in which part of the body is rendered functionally useless or is substantially reduced in efficiency," or "illnesses that could shorten life or significantly reduce physical or mental efficiency." A willful violation requires either that the employer have actual knowledge of the existence of the dangerous condition and that the condition violates a specific standard of the Act or the regulations, or that the employer act with plain indifference to worker safety. There is no requirement that the condition have potential consequences equivalent to those required for a serious violation; the challenged conduct must merely violate the Act or regulations.

To establish a willful violation, OSHA must meet a higher burden of proof than for a serious violation, because it must demonstrate that the employer actually knew that it was violating a duty. Accordingly, employers frequently raise lack of knowledge as a defense to such violations. Employee misconduct constitutes a good faith defense to a willful violation. To assert such a defense, an employer must prove that:

1. it was not aware of the employee's actions constituting noncompliance with the standard;
2. there was a company work rule that was uniformly enforced; and

3. employees were adequately trained and supervised with respect to specific hazards particular to the industry.[57]

Other factors considered by the court in deciding whether to accept this defense include whether the employer has a history of violations,[58] and whether appropriate corrective measures are taken when employees fail to comply with required precautions.

Some employers have also successfully asserted a defense based on their lack of knowledge about a hazardous condition and their resulting inability to prevent the harm. This defense has been successful in cases in which the employer could not have known of the particular danger, such as situations in which it has been misinformed about the hazards of a specific substance by the manufacturer.[59]

The Commission divides defenses into two broad categories: procedural defenses, which included challenges to the service, timing, issuance, and specifics of the citation, and constitutional and statutory challenges to inspections; and substantive defenses, which deal with the validity and applicability of a particular standard to the facts of the case, the employer's conduct, and the effects on the employees. Among the specific affirmative defenses raised successfully to date are the following:

1. greater hazard (that is, compliance with the standard will result in the creation of a greater hazard for employees);[60]
2. unpreventable employee misconduct;[61]
3. exemption under the Act;
4. failure to issue the citation with reasonable promptness;[62]
5. impossibility of compliance;[63]
6. invalidity of the cited standard;
7. preemption by a more specifically applicable standard;
8. res judicata; and
9. expiration of the six-month statute of limitations.[64]

In 1986, OSHA implemented a megafine strategy and began fining employers on a violation-by-violation basis instead of grouping violations together in one citation for flagrant violations. The policy has resulted in significantly higher penalties for employers. Furthermore, in 1990, Congress increased sevenfold the civil penalties that may be imposed under the Act.[65]

Using the Protections Afforded by Other Statutes

The National Labor Relations Act Like the OSH Act, the National Labor Relations Act (NLRA)[66] provides workers with a limited right to refuse to perform hazardous work. Properly exercised, this right can provide a measure of protection from retaliatory discharge or other discriminatory action for refusing such work, and incorporates a remedy providing for reinstatement and back pay. The nature of the right available to workers, however, depends upon whether the workplace is unionized or not, and, if it is unionized, the nature of the guarantees provided under the collective bargaining agreement.[67]

Section 7 of the NLRA[68] provides protection to employees who are not members of a union, and for union employees whose collective bargaining agreement excludes health and safety issues from its no-strike clause, if they choose to stage a safety walkout. The walkout must be based on the workers' good faith belief[69] that their working conditions are unsafe.[70]

Section 502 of the NLRA[71] provides similar protection for union employees who are covered under a comprehensive collective bargaining agreement. Under this provision, an individual employee has the right to leave the workplace if he or she is faced with an "abnormally dangerous condition" that can be *objectively* verified.[72] This requirement means that no protection is available should the employee's subjective determination prove to be incorrect. Furthermore, a worker seeking to invoke the protection of Section 502 must demonstrate that the danger was sufficiently "hazardous" to warrant a refusal to work. This limitation has been interpreted to mean that the hazardous conditions may not be a "normal" part of the job. Thus, Section 502 protection may not be available to those working in inherently dangerous jobs.

The Americans with Disabilities Act The Americans with Disabilities Act (ADA)[73] provides another source of protection for individuals subject to toxic exposures at work.[74] Title I of the ADA specifies that covered entitites, including employers,[75] labor organizations, and employment agencies,[76] cannot discriminate against a "qualified individual"[77] in employment application procedures, training, compensation, job advancement, working conditions, or termination because of the individual's disability.[78] In addition, the ADA prohibits retaliation, interference, coercion, or intimidation against anyone who asserts their rights under the Act.[79]

Employment discrimination is defined under Title I to include an employer's failure to make "reasonable accommodations"[80] to employees or job applicants suffering from known physical or mental disabilities who are otherwise qualified for their positions, as long as the accommodations do not impose an undue hardship on the employer.[81] Thus, under the ADA, employers are required not only to refrain from discrimination, but also must undertake efforts to provide access to those who are disabled within the meaning of the Act.

The ADA defines the term "disabled" to mean "a physical or mental impairment that substantially limits one or more of the major life activities of such individual. . . ."[82] The Act does not require an individual to explain the diagnosis, cause, or precise nature of his or her disability,[83] although it does require that the individual seeking accommodation establish the "real" disabling effects of his or her condition.[84] The type of medical evidence that will suffice varies because the ADA, like the Rehabilitation Act, does not delineate any requirement regarding the type of evidence or proof needed to support a claim.[85]

Given the Supreme Court's acceptance of a broad statutory definition of the term "handicapped" under the Rehabilitation Act regulations, and the similarity of the definition of "disabled" under the comparable ADA regulations,[86] there is good reason to believe that the scope of the ADA's coverage will be interpreted broadly as well. Thus, for example, an individual's chemical sensitivities may constitute a disability warranting protection and reasonable accommodation under the ADA.[87]

However, a number of hurdles remain before a court will find such an individual entitled to a reasonable accommodation. First, even if an employee's disability is recognized as legitimate, the individual will not be covered under the ADA unless the condition "substantially limits" a "major life activity"[88] of the employee such as walking, seeing, hearing, breathing, or working.[89] In cases in which a person is sensitive to exposures in the workplace, a showing must be made that the affected individual "is significantly restricted in the ability to perform either a class of jobs," a "broad range of jobs in various classes,"[90] or "the entire class of jobs for which he or she has been trained,"[91] for the disability to be recognized. An individual will not be deemed substantially impaired based on his or her inability to perform a particular job in a particular location.[92] Thus, those with chemical sensitivities will likely be successful in seeking an accommodation under the ADA when their reactions are severe enough to impair their functioning substantially, and the chemicals they respond to are common enough that their search for alternative employment is difficult.[93]

Second, while an employee with chemical sensitivities may need a reasonable accommodation to "qualify" for the position in question, and the ADA requires that the employer make the accommodations necessary to render the disabled employee "qualified," the employer is relieved of this obligation if the accommodation would result in an undue hardship[94] or if the accommodation would not enable the employee to perform the essential functions of the position.[95]

Third, although the employer must select "the accommodation that best serves the needs of the individual and the employer,"[96] it need not provide the best accommodation available, only an effective accommodation that enables the individual to enjoy the same "benefits and privileges of employment as are enjoyed by . . . other similarly situated employees without disabilities."[97]

The employer is ultimately responsible for determining how to accommodate his or her employee's disability, and the ADA contemplates a wide range of accommodations including not only physical alterations of the workplace but also changes in the manner in which the jobs are conducted. For those with chemical sensitivities, appropriate accommodations might include: removing the offending chemicals from the workplace, improving ventilation systems, offering personal protective equipment, transferring the employee to another area, or modifying the job to reduce exposure. In addition, an employer may be required to accommodate an individual by restructuring the position, modifying work schedules, or reassigning the individual to a comparable vacant position.[98]

Whistleblower Laws "Whistleblower" provisions in federal and state statutes, as well as state court decisions recognizing an employee's right to be free from retaliation, provide additional protection for workers who report safety violations, file compensation claims, or seek to avoid hazardous work. Federal whistleblower protections are found in seven environmental statutes, including the Resource Conservation and Recovery Act (RCRA),[99] which regulates the handling, treatment, storage, transportation, and disposal of solid and hazardous waste; the Asbestos Hazard Emergency Response Act;[100] the Toxic Substances Control Act (TSCA); the Energy Reorganization Act of 1974 (ERA); the Comprehensive Environmental Response, Compensation and Liability Act of 1980 (CERCLA); the Clean Water Act (CWA);[101] and the Clean Air Act (CAA).[102] These statutes all vary with regard to the range of protected activity, the adjudicatory agencies, statutes of limitation, exhaustion requirements, and the types of relief available. The administrative complaint process overseen by the United States Department of Labor moves quickly, requiring the filing of a written charge within 30 days of the unlawful discrimination.

The protection afforded by state statutes also varies widely.[103] Under New Jersey's Whistleblower statute,[104] for example, an employee may recover on a claim of wrongful discharge only if he or she can show that the unlawful act or practice was brought to the employer's attention, affording the employer a reasonable period of time in which to remedy the problem. This duty is excused, however, when the employee fears for his or her personal safety or the employer was already aware of the problem. A similar employer notification requirement is included in Maine's Whistleblower statute,[105] with the exception that there is no mandatory opportunity-to-cure period. The Maine law also provides that an employee is excused from the notification requirement when he or she can articulate a specific reason for believing that the employer would not correct the problem. Both New York's and Ohio's laws protect internal and external reporting, but impose a mandatory duty on employees to apprise their employers of the unlawful condition or practice before reporting the violation externally.[106] In contrast, other states merely require the employee to disclose the violation to the agency responsible for enforcing the underlying law.[107]

In addition to specific statutory protections, many state courts have recognized a public policy exception to the at-will doctrine, which prevents an employer from discharging an employee when the termination would be contrary to public policy. In some states, the scope of the exception is quite broad, recognizing "a safe working environment" as a clear public policy that supports a claim of wrongful discharge;[108] while in others, courts have required an employee to show that his or her discharge violates a specific statute.[109]

Achieving and Enforcing Contractual Obligations

Under the common law, the employer, and not the labor union, has an obligation to the employees to exercise reasonable care in providing safe working conditions.[110] A labor union, however, may assume some responsibility toward employees by accepting a duty of care through a contractual agreement. In most cases, the union's intent to assume this responsibility will be reflected in the relevant collective bargaining agreement or other ancillary agreements[111] between the employer and the union.[112] Given this fact, any attempt to assess the union's liability would inevitably require an interpretation of the terms of the collective bargaining agreement.[113] The Supreme Court's consistent position on the need for uniform interpretation of such agreements has now been conclusively applied in the context of state contract and tort law claims (as well as federal common law claims), to foreclose state common law negligence suits against unions.[114] Furthermore, even if a plaintiff could demonstrate that his or her union is subject to an independent state law duty of care unconnected to a collective bargaining agreement, such a direct state law obligation would be unlikely to survive the preemptive power of federal labor law.[115]

The decisional authority under federal labor law is clear—that a union's exclusive duty to its members under the collective bargaining agreement is that of fair representation.[116] Because no general due care obligation has been read into the duty of fair representation, the courts have stated that mere negligence will not support a claim of breach of the union's duty toward its members.[117] Accordingly, a union cannot be held liable for the negligent performance of a safety duty it may have assumed by virtue of the safety and health provisions of a collective bargaining agreement.[118]

That principle notwithstanding, the decisional authority to date has not precluded all claims against unions for failure to perform their obligations with respect to health and safety conditions in the workplace. To assert such a claim against a union under a duty of fair representation theory, a plaintiff must explicitly allege that the union implemented its health and safety functions in an arbitrary and discriminatory manner, marked by bad faith.[119] However, even in cases in which the collective bargaining agreement allows the union to exercise a significant role in the resolution of safety and health issues, courts have been reluctant to impose these duties on unions for fear that it would deter them from seeking to obtain any role in workplace safety enforcement and would permit the employers to shift losses to unions.[120]

By contrast, unions may, through the collective bargaining process, seek to augment the existing workplace safety and health protections afforded workers under the OSH Act and state analogs. Health and safety concerns are a mandatory subject of bargaining under federal law, and the contractual duties imposed upon an employer under a negotiated collective bargaining agreement are subject to enforcement under the NLRA[121] and any applicable arbitration agreement. Union contracts often include provisions protecting workers from retaliation and/or discipline from actions taken with regard to safety and health concerns,[122] but with less than 16 percent of the workforce enrolled as union members,[123] the vast majority of workers in the United States must rely on the meager coverage provided to them under the OSH Act.

Forcing Regulatory Standard-Setting Action

Employees can encourage agency action to implement the substantive protections provided under the OSH Act by petitioning OSHA for formal action under Sections 5(a)(1), 6(b), 6(c), or 13[124] to promulgate a permanent standard, implement an emergency temporary standard for toxic materials or harmful physical agents, or seek immediate injunctive relief against an "imminent danger." If the agency fails to act, employees can seek to compel the Secretary to meet his obligations under the Act.[125]

Under the Toxic Substances Control Act (TSCA),[126] manufacturers are responsible for reporting to the U.S. Environmental Protection Agency (EPA) the testing results of all potentially dangerous chemical substances it produces that "may present an unreasonable risk of injury to health or the environment," and those it produces in substantial quantities that "may reasonably be anticipated to enter the environment in substantial quantities" or may result in "significant or substantial human exposure."[127] The purpose of such testing is to provide the information necessary for the EPA to determine whether regulation of production and use is appropriate. The EPA administrator is required to develop a permanent standard or take other decisive action if there is "a reasonable basis to conclude" that a substance poses an "unreasonable risk of injury to health or the environment."[128]

Section 21 of TSCA[129] authorizes citizen petitions for issuing or amending production, use, or testing standards, and Section 20[130] authorizes citizens' suits to compel the EPA administrator to take nondiscretionary actions under the Act.

While the OSH Act and TSCA provide these mechanisms for pushing agency action in the standard-setting arena, in reality such lawsuits are rarely successful, given judicial deference to agency expertise.

The Power of Information: Using the OSH Act and Other "Right-to-Know" Laws

Enforcing the Duty to Generate Information Regarding Exposure and Effects Established by Federal Disclosure Statutes

For the workplace health and safety rights embodied in federal and state laws to be meaningful, workers must have access to scientific and technical information regarding the toxic substance exposures and other hazards they may face on the job. The assumption that mandatory sharing of information between management and labor will prompt activity that will improve worker health has lead to the development of "right-to-know" laws that build on the foundation laid by the OSH Act. Under such laws, enacted at the federal, state, and local levels,[131] manufacturers and employers must disclose information regarding toxic substance exposures and other hazardous conditions to workers, to unions in their capacity as worker representatives, and to governmental agencies charged with the responsibility of protecting public health.

The value of such information lies not only in its obvious use in providing evidentiary support for cases ranging from toxic torts to product liability, but also in its potential use for increasing public awareness, galvanizing community action, encouraging industry innovation, and building political consensus for additional toxics use reduction legislation.

Both the OSH Act and TSCA contain provisions requiring employers to generate and retain exposure and effects information and provisions requiring the disclosure of specific information. For example, OSHA's Hazard Communication Rule requires chemical manufacturers, importers, and distributors to provide employers with evaluations of all toxic or hazardous materials sold to them. Employers are then required to compile information regarding the ingredients of chemicals, their physical hazards, associated human health risks, and OSHA exposure limits in Material Safety Data Sheets (MSDS).[132]

Similarly, TSCA requires chemical manufacturers, processors, importers, and distributers to generate and retain information pertaining to "significant adverse reactions" to chemical exposures as well as information regarding the ingredients, general exposures, and product use for 300 specifically designated chemicals.[133]

The OSH Act provides an accompanying right of access for workers to the information generated by the employer.[134] Under both the Worker Access Rule and the Hazard Communication Rule, workers or their designated representatives are entitled to chemical identities, exposure, and effects information regarding a specific set of designated chemicals.[135] Under the Worker Access Rule, however, the access to effects data is limited to one's own medical record. No such limitation applies with regard to exposure data.

In addition to preparing and making available to employees the MSDSs for all hazardous chemicals on the worksite premises, the OSH Act requires employers to establish a hazard communication program that includes training designed to educate employees about OSHA regulations, the potential hazards of materials in the workplace, and the proper methods for using these materials safely.[136] Other specific OSHA standards, such as those for exposure to asbestos[137] and to blood-borne pathogens,[138] also mandate worker training regarding hazards and protective equipment and procedures. However, where OSHA has yet to issue standards, no training or warning is required by the Act. Given that OSHA has been able to issue only 30 comprehensive health standards,[139] and set permissible exposure limits for only about 630 chemicals in nearly 30 years, workers' health remains largely contingent on employers' concern and initiative.

Other sources of information about an employer's use of hazardous chemicals include toxic chemical release reports that must be filed by companies covered under the Emergency Planning and Community Right-to-Know Act of 1986 (EPCRA),[140] and the Toxic Release Inventory, the EPA database of release information for all facilities meeting the statute's reporting requirements. One of the main objectives of EPCRA is to provide the public with access to information concerning hazardous chemicals in the community. That goal is achieved through the mechanism of extensive reporting requirements in which covered facilities are required to relate detailed information about the presence, amounts, location, health effects, disposition, and releases of specified chemicals. Thus, under Section 313 of EPCRA,[141] subject facilities must submit a "toxic chemical"[142] release form annually, to EPA and a state-designated official, that covers releases to all environmental media, including air emissions, wastewater discharges, land disposal, transfers to publicly owned treatment facilities, and transfers to off-site facilities for transport, disposal, or storage. The Toxic Chemical Release Form, more commonly known as the Toxics Release Inventory, or Form R, summarizes all toxic releases made by a facility during the preceding 12 months, including those made legally pursuant to permits issued by EPA and the counterpart state environmental agency.

A second reporting form, the Hazardous Chemical Inventory, must also be filed annually, providing the location of each chemical in a facility and classifying the chemical within one of five hazard categories established by EPA. As part of the Inventory, a facility must submit an MSDS for any chemical on its premises that meets or exceeds a specified threshold quantity to the State Emergency Response Commission, the local emergency planning committee, and the local fire department.[143] The information generated by these reports must be made available to the public, but is subject to trade secret limitations.[144] The full scope of EPCRA is discussed in Chapter 8, "Access to Information," pages 230–55.

Taking Advantage of the Duty to Generate Information Embodied in State and Local Right-to-Know Laws

Beyond federal disclosure laws, state and local right-to-know laws may provide an additional avenue of employee access to information regarding workplace exposures. However, the degree of coverage provided by these laws and ordinances varies greatly with the particular statute or ordinance.[145]

In the wake of the 1992 Hamlet chicken processing plant fire, North Carolina became one of the first states to enact legislation intended to provide workers with both information and substantive protections.[146] The constellation of statutes:

1. requires the creation of safety and health programs and safety and health committees in all state agencies;[147]
2. requires the same of employers of 11 or more employees that have a workers' compensation "rate modifier" of 1.5 or above;[148]
3. provides the Commissioner of Labor with the authority to impose fines against every state, county, and municipal agency

that was previously exempt from compliance with the state's occupational safety and health regulations;[149]

4. directs the Department of Labor to set up a "special emphasis inspection program" to target employers with high rates of violations or high rates of injury, illness, or death;[150] and
5. prohibits retaliatory action against an employee for filing a workers' compensation claim, a wage and hour claim, or an OSH Act complaint, as long as the claim or complaint is made in good faith.[151]

In addition to "Right to Act" legislation of the type adopted in North Carolina, and more recently in New Jersey,[152] California has enacted another form of right-to-know/act legislation that provides both a means of gathering information and an avenue for recourse against businesses that fail to disclose their activities that may endanger public health. California's Safe Drinking Water and Toxic Enforcement Act of 1986, or Proposition 65,[153] which prohibits the discharge of known carcinogens and reproductive hazards into drinking water, also requires companies to provide clear and reasonable warnings whenever their products or activities expose people to any of the more than 650 toxic chemicals listed by the state.[154] This list is considered the most comprehensive of delineation of carcinogens developed by any government agency.[155] The implementing regulations for the statute require warnings for consumer product exposures, occupational exposures, and environmental exposures.[156]

For some chemicals found in the workplace, Proposition 65's warning threshold is more stringent than that of the OSH Act's Hazard Communication Standard. For example, when a chemical mixture contains a carcinogen, the Hazard Communication Standard is triggered only if the concentration of the carcinogen is greater than one-tenth of one percent, whereas Proposition 65's warning requirement is triggered by the actual level of worker exposure to the chemical. Despite its more stringent standards, relatively few lawsuits have been filed to enforce Proposition 65's workplace warning requirements.[157] Those filed, however, plainly show the law's potential to effect beneficial changes in workplace conditions.[158]

Employer Defenses

Two potential obstacles impair attempts to invoke the protection afforded by laws that require the disclosure of information regarding workplace hazards: claims of trade secrecy and confidentiality in personal information. An industrial employer's interest in maintaining its trade secrets entitles it to take reasonable steps to prevent the disclosure of information regarding manufacturing processes that give the company a commercial advantage over its competitors.

However, because much of the data subject to statutory disclosure requirements is not the type of information deemed exempt under such policies, an employer's defense based upon protection of its trade secrets generally is not a sufficient ground for disregarding disclosure requirements or requests for data on workplace exposures. Thus, the identity of a chemical substance may be exempt from disclosure under such a theory only if:

1. disclosure would reveal a technological process or functional characteristic that is not known to other companies;
2. the use of the chemical represents a clear advance in the field;
3. the use of the chemical provides the owner with a distinct competitive advantage; and
4. such use is not discoverable through reverse engineering or other fair investigative methods.[159]

Even in those instances in which all of these conditions are met and a claim of trade secrecy might therefore be valid, such a claim may be undermined by a union's ability to facilitate the release of the protected information by a means designed to prevent disclosure to third-party competitors. Thus, to the extent that a company's competitive advantage can be maintained in the wake of its compliance with disclosure requirements, trade secrecy no longer provides a valid basis for exemption.[160]

The second limitation on worker access to toxics exposure information is an employer's ability to assert an individual worker's right to confidentiality regarding his or her own medical history. Of course, such a defense cannot be raised when the worker specifically grants a right of access to personal medical or exposure information, nor when the risk of disclosure is eliminated by removal of identifiers or some other mechanism that permits the release of personal safety and health information without an invasion of privacy.[161]

Beyond these commercial and personal privacy restrictions on disclosure, some statutes contain specific provisions designed to protect trade secrets and therefore may pose an additional barrier to information access. For example, information obtained by the EPA pursuant to the reporting requirements of the TSCA is explicitly exempted from disclosure to the extent that it reveals either a chemical manufacturing process or the percentage composition of a chemical compound.[162]

The Benefits Available and Limitations Imposed Under State Workers' Compensation Schemes

With very few exceptions, state workers' compensation statutes prohibit an injured worker from pursuing a tort action against his or her employer.[163] The primary purpose of workers' compensation is to cover the costs of medical care and rehabilitation and to provide compensation for lost wages resulting from workplace injuries and illnesses.[164] The agreement embodied in the system entails the employee's relinquishment of the right to sue an employer and seek tort damages, in return for timely and adequate compensation for an occupational injury.[165]

Workers' compensation benefits have been held to be the exclusive remedy available to injured workers except in four narrowly circumscribed situations:

1. when the employer fails to maintain such coverage as required by law;
2. when the injury results from an intentional tort perpetrated by, or at the direction of, the employer;[166]
3. when the employer is responsible for impairing an employee's right to sue a third-party tortfeasor;[167] and
4. when the employer's business is illegal.[168]

The burden is placed on the employee seeking to avoid the exclusivity bar to establish that one of these exceptions applies. To plead an intentional tort that falls outside the scope of workers' compensation laws, an employee must prove an intentional or deliberate act by the employer that is directed at causing the specific harm flowing from the act to that particular employee.[169] Given these narrow parameters, an injured worker's recovery vis-a-vis an employer is essentially limited to filing a claim for benefits under the state's workers' compensation scheme.

While workers' compensation schemes remove the hurdle of suing an employer for injuries suffered on the job, they strictly prescribe the types of benefits provided and frequently delineate ceilings on the total recovery a worker may receive. Most state schemes provide for only two types of benefits: medical care and loss of earnings. Damages recoverable at common law, such as pain and suffering and loss of consortium, are not available under these statutes, and permissible claims of permanent disability can be challenged by the insurance company.[170] Loss of earnings benefits do not fully recompense a claimant for the actual monetary loss suffered as a result of the occupational injury or illness, but they are generally set at a rate equal to two thirds of the claimant's weekly wage,[171] with a maximum amount set by statute. Many states also set a maximum number of weeks for the collection of loss of earnings benefits.

Beyond the statutory limitations, there are serious deficiencies in workers' compensation schemes that operate unfairly to curtail compensation awards. Among the problems plaguing these systems is the complete lack of coverage for many employees, imposition of arbitrary limits on reimbursement for medical and physical rehabilitation services, inadequate cash benefits for all types of disabilities, and the deficient coverage of occupational diseases.[172]

According to a recent analysis, only 5 percent of occupational disease is covered by workers' compensation programs, and 21 states limit occupational disease coverage to those specific illnesses that are "peculiar to" or "characteristic of" a worker's occupation.[173] Moreover, because work-related diseases often have multiple vectors of causation, and long latency periods, they are frequently excluded from coverage. Compounding these problems are medical personnel unfamiliar with diseases that result from workplace exposure and the difficulty of pinpointing the precise time and place of exposure. Minimum exposure requirements (that workers must be exposed for a specific period of time before claiming that the agent is a source of an occupational disease) and short statutes of limitation exacerbate these weaknesses to create more serious disease compensation deficiencies.[174]

In situations where an employee is injured on the job due to the negligence of a person other than his or her employer or coworker, the employee may both file for workers' compensation benefits and bring suit against the third-party whose negligence caused the injury.[175] While such actions provide the opportunity to garner a wider range of monetary damages,[176] they are also subject to the traditional defenses of comparative negligence and assumption of risk not available under compensation schemes. Furthermore, when an individual is successful in winning a negligence claim against a third party, the compensation insurance carrier will, in most cases,[177] have a lien against the monies recovered by the claimant in the tort action.

The use of third-party liability claims in occupational disease cases is well established in a few areas such as asbestosis and black lung disease,[178] and is now being considered with regard to other types of chemical exposures. To date, decisional authority assessing such claims has focused on several key issues, including the manufacturers' awareness of the human health effects of their products, the severity of those effects, the technologic feasibility of reducing them, and the workers' assumption of the risk.[179] Third-party suits premised on injuries from occupational diseases are time-consuming and expensive, and rest primarily on the plaintiff's ability to demonstrate an established scientific basis for linking exposure to the harmful substance with the occupational disease. The absence of epidemiological studies showing these links for the wide range of chemicals used in the workplace makes such proof difficult to accomplish in many cases.[180]

The Situations of Special Classifications of Workers

The Unenviable Situation of Farm Workers

Of the more than 2.5 million[181] farm workers hired in the United States, approximately 90 percent are people of color. This population, comprised primarily of Mexican Americans, Puerto Ricans, African Americans, and Caribbean blacks, works in one of the least protected jobs in the country.[182] Farm workers were intentionally excluded from coverage under the three key federal statutes intended to ensure safe working conditions, fair wages, and the ability to bargain collectively: the OSH Act, the Fair Labor Standards Act (FLSA),[183] and the NLRA.[184] Although the passage of the Migrant and Seasonal Agricultural Worker Protection Act (AWPA)[185] in 1983 was intended to address some of these issues,[186] farm workers continue to face numerous hurdles in their efforts to achieve a safe and healthy working environment and encounter some of the most serious health hazards found in workplaces today.

While the health hazards confronting agricultural workers have not been comprehensively documented, many are widely recognized, such as infectious diseases from poor sanitation conditions in the fields and assigned living quarters, heat-related disorders, and repetitive stress injuries. In addition, farm workers also face significant health problems stemming from the pervasive use of pesticides by farmers in the United States.[187] Unable to invoke any of the protections afforded by the OSH Act, farm workers must rely upon the EPA's regulation of pesticide use under the Federal Insecticide Fungicide and Rodenticide Act (FIFRA),[188] but this statute is limited by its scope in the degree of protection that it provides. Intended to be a risk-benefit statute, FIFRA merely requires that a pesticide, when used for its intended purpose, must not cause "unreasonable adverse effects on the environment." While this balancing process must take into account "the economic, social, and environmental costs as well as the potential benefits of the use of any pesticide,"[189] many of the pesticides registered by the EPA pursuant to the statute are evaluated with regard to consumption—residue concentrations in foods—rather than human exposure in the fields.

In addition to those limitations, the EPA's assessment of the potential health effects of the 600 or more active ingredients in current pesticide products lags woefully behind the development of new products. Full safety assurances have been issued by the agency for less than 10 percent of these agents. Similarly, while FIFRA's chief purpose is to regulate pesticide use, "re-entry" times (the interval that must elapse between pesticide application and worker re-entry into the field) have been set for just 12 pesticides.[190] Poor enforcement of even those few requirements means that the rules are widely disregarded, so that pesticide spraying is frequently done while workers are in the fields harvesting crops.

Exacerbating these problems is the wholesale lack of information provided to workers. Because workers are rarely informed of the chemicals contained in the pesticides being used, they are unaware of the toxic substances they encounter on a daily basis and may not request protective clothing or equipment. The result of this lack of protection is nearly 313,000 pesticide-related illnesses, and nearly one thousand deaths among farm workers from pesticide exposure each year.[191]

Beyond the severe health effects associated with direct exposure, workers' families often suffer the effects of "take-home" contamination from workplace exposures to hazardous chemicals. Recognizing the seriousness of this problem, and the gap in knowledge about the extent of such exposures and the related health effects, the government enacted the 1992 Workers' Family Protection Act. It instructs the National Institute for Occupational Safety and Health (NIOSH) to "evaluate the potential for, prevalence of, and issues related to the contamination of workers' homes with hazardous chemicals and substances . . . transported from the workplaces of such workers." The task force established in 1994 to review NIOSH's report noted in February of 1998 that there is a total lack of information on the "types and levels of take-home exposures that are currently occurring in the U.S., the size and demographic composition of the populations at risk for exposure, types of illnesses associated with take-home exposures, and adequacy of exposure control methods in the workplace and in the home."[192]

The AWPA, which replaced the Farm Labor Contractor Registration Act of 1963 (FLCRA)[193] as part of the Congressional effort to "protect agricultural workers whose employment had been historically characterized by low wages, long hours and poor working conditions,"[194] provides little additional health and safety protection. The AWPA requires that all farm labor contractors, agricultural employers, and agricultural associations[195] pay migrant[196] and seasonal farm workers minimum wage and attempts to ensure that any housing provided to these workers meets federal and state health and safety standards.[197] All employing entities must also provide their workers with a written disclosure statement informing them of wage rates, the period of employment, where it is located, what the job entails, and whether housing, transportation, or any other benefits will be provided.[198]

Finally, the AWPA also includes motor vehicle safety and insurance requirements.[199] These provisions are among the most important protections afforded farm workers today. The Act imposes a duty upon farm contractors, agricultural workers, and agricultural associations to transport workers in safe vehicles and to provide insurance coverage for the workers while they are being transported.[200] Further, these obligations are imposed on the contractor, employer, or association whether they use, or cause to be used, any vehicle for worker transport.[201] While the accompanying regulations to the Act specifically exempt employers from liability resulting from car pool arrangements made solely among employees, that exception does not apply when a farm labor contractor participates in the transportation arrangement.[202]

Given the limitations imposed by the workers' compensation exclusivity rule, there are few promising avenues through which farm workers may seek to address pesticide exposure or other health and safety problems directly with employers. To the extent that it is available, a workers' compensation claim can, however, provide crucial financial support pending the resolution of a third-party products liability suit, and may also help to ensure the cooperation of the employer with the investigation of the suit against the third party.[203]

The AWPA establishes a private right of action in federal court for injured workers aggrieved by violations of the Act.[204] Upon a finding that a defendant has intentionally[205] violated any provision of the Act or an applicable regulation, the court may award actual damages or statutory damages of up to $500 per plaintiff per violation. In 1995, revisions to the AWPA were enacted to bar actions for actual damages when state workers' compensation coverage is provided to the injured worker.[206] In such situations, the Act provides for higher statutory damage awards of up to $10,000 per plaintiff per violation. The higher awards are available in four situations:

1. where the defendant knowingly required or permitted a driver to transport migrant or seasonal workers while under the influence of alcohol or a controlled substance;
2. where a defendant has been determined in a prior judicial or administrative proceeding to have violated one of the Act's motor vehicle safety requirements;
3. where the defendant willfully disabled a safety device or failed to provide a required safety device; and
4. where the defendant violated a safety standard prescribed under 29 U.S.C. § 1841(b) and utilizes the services of a farm labor contractor without taking reasonable steps to determine whether the contractor possesses a valid certificate of registration for the activities for which his or her services are requested.[207]

Because the AWPA does not contain a statute of limitations, and the uniform four-year limitations period for civil actions arising under federal statutes does not apply,[208] differing limitations periods have been applied to claims in different jurisdictions.[209] The migratory nature of the work may therefore pose problems for bringing an action for violation of the Act.

Employer Defenses

The AWPA provides protections for farm workers only to the extent that those workers are found to be "employees." Therefore, suits brought for violations of the Act have primarily been subject to two defenses: employer defendants contend either that the worker is an independent contractor or that he or she is employed solely by an independent contractor crew leader.[210] Either defense, if accepted by a court, will preclude farm workers from recovering under the Act. Given the lack of resources of most crew leaders and the transient nature of such work,[211] a finding that farm workers are employees of a crew leader, and holding him or her responsible for any injuries, has the same preclusive effect as the independent contractor defense. However, the recent codification in the regulations of the broad joint employer doctrine developed under the FLSA[212] may limit the effectiveness of such efforts to evade the responsibilities imposed by the Act. Under the AWPA regulatory test, a party's status as an independent contractor no longer negates the possibility of a finding of joint employment.[213]

Violations of the AWPA can also result in the imposition of criminal sanctions. The Department of Labor may bring a criminal action against any person who violates the Act, and both fines and prison terms are available as penalties, depending upon the severity and the circumstances of the violation.[214] In addition, the Secretary of Labor may petition the appropriate district court for injunctive relief if such relief from an AWPA violation is warranted.[215]

Under FIFRA, unlike the AWPA, most courts addressing the issue have determined that Congress did not intend to create a private right of action.[216] But courts that have considered whether state common law products liability claims asserted against manufacturers and distributors are preempted by federal law in the area have reached differing conclusions. Many courts have held that FIFRA preempts any state common law claim based on allegations of inadequate labeling or a failure to warn.[217] However, the courts in those jurisdictions have accepted state tort claims when they are based on theories of design defect, manufacturing flaws, inspection or inadequate testing.[218] Some courts have also upheld state common law claims premised on a failure to warn theory under strict liability[219] and common law negligence[220] principles. In those cases, the courts noted that the basic purpose of FIFRA is to regulate the labeling of pesticides to provide purchasers with assurance of the effectiveness and safety of the product when used in compliance with the manufacturer's instructions. The Act permits states to impose more stringent constraints on the use of EPA-approved pesticides than those imposed by the EPA, courts held, and Congress did not intend to immunize manufacturers from state tort claims because each regulatory scheme has distinct purposes, and state tort law may have broader compensatory goals. Third-party liability has also been established in suits lodged under theories of fraud and breach of express[221] and implied warranties.[222] Courts have found manufacturers jointly and severally liable for injuries from exposure in circumstances in which the plaintiffs could not identify the particular manufacturers of the chemical to which each person was exposed.[223] Finally, cases in which manufacturers complied with FIFRA labeling requirements and the consumer (farmer) misapplied the fungicide, injuring the employees of the distributor,[224] the manufacturer could be held responsible.

The defenses raised in third-party cases are the standard defenses generally interposed for each theory of liability. Thus, a manufacturer, seller, or distributor of a product cannot be held liable for injuries allegedly caused by a product absent proof that the product was defective when it left the defendant's possession or control and the injury was proximately caused by the product. Misuse of the product also bars recovery in a products liability case based on strict liability in tort. Contributory negligence or assumption of risk may be raised as defenses to an action for personal injury or death resulting from exposure in products liability claims predicated on negligence. In a statute of limitations defense against exposure lawsuits, the relevant date may be that of the last exposure, when the illness or disease was discovered, or when the plaintiff reasonably should have known of the causal relationship between the exposure and the harm. Finally, statutes of repose may require that the lawsuit be filed within a certain number of years from the date of a product's manufacture.

The person who applies a pesticide[225] and the person who recommends its improper use each may be liable under the FIFRA provision that prohibits using pesticides in a manner inconsistent with their labeling.[226] Criminal liability of a particular adviser for improper use depends on the extent of the adviser's involvement in the application of the pesticide and his or her knowledge of the facts surrounding that application. In evaluating claims of improper "exposure" in contravention of pesticide label instructions, courts have indicated that plaintiffs need not establish the defendant's actual contact with the produce to assert a claim under this provision.[227]

The Undefined Parameters of Protection for Workfare Participants

With the passage of the Personal Responsibility and Work Opportunity Reconciliation Act of 1996 (PRA),[228] federal entitlements to welfare[229] and the Aid to Families with Dependent Children[230] program were replaced by the Temporary Assistance for Needy Families (TANF)[231] state block grants program. This program mandates that beneficiaries of federal aid programs participate in state-sponsored work ventures to qualify for benefits. States are now required to place qualifying beneficiaries[232] in workfare[233] programs within twenty-four months of their receipt of such benefits[234] and to terminate federal aid to most people who have received benefits for a total of five years.[235] The ramifications of these changes are serious for welfare beneficiaries, as even those who cannot find work can be penalized for noncompliance with the PRA's work requirement.[236]

Across the country, hundreds of thousands of welfare recipients are being enrolled in workfare programs. Yet, in 27 states and the District of Columbia,[237] workfare participants have no legal protection from unsafe working conditions because state and municipal employees in those jurisdictions are covered neither by the OSH Act nor by state job safety and health laws.[238]

With no specific enforceable rights to safe and healthful working conditions, workfare participants face significant risks of physical harm.[239] Because they are not unionized, these workers are particularly vulnerable to placement in the most hazardous jobs available. These workers are more likely to be unfamiliar with the hazards they might face on the job and may not receive no substantive training on how to deal with the ones they do encounter. Preliminary assessments indicate that workfare participants are not generally given protective equipment appropriate for their work assignment; and in those few instances in which such equipment is provided, it is both ill-fitting and unsanitary, contributing further to the risk of injury and illness.[240] Basic requirements such as drinking water and access to bathroom facilities are often not provided. Workfare participants are often reluctant to refuse work or complain about conditions because they fear (or have been threatened with) retaliation in the form of dismissal from the job and expulsion from the assistance program.[241] Even those workfare participants who are covered under state safety and health laws face a significant hurdle in enforcing their rights because they must prove that actions taken against them for lodging complaints were retaliatory.[242]

States exacerbate these conditions by refusing to extend the benefits of existing basic labor law protections to these workers. They do not enforce prevailing wage protections and are silent while employers prohibit rest breaks or lunch hours, provide neither vacation nor sick leave, and fail to adhere to existing safety standards. Thus, while the Fair Labor Standards Act[243] entitles employees[244] to minimum wage, 150 percent of their regular pay for overtime hours, equal pay on the basis of gender, and protection against retaliation by employers for the filing of complaints, the question of whether states' workfare programs must adhere to it is as yet unresolved.[245] Similarly, the question of whether workfare workers have the right to organize, engage in concerted activity, and form a union is unsettled.[246] The National Labor Relations Board is currently considering several cases addressing the scope of the statutory independent contractor exemption and the definition of employee status under the NLRA.[247] Those decisions will undoubtedly frame the debate on the status of workfare participants.

Islands of protection for workfare participants can be found. Decisional authority addressing specific exemptions from NLRA coverage indicates that, in some circumstances, such workers may be treated as employees under the NLRA.[248] A recent study reported that, despite the uncertainty in this area, at least one private-sector collective bargaining agreement has included welfare workers.[249] Finally, while questions of coverage under the FLSA and the NLRA linger, most states extend workers' compensation coverage to workfare participants.[250]

Additional sources of protection for workfare participants can be found in the civil rights laws. Thus, when workers of color are systematically steered into the most hazardous jobs, or women are channeled from certain positions by employers who want to avoid potential liability for birth defects from fetal exposure to toxic substances, Title VII's protections against discrimination in employment may apply.[251]

To the extent that workfare participants are determined to be beneficiaries or trainees rather than employees for purposes of coverage under Title VII, Title VI[252] offers another avenue of relief from discriminatory treatment or conditions. The breadth of Title VI, which prohibits race and national origin discrimination in federally funded programs, may provide a needed recourse especially in situations in which "a primary objective of the Federal financial assistance is to provide employment."[253] In addition to these remedies, workfare workers who have disabilities that are exacerbated by a workplace condition may also assert a claim for discrimination and failure to provide a reasonable accommodation under the Americans with Disabilities

Act.[254] Similarly, state and local civil rights laws may add another layer of protection for these workers.[255]

Finally, federal environmental laws can provide avenues of recourse. Such statutes include the TSCA,[256] which requires the testing, screening, and regulation of all chemicals produced and imported into the United States; and the RCRA,[257] which governs the handling, storage, treatment, transportation, and disposal of solid and hazardous waste.[258] Under TSCA's citizen suit provisions, plaintiffs may bring a civil action against "any person" (including the government) for violating TSCA's provisions, regulations, rules, orders, or other requirements.[259] Similarly, RCRA authorizes "any person" to commence a civil action against any party (including the government) who has contributed to a situation that may present an imminent and substantial danger to human health or the environment.[260]

Criminal Prosecution for Hazardous Workplace Safety and Health Conditions

Federal Prosecutions Brought Under Occupational Health and Environmental Laws

Although the OSH Act provides for the imposition of criminal penalties upon employers, the prerequisites to prosecution, coupled with the limited number of situations in which such penalties may be imposed, means that OSHA has rarely used its authority in this fashion. Even when the agency has attempted to use its criminal prosecutorial power, it has had little success.[261] Indeed, the lack of successful federal prosecutions has led a number of states to attempt to fill the void by prosecuting employers under traditional penal statutes.[262]

Criminal liability, including possible imprisonment, may be imposed under the OSH Act in three situations:

1. where an employer has willfully violated an OSHA standard resulting in the death of a worker;[263]
2. where a person has given advance warning of an unannounced safety inspection;[264] and
3. where the employer has made false representations in a document filed with the agency pursuant to the Act.[265]

Significant hurdles hinder the establishment of criminal liability under the first scenario. First, the criminal penalty provisions do not authorize prosecution for violations of the "general duty" clause, no matter how many voluntary, egregious, and repeated hazardous acts occur. The agency can only prosecute employers that violate the provisions of a specific OSHA standard.[266] Second, courts have interpreted the term "employer" narrowly to include only those persons who are "engaged in a business affecting commerce who ha[ve] employees."[267] Individuals who do not meet this definition cannot be held liable.[268] Thus, even when supervisors and other individuals in management are personally responsible for the willful violations at issue, they are immune from prosecution under the Act by virtue of their subordinate position within the company. Third, the potential for prosecution is further reduced by the requirement that the violation be "willful." Courts have construed this term to mean that the act is "done knowingly and purposely by an employer who, having a free will or choice, either intentionally disregards the standard or is plainly indifferent to its requirement. An omission or failure to act is willfully done, if done voluntarily and intentionally."[269] The high standard of proof this requires has resulted in very few citations for willful violations of the Act.[270] Finally, even if all of these hurdles can be overcome, no prosecution can be commenced unless a worker dies as a result of the violation. Neither risk of death nor serious injury provides a basis for imposing criminal liability.

While the willful violation provision applies only to employers, criminal liability for providing advance notice of inspections and making false statements attaches to "any person" who violates those strictures. But OSHA has never referred a case to the Justice Department to prosecute an individual for providing advance notice of an OSHA inspection, and prosecutions for false statements have been only infrequently brought.[271]

In addition to the OSH Act provisions, congressional amendments incorporating the offense of knowing endangerment into the RCRA[272] and the CWA[273] now provide two more practical means for holding employers liable for actions or omissions that endanger workers.

Under RCRA, the government may prosecute "any person who knowingly transports, treats, stores, disposes of, or exports any hazardous waste . . . who knows at that time that he thereby places another person in imminent danger of death or serious bodily injury. . . ."[274] There is no requirement that the government prove harm to an individual; so the burden is significantly less stringent than under the OSH Act, where the government must show that the violation resulted in the death of a worker. Experts have noted that because "person[s]" in imminent danger is defined in the statute to include "individuals," it would seem to include workers.[275]

The knowing endangerment provision provides for criminal penalties of up to 15 years' imprisonment, as well as maximum fines of $250,000 for individuals and $1 million for companies.[276] A number of successful federal prosecutions have been brought under this provision,[277] although workers were the endangered party in only one of these cases.[278] To date, no other court has explicitly addressed the application of RCRA's knowing endangerment provision to workplace exposures.

The CWA contains a knowing endangerment provision that mirrors the RCRA provision.[279] Like RCRA, there are few reported decisions reporting prosecutions under the CWA's knowing endangerment provision.[280] However, unlike the decisions discussing RCRA, a recent circuit court decision addressing the CWA provision has cast doubt on the appropriateness of EPA's use of it to prosecute companies that place their workers at risk. In *United States v. Borowski*,[281] the First Circuit reversed the conviction of the president and owner of a company who "knew that [company] practices created serious health risks to the employees,"[282] and that such practices placed the employees in imminent danger, because the "danger was not caused by the knowing violation of Section 1317."[283] Specifically, the court noted that the employees would have been harmed even if there had been no violation of the CWA at all, and thus held that for the protections of the knowing endangerment provision to come into play, there must first be an independent and complete violation of the Act.[284]

Employer Defenses

The RCRA and the CWA knowing endangerment provisions each include the affirmative defense that the endangered person consented to the hazard identified, and that the danger and the conduct charged were reasonably foreseeable hazards of the occupation, business, or profession.[285] In certain industries, such as the hazardous waste industry, this defense may make prosecution difficult.

A mistake of fact may also excuse a violation under a knowing endangerment provision. Thus, where an employer incorrectly and innocently believes that he or she is treating, storing, or transporting a nonhazardous substance, such facts may mitigate culpability.[286]

State Prosecutions Under Occupational Health and Penal Laws

The dearth of criminal prosecutions brought under the OSH Act and the limited success of those actually pursued, led many states to apply their own more stringent criminal laws to the workplace conduct of individual corporate officers.[287] For example, in *People v. Pymm Thermometer Corp.*,[288] the New York state attorney general prosecuted a company, its owners, and the plant managers for criminal assault and reckless endangerment for exposing plant employees to mercury. According to a congressional report, OSHA had inspected the plant in 1981 in response to a worker's written complaint concerning the impact on employees' health of their constant exposure to mercury. Although the agency found serious violations at the time—"[n]o protective gear was being used to reduce workers' exposure to mercury—no respirator masks, no aprons, and no gloves. Work surfaces were covered with mercury, and even the area where workers ate their lunch was contaminated with mercury"[289]—the compliance deadline for the employer was repeatedly extended. In 1984, the New York City Health Department was alerted to the health risks faced by the Pymm plant workers when a doctor who had seen a Pymm worker notified the Department of the worker's elevated mercury levels. That situation, coupled with OSHA's discovery of a hidden cellar reclamation plant in 1985, prompted the attorney general's action.[290] The jury convicted the defendants, but the judge set aside the verdict on grounds of preemption. The verdict was subsequently reinstated by the appeals court. Similar charges were brought against corporate officers in *People v. Chicago Magnet Wire Corp.*[291] In that case, the Cook County district attorney successfully prosecuted a wire manufacturer and corporate officials for aggravated battery, reckless conduct, and conspiracy for exposing 42 employees to a range of hazardous substances used for coating wire. In *People v. O'Neil,*[292] the State of Illinois prosecuted the president, plant manager, and plant foreman of a silver reclamation company when a vat worker died after the company failed to inform workers or protect them from the effects of the cyanide they were using. The defendants were convicted of murder and sentenced to 25 years in prison.[293]

Beyond individual prosecutions for particularly egregious violations, some local jurisdictions have instituted occupational safety and health prosecution programs anchored in their own state penal laws. For example, California has two Labor Code provisions that impose criminal liability for the violation of safety and health regulations.[294] Employing these tools, in 1984 the Los Angeles district attorney commenced an aggressive program to identify and prosecute individuals and employers responsible for traumatic occupational injuries and fatalities. In the first five years of the program, the Los Angeles district attorney's office investigated more than 200 workplaces and filed 27 criminal cases.[295] The defendants in these prosecutions included small employers, supervisors, and plant managers, as well as large employers and high-level corporate officers.[296] Few prosecutions were brought on the ground that the existence of health hazards in the workplace endangered the lives of workers.[297]

Notes

* The author wishes to acknowledge the assistance of CUNY Law School student Craig S. Acorn, without whom this chapter could not have been written.

1. *See* North Carolina v. Roe, 22 O.S.H. Rep. (BNA) 561 (1992) (owner of plant pled guilty to involuntary manslaughter and received a nearly twenty-year prison sentence).

2. *See, e.g.,* George Friedman-Jimenez, *Achieving Environmental Justice: The Role of Occupational Health,* 21 FORDHAM URB. L. J. 604 (1994) [hereinafter Friedman-Jimenez, *Achieving Environmental Justice*].

3. *See* Friedman-Jimenez, *Achieving Environmental Justice, supra* note 2, at 606–07; *see also* Michael Fisher, *Environmental Racism Claims Brought Under Title VI of the Civil Rights Act,* 25 *Envtl.* L. 285, 297–98 (1995) (citing studies showing that the overwhelming majority of farm workers are workers of color, and these workers also suffer the highest incident rates of toxic poisoning of any occupational group in the United States). James C. Robinson, *Trends in Racial Inequality and Exposure to Work-Related Hazards, 1968–1986,* 65 MILBANK MEMORIAL FUND QUARTERLY 404–420 (1987) (documenting racial differences in risk of work-related injury and illness).

4. *See* M.E. DAVIS & A. ROWLAND, PROBLEMS FACED BY MINORITY WORKERS IN OCCUPATIONAL HEALTH: RECOGNIZING AND PREVENTING WORK-RELATED DISEASE" (Levy Wegman eds., 1983); James C. Robinson, *Hazard Pay in Unsafe Jobs: Theory, Evidence and Policy Implications,* 64 MILBANK MEMORIAL FUND QUARTERLY 65–67 (1986).

5. *See* Beverly Hendrix Wright & Robert D. Bullard, *Hazards in the Workplace and Black Health,* 4 NAT'L J. SOC. 45 (Spring 1990) (survey of available data on injury, illness, and death rates of black workers by occupational and industry category); Morris E. Davis, *Occupational Health Hazards and Black Workers,* URB. HEALTH 16, 17 (August 1977) (reviewing mortality studies of steelworkers, coke plant workers, rubber workers, and laundry and dry-cleaning workers); Morris E. Davis, *The Impact of Workplace Health and Safety on Black Workers: Assessment and Prognosis,* 31 LAB. L. J. 723, 725 (December 1980) (citing long-term health study of workers in the chromate-producing industry).

6. *See* C.A. Redlich et al., *Liver Disease Associated with Occupational Exposure to the Solvent Dimethylformamide,* 108 ANNALS OF INTERNAL MED. 680–86 (1988) (detailing epidemic of toxic liver disease among minority workers in a fabric coating factor); C. Martin & J. Higgins, *Byssinosis and Other Respiratory Ailments: A Survey of Cotton Textile Employees,* 18 J. OCCUPATIONAL MED. 455 (1976) (documenting that black workers employed in the textile mill industry were at higher risk of developing byssinosis than white workers because they were assigned to work areas with the highest concentrations of cotton, flax and hemp dust).

7. *See, e.g.,* James C. Robinson, *Exposure to Occupational Hazards Among Hispanics, Blacks and Non-Hispanic Whites in California,* 79 AM. J. PUB. HEALTH 629, 630 (May 1989).

8. The environmental justice movement has sparked a renewed public interest in these issues, but the problems pinpointed in recent studies are far from new, which prompts the question of why so little progress in this area has been made since the enactment of the Occupational Safety and Health Act in 1970. That question stands in bold relief when the few milestones achieved in the occupational health field are compared with the measurable progress made toward stemming the tide of degradation of the natural environment. Several scholars have recently noted that environmental laws aimed at protecting the air, water, and land are significantly more stringent than our substantive workplace protections, the physical environment is more diligently policied than our work environments, and environmental laws are more strictly enforced than those designed to remedy occupational hazards and exposures. *See, e.g.,* Lynn Rhine-

hart, *Would Workers Be Better Protected If They Were Declared an Endangered Species? A Comparison of Criminal Enforcement Under the Federal Workplace Safety and Environmental Protection Laws,* 31 AM. CRIM. L. REV. 351 (1994) [hereinafter Rhinehart, *Workplace Safety Enforcement*].

9. 29 U.S.C. §§ 651–678.

10. 29 U.S.C. § 651(b).

11. 29 U.S.C. § 654(a)(1).

12. *See* United States v. Sturm, Ruger & Co., Inc., 84 F.3d 1, 3–6 (9th Cir. 1996); *see also* Reich v. Montana Sulphur & Chem. Co., 32 F.3d 440, 445 (9th Cir. 1994), *cert. denied,* 514 U.S. 1015 (1995) (finding that even absent specific regulations, OSHA may still investigate a violation of the general duty clause).

13. *See* In the Matter of Establishment Inspection of the Kelly-Springfield Tire Co., 13 F.3d 1160, 1167 (7th Cir. 1994). *See also* David B. Darden et al., *Employment-Related Crimes,* 35 AM. CRIM. L. REV. 561, 563 & nn. 11–13 (1998).

14. *See* Pratt & Whitney Aircraft v. Secretary of Labor, 649 F.2d 96, 99–101 (2d Cir. 1981).

15. *See* Reich v. Montana Sulphur & Chem. Co., 32 F.3d 440, 445 (9th Cir. 1994) (holding that specific regulations do not obviate the need for OSHA's enforcement of the general duty clause as a minimum requirement); International Union, United Auto., Aerospace & Agric. Implement Workers of Am. v. General Dynamics Land Sys. Div., 815 F.2d 1570, 1577 (D.C. Cir. 1987) (holding that compliance with a specific standard will not fulfill an employer's obligations under the general duty clause if the employer knows that the standard will not protect its employees against the identified hazard).

16. *See* 29 U.S.C. §§ 655(a), (b), & (c).

17. *See* United Auto Workers v. Occupational Safety and Health Administration, 938 F.2d 1310 (D.C. Cir. 1991).

18. *See* International Union, United Automobile, Aerospace & Agricultural Implement Workers v. Occupational Safety and Health Administration, 37 F.3d 665 (D.C. Cir. 1994).

19. *See* Society of the Plastics Industry, Inc. v. Occupational Safety and Health Administration, 509 F.2d 1301 (2d Cir.), *cert. denied,* 421 U.S. 992 (1975).

20. For example, OSHA has promulgated specification requirements for guardrail protection in the construction industry. *See, e.g.,* 29 U.S.C. § 1926.500(d).

21. The performance standard for personal protective equipment, for example, states that employees shall be supplied with personal protective equipment whenever necessary because of the hazards they must encounter on the job. 29 U.S.C. § 1910.132.

22. 29 U.S.C. § 655(c).

23. *See, e.g.,* Organized Migrants in Communication Action v. Brennan, 520 F.2d 1161 (D.C. Cir. 1975).

24. 29 U.S.C. § 655(b)(3).

25. 29 U.S.C. § 655(b)(4).

26. 29 U.S.C. § 655(f).

27. These include: Alaska, Arizona, California, Connecticut, Hawaii, Indiana, Iowa, Kentucky, Maryland, Michigan, Minnesota, Nevada, New Mexico, New York, North Carolina, Oregon, Puerto Rico, South Carolina, Tennessee, Utah, Vermont, Virgin Islands, Virginia, Washington, and Wyoming. These states

have six months after the promulgation of a new federal standard to adopt an equivalent standard under their own rules.

28. For example, the state of Maryland enacted provisions limited exposure to lead in the construction industry 10 years before the federal standard was adopted and implemented.

29. *See* 29 C.F.R. § 1904. In addition, some states impose additional recordkeeping requirements.

30. Similar recordkeeping requirements are specified by a number of safety standards for the construction and maritime industries. *See, e.g.*, 29 C.F.R. § 1910.134 (respirators).

31. *See, e.g.*, 29 C.F.R. § 1910.95 (lead); Secretary v. American Sterilizer Co., 15 BNA OSHC 1476 (OSHRC 1992).

32. For example, as of 1997, there were approximately 1113 OSHA field inspectors available to monitor the more than six million workplaces at which over 100 million Americans work. OCCUPATIONAL SAFETY AND HEALTH ADMINISTRATION FACT SHEET NO. 98-13 (Jan. 1998). With these limited resources, each covered workplace would be inspected once every 80 years. Moreover, due to the limited funding and resources provided to the agency, OSHA has managed to regulate approximately 630 out of the more than 60,000 toxic chemicals used in the workplace.

33. An employee representative may be an official of a union or other labor organization, an attorney, or any other person acting as the bona fide representative of the employee.

34. *See* 29 C.F.R. § 1903.11.

35. The OSH Act requires the agency to maintain the confidentiality of the complaining employee if requested.

36. 29 U.S.C. § 657(e).

37. 29 U.S.C. § 659(c).

38. *See Pan American World Airways*, 11 OSHRC 2003 (1984). The OSHRC's decisions on this issue have been consistently upheld by the courts. *See, e.g.*, Donovan v. OSHRC, 713 F.2d 918 (2d Cir. 1983); Oil Chemical and Atomic Workers v. OSHRC, 671 F.2d 634 (D.C. Cir.), *cert. denied*, 459 U.S. 905 (1982).

39. *See* 29 C.F.R. § 2200.7.

40. *See* S.A. BOKAT & H.A. THOMPSON, OCCUPATIONAL SAFETY AND HEALTH LAW, ch. 17, 471–74 (BNA 1988).

41. *See Georgia Pacific Corp.*, 15 BNA OSHC 1127 (OSHRC 1991); *Ficks Reed Co.*, 14 BNA OSHC 2222 (1991), and cases cited therein.

42. Cuyahoga Valley Railway v. United Transportation Union, 474 U.S. 3 (1985).

43. 29 C.F.R. §§ 1977.12(b)(1)–(2).

44. These prerequisites were upheld by the Supreme Court in Whirlpool Corp. v. Marshall, 445 U.S. 1 (1980).

45. 29 U.S.C. § 660(c)(1).

46. *See* Donovan v. Diplomat Envelope Corp., 587 F. Supp. 1417 (E.D.N.Y. 1984).

47. Under Section 660(c)(2), an employee who believes that he or she has been discriminated against may file a complaint with the Secretary of Labor. The OSHA then conducts an investigation in conjunction with the Department of

Labor's Solicitor's Office. If the Department of Labor and OSHA find merit in the case, then the Secretary of Labor may bring an action in federal district court. Courts have reached conflicting conclusions on whether there is a private right of action for employees under this section. *Compare* Donovan v. Occupational Safety and Health Review Commission, 713 F.2d 918 (2d Cir. 1983) (finding no private right of action) *with* Schweiss v. Chrysler Motors, 992 F.2d 473 (8th Cir. 1990) (permitting private cause of action). An employee who has been the victim of retaliation has no recourse other than waiting for the conclusion of the litigation.

48. Some courts have held that there is an equitable tolling where the employer has concealed the adverse action from the employee. *See, e.g.,* Donovan v. Hahner, Foreman & Harness, Inc., 11 OSHC (10th Cir. 1984) (employer misled employee about termination by stating that employee was laid off for lack of work).

49. A citation must be contested within fifteen days of receipt. 29 U.S.C. § 659(a). By contesting a citation, an employer may be able to achieve any of the following:

(a) dismissal of the citation;
(b) modification of the citation (for example, to a lesser included offense);
(c) reduction or elimination of the fine proposed; and
(d) extension of the time in which to abate the hazard.

Employers should also note that failure to contest a citation for a willful violation in a case in which a worker has died may support a criminal charge.

50. 29 U.S.C. § 659(c).

51. 29 U.S.C. § 660.

52. 29 U.S.C. § 654.

53. *See, e.g., W.R. Mitchell Contractor, Inc.,* 13 BNA OSHC 1012 (OSHRC 1986), *aff'd,* 809 F.2d 161 (1st Cir. 1991).

54. Nonserious violations are those in which the potential consequences of the conduct are a minor injury or illness that does not rise to the level of serious physical harm. *See, e.g., Christian Roofing Co.,* 14 BNA OSHC 2206 (OSHRC 1991). Knowledge of the existence of the unlawful condition is required to prove the violation. *See, e.g., Williams Enterprises, Inc.,* 10 BNA OSHC 1260, 1262 (OSHRC 1981).

55. *See North American Rockwell Corp.,* 2 BNA OSHC 1710 (OSHRC 1975), *aff'd,* 540 F.2d 1283 (6th Cir. 1976) (serious violations); Brennan v. OSHRC & Raymond Hendrix, 511 F.2d 1139, 1143-44 (9th Cir. 1975) (nonserious violations).

56. 29 U.S.C. § 666(k). *See* Usery v. Hermitage Concrete Pipe Co., 584 F.2d 127, 132 (6th Cir. 1978).

57. *See Masonry Constr. Co.,* 12 BNA OSHC 1602 (OSHRC 1985); H.B. Zachry Co. v. OSHRC, 638 F.2d 812, 818 (5th Cir. 1981).

58. *See, e.g., Jensen Contr. Co.,* 7 BNA OSHC 1477 (OSHRC 1979); *Spaulding Lighting Inc.,* 13 BNA OSHC 1847 (OSHRC 1988).

59. *See, e.g., Morrison-Knudsen Indus. Serv. Inc.,* 14 BNA OSHC 1624 (OSHRC 1990) (employer not responsible for workers' exposure because manufacturer failed to specify that sandblasting grit contained lead and arsenic); *see also Mercury Consolidated,* 13 BNA OSHC 1519 (OSHRC 1987) (employer not responsible when employee suffered electric shock working on substation because wiring diagram failed to indicate additional underground supply); *Kut-Kwick Corp.,* 11 BNA OSHC

1864 (OSHRC 1984) (employer not liable when paint supplier failed to remove lead from paint formulation despite specific request and payment by employer).

60. To assert a greater hazard defense, an employer must demonstrate that:

1. the hazards of compliance are greater than those of noncompliance;
2. alternative means of protecting employees are unavailable; and, where there is a recurring situation,
3. a variance is inappropriate.

See Secretary of Labor v. Williams Enterprises, Inc., 1989 OSHD 28,554 (D.C. Cir. 1989); Modern Drop Forge Co. v. Secretary of Labor, 683 F.2d 1105, 1116 (7th Cir. 1982).

61. To assert this defense, the employer must show that:

1. it has implemented work rules intended to prevent the problem;
2. these rules have been communicated to the employees;
3. it has made an effort to discover violations; and
4. it has effectively enforced the rules when violations have been discovered.

See Jensen Construction Co., 7 OSHC 1477, 1979 OSHD 23,664 (OSHRC 1979).

62. This defense is rarely successful because it requires that employer demonstrate that it has been seriously prejudiced by the agency's delay.

63. *See, e.g., Cleveland Electric Illuminating Co.*, 13 OSHC 2209, 1989 OSHD 28,494 (OSHRC 1989) (employer asserted that compliance would have prevented it from performing its required work). Generally, employers have claimed difficulty of compliance rather than impossibility and have not been successful. *See, e.g., Walker Towing Corp., Daducah River Service*, 1991 OSHD 29, 239 (OSHRC 1991). In addition, to assert this defense, the employer must also demonstrate that alternative means of protection were being used or that no other protections were available. *See* Secretary of Labor v. Dun-Par Engineered Form Co., 843 F.2d 1135, 1138 (8th Cir. 1988).

64. 29 U.S.C. § 658(c).

65. The maximum allowable penalty is now $70,000 for each willful or repeated violation; and $7,000 for each serious or other-than-serious violation as well as $7,00 for each day beyond a stated abatement date for failure to correct a violation. Base penalties for posting requirement violations are:

- OSHA notice, $1,000;
- annual summary, $1,000; and
- failure to post citations, $3,000.

Base reporting and recordkeeping penalties are:

- failure to report a fatality or castastrophe within 48 hours, $5,000;
- denying access to records, $1,000; and
- failing to tell employees about advance notice of an inspection, $2,000.

OCCUPATIONAL SAFETY AND HEALTH ADMINISTRATION FACT SHEET NO. 92-36 (Jan. 1992).

66. 29 U.S.C. §§ 151–168.

67. *See* Nicholas A. Ashford & Charles C. Caldart, *The Control of Reproductive Hazards in the Workplace: A Prescription for Prevention*, 5 INDUS. REL. L. J. 523, 541 (1983).

68. 29 U.S.C. § 157.

69. Because Section 7 of the NLRA permits employee action based on one's subjective determination of workplace danger, it arguably provides the broadest protection of the refusal rights available under the NLRA and the OSH Act.

70. Section 7 of the NLRA provides that members of a collective bargaining unit may engage in concerted activity "for the purpose of collective bargaining or other mutual aid or protection." 29 U.S.C. § 157. In NLRB v. City Disposal Sys., Inc., 465 U.S. 82, 824–25 (1984), the Supreme Court held that an individual employee, who refused to drive a truck he believed to be unsafe pursuant to a provision of the collective bargaining agreement stating that the employer would not force employees to drive unsafe equipment, was engaged in "concerted activity" within the meaning of the NLRA. *Id.* at 826. An individual work stoppage may also qualify for Section 7 protection if the individual can show that it was intended to serve the interests of other workers as well. *See* NLRB v. Interboro Contractors, Inc., 388 F.2d 495, 499 (2d Cir. 1967). *But see* NLRB v. C & I Air Conditioning, Inc., 486 F.2d 977, 978 (9th Cir. 1973).

71. 29 U.S.C. § 143.

72. *See* Gateway Coal Co. v. UMW, 414 U.S. 368, 385–87 (1974).

73. 42 U.S.C. §§ 12,101–12,213. The Americans with Disabilities Act was passed by Congress in 1990 and took effect on July 26, 1992. The ADA was modeled closely on the Civil Rights Act of 1964, 42 U.S.C. § 2000a and Section 504 of the Rehabilitation Act of 1973, 29 U.S.C. § 794. In many ways, the protections afforded workers by the ADA are a logical extension of Section 504 of the Rehabilitation Act of 1973, which made it illegal to discriminate against disabled individuals under any program or activity receiving federal financial assistance.

74. The employment provisions of the ADA are enforced by the Equal Employment Opportunity Commission in accordance with the procedures established for Title VII of the Civil Rights Act of 1964. 42 U.S.C. § 12,117(a). Employees or job applicants who believe that they have been discriminated against in violation of the ADA must file a complaint with the EEOC within 180 days of the date of the alleged discriminatory act. 42 U.S.C. § 2000e-5(e)(1); 29 C.F.R. § 1601.13.

75. Employers with more than 15 employees are liable for discriminatory actions. *See* 42 U.S.C. § 12,111(5)(A).

76. 42 U.S.C. § 12,111(2).

77. Under the regulations promulgated by the Equal Employment Opportunity Commission of the United States Department of Justice (EEOC), a qualified individual is one with a disability who "satisfies the requisite skill, experience, education and other job-related requirements of the employment position such individual holds or desires, and who, with or without reasonable accommodation, can perform the essential functions of such position." 29 C.F.R. § 1630.2(m) (1992).

78. 42 U.S.C. § 12,112(a).

79. 42 U.S.C. § 12,203; 29 C.F.R. § 1630.12.

80. A "reasonable accommodation" is the means by which existing facilities are made accessible to and usable by qualified individuals. 42 U.S.C. § 12,111(9)(A).

81. 42 U.S.C. § 12,112(b)(5)(A).

82. 42 U.S.C. § 12,102(2).

83. However, because the ADA requires an employer to accommodate only a "known" disability, the individual desiring an accommodation is responsible

for notifying his or her employer when the disability is not obvious. EEOC AND THE UNITED STATES DEPARTMENT OF JUSTICE, AMERICANS WITH DISABILITIES ACT HANDBOOK [hereinafter I-61 ADA HANDBOOK].

84. *See* ADA HANDBOOK (Oct. 1991) I-1.

85. *Compare* Maulding v. Sullivan, 961 F.2d 695 (8th Cir. 1992) (holding that doctor's conclusory assertion that plaintiff could not work in a lab due to her chemical sensitivity were sufficient to demonstrate that she had the claimed sensitivity) *with* Langon v. Department of Health and Human Services, 959 F.2d 1053 (D.C. Cir. 1992) (holding that plaintiff did not supply sufficient medical evidence that multiple sclerosis required her to work at home).

86. *Compare* 41 C.F.R. 60-741.2 (Rehabilitation Act regulation defining "handicapped individual") *with* 29 C.F.R. 1630.2(g) (ADA regulation defining "disability").

87. *See, e.g.,* Rosiak v. United States Dept. of Army, 679 F. Supp. 444 (M.D. Pa. 1987) (accepting that plaintiff's claim of hypersensitivity to hydrocarbon fumes and dust, resulting from exposure to contact cement, is a handicap under the Rehabilitation Act); *San Diego Unified School District (Cal.),* 1 NAT'L DISABILITY L. REP. 311 ¶ 61 (May 24, 1990) (U.S. Department of Energy finding that a person with "chemical sensitivities" is "handicapped" under the Rehabilitation Act).

88. 29 C.F.R. 1630.2(I).

89. An impairment is substantially limiting if it "significantly restricts the duration, manner, or condition" in which an individual can perform the activity in comparison with the average person. *See* 29 C.F.R. 1630.2(j)(1). As one expert has pointed out, in this regard, the ADA helps only a portion of those who have chemical sensitivities. Those who are not sensitive enough will not be deemed "substantially impaired" and therefore will not qualify for protection under the ADA, while those who are too sensitive may not be able to find a reasonable accommodation that enables them to "qualify" for the position. *See* Alice Kaswan, *The Americans with Disabilities Act as a Weapon Against Indoor Air Pollution,* 4 ENVTL. L. N.Y., 110 (July 1993).

90. 29 C.F.R. 1630.2(j)(3)(I).

91. ADA HANDBOOK at I-31.

92. *See* ADA HANDBOOK at I-30–I-31.

93. *See* Kaswan, *supra* note 89, at 110.

94. Under the ADA, an accommodation will cause undue hardship if it is "unduly costly; extensive; substantial; disruptive; or . . . would fundamentally alter the nature or operation of the business." 42 U.S.C. § 12,111(10)(A). The cost to be considered is the actual cost of the accommodation to the employer, taking into account tax credits or deductions, or other sources of funding. Other considerations include the financial resources of the facility, the number of people employed, the effect of providing the accommodation on the facility's expenses, the impact of the accommodation on the nature of the business operation and on other employees. *See* 29 C.F.R. § 1630.2(p)(2)(ii) and (v).

95. *See* Guice-Mills v. Derwinski, 967 F.2d 794, 798 (2d Cir. 1992).

96. *See* EEOC, A TECHNICAL ASSISTANCE MANUAL ON THE EMPLOYMENT PROVISIONS OF THE AMERICANS WITH DISABILITIES ACT, III 7–8 (Jan. 1992) [hereinafter TECHNICAL ASSISTANCE MANUAL].

97. 29 C.F.R. § 1630.2(o)(iii).

98. 42 U.S.C. § 12,111(9)(B); 29 C.F.R. § 1630(o)(2)(ii); ADA HANDBOOK at I-42 to -43; TECHNICAL ASSISTANCE MANUAL at III-21 to -22.

99. 42 U.S.C. §§ 6901–6992k.

100. *See* 15 U.S.C. § 2651.

101. *See* 33 U.S.C. § 1367.

102. *See* 42 U.S.C. § 7622.

103. For a comprehensive compilation of state whistleblower protection laws, see INDIVIDUAL EMPLOYEE RIGHTS MANUAL, 9A LAB. REL. REP. ¶ 541:i–593:2 (BNA).

104. *See* N.J. REV. STAT. § 34:19-4.

105. *See* ME. REV. STAT. ANN. tit. 26, § 831.

106. *See* N.Y. LAB. LAW § 740(3); OHIO REV. CODE ANN. § 4113.52(A)(1)(a).

107. *See, e.g.,* CAL. LAB. CODE § 1102.5(a); CONN. GEN. STAT. ANN. 31-51m(b); HAW. REV. STAT. § 378-62(1) & (2); MICH. COMP. LAWS ANN. § 15.362(2); R.I. GEN. LAWS § 28-50-(1–9). Rhode Island's law protects private sector employees only in the waste disposal industry. *See* R.I. GEN. LAWS § 28-50-(1–9).

108. *See, e.g.,* Cloutier v. Great Atlantic & Pacific Tea Co., 121 N.H. 915, 923, 436 A.2d 1140, 1144-45 (1981); Miller v. Sevamp, Inc., 234 Va. 462, 362 S.E.2d 915 (1987); Parner v. Americana Hotels, Inc., 65 Haw. 370, 652 P.2d 625 (1982).

109. *See, e.g.,* Crockett v. Mid-American Health Servs., 780 S.W.2d 656 (Mo. 1989) (holding that plaintiff must allege that she was terminated because she refused to violate the law); Grzyb v. Evans, 700 S.W.2d 399 (Ky. 1985) (holding that the public policy exception may be invoked for a termination resulting from the employee's refusal to violate a statute or exercise of a statutory right); Campbell v. Eli Lilly & Co., 413 N.E.2d 1054 (Ind. 1980) (employee must show that he was terminated for exercising a statutory right or fulfilling a statutory duty).

In some states, even a violation of federal law will not support an employee's claim of wrongful discharge under the public policy exception. *See, e.g.,* Buethe v. Britt Airlines, Inc., 787 F.2d 1194, 1197 (7th Cir. 1986) (no cause of action exists for a termination resulting from an employee's refusal to fly an airplane that did not meet Federal Aviation Association standards); Guy v. Travenol Laboratories, 812 F.2d 911, 915 (4th Cir. 1987) (the state need not recognize a public policy exception for the violation of a federal statute).

Other states have refused to recognize any public policy exception to employment at will. *See, e.g.,* Ochab v. Morrison Inc., 517 So.2d 763 (Fla. Dist. Ct. App. 1987) (Florida); Taylor v. Foremost-McKesson, Inc., 656 F.2d 1029 (5th Cir. 1981) (Georgia); Maus v. National Living Centers, Inc., 633 S.W.2d 674 (Tex. Ct. App. 1982) (Texas); and Jones v. Keogh, 137 Vt. 562, 409 A.2d 581 (1979) (Vermont).

110. *See* International Brotherhood of Electrical Workers v. Hechler, 481 U.S. 851 (1987) (finding that a union may owe its members a duty to exercise due care in the performance of safety inspections that is sufficiently independent of the collective bargaining agreement to withstand the preemptive force of Section 301(a) of the Labor Management Relations Act of 1947, as amended, 29 U.S.C. §(a)).

111. A union member may also claim that he or she is owed a duty of reasonable care pursuant to the union's constitution. Skipper v. Hoff and Associates, 684 F. Supp. 707, 709–10 (S.D. Ga. 1987).

112. *See, e.g., Hechler,* 481 U.S. 851 (1987); Condon v. Local 2944, United Steelworkers, 683 F.2d 590 (1st Cir. 1982); Bryant v. United Mine Workers, 467

F.2d 1 (6th Cir. 1972); Pockalny v. Elwell Parker Electric Co., 608 F. Supp. 570 (W.D.N.Y. 1985); House v. Mine Safety Appliances Co., 417 F. Supp. 939 (D. Idaho 1976).

113. Allis-Chalmers Corp. v. Lueck, 471 U.S. 202, 218 (1985).

114. *See* Allis-Chalmers Corp. v. Lueck, 471 U.S. 202, 211 (1985).

115. Skipper v. Hoff and Associates, 684 F. Supp. 707, 711 n.9 (S.D. Ga. 1987).

116. *See* Condon v. Local 2944, United Steelworkers, 683 F.2d 590, 594 (1st Cir. 1982); Dente v. International Organization of Masters, Mates & Pilots, 492 F.2d 10 (9th Cir. 1974), *cert. denied*, 417 U.S. 910 (1974).

117. Bazarte v. United Transportation Union, 429 F.2d 868, 872 (3d Cir. 1970); *see* Vaca v. Sipes, 386 U.S. 171 (1967); Brough v. United Steelworkers, 437 F.2d 748, 750 (1st Cir. 1971). *But see* Helton v. Hake, 386 F. Supp. 1027 (W.D. Mo. 1974) (court found that the collective bargaining agreement required the union, through the shop steward, to enforce a safety rule relating to work in the area of high-tension power lines).

118. *See* Condon v. Local 2944, United Steelworkers, 683 F.2d 590 (1st Cir. 1982); Curran v. International Union of Oil, Chemical & Atomic Workers, 582 F. Supp. 420 (W.D.N.Y. 1984).

119. *See* Airline Pilots Association, International v. O'Neill, 499 U.S. 65, 67 (1991) (expanded rule to apply to all union activity including contract negotiation); Vaca v. Sipes, 386 U.S. 171, 190 (1967); *see also* Humphrey v. Moore 375 U.S. 335 (1964) (holding that the duty of fair representation includes the obligation to enforce fairly the provisions of any collective bargaining agreement).

120. *See, e.g.*, Bryant v. United Mine Workers, 467 F.2d 1 (6th Cir. 1972) (noting the problematic disincentives that would be created by imposing additional duties on unions).

121. *See* 29 U.S.C. §§ 151–168.

122. Currently, collective bargaining agreements negotiated by the Oil, Chemical and Atomic Workers Union provide for the establishment of joint worker-management committees as well.

123. Daily Labor Report (BNA) 1 (Feb. 9, 1993).

124. *See* 29 U.S.C. §§ 655(b), 655(c), and 662, respectively.

125. Section 13(d) of the Act provides a specific right of mandamus in situations in which the Secretary of Labor "arbitrarily or capriciously fails to seek relief" under the "imminent danger" provision of that section. 29 U.S.C. § 662(d). Similar mandamus relief can be achieved through the Administrative Procedure Act (APA), 5 U.S.C. §§ 702 *et seq.*, which provides for relief against "an agency or an officer or employee thereof [that] acted or *failed to act* in an official capacity or under color of legal authority." 5 U.S.C. § 702 (emphasis supplied). In addition, the APA provides for review of an agency's decision not to act on a particular hazard. *See* 5 U.S.C. §§ 704, 706.

126. 15 U.S.C. §§ 2601–2629.

127. 15 U.S.C. § 2603(a).

128. 15 U.S.C. §§ 2604(f), 2605(a). For carcinogens, mutagens, and teratogens, the EPA Administrator is required to "initiate appropriate action . . . to prevent or reduce to a sufficient extent such risk or publish in the Federal Register a finding that such risk is not unreasonable." 15 U.S.C. § 2603(f).

129. 15 U.S.C. § 2620.

130. 15 U.S.C. § 2619.

131. Although states have begun enacting such legislation, the primary sources of regulation governing toxics information transfer are three federal statutes: the Occupational Safety and Health Act, 29 U.S.C. §§ 651 *et seq.*, the Toxic Substances Control Act, 15 U.S.C. §§ 2601 *et seq.;* and the National Labor Relations Act, 29 U.S.C. §§ 151 *et seq. See* Nicholas A. Ashford & Charles C. Caldart, *The "Right To Know": Toxics Information Transfer in the Workplace*, 6 ANN. REV. OF PUB. HEALTH (1985) 385 [hereinafter referred to as *Toxics Information Transfer*].

132. *See* 29 C.F.R. § 1910.1200. Many have noted, however, that MSDSs are difficult to understand because of the abbreviations used, and provide little valuable data, and incomplete risk assessments. *See* Paulette L. Stenzel, *Right to Act: Advancing the Common Interests of Labor and Environmentalists,* 57 ALB. L. REV. 1, 9 (1993).

133. *See* 40 C.F.R. § 712, 717.

134. In contrast to OSHA, the TSCA provides solely for EPA access to information regarding reactions to chemical exposures or other scientific data that must be reported by employers. *See* § 8 and implementing regulation, 40 C.F.R. § 717, and § 11.

135. *See* Worker Access Rule, 29 C.F.R. § 1910.20; Hazard Communication Rule, 29 C.F.R. § 1910.1200. Under the Medical Records Rule, 29 C.F.R. § 1913.10, and a separate provision of the Worker Access Rule, 29 C.F.R. § 1910.1020(e)(3), the Occupational Safety and Health Administration is entitled to all exposure and effects data recorded by an employer.

136. *See* 29 C.F.R. § 1910.1200. According to OSHA, despite the specificity of the rule, many employers do not inform workers of the identity or dangers posed by the hazardous substances they are working with, and those employers that do attempt to comply often provide confusing and inadequate information. *See* U.S. DEPT. LAB. NEWS (Nov. 9, 1990); Rhinehart, *Workplace Safety Enforcement, supra* note 8, at 377.

137. *See* 29 C.F.R. § 1910.1001(j)(7) (requiring training on the hazards of asbestos).

138. *See* 29 C.F.R. § 1910.1030(g)(2) (requiring training on blood-borne infectious diseases for workers exposed to blood on the job).

139. *See* OCCUPATIONAL SAFETY AND HEALTH ADMINISTRATION FACT SHEET on 29 C.F.R. pt. 1910 Occupational Safety and Health Standards (Dec. 1998).

140. 42 U.S.C. §§ 11,001 *et seq.*

141. 42 U.S.C. § 11,023.

142. "Toxic Chemicals" are listed at 40 C.F.R. § 372 (subpt. D).

143. *See* 42 U.S.C. § 11,021(a)(1).

144. *See* 42 U.S.C. § 11,023(b); 40 C.F.R. § 350 *et seq.*

145. *See* "Toxics Information Transfer" at Table 1.

146. N.C. GEN. STAT. § 95-126.

147. N.C. GEN. STAT. § 95-148.

148. N.C. GEN. STAT. § 95-252. Other states also require the establishment of worker-management safety committees. *See, e.g.,* Wash. Admin. Order 78-22 (1978), Wash. Admin. Order 80-20 (1980) (executive orders); OR. WORKERS' COMP. LAW, OR. REV. STAT. §§ 656.001–656.990 (1991); CAL. LAB. CODE § 6401.7 (Deering Supp. 1993).

149. N.C. GEN. STAT. § 95-148.

150. N.C. GEN. STAT. § 95-136.1.

151. N.C. GEN. STAT. § 95-241.

152. N.J. STAT. ANN. § 34-5A.

153. CAL. HEALTH & SAFETY CODE §§ 25,249.5–25,249.13.

154. CAL. HEALTH & SAFETY CODE § 25,249.6.

155. *See* Clifford Rechtschaffen, *The Warning Game: Evaluating Warnings Under California's Proposition 65,* 23 ECOLOGY L. Q. 303, 307 n.14 (1996). Proposition 65 also includes an expedited process for the listing of additional chemicals: any chemical that has been found to cause cancer or reproductive toxicity by certain government agencies or scientific bodies is automatically included under the statute. CAL. HEALTH & SAFETY CODE § 25,249.8(a), (b).

156. CAL. CODE REGS. tit. 26, 22-12601(b), (c), and (d) (1995).

157. *See* Rechtschaffen, *supra* note 155, at 354–55.

158. *See, e.g.,* Gonzales v. Sam's Group, Inc., No. 714908-3 (Alameda County Super. Ct. *filed* Apr. 17, 1993) (rubber stamp manufacturer agreed to hire a consultant to review hazardous chemical warning and training programs and implement recommendations after suit brought for failure to provide warnings to workers regarding toluene).

159. *See* "Toxics Information Transfer" at 388.

160. *See* "Toxics Information Transfer" at 389.

161. G. J. Annas, *Legal Aspects of Medical Confidentiality in the Occupational Setting,* 18 J. OCCUP. MED. 537 (1976).

162. *See* 15 U.S.C. § 2613.

163. N. Y. Workers' Comp. Law § 11. *See also* Olsson v. Nyack Hospital, 598 N.Y.S.2d 348 (3d Dept. 1993) (reiterating the principle that workers' compensation remedies are the exclusive remedies for recompense to employees injured in the course of employment).

164. Workers' compensation statutes are intended to ensure that workers are compensated for injuries that "arise out of" and "in the course of" their employment. Such programs are also intended to spread the risk of catastrophic financial loss by means of an insurance pool, and to internalize the costs of workplace disease and injury to create an incentive for employers to improve safety and health conditions in their workplaces. These statutes mandate that employers obtain workers' compensation insurance and make failure to comply with this requirement a criminal offense. N. Y. Workers' Comp. Law § 11.

165. The presumptions included in most state workers' compensation schemes weigh in favor of coverage. Thus, in New York for example, the Workers' Compensation statute establishes the presumptions that:

1. the claim falls within the parameters of the Workers' Compensation Law;
2. sufficient notice was given;
3. the injury was not occasioned by the willful intent of the injured employee to bring about the injury;
4. the injury did not result solely from the intoxication of the injured employee while on duty; and
5. medical reports introduced are *prima facie* evidence of fact.

N. Y. Workers' Comp. Law § 21. The employer must affirmatively rebut these presumptions by substantial evidence to make use of the exceptions to its liability for compensation benefits.

166. *See, e.g.*, Jackson v. Frederick Richman & Co., 15 N.Y.2d 877, 258 N.Y.S.2d 414 (1965) (stating that the exclusive remedy provision of the Workers' Compensation Law does not apply to intentional torts); Acevedo v. Consolidated Edison, 596 N.Y.S.2d 68, 70–71 (1st Dept. 1993) (holding that there is an exception to the exclusivity rule "where injury is sustained to an employee due to an intentional tort perpetrated by the employer or at the employer's direction).

However, by accepting workers' compensation benefits, claimants will forfeit their rights to maintain an action against the employer for intentional torts. *See* Cunningham v. State of New York, 60 N.Y.2d 246, 252 n.2, 469 N.Y.S.2d 588, 590 n.2 (1983). Indeed, the acceptance of compensation benefits, regardless of whether a formal award is made, is generally deemed preclusive of any alternative civil remedy. *See* Hardie v. Attica Correctional Facility, 534 N.Y.S.2d 492, 494 (3d Dept. 1988) (noting that the commission of an intentional tort by employer creates "the initial option on the part of the injured employee to sue the employer for civil damages or, in the alternative, to obtain [workers'] compensation benefits," and that such remedies are "inconsistent and mutually exclusive").

167. *See, e.g.*, Weigel v. Quincy Specialities Co., 601 N.Y.S.2d 774 (Sup. Ct. N.Y. Cnty. 1993) (reaffirming the jurisdiction's recognition of a common law cause of action against an employer for negligently and intentionally impairing an employee's right to sue a third-party tortfeasor notwithstanding the employee's receipt of workers' compensation benefits); Caban v. Gottlieb Iron Works, 558 N.Y.S.2d 810 (1990) (same).

168. The fact that an employment situation or position is illegal does not remove either the employer or the employee from the scope of the Workers' Compensation law. However, when the parties are engaged in an unlawful occupation so that compensation is not available as a remedy, the employee may choose to sue in the courts for any injuries sustained. *See* Wasserman v. Josephson, 61 N.Y.S.2d 204 (1946), aff'd 84 N.Y.S.2d. When the manner of conducting the business is illegal, but not the nature of the business, no such option is provided. *Id.*

169. To circumvent the exclusivity rule, an employee must show that "the conduct must be engaged in with the desire to bring about the consequences of the act." Acevedo v. Con Edison, 596 N.Y.S.2d 68, 71 (1st Dept. 1993); *see also* Briggs v. Pymm Thermometer Corp., 537 N.Y.S.2d 553 (2nd Dept. 1989). This rule is also sometimes framed as requiring showing of either substantial certainty of injury or the employer's actual subjective intent to injure. Neither intentional concealment or misrepresentation, nor the failure to provide safe working conditions constitutes a cognizable intentional tort under the workers' compensation schemes.

170. Such challenges are handled by state compensation boards in an administrative proceeding in which the burden of proof is on the worker.

171. *See* Nicholas A. Ashford, CRISIS IN THE WORKPLACE: OCCUPATIONAL DISEASE AND INJURY, ch. 8 (Cambridge, MIT Press 1976).

172. *See* Nicholas A. Ashford, *Worker's Compensation*, in ENVIRONMENTAL AND OCCUPATIONAL MEDICINE at 1352 (2d ed. Little, Brown & Co. 1992) [hereinafter referred to as Ashford, *Worker's Compensation*]. In 1990, the American Public Health Association (APHA) estimated that approximately 50,000 to 70,000 persons die of diseases developed from toxic exposures on the job. The APHA fur-

ther estimated that 350,000 new cases of occupational disease develop each year from such toxic exposures.

173. Ashford, *Worker's Compensation, supra* note 172, at 1353.

174. Ashford, *Worker's Compensation, supra* note 172, at 1354.

175. Employers may also be able to sue manufacturers for the costs of employee compensation.

176. Third-party suits may provide compensation for lost wages, disfigurement, medical and legal expenses, and pain and suffering, and generally have the potential for higher awards than are available under workers' compensation statutes.

177. The states of Ohio, Georgia, and West Virginia have no such provision in their workers' compensation statutes, and the courts of these states have refused to grant a lien against such recovery when the statutory scheme does not specifically provide for one.

178. Compensation systems for specific diseases, such as that for black lung disease, operate as a no-fault compensation mechanism for those exposed and suffering from the illness in lieu of state workers' compensation benefits. *See* Ashford, *Worker's Compensation, supra* note 172, at 1355.

179. Johns-Manville Products Corporation v. Contra Costa Superior Court, 612 P.2d 948 (1981); *see also* McLandrich v. Southern California Edison Co., 145 F.3d 1339 (9th Cir. 1998).

180. *See* Ellen K. Silbergeld, *The Risks of Comparing Risks,* 3 N.Y.U. ENVTL. L.J. 405, 413–14 (1995) (noting that "[l]ittle has changed since the National Research Council (NRC) noted ten years ago that between seventy-three and eighty-nine percent of chemicals in commerce have almost no toxicity data upon which even a qualitative identification of hazard can be made. . . .").

181. *See generally* PHILIP A. MARTIN & DAVID A. MARTIN, THE ENDLESS QUEST 3 (1994). In 1994, approximately one-half of these workers were employed for more than one month but less than ten months, and earned an average of $5000 annually for six months of farm work. *Id.*

182. Ivette Perfecto & Baldemar Velasquez, *Farm Workers: Among the Least Protected,*" EPA JOURNAL at 13–14 (Mar./Apr. 1992) [hereinafter *Farm Workers*]. Agricultural workers are the most abused of all workers in the United States. *See* H.R. REP. NO. 97-885, *reprinted in* 1982 U.S.C.C.A.N. 4547.

183. 29 U.S.C. §§ 201–219.

184. Section 2 of the National Labor Relations Act, 29 U.S.C. § 152, removes agricultural workers from the protections of the Act. *See* 29 U.S.C. § 152(3) (1993).

185. 29 U.S.C. §§ 1801–1854.

186. In enacting the AWPA, Congress specifically adopted FLSA definitions and jurisprudence. H.R. REP. No. 97-885, 6 (1982), *reprinted in* 1982 U.S.C.C.A.N. 4547, 4552.

187. *See* George Friedman-Jimenez, *Occupational Disease Among Minority Workers: A Common and Preventable Problem,* 37 AAOHN JOURNAL 64–65 (Feb. 1989). According to EPA estimates, farmers use approximately 1.2 billion pounds of pesticides each year. *See Farm Workers, supra* note 182, at 13.

188. 7 U.S.C. §§ 136–136y Under FIFRA, pesticide use is controlled through a registration process administered by the EPA. A separate registration is required for each different use of a given pesticide, and EPA registration of each use and

approval of a label detailing the legally binding instructions for that use are required before a pesticide can be legally sold. For a pesticide to be registered, manufacturers must submit to EPA the data needed to support the product's registration, including substantiation of its usefulness and disclosure of its chemical and toxic properties, its likely distribution in the environment, and its possible effects on wildlife and plants. 7 U.S.C. §§ 136–136y.

189. 7 U.S.C. § 136(bb). *See also* Chapter 10, "Risk Assessment, Susceptible Subpopulations, and Environmental Justice," pages 307–356, for a discussion of risk assessment and balancing under FIFRA and other environmental statutes.

190. *See Farm Workers, supra* note 182, at 14.

191. *Id.*

192. The task force recommended that NIOSH and other federal agencies sponsor research into the sources, types, levels, and health effects of take-home exposures, and assess the effectiveness of current prevention and remediation methods. U.S. DEPT. OF HEALTH AND HUMAN SERVICES, REPORT OF THE WORKERS' FAMILY PROTECTION TASK FORCE, 63 Fed. Reg. 5952 (Feb. 5, 1998).

193. In 1963, Congress enacted the FLCRA to remedy the exploitation and abuse of farm workers by farm labor contractors, crew leaders who recruited workers for the growers and often underpaid the workers while collecting full wages from the growers. The FLCRA required crew leaders to register with the U.S. Department of Labor and to provide information regarding his method of operation, submit proof of public liability insurance for all vehicles used in the business, maintain payroll records, and inform workers about employment terms and anticipated earnings. Farm Labor Contractor Registration Act of 1963, Pub. L. No. 88-582, 78 Stat. 920 (repealed 1983).

194. H.R. REP. No. 97-885, *reprinted in* 1982 U.S.C.C.A.N. 4547.

195. 29 U.S.C. §§ 1821–44.

196. Both migrant and seasonal workers are employed in agricultural work of a temporary nature, but a migrant worker is one who is required to be absent overnight from his or her permanent place of residence. 29 U.S.C. § 1802(8)(A).

197. 29 U.S.C. §§ 1801–72.

198. 29 U.S.C. § 1821. Records indicating the wage rates, number of hours worked, total earnings, withholding and net pay for each period must be kept for three years. *Id.*

199. 29 U.S.C. §§ 1841–42.

200. 29 U.S.C. § 1841. The U.S. Department of Labor, in the regulations to the Act, enumerates many motor vehicle safety standards, including the width of seats, 29 C.F.R. § 500.105(b)(3)(vi)(D), and the spacing of footholds. 29 C.F.R. § 500.105(b)(3)(vi)(H). However, the regulations do not include any seat belt requirements. Because Article III standing principles require that a plaintiff prove that a violation of the Act caused his injuries, any claim for damages due to injuries resulting from the lack of seat belts must be based on an applicable state safety standard where such exists.

201. 29 C.F.R. § 500.100(a).

202. 29 C.F.R. § 500.100(c). *See, e.g.,* Saintida v. Tyre Jackor Super Picking, Inc., 783 F. Supp. 1368 (S.D. Fla. 1992) (holding employer liable for employees' lost wages due to accident resulting from farm labor contractor's lack of insurance coverage for vehicle used to transport workers).

203. Workers' compensation programs generally do not cover casual workers, domestic workers, self-employed workers, farm workers, some small business workers, and state and local government workers.

204. 29 U.S.C. § 1854(d).

205. "A violation is intentional under the Act if it is the natural result of one's conscious and deliberate acts." Osias v. Emerson Marc, 700 F. Supp. 842, 844 (D. Md. 1988) (*quoting* Bueno v. Mattner, 829 F.2d 1380, 1385–86 (6th Cir. 1987)).

206. *See* 29 U.S.C. § 1854.

207. 29 U.S.C. § 1854(e)(1)-(4).

208. *See* Barajas v. Bermudez, 43 F.3d 1251, 1255 (9th Cir. 1994).

209. *See, e.g.*, Rivera v. Anaya, 726 F.2d 564 (9th Cir. 1984) (applying a three-year limitations period for an AWPA case); Sanchez v. Morrison, 667 F. Supp. 536, 538 (W.D. Mich. 1987) (applying a six-year limitations period); Marquis v. United States Sugar Corp., 652 F. Supp. 598, 602 (S.D. Fla. 1987) (applying a four-year limitations period).

210. *See, e.g.*, Amiable v. Long & Scott Farms, Inc., 20 F.3d 434, 445 (11th Cir.) (finding that crew leader is sole employer of migrant workers), *cert. denied*, 115 S. Ct. 351 (1994); Howard v. Malcom, 852 F.2d 101, 105 (4th Cir. 1988) (crew leader is sole employer of migrant corn pickers); Donovan v. Brandel, 736 F.2d 1114, 1120 (6th Cir. 1984) (pickle harvesters are independent contractors); Charles v. Burton, 857 F. Supp. 1574, 1581–82 (M.D. Ga. 1994) (crew leader is sole employer of migrant workers).

211. *See* Marc Linder, *Employees, Not-So-Independent Contractors, and the Case of Migrant Workers: A Challenge to the "Law and Economics" Agency Doctrine*, 15 N.Y.U. Rev. L. & Soc. Change 435, 436–37 (1987).

212. The factors considered under this test include, but are not limited to, the following:

(i) the nature and degree of control of the workers;
(ii) the degree of supervision, direct or indirect, of the work;
(iii) the power to determine the pay rates or the methods of payment of the workers;
(iv) the right to hire, fire, or modify the employment conditions of the workers; and
(v) the preparation of payroll and the payment of wages.

29 C.F.R. § 500.20(h)(4)(ii).

213. The majority of courts have found that migrant workers are either employees of the grower or employees of both the crew leader and the grower. *See, e.g.*, Department of Labor v. Lauritzen, 835 F.2d 1529, 1536–38 (7th Cir. 1987), *cert. denied*, 488 U.S. 898 (1988), *rehearing denied*, 488 U.S. 987 (1988); Beliz v. W.H. McLeod & Sons Packing Co., 765 F.2d 1317, 1328 (5th Cir. 1985); Castillo v. Givens, 704 F.2d 181, 188 (5th Cir.), *cert. denied*, 464 U.S. 850 (1983); Real v. Driscoll Strawberry Assocs., 603 F.2d 748, 754 (9th Cir. 1979); Hodgson v. Okada, 472 F.2d 965, 968 (10th Cir. 1973); Alviso-Medrano v. Harloff, 868 F. Supp. 1367, 1374 (M.D. Fla. 1994); Aviles v. Kunkle, 765 F. Supp. 358 (S.D. Tex. 1991), *judgment vacated on other grounds*, 978 F.2d 201 (5th Cir. 1992); Maldonado v. Lucca, 629 F. Supp. 483, 487-88 (D.N.J. 1986); Haywood v. Barnes, 109 F.R.D. 568, 587 (E.D.N.C. 1986). *But see* Charles v. Burton, 857 F. Supp. 1574, 1579–81 (M.D. Ga. 1994) (holding that crew leader was the sole employer of migrant workers).

214. 29 U.S.C. §§ 1851-54.

215. 29 U.S.C. § 1852.

216. *See, e.g.*, Fiedler v. Clark, 714 F.2d 77 (9th Cir. 1983); *Re: "Agent Orange" Product Liability Litig.*, 506 F. Supp. 737 (EDNY 1979), *rev'd on other grounds*, 635 F.2d 987 (2d Cir. 1980); Turner v. United States Environmental Protection Agency, 848 F. Supp. 711, 7156-16 (S.D. Miss. 1994). *But see* Defenders of Wildlife v. Administrator, Environmental Protection Agency, 882 F.2d 1294 (8th Cir. 1989). However, the Ninth Circuit Court of Appeals has permitted environmental groups to sue the EPA under the Administrative Procedure Act, 5 U.S.C. §§ 501 *et seq*. for actions undertaken in contravention of FIFRA. *See* Oregon Environmental Council v. Kunzman, 714 F.2d 901 (9th Cir. 1983).

217. *See, e.g.*, Bice v. Leslie's Poolmart, 39 F.3d 887 (8th Cir. 1994) (state law claim dismissed with regard to swimming pool maintenance product which carried EPA approved label); Arkansas-Platte & Gulf Partnership v. Van Waters & Rogers, Inc., 959 F.2d 158 (10th Cir. 1992) (holding that plaintiffs' state law claims sounding in negligence and strict liability based on the manufacturer's failure to warn of the product's environmental hazard were preempted by FIFRA); Papas v. Upjohn Co., 926 F.2d 1019 (11th Cir. 1991) (finding that FIFRA impliedly preempts claims of inadequate labeling even if pesticide manufacturer failed to provide government with complete information about pesticide), *on remand*, 985 F.2d 516 (1993) (court stated that FIFRA expressly preempts claims based on inadequate labeling or packaging); Kennan v. Dow Chemical Co., 717 F. Supp. 799 (M.D. Fla. 1989) (widow's products liability claims against chemical manufacturers based on failure to warn adequately of dangers associated with the use of pesticide held preempted by FIFRA); Fitzgerald v. Malinckrodt, Inc., 681 F. Supp. 404 (E.D. Mich. 1987) (holding that products liability action brought by greenskeeper alleging injury due to fungicide manufacturer's failure to warn adequately of product's dangers was preempted by FIFRA); Ackles v. Luttrell, 252 Neb 273, 561 NW2d 573, *cert. denied*, 118 S. Ct. 329 (1997) (finding that plaintiff's common law strict liability claim alleging failure to warn users of toxic nature of insecticide was preempted by FIFRA, but striking plaintiff's negligence claim alleging failure to warn based on the insufficiency of the pleadings); Little v. Dow Chemical Co., 148 Misc. 2d 11, 559 N.Y.S.2d 788 (Sup. Ct. Erie Cnty. 1990) (dismissing worker's claims of improper labeling and failure to warn as in conflict with FIFRA, and plaintiff's remaining claims of design defect and breach of warranty because product registration with EPA is based on agency's finding that product is not unreasonably risky to human beings); Oakes v. E.I. Du Pont de Nemours & Co., 272 Cal. App. 2d 645, 77 Cal. Rptr. 709 (3d Dist. 1969) (holding that an action in strict liability could not be sustained where an injured party sought to recover damages from the manufacturer for a skin condition that was due to an allergy to an ingredient in the weed killer).

218. *See* MacDonald v. Monsanto Co., 27 F.3d 1021 (5th Cir. 1994) (stating that FIFRA preempts only those state laws that impose different or additional labeling requirements); Deshotel v. Rhone-Poulenc, Inc., 969 F. Supp. 397 (W.D. La. 1997) (same); DerGazarian v. Dow Chemical Co., 836 F. Supp. 1429 (W.D. Ark. 1993) (same). *See also* Worm v. American Cyanamid Co., 5 F.3d 744 (4th Cir. 1993) (holding that FIFRA does not preempt common law actions based on state-imposed standards of care relating to product design, manufacture, and testing);

Bingham v. Terminix Int'l Co., 850 F. Supp. 516 (SD Miss. 1994) (holding that FIFRA does not preempt claims that insecticide manufacturers were negligent in failing to test and inspect their products to ascertain dangers in their use); Kennan v. Dow Chemical Co., 717 F. Supp. 799 (M.D. Fla. 1989) (widow's products liability claims against chemical manufacturers based on failure to warn preempted, but claims based on design defect permitted to proceed).

219. *See* Ferebee v. Chevron Chemical Co., 736 F.2d 1529 (D.C. Cir.), *cert. denied*, 105 S. Ct. 545 (1984) (affirming judgment for plaintiffs, children of worker at agricultural center, in wrongful death action brought on theory of failure to warn that long-term skin exposure to herbicide paraquat could result in pulmonary fibrosis). In *Ferebee*, the District of Columbia Court of Appeals specifically noted that EPA's determination that the herbicide's label was adequate for purposes of FIFRA did not compel the jury to find that the label was adequate for purposes of state tort law. *See also* Peteet v. Dow Chemical Co., 868 F.2d 1428 (5th Cir. 1989), *cert. denied*, 493 U.S. 935 (1989) (affirming judgment in products liability action for surviving spouse, child and parents of U.S. forest service employee who developed Hodgkin's disease after participating in weed control project using 2,4-D herbicide); Hubbard-Hall Chemical Co. v. Silverman, 340 F.2d 402 (1st Cir. 1965) (holding manufacturers of Parathion insecticide liable for the death of two farm workers from contact with product because warning on label was not meaningful to all users of the product); *In re Dupont-Benlate Litig.*, 877 F. Supp. 779 (D.C. Puerto Rico 1995); Roberts v. Dow Chemical Co., 702 F. Supp. 195 (N.D. Ill. 1988) (holding that label in compliance with FIFRA did not compel finding of adequacy under state tort law because of failure to warn against significant risk of harm); Wilson v. Chevron Chemical Co., 1988 US Dist LEXIS 4457 (S.D.N.Y. 1988) (holding that widow's suit against paraquat manufacturer was not preempted by FIFRA); Macrie v. SDS Biotech Corp., 267 N.J. Super. 34, 630 A.2d 805 (App. Div. 1993) (summary judgment in favor of manufacturer reversed despite fact that label was in conformity with FIFRA holding that FIFRA does not preempt state law claims).

220. *See* Riden v. ICI Americas, Inc., 763 F. Supp. 1500 (W.D. Mo. 1991) (denying manufacturer's motion to dismiss negligence and failure to warn claims arising out of use of Havoc, a rat poison, by farm worker who suffered severe internal and external bleeding); Gonzalez v. Virginia-Carolina Chemical Co., 239 F. Supp. 567 (D.S.C. 1965) (holding that under South Carolina law manufacturer of defoliant was negligent in distributing a dangerous poison without adequate warning of its toxic effects, and that failure to comply with the labeling requirements of state and federal statutes was negligence per se). *But see* Daniels v. Atlantic Refining Co., 295 F. Supp. 125 (D.C. Del. 1968) (holding that manufacturer's failure to directly warn farm laborer of danger of flammability of solvent could not provide the basis for negligence claim when solvent ignited and burned plaintiff when it was emitted from a sprayer driven by fellow employee).

221. *See, e.g., In re Dupont-Benlate Litig.*, 859 F. Supp. 619 (D.C. Puerto Rico 1994) (holding that express warranties cannot be preempted by federal law because they are voluntarily imposed by the manufacturer); Higgins v. Monsanto Co., 862 F. Supp. 751 (N.D.N.Y. 1994) (same); McQuaide v. Bridgeport Brass Co., 190 F. Supp. 252 (D.C. Conn. 1960) (holding that consumer injured as a result of using insecticide spray could maintain an action for breach of implied

and express warranties even in the absence of privity of contract because the product was not fit for its intended purpose). In such cases, claims have been based on allegations regarding warranties made through advertisements, sales literature, and manufacturers' trade names.

222. *See* Wright v. Dow Chemical U.S.A., 845 F. Supp. 503 (M.D. Tenn. 1993) (claim of breach of implied warranty or merchantability permitted to proceed to trial).

223. *See Re: "Agent Orange" Product Liability Litig.*, 597 F. Supp. 740, 827–28 (E.D.N.Y. 1984).

224. *See* Macrie v. SDS Biotech Corp., 267 N.J. Super. 34, 630 A.2d 805 (App. Div. 1993).

225. *See* George's Pest Control Service v. United States Environmental Protection Agency, 572 F.2d 204 (9th Cir. 1977) (upholding fine imposed by EPA against pest control company).

226. 7 U.S.C. § 136j(a)(2)(G). *See* United States v. Corbin Farm Service, 444 F. Supp. 510 (ED Cal. 1978), *aff'd*, 578 F.2d 259 (9th Cir. 1979).

227. *See, e.g.*, Henderson v. Department of Agriculture, 128 Or. App. 169, 875 P.2d 487, *review denied*, 320 Or. 271 (1994).

228. Pub. L. No. 104-193, 110 Stat. 2105 (1996).

229. 42 U.S.C. § 601(b).

230. 42 U.S.C. §§ 604–19.

231. Personal Responsibility and Work Opportunity Reconciliation Act § 103 (new Section 402(a) of the Social Security Act).

232. The new law implements a "participation rate" requirement: States must place 25 percent of the individuals receiving welfare in jobs by the end of 1997, and 50 percent in jobs by 2002. *See* 42 U.S.C.A. § 607(a)(1).

233. The term "workfare" is generally used to refer to any work situation, in either the public or private sector, that is a condition of receiving welfare or AFDC benefits.

234. *See* 42 U.S.C.A. § 602(a)(1)(A)(ii).

235. *See* 42 U.S.C.A. § 608(a)(7). A state may extend a "hardship exception" to up to 20 percent of the "average monthly number of families" that receive TANF. *Id.* at 608(a)(7)(C)(ii).

236. *See* 18 Soc. Serv. § 387.1 (1996). The effects of implementing the new Temporary Assistance for Needy Families program have been documented in a number of sources. *See, e.g.*, Mary R. Mannix et al., *Implementation of the Temporary Assistance for Needy Families Block Grant: An Overview*, CLEARINGHOUSE REV., Jan.–Feb. 1997, at 868–901.

237. The jurisdictions include Alabama, Arkansas, Colorado, Delaware, Florida, Georgia, Idaho, Illinois, Kansas, Louisiana, Maine, Massachusetts, Mississippi, Montana, Nebraska, New Hampshire, New Jersey, North Dakota, Ohio, Oklahoma, Pennsylvania, Rhode Island, South Dakota, Texas, West Virginia, and Wisconsin.

238. Protection under existing state public employee health and safety laws is not certain in even those jurisdictions that have such statutes. For example, in New York State, coverage of workfare participants under the Public Employees Safety and Health Act, N.Y. LAB. LAW § 27-a(4)(a), is premised on a letter interpretation provided by the State Commission of Labor. *See* Letter to AFSCME,

District Council 37 from the New York State Department of Labor (Oct. 25, 1995) (on file with the author).

239. The hazards that workfare workers may encounter on the job include:

- asbestos exposure;
- blood-borne pathogen exposure and tuberculosis exposure in health care facilities;
- exposure to toxic cleaning agents, paint solvents, and lead;
- exposure to pesticides and other agricultural chemicals;
- the ill effects of extreme air temperatures;
- exposure to irritant dusts and hazardous materials;
- unguarded machinery;
- fall hazards from elevated work;
- inadequate or unsanitary personal protective equipment;
- inadequate supplies of drinking water; and
- unsanitary bathroom and eating facilities.

240. *See, e.g.,* Capers v. Giuliani, 677 N.Y.S.2d 353 (1st Dept. 1998) (reviewing factual record before trial court indicating unsanitary conditions at job sites).

241. For example, in New York, individuals who are deemed noncompliant with their work assignments are typically subjected to sanction and loss of their cash assistance, food stamp, and Medicaid benefits for extended periods of time. The length of the sanction imposed depends upon the number of infractions found. The first infraction garners a sanction of 75 days, the second infraction garners a 120-day sanction, and the third infraction garners a 180-day sanction. After three infractions, the worker's eligibility is permanently closed.

242. *See, e.g.,* Sorge v. Wright's Knitwear, 8 IER Cases 1274, 832 F. Supp. 118 (E.D. Pa. 1993); Lepore v. National Tool and Mfrg. Co., 540 A.2d 1296 (N.J. Super. Ct. App. Div. 1988).

243. 29 U.S.C. §§ 201–19. In May 1997, the United States Department of Labor issued guidance on this issue. *See* U.S. Department of Labor, *Department of Labor Guidance: How Workplace Laws Apply to Welfare Recipients,* 1997 DAILY LAB. REP. (BNA) No. 103, at E-3 (May 29, 1997). In the Guidance, the Department of Labor states that "the minimum wage and other FLSA requirements apply to welfare recipients as they apply to all other workers . . . if welfare recipients are 'employees' under the FLSA's broad definition, they must be compensated at the applicable minimum wage." *Id.* The Department has acknowledged that this language constitutes merely a restatement of the prevailing decisional authority evaluating whether a worker is an employee for FLSA purposes, and that the answer to this question is dependent upon the facts of each particular situation. *Id.*

244. The only decision to date to consider the question of the application of the FLSA to workfare participants is that rendered by the Tenth Circuit Court of Appeals in Johns v. Stewart, 57 F.3d 1544 (10th Cir. 1995). In that case, welfare beneficiaries participating in a workfare program contended that they were unlawfully compensated below the minimum wage for the hours they worked in the program. *Id.* at 1551. Applying the economic realities test, the *Johns* court noted the express purpose of the program and the differences between the working conditions of workfare participants and those of state employees—that is, salary, job security, career development potential, pension rights, Social Security and collective bargaining—and concluded that workfare does not qualify as

employment under the FLSA. *Id.* at 1558. In reaching this determination, however, the Tenth Circuit expressly stated that it was denying the plaintiffs employee status despite the fact that they were doing precisely the same work as the state employees they were working with. *Id.* at 1559.

There is also a long-recognized exception to the FLSA for work done as part of a training program for full employment. *See* Walling v. Portland Terminal Co., 330 U.S. 148 (1947). The U.S. Department of Labor has published guidelines that delineate the requirements that must be met in order for the work to be exempt from coverage as a training program. *See* U.S. DEPT. OF LABOR WAGE & HOUR MANUAL (BNA) 91:416 (1975). Courts applying these guidelines have deemed work activities in training programs exempt when the programs were clearly connected to specific job placement. *See, e.g.,* Walling v. Portland Terminal Co., 330 U.S. 148 (1947) (railroad yard brakemen); Reich v. Parker Fire Protection Dist., 992 F.2d 1023 (10th Cir. 1993) (firefighters); Donovan v. American Airlines, Inc., 686 F.2d 267 (5th Cir. 1982) (flight attendants). In light of the deference given by courts to the Department of Labor analysis, (*see* Craig L. Briskin & Kimberly A. Thomas, *The Waging of Welfare: All Work and No Pay?*, 33 HARV. C.R.-C.L. L. REV. 559, 573 (1998) [hereinafter *The Waging of Welfare*], it seems unlikely that courts will find the training exemption applicable to the work activities of workfare participants. *See* Archie v. Grand Central Partnership, Inc., 997 F. Supp. 504 (S.D.N.Y. 1998) (holding that an organization that employed homeless individuals through a contract with New York City could not pay its workers subminimum wages because the program did not focus on training and operated to the direct benefit of the employers). The *Archie* court's conclusion is further bolstered by the Supreme Court decision holding that there is a presumption of FLSA coverage when there is contemplated compensation, even if that compensation takes the form of in-kind benefits. *See* Tony & Susan Alamo Foundation v. Secretary of Labor, 471 U.S. 290, 301, 303–04 (1985).

245. While current federal law is silent as to whether the minimum wage is a required benchmark for welfare beneficiaries participating in workfare programs, [*see* Joel F. Handler, *"Ending Welfare As We Know It"—Wrong for Welfare, Wrong for Poverty,* 2 GEO. J. ON FIGHTING POVERTY 3, 29 (1994)], some states have prevailing wage statutes that permit workers to work off their benefits at the prevailing wage for the work they are performing. However, in many cases prevailing wage laws are disregarded, and as a result, such workers receive the minimum wage (or significantly less) despite their performance of work identical to that of union workers who are often paid 2 to 6 times the minimum wage. *See The Waging of Welfare supra* note 244, at 566 n.40.

246. *See The Waging of Welfare, supra* note 244, at 577.

247. *See The Waging of Welfare, supra* note 244 at 578.

248. *See, e.g.,* NLRB v. Chinatown Planning Council, 875 F.2d 395 (2d Cir. 1989) (holding that Chinese immigrants participating in a training program which taught "job skills" while providing counseling services to participants, were employees under the NLRA given that the employer provided periodic raises, paid social security and other taxes, and provided workers' compensation coverage). *But see* Arkansas Lighthouse for the Blind v. NLRB, 851 F.2d 180 (8th Cir. 1988) (finding that the NLRB erred in determining that blind workers employed in work training program were "employees" under the Act because the workers

were in a "rehabilitative relationship" with their employer and therefore exempt from coverage under the NLRA); *see also* Davis Memorial Goodwill Indus. v. NLRB, 108 F.3d 406, 410 (D.C. Cir. 1997) (stating that "the ultimate purpose of a rehabilitative job training program is to place participants in jobs elsewhere").

249. *See* The 1998 Hotel Employees and Restaurant Employees Local 11 collective bargaining agreement with six Los Angeles hotels (on file with the author). *See also The Waging of Welfare, supra* note 244, at 577.

250. *See, e.g.,* Allen v. New York, 554 N.Y.S.2d 789, 791 (1990) (holding that a workfare participant working for a municipal agency as a condition of receiving aid is an "employee" within the meaning of the workers' compensation law because the municipality receives the benefit of his or her labor); Polk County v. Steinbach, 374 N.W.2d 250 (Iowa 1985) (finding eligibility for workers' compensation benefits for a recipient of rent vouchers who was injured in a workfare program); Scissons v. City of Rapid City, 251 N.W.2d 681, 687 (S.D. 1977) (finding "no sound reason for discriminating against a poor relief worker who may be injured while working shoulder to shoulder with a regular county employee who would be entitled to benefits or even a volunteer who might be").

251. 42 U.S.C. §§ 2000e–2000e-17.

252. 42 U.S.C. §§ 2000d–2000d-7.

253. 42 U.S.C. § 2000d-3.

254. 42 U.S.C. § 12110.

255. *See, e.g.,* N.Y. EXEC. LAW § 296(1)(a); N.Y.C. ADMIN. CODE § 8-107 1(a); 18 NEW YORK CODE RULES & REGULATIONS § 303.3 (prohibiting discrimination on the basis of race, color, national origin, age, sex, religion, or handicap in the selection of participants for community work and training programs, in rates and forms of compensation, and all other treatment of participants).

256. 15 U.S.C. §§ 2601–2692.

257. 42 U.S.C. §§ 6971–6992k.

258. *See* 42 U.S.C. § 6972(a)(1)(B).

259. *See* 15 U.S.C. § 2619(a).

260. *See* 42 U.S.C. § 6972.

261. For the period from 1970 through 1994, OSHA referred ninety-five cases to the U.S. Department of Justice for criminal prosecution; of these, there were twenty-three convictions and one settlement. Only two employers served any jail time for their conduct. Rhinehart, *Workplace Safety Enforcement, supra* note 8, at 359.

262. *See* Rhinehart, *Workplace Safety Enforcement, supra* note 8, at 390 n.47. States that operate their own OSHA programs may enact criminal penalty provisions that are stronger than those of the OSH Act.

263. 29 U.S.C. § 666(e).

264. 29 U.S.C. § 666(f).

265. 29 U.S.C. § 666(g).

266. *See* United States v. Ladish Malting Co., 135 F.3d 484, 491–92 (7th Cir. 1998).

267. *See* United States v. Cusack, 806 F. Supp. 47, 49 (D.N.J. 1992) ("[A]n officer's or director's role in a corporate entity (particularly a small one) may be so pervasive and total that the officer or director is in fact the corporation and is therefore an employer").

268. *See, e.g.*, United States v. Shear, 962 F.2d 488 (5th Cir. 1992) (holding construction company superintendent not liable under the OSH Act); United States v. Doig, 950 F.2d 411 (7th Cir. 1991) (holding project manager not liable under the OSH Act for the death of three workers in an explosion resulting from failure to comply with regulations because he was "not a corporate officer, and thus not an employer"). The Seventh Circuit in *Doig* also noted that its ruling did not foreclose the possibility of "state law liability for an employee whose recklessness or criminal negligence causes the death of a co-worker." *Id.* at 414.

269. United States v. Dye Constr. Co., 510 F.2d 78, 81 (10th Cir. 1975).

270. *See* Rhinehart, *Workplace Safety Enforcement, supra* note 8, at 356–57. In 1992, OSHA issued fewer than 800 citations for willful violations. 22 O.S.H. REP. (BNA) 1454 (Jan. 20, 1993); 22 O.S.H. REP. (BNA) 1572 (Jan. 27, 1993).

271. *See, e.g.*, United States v. Mickey, 22 O.S.H. REP. (BNA) 1969 (N.D. Ohio 1993) (sentencing).

272. 42 U.S.C. § 6928(e) (1988).

273. 33 U.S.C. § 1319(c)(3)(A) (1988).

274. 42 U.S.C. § 6928(e) (1988). One commentator has suggested that the elements of the crime of knowing endangerment are as follows:

1. the defendant must violate one of the RCRA sections that are enumerated in the knowing endangerment provision;
2. the defendant must "know" that he has committed a predicate offense;
3. the predicate offense must expose another person to a high risk of physical injury; and
4. the defendant must "know" that he has created the proscribed risk of injury.

Robert G. Schwartz, Jr., *Criminalizing Occupational Safety Violations: The Use of "Knowing Endangerment" Statutes to Punish Employers Who Maintain Toxic Working Conditions*, 14 HARV. ENVTL. L. REV. 487, 495 (1990).

Predicate offenses that would trigger the protections of the knowing endangerment provision under RCRA include:

a) treating, storing, or disposing of any listed hazardous waste without a valid permit or violation of a permit condition or regulation;
b) making any false material statement or omitting material information in any relevant document;
c) altering, concealing, or failing to file any documentation required for RCRA compliance;
d) transporting any listed hazardous waste without a proper manifest; and
e) exporting a listed hazardous waste without the consent of the receiving country or in violation of an international agreement between the United States and the receiving country.

See 42 U.S.C. §§ 6928(d)(2)–(6).

275. *See* Rhinehart, *Workplace Safety Enforcement, supra* note 8, at 363–64.

276. 42 U.S.C. § 6928(e).

277. *See, e.g.*, United States v. Tumin, 19 ENV'T REP. (BNA) 1252 (E.D.N.Y. Oct. 28, 1988) (defendant sentenced to two years for his conviction of two felonies for the illegal disposal of ethyl ether drums in a densely populated

neighborhood on Long Island); United States v. Protex Industries, 874 F.2d 740 (10th Cir. 1989) (upholding conviction and $7.63 million criminal penalty imposed on company for knowingly exposing its employees to pesticide residues and solvents that caused central nervous system disorders); United States v. Metro Container Corp., No. 90-359 (E.D. Pa. June 17,1992), *reprinted in* U.S. ENVIRONMENTAL PROTECTION AGENCY, SUMMARY OF CRIMINAL PROSECUTIONS RESULTING FROM ENVIRONMENTAL INVESTIGATIONS 145 (1992) (conviction of supervisor and corporate officers for knowing endangerment in violation of RCRA). Other prosecutions resulted in acquittal. *See, e.g.*, United States v. Gershon, No. 89- 20074-01 (D. Kan. 1989), *reprinted in* U.S. ENVIRONMENTAL PROTECTION AGENCY, SUMMARY OF CRIMINAL PROSECUTIONS RESULTING FROM ENVIRONMENTAL INVESTIGATIONS 119 (1992) (indictment against company owner for knowingly endangering three employees by unlawfully disposing of hazardous waste dismissed in exchange for guilty pleas on other charges).

278. Only in United States v. Protex Industries, 874 F.2d 740 (10th Cir. 1989), was the issue of a company's knowing endangerment of its employees before the court.

279. 33 U.S.C. § 1319(c)(3). Predicate offenses that trigger the protections of the CWA knowing endangerment provision include:

a) discharge of any listed pollutant into navigable waters that is not in compliance with the Act;
b) violation of any established effluent limitation or water quality standard;
c) failure to maintain records required by the EPA Administrator;
d) violation of discharge permit conditions with regard to specific pollutants in connection with an aquaculture project;
e) discharge of sewage sludge from waste treatment facilities in violation of established standards; and
f) violation of any permit condition or limitation.

See 33 U.S.C. §§ 1311(a), 1312, 1313, 1316, 1317, 1318, 1328, 1345, and 1319(c)(3)(A), respectively.

280. *See, e.g.*, United States v. Borowski, 977 F.2d 27 (1st Cir. 1992) (reversing conviction of factory owner who directed employees to empty nickel plating and nitric acid baths into sinks thereby exposing them to nickel vapor); United States v. Rutana, 932 F.2d 1155 (6th Cir.), *cert. denied*, 112 S. Ct. 300 (1991) (defendant indicted for knowingly endangering wastewater treatment plant workers by disposing of substances that ultimately burned workers during sampling); United States v. Villegas, 784 F. Supp. 6 (E.D.N.Y. 1991), *aff'd*, 1993 U.S. App. LEXIS 22414 (2d Cir. Sept. 1, 1993) (defendant convicted under CWA's knowing endangerment provision for discarding glass vials containing human blood contaminated with the hepatitis B virus on the beach).

281. 977 F.2d 27 (1st Cir. 1992).

282. *Borowski*, 977 F.2d at 29.

283. *Borowski*, 977 F.2d at 30.

284. *Borowski*, 977 F.2d at 29–30. The First Circuit also noted that the CWA was not intended to protect worker exposure to harmful substances, but rather the nation's water. *Id.* at 30.

285. 42 U.S.C. § 6928(f)(3); 33 U.S.C. § 1319 (c)(3)(B)(ii).

286. *See* United States v. Hayes Int'l Corp., 786 F.2d 1499, 1505-06 (11th Cir. 1986).

287. Until recently, the question of OSH Act preemption of state criminal prosecutions seemed definitively settled given the holding in People v. Chicago Magnet Wire Corp., 534 N.E.2d 962 (Ill.), *cert. denied,* 493 U.S. 809 (1989) that the Act did not preempt state criminal prosecution of corporate officials even though their conduct was regulated by a federal safety and health standard. *See also* Sabine Consolidated, Inc. v. Texas, 756 S.W.2d 865 (Tex. Ct. App. 1988), *rev'd,* 806 S.W.2d 553 (Tex. Crim. App. 1991), *cert. denied,* 113 S. Ct. 364 (1992) (holding that state criminal prosecution of construction company president was not preempted). However, some commentators have noted that this proposition could be called into question by the recent Supreme Court decision in Gade v. National Solid Wastes Management Ass'n, 505 U.S. 88, 112 S. Ct. 2374, 2388 (1992), which held that state standards that "directly, substantially, and specifically regulate" an occupational safety and health issue for which there exists a federal standard are preempted by the OSH Act even if they are intended to protect the general public as well. Given the purposes behind criminal statutes and the fact that workers must be entitled to the same protections as those afforded other members of the general public, such an extension of the preemption doctrine seems unlikely. *See* Amelia Jean Uelmen, *Trashing State Criminal Sanctions?: OSHA Preemption Jurisprudence in Light of Gade v. National Solid Wastes Management Association,* 30 AM. CRIM. L. REV. 373, 409–11 (1993).

288. 151 A.D.2d 133, 546 N.Y.S.2d 871 (2d Dept. 1989), *aff'd,* 76 N.Y.2d 511, 563 N.E.2d 1990, *cert. denied,* 498 U.S. 105 (1991).

289. HOUSE COMM. GOV'T. OPERATIONS, GETTING AWAY WITH MURDER IN THE WORKPLACE: OSHA'S NONUSE OF CRIMINAL PENALTIES FOR SAFETY VIOLATIONS, at 4 (Oct. 4, 1988).

290. *Id.* at 6.

291. 126 Ill. 2d 356, 534 N.E.2d 962, *cert. denied sub nom.* Asta v. Illinois, 493 U.S. 809 (1989).

292. Nos. 4-C-5064 & 83-C-11091 (Cir. Ct. Cook County, Ill. June 14, 1985), *rev'd and remanded,* 550 N.E.2d 1090 (Ill. App. 1990) (holding judgments rendered illegally inconsistent). *See also* Sabine Consolidated, Inc. v. State, 756 S.W.2d 865 (Tex. Ct. App. 1988), *rev'd,* 806 S.W.2d 553 (Tex. Crim. App. 1991), *cert. denied,* 113 S. Ct. 364 (1992) (indicting construction company president for criminally negligent homicide when two employees were killed when walls of trench collapsed); People v. Hegedus, 425 N.W.2d 729 (Mich. Ct. App. 1988), *rev'd,* 443 N.W.2d 127 (Mich. 1989) (indicting employer for involuntary manslaughter after an employee died of carbon monoxide poisoning when a loose exhaust pipe leaked gas into company van).

293. The evidence introduced in the case showed that the managers knew of the hazards of cyanide and had ignored the recommendation that a ventilation system be installed. Moreover, when officer workers became ill from the fumes, they were moved to another building; in contrast, vat workers were required to work in the silver recovery area where large vats of cyanide were located. When the worker went into convulsions after repeated exposure to cyanide fumes, no antidote was administered. Despite the overwhelming evi-

dence, the convictions were reversed on appeal. People v. O'Neill, 550 N.E.2d 1090 (Ap. Ct. 1st Dist. 1990) (holding that defendants could not be held responsible for intentional and unintentional conduct [murder and reckless conduct] at the same time).

294. CAL. LAB. CODE § 6425 provides that it is a misdemeanor to violate willfully an OSHA regulation when the violation results in death or permanent or prolonged impairment. CAL. LAB. CODE § 6423(a) makes it a misdemeanor to violate a Cal-OSHA regulation knowingly or negligently, when that violation is serious. Under these sections, any individual that exercises responsibility, management, custody, or control of the workplace can be charged with a misdemeanor in addition to the corporate employer.

295. *See* Ira Reiner & Jan Chatten-Brown, *When It Is Not an Accident, But a Crime: Prosecutors Get Tough with OSHA Violations,* 17 N. KY. L. REV. 83, 96 (1989) [hereinafter Reiner & Chatten-Brown]. According to Reiner, only six of the twenty-seven cases did not involve fatalities. In a number of cases in which workers died, defendants entered pleas of nolo contendere to charges of involuntary manslaughter, and were sentenced to 60 to 90 days in county jail with a probation condition requiring the implementation of a comprehensive accident prevention plan. *Id. See, e.g.,* People v. Maggio, No. A780779 (Mar. 26, 1986); People v. Gonterman, No. A91972 (July 21, 1987).

296. *See* Reiner & Jan Chatten-Brown, *supra* note 295, at 98. *See, e.g.,* People v. Golden State Foods, No. 31386211 (June 11, 1985) (prosecution for violation of California lockout requirements, intended to prevent machine operation during cleaning, which resulted in death of an individual who was caught in a meat grinder).

297. During the first five years of the Los Angeles County OSHA program, only two such prosecutions were brought; one against the Dial Corporation for a chlorine gas leak that resulted in the hospitalization of more than eighty people, People v. Dial Corp., No. 87-M00849 (Feb. 21, 1986), and the other against Federated-Weiner Metals, Inc. for lead exposure. People v. Federated-Weiner Metals, No. 89M06086 (May 23, 1989).

CHAPTER 21

Protecting Citizens of Other Countries

JEFFREY B. GRACER

The domestic environmental justice movement seeks to promote decisions based not only on sound environmental criteria, but also on the social impacts of projects on poor and minority communities. A parallel movement is taking place on the international front, where "sustainable development" is increasingly understood to include a distinctly local emphasis on community acceptance and social sustainability. Poor and indigenous communities around the world are participating in the review, approval, and monitoring of international projects at an unprecedented level, often with the assistance of international environmental justice and human rights advocates. Just as the domestic environmental justice movement is requiring project proponents to consider and address broader civil rights concerns, the international environmental justice movement is promoting consideration of social issues and human rights concerns in conjunction with traditional environmental issues raised by major projects.

Unlike the domestic arena, where the EPA has created a specialized environmental justice complaint procedure, international advocates do not have recourse to a single, well-defined forum for resolving environmental justice claims. However, as is set forth below, environmental justice advocates have access to review panels created by international treaties and multilateral institutions, as well as the U.S. courts.[1]

Citizen Submissions Under NAFTA's Environmental Side Agreement

The citizen submission process created by the North American Agreement on Environmental Cooperation (the Environmental Side Agreement, or Agreement) provides advocates in the United States, Canada, and Mexico with an important avenue for raising environmental justice concerns.[2]

When the United States, Canada, and Mexico (the Parties) entered into the North American Free Trade Agreement (NAFTA) in 1992, they hailed it as the first trade agreement to link environmental protection explicitly with economic development.[3] That link was made only in NAFTA's preamble, however, and the agreement itself did not contain enforceable environmental commitments. As a result, many environmental organizations and community advocates opposed NAFTA's ratification, fearing it would result in a "race to the bottom" for environmental compliance and enforcement.

The ensuing debate on NAFTA ratification focused on the extensive environmental problems that have long impacted poor and indigenous communities on both sides of the U.S.–Mexican border, along with heightened concern that such impacts would intensify with increased trade arising from NAFTA. The potential adverse impacts at the center of the debate are quintessential environmental justice issues, including community impacts arising from illegal disposal of hazardous waste, discharge of untreated sewage and industrial wastewater, and air pollution.[4] The appearance of several cancer clusters in border communities lent particular immediacy to the debate. A report issued by the Clinton administration in 1993 recognized that "there are serious environmental problems in North America, particularly along the U.S.–Mexican border, that must be addressed in the context of expanded trade."[5]

The Environmental Side Agreement was conceived, negotiated, and executed by the Clinton administration in an attempt to address these concerns and to secure ratification of NAFTA.[6] The Agreement, which became effective on January 1, 1994, provides a unique international forum for individuals and organizations to allege that a governmental Party to NAFTA is failing to "effectively enforce" its environmental laws.[7] The term "environmental law" is defined broadly to include any statute or regulation whose primary purpose is prevention of danger to human life or health (other than those related directly to worker safety or health).[8] The Agreement does not by its terms encompass broader social justice concerns. However, it provides an avenue for communities to raise such concerns if they stem from an alleged failure to enforce an environmental law effectively.

The Commission for Environmental Cooperation (CEC), based in Montreal, administers the Environmental Side Agreement through a ministerial-level Council and a staff-level Secretariat.[9] The Council consists of the Ministers of the Environment of Canada and Mexico and the EPA administrator.[10] The Secretariat consists of an executive director and other professional staff.[11] In addition to providing technical, administrative, and operational support to the Council, the Secretariat has certain "special responsibilities," including authority to administer citizen submissions and to make recommendations to the Council regarding such submissions.

Article 14 of the Environmental Side Agreement governs citizen submissions asserting that a governmental Party has failed to enforce its environmental laws effectively.[12] The submission can be made by any nongovernmental organization (NGO) or by any person established or residing in the territory of a Party.[13] It must specifically identify the applicable environmental statutes or regulations at issue, include a succinct account of the underlying facts, establish that the matter has been communicated in writing to the relevant authorities of the Party in question, and indicate the Party's response, if any.[14] The submission must "appear to be aimed at promoting enforcement rather than harassing industry."[15] According to CEC Guidelines, the Secretariat determines whether this last requirement is met based on whether the submission focuses on the acts and omissions of a Party (as opposed to noncompliance by a particular company), whether the submission appears to be frivolous, and whether it is filed by competitors.[16] The Secretariat can terminate the process if it determines that the criteria for a proper submission are not met.[17]

If a submission is accepted, the Secretariat next determines whether the submission warrants a response from the Party at issue. That determination is based on:

1. whether the submission alleges harm that relates to the protection of the environment or the prevention of danger to human life or health (but not directly to worker safety or health);[18] and
2. whether the alleged harm "is due to" a Party's alleged failure to enforce an environmental law effectively.[19]

The Secretariat can terminate the process if it determines that no Party response is required.[20]

If the Secretariat requests a Party response, the Party must indicate:

1. whether the matter is the subject of pending (or prior) judicial or administrative proceedings;

2. whether private remedies have been pursued; and
3. whether environmental policies have been defined or actions taken in connection with the matter at issue.[21]

If the matter is the subject of a pending judicial or administrative proceeding, the Secretariat must terminate the process.[22]

Article 15 of the Environmental Side Agreement permits development of a Factual Record at the conclusion of the submission process established under Article 14.[23] If the Secretariat determines that development of a Factual Record is warranted, it must seek Council approval before it can proceed further.[24] If the Council determines by a two-thirds vote that a Factual Record is warranted, the Secretariat prepares the record. In doing so, the Secretariat may consider publicly available information, as well as information provided by a Party, citizen, or NGO.[25] The Secretariat also may develop its own information, and may rely on information developed by independent experts. Once finalized, the Factual Record consists of a summary of the submission, a summary of the response, a summary of other relevant factual information, facts presented by the Secretariat, and (as appropriate) Party comments.[26] The Council can authorize release of the Factual Record to the complainant and the public by a two-thirds vote.[27]

The effectiveness of the citizen submission process under the Environmental Side Agreement is the subject of continuing debate. Critics of the Agreement claim that it has not secured environmental improvement, and that environmental conditions, particularly along the U.S.–Mexican border, have deteriorated as a result of NAFTA's ratification.[28] A specific criticism focuses on the failure of the citizen submission process to result in effective corrective actions. The citizen submission process is not a trial type of adversarial process. Even if a Factual Record is developed, "no judgment is reached as to whether a Party has or has not effectively enforced its environmental law(s)."[29] A Factual Record's conclusions could lead one governmental Party to request formal consultation with another Party under Article 22 of the Environmental Side Agreement to address "whether there has been a persistent pattern of failure by that other Party to effectively enforce its environmental law."[30] A Factual Record also could cause a Party to initiate formal dispute resolution procedures under Part V of the Agreement.[31] However, the power to secure a concrete remedy resides with the governmental Parties. If the Parties do not act, the final result of the citizen submission process could be a Factual Record without any corresponding corrective actions.

Despite these limitations, an independent review panel recently concluded that the Environmental Side Agreement's citizen submission process is working reasonably well, and that the Secretariat's decisions have been objective, professional, and appropriate.[32] The process "provides some 350 million pairs of eyes to alert the Council of any 'race to the bottom' through lax environmental enforcement."[33] It also "empowers citizens, acting individually or through representatives groups, to initiate an international process."[34]

To date, the Environmental Side Agreement has not been explicitly utilized to promote the international environmental justice agenda. Submissions have been filed against each of the governmental Parties, including the United States. Some of these submissions have raised implicit environmental justice concerns. For example, one submission made by indigenous groups alleges that Canada has improperly permitted the destruction of native fish habitats.[35] Another submission alleges that Mexico has failed to require treatment of wastewater prior to its discharge into the Magdalena River, with resulting impacts on the surrounding community.[36] As environmental advocates gain experience with the Agreement's citizen submission process, it is reasonable to expect explicit integration of environmental justice issues into future submissions.

In addition to the above, Article 6 of the Environmental Side Agreement (entitled "Private Access to Remedies") requires each governmental Party to "ensure that interested persons may request the Party's competent authorities to investigate alleged violations of its environmental laws and regulations," and to "give such requests due consideration in accordance with law."[37] It also requires each governmental Party to "ensure that persons with a legally recognized interest under its law in a particular matter have appropriate access to administrative, quasi-judicial, or judicial proceedings for the enforcement of the Party's environmental laws and regulations."[38] Environmental advocates who feel that they have been denied access to remedies within their own country could allege that a governmental Party has violated this provision as well.

The Border Environmental Cooperation Agreement

In addition to NAFTA's Environmental Side Agreement, environmental issues along the 2,000 mile U.S.–Mexican border are impacted, as well, by the 1983 Agreement Between the United States of America and the United Mexican States on Cooperation for the Protection and Improvement of the Environment in the Border Area (the La Paz Agreement).[39] This bilateral Agreement provides a framework for cooperation between the United States and Mexico on border environmental issues. Annexes to the agreement address cross-border sewage impacts, joint responses to hazardous substance releases, transboundary shipment of hazardous waste, air emissions from copper smelters operating in the border area, and urban air pollution in border cities. In 1992, the environmental authorities of both governments issued an Integrated Environmental Plan for the Mexican–U.S. Border Area.[40]

Thereafter, a Border XXI Program was created by the United States and Mexico "to achieve a clean environment, protect public health and natural resources, and encourage sustainable development."[41] Nine binational workgroups have been formed to address:

1. water;
2. air;
3. hazardous and solid waste;
4. pollution prevention;
5. contingency planning and emergency response;
6. cooperative enforcement and compliance;
7. environmental information resources;
8. natural resources; and
9. environmental health.

Although a separate environmental justice workgroup has not been formed, many of the existing workgroups are addressing issues that encompass environmental justice concerns. It is reasonable to expect that such concerns will be integrated into the Border XXI framework. Indeed, disputes regarding the siting of controversial projects within the border area (including a low-level radioactive waste disposal facility) have explicitly raised environmental justice concerns.[42]

Citizen Submissions to the World Bank's Inspection Panel

In response to a campaign led by international NGOs, the World Bank Group (the Bank, or World Bank) established an independent Inspection Panel (Panel) in 1993 to provide a forum for citizens who believe their interests have been harmed by Bank-financed projects. The process applies only to projects funded by the International Bank for Reconstruction and Development (IBRD) and the International Development Association (IDA). The Panel receives and investigates complaints that such projects are materially harming communities based on the Bank's alleged failure to follow its own policies and procedures (including failure to enforce loan agreement requirements arising from such policies and procedures).

The Bank has formulated and issued several policies and procedures that are designed to protect against environmental and social injustices incident to Bank-financed projects. These policies and procedures address Involuntary Resettlement (Operational Directive [OD]

4.30), Indigenous Peoples (OD 4.20), Cultural Properties (OPN 11.03), Wildlands (OP 11.02), Involvement of NGOs in Bank-Supported Activities (OD 14.70), Environmental Assessment (OD 4.01), Environmental Aspects of Bank Work (OMS 2.36), Dam and Reservoir Projects (OD 4.00, Annex B), Forestry Projects (OD 4.36), Project Monitoring and Evaluation (OD 10.70), Project Supervision (OD 13.05), and Suspension of Disbursements (OD 13.40).

The Inspection Panel was created to promote compliance with these policies and procedures in connection with the design, appraisal, and/or implementation of Bank projects.[43] It consists of three members appointed by the Bank's Board of Executive Directors (the Board). Panel members are selected based on professional qualifications, knowledge, and experience, as well as independence from Bank operations.

The Panel's Operating Procedures govern citizen submissions.[44] A Request for Inspection (Request) can be filed by any group of two or more people in the country where the project is located; by a duly appointed local representative (or a foreign representative if no local representative is available); or by a Board member (collectively, a Requester).[45] In addition to describing the project at issue, the Request must identify acts or omissions by the Bank that are alleged to violate Bank policies, procedures, or contractual documents; indicate how the violation harms the complaining party; discuss steps taken to resolve the alleged violations with Bank staff; and explain why the Bank's response was inadequate.[46]

Upon receipt, the Panel reviews the Request and may ask for additional information.[47] If the Request was filed by an eligible party and is not "manifestly outside" the Panel's mandate, the Panel registers the Request.[48] Once registered, the Bank's management must provide a response.[49]

If the Panel is not satisfied that management has followed, or is taking adequate steps to follow, Bank policies and procedures, the Panel conducts a preliminary review. This review determines whether "the complaint is *prima facie* justified and warrants a full investigation."[50] At the Chair's request, a Panel member may conduct a preliminary study to assist in that determination.[51]

Based on its Preliminary Review, the Panel makes a recommendation to the Board about whether a full investigation is warranted.[52] If the Panel determines that management has "dealt appropriately with the subject matter" and has "demonstrated clearly" that it has followed required Bank policies and procedures, it will not recommend an investigation.[53] Similarly, if management admits that it has failed to follow required policies and procedures, but sets forth a specific remedial action plan with implementation timetables, the Panel may choose not to recommend an investigation.[54]

If the Panel recommends an investigation, that recommendation must be approved by the Bank's Board.[55] If the Board authorizes an investigation, the Panel can convene meetings with stakeholders, hold public hearings in the project area, conduct on-site project visits, receive oral and written submissions, and obtain input from independent consultants.[56] The Requester can participate in the investigation by submitting supplemental information.[57] The Panel may discuss its preliminary findings with the Requester "to facilitate understanding of specific points," but is not required to do so.[58] Any member of the public also may provide the Panel with supplemental information.[59]

The Panel's investigation culminates in a report submitted to the Bank's Board.[60] Each report must include a summary of the investigation and pertinent facts, along with the Panel's findings and conclusions regarding compliance with Bank policies and procedures.[61] The Bank's Management then has an opportunity to respond to the report and to submit its recommendations to the Board.[62] Thereafter, the Board determines whether any action should be taken and, if so, what that action should be.[63] The Panel's report, management's recommendations, and the Board's decision are provided to the Requester and are made publicly available.[64]

The creation of the Inspection Panel was widely viewed as a major advance. Its record has been somewhat more controversial. There is evidence that the Panel has affected Bank decisions in certain cases. For example, as a result of a Panel recommendation to conduct a full investigation of alleged violations of Bank policies in connection with a proposed hydroelectric dam project in Nepal, Bank management withdrew its support for the project.[65] A Panel recommendation for a full investigation of a natural resources management project in Brazil led to a management plan of action that was subject to continued Panel oversight.[66] The Panel later issued a report finding "mixed results," but recommended continued Bank involvement in the project based on input from "locally affected people."[67]

Perhaps the most controversial issue presented to the Panel thus far was a Request from a Chilean NGO alleging that the International Finance Corporation (IFC) had violated several IFC and World Bank policies in connection with its support of the Pangue hydroelectric project on the upper Bio Bio River.[68] The Inspection Panel concluded that its mandate was strictly limited to review of projects funded by the IBRD and the IDA, and that it did not have jurisdiction over projects financed by the IFC. Accordingly, it rejected the submission.[69] Advocates have argued that the Inspection Panel's jurisdiction should extend to all members of the World Bank Group, including the IFC.

The Pangue submission raised several significant environmental justice concerns. Among other things, the Requesters alleged that the IFC and private developers had violated the human rights of an indigenous people, the Pehuenche, who lived in the project area and were relocated from their tribal lands. The Pehuenche have been described as the last Chilean indigenous group to live by traditional means on traditional lands.[70] Critics charge that secret covenants were negotiated without the knowledge or participation of the Pehuenche or the government authorities responsible for indigenous affairs, that cumulative impacts of a related dam project (Ralco) were never considered, and that a report outlining these and other deficiencies was withheld from the Pehuenche. After the Inspection Panel decided it lacked jurisdiction over the dispute, the President of the World Bank commissioned an independent study by the President of the National Wildlife Federation. The full text of the resulting report was not released. According to advocates, it concluded that the IFC had failed to comply with several environmental and social directives in connection with the project.[71] The IFC has since adopted new social and environmental policy guidelines and has placed increased emphasis on these issues in connection with project review, approval, and implementation.[72]

For the moment, at least for projects funded by the IBRD or the IDA, indigenous groups and minority communities can utilize the Inspection Panel's procedures to promote environmental justice concerns. Private companies that receive financing from the IFC should anticipate continued scrutiny by NGOs and pressure to ensure that projects meet commitments made in loan documents and environmental mitigation plans.

Ex-Im and OPIC Environmental Reviews

As is the case with World Bank projects, an environmental review is required for most projects that receive assistance or guarantees from the Export-Import Bank of the United States (Ex-Im Bank, or Ex-Im) or the Overseas Private Investment Corporation (OPIC). Environmental justice advocates have begun to monitor submissions made to these agencies, and are submitting their own information regarding proposed projects.

The Ex-Im Bank is under a statutory mandate to ensure that its actions are environmentally responsible. Environmental review is required for any project seeking $10 million or more in long-term support where:

1. that support is "critical" to the project's implementation; and
2. the project "may have significant environmental effects upon the global commons or any country not participating in the

> project, or may produce an emission, an effluent, or a principal product that is prohibited or strictly regulated pursuant to Federal Environmental Law."[73]

Among other things, Ex-Im's procedures require a full-scale environmental review for projects that are located in or near areas reserved for ethnic minorities or indigenous peoples, and projects that will require large-scale resettlement.[74] The procedures explicitly require consideration of a proposed project's "socioeconomic and sociocultural effects" along with technical environmental concerns.[75] Proposed projects are posted on the Internet <www.exim.gov>. Interested parties can request copies of environmental materials submitted by a project proponent, and can submit their own materials to Ex-Im staff. This process does not confer legal standing to participate in Ex-Im's actual decision making or to appeal any resulting decisions. However, it does provide an opportunity to identify potential adverse impacts and influence the Ex-Im decisions.

OPIC is under a similar statutory mandate to consider the environmental effects of its decisions. It "shall . . . refuse to insure, reinsure, guarantee, or finance any investment in connection with a project which [OPIC] determines will pose an unreasonable or major environmental, health or safety hazard, or will result in the significant degradation of national parks or similar protected areas."[76] A full-scale environmental review is required for Category A projects, which include projects that will have significant impacts on "vulnerable population groups," involve "involuntary resettlement," or affect "cultural heritage sites."[77] Environmental and social aspects of a project are considered in an integrated fashion throughout the review process. Proposed Category A projects are posted on the Internet <www.opic.gov>. Interested parties can request a copy of the relevant environmental materials for a project, and submit their own comments and information. As is the case with Ex-Im, these procedures do not create a right to participate in OPIC's decision making. They do, however, provide an important opportunity for public consultation.

Companies that anticipate seeking financial assistance or guarantees from Ex-Im or OPIC should be prepared to address any potential environmental justice issues that may arise during the public comment period. They also should consult with Ex-Im or OPIC staff during initial scoping sessions to identify any environmental justice issues that might be of concern to staff.

Lawsuits in U.S. Courts Alleging Foreign Torts

Efforts by plaintiffs to litigate environmental claims arising from activities abroad have generally been dismissed by U.S. courts on forum non conveniens and comity grounds.[78] These decisions tend to presume that foreign courts are competent to adjudicate disputes arising within their national territories, including environmental disputes. However, when a corporate defendant is not amenable to suit in a foreign court, dismissal may be conditioned on voluntary submission to the jurisdiction of a foreign court.

In *Jota v. Texaco, Inc.*,[79] for example, several indigenous residents of the Oriente region of Ecuador sued Texaco in the Southern District of New York for environmental and personal injuries allegedly arising from exploration and development of Ecuador's oil fields between 1965 and 1992. Texaco, the only defendant in the US. lawsuit, was not amenable to suit in Ecuador. However, its fourth-level subsidiary (TexPet), which had conducted the actual operations in question, was amenable to suit, and was already involved in litigation in Ecuador. Texaco moved to dismiss the U.S. lawsuit on international comity and forum non conveniens grounds. After initially reserving decision, the District Court granted Texaco's motion in full.[80] The Second Circuit reversed, holding that it was an abuse of discretion for the District Court to dismiss the case "absent a commitment by Texaco to submit to the jurisdiction of the Ecuadorian courts for purposes of this action." The Second Circuit found it immaterial that TexPet was amenable to suit in Ecuador. Texaco was the only defendant in the lawsuit at hand. Unless Texaco voluntarily submitted to the jurisdiction of the Ecuadorian courts, there was no alternative forum available for the plaintiffs in their claim against Texaco.

The Texaco lawsuit underscores the need for great care by multinationals in their international operations. If a dispute arises regarding the operations of a foreign subsidiary, a parent corporation could find itself on the horns of a dilemma. It would either have to submit to the jurisdiction of a foreign court (where it otherwise might be beyond that court's reach) or litigate foreign claims in a U.S. court. A parent corporation could argue in a U.S. court that it is not legally responsible for the operations of its foreign subsidiaries under traditional corporate law doctrines of limited liability, but such arguments typically raise fact questions regarding whether the parent directly participated in liability-creating conduct, or whether there is a basis for piercing the corporate veil.

Foreign plaintiffs also can be expected to assert human rights claims under the Alien Tort Claims Act (ATCA), which vests federal district courts with original jurisdiction over "any civil action by an alien for a tort only, committed in violation of the law of nations or a treaty of the United States."[81] The federal courts have recognized that certain human rights violations (including state-sponsored torture, rape, murder, and disappearance) are violations of the law of nations and are thus actionable under the ATCA.[82] A plaintiff can assert a claim under the ATCA against a present or former governmental official who perpetrated or organized human rights violations under color of state law.[83] Plaintiffs also can sue private actors for a narrow class of human rights violations, such as slavery and genocide, even if the defendant did not engage in state action.[84]

Until recently, corporations were not typically named as defendants in ATCA cases. However, foreign plaintiffs are increasingly asserting ATCA claims against corporate defendants in connection with major international projects. In *John Doe v. Unocal Corp.*,[85] for example, farmers in rural Burma asserted ATCA claims against Unocal, alleging that the company conspired with the military government of Myanmar to commit human rights violations in furtherance of a gas pipeline project. The complaint alleged that the government enslaved farmers, utilized them as forced labor for the project, stole property and relocated entire villages, and engaged in systematic rape and torture.[86] The complaint further alleged that Unocal was aware of these violations, subsidized the government's activity, and perpetrated human rights abuses through its joint venture with the government. Unocal denied these allegations. Ruling on a motion to dismiss, the court held that such allegations were sufficient to establish, if true, that Unocal was jointly engaged in state action with the military government and was thus subject to suit under the ATCA.[87] The court also held that allegations of slavery through forced labor were actionable under the ATCA even if Unocal was not engaged in state action.

ATCA claims also were asserted in *Beanal v. Freeport-McMoran, Inc.*[88] in connection with a mining project in Indonesia, but those claims were ultimately dismissed. There, plaintiffs alleged that Freeport's private security forces committed torture and other human rights violations, including "cultural genocide," while forcibly relocating a tribe from the project area. Freeport denied these allegations. The court held that plaintiffs failed to allege that the claimed conduct of Freeport's private security forces constituted state action. It also held that plaintiffs' allegation of "cultural genocide" based on relocation from tribal lands did not state a claim for "genocide" as that term is defined under international law.

In *Beanal,* the court also rejected plaintiffs' argument that environmental damage arising from mining activity violated international law. Plaintiffs argued that broadly recognized principles requiring companies to prevent pollution and pay for its cleanup had been incorporated into customary international law, and that Freeport's alleged violation of these principles was actionable under the ATCA. The court disagreed, concluding that there was a lack of "universal consensus" regarding incorporation of nontreaty environmental principles into customary international law. The court also observed that any customary environmental principles would apply only to governments, and that the complaint pertained only to "corporate decisions, rather than state practices."[89] At least one court has suggested, however, that certain environmental violations might rise to the level of a violation of international law, and thus be actionable under the ATCA.[90]

U.S. courts have traditionally been reluctant to become the forum of choice for foreign plaintiffs, particularly in the environmental arena. Nonetheless, to the extent international environmental justice claims involve traditional human rights abuses, advocates can be expected to assert claims in U.S. courts under the ATCA. Under current case law, such claims could survive a motion to dismiss if plaintiffs make a compelling case that the courts of their own countries are effectively unavailable; the claims assert a very close connection between governmental human rights violations and corporate conduct; and the claims are premised on core human rights violations that are universally recognized under international law. As international environmental principles are more firmly incorporated into customary international law, or to the extent a complaint alleges a violation of a binding international environmental treaty, plaintiffs also may be able to assert environmental claims successfully under the ATCA.

Environmental Impact Review Under NEPA and Executive Order 12,114

The National Environmental Policy Act (NEPA) and its implementing regulations require preparation of an environmental impact statement (EIS) for all "major federal actions significantly affecting the environment,"[91] including "projects and programs entirely or partly financed, assisted, conducted, regulated, or approved by federal agencies."[92] (The domestic application of NEPA is discussed in Chapter 9, "Impact Assessment," pages 256–306).

Notwithstanding this apparently simple mandate, NEPA's applicability to decisions concerning federally funded projects abroad remains largely unsettled. Although NEPA directs federal agencies to "recognize the worldwide and long-range character of environmental problems,"[93] it does not expressly provide that its EIS requirements apply to federal actions that take place outside the United States. The U.S. Supreme Court has never decided the issue. Lower court decisions are highly fact-specific and of limited precedential value.

Initially, it was generally accepted that NEPA compliance was required whenever a foreign project could reasonably be expected to cause impacts in the United States. Thus, in *Sierra Club v. Adams*,[94] the D.C. Circuit held that an EIS was required for a highway project in Panama and Colombia because of the project's potential to spread disease to the United States. Similarly, in *National Organization for the Reform of Marijuana Laws (NORML) v. U.S. Dep't of State*,[95] a district court held that an EIS was required for a federally funded herbicide program to eradicate marijuana in Mexico because of anticipated health impacts in the United States.

In 1979, President Carter issued Executive Order 12,114 (Environmental Effects Abroad of Major Federal Actions), which explicitly requires federal agencies to consider the environmental impacts of actions "having significant effects on the environment outside the geographical borders of the United States."[96] The Executive Order states that countervailing policy considerations, such as national security, foreign relations, and international trade, can determine whether a federal agency must conduct a full environmental review for a foreign project, at least in specified cases. It also explicitly exempts entire categories of federal action from its requirements, including actions taken by the President; actions involving national security or armed conflict; intelligence activities and arms transfers; disaster and emergency relief; export licenses or permits or export approvals; certain actions related to nuclear activities; and votes and other actions taken in international organizations. The Executive Order also expressly provides that it does not create an enforceable cause of action.[97]

Although Executive Order 12,114 did not preempt NEPA, subsequent court decisions have implicitly deferred to the discretion it vests in federal agencies, and have been less willing to require strict compliance with NEPA for foreign projects, especially when countervailing policy concerns are present. Thus, in *Greenpeace USA v. Stone*,[98] a federal district court in Hawaii held that NEPA did not apply to munitions movements through Germany to the Johnston Atoll, based on political question and foreign policy considerations. This decision was consistent with other cases excusing federal agencies from NEPA's requirements when foreign policy interests were perceived to outweigh the benefits of an EIS.[99] The district court noted, however, that, "[i]n other circumstances, NEPA *may* require a federal agency to prepare an EIS for action taken abroad, especially where [the] United States agency's action abroad has direct environmental impacts within this country, or where there has clearly been a total lack of environmental assessment by the federal agency or foreign country involved.[100]

Opponents of NEPA's international reach cite the strong presumption against extraterritorial application of substantive federal law, and argue that NEPA does not explicitly apply to activity undertaken abroad.[101] Environmental groups assert, however, that federal agency decisions under NEPA are predominantly procedural in nature, and in any event are made in the United States. In *Environmental Defense Fund, Inc. v. Massey*,[102] the D.C. Circuit indicated that, because "NEPA is designed to regulate conduct occurring within the territory of the United States, and imposes no substantive requirements which could be interpreted to govern activity abroad, the presumption against extraterritoriality does not apply to this case."[103] It went on to hold that NEPA applied to the National Science Foundation's plan to incinerate waste food in Antarctica. That holding was premised, however, on the fact that Antarctica is not under the control of any sovereign state. The court expressly declined to decide "how NEPA might apply to actions in a case involving an actual foreign sovereign."[104] As a result, NEPA's application to federal agency decisions involving foreign projects in sovereign states remains unsettled. In *NEPA Coalition of Japan v. Aspin*,[105] for example, a federal district court held that NEPA did not apply to a decision involving a U.S. military base in Japan, citing foreign policy concerns.

As is discussed more fully in Chapter 9, EPA has adopted policies seeking to integrate environmental justice concerns into the NEPA review process. When major international projects receive federal funds, environmental justice advocates can be expected to argue that NEPA applies to federal agency decisions, that an EIS is required, and that the EIS should consider environmental justice concerns. It is difficult to predict given the current state of the law whether such arguments will ultimately be successful. While courts tend to afford substantial deference to federal agencies when they operate abroad, the outcome in any particular case will be far from clear, at least until the issue is decided by the Supreme Court. Accordingly, companies must remain attentive to potential NEPA arguments that might be raised by project opponents regarding international projects that receive federal funding. Ensuring that environmental impacts and environmental justice concerns are fully and fairly considered in connection with federally funded projects abroad will provide companies with substantial protection against possible adverse court rulings in the future.

Companies engaged in projects that could raise potential cross-border impacts among the NAFTA countries (Canada, Mexico, and the United States) also should be aware of an impending North American Agreement on Transboundary Environmental Impact Assessment. Article 10(7) of NAFTA's Environmental Side Agreement requires the CEC to develop recommendations for such an agreement. Once adopted, it will provide decision makers with timely information on the transboundary consequences of proposed projects, and provide a mechanism for potentially affected people and governments to participate in the review of such projects. As of September 1998, the Parties to the Environmental Side Agreement were negotiating a legally binding agreement that would govern the review of such projects.

Hazardous Waste Export

The improper disposal of hazardous wastes in developing countries has long been recognized as a core environmental justice concern. Among other things, such activity has been denounced as the "global poison trade" and "toxic imperialism."[106] Although existing law was designed to protect against indiscriminate foreign hazardous waste disposal by requiring prior notification and consent, EPA's enforcement authority is relatively narrow, and environmental justice advocates have few formal rights.

In response to several highly publicized events involving the dumping of waste abroad by U.S. companies, Congress amended the Resource Conservation and Recovery Act (RCRA) in 1984 to regulate hazardous waste exports.[107] Exporters must notify EPA of their intent to ship hazardous waste abroad at least 60 days prior to initial shipment.[108] Upon receipt, the EPA (in conjunction with the Secretary of State) transmits the notice to importing and transit countries.[109] Shipment cannot take place unless the importing country consents in writing to the export.[110] Consent is not required from a transit country, but in practice the EPA expects exporters to reroute shipments if an objection is received. Once the importing country's consent is received, the exporter is free to ship the waste but must comply with certain manifest, exception, and annual report requirements.[111] EPA has statutory authority to impose civil and criminal penalties of up to $50,000 per day for the export of hazardous waste to a receiving country without its prior consent or in violation of an international agreement between the United States and the receiving country.[112] However, it does not have authority to prevent the export of hazardous waste to a country that has consented to such export, even if the EPA has reason to believe that the waste will not be disposed of in an environmentally sound manner. The ability of environmental justice advocates to enforce EPA's waste export regulations has not been squarely decided at the appellate level. At least one federal district court has held that private plaintiffs cannot enforce RCRA's foreign export rules in federal court.[113]

In addition to EPA's waste export regulations, the United States has entered into bilateral agreements with Canada and Mexico that govern hazardous waste exports to those countries.[114] The United

States also is subject to a binding decision of the Organization for Economic Cooperation and Development (OECD) governing the export of waste for recovery in other OECD countries (which include the United States, most European countries, and Mexico).[115] The export of such waste is subject to special EPA regulation.[116] Export of waste to OECD countries for purposes other than recovery (such as incineration or disposal) is subject to general EPA waste export regulations.[117]

A company's ability to dispose of hazardous waste abroad also may be limited by the Basel Convention on the Control of Transboundary Movements of Hazardous Waste and Their Disposal (the Basel Convention).[118] The Convention entered into force in 1992 and has been ratified by approximately 122 countries. The United States is a signatory but has not yet ratified the treaty. The Senate has consented to ratification. Implementing legislation is expected to be introduced in the 1999 Congress.[119]

The Basel Convention prohibits the transboundary movement of hazardous waste between Parties and non-Parties unless there is a separate bilateral or multilateral agreement providing for the disposal of covered waste in an "environmentally sound manner."[120] Until the United States ratifies the Convention, countries that are Parties to the Convention are effectively precluded from accepting shipments of hazardous waste from U.S. companies, unless they have an "environmentally sound" waste export agreement with the United States.

The Basel Convention is more stringent than existing federal law in several significant respects. Among other things:

1. transit countries have the absolute right to reject a shipment of waste through their territory;
2. signatories can prohibit waste export if there is reason to believe the waste will not be managed in an "environmentally sound manner" within the importing country, even if the importing country consents; and
3. signatories have the power to compel the return of hazardous waste that is improperly disposed.[121]

It is expected that U.S. ratification of the Basel Convention will vest the EPA with broader authority to address these and other issues related to waste export.

Environmental advocates have focused their efforts on ratification of the so-called "Basel Ban," an amendment to the Convention that would ban waste exports from OECD countries to non-OECD countries. In February 1998, an agreement was reached at a conference of the Parties to modify the ban by prohibiting the export of certain high-risk wastes, while permitting the export of lower-risk wastes.[122] It remains to be seen whether this modified ban will be ratified. In addition to the Basel Ban, a resolution of the Organization of African Unity (OAU) bans member countries from accepting industrial waste products from abroad.[123]

Export of Pesticides and Industrial Chemicals

The export of pesticides and industrial chemicals also presents environmental justice concerns. Export of pesticides is governed by the Federal Insecticide, Fungicide and Rodenticide Act (FIFRA).[124] Export of chemicals is governed by the Toxic Substances Control Act (TSCA).[125]

FIFRA prohibits the distribution or sale of unregistered pesticides in the United States.[126] However, an unregistered pesticide can be exported if the foreign purchaser signs a written acknowledgment prior to export that it understands the pesticide is not registered and cannot be sold in the United States.[127] EPA regulations also impose recordkeeping, inspection, and annual reporting requirements for pesticide exports.[128]

Similarly, specified categories of chemical substances and mixtures are subject to TSCA's export notice provisions.[129] EPA maintains a list of chemicals and mixtures that are subject to export notification. An export notice must be filed with EPA within 7 days of export (or within 7 days of forming the intent to export).[130] EPA must then advise foreign governments of the shipments and indicate whether restrictions have been placed on the chemicals in the United States.[131]

Critics assert that the export notice provisions of FIFRA and TSCA are inadequate. In 1989, voluntary Prior Informed Consent (PIC) procedures were adopted by the Food and Agriculture Organization (FAO) and the United Nations Environment Programme (UNEP) to enable countries to ban the import of pesticides or chemicals that have been banned or severely restricted in another country. Under this system, when the EPA bans or severely restricts a pesticide or chemical through final regulatory action, it notifies the FAO, which in turn transmits notices of the action to participating countries. If a participating country indicates that it no longer wants to import the pesticide or chemical in question, the EPA notifies relevant U.S. industries of the action. Exporting industries, in turn, are expected to honor the decision of the importing countries.[132] In September 1998, this previously voluntary system was formalized in a Prior Informed Consent treaty.[133] Once the treaty is ratified and goes into effect, it will ban the export of pesticides and chemicals unless an importing country agrees to such exports.

EPA has imposed substantial fines for violations of FIFRA and TSCA export requirements. However, the right of private citizens to enforce existing export notification requirements is not well established. Companies that export pesticides and chemicals, particularly those that have been banned or restricted in the United States, should remain attentive to possible claims arising from environmental and health impacts that are felt abroad.

Voluntary Corporate Responses

In reaction to the Bhopal disaster and the Exxon Valdez oil spill, several industry groups and multinational corporations have formulated and adopted voluntary environmental policies and practices for the conduct of their business worldwide. These policies and practices have tended to focus on "traditional" environmental issues, such as emission standards and pollution prevention efforts. They have been less focused on formal integration of social concerns into corporate decision making.

As the environmental justice movement matures and takes on an increasingly international focus, many corporations are now concluding that the long-term sustainability of their ventures depends in large part on the informal "license to operate," which emanates from ongoing community support. Corporations also are increasingly sensitive about allegations that they are engaging in or condoning human rights abuses. As a result, several companies have adopted or are considering the adoption of worldwide social and human rights policies. Royal Dutch/Shell, for example, has adopted explicit policies addressing community and human rights issues, and has sought to integrate such considerations into project design and implementation, most notably in connection with the proposed Camisea project in Peru.[134]

These new corporate policies contain several common components, including aggressive outreach to affected communities, increased opportunities for consultation during project planning, creation of an appropriate infrastructure to support the project, ongoing monitoring of project commitments, and public reporting of monitoring results. Even if applicable law does not require such commitments, companies can expect environmental justice advocates to ask for them.

Notes

1. Environmental justice advocates in the United States also have access to international institutions. A coalition of U.S. environmental and human rights organizations recently petitioned the U.N. Commission on Human Rights to

investigate allegations that EPA and state environmental officials have violated the rights of minority and low-income persons. *See* "Groups Ask U.N. to Investigate Environmental Racism in Permitting," Superfund Report (May 26, 1999).

2. North American Agreement on Environmental Cooperation Between the Government of the United States of America, the Government of Canada and the Government of the United Mexican States, Sept. 13, 1993, 32 I.L.M. 1480 [hereinafter Environmental Side Agreement].

3. North American Free Trade Agreement Between the Government of the United States of America, the Government of Canada, and the Government of the United Mexican States, Dec. 17, 1992, 32 I.L.M. 289 (1993) [hereinafter NAFTA].

4. *See generally* Luis R. Vera-Morales, *Dumping in the International Backyard: Exportation of Hazardous Wastes to Mexico,* 7 Tul. Envtl. L.J. 353 (1994).

5. The NAFTA Report on Environmental Issues, prepared by the Clinton administration, Nov. 1993, at 4.

6. Environmental Side Agreement, *supra* note 2, at 1480.

7. Environmental Side Agreement, art. 14 (Submissions on Enforcement Matters), *supra* note 1.

8. Environmental Side Agreement, art. 45(2)(a), *supra* note 2.

9. Environmental Side Agreement, pt. 3, *supra* note 2.

10. Environmental Side Agreement, art. 9, *supra* note 2.

11. Environmental Side Agreement, art. 11, *supra* note 2.

12. Environmental Side Agreement, art. 14, *supra* note 2. *See also* Guidelines for Submissions on Enforcement Matters under arts. 14 & 15 of the North Agreement on Environmental Cooperation [hereinafter CEC Guidelines], available on the CEC web site at <www.cec.org>.

13. Environmental Side Agreement, art. 14(1)(f), *supra* note 2.

14. CEC Guidelines, § 5, *supra* note 12.

15. Environmental Side Agreement, art. 14(1)(d), *supra* note 2.

16. CEC Guidelines, § 5.4, *supra* note 12.

17. CEC Guidelines, §§ 6.1–6.3, *supra* note 12.

18. The Environmental Side Agreement does not reach on-site worker health and safety issues. To the extent a submission raised on-site health and safety issues along with off-site issues, the on-site health and safety issues would not be considered.

19. CEC Guidelines, § 7, *supra* note 12.

20. CEC Guidelines, § 8, *supra* note 12.

21. CEC Guidelines, § 9, *supra* note 12.

22. CEC Guidelines, § 9.4, *supra* note 11. It appears, therefore, that a governmental party could effectively terminate the process, even after a citizen complaint is filed, by initiating a judicial or administrative enforcement proceeding. At the conclusion of that judicial or administrative proceeding, the citizen could file a new complaint with the CEC.

23. Environmental Side Agreement, art. 15, *supra* note 2.

24. Environmental Side Agreement, art. 15(1) and (2), *supra* note 2.

25. CEC Guidelines, § 11, *supra* note 12.

26. CEC Guidelines, § 12, *supra* note 12.

27. CEC Guidelines, § 13, *supra* note 12. If the Council does not authorize release of the Factual Record, it must publicly state its reasons for that decision.

28. *See NAFTA's Broken Promises: The Border Betrayed, in* PUBLIC CITIZEN (Jan. 1996).

29. Four-Year Review of the North American Agreement on Environmental Cooperation: Report of the Independent Review Committee (June 1998) at 22 [hereinafter Four-Year Review], available on the CEC web site at <www.cec.org>.

30. Environmental Side Agreement, art. 22(1), *supra* note 2.

31. Environmental Side Agreement, arts. 23–36, *supra* note 2.

32. Four-Year Review, *supra* note 29, at 22.

33. Four-Year Review, *supra* note 29, at 22.

34. Four-Year Review, *supra* note 29, at 22–23.

35. B.C. Aboriginal Fisheries Commission, SEM 97-001.

36. Comite Pro Limpieza del Rio Magdalena, SEM 97-002.

37. Environmental Side Agreement, art. 6(1), *supra* note 2.

38. *Id.*

39. La Paz Agreement for Cooperation on Environmental Programs and Transboundary Problems, August 14, 1983, U.S.-Mex., 1 T.I.A.S. 10,827.

40. Integrated Environmental Plan for the Mexico–U.S. Border Area (First Stage, 1992–1994).

41. Border XXI Program Framework Document, Executive Summary.

42. *License Denied for Radioactive Dump,* Associated Press (Oct. 22, 1998).

43. Clarification of Certain Aspects of the Resolution Establishing the Inspection Panel [hereinafter Clarification] at 1, available on the Bank's web site at <www.worldbank.org/html/ins-panel/resolution.html>.

44. World Bank Inspection Panel Operating Procedures [hereinafter Operating Procedures], available on the World Bank's web site at <www.worldbank.org/html/ins-panel/oper.html>. These procedures were modified in a second clarification of the resolution establishing the panel dated April 20, 1999.

45. Operating Procedures, ¶ 4, *supra* note 44.

46. Operating Procedures, ¶ 5, *supra* note 44.

47. Operating Procedures, ¶ 16, *supra* note 44.

48. Operating Procedures, ¶ 16, 19, 22, 32, *supra* note 44.

49. Operating Procedures, ¶ 18(d), *supra* note 44.

50. Clarification at 1, *supra* note 43.

51. Operating Procedures, ¶ 36, *supra* note 44.

52. Operating Procedures, ¶ 37, *supra* note 44.

53. Operating Procedures, ¶ 33(a) and (b), *supra* note 44.

54. Operating Procedures, ¶ 33(c), *supra* note 44.

55. Operating Procedures, ¶ 39, *supra* note 44.

56. Operating Procedures, ¶ 45, *supra* note 44.

57. Operating Procedures, ¶ 47, *supra* note 44.

58. Operating Procedures, ¶ 49, *supra* note 44.

59. Operating Procedures, ¶ 51, *supra* note 44.

60. Operating Procedures, ¶ 52, *supra* note 44.

61. Operating Procedures, ¶ 52, *supra* note 44.

62. Operating Procedures, ¶ 53, *supra* note 44.

63. Operating Procedures, ¶ 55, *supra* note 44.

64. Operating Procedures, ¶¶ 55 and 56, *supra* note 44.

65. Request for Inspection Summary #1, available on the Bank's web site at <www.worldbank.org/html/ins-panel/overview.html>.

66. Request for Inspection Summary # 4, *supra* note 65.

67. Request for Inspection Summary #4, *supra* note 65.

68. Request for Inspection Summary #5, *supra* note 65.

69. Request for Inspection Summary #5, *supra* note 65. The World Bank consists of the IBRD and the IDA. The Multilateral Investment Guarantee Agency (MIGA) and the IFC are legally, financially, and operationally separate from the World Bank. Together, all four entities make up the World Bank Group.

70. The Pehuenche, the World Bank Group and ENDESA, S.A.: Report of the Committee for Human Rights, American Anthropological Association (Mar. 1998) [hereinafter AAA Report], available on the Internet at <www.ameranthassn.org/pehuenc.htm>.

71. AAA Report, *supra* note 70, at 9.

72. 1998 Social and Environmental Policy Guidelines for the International Finance Corporation, available on the World Bank web site at <www.worldbank.org>.

73. 12 U.S.C. § 635i-5(a).

74. Ex-Im Bank Environmental Procedures, available on the Internet at <www.exim.gov>.

75. Ex-Im Bank Environmental Procedures, *supra* note 74.

76. 22 U.S.C. § 2191(n).

77. OPIC Environmental Handbook, available on the Internet at <www.opic.gov>.

78. *See* Torres v. Southern Peru Copper Corp., 113 F.3d 540 (5th Cir. 1997) (affirming dismissal of toxic tort suit brought by 700 Peruvian citizens against copper company); *In re Union Carbide Corp. Gas Plant Disaster,* 634 F. Supp. 842 (S.D.N.Y. 1986), *aff'd in part, modified in part,* 809 F.2d 1295 (2d Cir. 1987), *cert. denied,* 485 U.S. 871 (1987) (affirming dismissal of 145 consolidated actions against Union Carbide arising from catastrophic leak of methyl icocyanate in Bhopal, India); Delgado v. Shell Oil Co., 890 F. Supp. 1324 (S.D. Tex. 1995) (dismissing actions brought by farmworkers from 23 foreign countries alleging chemical exposure); Sequihua v. Texaco, 847 F. Supp. 61 (S.D. Tex. 1994) (dismissing suit by residents of Ecuador alleging massive air, soil, and water contamination).

79. 157 F.3d 153, (2d Cir. 1998).

80. Aguinda v. Texaco, Inc., 945 F. Supp. 625 (S.D. N.Y. 1996).

81. 28 U.S.C. § 1350.

82. *See In re Estate of Ferdinand Marcos, Human Rights Litigation,* 25 F.3d 1467 (9th Cir.), *cert. denied,* 513 U.S. 1126 (1995); Filartica v. Pena-Irala, 630 F.2d 876 (2d Cir. 1980); *see also* Restatement (Third) of Foreign Relations Law of the United States §§ 701–02 (identifying state conduct that is recognized to violate international law).

83. Jurisdiction in these cases has generally been obtained through personal service on defendants while they are living or traveling in the United States.

84. Kadic v. Karadzic, 70 F.3d 232 (2d Cir. 1995).

85. 963 F. Supp. 880 (C.D. Cal. 1997).

86. *Id.* at 883–84.

87. *Id.* at 890.

88. 969 F. Supp. 362 (E.D. La. 1997).

89. 969 F. Supp. at 382–84. Although the federal case was dismissed, a case filed in state court is proceeding

90. Aguinda v. Texaco, 1994 U.S. Dist. LEXIS 4718 (S.D.N.Y. 1994).

91. 42 U.S.C. § 4332(2)(C).

92. 40 C.F.R. § 1508.18(a).

93. 42 U.S.C. § 4332(2)(F).

94. 578 F.2d 389 (D.C. Cir. 1978).

95. 452 F. Supp. 1226 (D. D.C. 1978).

96. Exec. Order No. 12,114, 44 Fed. Reg. 1957 (1979), *reprinted at* 42 U.S.C.A. § 4321.

97. Environmental Defense Fund, Inc. v. Massey, 986 F.2d 528, 530 (D.C. Cir. 1993).

98. 748 F. Supp. 749, 757 (D. Haw. 1990), *appeal dismissed as moot,* 924 F.2d 175 (9th Cir. 1991).

99. NRDC v. NRC, 647 F.2d 1345 (D.C. Cir. 1981); Committee for Nuclear Responsibility v. Seaborg, 463 F.2d 796 (D.C. Cir. 1971).

100. 748 F. Supp. at 761 (emphasis in original).

101. EEOC v. Arabian American Oil Co., 111 S. Ct. 1227 (1991).

102. 986 F.2d 528 (D.C. Cir. 1993).

103. 986 F.2d at 533.

104. 986 F.2d at 535.

105. 837 F. Supp. 466 (D. D.C. 1993).

106. Johnson, *The Basel Convention: The Shape of Things to Come for United States Waste Exports,* 21 ENVTL. L. 299 (1991).

107. Pub. L. No. 98-616, 98 Stat. 3224.

108. 40 C.F.R. § 262.53.

109. 40 C.F.R. § 262.53(e).

110. 40 C.F.R. § 262.52.

111. 40 C.F.R. § 262.54-56.

112. 42 U.S.C. § 6928(d)(6).

113. Amlon Metals, Inc. v. FMC Corporation, 775 F. Supp. 668 (S.D.N.Y. 1991) (dismissing RCRA claim alleging improper shipment of hazardous waste to a foreign corporation).

114. Agreement Concerning the Transboundary Movements of Hazardous Waste, Oct. 28, 1986, U. S.-Canada, *referenced in* 26 I.L.M. 593 (1987); Agreement of Cooperation Between the United States and United Mexican States Regarding the Transboundary Shipments of Hazardous Wastes and Hazardous Substances, Nov. 12, 1986, U. S.-Mexico, 26 I.L.M. 25 (1987).

115. Multilateral Arrangement for Transboundary Movements of Recyclables, May 5, 1992.

116. 40 C.F.R. § 262.58(b).

117. 40 C.F.R. § 262.58(b).

118. Basel Convention on the Control of Transboundary Movements of Hazardous Waste and Their Disposal, Mar. 22, 1989, 28 I.L.M. 649 (1989).

119. *Administration Commits to Begin Early Process of Implementing Basel Early Next Congress,* BNA DAILY ENV'T REP., Aug. 27, 1998, at AA-1.

120. Basel Convention, art. 4, § 1(e).

121. BNA DAILY ENV'T REP., Aug. 27, 1998, at AA-1.

122. BNA DAILY ENV'T REP., Aug. 27, 1998, at AA-1.

123. Resolution on the Control of Transboundary Movements of Hazardous Wastes and Their Disposal in Africa, OAU, CM/Res. 1225(L) (Mar. 22, 1989).

124. 7 U.S.C. §§ 136–136y.

125. 15 U.S.C. §§ 2601–2629.

126. 7 U.S.C. § 136a.

127. 7 U.S.C. § 136o(a).

128. 40 C.F.R. §§ 168.65–168.85.

129. 15 U.S.C. § 2611.

130. 40 C.F.R. § 707.60(a).

131. 40 C.F.R. § 707.70.

132. 55 Fed. Reg. 4959 (1990); 57 Fed. Reg. 58,390 (1992).

133. *Treaty on Prior Informed Consent Signed by 57 Countries at Rotterdam Meeting,* DAILY ENV'TL. REPORTER (BNA) Sept. 15, 1998.

134. For a detailed discussion of Shell's efforts in Peru, see the Camisea web site at <www.camisea.com>.

EXECUTIVE ORDER 12,898

Federal Actions To Address Environmental Justice in Minority Populations and Low-Income Populations

February 11, 1994

By the authority vested in me as President by the Constitution and the laws of the United States of America, it is hereby ordered as follows:

Section 1-1. Implementation.

1-101. Agency Responsibilities. To the greatest extent practicable and permitted by law, and consistent with the principles set forth in the report on the National Performance Review, each Federal agency shall make achieving environmental justice part of its mission by identifying and addressing, as appropriate, disproportionately high and adverse human health or environmental effects of its programs, policies, and activities on minority populations and low-income populations in the United States and its territories and possessions, the District of Columbia, the Commonwealth of Puerto Rico, and the Commonwealth of the Mariana Islands.

1-102. Creation of an Interagency Working Group on Environmental Justice. (a) Within 3 months of the date of this order, the Administrator of the Environmental Protection Agency ("Administrator") or the Administrator's designee shall convene an interagency Federal Working Group on Environmental Justice ("Working Group"). The Working Group shall comprise the heads of the following executive agencies and offices, or their designees: (a) Department of Defense; (b) Department of Health and Human Services; (c) Department of Housing and Urban Development; (d) Department of Labor; (e) Department of Agriculture; (f) Department of Transportation; (g) Department of Justice; (h) Department of the Interior; (i)

Department of Commerce; (j) Department of Energy; (k) Environmental Protection Agency; (l) Office of Management and Budget; (m) Office of Science and Technology Policy; (n) Office of the Deputy Assistant to the President for Environmental Policy; (o) Office of the Assistant to the President for Domestic Policy; (p) National Economic Council; (q) Council of Economic Advisers; and (r) such other Government officials as the President may designate. The Working Group shall report to the President through the Deputy Assistant to the President for Environmental Policy and the Assistant to the President for Domestic Policy.

(b) The Working Group shall: (1) provide guidance to Federal agencies on criteria for identifying disproportionately high and adverse human health or environmental effects on minority populations and low-income populations;

(2) coordinate with, provide guidance to, and serve as a clearinghouse for, each Federal agency as it develops an environmental justice strategy as required by section 1-103 of this order, in order to ensure that the administration, interpretation and enforcement of programs, activities and policies are undertaken in a consistent manner;

(3) assist in coordinating research by, and stimulating cooperation among, the Environmental Protection Agency, the Department of Health and Human Services, the Department of Housing and Urban Development, and other agencies conducting research or other activities in accordance with section 3-3 of this order;

(4) assist in coordinating data collection, required by this order;

(5) examine existing data and studies on environmental justice;

(6) hold public meetings as required in section 5-502(d) of this order; and

(7) develop interagency model projects on environmental justice that evidence cooperation among Federal agencies.

1-103. Development of Agency Strategies. (a) Except as provided in section 6- 605 of this order, each Federal agency shall develop an agency-wide environmental justice strategy, as set forth in subsections (b)-(e) of this section that identifies and addresses disproportionately high and adverse human health or environmental effects of its programs, policies, and activities on minority populations and low-income populations. The environmental justice strategy shall list programs, policies, planning and public participation processes, enforcement, and/or rulemakings related to human health or the environment that should be revised to, at a minimum: (1) promote enforcement of all health and environmental statutes in areas with minority populations and low-income populations; (2) ensure greater public participation; (3) improve research and data collection relating to the health of and environment of minority populations and low-income populations; and (4) identify differential patterns of consumption of natural resources among minority populations and low-income populations. In addition, the environmental justice strategy shall include, where appropriate, a timetable for undertaking identified revisions and consideration of economic and social implications of the revisions.

(b) Within 4 months of the date of this order, each Federal agency shall identify an internal administrative process for developing its environmental justice strategy, and shall inform the Working Group of the process.

(c) Within 6 months of the date of this order, each Federal agency shall provide the Working Group with an outline of its proposed environmental justice strategy.

(d) Within 10 months of the date of this order, each Federal agency shall provide the Working Group with its proposed environmental justice strategy.

(e) Within 12 months of the date of this order, each Federal agency shall finalize its environmental justice strategy and provide a copy and written description of its strategy to the Working Group. During the 12 month period from the date of this order, each Federal agency, as part of its environmental justice strategy, shall identify several specific projects that can be promptly undertaken to address particular concerns identified during the development of the proposed environmental justice strategy, and a schedule for implementing those projects.

(f) Within 24 months of the date of this order, each Federal agency shall report to the Working Group on its progress in implementing its agency-wide environmental justice strategy.

(g) Federal agencies shall provide additional periodic reports to the Working Group as requested by the Working Group.

1-104. Reports to the President. Within 14 months of the date of this order, the Working Group shall submit to the President, through the Office of the Deputy Assistant to the President for Environmental Policy and the Office of the Assistant to the President for Domestic Policy, a report that describes the implementation of this order, and includes the final environmental justice strategies described in section 1-103(e) of this order.

Sec. 2-2. Federal Agency Responsibilities for Federal Programs. Each Federal agency shall conduct its programs, policies, and activities that substantially affect human health or the environment, in a manner that ensures that such programs, policies, and activities do not have the effect of excluding persons (including populations) from participation in, denying persons (including populations) the benefits of, or subjecting persons (including populations) to discrimination under, such programs, policies, and activities, because of their race, color, or national origin.

Sec. 3-3. Research, Data Collection, and Analysis.

3-301. Human Health and Environmental Research and Analysis. (a) Environmental human health research, whenever practicable and appropriate, shall include diverse segments of the population in epidemiological and clinical studies, including segments at high risk from environmental hazards, such as minority populations, low-income populations and workers who may be exposed to substantial environmental hazards.

(b) Environmental human health analyses, whenever practicable and appropriate, shall identify multiple and cumulative exposures.

(c) Federal agencies shall provide minority populations and low-income populations the opportunity to comment on the development and design of research strategies undertaken pursuant to this order.

3-302. Human Health and Environmental Data Collection and Analysis. To the extent permitted by existing law, including the Privacy Act, as amended (5 U.S.C. section 552a): (a) each Federal agency, whenever practicable and appropriate, shall collect, maintain, and analyze information assessing and comparing environmental and human health risks borne by populations identified by race, national origin, or income. To the extent practical and appropriate, Federal agencies shall use this information to determine whether their programs, policies, and activities have disproportionately high and adverse human health or environmental effects on minority populations and low-income populations;

(b) In connection with the development and implementation of agency strategies in section 1-103 of this order, each Federal agency, whenever practicable and appropriate, shall collect, maintain and analyze information on the race, national origin, income level, and other readily accessible and appropriate information for areas surrounding facilities or sites expected to have a substantial environmental, human health, or economic effect on the surrounding populations, when such facilities or sites become the subject of a substantial Federal environmental administrative or judicial action. Such information shall be made available to the public, unless prohibited by law; and

(c) Each Federal agency, whenever practicable and appropriate, shall collect, maintain, and analyze information on the race, national origin, income level, and other readily accessible and appropriate information for areas surrounding Federal facilities that are: (1) subject to the reporting requirements under the Emergency Planning and Community Right-to-Know Act, 42 U.S.C. section 11001-11050 as mandated in Executive Order No. 12856; and (2) expected to have a substantial environmental, human health, or economic effect on surrounding populations. Such information shall be made available to the public, unless prohibited by law.

(d) In carrying out the responsibilities in this section, each Federal agency, whenever practicable and appropriate, shall share information and eliminate unnecessary duplication of efforts through the use of existing data systems and cooperative agreements among Federal agencies and with State, local, and tribal governments.

Sec. 4-4. Subsistence Consumption of Fish and Wildlife.

4-401. Consumption Patterns. In order to assist in identifying the need for ensuring protection of populations with differential patterns of subsistence consumption of fish and wildlife, Federal agencies, whenever practicable and appropriate, shall collect, maintain, and analyze information on the consumption patterns of populations who principally rely on fish and/or wildlife for subsistence. Federal agencies shall communicate to the public the risks of those consumption patterns.

4-402. Guidance. Federal agencies, whenever practicable and appropriate, shall work in a coordinated manner to publish guidance reflecting the latest scientific information available concerning methods for evaluating the human health risks associated with the consumption of pollutant-bearing fish or wildlife. Agencies shall consider such guidance in developing their policies and rules.

Sec. 5-5. Public Participation and Access to Information. (a) The public may submit recommendations to Federal agencies relating to the incorporation of environmental justice principles into Federal agency programs or policies. Each Federal agency shall convey such recommendations to the Working Group.

(b) Each Federal agency may, whenever practicable and appropriate, translate crucial public documents, notices, and hearings relating to human health or the environment for limited English speaking populations.

(c) Each Federal agency shall work to ensure that public documents, notices, and hearings relating to human health or the environment are concise, understandable, and readily accessible to the public.

(d) The Working Group shall hold public meetings, as appropriate, for the purpose of fact-finding, receiving public comments, and conducting inquiries concerning environmental justice. The Working Group shall prepare for public review a summary of the comments and recommendations discussed at the public meetings.

Sec. 6-6. General Provisions.

6-601. Responsibility for Agency Implementation. The head of each Federal agency shall be responsible for ensuring compliance with this order. Each Federal agency shall conduct internal reviews and take such other steps as may be necessary to monitor compliance with this order.

6-602. Executive Order No. 12250. This Executive order is intended to supplement but not supersede Executive Order No. 12250, which requires consistent and effective implementation of various laws prohibiting discriminatory practices in programs receiving Federal financial assistance. Nothing herein shall limit the effect or mandate of Executive Order No. 12250.

6-603. Executive Order No. 12875. This Executive order is not intended to limit the effect or mandate of Executive Order No. 12875.

6-604. Scope. For purposes of this order, Federal agency means any agency on the Working Group, and such other agencies as may be designated by the President, that conducts any Federal program or activity that substantially affects human health or the environment. Independent agencies are requested to comply with the provisions of this order.

6-605. Petitions for Exemptions. The head of a Federal agency may petition the President for an exemption from the requirements of this order on the grounds that all or some of the petitioning agency's programs or activities should not be subject to the requirements of this order.

6-606. Native American Programs. Each Federal agency responsibility set forth under this order shall apply equally to Native American programs. In addition, the Department of the Interior, in coordination with the Working Group, and, after consultation with tribal leaders, shall coordinate steps to be taken pursuant to this order that address Federally-recognized Indian Tribes.

6-607. Costs. Unless otherwise provided by law, Federal agencies shall assume the financial costs of complying with this order.

6-608. General. Federal agencies shall implement this order consistent with, and to the extent permitted by, existing law.

6-609. Judicial Review. This order is intended only to improve the internal management of the executive branch and is not intended to, nor does it create any right, benefit, or trust responsibility, substantive or procedural, enforceable at law or equity by a party against the United States, its agencies, its officers, or any person. This order shall not be construed to create any right to judicial review involving the compliance or noncompliance of the United States, its agencies, its officers, or any other person with this order.

WILLIAM CLINTON
THE WHITE HOUSE,
February 11, 1994.

TABLE OF CASES

A

Bedford, Town of v. Raytheon Co., 755 F. Supp. 469 (D. Mass. 1991), 556 n.76
Beliz v. W.H. McLeod & Sons Packing Co., 765 F.2d 1317 (5th Cir. 1985), 707 n.213
Belleville, Township of v. Federal Transit Administration, 30 F. Supp. 782 (D.N.J. 1998), 387 n.48
BellSouth Telecommunications v. W.R. Grace & Co., 77 F. 3d 603 (1995), 615 n.101
Benavie v. Baker, 420 N.Y.S.2d 735 (N.Y. A.D.2d 1979), 654 n.112
Bennett v. Mallinckrodt, Inc., 698 S.W.2d 854 (Mo. Ct. App. 1985), 650 n.37, 652 n.85
Bennett v. Spear, 520 U.S. 154 (1997), 359, 385 n.4, 385 n.6, 385 n.12, 385 n.14, 385 n.16, 386 nn.17–18, 389 n.105
Berry, 989 F.2d 822 (5th Cir. 1993), *cert. denied*, 510 U.S. 1117 (1994), 657 n.154
Bevan v. Honeywell, Inc., 118 F. 3d 603 (8th Cir. 1997), 423 n.5
Bice v. Leslie's Poolmart, 39 F. 3d 887 (8th Cir. 1994), 708 n.217
Bingham v. Terminix Int'l Co., 850 F. Supp. 516 (S.D. Miss. 1994), 709 n.218
Birch Corporation v. Nevada Instrument Holding, Inc., 1998 U.S. App. LEXIS 14923, 547
Bivens v. Six Unknown Named Agents, 403 U.S. 388 (1971), 22 n.69
Bixby Ranch Co. v. Spectrol Electronics Corp., No. BC-052566 8 TX L.R. 955 (Sup. Ct. L.A. County 1993), 656 n.149
Black Citizens Task Force v. City of Austin, Texas, Case No. [unavailable at publication date], 98 n.85
Black Hills Institute of Geological Research v. South Dakota School of Mines & Technology, 12 F. 3d 737 (8th Cir. 1993), *cert. denied*, 513 U.S. 810 (1994), 176 n.28
Black Jack, Mo., City of, United States v., 508 F.2d 1179 (8th Cir. 1974), *cert. denied*, 422 U.S. 1042 (1975), 90 n.13
Blanchard v. Bergeron, 489 U.S. 87 (1989), 391 n.146
Bliss, United States v., 667 F. Supp. 1289 (E.D. Mo. 1987), 517 n.45
Bloomington, City of v. Westinghouse Electric Corp., 891 F.2d 611 (7th Cir. 1989), 659 n.172
Blue Legs v. U.S. Bureau of Indian Affairs, 867 F.2d 1095 (8th Cir. 1989), 179 nn.97–98, 179 n.100
Blue Sky Advocates v. State, 727 P.2d 644 (Wash. 1986), 393 n.224
Blum v. Stenson, 465 U.S. 886 (1984), 391 n.162, 391 n.167
Board of County Comm'rs v. Slovek, 723 F.2d 1303 (Colo. 1986), 655 nn.125–129
Board of Managers of Glen Mills Schools v. West Chester Areas School District, 838 F.Supp. 1035 (E.D. Pa. 1993), *reversed in part, aff'd in part without opinion*, 52 F. 3d 313 (3d Cir. 1995), 18

D

E

F

G

I

K

L

M

N

O

P

Q

R

S

T

U

W

INDEX

E

F

I

O

U

V

W

Z

PUBLICATIONS ORDER FORM
Section of Environment, Energy, and Resources

Qty	Title	Section member price	Non-member price	Total $
	Brownfields: A Comprehensive Guide to Redeveloping Contaminated Property **5350056**	139.95	149.95	
	CERCLA Enforcement **5350053**	110.00	120.00	
	The Clean Air Act Handbook **5350063**	110.00	120.00	
	The Clean Water Act Handbook **5350045**	75.00	80.00	
	A Complete Guide to Environmental Audits **5350057**	75.00	85.00	
	Environmental Aspects of Real Estate Transactions **5350072**	149.95	159.95	
	The Environmental Crimes Case **5090075**	89.95	99.95	
	The EPCRA Compliance Manual **5350061**	105.00	115.00	
	Guide to RCRA Inspections **5350067**	49.95	59.95	
	Natural Gas Contracting **5350068**	49.95	59.95	
	NEPA Litigation Guide **5350070**	75.00	85.00	
	Prospective Purchaser Agreements **5350062**	85.00	95.00	
	RCRA Practice Manual **5350044**	84.95	94.95	
	RCRA Policy Documents **5350037**	55.00	60.00	
	Restoration of Oil Field Sites **5350066**	49.95	59.95	
	Underground Storage Tanks **5350048**	55.00	60.00	
	Water Law **5350050**	70.00	75.00	
	What to Do When the Environmental Client Calls **5350043**	55.00	60.00	
	TAX** In DC add 5.75%, in MD add 5%, in IL add 8.75%		**Subtotal**	
	HANDLING*		**Tax****	
	Orders up to $24.99, add $3.95; Orders from $25 to $49.99 add $5.95		**Handling***	
	Orders from $50 to $99.99 add $7.95; Orders $100+ add $9.95		**TOTAL**	

❑ Check enclosed payable to ABA ❑ VISA ❑ MasterCard ❑ American Express

Card number ______________________ Exp. Date ______________

Signature ______________________________________

Name/Firm/Org. ______________________________________

Address ______________________________________

Phone number ______________ E-mail ______________ *Source Code BOOK899*

Mail to: ABA Publication Orders, P.O. Box 10892, Chicago, IL 60610-0892
Phone: 1-800-285-2221 (ABA1) **Fax:** (312) 988-5568
E-mail: abasvcctr@abanet.org **Website:** http://www.abanet.org/abapubs